Agoston E. Eiben   Thomas Bäck
Marc Schoenauer   Hans-Paul Schwefel (Eds.)

Parallel Problem Solving from Nature – PPSN V

5th International Conference
Amsterdam, The Netherlands
September 27-30, 1998
Proceedings

Springer

Volume Editors

Agoston E. Eiben
Leiden University, Department of Mathematics and Computer Science
Niels Bohrweg 1, 2333 CA Leiden, The Netherlands
E-mail: gusz@wi.leidenuniv.nl

Thomas Bäck
Informatik Centrum Dortmund, CASA
Joseph-von-Fraunhofer-Str. 20, D-44227 Dortmund, Germany
E-mail: baeck@icd.de
and
Leiden University, Department of Mathematics and Computer Science
Niels Bohrweg 1, 2333 CA Leiden, The Netherlands
E-mail: baeck@wi.leidenuniv.nl

Marc Schoenauer
CMAP, Ecole Polytechnique
Route de Saclay, F-91128 Palaiseau Cedex, France
E-mail: marc.schoenauer@polytechnique.fr

Hans-Paul Schwefel
University of Dortmund, Department of Computer Science
D-44221 Dortmund, Germany
E-mail: hps@icd.de

Cataloging-in-Publication data applied for

Die Deutsche Bibliothek - CIP-Einheitsaufnahme

Parallel problem solving from nature : 5th international conference
; proceedings / PPSN V, Amsterdam, The Netherlands, September
27 - 30, 1998. Agoston E. Eiben ... (ed.). - Berlin ; Heidelberg ; New
York ; Barcelona ; Budapest ; Hong Kong ; London ; Milan ; Paris ;
Singapore ; Tokyo : Springer, 1998
  (Lecture notes in computer science ; Vol. 1498)
  ISBN 3-540-65078-4

CR Subject Classification (1991): C.1.2, D.1.3, F.1-2, I.2.6, I.2.8, I.2.11, J.3

ISSN 0302-9743
ISBN 3-540-65078-4 Springer-Verlag Berlin Heidelberg New York

© Springer-Verlag Berlin Heidelberg 1998
Printed in Germany

Typesetting: Camera-ready by author
SPIN 10638928   06/3142 – 5 4 3 2 1 0   Printed on acid-free paper

Preface

We are pleased to introduce the reader to the proceedings of the Fifth International Conference on Parallel Problem Solving from Nature, PPSN V – International Conference on Evolutionary Computation, held in Amsterdam, September 27-30, 1998. PPSN V is organized in cooperation with the International Society for Genetic Algorithms (ISGA) and the Evolutionary Programming Society (EPS), reflecting the beneficial interaction between the conference activities in Europe and the USA in the field of evolutionary computation.

Following the 1990 meeting in Dortmund [1], this biennial event was held in Brussels [2], Jerusalem [3], and Berlin [4], where it was decided that the 1998 location should be Amsterdam with Agoston E. Eiben as the general chair.

The scientific content of the PPSN conference focuses on the topic of problem solving paradigms gleaned from a natural model, including (but not limited to) organic evolution, neural network based learning processes, immune systems, life and its properties in general, DNA strands, and chemical and physical processes. The term *natural computing* perfectly summarizes the essential idea of the PPSN conference series, and the organizers of PPSN V are delighted that the Leiden Center for Natural Computation (LCNC) is involved in the organization of this conference.

As with the previous PPSN meetings, these proceedings also emphasize the topic of evolution, represented in computer science by the field of *evolutionary computation* with its evolutionary algorithms. Historically this field has been represented by areas such as genetic algorithms, evolution strategies, evolutionary programming, genetic programming, and classifier systems. In recent years these artificial terminological boundaries have been dropped to the benefit of a more general understanding of evolutionary principles applied to different search spaces with different aims, such as problem solving, investigating evolutionary principles, or understanding life. In these proceedings, the reader will find a variety of sections focusing on aspects of evolutionary algorithms, such as for instance Convergence Theory, Multi-Criteria and Constrained Optimization, Coevolution and Learning, just to name a few. Besides these evolutionary themes, there are also contributions on other aspects of natural computation, such as Cellular Automata, Fuzzy Systems and Neural Networks or Ant Colonies, Immune Systems, and Other Paradigms.

In total, these proceedings contain 100 contributions which were selected from 185 papers submitted to the conference organizers. The members of the program committee (listed on the following pages) undertook the extremely challenging task of submitting their scientific reviews to facilitate the final decision making for the acceptance of the top 54% of all submissions. We are very grateful to these reviewers for their willingness to volunteer their scientific expertise to ensure the decision making process was as fair as possible. We would also like to thank the EvoNet Electronic Communication Committee for its support with the Web-based submission and review procedure which greatly simplified the review process, facilitating a smooth exchange of papers and reviews. As this software was used for the very first time in a real conference setting, inevitably a few technical problems occured and a special thanks is owed to those reviewers who provided their reviews in a very short time. We are confident that the – debugged – system will provide a good support for future events.

Following the PPSN spirit, PPSN V is a poster-only conference, i.e., all papers are presented as posters to facilitate personal discussion and exchange of ideas between the presenter and the audience. Although this might imply a smaller audience than would be the case for an oral presentation, it gives presenters a better chance to communicate with the people most interested in their topic, and to chat with them in a more relaxed atmosphere. Consequently, posters are not "second-class" papers as in some other conferences – they are the preferred method of open presentation. The 100 papers presented at the conference are grouped into 5 groups of about 20 papers each. To simplify orientation within a session, and to allow the audience to get a good overview of posters, each poster session is introduced by a volunteer giving a brief overview. We believe that this is very helpful for the conference participants, and we appreciate the efforts of these volunteers for helping with this.

The conference includes oral presentations from three invited speakers including Grzegorz Rozenberg (DNA Computing), Nicholas Gessler (Artificial Culture: Experiments in Synthetic Anthropology), and Lawrence Davis (Commercial Applications of Evolutionary Algorithms: Some Case Studies), all addressing hot topics in the context of natural computation.

On the first day of the conference, September 27th, eight tutorials will be given by well-known experts in evolutionary computation and related fields. These tutorials are designed for an audience looking for some particular aspects of the state of the art. The list of tutorials and their presenters can be found on the introductory pages.

Finally, we would like to thank our sponsors, who helped in many different ways to make this conference possible. These sponsors are (in alphabetic order) the European Network of Excellence on Evolutionary Computation (EvoNet), Informatik Centrum Dortmund (ICD), Institute for Programming Technology and Algorithmics (IPA), International Society for Genetic Algorithms (ISGA), Leiden Center for Natural Computing (LCNC), the Municipality of Amsterdam, Philips, Siemens AG, and the Stichting European Evolutionary Computing Conferences (EECC), a Dutch-based non-profit-making organization aimed at the support of European research and organizational activities in the field of natural and evolutionary computation. The continuous support and invaluable help of Nathalie Limonta at Ecole Polytechnique was highly appreciated and we also would like to thank Ben Pechter for his efforts to make PPSN V a success.

We feel these proceedings bear witness to the fruitful cooperation and exchange of ideas between evolutionary computation groups from all parts of the world and mark some major progress in the field – and we look forward to seeing

how the Amsterdam environment with its coffee-shops and nightlife will help to
support this development, and smoothen the cultural barriers ...
Have fun at the conference, and with the proceedings !

July 1998   Agoston E. Eiben, General Chair
                           Thomas Bäck and Marc Schoenauer, Program Co-Chairs
                                       Hans-Paul Schwefel, Publication Chair

References

1. H.-P. Schwefel and R. Männer, editors. *Proceedings of the 1st Conference on Parallel Problem Solving from Nature*, number 496 in Lecture Notes in Computer Science. Springer-Verlag, 1991.
2. R. Männer and B. Manderick, editors. *Proceedings of the 2nd Conference on Parallel Problem Solving from Nature*. North-Holland, 1992.
3. Y. Davidor, H.-P. Schwefel, and R. Männer, editors. *Proceedings of the 3rd Conference on Parallel Problem Solving from Nature*, number 866 in Lecture Notes in Computer Science. Springer-Verlag, 1994.
4. H.-M. Voigt, W. Ebeling, I. Rechenberg, and H.-P. Schwefel, editors. *Proceedings of the 4th Conference on Parallel Problem Solving from Nature*, number 1141 in Lecture Notes in Computer Science. Springer, Berlin, 1996.

PPSN V Conference Committee

Agoston E. Eiben
Leiden University, The Netherlands
General Chair

Thomas Bäck
Informatik Centrum Dortmund, Germany
Leiden University, The Netherlands

and

Marc Schoenauer
CNRS, Ecole Polytechnique, France
Program Co-Chairs

Hans-Paul Schwefel
Universität Dortmund, Germany
Proceedings Chair

Hans-Michael Voigt
Gesellschaft zur Förderung angewandter Informatik e.V. (GFaI), Germany
Tutorial Chair

Terry Fogarty
Napier University, Scotland, UK
Publicity Chair

Thea van Wijk
Leids Congres Bureau, The Netherlands
Local Arrangements

PPSN Steering Committee

Yuval Davidor
Schema Ltd., Israel

Kenneth A. De Jong
George Mason University, USA

Agoston E. Eiben
Leiden University, The Netherlands

Hiroaki Kitano
Sony Computer Science Lab., Japan

Reinhard Männer
Universität Mannheim, Germany

Hans-Paul Schwefel
Universität Dortmund, Germany

Hans-Michael Voigt
Gesellschaft zur Förderung angewandter Informatik e.V. (GFaI), Germany

PPSN V Program Committee

PPSN V Tutorials

Hans-Georg Beyer,
Universität Dortmund, Germany:
An Introduction into ES-Theory

Kalyanmoy Deb and Jeffrey Horn,
Indian Institute of Technology, Kanpur, India, and
Northern Michigan University, Marquette, USA:
Evolutionary Computation for Multiobjective Optimization

Marco Dorigo,
Université Libre de Bruxelles, Belgium:
Ant Colony Optimization

Agoston E. Eiben and Zbigniew Michalewicz,
Leiden University, The Netherlands, and
University of North Carolina, Charlotte, USA:
Parameter Control, Adaptation, and Self-Adaptation in Evolutionary Algorithms

Christian Jacob,
Friedrich-Alexander-Universität Erlangen-Nürnberg, Germany:
Evolutionary Algorithms and Agent-Based Distributed Systems

Riccardo Poli and William B. Langdon,
The University of Birmingham, UK:
Introduction to Genetic Programming

Joachim Sprave,
Universität Dortmund, Germany:
Evolutionary Algorithms: Spatially Structured Populations and Parallelism

Hans-Michael Voigt,
Gesellschaft zur Förderung angewandter Informatik e.V., Berlin, Germany:
Introduction to Quantitative Genetics with Applications to Evolutionary Computation

PPSN V Tutorials

Hans-Georg Beyer
Informatik Centrum Dortmund
An Introduction to ES Theory

Kalyanmoy Deb and Jeffrey Horn
...Basics of Technology, Kanpur, India and
...of Minnesota, Minneapolis, USA
Evolutionary Computation for Multi-Criteria Optimization

Marco Dorigo
University Libre de Bruxelles, Belgium
Ant Colony Optimization

Agoston E. Eiben and Zbigniew Michalewicz
Leiden University, The Netherlands and
University of North Carolina, Charlotte, USA
Parameter Control, Adaptation, and Self-Adaptation in Evolutionary Algorithms

Claudio Rocco
Fraunhofer ... Intelligent Systems, Germany
Evolutionary Algorithms and Agent-Based Distributed Systems

John Fitzgerald and William L. Langdon
The University of Birmingham, UK
Introduction to Genetic Programming

Stefan Voget
Fraunhofer ..., Germany
Evolutionary Algorithms: Analysis, Predictions and Results

Hans-Michael Voigt
...and Environment ...
Introduction to Population Genetics with Application to Evolutionary Algorithms

Table of Contents

Convergence Theory

Modelling Genetic Algorithms: From Markov Chains to
Dependence with Complete Connections
A. Agapie — 3

On the Optimization of Unimodal Functions with the (1+1)
Evolutionary Algorithm
S. Droste, Th. Jansen, and I. Wegener — 13

A Timing Analysis of Convergence to Fitness Sharing Equilibrium — 23
J. Horn and D.E. Goldberg

Where Elitists Start Limping: Evolution Strategies at Ridge
Functions
A.I. Oyman, H.-G. Beyer, H.-P. Schwefel — 34

Fitness Landscapes and Problem Difficulty

A Bit-Wise Epistasis Measure for Binary Search Spaces — 47
C. Fonlupt, D. Robilliard, and P. Preux

Inside GA Dynamics: Ground Basis for Comparison — 57
L. Kallel

The Effect of Spin-Flip Symmetry on the Performance of the
Simple GA — 67
B. Naudts and J. Naudts

Fitness Distance Correlation and Ridge Functions — 77
R.J. Quick, V.J. Rayward-Smith, and G.D. Smith

Accelerating the Convergence of Evolutionary Algorithms by
Fitness Landscape Approximation — 87
A. Ratle

Modeling Building-Block Interdependency — 97
R. A. Watson, G. S. Hornby, and J. B. Pollack

Noisy and Non-stationary Objective Functions

Mutate Large, But Inherit Small! On the Analysis of Rescaled
Mutations in $(\bar{1}, \bar{\lambda})$-ES with Noisy Fitness Data   109
H.-G. Beyer

Creating Robust Solutions by Means of Evolutionary Algorithms   119
J. Branke

Analytic Curve Detection from a Noisy Binary Edge Map Using
Genetic Algorithm   129
S. Chakraborty and K. Deb

A Comparison of Dominance Mechanisms and Simple Mutation
on Non-stationary Problems   139
J. Lewis, E. Hart, and G. Ritchie

Adaptation to a Changing Environment by Means of the Feedback
Thermodynamical Genetic Algorithm   149
N. Mori, H. Kita, and Y. Nishikawa

Optimization with Noisy Function Evaluations   159
V. Nissen and J. Propach

On Risky Methods for Local Selection under Noise   169
G. Rudolph

Polygenic Inheritance - A Haploid Scheme that Can Outperform
Diploidy   178
C. Ryan and J.J. Collins

Averaging Efficiently in the Presence of Noise   188
P. Stagge

Multi-criteria and Constrained Optimization

Solving Binary Constraint Satisfaction Problems Using
Evolutionary Algorithms with an Adaptive Fitness Function   201
A.E. Eiben, J.I. van Hemert, E. Marchiori, and A.G. Steenbeek

Varying Fitness Functions in Genetic Algorithms: Studying the
Rate of Increase of the Dynamic Penalty Terms   211
S. Kazarlis and V. Petridis

Landscape Changes and the Performance of Mapping Based
Constraint Handling Methods   221
D.G. Kim and P. Husbands

A Decoder-Based Evolutionary Algorithm for Constrained
Parameter Optimization Problems   231
S. Kozieł and Z. Michalewicz

A Spatial Predator-Prey Approach to Multi-objective
Optimization: A Preliminary Study   241
M. Laumanns, G. Rudolph, and H.-P. Schwefel

Selective Breeding in a Multiobjective Genetic Algorithm   250
G.T. Parks and I. Miller

Niching and Elitist Models for MOGAs   260
S. Obayashi, S. Takahashi, and Y. Takeguchi

Parallel Evolutionary Optimisation with Constraint Propagation 270
A. Ruiz-Andino, L. Araujo, J. Ruz, and F. Sáenz

Methods to Evolve Legal Phenotypes   280
T. Yu and P. Bentley

Multiobjective Optimization Using Evolutionary Algorithms –
A Comparative Case Study   292
E. Zitzler, L. Thiele

Representation Issues

Utilising Dynastically Optimal Forma Recombination in Hybrid
Genetic Algorithms   305
C. Cotta, E. Alba, and J.M. Troya

Further Experimentations on the Scalability of the GEMGA   315
H. Kargupta and S. Bandyopadhyay

Indexed Memory as a Generic Protocol for Handling Vectors of
Data in Genetic Programming   325
I.S. Lim and D. Thalmann

On Genetic Algorithms and Lindenmayer Systems   335
G. Ochoa

Genome Length as an Evolutionary Self-Adaptation   345
C.L. Ramsey, K.A. De Jong, J.J. Grefenstette, A.S. Wu, and D.S. Burke

Selection, Operators and Evolution Schemes

Restart Scheduling for Genetic Algorithms 357
A.S. Fukunaga

A Comparative Study of Global and Local Selection in Evolution
Strategies 367
M. Gorges-Schleuter

UEGO, an Abstract Niching Technique for Global Optimization 378
M. Jelasity

Development of Problem-Specific Evolutionary Algorithms 388
A. Leonhardi, W. Reissenberger, T. Schmelmer, K. Weicker,
and N. Weicker

The Effects of Control Parameters and Restarts on Search
Stagnation in Evolutionary Programming 398
K.E. Mathias, J.D. Schaffer, L.J. Eshelman, and M. Mani

Accelerating the Evolutionary-Gradient-Search Procedure:
Individual Step Sizes 408
R. Salomon

Extending Population-Based Incremental Learning to Continuous
Search Spaces 418
M. Sebag and A. Ducoulombier

Multi-parent Recombination in Genetic Algorithms with Search
Space Boundary Extension by Mirroring 428
S. Tsutsui

Selective Crossover in Genetic Algorithms: An Empirical Study 438
K. Vekaria and C. Clack

Line-Breeding Schemes for Combinatorial Optimization 448
R. Yang

Coevolution and Learning

Finding Regions of Uncertainty in Learned Models:
An Application to Face Detection 461
S. Baluja

On ZCS in Multi-agent Environments 471
L. Bull

Empirical Analysis of the Factors that Affect the Baldwin Effect 481
K.W.C. Ku and M.W. Mak

Promoting Generalization of Learned Behaviours in Genetic
Programming 491
I. Kuscu

Generalization in Wilson's Classifier System 501
P.L. Lanzi

Symbiotic Coevolution of Artificial Neural Networks and Training
Data Sets 511
H.A. Mayer

Information-Theoretic Analysis of a Mobile Agent's Learning in a
Discrete State Space 521
C. Pötter

The Coevolution of Antibodies for Concept Learning 530
M.A. Potter and K.A. De Jong

Does Data-Model Co-evolution Improve Generalization
Performance of Evolving Learners? 540
J.L. Shapiro

A Corporate Classifier System 550
A. Tomlinson and L. Bull

Applying Diffusion to a Cooperative Coevolutionary Model 560
R.P. Wiegand

Cellular Automata, Fuzzy Systems and Neural Networks

Studying Parallel Evolutionary Algorithms: The Cellular
Programming Case 573
M. Capcarrère, A. Tettamanzi, M. Tomassini, and M. Sipper

Learning to Avoid Moving Obstacles Optimally for Mobile Robots
Using a Genetic-Fuzzy Approach 583
K. Deb, D.K. Pratihar, and A. Ghosh

Evolutionary Neural Networks for Nonlinear Dynamics Modeling 593
I. De Falco, A. Iazzetta, P. Natale, and E. Tarantino

Hybrid Distributed Real-Coded Genetic Algorithms 603
F. Herrera, M. Lozano, and C. Moraga

Mechanisms of Emergent Computation in Cellular Automata   613
W. Hordijk, J.P. Crutchfield, and M. Mitchell

Towards Designing Neural Network Ensembles by Evolution   623
Y. Liu and X. Yao

Selection of Training Data for Neural Networks by a Genetic
Algorithm   633
C.R. Reeves and S.J. Taylor

Discovery with Genetic Algorithm Scheduling Strategies for
Cellular Automata   643
F. Seredyński

Simple + Parallel + Local = Cellular Computing   653
M. Sipper

Evolution, Learning and Speech Recognition in Changing
Acoustic Environments   663
A. Spalanzani and H. Kabré

Ant Colonies, Immune Systems, and Other Paradigms

Ant Colonies for Adaptive Routing in Packet-Switched
Communications Networks   673
G. Di Caro and M. Dorigo

The Stud GA: A Mini Revolution?   683
W. Khatib and P.J. Fleming

An Island Model Based Ant System with Lookahead for the
Shortest Supersequence Problem   692
R. Michel and M. Middendorf

Parameter-Free Genetic Algorithm Inspired by "Disparity Theory
of Evolution"   702
H. Sawai and S. Kizu

Immune Network Dynamics for Inductive Problem Solving   712
V. Slavov and N.I. Nikolaev

Parallelization Strategies for Ant Colony Optimization   722
Th. Stützle

Self-Organizing Pattern Formation: Fruit Flies and Cellular
Phones.   732
R. Tateson

Applications

TSP, Graphs and Satisfiability

A New Genetic Local Search Algorithm for Graph Coloring   745
R. Dorne and J.-K. Hao

Improving the Performance of Evolutionary Algorithms for the
Satisfiability Problem by Refining Functions   755
J. Gottlieb and N. Voss

Memetic Algorithms and the Fitness Landscape of the Graph
Bi-partitioning Problem   765
P. Merz and B. Freisleben

Investigating Evolutionary Approaches to Adaptive Database
Management Against Various Quality of Service Metrics   775
M.J. Oates and D. Corne

Genetic Algorithm Behavior in the MAXSAT Domain   785
S. Rana and D. Whitley

An Adaptive Mutation Scheme for a Penalty-Based Graph-
Colouring GA   795
P. Ross and E. Hart

Inver-over Operator for the TSP   803
G. Tao and Z. Michalewicz

Repair and Brood Selection in the Traveling Salesman Problem   813
T. Walters

The Traveling Salesrep Problem, Edge Assembly Crossover, and
2-opt   823
J.-P. Watson, C. Ross, V. Eisele, J. Denton, J. Bins, C. Guerra,
D. Whitley, and A. Howe

Scheduling, Partitioning and Packing

Load Balancing in Parallel Circuit Testing with Annealing-Based
and Genetic Algorithms   835
C. Gil, J. Ortega, A.F. Díaz, M.G. Montoya, and A. Prieto

A Heuristic Combination Method for Solving Job-Shop Scheduling
Problems   845
E. Hart and P. Ross

Reduction of Air Traffic Congestion by Genetic Algorithms   855
S. Oussedik and D. Delahaye

Timetabling the Classes of an Entire University with an
Evolutionary Algorithm   865
B. Paechter, R.C. Rankin, A. Cumming, and T.C. Fogarty

Genetic Algorithms for the Multiple Container Packing Problem   875
G.R. Raidl, and G. Kodydek

Buffer Memory Optimization in DSP Applications –
An Evolutionary Approach   885
J. Teich, E. Zitzler, and S. Bhattacharyya

Design and Telecommunications

The Breeder Genetic Algorithm for Frequency Assignment   897
C. Crisan and H. Mühlenbein

A Permutation Based Genetic Algorithm for Minimum Span
Frequency Assignment   907
C. Valenzuela, S. Hurley, and D. Smith

Comparison of Evolutionary Algorithms for Design Optimization   917
W. Jakob, M. Gorges-Schleuter, and I. Sieber

Aspects of Digital Evolution: Evolvability and Architecture   927
J.F. Miller and P. Thomson

Integrated Facility Design Using an Evolutionary Approach with
a Subordinate Network Algorithm   937
B.A. Norman, A.E. Smith, and R.A. Arapoglu

An Evolutionary Algorithm for Synthesizing Optical Thin-Film
Designs   947
J.-M. Yang and C.-Y. Kao

Model Estimations and Layout Problems

Implementing Genetic Algorithms with Sterical Constraints for
Protein Structure Prediction   959
E. Bindewald, J. Hesser, and R. Männer

Optimal Placements of Flexible Objects:. An Adaptive Simulated
Annealing Approach   968
S.K. Cheung, K.S. Leung, A. Albrecht, and C.K. Wong

Encapsulated Evolution Strategies for the Determination of
Group Contribution Model Parameters in Order to Predict
Thermodynamic Properties   978
H. Geyer, P. Ulbig, and S. Schulz

Recombination Operators for Evolutionary Graph Drawing   988
D. Kobler and A.G B. Tettamanzi

Optimisation of Density Estimation Models with Evolutionary
Algorithms   998
M. Kreutz, A.M. Reimetz, B. Sendhoff, C. Weihs, and W. von Seelen

Genetic Algorithm in Parameter Estimation of Nonlinear
Dynamic Systems   1008
E. Paterakis, V. Petridis, and A. Kehagias

Optimizing Web Page Layout Using an Annealed Genetic
Algorithm as Client-Side Script   1018
J. González Peñalver and J. J. Merelo

Solving the Capacitor Placement Problem in a Radial Distribution
System Using an Adaptive Genetic Algorithm   1028
K. Hatta, M. Suzuki, S. Wakabayashi, and T. Koide

Author Index   1039

Convergence Theory

Modelling Genetic Algorithms:
From Markov Chains to Dependence
with Complete Connections

Alexandru Agapie

Computational Intelligence Lab., National Institute of Microtechnology
PO Box 38-160, 72225, Bucharest, Romania
E-mail: agapie@oblio.imt.pub.ro

Abstract. The paper deals with homogeneous stochastic models of the binary, finite-population Genetic Algorithm. Previous research brought the Markov chain analysis up to sufficient convergence conditions for the elitist case. In addition, we point out a condition that is both necessary and sufficient, for the general case convergence. Next, we present an example of algorithm, which is globally convergent yet not elitist. Considering this type of Markov chain analysis reached its end, we indicate another type of random systems - *with complete connections* - promising better results in real Genetic Algorithms modelling.

1 Introduction

Genetic algorithms (GAs) are probabilistic techniques for optimization [1], operating on populations of strings (called *chromosomes*) coded to represent some underlying parameter set. Some operators, called *selection, crossover* and *mutation* are applied to successive generations of chromosomes to create new, better-valued populations.

Several studies explored the GA convergence from different perspectives. When the schema theorem - established in [8], and consecutively revised [22] - proved to be insufficient for analyzing the GA, most of the theoretical approaches moved onto the convergence theorems of stochastic processes, and especially to the ergodic theorems from Markov chain theory. Mostly, the attempts were concerning the theory of finite, homogenous Markov chains [1, 2, 4-7, 9, 15-17, 22-24], but they evolved also to the study of infinite [18], or inhomogeneous models [1, 4, 5]. Additionally, some work built on basic probabilities [1, 5] - or even on the Banach fixpoint theorem [13]. The Markov chain models vary from the *simple* GA [6, 7, 15], to *elitist* [2, 16], *adaptive* [4, 9], and even *hybrid* GA [24].

Basically, the research performed up to this moment was looking for sufficient convergence conditions, only - except [17], where a necessary condition was pointed out for the elitist GA. The aim of the present analysis is to provide a condition, both necessary and sufficient, for the GA convergence.

---

[1] The optimization task is assumed to be *maximization*, all over the paper

Modelling the GA as a finite, homogenous Markov chain, Sect.2 proves that the GA convergence is equivalent to the condition below.

> *Each Sub-Optimal state is INessential*   *(SO-IN)*

This means that each sub-optimal state leads to a "one way" path, at least. We notice that (SO-IN) is equivalent to:

> *Each ESsential state is Optimal*   *(ES-O)*

The convergence is assumed to be *regardless of the initial population*. According to this equivalence result, one has to design a GA for which (SO-IN) holds and the convergence is assured. Vice versa, if a GA model does not satisfy (SO-IN), there is no theoretical support for its convergence regardless of initialization. Nevertheless, the convergence may occur on practical problems and particular initial populations.

Section 3 consolidates the analysis by showing how (SO-IN) appears as a consequence - even if not explicitly stressed - of the convergence results from [1, 5], [13] and [17]. Therefore, all the central theorems from those papers appear to provide sufficient, yet not necessary convergence conditions. In this regard, the analysis performed below is unifying in content and simplifying in form.

Section 4 emphasizes the generality of the (SO-IN) condition, by making the difference between the general case convergence (introduced in this paper) and the elitist case convergence introduced in [16] and successively revised in [17] and [2]. Actually, this section provides a positive answer to the justified question: *Is it possible to obtain global convergence without elitism?*

Section 5 presents the concept of *random systems with complete connections*, as introduced in [12] and gives a hint of the way they can be applied to GA modelling. A critique of the analysis completes the paper.

2 GA Convergence - Equivalent Condition

This study adopts the following formalism:

- The optimization task is: max $\{f(x) \mid x \in \{0,1\}^l\}$, where f, the *fitness function*, satisfies $f(x) > 0 \ \forall x$.
- The current GA consists of an n-tuple (called *population*) of binary strings (*chromosomes*), each of them of length l. The transition between successive populations is performed by applying the genetic operators of *crossover, mutation* and *selection*; crossover and mutation are applied with some probabilities - p_c, resp. p_m - which are considered fixed all over the algorithm, in the homogenous case. No other restrictions are imposed to these operators within this section.
- The k chromosome from population i at time t can be accessed by the projection function, $\pi_k^t(i)$.

- The Markov chain's state space (denoted S) is finite, containing all the possible populations of chromosomes. In this regard, the GA may be seen as a stochastic process $\{X_t\}_{t \geq 0}$ - where X_t is the random variable corresponding to the GA population at time t. Considering populations and not single chromosomes as states in the Markov chain model is a fundamental assumption for the GA analysis - similar models are presented in [2, 4, 15 - 17, 23, 24]. The Markov chain matrix is the square, non-negative, stochastic matrix of transition probabilities between states. The model is assumed to be homogenous, *i.e.* the transition matrix is time independent.

Next, let us recall some definitions and results from the theory of non-negative matrices and Markov chains.

Definition 1 (*State classification in Markov chains*). a. A non-negative matrix $A = (aij)_{i,j=1,\ldots,n}$ is said to be stochastic if $\sum_{j=1}^{n} a_{ij} = 1$, for each $i = 1, \ldots, n$.

b. Let i and j be two states from a Markov chain with stochastic transition matrix P. We say that i *leads to* j (write $i \to j$) if there is a chain of states $(i, i_1, i_2, \ldots, i_k, j)$ s.t. $p_{i,i_1} p_{i_1,i_2} \ldots p_{i_k,j} > 0$. Equivalently: there is an integer t s.t. the (i, j) element from P^t - denoted p_{ij}^t - is positive.

c. A state i is said to be *essential* if $j \to i$, for each j satisfying $i \to j$. Otherwise, (*i.e.* if there exists some j s.t. $i \to j$ but $j \not\to i$) i is said to be *inessential*.

d. A state i is said to be *absorbing* if $p_{ii} = 1$.

e. A square matrix $P = (aij)_{i,j=1,\ldots,n}$ is said to be *irreducible* if for each pair of states $i, j \leq n$ there exists an integer t s.t. $p_{ij}^t > 0$. Equivalently, P is *irreducible* if $i \to j$ for each pair (i, j). Otherwise P is said to be *reducible* (see [19, p. 12, 18] for Definition 1.a-e).

f. A state i is said to be *recurrent* if the probability of returning to i infinitely often is 1. If the probability of returning infinitely often is 0, the state is said to be *transient*.(see [11, p.88] for this definition).

g. A state i is said to be *optimal* (for the GA problem) if the corresponding population contains (at least) one global-optimal chromosome. Otherwise, i is said to be *sub-optimal*.

Lemma 2. *A state is recurrent if and only if it is essential. Equivalently: a state is transient if and only if it is inessential.*

Definition 3 (*GA convergence*). a. Let $Z_t = \max\{f(\pi_k^t(i)), k = 1, \cdots, n\}$ be a sequence of random variables representing the best fitness within a population represented by state i at time t. The GA *converges* to the global optimum if $\lim_{t \to \infty} P\{Z_t = f^*\} = 1$, where $f^* = \max\{f(x)|x \in \{0,1\}^l\}$ is the global optimum of the problem.

b. Additionally, the convergence is *regardless of initialization* if the choice of the initial population (initial distribution of the Markov chain) does not affect the limit behavior.

Theorem 4 ([19], p.16). *There is at least one essential state in each Markov chain.*

Theorem 5 ([19], p.120). *Let P be the transition matrix of a Markov chain containing at least one inessential state, let Q be the square sub-matrix of P associated to the (transitions between the) inessential states and let T be the square sub-matrix associated to the essential states: $P = \begin{pmatrix} T & 0 \\ R & Q \end{pmatrix}$. Then the following holds: $Q^t \to 0$, geometrically fast, as $t \to \infty$.*

Considering the GA modeled by a Markov chain with state space S in the previous manner, now we are able to introduce the equivalence condition - the central issue of this analysis:

Theorem 6. *The GA is convergent regardless of initialization if and only if i is Sub-Optimal $\Rightarrow i$ is INessential , for all $i \in S$*   *(SO-IN)*

Proof. The proof we present below relies on the equivalence *recurrent - essential*, for the states of the Markov chain.

Recall -from Markov chain theory - that recurrence is a class property, so one can partition the state space of the Markov chain into two non-overlapping sets: the recurrent set (which may consist of several disjoint, closed classes) and the transient set. The chain can pass from the transient set of states to the recurrent one, but **not** vice versa.

So, each initial population of the GA is either transient or recurrent. If it is transient, the population will finally enter some recurrent class. Therefore, we need only consider the properties of the recurrent classes. Since it is generally open in which recurrent class the population will be trapped, the desired property must be present in each recurrent class. So, which property is desired for convergence?

Let the GA be in some recurrent class (which cannot be left).

(a) Assume each state is optimal. Trivially, we obtain convergence to the optimum.
(b) Assume there exist non-optimal states. Since the Markov chain visits every recurrent state of this class infinitely often, it will also visit the non-optimal states infinitely often. As a consequence, the sequence of the best objective function value will oscillate such that convergence is excluded.

Summing up: Global convergence if and only if each recurrent state is optimal, which - according to Lemma 2 is equivalent to (ES-O) and to (SO-IN).

3 Application of the Equivalence Condition

Theorem 6 from the previous section provides a necessary and sufficient condition for the GA's convergence to global-optimum, regardless of the initial population. At this point, it would be interesting to make the connection to other convergence results in the GA's literature, and to prove that (SO-IN) is satisfied by the sufficient conditions introduced in those papers. This is our next goal, which will be detailed by separately analyzing the papers [1, 5], [13] and [17].

3.1 Application to [1, 5]

Let us recall first the general convergence theorem for genetic algorithms, as it appears in [1].

Theorem 7 (*Theorem 2 - from [1] or [5]*). *Let $x \in S_a$ and the following conditions be satisfied:*

a) $\{X_n : n \in N\}_x$ *is monotone, and*
b) $\{X_n : n \in N\}_x$ *is homogenous, and*
c) *for every* $y \in \{\bar{x}\}$ *there exists at least one accessible optimum.*

Then $\{X_n : n \in N\}_x$ *surely reaches an optimum.*

Where

- $\{X_n : n \in N\}_x$ *stands for a Markov chain starting from state* x *(i.e.* $P\{X_0 = x\} = 1$*),*
- S_a *stands for the set of all possible populations of size* a*,*
- $\{\bar{x}\}$ *stands for the set of all states* j *s.t.* $x \to j$*,*
- $\{X_n : n \in N\}_x$ *surely reaches an optimum* $\Leftrightarrow$ *Definition 3.a, Sect.2 (this equivalence is proved in Lemma 4 from [1]),*
- *the optimization task in [1] is assumed to be minimization - this yields minor changes to definitions and theorems, only.*

One will see in the following how the hypothesis from Theorem 7 imply the (SO-IN) condition from Theorem 6.

Theorem 8. *Let* $x \in S_a$ *and the conditions (a), (b) and (c) from Theorem 7 be satisfied. Then (SO-IN) holds.*

Proof. Let y be a sub-optimal state, s.t. $y \in \{\bar{x}\}$. Notice that $y \in \{\bar{x}\}$ corresponds to the only situation we concern, as long as the chain starts from x.

By *(c)*, there exists an optimal state z s.t. $z \in \{\bar{y}\}$, thus $y \to z$. As y is sub-optimal, the following holds: $f(y) < f(z)$, where f denotes the fitness function (and we revert to a maximization task, for convenience). From (a) we obtain $z \not\to y$, thus y is inessential.

3.2 Application to [13]

In [13], a *Contractive Mapping GA* (CM-GA) is introduced. Imposing the CM-GA to fit the hypothesis from Banach fixpoint theorem, the author builds the model on a very strong (yet not so well stated, and not explicitly presented) assumption:

*Let the CM-GA be in the sub-optimal state i, at generation t. At least one state j exists, s.t. $f(i) < f(j)$ and $i \to j$ **in one step** (this is, in the Markov chains' formalism: $p_{ij} > 0$). Supplementary, the probability of choosing such a state j is one. (A)*

In short, [13] shows that the CM-GA satisfies the assumptions of Banach fixpoint theorem and consequently the algorithm converges to a population P^*, which is a unique fixed point in the space of all populations. Moreover, P^* is filled with copies of the same (global) optimal value, and the convergence is regardless of initialization. One must notice that assumption (A) is stronger than assumptions *(a)-(c)* from Sect.3.1, and than the elitist assumption from Sect.3.2.

Let us make the connection between the CM-GA and our (SO-IN) condition.

Theorem 9. *The Contractive Mapping GA satisfies (SO-IN).*

Proof. Let i be a sub-optimal population. By condition *(A)*, the i-th row from the transition matrix must have the following form: $p_{ij} > 0$ for states j with $f(i) < f(j)$; $p_{ik} = 0$ for all the other states k.

Obviously, this implies $i \to j$, but $j \not\to i$ and (SO-IN) is satisfied.

3.3 Application to [17]

In [17], the results that can be related to this analysis are the convergence theorems in *Binary Search Space - pp. 81-157*. Even if those theorems concern a larger class of algorithms (namely Evolutionary Algorithms (EA) - which include GA as a particular class), one can easily prove that (SO-IN)is still consistent for the EA Markov chain model. Moreover, (SO-IN) appears explicitly as a sufficient convergence condition, as in the following:

Theorem 10 ([17], p.119). *If the transition matrix of the EA is reducible and the set of recurrent states is a subset of X^* (the set of optimal states), then the EA converges to optimum, regardless of the initial distribution.*

Theorem 11 ([17], p.85). *Let (X_t) be a homogenous finite Markov chain generated by some elitist EA. If for each $i \in S$ there exists a finite constant t_0 that may depend on state $i \in S$ such that $P(X_{t_0} \in X^*/X_0 = i) > 0$, then X_t converges to optimum, regardless of the initial distribution.*

Actually, the underlined condition implies $i \to j$, for i sub-optimal and j optimal, while the elitism makes sure there is no way back ($j \not\to i$). Thus, again, (SO-IN).

We must acknowledge the fact that (SO-IN) was also pointed out as a necessary convergence condition, [17, p.85], but for the elitist EA only. Actually, the reasoning from [17] can be seen as an intrinsic part of Theorem 6 above, while our analysis proved that (SO-IN) is an equivalent condition for the convergence of the general algorithm, imposing no restriction like *elitism*. Nevertheless, elitist evolutionary algorithms constitute a very important class of optimization algorithms, extensively used in practice, and - as all this analysis witnesses - a major source of theoretical developments.

4 Is it Possible to Obtain Convergence without Elitism? Yes, it is

In order to make the difference between our convergence approach and the classical elitist case - presented by Rudolph in [16-17], we should provide at least one algorithm, which is convergent but not elitist. Consider the so-called *threshold acceptance algorithm*:

$$X(k+1) = \begin{cases} X(k) + Z(k) \text{ if} f(X(k) + Z(k)) \le f(X(k)) + T \\ X(k) \qquad\qquad\qquad \text{otherwise} \end{cases}$$

where threshold $T > 0$ (we are minimizing here!) and $Z(k)$ is a binary random vector.

Let $|x|$ denote the number of *ones* in bit string x (which is considered to be of length 10). The objective function is the following:

$|x|$	0	1	2	3	4	5	6	7	8	9	10
$f(x)$	3.0	1.0	3.0	2.1	2.4	2.3	2.9	2.5	2.2	2.1	2.8

One can notice that there exist 10 optimal bit strings with $|x| = 1$. The threshold algorithm is not elitist in the classical sense (worse solutions are accepted!).

The Markov chain associated to this algorithm and f and $T = 1$ has only one recurrent class and one transient class. All recurrent states are optimal; thus, we can get global convergence without elitism.

Next, one can use the threshold acceptance algorithm as the selection procedure for a GA (or, more generally, for any type of evolutionary algorithm - as one can easily notice that the whole convergence analysis presented above remains consistent for any finite-space probabilistic optimization algorithm). Assuming that condition (SO-IN) still holds after incorporating mutation and crossover into the algorithm (which is easy to prove by a "matrix product" type reasoning, similar to those performed in [2] or [16]), we obtain a GA which is convergent but not elitist.

5 Dependence with Complete Connections

We state that Markov chains cannot provide any fruitful results from this point further - confining this claim to finite state time-homogeneous Markov chains and to the limit behavior of GAs associated to those Markov chains. This comes for the following reasons:

1. The homogeneous model is not able to avoid stagnation of practical GA in sub-optimal points.
2. The inhomogeneous model is able to avoid stagnation but it does not know how to do it (without additional on-line help from the GA user).

At a closer look, one will see these deficits originating from the very definition of the Markov chain: the transition to position j at time $n+1$ is conditioned by the chain's position at time n, alone. Referring to our GA, this means that evolution from a population to another is conditioned only by the current population - in the homogeneous case, with the unpredictable (thus useless) aid of time changing the transition matrix - in the inhomogeneous case. Obviously, such a model offers too less information for avoiding stagnation in sub-optimal points. Making a step further in the theory of stochastic processes, we propose the use of *random systems with complete connections*, a non-trivial extension of Markovian dependence taking into account not only the last experience, but also the whole process' evolution.

Definition 12 ([12], p.5). A random system with complete connections (RSCC for short) is a quadruple $\{(W, W), (X, X), u, P\}$, where

(i) (W, W) and (X, X) are arbitrary measurable spaces;
(ii) $u : W \times X \to W$ is a $(W \otimes X, W)$ measurable map;
(iii) P is a transition probability function from (W, W) to (X, X).

In our case, X should be the set of all possible GA populations and W the set of probability vectors of a *certain* length (for example l - the chromosome length). Two sequences of random variables $(\zeta_n)_{n \in N}$ and $(\xi_n)_{n \in N}$ are associated with the RSCC. The variable ζ_{n-1} is the (random) probability vector according to which we select a population at time n, while ξ_n is the population itself, so that:

$$\zeta_n = u_{n-1}(\zeta_{n-1}, \xi_n), n \in N^*$$

$$P(\xi_1 = i | \zeta_0) = P(\zeta_0, i)$$

$$P(\xi_{n+1} = i | \xi_n, \zeta_n, \cdots, \xi_1, \zeta_1, \zeta_0) = P(\zeta_n, i)$$

We state that the RSCC can be used in modelling a "smarter" GA - an algorithm able to avoid tracking in sub-optimal points by redirecting the search in case of stagnation. At this point of our research, the key-problem seems to be the definition of function u. Next, it would be interesting to find whether condition SO-IN is equivalent to convergence, or not (under some special assumptions permitting a state classification for the RSCC, of course).

Conclusions

Basically, the research performed up to this moment on the GA convergence was either:

- looking for better theoretical models, better fitting the practical GA, or
- looking for sufficient convergence conditions.

With respect to the theory of finite, homogeneous Markov chains, we proved that convergence is equivalent to the following condition: *each sub-optimal state is inessential (SO-IN)*. This is, each sub-optimal state must lead to a "one way" path, at least.

The most interesting part of our analysis proved to be the *necessity* implication; by this result, a further convergence research on special GA models should verify if condition (SO-IN) is fulfilled, instead of dealing with ergodic theorems from Markov chain theory.

A survey of some *sufficient* conditions from GA literature was performed in Sect.3, now from a new prospect. This analysis was instructive, showing how (SO-IN) was more or less hidden in all the previous convergence theorems (for finite, homogeneous GA models). It could be no other way, as the condition is *necessary*. An example of algorithm which enlightens the subtle difference between elitism and (SO-IN) convergence is provided in Sect.4.

Two generalizations seem to be of interest at this point: for the inhomogeneous model and for other types of evolutionary algorithms, following [17].

However, the convergence theorem proposed in this paper shows the same deficit as most of the previous theoretical results in the area: *it is too general*. This occurs, for it does not use the particular form of *crossover*, *mutation* and *selection*. Practically, it makes no difference between elitist genetic algorithms and, e.g., elitist *random walk*. Both are convergent, regardless of initialization, under these circumstances. And this is not the practical situation, where GAs perform better. Consequently, the further analysis must withdraw the hopeless goal of generality, facing the recent *no free lunch theorem* [25] and other attempts *raising theoretical questions on the utility of GAs* [20].

Nevertheless, some important steps in this direction have been already made - e.g., in [3] and [14] the time complexity of reaching the optimal point is considered, while in [17] topics like *convergence rates* and *special problem classes* are analyzed.

Another promising tool in modelling GAs seem to be the *random system with complete connections* [12] - a model taking into account the whole evolution, not only the last generation. This analysis is still in work.

Acknowledgements

The author would like to thank Marc Schoenauer and reviewer 129 for providing some important references in Markov chain modelling of GA - hence opening the way for further results and comparisons on the convergence matter. A very special debt is owed to reviewer 85, for providing the present proof of Theorem 6 (considerably shorter than its first version) and also for providing the threshold acceptance algorithm (Sec.3), raising in this way the value of the entire approach.

References

1. Aarts, E.H.L., Eiben, A.E., Van Hee, K.M.: A General Theory of Genetic Algorithms. Computing Science Notes, Eindhoven University of Technology, (1989)

2. Agapie, A.: Genetic Algorithms: Minimal Conditions for Convergence. LNCS series **1363**, Artificial Evolution, Springer (1998) 183–193.

3. Bäck, T.: The interaction of mutation rate, selection, and self-adaptation within a genetic algorithm. PPSN 2, Amsterdam: North Holland (1992) 85–94

4. Davis, T.E., Principe, J.C.: A Markov Chain Framework for the Simple Genetic Algorithm. Evol. Comp. **1**, Vol. 3 (1993) 269–288

5. Eiben, A.E., Aarts, E.H.L, Van Hee, K.M.: Global Convergence of Genetic Algorithms: a Markov Chain Analysis. PPSN 1, Springer, Berlin (1990) 4–12

6. Fogel, D.B.: Evolutionary Computation - Toward a New Philosophy of Machine Intelligence. IEEE Press (1995) 121–143

7. Goldberg, D.E., Segrest, P.: Finite Markov chain analysis of genetic algortihms. Proc. ICGA '87 (1987) 1–8

8. Holland, J.H.: Adaptation in natural and artificial systems. Ann. Arbor, The Univ. of Michigan Press (1975)

9. Horn, J.: Finite Markov Chain Analysis of Genetic Algorithms with Niching. Proc. ICGA '93 (1993) 110–117

10. Iosifescu, M.: Finite Markov chains and applications. Techn. Publ., Bucharest, (1977)

11. Iosifescu, M.: Finite Markov Processes and Their Applications. Chichester: Wiley (1980)

12. Iosifescu, M., Grigorescu, S.: Dependence with complete connections and its applications. Cambridge Univ. Press (1990)

13. Michalewicz, Z.: Genetic Algorithms + Data Structures = Evolution Programs. 2nd ed., Springer-Verlag (1994) 64–69

14. Muehlenbein, H.: How genetic algorithms really work I: Mutation and hillclimbing. PPSN 2, Amsterdam: North Holland (1992) 15–25

15. Nix, A.E., Vose, M.D.: Modelling genetic algorithms with Markov chains. Ann. Math. and AI **5** (1992) 79–88

16. Rudolph, G.: Convergence Analysis of Canonical Genetic Algorithms. IEEE Tr. on NN. 1, Vol. 5 (1994) 98–101

17. Rudolph, G.: Convergence Properties of Evolutionary Algorithms. Verlag Kovac, Hamburg (1997)

18. Qi, X., Palmieri, F.: Theoretical Analysis of Evolutionary Algorithms, I-II. IEEE Tr. on NN. 1, Vol. 5 (1994) 102–129

19. Seneta, E.: Non-negative Matrices and Markov Chains. 2nd ed. Springer, New York (1981)

20. Salomon, R.: Raising Theoretical Questions about the Utility of Genetic Algorithms. Proc. EP '97, LNCS Series, Springer (1997) 275–284

21. Suzuki, J.: A Markov Chain Analysis of a Genetic Algorithm. Proc. ICGA'93, Urbana Illinois, Morgan Kaufmann (1993) 46–153 bibitem22 Uesaka, Y.: Convergence of algorithm and the schema theorem in genetic algorithms Proc. ICANGA (1995) 210–213

22. Vose, M.D.: Modelling Simple Genetic Algorithms. Foundations of Genetic Algorithms II, San Mateo, CA: Morgan Kaufmann (1993) 63–73

23. Whitley, D.: Modelling Hybrid Genetic Algorithms. Genetic Algorithms in Engineering and Computer Science, Wiley (1995) 191–201

24. Wolpert D., Macready, W.: No Free Lunch Theorems for Optimization. IEEE Tr. on EC. 1, Vol. 1 (1997) 67–82

On the Optimization of Unimodal Functions with the (1 + 1) Evolutionary Algorithm⋆

Stefan Droste, Thomas Jansen, and Ingo Wegener

FB Informatik, LS 2, Univ. Dortmund, 44221 Dortmund, Germany
droste, jansen, wegener@ls2.cs.uni-dortmund.de

Abstract. We investigate the expected running time of the (1 + 1) EA, a very simple Evolutionary Algorithm, on the class of unimodal fitness functions with Boolean inputs. We analyze the behavior on a generalized version of long paths [6, 10] and prove an exponential lower bound on the expected running time. Thereby we show that unimodal functions can be very difficult to be optimized for the (1 + 1) EA. Furthermore, we prove that a little modification in the selection method can lead to huge changes in the expected running time.

1 Introduction

Evolutionary Algorithms are a class of search algorithms that comprises Evolution Strategies [9, 12], Evolutionary Programming [2], Genetic Algorithms [5, 3], and Genetic Programming [7]. Often these general search methods are used for the optimization of static objective functions. Evolutionary Algorithms are typically applied to problems that at least appear to be difficult and have not been subject to intense research, yet. Most research in this area is led by strongly practical interests, so only a few results concerning the expected performance of Evolutionary Algorithms, that have been gained by theoretical analysis rather than experimental practice, are known. In order to make first steps towards a unified theory of expected performance of Evolutionary Algorithms used for function optimization, it is reasonable to investigate the properties of a Evolutionary Algorithm, that is kept as simple as possible. This approach leads to the so called (1 + 1) Evolutionary Algorithm ((1 + 1) EA), that is applied to Boolean fitness functions $f : \{0,1\}^n \to \mathbb{R}$ and can be formally described as follows, assuming that maximization of f is our objective.

Algorithm 1. 1. Set $p_m := 1/n$.
2. Choose randomly an initial bit string $x \in \{0, 1\}^n$.
3. Repeat the following mutation step: Compute x' by flipping independently each bit x_i with probability p_m. Replace x by x' iff $f(x') \geq f(x)$.

⋆ This work was supported by the Deutsche Forschungsgemeinschaft (DFG) as part of the Collaborative Research Center "Computational Intelligence" (531).

This algorithm combines a binary representation and bitwise mutation with a fixed mutation rate, both typical for GAs, with the $(1 + 1)$-selection method from ESs. As Rudolph [10] we consider it to be the most simple EA and adopt his term "$(1 + 1)$ EA" for it. The $(1 + 1)$ EA has been subject to various studies, see, e.g., [1, 6, 8, 10]. One cannot expect that a single optimization algorithm can find a global optimum efficiently on all fitness functions [14]. So it is reasonable to concentrate on some class of functions and try to find upper and lower bounds on the expected running time of the $(1 + 1)$ EA, i.e., the expected number of evaluations of f.

Since it is quite easy to construct functions that are difficult for this simple algorithm one is more interested in identifying function classes that can be optimized efficiently by the $(1 + 1)$ EA. A class of functions that the $(1 + 1)$ EA optimizes easily are linear functions, i.e., functions $f : \{0, 1\}^n \to \mathbb{R}$ that can be written as $f(x) = \sum_{i=1}^{n} g_i(x_i)$. The expected number of steps until the $(1 + 1)$ EA finds a global optimum of a linear function f is $O(n \ln n)$, if the mutation rate p_m is $\Theta(1/n)$ [1]. Since $p_m = 1/n$ is the most common choice for the constant mutation rate and is vital for the success of the $(1 + 1)$ EA on linear functions, we stick to this choice.

A larger class of functions, that contains the class of linear functions, that depend essentially on all variables as a proper subclass, are unimodal functions. Since we consider Boolean fitness functions, it is not totally obvious, how "unimodal" should be defined. In fact, different definitions can be found in the literature yielding quite different classes of functions. For a definition of unimodality one needs some notion of neighborhood. We use Hamming distances to define our neighborhood and therefore consider the following definition to be the most natural one.

Definition 2. For two bit strings $x, y \in \{0, 1\}^n$ we define the *Hamming distance* of x and y by $H(x, y) := \sum_{i=1}^{n} |x_i - y_i|$.

Let $f : \{0, 1\}^n \to \mathbb{R}$ be a fitness function. We call $x \in \{0, 1\}^n$ a *local maximum*, iff $\forall y \in \{0, 1\}^n : H(x, y) = 1 \Rightarrow f(x) \geq f(y)$. The function f is *unimodal*, iff f has exactly one local maximum.

2 First Intuitions

The definition of unimodal functions implies, that for all $x \in \{0, 1\}^n$ different from the global optimum there is always another point with Hamming distance 1 and greater fitness. So there is always a mutation of exactly one bit that improves the function value. Since linear functions, that depend essentially on all variables, are unimodal, this holds for such linear functions, too. It is this property, that is usually exploited in the analysis of the expected running time of the $(1 + 1)$ EA on simple linear functions. This leads Mühlenbein [8], who carries out such an analysis for the linear function $\text{ONEMAX} = \sum_{i=1}^{n} x_i$, to the remark, that all unimodal functions can be optimized by the $(1 + 1)$ EA in expected $O(n \log n)$ steps.

At first sight it is obvious, that the expected running time of the $(1 + 1)$ EA on a unimodal function with k different function values is $O(kn)$. Either the current bit string x is the global optimum, or a bit string y with Hamming distance 1 to x exists, that has greater fitness. Since the probability for a mutation from x to y equals $n^{-1}(1 - 1/n)^{n-1}$, the expected number of steps, until y or another bit string with function value greater than $f(x)$ is reached, is bounded above by $\exp(1)n$. But a unimodal function may have 2^n different function values, so it is not clear whether a general upper bound of $O(n \ln n)$ holds.

In fact, Rudolph [10] doubts that such an upper bound is valid. He introduces the function LEADINGONES : $\{0, 1\}^n \to \mathbb{R}$ with

$$\text{LEADINGONES}(x) := \sum_{i=1}^{n} \prod_{j=1}^{i} x_i,$$

that counts the number of leading ones in x. He proves an upper bound of $O(n^2)$ and presents experiments that indicate a lower bound of $\Omega(n^2)$. Indeed, a bound of $\Theta(n^2)$ can be formally proven, though we omit the proof here.

If $f : \{0, 1\}^n \to \mathbb{R}$ is unimodal, then for any $x_0 \in \{0, 1\}^n$ there is always a sequence of points $(x_0, x_1, \ldots, x_l)$, such that $H(x_i, x_{i+1}) = 1$ and $f(x_i) < f(x_{i+1})$ hold for all i with $0 \le i < l$ and x_l is the global optimum. We call such a sequence of points a *path*. If we seek unimodal functions, such that the $(1 + 1)$ EA has large expected running times, we have to find functions, where many bit strings only have long paths to the optimum. According to this understanding Horn, Goldberg, and Deb [6] define long path functions, where many points only have exponential long paths to the global optimum. They perform several experiments on such long paths and are confirmed to observe exponential running times for the $(1 + 1)$ EA. Höhn and Reeves [4] carry out analytical investigations and, finally, Rudolph [11] proves that the expected running time of the $(1 + 1)$ EA on these long paths is $O(n^3)$. The problem is, that though exponentially many mutations of exactly one mutating bit are needed to reach the optimum, only a small polynomial number of mutations of exactly two simultaneously mutating bits is sufficient for optimization. Since the expected time until a mutation of k bits flipping simultaneously occurs is $O(n^k)$, it is necessary, that for sufficiently many bit strings no polynomial number of mutations with a constant number of bits flipping simultaneously can lead to the optimum, if we want to have an exponentially lower bounded running time. A generalization of long paths, informally described in [6] and formally defined in [10], can achieve this and therefore is a candidate for being a hard fitness function for the $(1 + 1)$ EA. We prove an exponential lower bound on such long path functions now.

3 A Unimodal Function With Exponential Expected Running Time

Rudolph [10] formally defines a more general version of long paths (already informally described by Horn, Goldberg, and Deb [6]), such that no mutation of at most k bits is sufficient to take a short cut. These paths are called long k-paths. The parameter k can be chosen, though with increasing k the length of the path decreases. We start with defining long k-paths and a few simple statements about them, that are taken from [10].

Definition 3. Let $n \geq 1$ hold. For all $k > 1$, that fulfill $(n-1)/k \in \mathbb{N}$, the long k-path of dimension n is a sequence of bit strings from $\{0,1\}^n$. The long k-path of dimension 1 is defined as $P_1^k := (0,1)$. The long k-path of dimension n is defined using the long k-path of dimension $n-k$ as basis as follows. Let the long k-path of dimension $n-k$ be given by $P_{n-k}^k = (v_1, \ldots, v_l)$. Then we define the sequences of bit strings S_0, B_n, and S_1 from $\{0,1\}^n$, where $S_0 := (0^k v_1, 0^k v_2, \ldots, 0^k v_l)$, $S_1 := (1^k v_l, 1^k v_{l-1}, \ldots, 1^k v_1)$, and $B_n := (0^{k-1}1 v_l, 0^{k-2}11 v_l, \ldots, 01^{k-1} v_l)$. The points in B_n build a bridge between the points in S_0 and S_1, that differ in the k leading bits. Therefore, the points in B_n are called *bridge points*. The resulting long k-path P_n^k is constructed by appending S_0, B_n, and S_1, so P_n^k is a sequence of $|P_n^k| = |S_0| + |B_n| + |S_1|$ points. We call $|P_n^k|$ the length of P_n^k. The i-th point on the path P_n^k is denoted as p_i, p_{i+j} is called the j-th successor of p_i.

The recursive definition of long k-paths allows us to determine the length of the paths easily. A proof of the following lemma can be found in [10].

Lemma 4. *The long k-path of dimension n has length $|P_n^k| = (k+1)2^{(n-1)/k} - k + 1$. All points of the path are different.*

The most important property of long k-paths are the regular rules, that hold for the Hamming distances between each point and its successors.

Lemma 5. *Let n and k be given, such that the long k-path P_n^k is well defined. For all i with $0 < i < k$ the following holds. If $x \in P_n^k$ has at least i different successors on the path, then the i-th successor of x has Hamming distance i of x and all other points on the path, that are successors of x, have Hamming distances different from i.*

We omit the lengthy proof, that can be carried out via induction without any difficulties. We are interested in unimodal fitness functions, so for a fitness function $f : \{0,1\}^n \to \mathbb{R}$ exactly 2^n function values have to be defined. Since the long k-path of dimension n consists of only $(k+1)2^{(n-1)/k} - k + 1$ points, we have to embed this path in a unimodal function. The following definition differs from the one given in [10] in the way, that bit strings not belonging to the long k-path are treated. This little modification helps us to establish the lower bound, while it does not matter for the upper bounds, that were already given by Rudolph.

Definition 6. Let $n \geq 1$ hold, let $k > 1$ be given, such that k fulfills $(n-1)/k \in \mathbb{N}$. The long k-path function of dimension n is called $\text{PATH}_k : \{0,1\}^n \to \mathbb{N}$ and is defined by

$$\text{PATH}_k(x) = \begin{cases} n^2 + l & \text{if } x \text{ is the } l\text{-th point of } P_n^k \\ n^2 - n\sum_{i=1}^k x_i - \sum_{i=k+1}^n x_i & \text{if } x \notin P_n^k \end{cases}.$$

We have already mentioned, that a fitness function f is unimodal, iff for all points $x \in \{0,1\}^n$ we have, that either x is the global maximum or there exists $y \in \{0,1\}^n$ with $H(x,y) = 1$, such that $f(x) < f(y)$ holds. For PATH$_k$ this is obviously the case. For all points on the path except the last one, which is the global optimum, this holds, since there is always one successor on the path with Hamming distance exactly 1 according to Lemma 5. For points not on the path decreasing the number of ones by 1 always yields a bit string with increased function value. By Definition 3 it is obvious, that the all zero bit string is the first point on the path.

Rudolph [10] establishes two different upper bounds on the expected running time, that both yield exponential values for $k = \sqrt{n-1}$, so he speculates, that the expected running time may in fact be exponential for this choice of k. We prove this here, and thereby answer the open question, whether unimodal functions exist, on which the $(1+1)$ EA has exponential expected running time.

Lemma 7 (Rudolph [10]). *The expected running time of the $(1+1)$ EA on* PATH$_k$ *is bounded above by $O\left(n^{k+1}/k\right)$ and $O\left(n\left|P_n^k\right|\right)$.*

Proof. We distinguish two different ways to reach the optimum. If we assume, that the $(1+1)$ EA advances by mutations of exactly one bit only, we see, that at most $\left|P_n^k\right| + n$ such mutations are necessary, so the upper bound $O\left(n\left|P_n^k\right|\right)$ follows. If we assume, that mutations of k bits flipping simultaneously are taken to reach the optimum, i.e., the $(1+1)$ EA takes shortcuts, then we notice that n/k such mutations are sufficient, implying the other upper bound. $\square$

Theorem 8. *The expected running time of the $(1+1)$ EA on* PATH$_{\sqrt{n-1}}$ *is* $\Theta\left(n^{3/2}2^{\sqrt{n}}\right)$.

Proof. For $k = \sqrt{n-1}$ we have $\left|P_n^{\sqrt{n-1}}\right| = (\sqrt{n-1}+1)2^{\sqrt{n-1}} - \sqrt{n-1}+1$ according to Lemma 4, so the upper bound follows directly from Lemma 7.

The idea for the proof of the lower bound is roughly speaking the following. We assume, that the $(1+1)$ EA reaches the path somewhere in the first half of the bridge points. If only mutations with at most $\sqrt{n-1}-1$ bits flipping simultaneously occur, the $(1+1)$ EA has to follow the long path, so the expected number of steps is about $n\left|P_{\sqrt{n-1}}^n\right|/2$. Furthermore, the probability, that a mutation with at least $\sqrt{n-1}$ bits flipping simultaneously occurs before the optimum is reached, is small.

Let T denote the number of steps until the $(1+1)$ EA reaches the optimum. Let T_i denote the number of steps until the $(1+1)$ EA reaches the optimum, if it is started in the i-th point on the path. Let E_t be the event, that in t steps no mutation of at least $\sqrt{n-1}$ simultaneously flipping bits occurs. Since the future steps of the $(1+1)$ EA depend only on the current state and not on the "history" of the current run, T_i describes the number of steps until the optimum is reached after the i-th point of the path is reached, too. We use the notation "$i \in I$" to describe the event, that the $(1+1)$ EA reaches at least one of the points on the path with index in I. By I_m we denote the set of integers from 1 to m, i.e., $I_m = \{1, \ldots, m\}$.

By Definition 3 we have, that $\left|P_n^{\sqrt{n-1}}\right| = 2\left|P_{n-\sqrt{n-1}}^{\sqrt{n-1}}\right| + \sqrt{n-1} - 1$ holds for the length of $P_n^{\sqrt{n-1}}$. We want to estimate the expected running time of the $(1+1)$ EA, if the first point on the path does not belong to S_1, i.e., it does belong to the first $a := \left|P_{n-\sqrt{n-1}}^{\sqrt{n-1}}\right| + \sqrt{n-1} - 1$ points on $P_n^{\sqrt{n-1}}$.

Therefore, we have

$$E(T) \geq \mathrm{Prob}\,(i \in I_a) \cdot \min\left\{E\,(T_i \mid E_t) \mid i \in I_a\right\} \cdot \mathrm{Prob}\,(E_t).$$

We start with estimations for the two probabilities. For any k the probability that at least k bits mutate simultaneously is bounded above by $\binom{n}{k}n^{-k}$, so this happens at least once in t steps with probability at most $t\binom{n}{k}n^{-k}$. We can use $\binom{n}{k} \leq n^k/k!$ and Stirling's formula for the bound $\sqrt{2\pi k}k^k/\exp(k) \leq k!$ to get $t\exp(k)/(\sqrt{2\pi k}k^k)$ as upper bound. So for $k = \sqrt{n-1}$ we have

$$\mathrm{Prob}\,(E_t) \geq 1 - \frac{t\exp(\sqrt{n-1})}{\sqrt{2\pi\sqrt{n-1}}\sqrt{n-1}^{\sqrt{n-1}}}.$$

We know, that P_n^k is constructed from S_0, S_1, and B_n as described in Definition 3. We are interested in the first point on the path, that the $(1+1)$ EA reaches after random initialization. In particular we are looking for a lower bound on the probability, that this point belongs to S_0 or B_n.

If the initial bit string is on the path, then the probability, that this string does not belong to S_1 is $1 - \left|P_{n-k}^k\right|/\left|P_n^k\right| > 1/2$. Now we are left with the case that the initial bit string is off the path. In this case a mutation is accepted, iff

1. the path is reached,
2. the number of ones in the first k bits is decreased, or
3. the number of ones in the first k bits remains unchanged and the number of ones in the bit string is not increased.

Since the probability of reaching a point in S_1 as first point on the path decreases with increasing number of zeros in the first k bits, we are overestimating the probability of first reaching S_1, if we assume that no mutation steps off the path are accepted. After random initialization before the first step the probability of reaching S_0 is obviously equal to the probability of reaching S_1 for symmetry reasons. It follows, that the probability, that the first bit string on the path belongs to S_0 or B_n, is greater than $1/2$. So in any case we have $\mathrm{Prob}\,(i \in I_a) > 1/2$.

Now we need a lower bound for $E(T_i \mid E_t)$ for $i \in I_a$. We call the number of points on the path between the i-th point (our starting point) and the global optimum the distance d and have $d = \left|P_n^{\sqrt{n-1}}\right| - i + 1$. We denote the number of points between the i-th point on the path and the current point on the path after j steps by a_j. Using these notions we have

$$E\left(T_i \mid E_t\right) \geq t \cdot \text{Prob}\left(T_i \geq t \mid E_t\right) = t \cdot \text{Prob}\left(a_t < d \mid E_t\right)$$
$$= t \cdot \left(1 - \text{Prob}\left(a_t \geq d \mid E_t\right)\right).$$

Using Markoff's inequality we get $E\left(T_i \mid E_t\right) \geq t \cdot \left(1 - E\left(a_t \mid E_t\right)/d\right)$.

The most important property of long $\sqrt{n-1}$-paths is, that a mutation of j bits simultaneously (with $j < \sqrt{n-1}$) implies an advance of at most j points (Lemma 5). This yields

$$E\left(a_t \mid E_t\right) \leq t \cdot E\left(a_1 \mid E_t\right),$$

so we have $E\left(T_i \mid E_t\right) \geq t \cdot \left(1 - \left(t \cdot E\left(a_1 \mid E_t\right)\right)/d\right)$. Since we want an upper bound for the expected gain in one step under the condition, that only mutations with less than $\sqrt{n-1}$ simultaneously flipping bits occur, we have

$$E\left(a_1 \mid E_t\right) = \sum_{i=1}^{\sqrt{n-1}-1} i \cdot \text{Prob}(M_i),$$

if M_i denotes the event, that the only accepted mutation of exactly i simultaneously flipping bits occurs. According to Lemma 5 there is always exactly one accepted mutation of exactly i bits. It follows, that the probability of the "correct" i-bit mutation equals $n^{-i}(1 - 1/n)^{n-i}$. This implies

$$E\left(a_1 \mid E_t\right) \leq \sum_{i=1}^{\sqrt{n-1}-1} \frac{i}{n^i} < \sum_{i=1}^{\infty} \frac{i}{n^i} = \sum_{i=1}^{\infty}\sum_{j=i}^{\infty} n^{-j} = \frac{n}{(n-1)^2} \leq \frac{2}{n},$$

for $n \geq 4$. The last equality follows from an easy calculation using the fact, that $\sum_{s=0}^{t-1} q^s = (1 - q^t)/(1 - q)$ holds for $|q| < 1$ and all integers $t > 1$.

So we have

$$E\left(T_i \mid E_t\right) \geq t \cdot \left(1 - \frac{2t}{nd}\right).$$

We know, that $d = \left|P_n^{\sqrt{n-1}}\right| - i + 1$ and $i \leq \left|P_{n-\sqrt{n-1}}^{\sqrt{n-1}}\right| + \sqrt{n-1} - 1$, so we have

$$d \geq \left|P_{n-\sqrt{n-1}}^{\sqrt{n-1}}\right| + 2 = \left(\sqrt{n-1}+1\right)2^{\sqrt{n-1}-1} - \sqrt{n-1} + 1.$$

For $t = n^{3/2}2^{\sqrt{n}-5}$ we get $E\left(T_i \mid E_t\right) = \Omega\left(n^{3/2}2^{\sqrt{n}}\right)$ and together with the upper bound this finishes the proof. □

We can visualize the quality of our asymptotically tight bound for the expected running time by experiments. We compare the number of function evaluation of the $(1+1)$ EA before the global optimum is reached, averaged over 100 runs with $3 \cdot n^{3/2} \cdot 2^{\sqrt{n}}$. The constant 3 is chosen, since it fits well with our experimental data. Since the expected running time is exponential and we can only use values of n with $\sqrt{n-1} \in \mathbb{N}$, we are restricted to $n \in \{5, 10, 17, 26, 37, 50, 65, 82, 101, 122, 145, 170\}$. The results can be found in Fig. 1.

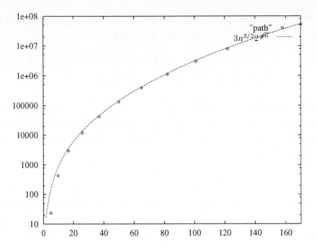

Fig. 1. $(1+1)$ EA on $\text{PATH}_{\sqrt{n-1}}$ and bound $3n^{3/2}2^{\sqrt{n}}$

4 A Variant of the $(1+1)$ EA

We already mentioned in Sect. 1, that different definitions of local maxima can be found in the literature, resulting in different definitions of unimodality. For instance, Horn, Goldberg, and Deb [6] define a local optimum as a point or region of the search space with strictly higher fitness than all neighbors. This means, that even functions, which are constant for all points but the global maximum, are unimodal. The standard example of such a function is $\text{PEAK} : \{0,1\}^n \to \mathbb{R}$, defined by

$$\text{PEAK}(x_1,\ldots,x_n) := \prod_{i=1}^{n} x_i.$$

As all bit strings of $\{0,1\}^n \setminus \{(1,\ldots,1)\}$ form one plateau, i.e., one set of neighboring bit strings with equal fitness value, every mutation starting from one of these bit strings is accepted. Hence, the $(1+1)$ EA does a random walk on this plateau, until the peak $(1,\ldots,1)$ is reached. This random walk is only possible, because an old bit string x is replaced by a new bit string x', even if $f(x) = f(x')$.

This strategy of *accepting equal-valued bit strings* is often used in many Evolutionary Algorithms, as it is assumed to help the algorithm to escape from plateaus [13]: if the actual bit string is "surrounded" by bit strings of the same fitness value and the $(1+1)$ EA accepts only bit strings with higher fitness, it would need a long time to make an improvement. By accepting bit strings with the same fitness, the $(1+1)$ EA can make random steps on this plateau, which can bring it nearer to bit strings with higher fitness, therefore making it more likely to escape from this plateau.

Now we will show, that this common-sense argumentation for the strategy of accepting equal-valued bit strings can be rigorously proven to lower the growth of the expected running time of the $(1+1)$ EA for PEAK substantially. The PEAK-function should be well suited for our purpose, as it has only one peak, while all other bit strings form one big plateau, therefore giving no "hints" about the peak.

Theorem 9. *If equal-valued bit strings are accepted, the expected running time of the $(1+1)$ EA for* PEAK *is* $O(\exp(2n + \ln(n)/2))$. *If the $(1+1)$ EA only accepts bit strings with higher fitness, the expected running time for* PEAK *is* $\Theta(\exp(n\ln(n) - n\ln(2)))$.

Proof. Let us first take a look at the expected running time of the original form of the $(1+1)$ EA. In order to upper bound this for PEAK, we lower bound the probability of reaching the global optimum $(1, \ldots, 1)$ after n steps independent of the initial bit string. A sufficient condition to mutate from a bit string with $k < n$ ones to $(1, \ldots, 1)$ is, that in every step exactly one of the zeros mutates, but no other bit. This event has probability

$$\prod_{i=k}^{n-1} \binom{n-i}{1} \cdot \frac{1}{n} \cdot \left(1 - \frac{1}{n}\right)^{n-1} \geq \frac{n!}{n^n} \cdot \left(1 - \frac{1}{n}\right)^{n(n-1)} \geq \frac{\sqrt{2\pi n}}{\exp(2n)}.$$

So we have to wait at most $\exp(2n)/\sqrt{2\pi n}$ blocks of n steps each in the expected case until the $(1+1)$ EA reaches the global optimum, independent of the initial bit string. Hence, the expected running time of the $(1+1)$ EA for PEAK is at most

$$\sqrt{\frac{n}{2\pi}} \cdot \exp(2n) = O(\exp(2n + \ln(n)/2)).$$

If the $(1+1)$ EA is changed in such a way, that it only accepts bit strings with higher fitness the expected running time can be computed exactly. Because now the expected running time of the $(1+1)$ EA is $n^k \cdot (n/(n-1))^{n-k}$, if the initial bit string has k zeros. As the initial bit string is chosen randomly, the expected running time is now

$$\sum_{k=1}^{n} \binom{n}{k} \cdot 2^{-n} \cdot n^k \cdot \left(\frac{n}{n-1}\right)^{n-k} = 2^{-n} \cdot \left(\left(n + \frac{n}{n-1}\right)^n - \left(\frac{n}{n-1}\right)^n\right)$$

$$= \Theta\left(\left(\frac{n}{2}\right)^n\right) = \Theta(\exp(n\ln(n) - n\ln(2))).$$

$\square$

So we have proven, that the strategy of accepting equal-valued bit strings can improve the order of growth of the expected running time. But do functions exist, where the expected running time of the $(1+1)$ EA increases, when equal-valued bit strings are accepted? It is known, that there are functions, where for explicit values of n the expected running time is worse when equal-valued bit strings are accepted, but it is an open question, if there are functions, so that the order of growth of the expected running time increases, when accepting equal-valued bit strings, too.

5 Conclusion

We proved, that the $(1 + 1)$ EA can have exponential expected running time on unimodal functions. This confirms, at least for the $(1 + 1)$ EA, the conjecture of Horn, Goldberg, and Deb [6], that the modality of the fitness landscape is not a sufficient indicator for the hardness of the function. It is an open question, whether $\sqrt{n-1}$-long paths can be optimized in expected polynomial time by Genetic Algorithms, but it can be doubted, that the use of a larger population and crossover can be helpful in this situation.

The enormous difference in the expected running time on PEAK between the $(1 + 1)$ EA as it is used here and the version where equal-valued bit strings are not accepted is surprising. It demonstrates, that Evolutionary Algorithms are not so robust in general as is often assumed and that they can be very sensitive to some seemingly small changes.

References

1. Droste, S., Jansen, Th., and Wegener, I. (1998). A rigorous complexity analysis of the $(1 + 1)$ Evolutionary Algorithm for linear functions with Boolean inputs. In Proceedings of the IEEE Congress on Evolutionary Computation (ICEC'98), 499-504. IEEE Press, Piscataway, NJ.
2. Fogel, D. B. (1995). Evolutionary Computation: Toward a New Philosophy of Machine Intelligence. IEEE Press, Piscataway, NJ.
3. Goldberg, D. E. (1989). Genetic Algorithms in Search, Optimization, and Machine Learning. Addison-Wesley, Reading, Mass.
4. Höhn, C. and Reeves, C. (1996). Are long path problems hard for Genetic Algorithms? In Voigt, H.-M., Ebelin, W., Rechenberg, I., and Schwefel, H.-P. (Eds.): Parallel Problem Solving from Nature (PPSN IV), 134–143. Springer, Berlin. LNCS 1141.
5. Holland, J. H. (1975). Adaption in Natural and Artificial Systems. University of Michigan, Michigan.
6. Horn, J., Goldberg, D. E., and Deb, K. (1994). Long path problems. In Davidor, Y., Schwefel, H.-P., and Männer, R. (Eds.): Parallel Problem Solving From Nature (PPSN III), 149–158. Springer, Berlin. LNCS 866.
7. Koza, J. R. (1992). Genetic Programming: On the Programming of Computers by Means of Natural Selection. MIT Press, Cambridge, Mass.
8. Mühlenbein, H. (1992). How Genetic Algorithms really work. Mutation and hill-climbing. In Männer, R. and Manderick, R. (Eds.), Parallel Problem Solving from Nature (PPSN II), 15–25. North-Holland, Amsterdam.
9. Rechenberg, I. (1994). Evolutionsstrategie '94. Frommann-Holzboog, Stuttgart.
10. Rudolph, G. (1997). Convergence Properties of Evolutionary Algorithms. Ph. D. Thesis. Verlag Dr. Kovač, Hamburg.
11. Rudolph, G. (1997b). How mutation and selection solve long-path problems in polynomial expected time. Evolutionary Computation 4(2), 195–205.
12. Schwefel, H.-P. (1995). Evolution and Optimum Seeking. Wiley, New York.
13. Schwefel, H.-P. (1997). Personal communication.
14. Wolpert, D. H. and Macready, W. G. (1997). No free lunch theorems for optimization. IEEE Transactions on Evolutionary Computation 1(1), 67–72.

A Timing Analysis of Convergence to Fitness Sharing Equilibrium

Jeffrey Horn[1] and David E. Goldberg[2]*

[1] Northern Michigan University, Marquette, MI, 49855, USA
jhorn@nmu.edu (http://aki.nmu.edu)
[2] Illinois Genetic Algorithms Laboratory, University of Illinois at
Urbana-Champaign, IL, 61801, USA
deg@uiuc.edu (http://www-illigal.ge.uiuc.edu)

Abstract. Fitness sharing has been shown to be an effective niching
mechanism in genetic algorithms (GAs). Sharing allows GAs to maintain
multiple, cooperating "species" in a single population for many generations under severe selective pressure. While recent studies have shown
that the *maintenance* time for *niching equilibrium* is long, it has never
been shown that the time it takes to reach equilibrium is sufficiently fast.
While experiments indicate that selection under fitness sharing drives
the population to equilibrium just as fast and as effectively as selection
alone drives the simple GA to a uniform population, we can now show
analytically that this is the case.

1 Introduction and Background

Fitness sharing is only one type of niching mechanism, but it has gained acceptance as a well-tested, successful nicher with a growing body of analysis. Before
attempting to contribute to fitness sharing theory, we provide some motivation
for niching and a brief description of the algorithm itself. We review earlier analyses of fitness sharing equilibrium and niche maintenance times, then give our
analysis of convergence under fitness sharing.

1.1 The Need For Niching

In a GA, selection drives the evolving population toward a uniform distribution of N copies of the most highly fit individual. Mutation and non-stationary

---

* Professor Horn's efforts were supported by NASA under contract number NGT-
50873. Professor Goldberg's contribution was sponsored by the Air Force Office of
Scientific Research, Air Force Materiel Command, USAF, under grants F49620-94-
1-0103, F49620-95-1-0338, and F49620-97-1-0050. The US Government is authorized
to reproduce and distribute reprints for Government purposes notwithstanding any
copyright notation thereon. The views and conclusions contained herein are the authors' and should not be interpreted as necessarily representing the official policies
or endorsements, either expressed or implied, of the Air Force Office of Scientific
Research or the U. S. Government.

fitness functions might stave off 100% convergence, but it is unarguable that the first-order effect of the first-order operator, selection, is the loss of diversity. In many applications of the GA, uniform convergence is undesirable. In multi-objective GA problems, for example, we might want to find a number of solutions with different tradeoffs among the multiple objectives [11]. Even with single objective (scalar fitness function) GAs, we might want to avoid premature convergence, or discover alternative "runner-up" solutions, by maintaining high quality diversity [7]. And in classifier systems [16, 10, 9], we ask the GA to search through the space of all possible rules to find and maintain a diverse, cooperative subpopulation.

To prevent the best individual in the population from replacing all copies of competing rivals, some kind of *niching* (a.k.a. *speciation*) is necessary. Niching induces *restorative pressure* to balance the *convergence pressure* of selection [9].

1.2   Fitness Sharing

Fitness sharing [7] accomplishes niching by degrading the *objective* fitness (i.e., the unshared fitness) of an individual according to the presence of nearby (similar) individuals. Thus this type of niching requires a distance metric on the phenotype or genotype of the individuals. In this study we use the Hamming distance between the binary encodings (genotypes) of individuals. We degrade the objective fitness f_i of an individual i by first summing all of the *share values* $Sh(d)$ of individuals within a fixed radius σ_{sh} of that individual, and then dividing f_i by this sum, which is known as the *niche count* $m_i = \sum Sh(d)$ for that individual. More specifically, if two individuals, i and j, are separated by Hamming distance $d_{i,j}$, then we add a share value

$$Sh(d_{i,j}) = \begin{cases} 1 - (\frac{d_{i,j}}{\sigma_{sh}})^{\alpha_{sh}} & \text{if } d_{i,j} < \sigma_{sh} \\ 0 & \text{otherwise} \end{cases} \tag{1}$$

to both of their niche counts, m_i and m_j. Here, σ_{sh} is the fixed radius of our *estimated niches*. Individuals separated by σ_{sh}, or more, do not degrade each other's fitness. The parameters α_{sh} and σ_{sh} are chosen by the user of the niched GA based on some *a priori* knowledge of the fitness landscape or a specific user objective (e.g., minimum separation σ_{sh} of alternative solutions). The effect of varying α_{sh} has not been studied to the same extent as has been the effect of changing σ_{sh}. For this reason, α_{sh} is often set to one, yielding the *triangular sharing function*. The contribution to the niche count, $Sh(d)$, always decreases monotonically from one to zero as the distance d between the pair of individuals goes from zero to σ_{sh}.

For an individual i, the niche count m_i is calculated as $m_i = \sum_{j=1}^{N} Sh(d_{i,j})$, where N is the size of the population. The *shared fitness* of individual i is then given by $f_{sh,i} = \frac{f_i}{m_i}$. In the case of no niche overlap (a.k.a., *perfect sharing* [8]) the niche count for individual i reduces to the number of copies of i ($m_i = n_i$), and i's shared fitness becomes independent of other niches: $f_{sh,i} = \frac{f_i}{n_i}$.

Fitness sharing tends to spread the population out over multiple peaks (niches) in proportion to the height of the peaks. GAs with proportionate selection and fitness sharing have been successfully used to solve a variety of multimodal functions [3].

1.3 Stable Niching Equilibrium

Deb and Goldberg [3] calculate equilibrium for the more general fitness sharing case (i.e., niche overlap) by setting shared fitnesses equal to each other:

$$\frac{f_A}{m_A} = \frac{f_B}{m_B}. \tag{2}$$

Recall the calculation of niche counts m_i in Equation 1. (We simplify our calculations by assuming $\alpha_{sh} = 1$.) For our two niches **A** and **B**, we normalize the inter-niche distance, $d(A, B) = 1$, without loss of generality. Since $n_A + n_B = N$ (population size), the niche count of **A** becomes $m_A = n_A * Sh(A, A) + n_B * Sh(A, B)$. Now since $d(A, A) = 0$, then $Sh(A, A) = 1$, while $Sh(A, B) = 1 - \frac{1}{\sigma_{sh}}$. Thus the niche count becomes $m_A = n_A + (N - n_A)(1 - \frac{1}{\sigma_{sh}})$. Similarly for **B**, $m_B = (N - n_A) + n_A(1 - \frac{1}{\sigma_{sh}})$. Substituting m_A and m_B into Equation 2 above, yields

$$\frac{f_A}{n_A + (N - n_A)(1 - \frac{1}{\sigma_{sh}})} = \frac{f_B}{(N - n_A) + n_A(1 - \frac{1}{\sigma_{sh}})}. \tag{3}$$

Solving for n_A and calling it $n_{A,eq}$ for "n_A at equilibrium", and also defining the ratio of fitness $r_f \equiv \frac{f_A}{f_B}$, results in

$$n_{A,eq} = \frac{r_f \sigma_{sh} - \sigma_{sh} + 1}{1 + r_f} N. \tag{4}$$

We recast our equations in terms of proportions of **A** at time t, by defining $P_{A,t} \equiv \frac{n_{A,t}}{N}$. At equilibrium, the expected proportion of **A**s is $P_{A,eq} \equiv \frac{n_{A,eq}}{N}$. Thus we rewrite Equation 4 as

$$P_{A,eq} = \frac{r_f \sigma_{sh} - \sigma_{sh} + 1}{1 + r_f}. \tag{5}$$

1.4 Exponential Niche Maintenance Times

Fitness sharing tends to *maintain* multiple high-quality niches for long periods of time. Expected times to loss of one or more niches have been shown to grow exponentially with increasing population size N [8, 12]. Mahfoud [12], and Horn, Goldberg, and Deb [10] developed a closed-form expression for the case of non-overlapping niches (perfect sharing):

$$E[t_{abs}] = \frac{(r_f + 1)^N}{r_f^N + 1}. \tag{6}$$

The expected absorption time above grows exponentially in N for any $r_f > 0$.

2 Fast Convergence to Niching Equilibrium

Now that we have an upper bound on the (very long) expected lifetimes of niches, we turn to the question of how such steady-states are reached, and in particular, how quickly they are reached. Under normal selection (e.g., in a simple GA) it has been shown that convergence to the "equilibrium point" of a uniform population takes place very quickly [6]. In the case of selective preference (i.e., $r_f \neq 1$) the convergence time grows logarithmically in population size N, while under genetic drift (i.e., $r_f = 1$), the expected convergence time grows linearly in N. Can we expect similarly quick convergence to "niching equilibrium"?

2.1 Background: Expected Proportions Analysis

To answer such questions, we use the simple, well-known method of *expected proportion equations* to model niche convergence. This method of tracking the expected next generation *population* only (rather than tracking the entire *distribution* over all possible populations) has been put to good use many times in the GA literature (e.g., [14, 6, 13]). The methodology has acquired several names: the *infinite population model* [15], the *virtual average population* [13], or the *local expected path*[3] [4].

2.2 Example: Simple GA Convergence

To illustrate the expected proportions analysis, and to provide a basis for comparison with our niching results later, we review some of the work done on convergence time in simple GAs (i.e., no niching). The technique has been applied to a simple GA under proportionate selection by several authors in the literature, including Goldberg [5], Ankenbrandt [1], and Goldberg and Deb [6]. Here we follow our own derivation, to arrive at the same kind of result: a closed-form expression for the expected proportion at generation t, with a logarithmic growth in convergence time with increasing population size N.

Under proportionate selection, the expected proportion of the next generation's population given to an individual is *equal* to the probability of selecting that individual for reproduction in the current generation's population. Thus if $P_{A,t}$ is the proportion of the current population, at time t, consisting of copies of rule **A**, then $E[P_{A,t+1}] = p_A$, where p_A is calculated at time (generation) t. That is, p_A is the probability of selecting a single individual copy of rule **A** for reproduction from a particular population with $n_A = N P_{A,t}$ copies of rule **A** and $n_B = N(1 - P_{A,t})$ copies of rule **B**. So in general

$$E[P_{A,t+1}] = p_A = \frac{n_A f_A}{n_A f_A + (N - n_A) f_B}. \tag{7}$$

---

[3] See [4], Appendix 1, or [15], for in-depth consideration of the accuracy of these models for finite populations.

Dividing numerator and denominator by population size N, and by f_B, and then substituting $r_f \equiv \frac{f_A}{f_B}$, yields

$$E[P_{A,t+1}] = \frac{P_{A,t}\, r_f}{P_{A,t}(r_f - 1) + 1}. \tag{8}$$

Now we make the major assumption that is key to this type of analysis: we assume that $E[P_{A,t+1}] \approx P_{A,t+1}$. That is, we allow ourselves to plug the expected proportion for the next generation back into our Equation 8 to get the expected proportion for the $t+2$ generation, and so on[4]. Substituting $E[P_{A,t+1}]$ for $P_{A,t+1}$, we derive a simple linear recurrence relation on $P_{A,t}$:

$$P_{A,t+1} = \frac{P_{A,t}\, r_f}{P_{A,t}(r_f - 1) + 1}. \tag{9}$$

The Convergence Equation. Solving the recurrence relation in Equation 9 results in

$$P_{A,t} = \frac{P_{A,0}\, r_f^t}{P_{A,0}\, r_f^t - P_{A,0} + 1}, \tag{10}$$

which is equivalent to Equation 7 of [6] with only $k = 2$ types of individuals (i.e., niches). In Figure 1 we plot an example expected convergence using Equation 10 with a fitness ratio of $r_f = 2$ so that the population quickly converges to all **A**s. The initial proportion is $P_{A,0} = \frac{1}{100}$ (e.g., for a population size $N = 100$ and only a single copy of **A** in the initial population).

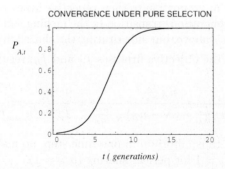

CONVERGENCE UNDER PURE SELECTION

t (generations)

Fig. 1. Expected proportion of **A**s in a simple GA under proportionate selection.

---

[4] Of course, $E[P_{A,t+1}] \approx P_{A,t+1}$ is a strict equality only for deterministic selection operators or for infinite populations [15]. But we use it to model our finite population, stochastic selection GA here.

Convergence Times. We can solve Equation 10 for time (generations) t:

$$t = \frac{1}{\ln r_f}(\ln \frac{P_{A,t}}{P_{A,0}} + \ln \frac{1 - P_{A,0}}{1 - P_{A,t}}). \tag{11}$$

We can see from this equation that increasing fitness difference speeds up convergence time, in agreement with our intuition.

Equation 11 is written in terms of proportions, and so is general to all population sizes, including infinite N. To add in the effects of finite populations, let's assume population size N and look for the time to go from a single copy of **A**, which is the worst case (i.e., longest time), to *almost* (one less than) full convergence[5]. In other words, we set $P_{A,0} = \frac{1}{N}$ and $P_{A,t_{conv}} = \frac{N-1}{N} = 1 - \frac{1}{N}$. Plugging these into Equation 11, and simplifying, we find that

$$t_{conv} = \frac{2}{\ln r_f} \ln(N - 1). \tag{12}$$

Clearly then convergence time in the simple GA grows logarithmically in population size. But convergence time here in the "selective case" of the simple GA is the time for a single species to take over the entire population. Will convergence time for niching, to arrive at some non-uniform population equilibrium, be different?

2.3 Perfect Sharing Convergence (no overlap)

We already know that the case of perfect sharing is special under proportionate selection [9]. Sharing (with no overlap) allocates objective fitness to individuals in proportion to the numbers of individuals, while proportionate selection allocates numbers of individuals in proportion to their objective fitnesses. The result is an "instantaneous" (one generation) transition to the niching equilibrium, in expectation. Using Equation 7 above, but substituting the shared fitnesses $f_{A,sh} = \frac{f_A}{n_A}$ and $f_{B,sh} = \frac{f_B}{N-n_A}$ for the objective fitnesses f_A and f_B, results in

$$E[P_{A,t+1}] = p_A = \frac{n_A \frac{f_A}{n_A}}{n_A \frac{f_A}{n_A} + (N - n_A)\frac{f_B}{N-n_A}} = \frac{f_A}{f_A + f_B} = \frac{r_f}{r_f + 1} = P_{A,eq}.$$

Thus we expect to get to equilibrium in one time step, no matter in what state $P_{A,0}$ we begin. So $t_{conv} = 1$ for perfect sharing ($\sigma_{sh} = 1$).

2.4 Fitness Sharing Convergence (with niche overlap)

Next we examine convergence time for fitness sharing with two overlapping niches ($1 < \sigma_{sh}$).

---

[5] Note that even our finite model will approach N only asymptotically. So we consider convergence to be $N - 1$ to allow us to compute a finite convergence time t.

The Convergence Equation. We start with the probability of selecting an **A** under fitness sharing,

$$p_A = \frac{n_A f_{A,sh}}{n_A f_{A,sh} + n_B f_{B,sh}}. \tag{13}$$

We recall that **A**'s shared fitness $f_{A,sh}$ is its objective fitness f_A divided by its niche count. Since we only have two types of individuals, **A** and **B**, we only have two possible contributions to the niche count: 1 for each **A** and $(1 - \frac{1}{\sigma_{sh}})$ for each **B**:

$$f_{A,sh} = \frac{f_A}{n_A + n_B(1 - \frac{1}{\sigma_{sh}})}.$$

Let's define $\mathcal{S} \equiv (1 - \frac{1}{\sigma_{sh}})$ (that is, the sharing function Sh). Now we can rewrite the probability of selecting an **A** under fitness sharing:

$$p_A = \frac{n_A \frac{f_A}{n_A + n_B \mathcal{S}}}{n_A \frac{f_A}{n_A + (N - n_A)\mathcal{S}} + n_B \frac{f_B}{n_B + n_A \mathcal{S}}}. \tag{14}$$

Dividing numerator and denominator by N to get proportions and by f_B to get the fitness ratio r_f, then substituting p_A into Equation 7,

$$E[P_{A,t+1}] = p_A = \frac{\frac{P_{A,t} r_f}{P_{A,t} + (1 - P_{A,t})\mathcal{S}}}{\frac{P_{A,t} r_f}{P_{A,t} + (1 - P_{A,t})\mathcal{S}} + \frac{1 - P_{A,t}}{1 - P_{A,t} + P_{A,t}\mathcal{S}}}. \tag{15}$$

This is a rather messy equation that can't be simplified much nor can it be solved (as a recurrence relation) directly for $P_{A,t}$. However, we can solve for something just as useful, the ratio of **A**s to **B**s: $\frac{n_A}{n_B}$. Note that the ratio of numbers is the same as the ratio of proportions: $\frac{P_{A,t}}{P_{B,t}} = \frac{n_A}{n_B}$. We'll name the proportion ratio $P_{r,t} \equiv \frac{P_{A,t}}{P_{B,t}}$ for short. Now since $P_{r,t+1} = \frac{P_{A,t+1}}{P_{B,t+1}} = \frac{P_{A,t+1}}{1 - P_{A,t+1}}$, we can just divide both sides of Equation 15 above by $(1 - P_{A,t+1})$. On the left hand side this gives us:

$$\frac{E[P_{A,t+1}]}{1 - P_{A,t+1}} \Rightarrow \frac{P_{A,t+1}}{1 - P_{A,t+1}} \Rightarrow P_{r,t+1} \Rightarrow E[P_{r,t+1}].$$

Dividing the right hand side of Equation 15 by $(1 - P_{A,t+1})$, and simplifying, we now have

$$E[P_{r,t+1}] = \frac{P_{A,t} r_f}{P_{A,t} + (1 - P_{A,t})\mathcal{S}} \frac{1 - P_{A,t} + P_{A,t}\mathcal{S}}{1 - P_{A,t}}. \tag{16}$$

Making our key assumption that $E[P_{r,t+1}] \approx P_{r,t+1}$ for the right hand side, and substituting our defined ratio of proportions $P_{r,t} \equiv \frac{P_{A,t}}{1 - P_{A,t}}$ on the left hand side, we derive

$$P_{r,t+1} = r_f \frac{1 + P_{r,t} \mathcal{S}}{1 + \frac{\mathcal{S}}{P_{r,t}}}. \tag{17}$$

Equation 17 appears simple in form, but unfortunately it is difficult to solve exactly. To obtain a closed-form, we use the continuous approximation method.

That is, we set up a differential equation approximating the difference equation 17 and then integrate the differential equation. Subtracting $P_{r,t}$ from both sides of Equation 17 above, we obtain

$$P_{r,t+1} - P_{r,t} = r_f \frac{1 + P_{r,t} S}{1 + \frac{S}{P_{r,t}}} - P_{r,t},$$

which we can then approximate by the differential equation

$$\frac{dP_{r,t}}{dt} = r_f \frac{1 + P_{r,t}S}{1 + \frac{S}{P_{r,t}}} - P_{r,t},$$

which upon integration yields

$$t + \frac{S \ln P_{r,t}}{S - r_f} + \frac{(S^2 r_f - r_f) \ln(S - r_f + P_{r,t} - S r_f P_{r,t})}{S - r_f - S^2 r_f + S r_f^2} = C. \qquad (18)$$

We can solve for the constant C if we substitute the initial proportion ratio $P_{r,0}$ for the first generation ($t = 0$):

$$C = 0 + \frac{S \ln P_{r,t}}{S - r_f} + \frac{(S^2 r_f - r_f) \ln(S - r_f + P_{r,t} - S r_f P_{r,t})}{S - r_f - S^2 r_f + S r_f^2}.$$

Plugging this C back into Equation 18, we can solve for t as a function of proportion ratio "desired", $P_{r,t}$, (as well as of the initial proportion ratio $P_{r,0}$):

$$t[P_{r,t}] = \frac{\ln(\frac{P_{r,0}}{P_{r,t}})}{1 - \frac{r_f}{S}} + \frac{(S - \frac{1}{S}) \ln(\frac{S - r_f + P_{r,0} - S r_f P_{r,0}}{S - r_f + P_{r,t} - S r_f P_{r,t}})}{1 + r_f - S - \frac{1}{S}}. \qquad (19)$$

So now we have in Equation 19 a closed-form equation relating time (generations) to proportion ratio ($P_{r,t} = \frac{P_A}{P_B}$). Unfortunately, we cannot solve this equation generally for $P_{r,t}$ in terms of t, but we can always solve it numerically for any particular values of t, r_f, and $P_{r,0}$. For now we compare our continuous approximation, Equation 19, to our more accurate discrete model, Equation 17, in Figure 2. We assume equal fitness $r_f = 1$, and an overlap ($\sigma_{sh} = 2$ so that $S = 1 - \frac{d}{\sigma_{sh}} = 0.5$). Note how the population asymptotically approaches the niching equilibrium proportion ratio ($\frac{n_A}{n_B} = P_{r,eq} = 1$). Note also how the curve of this plot is similar in form to the curve for simple GA convergence (Figure 1).

Convergence Times. Equation 19 is already solved for time t (in generations), but since it is uses only proportions (as in Equation 11 for simple GA convergence times), it implicitly models infinite population sizes. We now introduce into Equation 19 the discrete nature of a finite population size N by re-defining the two proportion ratios $P_{r,0}$ (the initial proportions) and $P_{r,t}$ (the proportions at time t). We model the bounding case of growing from a single copy of species **A** to within one copy of the niching equilibrium.

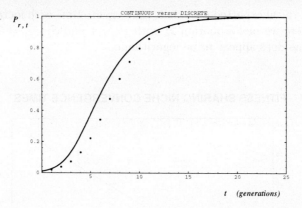

t *(generations)*

Fig. 2. Expected convergence under fitness sharing. The predictions of the discrete model are the solid dots, while the continuous model predicts the solid line.

With $n_{A,0} = 1$, the initial proportion of **A**s is $P_{A,0} = \frac{1}{N}$, and $P_{B,t} = \frac{N-1}{N}$. It follows that the initial proportion *ratio* $P_{r,0} = \frac{P_{A,0}}{P_{B,0}} = \frac{1}{N} / \frac{N-1}{N} = \frac{1}{N-1}$. For equilibrium, we rewrite Equation 5, substituting our sharing function $S = 1 - \frac{1}{\sigma_{sh}}$ for σ_{sh} (by using $\sigma_{sh} = \frac{1}{1-S}$):

$$P_{A,eq} = \frac{\frac{r_f - 1}{1-S} + 1}{r_f + 1}.$$

When we are just one (copy of **A**) less than the equilibrium:

$$P'_{r,eq} = \frac{P_{A,eq} - \frac{1}{N}}{P_{B,eq} + \frac{1}{N}} = \frac{P_{A,eq} - \frac{1}{N}}{1 - P_{A,eq} + \frac{1}{N}},$$

where $P'_{r,eq}$ is our symbol for *near* (within one of) equilibrium. Now we can substitute in $P_{A,eq}$ from Equation 5 and simplify:

$$P'_{r,eq} = \frac{N \frac{r_f - 1}{1-S} + N - r_f - 1}{(N+1)(r_f + 1) + N \frac{1-r_f}{1-S} - N}. \tag{20}$$

We want to know the expected time to go from $P_{r,0} = \frac{1}{N-1}$ to $P_{r,t} = P'_{r,eq}$. Plugging these two proportion ratios into Equation 19 above, and solving, yields:

$$t_{conv} = \frac{(S^2 - 1)}{r_f S - S^2 + S - 1} \ln\left(\frac{(\frac{1}{N-1} - r_f + S + \frac{r_f S}{1-N})(N r_f S + r_f S + S - r_f - N - 1)}{(r_f + 1)^2 (S-1)^2}\right)$$
$$+ \frac{S}{S - r_f} \ln\left(\frac{N - N r_f S - r_f S - S + r_f + 1}{(N-1)(r_f S - N S + S + N r_f - r_f - 1)}\right). \tag{21}$$

Although not a very simple formula, this expression for expected niche convergence time is clearly logarithmic in population size N, as predicted. Figure 3 illustrates a typical expected growth in convergence time with increasing N from 1 to 1000. Here we plot Equation 21 with $r_f = 1$ and $\mathcal{S} = \frac{1}{2} \Rightarrow \sigma_{sh} = \frac{1}{2}$. The growth in time does appear to be logarithmic.

FITNESS SHARING NICHE CONVERGENCE TIMES

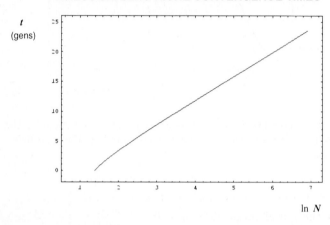

Fig. 3. Expected convergence times under fitness sharing grow logarithmically in N.

3 Summary

In this paper we have shown that convergence to niching equilibrium is fast, as we suspected. It is immediate for perfect sharing, and grows slowly, logarithmically, in population size N for overlapped niches. This fast convergence time means that not only is niching equilibrium reached quickly initially, but that perturbations from equilibrium are quickly compensated for. This fact supports our intuition that the GA will maintain the population at or very near equilibrium most of the time. Contrasting the fast (logarithmic) convergence times with the long (exponential) niche loss times, we can see that niching equilibrium dominates the evolutionary time scale.

We note, however, that increasing fitness difference r_f and increasing overlap σ_{sh} slow niche convergence time while also speeding up niche loss. We conjecture that when these two characteristic niching times are similar, perhaps differing only by an order of magnitude, niching fails. Applying this conjecture, and solving for the combinations of fitness difference and overlap that give us these niche failure conditions, we hope to plot the "boundary" between niching failure (i.e., competition) and success (i.e., cooperation), in future work.

References

1. Ankenbrandt, C. A. (1991). An extension to the theory of convergence and a proof of the time complexity of genetic algorithms. In G. E. Rawlins (Ed.), *Foundations of Genetic Algorithms*. San Mateo, CA: Morgan Kaufmann, 53–68.
2. Deb, K. (1989). *Genetic algorithms in multimodal function optimization*. Masters thesis and TCGA Report No. 89002. Tuscaloosa, AL: Department of Engineering Mechanics, University of Alabama.
3. Deb, K., & Goldberg, D. E. (1989). An investigation of niche and species formation in genetic function optimization. In J. D. Schaffer (Ed.), *Proceedings of the Third International Conference on Genetic Algorithms*. San Mateo, CA: Morgan Kaufmann, 42–50.
4. Goertzel, B. (1993). *The Evolving Mind*. Langhorne, PA: Gordon and Breach.
5. Goldberg, D. E. (1989). *Genetic algorithms in search, optimization, and machine learning*. Reading, MA: Addison-Wesley.
6. Goldberg, D. E., & Deb, K. (1991). A comparative analysis of selection schemes used in genetic algorithms. In G. E. Rawlins (Ed.), *Foundations of Genetic Algorithms* (FOGA). San Mateo, CA: Morgan Kaufmann. 69–93.
7. Goldberg, D. E., & Richardson, J. (1987). Genetic algorithms with sharing for multimodal function optimization. In J. Grefenstette, (Ed.), *Proceedings of the Second International Conference on Genetic Algorithms*, Hillsdale, NJ: Lawrence Erlbaum Associates, 41–49.
8. Horn, J. (1993). Finite Markov chain analysis of genetic algorithms with niching. In S. Forrest, (Ed.), *Proceedings of the Fifth International Conference on Genetic Algorithms*. San Mateo, CA: Morgan Kaufmann, 110–117.
9. Horn, J. (1997). *The Nature of Niching: Genetic Algorithms and the Evolution of Optimal, Cooperative Populations*. Ph.D. thesis, University of Illinois at Urbana-Champaign, (UMI Dissertation Services, No. 9812622).
10. Horn, J., Goldberg, D. E., & Deb, K. (1994). Implicit niching in a learning classifier system: nature's way. *Evolutionary Computation, 2*(1). 37–66.
11. Horn, J., Nafpliotis, N., & Goldberg, D. E. (1994). A niched Pareto genetic algorithm for multiobjective optimization. *Proceedings of the first IEEE conference on evolutionary computation, IEEE world congress on computational intelligence, volume 1*. Piscataway, NJ: IEEE Service Center, 82–87.
12. Mahfoud, S. W. (1994). Genetic drift in sharing methods. *Proceedings of the first IEEE conference on evolutionary computation, IEEE world congress on computational intelligence, volume 1*. Piscataway, NJ: IEEE Service Center, 67–72.
13. Neri, F., & Saitta, L. (1995). Analysis of genetic algorithms evolution under pure selection. In L. J. Eshelman, (Ed.), *Proceedings of the Sixth International Conference on Genetic Algorithms*. San Francisco, CA: Morgan Kaufmann. 32–39.
14. Smith, R. E., & Valenzuela-Rendón, M. (1989). A study of rule set development in a learning classifier system. In J. D. Schaffer, (Ed.), *Proceedings of the Third International Conference on Genetic Algorithms*, San Mateo, CA: Morgan Kaufmann, 340–346.
15. Vose, M. D. (1995). Modeling simple genetic algorithms. *Evolutionary Computation, 3*(4). 453–472.
16. Wilson, S. W. (1987). Classifier systems and the animat problem. *Machine Learning, 2*. 199–228.

Where Elitists Start Limping
Evolution Strategies at Ridge Functions

Ahmet Irfan Oyman, Hans-Georg Beyer, Hans-Paul Schwefel

University of Dortmund, Germany,
{oyman, beyer, schwefel}@LS11.cs.uni-dortmund.de

Abstract. How well an optimization algorithm satisfies short-term and long-term goals, can be verified using appropriate test functions, respective convergence measures, theoretical analysis, and simulations. This paper analyses the convergence behavior of the evolution strategy (ES) at the parabolic ridge function using the standard $(1 \overset{+}{,} \lambda)$-ES. Some further results are given for the case of more general ridge functions. The results obtained are counter-intuitive and different from if not contrary to those obtained from the sphere model theory. Furthermore, using static analysis, we show that the progress rate and the quality gain possess entirely different characteristics.

Keywords. ridge functions, Evolution Strategy, elitist ES, progress rate, quality gain, convergence behavior.

1 Introduction

Short-term gains are normally *not* expected to be coherent with the long-term gain or success. In order to be able to measure these two kinds of gains, one needs local and global performance measures. These measures are called "quality gain" and "progress rate", respectively, in the terminology of the evolution strategies. Both of these measures are actually measured locally; however, they are of different nature. The consequences are noticeable e.g. at the performance of the elitist strategies.

The static as well as the dynamic behavior of the elitist and non-elitist Evolution Strategies with one parent are investigated at the parabolic ridge in this paper. Furthermore, some important results on the general case of ridge functions are mentioned. Simulation results are given and compared with those of the sphere model, where appropriate.

The following section (Section 2) serves as historical basis. The background for the optimization algorithms used is given in Section 3. Section 4 is devoted to the test function used in the analysis (parabolic ridge) and to other related functions. Section 5 introduces the convergence measures used, for some of which analytical formulae are derived in Section 6 (theory). These are compared with simulation results in Section 7. A summary is given in Section 8.

2 The historical basis

Evolution Strategies were first devised for solving experimental optimization problems with *discrete* variables, the numbers of which may be variable as well [Rec65,KS70]. Theoretical results, however, were first obtained for a fixed number of real variables [Rec71,Sch75]. For a detailed history see [BFM97].

Rechenberg introduced two types of N-dimensional functions in order to investigate the progress rate φ mainly depending on the problem size N and isotropic mutation strength σ, and to find rules for adjusting σ so that φ is maximized. These two functions, namely sphere model and corridor model, form the basis of the functions analysed in this paper: Ridge functions are closely related with the former one in their definition, and with the latter one by having an open success region. From another point of view, the latter one was formulated to model situations far from the optimum, and the former in its vicinity, respectively. In case of the spherical model, the mutation strength must be decreased permanently in order to come ever closer to the optimum, on the ridge it is sufficient to adjust σ once and for all.

The first $(1+1)$-ES was conceived with one parent and one descendant per generation, in an elitist manner. Later, algorithms with multiple parents, recombination (both intermediary and dominant) and even multiple parallel populations were introduced [Rec78,Her92]. All variables are mutated using normal distributions for real-valued ones, or using geometric distributions for integer variables, respectively. Furthermore, from the beginning, *self-adaptation* of the mutation strength σ was included in the algorithm.

Schwefel argued that a finite life span is advantageous for collectively self-adapting σ, and he devised a more general scheme which comprises plus and comma selection strategies as extreme cases [SR95]. *Aging* and self-adaptation are not considered in this paper.

3 Algorithms

Only the $(1, \lambda)$-ES and the $(1+\lambda)$-ES are considered in this paper. The self-adaptation and recombination mechanisms are not used. The algorithm starts at a random or user-defined location in the search space, $\mathbb{R}^N$. This initial parent generates λ descendants in its neighborhood. Mutations occur according to a Gaussian distribution with zero mean and standard deviation σ for all N variables. The fitness function values obtained for the isotropically scattered offspring are used in the selection. In the $(1, \lambda)$-ES, the descendant with the best fitness substitutes the parent, no matter whether it is better than the parent or not. In the elitist $(1+\lambda)$-ES, however, the parent survives if none of the descendants leads to an improvement. These steps (mutation, evaluation, and selection) are repeated until a termination criterion is satisfied.

4   Problems, test functions

The case of maximization is considered in this paper w.l.o.g. In the ES literature, the *sphere model* test function has been used for most theoretical studies, either *statically* [Bey93], i.e. keeping the parent individual fixed in the search space, or *dynamically*, i.e. over many generations in time and space, if self-adaptation is applied (see [Bey96,Rec94] among others):

$$F(\boldsymbol{x}) := -W\left(\sqrt{\sum_{i=1}^{N}(x_i - \hat{x}_i)^2}\right) =: -W(R) \qquad (1)$$

NB, $\hat{x}_i$ are the coordinates of the optimizer, R denotes the Euclidean distance to the optimum, and N is the number of variables: Normally, $N \to \infty$ is assumed in the theoretical analysis; however, the results may serve as approximation for $N \geq 30$. $W(.)$ stands for an arbitrary monotonically increasing function. W.l.o.g., the origin ($\hat{\boldsymbol{x}} = \boldsymbol{0}$) can be used as optimizer.

The general case of the *ridge functions*[1] studied here can be stated as

$$F(\boldsymbol{x}) := x_0 - d\left(\sum_{i=1}^{N-1} x_i^2\right)^{\frac{\alpha}{2}} =: x_0 - dr^\alpha, \qquad \alpha \in \mathbb{R},\, d \in \mathbb{R}^+, N \in \mathbb{N} , \quad (2)$$

having the optimizer at $\hat{x}_0 = +\infty$ (therefore, the x_0-axis can be called *ridge axis* along which the progress is measured) and $\hat{x}_i = 0$, $\forall i \neq 0$, where r is the actual distance from the ridge axis. It has an open success region. Movements in

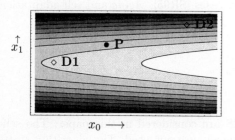

Fig. 1. Contour plot of the parabolic ridge test function, for $N = 2$. The brighter areas have higher fitness values, indicating that the optimum is at far right. The parent **P** and two descendants, **D1** and **D2**, are shown. No matter whether one uses a $(1+2)$-ES or $(1,2)$-ES, **D1** will be selected as the next parent because it has the best fitness value, although **D2** is the nearest one to the optimum.

x_0 direction are privileged linearly, whereas all deviations in other directions are punished by a multiplicative weight d and by a further weight α at the exponent. As α becomes larger, the optimum seeking process resembles an inclined razor riding process. Figure 1 shows a gentle case for $\alpha = 2$ (parabolic ridge). For $\alpha = 0$, one gets the *hyperplane* as the *limit* case, for $\alpha = 1$ the *sharp ridge*.

---

[1] NB, mathematicians use the same name for *another* function family [Pin97].

Due to the isotropy of the ES mutations chosen, epistatic effects do not degrade the performance even if the ridge or progress axis is *not* aligned with one of the coordinate axes [Sal96].

5 The convergence measures

Strictly speaking, the long-term behavior of an algorithm is of utmost interest in convergence analysis: One wants to know about the number of iterations that are necessary to reach (or come close to) the optimum (or the optimizer). Due to the simple Markovian character of ES, easier to achieve local measures may be used for estimating the long-term behavior. There are at least two of such measures:

$$\varphi^{(g)} := \mathrm{E}\{\|\hat{x} - x^{(g)}\| - \|\hat{x} - x^{(g+1)}\|\} , \tag{3}$$

the *progress rate* as defined by Rechenberg [Rec71], which measures the useful Euclidean distance traveled *toward* the optimum in the parameter space within one generation, where $\hat{x}$ denotes the optimum vector. Due to the stochastic character of the process, one has to consider its expected value, of course. This progress rate varies not only over time, but also depends on the current position in the search space. Another measure,

$$\overline{Q}^{(g)} := \mathrm{E}\{F^{(g+1)} - F^{(g)}\} , \tag{4}$$

not less dependent from time and local position, is called the average *quality gain*. It has been analysed in [Bey94] for a wide class of fitness functions and mutation operators. The special case of uniform sphere mutations on the special case of $F(x) = -\sum_{i=1}^{N} x_i^2$ has been analysed in [Rud97], too.

For the sphere model, both φ and $\overline{Q}$ only depend on σ, N, and R, for the ridge models introduced in (2) they depend on σ, N, d, α, and r.

The *success rate* ω is the probability of getting a descendant with a better fitness function value than the parent in a *single* trial. For the calculation of ω we need the first two moments of the *quality difference* $\Delta F(z) := F(x_P + z) - F(x_P)$, of the parent at position x_P and all possible descendants at $x_P + z$. Let $M_{\Delta F} := \mathrm{E}\{\Delta F(z)\}$ and $S_{\Delta F} := \sqrt{\mathrm{E}\{\Delta F^2(z)\} - [\mathrm{E}\{\Delta F(z)\}]^2}$, respectively. ω can be approximated by (see [Bey94])

$$\omega \approx 1 - \Phi\left(\frac{0 - M_{\Delta F}}{S_{\Delta F}}\right) = \Phi\left(\frac{M_{\Delta F}}{S_{\Delta F}}\right) , \tag{5}$$

where "$\Phi(.)$" denotes the cumulative distribution function of the standard normal distribution, $\mathcal{N}(0,1)$.

6 Theory

We first look closer to the formulation of ridge functions to explain the derivation semantically. The required stationary value for r is derived next. The approximate progress and success rate formulae will be derived in this section using simple local models.

The long-term and short-term aims can be formulated more precisely using (2): Minimization of r causes a short term gain, maximization of x_0 is a long term gain. The reason is simple: r can only be decreased to 0, whereas the values for x_0 are unlimited, but r has normally a greater effect on $\Delta F(z)$ than x_0.

Rechenberg already investigated the parabolic ridge ($\alpha = 2$). Under the condition $r = const$, he presents an approximate quality gain ($\overline{Q}$) formula for the $(1, \lambda)$-ES without derivation [Rec94, p. 66], and reasons about local and global progress [Rec94, p. 77]. In [OBS97], we provide derivations for φ, $\overline{Q}$, and ω, as well as the average distance to the ridge axis ($R^{(\infty)}$) for the $(1, \lambda)$-ES, and simulation results for the $(1+\lambda)$-ES, together with confirming simulation results for the $(1, \lambda)$-ES. Extensions to values other than $\alpha = 2$ and asymptotic results for $N \to \infty$ may be found in [OBS98]. The theoretical part of his paper is partially established on these results previously obtained.

A few words can be said here about r at ridge functions. If we start at an arbitrary $r^{(0)}$ value and apply the $(1, \lambda)$-ES algorithm for many generations, keeping σ constant, the $r^{(g)}$ value finally fluctuates around a typical mean value, which we will denote as $R^{(\infty)}$. A similar phenomenon is also observed at the sphere model for dynamic evaluation *without* self-adaptation. The $r \approx R^{(\infty)}$ case is called *stationary* in this paper. The number of generations required for this process within an $(1, \lambda)$-ES can be estimated for the case $\alpha = 2$ [OBS97, Subsection 13.10].

If the x_0 component of ridge functions could be neglected, (2) becomes a special case of the sphere model with $W(r) = dr^\alpha$, $\hat{x} = \mathbf{0}$, in $(N-1)$ dimensions. The $R^{(\infty)}$ value for large σ and d will be derived here for considering x_0 as *noise*. For the sphere model in case $\varphi^*_{sphere} \stackrel{!}{=} 0$, we obtain from the asymptotically $(N \to \infty)$ exact $\varphi^*_{sphere} = c_{1,\lambda}\sigma^* - \sigma^{*2}/2$ for the $(1, \lambda)$-ES [Rec78,Bey93]

$$0 = c_{1,\lambda} - \frac{\sigma^*}{2}, \qquad \sigma \frac{N}{R} =: \sigma^* = 2c_{1,\lambda} \ , \tag{6}$$

($\varphi^* := \varphi N/R$, $\sigma^* := \sigma N/R$ are normalized, dimensionless items) and therefore $R^{(\infty)}_{sphere} = N\sigma/2c_{1,\lambda}$. Using $(N-1)$ instead of N, the corresponding $R^{(\infty)}$ limit for ridge functions reads

$$R^{(\infty)} \approx \frac{(N-1)\sigma}{2c_{1,\lambda}} \ , \tag{7}$$

The progress coefficient $c_{1,\lambda}$ for the $(1, \lambda)$-ES is the λ-th order statistics of λ samples generated using the standard normal distribution,

$$c_{1,\lambda} = \frac{\lambda}{\sqrt{2\pi}} \int_{-\infty}^{\infty} t e^{-\frac{1}{2}t^2} [\Phi(t)]^{\lambda-1} dt \ . \tag{8}$$

The progress rate will be calculated next, where the $R^{(\infty)}$ value will be used to compute the asymptotic ($\sigma \to \infty$) value of φ. For the derivation of approximate φ, the local model is considered first.

The isometric surfaces of ridge functions can locally be approximated by *hyperplanes* for $r \approx R^{(\infty)}$ and corresponding σ (see Fig. 1). Consequently, we have a stationary progress in the direction of the gradient vector $\boldsymbol{a}$ as large as φ at the hyperplane, i.e. $\varphi_{\boldsymbol{a}} \approx c_{1,\lambda}\sigma\boldsymbol{a}/\|\boldsymbol{a}\|$. If we call the unit vector in x_0 direction as $\boldsymbol{e}_0$, one obtains $\varphi_{ridge} \approx \boldsymbol{e}_0^T \cdot \varphi_{\boldsymbol{a}}$. By partially differentiating (2) with respect to x_0 and r, the gradient vector $\boldsymbol{a}$ at the location (x_0, r) is obtained as

$$\boldsymbol{a} = \begin{pmatrix} \frac{\partial F}{\partial x_0} \\ \frac{\partial F}{\partial r} \end{pmatrix} = \begin{pmatrix} 1 \\ -d\alpha r^{\alpha-1} \end{pmatrix} , \text{ therefore} \tag{9}$$

$$\varphi_{ridge} \approx \boldsymbol{e}_0^T \cdot \varphi_{\boldsymbol{a}} = \frac{c_{1,\lambda}\sigma}{\|\boldsymbol{a}\|}\boldsymbol{e}_0^T \cdot \boldsymbol{a} = \frac{c_{1,\lambda}\sigma}{\|\boldsymbol{a}\|} = \frac{c_{1,\lambda}\sigma}{\sqrt{1 + (\alpha d r^{\alpha-1})^2}} ; \tag{10}$$

$$\varphi_{ridge}\big|_{\alpha=2} = \frac{c_{1,\lambda}\sigma}{\sqrt{1 + (2dr)^2}} . \tag{11}$$

It is very remarkable that the negative quadratic term in the asymptotically ($N \to \infty$) exact $\varphi_{1,\lambda}$ formula for the sphere model does not appear for the ridge function case.

The investigation of the φ limit for very large mutation strengths yields other remarkable results. Replacing r by $R^{(\infty)}$, i.e. inserting (7) into (10), one gets the asymptotic ($\sigma \to \infty$) value of (10) as $\varphi_{ridge} = \infty$ for $\alpha < 2$, and $\varphi_{ridge} = 0$ for $\alpha > 2$, respectively. Using the normalizations

$$\varphi^* := d(N-1)\varphi \quad \text{and} \quad \sigma^* := d(N-1)\sigma , \tag{12}$$

one gets from (11)

$$\lim_{\sigma \to \infty} \varphi_{ridge}\big|_{\alpha=2} = \frac{c_{1,\lambda}^2}{d(N-1)}, \quad \lim_{\sigma^* \to \infty} \varphi_{ridge}^*\big|_{\alpha=2} = \hat{\varphi}^* = c_{1,\lambda}^2 , \tag{13}$$

and $\hat{\sigma} = \hat{\sigma}^* = +\infty$, where the hat symbol denotes optimal values. The results in (13) are completely independent from σ or σ^*. This is in contrast to the sphere model, where $\lim_{\sigma^* \to \infty} \varphi_{sphere}^* = -\infty$, $\hat{\varphi}_{sphere}^* = c_{1,\lambda}^2/2$, and $\hat{\sigma}_{sphere}^* = c_{1,\lambda}$.

The computation of the success rate ω for the $(1, \lambda)$-ES and $\alpha = 2$ is straightforward. For the calculations, assuming $z_i \sim \mathcal{N}(0, \sigma^2)$, one has $\mathrm{E}\{z_i\} = \mathrm{E}\{z_i^3\} = 0$, $\mathrm{E}\{z_i^2\} = \sigma^2$, $\mathrm{E}\{z_i^4\} = 3\sigma^4$. Using the definition (5), one obtains step by step

$$\Delta F(\boldsymbol{z}) = F(\boldsymbol{x}_{\mathrm{P}} + \boldsymbol{z}) - F(\boldsymbol{x}_{\mathrm{P}}) = z_0 - d \sum_{i=1}^{N-1} (2x_i z_i + z_i^2) \tag{14}$$

$$M_{\Delta F} = -d(N-1)\sigma^2 \tag{15}$$

$$S_{\Delta F} = \sigma\sqrt{1 + (2dr)^2 + 2d^2(N-1)\sigma^2} \tag{16}$$

$$\omega \approx \Phi\left(\frac{M_{\Delta F}}{S_{\Delta F}}\right) = \Phi\left(-\frac{d(N-1)\sigma}{\sqrt{1 + (2dr)^2 + 2d^2(N-1)\sigma^2}}\right) . \tag{17}$$

In (16), we used the statistical independence of the z_i. Asymptotically, after inserting (7) into (17), and using (12) one gets $\lim_{\sigma^* \to \infty} \omega = \Phi(-c_{1,\lambda})$. The theoretical results expressed in this section are valid for $N \geq 100$ and $r \approx R^{(\infty)}$.

7 Simulation results

All following simulation results were obtained for $\alpha = 2$, $d = 0.01$, $N = 100$, and $\lambda = 10$; $c_{1,10} \approx 1.54$. Mean values and error bars for $100\,000$ generations (after a transition phase of 2000 generations to reach stationarity) are plotted as dots for both versions of $(1 \stackrel{+}{,} 10)$-ES in Fig. 2 and Fig. 3. Continuous lines show the

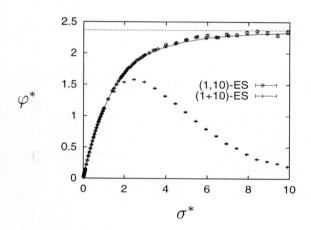

Fig. 2. Normalized progress rate φ^* versus normalized mutation strength σ^* curves for the $(1 \stackrel{+}{,} 10)$-ES. $d = 0.01$, $N = 100$. For increasing σ^*, the non-elitist strategy attains larger progress rates.

approximate theoretical results for the $(1, 10)$-ES, dotted horizontal lines limits. For the calculation of φ^* and ω over σ^* we did not use the $R^{(\infty)}$ formula (7), but the differing simulation results (right part of Fig. 3). Otherwise, theory and simulation results do not fit as well as they do in the range $2 < \sigma^* < 7$.

The most surprising overall result is the obvious superiority of the non-elitist ES over the elitist one. Whereas the progress rate of the latter goes down to zero as usual after a climax at the optimal mutation strength $\hat{\varphi}^* \approx 2.5$, it goes further up and never down for the comma version. This phenomenon is coupled with linearly increasing $R^{(\infty)}$ and a leveling out of the success rate at a constant limit. A closer investigation reveals the mechanism: The forgetting principle of non-elitism enhances larger, more frequent side steps from the ridge axis with short-term recessions, but better long-term chances to ride along the ridge that is more and more razor-like the larger N becomes.

To further clarify the situation, we use a static analysis in the following, i.e., we fix the distance r to the ridge axis and measure success rates and quality gains for a fixed mutation strength $\sigma = 2$ during $100\,000$ generations, all starting from the same position, and we do so for both $(1 \stackrel{+}{,} 10)$-ES under otherwise same conditions as before. Qualitative results of this experiment series are shown in Fig. 4. The theoretically upper limit $\varphi_{hyperplane}|_{\sigma=2} = 2c_{1,10}$ is also shown, as

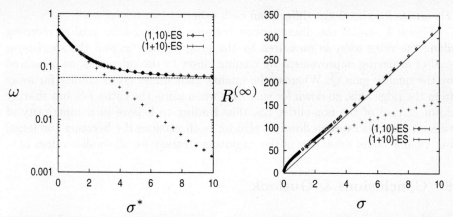

Fig. 3. Success rate ω versus normalized mutation strength σ^* (left picture) and stationary distance to ridge axis $R^{(\infty)}$ versus mutation strength σ curves (right picture) for the $(1 \overset{+}{,} 10)$-ES, obtained from the same simulation as for Fig. 2.

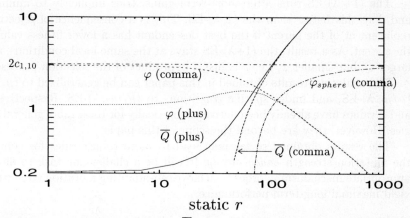

Fig. 4. Progress rate φ and quality gain $\overline{Q}$ over $r = const.$ *Static* analysis for given $\sigma = 2$, otherwise same conditions as before. Both axes are logarithmic. For the parabolic ridge, $\varphi \neq \overline{Q}$ if $r \neq R^{(\infty)}$, furthermore, φ and $\overline{Q}$ behave inversely over r. φ_{sphere} for the $(1, 10)$-ES is given for comparison.

well as the unnormalized, asymptotically $(N \to \infty)$ exact $\varphi_{sphere} = c_{1,10}\sigma - N\sigma^2/2R$ for the $(1, 10)$-ES. Obviously, $\varphi \neq \overline{Q}$ except for $r = R^{(\infty)}$. Remember that for $\sigma = 2$ or $\sigma^* = \sigma d(N - 1) \approx 2$ (see Fig. 2) both ES versions yield nearly identical progress rates φ^* (or φ). However, the static analysis gives different results for the two progress measures:

$$\varphi_{1,\lambda} \geq \varphi_{1+\lambda}, \qquad \lim_{r \to \infty} \varphi_{1 \overset{+}{,} \lambda} = 0, \qquad \lim_{r \to \infty} \overline{Q}_{1 \overset{+}{,} \lambda} = +\infty \qquad (18)$$

$$\overline{Q}_{1,\lambda} \leq \overline{Q}_{1+\lambda}, \qquad \overline{Q}_{1,\lambda} \neq \varphi_{1,\lambda}, \qquad \overline{Q}_{1+\lambda} \neq \varphi_{1+\lambda} \qquad (19)$$

The limits for $r \to 0$ also differ from each other.

Figure 4 reveals the discrepancies between the long-term goal of creeping along the ridge axis, as measured by the progress rate φ, and the short-term goal of achieving improvement by coming closer to the ridge axis, as measured by the quality gain $\overline{Q}$: Whereas the quality gain values go to infinity far away from the ridge axis, go down for smaller r when using the elitist ES, but sharply down in case of the non-elitist ES, thus leading to believe in a superiority of elitism, progress rates go down to zero for both versions if r becomes too large, but yield a *sound advantage* of the forgetting strategy for all smaller values of r.

8 Conclusions & Outlook

For the parabolic ridge, one obtains $\hat{\varphi}^*_{1,\lambda} > \hat{\varphi}^*_{1+\lambda}$, $\lim_{\sigma^* \to \infty} \varphi^*_{1,\lambda} = \hat{\varphi}^*_{1,\lambda} = c^2_{1,\lambda}$, and $\hat{\omega} = \Phi(-c_{1,\lambda})$ using dynamic analysis. If the static case is considered, $\overline{Q}$ is not convertible to φ (except for $r = R^{(\infty)}$). At ridge functions, $\varphi_{1,\lambda} \geq 0$. All of these results are new with respect to the sphere model theory.

The $(1+\lambda)$-ES runs after short-term gains, tries implicitly to minimize r, and does this better than the $(1,\lambda)$-ES. This is a consequence of rejecting the replacement of the parent if the best descendant has a lower fitness value than the parent. As a result, the $(1+\lambda)$-ES stays at the same local conditions, attains larger $\overline{Q}$, but smaller φ. I.e. φ is just a byproduct of the selection process.

The analytical results obtained in this paper can be generalized to (μ, λ)-ES, $(\mu/\mu_\mathrm{I}, \lambda)$-ES, and under specific conditions to $(\mu/\mu_\mathrm{D}, \lambda)$-ES. Respective $R^{(\infty)}$ and φ values have already been derived analytically for these more general strategies. However, they are beyond the scope of this paper.

The results obtained so far may lead to more robust rules for controlling the mutation strength *endogenously*. It will be a challenging task to devise an appropriate mechanism in order to achieve self-adapting mutation strengths that yield maximal long-term performance.

9 Acknowledgments

This research is funded by a PhD scholarship of DAAD (German Academic Exchange Service), grant number A/95/11445. The second author is a Heisenberg fellow of the DFG (German Science Foundation) under grant Be 1578/4-1, and the third one is spokesman of the Collaborative Research Center on Computational Intelligence (SFB 531), sponsored by the DFG, as well. We are grateful to Peter Dittrich for helpful comments.

References

[Bey93] H.-G. Beyer. Toward a Theory of Evolution Strategies: Some Asymptotical Results from the $(1 \overset{+}{,} \lambda)$–Theory. *Evolutionary Computation*, 1(2):165–188, 1993.

[Bey94]   H.-G. Beyer. Towards a Theory of 'Evolution Strategies': Progress Rates and Quality Gain for $(1,^+ \lambda)$-Strategies on (Nearly) Arbitrary Fitness Functions. In Y. Davidor, R. Männer, and H.-P. Schwefel, editors, *Parallel Problem Solving from Nature, 3*, pages 58–67, Heidelberg, 1994. Springer.

[Bey96]   H.-G. Beyer. Toward a Theory of Evolution Strategies: Self-Adaptation. *Evolutionary Computation*, 3(3):311–347, 1996.

[BFM97]   Th. Bäck, D. B. Fogel, and Z. Michalewicz. *Handbook of Evolutionary Computation*. Oxford University Press, New York, and Institute of Physics Publishing, Bristol, 1997.

[Her92]   M. Herdy. Reproductive Isolation as Strategy Parameter in Hierarchically Organized Evolution Strategies. In R. Männer and B. Manderick, editors, *Parallel Problem Solving from Nature, 2*, pages 207–217, Amsterdam, 1992. Elsevier.

[KS70]   J. Klockgether and H.-P. Schwefel. Two-phase nozzle and hollow core jet experiments. In D. G. Elliott, editor, *Proc. Eleventh Symp. Engineering Aspects of Magnetohydrodynamics*, pages 141–148, Pasadena CA, March 24-26 1970. California Institute of Technology.

[OBS97]   A. I. Oyman, H.-G. Beyer, and H.-P. Schwefel. Analysis of a Simple ES on the "Parabolic Ridge". Technical Report SyS-2/97, University of Dortmund, Department of Computer Science, Systems Analysis Research Group, August 1997. http://ls11-www.cs.uni-dortmund.de/people/oyman/TR.ps.gz.

[OBS98]   A. I. Oyman, H.-G. Beyer, and H.-P. Schwefel. Convergence Behavior of the $(1 \overset{+}{,} \lambda)$ Evolution Strategy on the Ridge Functions. Technical Report SyS–1/98, University of Dortmund, Department of Computer Science, Systems Analysis Research Group, February 1998. http://ls11-www.cs.uni-dortmund.de/people/oyman/TR/TR2.ps.gz.

[Pin97]   A. Pinkus. Approximating by Ridge Functions. In A. Le Mehaute, C. Rabut, and L. L. Schumaker, editors, *Surface Fitting and Multiresolution Methods*, pages 279–292. Vanderbilt University Press, Nashville, 1997.

[Rec65]   I. Rechenberg. Cybernetic solution path of an experimental problem. Library translation 1122, Royal Aircraft Establishment, Farnborough, 1965.

[Rec71]   I. Rechenberg. *Optimierung technischer Systeme nach Prinzipien der biologischen Evolution*. Dr.-Ing. Dissertation (PhD Thesis), Technical University of Berlin, Department of Process Engineering, 1971.

[Rec78]   I. Rechenberg. Evolutionstrategien. In B. Schneider and U. Ranft, editors, *Simulationsmethoden in der Medizin und Biologie*, pages 83–114. Springer, Berlin, 1978.

[Rec94]   I. Rechenberg. *Evolutionsstrategie '94*, volume 1 of *Werkstatt Bionik und Evolutionstechnik*. Frommann–Holzboog, Stuttgart, 1994.

[Rud97]   G. Rudolph. *Convergence Properties of Evolutionary Algorithms*. Verlag Dr. Kovač, Hamburg, 1997.

[Sal96]   R. Salomon. Re-evaluating genetic algorithm performance under coordinate rotation of benchmark functions. A survey of some theoretical and practical aspects of genetic algorithms. *BioSystems*, 39(3):263–278, 1996.

[Sch75]   H.-P. Schwefel. *Evolutionsstrategie und numerische Optimierung*. Dr.-Ing. Dissertation (PhD Thesis), Technical University of Berlin, Department of Process Engineering, 1975.

[SR95]   H.-P. Schwefel and G. Rudolph. Contemporary Evolution Strategies. In F. Morán, A. Moreno, J. J. Merelo, and P. Chacón, editors, *Advances in Artificial Life. Third International Conference on Artificial Life*, pages 893–907. Springer, Berlin, 1995.

Fitness Landscapes and Problem Difficulty

A Bit-Wise Epistasis Measure
for Binary Search Spaces

Cyril Fonlupt, Denis Robilliard, Philippe Preux

Laboratoire d'Informatique du Littoral
BP 719
62228 Calais Cedex, France
e-mail: {fonlupt,robillia}@lil.univ-littoral.fr

Abstract. The epistatic variance has been introduced by Davidor as a tool for the evaluation of interdependences between genes, thus possibly giving clues about the difficulty of optimizing functions with genetic algorithms (GAs). Despite its theoretical grounding in Walsh function analysis, several studies have shown its weakness as a predictor of GAs results. In this paper, we focus on binary search spaces and propose to measure epistatic effect on the level of individual genes, an approach that we call *bit-wise epistasis*. We give examples of this measure on several well-known test problems, then we take into account this supplementary information to improve the performances of evolutionary algorithms. We conclude by pointing towards possible extensions of this concept to real size problems.

1 Introduction

An important issue tackled by epistasis studies, in genetic algorithms (GAs), is understanding and characterizing the difficulty to optimize functions. In other words, how well are epistatic measures able to predict the difficulty of problems? Can they help in finding better solutions? There have been a lot of works dealing with this problem, both theoretical and empirical studies, initiated by a seminal paper by Davidor [1]. His epistasis variance have been shown to have a strong mathematical foundation, based on Walsh functions analysis (see [2–4] and also [5,6]), but still the correlation between problem hardness and epistasis is not straightforward. As it was argued in [3], even if it may provide some guidance for this matter, no definitive conclusion can be drawn. This is also confirmed by recent works from Rochet and Venturini [7], showing that one can change the representation of a problem, and thus achieve a lower epistasis, *without* changing the problem hardness. We think that this lack of accuracy may come from the global nature of this measure, which computation involves two levels of averaging. In this paper, we do not hope to provide a definitive answer to this question. Rather we propose a different measure of epistatic effects in binary search spaces, that we call *bit-wise epistasis*. We think our measure provides an increased accuracy over Davidor's proposition and we show that this may give another point of vue on the matter of problems hardness. This accuracy is especially clear when dealing with and explaining the unsuccessful remappings of search space proposed in [7]. We present the definition and the principles of our epistasis measure in Sect. 2. We give examples of computations, applied to NK-landscapes, in Sect. 3. Then we study a set of common functions in Sect. 4, and explain why some proposed remapping have failed in Sect. 5. In Sect. 5, we use the information provided by our measures in order to enhance the quality of solutions found by evolutionary algorithms. This improvement is obtained through adding a simple stochastic mutation operator which rate is based on bit-wise epistasis values. This work is too preliminary to allow us to report improvements on real world problems, but we give hints at how one could use the concept of bit-wise epistasis in GAs.

2   A Definition of Bit-Wise Epistasis

Our approach is based on the fact that a strong epistatic relation may exist only on some genes within a genotype, the other genes being much more independent. We think that it may be interesting to have a detailed view of such interactions rather than mixing and merging them like it is done in the epistatic variance defined by Davidor. In the following, we assume the reader is familiar with the notion of *schema* (see also [8,9]).

Let f be the fitness function from a binary search space $B = \{0,1\}^l$ in the set of reals $\mathbb{R}$ with l the length of genotypes.

Let $B' = \{0,1,\#\}^l$ the set of schemata associated with B. Let Σ_i the set of schemata of order $l-1$ such that their unique undefined loci is at the ith position in the schema, i.e. $\Sigma_i = \{\sigma_0\sigma_1\ldots\sigma_i\ldots\sigma_{l-1} \in B' \mid \sigma_{j \neq i} \in \{0,1\} \text{ and } \sigma_i = \#\}$.

Let $\alpha = \alpha_0\alpha_1\ldots\alpha_{i-1}\#\alpha_{i+1}\ldots\alpha_{l+1}$ a schema in Σ_i. Let $X_\alpha, \bar{X}_\alpha$ be genotypes in B, members of α, with $X_\alpha = \alpha_0\alpha_1\ldots\alpha_{i-1}0\alpha_{i+1}\ldots\alpha_{l-1}$ and $\bar{X}_\alpha = \alpha_0\alpha_1\ldots\alpha_{i-1}1\alpha_{i+1}\ldots\alpha_{l-1}$. We call $d_i(\alpha)$ the *fitness difference*[1] *at gene i*:

$$d_i(\alpha) = f(X_\alpha) - f(\bar{X}_\alpha)$$

We define the *mean fitness difference at gene i* as the mean $d_i(\alpha)$ for all schemata $\alpha \in \Sigma_i$:

$$M_i = \frac{1}{2^{l-1}} \sum_{\alpha \in \Sigma_i} d_i(\alpha)$$

We call *bit-wise epistasis at gene i* the variance of the fitness difference at gene i:

$$\sigma_i^2 = \frac{1}{2^{l-1}} \sum_{\alpha \in \Sigma_i} [M_i - d_i(\alpha)]^2$$

---

[1] An alternative definition could be the absolute value $|d_i(\alpha)|$. We intend to discuss the reasons underlying our choice in a forthcoming paper.

When the search space is too big for such a computation (as is usually the case), we approximate bit-wise epistasis on a sample of schemata. This raises the same kind of problems as for Davidor's variance relatively to sampling error and cost of epistasis computation. To allow comparison between different problems, we have followed a suggestion in [2], and normalized numerical results on the fitness variance of our samples. Obviously, a bit-wise epistasis equals to 0 for all genes is associated with a problem where there is no dependency between genes.

3   An Illustration of Bit-Wise Epistasis: the *NK* Landscapes

In this section we use *NK* landscapes as an illustration of bit-wise epistasis measures. We do not define *NK* landscapes but refer the reader to [10]. Let us say that these are artificial problems where the degree of epistasis can be tuned in a wide range of values. We generate different NK landscapes using the guidelines provided in [11]. Our measures were computed on landscapes characterized by $N = 24$ and four different values for parameter K : 1, 4, 12, 23 (the higher the value of K, the higher the level of epistatic dependencies). Bit-wise epistasis measures are plotted in Fig. 1 and consistent with what we expected: the higher the value of K, the higher the curve on the plot; also notice that the level of bit-wise epistasis is evenly distributed on the whole range of 24 bits with no peak of epistasis.

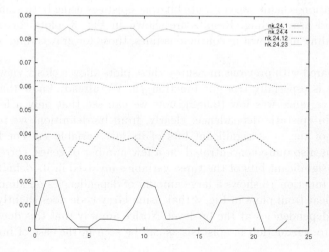

Fig. 1. Comparison of bit-wise epistasis in different NK landscapes.

4 Bit-Wise Epistasis Measures for a Set of Common Problems

In this section, we look at 4 functions taken from a set of problems widely studied in the GA community, proposed in [12, 13]. Figure 2 sums-up the characteristics of the functions we have studied. We have added the Davidor's epistasis variance computed on a sample of 2000 points and normalized on the fitness variance of the sample (as proposed in [2]).

Functions		Range of x_i	x_i coded on	Davidor's Epistasis
f1	$x_1^2 + x_2^2 + x_3^2$	$[-5.12, 5.11]$	10 bits	0.984
f2	$100(x_1^2 - x_2)^2 + (1 - x_1)^2$	$[-2.048, 2.047]$	12 bits	0.728
f6	$0.5 + \frac{\sin^2(\sqrt{x_1^2 + x_2^2}) - 0.5}{1 + 0.001(x_1^2 + x_2^2)}$	$[-100, 100]$	10 bits	0.994
f9	$x_1 + 2x_2 + 3x_3 + x_4^2$	$[0, 100]$	10 bits	0.082

Fig. 2. The set of test functions.

There have been for some time, a debate about the interest of using Gray coding as a general way to improve GAs performances (a general presentation can be found in [14]). Gray coding greatly reduces the "Hamming cliffs" that exist between consecutive integers around powers of 2 (e.g. $2^x - 1$ and 2^x are separated by a Hamming distance equal to $x + 1$ in binary coding, and only 1 in Gray coding). To allow the monitoring of differences introduced by this alternative representation scheme, we compute bit-wise epistasis using both standard binary coding and gray coding. Results are shown in Fig. 3, plots corresponding to binary coding are shown in continuous lines, those for gray coding are in dotted lines.

Compared with previous measures, these plots allow a closer view at epistatic effects. It is especially true for function $f9$. We already know that its overall epistatic variance was low (0.082), now we can see that only a few genes are involved in epistatic dependence: clearly, from its definition, we recognize the influence of the most significant bits of its last variable x_4. For function $f1$, epistasis is also quite concentrated on a few number of genes, corresponding to the most significant bits of the three variables involved in its definition. On the opposite, function $f6$ shows a large amount of dependencies on almost every bit.

It is clear from plots in Fig. 3 that using Gray code does slightly change the epistatic dependencies at the bit level. Notice anyway that this does not always amounts to a reduction in epistasis as can be seen in the case of function $f9$.

5 What is Bit-Wise Epistasis Good for ?

Through this section we propose to use the bit-wise epistasis measure to:

51

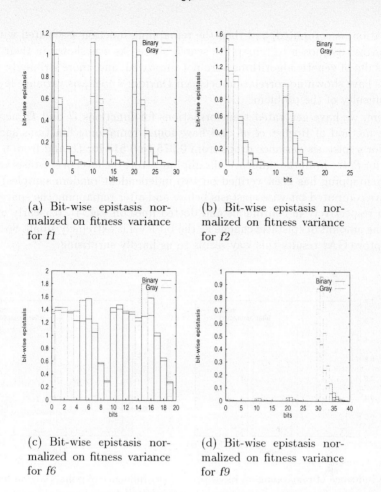

(a) Bit-wise epistasis normalized on fitness variance
for *f1*

(b) Bit-wise epistasis normalized on fitness variance
for *f2*

(c) Bit-wise epistasis normalized on fitness variance
for *f6*

(d) Bit-wise epistasis normalized on fitness variance
for *f9*

Fig. 3. Bit-wise epistasis for some test functions using binary and Gray coding.

- understand why remapping the binary search space does not always improve GA performance;
- improve the evolutionary algorithms by using the supplementary information gained through bit-wise epistasis computation.

5.1 Remapping

Remapping a function is known to be a very difficult problem (see [15]), but nonetheless some interesting attempts have been made to find other representations, notably in [16,17]. Here we focus on the method proposed in [7], where Rochet *et al* have proposed to randomly generate transformations in binary search spaces that remap bits 3 by 3. A random sample of such remapping functions is generated, their associated epistasis variance (or the derived epistasis correlation) is computed, and then the remapping function associated with lowest epistasis is chosen to remap the search space. As was shown in their paper, the results of genetic algorithms were not improved, and, more strikingly, experiments have shown no correlation between Davidor's epistasis variance level and the difficulty of the problem.

Here, we have generated transformations for functions *f1* and *f2*, according to the method of Rochet *et al.* and have found remapping functions such that Davidor's epistasis variance drops from 0.975 to 0.513 for *f1*, and from 0.713 to 0.431 for *f2* (to limit the influence of sampling error, the level of epistasis variance after remapping has been verified on two independent random samples). Then we have computed bit-wise epistasis before and after remapping the space (plots shown respectively in continuous and dotted lines on Fig. 4). It clearly appears that the amount of epistatic change at the bit level is extremely small. So, failing to improve GAs results this way seems to us hardly surprising.

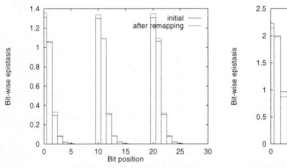 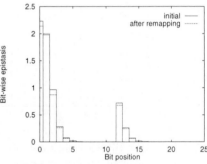

(a) Influence of remapping on bit-wise epistasis for *f1*

(b) Influence of remapping on bit-wise epistasis for *f2*

Fig. 4. Bit-wise epistasis before and after remapping.

5.2 Hints at Building Epistasis-Based Hybrid Algorithms

Now we intend to show how our epistasis measure can be used to improve evolutionary algorithms. First, we have focused our experiments on a basic hill-climber exploring the standard bit flipping neighborhood, to which a probabilistic mutation phase is added. The mutation rate is set independently for every gene, proportionally to the bit-wise epistasis value. Next we apply the same idea to a genetic algorithm, where we replace the usual unique mutation rate by computing for every gene a rate that depends on its bit-wise epistasis value. We do not claim to have devised algorithms that fully exploit bit-wise epistasis information.

We only show that a very simple scheme, changing probability of mutation on the basis of this information, is enough to obtain better results.

Accordingly, we don't have formal proofs of the underlying mechanics behind our scheme. An intuitive idea is that genes with few epistatic dependencies don't need to be changed very often. Indeed if the algorithm finds an allele that increases fitness, it is not useful to question this choice in the future: changing others genes values doesn't have much impact on this choice. On the opposite, highly epistatic genes should be mutated at a higher rate, due to the fact that their contribution to the global fitness is very dependent on other genes values: the more combinations we evaluate, the more chances we have to find a good set of alleles and jump away from local optimum (see also [18]).

Experimental Setting We present here three other problems that were used as benchmarks in our experiments.

The two first functions, taken from Sebag and Schoenauer in [19], are known to be difficult to solve.

$$y_1 = x_1$$
$$y_i = x_i + y_{i-1}, \; i \geq 2 \qquad F'_1 = \frac{100}{10^{-5} + \sum_i |y_i|}$$

$$F'_2 = \frac{100}{10^{-5} + \sum_i |.024 \times (i+1) - x_i|}$$

All these two functions involve 100 numerical variables x_i coded on 9 bits each and varying in $[-2.56, 2.56]$. The maximum for $F'1$ is 10^7, the maximum for $F'2$ is 416.64.

The third problem is a special version of the NK problem, with the following modifications:

- each even bit is involved in the NK epistatic dependencies;
- each odd bit brings an independent fitness contribution (like in the well-known OneMax problem).

We call this last problem *semi-nk*. In our experiments, the length of the chromosome was 100 and $K = 50$.

Hill-Climber Experiments In this section, a gene is said to be *epistatic* if its bit-wise epistatic measure is over the average bit-wise epistasis measure for all genes. In order to improve the hill-climber, we hybridize the standard hill-climbing method with a high rate mutation operator working only on epistatic genes. We do not detail this algorithm, due to lack of space.

Shapes of the $F'1$ and $F'2$ problems in Fig. 5 clearly indicate that we face very epistatic problems. The fitness contribution of each bit except the last one depends on the other ones. Furthermore, $F'1$ problem can be seen as a deceptive problem because for each numerical variable coded on 9 bits the optimal solution is 100000000 (binary coding) while a basic hill-climbing method will improve the fitness by flipping a 1 to the last eight positions.

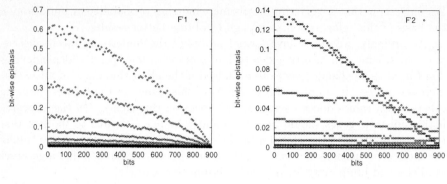

(a) Bit-wise epistasis for the $F'1$ problem. The average epistasis is 0.11

(b) Bit-wise epistasis for the $F'2$ problem. The average epistasis is 0.026

Fig. 5. Bit-wise epistasis for our experiments

Our results are compared with a basic multi-start hill-climber (HC), which explores the neighborhood defined by flipping one bit of the current solution. We allow 200000 functions evaluations.

Problems	HC	Hybrid HC
$F'1$ binary	1.04	1.37
$F'2$ binary	8.07	9.7
semi-nk binary	1.605	1.63

Table 1. Average best fitness for the 3 problems

Using bit-wise epistasis information improves the results. For the *semi-nk* problem, the smallness of the improvement may be explained by the relative easiness of this problem.

GAs Experiments In this section we show how bit-wise epistasis information can be used within the GAs frame. Experiments have been done on problems known to be hard for GAs : maximizing Schoenauer's *et al.* function $F'1$, mini-mizing Whitley's functions $F3$ and $F7$ (in [12]). We have used a standard GA, with ranked selection, 1-points crossover with a probability of 0.8, the size of the population being respectively 50, 20 and 30, the number of generations respec-tively 1000, 2000 and 5000, and the mutation operator the classical bit-flipping. There was two versions of this GA that differed from each other by mutation rates. In version 1 of our algorithm, half of the genes, those with lower bit-wise epistasis values, were associated with a mutation rate of $2e - 3$, the other half (higher bit-wise epistasis genes) using a rate of $1e - 3$. Version 2 of the GA used the opposite setting : lower mutation rate associated with lower bit-wise epistasis, higher rates with higher epistasis. The average best results other 20 independent runs of each GA is shown in Tab. 2, with other statistics.

	maximizing $F'1$		minimizing $F3$		minimizing $F7$	
	GA 1	GA 2	GA 1	GA 2	GA 1	GA 2
Min	1.107	1.306	4.431	3.647	0.599	0.599
Average	1.349	1.568	11.471	8.542	1.059	0.834
Max	1.533	1.770	25.394	16.044	3.093	2.511
Std Deviation	0.106	0.112	4.769	3.613	0.864	0.580

Table 2. Best results on 20 independent runs: GA1 works with low mutation on epistatic genes, GA2 with high mutation on epistatic genes.

We can see that GA2 is ahead of GA1, so putting higher mutation rates on genes with high bit-wise epistasis is worthwhile. Nonetheless we warn the reader that this effect appears on rather long runs (1000 generations or more). Work is still needed to show if easier problems or shorter runs may benefit from "bit-wise epistasis aware" schemes.

6 Conclusion

In this article, we have introduced the notion of bit-wise epistasis measure. We think this notion is a tool that is useful to understand epistatic interactions at a detailed level. This measure gives clues in explaining the failure of some remapping techniques which decreases the amount of Davidor's epistasis but seemingly with very few effects at the bit level. We have applied this tool to devise simple improvement schemes to a hill-climber and a GA. Work is still needed to understand how to use this information in better ways.

We are currently working on an extension of this technique to address non binary problems, like Traveling Salesman and Quadratic Assignment Problems. We think this concept deserves an in-depth theoretical study, in order to precise its relationship with Davidor's epistasis and also with the notion of ruggedness in fitness landscapes.

Note: we acknowledge the anonymous referree's suggestions that helped us in improving the presentation of our results.

References

1. Yuva Davidor. Epistasis variance: A viewpoint on GA-hardness. In [20], pages 23–35, 1991.
2. Mauro Manela and J.A. Campbell. Harmonic analysis, epistasis and genetic algorithms. In [21], 1992.

3. C.R. Reeves and C.C. Wright. Epistasis in genetic algorithms: An experimental design perspective. In *[22]*, pages 217–224, 1995.

4. S. Rochet, M. Slimane, and G. Venturini. Epistasis for real encoding in genetic algorithms. In *IEEE ANZIIS'96*, pages 268–271, 1996.

5. David E. Goldberg. Genetic algorithms and Walsh functions: Part I, a gentle introduction. *Complex Systems*, 3:129–152, 1989.

6. David E. Goldberg. Genetic algorithms and Walsh functions: Part II, deception and its analysis. *Complex Systems*, 3:153–171, 1989.

7. S. Rochet, G. Venturini, M. Slimane, and E. M. El Kharoubi. A critical and empirical study of epistasis measures for predicting GA performances: a summary. In *Evolution Artificielle 97*, pages 331–341, Nimes, Frances, October 1997.

8. David E. Goldberg. *Genetic Algorithms in Search, Optimization and Machine Learning*. Addison Wesley, 1989.

9. John H. Holland. *Adaptation in Natural and Artificial Systems*. Michigan Press University, 1975.

10. S.A. Kauffman. Adaptation on rugged fitness landscapes. *Lecture in the Sciences of Complexity*, pages 527–618, 1989.

11. Kenneth A. De Jong, Mitchell A. Potter, and William M. Spears. Using problem generators to explore the effects of epistasis. In *[23]*, pages 338–345, 1997.

12. D. Whitley, K. Mathias, S. Rana, and J. Dzubera. Building better test functions. In *in [22]*, pages 239–246, 1995.

13. K. A. De Jong. *An analysis of the behavior of a class of genetic adaptive systems*. PhD thesis, University of Michigan, MI, USA, 1975.

14. David Goldberg. *Genetic Algorithms in Search, Optimization and Machine Learning*. Addison-Wesley, 1989.

15. G.E. Liepins and M.D. Vose. Representational issues in genetic optimization. *Journal of Experimental and Theoretical AI*, 2:1–15, 1990.

16. Keith Mathias and Darrell Whitley. Remapping hyperspace during genetic search: Canonical delta folding. In *[24]*, pages 167–186, 1993.

17. Keith E. Mathias and Darrell Whitley. Changing representations during search: A comparative study of delta coding. *Evolutionary Computation*, 2, 1994.

18. J. David Schaffer and Larry J. Eshelman. On crossover as an evolutionarily viable strategy. In *[25]*, pages 61–67, 1991.

19. Michèle Sebag and Marc Schoenauer. A society of hill-climbers. In *[26]*, 1997.

20. Gregory J.E. Rawlins, editor. *Workshop on the Foundations of Genetic Algorithms and Classifiers*, Bloomington, IN, USA, July 1991. Morgan Kaufmann.

21. Reinhard Manner and Bernard Manderick, editors. *Proceedings of the second Conference on Parallel Problem Solving from Nature*, Free University of Brussels, Belgium, September 1992. Elsevier Science.

22. Philips Laboratories Larry J. Eshelman, editor. *Proceedings of the 6th International Conference on Genetic Algorithms*, University of Pittsburgh, USA, July 1995. Morgan Kaufmann.

23. *Proceedings of the 7th International Conference on Genetic Algorithms*, East Lansing, Michigan, USA, July 1997. Morgan Kaufmann.

24. Darrell Whitley, editor. *Proc. of the Workshop on Foundations of Genetic Algorithms*, Vail, CO, USA, 1993. Morgan Kaufmann.

25. Richard K. Belew and Lashon B. Booker, editors. *Proceedings of the 4th International Conference on Genetic Algorithms*, La Jolla, California, USA, July 1991. Morgan Kaufmann.

26. *International Conference on Evolutionary Computation*, Anchorage, USA, 1997.

Inside GA Dynamics: Ground Basis for Comparison

Leila Kallel

CMAP – UMR CNRS 7641
Ecole Polytechnique
Palaiseau 91128, France
kallel@cmapx.polytechnique.fr

Abstract. Much attention has been paid in the GA literature to understand, characterize or to predict the notion of difficulty for genetic algorithms. Formal or informal ways of handling difficulty in previous work are commented. This points out a major problem of scaling especially when comparing differently distributed fitness functions.
Hamming fitness functions are proposed as a basis to scale difficulty measures, and to account for GA parameters bias. The use of a basis relaxes the dependence on fitness scale or distribution. Different measures are also proposed to characterize GA behavior, distinguishing convergence time and on-line GA radial and effective trajectory distance in Hamming space.

Introduction

As far as optimization problems and GAs are concerned, no rigorous definition of the concept of difficulty is available. Yet, many papers use implicit definitions in many cases. For example, when two instances of algorithm parameters are compared on some problem, or when two different problems are compared. Also, when tools are developed (and validated) in order to measure problem difficulty. Examples of such tools are fitness distance correlation [12], correlation length, operator correlation [16] , epistasis [5], schema variance [19], hyperplane ranking [4] ...

The early attempts to characterize difficulty propose criteria based on: Isolation (needle in a haystack), Deception (schema analysis) and Multimodality [9] [8] [7]. It seems clear that these criterion certainly contribute to problem difficulty. However, there exist examples showing that the latter two criterion (deception and multimodality) are neither necessary nor sufficient: Vose and Wright in [23] present the extreme case of a fully non deceptive function that is difficult for a GA because of an exponential number (in string length l) of stable suboptimal attractors. Wilson proposes a deceptive function, yet straightforward to optimize for a GA [25]. Horn and Goldberg [10] construct an easy maximally multimodal function. They also stress the fact that modality and schema-GA-easy analysis are not at all enough to describe GA-behavior. Finally, longpath problems [11] have been designed to show that unimodal functions can be difficult because of an exponential path length.

Many papers use the word 'difficult problem for GA' when the fitness land-scape presents a large number of local optima with large basins of attraction and high barriers between them, as with the NK landscapes when K value increases (1989, [15]).

Apart from such fitness landscape analysis, practical methods have been used to compare genetic algorithms with different sets of parameters or on different problems. Some examples of commonly used methods (often named differently) are presented in the following. These methods are mainly based on results of intensive GA runs, as Shaffer's (1989,[21]) 'brute force' comparisons :

In Tanese's doctoral dissertation (1989), GA performance is related to its *success rate*, defined as the fraction of runs that find the global optimum. Collins and Jefferson define two notions (1991, [2]): The *speed of evolution* is the number of generations necessary to discover an *acceptable solution* (user-defined). The *robustness of evolution* is the fraction of runs that find at least one acceptable solution (within 1000 generations).

As early as 1991, some attempt was made to formalize the properties that all performance measures should follow [6] *'(1) they should be normalized so that performance can be compared on different problems and with different optimizers, (2) they should reflect problem difficulty, and (3) they should indicate how far the optimizer got, not just whether or not it reached the global optimum.'*

A different point of view on difficulty is encountered in [14] (1996) concerning SEARCH, a particular optimization algorithm: difficulty is not only related to some measure, but also to the way the measure evolves with some parameter (problem size, solution quality or success probability requirement).

Recently, Rochet et al. define a measure of difficulty to compare different minimization problems [20]: The ratio of best fitnesses found by GA and random search, after the same number of evaluations.

All these methods may be helpful when comparing two sets of parameters on the same problem and algorithm. To compare problems with different fitness distributions, fitness values or improvements are completely unreliable. And the main weakness of probability of success or convergence time is that 1- they don't give information about what happened during the run. 2- they don't take into account initialization and operators bias. These points define the context of the difficulty measure proposed in the following.

The first section defines the point of view on difficulty considered in this paper, and motivates the proposed approach: using *Hamming functions* as a basis to compare GA behaviors. Section 1 proposes different characterizations of GA behaviors distinguishing time and trajectory. The last section illustrates the method on some well known problems of GA literature. Special attention is paid to GA dynamics with the difficult Baluja F1 problem.

1   Method

In the following we stick to the binary space $E = \{0,1\}^l$ and note d the normalized Hamming distance between strings. Before presenting the comparison method, we discuss two different points of view on difficulty.

1.1   Difficulty of landscapes versus GA difficulty

Two notions have to be distinguished: the measure of intrinsic problem difficulty, and the measure of difficulty (or adequacy) of some algorithm with a fixed set of parameters.

It is not clear whether any known landscape based measure (as Epistasis and Fitness Distance Correlation ..) would characterize intrinsic problem difficulty. It is demonstrated in [18] that, among other limitations, the sensitivity of such measures to scaling, makes their values unreliable. It is even more unlikely that such landscape based measures would characterize problem difficulty for some algorithm. In the same paper, simple examples show that epistasis and correlation are completely unrelated to convergence quality (find the solution or not) and speed of GAs, even without any problem of scaling.

Many papers [3], [22] stress the nonsense of speaking of problem difficulty without considering all the parameters of the algorithm at hand: [3] presents two unimodal functions on the binary space: depending on whether elitism is used or not, the same sampling technique (ex. steepest ascent hill climber) yields an exponential difference –in both directions– in convergence time. Authors explain that the potentialities of an operator are not necessarily exploited by the algorithm. Such differences are unmeasurable, with any landscape based measure.

Now let's consider the notion of problem difficulty as directly related to some particular run of a given algorithm.

1.2   Hamming functions basis

Accounting for initialization, and other parameters bias is certainly impossible if we refer only to fitness values, because we have no idea of their distribution. In the following we propose a basis that should account for this bias.

Given some fitness function f, suppose the GA found the optimum of f. To characterize GA behavior for this particular run, the question one can ask is: 'What this same algorithm -starting from the same population- would have done if for each x the fitness function were simply the distance to the optimum of f?' Let's call such a fitness function a Hamming function to optimum. Then h is *Hamming function to y*, if for each $x \in E$, $h(x) = d(x,y)$.

Comparing GA *behavior* to its behavior with a Hamming function to the optimum, allows us to get rid of initialization and other parameters bias, mainly keeping the difficulty introduced by fitness function.

GA *behavior* includes both temporal and spatial issues. If time is rather straightforward to define, it is not the case with trajectory.

1.3 Definition of GA trajectory

The effective trajectory of the GA is the succession of populations from one generation to the other. To measure the length of this trajectory, one can use a distance between two populations considered as sets of elements of E, replacing the Hamming distance with the adequate distance function. For example the *Hausdorff*'s metric: $\Delta(A, B) = max\{\delta(a, B) : a \in A\} + max\{\delta(b, A) : b \in B\}$, where $\delta(a, b)$ is any metric distance on E, and the distance of a point $a \in E$ to a set B is $\delta(a, B) = min\{\delta(a, b), b \in B\}$.

But in the context of optimization, we may be interested in the trajectory of the upper tail of the successive populations, viewed as sampling of the fitness distribution, rather than some average distance that hides what happens with the fittest individuals. Thus, GA trajectory will be reduced to the fittest so far individual known to the GA at each generation. The following approach can be generalized to different definitions of the GA trajectory, by simply replacing the Hamming distance with the adequate distance.

1.4 Summary measures of GA behavior

In the following, we present some measures that characterize on-line GA behavior (of a given run) when maximizing a fitness function f with a unique global optimum on the binary space. Let's note $\hat{X}_i$ the -so far- best individual at generation i for a given run, N_c the number of generations to reach $\hat{X}_i$, and d the Hamming distance normalized to string length.

In order to compare some fitness f to another one, the significant amount is the ratio (ρ_m) of the measure m obtained when f is used as fitness function, and the measure obtained when a Hamming function to the $\hat{X}_{N_c}$ is used. Both runs starting at the same initial population.

The measures presented below, characterize on-line GA behavior (of a given run) to reach $\hat{X}_{N_c}$. In case $\hat{X}_{N_c}$ is not the optimum, the measures characterize GA dynamic to reach this local optimum. In case the GA converged to the optimum $(\hat{X}_{N_c} = X^*)$, we get the desired information about optimization difficulty for the considered GA.

1. **Convergence time: N_c** = Number of generations

2. **Distance to $\hat{X}_{N_c}$: D** $= \dfrac{\sum_{1,N_c} d(\hat{X}_i, \hat{X}_{N_c})}{N_c}$
   This is the average distance to $\hat{X}_{N_c}$ during the run.

3. **Trajectory distance:** $\theta = \sum_{1,N_c-1} d(\hat{X}_i, \hat{X}_{i+1})$
   θ characterizes the amount of exploration within the fittest points 'seen by the GA'. θ is minimum and equals $d(\hat{X}_1, \hat{X}_{N_c})$, if each time an allele of the optimum is found, it remains fixed until the end of the run. Hence, there are no more than l improvement steps.

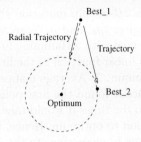

Fig. 1. *Two points of view on GA trajectory distance: the distance between best individuals at successive generations, or their difference in distance to optimum.*

4. **Radial Trajectory distance:** $\theta_{\mathbf{r}} = \sum_{1, N_c - 1} |d(\hat{X}_i, \hat{X}_{N_c}) - d(\hat{X}_{i+1}, \hat{X}_{N_c})|$

Replacing the distance between $\hat{X}_i$ and $\hat{X}_{i+1}$ by their difference in distance to $\hat{X}_{N_c}$ gives the point of view on GA trajectory 'as seen from $\hat{X}_{N_c}$'.
θ_r is minimal and equals $d(\hat{X}_1, \hat{X}_{N_c})$, if the GA comes closer to $\hat{X}_{N_c}$ at each step. This is always the case with Hamming functions.

Note that θ and θ_r (Fig. 1) are not necessarily correlated: θ_r can be minimal, with arbitrary θ values. For Hamming functions, experiments (next section) show that θ often equals 5 to 10 times θ_r. On the other hand, the unrealistic case of minimal θ_r implies necessarily a minimal θ.

2 Experiments

To illustrate the method, we propose to focus on comparing the same function with different GA instances. For each function, only the most significant cases (in relation to the measures) are presented. In the last experiment, the case of the difficult Baluja F1 problem is studied with different algorithms.

Otherwise mentioned, a generational GA with a population size of 100, linear ranking selection, crossover rate 0.6 and mutation rate per individual 0.4, is used. Mutation independently flips each bit of a string with probability $1/l$. Stopping criterion is 1000 generations with no improvement or 200 000 generations. Results are averaged over 10 runs.

2.1 Longpath: large θ_r

As expected, longpath problem [10] with $1/l$-bit flip mutation (Fig. 2) shows a particularly high Radial trajectory ($\rho_{\theta_r} = 7$): the GA -partially following the path- makes big movements getting closer then further to the optimum. These movements are responsible for the increase in average distance to optimum ($\rho_D = 2$), as well as for the large time ratio($\rho_{N_c} = 39$).

Longpath problem with a $2/l$-bit flip mutation shows a completely different behavior: 1- Trajectory measures (ρ_θ, and ρ_{θ_r}) are rather close to one: GA trajectory is similar to that obtained with a Hamming function to optimum. In fact, the search begins almost as a linear function to the first point on the path, which is two bits distant from optimum. 2- Average distance to optimum ($D = 0.66$) is even smaller than one: Once it found the first point on the path, it takes the GA a large time -relatively to the times it would take with a Hamming function- to find the right 2-bit mutation to optimum. Hence, the GA spends a relatively large amount of time searching in close areas to the optimum.

	N_c	D	θ	θ_r
longpath 1/l-mut	2466(914)	0.2(0.08)	5.7(1.6)	2.7(1)
Hamming	63(9)	0.1(0.01)	2.9(0.6)	0.3(0.02)
ρ	**39**(15)	**1.9**(0.7)	**2**(0.6)	**7.5**(2.8)
longpath 2/l-mut	271(142)	0.07(0.01)	3.5(0.7)	0.5(0.1)
Hamming	65(11)	0.1(0.01)	2.4	0.3(0.02)
ρ	**4.3**(2.4)	**0.66** (0.13)	**1.2** (0.4)	**1.54**(0.3)

Fig. 2. *GA results on the 91-bits longpath problem, using mutation at 1/l and 2/l-bit-flip probability. ρ is the ratio of the two upper lines (longpath and Hamming measures).*

2.2 F1g,F3g: influence of problem size

Gray coded F1 problem [1] is very sensitive to the choice of problem and population size. For example, Fig. 3 shows that convergence time ratio ρ_{N_c} increases at a more than linear rate (wrt. problem size). Yet, F1g trajectory is -in average distance- as close to optimum as the Hamming run is ($\rho_D = 1$). Hence, the big radial trajectory ($\rho_{\theta_r} >= 3$) is not due to big deviations far away from optimum (as for longpaths), but due to small oscillating movements.

On the other hand, Gray F3 problem [1] is an easy problem that have a close behavior to that of Hamming functions for different population and problem sizes (Fig. 3). The difference in convergence time $\rho_{N_c} = 2$ is mainly due to small oscillating movements as witnessed by radial trajectory $\rho_{\theta_r} = 3$.

2.3 Ugly and royal problems: initialization bias

Two initialization procedures are compared on ugly [24] and Royal Road (RR) [17] problems. The second initialization -defined and studied in [13]- is biased to enhance density of ones in a bitstring. Although both problems have the same optimum (all ones string), the resulting initialization bias is not the same:

The 2nd initialization, generates individuals closer to optimum than the first, standard initialization. For instance, initial distance to optimum drops form

	N_c	D	θ	θ_r
45-F3g 100-GA	**2.102** (0.3)	**1.4** (0.16)	**2.3** (1.1)	**3** (0.47)
90-F3g 100-GA	**2.039** (0.3)	**1.3** (0.14)	**1.6** (0.44)	**2.9** (0.29)
90-F3g 200-GA	**2.019** (0.35)	**1.3** (0.13)	**1.8** (0.41)	**2.9** (0.52)

	N_c	D	θ	θ_r
45-F1g 100-GA	**16.68** (14)	**1.1** (0.29)	**1.9** (0.87)	**3.1** (0.86)
90-F1g 100-GA	**47.46** (24)	**1.1** (0.15)	**1.8** (0.3)	**4.5** (0.4)
90-F1g 200-GA	**34.8** (27)	**1.1** (0.24)	**2.2** (0.86)	**5** (1.3)

Fig. 3. *Influence of problem size (*-F1), with different population sizes (*-GA). Only ratios of the measures are presented. At the difference with F1g, F3g ratios scarcely vary.*

about 0.35 (init1) to 0.15 (init2) (values given by θ_r values of the Hamming problems in Fig. 4). As expected, when using the 2nd initialization, convergence is a lot faster for both RR and ugly problems. But Hamming functions also get quicker, and only the RR ratio of time drops. This is not surprising since the 2nd initialization enhances the emergence of the building blocks (blocks of 1s) of the RR function. On the other hand, the ugly landscape is invariably deceptive with both initializations, hence beginning closer to optimum scarcely changes the time ratio ($\rho_{N_c} = 7$).

	N_c	D	θ	θ_r
ugly init1	**7.947** (3.9)	**0.89** (0.25)	**1.2** (0.55)	**2** (0.52)
ugly init2	**6.8** (4.2)	**0.95** (0.36)	**2.4** (1.1)	**3.1** (0.93)

	N_c	D	θ	θ_r
royal init1	**16.3** (8.7)	**1** (0.18)	**0.7** (0.21)	**1.3** (0.19)
royal init2	**7.2** (7.8)	**1.2** (0.26)	**1.8** (0.76)	**2.4** (1.1)

Fig. 4. *Influence of initialization on 90-bits ugly and 64-bits royal problems. Only ratios are presented. The second initialization is biased to enhance density of ones in a bitstring. Note that we easily compare different problem sizes here.*

2.4 F1b: comparison of different algorithms

Different algorithms are studied on Blauja's binary F1 [1] problem with $l = 45$. Most algorithms (denoted F1b* in Fig. 5) fail to find the optimum. Only a GA using one-point complementary crossover (CX) between a string and its bit-wise complement finds the optimum. Note that this crossover seriously weakens the linear run to optimum (807 generations!!), resulting in a small ρ_{N_c} of 2 in average.

Fig. 6-a shows GA trajectory over the course of the GA. 1C-GA gets stuck in a local optimum far away from optimum. As witnessed by the particularly

	N_c	D	θ	θ_r
F1b* (1+200)-ES : ρ	**32.55** (45)	**0.83** (0.24)	**1.8** (0.55)	**1.2** (0.27)
F1b* (1,200)-ES : ρ	**49.1** (42)	**0.78** (0.33)	**1.7** (0.48)	**1.2** (0.32)
F1b* 200-GA : ρ	**4.338** (1.8)	**1.8** (0.67)	**3.1** (1.5)	**6.9** (3.2)

F1b 100-CX-GA	1356 (490)	0.3 (0.049)	11 (1.9)	3.1 (0.64)
Hamming	807.9 (320)	0.066 (0.018)	1.3 (0.67)	0.3 (0.044)
ρ	**1.904** (1.1)	**5** (1.7)	**12** (8.8)	**11** (2.7)

Fig. 5. *Study of Baluja's binary F1 problem with $l = 45$. F1b* means all runs failed to find the optimum. Then measures are calculated with respect to $\hat{X}_{N_c}$. Last case shows results with complementary crossover (CX): 8 GA runs out of 20 found the optimum, and results are averaged among successful runs only.*

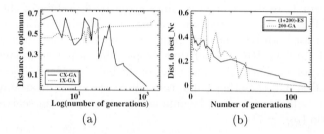

(a)   (b)

Fig. 6. *Binary F1 problem (a) GA trajectory with one point and complementary crossover plotted in distance to optimum: 1C-GA gets stuck in a local optimum. (b) ES and GA trajectories plotted in distance to local optimum: ES trajectory is almost monotone decreasing.*

high $\rho_{\theta_r} = 7$, its trajectory makes big movements further and closer to the local optimum it finally converges to (Fig. 6-b). At the difference with GA, both evolution strategies have a close to Hamming trajectory distance (ratios are often close to one).

Conclusion and further directions

Different measures have been proposed to characterize GA behavior. Both time and on-line GA trajectory distance in Hamming space are involved. Hamming fitness functions are proposed as a basis to scale the measures values, and to account for GA parameters bias. The measures ratios don't depend directly on fitness scale or distribution, therefore, they can be used to compare GA behaviors on different fitness functions. For instance, results of the measures would be the same if we compare a ranking selection GA optimizing f or $g(f)$ for any monotone increasing function g.

Moreover, this method can also be used to study the influence of problem size, or to evaluate initialization bias on some problem, and more generally, to compare different problems at different problem sizes and with different algorithms. For example, if we stick to the temporal point of view, 45-bits F1g problem is as difficult as 64-bits royal problem, and (4 times) more difficult than 2-bits mutation 91-bits longpath problem.

The case of F1b problem is very instructive : we observe a low θ_r value (for evolution strategies), and globally a similar to linear behavior. Though, this situation reflects the presence of strong local optima and certainly not problem easiness. A close look at the solutions, clearly shows they vary in fitness and in genotype from one run to the other.

The method presented in this paper can easily be generalized to different representations, simply by replacing *Hamming functions basis* with the appropriate *genotypic-distance functions basis*. Alternatively the basis can be defined with a phenotypic distance. Then, a possible comparison of results obtained with genotypic and phenotypic basis, may give insights in the dynamic of the search linked to representational issues.

The choice of Hamming functions as a basis is though rather arbitrary, and may be too weak when taken alone. One can imagine that a sequence of basis would allow to identify different GA-like behavior, rather than simply detect the differences from some fixed basis. The NK-Landscapes for example, can provide such a sequence indexed by K values. In this case, note that Hamming functions correspond to a null K value.

References

1. S. Baluja. An empirical comparison of seven iterative and evolutionary function optimization heuristics. Technical Report CMU-CS-95-193, Carnegie Mellon University, 1995.
2. Robert J. Collins and David R. Jefferson. Selection in massively parallel genetic algorithm. In R. K. Belew and L. B. Booker, editors, *Proc. of the 4th ICGA*, pages 249–256. Morgan Kaufmann, 1991.
3. J. Culberson and Jonathan Lichtner. On searching 'alpha'-ary hypercubes and related graphs. In R. K. Belew and M. D. Vose, editors, *FOGA 4*, pages 263–290. Morgan Kaufmann, 1996.
4. K. Mathias D. Whitley and L. Pyeatt. Hyperplane ranking in simple genetic alghoritms. In L. J. Eshelman, editor, *Proc. of the 6th ICGA*, pages 231–238. Morgan Kaufmann, 1995.
5. Y. Davidor. Epistasis variance: a viewpoint on ga-hardness. In G. J. E. Rawlins, editor, *FOGA*, pages 23–35. Morgan Kaufmann, 1991.
6. S. Forrest and M. Mitchell. The performance of genetic algorithms on walsh polynomials: Some anomalous results and their explanation. In R. K. Belew and L. B. Booker, editors, *Proc. of the 4th ICGA*, pages 182–189. Morgan Kaufmann, 1991.
7. S. Forrest and M. Mitchell. Relative building-block fitness and the building-block hypothesis. *FOGA 2*, pages 109–126, 1993.
8. D. E. Goldberg. *Genetic algorithms in search, optimization and machine learning*. Addison Wesley, 1989.

9. D. E. Goldberg. Making genetic algorithms fly:a lesson from the wright brothers. *Advanced Technology for Developpers*, 2:1–8, February 1993.

10. J. Horn and D.E. Goldberg. Genetic algorithms difficulty and the modality of fitness landscapes. In L. D. Whitley and M. D. Vose, editors, *FOGA 3*, pages 243–269. Morgan Kaufmann, 1995.

11. J. Horn, D.E. Goldberg, and K. Deb. Long path problems. In Y. Davidor, H.-P. Schwefel, and R. Manner, editors, *Proc. of the 3rd Conference on Parallel Problems Solving from Nature*, pages 149–158. Springer Verlag, 1994.

12. T. Jones and S. Forrest. Fitness distance correlation as a measure of problem difficulty for genetic algorithms. In L. J. Eshelman, editor, *Proc. of the 6th ICGA*, pages 184–192. Morgan Kaufmann, 1995.

13. L. Kallel and M. Schoenauer. Alternative random initialization in genetic algorithms. In Th. Bäeck, editor, *Proc. of the 7th ICGA*. Morgan Kaufmann, 1997.

14. H. Kargupta and D. E. Goldberg. Serch, blackbox optimisation, and sample complexity. In R. K. Belew and M. D. Vose, editors, *FOGA 4*, pages 291–324. Morgan Kaufmann, 1996.

15. S. A. Kauffman. *Lectures in the Sciences of Complexity*, volume I of *SFI studies*, chapter Adaptation on Rugged Fitness Landscape, pages 619–712. Addison Wesley, 1989.

16. B. Manderick, M. de Weger, and P. Spiessens. The genetic algorithm and the structure of the fitness landscape. In R. K. Belew and L. B. Booker, editors, *Proc. of the 4th ICGA*, pages 143–150. Morgan Kaufmann, 1991.

17. M. Mitchell and J.H. Holland. When will a genetic algorithm outperform hill-climbing ? In S. Forrest, editor, *Proc. of the 5th ICGA*, page 647, 1993.

18. B. Naudts and L.Kallel. Some facts about so called ga-hardness measures. Technical Report 379, CMAP, Ecole Polytechnique, Mars 1998. submitted.

19. N. J. Radcliffe and P. D. Surry. Fitness variance of formae and performance prediction. In L. D. Whitley and M. D. Vose, editors, *FOGA 3*, pages 51–72. Morgan Kaufmann, 1995.

20. S. Rochet, G. Venturini, M. Slimane, and E.M El Kharoubi. A critical and empirical study of epistasis measures for predicting ga performances: a summary. In J.-K. Hao, E. Lutton, E. Ronald, M. Schoenauer, and D. Snyers, editors, *Artificial Evolution'97*, LNCS, pages 287–299. Springer Verlag, 1997.

21. J. D. Schaffer, R. A. Caruana, L. Eshelman, and R. Das. A study of control parameters affecting on-line performance of genetic algorithms for function optimization. In J. D. Schaffer, editor, *Proc. of the 3rd ICGA*, pages 51–60. Morgan Kaufmann, 1989.

22. K. A. DeJong W. M. Spears and D. M. Gordon. Using markov chains to analyse gafos. In L. D. Whitley and M. D. Vose, editors, *FOGA 3*, pages 115–137. Morgan Kaufmann, 1995.

23. Michael D. Vose and Alden H. Wright. Stability of vertex fixed points and applications. In L. D. Whitley and M. D. Vose, editors, *FOGA 3*, pages 103–11. Morgan Kaufmann, 1995.

24. D. Whitley. Fundamental principles of deception in genetic search. In G. J. E. Rawlins, editor, *FOGA*. Morgan Kaufmann, 1991.

25. S.W. Wilson. Ga-easy does not imply steepest-ascent optimizable. In R. K. Belew and L. B. Booker, editors, *Proc. of the 4th ICGA*. mk, 1991.

The Effect of Spin-Flip Symmetry on the Performance of the Simple GA

Bart Naudts[1] and Jan Naudts[2]

[1] Department of Mathematics and Computer Science, University of Antwerp, RUCA, Groenenborgerlaan 171, B-2020 Antwerpen, Belgium. E-mail: *bnaudts@ruca.ua.ac.be*
[2] Department of Physics, University of Antwerp, UIA, Universiteitsplein 1, B-2610 Antwerpen, Belgium. E-mail: *naudts@uia.ua.ac.be*

Abstract. We use the one-dimensional nearest neighbor interaction functions (NNIs) to show how the presence of symmetry in a fitness function greatly influences the convergence behavior of the simple genetic algorithm (SGA). The effect of symmetry on the SGA supports the statement that it is not the amount of interaction present in a fitness function, measured e.g. by Davidor's epistasis variance and the experimental design techniques introduced by Reeves and Wright, which is important, but the kind of interaction. The NNI functions exhibit a minimal amount of second order interaction, are trivial to optimize deterministically and yet show a wide range of SGA behavior. They have been extensively studied in statistical physics; results from this field explain the negative effect of symmetry on the convergence behavior of the SGA. This note intends to introduce them to the GA-community.

Introduction

One factor influencing the convergence behavior of the simple genetic algorithm (SGA) is the presence of dependencies between the sites (or bit positions) of the strings, called *epistasis*. An example of a class of epistatically free functions is the class of first order or linear functions, whose members are of the form

$$f : \{0,1\}^L \to \mathbb{R} : s \mapsto \sum_{i \in L}(k_i s_i + l_i(1 - s_i)), \tag{1}$$

where k_i and l_i are constants. Notationally, we use $L = \{0, \ldots, \ell - 1\}$ to index the sites within a string, i.e., $s = s_0 s_1 \ldots s_{\ell-1}$, with $s_i \in \{0,1\}$ for all $i \in L$.

Kauffman's *NK-landscapes* [5], to give an example of the other side of the epistatical spectrum, are fitness functions featuring a fixed number of dependencies of order $K + 1$. They are typically written in the form

$$s \mapsto \frac{1}{N} \sum_{i \in L} g_i(\pi_{\Gamma_i}(s)). \tag{2}$$

Here, the Γ_i are subsets of L containing i and K randomly chosen other sites. The operator $\pi_{\Gamma_i} : \Sigma^L \to \Sigma^{\Gamma_i}$ projects strings to the substrings on which the $g_i : \Sigma^{\Gamma_i} \to R$ are defined.

Davidor's *epistasis variance* [2] and the *Anova tables* proposed by Reeves and Wright [12] are techniques to measure the amount of epistasis present in a fitness function. The former only detects the presence of second or higher order dependencies, more precisely, it computes the distance between a function and the class of first order functions. The latter can quantify the amount of first, second, third, and higher order dependencies.

The main point of this paper is to show that it is not the amount of higher order interaction but the type of interaction which determines the convergence behavior of the genetic algorithm (and also of simulated annealing and other stochastic search algorithms). The fact that the optimization of second order functions (functions where only first and second order dependencies are present) is an NP-hard problem already supports this statement: third and higher order interactions are not needed to make optimization problems really hard.

From the study of interacting particle systems (e.g., Liggett [7]) we deduce that there are at least three factors which seriously influence the convergence behavior of the SGA: the *dimension* of the problem, the presence of *frustration* in the problem and the *symmetry* of the problem. By means of the one-dimensional nearest neighbor interaction functions (NNIs), we show in this paper that symmetry on its own is enough to stop the SGA from converging to the global optimum. The NNIs exhibit only a small amount of second order interaction and are trivially optimized deterministically, yet their symmetry can force the SGA to drift for long time in sub-optimal fitness areas.

Some macroscopic properties of the dynamics of the SGA on a slight generalization of the NNIs are described in by Prügel-Bennett and Shapiro in [11]. The approach they take, however, is not suited to capture the effects of symmetry we will discuss in this paper.

In a way this paper is complementary to Altenberg's [1]. He presents the simplest form of symmetrical NNIs as an example which defeats fitness distance correlation, and analyzes this function using the "one operator, one landscape" paradigm. Whereas he mainly concentrates on crossover landscapes, we concentrate on hill-climber behavior, i.e., on the effect of mutation.

1   One-Dimensional Nearest Neighbor Interaction Functions

1.1   Optimization point of view

Optimization in the context of genetic algorithms usually involves the search for a string $s \in S = \{0,1\}^L$ for which a given fitness function $f : S \to \mathbb{R}$ yields a (near to) maximal value.

In the previous section we introduced the first order functions. Their main characteristic is the absence of terms in the fitness function sum which depend on the values of more than one site. Because of their simple form, the first order functions appear often in theoretical GA works.

The *second order functions* generalize the first order functions in a canonical way by allowing terms in the fitness value sum which depend on the values of two sites. Their generic form is

$$f : s \mapsto \sum_{i<j \in L} g_{ij}(s_i, s_j) + \sum_{i \in L} (k_i s_i + l_i(1 - s_i)). \tag{3}$$

It is of course also possible to construct fitness functions where terms which are dependent on the value of three or more sites are present. Since the deterministic optimization of second order functions is an NP-hard problem (see [8] for a proof), we are not too much interested in dependencies of order three and higher: second order dependencies make the optimization hard enough. For essentially the same reason, statistical physics does not pay much attention to higher order interactions.

The number of second order dependencies of a second order function can be reduced by a factor of 4 with the problem remaining NP-hard. We obtain the class of *asymmetric interaction functions*, studied in [9], with generic form

$$f : s \mapsto \sum_{i<j \in L} g_{ij}(1 - s_i)s_j + \sum_{i \in L} (k_i s_i + l_i(1 - s_i)). \tag{4}$$

Note that the problem difficulty of optimizing the second order functions does not depend on the cardinality of the range of their components: all g_{ij}, k_i and l_i can take natural values without loss of problem difficulty. In what follows, we will assume that they do indeed.

Restricting the class of asymmetric interaction even further, we obtain the asymmetric one-dimensional nearest neighbor interaction functions, on which we will focus in this paper. They are of the form

$$f : s \mapsto \sum_{i \in L} g_i(1 - s_i)s_{i+1} + \sum_{i \in L} (k_i s_i + l_i(1 - s_i)), \tag{5}$$

where we assume periodic boundary conditions, i.e., we let $s_0 \equiv s_\ell$. To lessen the burden of terminology, we will call functions of the form of Eq. 5 *NNI functions* (or *NNI problems* if we see them in the context of optimization).

In [8], a deterministic *divide and conquer* algorithm is presented which optimizes the NNI problems in linear time.

1.2 Statistical physics point of view

A classical model for magnetism is the *generalized Ising model* described by the energy functional (Hamiltonian)

$$H = - \sum_{i<j \in L} J_{ij} \sigma_i \sigma_j - \sum_{i \in L} h_i \sigma_i. \tag{6}$$

Here L is again the set of sites. Each spin variable σ_i at site $i \in L$ either takes the value 1 or the value -1, representing either the north or the south pole of a little magnet. A specific choice of values for the spin variables is called a configuration. The constants J_{ij} are called the interaction coefficients, the constants h_i the external magnetic field strengths. The problem central to statistical physics is the description of all configurations typical for a given value of the energy functional (typical in the stochastic sense not explained here). A ground state, as a special case, is any configuration for which the energy is minimal.

The case where $J_{ij} = J\delta_{j,i+1}$ for all $i < j \in L$ (with $\delta_{i,j}$ the Kronecker delta, yielding 1 if $i = j$ and 0 otherwise) and $h_i = h$ for all $i \in L$ is the original one-dimensional Ising model [3]. One speaks of a one-dimensional model here because the interaction between the sites is restricted to neighboring sites due to the Kronecker delta. A slight generalization of the standard one-dimensional Ising model is the *one-dimensional nearest neighbor model with arbitrary coefficients*. It is described by the energy functional

$$H = -\sum_{i \in L} J_i \sigma_i \sigma_{i+1} - \sum_{i \in L} h_i \sigma_i. \tag{7}$$

In this equation we assume periodic boundary conditions, i.e., we let $\sigma_\ell \equiv \sigma_0$.

When all the J_{ij} of the generalized Ising model are non-negative the model is called ferromagnetic. Most of the theoretical results of statistical physics have been obtained for models with this property, including the famous result by Onsager on the phase transition of the standard two-dimensional Ising model [10]. Less understood and much harder to tackle are the random field models and spin glass models for which either the h_i resp. the J_{ij} take arbitrary values or are replaced by stochastic variables. The model without interaction, leaving only the external magnetic field, is called an ideal paramagnet and is easily analyzed. Its energy functional is $H = -\sum_{i \in L} h_i \sigma_i$. It is easy to see the correspondence between the ideal paramagnet and the first order functions.

In what follows, we will study a model of moderate difficulty involving one-dimensional anti-ferromagnetic nearest neighbor interaction coefficients whose values depend on the sites in a periodic manner. The term anti-ferromagnetic implies that the interaction coefficients cannot take positive values. Any model with anti-ferromagnetic nearest neighbor interaction and an even number of sites can easily be transformed into a model with ferromagnetic interaction coefficients by flipping $(1 \leftrightarrow -1)$ every second spin.

Using the transfer matrix technique of Kramers and Wannier [6], one is able to compute the minimal energy of the one-dimensional nearest neighbor model.

A final word on notations. A configuration will be represented by a chain of arrows indicating either spin up ($\uparrow$, north pole, value 1) or spin down ($\downarrow$, south pole, value -1). One easily sees, for example, that the chains

$$\uparrow \downarrow \uparrow \downarrow \uparrow \ldots \uparrow \downarrow \quad \text{and} \quad \downarrow \uparrow \downarrow \uparrow \downarrow \ldots \downarrow \uparrow \tag{8}$$

represent the only two ground states of the model with Hamiltonian

$$H = -J \sum_{i \in L} \sigma_i \sigma_{i+1} \tag{9}$$

with $J < 0$ and periodic boundary conditions.

1.3 The correspondence

The problem of finding the ground states of the one-dimensional anti-ferromagnetic nearest neighbor model corresponds to the problem of optimizing the NNI functions. Starting from Eq. 6, we substitute σ_i by $2s_i - 1$, we change the sign of the Hamiltonian to switch from minimization to maximization, we set $J_{ij} = J_i \delta_{i+1,j}$, we assume periodic boundary conditions and we drop constant terms to obtain

$$-H = -4 \sum_{i \in L} J_i(1 - s_i)s_{i+1} - 2 \sum_{i \in L} s_i(J_i - J_{i-1} - h_i). \tag{10}$$

If we now take an anti-ferromagnetic model, i.e., all $J_i \leq 0$, then we are assured of non-negative components g_i in the corresponding class of NNI functions. Also requiring non-negative components k_i and l_i, we obtain the relationship

$$g_i = -4J_i, \tag{11}$$

$$k_i = \max\{-2(J_i - J_{i-1} - h_i), 0\}, \tag{12}$$

$$l_i = \max\{2(J_i - J_{i-1} - h_i), 0\}. \tag{13}$$

Conversely, starting from the NNI functions we obtain instances of the one-dimensional anti-ferromagnetic nearest neighbor model.

2 Adding Symmetry: Balancing

Motivated by the construction of the heuristic for the asymmetric interaction functions described in [9], we propose to add symmetry to the NNI functions by making all sites equal with respect to local changes. More precisely, we want to make sure that the expected contribution of any site to the total fitness value sum is independent of the value at this site.

This symmetry is easily achieved by changing the first order component of the NNI function. If we ensure that $g_{i-1} + 2k_i = g_i + 2l_i$, using the notations of Eq. 5, then we obtain that the expected contribution of site i with value 0 to the total fitness sum, namely $g_{i-1}/2 + k_i$, equals that of site i with value 1, namely $g_i/2 + l_i$. This procedure of changing the first order component of an NNI function will be called *balancing the NNI function*.

A consequence of balancing is that none of the first order schema competitions can be decided; it is easy to verify that

$$\frac{1}{2^{\ell-1}} \sum_{s \in S, \, s_i = 0} f(s) = \frac{1}{2^{\ell-1}} \sum_{s \in S, \, s_i = 1} f(s). \tag{14}$$

or, in traditional schema notation, $f(\# \ldots \#0\# \ldots \#) = f(\# \ldots \#1\# \ldots \#)$.

It is easy to verify that the balanced NNI functions correspond to the instances of the one-dimensional anti-ferromagnetic nearest neighbor model without external magnetic field.

Note that the balancing procedure can easily be extended to the asymmetric interaction functions, and even to functions with higher order dependencies. The same can of course be achieved in the generalized Ising model.

3   Balanced NNIs

In this section we study the dynamics of single-bit-flip hill-climbers (like simulated annealing) on the balanced NNI functions. For visual reasons we use the notations of statistical physics to explain the dynamics.

3.1   The random walk of the domain walls

Equation 8 gives the two ground states of the model with Hamiltonian $H = -J \sum_{i \in L} \sigma_i \sigma_{i+1}$. Now consider the following configuration

$$\uparrow \downarrow \uparrow \downarrow \uparrow \underset{W}{\downarrow} \downarrow \uparrow \downarrow \uparrow \downarrow \uparrow \downarrow \uparrow \underset{W}{\uparrow} \downarrow \uparrow \downarrow \uparrow \downarrow \,. \tag{15}$$

In the case of $J = -1$, it is in energy only 4 apart from the energy of the ground states. Only the interactions indicated with a W increase the energy. Yet in Hamming distance this configuration is very far from the ground states, because it contains a large chunk of out-of-phase down-up spins, the rest of the configuration being an up-down sequence. Sequences of alternating spins are called *domains*, the combinations of two up or two down spins are called *domain walls*.

What can a single-bit-flip (or *spin-flip*) hill-climber do when it has arrived in such a configuration? If it flips a spin inside one of the domains, it introduces a sequence of 3 spins in the same direction, which causes an unwanted rise in energy. The only alternative it has is to flip one of the spins of a domain wall, moving the wall to the left or the right with the configuration staying at the same energy. Only when two domain walls collide, they can disappear. In this way, the domain walls undergo a random walk, until all of them disappear.

3.2   Pinning

When not all the J_i are equal, a phenomenon called *pinning* can occur (see Jäckle et al. [4]). Domain walls which first were free to walk until they met another wall, are now pinned down to some restricted area. The following example shows how this happens in the presence of two interactions whose J_i value is significantly higher than the others:

$$\uparrow \downarrow \uparrow \downarrow \overset{9}{\uparrow} \downarrow \uparrow \downarrow \underset{W}{\uparrow} \uparrow \downarrow \uparrow \downarrow \overset{9}{\uparrow} \downarrow \uparrow \downarrow \,. \tag{16}$$

The wall can move three positions to the right, but not a fourth, because then the interaction with value 9 will be involved, resulting in a significant rise in energy. The same situation applies to a walk in the other direction. The probability that the wall of the example disappears is thus determined by the probability that both spins involved in one of the expensive interactions are flipped.

Assuming that pinned walls can only be removed by waiting a substantial amount of iterations of a spin-flip hill-climber, it is straightforward to show that pinning can turn the balanced NNI problem into a needle-in-a-haystack problem. Consider the following periodic assignment of J_i values: the interaction between sites i and $i+1$ is set to 1 when $i \bmod \sqrt{\ell}$ is non-zero, and to 9 when it is zero. In the case of $\ell = 16$, we have

$$\underset{\downarrow}{\overset{9}{\frown}}\uparrow\downarrow\uparrow\underset{\downarrow}{\overset{9}{\frown}}\uparrow\downarrow\uparrow\underset{\downarrow}{\overset{9}{\frown}}\uparrow\downarrow\uparrow\underset{\downarrow}{\overset{9}{\frown}}\uparrow\downarrow\uparrow \tag{17}$$

as one of the two optimal configurations.

To achieve an optimal configuration starting from a sub-optimal one, we need that each couple of spins involved in one the $\sqrt{\ell}$ interactions with value 9 is either in spin-up spin-down or spin-down spin-up; moreover, all couples have to be at the same time in spin-down spin-up (as in the example) or in spin-up spin-down, or we are faced with the presence of domain walls. Assuming that once the spins of a high-valued interaction are in spin-up spin-down or spin-down spin-up, it takes a long time to switch between one of these two, and that the choice of spin-up spin-down or spin-down spin-up is independent for each of the expensive interactions (and this is the case for the spin-flip hill-climber), we have a probability of 2 out of $2^{\sqrt{\ell}}$ of finding the correct path to the optimum.

3.3 Experimental results

For our experiments with the SGA and balanced NNIs, we select a set of NNI functions on 80 sites with interaction coefficients which are assigned periodically with respect to the sites. In particular, we set

$$g_i = 1 + (a(i+1) \bmod b) \tag{18}$$

for all $i \in L$, and we concentrate on the balanced versions of the functions arising from the 28 parameter couples $(1,2)$, $(1,3)$, $(2,3)$, $(1,4)$, $\ldots$, $(7,8)$. The SGA is equipped with quadratic ranking selection (i.e., the strings are ordered according to their fitness and proportional selection on the square of the ordering is performed), one-point crossover with rate 1, ordinary mutation with rate $1/20$, and a population of size 80. We take the number of successful runs out of 21 as an empirical measure of GA-hardness of an instance; a successful run is defined as a run where the SGA finds the optimum within the specified number of iterations. Table 1 shows the results.

To get a better idea of the effects of pinning, we change the rule of Eq. 18 to

$$g_i = \begin{cases} a & \text{when } i \bmod b = 0, \\ 1/2 & \text{otherwise,} \end{cases} \tag{19}$$

which allows us to use the same set of parameters. Clearly a represents the cost of an expensive interaction, and b the distance between expensive interactions. Table 1 shows that when the cost of the expensive interaction increases, the SGA performance drops; raising the maximal number of iterations does not significantly change the results.

rule: a, b	periodic 15000	pinning 15000	pinning 30000
1, 2	14	14	18
1, 3	9	14	20
2, 3	8	0	3
1, 4	6	17	20
2, 4	8	2	6
3, 4	6	0	0
1, 5	4	16	21
2, 5	4	3	3
3, 5	7	0	0
4, 5	8	0	0
1, 6	1	19	20
2, 6	5	2	7
3, 6	0	0	0
4, 6	0	0	0
5, 6	3	0	0

rule: a, b	periodic 15000	pinning 15000	pinning 30000
1, 7	2	15	20
2, 7	2	4	4
3, 7	2	0	0
4, 7	2	0	0
5, 7	3	0	0
6, 7	0	0	0
1, 8	4	14	20
2, 8	4	7	15
3, 8	7	3	2
4, 8	8	0	0
5, 8	1	0	0
6, 8	5	0	0
7, 8	0	0	0

Table 1. The number of successful runs out of 21 of the SGA on a selection of 28 balanced NNI functions on 80 bits. This table shows results for the first rule (Eq. 18) and the second rule (Eq. 19), with a varying maximal number of iterations.

3.4 Breaking the symmetry

The symmetry of the balanced NNI problem with pinning can be broken by making the choice of spin-up spin-down or spin-down spin-up for the expensive interactions dependent on the choice for other interactions. Once one of the expensive interactions has fallen into spin-up spin-down, all the others follow correctly to spin-up spin-down as well. The heuristic defined in [9] breaks the symmetry by fixing spin after spin, and reaches the optimum in quadratic time.

4 Unbalanced NNIs

To investigate the behavior of the SGA on unbalanced NNIs, we consider the 28 instances generated by the rule of Eq. 18 and the same set of parameter couples. Since the unbalanced functions are expected to be easier for the GA, we set the number of iterations within which the optimum has to be reached at 1000.

Summarizing the results of Table 2, we find that not all instances are equally hard, the combinations $(a, b) = (1, 5)$ and $(a, b) = (6, 7)$ being the hardest and the combination $(1, 2)$ and the group $(2, 4)$, $(3, 6)$ and $(4, 8)$ the easiest. Much depends on the choice of genetic operators and parameter settings. The combination $(6, 7)$, for example, is very hard unless the mutation rate is set to at least $1/\ell$. The unbalanced instances are much easier than their balanced counterparts.

crossover: rate: mutation rate: a, b	1PT 0.9 $1/\ell$	1PT 0.9 $1/10\ell$	1PT 0.9 -	1PT 0.45 $1/\ell$	1PT 0.45 $1/10\ell$	UX 0.9 $1/\ell$	UX 0.9 $1/10\ell$	UX 0.9 -	UX 0.45 $1/\ell$	UX 0.45 $1/10\ell$	- - $1/\ell$
1, 2	21	16	0	21	11	21	20	4	21	14	21
1, 3	21	18	1	19	14	20	18	14	20	17	20
2, 3	20	19	2	20	18	20	18	14	20	17	19
1, 4	21	6	0	21	3	21	10	0	21	7	21
2, 4	21	16	0	21	10	21	21	8	21	18	21
3, 4	21	7	0	21	4	21	8	0	21	3	21
1, 5	5	0	0	7	0	9	1	0	2	1	3
2, 5	21	12	0	20	3	20	16	4	20	9	21
3, 5	21	10	0	20	4	18	17	3	21	8	19
4, 5	12	2	0	7	0	6	0	0	4	1	1
1, 6	20	0	0	19	0	20	0	0	14	0	18
2, 6	21	1	0	21	0	19	3	6	19	1	18
3, 6	21	18	0	21	15	21	21	9	21	18	21
4, 6	21	1	0	19	0	18	11	6	18	1	19
5, 6	21	6	0	21	2	20	2	0	21	1	20
1, 7	15	2	0	11	0	15	0	0	9	0	7
2, 7	15	5	0	11	2	11	3	0	7	1	3
3, 7	21	16	0	21	6	21	17	8	21	9	21
4, 7	21	6	0	21	6	21	17	3	21	6	21
5, 7	13	5	0	10	3	10	6	0	5	1	4
6, 7	4	0	0	6	0	4	1	0	2	0	5
1, 8	21	1	0	21	0	19	0	0	19	1	20
2, 8	21	11	0	21	2	21	15	1	21	7	21
3, 8	21	2	1	20	0	20	5	2	20	4	20
4, 8	21	19	0	21	19	21	21	8	21	20	21
5, 8	21	1	0	21	2	19	9	9	18	4	20
6, 8	21	4	0	21	3	21	11	0	21	7	21
7, 8	21	1	0	21	0	20	1	0	18	0	16

Table 2. The number of successful runs out of 21 of the SGA on a selection of 28 unbalanced NNI functions. This table shows the dependence of the convergence quality on the choice of genetic operators (1PT is one-point crossover, UX is uniform crossover, selection is linear ranking selection, population size is 80). The NNI functions are defined on 80 bits using the parameters of the leftmost column, using the rule $g_i = 1 + (a(1 + i) \bmod b)$ and the notations of Eq. 5. A run is called successful when the optimum is found by the GA with given parameters within 1000 iterations. It is clear from the table that mutation is the dominant genetic operator, that more crossover helps, and that there is no significant difference between uniform crossover and one-point crossover.

Conclusions

We have shown that the presence of symmetry in a fitness function can have a negative effect on the convergence quality of the SGA. We used the one-dimensional nearest neighbor functions, which are extensively studied in statistical physics, to show this. The results support the claim that it is not the amount of interaction present in a fitness function which is the major cause of GA-hardness, but other features like the symmetry of interaction.

The unbalanced NNI functions exhibit a wide range of GA behavior and can hence serve as a class of test functions. The balanced NNIs are examples of deterministically simple functions which make the SGA's life extremely hard.

Acknowledgements

The first author is a research assistant of the Fund for Scientific Research – Flanders (Belgium) (F.W.O.). He wishes to thank his PhD promoter Alain Verschoren (University of Antwerp, RUCA) for his continuing support. The research of the second author is also funded by the F.W.O. The authors acknowledge the reviewers' comments which improved this paper.

References

1. L. Altenberg. Fitness distance correlation analysis: an instructive counterexample. In Th. Bäck, editor, *Proceedings of the 7th International Conference on Genetic Algorithms*, pages 57–64. Morgan Kaufmann Publishers, 1997.
2. Y. Davidor. Epistasis variance: a viewpoint on GA-hardness. In G. J. E. Rawlins, editor, *Foundations of Genetic Algorithms*, pages 23–35. Morgan Kaufmann Publishers, 1991.
3. E. Ising. Beitrag zur Theorie des Ferromagnetismus. *Z. Physik*, 31:235, 1924.
4. J. Jäckle, R. B. Stinchcombe, and S. Cornell. Freezing of nonequilibrium domain structures in a kinetic Ising model. *J. Stat. Phys.*, 62:425–433, 1991.
5. S. A. Kauffman. Adaptation on rugged fitness landscapes. In *Lectures in the Sciences of Complexity*, volume I of *SFI studies*, pages 619–712. Addison Wesley, 1989.
6. H. A. Kramers and G. H. Wannier. Statistics of the two-dimensional ferromagnet. Part I. *Phys. Rev.*, 60:252–262, 1941.
7. T. M. Liggett. *Interacting Particle Systems*. Springer Verlag, 1985.
8. B. Naudts. *Measuring GA-hardness*. PhD thesis, University of Antwerp, RUCA, Belgium, 1998.
9. B. Naudts and A. Verschoren. SGA search dynamics on second order functions. In J.-K. Hao, E. Lutton, E. Ronald, M. Schoenauer, and D. Snyers, editors, *Artificial Evolution 97*. Springer Verlag, 1998.
10. Lars Onsager. Crystal statistics. I. A two-dimensional model with an order–disorder transition. *Physical Review*, 65(3):117–149, feb 1944.
11. A. Prügel-Bennett and J. L. Shapiro. The dynamics of a genetic algorithm for simple Ising systems. *Physica D*, 104:75–114, 1997.
12. C. Reeves and C. Wright. An experimental design perspective on genetic algorithms. In L. D. Whitley and M. D. Vose, editors, *Foundations of Genetic Algorithms 3*, pages 7–22. Morgan Kaufmann Publishers, 1995.

Fitness Distance Correlation and Ridge Functions

R.J.Quick, V.J.Rayward-Smith and G.D.Smith

University of East Anglia, Norwich, UK

Abstract. Fitness Distance Correlation has been proposed as a measure of function optimization difficulty. This paper describes a class of functions, named the Ridge Functions which, according to the measure, should be highly misleading. However, all functions tested were optimized easily by both a GA and a simple hill climbing algorithm. Scatter graph analysis of Ridge functions gave little guidance due to the large number of functions with an identical scatter graph, the majority of which are not in the class of Ridge functions and are not simple to optimize.

1 Fitness Distance Correlation

1.1 Introduction

Fitness distance correlation (FDC) introduced by Jones and Forrest [6] is a measure of problem difficulty for genetic algorithms. FDC measures the correlation between the fitness values of a function under investigation and the distance to the goal of the search. The choice of metric used for distance may be crucial to the study.

Given a set $F = \{f_1, f_2, ..., f_n\}$ representing the evaluations of the points in the search space and a set $D = \{d_1, d_2, ..., d_n\}$ representing the corresponding distance of those points from the optimal solution, the correlation coefficient, r, is calculated as

$$r = \frac{C_{FD}}{\sigma_F \sigma_D}, \tag{1}$$

where

$$C_{FD} = \frac{1}{n}\sum_{i=1}^{n}(f_i - \overline{f})(d_i - \overline{d}), \tag{2}$$

is the covariance of F and D and σ_F, σ_D, $\overline{f}$ and $\overline{d}$ are the standard deviation and means of F and D, respectively.

For a maximization problem, the ideal value of r is -1.0 which implies a perfect negative correlation between the function values of the points in the search space and their distances to the optimal. Such a function should be easy to optimize as each function value gives a perfect measure of each point's distance from the optimal. An r value of 1.0, for a maximization problem, implies that the distance of points from the optimal decreases as the function values decrease. Thus, the function should be very deceptive. An r value of 0.0 implies that there is no correlation between the function values and distances of points from the optimal.

Jones and Forrest make several conjectures with reference to the FDC correlation statistic.

- If $r \leq -0.15$, the function should be straightforward and the global optimal will be found easily.

- If $-0.15 < r < 0.15$, the prediction is indeterminate.

- If $r \geq 0.15$, the function is misleading and the search will be led away from the global optimal.

As a secondary measure, Jones and Forrest suggest that a scatter diagram of fitness against distance can be helpful for spotting the structure of a function otherwise missed by the correlation statistic, which will indicate if the function is straightforward, misleading or otherwise.

In [1], Altenberg describes a function which has an indeterminate correlation value, yields no structure in the scatter diagram and yet is GA-easy. In his paper, Altenberg asks if a GA-easy function can be found which has a large positive correlation value. The first part of this paper describes such a function.

1.2 Previous Work

It has been shown [6] using Hamming distance as the relevant distance measure, that FDC provides a "reliable although not infallible indicator of GA performance" when tested on a set of well known functions. It was acknowledged that the FDC statistic would be more accurate if distance was determined "according to the operator in use by the algorithm" [6]; however, "the Hamming distance is the first approximation to distance under the actual operators of a Genetic Algorithm". In short, Jones and Forrest claim that the use of the FDC statistic using Hamming Distance as the relevant measure of distance is a good indicator of the performance of a genetic algorithm.

Altenberg [1] describes the construction of a function which, although having an r value of zero, is easy for a genetic algorithm to optimize. This function is offered as a counterexample to the claim that the FDC statistic is a good measure of optimization difficulty when using a genetic algorithm in the cases when r is approximately 0. Altenberg achieves this result by concentrating on the mechanics of the crossover operator whilst still using Hamming distance as the measure of distance. Altenberg's paper questions the relevance of the FDC measure of difficulty with reference to genetic algorithms when the measure of distance is based upon Hamming distance. However, he states that if the measure of distance used matched the actual operator used, i.e. crossover, then the FDC coefficient will predict accurately that Altenberg's function will be straightforward to optimize.

In this paper, we provide a function in which, although the measure of distance used by the statistic and the measure of distance defined by the operator are the same, the FDC statistic indicates a deceptive/difficult search and yet is simple for a genetic algorithm or hill climber to optimize.

2 Ridge Functions

2.1 Description of the Function

The maximization version of the function is formed in the following manner. Consider a function $y = f(x)$ defined over a binary string $x \in \{0, 1\}^n$, where n is the bit string length.

A string is chosen to represent the optimal, without loss of generality, say $s_{opt} = 111...111$. A very specific path is then formed from the complement of the optimal string to the optimal, $(00...00, 10...00, 11...00, ..., 11...10, 11...11)$. Each string on the path is one bit different to the previous string on the path and is of successively decreasing Hamming distance from the optimal solution. The path is denoted $s_1, s_2, s_3, ..., s_n, s_{n+1}$, where s_{n+1} represents the optimal point and the bit string is of length n.

The points on the path are given successively higher evaluations from the complement to the optimal. Thus $f(s_i) < f(s_{i+1})$ for $1 \leq i \leq n$.

All other strings are allocated function values as a function of the number of "0"s in the string. The greater the number of "0"s the higher the evaluation of the string. All these strings will have a function value smaller than $f(s_1)$. Given that we are trying to maximize the number of "1"s, such a method of calculating string evaluations will be deceptive.

2.2 Specific Evaluation Function and Corresponding FDC Statistic Value

Evaluation of String. For any given string s of length n, let the number of contiguous "1"s from the left hand side equal q. Let the number of "0"s in the string equal p and the number of "1"s in the string equal m. For the sample string, 111011111000, $q=3$, $p=4$ and $m = 8$. The evaluation $f(s)$ is determined as follows:-

$$\text{if } ((q > 0) \wedge (m = q))$$
$$f(s) = \text{n + q};$$
$$\text{else}$$
$$f(s) = \text{p};$$

Some sample strings of size $n = 20$ and their evaluations are shown in Table 1.

Table 1. Example string evaluations for a bit string of length 20

	Bit String	Eval
	10111111111111111110	2
Off-path	00000011111111111111	6
	00111111000000000000	14
	11000000000000000011	16
	00000000000000000000	20
On-path	10000000000000000000	21
	11100000000000000000	23
	11111111111111111111	40

Correlation Coefficient Value of Functions. For a function defined on strings of length n, the search space is equal to 2^n. The smallest function used in the experimentation is defined on strings of length $n = 20$, for which the correlation coefficient r is equal to 0.998906, where the whole search space is used in the calculation. The value of r tends to 1 as n tends to ∞, thus all Ridge functions used in this paper have r values of approximately 1. For a maximization problem, a coefficient value of near 1 would suggest that the function should be very difficult to solve.

2.3 Experimentation

Experimentation relating to optimization of the Ridge functions was conducted in two sections. The first set of experiments were conducted using a simple hill climber, the second using genetic algorithms.

Optimization by Hill Climber. A single bit hill climber (HC) was used as the optimization algorithm. It should be noted that the measure of distance used in the calculation of the FDC statistic is identical to the operator distance as defined by the HC algorithm.

The manner in which a single bit hill climber will direct search on the landscape formed by this function is fairly obvious. Search will be quickly drawn towards the point represented by the complement of the optimal string where the start of the ridge path will be discovered, subsequently directing search to the optimal.

The landscape formed by this function as viewed by the hill climber can be visualized, dangerous as this can be, in the following way. The total terrain under consideration can be considered to be in the shape of circle. The landscape on this terrain consists mainly of a large hill rising from all directions to a point on the edge of the circle. This peak is represented by the complement of the optimal string. From this point a thin rising ridge one bit wide extends across the landscape to the opposite edge of the circle. The last point on this ridge on the edge of the terrain represents the optimal point.

Results of Experimentation. Experimentation was conducted on three Ridge functions of different sizes. Table 2 records data showing the bit string length, search space size, correlation coefficient r and the number of evaluations taken to reach the optimal solution. #Evaluations represents the average number of evaluations taken to reach the optimum in 20 runs.

The experimental results described in Table 2 show that, as expected, the hill climber was able to optimize these functions extremely easily, requiring a number of evaluations amounting to a small fraction of the search space.

Table 2. Experimental results

Function			#Evaluations		
Len	Size	r	HC	GA-SIM	GA-NM
20	2^{20}	0.999	446	2893	6148
25	2^{25}	~ 1	727	4869	9704
30	2^{30}	~ 1	932	6921	14069

Optimization by Genetic Algorithm. A second set of experiments were conducted using genetic algorithms. Initial experimentation was conducted using a basic genetic algorithm (GA-SIM) using Roulette selection, a population of 100, 1pt crossover, best fit merge and a mutation rate of $1/n$ where n is the length of the bit string. Best fit merge only accepts solutions better than the poorest solution in the pool. As shown in Table 2 the function once again proved simple to optimize. It is obvious that any genetic algorithm using a reasonable mutation rate will be able to optimize these functions. The nearer a genetic algorithm comes to mimicking a single bit hill climber the better the results.

Further experimentation was conducted using genetic algorithms with no mutation operator. The best results obtained during this investigation were obtained using a genetic algorithm with rank selection, a population of 100, one point crossover, and a best fit merge mechanism using a high degree of inaccuracy, where solutions with fitnesses worse than the poorest solution in the pool were accepted 80% of the time. This genetic algorithm uses an unconventional merge mechanism in order to retain genetic diversity in the population. The results for this algorithm, GA-NM, are also shown in Table 2. Though the algorithm's performance was not as good as the genetic algorithm using mutation, the algorithm still had very little difficulty in obtaining the optimal solution quickly. As the string size increases, the number of evaluations taken to reach the optimal point decreases significantly as a fraction of the search space.

2.4   Scatter Diagram of Function

Figure 1 displays a scatter graph of fitness against distance relating to points from a Ridge function of size $n = 7$. After [1, 6], noise has been added to the function distances and fitnesses so that identical points can be distinguished. The striking structure present in scatter graphs of all Ridge functions is apparent. The scatter plot consists of the "deceptive" line with positive gradient constructed from the $(2^7 - 8)$ off-path points and the perfect negative correlation of the on-path points.

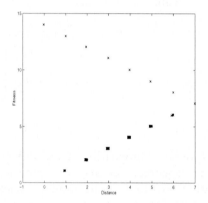

Fig. 1. Scatter plot of Ridge function, n=7

It might be thought that the structure shown in the scatter graph would help us to assess the difficulty of the problem. However, it is possible to form a great number of functions with an *identical* scatter diagram and correlation value which will be impossible for the hill climber to optimize.

Consider the following class of functions ϵ. The members of this class are formed in a similar manner to a Ridge function of the same size n. However, for the members of ϵ, the $n + 1$ strings which represent the steps on the path can take any form as long as the string at step s_i contains $i - 1$ "1"s. The evaluation of each string on the path is equal to $n + (i - 1)$, where i is the position on the path of that string. All members of ϵ, for a given n, have an identical set of fitness distance pairs and the Ridge functions are a subset of this class.

An example path which defines a member of ϵ is shown in Table 3. A single bit hill climber will be unable to climb to the optimal on this path as there is more than a single bit difference between the second and third steps on the path. As this function has identical fitness distance pairs to a Ridge function of the same size it will consequently have the same scatter diagram and r correlation value. In fact, the number of members of ϵ for which the hill climber will be unable to reach the optimal will be vastly greater than the number for which it will.

Table 3. Example path for function from class ϵ of size $n = 20$

Step	Bit String	Eval
1	00000000000000000000	20
2	01000000000000000000	21
3	00110000000000000000	22
4	00001110000000000000	23
21	11111111111111111111	40

Thus, in this case, the scatter diagram is not a good indicator of the algorithm's performance. It is likely that this scenario will occur for many classes of functions that display the same scatter plot.

A function generator was created which forms random functions from the class of ϵ. Experimentation was conducted on a randomly generated set of 20 functions from this class. For this set of functions the hill climber was unable to get beyond the lowest steps on the path. Experimentation using a genetic algorithm was marginally more successful due to its ability to flip more than 1 bit, however it was impossible to maintain the diversity in the population necessary to make any real progress towards the optimal for this set of test functions.

2.5 Discussion of Results

It is claimed [6] that there is a relationship between the optimization difficulty of a function and the FDC statistic relating to that function. The measure should be most accurate when the measure of distance is based on the operator used by the algorithm attempting optimization. The FDC statistic using Hamming distance predicts that Ridge functions should be very misleading to a single bit flip hill climbing algorithm. However, the algorithm easily optimizes the function, in contradiction to the prediction of the FDC statistic, without the use of any special operators to take advantage of the overall deceptive nature of the function. Deceptive landscapes are usually seen as being unhelpful to search. However, given that the path defined by the points evaluated in the course of the search is so short and consists of constantly increasing evaluations it is difficult to consider the algorithm as being in any way deceived.

The basic aim of heuristic search algorithms is to find a (near) goal state as quickly as possible. The value or characteristic of non-goal states examined are only important in so much as they provide information as to the whereabouts of a goal state. With respect to Ridge functions, the hill climbing algorithm is very deliberate and efficient in its movements. The off-path points all accurately predict the location of the complement and thus the beginning of the path to the optimal.

In a similar way to how Long Path Functions [2] show that a hill climbing algorithm which always discovers the optimal does not always mean efficient search, Ridge functions show that an algorithm which spends a good proportion of its search heading in the "wrong" direction is not necessarily inefficient.

3 Long Path Functions

Long Path functions (LPF) [2] are functions which, when maximized by a simple hill climber, result in the formation of a search path through the search space which consists of points of increasing function evaluation leading to the optimal. The path created is, however, infeasibly long. Such functions demonstrate that, just because the function can be optimized by a simple hill climber this does not necessarily mean that it is an efficient search strategy.

For a given LPF the length of the path is equal to: (see [2])

$$|P_n| = 3.2^{\lfloor (n-1)/2) \rfloor} - 1, \tag{3}$$

where n is the length of the bit string on which the function is defined. Thus, it can be seen that the growth in the length of a LPF path length, $|P_n|$, is exponential with respect to n, the size of the bit string.

The suggested evaluation function allocates values to strings according to their position on the path, where the point 000...000 is considered to be at position 0 on the path. All off-path points are allocated values equal to the number of "0"s in the string.

Thus, let P denote all the binary strings on the path and the function $g(s)$ return the position on the path of each of these strings. Let the function $p(s)$ represent the number of "0"s in a string. Then the evaluation, $f(s)$, of a string s of length n, is as follows.

$$
\begin{aligned}
&\text{if } s \in P \\
&\qquad \text{f(s) = g(s)+ } n; \\
&\text{else} \\
&\qquad \text{f(s) = p(s);}
\end{aligned}
$$

This function is solved by a simple hill climber such as the HC hill climber described in section 2.3.

The search is initially drawn towards the beginning of the path until an on-path point is encountered. Once on the path, search will move up the path until the optimal is found. It is shown [2] that the number of evaluations taken to reach the optimal by such an algorithm is prohibitively long.

3.1 Similarities between Long Path and Ridge Functions

There are certain similarities between LPFs and Ridge functions. They both direct search towards the beginning of a path. Once an on-path point is found, search is directed along the path towards the optimal point. The basic difference between the two types of function is that the Ridge function path is designed to be as short as possible whilst the LPF path is, as the name suggests, designed to be as long as possible.

For a given Ridge function the path length is equal to n. As the size of Ridge functions increase, the growth in the path length is linear with respect to the growth of n. As described in section 3, as the size of LPFs increase the growth of the path length is exponential with respect to n.

In [6] it was indicated that the FDC values of LPFs were near to zero which implies that such functions should be difficult to optimize, which is indeed the case for the single bit hill climber for which it is designed. The FDC values of some different sized LPFs are shown in Table 4. The table shows that the number of evaluations taken to optimize the function appears to be rising at an exponential rate with respect to the growth of the string length.

Table 4. Correlation values of LPF and ALPF

	Len	Size	r	# Eval (HC)
LPF	15	2^{15}	0.08	4838
	17	2^{17}	0.06	11244
	19	2^{19}	0.05	25742
ALPF	15	2^{15}	-0.94	3465
	17	2^{17}	-0.97	7472
	19	2^{19}	-0.98	16576

3.2 Amended Long Path Functions

The similarities between Long Path and Ridge functions lead us to believe that the correlation value of a LPF was somewhat arbitrary. It was considered likely that it would be easy to create a function whose FDC value tended to -1 as n tended to ∞ whilst retaining the original qualities of the LPF.

The Amended Long Path Functions (ALPF) of dimension n is formed simply by taking a LPF of dimension n, defining the string 111...111 to be the optimal string and all strings on the path beyond that optimal string to represent off-path points.

The calculation of the ALPF path length is not obvious. However, the optimal string 111...111 will always be in the second half of the corresponding Long Path path. Thus, there is an obvious lower bound for the path length of an ALPF,

$$|P_n| > \frac{(3.2^{\lfloor (n-1)/2 \rfloor} - 1)}{2} \tag{4}$$

Although the path formed by this amended function might only be half the size of the original path, the path still grows at an exponential rate and thus will still be prohibitively hard for a hill climber to solve.

For the ALPF the evaluation, $f(s)$, of a string s, of length n, is identical to the LPF except that n and $p(n)$, but not $g(n)$, are scaled by 1000 to flatten the landscape.

The results are shown in Table 4. The functions produced have correlation values which tend to -1 as n tends to ∞. The original qualities of the LPFs are retained as the number of evaluations taken by a hill climber to reach the optimal still appears to be growing at an exponential rate.

This section shows that the FDC value of the whole search space is not a good judge of the difficulty of optimizing the wider set of LPFs described in this section.

The failure of the FDC statistic to correctly predict the performance of the Ridge functions and ALPFs led to a search to find a measure which would correctly predict the performance of the functions. In [5], the use of parent offspring predictive measures is discussed and it is shown that the application of the FDC statistic to the points typically sampled by Ridge functions, LPFs and ALPFs provides a more accurate predictor of function difficulty. The success of this predictive measure is likely to be a feature of the classes of functions under investigation. In [3] Kallel and Schoenauer describe the general inadequacy of parent offspring type statistics.

4 Conclusion

It is apparent from the above analysis that neither the FDC statistic nor the scatter plot are reliable indicators of optimization difficulty. This is also one of the conclusions of Naudts and Kallel [4] who analysed predictive measures in a more general context.

References

1. L. Altenberg. Fitness distance correlation analysis: An instructive counterexample. In *Proceedings of the Seventh International Conference on Genetic Algorithms*, pages 57–64. Morgan Kaufmann, 1997.
2. D. E. Goldberg J. Horn and K. Deb. Long path problems. In *Parallel Problem Solving from Nature*. Springer, 1994.
3. L. Kallel and M. Schoenauer. A priori comparison of binary crossover operators: No universal statistical measure, but a set of hints. In *Proceedings of the third Artificial Evolution*, pages 287–299. Springer, 1997.
4. B. Naudts and L. Kallel. Some facts about so called GA-hardness measures. Technical report, University of Antwerp, 1998.
5. V. J. Rayward-Smith R. J. Quick and G. D. Smith. Ridge functions. Technical Report 98-005, University of East Anglia, 1998.
6. T.Jones. *Evolutionary Algorithms, Fitness Landscapes and Search*. PhD thesis, Massachusetts Institute of Technology, 1994.

Accelerating the Convergence of Evolutionary Algorithms by Fitness Landscape Approximation

Alain Ratle

Département de génie mécanique,
Université de Sherbrooke,
Sherbrooke, Québec, J1K 2R1 Canada

Abstract. A new algorithm is presented for accelerating the convergence of evolutionary optimization methods through a reduction in the number of fitness function calls. Such a reduction is obtained by 1) creating an approximate model of the fitness landscape using kriging interpolation, and 2) using this model instead of the original fitness function for evaluating some of the next generations. The main interest of the presented approach lies in problems for which the computational costs associated with fitness function evaluation is very high, such as in the case of most engineering design problems. Numerical results presented for a test case show that the reconstruction algorithm can effectively reduces the number of fitness function calls for simple problems as well as for difficult multidimensional ones.

1 Introduction

Evolutionary algorithms in general, are increasingly popular for solving complex parameter optimization problems where classical deterministic methods are known to have failed [1]. In several areas, including engineering design problems, genetic algorithms as well as evolution strategies and evolutionary programming, among others, have been used with success [2–4]. However, a major barrier to the use of evolutionary optimization methods for solving engineering design problems is the sometime prohibitively large number of fitness function calls required, since this function often represents a quite heavy computational load [4]. It seems clear that a faster algorithm requiring a smaller number of fitness function calls would be really helpful for problems where the computational cost associated with the fitness function is high.

The approach presented for solving this problem consists of building up a statistical model of the fitness landscape from a small number of data points. These data points are obtained during one or more generations of a classical evolutionary method. The statistical model is then exploited by the evolutionary algorithm as an auxiliary fitness function in order to get the maximum amount of information out of the initial data points. Once a convergence criteria has been reached, the algorithm can get back once more to the true fitness landscape for updating the statistical model with new data points, expected to be closer to the global optimum. A great care must be taken in the choice of a suitable modelisation technique. In order to be efficient for numerical optimization purposes, the selected model should retain some characteristics:

1. A small computational complexity, compared to the real fitness function;
2. An adequate representation of the global trends on the fitness landscape;
3. Considerations for the local fluctuations around data points, in order to detect emerging locally optimal points.
4. A minimal number of initial hypothesis on the morphological characteristics of the fitness landscape.

From the various existing modelisation techniques, kriging interpolation is chosen since it retains the aforementioned features. Sect. 2 is a general presentation of the theoretical developments of kriging interpolation. Sect. 3 presents an evolutionary optimization algorithm using kriging interpolation as a fitness landscape approximation. Sect. 4 finally presents some results obtained on a test problem recently proposed by Keane [1].

2 Theory of Kriging

2.1 General Principles

Kriging has emerged in mining geostatistics as a powerful tool for modelisation and estimation of geophysical resources, based on a set of N non-uniformly distributed experimental data points [7]. The original method was formulated for dealing with one, two or three dimensional problems, reflecting real-world physical phenomena. However, in the function optimization framework, it must be generalized for an L dimensional problem. Denoting by x a vector representing a point in the search space, kriging allows to create a statistical model $U(x)$ of the function $f(x)$ defined as:

$$U(x) = a(x) + b(x), \quad \text{with} \quad x = \{x_1, x_2, \ldots, x_L\} \tag{1}$$

The function $a(x)$, denoted *drift* function, represents the average long range behavior, or the expected value of the true function, e.g.: $a(x) = E[F(x)]$. The drift function can be modeled in various ways, such as polynomial or trigonometric series. While almost any representation may gives interesting results, a polynomial serie of order R in the L dimensions is retained for the present case, giving a drift function depending on $(1 + RL)$ coefficients a_0 and a_{ij}:

$$a(x) = a_0 + \sum_{i=1}^{L} \sum_{j=1}^{R} a_{ij}(x_i)^j \tag{2}$$

The present model contains no coupling terms between the x_i's. It is chosen here for its simplicity, although for some problems, a complete polynomial basis including coupling terms might be more suitable. The second part of $U(\boldsymbol{x})$ is the covariance function $b(\boldsymbol{x})$. This function represents a short-distance influence of every data point over the global model. The general formulation for $b(\boldsymbol{x})$ is a weighted sum of N functions, $K_n(\boldsymbol{x})$, $n = 1 \ldots N$. These functions represent the covariance functions between the nth data point $\boldsymbol{x}_n$ and any point $\boldsymbol{x}$. The fundamental hypothesis of kriging, called the *intrinsic hypothesis*, states that no data point has any particularly significant value compared to another. Therefore, a standard covariance function $K(h)$ is taken, depending only on the distance h between $\boldsymbol{x}_n$ and $\boldsymbol{x}$. For the sake of generality, h is taken as a normalized value, dividing each of its components by the length of the search space over that dimension:

$$b(\boldsymbol{x}) = \sum_{n=1}^{N} b_n K(h(\boldsymbol{x}, \boldsymbol{x}_n)) \quad \text{and} \quad h(\boldsymbol{x}, \boldsymbol{x}_n) = \sqrt{\sum_{i=1}^{L} \left(\frac{x_i - x_{in}}{x_i^{max} - x_i^{min}} \right)^2} \quad (3)$$

where x_i^{min} and x_i^{max} are the lower and upper bounds of the search space over the ith dimension and x_{in} denotes the ith component of the data point $\boldsymbol{x}_n$. In a similar fashion as for the drift function, one might choose any set of basis functions for the covariance function, as long as the desired continuity conditions are followed. However, the shape of $K(h)$ has a strong influence on the resulting aspect of the statistical model. For example, as shown by Matheron [8], kriging is exactly equivalent to spline interpolation for some particular cases of $K(h)$. Using an estimation of the true covariance inferred from the data points, kriging is said to be used as an *estimator*. Using any pre-defined basis function, as it is the chosen here, kriging is said to be an *interpolator* [9].

2.2 Kriging System

Building up the kriging function in the format described above requires N covariance coefficients and $(1+RL)$ drift coefficients. There are therefore, $(N+1+RL)$ independent equations that must be stated. A first set of N equations is given by applying Eq. (1) to the sample points:

$$\sum_{m=1}^{N} b_m K(h(\boldsymbol{x}_m, \boldsymbol{x}_n)) + a_0 + \sum_{i=1}^{L} \sum_{j=1}^{R} a_{ij} (x_{in})^r = F(\boldsymbol{x}_n), \quad \text{for } n = 1 \ldots N \quad (4)$$

The next $(1 + RL)$ equations are found using the statement that the drift function represents the expected value of the true fitness landscape. The covariance function must therefore be of zero expected value over the domain. This is called the *no-bias* condition of the estimator. Applying this condition gives the required $(1 + RL)$ equations:

$$\sum_{n=1}^{N} b_n = 0 \quad \text{and} \quad \sum_{n=1}^{N} b_n (x_{in})^j = 0 \quad \text{with } i = 1 \ldots R, \ j = 1 \ldots L \quad (5)$$

The $(N + 1 + RL)$ kriging coefficients are determined by solving the matrix system defined by Eq. (4) and (5).

2.3 Distance of Influence

The concept of distance of influence, as introduced by Trochu [9], reflects the notion that the actual covariance between two very distant points in the search space is often small enough that the covariance function value between these points can be assumed to be zero. The general covariance function $K(h)$ may therefore be designed in such a way that $K(h) = 0$ whenever $h > d$, where d is a predefined threshold. This however does not means that the function contains no long distance influence terms, since long distance effects are already taken into account by the drift function. Covariance is intended to be nothing but a local perturbation. In cases where the fitness landscape is smooth enough, a close to zero covariance may be found on every point, provided that the drift function basis has enough degrees of freedom for that particular fitness landscape.

Using the previous definition of the normalized distance h, the distance of influence d must be a normalized value lying between zero and one. This strategy results in a sparse kriging matrix, instead of a full matrix, allowing a faster computation by making use of sparse matrix solving algorithms when dealing with large sets of data. Designing an appropriate covariance function is a crucial part of the whole process. The simplest model, called linear covariance, is defined as follow:

$$K^0(h) = \begin{cases} 1 - \left(\dfrac{h}{d}\right) & \text{if } h < d, \\ 0 & \text{otherwise.} \end{cases} \tag{6}$$

A second example implies the choice of having a "smooth" statistical model, e.g. a C^1 continuity is ensured by imposing the following four conditions over the covariance function and it's first derivative:

$$K(0) = 1, \quad K(d) = 0, \quad \left(\frac{\partial K}{\partial h}\right)_{h=0} = \left(\frac{\partial K}{\partial h}\right)_{h=d} = 0 \tag{7}$$

Solving the 4×4 system given by applying Eq. (7) to a cubic polynomial, the covariance function is defined as:

$$K^1(h) = \begin{cases} 1 - 3\left(\dfrac{h}{d}\right)^2 + 2\left(\dfrac{h}{d}\right)^3 & \text{if } h < d, \\ 0 & \text{otherwise.} \end{cases} \tag{8}$$

2.4   Controlling the Influence of Local Perturbations

The kriging interpolation model, as presented up to this point, is an exact interpolator that passes exactly through all the data points. However, this situation
is not desirable unless all the sample points are error free and highly correlated
one with another. Taking into account experimental error or uncorrelated noise
over the data point, the most probable estimator should tends more or less toward the average behavior rather than passing exactly through the data points.
Such an adjustment of the local versus global behavior is known as the *nugget
effect* in geostatistical estimation.

In gold ore estimation, point samples are either 100% gold, if taken from a
nugget, or 0% gold, if taken from the surrounding material. However, samples
that are averaged over a non-zero volume always lies somewhere between 0%
and 100% in gold content. This means that although the covariance between
two very close points is high, it drops to a very small value when the distance
increase of only a small amount. The limit case of *pure nugget effect* covariance
is modeled by nothing but a discontinuity at the origin:

$$K(h) = \begin{cases} 1 & \text{if } h = 0, \\ 0 & \text{otherwise.} \end{cases} \tag{9}$$

In this case, kriging interpolation reduces to a simple regression on the drift
function basis (polynomial or other). Intermediate cases between pure nugget
effect and continuous covariance are implemented by adding a constant value P
on the N first diagonal elements of the kriging system defined by Eq. (4) and (5).
These elements correspond to covariance functions where $h = 0$.

3   Optimization Algorithm

3.1   General Layout

The proposed optimization algorithm is based on a classical genetic algorithm
using a real-valued encoding. The basic genetic algorithm will not be described
here, the reader is rather refereed to [10]. Figure 1 shows the proposed modified
algorithm using a fitness landscape approximation. The first generation is randomly initiated like in a basic genetic algorithm. Fitness is evaluated using the
true fitness function. Solutions found in the first generation are used for building up a first fitness landscape approximation by kriging interpolation. This new
fitness function is then exploited for several generations until a convergence criterion is reached. The next generation is evaluated using the true fitness function
and the kriging interpolation model is updated using these new data points. The
process is repeated as long as the global stopping criterion is not attained.

3.2 Convergence Criteria

Using the presented algorithm, a local convergence criteria has to be defined, in order to decide whenever the statistical model must be updated with new sample points. Such a criteria is to be defined using the stability of the best value found over several generations. Convergence is obtained when the best solution of the last Δt generations has not changed by more than ε, an user-defined value.

3.3 Dynamic Adaptation

As it was mentioned in Sect. 2.4, kriging allows an adaptation of the relative weights of the drift function and the local fluctuations around each data point. In order to adapt the reconstruction algorithm to the most probable behavior of an evolutionary algorithm, a fundamental hypothesis is stated here. It is assumed that the first sets of data points obtained in early generations are weakly correlated with the global optimum and that those obtained in later stages are more and more correlated. A reasonable strategy is to use a high value of nugget effect in the early stages of optimization, and to reduce this value to zero in the later generations. The proposed adaptation model for the nugget effect is hence:

$$P = P_{max} \left(1 - \frac{t}{t_{max}} \right)^b \tag{10}$$

where P_{max} is the initial value of P at time $t = 0$, t_{max} is the maximum number of generations allowed and b is a control parameter. The model depends upon two control parameters, and a thorough study on the influence of these parameters would be necessary to better understand the underlying phenomena.

4 Numerical Results

4.1 Test Case

In order to demonstrate the possibilities of the fitness landscape reconstruction algorithm, the method has been applied on a mathematically simple but hard to optimize problem, prior to attack real-world engineering design problems. An interesting case has been recently proposed by Keane [1]. This problem is scaleable to an arbitrary number L of variables:

$$\text{maximize } f(\boldsymbol{x}) = \left| \frac{\sum_{i=1}^{L} \cos^4(x_i) - 2 \prod_{i=1}^{L} \cos^2(x_i)}{\sqrt{\sum_{i=1}^{L} ix_i^2}} \right| \tag{11}$$

The optimal solution, as originally proposed by Keane [1], must respect the two following constraints:

$$\prod_{i=1}^{L} x_i > 0.75, \quad \text{and} \quad \sum_{i=1}^{L} x_i < 7.5L \tag{12}$$

Begin
  Random initialization
  Evaluation of N individuals
  Construction of the statistical model
  fitness function := statistical model
  while not(stopping criterion)
    if (convergence over statistical model) **then**
      fitness function := original function
    else
      fitness function := statistical model
    end if
    for i = 1 **to** population size
      Selection
      Crossover
      Mutation
      Evaluation
    end for
    if fitness function == original function
      Updating of statistical model
      function := statistical model
    end if
  end while
End

Fig. 1. Evolutionary optimization algorithm using an approximated fitness function

4.2 2-Dimensional Problem

The test function f_1 is plotted on Fig. 2, for the 2-dimensional case without considering the constraints. This function has an absolute maximum of 0.67367 at the point $(x_1, x_2) = (1.3932, 0)$.

A real-coded genetic algorithm has been used, with tournament selection of size 4, uniformly-distributed time-dependent mutation operator and linear arithmetical 2-parents crossover. 50 generations were allowed with a population size of 50. For the reconstruction algorithm, the same basic scheme was used with a quadratic drift function, a C^1 continuous covariance, a normalized distance of influence $d = 0.2$ and an initial nugget effect $P_{max} = 1.0$. The time adaptation parameter of the nugget effect control function was set to $b = 2.0$. A minimum of four generations were performed over the reconstructed fitness function before updating the model with new data points. These parameter values where found to be the best ones after a few trial and errors, but a systematic study is awaiting. Results are presented on Fig. 3, showing a significant increase in the convergence rate for the reconstruction algorithm. It should be noted that all the results presented in this paper were calculated from an average of five runs.

On the other hand, the constrained 2-dimensional problem described by Eq. (11) and (12) has an absolute maximum lying on the surface defined by $\prod_{i=1}^{L} x_i = 0.75$. The best value found by the genetic algorithm was 0.3709 at the

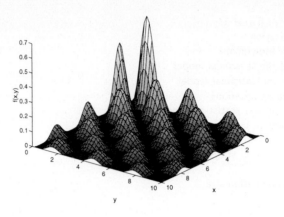

Fig. 2. Test function $f1$ for the 2-dimensional case

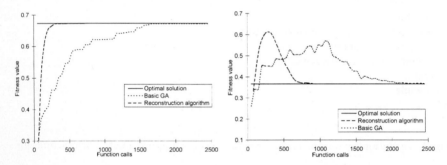

Fig. 3. Fitness value versus number of true fitness function calls, for the unconstrained 2-D problem

Fig. 4. Fitness value versus number of true fitness function calls, for the constrained 2-D problem

point $(x_1, x_2) = (1.59898, 0.462155)$. The problem was handled using a dynamically adapting penalty function algorithm. This penalty function takes a zero value at $t = 0$ and a maximal value at $t = t_{max}$, the predetermined number of generations:

$$f'(x) = f(x) - \frac{t}{t_{max}}\text{pen}(x) \qquad (13)$$

$$\text{pen}(x) = \begin{cases} 1 - \frac{4}{3}\prod_{i=1}^{L} x_i & \text{if } \prod_{i=1}^{L} x_i < 0.75 \\ 0 & \text{otherwise.} \end{cases} \qquad (14)$$

Results are presented on Fig. 4 for the basic genetic algorithm and for the reconstruction algorithm. Since the penalty function always has a zero value at the beginning of the process, the algorithm first tends to reach the unconstrained optimal solution. As time goes by, the weight given to the penalty function increases, redirecting the population toward the constrained optimal solution.

4.3   20-Dimensional Problem

The 20-dimensional case for the constrained $f1$ function is considered to be a difficult optimization problem, where no standard method have given satisfactory results, as pointed out by Michalewicz and Schoenauer [5]. Using dedicated operators that restrict the search only to the constraint surface, some good solutions have been found [5,6]. A similar approach has been used together with the fitness landscape approximation algorithm. A population size of 300 individuals was found to be necessary in order to get reliable modelisation and optimization results. Smaller population size resulted in unstable or divergent optimization paths. There is obviously a minimal number of data points required to ensures a correct reconstruction. This minimal population size remains to be investigated. Results for the 20-D problem are presented on Fig. 5. Although the increase in convergence rate is smaller compared to the 2-D cases, the proposed algorithm seems to be appropriate for obtaining rapidly a moderately good solution.

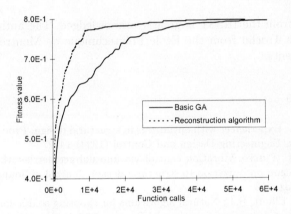

Fig. 5. Fitness value versus number of true fitness function calls, for the constrained 20-D problem

5   Conclusion

The aim of this paper was to introduce a new approach for speeding up the convergence of evolutionary algorithms in the case of numerically heavy fitness functions. Results presented on a test case have shown the potential use of this approach, for relatively simple 2-dimensional problems and for a difficult 20-dimensional multimodal problem. The results demonstrate that it is possible to extract more information from a finite set of data points than a basic evolutionary algorithm does, by using statistical techniques for estimating the whole fitness landscape from these data points. Although this approach might represents a strong disruption from the underlying paradigm of "decentralized intelligence" in evolutionary algorithms, it gave useful results as an optimization tool. The presented approach can be associated with a mechanism of "group learning", emerging from matching together all the individual experiences, instead of the more usual concept of "individual learning".

However, some points regarding the conditions for a correct reconstruction of the fitness landscape remains to be explained. These points are mainly the effect of the number of dimensions over the minimal number of data points ensuring convergence, and the influence of the basis functions for drift and covariance functions. A more general tool for automated reconstruction should includes several features such as an experimental inference of a covariance model, rather than a theoretically imposed one, and a goodness-of-fit criteria for the drift and covariance models. The effect of weighting the local influence functions versus the drift function on the rate of convergence should also be investigated carefully.

Acknowledgments

The support from the IRSST is greatly acknowledged. The author also thanks Prof. François Trochu from the Ecole Polytechnique de Montréal for his very helpful comments.

References

1. Keane, A. J.: Experiences with optimizers in structural design. Proc. Conf. Adaptive Computing in Engineering Design and Control (1994) 14–27
2. Keane, A. J.: Passive vibration control via unusual geometries: the application of genetic algorithm optimization to structural design. Journal of Sound and Vibration **185** (1995) 441–453
3. Baek, K.H., Elliott, S.J.: Natural algorithms for choosing source locations in active control systems. Journal of Sound and Vibration **186** (1995) 245–267
4. Ratle, A., Berry, A.: Use of genetic algorithms for the vibroacoustic optimization of plate response. Submitted to the Journal of the Acoustical Society of America.
5. Michalewicz, Z., Schoenauer, M.: Evolutionary Algorithms for Constrained Parameter Optimization Problems. Evolutionary Computation **4** (1996) 1–32
6. Michalewicz, Z.: Genetic Algorithms + Data Structure = Evolution Programs, 2nd ed. Berlin, Springer-Verlag (1994)
7. Matheron, G.: The intrinsic random functions and their applications. Adv. Appl. Prob. **5** (1973) 439–468
8. Matheron, G.: Splines et krigeage: leur équivalence formelle. Technical Report N–667, Centre de Géostatistique, École des Mines de Paris (1980)
9. Trochu, F.: A contouring program based on dual kriging interpolation. Engineering with Computers **9** (1993) 160–177
10. Bäck, T., Schwefel, H.-P.: An Overview of Evolutionary Algorithms for Parameter Optimization. Evolutionary Computation **1** (1993) 1–23

Modeling Building-Block Interdependency

Richard A. Watson   Gregory S. Hornby   Jordan B. Pollack

Dynamical and Evolutionary Machine Organization Group
Volen Center for Complex Systems – Brandeis University – Waltham, MA – USA

Abstract. The Building-Block Hypothesis appeals to the notion of problem decomposition and the assembly of solutions from sub-solutions. Accordingly, there have been many varieties of GA test problems with a structure based on building-blocks. Many of these problems use deceptive fitness functions to model interdependency between the bits within a block. However, very few have any model of interdependency between building-blocks; those that do are not consistent in the type of interaction used intra-block and inter-block. This paper discusses the inadequacies of the various test problems in the literature and clarifies the concept of building-block interdependency. We formulate a principled model of hierarchical interdependency that can be applied through many levels in a consistent manner and introduce *Hierarchical If-and-only-if* (H-IFF) as a canonical example. We present some empirical results of GAs on H-IFF showing that if population diversity is maintained and *linkage* is tight then the GA is able to identify and manipulate building-blocks over many levels of assembly, as the Building-Block Hypothesis suggests.

1 Introduction

Problem decomposition – the method of forming solutions by first breaking down a problem into sub-problems – is a central tenet behind the Building-Block Hypothesis ((Holland, 1975), (Goldberg , 1989)). Yet there has been much controversy over whether the GA can identify and manipulate sub-solutions or building-blocks appropriately ((Forrest & Mitchell, 1993b), (Goldberg and Horn, 1994), (Mitchell *et al.*, 1995)). Much of this controversy arises from the inadequacy of test problems in the literature and in turn this inadequacy arises from lack of clarity on the seemingly straight-forward concept of problem decomposition. More specifically, although problem decomposition implies some form of modularity it does not require that sub-problems be independent from each other. However, most building-block problems in the literature have no model of dependency between the building-blocks. This paper offers clarification on the issues of problem decomposition and in particular discusses how a problem may be decomposable into sub-problems and yet have strong non-linear interdependencies between these sub-problems. We define a construction method for a new class of problems, hierarchically decomposable problems, which exemplify those for which GAs should be well-suited according to the intuition of the Building-Block Hypothesis.

Before we proceed further we must define some terms. Although the basic concept of decomposing a problem into sub-problems may seem clear there are many ways that our straight-forward interpretation may be inadequate. Firstly, we clarify that a *separable* problem is a problem which can be divided into sub-problems each of which has a fixed optimal solution that is independent of how other sub-problems are solved. We define a *decomposable* problem to be something more general: simply a problem that has sub-problems, and we specifically allow that these sub-problems need not be separable - i.e. the optimal solution to one sub-problem may be different according to the solution of another sub-problem. In this case we say that a sub-problem is *dependent* on another, or in the bi-directional case, the sub-problems are *interdependent*. Included in the term decomposable is the notion of identifiable component parts, i.e. *modularity*, so a system of uniformly related variables with no modular structure is excluded from the term decomposable. Next we look at the notion of hierarchy. The Building-Block Hypothesis describes the assembly of bits into blocks, blocks into bigger blocks, and so on to provide a complete solution - the hierarchical aspect of the process is clear in our intuitions. Our general notions of GAs, building-blocks and the Building-Block Hypothesis all imply that the process continues over many levels *in the same fashion*. We define a *consistent* hierarchical problem as one where the nature of the problem at all levels is the same. In a consistent problem, the difficulty of solving a sub-problem and the difficulty of the solving the whole problem (given the solutions to the sub-problems) should be the same. This will be a central characteristic of our new problem class.

The following section discusses the properties of test problems in the literature in the light of the concepts defined above. Section 3 describes the general class of functions that can be used to construct principled decomposable problems, and 3.1 introduces the *Hierarchical If-and-only-if* (H-IFF) function as the canonical example of this class. Section 4 discusses the properties of H-IFF and adds justification for our construction method. Section 5 describes empirical results of GA trials using H-IFF.

2   Existing test problems from the GA literature

Before introducing our new problem class we first review some common test problems from the GA literature. We will be looking for a consistent hierarchical problem that exhibits modular sub-problems and interdependency between these sub-problems.

Whitley *et al.* (1995 and 1995b), provide a review of test-problems from the GA literature and summarize, "most common test problems used in the past to evaluate genetic algorithms lack" the inclusion of "strong non-linear dependencies between state variables." That is, although, the contribution of a single variable to the overall evaluation may be non-linear, there may be no non-linear interactions *between* variables, and therefore the optimal value for each parameter can be determined independently of all other parameters.

There are several building-block style functions - the Royal Road (RR) functions (Mitchell *et al.*, 1992, Forrest & Mitchell, 1993), revised Royal Road functions (Holland 1993), (see also, Jones, 1995), concatenated trap functions (Deb & Goldberg, 1992), and others - that clearly emphasize a gross-scale building-block structure. But, like the real-valued functions that Whitley investigated, these consist of concatenated blocks, each of which may be optimized independently in a cumulative fashion. The R1 version of the Royal Roads problem (Forrest & Mitchell, 1993), for example, can be imagined as a staircase leading search in a stepwise fashion in the correct direction. In concatenated trap functions and the revised Royal Road functions, the fitness gradient leads search away from the solution to each block. But, whereas the bit-wise landscape is fully deceptive, the 'block-wise landscape' is fully non-deceptive. That is, within a block the bits are not separable but each block is still separable from every other block (i.e. the optimal setting for a bit remains the same regardless of the setting of bits in other blocks) and again the sub-solutions accumulate linearly. To continue the analogy, although each tread on the stair is inclined unfavorably the whole staircase still leads to the global optima.

The R2 function, (Forrest & Mitchell, 1993), and the revised Royal Road functions make hierarchy explicit. However the interactions between bits within the first level blocks are very different from the interactions between blocks in subsequent levels. Although the fitness contributions of the base-level blocks accumulate non-linearly because of 'bonus' contributions from higher levels the blocks are still separable in that the optimal bit-setting for a block does not change.

Goldberg *et al.* (1993) acknowledge that they have "temporarily ignored the possibility of subfunction crosstalk". *Crosstalk*, is defined by Kargupta (1995) as "a property of both the algorithm and the landscape" and appeals to the idea that the algorithm may be misled in identifying building-blocks by changes in fitness contribution. Accordingly, Goldberg et al. suggest that noise in the fitness function may be an appropriate model for crosstalk. But this interpretation of crosstalk is not interdependency as we have defined it. We favor a definition of building-block dependency that is not reliant on the algorithm being used - specifically, the observation that the optimal bit-setting for a block is different in one context than in another is algorithm independent.

Whitley *et al.* (1995) argue for test-problems that have non-separable components, and propose an "expansion" method for constructing scaleable non-separable functions from a non-linear base function of two variables. By selecting pairs of variables in an overlapping fashion and summing the results they create a non-separable function over an arbitrarily large set of variables. They also propose that using all possible pairs, rather than a minimal set of overlapping pairs, provides a method to vary the amount of inter-dependency. This notion has some similarities with the NK landscapes of Kauffman (1993). The NK landscapes certainly do model the interdependency of variables - the contribution of each of N variables is defined as a random look-up function of itself and k other variables. The expanded functions of Whitley are analogous to NK landscapes with k=2 (and with a repeated base-function instead of random lookup tables). Using additional pairs is not wholly different from increasing k. This seems like a step in the right direction especially since the value of k, in some sense, defines the degree of interdependence.

But this is still not wholly satisfying for now we cannot see the building-blocks. In the NK model (and the expanded function method) the dependencies form a uniform network; there is no modularity. Our preliminary work explored varieties of the NK model that cluster the variables into groups with many intra-group dependencies and few inter-group dependencies- an idea inspired by the dependency matrices used by Simon (1969). Goldberg *et al* (1993), also suggests adding changes in fitness according to "the presence or absence of bit combinations across subfunction boundaries". But this method does not provide a principled hierarchical structure - merely a clustered, single-level one. To be consistent the interdependency of building-blocks should be defined as a function of the blocks as wholes not as a function of particular bits within the blocks.

Thus, none of these problems from the literature model building-block interdependency in a consistent hierarchical fashion.

3   Hierarchically   decomposable   problems

In this section we introduce a recursive construction for defining hierarchically consistent decomposable fitness functions from two base functions. Section 3.1 gives our canonical example, Hierarchical-if-and-only-if (H-IFF). This enables the construction of a problem, reminiscent of R2, that exhibits a gross-scale hierarchical building-block structure. But unlike R2, the blocks in this function are not separable.

The construction we will use defines the fitness contribution of a building-block separately from the *meaning* of the block. The meaning of a block is given by a *transform* function that defines what kind of block results from a particular combination of sub-blocks. The transform function 'decodes' or 'interprets' a block, and it is this that defines the interdependencies between sub-blocks. By making the definition of interdependencies separate from the fitness contributions we will be able to define two (or more) blocks that are indistinguishable from each other in respect of their individual fitness contributions yet which may have different results when put together with other blocks at the next level of the hierarchy.

A string of symbols $B = \{b_1,...,b_n\}$, over an alphabet S, where $n=k^p$, represents a hierarchical block structure, where k is the number of sub-blocks in a block, and p is the number of levels in the hierarchy. Each block at the bottom level of this hierarchy, consisting of k symbols each, will be converted into a single symbol by a *transform* function, t. This transform function defines the meaning of each block. This creates a new string (with length $k^{(p-1)}$) that is the decoding of the block structure to the first level. This process is repeated for each level in the hierarchy to give the single symbol that is the meaning of the whole structure. Thus, the recursive transform function, T, transforms any block structure to its meaning, a single symbol:

$$T(B) = \begin{cases} b_1 & if \mid B \mid = 1, \\ t(T(B^1),...,T(B^k)) & otherwise. \end{cases}$$

where t is a base function, $t:S^k \rightarrow S$, that defines the resultant symbol from a block of k symbols, $|B|$ is the number of symbols in B, and B^i is the ith sub-block of B i.e. $\{b_{(i-1)d+1},...,b_{id}\}$ (where $d=|B|/k$).

Now we may use $T(B)$ to construct $F(B)$, the fitness of a block structure. Specifically, the fitness of a block structure will be the fitness contribution of its transform (scaled for its size) plus the sum of the fitnesses of its sub-blocks. Hence the recursive function, F, defined using the base function f:

$$F(B) = \begin{cases} f(B) & if \mid B \mid = 1, \\ \mid B \mid f(T(B)) + \sum_{i=1}^{k} F(B^i) & otherwise. \end{cases}$$

where f is a base function, $f:S \rightarrow \Re$, giving the fitness of a single symbol.

The recursive constructions ensure that the fitness function is hierarchical and consistent. To illustrate, we can 'unroll' F(B) for a four variable problem with blocks formed from pairs (i.e. k=2, p=2) to give:

$$F(a,b,c,d) = 4f(t(t(t(a,b),t(c,d)))) + 2f(t(a,b)) + 2f(t(c,d)) + f(a) + f(b) + f(c) + f(d).\ ^1$$

3.1 Hierarchical-If-and-only-if (H-IFF)

We now need to give examples of the base functions, f and t, that provide an interesting fitness landscape. Our canonical example is provided for a k=2 problem by the logical relation if-and-only-if (IFF), or equality. First we define $t(\{A,B\})$ by arbitrarily assigning 0 and 1 to the two solutions of IFF (i.e. $t(\{0,0\})$=0 and $t(\{1,1\})$=1), and null to the non-solutions (i.e. $t(\{0,1\})$=$t(\{1,0\})$=null). But since t should map $S^k \rightarrow S$ so that it can be used in the recursive construction, we must expand its definition to a pair of tertiary variables {0,1, and null} instead of binary variables (Table 1). Then f(A) naturally defines the two non-null transform values as desirable and null as undesirable, (Table 2). F(B), T(B) and our two base functions, f and t, complete our definition of Hierarchical-If-and-only-if (H-IFF).

A	B	$t(\{A,B\})$
0	0	0
0	-	-
0	1	-
-	0	-
-	-	-
-	1	-
1	0	-
1	-	-
1	1	1

Table 1, left, and Table 2, right, define the two base functions, f and t, for Hierarchical-IFF. (nulls are shown as "-")

A	f(A)
0	1
-	0
1	1

4 Properties of H-IFF: deception and dimensional reduction

Our general construction and our choice of base functions warrants some explanation, but let us first examine some of the interesting properties of H-IFF. Blocks of two bits assemble into blocks of four, then eight, and so on. There are two solutions to every block and, similarly, two global optima. These solution pairs for each block are always maximally distinct, i.e. all-ones or all-zeros. Also, notice that any setting of any bit can be included in one of the two global optima – there is no preference for any particular bit settings *per se*, only for particular *combinations* of bit settings. Further, suppose the

---

[1] This can be contrasted with the R1 function and the concatenated trap functions which have the form F(a,b,c,d)=f(a,b)+f(c,d), which is separable and has only one level; and it is also distinct from the R2 function which has the form: F(a,b,c,d)= f(a,b,c,d)+g(a,b)+g(c,d), which is multi-level but not consistent; and distinct from Whitley's expanded functions of the form: F(a,b,c,d)= f(a,b)+f(b,c)+f(c,d)+f(d,a), which is non-separable and shows some consistency but is not hierarchical or modular; and lastly distinct from the Nk functions which have the form F(a,b,c,d)= f_1(a,b)+f_2(b,c)+f_3(c,d)+f_4(d,a), which is like Whitley's function but less consistent.

fitness base function were modified so that $f(0)=0$ – in this case a search would find a staircase in the fitness landscape that would lead to the global optimum at all-ones (see Figure 1, "all null to all 1s"). Notice the small steps in fitness at each block of 4, and larger jumps at each block of 8, etc. (similar to the higher levels of R2). Similarly, a corresponding curve exists for the all-zeros solutions if $f(1)=0$ (with $f(0)=1$ and $f($null$)=0$ as before). To illustrate that the all-zeros maximum is mutually exclusive with the all-ones maximum it is shown at the opposite extreme. But, in H-IFF, both blocks of zeros and blocks of ones are rewarded, and the "all 0s to all 1s" curve indicates the combination of the previous two. We can see that the best local-optima (with 32-ones and 32-zeros) are maximally distant from both global optima, and the next best are maximally distant from them and the global optima, and so on. This, as we will demonstrate, makes H-IFF very hard for hill-climbers.

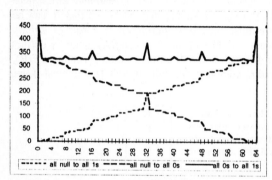

Figure 1: Three sections through the 64-bit H-IFF landscape (as used in the following experiments) showing two maximally distinct global optima (max. fit = 448) and illustrating the fractal structure for the local optima arising from the (consistent) hierarchical interdependencies. Bear in mind that we are only viewing 65 points out of a total 2^{64}. See text.

Consider the local optimum 00001111 for an 8-bit H-IFF. This string confers fitness for each of the two sub-blocks, 0000 and 1111, but no fitness contribution for the top level. Each substring that is rewarded is a substring of a global optima and *in this sense* the fitness contributions are not 'misleading'. Deceptive fitness functions such as the concatenated trap functions are conceptually different. These fitness functions create artificial local optima that represent erroneous elements of a fitness function. They are completely (and deliberately) wrong in their assessment of low-order schema, but improve as schema increase in size. It does not make sense to apply this kind of misleadingness consistently through many levels of a hierarchy - the fitness function cannot be completely wrong at the top level.

A more informative point of view with which to understand the problem difficulty is to imagine that the fitness of a local optima is not so much 'wrong' as 'incomplete'. That is, it does not apply any knowledge of subsequent levels - substrings are rewarded for what they are, even if they are not used in the best context. From this perspective the fitness contribution of a block may be misleading not because of its incompatibility with the global optima but rather because it is incompatible with its context.

How is it that we can make sense of a fitness contribution when it does not take account of context? After all, in H-IFF, a block might be completely right for one context and completely wrong for another! The information provided by the fitness contributions enables search to identify how to reduce the dimensionality of the problem space. In this manner search can progress from the combination of bits to the combination of low-order schema, to the combination of higher-order schema, and so on, exactly as the building-block hypothesis suggests. This does not mean that finding the right combinations will not be problematic at each and every level - it simply means that at each level the search process has bigger building-blocks to experiment with. This dimensional reduction is the only way to make sense of problem decomposition when sub-problems are strongly interdependent. If there is only one solution to a building-block then finding the right combination of blocks cannot be problematic. Hence, we arrive at a fundamental requirement for a (non-trivial) decomposable problem - there has to be *more than one way to solve a (sub-)problem*. This is the motivation that leads us to conceptually separate the way in which a problem is solved from the fact that the solution is good - to separate meaning from fitness. It is, perhaps, the lack of this simple distinction between meaning and fitness, and the resultant tendency to try and define interdependency using functions that manipulate fitness values, that has prevented the prior formulation of a principled model for building-block interdependency.

To represent the two ways to solve a problem and one non-solution we need an alphabet of three symbols and accordingly f has two high-fitness entries and one low-fitness entry. Then we must ensure that these two high-fitness blocks arise from certain combinations of the high-fitness sub-blocks but not all combinations - hence, t is based on IFF where two out of four possible combinations provide non-nulls for use in the next level. Logical exclusive-or (being the negation of IFF) will suffice equally well in formulating a Hierarchical-XOR[2]. Other Boolean functions of two variables are not suitable since they either have only one solution, or solutions dependent on only one variable. Other base functions over larger alphabets, and different values of k and p, may be used to produce asymmetric, biased, or possibly noisy fitness landscapes that have a consistent hierarchical decomposability.

5 Experiments using H-IFF

The following experiments use H-IFF to verify the GA's ability to identify building-blocks, resolve their interdependencies, and (re)combine them, as described by the Building-Block Hypothesis. Forrest and Mitchell (1993b, and Mitchell *et al*, 1995) use random mutation hill-climbing (RMHC) to demonstrate that the RR functions are not appropriate test-functions for GAs. Likewise, Jones (1993 pp. 57-58) demonstrates that the revised RR functions and the concatenated trap-functions are inappropriate by applying the "Headless Chicken Test" (HCT) (a hill-climber that uses macro-mutations). Thus RMHC and HCT are chosen for comparison against the standard GA (both two-point and uniform crossover). These algorithms are each applied to a standard 64-bit H-IFF and a bit-shuffled H-IFF, both with and without fitness-sharing. The bit-shuffled H-IFF (a standard H-IFF with random bit-ordering) demonstrates that the GA's ability to manipulate building-blocks with crossover is dependent on the heuristic of bit-adjacency (see linkage disequalibrium, Altenberg 1995). The fitness-sharing method is used to enforce diversity since any algorithm that is to explore the space of solutions properly will need to maintain both solutions to a block at least as long as it takes to find the solution at the next level. We use a resource-based fitness-sharing method (similar to implicit fitness sharing) that uses explicit knowledge of the block-structure, and is

---

[2] It was tempting to give H-XOR as the canonical example of the class since this name perhaps reveals more of the difficulty in the resultant landscape - however, although the problem difficulty of hierarchical-equality (H-IFF) is exactly the same as that of hierarchical-inequality (H-XOR), a solution like 11111111 is much easier on the eye than 01101001.

therefore not a general purpose fitness-sharing method. Rather, it simply provides a tool for enforcing diversity, so that we can investigate the GA's ability to combine building-blocks when diversity is maintained. All four algorithms (1-4 detailed below) are applied to each of the 4 different varieties of H-IFF (a - d) in Figure 2.

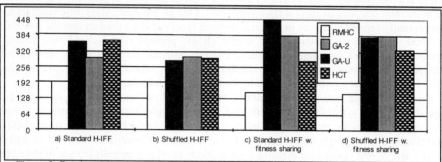

Figure 2: Random Mutation Hill Climbing (RMHC), GA with 2 point crossover (GA-2), GA with uniform crossover (GA-U), and the Headless Chicken Test (HCT), each applied to a) Standard 64-bit H-IFF, b) Shuffled H-IFF (H-IFF with random bit-ordering), c) Standard H-IFF with fitness sharing, d) Shuffled H-IFF with fitness sharing. Each point is the best fitness from the last generation, averaged over 10 runs. In all runs there was no significant improvement in the best fitness after approximately 400 generations. A 64-bit H-IFF is used which has a maximum fitness solution of 448. a) As expected, RMHC performs poorly, becoming trapped in local optima. GAs do better but also become trapped. Although the 2-point cross-over performs better than uniform, the HCT suggests that the GA gets as far as it does because of macro mutations rather than the combination of pre-adapted blocks. From comparison with the HCT performance we see that the GA performance is not very impressive. b) When the bits of a H-IFF problem are randomly shuffled the problem is even harder - all algorithms perform as poorly as uniform cross-over performed on the standard H-IFF. This strengthens the hypothesis that the GAs representation of blocks in the standard H-IFF does add to the GA performance. c) When we enforce diversity in the population the standard 2 point GA succeeds easily. The HCT shows that the success of the regular GA is not because of macro mutations (as it is in the previous two graphs). The hill-climber performs even worse now; when it finds one block the resources are depleted and it has to move to another - so, although it can escape from local optima, the next block it finds is usually no better. This and the HCT confirms that the fitness-sharing methods did not trivialize the problem, and that the population of the GA is necessary. d) demonstrates that the heuristic of bit-adjacency in identifying building-blocks is required for GA success as expected. Poor linkage reduces the performance of the GA with 2 point crossover to the performance of uniform crossover.

1) **RMHC: Random Mutation Hill-Climbing:** Mutation rate is 2/64 probability of assigning a new random value. RMHC is run for 10^6 evaluations.
2) **GA-2: GA with 2 point crossover:** 1000 individuals are run for 1000 generations. Elitism of 1% is used. The ranking function uses Michalewicz's exponential scaling with 0.01 for the value that determines the selection pressure (Michalewicz, 1995). Two-point crossover is used with a probability of 0.3. Mutation as per RMHC.
3) **GA-U: GA with uniform crossover:** Other parameters as per GA-2.

4)   **HCT: Headless Chicken Test:** The headless chicken test (Jones, 1995) is a GA in all respects except that when cross-over is performed one of the parents is an entirely random string which thus replaces whole chunks of the genotype with random bits whilst leaving other sections intact. If a regular GA performs no better than the HCT then the crossover operator is not providing any useful advantage. All other parameters are the same as GA-2.

The results in Figure 2 show that the GA is able to identify building-blocks and combine them appropriately as the Building-Block Hypothesis suggests. The results demonstrate that the success of the GA is not attainable with RMHC or with macro-mutation hill-climbing (HCT). They also show that this success is dependent on maintaining diversity and on good linkage. Together these results indicate that H-IFF is exemplary of the class of functions that GAs are good for.

6   Conclusions

This paper has reviewed the inadequacies of current GA test-problems. In particular, the emphasis has been on the modeling of problems with a hierarchical decomposable structure where sub-problems are not separable. The concept of a transform function that can be applied recursively to construct a multi-level problem with strong non-linear interdependencies is identified and separated from the concept of a fitness function. The recursive constructions can be parameterized by the size of the alphabet, the number of sub-blocks per block, and the number of hierarchy levels. Also, the characteristics of the landscape can be modified by the choice of base functions. The Hierarchical-IF-and-only-IF function is introduced as a canonical example of the class.

The experimental results using H-IFF demonstrate that the GA can assemble blocks hierarchically, as per the Building-Block Hypothesis, but only when allowed to use the heuristic of bit-adjacency and when diversity can be maintained. This indicates that H-IFF is exemplary of the class of problems that GAs are good for. Also H-IFF provides a good test-problem for investigating linkage-learning algorithms and fitness-sharing methods.[3]

We have seen that interdependency (where the contribution of a block may be misleading because of its incompatibility with other blocks) may be a more fruitful perspective on GA-difficulty than deception (based on incompatibility with a global optimum). Also, H-IFF demonstrates that interdependency can be modeled deterministically and that noisy fitness functions are not required for modeling building-block interdependency. Lastly, H-IFF is highly multi-modal but is amenable to GAs - which verifies that the structure of a landscape is more important than the number of local-optima (Goldberg et al. 1994). So although H-IFF is not a complete model of problem difficulty it is relevant to the issues of deception, noise, and multi-modality as well as building-block interdependency.

---

[3]   Although this paper has focused on introducing H-IFF, other research has developed a variant of the Messy GA which (unlike the algorithms tested here) solves the shuffled H-IFF in approximately 500 generations. However, this is a rather non-standard algorithm (interestingly, we only use a 'splice' genetic operator with no mutation or cross-over) and it is not yet clear which of the new features are essential to success.

Acknowledgments

The first author thanks Inman Harvey for providing the impetus to pursue these concepts and laying the challenge to ground them in a concrete model. Many thanks also to Una-May O'Reilly for her valuable clarifying discussion and assistance in reviewing the literature. To the members of the DEMO group, especially, Sevan Ficici and Pablo Funes appreciation for assisting us in the research process. And, thanks to the reviewers for their suggestions.

References

1. Altenberg, L, 1995 "The Schema Theorem and Price's Theorem", FOGA3, editors Whitley & Vose, pp 23-49, Morgan Kauffmann, San Francisco.
2. Deb, K & Goldberg, DE, 1989, "An investigation of Niche and Species Formation in genetic Function Optimization", ICGA3, San Mateo, CA: Morgan Kauffman.
3. Deb, K & Goldberg, DE, 1992, "Sufficient conditions for deceptive and easy binary functions", (IlliGAL Report No. 91009), University of Illinois, IL.
4. Forrest, S & Mitchell, M, 1993 "Relative Building-block fitness and the Building-block Hypothesis", in Foundations of Genetic Algorithms 2, Morgan Kaufmann, San Mateo, CA.
5. Forrest, S & Mitchell, M, 1993b "What makes a problem hard for a Genetic Algorithm? Some anomalous results and their explanation" Machine Learning 13, pp.285-319.
6. Goldberg, DE, 1989 "Genetic Algorithms in Search, Optimisation and Machine Learning", Reading Massachusetts, Addison-Wesley.
7. Goldberg, DE, & Horn, J, 1994 "Genetic Algorithm Difficulty and the Modality of Fitness Landscapes", in Foundations of Genetic Algorithms 3, Morgan Kaufmann, San Mateo, CA.
8. Goldberg, DE, Deb, K, Kargupta, H, & Harik, G, 1993 "Rapid, Accurate Optimization of Difficult Problems Using Fast Messy GAs", IlliGAL Report No. 93004, U. of Illinois, IL.
9. Goldberg, DE, Deb, K, & Korb, B, 1989 "Messy Genetic Algorithms: Motivation, Analysis and first results", Complex Systems, 3, 493-530.
10. Holland, JH, 1975 "Adaptation in Natural and Artificial Systems", Ann Arbor, MI: The University of Michigan Press.
11. Holland, JH, 1993 "Royal Road Functions", Internet Genetic Algorithms Digest v7n22.
12. Jones, T, 1995, Evolutionary Algorithms, Fitness Landscapes and Search, PhD dissertation, 95-05-048, University of New Mexico, Albuquerque. pp. 62-65.
13. Jones, T, & Forrest, S, 1995 "Fitness Distance Correlation as a Measure of Problem Difficulty for Genetic Algorithms" ICGA 6, Morgan & Kauffman.
14. Kauffman, SA, 1993 "The Origins of Order", Oxford University Press.
15. Michalewicz, Z, 1992, "Genetic Algorithms + Data Structures = Evolution Programs" Springer-Verlag, New York, 1992.
16. Mitchell, M, Holland, JH, & Forrest, S, 1995 "When will a Genetic Algorithm Outperform Hill-climbing?" to appear in Advances in NIPS 6, Mogan Kaufmann, San Mateo, CA.
17. Mitchell, M, Forrest, S, & Holland, JH, 1992 "The royal road for genetic algorithms: Fitness landscapes and GA performance", Procs. of first ECAL, Camb., MA. MIT Press.
18. Simon, HA, 1969 "The Sciences of the Artificial" Cambridge, MA. MIT Press.
19. Smith, RE, Forrest, S, & Perelson, A, 1993 "Searching for Diverse, Cooperative Populations with Genetic Algorithms", Evolutionary Computation 1(2), pp127-149.
20. Whitley, D, Mathias, K, Rana, S & Dzubera, J, 1995 "Building Better Test Functions", ICGA-6, editor Eshelman, pp239-246, Morgan Kauffmann, San Francisco.
21. Whitley, D, Beveridge, R, Graves, C, & Mathias, K, 1995b "Test Driving Three 1995 Genetic Algorithms: New Test Functions and Geometric Matching", Heuristics, 1:77-104.

Noisy and Non-stationary
Objective Functions

Mutate Large, But Inherit Small!
On the Analysis of Rescaled Mutations in
$(\tilde{1}, \tilde{\lambda})$-ES with Noisy Fitness Data

Hans-Georg Beyer*

University of Dortmund, Department of Computer Science XI
D-44221 Dortmund, Germany

Abstract. The paper presents the asymptotical analysis of a technique for improving the convergence of evolution strategies (ES) on noisy fitness data. This technique that may be called "Mutate large, but inherit small", is discussed in light of the EPP (evolutionary progress principle). The derivation of the progress rate formula is sketched, its predictions are compared with experiments, and its limitations are shown. The dynamical behavior of the ES is investigated. It will be shown that standard self-adaptation has considerable problems to drive the ES in its optimum working regime. Remedies are provided to improve the self-adaptation.

1   Introduction

The evolution in noisy environments has some peculiarities over the non-perturbed fitness case. This is due to the deception introduced by the noisy fitness data, denoted by $\tilde{Q}$, which randomly mislead the selection process in the evolutionary algorithms. The deception can be so strong that even elitist selection schemes may exhibit divergence behavior. That is, the initial distance $R^{(0)}$ of the population to the optimum grows with increasing time g, $R^{(g)} > R^{(0)}$. This remarkable behavior has been first derived and experimentally verified in [1] for the $(\tilde{1}\overset{+}{,}\tilde{\lambda})$-ES[1] on the sphere model. In this paper we will resume the analysis of the $(\tilde{1}, \tilde{\lambda})$-ES. According to the work of Ostermeier and Rechenberg published in [6], there is a new technique for coping with noise deception, which is worth investigating here. The paper is organized as follows. The next section re-examines the $(\tilde{1}, \tilde{\lambda})$-ES progress rate theory in the light of the *evolutionary progress principle* (EPP) leading us to the idea of rescaled mutations in an natural way. Section 3 is devoted to the asymptotical analysis. Section 4 relates these results to the real time behavior of the $(\tilde{1}, \tilde{\lambda})$-ES including self-adaptation. We will see that *current σ-self-adaptation (σSA) methods do work for $(\tilde{1}, \tilde{\lambda})$-ES*, but that *they are not able to reach the domain of optimum performance* (i.e. the vicinity of the theoretically predicted maximal progress rate).

---

* e-mail: beyer@ludo.cs.uni-dortmund.de
[1] The tilde indicates that the parental fitness data ($\tilde{1}$: there is only one parent) and the offspring values ($\tilde{\lambda}$: there are λ offspring) are disturbed by noise.

2   The $(\tilde{1}, \tilde{\lambda})$-ES, the EPP, and Rescaled Mutations

2.1   The $(\tilde{1}, \tilde{\lambda})$-ES Re-examined

Let us first reconsider the $(\tilde{1}, \tilde{\lambda})$-ES. It is assumed that the reader is familiar with the ES and the progress rate theory on the sphere model. Therefore, only a short summary is given here. The parent $\mathbf{y}_p$ at generation $g + 1$ is the best offspring of generation g which is obtained by the mutation $\mathbf{z}_{\tilde{1};\tilde{\lambda}}$ that has produced the fittest individual, i.e. $\mathbf{y}_p^{(g+1)} := \mathbf{y}_p^{(g)} + \mathbf{z}_{\tilde{1};\tilde{\lambda}}$. The vectors $\mathbf{y}$ and $\mathbf{z}$ are from the N-dimensional real-valued space $\mathbb{R}^N$. The mutations are isotropic and Gaussian distributed with each component sampling from $\mathcal{N}(0, \sigma^2)$. As fitness model, the noisy sphere is considered, i.e., $\tilde{Q}(\mathbf{y}) = Q(R) + \varepsilon_Q$, with $R = \|\mathbf{y}\|$ the distance to the optimum and ε_Q a noise source which is assumed to be normally distributed $\varepsilon_Q \sim \mathcal{N}(0, \sigma_{\varepsilon_Q}^2)$, where σ_{ε_Q} can be a function of R. For this model, the progress rate φ, i.e., the expected distance change toward the optimum, can be calculated [1] (for the definition of φ, see Section 3). Using normalized quantities

$$\varphi^* := \varphi \frac{N}{R}, \quad \sigma^* := \sigma \frac{N}{R}, \quad \sigma_\varepsilon^* := \frac{\sigma_{\varepsilon_Q}(R)}{|Q'(R)|} \frac{N}{R} \quad \text{with} \quad Q'(R) := \frac{dQ}{dR} \qquad (1)$$

the normalized progress rate reads

$$\varphi_{\tilde{1},\tilde{\lambda}}^*(\sigma^*, \sigma_\varepsilon^*) = c_{1,\lambda} \sigma^* \frac{1}{\sqrt{1 + (\sigma_\varepsilon^*/\sigma^*)^2}} - \frac{\sigma^{*2}}{2} + \mathcal{O}\left(\frac{1}{N}\right). \qquad (2)$$

Here, $c_{1,\lambda}$ is the progress coefficient being the expectation of the λth order statistics of the standard normal variate (see [1], p. 171).[2]

2.2   The EPP and Convergence Improvement Techniques

It is interesting to discuss Eq. (2) from the viewpoint of the evolutionary progress principle (EPP), proposed in [4]. This principle states that the evolutionary progress toward the optimum is the result of two opposite forces:

EVOLUTIONARY PROGRESS	=	PROGRESS GAIN	−	PROGRESS LOSS

---

[2] A simple, but good approximation for $c_{1,\lambda}$ has been proposed by Rechenberg [5] $c_{1,\lambda} \approx \Phi^{-1}(\sqrt[\lambda]{1/2})$, with Φ^{-1} the inverse to the cdf (i.e., the quantile function) of the standard normal variate. The relative error is less than 3.5%.

As to the asymptotical ($N \to \infty$) formula (2), one can see that the *loss part* is a quadratic function of σ^*, whereas the *gain part* is given by $c_{1,\lambda}\sigma^*/\sqrt{1 + (\sigma_\varepsilon^*/\sigma^*)^2}$. An important observation is that selection influences the gain part, but not the loss part. Because $\sigma_\varepsilon^* = 0$ yields as gain $c_{1,\lambda}\sigma^*$, one can further conclude that the effectiveness of selection is degraded by increasing the noise level σ_ε^*. If a fixed normalized mutation strength ($\sigma^* = $ const.) is assumed then there are two possibilities to improve the convergence rate of the standard $(\tilde{1}, \tilde{\lambda})$-ES [1]:

a) Increase "selection pressure" by increasing λ, because $c_{1,\lambda} \sim \sqrt{2\ln(\lambda)}$.
b) Improve the effectiveness of the selection by reduction of σ_ε^* using m-times repeated fitness measurements with averaging. This produces a $\sigma_\varepsilon^{*\prime} = \sigma_\varepsilon^*/\sqrt{m}$.

It is to notice that both methods are not for free because they both afford additional fitness calculations and in case a) mutation and selection costs.

The aforementioned techniques work through the increase of the gain part; however, there are also methods for reducing the loss part of the EPP. Actually, recombination is such a technique; in case of intermediate (μ/μ) multi-parent recombination, the loss part reduces up to a factor of μ, however, recombination will not be considered here. As another approach, one could perhaps take advantage of the nonlinearity of the loss part in Eq. (2). Since the gain part is for small σ_ε^* ($\sigma_\varepsilon^*/\sigma^* \ll 1$) almost linear in σ^*, a reduction of σ^* by a factor of $1/\kappa$ reduces much more the loss part than the gain part, thus, providing a positive net progress. This is exactly the effect of a modified ES proposed by Ostermeier and Rechenberg [6] that follows the slogan: *"mutate large, but inherit small"*. That is, one produces λ offspring in the usual way by z_l mutations applied to the parent $\mathbf{y}_p^{(g)}$. The mutation $\mathbf{z}_{\tilde{1};\tilde{\lambda}}$ that generates the best offspring; however, is *rescaled* by a factor $1/\kappa$. This rescaled mutation is then added to the parent of generation g to produce the new $\mathbf{y}_p^{(g+1)}$. The algorithm reads

$$\mathbf{y}_p^{(g+1)} := \mathbf{y}_p^{(g)} + \frac{1}{\kappa}\mathbf{z}_{\tilde{1};\tilde{\lambda}}, \qquad \kappa \geq 1. \tag{3}$$

In the following section, it will be shown that the algorithm (3) indeed reduces the loss part of the progress rate formula.

3 Asymptotical Analysis

3.1 Derivation of the φ^* Formula

Due to space limitations only a sketch can be given that reflects the main ideas for the derivation of the asymptotically ($N \to \infty$) correct φ^* formula (see [3] for details). Let R be the distance of $\mathbf{y}_p^{(g)}$ to the optimum and $\tilde{R}$ that of $\mathbf{y}_p^{(g+1)}$. The progress rate φ is defined as the expectation $\varphi := \mathrm{E}\{R - \tilde{R}\}$. In order to calculate $\tilde{R}$ produced by $\mathbf{z}_{\tilde{1};\tilde{\lambda}}/\kappa$, according to (3), the mutations z_l are decomposed in such

Fig. 1. Decomposition of the $\mathbf{z}$ mutation in a part x in optimum direction and a perpendicular $\mathbf{h}$-vector, i.e., $\mathbf{z} = -x\mathbf{e}_R + \mathbf{h}$. R is the parental distance $\|\mathbf{y}_p^{(g)} - \hat{\mathbf{y}}\|$ to the optimum $\hat{\mathbf{y}}$. $\tilde{R}$ is the parental distance $\tilde{R} = \|\mathbf{y}_p^{(g+1)} - \hat{\mathbf{y}}\|$ for generation $g+1$ obtained *after* rescaling of that mutation which belongs to the best offspring. Due to the isotropy of the mutations, the x as well as the components of $\mathbf{h}$ are $\mathcal{N}(0, \sigma^2)$ distributed.

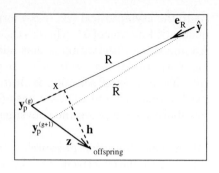

a way that one component, say x, points in optimum direction $-\mathbf{e}_R$ and the rest is carried by a vector $\mathbf{h}$. From Fig. 1, we read $\mathbf{y}_p^{(g)} - \hat{\mathbf{y}} = R\mathbf{e}_R$. Thus, we get for $\tilde{R} = \|\mathbf{y}_p^{(g+1)} - \hat{\mathbf{y}}\|$, using (3) and $\mathbf{z}_{\tilde{1};\tilde{\lambda}} = -x_{\tilde{1};\tilde{\lambda}}\mathbf{e}_R + \mathbf{h}_{\tilde{1};\tilde{\lambda}}$, the expression $\tilde{R} = \|(R - \frac{1}{\kappa}x_{\tilde{1};\tilde{\lambda}})\mathbf{e}_R + \frac{1}{\kappa}\mathbf{h}_{\tilde{1};\tilde{\lambda}}\|$. Therefore the progress rate is

$$\varphi_{\tilde{1},\tilde{\lambda}} = \mathrm{E}\left\{R - \sqrt{\left(R - x_{\tilde{1};\tilde{\lambda}}/\kappa\right)^2 + \mathbf{h}_{\tilde{1};\tilde{\lambda}}^2/\kappa^2}\right\}. \tag{4}$$

This expression can be further simplified if one takes the symmetry of the spherical model into account: The $\mathbf{h}$ parts of the mutations are selectively neutral as to their orientations in the $(N-1)$-dimensional subspace (isotropy). Therefore, the $\mathbf{h}^2$ of a single mutation is simply the sum over $N-1$ independent and squared $\mathcal{N}(0, \sigma^2)$ variates, i.e., $\mathbf{h}^2$ is χ^2 distributed with expectation $\mathrm{E}\{\mathbf{h}^2\} = (N-1)\sigma^2$ and standard deviation $\mathrm{D}\{\mathbf{h}^2\} = \sqrt{2(N-1)}\sigma^2$. Since $\mathrm{D}\{\mathbf{h}^2\}/\mathrm{E}\{\mathbf{h}^2\} \to 0$ for $N \to \infty$, the simplification $\mathbf{h}_{\tilde{1};\tilde{\lambda}}^2 \sim \mathrm{E}\{\mathbf{h}^2\} = (N-1)\sigma^2 \sim N\sigma^2$ is justified. If this is inserted in (4), one obtains after a short calculation $\varphi_{\tilde{1},\tilde{\lambda}} \simeq RE\left\{1 - \sqrt{1 - \frac{2x_{\tilde{1}:\tilde{\lambda}}}{R\kappa} + \frac{x_{\tilde{1}:\tilde{\lambda}}^2}{R^2\kappa^2} + \frac{N\sigma^2}{R^2\kappa^2}}\right\}$. Now, the square root is expanded into a Taylor series, i.e., $1 - \sqrt{1-2y} = y + \mathcal{O}(y^2)$, and the $(x_{\tilde{1};\tilde{\lambda}}/\kappa R)^2$ term is neglected. As result $\varphi_{\tilde{1},\tilde{\lambda}} \simeq RE\left\{\frac{x_{\tilde{1}:\tilde{\lambda}}}{R\kappa} - \frac{N\sigma^2}{R^2}\frac{1}{2\kappa^2}\right\}$ is obtained. Using the normalization from Eq. (1) we arrive at $\varphi_{\tilde{1},\tilde{\lambda}}^* \simeq \frac{N}{R}\frac{1}{\kappa}\mathrm{E}\{x_{\tilde{1};\tilde{\lambda}}\} - \frac{\sigma^{*2}}{2\kappa^2}$. As one can see, the rescaling technique (3) produces just the desired effect: The loss part is reduced by κ^2, whereas the gain part only by κ.

Due to space limitations, the calculation of $\mathrm{E}\{x_{\tilde{1};\tilde{\lambda}}\}$ must be omitted here. One finds $\mathrm{E}\{x_{\tilde{1};\tilde{\lambda}}\} = c_{1,\lambda}\sigma/\sqrt{1 + (\sigma_\varepsilon^*/\sigma^*)^2}$ which is similar to the linear part of Eq. (2). Thus, one finally obtains the asymptotical φ^* formula

$$\varphi_{\tilde{1},\tilde{\lambda}}^*(\sigma^*, \sigma_\varepsilon^*) = \frac{1}{\kappa}\left[c_{1,\lambda}\sigma^* \frac{1}{\sqrt{1 + (\sigma_\varepsilon^*/\sigma^*)^2}} - \frac{\sigma^{*2}}{2\kappa}\right]. \tag{5}$$

3.2 Comparison with Experiments and Discussion

The progress rate formula (5) has been extensively tested. As an example the $(\tilde{1}, \tilde{5})$-ES will be simulated using 1-generation experiments. That is, for a fixed mutation strength σ the parent is randomly placed at distance R to the optimum. Then, algorithm (3) is performed for *one* generation and the parental distance change is calculated. This 1-generation experiment is repeated T times and the average distance change serves as an estimate for $\varphi(\sigma)$. Figures 2 and 3 show simulation results for a noise level $\sigma_\varepsilon^* = 3.5$ and different values of N and κ. The

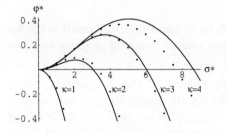

Fig. 2. On the approximation quality of the φ^* formula (5). The dots are obtained from the simulations of a $(\tilde{1}, \tilde{5})$-ES. Each dot is the average over $T = 100,000$ 1-generation experiments. The case $N = 30$ (parameter space dimensions) is displayed. For the cases $N = 100$ and $N = 500$, see Fig. 3.

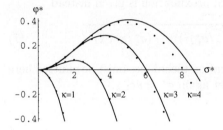
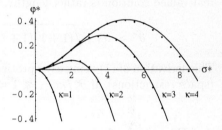

Fig. 3. Left picture: $N = 100$, $T = 100,000$. Right picture: $N = 500$, $T = 50,000$.

progress coefficient $c_{1,5} \approx 1.163$ and as fitness function $Q(\mathbf{y}) = \|\mathbf{y}\|^2$ has been chosen. As one can see, the approximation quality increases with larger N and decreases with increasing σ^*. Since there are considerable deviations for larger κ and σ^* there is still a demand for an N-dependent φ^* formula.

Let us discuss Eq. (5) in detail. Again for the $(\tilde{1}, \tilde{5})$-ES, φ^* is plotted by contour lines in Fig. 4. It seems that φ^* increases monotonously when κ and σ^* are appropriately increased. This can be shown analytically by maximizing (5) with respect to κ and fixed σ^*. One finds

$$\kappa_{\text{opt}} = \frac{1}{c_{1,\lambda}} \sqrt{\sigma^{*2} + \sigma_\varepsilon^{*2}} \quad \Longrightarrow \quad \hat{\varphi}_{\tilde{1},\tilde{\lambda}}^* = \frac{1}{1 + (\sigma_\varepsilon^*/\sigma^*)^2} \frac{c_{1,\lambda}^2}{2}. \quad (6)$$

The limit case $\kappa_{\text{opt}} \to \infty$ yields $\hat{\varphi}^* \to c_{1,\lambda}^2/2$. That is, for the asymptotical limit, the progress rate of the noisy ES approaches the performance of the ES without

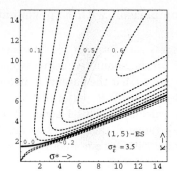

Fig. 4. Contour plot of $\varphi^*_{\tilde{1},5}(\sigma^*,\kappa)$. The solid curve $\varphi^* = 0.0$ separates the domain of convergence from the domain of divergence.

noise! However, it is really important to keep in mind that this result holds for $N \to \infty$. The real-world case $N < \infty$ gives smaller maximal progress and κ is to be chosen appropriately.

As for each ES, the optimum mutation strength $\hat{\sigma}^*$ that maximizes φ^* is of interest. Unlike the determination of κ_{opt} by Eq. (6), maximizing φ^* with respect to σ^* requires a third order equation $y^3 - \kappa c_{1,\lambda} y^2 - \kappa c_{1,\lambda} \sigma_\varepsilon^{*2} = 0$ to be solved for y. The optimal $\sigma^* = \hat{\sigma}^*$ is then obtained by $\hat{\sigma}^* = \sqrt{y^2 - \sigma_\varepsilon^{*2}}$. Since the only real-valued solution is rather lengthy, an approximation is given instead

$$\hat{\sigma}^* \approx \kappa c_{1,\lambda} \sqrt{(1 + 1/(1 + (\kappa c_{1,\lambda}/\sigma_\varepsilon^*)^2))^2 - (\sigma_\varepsilon^*/\kappa c_{1,\lambda})^2}. \tag{7}$$

The derivation of (7) using asymptotic iteration techniques must be omitted here (space restrictions). If $\sigma_\varepsilon^*/\kappa c_{1,\lambda} \ll 1$ we get again $\hat{\sigma}^* \approx \kappa c_{1,\lambda}$.

4 Dynamical Aspects

4.1 The Thales Criterion of Evolution

As we will see later on, one cannot always expect the ES working in its optimal performance interval $\sigma^* \approx \hat{\sigma}^*$. Therefore, an *evolution criterion* can be helpful to estimate the convergence/divergence of the ES. Such a criterion is easily obtained from the condition $\forall g,\ g > g_0 : R^{(g+1)} < R^{(g)}$. Since $R^{(g+1)} = \mathrm{E}\{\tilde{R}\}$, we have $R^{(g+1)} < R^{(g)} \Leftrightarrow \mathrm{E}\{\tilde{R}\} < R^{(g)} \Leftrightarrow \mathrm{E}\{R - \tilde{R}\} > 0 \Leftrightarrow \varphi^* > 0$. Thus, by means of Eq. (5) one obtains the

EVOLUTION CRITERION: $\qquad 4\kappa^2 c_{1,\lambda}^2 > \sigma^{*2} + \sigma_\varepsilon^{*2}.$ $\qquad\qquad$ (8)

If the relation sign in (8) is substituted by an equal sign, a Thales circle with radius $\kappa c_{1,\lambda}$ is prescribed. This allows for a graphical interpretation of the $(\tilde{1}, \tilde{\lambda})$ convergence properties, given in Fig. 5. As one can see, the normalized σ_ε must *necessarily fulfill the condition* $\sigma_\varepsilon^* < 2\kappa c_{1,\lambda}$ in order to have convergence. If

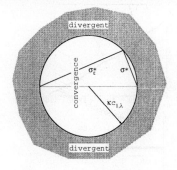

Fig. 5. The Thales criterion of convergence. All σ^*-, σ_ε^*-length combinations lying within the circle of radius $\kappa c_{1,\lambda}$ are convergent states, i.e., the ES reduces on average the distance to the optimum. All states outside are divergent.

this necessary condition is fulfilled, convergence depends on the actual mutation strength σ. That is, one needs a technique that tunes σ in such a way that σ^* and σ_ε^* are in the Thales circle. σ-self-adaptation (σSA) can be used for this purpose.

4.2 Experiments with σ-Self-Adaptation (σSA)

The self-adaptation theory is still in the beginning. Up to now, only the $(1, \lambda)$-ES without noise and $\kappa = 1$ has been analyzed [2]. It is assumed that the reader is familiar with the σSA-algorithm and the notations used in [2]. The mutation of the σ values is performed by multiplying the parental σ with a random number ξ. The ξ variates which have been investigated are the log-normal mutation ξ_{LN} with learning parameter τ [7] and the *generalized two-point mutation* ξ_γ [2] with τ (defined below) and probability parameter γ

$$\xi_{\mathrm{LN}} := e^{\tau \mathcal{N}(0,1)} \quad \text{and} \quad \xi_\gamma := \begin{cases} 1 + \tau, & \text{if} \quad u(0,1] > \gamma \\ 1/(1+\tau), & \text{if} \quad u(0,1] \leq \gamma \end{cases}. \tag{9}$$

$\mathcal{N}(0,1)$ is a standard normal random number and $u(0,1]$ is a sample from the uniform distribution $0 < u \leq 1$. As learning parameter, $\tau = c_{1,\lambda}/\sqrt{N}$ has been chosen and $\gamma = 1/2$ (symmetrical two-point mutations).

All experiments minimize a fitness function $Q(\mathbf{y}) = \|\mathbf{y}\|^2$ using a $(\tilde{1}, \tilde{5})$-ES in an $N = 100$-dimensional space, $\sigma_\varepsilon^* = 3.5$, with the initial conditions $\mathbf{y}^{(0)} = (1.5, \ldots, 1.5)$ and $\sigma^{(0)} = 1$. As rescaling factor, $\kappa = 3$ has been chosen (if not explicitly stated). All figures show the evolution of the residual distance to the optimum and the effect of the σSA by displaying the *normalized* mutation strength σ^*. The left picture of Fig. 6 shows the standard σSA with log-normal mutation of σ and *no* rescaling, i.e., $\kappa = 1$. Since $\sigma_\varepsilon^* = 3.5 > 2c_{1,5} \approx 2.3$, Eq. (8) is not fulfilled and the ES *must* diverge, however, *the σSA does work*: It reduces σ in such a way that $\sigma^* \approx 0$. The right picture shows the ES with rescaling $\kappa = 3$. Unlike the left picture *no* σSA was used, instead an "evolution daemon" tunes the σ by measuring the actual distance $R^{(g)}$ such that $\sigma^{(g)} = \hat{\sigma}^* R^{(g)}/N$ (in real applications this is, of course, excluded). As one can see, the use of the

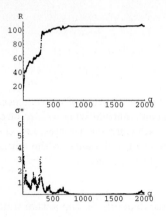 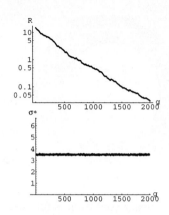

Fig. 6. Left picture: performance of the $(\tilde{1}, \tilde{5})$-σSA-ES with $\kappa = 1$ applying ξ_{LN}. Right picture: performance of the $(\tilde{1}, \tilde{5})$-ES with $\kappa = 3$, *but* σ is dynamically tuned such that $\sigma^* \approx \hat{\sigma}^* \approx \kappa c_{1,5} \approx 3.49$. $\varphi^* \approx 0.28$, measured over $g = 1 \ldots 2000$.

right mutation strength guarantees nearly optimal performance (measured, as well as theoretically: $\varphi^* \approx \hat{\varphi}^* \approx 0.28$).

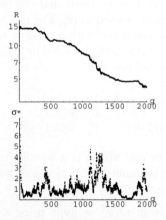 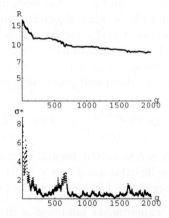

Fig. 7. General setup: $\tau = c_{1,5}/\sqrt{100} \approx 0.116$, $\kappa = 3$. Left picture: σSA with ξ_{LN}. $\varphi^* \approx 0.078$, average of $\sigma^* \approx 1.18$ (measured over $g = 501 \ldots 2000$). Right picture: σSA with $\xi_{\gamma=1/2}$. $\varphi^* \approx 0.014$, average of $\sigma^* \approx 0.60$ (measured over $g = 501 \ldots 2000$).

In Fig. 7 the performance of the σSA using log-normal ξ_{LN}, left picture, and symmetrical two-point ξ_γ (i.e. $\gamma = 1/2$), right picture, for $\kappa = 3$ is compared. By using rescaled mutations, the σSA is able to drive the ES into the convergence regime. However, the progress rates obtained are rather disappointing when compared with the theoretical optimum $\hat{\varphi}^* \approx 0.28$. It seems that the log-normal mutation rule is superior to the symmetrical two-point variant.

4.3 Thoughts About the Poor σSA Performance and Remedies

Let us look once more at Fig. 7. The average performance is well predicted by Eq. (5) if the actually measured averages of σ^* are used. Therefore, the poor performance of the ES is due to the too small steady state σ^* averages of 1.18 and 0.6, respectively, instead of the desirable $\sigma^* = \hat{\sigma}^* \approx 3.49$. Obviously, σSA is not able to drive the ES into the vicinity of the optimum σ^*. Since there is no theory for σSA in noisy environments, only a qualitative explanation for this failure can be given here. To understand the stationary σ^* value (to be more correct, one should speak of the steady state σ^* distribution) one has to recall that the actual parental σ^* is inherited from the offspring with the best $\tilde{Q}$ value obtained by $(1, \lambda)$-selection. However, the rescaling takes place *after* the selection. That is, there is no feedback from the fitness of the parent actually produced by the rescaling Eq. (3). Thus, the σSA learns the optimum σ^* *without* rescaling. Up to now there is no simple way – other than Meta-ES – to learn the optimal σ^* of the rescaling algorithm. However, two "remedies" aiming at an increase of the steady state σ^* shall be mentioned and discussed in short.

The first technique is after an idea of Rechenberg [6], however slightly modified, and uses a rescaling approach similar to Eq. (3). Since the mutation of σ is done by multiplication that maps to the addition when the logarithm is taken, $\ln \tilde{\sigma}_l := \ln \sigma_p^{(g)} + \ln \xi$, the slogan "mutate large, but inherit small" leads to $\ln \tilde{\sigma}_p^{(g+1)} := \ln \sigma_p^{(g)} + \frac{1}{\kappa_\sigma} \ln \xi_{\tilde{1};\tilde{\lambda}}$. Therefore, the new σ update rule reads

$$\tilde{\sigma}_p^{(g+1)} := \sigma_p^{(g)} \cdot \xi_{\tilde{1};\tilde{\lambda}}^{1/\kappa_\sigma}, \qquad \kappa_\sigma \geq 1. \tag{10}$$

The second technique, proposed in this paper, uses ξ_γ mutations with $\gamma < 1/2$. That is, the probability of a σ-increase is greater than that of a σ-decrease. Thus, the steady state σ is shifted toward larger mutation strengths. Both techniques are displayed in Fig. 8. The left picture is a sample generated by an ES using rule (10). The right picture applies non-symmetrical two-point mutations. Both techniques can produce a larger average σ^* than the standard σSA. Up until now there is no theory how to choose the new strategy parameters κ_σ and γ. Also the idea of combining both techniques seems promising; however, this "hybridism" is still under investigation.

5 Outlook

The theoretical investigation of the ES in noisy fitness landscapes as well as the σSA and the rescaling techniques are still *in statu nascendi*. As to the $(\tilde{1}, \tilde{\lambda})$-ES, there are two main directions which should be followed in future research. First, the investigation of the rescaling Eq. (3) in case of finite N. This will allow for the estimation of optimal κ not available from the asymptotic theory. Second, the analysis of the σSA with noisy fitness and generalized σ update rules (10)

118

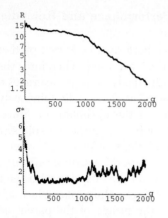 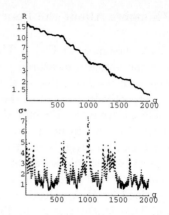

Fig. 8. General setup: $\tau \approx 0.116$, $\kappa = 3$. Left picture: σSA with ξ_γ, $\gamma = 1/2$, $\kappa_\sigma = 3$. $\varphi^* \approx 0.17$, average of $\sigma^* \approx 1.92$. Right picture: σSA with ξ_γ, $\gamma = 0.45$, $\kappa_\sigma = 1$. $\varphi^* \approx 0.15$, average of $\sigma^* \approx 2.01$. Interval of measurement: $g = 1000 \ldots 2000$.

and/or non-symmetrical two-point rules. A progress in this direction would open the possibility to determine γ and κ_σ on a solid ground.

6 Acknowledgments

The author is grateful to A. Irfan Oyman and Ralf Salomon for helpful comments. The author is Heisenberg fellow of the DFG, grant Be 1578/4-1.

References

1. H.-G. Beyer. Toward a Theory of Evolution Strategies: Some Asymptotical Results from the $(1, {}^+ \lambda)$-Theory. *Evolutionary Computation*, 1(2):165–188, 1993.
2. H.-G. Beyer. Toward a Theory of Evolution Strategies: Self-Adaptation. *Evolutionary Computation*, 3(3):311–347, 1996.
3. H.-G. Beyer. *Zur Analyse der Evolutionsstrategien*. Habilitationsschrift, University of Dortmund, 1996.
4. H.-G. Beyer. An Alternative Explanation for the Manner in which Genetic Algorithms Operate. *BioSystems*, 41:1–15, 1997.
5. I. Rechenberg. Evolutionsstrategien. In B. Schneider and U. Ranft, editors, *Simulationsmethoden in der Medizin und Biologie*, pages 83–114. Springer-Verlag, Berlin, 1978.
6. I. Rechenberg. *Evolutionsstrategie '94*. Frommann–Holzboog Verlag, Stuttgart, 1994.
7. H.-P. Schwefel. *Evolution and Optimum Seeking*. Wiley, New York, NY, 1995.

Creating Robust Solutions by Means of Evolutionary Algorithms

Jürgen Branke

Institute AIFB
University of Karlsruhe
D-76128 Karlsruhe, Germany
branke@aifb.uni-karlsruhe.de

Abstract. For real world problems it is often not sufficient to find solutions of high quality, but the solutions should also be robust. By robust we mean that the quality of the solution does not falter completely when a slight change of the environment occurs, or that certain deviations from the solution should be tolerated without a total loss of quality.

In this paper, a number of modifications to the standard evolutionary algorithm (EA) are suggested that are supposed to lead the EA to produce more robust solutions. Some preliminary experiments are reported where the proposed approaches are compared to a standard model. As it turns out, the EA's ability to create robust solutions can be greatly enhanced even without additional function evaluations.

Keywords: evolutionary algorithm, robust solution

1 Introduction

For real world problems, it is often important to create robust solutions to a problem, i.e. solutions that are insensitive to changes in the environment or noise in the decision variables.

Some examples for applications include:

- in scheduling problems, solutions are sought that allow e.g. slight variation in processing times, time for machine breakdowns or the incorporation of an additional urgent job without requiring a total reordering of the production plan.
- for many control problems, the environment may change slowly, e.g. machines can slowly wear out or the composition/quality of the raw material can change slightly. Often it is not possible to constantly monitor and control the process, thus it is advantageous to implement solutions that yield good results over a certain range of environmental conditions.
- often, certain tolerances have to be allowed for production. Solutions are sought that give good results over all settings within these tolerances.

From a more abstract perspective, this means that not only the solution should be good, but also that the (phenotypic) neighborhood of the solution should have a high average quality. Looking at the fitness landscape, a solution on a high plateau should be preferred over a solution on a thin peak: if the environment changes slightly (e.g. shifts in a random direction) or if it can not be guaranteed that the exact parameters of the solution are actually implemented (but a solution close to the original solution), the solution on the plateau will yield much better expected quality than the solution on the peak. This *effective* fitness function, $f_{eff}(x)$, depends on the distribution of the noise added to the input and could be calculated as $\int_{-\infty}^{\infty} p(\delta) \cdot f(x + \delta) \, d\delta$, with $p(\delta)$ being the probability density function for the disturbance δ. Of course, for problems of relevant complexity, this calculation will not be possible, thus $f_{eff}(x)$ has to be estimated.

In this paper, it is tried to tune evolutionary algorithms (cf. e.g. [3,7]) to produce robust solutions. All suggested approaches use a modified fitness value f_{mod} for selection that is designed to be a reasonable estimate of the effective fitness function f_{eff}.

Some related work, developed independently of the work presented here, has recently been published in [12]. Earlier related work includes [6,8–10] and [11].

We apply a rather simplistic setting for investigating the robustness of solutions: a simple multi-modal mathematical function is maximized by the EA. To determine the final solution's quality (i.e. to obtain a good estimate of its effective fitness), the average of 100 disturbed evaluations is used. For disturbance, a normally distributed noise is added to the phenotypic values of the solution. Assuming that these disturbances might actually be experienced in practice, the solution is evaluated according to its expected performance in that environment.

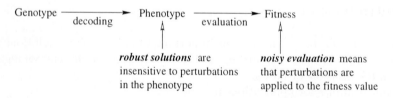

Fig. 1. Robust solutions vs. noisy fitness evaluation

Note that the problem of creating robust solutions as defined here has some similarities to optimizing noisy functions, which have already been examined in combination with EAs (e.g. [1,2,4]). However there are two main differences:

- with noisy functions, some noise is added to the output (quality) of the solution. In the settings regarded here, noise is added to the decision variables (or phenotype) of the solution. I.e. if $f(x)$ is the fitness function and δ is some (normally distributed) noise, then a noisy fitness function would mean $f'(x) = f(x) + \delta$, while in our case $f'(x) = f(x + \delta)$ (cf. Fig. 1 for illustration).
- noisy functions can not be evaluated without noise, the EA has to find good solutions despite the noise. In the settings considered in this paper, it is

assumed that only the decision variables of the final solution are disturbed, usual function evaluations during the EA run can be performed without disturbance. This is justified because that evaluation is usually done on the basis of a theoretical, computerized model, while the final solution is then actually implemented and has to face all the uncertainties present in reality.

The outline of the paper is as follows:
Section 2 describes in more detail the environments used for testing. In Section 3 we propose a number of modifications to the standard EA, aimed at delivering robust solutions. These approaches are evaluated empirically, the results obtained can be found in Section 4. The paper concludes with a summary and a number of ideas for future work.

2 Test Functions

For testing the approaches presented in Section 3, the following two 10-dimensional test functions have been used:

$$f_1(x) = \sum_{i=1}^{10} \sin \sqrt{|40x_i|} + \frac{20 - |x_i|}{b} \qquad -20 \le x_i < 20 \qquad (1)$$

and

$$f_2(x) = \sum_{i=1}^{10} g(x_i) \quad \text{with} \quad g(x_i) = \begin{cases} -(x_i + 1)^2 + 1 & : & -2 \le x_i < 0 \\ c \cdot 2^{-8|x_i - 1|} & : & 0 \le x_i < 2 \end{cases} \qquad (2)$$

Plots of the two functions along one dimension are shown in Fig. 2. The parameters b resp. c allow to influence the height of the sharp peaks relative to the smoother hills. In the experiments, $b = 20$ and $c = 1.3$ were used.

Function f_1 has been designed to allow the EA to choose between a number of alternatives concerning the tradeoff between robustness and quality. Function f_2 is much simpler, having only one hill and one peak in each dimension, while the basin of attraction for both, hill and peak, is of equal size.

The final solution of the EA is then tested 100 times, perturbed before each evaluation. As perturbation, the individual is shifted slightly by adding to each decision variable (in our case equivalent to a gene) a randomly chosen value from a normal distribution with mean 0 and standard deviation 0.5 for function f_1 resp. a standard deviation of 0.1 for function f_2. The resulting effective fitness functions $f_{1,eff}(x)$ and $f_{2,eff}(x)$ are displayed in Fig. 3.

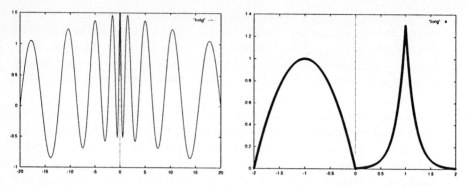

Fig. 2. Test function $f_1(x)$ with b=20 (left) and $f_2(x)$ with c = 1.3 (right)

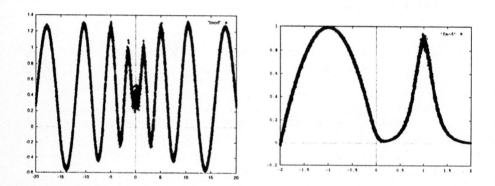

Fig. 3. Effective test functions $f_{1,eff}(x)$ (left) and $f_{2,eff}$ (right) when disturbed.

3   Tested Approaches

3.1   Simple EA

The standard EA by nature favors hills over peaks, since usually the probability that some individuals of the initial population are somewhere in the basin of attraction of a hill is higher, also the average fitness of individuals in the hill area is higher.

Thus, when for example in Fig. 2 (right) the two maxima are made equally high by setting c in Eq. (2) to 1.0, the standard EA will turn to the smooth hill rather than to the peak in 99% of the trials.

But as the experiments show, the higher the peak compared to the hill, the more often the standard EA will choose the peak, although this may not be advantageous in the environment considered in this paper. In this case, significant improvements can be obtained by slight modifications to the standard model.

As simple EA we use real-valued, direct encoding of the decision variables, generational replacement with elitism (i.e. the best individual survives), ranking selection, two-point-crossover, mutation rate of 0.1, and an island model[1] with 5 subpopulations, 50 individuals each, run for 500 generations. The same settings are used throughout all experiments unless stated otherwise.

3.2 Mean of several evaluations

To estimate the average quality of an individual's neighborhood, one possibility is to probe the fitness landscape at several random points in the neighborhood and calculate the mean. This value may then be used as that individual's fitness f_{mod}. The effect is a smoothing of the fitness landscape, with sharp peaks being flattened and smooth hills being almost non-affected.

Major drawback of this method is the increased computation time: since usually evaluation is the time determining factor, evaluating several points for one individual is very expensive. Furthermore, one has to decide how many probes in the neighborhood are necessary and how this neighborhood should be defined.

To investigate the first question, a number of experiments are conducted with different numbers of evaluations per individual. Concerning the definition of the neighborhood, it seems best to approximate the distribution of noise expected for the final solution, and use the same distribution for adding noise to the individuals during the run.

In the experiments reported below, it is assumed that the distribution of the noise finally applied to the solution is known, thus the same noise is applied to the decision variables when an individual is evaluated several times. The same assumption has been used in the approaches of Section 3.3 and Section 3.4.

3.3 Single disturbed evaluations

Instead of reevaluating several times with disturbed decision variables, one might as well just evaluate once at a disturbed position. If the input (i.e. the individual's phenotype as described by its genes) to the evaluation function is disturbed randomly for every evaluation, the *expected* returned value at every point in the search space is just equivalent to the mean over it's neighborhood. Since in EAs, promising areas are probed more often, this might be sufficient. In fact, Tsutsui and Gosh [12] showed, using the schema theorem, that given an infinitely large population size, an EA with disturbed evaluations is actually performing as if it would work on the effective fitness function.

Additionally, evaluation results in flat areas will be more consistent over time thus it could be easier for the EA to focus on these areas.

---

[1] from our experiences with EAs (e.g. [5]), the island model usually performs better than a single population model, thus we meanwhile use the island model as standard

3.4   Reevaluating only the best

As has been mentioned above, repeatedly evaluating the same (disturbed) individual may be extremely expensive. Thus it seems reasonable to try to achieve the same results by evaluating each individual once without disturbance, and then reevaluate only the best individuals several times. It may not be necessary to repeatedly evaluate mediocre individuals, since they won't be implemented in practice anyway.

In the experiments reported below, three settings were tested:

- the best individual is evaluated another 4 times
- the best 20% of the population (i.e. 10 individuals in our experiments) are evaluated another 2 times
- the best 20% individuals of the population are evaluated another 4 times, the next 20 % are evaluated another 3 times, etc. Note that the sum of function evaluations for this approach is just equal to the number of function evaluations necessary when each individual is evaluated 3 times (Section 3.2).

3.5   Looking at other individuals in the neighborhood

Even if only a part of the population is evaluated repeatedly, additional computational cost is incurred. To avoid additional evaluations, one might also use the information available anyway: the individuals evaluated so far.

Thus, the idea of this approach is to calculate a weighted mean of the fitness of the current individual and the fitnesses of other (previously evaluated) individuals in its neighborhood.

As individuals that could be taken into account, one might at least consider the current population, but it is certainly helpful to store a selection of individuals from previous generations as well. Appropriate strategies for selecting which individuals to keep in the memory are currently under investigation.

For this paper, two simple strategies have been implemented:

- use the current population only
- use a memory, in which the last 5000 individuals are stored.

Since both approaches suffer from the potential problem that when the population converges, there are too many equivalent individuals that do not provide any additional information, a variant with duplicate avoidance has also been tested. In these cases, an individual is mutated again when it already exists in the population.

Each individual x is compared with all individuals y in the population resp. the memory, and its modified fitness, $f_{mod}(x)$, is calculated as:

$$f_{mod}(x) = \frac{\sum_y w(y) \cdot f(y)}{\sum_y w(y)} \tag{3}$$

Ideally, the weight function $w(y)$ should reflect the probability that x is turned into y by a disturbance, i.e. $w(y) \propto p(\delta)$ such that $y = x + \delta$.

However in the experiments described in this paper, for reasons of computational simplicity, not the actual noise distribution has been used for weighting (which would have been the equivalent to the previous approaches). Instead, the following simple ad hoc neighborhood function was chosen.

$$w(y) = max\{0, 1 - d * b\} \qquad (4)$$

with $w(y)$ being the weight of the individual y, b being a parameter that has been set to 4 in function f_1 and to 1 in function f_2 (see above), and d the distance from y to the reference individual x currently being evaluated.

Note that this approach is based on the assumptions that the distance between individuals can be measured and the evaluation of an individual is much more expensive than the calculation of the weighted mean.

4 Results and Discussion

In the first set of experiments, only the method from Section 3.2, where the modified fitness is calculated as the average from n disturbed evaluations, has been tested, and only on Function f_2. As expected, the resulting effective quality increases with the number of function evaluations, while the benefit from an additional evaluation decreases with the number of function evaluations. The result is depicted in Fig. 4.

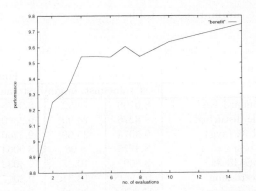

Fig. 4. Quality vs. number of trials per evaluation, averages over 10 runs

For comparisons between the different proposed approaches, extensive tests with both test function have been performed.

As performance measure, besides using the effective fitness from the final evaluation, we recorded the individual's distance from the origin in function f_1, with larger distance indicating that more flat hills were chosen, and the percentage of negative gene values in function f_2, with more negative values indicating that the hill was favored over the peak. All results reported are the averages over 10 runs with different random seeds.

Altogether, the following 10 approaches have been tested and compared:

1. a standard EA

2. a single evaluation with disturbed parameters

3. evaluate all individuals three times

4. evaluate the best individual another 4 times

5. evaluate the best 20% of the individuals another 2 times

6. evaluate the best 20% of the individuals another 4 times, the next 20% another 3 times etc.

7. use the current population to calculate a weighted fitness

8. same as 7., but with duplicate avoidance

9. use a memory of the last 5000 individuals to calculate weighted fitness

10. same as 9., but with duplicate avoidance.

The results are summarized in Table 1.

		Function 1		Function 2	
		best value	dist. origin	best value	genes < 0
1	standard EA	8.0798	7.692	8.9678	19%
2	single disturbed	8.8276	24.99	9.2360	69%
3	all 3x (avg)	9.5074	25.69	9.3260	79%
4	best 5x	8.4775	8.08	8.9064	50%
5	best10 3x	8.8699	10.37	9.4032	81%
6	decreasing	10.2495	13.31	9.8067	98%
7	pop weighted	10.2704	20.39	9.2730	47%
8	pop weighted, no doubles	10.2396	27.79	9.2541	50%
9	depot weighted	10.3613	39.46	9.8432	96%
10	depot weighted, no doubles	10.3233	41.95	9.7866	95%

Table 1. Results, each value is averaged over 10 runs

Figure 5 displays the tradeoff between cost (measured in the number of function evaluations) and performance (final effective quality achieved) of the different approaches for function f_1 (left) resp. function f_2 (right).

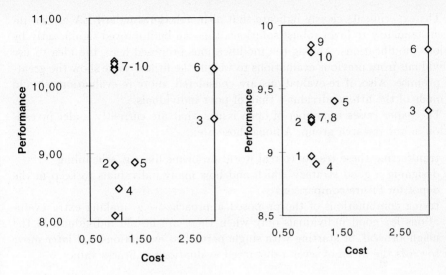

Fig. 5. Cost vs. performance comparison of different approaches on Function f_1 (left) resp. function f_2 (right)

From these preliminary results, the following conclusions may be drawn:

- Method 6 clearly outperforms Method 3, so the idea to distribute more function evaluations on the better individuals seems to give a significant advantage.
- the duplicate avoidance strategy does not seem to help much in the weighting approach (Methods 7 and 8 resp. 9 and 10 are almost equivalent).
- just disturbing the input for one evaluation (Method 2) performs comparatively well, at no additional cost.
- reevaluating just the best (Method 4) does not seem to be sufficient. At least the best fifth of the population (Method 5) has to be reevaluated to yield a noticeable effect.
- the idea to use individuals from previous evaluations in order to compute a weighted fitness vastly improves performance without requiring additional function evaluations. Of course the large memory base used in Method 9 and 10 incurs other computational overhead that has to be considered unless the function evaluations are the determining time factor. Anyway, it seems to be worth to investigate good strategies concerning which individuals to keep in the memory in order to obtain maximum benefit with minimum cost for weighting.

5   Conclusion

This paper pointed out the importance of creating robust solutions and compared a number of novel approaches to help the EA take into account the robustness of a solution.

The experiments clearly indicate that although the standard EA has an inherent tendency to favor robust solutions, this can be improved significantly by various modifications. Among the modifications proposed here, the idea to use individuals from previous evaluations to weight the fitness value show the greatest promise. Also, if re-evaluations are considered, more re-evaluations should be made of the fitter individuals than of poor individuals.

The paper raises a number of open issues, that are currently under investigation in our research group. Among those are:

- transferring these results to real world problems like e.g. scheduling
- designing a good strategy which and how many individuals to keep in the depot for future comparisons
- trying combinations of the proposed approaches, e.g. making extra evaluations for good individuals only when there are no old individuals in the neighborhood, or starting with single perturbed evaluations and later move towards the mean of several disturbed evaluations as fitness values.

References

1. A. N. Aizawa and B. W. Wah. Scheduling of genetic algorithms in a noisy environment. *Evolutionary Computation*, pages 97–122, 1994.
2. J. Michael Fitzpatrick and John J. Greffenstette. Genetic algorithms in noisy environments. *Machine Learning*, 3:101–120, 1988.
3. D. E. Goldberg. *Genetic Algorithms*. Addison-Wesley, 1989.
4. U. Hammel and T. Bäck. Evolution strategies on noisy functions, how to improve convergence properties. In Y. Davidor, H. P. Schwefel, and R. Männer, editors, *Parallel Problem Solving from Nature*, number 866 in LNCS. Springer, 1994.
5. U. Kohlmorgen, H. Schmeck, and K. Haase. Experiences with fine-grained parallel genetic algorithms. *Annals of Operations Research*, to appear.
6. M. McIlhagga, P. Husbands, and R. Ives. A comparison of search techniques on a wing-box optimisation problem. In H.-M. Voigt, editor, *Parallel Problem Solving from Nature 4*, number 1141 in LNCS, pages 614–623. Springer Verlag, 1996.
7. Z. Michalewicz. *Genetic Algorithms + Data Structures = Evolution Programs*. Springer Verlag, 3rd edition, 1996.
8. I. C. Parmee. Cluster-oriented genetic algorithms for the identification of high-performance regions of design spaces. In *EvCA96*, 1996.
9. C. R. Reeves. A genetic algorithm approach to stochastic flowshop sequencing. In *IEE Colloquium on Genetic Algorithms for Control and Systems Engineering*, number 1992/106 in Digest, pages 13/1–13/4. IEE, London, 1992.
10. R. Roy, I. C. Parmee, and G. Purchase. Integrating the genetic algorithm with the preliminary design of gas turbine blade cooling systems. In *ACEDC'96*, 1996.
11. A.V. Sebald and D.B. Fogel. Design of fault tolerant neural networks for pattern classification. In D.B. Fogel and W. Atmar, editors, *1st Annual Conf. on Evolutionary Programming*, pages 90–99, 1992.
12. S. Tsutsui and A. Ghosh. Genetic algorithms with a robust solution searching scheme. *IEEE Transactions on Evolutionary Computation*, 1(3):201–208, 1997.

Analytic Curve Detection from a Noisy Binary Edge Map Using Genetic Algorithm

Samarjit Chakraborty[1] and Kalyanmoy Deb[*2]

[1] Department of Computer Science and Engineering
[2] Department of Mechanical Engineering
Indian Institute of Technology Kanpur
Kanpur 208016, India

Abstract. Currently Hough transform and its variants are the most common methods for detecting analytic curves from a binary edge image. However, these methods do not scale well when applied to complex noisy images where correct data is very small compared to the amount of incorrect data. We propose a Genetic Algorithm in combination with the Randomized Hough Transform, along with a different scoring function, to deal with such environments. This approach is also an improvement over random search and in contrast to standard Hough transform algorithms, is not limited to simple curves like straight line or circle.

1 Introduction

Extracting curves from a binary edge image is an important problem in computer vision and robotics. The Hough transform (HT) [7, 21] is recognized as a powerful tool to handle this. Although it gives good results in the presence of small amounts of noise and occlusion, it does not scale well when applied to complex, cluttered scenes, with lot of noise. In a study on the noise sensitivity of the generalized HT by Grimson and Huttenlocher [5], it was concluded that even for moderate amounts of noise and occlusion, these methods can hypothesize many false solutions, and their effectiveness is dramatically reduced. So these techniques are reliable only for relatively simple tasks, where the edge data corresponding to correct solutions is a large fraction of the total data. We confirm this finding in the case of simpler Hough transforms also, used for detecting analytic curves like straight lines and circles. Based on this, we propose a different approach, using a Genetic Algorithm (GA) [4] in combination with the Randomized Hough Transform (RHT) [25, 26] but using a different scoring function than usual. A number of other researchers have considered the problem of detecting lines or other simple curves in noisy images [3, 8, 19, 22, 24]. However, all of them assume a uniform noise distribution and in some cases knowledge about the distribution. Califano et al. [2] and Leavers [17] attempted to deal with the effects of correlated noise by preferential segmentation of the image with respect to the shape under detection. Connective HT [27] is another method used in the case of correlated noise. But the method that we present is much more robust

---

[*] Author to whom all correspondence should be directed.

than any of these and makes no assumption about the noise distribution. It is particularly effective in the case of complex, cluttered and noisy images where the number of pixels belonging to genuine curves is a very small fraction of the total data.

Another problem of the HT is that its computational complexity and storage requirements increase exponentially with the number of parameters of the curve to be detected. In spite of the large number of papers which address this issue, straight lines and circles are still the only curves for which HT can be effectively used. Comprehensive reviews of the development in this field can be found in references [9] and [16].

To alleviate these problems, recently a new kind of approach in the form of a set of methods called Probabilistic Hough Transforms has been developed. Most of them use random sampling of the image data in various ways. A good review of these techniques along with comparisons with standard methods is done in reference [11]. However our method can be used for any analytic curve detection without incurring any additional computational or storage requirements, over those required for simple curves like straight line and circle. The method can be used independently of the RHT, but in the case of images with low noise, combination with RHT yields a considerable speedup.

The concept of using GA for curve extraction has been explored in the past [6, 23]. However the problem of noise was not addressed. Moreover, much simpler cases were considered than we do in this paper.

In the next section we briefly describe the Hough transform, its randomized variant, the RHT, and identify cases where these methods fail due to the presence of excessive noise and clutter, following which we describe our method. In Section 4 we give test results with a complex noisy image and compare the performance with known methods. Section 5 concludes the paper.

2   Motivation

In the conventional implementation, the Hough transform essentially consists of two stages. The first stage is based on a transformation mapping from each edge point to points in the parameter space, represented by an accumulator array, and a voting rule which determines how the transformation mapping affects the contents of the accumulator array. The second stage is an exhaustive search for parameters in the accumulator array which are local maxima. Each such local maximum represents a candidate curve in the edge map.

In the probabilistic versions of the Hough transform, mainly two approaches are used. In the first, due to Kiryati et al. [15], image data are randomly sampled and only the sampled subset of points is transformed. In the second approach due to Xu et al. [25, 26], Leavers et al. [17], Bergen et al. [1], and Califano et al. [2], for a curve with n parameters, n image points are sampled, the equation of the curve passing through these n points is determined and the corresponding point in the parameter space is incremented.

In all these approaches, points on the same curve result in points in the parameter space which are close together, whereas noise points result in randomly distributed points in the parameter space. Thus a large cluster of points in the parameter space represent a curve in the edge map. The validity of this assumption, however, depends on there being a low likelihood that clusters due to noise points will be comparable or larger in size than clusters due to points on genuine curves. We believe that in many real life images, this assumption does not hold. Fig. 1(a) shows two straight lines L_1 and L_2, where each line is composed of a small number of disconnected points. In Fig. 1(b), random noise is superimposed on the line L_1 (Fig. 4 in Section 4 shows one example where such a situation really arises in practice). Let us call the lines in Fig. 1(a) as *true lines* and the line in Fig. 1(b) that corresponds to line L_1 of Fig. 1(a), as a *pseudo line*. Line L_2 in this figure still remains a true line. Ideally the detection algorithm should detect both L_1 and L_2 from Fig. 1(a) but only L_2 from Fig. 1(b). Note that there are a large number of pseudo lines in the noise region in Fig. 1(b). Since the number of points on each of these pseudo lines is comparable or more than than the number of points on the line L_2, it gets masked in the parameter space by these pseudo lines.

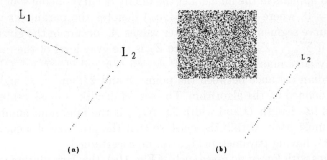

Fig. 1. A binary edge image (a) Two straight lines (b) Noise superimposed on one of the lines

To overcome the effects of noise, extensions of the basic Randomized Hough Transform has been proposed in [10]. These are Window RHT and Random Window RHT. Both of them randomly place a window on an edge point and try to locate a curve within the window. Although it is possible that they will work in Fig. 1(b), the probability that the window is placed on the line L_2 is extremely small. Moreover, when the window is placed on the noise region, pseudo lines will be detected.

The Connective Hough Transform [17, 18, 27] and its randomized version, the Connective Randomized Hough Transform [13, 14] tries to make use of the connectivity between points on a true curve to distinguish between true and pseudo curves. So they fail when the points on the curve are not connected i.e. there are gaps between the edge points, as in the case of line L_2. Such cases do arise in practice, for example in bubble-chamber photographs of particle tracks.

3 A Genetic Algorithm for Analytic Curve Detection

The kernel of our algorithm is conceptually similar to the Window RHT of Kälviäinen *et al.* [10]. But instead of placing a 'window' on a randomly chosen edge point, we place a weighted mask on the edge point. The mask measures the weighted difference between pixels on a real curve and the noise surrounding the curve. The placement of the mask is guided by a genetic algorithm. Since we are considering cases where the number of edge points on real curves is very small compared to the total number of edge points, this leads to an improvement over a simple random search. A Randomized Hough Transform with a very low parameter resolution and a smaller number of sample points than usual, is used to identify prospective regions of the parameter space. The genetic algorithm searches the entire parameter space with a bias towards these regions. For simple curves with low noise, this leads to a considerable speedup.

3.1 The Weighted Mask

Given a binary edge map and the family of curves being sought (such as straight line, circle, ellipse, etc.), the algorithm should produce the set of curves from that family which appears in the image. Let the family of curves being sought be given by $f(\mathcal{A}, \bar{x}) = 0$, where $\mathcal{A} = (a_1, a_2, \ldots, a_n)$ denotes the parameter vector. We say that a curve segment with parameter values $\mathcal{A}_\alpha$ occurs in the given image at location $\bar{x}'$ if $\sum_{\bar{x} \in \mathcal{M}} Z_{\bar{x}} \geq N_{min}$, where $Z_{\bar{x}}$ is the gray level of the pixel $\bar{x}$ (0 or 1 in a binary edge map), $\mathcal{M} = \{\bar{x} : |f(\mathcal{A}_\alpha, \bar{x})| \leq \delta \text{ and } d(\bar{x}, \bar{x}') \leq D\}$, $d(\bar{x}, \bar{x}')$ is the Euclidian distance between the points $\bar{x}$ and $\bar{x}'$, and δ, D and N_{min} are parameters defined by the algorithm. The set $\mathcal{M}$ denotes a mask centered on the pixel $\bar{x}'$ and has length D and width 2δ. N_{min} is the minimum number of edge points that must occur within the mask so that the presence of a curve segment located at $\bar{x}'$, having parameters $\mathcal{A}_\alpha$, can be ascertained.

For images with low or no noise such as Fig. 1(a), this formulation is sufficient, and is in fact similar to the Window RHT, except for the fact that we do not use any transformation from the image to the parameter space but rather simply count the number of points lying within the window or mask. But in the case of noisy images such a Fig. 1(b), whenever the mask is placed on the noise region, pseudo curves will be detected. To extend this method to include such images, we use a weighted mask rather than a simple one. The response of the mask defined with respect to its center location is given by $R = \sum_{\bar{x} \in \mathcal{M}} W_{\bar{x}} Z_{\bar{x}}$, where $W_{\bar{x}}$ is the mask coefficient of the pixel $\bar{x}$. We shall say that a curve segment with parameter values $\mathcal{A}_\alpha$ occurs in the edge map at $\bar{x}'$ if the response, R, of the mask centered at $\bar{x}'$ is greater than a constant R_{min}, fixed, depending on the mask length, width and coefficients. The mask coefficients of the pixels that lie away from the curve $f(\mathcal{A}_\alpha, \bar{x}') = 0$ are assigned negative values. So when a lot of noise is present near a curve, as in the case of pseudo curves, the positive response due to the points on and near the curve is offset by the negative response due to the noise points surrounding it. Hence pseudo curves are not detected. An example of a weighted mask for straight line detection is shown in Fig. 3 in Section 4.

3.2 Using Genetic Algorithm

Instead of placing the mask on a randomly chosen edge point, as done in Window RHT, we use a genetic algorithm to search the space $(\mathcal{A}, \bar{x})$ for all instances of curve segments for which the response of the mask is greater than R_{min}. For this, each of the parameters $a_1, a_2, \ldots, a_n$ of $\mathcal{A}$ and x of $\bar{x}$ are coded as fixed length binary strings. Since the y-coordinate of $\bar{x}$ is the dependent variable, it is not included in the string. The resulting string, obtained by concatenating all these strings, gives the chromosomal representation of a solution to the problem. Note that the domains of each of the parameters may be different and the length of the string coding for a given parameter depends on the required parameter resolution. The fitness of a solution $(\mathcal{A}_\alpha, \bar{x}')$ is taken to be the response of the weighted mask, centered at $\bar{x}'$, as described in the previous section.

[Step 1] **Creation of initial population and the use of Randomized Hough Transform.** In most GA applications, the initial population consists of entirely random structures to avoid convergence to a local optima. But in this problem, the question is not of finding the global optima, but of finding all solutions with fitness greater than R_{min}. To identify prospective regions of the search space, Randomized Hough Transform with a low parameter resolution and a smaller number of trials than usual, is used.

For a curve expressed by a n-parameter equation, n points are randomly chosen from the edge data and n joint equations are solved to determine one parameter point $\mathcal{A}_\alpha$. In the accumulator corresponding to the parameter space, the *count* of $\mathcal{A}_\alpha$ is then incremented by one. After repeating this process for a predefined number of times, points in the parameter space with counts exceeding a predefined threshold, indicate prospective curves in the image space. Whereas only the global maximum of the parameter space is used in RHT, here, all points with counts exceeding a specific threshold are used. So, the threshold value used here is much less than what is used in RHT. Corresponding to each of these points in the parameter space, a suitable number of solutions, proportional to the count values, with the x-coordinates randomly chosen, are introduced into the initial population. To reduce the effect of the sampling error, due to the low threshold value and hence smaller number of samples, a fixed number of random samples from the solution space are also introduced. The total number of solutions is kept fixed over all the generations.

[Step 2] **Selection.** The selection used here falls into the category of dynamic, generational, preservative, elitist selection [20]. Let there be M distinct solutions in a given generation, denoted by $S_1, S_2, \ldots, S_M$. The probability of selecting a solution S_i into the mating pool is given by :

$$P(S_i) = \frac{\mathcal{F}(S_i)}{\sum_{j=1}^{M} \mathcal{F}(S_i)}$$

Where $\mathcal{F}(S_i)$ is the fitness of the solution S_i. A fixed number of solutions are copied into the mating pool according to this rule and the remaining solutions are newly created from parameter values indicated by the RHT with the x-

coordinate randomly chosen. In each generation, a fixed number of best solutions of the previous generation are copied in place of the present worst solutions, if they happen to be less fit compared to the former. This is a slight modification of the Elitist model where only the best solution is preserved.

[Step 3] **Crossover.** Since the number of parameters may not be small, it is intuitive that the single point crossover operation may not be useful. So crossover is applied to each substring corresponding to each of the parameters $a_1, a_2, \ldots, a_n$, and x, the operation being the usual swapping of all bits from a randomly chosen crossover site of the two parents, chosen randomly from the mating pool [4]. Hence this crossover is similar to the standard single-point crossover operator, but operated on substrings of each parameter. Therefore, there are $n + 1$ single-point crossovers taking place between two parent strings.

[Step 4] **Mutation.** We have used two mutation operators. The first is the classical mutation operation in which each bit position of the solution strings is complemented with a small mutation probability p_{mut1}. The second operation is as follows : let $b_l \, b_{l-1} \ldots b_0$ be the binary substring corresponding to a parameter a_i whose domain is $[\alpha_i, \beta_i]$, and whose real value is decoded as c. In the parameter space corresponding to the RHT implementation, let the parameter a_i be quantized as $q_1, q_2, \ldots, q_{i_N}$ ($\alpha_i \leq q_1$ and $q_{i_N} \leq \beta_i$) and let $c \in [q_j, q_{j+1}]$. Then after mutation we get c', where c' is chosen uniformly from $[q_j, q_{j+1}]$. So, the mutation of the binary string $b_l \, b_{l-1} \ldots b_0$ results in the binary string corresponding to the real value c'. This mutation operation is applied with a probability p_{mut2} on each substring corresponding to the parameters $a_1, a_2, \ldots, a_n$, to take care of the low parameter resolution used in the RHT.

The overall algorithm. The initial population consisting of a fixed number of solutions is created as already described. In each generation, the entire population is subjected to selection, crossover and the first mutation. The second mutation operation is applied just after the selection process, only to the solutions generated by the RHT technique.

At the end of each generation, curve segments corresponding to solutions having fitness greater than R_{min} are removed from the edge map and after fixed number of generations, the accumulators are reset and RHT is again applied to the current edge map, so that the solutions corresponding to the removed curve segments are dropped from the population. This iteration is continued until no new curve segments are extracted for a given number of generations, which in our experiments was set to 200. A schematic diagram explaining the algorithm is shown in Fig. 2.

4   Test Results and Comparisons

We have experimented with a complex real world image containing a lot of noise points and a few straight lines. Although the simplest, straight line detection

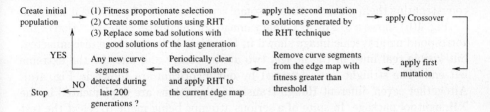

Fig. 2. The proposed algorithm

was chosen for ease of comparison with the various Hough transform algorithms. However, as evident from the previous section, our algorithm is blind to this fact. For comparing the performance of our method with HT, we used a public domain software package for line detection, XHoughtool [12], where a number of non-probabilistic and probabilistic Hough transform algorithms have been implemented.

As indicated in the previous section, there are various parameters that our algorithm uses. Parameters related to the mask are its dimensions, mask coefficients and the threshold response R_{min}. The mask length has an effect on the minimum allowable size of a curve segment, and the quality of the curves detected are determined by the mask coefficients and its width. A wide mask with more than one row of positive coefficients will detect curves whose pixels are spread out along its width. Thus a suitably designed mask, along with a proper threshold value, will be able to distinguish between fuzzy and spread out curves, and noise regions. We have used a mask length of 100 and width 3, to detect only perfect straight lines. The coefficients of all pixels lying on the straight line were set to 2 and the others to -1 as shown in Fig. 3. Too low a value, R_{min}, of the threshold might detect a pseudo line whereas a too high value might miss a faint, disconnected, but visually detectable line. The results shown in this section were obtained with R_{min} set to 100.

-1	-1	-1	....	-1	-1	-1
2	2	2	....	2	2	2
-1	-1	-1	....	-1	-1	-1

Fig. 3. A mask of length 100 and width 3

For the GA parameters, we used mutation probabilities p_{mut1} and p_{mut2} to be 0.1 and 0.5 respectively. Any population size around 100 was found to work well, and in each generation, 25% of the solutions were created using the RHT and the rest copied from the mating pool in accordance with the fitness proportional selection. Further, the best 10% solutions of the previous generation were copied in place of the worst solutions of the current generation. We used the ρ, θ parametric representation of a line, where each line is represented by $x\cos(\theta) + y\sin(\theta) = \rho$. Each of θ, ρ and x were coded as binary strings and concatenating them gives the chromosomal representation of a potential solution.

Fig. 4(b) shows a 512 by 512 binary image obtained after edge detection of the corresponding grayscale image shown in Fig. 4(a). Note the three disconnected, but visible real lines in the image, two at the centre and one the the extreme left end. The straight lines detected by our algorithm are shown in Fig. 4(c). Altogether seven different Hough transform algorithms are implemented in the XHoughtool package. In spite of a serious attempt being made to select the test parameters for each method as optimally as possibly, none of the algorithms gave useful results because a large number of pseudo lines were detected. A typical result is shown in Fig. 4(d). Since the number of edge points lying on the real lines are much less compared to those lying on many of the pseudo lines, no suitable accumulator threshold value exists which can detect only the real lines. Generally these algorithms work well even in the case of noisy images, where the lines are connected and the number of edge points lying on these lines are atleast comparable to the number of noise points.

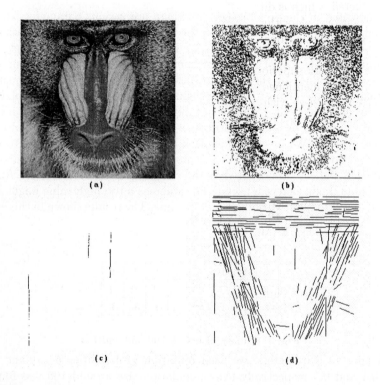

(a)

(b)

(c)

(d)

Fig. 4. Test results (a) A 512 by 512 gray scale image (b) The corresponding binary edge map obtained after edge detection (c) Straight lines detected by the proposed method (d) A typical result obtained using a Hough transform algorithm

This example was executed on a moderately loaded DEC Alpha 2000 4/233

(Dual Processor system) workstation and required around ten seconds to complete.

5 Conclusion

The Hough transform and its variants are still the most popular methods for detecting analytic curves from binary edge data. However, we conclude that they can be effectively used only in cases where the noise ratio is not too high. The main bottlenecks of the standard Hough transform are its computational complexity and storage requirements. Hence it is rarely used beyond circle detection. Some efforts to deal with these problems have led to parameter space decomposition, parallel architectures, and probabilistic techniques. In this paper we have seen that apart from its use in complex noisy images, the GA approach can also help to deal with these problems to some extent. Moreover, the concept of using the weighted mask introduced a flexibility in the quality of the curves to be detected, which is difficult, if not impossible to achieve using conventional Hough transform algorithms.

The probabilistic Hough transforms work well in the case of complex images; however, in the kind of data we considered in this paper, a search guided by a GA is probably superior to a simple random search for good edge points. Further, as also mentioned by Roth and Levine [23], another main advantage of using GA is the ease with which it can be implemented over a wide variety of parallel architectures compared to Hough transform, which is more difficult to parallelize.

References

1. Bergen, J. R., Shvaytser, H. : A probabilistic algorithm for computing Hough transforms. J. Algorithms, **12**, 4 (1991) 639–656
2. Califano, A., Bolle, R. M., Taylor, R. W. : Generalized neighbourhoods : A new approach to complex parameter feature extraction. Proc. IEEE Conference on Computer Vision and Pattern Recognition, (1989) 192–199
3. Cohen, M., Toussaint, G. T. : On the detection of structures in noisy pictures. Pattern Recognition, **9**, (1977) 95–98
4. Goldberg, D. E. : Genetic Algorithms in Search, Optimization and Machine Learning. Addison-Wesley, Reading, M.A. (1989)
5. Grimson, W. E. L., Huttenlocher, D. P. : On the sensitivity of the Hough transform for object recognition. IEEE Trans. Pattern Anal. Machine Intell., **PAMI-12**, (1990) 255–274
6. Hill, A., Taylor, C. J. : Model-based image interpretation using genetic algorithms. Image and Vision Computing, **10**, (1992) 295–300
7. Hough, P. V. C. : Method and means for recognizing complex patterns. U.S. Patent No. 3069654 (1962)
8. Hunt, D. J., Nolte, L. W., Reibman, A. R., Ruedger, W. H. : Hough transform and signal detection theory performance for images with additive noise. Computer Vision, Graphics and Image Processing, **52**, 3 (1990) 386–401

9. Illingworth, J. and Kittler, J. : A survey of the Hough transform. Computer Vision, Graphics and Image Processing, **44**, (1988) 87–116
10. Kälviäinen, H., Xu, L., Oja, E. : Recent versions of the Hough transform and the randomized Hough transform : Overview and comparisons. Research Report No. 37, Department of Information Technology, Lappeenranta University of Technology, Finland (1993)
11. Kälviäinen, H., Hirvonen, P., Xu, L., Oja, E. : Probabilistic and non-probabilistic Hough transforms : overview and comparisons. Image and Vision Computing, **13**, 4 (1995) 239–252
12. Kälviäinen, H., Hirvonen, P., Oja, E. : Houghtool–a Software Package for Hough Transform Calculation. Proceedings of the 9th Scandinavian Conference on Image Analysis, Uppsala, Sweden, (June 1995) 841–848 (http://www.lut.fi/dep/tite/XHoughtool/xhoughtool.html)
13. Kälviäinen, H., Hirvonen, P. : Connective Randomized Hough Transform (CRHT). Proc. 9th. Scandinavian Conference on Image Analysis, Uppsala, Sweden (June 1995).
14. Kälviäinen, H., Hirvonen, P. : An extension to the Randomized Hough Transform exploiting connectivity. Pattern Recognition Letters, **18**, 1 (1997) 77–85
15. Kiryati, N., Eldar, Y. Bruckenstein, A. : A probabilistic Hough transform. Pattern Recognition, **24**, 4 (1991) 303-316
16. Leavers, V. F. : Which Hough Transform ? CVGIP: Image Understanding, **58**, 2 (1993) 250–264
17. Leavers, V. F. : It's probably a Hough: The dynamic generalized hough transform, its relationship to the probabilistic Hough transforms, and an application to the concurrent detection of circles and ellipses. CVGIP: Image Understanding, **56**, 3, (1992) 381–398
18. Liang, P. : A new and efficient transform for curve deection. J. of Robotic Systems, **8**, 6 (1991) 841–847
19. Maitre, H. : Contribution to the prediction of performances of the Hough transform. IEEE Trans. Pattern Anal. Machine Intell., **PAMI-8**, 5 (1986) 669–674
20. Michalewicz, Z. : Genetic Algorithms + Data Structutes = Evolution Programs. Springer Verlag, Berlin (1992)
21. Princen, J., Illingworth, J., Kittler, J. : A formal definition of the Hough transform : properties and relationships. J. Math. Imaging Vision, **1**, (1992) 153–168
22. Risse, T. : Hough transform for the line recognition: complexity of evidence accumulation and cluster detection. Computer Vision, Graphics and Image Processing, **46**, (1989) 327
23. Roth, G., Levine, M. D. : Geometric primitive extraction using a genetic algorithm. IEEE Trans. Pattern Anal. Machine Intell., **PAMI-16**, 9 (1994) 901–905
24. Shapiro, S. D. : Transformations for the computer detection of curves in noisy pictures. Computer Graphics Image Processing, **4**, (1975) 328–338
25. Xu, L., Oja, E., Kultanen, P. : A new curve detection method : Randomized Hough transform (RHT). Pattern Recognition Letters, **11**, 5 (1990) 331–338
26. Xu, L., Oja, E. : Randomized Hough Transform (RHT) : Basic mechanisms, algorithms, and computational complexities. CVGIP : Image Understanding, **57**, 2 (1993) 131–154
27. Yuen, K. S. Y., Lam, L. T. S., Leung, D. N. K.: Connective Hough Transform. Image and Vision Computing, **11**, 5 (1993) 295–301

A Comparison of Dominance Mechanisms and Simple Mutation on Non-stationary Problems

Jonathan Lewis,* Emma Hart, Graeme Ritchie

Department of Artificial Intelligence, University of Edinburgh,
Edinburgh EH1 2QL, Scotland

Abstract. It is sometimes claimed that genetic algorithms using diploid representations will be more suitable for problems in which the environment changes from time to time, as the additional information stored in the double chromosome will ensure diversity, which in turn allows the system to respond more quickly and robustly to a change in the fitness function. We have tested various diploid algorithms, with and without mechanisms for dominance change, on non-stationary problems, and conclude that some form of dominance change is essential, as a diploid encoding is not enough in itself to allow flexible response to change. Moreover, a haploid method which randomly mutates chromosomes whose fitness has fallen sharply also performs well on these problems.

1   Introduction

Genetic algorithms (GAs) are often used to tackle problems which are *stationary*, in that the success criteria embodied in the fitness function do not change in the course of the computation. In a *non-stationary* problem, the environment may fluctuate, resulting in sharp changes in the fitness of a chromosome from one cycle to the next. It is sometimes claimed that a diploid encoding of a problem is particularly suited to non-stationary situations, as the additional information stored in the genotype provides a latent source of *diversity* in the population, even where the phenotypes may show very little diversity. This genotypic diversity, it is argued, will allow the population to respond more quickly and effectively when the fitness function changes. As well as incorporating diversity, it may be possible for a diploid to maintain some kind of long term *memory*, which enables it to quickly adapt to changing environments by remembering past solutions.

The effectiveness of a diploid GA may depend on the exact details of its dominance scheme. Moreover, where a changing environment is the central issue, it is important to consider changes which affect the dominance behaviour of chromosomes over time, as this may provide added flexibility.

We have carried out tests on a number of diploid methods, including some where dominance change can occur. We found that diploid schemes without some form of dominance change are not significantly better than haploid GAs

---

* Now at School of Mathematical and Computational Sciences, University of St Andrews, St Andrews KY16 9SS, Scotland.

for non-stationary problems, but certain dominance change mechanisms produce a distinct improvement. Also, certain representations are very effective at maintaining memory, whilst others are more effective at maintaining diversity. Thus, the nature of the non-stationary problem may influence the methodology chosen. Furthermore, we show that in some situations, a haploid GA with a suitable mutation mechanism is equally effective.

2 Previous work

Ng and Wong[4] describe a diploid representation with simple dominance change, as follows (for simplicity, we will confine our attention to phenotypes which are strings of 0s and 1s). There are 4 genotypic alleles: 1, 0(dominant) and i, o(recessive). The expressed gene always takes the value of the dominant allele. If there is a contention between two dominant or two recessive alleles, then one of the two alleles is arbitrarily chosen to be expressed. The dominance mapping to compute phenotype from genotype is shown in figure 1, where "0/1" indicates an equal probability of either value. The occurrence of $1i$ or $0o$ is prohibited — if this does occur, the recessive gene is promoted to be dominant in the genotype. This last stipulation is a simple form of dominance change observed in nature in which recessive genes tend to be eliminated, over time, in favour of their dominant counterparts. We will refer to this arrangement as *"basic Ng-Wong"*.

	0	o	1	i
0	0	0	0/1	0
o	0	0	1	0/1
1	0/1	1	1	1
i	0	0/1	1	1

	A	B	C	D
A	0	0	0	1
B	0	0	0	1
C	0	0	1	1
D	1	1	1	1

Fig. 1. Ng-Wong

Fig. 2. Additive

Ryan [5] proposed a notion of *additive dominance*. In this scheme, the genotypic alleles are regarded as having quasi-numeric (or at least ordered) values, and these values are combined using some suitably designed form of pseudo-arithmetic, with the resulting phenotypic allele depending on the value of this "addition". One way to effect this scheme is to associate actual numbers with the genotype alleles, and then apply some threshold to the result. Ryan uses 4 genotypic values A, B, C, D, and allocates these the values 2, 3, 7 and 9 respectively, with any result greater than 10 being mapped to 1 and lower values mapped to 0. The resulting dominance map is shown in figure 2.

In both these schemes, the probability of creating a phenotypic 0 is exactly 0.5, and hence the mapping in each case is unbiased.

Other forms of dominance exist which are not explored in this paper. These include using a "dominance mask", for instance, [1, 2], or implementing a form of meiosis, as observed in natural systems, in which a haploid chromosome is produced from a chromosome pair via recombination operators, for instance [6]. See [3] for further discussion of some of the issues.

3 Dominance Change

In natural systems, dominance can change over time, as a result of the presence or absence of particular enzymes. Ng and Wong [4] define a specific condition for dominance change to occur (which we adopt in this paper for all our dominance change methods): if the fitness of a population member drops by a particular percentage Δ between successive evaluation cycles, then the dominance status of the alleles in the genotype of that member is altered. That is, the dominance *mapping* for computing the phenotype does not change, but the allele values alter their dominance characteristics.

Dominance change is achieved in the Ng-Wong diploid by inverting the dominance values of all allele-pairs, such that 11 becomes ii, 00 becomes oo, 1o becomes i0 and vice versa. It can be shown that this results in a probability 3/8 of obtaining a 1 in the phenotype where there was originally a 0, after applying the inversion. We will refer to this method as *"Full-Ng-Wong"*.

We have extended Ryan's additive GA by adding a similar dominance change mechanism, in which the genotypic alleles are promoted or demoted by a single grade. Thus demoting 'B' by 1 grade makes it an 'A' whereas promoting it makes it a 'C'. Furthermore 'A' cannot be demoted, and 'D' cannot be promoted. For each locus, we choose at random one of the two genotypic alleles and then use the following procedure:

- If the phenotypic expression at this locus is '1' then demote the chosen genotypic allele by one grade, unless it is an 'A'.
- If the phenotypic expression at this locus is '0' then promote the chosen genotypic allele by one grade, unless it is 'D'

It can be proved that this *"Extended-Additive"* method results in a 3/8 probability of changing a phenotypic 0 to a phenotypic 1.

Finally, we introduce a comparable "recovery" mechanism for the haploid GA, in which a bit-flip mutation operator is applied to each locus of the haploid genotype with probability 3/8, whenever a decrease of Δ in the fitness of that individual is observed between successive generations.

The Extended-Additive and Haploid-Recovery schemes have been designed with a 3/8 probability of flipping a phenotypic 0 to a 1 after a change in dominance so as to make them exactly comparable with the Full-Ng-Wong method.

4 Experiments

Methods tested. To investigate the benefit of a dominance change mechanism, we tested the Simple Additive and Basic Ng-Wong GAs (Section 2 above) *without* dominance change, and also an ordinary haploid GA with mutation rate 0.01. The dominance change GAs tested were those described in Section 3 above: Full-Ng-Wong, Extended-Additive and Haploid-Recover.

Parameters. All GAs were run with population size 150. Rank selection was used, with uniform cross-over, steady-state reproduction, and mutation rate 0.01. During crossover of diploid genotypes, chromosome I of the first parent diploid was always crossed with chromosome I of the second parent diploid. The threshold Δ for applying dominance change (Full-Ng-Wong and Extended-Additive) or recovery mutation (for Haploid-Recover) was a drop of 20% in the fitness of a phenotype. The modified version of an individual replaced the original with probability 1.0 if the modified version was no less fit; otherwise with probability 0.5. Each experiment was repeated 50 times, and the results averaged.

Test Problems. The GAs were tested on an oscillating version of the commonly known single knapsack problem. The object is to fill a knapsack using a subset of objects from an available set of size n, such that the sum of object weights is as close as possible to the target weight t. In the oscillating version, the target oscillates between two values t_1 and t_2 every o generations. A solution is represented by a phenotype of length n, where each gene x_i has a value 0 or 1, indicating if the object is to be included in the knapsack. The fitness f of any solution $\bar{x}$ is defined by

$$f(\bar{x}) = \frac{1}{1 + |target - \sum_{i=1}^{n} w_i x_i|}$$

In the following experiments, 14 objects were used. Each object had a weight $w_i = 2^i$, where i ranged from 0 to 13. This ensures that any randomly chosen target is attainable by a unique combination of objects. Two targets were chosen at random, given the condition that at least half their bits should differ. The actual targets used were 12643 and 2837, which have a Hamming separation of 9. The target weight was changed every 1500 generations. Each period of 1500 generations is referred to as an *oscillatory period* in the remainder of the text.

5   Results

5.1   Oscillating Knapsack, Fixed Targets – Simple Diploidy

The results for the basic GAs are shown in figures 3, 4 and 5. Simple Additive and the haploid GA perform very poorly for both targets after the first target change. The Basic Ng-Wong GA makes better progress towards finding a solution for the first target value, but never manages to find a solution for the second target that has fitness greater than 0.05. Clearly, diploidy alone does not maintain sufficient diversity to allow readjustment to a new target.

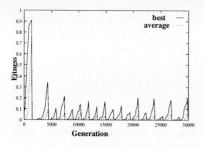

Fig. 3. Simple Haploid GA with Fixed Target Oscillation

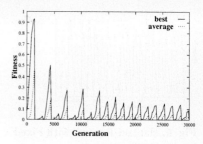

Fig. 4. Ryan's Additive GA with Fixed Target Oscillation

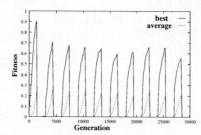

Fig. 5. Basic Ng-Wong with Fixed Target Oscillation

5.2 Oscillating Knapsack, Fixed Targets – Dominance Change

Figures 6, 7, and 8 show the averaged fitness over the 50 runs, plotted against generation for each of the 3 GAs. Each graph shows the best and average fitness of the population at each generation. Table 1 shows the number of the 50 ex-

	Oscillation Period									
	1	*2*	3	*4*	5	*6*	7	*8*	9	*10*
Haploid-Recover	45	*44*	33	*45*	33	*44*	29	*43*	37	*47*
Extended-Additive	43	*29*	44	*42*	39	*40*	45	*37*	39	*40*
Ng-Wong	32	*21*	41	*25*	34	*27*	32	*26*	32	*27*

Table 1. Number of instances in which optimum was achieved in each period. Periods in which the target was 2837 (low) are shown in italics.

periments in which the optimal fitness of 1 was attained during each oscillatory period.

Comparison of the graphs obtained for Extended-Additive and Haploid-Recover show very similar performance. Extended-Additive finds a solution within 20% of the optimal fitness (i.e. > 0.8)in 90% of oscillation periods, compared to

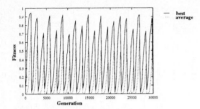

Fig. 6. Haploid-Recover with Fixed Target Oscillation

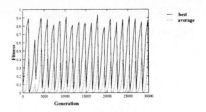

Fig. 7. Extended-Additive with Fixed Target Oscillation

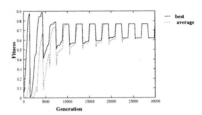

Fig. 8. Full-Ng-Wong with Fixed Target Oscillation

the haploid which finds a solution within 20% of optimum in 60% of periods. However, if we look at periods in which the solution obtained was within 10% of optimum, (i.e. > 0.9), then we find that Haploid-Recover outperforms Extended-Additive, with success rates of 35% and 15% respectively. Both methods show a rapid response to the change in environment, where the GA rapidly improves the quality of the new, poorly fit, solutions that are produced as a result of the environment change. This suggests that sufficient diversity is created in the population as a result of the dominance change of recovery mutation to allow evolution to continue efficiently.

The Full-Ng-Wong GA behaves very differently however. Firstly, we notice a incremental improvement in the best fitness obtained for the lower, 2nd target. A clear "learning curve" is observed, until after 12 complete oscillatory periods the GA is able to maintain a constant value for this target immediately after the environment changes. Secondly, the GA quickly finds a good solution for the high target, and this solution is rapidly reverted to each time the target switches. Thirdly, after 2 periods, there is no decrease in fitness for the population when the target switches from the low target to the high target. Finally, best solutions achieved for both targets are poor when compared to the haploid-recover and additive-recovery GAs — 0.62 for the low target and 0.77 for the high target.

The performance of Full-Ng-Wong can be explained by examining the dominance mechanism. If no '10' or 'io' contentions exist, then a genotype can encode two arbitrary solutions, changing from one solution to another by merely applying the dominance change mechanism. Thus, it is possible to encode a genotype that represents the perfect solution to both targets, and flip between the two by inverting the dominance, without any requirement for further evolution. Thus the gradient shown in figure 8 is due to the population simply "learning" a sequence of dominance values that enables this rapid change to take place. Notice that this mechanism allows the "remembering" of only 2 solutions in the genotype, so this mechanism will not be useful in an environment where there are more than 2 possible situations, or, more generally, where environmental change results in a completely new fitness function, or target in this case. To confirm this and to investigate the ability of the other GAs to cope with such changes, we repeated the experiments using a random-oscillating knapsack problem.

5.3 Knapsack with Randomly Changing Targets

The 14-object knapsack problem was repeated, but this time a random new target was chosen at the end of each oscillation period of 1500 generations. Target values were confined to the range 0 to 16383. Figures 9, 10 and 11 illustrate the performance of the three GAs on this problem.

The results show that Full-Ng-Wong performs poorly compared to the other two methods. Maintaining a memory of the environment is not useful in the random target case, and any GA must rely on maintaining a sufficiently diverse population to be able to adapt to the changing conditions. The results imply that the dominance change mechanism in the Full-Ng-Wong case does not reintroduce diversity into the population, whereas the use of straightforward mutation can be extremely useful.

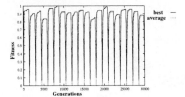

Fig. 9. Haploid-Recover with Random Target Oscillation

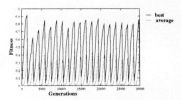

Fig. 10. Extended-Additive with Random Target Oscillation

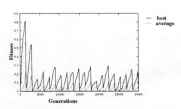

Fig. 11. Full-Ng-Wong with Random Target Oscillation

5.4   Analysis of Population Variance

In order to analyse the performance of each GA in more detail, we can look at the phenotypic variance in the population as each GA evolves, and for Full-Ng-Wong and Extended-Additive we can compare the phenotypic diversity to the genotypic diversity. Figures 12, 13 and 14 show the phenotypic gene-variance across the population at each locus in the phenotype plotted against generation for the fixed target experiments. For each type of GA, two graphs are plotted showing the variance (vertical axis) either side of the two target changes (low to high, generation 3000; high to low, generation 4500).

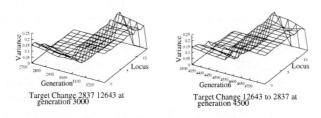

Fig. 12. Phenotypic Population Variance: Haploid-Recover

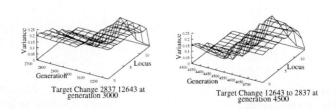

Fig. 13. Phenotypic Population Variance: Extended-Additive

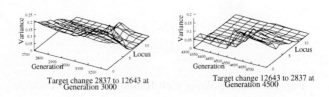

Fig. 14. Phenotypic Population Variance: Full-Ng-Wong

Figure 12 shows that Haploid-Recover has almost converged each time the target changes, but diversity is rapidly introduced due to the recovery mutation. Extended-Additive maintains slightly more phenotypic diversity in its population throughout the run than Haploid-Recover. This is unsurprising as a diploid GA would be expected to converge more slowly than a haploid. The effect of the dominance change is the same however. Full-Ng-Wong shows a slightly different picture. Just before the change from the low to high target, diversity in the population is high. However, the next time the target switches, phenotypic diversity is low across all loci and only a small increase is gained as a result of applying the dominance change mechanism. The effect becomes more pronounced as the number of target switches the population is exposed to increases.

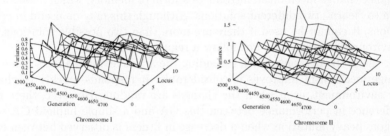

Fig. 15. Genotypic Population Variance for Extended-Additive

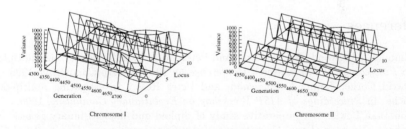

Fig. 16. Genotypic Population Variance for Full-Ng-Wong

We examine the genotypic diversity by plotting a similar graph for each of the two strings that make up the diploid genotype. Figures 15 and 16 show the *genotypic* diversity for Full-Ng-Wong and Extended-Additive either side of the 3rd target change, at generation 4500. For Extended-Additive, both parts of the genotype retain diversity, but the mapping from genotype to phenotype results in a less diverse phenotype than genotype. The genotypic diversity for Full-Ng-Wong shows a series of peaks running parallel to the generation axis, indicating some loci with very diverse genotypes and others that have completely converged. Closer examination reveals that those loci with little variance are exactly those loci in which the phenotype remains invariant from the optimal solution of target 1 to the optimal solution of target 2, hence even at generation 4500 the population is already starting to learn the two different solutions.

6   Conclusions

Using two variations of a non-stationary problem, we have shown that a simple diploid scheme does not perform well in either case. Adding some form of dominance change mechanism considerably improves matters, but the form of the change mechanism can have a significant effect. In the case of Full-Ng-Wong, the dominance change mechanism introduces a form of memory, which allows a population to "learn" two different solutions. Although this may be useful in certain situations, it cannot be used if there are more than two possible solutions, or if the environment changes do not follow a regular pattern.

For the problems considered, extending the additive dominance scheme with a change mechanism improves it considerably. It responds quickly to changes in the environment, even when the changes are random. However, there is little difference in performance between this GA and a simple haploid GA which undergoes heavy mutation when a decrease in fitness is observed between evaluations. Future experimentation with other non-stationary problems will make it possible to observe if these results can be generalised across this class of problems. If so, then the case for implementing a diploid mechanism as opposed to a simple mutation operator may be weakened, given that diploid schemes require more storage space and extra evaluations to decode genotype into phenotype.

References

1. Emma Collingwood, David Corne, and Peter Ross. Useful diversity via multiploidy. In *Proceedings of International Conference on Evolutionary Computing*, 1996.
2. David Corne, Emma Collingwood, and Peter Ross. Investigating multiploidy's niche. In *Proceedings of AISB Workshop on Evolutionary Computing*, 1996.
3. Jonathan Lewis. A comparative study of diploid and haploid binary genetic algorithms. Master's thesis, Department of Artificial Intelligence, University of Edinburgh, Edinburgh, Scotland, 1997.
4. Khim Peow Ng and Kok Cheong Wong. A new diploid sceme and dominance change mechanism for non-stationary function optimisation. In *Proceedings of the Sixth International Conference on Genetic Algorithms*, 1995.
5. Conor Ryan. The degree of oneness. In *Proceedings of the ECAI workshop on Genetic Algorithms*. Springer-Verlag, 1996.
6. Kukiko Yoshida and Nobue Adachi. A diploid genetic algorithm for preserving population diversity. In *Parallel Problem Solving from Nature: PPSN III*, pages 36–45. Springer Verlag, 1994.

Adaptation to a Changing Environment by Means of the Feedback Thermodynamical Genetic Algorithm

Naoki MORI[1], Hajime KITA[2] and Yoshikazu NISHIKAWA[3]

[1] College of Engineering, Osaka Prefecture University, Sakai 599-8531, JAPAN
[2] Interdisciplinary Graduate School of Science and Engineering,
Tokyo Institute of Technology, Yokohama 226-8502, JAPAN
[3] Faculty of Information Science, Osaka Institute of Technology,
Hirakata 573-0171, JAPAN

Abstract. In applications of the genetic algorithms (GA) to problems of adaptation to changing environments, maintenance of the diversity of the population is an essential requirement. Taking this point into consideration, the authors have proposed to utilize the thermodynamical genetic algorithm (TDGA) for the problems of adaptation to changing environments. The TDGA is a genetic algorithm that uses a selection rule inspired by the principle of the minimal free energy in thermodynamical systems. In the present paper, the authors propose a control method of the temperature, an adjustable parameter in the TDGA. The temperature is controlled by a feedback technique so as to regulate the level of the diversity of the population measured by entropy. The adaptation ability of the proposed method is confirmed by computer simulation taking time-varying knapsack problems as examples.

1 Introduction

Genetic Algorithms (GAs) are search and optimization techniques[1, 2] based on the mechanism of evolution by natural selection. Adaptation to changing environments is one of the most important applications of the GAs.

The GA approaches for adaptation to changing environments proposed so far are categorized into two types: If a environmental change is recurrent, i.e., if the environment appeared in the past reappears repetitively, to memorize the results of past adaptations and to utilize them as candidates of the solutions will be an effective strategy. We call such an approach *the memory-based approach*. In the context of GA research, several studies on this approach have been proposed. For example, methods using diploidy, structured gene have been proposed[2, 3]. The authors have also proposed a method taking this approach[4].

On the other hand, if an environmental change is unpredictable, GAs have to adapt to a novel environment using only their search ability. We call such an approach *the search-based approach*. If the environmental change is completely random, no method will be better than the method of restarting the GA for each environment. However, if the environmental change is moderate, to search the neighborhood of the recent solution will be an effective way. To achieve this strategy, maintenance of the diversity of the population plays an important role. That is, a GA must keep the results of adaptation to recent environments on one hand, and on the other hand, it must keep the diversity of the population to ensure their search ability.

There have been proposed several methods of the search-based approach. Grefenstette has proposed *the random immigrants*[5] where the population is partially replaced by randomly generated individuals in every generation. Since the randomly generated individuals are usually poor solutions, this method faces a difficulty of low online performance. Cobb has proposed the method of controlling the mutation rate called *the triggered hypermutation*[6], where the mutation rate is temporarily increased to a high value (called the hypermutation rate) whenever the time-averaged best performance of the GA declines. Since this method detects the environmental change using an assumption that the optimal value is always kept constant, its applicability is limited.

Both the random immigrants and the triggered hypermutation utilize random perturbation to increase the diversity of the population. We can generalize these two methods as *the random perturbation method* as follows:

1. The population is perturbed when the GA system receives *a perturbation signal* from environment.
2. Perturbation to the population is given by applying hypermutation with the hypermutation rate m_H to some individuals in the population specified by *the perturbation rate γ*.

Assuming that binary string representation and locus-wise mutation, the random immigrants is represented by a case that the perturbation signal occurs in every generation, $m_H = 0.5$ and γ is taken as an adjustable parameter. The triggered hypermutation is a case that the perturbation signal occurs when the time-averaged best performance declines, m_H is adjustable and $\gamma = 1$. We call the simple genetic algorithm which uses this method *the Perturbation SGA* (PSGA).

The authors have proposed another method categorized into this approach[7]. That is, the selection operation of the GAs is designed so as to keep the diversity of the population systematically. It is called the thermodynamical genetic algorithm (TDGA)[8].

This paper proposes a modified TDGA called *the Feedback Thermodynamical Genetic Algorithm* (FTDGA) which controls the temperature, an adjustable parameter of the TDGA, so as to regulate the level of the entropy of the population.

2   Feedback Thermodynamical Genetic Algorithm

2.1   Thermodynamical Genetic Algorithm (TDGA)

In the selection operation used in the conventional GA, an individual having the larger fitness value is allowed to yield the more offspring in the next generation.

While it is a basic mechanism to find the optimal solution by focusing search on the neighborhood of good solutions, it also brings about the problem of premature convergence.

In the TDGA, the selection operation is designed to minimize the free energy of the population. The free energy F is defined by:

$$F = \langle E \rangle - HT, \tag{1}$$

where $\langle E \rangle$ is the mean energy of the system, H is the entropy and T is a parameter called the temperature. Minimization of the free energy can be interpreted as taking a balance between minimization of the energy function (the first term in the RHS of Eq. (1), or equivalently maximization of the fitness function in GAs by regarding $-E$ as the fitness function) and maintenance of the diversity measured by the entropy (the second term in the RHS of Eq. (1)).

Hence, individuals having relatively small energy (or relatively large fitness) values will be given priorities to survive in the next generation. At the same time, individuals having rare genes will also be preserved owing to their contribution to minimization of the free energy via increase in the entropy term HT of Eq. (1). Thus, the diversity of the population can be controlled by adjusting the temperature T explicitly.

2.2 Adaptation to Changing Environments by TDGA

We have proposed to utilize the TDGA to problems of adaptation to changing environments[7]. In that paper, we have set the temperature constant, and its value was adjusted by a trial-and-error manner.

However, in some cases, the TDGA with a constant temperature could not follow the environmental change well. Suppose a situation that variance of the energy function decreases as an environmental change. Then, in the definition of the free energy given by Eq. (1), the entropy term TH becomes more dominant. Consequently, the selection mechanism of the TDGA tries to make the ratio of alleles in each locus more even. However, it will be harmful in finding good solutions for the new situation if it requires a biased allele ratio.

In the previous study[7], such a situation was observed in an application of the TDGA to a time-varying constrained optimization problem. The constraint was treated by a penalty function. When the constraint became severer as an environmental change, all the individuals became infeasible solutions, and the variance of the energy function decreased remarkably due to the penalty function. Then, the TDGA faced difficulty in recovering the feasibility of populations because of the mechanism mentioned above.

2.3 Feedback Control Method of Temperature

To overcome the aforesaid difficulty of the TDGA, the temperature should be controlled adaptively. This paper proposes the following feedback control method of the temperature. The temperature at generation t, T_t is controlled by the following equation:

$$T_t = \exp(\tau(H^* - H)) \times T_{t-1} \tag{2}$$

or taking logarithm of the both sides of Eq. (2), we obtain the following equation:

$$\log T_t = \log T_{t-1} + \tau(H^* - H) \tag{3}$$

where τ is a constant representing the feedback gain, H^* is the target entropy and H is the entropy of the current population. If $H > H^*$, this rule decreases the temperature, and if $H < H^*$, it increases the temperature keeping its positiveness. With this feedback mechanism, the diversity of the population in the genotypic level will be kept well even when the energy function changes largely.

We call the TDGA which uses this feedback control method *the feedback TDGA* (FTDGA). In the FTDGA, the feedback gain τ and the target entropy H^* are adjustable parameters.

2.4 Algorithm of FTDGA

The algorithm of FTDGA is as follows:

1. Select appropriate values for
   N_p: the population size,
   N_g: the maximum number of generations,
   T_{init}: the initial temperature,
   τ: the feedback gain, and
   H^*: the target entropy.
2. Let $t = 0$, $T_{-1} = T_{\text{init}}$, and construct the initial population $\mathcal{P}(0)$ randomly.
3. Observe the entropy H of $\mathcal{P}(t)$, and set T_t by the following equation:

$$T_t = \exp(\tau(H^* - H)) \times T_{t-1}$$

4. Preserve the individual having the minimum energy function value as an elite.
5. Pair all the individuals in $\mathcal{P}(t)$ randomly. Apply the crossover operator to all the pairs, and obtain N_p offsprings. Then, apply the mutation operator to all the N_p parents and N_p offsprings. Let $\mathcal{P}'(t)$ be the population consisting of the above $2N_p$ individuals and the elite preserved in Step 4.
6. Let $i = 1$, and make the population $\mathcal{P}(t+1)$ at the next generation empty.
7. We refer to an individual in $\mathcal{P}'(t)$ by its number $h = 1, \cdots, 2N_p + 1$. Let $\mathcal{P}(t+1, i, h)$ be the population which consists of already selected $i - 1$ individuals for $\mathcal{P}(t+1)$ and the h-th individual of $\mathcal{P}'(t)$. Calculate the free energy of $\mathcal{P}(t+1, i, h)$ for all individuals $h = 1, \cdots, 2N_p + 1$:

$$F = \langle E \rangle - T_t \sum_k H_k = \frac{\sum_{l=1}^{i-1} E_l + E_h'}{i} - T_t \sum_{k=1}^{M} H_k(i, h), \tag{4}$$

where $H_k(i, h)$ is the entropy evaluated as follows[1]:

$$H_k(i, h) = - \sum_{j \in \{0,1\}} P_j^k(i, h) \log P_j^k(i, h), \qquad (5)$$

E_l is the energy of the l-th individual of $\mathcal{P}(t+1)$, E_h' is the energy of the h-th individual of $\mathcal{P}'(t)$, $H_k(i, h)$ is the entropy of the k-th locus of $\mathcal{P}(t+1, i, h)$, and $P_j^k(i, h)$ is the ratio of gene j on the locus k of $\mathcal{P}(t+1, i, h)$. Find the individual h that minimizes the free energy F given by Eq. (4) from $\mathcal{P}'(t)$, and add it to $\mathcal{P}(t+1)$ as the i-th individual.

Repeated selection of the same individual in $\mathcal{P}'(t)$ is allowed.

8. Let $i = i + 1$. If $i \le N_\mathrm{p}$, go to Step 7.
9. Let $t = t + 1$. If $t < N_\mathrm{g}$, go to Step 3, otherwise terminate the algorithm.

3　Computer Simulation

3.1　Time-varying Knapsack Problem

We use the following time-varying knapsack problem[7] (TVKP) as an example:

$$\max_{x_i(t) \in \{0,1\}} z = \sum_{i=1}^{N} c_i(t) x_i(t), \quad \text{sub. to} \sum_{i=1}^{N} a_i(t) x_i(t) \le b(t), \quad t = 1, 2, \cdots, \qquad (6)$$

where N is the number of items, a_i and c_i are the weight and the value of item i, respectively, b is the weight limit and t is discrete time. In this paper, the following TVKP is used to examine the adaptation performance of FTDGA.

The number of items N is 30. The weight a_i and the value c_i are set randomly in the range $1 \sim 500$. These parameters are kept constant. The weight limit $b(t)$ is always reduced. Since the optimal solution is usually located near the boundary of the constraint, this environmental change makes the good solution infeasible suddenly. Thus the adaptation problem becomes difficult.

Following three reduction patterns of $b(t)$ are used.

Case 1 $b(t)$ is reduced from 90% of b_sum to 50% of b_sum by 10% of b_sum,
Case 2 $b(t)$ is reduced from 50% of b_sum to 10% of b_sum by 10% of b_sum,
Case 3 $b(t)$ is reduced from 90% of b_sum to 10% of b_sum by 20% of b_sum,

where $b_\mathrm{sum} = \sum_{i=1}^{N} a_i$. Fig. 1 shows the variation of the weight limit $b(t)$ and the optimal value in each generation. In the used TVKP, a_i and c_i are chosen so that the optimal solution is not found by a greedy algorithm in all the generations.

---

[1] The entropy is evaluated in a locus-wise manner to cope with the problem that the population size is much smaller than the number of the possible species[8].

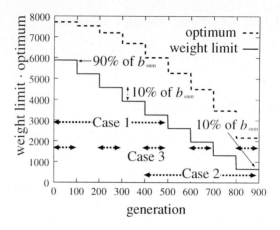

Fig. 1. The variation of TVKP

3.2 Setup of GAs

The genetic representation for the problems is a 30 bit binary code. The fitness of an individual which satisfies the constraint is the value of the objective function itself. The fitness of an infeasible individual is given by:

$$f = \left(b_{\text{sum}} - \sum_{i=1}^{N} a_i(t)x_i(t) \right) \times 0.01, \tag{7}$$

which is much smaller than the fitness of feasible individuals because of the factor 0.01. We use the following index I to measure adaptation performance:

$$I = \frac{1}{T_{\text{max}}} \sum_{t=1}^{T_{\text{max}}} \alpha \times \frac{f_{\text{best}}(t)}{f_{\text{opt}}(t)}, \quad \alpha = \begin{cases} 1, & f_{\text{best}}(t) = f_{\text{opt}}(t) \\ 0.5, & f_{\text{best}}(t) < f_{\text{opt}}(t) \end{cases} \tag{8}$$

where T_{max} is the maximum number of generations, $f_{\text{best}}(t)$ is the best objective function value in the population in the generation t, and $f_{\text{opt}}(t)$ is the value of the optimal solution in generation t. We introduce a weight parameter α so as to enhance finding of the optimal solution.

TVKP is solved by FTDGA, TDGA and PSGA. Setup of PSGA is the same as the triggered hypermutation except the trigger mechanism. The perturbation signal of PSGA is given whenever an environmental change occurs. The PSGA uses hypermutation in only one generation after an environmental change. Thus, the PSGA is given advantage of knowing that the environment is changed while the FTDGA and the TDGA receive no direct information about the environmental change.

In PSGA, the following liner scaling of the fitness function is used:

Table 1. Parameter List

Case	FTDGA	TDGA	PSGA
1	$H^* = 7$, $\tau = 0.1$, $m = 0.02$	$T = 40$, $m = 0.05$	$m = 0.02$, $m_H = 0.02$, $A = 3$
2	$H^* = 7$, $\tau = 0.2$, $m = 0.02$	$T = 50$, $m = 0.02$	$m = 0.02$, $m_H = 0.05$, $A = 3$
3	$H^* = 7$, $\tau = 0.5$, $m = 0.02$	$T = 30$, $m = 0.05$	$m = 0.01$, $m_H = 0.05$, $A = 3$

m: mutation rate, H^*: target entropy, τ: feedback gain, T: temperature
m_H: hypermutation rate ($m_H \geq m$), A: scaling parameter of Eq. (9)

$$f_{new} = \frac{A - B}{f_{max} - \bar{f}} f_{old} + \frac{B \cdot f_{max} - A \cdot \bar{f}}{f_{max} - \bar{f}} \qquad (9)$$

where f_{old} and f_{new} are the fitness values before and after scaling, respectively, f_{max} and $\bar{f}$ are the maximum and the mean fitness values, respectively, and A and B are constant parameters. In the following simulation, we set $B = 1$ and adjust A. If $f_{new} < 0$, we set $f_{new} = 0$. In the TDGA, the temperature is fixed. The uniform crossover is used in all the algorithms with unity crossover rate. In the PSGA, we set the population size to 100, i.e., twice as large as those in the TDGA and the FTDGA where the population size is 50 in order to make the number of fitness evaluation equal. We set the maximum number of generations N_g to 500 and fluctuation interval to 100. We have applied elitism to all the algorithms.

3.3 Simulation Results

The adjustable parameters of FTDGA, TDGA and PSGA have been set to the best values after preliminary experiments. These parameters are shown in Table 1. The mutation and hypermutation rates represent the probabilities of flip in each locus.

In the FTDGA, the best target entropy H^* is same in all the cases. It shows that suitable diversity is almost constant in these environmental changes. The best feedback gain τ becomes larger in the order of Case 1, 2 and 3. Since the weight limits in Case 2 are smaller than those in Case 1, and the change rate of $b(t)$ in Case 3 is larger than that of the other cases, large τ may be needed in these cases to achieve quick adaptation. It also should be noted that we have observed that instability such as oscillation with too large τ.

In the TDGA, the performance of $T = 40$ is the second highest value in Case 2 and Case 3 and these second values are almost the same as the best values in each case. Therefore the best temperature T is almost the same in all the cases like H^*. This result shows that the characteristic of T is similar to that of H^*.

In the PSGA, hypermutation works well in Case 2 and Case 3 because the hypermutation rate m_H is larger than the mutation rate m. However, the best

m_H is not much larger than m. In Case 1, m_H is equal to m, which means that the hypermutation is ineffective. These results show that large perturbation worsens the search performance.

Figs. 2 (a) ~ (f) show the search process of FTDGA, TDGA and PSGA in Case 2 respectively. The upper panels show the evolution of the fitness values, and the lower panels show the entropy variation.

It is shown in Fig. 2 (a) that the search by FTDGA follows the environmental change well. The search by TDGA shown in Fig. 2 (b) can not follow the environmental change around generation 300 because all individuals become infeasible and the problem discussed in 2.2 occurs. Fig. 2 (c) shows that the search by PSGA almost follows the environmental change. However the PSGA fails in finding the optimal solution in many periods, especially in generation 400 ~ 500.

Figs. 2 (d) ~ (f) show that the entropy values of the search are almost same in the three algorithms, which is the result of the parameter tuning for each algorithm. Fig. 2 (d) shows that the entropy of the FTDGA is controlled well to the target entropy value. When the environmental change occurs, the entropy value deviates from the target value, but it returns quickly. Fig. 2 (e) shows that the entropy of TDGA is more disordered than that of FTDGA. Fig. 2 (f) shows that the entropy of PSGA gets down in the generation 400 ~ 500. This decline means that convergence of the population occurs in this period, where the PSGA failed in finding the optimal solution.

Looking at the fitness distribution shown in Figs. 2 (a) ~ (c), it may seem that the PSGA maintains the diversity more than the FTDGA and the TDGA because the mean fitness value is much closer to the best one in the FTDGA and the TDGA than in the PSGA. However, looking at the entropy shown in Figs. 2 (d) ~ (f), the FTDGA and the TDGA maintain the diversity well. This result is explained as follows. The fitness distribution indicates *the phenotypic diversity*, while, the entropy indicates *the genotypic diversity*. In the knapsack problem taken as an example, there exist many suboptimal solutions. Hence, by careful selection operation such as FTDGA and TDGA, maintenance of the diversity can be achieved keeping the fitness value high. It ensures the good adaptation by crossover operation to the environmental change.

Fig. 3 shows performance variation of FTDGA with various target entropy H^*. It is shown in Fig. 3 that the performance of FTDGA has a peak at $H^* = 7$. At a low H^*, the FTDGA puts more emphasis on selecting good individuals than maintaining diversity which is important to follow the environmental change. On the other hand, at a high H^*, the FTDGA maintains diversity well, but the search performance in stationary periods becomes worse.

Fig. 4 shows performance comparison of FTDGA, TDGA and PSGA. The abscissa indicates the case number, and the ordinate indicates the performance index I, which is the mean value of 50 trials. Fig. 4 shows that the best performance is obtained by FTDGA in all the cases. The performance of TDGA falls down remarkably in Case 2 and Case 3 because the environmental change that makes all individuals infeasible occurs many times in these Cases. These results show the effectiveness of the feedback control of the temperature. The performance of PSGA is the lowest in all the cases, although the PSGA is given the advantage of detecting the environmental changes.

4   Conclusion

In this paper, the authors propose a modified thermodynamical genetic algorithm called the *Feedback Thermodynamical Genetic Algorithm* (FTDGA), in which the feedback control method of the temperature is introduced into the TDGA. The comparative study of FTDGA with TDGA and the triggered hypermutation through computer simulation shows that a satisfactory performance is obtained by FTDGA.

To combine memory-based approach[4] with the FTDGA and analysis of the stability of the feedback control are subjects of further study.

Finally, the authors would like to acknowledge helpful discussions by Prof. Keinosuke Matsumoto of Osaka Prefecture University. This research was supported by "The Research for the Future" program, 'Biologically Inspired Adaptive Systems (JSPS-RFTF96I00105)' of The Japan Society for the Promotion of Science.

References

1. J. H. Holland: Adaptation in Natural and Artificial Systems, The University of Michigan (1975).
2. D. E. Goldberg: Genetic Algorithms in Search, Optimization, and Machine Learning, Addison-Wesley (1989).
3. D. Dasgupta and D. R. McGregor: Nonstationary function optimization using the structured genetic algorithm, *Proc. of 2nd PPSN*, Vol. 2, pp. 145-154, (1992).
4. N. Mori, S. Imanishi, H. Kita, Y. Nishikawa: Adaptation to Changing Environments by Means of the Memory Based Thermodynamical Genetic Algorithm, *Proc. of 7th ICGA*, pp. 299-306 (1997).
5. J. J. Grefenstette : Genetic algorithms for changing environments, *Proc. of 2nd PPSN*, Vol. 2, pp.137-144 (1992).
6. H. G. Cobb : An investigation into the use of hypermutation as an adaptive operator in genetic algorithms having continuous, time-dependent nonstationary environments, *NRL Memorandum Report 6760* 523-529 (1990).
7. N. Mori, H. Kita and Y. Nishikawa: Adaptation to a Changing Environment by Means of the Thermodynamical Genetic Algorithm, *Proc. of 4th PPSN*, Vol. 4, pp. 513-522 (1996).
8. N. Mori, J. Yoshida, H. Tamaki, H. Kita and Y. Nishikawa: A Thermodynamical Selection Rule for the Genetic Algorithm, *Proc. of 2nd IEEE Conference on Evolutionary Computation*, pp. 188-192 (1995).

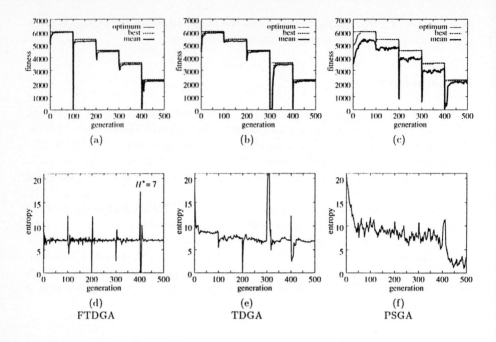

Fig. 2. Search processes of FTDGA, TDGA and PSGA in Case 2.

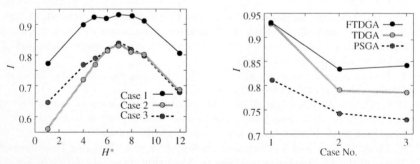

Fig. 3. Variation of performance index I w.r.t target entropy H^*.

Fig. 4. Performance comparison of FTDGA, TDGA and PSGA.

Optimization with Noisy Function Evaluations

Volker Nissen[1] and Jörn Propach[2]

[1]IDS Prof. Scheer GmbH - Altenkesseler Str. 17, D-66115 Saarbrücken
[2]Universität Göttingen, Abt. Wirtschaftsinformatik I, D-37073 Göttingen

Abstract. In the optimization literature it is frequently assumed that the quality of solutions can be determined by calculating deterministic objective function values. Practical optimization problems, however, often require the evaluation of solutions through experimentation, stochastic simulation, sampling, or even interaction with the user. Thus, most practical problems involve noise. We empirically investigate the robustness of population-based versus point-based optimization methods on a range of parameter optimization problems when noise is added. Our results favor population-based optimization, and the evolution strategy in particular.

0. Introduction

Practical problems frequently involve noisy evaluations. For complex real systems, building a stochastic simulation model is often a useful first step in optimization. While searching for a good setting of the model's decision variables we are faced with the problem that even for identical decisions the simulation will not return identical results due to stochastic influence in the model. Hence, we have to account for noisy evaluations. In other circumstances, assessing the quality of a solution might require an experiment, or even interaction with the user. Sometimes, the exact evaluation of a solution can be so time-consuming that sampling is a necessary measure. Again, one has to account for noise in the evaluation.

In this paper, we investigate the robustness of some well-known population-based heuristics versus some common point-based optimization methods on three high-dimensional standard test functions in the face of noise. While optimization under noisy conditions has received relatively little attention within evolutionary computation, there are important predecessors of this work, such as Grefenstette and Fitzpatrick (1985, 1988), Goldberg et al. (1992), Beyer (1993), Hammel and Bäck (1994), Nissen and Biethahn (1995), Rana et al. (1996), Miller (1997), Fogel and Ghozeil (1997), and others. Due to space limitations, we can only briefly mention these works here. For some more details see Nissen and Propach (1998).

Section 1 outlines the methodology used in our practical experiments. In Section 2 the results are presented, while Section 3 contains the discussion and conclusions.

1. Method

We compare two population-based optimization techniques, a Genetic Algorithm (GA) and an Evolution Strategy (ES), with two point-based methods, the classical Pattern Search (PS), and the modern Threshold Accepting (TA). Our focus of attention is the convergence precision of each heuristic, i.e. the exactness with which the optimum is located, when they are allowed to inspect a similar fraction of the search space in the sense of a fixed total number of evaluated solutions.

Every test function is first used in its standard deterministic form, and thereafter with an additive normally-distributed noise component of zero mean and varying standard deviation to create different levels of noise as would be typical for stochastic system simulation. Every heuristic is implemented in standard C and run 30 times on each test function and noise level. Thus, the results presented in Section 2 are based on several thousand individual runs. A run consists of 100,000 evaluated solutions in the case of the relatively straightforward test functions (1) and (2), and 200,000 evaluated solutions for test function (3). The experiments are performed on standard Pentium PCs with numerical co-processor, and consume many days of CPU-time. No optimization method is tuned to treat the noise.

We employ the following (piecewise) continuous test functions to be minimized (used, for instance in Bäck, 1996), with n being the dimensionality of the function. The global optimum of each function has an objective function value of zero:

(1) Sphere Function $\qquad F(x_i \mid i = 1,2,...,n) = \displaystyle\sum_{i=1}^{n} x_i^2 \qquad x_i \in [-40, 60]$

(2) Step Function $\qquad F(x_i \mid i = 1,2,...,n) = \displaystyle\sum_{i=1}^{n} \lfloor x_i + 0.5 \rfloor^2 \qquad x_i \in [-40, 60]$

(3) Ackley's Function

$$F(x_i \mid i = 1,2,...,n) = -c_1 \cdot \exp\left(-c_2 \sqrt{\frac{1}{n}\sum_{i=1}^{n} x_i^2}\right) - \exp\left(\frac{1}{n}\cdot\sum_{i=1}^{n} \cos(c_3 \cdot x_i)\right) + c_1 + e$$

$c_1 = 20$; $c_2 = 0.2$; $c_3 = 2\pi$; $\qquad x_i \in [-20, 30]$

Intuitively, when one function returns values in the range [0, 50000] and a second function in the range [0, 200] this should be reflected in the noise component. Hence, we choose the standard deviation of our additive Gaussian noise-component in the following way: First, we determine the average objective function value of a random sample of 100 solutions from the function in question. The standard deviation of the noise component is then set to certain fractions of this average objective function value to produce different noise levels. This noise is fitness-independent in the sense that it is not a function of the deterministic function value of a particular solution.

Of course, this procedure is purely heuristic, and many other schemes are possible. One should note that the global optimum of all test functions has a function value of zero, so that in a more general context we would actually take the difference between the best known function value and an average initial function value as a basis for modeling our noise levels. More formally the noisy objective function $\Phi: \mathbf{R}^n \rightarrow \mathbf{R}$ of our experiments is composed in the following way, where S is the search space, $N(0,\sigma)$ represents a normally distributed random variable and $\vec{x}^*$ is the best-known solution for the actual test function:

$$\Phi(\vec{x},\sigma) = F(\vec{x}) + N(0,\sigma)$$

$$\sigma = \alpha \cdot \left| \overline{m} - F(\vec{x}^*) \right| \qquad \overline{m} = \frac{1}{100} \sum_{j=1}^{100} F(\vec{x}_j) \quad \vec{x}_j \in S, \vec{x}_j \text{ chosen randomly}$$

By setting the parameter α to different values we can tune the amount of noise. We employ the following noise levels: $\alpha \in \{0.2\%, 0.5\%, 2\%, 5\%, 10\%\}$

The stream of random numbers used is identical for corresponding runs at different levels of noise. For the test functions (1) and (2), which are characterized by a very high difference between the optimum and an average objective function value, only the first three levels of noise are used. Furthermore, for each noise level we perform two sets of experiments. First, we evaluate each solution only a single time. This amounts to ignoring the fact that we deal with a stochastic problem during evaluation. The second set of experiments evaluates each solution with a sample size of ten and takes the mean objective function value as the 'true' fitness of the tested solution. Thereby, uncertainty is reduced as compared to the evaluation with a sample size of only one. The idea is to investigate how robustness is affected by different amounts of uncertainty in the evaluation under various levels of noise.

The implementation of our four optimization methods is fairly standard. The GA was implemented following Bäck (1996). We employ a population size of 100 using generational replacement and a random initialization. Each variable is Gray coded with 30 bits. The search operators are two-point crossover with $p_c = 0.6$ and bit mutation with $p_m = 0.001$. We use deterministic tournament selection with a tournament size of $q = 7$ for the test functions (1) and (2). For test function (3) linear ranking provides better results. The maximum and minimum expected values are set to $E_{max} = 1.5$ and $E_{min} = 0.5$ respectively. Stochastic Universal Sampling (Baker, 1987) is used as the sampling algorithm.

The ES-implementation again follows Bäck (1996). We use a (15,100)-strategy with n mutation step sizes corresponding to the problem dimensionality. Mutations of different object variables are not correlated. Discrete recombination is employed for the object variables while panmictic (global) intermediate recombination is used for the step sizes. The population is randomly initialized.

The classical Pattern Search (PS) is implemented after Schwefel (1995). We use a *multistart* version that begins in different random initial points. It is necessary to rely on a multistart strategy since in contrast to the other methods PS can not be tuned for a particular run length. We restart PS on a test function so often that the total number of evaluated solutions roughly equals the other optimization techniques. This means that for PS the result of an individual 'run' as refered to in Section 2 is actually the best result obtained from some multistarts. Depending on the test function, initial step sizes of PS are in the range [0.1, 10] and final step sizes in the interval $[10^{-10}, 10^{-3}]$.

Threshold Accepting (TA) is a simplification of Simulated Annealing (SA), and was first presented in Dueck and Scheuer (1990). Starting from a random initial solution, each TA-step consists of a slight change of the old solution in a new one. TA accepts every new solution that is either better than the old one or that deteriorates the old objective function value by less than a given threshold level T. The threshold will be relatively large in the beginning of the search to allow for a full exploration of the search space. As the search continues, T is lowered in a stepwise manner. Generally, an increasing number of trials is performed at successive levels of T until some minimum threshold level is reached. Our TA-implementation follows Nissen and Paul (1995).

Since TA was originally designed for combinatorial optimization with clearly defined neighborhood structures surrounding each solution, it was necessary to decide how a new solution should be created from an old one in the case of the continuous test functions used here. In our TA-implementation each variable has an identical probability to be modified in the transition from the old to a new solution. An expected 1.5 variables are modified in each TA-step to produce a new solution, keeping the idea of local neighborhood search. The modification itself is achieved by adding the realization of a normally-distributed random variable to the current value of an object variable. The random variable has zero mean and a standard deviation that has been manually tuned to work well on the given deterministic test function. The initial and final thresholds of TA are 5% and 0.01%, respectively.

In the following section we discuss experimental results obtained with these heuristics on standard test functions under conditions of various levels of noise. An important point is that all heuristics work on an acceptable level in the deterministic case, so that one has a basis for judging performance losses in the stochastic cases.

2.   Results

The deterministic unimodal Sphere Function is a simple task for all heuristics tested here as can be seen from the results in Table 1. All heuristics reliably find solutions near the global optimum. It is worth mentioning that the mean objective function value from a random sample of 100 solutions is as high as 28,140 resulting in high absolute amounts of noise during our experiments with noisy evaluations. The classical PS gives the best mean result over 30 runs in the deterministic case.

It should be noted that results for stochastic functions as stated in tables and figures always refer to the *deterministic* objective function value (without noise component) of the best solution discovered during each optimization run, averaged over 30 runs. This means, we give the average true quality of solutions found by each heuristic under conditions of noise, and so results become comparable to the deterministic case.

eval.	GA		ES		PS		TA	
	$\overline{F}$	σ	$\overline{F}$	σ	$\overline{F}$	σ	$\overline{F}$	σ
determ.	2.01 E−12	1.70 E−12	8.01 E−15	8.40 E−16	1.44 E−20	1.30 E−21	9.02 E−04	2.92 E−04
0.2 % 1 eval.	1.38 E+01	3.03 E+00	1.36 E+01	2.91 E+00	7.08 E+02	1.12 E+02	5.09 E+03	7.87 E+02
0.2 % 10 eval.	6.25 E+00	2.29 E+00	4.44 E+00	0.97 E+00	7.98 E+01	1.29 E+01	1.43 E+02	2.76 E+01
0.5 % 1 eval.	4.20 E+01	8.63 E+00	3.26 E+01	6.75 E+00	3.39 E+03	5.12 E+02	1.16 E+04	1.84 E+03
0.5 % 10 eval.	1.26 E+01	3.96 E+00	9.50 E+00	1.92 E+00	4.34 E+02	7.97 E+01	5.41 E+02	8.47 E+01
2.0 % 1 eval.	1.44 E+02	4.99 E+01	1.26 E+02	2.12 E+01	1.81 E+04	2.33 E+03	1.59 E+04	2.49 E+03
2.0 % 10 eval.	5.76 E+01	2.05 E+01	4.35 E+01	8.66 E+00	4.96 E+03	7.40 E+02	4.86 E+03	1.04 E+03

Tab. 1. Results for the Sphere Function (mean and std.dev. of 30 independent runs; 100,000 evaluated solutions per run)

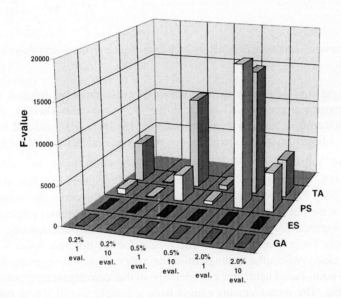

Fig. 1. Results for the stochastic Sphere Function ($n = 30$, $x_i \in [60,-40]$, F-value is deterministic objective function value of the best solution averaged over 30 independent runs)

In Figure 1, it is quite interesting to see how the different heuristics cope with increasing levels of noise under 1 and 10 evaluations per individual solution. The Sphere Function that appeared so easy in the deterministic case turns into a 'real nightmare' for the point-based methods when noise is added. As one would expect, increasing the amount of noise deteriorates the performance of all heuristics.

However, the population-based GA and ES are remarkably robust in the presence of noise and even produce reasonable results for the highest noise level and a sample size of only one evaluation per solution.

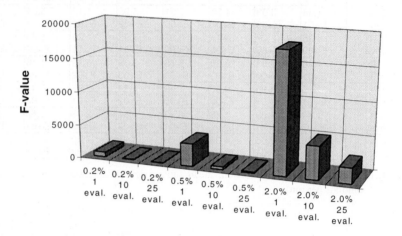

Fig. 2. Increasing evaluations per solution for Pattern Search on the Sphere Function

One might suggest increasing the number of evaluations per solution to improve the performance of point-based search in the stochastic case. Thereby, the level of uncertainty during evaluation would be reduced. However, Hammel and Bäck (1994) noted that t-times sampling increases run-time requirements considerably (up to t-times), but indeed can only reduce the observation error by $\sqrt{t}$. This is experimentally confirmed for the example of PS on the Sphere Function in Figure 2.

For the Step Function, a modification of the Sphere Function, the global optimum is located at the plateau $x_i \in [-0.5, 0, 5]$ i = 1,2,..,n . All heuristics reliably achieve a high convergence precision on this test function for the deterministic case as is evident from Table 2 and Figure 3. The results for the different noise levels in the stochastic case confirm the findings from the Sphere Function. Even moderate noise affects the point-based heuristics considerably so that convergence precision becomes unacceptable. The improvements gained from a sample size of ten as opposed to a sample size of one are not sufficient to compensate the much increased computational requirements that follow from multiple sampling. Again, the population-based GA and ES appear far more robust in the presence of noise.

Test function (3), the Ackley Function, has a highly multimodal fitness landscape. The mean objective function value from a random sample of 100 solutions was 20.73. Optimization results are documented in Table 3 and Figure 4. On the deterministic function, ES and PS achieve a higher convergence precision than GA and TA, but it is fair to state that all four heuristics work reasonably well in the deterministic case. When noise is added, the point-based PS and TA can deal with up to a noise-level of

0.5 % when each solution is evaluated with a sample size of ten. Both methods are unable to identify good solutions when higher noise levels are employed. The population-based GA and ES are much more robust, and give reasonable performance even at the very high noise level of 10 %, particularly when a sample size of ten is used. For low and medium noise the ES achieves superior results over the GA.

eval.	GA		ES		PS		TA	
	$\overline{F}$	σ	$\overline{F}$	σ	$\overline{F}$	σ	$\overline{F}$	σ
determ.	1.00 E–01	1.80 E–01	0	0	0	0	0	0
0.2 % 1 eval.	1.43 E+01	3.80 E+00	1.28 E+01	2.16 E+00	7.16 E+02	1.59 E+02	5.22 E+03	7.27 E+02
0.2 % 10 eval.	7.83 E+00	6.50 E+00	3.43 E+00	1.25 E+00	8.15 E+01	1.46 E+01	1.45 E+02	2.03 E+01
0.5 % 1 eval.	4.64 E+01	2.09 E+01	3.44 E+01	9.93 E+00	3.40 E+03	4.92 E+02	1.10 E+04	1.84 E+03
0.5 % 10 eval.	1.68 E+01	1.07 E+01	1.01 E+01	2.28 E+00	4.60 E+02	9.08 E+01	5.32 E+02	9.02 E+01
2.0 % 1 eval.	1.31 E+02	4.32 E+01	1.33 E+02	2.84 E+01	1.83 E+04	2.03 E+03	1.63 E+04	2.25 E+03
2.0 % 10 eval.	6.31 E+01	3.02 E+01	4.03 E+01	1.04 E+01	4.98 E+03	5.37 E+02	4.86 E+03	1.04 E+03

Tab. 2. Results for the Step Function (mean and std.dev. of 30 independent runs; 100,000 evaluated solutions per run)

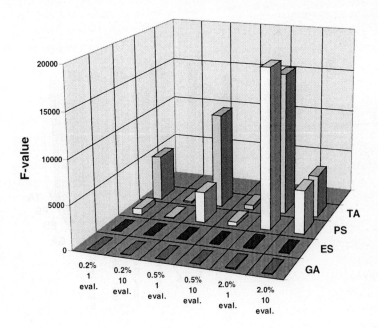

Fig. 3. Results for the Step Function ($n = 30$, $x_i \in [60, -40]$)

eval.	GA		ES		PS		TA	
	$\overline{F}$	σ	$\overline{F}$	σ	$\overline{F}$	σ	$\overline{F}$	σ
determ.	8.86 E–03	2.29 E–03	6.13 E–08	1.97 E–09	8.47 E–11	3.57 E–12	6.59 E–03	1.14 E–03
0.2 % 1 eval.	4,29 E–01	0.54 E+00	3,04 E–02	4.23 E–03	0.27 E+00	0.34 E–01	1.62 E+01	4.40 E+00
0.2 % 10 eval.	4,34 E–01	0.58 E+00	9,95 E–03	1.75 E–03	8.48 E–02	0.72 E–02	0.22 E+00	3.83 E–02
0.5 % 1 eval.	3,76 E–01	0.42 E+00	5,62 E–02	6.51 E–03	1.72 E+01	2.79 E+00	1.92 E+01	3.67 E–01
0.5 % 10 eval.	4,76 E–01	0.67 E+00	2,40 E–02	4.29 E–03	0.21 E+00	0.19 E–01	0.43 E+00	6.74 E–02
2.0 % 1 eval.	6,06 E–01	0.68 E+00	2,99 E–01	1.57 E–01	2.05 E+01	0.34 E+00	1.98 E+01	2.63 E–01
2.0 % 10 eval.	3,52 E–01	0.43 E+00	7,79 E–02	1.34 E–02	1.86 E+01	1.33 E+00	1.65 E+01	3.02 E+00
5.0 % 1 eval.	7,53 E–01	5.81 E–01	1,38 E+00	4.39 E–01	2.12 E+01	0.16 E+00	2.03 E+01	2.29 E–01
5.0 % 10 eval.	3,50 E–01	2.97 E–01	2,05 E–01	7.47 E–01	2.03 E+01	0.20 E+00	1.94 E+01	3.43 E–01
10.0 % 1 eval.	1,85 E+00	7.53 E–01	4,42 E+00	8.87 E–01	2.13 E+01	0.16 E+00	2.04 E+01	2.38 E–01
10.0 % 10 eval.	6.83 E–01	6.69 E–01	0.55 E+00	2.16 E–01	2.11 E+01	0.19 E+00	1.98 E+01	2.71 E–01

Tab. 3. Results for the Ackley Function (mean and std.dev. of 30 independent runs; 200,000 evaluated solutions per run)

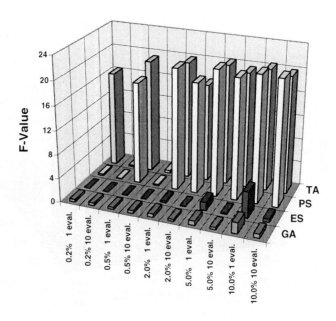

Fig. 4. Results for the Ackley Function ($n = 30$, $x_i \in [30, -20]$)

We have also investigated three standard low-dimensional test functions, the well-known Rosenbrock Function, Griewank Function, and Schaffer Function. Due to space limitations, we can only briefly state that the results are similar to those presented here. Raising the noise-level clearly affects the ability of point-based search to locate good solutions. For the GA and ES, we again find a very stable performance. More detailed results will be published elsewhere (Nissen and Propach, 1998). Finally, it should be stressed that we have focused on convergence precision of different heuristics given a total number of evaluated solutions, but we do not consider run times, which are much higher for GA, ES, and TA than for PS.

3. Discussion and Conclusions

As could be expected, increasing the amount of noise generally deteriorates heuristic performance while increasing the sample size per individual solution generally improves performance by reducing the amount of uncertainty in the evaluation. It appears that the point-based PS and TA take a greater advantage of increased sample size than do the population-based GA and ES. This is conceivable as reducing the observation error more immediately influences the course of the process for a path-oriented search (as in PS and TA). For test functions (1) - (3) the point-based methods PS and TA already had difficulties with moderate levels of noise. The population-based GA and ES showed a remarkable robustness at all noise levels. In particular, for medium and high levels of noise, even a sample size of one frequently produced better results than a sample size of ten for the point-based techniques.

PS and TA seem to suffer more than GA and ES from 'lucky evaluations' of mediocre solutions. This means that a solution of only moderate quality can appear better when evaluated under conditions of noise. Since point-based optimization methods search locally for improvements they are severely affected when a mediocre solution appears better than it is, as this introduces false local optima (c.f. Rana et al. 1996). In the case of PS, the search terminates when no improvements are found and the minimum step length has been reached. For TA, such a lucky evaluation will, at least for some time, concentrate the search effort on a mediocre region of the search space and, thus, waste computational ressources. For both heuristics, accepting a mediocre solution as an 'improvement' destroys much previous optimization effort.

Explanations of the robustness of population-based search cannot, in our view, rely on schema theory (see criticism in Mühlenbein 1991, Grefenstette 1993, Fogel and Ghozeil 1997). We do not attempt to give a unified theoretical explanation, but rather we would like to point out that population-based optimization is by design less dependent on the quality of individual solutions. It moves from one *set* of solutions to the next, and is, consequently, not so much affected when a mediocre solution receives a good evaluation due to stochastic influence.

Summarizing, our results seem to indicate that population-based search has an advantage in convergence precision and reliability over point-based search when a reasonably complex (piecewise) continuous function is optimized under conditions of fitness-independent noise. This difference is particularly pronounced when a sample size of one is employed in the evaluation, but is also present with increased sample size.This is a hint that population-based techniques may be the method of choice for the optimization of continuous parameters in noisy environments. An important area of application is the optimization of decision variables in stochastic simulation.

Finally, our results support attempts which aim at transfering the population concept to optimization methods other than EC (see, for instance, Rudolph 1993).

Acknowledgments

The authors appreciate helpful comments by the anonymous reviewers. The views and conclusions contained in this document are those of the authors and should not be interpreted as necessarily representing the opinion of IDS Prof. Scheer GmbH.

References

1. Bäck, T.: *Evolutionary Algorithms in Theory and Practice.* Oxf. Univ. Press, N.Y. (1996)
2. Baker, J.E.: *Reducing Bias and Inefficiency in the Selection Algorithm.* In: Proceedings ICGA II, Lawrence Erlbaum, Hillsdale (1987) 14-21
3. Beyer, H.-G.: *Toward a Theory of ES: Some Asymptotical Results from the $(1,+\lambda)$-Theory.* Evolutionary Computation 1 (2) (1993) 165-188
4. Dueck, G.; Scheuer, T.: *Threshold Accepting: A General Purpose Optimization Algorithm Appearing Superior to Simulated Annealing.* Journal of Comp. Physics 90 (1990) 161-175
5. Fitzpatrick, J.M.; Grefenstette, J.J.: *GA in Noisy Environments.* Machine Learning 3 (1988) 101-120
6. Fogel, D.B.; Ghozeil, A.: *Schema Processing Under Proportional Selection in the Presence of Random Effects.* IEEE Transactions on Evolutionary Computation 1 (4) (1997) 290-293
7. Goldberg, D.E.; Deb, K.; Clark, J.H.: *Genetic Algorithms, Noise, and the Sizing of Populations.* Complex Systems 6 (1992) 333-362
8. Grefenstette, J.J.; Fitzpatrick, J.M.: *Genetic Search with Approximate Function Evaluations.* In: Proceedings ICGA I, Lawrence Erlbaum, Hillsdale (1985) 112-120
9. Grefenstette, J.J.: *Deception Considered Harmful.* In: Whitley, D. (Ed.): Foundations of Genetic Algorithms 2, Morgan Kaufmann, San Mateo (1993) 75-91
10. Hammel, U.; Bäck, T.: *Evolution Strategies on Noisy Functions.* How to Improve Convergence Properties. In: Proceedings PPSN III, Springer, Berlin (1994) 159-168
11. Miller, B.: *Noise, Sampling, and Efficient GAs*, Doctoral Thesis, Urbana, Illinois (1997)
12. Mühlenbein, H.: *Evolution in Time and Space.* In: Rawlins, G. (ed.): Foundations of Genetic Algorithms, Morgan Kaufmann, San Mateo (1991) 316-337
13. Nissen, V.; Biethahn, J.: *Determining a Good Inventory Policy with a GA.* In: Biethahn and Nissen (eds.): Evolutionary Algorithms in Management Applications. Springer, Berlin (1995) 240-249
14. Nissen, V.; Paul, H.: *A Modification of Threshold Accepting and its Application to the Quadratic Assignment Problem.* OR Spektrum 17 (1995) 205-210
15. Nissen, V.; Propach, J.: *On the Robustness of Population-Based Versus Point-Based Optimization in the Presence of Noise.* To appear in IEEE Transactions on EC
16. Rana, S.; Whitley, D.; Cogswell, R.: *Searching in the Presence of Noise.* In: Proceedings PPSN IV, Springer, Berlin (1996) 198-207
17. Rudolph, G.: *Massively Parallel Simulated Annealing and Its Relation to Evolutionary Algorithms.* Evolutionary Computation 1 (1993) 361-383
18. Schwefel, H.-P.: *Evolution and Optimum Seeking.* Wiley&Sons, New York (1995)

On Risky Methods for Local Selection under Noise

Günter Rudolph

Universität Dortmund, Fachbereich Informatik, D–44221 Dortmund / Germany

Abstract. The choice of the selection method used in an evolutionary algorithm may have considerable impacts on the behavior of the entire algorithm. There-fore, earlier work was devoted to the characterization of selection methods by means of certain distinguishing measures that may guide the design of an evo-lutionary algorithm for a specific task. Here, a complementary characterization of selection methods is proposed, which is useful in the presence of noise. This characterization is derived from the interpretation of iterated selection procedures as sequential non-parametric statistical tests. From this point of view, a selection method is risky if there exists a parameterization of the noise distributions, such that the population is more often directed into the wrong than into the correct direction, i.e., if the error probability is larger than $1/2$. It is shown that this char-acterization actually partitions the set of selection methods into two non-empty sets by presenting an element of each set.

1 Introduction

Selection methods may occur on two occasions during the population's life cycle of an evolutionary algorithm. They are used for choosing mating partners if recombination operators are used, and if the parents produce a surplus of offspring then they are used for keeping the population at a constant size. In both cases, these selection methods are responsible for moving the population towards regions with better fitness values. Since this happens differently fast or reliable for the variety of selection methods com-monly in use, it has been tried to characterize these selection methods by quantities like takeover time, takeover probability, selection intensity, and related metrics [1–5]. Recently, it was also examined to which extent these measures are affected by noisy fitness functions [6–8]. Here, a complementary characterization of selection methods in the presence of noise is proposed. The key idea rests on the observation that the re-peated application of some selection method to a population of random elements may be interpreted as a sequential non-parametric statistical test [9]. From this point of view, there are many measures that may serve to characterize the statistical power of a selec-tion method. For example, a first simple distinguishing feature of a selection method might be based on its ability of keeping the error probability below $1/2$. Remarkably, this type of characterization actually partitions the set of selection methods into two non-empty sets. This is shown in sections 3 and 4 by presenting a member of each class. The theoretical foundation of these sections is introduced next.

2 Theoretical Framework

Suppose that the determination of the fitness value (to be maximized) is stochastically perturbed by additive noise which continuous distribution (with support $\mathbb{R}$) is symmetrical with respect to zero. More specifically, let μ be the true, unperturbed fitness value of some individual. Then the perturbed fitness value is given by $\mu + \sigma Z$ where $\sigma > 0$ and the median of random variable Z is zero. If $\mathsf{E}[|Z|] < \infty$ then also $\mathsf{E}[Z] = 0$, otherwise the expectation of Z does not exist. An assumption regarding the scale of Z is not yet necessary.

Let the initial population consist of n individuals (n even) where $n/2$ individuals are of type x and the remaining half of type y. An individual is said to be of type x (resp. y) if its random fitness value X (resp. Y) possesses the distribution function

$$F_X(z) = F_Z\left(\frac{z - \mu_x}{\sigma_x}\right) \quad \text{resp.} \quad F_Y(z) = F_Z\left(\frac{z - \mu_y}{\sigma_y}\right). \tag{1}$$

Without loss of generality it is assumed that $\mu_x > \mu_y$. In this case, $\mu_x > \mu_y$ if and only if $\mathsf{P}\{X < Y\} < 1/2$. Repeated application of some selection method will lead to a uniform population with probability one, i.e., each individual is either of type x or of type y. One might expect that a proper selection method leads more often to a uniform population of type x individuals than to type y individuals. As it is shown in the subsequent sections this property is not valid for all selection methods commonly used in evolutionary algorithms.

In general, this scenario can be modeled by homogeneous finite Markov chains which state space and transition probabilities depend on the selection method under consideration and on the spatial structure, if any, of the population. In any case, the resulting Markov chain has only two absorbing states, namely, the states representing uniform populations.

Definition

Let the initial population consists of $n/2$ individuals of type x and $n/2$ individuals of type y with distribution functions as specified in equation (1). A selection method is called *risky* if there exists a parameterization of the distributions, i.e., parameter values $(\mu_x, \mu_y, \sigma_x, \sigma_y)$ with $\mu_x > \mu_y$, such that the absorption probability to a uniform population with lower median μ_y is larger than the absorption probability to a uniform population with higher median μ_x. □

For the sake of brevity, only three local selection methods on a certain spatially structured population will be investigated. The imposition of this limitation has the compensating advantage that the associated Markov chain models reduce to less complex random walk models. Suppose that the individuals are arranged in a one-dimensional array of size n. Initially, the first $n/2$ cells of the array are filled with individuals of type x and the remaining cells with individuals of type y. Prior to selection the random fitness values of the individuals are calculated. The type of each cell after selection only depends on the fitness values before selection of the cell itself and its nearest neighbors. It is clear that the type of a cell is unaltered if its type is identical to the type of both neighboring cells. Therefore, it is sufficient to restrict the attention to the section of the array where type x individuals meet type y individuals. For this purpose consider the 4-tuple (X_1, X_2, Y_1, Y_2) of independent random variables. Notice that the leftmost and rightmost cell will not alter their type since there are further type x cells to the left and type y cells to the right. Only the two cells in between can change their type. Thus, there are four possible arrangements after selection: $(xyyy)$, $(xxxy)$, $(xxyy)$, and $(xyxy)$. Assume that the probability of the last outcome is zero whereas

$$\left. \begin{array}{l} \mathsf{P}\{\,(xxyy) \rightarrow (xyyy)\,\} = \alpha > 0 \\ \mathsf{P}\{\,(xxyy) \rightarrow (xxxy)\,\} = \beta > 0 \\ \mathsf{P}\{\,(xxyy) \rightarrow (xxyy)\,\} = 1 - (\alpha + \beta). \end{array} \right\} \qquad (2)$$

Let N_k be the random number of type x cells at step $k \geq 0$. Then N_k performs a random walk on the state space $\{0, 1, \ldots, n\}$ so that the transition probabilities given in equation (2) are now expressible by

$$\mathsf{P}\{\,N_{k+1} = i - 1 \mid N_k = i\} = \alpha$$
$$\mathsf{P}\{\,N_{k+1} = i + 1 \mid N_k = i\} = \beta$$
$$\mathsf{P}\{\,N_{k+1} = i \mid N_k = i\} \quad = 1 - (\alpha + \beta)$$

for $i = 2, \ldots, n - 2$. If $i \in \{1, n - 1\}$ then the transition probabilities will generally be different from α and β, but these differences may be neglected if the population size is large enough. A formal proof of this claim will be published in a subsequent paper. Under the assumption that the population size is sufficiently large the probability of absorption a_n from initial state $n/2$ to state n is

$$a_n = \frac{1}{1 + (\alpha/\beta)^{n/2}}$$

whereas the probability of absorption to state zero is $a_0 = 1 - a_n$ [10]. Thus, $a_0 > a_n$ if $\alpha > \beta$ or, equivalently, if the *replacement error* $\rho = \alpha/(\alpha + \beta) > 1/2$. If this case may occur for some local selection method then it will be classified *risky*.

3 A Risky Local Selection Method

3.1 Characteristics of Local Best Offspring Selection

The local best offspring selection method works as follows: Each cell adopts the type of that cell with largest fitness value among the cell itself and its nearest neighbors. To determine the transition probabilities α and β consider the random tuple (X_1, X_2, Y_1, Y_2). The second cell changes its type if and only if $\max\{X_1, X_2\} < Y_1$ whereas the third cell changes its type if and only if $\max\{Y_1, Y_2\} < X_2$. Notice that these events are mutual exclusive. As a consequence, one obtains

$$\alpha = \mathsf{P}\{\,X_{2:2} < Y\,\} \qquad \text{and} \qquad \beta = \mathsf{P}\{\,Y_{2:2} < X\,\}$$

where $X_{2:2} = \max\{X_1, X_2\}$ and $Y_{2:2} = \max\{Y_1, Y_2\}$. These probabilities can be calculated via

$$\alpha = \mathsf{P}\{\,X_{2:2} < Y\,\} = F_{X_{2:2}}(Y) = const. = \mathsf{E}[\,F_{X_{2:2}}(Y)\,]$$

$$= \int_{-\infty}^{\infty} F_{X_{2:2}}(y)\, f_Y(y)\, dy = \int_{-\infty}^{\infty} F_X^2(y)\, f_Y(y)\, dy \tag{3}$$

where $f_Y(y) = \frac{d}{dy} F_Y(y)$, and analogously for β. In general, the inequality $\alpha < \beta$ is nonlinear and can be solved only in exceptional cases. For example, the integrals can be used to consider the case $\sigma_x = \sigma_y = \eta > 0$. Owing to equations (1) and (3) one easily obtains

$$\alpha = \int_{-\infty}^{\infty} F_Z^2(z - \xi)\, f_Z(z)\, dz < \int_{-\infty}^{\infty} F_Z^2(z + \xi)\, f_Z(z)\, dz = \beta$$

where $\xi = (\mu_x - \mu_y)/\eta > 0$. The situation changes if σ_y is sufficiently larger than σ_x.

3.2 Determination of Critical Parameter Ranges

Unless the distribution of the noise is specified it is hardly possible to determine the parameter ranges for which $\alpha > \beta$. A parameterization with this property will be termed critical.

To consider the most usual case let $G_i \sim N(\mu, \sigma^2)$ and $Z_i \sim N(0, 1)$ with $i = 1, 2$ be independent normal random variables. As usual, the symbol "$\sim$" means that the random variable on its left hand side possesses the distribution specified on its right hand side. Similarly, the symbol "$\sim_a$" indicates that the distributional relationship is approximately valid.

Since $G_i \overset{d}{=} \mu + \sigma Z_i$ it follows that $G_{2:2} \overset{d}{=} \mu + \sigma Z_{2:2}$ and hence

$$\mathsf{E}[\,G_{2:2}\,] = \mu + \sigma\, \mathsf{E}[\,Z_{2:2}\,] = \mu + \frac{\sigma}{\sqrt{\pi}} \quad \text{and} \quad \mathsf{V}[\,G_{2:2}\,] = \sigma^2\, \mathsf{V}[\,Z_{2:2}\,] = \sigma^2\, \frac{\pi - 1}{\pi}$$

where the operator $\overset{d}{=}$ indicates that the random variables on its left and right hand side possess the same distribution. The approximation of the replacement error rests on the observation that the distribution of $G_{2:2}$ is well approximated by a normal distribution with expectation $\mathsf{E}[\,G_{2:2}\,]$ and variance $\mathsf{V}[\,G_{2:2}\,]$. As a consequence, if $X_i \sim N(\mu_x, \sigma_x^2)$ and $Y_i \sim N(\mu_y, \sigma_y^2)$ are normally distributed random variables with $\mu_x > \mu_y$ then

$$X_{2:2} - Y \sim_a N\left(\mu_x - \mu_y + \frac{\sigma_x}{\sqrt{\pi}}, \sigma_x^2\, \frac{\pi - 1}{\pi} + \sigma_y^2\right)$$

$$Y_{2:2} - X \sim_a N\left(\mu_y - \mu_x + \frac{\sigma_y}{\sqrt{\pi}}, \sigma_x^2 + \sigma_y^2\, \frac{\pi - 1}{\pi}\right)$$

and hence

$$\alpha = \mathsf{P}\{X_{2:2} - Y < 0\} \approx 1 - \Phi\left(\frac{\delta\, \pi^{1/2} + \eta}{\eta\, (\pi - 1 + c^2\, \pi)^{1/2}}\right)$$

$$\beta = \mathsf{P}\{Y_{2:2} - X < 0\} \approx \Phi\left(\frac{\delta\, \pi^{1/2} - c\,\eta}{\eta\, (\pi + c^2\, (\pi - 1))^{1/2}}\right)$$

where $\delta = \mu_x - \mu_y > 0$, $\eta = \sigma_x$, and $\sigma_y = c\,\sigma_x$ with $c > 0$. Assume that δ and η are fixed. Since

$$\alpha \to 1 - \Phi(0) = \frac{1}{2} \quad \text{strictly monotonically increasing whereas}$$

$$\beta \to 1 - \Phi((\pi - 1)^{-1/2}) < \frac{1}{4} \quad \text{strictly monotonically decreasing}$$

as $c \to \infty$ there must exist a value $c_0 > 0$ such that $\alpha > \beta$ and therefore $\rho > 1/2$ for all $c > c_0$. It remains to ensure that this property is not an artifact of the approximation via the normal distribution above. Owing to equation (3) the values for α and β can be reliably calculated via numerical integration. For this purpose let $\mu_x = 1$, $\mu_y = 0$, and $\eta = 1$. Figure 1 reveals that $c_0 \approx 4.2$ for this particular choice of parameters. Thus, the approximation via the normal distribution already offers considerable insight into the situation. One may conclude that for every choice of the triple (μ_x, μ_y, σ_x) with $\mu_x > \mu_y$ there exists a critical value $c_0 > 0$ such that the replacement error ρ is larger than $1/2$ for every $\sigma_y = c\,\sigma_x$ with $c > c_0$. As a consequence, this type of local selection may lead more often into the wrong than into the correct direction—at least for the specific initial population considered here.

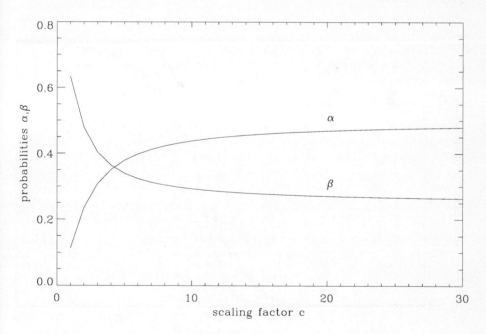

Fig. 1. Probabilities α and β for $(\mu_x, \mu_y, \sigma_x, \sigma_y) = (1, 0, 1, c)$ and varying scaling factor c.

3.3 Numerical Validation for Random Initial Populations

The analysis presented so far presupposes a very special initial population: The first $n/2$ cells are of type x whereas the last $n/2$ cells are of type y. It is by no means obvious that the results remain valid if the initial population is a random permutation of the initial population considered previously. In this case there are

$$\binom{n}{n/2} \sim 2^{n+1/2}/\sqrt{n\,\pi}$$

equally likely initial populations with $n/2$ cells of each type x and y. The existence of the critical scale parameter c_0 in this more general situation may be validated by numerical experiments with random initial populations. More specifically, for each population size $n \in \{50, 100\}$ and scale parameter $c = 2(0.05)6$ the process was run 1000 times with random initial populations. The relative frequency of the event "absorption at uniform population of type y cells" is an estimator of the absorption probability a_0. Figure 2 reveals that there actually exists a value c_0 for which $a_0 > 1/2$ if $c > c_0$ and vice versa. Moreover, the value of c_0 is apparently between 4.20 and 4.25, which is in agreement with the value found in the previous subsection. This observation provides evidence that the random walk model is an appropriate approximation of the more general situation.

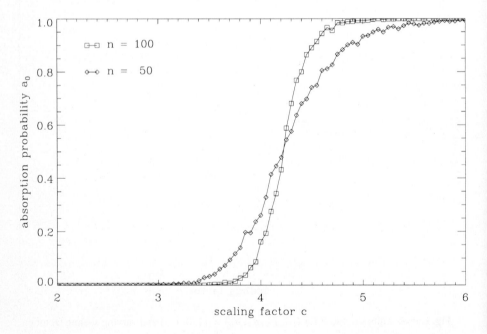

Fig. 2. Empirical absorption probability a_0 based on 1000 experiments per population size $n \in \{50, 100\}$ with parameters $(\mu_x, \mu_y, \sigma_x, \sigma_y) = (1, 0, 1, c)$ and random initial population.

To sum up, we can say that this selection method may become risky if the scale of the noise is a strictly monotonous increasing function of the distance between the individual's fitness value μ and the maximum fitness value μ^*, i.e., $\sigma = h(\mu^* - \mu)$ for some strictly monotonous increasing function $h : \mathbb{R}_+ \to \mathbb{R}_+$ with $h(x) = 0$ if and only if $x = 0$. In this case it is ensured that individuals with low true fitness will encounter larger additive noise than individuals with high true fitness. Notice that this is exactly the situation which may lead to predominantly wrong selection decisions.

4 Are there Non-Risky Local Selection Methods?

4.1 Characteristics of Local Random Neighbor Tournament Selection

Local random neighbor tournament selection [9] works as follows: For each cell the individual chooses either its left or right neighbor with the same probability and adopts the chosen neighbor's type if this neighbor's fitness value is larger than the fitness value of the cell itself. Again, consider the random tuple (X_1, X_2, Y_1, Y_2) of fitness values. Only the second and third cell may change their type. The second cell changes its type if and only if it competes with its right neighbor and $X_2 < Y_1$ whereas the third cell changes its type if and only if it competes with its left neighbor and $X_2 > Y_1$. Notice that these event are mutual exclusive. As a consequence, one obtains

$$\alpha = \frac{\gamma}{2} \qquad \text{and} \qquad \beta = \frac{1 - \gamma}{2}$$

where $\gamma = \mathsf{P}\{X < Y\} < 1/2$ (because of $\mu_x > \mu_y$; see section 2). Since $\alpha < \beta$ (or $\rho < 1/2$) this leads to $a_n > a_0$ regardless of the scaling parameters σ_x and σ_y, i.e., despite potentially arbitrarily scaled noise the local random neighbor tournament selection method leads more often into the correct than into the wrong direction.

If the initial population is drawn at random then the situation is considerably more complicated since the probability distribution of the number of type x cells may now depend on the ordering of all n in lieu of only four random variables. A formal analysis of this situation is beyond the scope of this paper. Needless to say, the non-existence of a critical parameterization for random initial populations cannot be proven by numerical experiments. But as shown next, there is a similar local selection method that is certainly non-risky.

4.2 Characteristics of Alternating Local Binary Tournament Selection

Let the population be arranged on a ring instead of a linear array and let $c_i \in \{x, y\}$ denote the type of cell $i \in \{0, 1, \ldots, n-1\}$. At iteration $k \geq 0$ the population is grouped into pairs (c_i, c_{i+1}) such that $i \in \mathbb{Z}_n$ is odd if k is even and vice versa. Each pair performs a binary tournament and the types of the pair are set to that of the winner. Thus, there are $n/2$ *independent* binary tournaments. Let the initial population be drawn at random and let $d > 0$ be the number[1] of pairs with type (x, y) or (y, x)

---

[1] If $d = 0$ then the frequencies of type x and y cells is not changed. Notice that this event does not affect the absorption probabilities. But if this event has been occurred then $d > 0$ for the next iteration—or the population is uniform.

of the current population. The probability that such a pair transitions to a pair of type (y, y) is $\gamma = \mathsf{P}\{X < Y\} < 1/2$ so that the probability distribution of the number D of (y, y)-pairs after selection is binomially distributed with parameters (d, γ). Since $\mathsf{P}\{D = i\} > \mathsf{P}\{D = d - i\}$ for $0 \leq i < d/2$ if and only if $\gamma < 1/2$ it follows that a decrease of type y cells is uniformly more likely than an increase, regardless of the current state of the population. Since the initial population has the same number of type x and y cells the property above ensures that $a_n > a_0$. As a consequence, this selection method leads more often into the correct than into the wrong direction.

5 Conclusions

The distinction between risky and non-risky methods for selection under noise leads to a clear recommendation which selection methods should be avoided in the presence of additive noise. A quantitative determination of the absorption probabilities, however, may become a very complex task. Therefore, it should be aimed at developing simpler yet sufficient conditions permitting a distinction between risky and non-risky methods.

The observation that the local best offspring selection rule is risky only for state-dependent noise might lead to the conjecture that all selection methods commonly used in evolutionary algorithms are non-risky under constant additive noise. Its verification would be a pleasant result.

The interpretation of repeated selection as a sequential statistical test offers the opportunity of transferring typical measures known from statistical test theory to selection methods under noise. This may open the door to more detailed guidelines for the design of evolutionary algorithms that operate in the presence of noise.

Acknowledgments

This work is a result of the *Collaborative Research Center "Computational Intelligence" (SFB 531)* supported by the German Research Foundation (DFG).

References

1. D. E. Goldberg and K. Deb. A comparative analysis of selection schemes used in genetic algorithms. In G. J. E. Rawlins, editor, *Foundations of Genetic Algorithms*, pages 69–93. Morgan Kaufmann, San Mateo (CA), 1991.
2. M. de la Maza and B. Tidor. An analysis of selection procedures with particular attention paid to proportional and Boltzman selection. In S. Forrest, editor, *Proceedings of the Fifth International Conference on Genetic Algorithms*, pages 124–131. Morgan Kaufmann, San Mateo (CA), 1993.
3. T. Bäck. Selective pressure in evolutionary algorithms: A characterization of selection mechanisms. In *Proceedings of the First IEEE Conference on Evolutionary Computation, Vol. 1*, pages 57–62. IEEE Press, Piscataway (NJ), 1994.
4. T. Blickle and L. Thiele. A comparison of selection schemes used in evolutionary algorithms. *Evolutionary Computation*, 4(4):361–394, 1996.

5. U. Chakraborty, K. Deb, and M. Chakraborty. Analysis of selection algorithms: A Markov chain approach. *Evolutionary Computation*, 4(2):133–167, 1996.
6. B. L. Miller and D. E. Goldberg. Genetic algorithms, selection schemes, and the varying effects of noise. *Evolutionary Computation*, 4(2):113–131, 1996.
7. Y. Sakamoto and D. E. Goldberg. Takeover time in a noisy environment. In T. Bäck, editor, *Proceedings of the 7th International Conference on Genetic Algorithms*, pages 160–165. Morgan Kaufmann, San Francisco (CA), 1997.
8. D.B. Fogel and A. Ghozeil. The schema theorem and the misallocation of trials in the presence of stochastic effects. In *Proceedings of the 7th Annual Conference on Evolutionary Programming*. Springer, Berlin, 1998.
9. G. Rudolph. Reflections on bandit problems and selection methods in uncertain environments. In T. Bäck, editor, *Proceedings of the 7th International Conference on Genetic Algorithms*, pages 166–173. Morgan Kaufmann, San Fransisco (CA), 1997.
10. M. Iosifescu. *Finite Markov Processes and Their Applications*. Wiley, Chichester, 1980.

Polygenic Inheritance - A Haploid Scheme That Can Outperform Diploidy*

Conor Ryan and J.J. Collins

Dept. of Computer Science and Information Systems
University of Limerick. Ireland
conor.ryan@ul.ie   j.j.collins@ul.ie

Abstract. Nonstationary function optimisation has proved a difficult area for Genetic Algorithms. Standard haploid populations find it difficult to track a moving target and tend to converge to a local optimum that appears early in a run. While it is generally accepted that various approaches involving diploidy can cope better with these kinds of problems, none of these have gained wide acceptance in the GA community. We survey a number of diploid GAs and outline some possible reasons why they have failed to gain wide acceptance, before describing a new haploid system which uses Polygenic Inheritance. Polygenic inheritance differs from most implementations of GAs in that several genes contribute to each phenotypic trait. A nonstationary function optmisation problem from the literature is described, and it is shown how various represenation scheme affect the performance of GAs on this problem.

1   Introduction

Evolutionary Algorithms (EAs) are biological models only at the most coarse and abstract of levels. This is a consequence of the highly structured and correlated nature of the application domains, as well as constraints on computing power. Theoretical modelling and analysis of the evolution of genetic systems has made great advances of late i.e. molecular phylogeny [2]. However, there are many phenomonen that lack understanding due to the large time scales involved [8] As a result, when trying to solve difficult problems using EAs, the implementator is often faced with imposing his/her own interpretation on the computer simulation. Such interpretations include genotype to phenotye mapping and more subjectively, the recessive-dominant relationship of alleles in diploid implementations. In the absense of a first order theory of simplified EAs, the underlying methodology is prescriptive/conceptual as opposed to the descriptive/material [4].

Diploidy is one such phenomonen which suffers from the weaknesses mentioned above, and hence lacks wider coverage and research in the EA community[3]. The idea is an attractive one, most higher animals and many higher plants[2] employ diploid structures, and this suggests that a more complex genetic structure can yield a more complex phenotype. The crucial difference between diploid and

---

* This work is support in part by the University of Limerick Foundation

haploid genotypes is that diploid structures maintain two copies of each gene at a particular locus. Some method, as described in the following section, is used to decide which gene will be used to generate the phenotype. When reproducing, both genes are passed on so that in this manner, a gene can be held in abeyance, with the possibility of being expressed in future generations. This endows the population with a "genetic memory" [9] which allows it to react more quickly to changes in the environment.

The promise of faster adaptation through diploidy is particularly useful when a GA is being applied to a dynamic environment[5]. The implications for this are enormous, from applying EAs to dynamic or even chaotic environments, to forcing a static environment to become dynamic through varying the testcases from generation to generation. As was shown by Hillis [5], this not only can have the effect of speeding up each generation, but also can be used to force a population to evolve faster, by using the so called "Red Queen Hypothesis" [12].

This paper reviews some of the more well known diploid schemes and offers some thoughts on their implicit weakness. A haploid scheme, Shades, based on ploygeneic inheritance is then described as an alternative to diploidy. Empirical analysis of Shades versus a newer diploid scheme[10] is carried out, on a dynamic problem domain. The results demonstrate the power of Shades. In addition it is argued that Shades will better facilitate the use of GAs in a dynamic environment because of the focus of theoretical modelling and analysis on deriving a first order theory of simple EAs using a haploid representation [17].

2 Dominance and Diploidy

Diploid GAs maintain two copies of each gene, known as alleles, typically chosing one of them to express as the phenotype. In Mendel's experiments, two alleles were described for each gene, one *recessive* and the other *dominant*. In the case of a homozygous location, i.e. both forms the same, the expressed allele is selected at random. However, in the case of a heterozygous location, where there are two different forms of the gene, the dominant form is expressed. See figure 1. Virtually all higher life forms have diploid structures, and it is no surprise that they are the most well adapted. Diploidy can shield genes from selection by holding them in abeyance, i.e. the gene is present but not expressed in the phenotype. This ability to "remember" genes that permits diploid structures to react to changes.

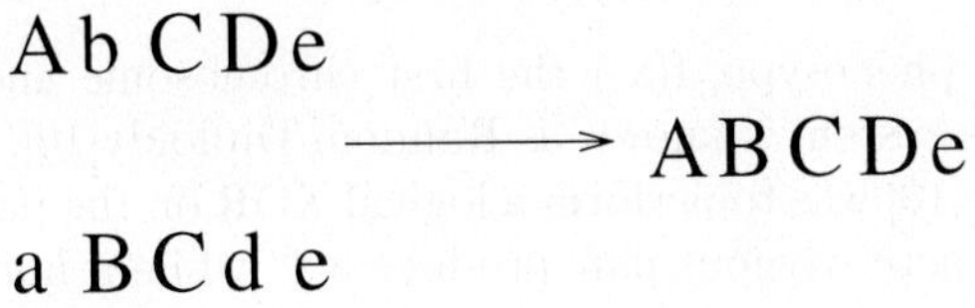

$$
\begin{array}{c}
\text{Ab C D e} \\
\\
\text{a B C d e}
\end{array}
\longrightarrow
\text{A B C D e}
$$

Fig. 1. A simple dominance scheme. Upper case letters represent dominant genes, lower case recessive ones.

Goldberg[3] showed a scheme known as the triallelic scheme[6] vastly outperformed a traditional haploid scheme. Despite the extremely encouraging signs, the triallelic scheme has enjoyed very little use in mainstream GA applications. This lack of popularity is a result of one inherent flaw in the scheme, that is, it biases the search to a particular allele, i.e. an individual is more likely to have a 1 expressed than a 0. The scheme, as described in table 1 employs three alleles, namely 1, 0 and 1_0. In this scheme, 1 dominates 0 and 1_0, while 0 dominates 1_0.

	1	1_0	0
1	1	1	1
1_0	1	1	0
0	1	0	0

Table 1. Triallelic dominance map

This bias has recently come in for criticism [16] [9]. It has also been described as being somewhat biologically implausible [9], as there are no examples in nature of an allele being both dominant and recessive[2]. Notice that this is quite different from codominance, in which both alleles are expressed, as in human blood.

2.1 Diploidy without Dominance

Another approach is try and switch dominance using the Dominance Change Mechanism[9], however, this method relies on much implementation specific knowledge for the system to be able to correctly switch dominance. A different approach to diploidy avoids the use of dominance by randomly choosing which chromosome to choose a bit from[10]. While there is a large degree of randomness in calculating the phenotype, the intention is to guide the randomness to some extent. In a locus in which a 1 contributes to the overall fitness, it is likely that a homozygous 11 pair will appear, and similar for the case where a 0 is required. In the case where the most desirable bit varies from generation to generation, a heterozygous pair is expected. Thus, the scheme can be summarised as

$$f(x) = rand(f(x'), f(x''))$$

where f(x) is the phenotype, f(x') the first chromosome and f(x") the second chromosome. This system is known as Random Diploidy[10]. A second proposal offered by Osmera[10] was to perform a logical XOR on the pair of chromosomes. In this scheme, a heterozygous pair produce a 1, while a homozygous pair produce a 0. This scheme is interesting in that it has two representations for each phenotype, in the case of 1, 10 and 01. This is useful because it means it is possible to mate two individuals of identical phenotypes and produce an offspring of a different phenotype. A property which is crucial if a diploidy scheme is to be able to adapt. The XOR scheme can be summarised as below

$$f(x) = f(x') \bigoplus f(x'')$$

This scheme was tested on an objective function which varied with time, which is described in section 5.1.

3 Polygenic Inheritance

There is no particular reason why any trait should be controlled by a single gene, or gene pair. The first instance of this in natural biology was discovered in 1909 by Nilsson-Ehle[11] when he showed that the kernel colour in wheat, an additive trait, was in fact managed by two pairs of genes. Inheritance of genes of this type is known as polygenic inheritance. Polygenic inheritance could be of interest in this case because the more loci involved in the calculation of a trait, the more difficult it is to distinguish between various phenotypes - clearly a situation which would benefit GAs being applied to nonstationary functions.

An additive effect occurs when the alleles concerned with the trait all contribute to it, rather than simply choosing one. An example of this from nature was described by Pai [11] who used Four o'clock flowers to illustrate the point. In these flowers, the colour is controlled by a gene pair, and there are two alleles, G_r which corresponds to a red gene, and G_w which corresponds to a white gene. If the pair is G_rG_r the flower is red, and if the pair is G_wG_w the flower is white. However, if, a white parent and a red parent are mated, all the children will have the heterozygous G_rG_w pair. Unlike the other schemes where a conflict is resolved by chosing one of the alleles, *both* contribute to the colour, resulting in an intermediate form, pink.

Using polygenic inheritence in a haploid GA can effectively be the same as using a diploid GA. Using two genes to control each trait, we get a range of values as in table 2. We say that each trait is a "shade" of 1. Thus, a phenotype of 0 is a lighter shade of 1. and the darker the shade of 1, the more likely the phenotype is to be 1.

	A	B	C
A	0	0	
B	0		1
C		1	1

Table 2. Dominance map for the Shades scheme

Using the polygenic system, the population can still fixate on certain alleles. Figure 2 illustrates the problem, once every individual in the population had a homozygous pair for a particular trait, it cannot change. In this case, all individuals have a homozygous AA pair controlling the first trait. The pairs that caused this problem were AA and CC, as these are at the extreme of the phentoypic space.

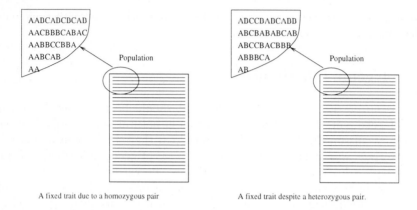

AADCADCDCAD
AACBBBCABAC
AABBCCBBA
AABCAB
AA
Population

ADCCDADCADD
ABCBABABCAB
ABCCBACBBB
ABBBCA
AB
Population

A fixed trait due to a homozygous pair   A fixed trait despite a heterozygous pair.

Fig. 2. Traits in a population being fixed due to lack of diversity

A second problem also occurs at a pair-level. Even the heterozygous pairs can fixate, due to each pair having its genes in the same order, also illustrated in figure 2. This is a particularly interesting problem, as a simple examination of the gene distribution can suggest that there are ample numbers of each gene to permit a change of phenotype. Again, taking the example in figure 2, the gene pair controlling the first trait (AB) is identical throughout the population. Despite being heterozygous, the phenotype cannot change, due to the positions of the alleles. If two parents, both of the form AB mated, one would expect that the possible offspring would be AA, AB and BB. However, the fixed order of haploid crossover prevents this from happenning. All children will have A in the first position and a B in the second. This effectively stops evolution of that pair. Both these problems were solved by the introduction of simple operators.

3.1 The Force Operator

The most attractive aspect of additive effects is how the phenotypic space becomes a continuous one. However, despite this continuous nature, only those shades near the threshold enjoy the ability to change. Values at the extreme cannot change when crossed over with identical pairs. To solve this problem, we introduce a new operator, the **force** operator. **Force** is applied to any homozygous pair that occurs at an extreme of the phenotypic space, and forces the mutation of one of the alleles. The mutation is always such that while the phenotype does *not* change, if the pair is crossed over with an identical pair, the parents can produce offspring of a different phenotype. It is still possible for them to produce offspring of the same phenotype as themselves. **Force** is applied to every occurence of extreme homozygotes in Shades scheme.

3.2 The Perturb Operator

Perturb operates in a similar manner to the rather unpopular inversion operator, but at a much more limited scale of disruption, hence its gentler title. **Perturb** swaps a pair that control a single trait, and therefore doesn't affect the phenotype. **Perturb** is applied randomly to possible candidate locations, and helps alleviate the fixed position problem. Neither the **force** or the **perturb** operator modify the phenotype of the individual affected.

4 Shades³

Shades is better than an ordinary haploid scheme because of the smoothening effect of polygenic inheritance on the phenotypic landscape. Adding another extra gene to each trait should make the phenotypic space smoother again. In general, the more genes involved in the calculation of a trait, the more difficult it is to distinguish between the phenotypes. This could be useful for the kind of problem we are concerned with, as it creates extremely smooth progression between phenotypes. A further experiment was conducted, in which there are three genes controlling each trait. We call this scheme Shades³. The three alleles yield ten possible combinations, see table 3 for details, again, the blank entries are decided randomly. Each allele has the same value as before, and the overall value is still their sum. In this case the threshold value is 3.

Combination	AAA	AAB	AAC	ABB	ABC	BBB	ACC	BBC	BCC	CCC
Shade	0	1	2	2	3	3	4	4	5	6
Phenotype	0	0	0	0			1	1	1	1

Table 3. Genotype to phenotype mapping using 3 alleles, the order of alleles doesn't affect the shade

In the Shades³ system, **force** operates slightly differently. Phenotypes at the extremeties have their shades adjusted up or down by 2, those near the extremeties are adjusted up or down by 1. This ensures that if the individual subsequently mates with another individual of the same phenotype, they can produce an offspring of a different appearance. Table 4 shows the action taken on each genotype in the Shades³ scheme. Notice that the order for **force** is not important.

For **perturb**, two of the three genes controlling a trait are selected at random and swapped. Shades³ has been shown[15] to be considerably quicker to react to a change in the environment than any of the other methods, tracking each change in the environment immediately.

Genotype	After Force
AAA	ABB or AAC
AAB	ABB or AAC
BCC	BBC or ACC
CCC	BBC or ACC

Table 4. Using the force operator on three alleles. For the extreme values, two mutations take place.

5 Comparison

Shades[3] has been shown to outperform both the triallelic and Dominance Change Mechanism schemes for diploidy[15]. It was quicker to react to a change in the environment and consistently found new optima following a change. We now examine Osmera's scheme, using the problem introduced in his paper and described in Section2.1. Examination of the problem shows that it displays quite a predictable pattern, with the possibility of certain loci becoming fixed at 1 without incurring any penalties.

5.1 Dynamic Problem Domain

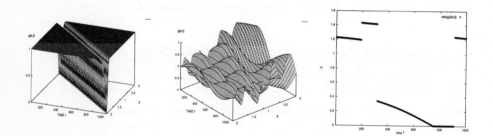

Fig. 3. Dynamic problem domain.

The test environment is specified by the function:

$$g_1(x,t) = 1 - e^{-200(x-c(t))^2} \quad \text{where} \quad c(t) = 0.04(\lfloor t/20 \rfloor) \tag{1}$$

$$g_2(x,t) = e^{-0.25x^2} \cdot \sin\left(2\pi x + 2\pi \frac{t}{100}\right) \cdot \cos\left(2\pi x^2\right) \tag{2}$$

where $x \in \{0.000, \ldots, 2.000\}$ and $t \in \{0, 1000\}$, where t is the time step and each is equal to one generation. Fig. 3 shows a 2 dimensional view of the domain, with x varying linearly with t. Solutions to the problem are derived by finding a value of x at time t that minimises $g(x,t)$.

A bit string of length 31 was used to represent the parameter, and normalised to yield a value in the range $\{0, 2\}$. A generation gap of 1.0 was set as the replacement parameter. Test parameters used are $P_{mut} = 0.01, P_{cross} = 0.7$, and population size $p = 400$. Each run terminated after 1000 generations; and a test result was derived by taking the mean of 50 runs.

5.2 Diploidy and Shades

Figure ?? demonstrates the performance of the two diploid schemes, while figure 4 shows the results of the Shades schemes. The Xor scheme doesn't perform particularly well, but the random scheme is surprisingly good for such an unstructured approach. However, each of the Shades schemes performed better on this problem than any of the other schemes, getting a mean tracking error of 0.024% and 0.017% for $Shades^2$ and $Shades^3$ respectively. After a change in the environment, $Shades^3$ suffered from the lowest drop in fitness, and was the quickest to find the new optimum. A summary of the performance of each of the coding schemes can be found in table 5.

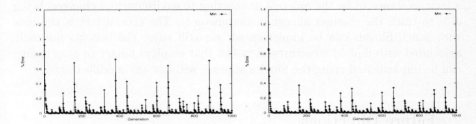

Fig. 4. % error for haploid polygenic inheritance using Gray encoding, $Shades^2$ (left)and $Shades^3$ (right).

Genotype	Encoding Scheme	Additional Parameters	Mean % Tracking Error
Diploid	Binary	XOR	0.191
Diploid	Binary	Random	20.767
Diploid	Gray	XOR	0.173
Diploid	Gray	Random	0.026
$Shades^2$	Gray		0.024
$Shades^3$	Gray		0.017

Table 5. Mean tracking error.

6   Conclusion

We have described the results of a number of experiments on a non-stationary optimization function using a number of different coding schemes. The enormous difficulty in overcoming the problem of a Hamming cliff in a problem such as this has been again demonstrated. Shades, a new version of haploidy, coarsely modelled on naturally occuring phenomena, has been described, as have its associated functions. Two versions are described, each using a different number of genes to control a single trait.

While space doesn't permit us to show all our results, we present a representative sample in this paper. These show that diploid genetic structures are not a prerequisite for a population to survive in a dynamic problem space. Our experimental evidence shows that it is perfectly possible for a haploid population to flourish in such an environment. Indeed, Shades[3], the best performer on this problem had a mean tracking error that was 35% less than the next best. It is also shown that the more genes controlling a trait, the quicker a system is to react to changes in the environment. Shades[3], which uses three genes to control a trait, is shown to be the quickest at reacting to environmental changes, being able to track the changes almost instantaneously. The crucial fact is the ease with which Shades can be implemented, yet still enjoy the benefits normally associated with diploid structures. Any GA that employs binary or gray coding can be implemented using the Shades scheme, without any modifications.

7   Future Directions

The potential benefits of using dynamic environments have yet to be realised. By providing an unbiased scheme that can react to environmental changes, we hope to be able to convert static environments, e.g. sets of testcases to dynamic environments. This could lead to quicker evaluations of generations and to more powerful evolution, by coevolving the testcases in parallel with the solution.

There is still quite some work to be done to discover the optimal parameters of Shades, if they actually exist. We discovered that adding an extra gene improved the performance of the scheme, but have not yet experiment with using four or more genes. Possibly, higher numbers will continue to add to performance, but may be subject to a law of diminishing returns when the cost is examined. Furthermore, Shades works by making the phenotypic space continuous, and could be complentary to Evolutionary Strategie s or Evolutionary Programming which operate in a somewhat similar way.

Thus far, all work on Shades has concentrated on dynamic environments. Our experience suggests that Shades population is less likely to converge on a (possibly less than optimal) solution than other schemes. It is possible that employing Shades in standard, stationary GA optimisation problems that this will be of benefit.

References

1. Collins, J.J. & Eaton, M. (1997) *Genocodes for Genetic Algorithms* Procs. of Mendel '97, Czech Republic.
2. Elseth, G. and Baumgardner, K. (1995) *Principles of Modern Genetics*. West Publishing Company, MN.
3. Goldberg, D. (1987) *Nonstationary function optimisation with dominance and diploidy* Procs. of ICGA2.
4. Goldberg, D. (1995) *Towards a Mechanics of Conceptual Machines*. IlliGAL Report # 95011.
5. Hillis, D. (1989) *Coevolving parasites improves simulated evolution as an optmisation procedure*. Proceedings of ALife II
6. Hollstein, R. B. (1971) *Artificial genetic adaptation in computer control systems*. PhD Dissertation, University of Michigan.
7. Mathias, K. E. and Whitley, L. D. (1994) *Transforming the search space with gray coding*. In Proc. of IEEE Int. Conf. on Evolutionary Computing.
8. Majerus, M. et al. *Evolution - The Four Billion Year War*. Addison Wesley Longman. 1997
9. Ng, K. and Wong, K (1995) *A new diploid scheme and dominance change mechanism for non-stationary function optimisation*. Proceedings of ICGA5.
10. Osmera, P. et al. (1997) Genetic Algorithms with Diploid Chromosomes Proceedings of Mendel '97, Czech Republic.
11. Pai, A. (1989) *Foundations of Genetics : A science for society*. McGraw-Hill.
12. Ridley, M. (1993). The Red Queen: Sex and the Evolution of Human Nature. Viking London.
13. Ryan, C. (1996) *The Degree of Oneness*. Proceedings of Workshop on Soft Computing.
14. Ryan, C. (1996) *Reducing Premature Convergence in Evolutionary Algorithms*. PhD Dissertation, University College Cork, Ireland.
15. Ryan, C. (1997) *Shades : A Polygenic Inheritance Scheme* Proceedings of Mendel '97, Czech Republic.
16. Ryan, C. (1997) *Diploidy without Dominance* Procdings of the Third Nordic Workshop on Genetic Algorithms, Finland.
17. Thierens, D. and Goldberg, G. (1993). Mixing in Genetic Algorithms. In *Procs. of the Fifth Int. Conf. on Genetic Algorithms*, University of Illinois at Urbana-Champaign.

Averaging Efficiently in the Presence of Noise

Peter Stagge*

Institut für Neuroinformatik
Ruhr-Universität-Bochum
44780 Bochum, Germany

Abstract In this paper the problem of averaging because of noise on the fitness function is addressed. In simulations noise is mostly restricted to the finite precision of the numbers and can often be neglected. However in biology fluctuations are ubiquitous and also in real world applications, where evolutionary methods are used as optimization tools, the presence of noise has to be coped with [1]. This article originated from the second point: Optimizing the structure of Neural Networks their fitness is the result of a learning process. This value depends on the stochastic initialization of the connection strengths and thus represents a noisy fitness value. To reduce noise one can average over several evaluations per individual which is costly. The aim of this work is to introduce a method to reduce the number of evaluations per individual.

1 Introduction

Evolutionary algorithms can cope with noisy objective functions because the search direction of such algorithms evolves due to a population of individuals; erroneously misclassified individuals, when esteemed too good, will not lead to absolutely wrong search directions and the information of mistakenly underestimated individuals will not necessarily be dismissed. As it is notoriously difficult to estimate numerical differences in the presence of noise, the gradient information in purely local search techniques may lead to a wrong search direction. This is also a problem in many other domains, e.g. non–linear time series analysis [2]. (Estimating Liapunov Exponents.) On the other hand, even in a gradient based optimization procedure a stochastic component may sometimes be of advantage: For example in learning weights in Neural Networks the gradient is a sum of gradients for each training pattern. Calculating and using each summand individually often helps avoiding local extrema [3].

When thinking about fluctuations on the fitness function, the term "noisy fitness landscape" is not adequate: a landscape is thought to be static, whereas for a noisy fitness function one can just get a snapshot of the fitness; in the next moment it will have changed. Therefore, a small–scale rugged contribution superposed on an otherwise "normal" landscape, for example the fractal function introduced in [4], should not be confused with a fitness with noise of the same scale. On a rugged fitness landscape one can keep an elitist and definitively

---

* e-mail:peter.stagge@neuroinformatik.ruhr-uni-bochum.de

knows its correct fitness, which can be quite important [4]. On a noisy fitness function this is not possible. This is due to the fact that an evaluation on a noisy fitness function merely is an estimation for the true fitness. By averaging over several evaluations the confidence increases, but it still remains an estimation. The uncertain fitness values obstruct the selection mechanism, as this part of the evolutionary algorithm is based on the individuals' fitness values. Proportionate–based selection selects individuals on the basis of their fitness values relative to the fitness of the other individuals in the population. Ordinate–based selection schemes work on a weaker description level. They depend on the individuals' rank in the population. Extinctive selection schemes assign a reproduction probability $\neq 0$ only to the best individuals. One common used example for an ordinate–based extinctive selection scheme is the (μ, λ)–selection. In this case, which as also used in the presented work, it is only necessary to know which are the best μ individuals, e.g. in a large population it does not matter whether an individual is ultimate or penultimate. In either case it's reproduction probability is 0.

At this level of abstraction methods from statistics can be employed to answer the question over how many evaluations it has to be averaged to decide with a certain amount of confidence which individuals will serve as parents for the next generation. The number of evaluations need not be equal for all individuals. Some might easily be detected to be too bad without further computation.

For evolutionary algorithms there exists some fundamental theory about noisy fitness functions, for example from Rechenberg and Beyer [5,6]. Beyer also studies the effect of averaging, but does not discuss ways to organize this process. Miller and Goldberg took another approach to analyze the effect of noise on different selection mechanisms [7]. As the results yield some insight into the problem with noise some of them will be described. Thereafter the testing of hypotheses – the statistical method that will be used – is briefly reviewed. Simulations will show results for the well–known sphere problem, and a short comment on the issue of genotype–phenotype mapping will be followed by the conclusion.

2 Some Theory for Evolution Strategies

The aim is to find an individual x^*, for which holds (minimization task) :

$$f(x^*) \leq f(x) \quad \forall \text{ individuals } x \tag{1}$$

The measured fitness value is:

$$\tilde{f}(x) = f(x) + \delta , \quad \delta \in \mathcal{N}(0, \sigma_\delta) \tag{2}$$

Where δ is white noise with mean $= 0$ and standard-deviation $= \sigma_\delta$. During the part of the evolutionary process where rapid progress is made it may happen that some other individual than the best is chosen as parent for the next generation. This leads to a decrease in progress velocity but there will still be some progress. Concerning the $ES(1,\lambda)$ with linear fitness increase in direction of one variable and no change in the others, $f(x) = a \times x$, Rechenberg could derive an equation for the decrease in fitness velocity:

$$h = \sqrt{\frac{1}{1 + \frac{\sigma_\delta^2}{a\sigma^2}}} \quad , \tag{3}$$

where σ is the parameter for the mutation size in th ES. Noise much smaller than the step size, $\sigma_\delta \ll \sigma$, will hardly effect the velocity. In [5] there is a complete reprint of Rechenberg's book from 73, where this result is stated; in the new part of the book h is related to the biological quantity *heritability*. The case of linear fitness increase may be a very simple model for the region far from the optimum.

In the vicinity of an optimum one might think of the fitness function as being a sphere.

$$f(x) = \sum_{i=1}^{n} x_i^2 \tag{4}$$

In this situation it is evident that for an individual being very close to the optimum an advantageous mutation will easily be corrupted by noise. Therefore, the process will not maintain the optimum if started there and it will not reach the optimum if started somewhere else. Theory for this case is given by [5] and in much more detail by Beyer [6]. Experimental results for this domain was presented in [8]. Beyer [6] gives following theoretical results for a $(1,\lambda)$–ES applied to the sphere problem, equation 4, in the case of $n \longrightarrow \infty$ and with one self–adapted strategy parameter:

$$\frac{dR}{dg} = \sigma^2 \left[\frac{n}{2R} - \frac{2Rc_{1,\lambda}}{\sqrt{\sigma_\delta^2 + (2R\sigma)^2}} \right] \quad , \tag{5}$$

where $R = \|x - x^*\|$ and g is the number of the generation.

Equation 5 can be used to calculate the optimal step size, and also to find R_∞, the finally remaining distance from the individual to the optimum, namely by setting

$$\frac{dR}{dg} = 0 \quad \text{and} \quad \sigma \longrightarrow 0 , \tag{6}$$

which results in:

$$R_\infty = \sqrt{\frac{n\sigma_\delta}{4c_{1,\lambda}}} \propto \sqrt{\sigma_\delta} . \tag{7}$$

When $\sigma \neq 0$, equation 5 leads to a final distance

$$R_\infty = \frac{1}{\sqrt{2}} \frac{\sigma}{2c_{1,\lambda}} \sqrt{1 + \sqrt{1 + \left(\frac{2c_{1,\lambda}\sigma_\delta}{n\sigma^2} \right)^2}} . \tag{8}$$

The two final equations show the dependence of the final distance from the optimum and the level of noise on the fitness function.

The two main ideas from theory will hopefully carry over to other Evolutionary algorithms as they manifest firstly that noise leads to the choice of individuals as parents which are not optimal and thus slows down the evolutionary process and secondly that noise hinders the final convergence to the optimum.

3 Some Theory for Tests

One well known way to reduce noise on the fitness function is to decrease the noise by averaging over several fitness evaluations for each individual. This statistical method yields a decreased effective noise–level of

$$\sigma_{\text{eff}} = \frac{\sigma}{\sqrt{N}} \tag{9}$$

when averaging N times.

As mentioned in the introduction it is not necessary to reduce the noise level for every individual it is just necessary to do this for the best one and to have a mean to find the best one.

The fitness of individual k is estimated as:

$$\hat{f}(x_k) = \frac{1}{N_k} \sum_{i=1}^{N_k} \tilde{f}_i(x_k) \,, \tag{10}$$

where N_k is the number of evaluations $\tilde{f}(x_k)$ on the noisy fitness function. If say $\hat{f}(x_k) > \hat{f}(x_j)$ and the noise is assumed to be Gaussian, possibly different for the two individuals, the hypotheses

$$H_0 : \hat{f}(x_k) - \hat{f}(x_j) \leq 0 \tag{11}$$

can be tested against its alternative

$$H_1 : \hat{f}(x_k) - \hat{f}(x_j) > 0 \,. \tag{12}$$

A one–sided t–test to significance $\alpha \in [0, 1]$ answers the question whether H_0 can be rejected with an error probability $\leq \alpha$. In this way the order between $\hat{f}(x_k)$ and $\hat{f}(x_j)$ can possibly be deduced without too many evaluations. If H_0 can not be rejected more evaluations of either one or the other (or both) individual(s) have to be made. As already mentioned, it is important to find the parents for the next generation; when using extinctive selection in a large population the order of the bad individuals does not matter.

The proposed tests rely on the assumption of Gaussian noise on the fitness. Although this will hardly ever be proven the tests are said to be rather robust against deviations from this assumption. If one has a better knowledge of the underlying noise distribution one can adopt other tests. For example the learning process of neural networks sometimes yields poor results even for good networks. Non–parametric tests, like the Mann–Whitney–U test [9] may also be an alternative to the t–test.

4 Experiments

Using the introduced ideas, notations and the sphere model as an example several experimental results are obtained. The dimension of the sphere model is $n = 10$, every coordinate is coded with 10 bits, Gray code is used and the range is mapped onto the interval $[-3; 5]$. There is standard mutation and crossover. (Mutation probability $= 1/\#$bits, crossover probability $= 0.6$, with 2 crossover points.) In the selection procedure the μ best individuals are selected out of a population with λ individuals. The number of evaluations of an individual is determined via the introduced test at level α but of course restricted to a maximum, called $N_{\max}$. σ denotes the standard-deviation of the noise. Each of the following results is obtained by averaging over 200 runs.

The distance from the optimum, given in the results, is:

$$f(x) = R^2 = \|x - x^*\|^2 = \|x\|^2 \ , \text{ as } x^* = 0. \tag{13}$$

The results shall answer two questions:

The maximum number of evaluations per generation is $(N_{\max} \cdot \lambda)$. In how far is this computational cost reduced if the testing procedure is included at different test–levels α. This will be shown as the average *number of evaluations / generation* during the evolutionary run for several α's.

On the other hand reducing the number of fitness evaluations will influence the achieved fitness, this is shown as average *distance from the optimum*.

$N_{\max}$ and α are varied ($N_{\max} \in \{2, 3, 4, 5, 7\}$, $\alpha \in \{0, 0.025, 0.05, 0.1, 0.2\}$). While for a very restrictive test, $\alpha \in \{0.025\}$, just a small effect is expected, $\alpha \in \{0.05, 0.1, 0.2\}$ reduces the number of evaluations but influences the achieved distance from optimum only slightly.

4.1 Experiment with a large population

In this case, $\mu = 10$, $\lambda = 50$ and $\sigma = 0.1$. Fig. 1 shows the average fitness for varying $N_{\max}$ and $\alpha = 0$ and for $\alpha = 0.2$. Fig. 2, 3 show the corrsponding effect of the tests on the average *number of evaluations/generation*. $\alpha = 0$ stands for no testing at all, as an error probability of $\alpha = 0$ can never be guaranteed.

All the experimental fitness runs look similar to those in Figure 1 . The interesting value is f_∞, which is the square of the final distance from the best individual to the optimum. Figure 1 shall serve as an example that the two situations yield very similar results concerning both the final distance and the progress/generation, although in one case every individual is evaluated as often as possible, in the other case it is not. Table 1 makes the results more precise.

For increased $N_{\max}$ an increasing fraction of evaluations can be spared and the *number of evaluations/generation* quickly reaches a stable level. The results for these experiments, which are plotted in Fig. 2, 3 are summarized in Table 2.

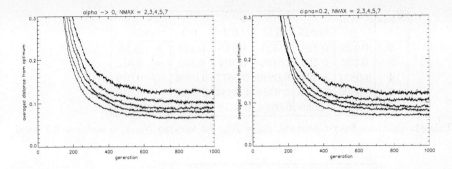

Figure1. *Distance to the optimum*; on the left no testing takes place, on the right it is tested with $\alpha = 0.2$; $N_{\max} = 2$ yields the upper curve, $N_{\max} = 7$ the lower one.

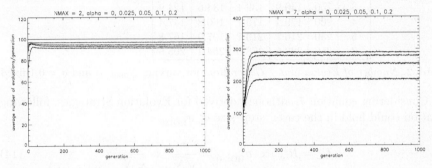

Figure2. *Average number of evaluations/generation*, several test levels α; on the left $N_{\max} = 2$, a large reduction is not expected; on the right $N_{\max} = 7$, a large reduction can be achieved. ($\alpha = 0$ yields the upper, $\alpha = 0.2$ the lower curve.)

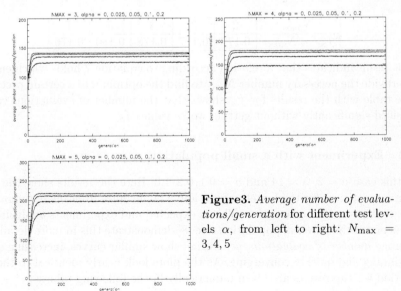

Figure3. *Average number of evaluations/generation* for different test levels α, from left to right: $N_{\max} = 3, 4, 5$

N_{max}	α					
	0	0.025	0.05	0.1	0.2	error
2	0.125	0.125	0.121	0.125	0.122	+/- 0.01
3	0.102	0.104	0.105	0.104	0.106	+/- 0.012
4	0.0894	0.894	0.0890	0.0877	0.0904	+/- 0.010
5	0.0806	0.0790	0.0782	0.0834	0.0822	+/ 0.010
7	0.0666	0.0685	0.0694	0.0658	0.0714	+/- 0.0013

Table1. *Distance from Optimum,* $f_\infty = R_\infty^2$, *for varying* N_{max}, α *and* $\sigma = 0.1$ *fixed*

N_{max}	α				
	0	0.025	0.05	0.1	0.2
2	100	96.80	94.52	93.04	91.55
3	150	140.9	139.1	134.6	124.9
4	200	179.4	175.7	166.8	147.4
5	250	216.7	210.7	197.0	167.8
7	350	289.6	278.5	254.4	205.5

Table2. *Number of Evaluations / Generation, for varying* N_{max}, α *and* $\sigma = 0.1$ *fixed*

Considering equation 7, although derived for Evolution Strategies, following relation could hold in the case: step–size $\ll \sigma_{noise}$:

$$f_\infty = R_\infty^2 \propto \sigma_{noise} = \frac{\sigma}{\sqrt{N}} \propto \frac{1}{\sqrt{N}}, \qquad (14)$$

where N is the number of evaluations per individual.
For $\alpha = 0$ and $N_{max} = 2, 3, 4, 5, 7$ this is shown in the following table:

N_{max}	2	3	4	5	7
$f_\infty \cdot \sqrt{N_{max}}$	0.177	0.177	0.178	0.180	0.176

This result indicates that a relation according to equation 7 holds which enables to provide the necessary number N_{max} to find the optimum to a certain precision. The table with the results for f_∞ shows that the number of evaluations can be reduced significantly without getting worse values f_∞.

4.2 Experiment with a small population

In this case $\mu = 2$, $\lambda = 14$ and $\sigma = 0.1, 0.2, 1.0$. Here the results show the same characteristics as for the larger population: The *distance from the optimum* converges, but onto a higher value; This is expected and experiments analyzing the influence of the parental population size [8] demonstrate this in more detail. The average *number of evaluations/generation* show similar curves, increasing at the beginning and quickly converging. As the plots look nearly identical to those in Section 4.1 the results are given numerically in the following tables:

For $\sigma = 0.1$:

N_{max}	α					
	0	0.025	0.05	0.1	0.2	error
2	0.444	0.463	0.449	0.453	0.478	+/- 0.01
3	0.359	0.371	0.374	0.389	0.403	+/- 0.01
4	0.323	0.344	0.332	0.339	0.352	+/- 0.008
5	0.291	0.290	0.308	0.310	0.323	+/- 0.007
7	0.248	0.242	0.248	0.256	0.284	+/- 0.006

Table3. *Distance from Optimum, $f_\infty = R_\infty^2$, for varying N_{max}, α and $\sigma = 0.1$ fixed*

N_{max}	α				
	0	0.025	0.05	0.1	0.2
2	28	26.75	26.13	25.51	24.81
3	42	37.87	36.62	34.74	32.08
4	56	47.46	45.13	41.57	36.64
5	70	56.71	53.34	48.11	40.90
7	98	74.73	68.94	60.60	48.81

Table4. *Number of Evaluations / Generation, for varying N_{max}, α and $\sigma = 0.1$ fixed*

And for $\sigma = 1.0$:

N_{max}	α					
	0	0.025	0.05	0.1	0.2	error
2	1.412	1.440	1.427	1.401	1.480	+/- 0.0310
3	1.154	1.135	1.163	1.183	1.264	+/- 0.0269
4	0.9820	1.004	1.0124	1.043	1.095	+/- 0.0219
5	0.8837	0.9122	0.9084	0.9198	0.9925	+/- 0.0195
7	0.7756	0.7667	0.7853	0.7903	0.8730	+/- 0.0183

Table5. *Distance from Optimum, $f_\infty = R_\infty^2$, for varying N_{max}, α and $\sigma = 1.0$ fixed*

N_{max}	α				
	0	0.025	0.05	0.1	0.2
2	28	26.35	25.58	24.33	21.80
3	42	38.47	36.95	34.48	31.02
4	56	48.78	45.90	42.02	36.17
5	70	58.88	54.88	48.93	40.77
7	98	77.98	71.42	61.87	49.29

Table6. *Number of Evaluations / Generation, , for varying N_{max}, α and $\sigma = 1.0$ fixed*

The effect of the tests on the overall computing time may be illustrated by plotting the distance from the optimum versus evaluations during the entire run. Figure 4 shows one example in the case of $N_{\max} = 5$. For $N_{\max}$ less than five the effect will become smaller for $N_{\max} = 7$ it is larger.

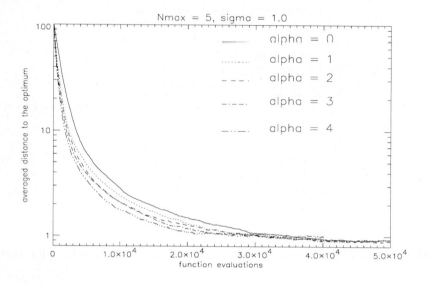

Figure4. Distance from the optimum as a function of the total sum of evaluations, here for $\sigma = 1.0$, $N_{\max} = 5$

In these experiments the step sizes of the individuals in the genotype space and in the fitness space are due to the crossover and mutation process and the transformation of these changes according to the used Gray code. The benefits of the testing procedure relies on the early recognition of – most probably – bad individuals. Besides in parameter optimization by Evolution Strategies the effect of the search operators and the code on the step–size in fitness space, i.e. the causality of the evolutionary process [10], seems often very hard to analyze. Therefore the used set of {search operators; genotype–phenotype mapping} may yield large jumps in fitness–space. As an explicit self–adaptation of the search operators in GA is rarely used, the mutation operator will produce large jumps in fitness–space during the entire optimization run. This is inevitable and leads to individuals which are easily recognized as being insufficient. So if one can not make the step–size in fitness space smaller one can still avoid to evaluate bad individuals too often.

The number of evaluations that can be spared depends on the noise distribution and the distribution of the offsprings' fitness values. This was additionally tested by studying simulations with an increased mutation probability. So the distribution of the offsprings' fitness values was changed (it was made broader with respect to the noise distribution) and the number of evaluations that could be spared increased.

5 Conclusion

In real world applications evolutionary algorithms will often have to cope with noise and their robustness against noise is possibly one of their major advantages. Theoretical considerations [6] and experimental work [8] have shown that increasing the size of the parental population and averaging over several fitness evaluations help to manage fluctuations on the fitness function. This produces computational costs. The main idea behind this work is the fact that a reduction of noise is not necessary for every individual but only for the best ones. The decision which ones are the best is facilitated by averaging but possibly a small number of evaluations is enough for that decision. The results show that this simple idea can reduce the number of function evaluations significantly. There are certainly some algorithmic problems, for example if the order between two individuals can not be decided upon, which one is to be evaluated anew. Unfortunately the method also reveals a theoretical problem: Working on a real problem one can chose a combination out of several methods for dealing with noise, such as increasing the population size, allowing more evaluations or taking a different test, etc., but nobody can tell the best way.

References

1. S. Rana, L.D. Whitley, and R. Cogswell. Searching in the Presence of Noise. In *Parallel Problem Solving from Nature,4*, pages 198 – 207. Springer Verlag, 1996.
2. H. Abarbanel, R. Brown, J. Sidorowich, and L. Tsimring. Analysis of observed chaotic data in physical systems. *Rev. Mod. Phys.*, 65:1331 – 1392, 1993.
3. Simon Haykin. *Neural Networks*. Macmillan College Publishing Company, New York, 1994.
4. Thomas Bäck. *Evolutionary Algorithms in Theory and Practice*. Oxford University Press, 1996.
5. Ingo Rechenberg. *Evolutionsstrategie '94*. Friedrich Frommann Holzboog Verlag, Stuttgart, 1994.
6. Hans-Georg Beyer. Toward a Theory of Evolution Strategies: Some Asymptotical Results from $(1,^+ \lambda)$–theory. *Evolutionary Computation*, 1(2):165 – 188, 1993.
7. B. Miller and D. Goldberg. Genetic Algorithms, Selection Schemes, and the Varying Effects of Noise. *Evolutionary Computation*, 4(2):113 – 131, 1997.
8. Ulrich Hammel and Thomas Bäck. Evolution Strategies on Noisy Functions How to Improve Convergence Properties. In Y. Davidor, H.P. Schwefel, and R. Manner, editors, *Parallel Problem Solving from Nature,3*, pages 159 – 168. Springer Verlag, 1994.
9. Herbert Büning and Götz Trenkler. *Nichtparametrische statistische Methoden*. Walter de Gruyter, Berlin, 1994.
10. Bernhard Sendhoff, Martin Kreutz, and Werner von Seelen. A condition for the genotype–phenotype mapping: Causality. In Thomas Bäck, editor, *International Conference on Genetic Algorithms*. Morgan Kaufman, July 1997.

Multi-criteria and Constrained Optimization

Solving Binary Constraint Satisfaction Problems Using Evolutionary Algorithms with an Adaptive Fitness Function

A.E. Eiben[1,2], J.I. van Hemert[1], E. Marchiori[1,2] and A.G. Steenbeek[2]

[1] Dept. of Comp. Science, Leiden University, P.O. Box 9512, 2300 RA Leiden, NL
[2] CWI, P.O. Box 94079, 1090 GB Amsterdam, NL

Abstract. This paper presents a comparative study of Evolutionary Algorithms (EAs) for Constraint Satisfaction Problems (CSPs). We focus on EAs where fitness is based on penalization of constraint violations and the penalties are adapted during the execution. Three different EAs based on this approach are implemented. For highly connected constraint networks, the results provide further empirical support to the theoretical prediction of the phase transition in binary CSPs.

1 Introduction

Evolutionary algorithms are usually considered to be ill-suited for solving constraint satisfaction problems. Namely, the traditional search operators (mutation and recombination) are 'blind' to the constraints, that is, parents satisfying a certain constraint may very well result in an offspring that violates it. Furthermore, while EAs have a 'basic instinct' to optimize, there is no objective function in a CSP – just a set of constraints to be satisfied. Despite such general arguments, in the last years there have been reports on quite a few EAs for solving CSPs having a satisfactory performance. Roughly speaking, these EAs can be divided into two categories: those based on exploiting heuristic information on the constraint network [6, 14, 21, 22], and those using a fitness function (penalty function) that is adapted during the search [2, 4, 5, 7, 9, 10, 17, 18]. In this paper we investigate three methods from the second category: the co-evolutionary method by Paredis [17], the heuristic-based microgenetic algorithm by Dozier et al [4], and the EA with stepwise adaptation of weights by Eiben et al. [10]. We implement three specific evolutionary algorithms based on the corresponding methods, called COE, SAW, and MID, respectively, and compare them on a test suite consisting of randomly generated binary CSPs with finite domains.

The results of the experiments are used to assess empirically the relative performance of the three different methods within the same category, thereby providing suggestions as to which implementation of the same general idea is the most promising. We use randomly generated problem instances for the experiments, where the hardness of the problem instances is influenced by two parameters: constraint density and constraint tightness. By running experiments on 25 different combinations of these parameters we gain detailed feedback on EA behavior and can validate theoretical predictions on the location of the phase transition. In summary, on the 625 problem instances considered, MID performs better than the other two EAs with respect to the success rate (i.e., how many times a solution is found). The success rate of SAW is slightly worse on harder problem instances corresponding to higher constraint density and tightness, while the performance of COE is rather unsatisfactory when compared with the performance of one of the other two algorithms. Concerning the computational effort, it is worthwhile to note that SAW requires fewer fitness evaluations to find a solution than the other two EAs. The obtained results show that for higher constraint density and tightness, all three EAs are unable to find a solution. This behavior is in accordance with theoretical predictions on the phase transition in binary CSPs (cf. [23]).

The paper is organized as follows: the next section describes the notion of constrained problems and it deals more specifically with random binary CSPs. In Section 3 various evolutionary approaches for solving CSPs are discussed and the three EAs COE, SAW, and MID are introduced. In Section 4 the experimental setup is given, followed by the results. Finally, in Section 5 we summarize our conclusions and we give some hints on future work.

2   Constraint satisfaction problems

A *constraint satisfaction problem* (CSP) is a pair $\langle S, \phi \rangle$, where S is a free search space and ϕ is a formula (Boolean function on S). A *solution of a constraint satisfaction problem* is an $s \in S$ with $\phi(s) = true$. Usually a CSP is stated as a problem of finding an instantiation of variables $v_1, \ldots, v_n$ within the finite domains $D_1, \ldots, D_n$ such that constraints (relations) $c_1, \ldots, c_m$ hold. The formula ϕ is then the conjunction of the given constraints. One may be interested in one, some or all solutions, or only in the existence of a solution. We restrict our discussion to finding one solution.

More specifically, we consider binary constraint satisfaction problems over finite domains, where constraints act between pairs of variables. This is not restrictive since any CSP can be reduced to a binary CSP by means of a suitable transformation which involves the definition of more complex domains (cf. [24]). A class of random binary CSPs can be specified by means of four parameters $\langle n, m, d, t \rangle$, where n is the number of variables, m is the uniform domain size, d is the probability that a constraint exists between two variables, and t is the probability of a conflict between two values across a constraint. CSPs exhibit a *phase transition* when a parameter is varied. At the phase transition, problems change from being relatively easy to solve (i.e., almost all problems have many solutions) to being very easy to prove unsolvable (i.e., almost all problems have no solutions). The term *mushy region* is used to indicate that region where the probability that a problem is soluble changes from almost zero to almost one. Within the mushy region, problems are in general difficult to solve or to prove unsolvable. An important issue in the study of binary CSPs is to identify those problem instances which are very hard to solve [3]. Recent theoretical investigations ([23, 26]) allow one to predict where the hardest problem instances should occur. Williams and Hogg in [26] develop a theory that predicts that the phase transition occurs when per variable there are a critical number of nogoods (i.e., of conflicts between that variable and all other ones)[3]. Smith in [23] conjectures that the phase transition occurs when problems have, on average, just one solution.

An experimental investigation with a complete algorithm (i.e., an algorithm that finds a solution or detects unsatisfiability) based on forward checking and on conflict-directed backjumping, is given by Prosser in [20], which provides empirical support to the theoretical prediction given in [23, 26] for higher density/tightness of the constraint networks. We will see that this trend is supported also by our experimental investigation on three specific evolutionary algorithms for CSPs. Being stochastic techniques, EAs are in general unable to detect inconsistency, so our analysis of hard instances for these algorithms will necessarily be incomplete. However, we will see that the success rate of the three EAs on the considered problems provides a neat indication of which (d, t) regions contain hard problems for these EAs, indicating a phase transition which is in accordance with the one identified using the theoretical prediction in [23, 26] for relatively high values of d and t.

3 Constraint handling by penalties in EAs

There are several ways to handle constraints in an EA. At a high conceptual level we can distinguish two cases, depending on whether they are handled *indirectly* or *directly*. Indirect constraint handling means that the constraints are incorporated in the fitness function f such that the optimality of f implies that the constraints are satisfied. Then the optimization power of the EA can be used to find a solution. By direct constraint handling here we mean that the constraints are left as they are and 'something' is done in the EA to enforce them. Some commonly used options are repair mechanisms, decoding algorithms and using special reproduction operators [8, 15].

In the case of indirect constraint handling a lot of different fitness functions can satisfy the above requirement. A common way of defining a suitable fitness function is based on using penalties, usually penalizing the violation of each constraint and making the fitness function (to be minimized) the sum of such penalties. In the simplest case, each constraint violation scores one penalty point, hence the fitness function is just counting the number of violated constraints. A weighted sum, however, allows more appropriate measurement of quality, for instance harder constraints can be given higher weights. This would give a relatively high reward when satisfying them, thus directing the EAs attention to such constraints. Natural as it may sound, this idea is not so trivial to implement. The two main problems are that 1) estimating constraint hardness a priori for setting the weight appropriately may require substantial problem specific knowledge or computational efforts, 2) the appropriate weights may change

---

[3] Note that the expected number of nogoods per variable is $dtm^2(n-1)$.

during the problem solving process. A possible treatment for both problems is to have the algorithm setting the weights (penalties) itself and re-adjusting the weights during the search process.

In this paper we investigate three evolutionary algorithms that represent constraints by penalties and update the penalty function during the run. We retrieve the specification of these EAs from the literature and maintain the original parameter settings, whenever possible. Therefore, here we describe only the main features of the algorithms and refer to the cited articles for further details.

The first EA we consider is a heuristic-based microgenetic algorithm introduced by Dozier et al in [4]. It is called microgenetic because it employs a small population. Moreover, it incorporates heuristics in the reproduction mechanism and in the fitness function in order to direct the search towards better individuals. More precisely, the EA we implement works on a pool of 8 individuals. It uses a roulette-wheel based selection mechanism, and the steady state reproduction mechanism where at each generation an offspring is created by mutating a specific gene of the selected chromosome, called pivot gene, and that offspring replaces the worse individual of the actual population. Roughly, the fitness function of a chromosome is determined by adding a suitable penalty term to the number of constraint violations the chromosome is involved in. The penalty term depends on the set of breakouts[4] whose values occur in the chromosome. The set of breakouts is initially empty and it is modified during the execution by increasing the weights of breakouts and by adding new breakouts according to the technique used in the Iterative Descent Method ([16]). Therefore we have named this algorithm MID, standing for Microgenetic Iterative Descent.

The basic concept behind the *co-evolutionary approach* is the idea of having two populations constantly in battle with each other. This approach has been tested by Paredis on different problems, such as neural net learning [18], constraint satisfaction [17, 18] and searching for cellular automata that solve the density classification task [19]. The evolutionary algorithm used in the experiments, denoted as COE, is a steady-state EA, it has two populations, one is called the *solution population* and the other is called the *constraint population*. The fitness of an individual in either of these populations is based on a history of encounters. An *encounter* means that an individual from the constraint population is matched with an individual from the solution population. If the constraint is not violated by the solution, the individual from the solution population gets a point. If the constraint is violated the individual from the constraint population gets a point. The fitness of an individual is the amount of points it has obtained in the last 25 encounters. Every generation of the EA, 20 encounters are executed by repeatedly selecting an individual from each population. Then two parents are selected using linear ranked selection, with a bias of 1.5, as described by Whitley [25]. The two parents are crossed using a two-point reduced surrogate parents crossover, this makes sure that the children are different when

---

[4] A breakout consists of two parts: 1) a pair of values that violates a constraint; 2) a weight associated to that pair.

the parents differ. The two resulting children are then mutated using adaptive mutation. This means every allele has a chance of 0.001 of mutating, unless the two children are the same then the chance is increased to 0.01. The size of the constraint population is determined by the amount of constraints in the problem, the solution population however has a fixed size of 50 individuals.

The third EA we are studying is the so-called SAW-ing EA. The Stepwise Adaptation of Weights (SAW) mechanism has been introduced by Eiben and van der Hauw [9] as an improved version of the weight adaptation mechanism of Eiben, Raué and Ruttkay [6, 7]. In several comparisons the SAW-ing EA proved to be a superior technique for solving specific CSPs [1, 10]. The basic idea behind the SAW-ing mechanism is that constraints that are not satisfied after a certain number of steps must be hard, thus must be given a high weight (penalty). The realization of this idea constitutes of initializing the weights at 1 and re-setting them by adding a value $\triangle w$ after a certain period. Re-setting is only applied to those constraints that are violated by the best individual of the given population. Earlier studies indicated the good performance of a simple (1+1) scheme, using a singleton population and exclusively mutation to create offspring. The representation is based on a permutation of the problem variables; a permutation is transformed to a partial instantiation by a simple decoder that considers the variables in the order they occur in the chromosome and assigns the first possible domain value to that variable. If no value is possible without introducing constraint violation, the variable is left uninstantiated. Uninstantiated variables are, then, penalized and the fitness of the chromosome (a permutation) is the total of these penalties. Let us note that penalizing uninstantiated variables is a much rougher estimation of solution quality than penalizing violated constraints. Yet, this option worked well for graph coloring, therefore we test it here without much modification.

4 Experimental Setup and Results

To generate a test suite we have used a problem instance generator that was loosely based on the generator of Gerry Dozier [2]. The generator first calculates the number of constraints that will be produced using the equation $\frac{n(n-1)}{2} \cdot d$. It then starts producing constraints by randomly choosing two variables and assigning a constraint between them. When a constraint is assigned between variable v_i and v_j, a table of conflicting values is generated. To produce a conflict two values are chosen randomly, one for the first and one for the second variable. When no conflict is present between the two values for the variables, a conflict is produced. The number of conflicts in this table is determined in advance by the equation $m(v_i) \cdot m(v_j) \cdot t$ where $m(v_i)$ is the domain size of variable i.

We have considered random binary constraints with $n = 15$ variables and uniform domains of $m = 15$ elements. These values are common in the empirical study of (random) CSPs. Later on we will discuss the effect of the varying of the number of variables. Each algorithm has been tested on the same 625 problem instances: for each combination of density d and tightness t (25 in total), we have generated 25 instances and executed 10 independent runs on each instance. The algorithm performance is evaluated by two measures. The *Success Rate* (SR) is the percentage of instances where a solution has been found. The *Average number of Evaluations to Solution* (AES) is the number of fitness evaluations, i.e. the number of newly generated candidate solutions, in *successful* runs. Note, that if a run did not find a solution, the number of steps to a solution is not defined, consequently if for a certain combination of d and t SR $= 0$, then the AES is not defined. The specific details of the three EAs used in this comparison are mentioned in the previous section. Recall, that each variant is allowed to generate 100000 candidate solutions, i.e., the algorithms terminate if a solution is found or the limit of 100000 is reached.

density	alg.	tightness				
		0.1	0.3	0.5	0.7	0.9
0.1	COE	1.00 (3)	1.00 (15)	1.00 (449)	1.00 (2789)	0.62 (30852)
	MID	1.00 (1)	1.00 (4)	1.00 (21)	1.00 (87)	0.96 (2923)
	SAW	1.00 (1)	1.00 (1)	1.00 (2)	1.00 (9)	0.64 (1159)
0.3	COE	1.00 (96)	1.00 (11778)	0.18 (43217)	0.00 (-)	0.00 (-)
	MID	1.00 (3)	1.00 (50)	1.00 (323)	0.52 (32412)	0.00 (-)
	SAW	1.00 (1)	1.00 (2)	1.00 (36)	0.23 (21281)	0.00 (-)
0.5	COE	1.00 (1547)	0.08 (39679)	0.00 (-)	0.00 (-)	0.00 (-)
	MID	1.00 (10)	1.00 (177)	0.90 (26792)	0.00 (-)	0.00 (-)
	SAW	1.00 (1)	1.00 (8)	0.74 (10722)	0.00 (-)	0.00 (-)
0.7	COE	1.00 (9056)	0.00 (-)	0.00 (-)	0.00 (-)	0.00 (-)
	MID	1.00 (20)	1.00 (604)	0.00 (-)	0.00 (-)	0.00 (-)
	SAW	1.00 (1)	1.00 (73)	0.00 (-)	0.00 (-)	0.00 (-)
0.9	COE	0.912 (28427)	0.00 (-)	0.00 (-)	0.00 (-)	0.00 (-)
	MID	1.00 (33)	1.00 (8136)	0.00 (-)	0.00 (-)	0.00 (-)
	SAW	1.00 (1)	1.00 (3848)	0.00 (-)	0.00 (-)	0.00 (-)

Table 1. Sucess rates and the corresponding AES values (within brackets) for the co-evolutionary GA (COE), the Micro-genetic algorithm with Iterative Descent (MID), and the SAW-ing GA (SAW)

Table 1 summarizes the results of our experiments. Considering the success rate it is clear that MID performs equally or better than the other two EAs in all classes of instances. SAW has a lower SR than MID on harder problem instances, namely for the classes $(d = 0.1, t = 0.9)$, $(d = 0.3, t = 0.7)$, and $(d = 0.5, t = 0.5)$, but on two of these three $((d = 0.1, t = 0.9)$ and $(d = 0.5, t = 0.5))$ it is more than twice as fast as MID, while being only approximately 30% less successful. The performance of COE is rather unsatisfactory also in relatively 'easy' classes, like for example the one characterized by $(d = 0.7, t = 0.3)$.

These observations can be explained by observing that MID employs a strong heuristic technique based on hill-climbing *and* an adaptive fitness function, while SAW and COE try to bias the search towards harder constraints in a more naive way. Recall that the version of SAW we are testing here considers only the uninstantiated variables, not the violated constraints, as the basis of the fitness function. This gives a very rough quality estimate as compared to the constraint based penalties of MID, i.e. using n variables instead of $\frac{n(n-1)}{2} \cdot d$ constraints. In this light, the exhibited performance of SAW can be seen as remarkably good. The method used in COE for dealing with harder constraints does not prove to be very effective. Concerning the computational effort (AES), it is worth noting that SAW usually requires much less evaluations to find a solution than the other two EAs. A possible reason for this fact could lay in the decoding mechanism SAW is using. Simple and unbiased as this decoder may seem, it could represent a successful heuristic.

The results of the experiments reported in Table 1 consider $n = 15$ variables and $m = 15$ domain size. It is interesting to investigate how the results scale up when we vary the number of variables n. The question of scaling up is interesting already for its own sake, but here we also have a special reason to look at it. In particular, measuring the performance of EAs by the AES is not as unbiased as it may look at the first glance. Namely, the use of the hill-climbing heuristic in MID, and the efforts spend on decoding in SAW are important for their good performance, but are invisible for the measure AES. In order to obtain a more fair comparison, we look at the steepness of the AES curve when increasing the problem size (n). We do not consider the CPU times, since it is much dependent on implementational details, network load, etc. Figure 1 illustrates how the performance of MID and SAW is affected by increasing n, when the other parameters are set to $m = 15$, $d = 0.3$, and $t = 0.3$. (Note that we do not consider COE because of its poor performance.) We consider values of n ranging from 10 till 40 with step 5 and observe that increasing the number of variables does not affect the success rates in this range of n values. The number of iterations that are needed in order to find a solution, however, is heavily affected and for both algorithms it exhibits a super-linear growth. Recall, that the exact heights of the data points on the curves are not relevant, it is the growth rate we are looking at. The two curves are similar in this respect, although up to $n = 35$ SAW is growing at a visibly slower rate. However, since the two curves are crossing at the end, we do not want to suggest a better scale-up behavior for either algorithms.

Considering the results in Table 1 from the point of view of the problem instances, we can observe success rates SR $= 1$ in the upper left corner, while SR $= 0$ is typical in the lower right corner, separated by a 'diagonal' indicating the mushy region. Technically, for higher constraint density and tightness, all three EAs are unable to find any solution. This is not surprising, because higher density and tightness yield problems that are almost always unsatisfiable. An other interesting aspect of the behavior of these algorithms is for which problem instances their performance rapidly degrade. The most difficult CSPs seem to

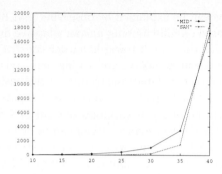

Fig. 1. Scale-up values for the SAW and MID algorithms.

start in the classes where $d \geq 0.3$ and $t = 0.7$, and where $d \geq 0.5$ and $t = 0.5$. These results are in accordance with theoretical predictions of the phase transition for binary CSP problems ([23, 26]). In fact, according to e.g. Smith prediction, for $n = m = 15$, the phase transition for binary CSPs is located to $t_{crit} = 0.725$ for $d = 0.3$, and to $t_{crit} = 0.539$ for $d = 0.5$.

We conclude this section with some observations on the behavior of the fitness function during the execution of these EAs. Figure 2 shows one typical run of each of the two winning methods SAW and MID, plotting the fitness of the best individual in the population during a run. The course of the fitness function in a typical run of MID suggests that the in the first generations a relatively good solution is found, where only few constraints remain to be satisfied. Then the fitness starts to go up and down by the adaptive mechanism on breakouts, and finally it jumps to zero (a solution). For SAW we see the penalty growing in the beginning, because of the increasing weights. Seemingly things get only worse, but then a solution is reached in just a few steps. A plausible interpretation of this behavior is that the algorithm is first looking for well-suited weights that make the problem 'easy', and solves the resulting problem (that is optimizes the resulting 'easy' function) afterwards.

5 Conclusion

In this paper we have performed a comparative experimental study on three EAs for solving CSPs, which have the common feature of employing an adaptive fitness function in order to direct the search.

Current work concerns investigating the performance of SAW if the same representation is used as in MID, i.e. integers instead of permutations, and if the fitness function is based on constraint violations instead of uninstantiated variables. Recall, that MID keeps the penalty term on violated constraints identical during the search and is adapting the penalty term on breakouts only. SAW and MID can thus be easily combined, if SAW-ing is applied to the first penalty term

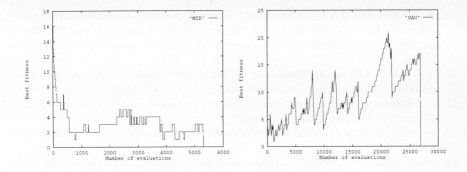

Fig. 2. Fitness (to be minimized) of the best individual in the population during a run of `MID` (left) and `SAW` (right).

and the `MID` mechanism is used to tune the breakouts during the run.

Future work will also involve comparison of EAs of the second group mentioned in the Introduction, those based on using information on the given constraint network.

References

1. Th. Bäck, A.E. Eiben, and M.E. Vink. A superior evolutionary algorithm for 3-SAT. In D. Waagen N. Saravanan and A.E. Eiben, editors, *Proceedings of the 7th Annual Conference on Evolutionary Programming*, Lecture Notes in Computer Science. Springer, 1998. in press.
2. J. Bowen and G. Dozier. Solving constraint satisfaction problems using a genetic/systematic search hybride that realizes when to quit. In Eshelman [11], pages 122–129.
3. P. Cheeseman, B. Kanefsky, and W.M. Taylor. Where the really hard problems are. In *Proceedings of the 12th International Conference on Artificial Intelligence*, pages 331–337. Morgan Kaufmann, 1991.
4. G. Dozier, J. Bowen, and D. Bahler. Solving small and large constraint satisfaction problems using a heuristic-based microgenetic algorithms. In IEEE [12], pages 306–311.
5. G. Dozier, J. Bowen, and D. Bahler. Solving randomly generated constraint satisfaction problems using a micro-evolutionary hybrid that evolves a population of hill-climbers. In *Proceedings of the 2nd IEEE Conference on Evolutionary Computation*, pages 614–619. IEEE Press, 1995.
6. A.E. Eiben, P.-E. Raué, and Zs. Ruttkay. Constrained problems. In L. Chambers, editor, *Practical Handbook of Genetic Algorithms*, pages 307–365. CRC Press, 1995.
7. A.E. Eiben and Zs. Ruttkay. Self-adaptivity for constraint satisfaction: Learning penalty functions. In *Proceedings of the 3rd IEEE Conference on Evolutionary Computation*, pages 258–261. IEEE Press, 1996.
8. A.E. Eiben and Zs. Ruttkay. Constraint satisfaction problems. In Th. Bäck, D. Fogel, and M. Michalewicz, editors, *Handbook of Evolutionary Algorithms*, pages C5.7:1–C5.7:8. IOP Publishing Ltd. and Oxford University Press, 1997.

9. A.E. Eiben and J.K. van der Hauw. Adaptive penalties for evolutionary graph-coloring. In J.-K. Hao, E. Lutton, E. Ronald, M. Schoenauer, and D. Snyers, editors, *Artificial Evolution'97*, number 1363 in LNCS, pages 95–106. Springer, Berlin, 1997.

10. A.E. Eiben, J.K. van der Hauw, and J.I. van Hemert. Graph coloring with adaptive evolutionary algorithms. *Journal of Heuristics*, 4:25–46, 1998.

11. L.J. Eshelman, editor. *Proceedings of the 6th International Conference on Genetic Algorithms*. Morgan Kaufmann, 1995.

12. *Proceedings of the 1st IEEE Conference on Evolutionary Computation*. IEEE Press, 1994.

13. *Proceedings of the 4th IEEE Conference on Evolutionary Computation*. IEEE Press, 1997.

14. E. Marchiori. Combining constraint processing and genetic algorithms for constraint satisfaction problems. In Th. Bäck, editor, *Proceedings of the 7th International Conference on Genetic Algorithms*, pages 330–337. Morgan Kaufmann, 1997.

15. Z. Michalewicz and M. Michalewicz. Pro-life versus pro-choice strategies in evolutionary computation techniques. In Palaniswami M., Attikiouzel Y., Marks R.J., Fogel D., and Fukuda T., editors, *Computational Intelligence: A Dynamic System Perspective*, pages 137–151. IEEE Press, 1995.

16. P. Morris. The breakout method for escaping from local minima. In *Proceedings of the 11th National Conference on Artificial Intelligence, AAAI-93*, pages 40–45. AAAI Press/The MIT Press, 1993.

17. J. Paredis. Co-evolutionary constraint satisfaction. In Y. Davidor, H.-P. Schwefel, and R. Männer, editors, *Proceedings of the 3rd Conference on Parallel Problem Solving from Nature*, number 866 in Lecture Notes in Computer Science, pages 46–56. Springer-Verlag, 1994.

18. J. Paredis. Co-evolutionary computation. *Artificial Life*, 2(4):355–375, 1995.

19. J. Paredis. Coevolving cellular automata: Be aware of the red queen. In Thomas Bäck, editor, *Proceedings of the Seventh International Conference on Genetic Algorithms (ICGA97)*, San Francisco, CA, 1997. Morgan Kaufmann.

20. P. Prosser. An empirical study of phase transitions in binary constraint satisfaction problems. *Artificial Intelligence*, 81:81–109, 1996.

21. M.C. Riff-Rojas. Using the knowledge of the constraint network to design an evolutionary algorithm that solves CSP. In IEEE [13], pages 279–284.

22. M.C. Riff-Rojas. Evolutionary search guided by the constraint network to solve CSP. In IEEE [13], pages 337–348.

23. B.M. Smith. Phase transition and the mushy region in constraint satisfaction problems. In A. G. Cohn, editor, *Proceedings of the 11th European Conference on Artificial Intelligence*, pages 100–104. Wiley, 1994.

24. E. Tsang. *Foundation of Constraint Satisfaction*. Academic Press, 1993.

25. D. Whitley. The GENITOR algorithm and selection pressure: Why rank-based allocation of reproductive trials is best. In J. David Schaffer, editor, *Proceedings of the Third International Conference on Genetic Algorithms (ICGA'89)*, pages 116–123, San Mateo, California, 1989. Morgan Kaufmann Publishers, Inc.

26. C.P. Williams and T. Hogg. Exploiting the deep structure of constraint problems. *Artificial Intelligence*, 70:73–117, 1994.

Varying Fitness Functions in Genetic Algorithms : Studying the Rate of Increase of the Dynamic Penalty Terms

S. Kazarlis and V. Petridis

Department of Electrical and Computer Engineering, Faculty of Engineering,
Aristotle University of Thessaloniki, 54006, Greece

Abstract. In this paper we present a promising technique that enhances the efficiency of GAs, when they are applied to constrained optimisation problems. According to this technique, the problem constraints are included in the fitness function as penalty terms, that vary during the GA evolution, facilitating thus the location of the global optimum and the avoidance of local optima. Moreover we proceed to test the effect that the rate of change in the fitness function has on GA performance. The tests are performed on two well-known real-world optimisation problems : the Cutting Stock problem and the Unit Commitment problem. Comparative results are reported.

0. Introduction

In real-world optimisation problems together with the optimisation of the problem's objective function there is usually a number of constraints that must also be satisfied. GAs unfortunately do not incorporate a default mechanism for handling such constraints. This deficiency is alleviated by a number of methods proposed in the literature [5], [6], [7], [9], [11], [12], [13]. The most important of these methods is the Penalty Assignment method [5], according to which penalty terms are added to the fitness function that depend on the constraint violation of the specific solution. In this way the invalid solutions are considered as valid but they are penalised according to the degree of violation of the constraints. For a minimisation problem the resulting fitness function is of the form:

$$Q(S) = O(S) + P(S) \tag{1}$$

where $O(S)$ is the objective function to be minimised and $P(S)$ is the penalty function that depends on the degree of constraint violation introduced by solution S.

This method is probably the most commonly used method for handling problem constraints with GAs and is implemented in many variations. However, it exhibits the problem of building a suitable penalty function for the specific problem, based on the violation of the problem's constraints, that will lead the GA to avoid infeasible solutions and converge to a feasible (and hopefully the optimal) one. This problem arises from the fact that high penalty values generally increase the complexity of the fitness function and the resulting search hypersurface, while low penalty values increase the possibility for the GA to converge to an infeasible solution.

In order to enhance the efficiency of the GAs in such real-world constrained optimisation problems we have introduced a new technique : the Varying Fitness Function Technique (VFF) [7], [11], [12]. According to this technique the penalty terms are not static functions of the amount of constraint violation but are dynamic functions of the constraint violation as well as the "evolution time", expressed by the generation index. Relating the penalties with time it is possible to construct a penalty function that relaxes the constraints at the beginning of the evolution process, simplifying thus the fitness landscape, and increases them later to separate the areas of valid and invalid solutions. This dynamic landscape facilitates the GA search in avoiding the local traps and locating the global optimum. For a minimisation problem a general Varying Fitness Function could be of the form:

$$Q_v(S,g) = O(S) + P_v(S,g) \tag{2}$$

where $O(S)$ is the objective function to be minimised and $P_v(S,g)$ is the varying penalty function that depends on the degree of constraint violation introduced by solution S and the generation index g.

The properties of the dynamic penalty function seem to be critical to the success of the VFF technique. In order to extract useful conclusions for the effectiveness of the VFF technique and its dependencies upon the shape of the increasing penalty function, we have tested its performance using seven different penalty functions on two different real-world problems.

The problems chosen are : (a) the Cutting Stock problem, that consists in cutting a number of predefined two-dimensional shapes out of a piece of stock material with minimum waste [2], [4], [11], [12], [15] and (b) the Unit Commitment problem, that consists in the determination of the optimum operating schedule of a number of electric power production units, in order to meet the forecasted demand over a short term period, with the minimum total operating cost [7], [8], [12], [16].

An introduction to the VFF technique is provided in Section 1. Section 2 describes the chosen penalty functions for the comparison tests. Sections 3 and 4 describe the two optimisation problems and the corresponding simulation tests performed, respectively. Finally conclusions are presented in Section 5.

1. The Varying Fitness Function technique

The VFF technique consists in adjusting the penalty factors dynamically during the search procedure. At the beginning of the GA search the penalty factors are kept low in order to simplify the search and give the GA the opportunity to explore the search space more efficiently. As the evolution proceeds the penalty factors increase according to an increasing penalty function, so that at the end of the run they reach appropriately large values, which result in the separation of valid solutions from invalid ones. This technique facilitates the GA to locate the general area of the global optimum at the early stages of the search. As the search proceeds, the penalty factors increase and the GA adapts to the changing search hypersurface. Near the end of the run, when the penalty factors reach their appropriately large values, the final search hypersurface is formed, preventing thus the GA from converging to invalid solutions.

In a constrained minimisation problem the normal (static) fitness function, built according to the Penalty Assignment Method, could be of the form:

$$Q(S) = O(S) + P(S) = O(S) + A \cdot \sum_{i=1}^{NC} (\delta_i \cdot w_i \cdot \Phi_i(d_i(S))) + B) \cdot \delta_S \qquad (3)$$

where : A is a "severity" factor, NC is the number of the problem constraints, δ_i is a binary factor (δ_i =1 if constraint i is violated and δ_i =0 otherwise), w_i is a "weight" factor for constraint i, $d_i(S)$ is a measure of the degree of violation of constraint i introduced by S, $\Phi_i(.)$ is a function of this measure, B is a penalty threshold factor and δ_S is a binary factor (δ_S =1 if S is infeasible and δ_S =0 otherwise).

In a Varying Fitness Function scheme the static penalty factor must be replaced with a function depending on the evolution time (i.e. the generation index). So, the corresponding Varying Fitness Function $Q_v(S,g)$ could be of the following form :

$$Q_v(S,g) = O(S) + P_v(S,g) = O(S) + V(g) \cdot (A \cdot \sum_{i=1}^{NC} (\delta_i \cdot w_i \cdot \Phi_i(d_i(S))) + B) \cdot \delta_S)$$

$$(4)$$

where $V(g)$ is an increasing function of g in the range (0..1).

2. Penalty Functions

The shape of the function $V(g)$ determines the rate of change in the penalty term of the fitness function. Linear functions have been used in the past [7], [11], [12] of the form :

$$V(g) = g/G \qquad (5)$$

where G is the total number of generations the GA is allowed to run.

In this paper seven shapes for the function $V(g)$ have been tested while all the other quality function parameters have been kept constant. The chosen functions are designed for an arbitrary run limit of G generations :

1) Exponential function 1: $V(g)=1-e^{-10 \cdot g/G}$ 5) Cubic function: $V(g)=(g/G)^3$
2) Exponential function 2: $V(g)=1-e^{-5 \cdot g/G}$ 6) Quartic function: $V(g)=(g/G)^4$
3) Linear function : $V(g)=g/G$ 7) 5-step function: $V(g) = int(5 \cdot g/G)/5$
4) Square function : $V(g)=(g/G)^2$ (where int is truncating the decimal part)

3. Simulation tests on the Cutting Stock problem

The problem addressed in this section belongs to the category of Cutting and Packing problems [2], [4], [11], [12], [15]. The common objective of such problems is the determination of an optimal arrangement of a set of predefined objects (pieces) so that they fit within a container or stock material with minimum waste. Problems of this category can be found in many industries such as the clothing and the furniture industry. The specific problem addressed in this section is a two-dimensional Cutting Stock problem [11], [12]. It consists in finding the best position for a set of pieces or shapes within a large piece of material with standard width W and infinite length so as to minimise the material waste. Rotation of the shapes, in any angle, is not allowed. As "material waste" we define the area of material not covered by the shapes, within the bounds of the smallest rectangle that contains the shapes (bounding rectangle). Overlapping of shapes is of course prohibited, and eventually this is the constraint of this problem.

Figure 1. The optimum arrangement of the 13 shapes of the two-dimensional Cutting Stock problem.

In the simulation tests we used a 13-shapes problem containing convex and non-convex shapes. The 13 shapes were chosen so as to leave no material waste in the optimum solution (Figure 1).

In order to represent a solution as a binary string we first considered a x and a y coordinate for each shape, with the origin taken at the bottom left corner of the material. So a single solution is described by 13 pairs of shape coordinates (x_i, y_i) $i=1..13$ which represent a specific cutting pattern. A solution can be considered as a point in a $2x13 = 26$ - dimensional space. A 10-bit integer is used to encode a single coordinate, resulting in a genotype string of $2x10x13 = 260$ bits in length, producing a search space of 2^{260} or $1.853x10^{78}$ different solutions.

For the construction of the quality function, instead of measuring directly the area of material waste, we chose to build a different objective function that embodies gradients towards the optimum :

$$O(S) = \sum_{i=1}^{13} ((x_i \cdot A_i) + y_i) \qquad (6)$$

where A_i is the area of shape i. This function creates a gradient towards positions with small x and y values, with more emphasis to the x coordinate. The constraint of no shape overlapping is incorporated into the quality function by a penalty term added to it. Thus, the following quality function is formed:

$$Q(S) = \sum_{i=1}^{13} ((x_i \cdot A_i) + y_i) + V(g) \cdot (A \cdot d(S)) \qquad (7), \qquad d(S) = \sum_{i=1}^{12} \sum_{j=i+1}^{13} OL(i,j) \qquad (8)$$

where A is taken equal to 1000 (B of eq. 4 is taken equal to 0), d(S) is the total shape overlapping area and OL(i,j) is the overlapping area concerning shapes i and j.

The GA used on this problem included the following characteristics : 13-point

Crossover [14], Bit Mutation, adaptive crossover-mutation probabilities (Crossover 0.4-0.9, mutation 0.004-0.024) [1], [3], [7], [11], [12] in order to control pre-mature convergence and excessive diversity, Roulette Wheel Parent Selection [5], Generational Replacement (replacement of the whole population at every generation) [5], elitism [5], population of 50 genotypes, final run limit of 500 generations, application of problem specific recombination operators [11], [12] to the whole population and application of hill climbing operators [10], [11], [12] to the best genotype of every generation.

For every one of the 7 penalty functions 20 GA runs have been performed, with different random seed at every run. In this problem, due to the design of the 13 shapes, the optimum was known and was equal to 12666. So we have set a success limit of quality 13000, that practically means that a run was considered successful only if it converged to the global optimum. The test results can be seen in Table I, Figure 2 and Figure 3. The bar chart with the Average Best Quality in Figure 3 shows the mean value of the final solution of the 20 runs, for each of the penalty functions. The horizontal line shows the global optimum value (12666).

Table I : Success percentage and average quality over 20 runs of the seven rates of increase on the Cutting Stock problem.

Function	Expon. 1	Expon. 2	Linear	Square	Cubic	Quartic	5-step
Success	10%	5%	15%	30%	10%	0%	0%
Avg.Qual.	13805	14257	18251	17184	28252	32013	29863

The test results clearly show that the GA performance is greatly affected by the penalty function chosen. The functions Exponential 1 and 2 that tend to apply a large proportion of the penalty at the beginning, generally converge to good solutions but they cannot make it to the top, because they get trapped to local minima. On the other hand the extremely sub-linear functions Cubic and Quartic do not allow the GA to distinguish valid and invalid areas early, so they have poor success rates and poor average best quality.

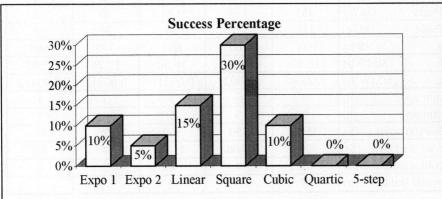

Figure 2. Success percentage over 20 runs of the seven rates of increase on the Cutting Stock problem

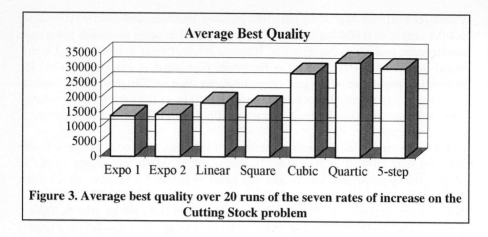

Figure 3. Average best quality over 20 runs of the seven rates of increase on the Cutting Stock problem

The best performance though is shown by the Square function, while the Step function performs poorly also.

4. Simulation tests on the Unit Commitment Problem

The Unit Commitment problem [7], [8], [12], [16] comes from the Power Systems Engineering and consists in the determination of the start-up and shut down schedules of thermal units, to meet forecasted demand over a future short term (24-168 hour) period. The objective is to minimise the total production cost of the operating units while satisfying a large set of operating constraints. The problem of Unit Commitment involves both combinatorial and continuous variable optimisation and can be also characterised as a scheduling problem.

Table II : Parameters of the 5 units of the Unit Commitment problem.

		Unit 1	Unit 2	Unit3	Unit 4	Unit 5
Pmax	(MW)	455	130	130	80	55
Pmin	(MW)	150	20	20	20	55
a	($/h)	1000	700	680	370	660
b	($/MWh)	16.19	16.60	16.50	22.26	25.92
c	($/MW^{2}h)	0.00048	0.002	0.00211	0.00712	0.00413
min up	(h)	8	5	5	3	1
min dn	(h)	8	5	5	3	1
hot start cost	($)	4500	550	560	170	30
cold start cost	($)	9000	1100	1120	340	60
cold start hrs	(h)	5	4	4	2	0
initial status	(h)	8	-5	-5	-3	-1

The a, b and c figures are the coefficients of the fuel cost function which is of the form : $fc=a+b{\cdot}P+c{\cdot}P^2$ where P is the power output of the unit. The min-up and min-dn hour figures are the continuously up time limit and the continuously down time limit respectively. The "hot start cost" is considered when the unit has been down for less than the "cold start hours" figure, otherwise the "cold start cost" is used. The initial status shows the number of hours the unit is already up (positive number) or down (negative number).

Table III : The demand for the 24 hours of the scheduling period of the Unit Commitment problem

Hour	1	2	3	4	5	6	7	8	9	10	11	12
Demand (MW)	400	450	480	500	530	550	580	600	620	650	680	700
Hour	13	14	15	16	17	18	19	20	21	22	23	24
Demand (MW)	650	620	600	550	500	550	600	650	600	550	500	450

The problem used for our tests consisted of 5 units and 24 hours scheduling horizon. The units' parameters are shown in Table II and the demand values are shown in Table III. For this problem, a $5 \times 24 = 120$ bit sting is used to encode a single solution resulting in a search space of $2^{120} = 1.329 \times 10^{36}$ different solutions. The constraints which must be satisfied during the optimisation process are: (a) System power balance (power output = demand+losses+exports), (b) System reserve requirements, (c) Unit initial conditions, (d) Unit high and low MegaWatt (MW) limits (economic/operating), (e) Unit minimum up-time and (f) Unit minimum down-time.

The fitness function is built as follows : with a given operating schedule, for every hour t, a dispatch algorithm [1] calculates the optimum power output values, P_i^t, for every operating unit i in order to meet the given forecasted demand (D^t) at that hour. The operating units are the ones that have, according to the schedule, their genotype bit, corresponding to hour t, equal to "1". The high and low limits of the units are also taken into account. The quality function is then calculated as follows:

a) The total fuel cost FC(S) of the operating units is calculated by:

$$FC(S) = \sum_{i=1}^{5} \sum_{t=1}^{24} u_i^t \cdot fc_i(P_i^t) \tag{9}$$

where u_i^t is the state (0,1) of unit i at time t and $fc_i(\cdot)$ is the unit's fuel cost function.

b) The units' start-up cost SC(S) and shut-down cost DC(S) are calculated by:

$$SC(S) = \sum_{i=1}^{5} \sum_{t=1}^{24} u_i^t \cdot (1-u_i^{t-1}) \cdot SU_i(x_i^t) \tag{10}$$

$$DC(S) = \sum_{i=1}^{5} \sum_{t=1}^{24} u_i^{t-1} \cdot (1-u_i^t) \cdot SD_i \tag{11}$$

where x_i^t is the number of hours the unit i has been down at time t, $SU_i(\cdot)$ is the start-up cost function of unit i and SD_i is the shut-down cost of unit i, and they are both calculated from the units' parameters of Table II. The final Varying Fitness Function is built by summing all the cost and penalty factors :

$$Q_v(S,g) = FC(S) + SC(S) + DC(S) + V(g) \cdot (A \cdot \sum_{i=1}^{NC} (\delta_i \cdot \Phi_i(d_i(S)))) \tag{12}$$

where A is taken equal to 1000 and B (of eq. 4) equal to 0.

The GA used on this problem, included the following characteristics : 5-point Crossover, Bit Mutation, adaptive crossover-mutation probabilities (Crossover 0.4-0.9, mutation 0.004-0.024) in order to control pre-mature convergence and excessive diversity, Roulette Wheel Parent Selection, Generational Replacement (replacement of the whole population at every generation), elitism, population of 50 genotypes, final run limit of 500 generations, application of problem specific recombination operators to the whole population [7], [12] and application of hill climbing operators to the best genotype of every generation [7], [12].

Table IV : Success percentage and average quality over 20 runs of the seven rates of increase on the Unit Commitment problem

Function	Expon. 1	Expon. 2	Linear	Square	Cubic	Quartic	5-step
Success	35%	25%	55%	95%	95%	90%	95%
Avg.Qual.	272180	272549	272051	271597	271549	271553	271597

For every one of the 7 penalty functions 20 GA runs have been performed, with different random seed at every run. In this problem, a Dynamic Programming algorithm was also used and gave the optimum quality of 271535 ($). So we have set as a success limit the quality 271540, that practically means that a GA run was considered successful only if it converged to the global optimum.

The test results can be seen in Table IV, Figure 4 and Figure 5. The bar chart with the Average Best Quality in Figure 5 shows the mean value of the final solution of the 20 runs, for each of the penalty functions. The horizontal line shows the global optimum value (271535).

The test results clearly show that, in this problem also, the GA performance is greatly affected by the penalty function chosen. The functions Exponential 1 and 2 perform poorly in this case as well, while the sub-linear functions do better than the Linear function. The best performance though is exhibited by the Square and the Cubic functions, while the 5-step function performs satisfactorily in this problem.

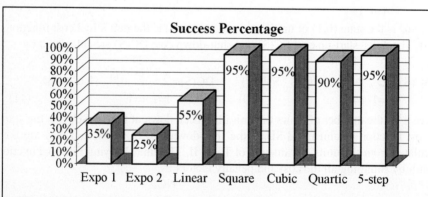

Figure 4. Success percentage over 20 runs of the seven rates of increase on the Unit Commitment problem

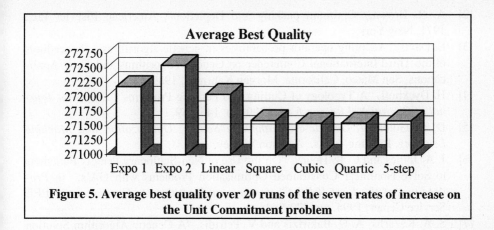

Figure 5. Average best quality over 20 runs of the seven rates of increase on the Unit Commitment problem

5. Conclusions

Comparing the test results of the seven increase rates of the varying penalty function on the two problems some general observations can be made :

- In the application of the VFF technique, the increase rate of the penalty terms, during the GA run, directly affects the overall GA performance and must be selected carefully to suit the specific GA application.
- The gradual application of the penalties for constraint violations, is critical for the success of the GA. The penalty functions Exponential 1 and Exponential 2 that quickly reach the maximum value of the penalty function, perform very poorly in the comparison tests.
- The optimum increase rate of the penalty term seems to be that of the Square function over the two problems considered, and not the Linear function which could be seen as an obvious choice.
- The extreme sub-linear increase rates (Cubic and Quartic functions) perform very well in the case of the Unit Commitment problem though they exhibit a poor performance in the case of the Cutting Stock problem.
- The 5-step function exhibits very good characteristics on the Unit Commitment problem but not on the Cutting Stock problem a fact that is partly due to the problem specific operators used in the Cutting Stock problem.

Further research is required in using the VFF technique on other constrained optimisation problems. Also other types of penalty functions could be used and tested (e.g. bimodal functions etc.).

References

[1] A. Bakirtzis, V. Petridis and S. Kazarlis, "A Genetic Algorithm Solution to the Economic Dispatch Problem", IEE Proceedings - Generation Transmission Distribution, Vol. 141, No. 4, July 1994, p.p. 377-382.

[2]   A. R. Brown, "Optimum packing and Depletion", American Elsevier Inc., 1971, New York.

[3]   L. Davis, "Adapting operator probabilities in genetic algorithms", Proceedings of the Third International Conference on Genetic Algorithms and Their Applications, San Mateo, California, Morgan Kaufman, 1989.

[4]   H. Dyckhoff, "A Typology of Cutting and Packing Problems", *European Journal of Operational Research* 44, 1990, pp. 145-159.

[5]   D. E. Goldberg, *Genetic Algorithms in Search, Optimization and Machine Learning,* Reading, Mass.: Addison Wesley, 1989.

[6]   J. A. Joines and C. R. Houck, "On the Use of Non-Stationary Penalty Functions to Solve Nonlinear Constrained Optimisation Problems with GA's," in *Proceedings of the First IEEE Conference on Evolutionary Computation*, IEEE Service Center, 1994, pp. 579-584.

[7]   S. A. Kazarlis, A. G. Bakirtzis and V. Petridis, "A Genetic Algorithm Solution to the Unit Commitment Problem," *IEEE Transactions on Power Systems*, Vol. 11, No. 1, February 1996, pp. 83-92.

[8]   D. Dasgupta and D. R. McGregor, "Thermal Unit Commitment using Genetic Algorithms," IEE Proceedings - Part C: Generation, Transmission and Distribution, Vol. 141, No. 5, September 1994, pp. 459-465.

[9]   Z. Michalewicz and G. Nazhiyath, "Genocop III: A Co-evolutionary Algorithm for Numerical Optimisation Problems with Nonlinear Constraints," in *Proceedings of the 2nd IEEE International Conference on Evolutionary Computation*, Vol. 2, Perth-Australia, 29 Nov. - 1 Dec. 1995, pp. 647-651.

[10] J. A. Miller. W. D. Potter, R. V. Gandham and C. N. Lapena, "An Evaluation of Local Improvement Operators for Genetic Algorithms", in *IEEE Transactions on Systems, Man, and Cybernetics*, Vol. 23, No. 5, Sep./Oct. 1993.

[11] V. Petridis and S. Kazarlis "Varying Quality Function in Genetic Algorithms and the Cutting Problem", in *Proceedings of the First IEEE Conference on Evolutionary Computation (ICEC '94 as part of WCCI'94)*, IEEE Service Center, 1994, Vol. 1, pp. 166-169.

[12] V. Petridis, S. Kazarlis and A. Bakirtzis, "Varying Fitness Functions in Genetic Algorithm Constrained Optimisation: The Cutting Stock and Unit Commitment Problems," accepted for publication at the IEEE Transactions on Systems, Man, and Cybernetics, Vol 28 Part B No 5 issue of October 1998.

[13] A. E. Smith and D. M. Tate, "Genetic Optimisation Using A Penalty Function," in *Proceedings of the Fifth International Conference on Genetic Algorithms*, S. Forrest, Ed. Los Altos, CA: Morgan Kaufmann, 1993, pp. 499-505.

[14] W.M. Spears and K.A. De Jong, "An Analysis of Multi-Point Crossover" in Foundations of Genetic Algorithms, San Mateo California, Morgan Kaufman, 1991, pp. 301-315.

[15] Paul. E. Sweeney, Elizabeth Ridenour Paternoster, "Cutting and Packing Problems: A categorized Application - Oriented Research Bibliography", *Journal of the Operational Research Society*, Vol. 43, No. 7, p.p. 691-706.

[16] A.J. Wood and B.F. Wollenberg, *Power Generation Operation and Control*, 1984, John Wiley, New York.

Landscape Changes and the Performance of Mapping Based Constraint Handling Methods

Dae Gyu Kim[†‡]

Ship & Ocean R & D Center[†]
DAEWOO Heavy Industries Ltd.
Koje, Kyungnam, Korea, 656-714
daegyu@daewoo.dhi.co.kr

Phil Husbands[‡]

School of Cognitive and Computing Sciences[‡]
University of Sussex
Falmer, Brighton, UK, BN1 9QH
{dgkim, philh}@cogs.susx.ac.uk

Abstract. The Mapping Based Constraint handling (MBC) method for evolutionary search methods was suggested and shown as a promising constraint handling method, [4]. The MBC method is based on an assumption that feasible solution domains can be mapped into a simple hypercubic domain. The MBC method makes a new unconstrained optimisation problem out of the originally constrained problem.

Transforming domains using the MBC method inevitably changes the landscape. When using the MBC method, two types of changes on the landscapes are expected: in the search point distribution pattern, and in the structure of the genotype domain. Preliminary test results on this suggests that the alterations to the landscape make little difference to the search performance.

1 Introduction

Constrained optimisation problems, one of the application areas of Evolutionary Search (ES) methods, has drawn a great deal of attention. Most of the research is about handling constraints for better search performance. Penalty based, repair based, and specialised encoding based approaches are some of the constraint handling methods listed in [7] and [8]. Most of the constraint handling methods steer the search away from infeasible regions, which in a sense is an indirect way of enforcing the constraints. These efforts are needed because the topology of the feasible solution domain is usually not a hypercubic shape where ES can work without producing infeasible solutions.

The Mapping Based Constraint handling (MBC) method turns a constrained optimisation problem into an unconstrained optimisation problem by mapping the feasible solution domain(s) into a hypercubic domain. A brief description of the MBC method is given in Section 2, followed by an example of applying a GA using the MBC method on a problem taken from [10]. One of the flexibilities of the MBC method is that various numerical mapping methods can be used as the tool for making mappings: for instance, Thurston's Circle Packing, Appendix B of [11], the homogeneous Thompson-Thames-Mastin (TTM) grid generator, [5], and some analytic mapping functions depending on the topology of the domain.

Using the MBC method inevitably changes the landscape, especially in two senses: 1) The distribution pattern of search points, 2) The structure of the genotype domain. Section 3 discusses the change in the search performance due to the changes on the landscapes, experimental test results are given.

2   Mapping Based Constraint handling (MBC)

Evolutionary Search Methods rely on a set of variables that encode solutions. Such variables are randomly initialised within their bounds during the population initialisation. When the feasible solution domain is not a hypercubic shape, as for most constrained problems, it is hard to avoid producing infeasible solutions during the initialization phase. Also, modification of valid solutions during the reproduction process does not guarantee producing feasible solutions either. Heuristics are needed to control the initialisation and the reproduction process, which are usually referred to as *constraint handling* methods.

Three main approaches to handling constraints are,

- Penalty Based constraint handling
- Repair based constraint handling
- Constraint handling using tailored encoding

In addition to the above, a mapping based constraint handling (MBC) method as another approach is discussed here.

2.1   Mapping Based Constraint Handling method

The MBC method, introduced in [4], maps feasible solution domain(s) into a hypercube, which turns the originally constrained problem into a new unconstrained problem. There are some properties that mappings should possess to be used as a tool for the MBC method[1].

a. Original domains   b. Mapped domains   c. Mapped domain
keeping the area ratio

Fig. 1. Handling multiple disjoint feasible domains using the MBC

The basic idea of the MBC is represented in Figure 1; feasible solution domains are mapped into a single hypercubic domain within which evolutionary search can work in a straight forward manner without generating infeasible solutions. Feasible solution domains are mapped into hypercubic domains which

---

[1] Michalewicz has proposed some properties in [7] that such a mapping is expected to have, "(1) for each solution $s \in \mathcal{F}$, $\mathcal{F}$ is the feasible solution domain, there is a decoded solution, $d \in \mathcal{S}$, (2) each decoded solution d corresponds to a feasible solution s, and (3) all solutions in $\mathcal{F}$ should be represented by the same number of decodings d. ... (4) the transformation T is computationally fast and (5) it has locality feature. ... ".

are then adjusted to keep their area ratio the same as in the original domains (a → b in Figure 1). The domains are put together to make a single hypercubic domain (b → c in Figure 1). The hypercubic domain in Figure 1.c is the feasible solution domain of the newly defined unconstrained problem, and the inverse mapping to the original domains is used for fitness evaluations of the individuals in the newly made domain.

Some questions can be raised following the idea of the MBC method; "do such mappings exists in general cases?", "how can such a mapping be found in general cases?", "how will the manipulation of domain topology affect the search performance?"

The *Riemann Mapping Theorem*, [2], proves the existence and the uniqueness of a one-to-one conformal mapping between two arbitrary planar domains. The proof is on a mapping between a simply-connected arbitrary planar domain and a unit circle. The unit circle then works as the intermediate domain connecting two arbitrary domains.

An analytic mapping function and its inverse between two domains can be easily used as a mapping tool for the MBC method if they exist. The mapping will define a new unconstrained problem. The inverse mapping can find matching points in the original domain from the search points in the mapped domain, through which fitness values of search points can be assigned from their matching points. A commonly used method to find conformal mappings between two domains is the *bilinear transformation*, [6], which has only four adjustable variables to define the domain boundary, which is very restrictive in the domain topologies that can be handled.

Instead of analytic functions, some numerical methods that approximate such a mapping can be used as tools for the MBC method. *Thurston's circle packing algorithm*, Appendix B of [11], is a numerical approximation of the Riemann mapping, which maps a domain to a unit circle[2]. *Structured grid generators* like the Thompson-Thames-Mastin (TTM) grid generator, [5], can be considered as performing mappings between domains. When using numerical mapping methods, linear interpolations will be used to find the matching points.

Thurston's circle packing algorithm starts with an approximation of a domain using a hexagonal circle packing (Figure 4.a shows an example). The algorithm then maps all the involved circles into a unit circle (shown in Figure 4.b) in two steps; *radii iteration* and a series of *bilinear transformations* (see Appendix A). The radii iteration adjusts radii of all the circles so that they can be placed outside a unit circle, while all the circles are disjoint and circles at the boundary of the hexagonal packing are tangential to the unit circle. An *inversion* transformation sends all the circles into the unit circle, and *scaling* adjusts radii of circles so that they can fit into the unit circle. More details on the steps are given in Appendix A.

---

[2] A unit circle in the Cartesian coordinate system can be interpreted as a rectangular domain in the polar coordinate system, which makes the use of the circle packing algorithm possible for the MBC method as illustrated in Figure 1.

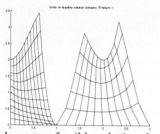 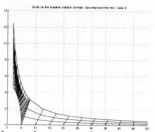

a. Grids on two feasible solution domains   b. Grids on decomposed solution domains

Fig. 2. Two examples of domain approximations using the homogeneous TTM grid generation

Figure 2 shows two examples of grids approximating the feasible solution domain(s) of two test problems from [1] and [7], the homogeneous TTM grid generator, [5], is used for the grid generation. Grids in Figure 2.a uses 10x10 and 10x5 grids for the approximation of the two domains. Both the domains will be interpreted as two rectangular domains with the same grid structures, adjusted, and put together to form a single hypercubic domain as shown in Figure 1, which is a new unconstrained problem.

The TTM grid generator produces a *spillover*[3] when applied on the whole domain of Figure 2.b, which is one of the weakness of the grid generator. To avoid the spillover, the domain is cut into two subdomains. Both of them are treated as separate feasible domains as in Figure 2.a. The decomposition of a single domain changes the domain landscape, and the influence on the search performance will be discussed in Section 3.

2.2   Example: Optimum fuel allocations to generators

This is an example of using three dimensional grids to solve a constrained optimisation problem, Example 7.6 in [10], with a GA using the MBC. The problem is to find an optimal fuel mixture for two oil-gas fired generators to produce a predefined power output while minimising the gas consumption. The power outputs and the fuel mixing rates for each generator make four independent variables. One linear equality constraint that require the sum of the power outputs from both generators to be a predefined value reduces one independent variable and leave three variable. (See [10] for a detailed formulation of the problem.)

Figure 3 shows the feasible solution domain and its three dimensional grid surfaces from two different viewing angles made using the TTM grid generator. The display is made using *chalmesh*, [9]. Three variables, x, y, z represent output from the first generator, mixing rates of the first and second generator respectively.

The feasible solution domain is approximated with three dimensional structured grids using the TTM grid generator. It uses a 10x10x5 meshes along x-y-z

---

[3] A spillover is when some of the grid points that should stay within the domain are located outside the domain.

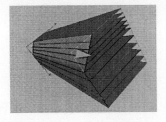 

Fig. 3. Feasible solution domain and grid surfaces of the fuel allocation problem

axis, and the domain is mapped to a unit cube with 10x10x5 meshes. Figure 3 shows 11 grid planes along the y direction.

A GA using the MBC method then works within the unit cube while getting fitness values from the original domain. A linear interpolation finds matching points in the original domain of search points in the cube. In [10] the solution to this problem was found after testing **8600** trial points using the *"Direct Sampling Procedures"*. The MBC based GA found the same solution, but with fewer trials; the average number of evaluations was **1409** with a standard deviation of 252 out of 100 test runs.

More test examples are in [4], which demonstrate a superior search performance of a GA using the MBC method over other constraint handling methods.

3 Changes on landscapes and the search performance

The MBC method alters the landscape of the feasible solution domain by transforming it to a simple hypercubic domain. Both the (visible) domains are *phenotype domains*, and each of them have associated *genotype domains* whose structure depends on the choice of the search operators, [3]. The genotype domain is where the actual search takes place, and its structure defines the paths through which the search explores. Two types of changes are made on the landscape when the MBC method is used to handle constraints; to the search point distribution pattern, and to the structure of the genotype domains.

3.1 Changes on the distribution pattern of search points

The mapping methods used for the MBC method possess a *locality* feature, therefore changes on the domain topology is like expanding and squeezing various parts of the domain until it becomes the desired shape. Search points in some parts may become concentrated and some may become dispersed. Figure 4 shows a mapping between two domains using the Thurston's circle packing. Circles of equal radius in Figure 4.a are packed into a unit circle by having different radii values.

Suppose random points are uniformly distributed in the unit circle, Figure 4.b , then the larger circles at the right may contain more random points than the smaller circles at other parts. Some of the smaller circles may not include any of the points. Mapping the points into the original domain of Figure 4.a will result

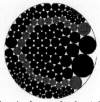

a. A domain with hexagonal circle packing   b. A unit circle packed with circles

Fig. 4. Example of the Thurston's circle packing

in uneven distribution of the points; points will be concentrated at the central parts and they will be dispersed at the upper-right and lower right tips whose matching circles are small in the unit circle. The neighbouring relationships between search points will remain the same in both domains, but their Euclidean distance measure will be changed. Figure 5 is an example of neighbouring points with Euclidean distance change by a mapping.

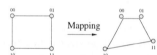

Fig. 5. Changes on the search point distribution pattern.

Supposing that the two graphs in Figure 5 show the structure of a genotype domain viewed from a *one-bit-flipping* operator, nothing has been changed from the operator's point of view. Therefore, there should be no changes on the search performance if it uses the *one-bit-flipping* operator. In the same way, the structure of genotype domains won't change only because the search point distribution pattern is changed.

An extreme dispersion of search points is what can prevent the search from exploring properly into a region for example the upper-right and lower-right tips of Figure 4.a. It can happen depending on the topology of the original domain; the aspect ratio is either very low or very high, or the domain has sharp corners. One cure to this problem is to increase the encoding precision; for a GA using binary string representation, increase the length of each binary string. By having higher precision, the search can explore into the region better than before, but the trade off is slowing down the search performance.

Other than increasing the encoding precision, decomposing the original domain may be another cure to the problem regarding to the changes on the search point distribution pattern. Cut the original domain into as many subdomains until each of them have a moderate aspect ratio and no sharp corners, and then apply mappings separately and put them together as disjoint feasible domains are handled in Figure 1. Another merit of doing decompositions is in reducing the burden on the mapping method being highly robust. As shown in Figure 2.b, the *spillover* could be mended by decomposing the original domain into two.

3.2 Changes on the structure of the genotype domain

The consequence of the domain decomposition is very serious in one sense; it changes the structure of the genotype domain. This alteration may affect the search performance. This is the second type of changes on the landscape made by the MBC method to be discussed here.

The genotype domain structure depends on the choice of search method, and operators[4]. Decomposition of a domain will cut some existing connections between genotypes, and recombining subdomains will make new connections between them, which means changes on the genotype domain.

Figure 6 shows two test sets of some possible decomposition and recombinations of two phenotype domains given in case **a**. Phenotype domains in both cases are one dimensional line segments of $[0, 1]$ along the x-axis. The phenotype domains are decomposed into two pieces and recombined to make cases **b** and **c**. Cases **d**, **e**, **f** are recombined results after decomposing into four subdomains. These test setups are similar to what the MBC method will do during either decomposition of a phenotype domain or when handling multiple feasible solution domains.

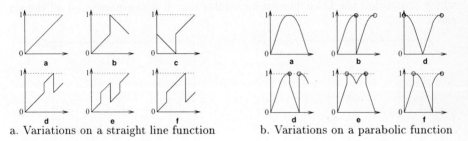

a. Variations on a straight line function   b. Variations on a parabolic function

Fig. 6. Maximising a linear and a parabola function and their permuted cases (Filled circles at b. show the locations of the maximum point.)

Table 1 summarises the search performance comparison of GAs applied to the two test sets shown in Figure 6. The GA tool PGA, [12], has been used with two different parameter settings. "GA Setting A" uses 5 sets of populations and each population set has 50 individuals, and "GA Setting B" uses 5 sets of populations and each population set has 10 individuals. Although the fitness functions are simple in the two test cases, applying GAs and comparing the search performance will give some idea about how the search performance will be affected from the changes of the phenotype domain. The performance comparison was done using the number of evaluations until they converge and given as ranks in the table, because the GAs found the solutions without failing.

---

[4] According to [3], the genotype domain of a *one-bit flipping* operator is a graph where every vertex has n neighbouring vertices if a genotype is an n-bit binary string. The genotype domain of a *mutation* operator is a complete graph, and a *crossover* operator experiences lots of disconnected graphs.

Decomp.-Recomb. Cases	Test Set 1				Test Set 2			
	GA Setting A		GA Setting B		GA Setting A		GA Setting B	
	# of Evals.	Rank	# of Evals.	Rank	# of Evals.	Rank	# of Evals.	Rank
a	5685	1	1606	3	2960	4	849	2
b	5843	4	1566	1	2530	1	805	1
c	5692	2	1648	5	2630	2	926	6
d	5936	6	1619	4	2996	5	885	5
e	5737	3	1593	2	3008	6	873	4
f	5879	5	1659	6	2872	3	870	3

Table 1. Number of evaluations for a MBC based GA to find solutions with permuted phenotype domains as in Figure 6

For "Test Set 1", the original phenotype, **a**, is ranked with "GA setting A" 1, but "GA setting B" works best on case **b**. The order of the ranks of case **a** and **b** is changed with the change of the GA parameter settings. Cases **c** and **d** also show reversed rank orders with the changed parameter settings. More importantly, averaged number of evaluations and their standard deviations show that all the cases are not that different from each other. Figure 7.a is a graph showing the averaged number of evaluations and the standard deviations in error-bar format, which shows that the GAs show quite similar search performances on all the six cases.

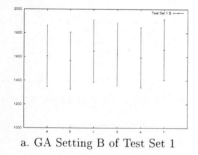 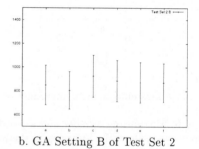

a. GA Setting B of Test Set 1   b. GA Setting B of Test Set 2

Fig. 7. Averaged number of evaluations and the standard deviations in error-bar graph.

In "Test Set 2", similar result as from "Test Set 1" can be drawn. Although the ranks of the three cases of **b**, **d**, and **f** remain unchanged with the two different parameter settings, the ranks of the others changes as the GA parameter setting changes. From Figure 7.b showing the averaged number of evaluations and their standard deviations, the search performances of the six cases are similar to each other.

4   Conclusion

The mapping based constraint handling (MBC) method is a new and promising approach of handling constraints for evolutionary search methods solving constrained function optimisation problems. The MBC method maps feasible solution domain(s) into a hypercubic domain, which turning the originally constrained problem into an unconstrained problem. With the new problem, evolutionary search methods can work without generating infeasible solutions while getting fitness information of individuals from the original feasible solution domain(s) using an inverse mapping.

The mapping between domains introduces two types of changes to the problem landscape: changes on the search point distribution pattern, and the structure of the genotype domain. Excessive dispersion of search points may worsen the search performance as it requires higher encoding precision. Decomposition and recombination of a single domain is suggested as a cure for the problem regarding to the search point distribution pattern change. Also, this may reduce the burden on the mapping method being highly robust. The decomposition in turn changes the structure of the genotype domain within which the actual search takes place. Two test sets to show the effect of modified phenotype domain on the search performance were invested. It was found that although the search performance changes a little depending on the mode of the decomposition and recombinations, it was not significantly affected.

References

1. C. A. Floudas and P. M. Pardalos. *A Collection of Test Problems for Constrained Global Optimization Algorithms.* Number 455 in Lecture Notes in Computer Science. Springer-Verlag, 1990.
2. Mario O. Gonzalez. *Complex Analysis: Selected Topics.* Marcel Dekker, Inc., 1992.
3. Terry Jones. A Model of Landscapes. ftp.teclata.es/pub/terry/model-of-landscapes.ps.gz, 1994.
4. Dae Gyu Kim and Phil Husbands. Mapping Based Constraint Handling For Evolutionary Search; Thurston's Circle Packing and Grid Generation. In I.C.Parmee, editor, *Adaptive Computing in Design and Manufacture*, pages 161–173. Third International Conference in Design and Manufacture, Springer-Verlag, 1998.
5. P. Knupp and S. Steinberg. *Fundamentals of Grid Generation.* CRC Press Inc., 1993.
6. H. Kober. *Dictionary of Conformal Representations.* Dover, 2nd edition, 1957.
7. Zbigniew Michalewicz. *Genetic Algorithms + Data Structures = Evolutionary Programs.* Springer-Verlag, 3rd edition, 1996.
8. Zbigniew Michalewicz and Marc Schoenauer. Evolutionary Algorithms for Constrained Parameter Optimisation Problems. *Evolutionary Computation*, 4(1), 1996.
9. N. Anders Petersson. User's guide to Chalmesh, version 1.0. Technical report, Department of Naval Architecture and Ocean Engineering, Chalmers University of Technology, July 1997. http://www.na.chalmers.se/ ~andersp/chalmesh/chalmesh.html.
10. G. V. Reklaitis, A. Ravindran, and K. M. Ragsdell. *Engineering Optimization: Methods and Applications.* John Wiley & Sons, Inc., 1983.
11. Burt Rodin and Dennis Sullivan. The convergence of Circle packing to the Riemann Mapping. *Journal of Differential Geometry*, 26:349–360, 1987.
12. Peter Ross and Geoffrey H. Ballinger. PGA - Parallel Genetic Algorithm Testbed. Technical report, Department of Artificial Intelligence, University of Edinburgh, UK, June 1996. ftp.dai.ed.ac.uk/pub/pga-2.9/pga-2.9.1.tar.gz.

Appendix A Two steps in Thurston's Circle Packing

Radii iteration (RI) and a series of *bilinear transformations* packs all the circles in a hexagonal circle packing (HCP) to a unit circle.

The process of radii iteration is to make the *curvature* of $r_k = (r_{k1}, r_{k2}, \ldots, r_{kn})$ vanish. r_k is a vector of positive n real numbers of radii of circles at the k-th iteration, n is the number of circles involved in a HCP. To start the iteration, radii of two circles are fixed as unit, $r_{k(n-1)} = r_{kn} = 1$, and one imaginary circle is introduced to the HCP with a unit radius, $r_{k(n+1)} = 1$. The three radii are fixed through out the iteration. An example of the unit circle is shown as circle 8 in Figure 8. The curvature of circle i, C_i, $(1 \leq i \leq n-2)$ is defined as $C_i = 2\pi - \sum_{j=1}^{l} \theta_{ij}$, $(4 \leq l \leq 6)$, l is the number of neighbouring circles of circle i. $\theta(j)$ is an angle of a triangle formed by two centre points of two neighbouring circles and the centre of the circle i Circle 1 in Figure 8 has four neighbours (circle 2, 4, 3, 8) including the imaginary circle, and four of the angles used to calculate the curvature are $\angle 2 - 1 - 4$, $\angle 4 - 1 - 3$, $\angle 3 - 1 - 8$, $\angle 8 - 1 - 2$.

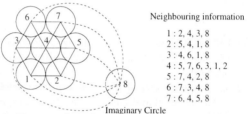

Neighbouring information

1 : 2, 4, 3, 8
2 : 5, 4, 1, 8
3 : 4, 6, 1, 8
4 : 5, 7, 6, 3, 1, 2
5 : 7, 4, 2, 8
6 : 7, 3, 4, 8
7 : 6, 4, 5, 8

Imaginary Circle

Fig. 8. Hexagonal circle packing and an imaginary circle

The *inversion* transformation sends all the circles into the unit circle. $v_i'.x = -\frac{v_i.x}{(v_i.x)^2 + (v_i.y)^2 - r_i^2}$, $v_i'.y = \frac{v_i.y}{(v_i.x)^2 + (v_i.y)^2 - r_i^2}$, and $r_i' = \left| \frac{r_i}{(v_i.x)^2 + (v_i.y)^2 - r_i^2} \right|$. Where, $v_i'.x$, $v_i'.y$, r_i' are new centre points of the circles inside the unit circle and their radii, and $v_i.x$, $v_i.y$, r_i are the centre points and radii in the Thurston's packing. $.x$, and $.y$ represent x and y coordinate of a point.

Inverted circles inside the unit circle are adjusted so that they can fit the unit circle. This transformation firstly chooses a circle, *null circle*, to be located at the centre of the unit circle, and the distance from the null circle to other circles especially to boundary circles are adjusted. $v_i'.x = \frac{-x + v_i.xx^2 + v_i.x - x((v_i.x)^2 + (v_i.y)^2 - (v_i.r)^2)}{1 - 2xv_i.x + x^2((v_i.x)^2 + (v_i.y)^2 - (v_i.r)^2)}$, $v_i'.y = \frac{v_i.yx^2 - v_i.y}{1 - 2xv_i.x + x^2((v_i.x)^2 + (v_i.y)^2 - (v_i.r)^2)}$, and $r_i' = \left| \frac{v_i.r(1 - x^2)}{((-\frac{1}{x} + h)^2 + (v_i.y)^2 - (v_i.r)^2)x^2} \right|$. Where, $x = \frac{2v_i.r(1+\rho) + 2(v_{null}.x + v_i.r)(v_{null}.x - v_i.r - 1)}{2(v_{null}.x - v_i.r - 1) + 2v_i.r(1+\rho)}$, and $\rho = -t - \sqrt{|t^2 - 4r^2|}$ if, $t - \sqrt{|t^2 - 4r^2|} < 0$, $(\rho = -t + \sqrt{|t^2 - 4r^2|}$ if, $t - \sqrt{|t^2 - 4r^2|} > 0)$, $t = 2v_i.r - (1 + v_i.r + v_{null}.x)(1 + v_i.r - v_{null}.x)$.

Rotation of circles in the unit circle is done using a simple transformation of $v_i' = \frac{A}{|A|} v_i$, where A is a complex number. If $A = x + iy$ then the rotation angle, θ, is $\theta = tan^{-1}(\frac{y}{x})$.□

A Decoder-Based Evolutionary Algorithm for Constrained Parameter Optimization Problems

Sławomir Koziel[1] and Zbigniew Michalewicz[2]

[1]Department of Electronics,
Telecommunication and Informatics
Technical University of Gdańsk
ul. Narutowicza 11/12, 80-952 Gdańsk, Poland
koziel@ue.eti.pg.gda.pl

[2]Department of Computer Science,
University of North Carolina,
Charlotte, NC 28223, USA
zbyszek@uncc.edu

Abstract. Several methods have been proposed for handling nonlinear constraints by evolutionary algorithms for numerical optimization problems; a survey paper [7] provides an overview of various techniques and some experimental results, as well as proposes a set of eleven test problems. Recently a new, decoder-based approach for solving constrained numerical optimization problems was proposed [2, 3]. The proposed method defines a homomorphous mapping between n-dimensional cube and a feasible search space. In [3] we have demonstrated the power of this new approach on several test cases. However, it is possible to enhance the performance of the system even further by introducing additional concepts of (1) nonlinear mappings with an adaptive parameter, and (2) adaptive location of the reference point of the mapping.

1 Introduction

The nonlinear parameter optimization problem is defined as

$$\text{Find } x \in \mathcal{S} \subset R^n \text{ such that } \begin{cases} f(\boldsymbol{x}) = \min\{f(\boldsymbol{y}); \ \boldsymbol{y} \in \mathcal{S}\}, & (1) \\ g_j(\boldsymbol{x}) \leq 0, \text{for } j = 1, \ldots, q, & (2) \end{cases}$$

where f and g_i are real-valued functions on $\mathcal{S}$; $\mathcal{S}$ is a search space defined as a Cartesian product of domains of variables x_i's ($1 \leq i \leq n$). The set of feasible points (i.e., points satisfying the constraints (2)) is denoted $\mathcal{F}$.[1]

Several methods have been proposed for handling nonlinear constraints by evolutionary algorithms for numerical optimization problems. The recent survey paper [7] classifies them into four categories (preservation of feasibility, penalty functions, searching for feasibility, and other hybrids). However, there is one central issue that all these methods have to address, which is, whether to allow processing of infeasible solutions? This is the most important issue to resolve. Many constraint-handling methods process infeasible solutions (e.g., various penalty-based methods), on the other hand, many other techniques process only feasible solutions (e.g., methods based on feasibility-preserving operators).

---

[1] Note, that we do not consider equality constraints; if necessary, an equality $h(\boldsymbol{x}) = 0$ can be replaced by a pair of inequalities $-\epsilon \leq h(\boldsymbol{x}) \leq \epsilon$ for some small $\epsilon > 0$.

In general, restricting the search to the feasible region seems a very elegant way to treat constrained problems. For example, in [5], the algorithm maintains feasibility of linear constraints using a set of closed operators which convert a feasible solution into another feasible solution. Similar approach for the nonlinear transportation problem is described in [4], where specialized operators transform a feasible solution matrix (or matrices) into another feasible solution. This is also the case for many evolutionary systems developed for the traveling salesman problem [4], where specialized operators maintain feasibility of permutations, as well as for many other combinatorial optimization problems.

However, for numerical optimization problems only special cases allowed the use of either specialized operators which preserve feasibility of solutions or repair algorithms, which attempt to convert an infeasible solution into feasible one. For example, a possible use of a repair algorithm was described in [6], but in that approach it was necessary to maintain two separate populations with feasible and infeasible solutions: a set of reference feasible points was used to repair infeasible points. Consequently, most evolutionary techniques for numerical optimization problems with constraints are based on penalties. However, highly nonlinear constraints still present difficulties for evolutionary algorithms, as penalty parameters or strategies are then difficult to adjust.

In this paper we investigate some properties of a recently proposed approach [3] for solving constrained numerical optimization problems which is based on a homomorphous mapping between n-dimensional cube $[-1, 1]^n$ and a feasible search space. This approach constitutes an example of decoder-based approach[2] where the mapping allows to process feasible solutions only. The first results [3] indicated a huge potential of this approach; the proposed method does not require any additional parameters, does not require evaluation of infeasible solutions, does not require any specialized operators to maintain feasibility—or to search the boundary of the feasible region [9], [8]. Moreover, any standard evolutionary algorithm (e.g., binary-coded genetic algorithm or evolution strategy) can be used in connection with the mapping. On the top of that, the method *guarantees* a feasible solution, which is not always the case for other methods.

The paper is organized as follows. The following section presents the new method, whereas section 3 discusses the research issues of this paper. Section 4 presents some experimental results and section 5 concludes the paper.

2   The homomorphous mapping

The idea behind this technique is to develop a homomorphous mapping φ, which transforms the n-dimensional cube $[-1, 1]^n$ into the feasible region $\mathcal{F}$ of the problem [3]. Note, that $\mathcal{F}$ need not be convex; it might be concave or even can consist of disjoint (non-convex) regions.

The search space $\mathcal{S}$ is defined as a Cartesian product of domains of variables of the problem, $l(i) \leq x_i \leq u(i)$, for $1 \leq i \leq n$, whereas a feasible part $\mathcal{F}$ of

---

[2] Actually, this is the first approach of this type; until recently, mappings (or decoders) were applied only to discrete optimization problems.

the search space is defined by problem specific constraints: inequalities (2) from the previous section. Assume, a solution r_0 is feasible (i.e., $r_0 \in \mathcal{F}$). Then any boundary point s of the search space $\mathcal{S}$ defines a line segment L between r_0 and s (figure 1 illustrates the case). Note that such a line segment may intersect a boundary of the feasible search space $\mathcal{F}$ in more than just one point.

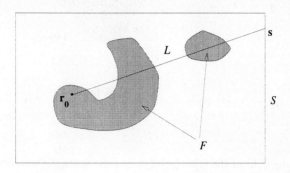

Fig. 1. A line segment in a non-convex space $\mathcal{F}$ (two-dimensional case)

Let us define an additional one-to-one mapping g between the cube $[-1,1]^n$ and the search space $\mathcal{S}$. Then the mapping $g : [-1,1]^n \to S$ can be defined as

$$g(\boldsymbol{y}) = \boldsymbol{x}, \text{ where } x_i = y_i \frac{u(i)-l(i)}{2} + \frac{u(i)+l(i)}{2}, \text{ for } i = 1, \ldots, n.$$

Indeed, for $y_i = -1$ the corresponding $x_i = l(i)$, and for $y_i = 1$, $x_i = u(i)$.

A line segment L between any reference point $r_0 \in \mathcal{F}$ and a point s at the boundary of the search space $\mathcal{S}$, is defined as

$$L(r_0, s) = r_0 + t \cdot (s - r_0), \text{ for } 0 \le t \le 1.$$

Clearly, if the feasible search space $\mathcal{F}$ is convex,[3] then the above line segment intersects the boundary of $\mathcal{F}$ in precisely one point, for some $t_0 \in [0,1]$. Consequently, for convex feasible search spaces $\mathcal{F}$, it is possible to establish a one-to-one mapping $\varphi : [-1,1]^n \to \mathcal{F}$ as follows:

$$\varphi(\boldsymbol{y}) = \begin{cases} r_0 + y_{max} \cdot t_0 \cdot (g(\boldsymbol{y}/y_{max}) - r_0) & \text{if } \boldsymbol{y} \ne 0 \\ r_0 & \text{if } \boldsymbol{y} = 0 \end{cases}$$

where $r_0 \in \mathcal{F}$ is a reference point, and $y_{max} = \max_{i=1}^n |y_i|$. Figure 2 illustrates the transformation φ.

On the other hand, if the feasible search space $\mathcal{F}$ is not convex, then the line segment L may intersect the boundary of $\mathcal{F}$ in many points (see figure 1).

---

[3] Note, that the convexity of the feasible search space $\mathcal{F}$ is not necessary; it is sufficient if we assume the existence of the reference point r_0, such that every line segment originating in r_0 intersects the boundary of $\mathcal{F}$ in precisely one point. This requirement is satisfied, of course, for any convex set $\mathcal{F}$.

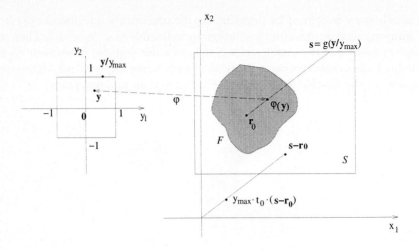

Fig. 2. A mapping φ from the cube $[-1,1]^n$ into the space $\mathcal{F}$ (two-dimensional case), with particular steps of the transformation

Let us consider an arbitrary point $\boldsymbol{y} \in [-1,1]^n$ and a reference point $\boldsymbol{r_0} \in \mathcal{F}$. A line segment L between the reference point $\boldsymbol{r_0}$ and the point $\boldsymbol{s} = g(\boldsymbol{y}/y_{max})$ at the boundary of the search space $\mathcal{S}$, is defined as before, however, instead of a single interval of feasibility $[0, t_0]$ for convex search spaces, we may have several intervals of feasibility: $[t_1, t_2], \ldots, [t_{2k-1}, t_{2k}]$. Assume there are altogether k subintervals of feasibility for a such line segment and t_i's mark their limits. Clearly, $t_1 = 0$, $t_i < t_{i+1}$ for $i = 1, \ldots, 2k-1$, and $t_{2k} \le 1$. Thus, it is necessary to introduce an additional mapping γ, which transforms interval $[0, 1]$ into sum of intervals $[t_{2i-1}, t_{2i}]$. However, we define such a mapping γ between $(0, 1]$ and the sum of intervals $(t_{2i-1}, t_{2i}]$:

$$\gamma : (0, 1] \rightarrow \bigcup_{i=1}^{k} (t_{2i-1}, t_{2i}].$$

Note, that due to this change, one boundary point (from each interval $1 \le i \le k$) is lost. However, this is not a serious problem, since we can approach the lost points with arbitrary precision. On the other hand, the benefits are clear: it is possible to "glue together" intervals which are open at one end and closed at another; additionally, such a mapping is one-to-one. There are many possibilities for defining such a mapping; we have used the following. First, let us define a reverse mapping δ:

$$\delta : \bigcup_{i=1}^{k} (t_{2i-1}, t_{2i}] \rightarrow (0, 1] \text{ as follows: } \delta(t) = (t - t_{2i-1} + \textstyle\sum_{j=1}^{i-1} d_j)/d,$$

where $d_j = t_{2j} - t_{2j-1}$, $d = \sum_{j=1}^{k} d_j$, and $t_{2i-1} < t \le t_{2i}$. Clearly, the mapping γ is reverse of δ:

$$\gamma(a) = t_{2j-1} + d_j \frac{a - \delta(t_{2j-1})}{\delta(t_{2j}) - \delta(t_{2j-1})},$$

where j is the smallest index such that $a \leq \delta(t_{2j})$.

Now we are ready to define the mapping φ, which is the essence of the method of transformation of constrained optimization problem to the unconstrained one for every feasible set $\mathcal{F}$. The mapping φ is given by the following formula:

$$\varphi(y) = \begin{cases} r_0 + t_0 \cdot (g(y/y_{max}) - r_0) & \text{if } y \neq 0, \\ r_0 & \text{if } y = 0, \end{cases}$$

where $r_0 \in \mathcal{F}$ is a reference point, $y_{max} = \max_{i=1}^{n} |y_i|$, and $t_0 = \gamma(|y_{max}|)$.

Finally, it is necessary to consider a method of finding points of intersections t_i. Let us consider any boundary point s of $\mathcal{S}$ and the line segment L determined by this point and a reference point $r_0 \in \mathcal{F}$. There are m constraints $g_i(x) \leq 0$ and each of them can be represented as a function β_i of one independent variable t (for fixed reference point $r_0 \in \mathcal{F}$ and the boundary point s of $\mathcal{S}$):

$$\beta_i(t) = g_i(L(r_0, s)) = g_i(r_0 + t \cdot (s - r_0)), \text{ for } 0 \leq t \leq 1 \text{ and } i = 1, \ldots, m.$$

As stated earlier, the feasible region need not be convex, so it may have more than one point of intersection of the segment L and the boundary of the set $\mathcal{F}$. Therefore, let us partition the interval $[0, 1]$ into v subintervals $[v_{j-1}, v_j]$, where $v_j - v_{j-1} = 1/v$ $(1 \leq j \leq v)$, so that equations $\beta_i(t) = 0$ have at most one solution in every subinterval.[4] In that case the points of intersection can be determined by a binary search.

Once the intersection points between a line segment L and all constraints $g_i(x) \leq 0$ are known, it is quite easy to determine intersection points between this line segment L and the boundary of the feasible set $\mathcal{F}$.

3   Adaptation issues

In [3] we reported on experimental results of the system based on the mapping described in the previous section. The system was based on Gray coding with 25 bits per variable, and incorporated proportional selection (no elitism), function scaling, and standard operators (flip mutation and 1-point crossover). All parameters were fixed: pop_size $= 70$, generation gap $= 100\%$, and $p_c = 0.9$. The only non-standard feature incorporated into the system (to increase fine tuning capabilities of the system [1]) was a variable probability of mutation.[5] In all experiments, $p_m(0) = 0.005$, $r = 4$, and $p_m(T) = 0.00005$.

The system provided very good results [3], which were better than for any other constraint handling method reported in literature. Yet there were some additional possibilities for a further improvement and unresolved issues which we address in this paper.

First of all, it is important to investigate the role of the reference point r_0. Note that instead of keeping this point static during the evolutionary process,

---

[4] Density of the partition is determined by parameter v, which is adjusted experimentally (in all experiments reported in section 4, $v = 20$).

[5] $p_m(t) = p_m(0) - (p_m(0) - p_m(T)) \cdot (t/T)^r$, where t and T are the current and maximal generation numbers, respectively.

it can change its location. In particular, it can "follow" the best solution found so far. In that way, the reference point can "adapt" itself to the current state of the search. One of the aims of this paper is to compare the proposed method with static versus dynamic reference point. In the latter case, the quotient of the total number of generations and the number of changes of the reference point during the run, gives the number of generations between each change; the new reference point is the best individual of the current generation.

Note that a change of the reference point r_0 changes the phenotypes of the genotypes in the population. Thus it might be worthwhile to consider an additional option: after each change of the reference point, all genotypes in the population are modified accordingly to yield the same phenotype as before the change. For example, if a genotype $(0101101...0111)$ corresponded to the phenotype $(-2.46610039, 1.09535518)$ just before the change of the reference point r_0, then, after the change, the genotype is changed in such a way, that its phenotype is still $(-2.46610039, 1.09535518)$ for a new reference point.

Also, in the proposed method it is important to investigate a non-uniform distribution of values of vectors $y \in [-1,1]^n$; this can be achieved, for example, by introducing an additional mapping $\omega : [-1,1]^n \to [-1,1]^n$:

$$\omega(y) = y', \text{ where } y_i' = a \cdot y_i,$$

where a is a parameter of the mapping, and $0 < a \leq 1/y_{max}$. Such exploration of non-uniform distribution of y provides additional possibilities for tuning the search:

- an increase in value of parameter a would result in selecting new vectors y' closer to a boundary of the feasible part of the search space. Thus, it is possible to use this approach to search the boundary of the feasible search space (e.g., instead of using specialized boundary operators [9]).[6]
- a decrease in value of parameter a would result in selecting new vectors y' closer to zero (i.e., the corresponding new search point would be closer to the reference point). This may work very well with the mechanism of adaptive change of the reference point: the system explores points closer to the reference point which, in turn, "follows" the best solution found so far.

Of course, there are many mappings which introduce a non-uniform distribution of values of vectors y; in this paper we experimented with the following mapping:

$$\omega(y) = y', \text{ where } y_i' = y_i \cdot y_{max}^{k-1},$$

where $k > 1$ is a parameter. Clearly, larger k would move new search points closer to the reference point (this corresponds to a decrease in value of parameter a, of course). However, such a mapping concentrates the search around the reference point, hence is not helpful in cases where the optimum solution is located on the boundary of the feasible part of the search space. Thus an additional option

---

[6] Note, however, that in general (e.g., non-convex feasible search spaces) only a part of the boundary will be explored.

(direction of change) was considered: if a vector c represents the normalized direction vector of the last change of the reference point, then the constant parameter k is replaced by a variable k' calculated (for every vector y) as follows:

$$k' = \begin{cases} 1 + (k-1) \cdot (1 - \cos^2(c, y)) & \text{if } \cos(c, y) > 0 \\ k & \text{if } \cos(c, y) \le 0, \end{cases}$$

Note that if the angle between c and y is close to zero, then $\cos(c, y)$ is close to one, and, consequently, the value of parameter k is close to one.

4 Experimental results

Ten versions of an evolutionary system were considered (see Table 1).

Version number	Number of changes of r_0 during run	Change of genotype	Value of k	Option: direction of change
1	0	N/A	1.0	N/A
2	3	N	1.0	N
3	3	N	3.0	N
4	3	N	3.0	Y
5	20	N	1.0	N
6	20	N	3.0	N
7	20	N	3.0	Y
8	3	Y	1.0	N
9	20	Y	3.0	N
10	20	Y	3.0	Y

Table 1. Ten versions of the evolutionary system. For each version we report the number of changes of the reference point during the run (0 corresponds to the case where is no change, thus some other options are not applicable N/A), whether an option of re-coding the genotype was used (Yes or No), the value of scaling parameter k, and whether the option (direction of change) was used (Y) or not (N).

The experiments were made for four functions: $G6$, $G7$, $G9$, and $G10$ from [7].[7] All results are given in Tables 2–3. For each function 10 runs were performed; the tables report the best solution found in all runs, the average value, and the worst one. For $G6$, all runs had 500 generations, whereas all runs for remaining functions had 5,000 generations.

It was interesting to see that:

[7] These functions have 2, 10, 7, and 8 variables, respectively, which a number (between 2 and 8) of (mainly) nonlinear constraints. Most constraints are active at the optimum.

	$G6$			$G7$		
Version number	Minimum value	Average value	Maximum value	Minimum value	Average value	Maximum value
1	−6961.806423	−6403.744816	−5658.854943	26.156504	34.014132	62.015826
2	−6961.813810	−6949.220321	−6880.366641	24.823462	29.702066	37.593063
3	−6961.813769	−6961.616254	−6959.862901	25.667881	31.635635	41.275908
4	−6961.811700	−6961.119165	−6955.609490	24.456143	27.501678	34.224130
5	−6961.813810	−6959.199162	−6936.007217	24.923346	29.034924	36.600579
6	−6962.041796	−6954.089593	−6887.142350	24.493854	27.846996	37.850277
7	−6961.813805	−6961.814303	−6961.813735	25.604691	27.765957	33.025607
8	−6961.813754	−6926.097556	−6605.883742	24.449495	27.451748	34.651248
9	−6961.689228	−6960.275484	−6953.448863	24.987889	27.657595	31.823738
10	−6961.813247	−6960.794588	−6958.289256	26.119342	27.744277	29.447646

Table 2. Results for $G6$ and $G7$. These are minimization problems and the optimum values of these functions are −6961.81381 and 24.3062091, respectively.

	$G9$			$G10$		
Version number	Minimum value	Average value	Maximum value	Minimum value	Average value	Maximum value
1	680.630511	680.660238	680.729387	7160.262971	8592.392352	11511.072437
2	680.630542	680.636662	680.647153	7059.228161	7464.926353	8229.071491
3	680.630181	680.636573	680.664618	7086.430306	7591.768786	9225.975846
4	680.630392	680.637875	680.661187	7197.628211	7819.787329	8827.143414
5	680.631795	680.633758	680.636254	7058.405010	7492.697550	8995.685583
6	680.631554	680.644804	680.703939	7081.945176	7888.418244	9656.438311
7	680.630826	680.634730	680.643466	7078.900133	7607.775554	8695.147494
8	680.631036	680.677782	680.965273	7089.686242	7994.728714	9734.441891
9	680.632734	680.635818	680.639192	7230.799808	7695.850259	8813.595674
10	680.630492	680.638832	680.668193	7063.878216	7597.675949	8637.628629

Table 3. Results for $G9$ and $G10$. These are minimization problems and the optimum values of these functions are 680.6300573 and 7049.330923, respectively.

- for the test case $G6$ the best results were obtained for versions 3, 4, 7, 9, and 10. In all these five versions, the value of the parameter k was set to 3.0; it seems that this factor had a major influence on the quality of the results. Note also, that these five versions include all three versions where the option of "changing directions" was used (versions 4, 7, and 10). Also, the difference between versions 6 and 7 was only in the use of the above option: note the average scores of these two versions. In this case this option proved its usefulness. Similarly, the only difference between versions 3 and 6 was in the number of changes of the reference point made during the run. For this particular test case, a higher value of this parameter was better in combination with the option of changing the genotype, and a lower value was better without this option (see versions 9 and 10 for the former case, and versions 3 and 4, for the latter).

- it is difficult to evaluate the performance of these versions for the test case G7. Note, that a few versions reported good *best* results (out of ten runs), however, the *average* values were less impressive. It seems that slightly better results were obtained for versions 4, 6, 8, and 9, but no interesting patterns emerged. For two of these versions, the number of changes of the reference point during the run was 3, whereas for the other two, it was 20. Two of these versions used the option of changing the genotype, and two others did not. Three versions used a higher value of parameter $k = 3$ and one version used $k = 1$. One version used the "direction of change" option.

- for the test case G9 all versions gave very good results, so it was possible to judge the performance of these version only on the basis of precision. The best versions (i.e., versions whose the best result was smaller than 680.631 and the average result smaller than 680.64) were versions 2, 3, 4, 7, and 10. This is consistent with our observations made in connection with the test case G6, where almost the same subset was selected.

- for the (hardest) test case G10, the best versions were selected on the following basis: the best solution was smaller than 7100 and the average solution was smaller than 7700. Only 5 versions satisfied these criterion; these were versions 2, 3, 5, 7, and 10. Again, as for test cases G6 and G9, versions 3, 7, and 10 are among the best.

It seems that the three versions which gave the best performance overall are versions 3, 7, and 10. Judging from the characteristics of these versions, we may conclude that generally:

- the higher value of parapeter k ($k = 3$) gives better results,
- small number of changes of the reference point does not require changes of genotypes nor the "direction of change" option,
- if the number of changes of the reference point is larger, it is not important whether genotypes in the population are adjusted (for each change) or not. However, it is important to keep "direction of change" option.

5 Conclusions

The results of these preliminary experiments are not, of course, conclusive. It is necessary to conduct a larger number of runs for a larger set of test cases (e.g., G1–G11, see [7]) to understand better the interactions among various options available. It is also necessary to extend this preliminary study for a larger set of parameters values (different values of k, different values of a number of changes of the reference point, etc). Further, a connection between the type of the problem (size of the feasible search space, number of active constraints at the optimum, modality of the objective function) and the characteristics of various versions discussed earlier, must be studied carefully.

Results of some further experiments performed for problems G2 and G3 suggest that the change of the reference point is not always beneficial. For these functions, version #1 (no change of reference point) gave the best results among all versions. It seems that a change of the reference point is beneficial only for some types of functions: thus such a change should be controlled by a feedback from the search process. A preliminary version of a new system with adaptive change of the reference point gave the best performance on all mentioned problems (from $G2$ to $G10$), making appropriate number of changes (e.g., zero changes for $G2$ and $G3$) for different problems. A connection between number of changes and the characteristic of the problem will be studied and reported in the next (full) version of the paper.

Also, currently a new version of the system based on floating point representation is being developed. Note that for such a system there would be no need for adjusting genotypes in the population, as the algorithm operates on phenotypes. A comparison between these systems (i.e., based on binary and floating point representations) should provide additional clues.

Acknowledgments:

This material is based upon work supported by the the grant 8 T11B 049 10 from the Polish State Committee for Scientific Research (KBN) and the grant IRI-9725424 from the National Science Foundation.

References

1. Kozieł, S. (1996). Non-uniform and non-stationary mutation in numerical optimization using genetic algorithms. Electronics and Telecomm. Quarterly, 42 (3), pp. 273–285.
2. Kozieł, S. (1997). Evolutionary algorithms in constrained numerical optimization problems on convex spaces. Electronics and Telecomm. Quarterly, 43 (1), pp. 5–18.
3. Kozieł, S. and Michalewicz, Z. (1997). Evolutionary algorithms, homomorphous mappings, and constrained parameter optimization. To appear in Evolutionary Computation, 1998.
4. Michalewicz, Z. (1996). *Genetic Algorithms+Data Structures=Evolution Programs*. New-York: Springer Verlag. 3rd edition.
5. Michalewicz, Z. and C. Z. Janikow (1991). Handling constraints in genetic algorithms. In R. K. Belew and L. B. Booker (Eds.), *Proceedings of the 4th International Conference on Genetic Algorithms*, pp. 151–157. Morgan Kaufmann.
6. Michalewicz, Z. and G. Nazhiyath (1995). Genocop III: A co-evolutionary algorithm for numerical optimization problems with nonlinear constraints. In D. B. Fogel (Ed.), *Proceedings of the Second IEEE International Conference on Evolutionary Computation*, pp. 647–651. IEEE Press.
7. Michalewicz, Z. and Schoenauer, M. (1996). Evolutionary computation for constrained parameter optimization problems. Evolutionary Computation, Vol.4, No.1, pp.1–32.
8. Schoenauer, M. and Z. Michalewicz (1996). Evolutionary computation at the edge of feasibility. W. Ebeling, and H.-M. Voigt (Eds.), *Proceedings of the 4th Conference on Parallel Problems Solving from Nature*, pp.245–254, Springer Verlag.
9. Schoenauer, M. and Z. Michalewicz (1997). Boundary Operators for Constrained Parameter Optimization Problems. Proceedings of the 7th International Conference on Genetic Algorithms, pp.320–329, July 1997.

A Spatial Predator-Prey Approach to Multi-objective Optimization: A Preliminary Study

Marco Laumanns, Günter Rudolph, and Hans-Paul Schwefel

Universität Dortmund, Fachbereich Informatik, D–44221 Dortmund / Germany

Abstract. This paper presents a novel evolutionary approach of approximating the shape of the Pareto-optimal set of multi-objective optimization problems. The evolutionary algorithm (EA) uses the predator-prey model from ecology. The prey are the usual individuals of an EA that represent possible solutions to the optimization task. They are placed at vertices of a graph, remain stationary, reproduce, and are chased by predators that traverse the graph. The predators chase the prey only within its current neighborhood and according to one of the optimization criteria. Because there are several predators with different selection criteria, those prey individuals, which perform best with respect to all objectives, are able to produce more descendants than inferior ones. As soon as a vertex for the prey becomes free, it is refilled by descendants from alive parents in the usual way of EA, i.e., by inheriting slightly altered attributes. After a while, the prey concentrate at Pareto-optimal positions. The main objective of this preliminary study is the answer to the question whether the predator-prey approach to multi-objective optimization works at all. The performance of this evolutionary algorithm is examined under several step-size adaptation rules.

1 Introduction

It may be discussed controversially, whether organic evolution is an adaptation or an amelioration process, or neither of those. But, mimicking some rules of that "game of life" has led to powerful optimum seeking algorithms [1]. Three different approaches that emerged in the 1960s have been given the common denominator *Evolutionary Algorithm* (EA) or *Evolutionary Computation* (EC) [2]. Together with Neural and Fuzzy Computation, EC has become part of the new field called *Computational Intelligence* (CI) [3]. The common feature of CI methods is their emphasis on "imitating life" by subsymbolic information processing.

In many if not most cases, EAs are used to solve optimization tasks with just one objective, where the (global) optimizer often turns out to be a unique position in the decision parameter space. However, if several conflicting objectives are given, there is a larger set of interesting solutions: the non-dominated or Pareto-optimal set. Tradeoff-curves for two objectives at a time show how far one has to concede with respect to one goal in order to win with respect to the other.

A couple of conventional approaches to multi-objective optimization have been adopted to EAs [4–6]. In most cases, ambiguities are eliminated before the Pareto-set is known, e.g., by weighting the criteria or Euclidean distances to the single-criteria optimizers.

A novel approach of identifying the whole Pareto-optimal set within one run is presented in the following, using the predator-prey model from ecology. The prey are the usual individuals of an EA that represent possible solutions to the optimization task. They are placed, e.g., on a toroidal grid, reproduce, die off after a while, and are challenged by predators that might cut down their life span. While the prey remain stationary on the vertices, each predator performs a random walk on the grid, chases the prey only within its current neighborhood and according to one of the optimization criteria. Because there are several predators with different selection criteria, those prey individuals, which perform best with respect to all objectives, are able to produce more descendants than inferior ones. As soon as a grid place for the prey becomes free, it is refilled by descendants from alive parents in the usual way of EA, i.e., by inheriting slightly altered attributes. After a while, the prey are expected to concentrate at Pareto-optimal positions. The principally asynchronous concept without global observer should ease the use of parallel processing systems substantially.

The organization of this paper is as follows. After the introduction of the basic terminology associated with the multi-objective optimization problem given in section 2, we present the spatial predator-prey model in section 3. To get a first assessment of the behavior of this evolutionary algorithm, we describe some initial numerical experiments and discuss the results in section 4. Finally, section 5 summarizes our preliminary conclusions.

2   Multi-Objective Optimization

Let $f : \mathcal{X} \to \mathbb{R}^q$ with $\mathcal{X} \subseteq \mathbb{R}^\ell$ and $q \geq 2$ be a vector-valued function that maps a decision vector $x \in \mathcal{X}$ to an objective vector $y = f(x) \in \mathbb{R}^q$. In the ideal case the objective functions $f_i : \mathcal{X} \to \mathbb{R}$ should be minimized simultaneously for $i = 1, \ldots, q$. The problem is, however, that the set of objective vectors is not totally ordered. To understand the problem to full extent it is important to keep in mind that the values $f_1(x), \ldots, f_q(x)$ of the $q \geq 2$ objective functions are *incommensurable* quantities and that the objectives themselves are conflicting in general: While f_1 may measure the costs of producing a car, f_2 may measure the level of pollution, f_3 the total weight, f_4 the probability of a lethal injury in case of a frontal crash, and so forth. As a consequence, the notion of the "optimality" of some solution needs a more general formulation than in single-objective optimization. It seems reasonable to regard those decisions as being optimal which cannot be improved with respect to one criterion without getting a worse value in another criterion. Formally, this concept of optimality may be stated as follows.

Let $\mathcal{F} = \{f(x) : x \in \mathcal{X} \subseteq \mathbb{R}^\ell\} \subset \mathbb{R}^q$ be the set of objective vectors that are attainable under the mapping f. An objective vector $y^* \in \mathcal{F}$ is said to be *Pareto-optimal* with respect to f if there is no $y \in \mathcal{F}$ with $y \neq y^*$ such that $y_i \leq y_i^*$ for all $i = 1, \ldots, q$. The set $\mathcal{F}^*$ of all Pareto-optimal objective vectors is called the *Pareto set*. Each decision vector $x^* \in \mathcal{X}^* = \{x \in \mathcal{X} \subseteq \mathbb{R}^\ell : f(x) \in \mathcal{F}^*\}$ is termed an *efficient solution* or a *Pareto-optimal decision vector* of the multi-objective optimization problem. Since the sets $\mathcal{X}^*$ and $\mathcal{F}^*$ can be analytically determined only in exceptional cases and since the dimension of $\mathcal{X}^*$ as well as $\mathcal{F}^*$ may be as large as $\min\{\ell, q - 1\}$, numerical methods for finding the set of Pareto-optimal decisions are generally restricted to approximating the shape of the set $\mathcal{X}^*$. Needless to say, this will also be the goal of the evolutionary algorithm to be presented shortly.

3 The Predator-Prey Model

3.1 Model Description

Let $G = (V, E)$ be an undirected connected graph with $|V| = n$ vertices and $|E| = m$ edges. Each vertex is associated with a prey which is represented by a decision vector. The predator makes a random walk on graph G, i.e., a predator on some vertex v moves with probability $1/d(v)$ to one of its nearest neighbors where $d(v)$ denotes the degree of vertex $v \in V$. More specifically, the transition probabilities of the predator's random walk are

$$p_{vw} = \begin{cases} 1/d(v) & \text{if } (v, w) \in E \\ 0 & \text{otherwise.} \end{cases}$$

Each predator chases the prey with respect to a single specific objective only. Thus, there are at least q predators simultaneously chasing the prey with respect to the q different criteria. An i-predator at vertex $v \in V$ will "catch" the prey in the neighborhood of v which is worst with respect to objective function f_i. If a prey has been caught by a predator then it is erased from this vertex and successively replaced by a new individual that is produced by mutation and possibly recombination of adjacent individuals.

3.2 Choice of Spatial Structure

If the evolutionary process is not stopped then each predator will visit every vertex/prey infinitely often. This is an immediate consequence of the fact that a predator moves through the graph according to a random walk. It seems reasonable to choose a graph structure such that the predator visits every vertex equally often in the limit (there is at least no obvious objection against this postulation). To identify the class of graphs satisfying this requirement let $N(v, k)$ be the number of times the random walk visits vertex $v \in V$ in k steps. If the graph is non-bipartite then

$$\lim_{k \to \infty} \frac{N(v, k)}{k} = \frac{d(v)}{2|E|} \tag{1}$$

for every $v \in V$ [7]. Thus, non-bipartite regular graphs are appropriate candidates. But bipartite d-regular graphs with bipartition $\{V_1, V_2\}$ are acceptable as well, since the distribution of the random walk oscillates between "almost uniform on V_1" and "almost uniform on V_2" as $k \to \infty$.

The inverse of the limit in (1) is the expected time until a random walk starting at $v \in V$ returns to v for the first time. Thus, for d-regular non-bipartite graphs the expected *recurrence time* is $h_v = 2m/d$ for all $v \in V$. This value is also approximately valid for bipartite d-regular graphs.

Evidently, the frequency of selecting a prey with respect to the different criteria depends on the graph structure on the one hand and on the number of predators per criterion on the other hand. Since the graph structure will be kept fixed we need a measure permitting an assessment of this relationship.

The mean *cover time* $\mathsf{E}[C(G)]$ of a graph G represents the maximum expected number of steps required by a predator until each vertex has been visited at least once. For arbitrary graphs the mean cover time can be bracketed by $(1 + o(1))\, n \log n \leq \mathsf{E}[C(G)] \leq \frac{4}{27} n^3 + o(n^3)$ [8,9]. A cubic increase in the number of vertices is certainly prohibitive for practical use. But the cubic upper bound decreases to a quadratic one for vertex- and edge-symmetric graphs [10]. More specifically, $(n-1)\, H_n \leq \mathsf{E}[C(G)] \leq 2\,(n-1)^2$ where H_n is the nth Harmonic number. The lower bound can be sharpened for a specific symmetric graph, namely, the two-dimensional torus. In this case one obtains $\mathsf{E}[C(G)] = \Omega(n \log^2 n)$ [11].

Thus, if the graph is a two-dimensional torus then the expected recurrence time per predator is $1/n$ and between $n \log^2 n$ and $2\,(n-1)^2$ random steps have to be waited for until a predator has visited each prey. Larger cover times are easy to achieve— but this would slow down the evolutionary process. Therefore, we have chosen the two-dimensional torus for our experiments. A perhaps fruitful generalization for future experiments is the introduction of different neighborhood graphs for reproducing prey and for the random walk of the predators.

3.3 Step Size Control

The development of an appropriate step size control in case of multi-objective opti-mization has received only little attention up to now. The few experiments made in [12] reveal that the step size rules used in single-criterion EAs do not work very well in the multi-criterion case. Actually, it is an open question of how to choose the step size—especially for the evolutionary model considered here.

Apart from a fixed step size, we also experimented with the external step size rule $\sigma_{k+1} = \gamma\, \sigma_k$ where $\gamma \in (0,1)$ and the index k is incremented whenever a prey produces an offspring. We conjecture that it is not possible to devise an internal step size rule (self-adaptation) for this type of evolutionary algorithm. This assessment is supported by the following observation: The predator-prey model may be seen as a generalization of the steady state or $(n+1)$-evolutionary algorithm for single-criterion optimization, and there is well-founded empirical evidence that the usual self-adaptation mechanism does not work satisfactorily for this type of evolutionary algorithms.

4 Preliminary Experimental Results

4.1 Test Problems and Parameter Settings

The neighborhood graph used in the experiments was a toroidal grid of size 30×30, i.e., with 900 prey. The two test problems have two objectives and were chosen as follows:

$$f(x) = \begin{pmatrix} x_1^2 + x_2^2 \\ (x_1 + 2)^2 + x_2^2 \end{pmatrix}$$

$$g(x) = \begin{pmatrix} -10 \exp(-0.2\sqrt{x_1^2 + x_2^2}) \\ |x_1|^{4/5} + |x_2|^{4/5} + 5\,(\sin^3 x_1 + \sin^3 x_2) \end{pmatrix}$$

The set of efficient solutions $\mathcal{X}^*$ associated with problem $f(\cdot)$ can be determined analytically. It is the straight line between the optima of both objective functions, namely, $\mathcal{X}^* = \{x \in \mathbb{R}^2 : (x_1, 0)' \text{ with } -2 \leq x_1 \leq 0\}$. Consequently, the Pareto set is

$$\mathcal{F}^* = f(\mathcal{X}^*) = \{(f_1, f_2)' \in \mathbb{R}_+^2 : f_2 = (2 - \sqrt{f_1})^2 \text{ where } 0 \leq f_1 \leq 4\}.$$

We have chosen this test problem since it possesses no locally efficient solutions apart from those which are also globally efficient. The second test problem $g(\cdot)$ is more difficult since there are also locally efficient solutions that are not globally efficient. Needless to say, our selection of test problems is somewhat arbitrary—but the main objective of this preliminary study is the answer to the question whether the predator-prey approach to multi-objective optimization is feasible or not.

For this purpose the initial individuals were drawn at random within the region $[-50, 50]^2 \subset \mathbb{R}^2$ and the predators were randomly placed at vertices of the graph. The standard deviations of the Gaussian mutations (the "step sizes") were either kept fixed with $\sigma = 0.5$ and $\sigma = 0.05$, or decreased by the schedule $\sigma_{k+1} = 0.99\,\sigma_k$. For each objective there was one predator, except for the decreasing schedule where we also experimented with up to 100 predators per objective.

4.2 Discussion

The first surprising observation that can be drawn from our experiments is that the recombination of the decision vectors leads to a significantly worse approximation of the Pareto-set than the usage of mutation alone. This phenomenon deserves further exploration which is however beyond the scope of this preliminary study. As a consequence, we have only employed mutations in our numerical experiments presented here.

Figure 1 shows the approximation of the Pareto-set and its associated decision vectors for the first test problem $f(\cdot)$. The top two rows represent the state of the predator-prey EA with fixed step sizes $\sigma = 0.5$ and $\sigma = 0.05$ for one predator per objective after $100,000$ random steps of each predator. Needless to say, the EA cannot stochastically converge to the Pareto-set if the step sizes are fixed. But the prey individuals are closely distributed in the vicinity of the Pareto-set, and the distribution becomes the more concentrated the smaller is the step size. Since small step sizes require more iterations than large step size in order to reach the stationary distribution, it seems reasonable to begin with large step sizes and to decrease them in the course of the evolution. We have experimented with various decreasing schedules—a good one was the choice $\sigma_{k+1} = 0.99\,\sigma_k$. The lower two rows show the state of the EA with this decreasing schedule after $380,000$ random steps per predator (one predator per objective) and $3,800$ random steps per predator in case of 100 predators per objective (last row). Evidently, the population of prey decomposes into several isolated subsets if there is only one predator per objective. We conjecture that this phenomenon is due to the fact that the predators stay too long in the vicinity of a certain vertex (so that these prey are pushed towards the solutions of only one criterion) and need too much time to commute between far distant vertices. If there are several predators per objective (last row) then each prey is more frequently evaluated by both objectives alternately. Apparently, this leads to a more accurate approximation of the Pareto-set.

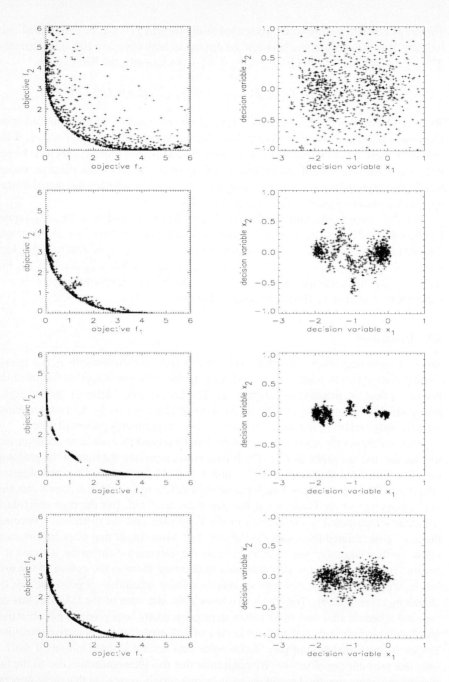

Fig. 1. Approximation of the Pareto-set and its associated set of decision vectors of problem $f(\cdot)$ with two predators and constant $\sigma = 0.5$ (row 1), $\sigma = 0.05$ (row 2), decreasing schedule $\sigma_{k+1} = 0.99\,\sigma_k$ (row 3), and decreasing schedule in case of 200 predators (row 4).

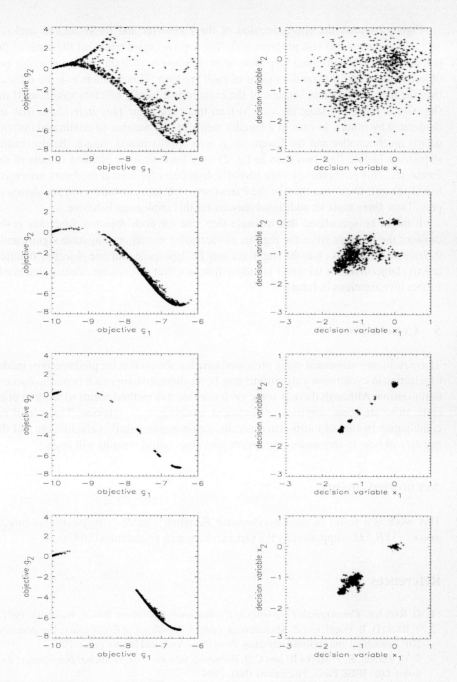

Fig. 2. Approximation of the Pareto-set and its associated set of decision vectors of problem $g(\cdot)$ with two predators and constant $\sigma = 0.5$ (row 1), $\sigma = 0.05$ (row 2), decreasing schedule $\sigma_{k+1} = 0.99\,\sigma_k$ (row 3), and decreasing schedule in case of 200 predators (row 4).

Figure 2 shows the approximation of the Pareto-set and its associated decision vectors for the second test problem $g(\cdot)$. The top two rows represent the state of the predator-prey EA with fixed step sizes $\sigma = 0.5$ and $\sigma = 0.05$ for one predator per objective after $100,000$ random steps of each predator. This problem is more difficult than the first test problem because of the existence of locally efficient solutions. If the step size is relatively large ($\sigma = 0.5$) then there are many prey individuals that are dominated by others. In case of a smaller step size, the number of dominated individuals is much smaller and the Pareto-set is well approximated. Again, the decreasing step size schedule (last two rows in fig. 2) only leads to some isolated subsets of the Pareto-set. This phenomenon only partially disappears for several predators per objective (last row): about one third of the Pareto-set is not represented by the population of prey. Thus, there must be additional reasons for this unpleasant behavior.

It might be speculated that a single step size for both objective functions is the cause of the problem since the regions of successful mutations may have significantly different sizes. In this case, the step sizes may be appropriate for one objective function and too large/small for the other objective function. But this is a speculation that needs further investigations in future.

5 Conclusions

The preliminary numerical study presented here has shown that the predator-prey model of selection in evolutionary algorithms may be an alternative approach in multi-objective optimization. Although there is some evidence that this method seems to work in principle, there are some surprising phenomena awaiting an explanation. The role of recombination in case of multi-criteria optimization requires further elucidation, and the question of how to choose an appropriate step size control remains still open.

Acknowledgments

This work is a result of the *Collaborative Research Center "Computational Intelligence" (SFB 531)* supported by the German Research Foundation (DFG).

References

1. G. Rudolph. *Convergence Properties of Evolutionary Algorithms*. Kovač, Hamburg, 1997.
2. T. Bäck, D. B. Fogel, and Z. Michalewicz, editors. *Handbook of Evolutionary Computation*. IOP Publishing and Oxford University Press, New York and Bristol (UK), 1997.
3. J. M. Zurada, R. J. Marks II, and C. J. Robinson, editors. *Computational Intelligence: Imitating Life*. IEEE Press, Piscataway (NJ), 1994.
4. C. M. Fonseca and P. J. Fleming. An overview of evolutionary algorithms in multiobjective optimization. *Evolutionary Computation*, 3(1):1–16, 1995.
5. H. Tamaki, H. Kita, and S. Kobayashi. Multi–objective optimization by genetic algorithms: a review. In *Proceedings of the 3rd IEEE International Conference on Evolutionary Computation*, pages 517–522. IEEE Press, Piscataway (NJ), 1996.

6. J. Horn. Multicriterion decision making. In T. Bäck, D. B. Fogel, and Z. Michalewicz, editors, *Handbook of Evolutionary Computation*, pages F1.9:1–15. IOP Publishing and Oxford University Press, New York and Bristol (UK), 1997.

7. R. Motwani and P. Raghavan. *Randomized Algorithms*. Cambridge University Press, New York (NY), 1995.

8. U. Feige. A tight upper bound on the cover time for random walks on graphs. *Random Structures and Algorithms*, 6(1):51–54, 1995.

9. U. Feige. A tight lower bound on the cover time for random walks on graphs. *Random Structures and Algorithms*, 6(4):433–438, 1995.

10. J. L. Palacios. Expected cover times of random walks on symmetric graphs. *Journal of Theoretical Probability*, 5(3):597–600, 1992.

11. D. Zuckermann. A technique for lower bounding the cover time. *SIAM Journal of Discrete Mathematics*, 5(1):81–87, 1992.

12. G. Rudolph. On a multi–objective evolutionary algorithm and its convergence to the pareto set. In *Proceedings of the 1998 IEEE International Conference on Evolutionary Computation*, pages 511–516. IEEE Press, Piscataway (NJ), 1998.

Selective Breeding in a Multiobjective Genetic Algorithm

G.T. Parks and I. Miller[1]

[1] Engineering Design Centre, Cambridge University Engineering Department,
Trumpington Street, Cambridge CB2 1PZ, UK

Abstract. This paper describes an investigation of the efficacy of various elitist selection strategies in a multiobjective Genetic Algorithm implementation, with parents being selected both from the current population and from the archive record of nondominated solutions encountered during search. It is concluded that, because the multiobjective optimization process naturally maintains diversity in the population, it is possible to improve the performance of the algorithm through the use of strong elitism and high selection pressures without suffering the disadvantages of genetic convergence which such strategies would bring in single objective optimization.

1   Introduction

Many (perhaps most) real-world design problems are, in fact, multiobjective optimization problems in which the designer seeks to optimize simultaneously several conflicting performance attributes of the design. There are two standard methods for treating multiobjective problems, if a traditional optimization algorithm which minimizes a single objective is to be employed. One is to construct a composite objective through a weighted summation of the individual objectives. The other is to place constraints on all but one of the objectives and to optimize the remaining one. Whichever method is used, the solution of the resulting single objective problem leads to the identification of just one point on the trade-off surface, the position of which depends on the designer's preconceptions. To explore the trade-off surface further a large number of different optimization runs must be executed each with different weightings or constraints — a potentially time-consuming and computationally expensive exercise if even attempted.

Evolutionary Algorithms are well suited to multiobjective optimization and a number of different multiobjective Genetic Algorithms (GAs) have been developed [1]. Multiobjective GAs provide the means to expose the trade-off surface between competing objectives in a single optimization and are therefore a very attractive tool for the designer.

It is well established that an elitist strategy, in which the best solution found thus far is always selected as a parent, can be advantageous in single objective GA optimization. In multiobjective optimization there may well be more than one 'best' solution. A solution X can be said to be *dominated* by solution Y if Y is better on all counts (objectives). Any solution found which is not dominated by any other solution yet encountered can therefore be said to be *nondominated* and, from a multiobjective viewpoint, equally good.

This paper investigates the benefits of various elitist selection strategies in a multiobjective GA developed to optimize Pressurized Water Reactor (PWR) reload cores.

2 Pressurized Water Reactor Reload Design

A typical PWR core contains 193 fuel assemblies arranged with quarter core symmetry. At each refuelling one third or one quarter of these may be replaced. It is common practice for fresh fuel assemblies to carry a number of burnable poisons (BP) pins (control material). It is also usual to rearrange old fuel in order to improve the characteristics of the new core. This shuffling can entail the exchange of corresponding assemblies between core quadrants, which is equivalent to changing the assembly 'orientations', or the exchange of different assemblies, which changes their locations and possibly their orientations also.

Thus, a candidate loading pattern (LP) of predetermined symmetry must specify:
- the fuel assembly to be loaded in each core location,
- the BP loading with each fresh fuel assembly, and
- the orientation of each assembly.

It is readily apparent that the search for the best LP is a formidable combinatorial optimization problem.

The PWR reload core design problem has been tackled in many different ways [2] and one interesting point to emerge from a review of past work is the diversity in objective functions chosen. It is clear that the PWR reload core design problem is in reality a multiobjective optimization problem, where an improvement in one objective is often only gained at the cost of deteriorations in others.

3 A Multiobjective GA for PWR Reload Design

A multiobjective GA which attempts to solve the PWR reload core design problem has been developed [3]. The structure of the GA is shown in Fig. 1 and is fairly standard. The details of the implementation are, however, problem specific.

3.1 Coding

Each solution is represented by three two-dimensional arrays, corresponding to the physical layout of the fuel assemblies, their BP loadings and their orientations respectively.

3.2 Crossover Operator

For this application Poon's Heuristic Tie-Breaking Crossover (HTBX) operator [4] is used. HTBX maps the parent fuel arrays to reactivity-ranked arrays based on the assemblies' reactivities (reactivity being a parameter related to the amount of fissile material in the fuel and thus a convenient indicator of other attributes of interest.). HTBX then combines randomly selected complementary parts of these arrays through a 'cut and paste' operation, and uses a simple tie-breaking algorithm to produce valid offspring reactivity-ranked arrays. Finally the assembly-ranking mapping is reversed to produce the

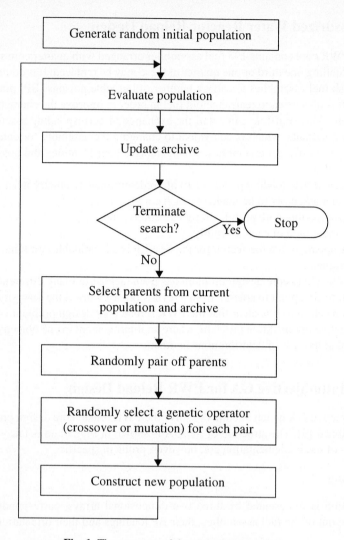

Fig. 1. The structure of the multiobjective GA

offspring assembly LPs. The BP loadings and assembly orientations are all inherited from one or other parent. Thus, the reactivity distribution (and it is hoped, in consequence, other attributes) of an offspring LP resembles, but is not necessarily identical to, parts of both parents.

3.3 Mutation Operator

For this application the mutation operator performs one, two or three fuel assembly shuffles, randomly allocating allowed BP loadings and orientations to the assemblies affected. It is used as an alternative to crossover, i.e. offspring are produced using either mutation or crossover but not both, the choice between operators being made randomly.

The relative frequencies with which these operators are chosen are approximately 25% and 75% respectively, this ratio having been determined (by extensive testing) to give good performance in this application.

3.4 Population Evaluation

In the examples which follow the Generalized Perturbation Theory based reactor model employed in FORMOSA-P [5] was used to evaluate LPs, but, in principle, the evaluation of objectives can be performed using any appropriate reactor physics code.

3.5 Archiving

While the GA is running an *archive* of nondominated solutions is maintained. After each LP has been evaluated it is compared with existing members of the archive. If it dominates any members of the archive, those are removed and the new solution is added. If the new solution is dominated by any members of the archive, it is not archived. If it neither dominates nor is dominated by any members of the archive, it is archived if it is sufficiently 'dissimilar' to existing archive members, where, for this application, the degree of dissimilarity between two LPs is defined in terms of their reactivity distributions [5]. This dissimilarity requirement helps to maintain diversity in the archive.

The archiving logic is such that the solutions are arrayed by age, i.e. the first solution in the archive is earliest nondominated solution found and the last solution in the archive is the most recent nondominated solution found.

3.6 Selection

The current population is ranked by sorting through to identify all nondominated solutions, ranking these appropriately, then removing them from consideration, and repeating the procedure until all solutions have been ranked — a procedure first proposed by Goldberg [7] and implemented by Srinivas and Deb [8]. A selection probability is then assigned to each solution based on its ranking in a manner similar to Baker's single criterion ranking selection procedure [9]. The probability of a rank n member of the current population being selected is given by:

$$p_n = \frac{S(N + 1 - R_n) + R_n - 2}{N(N-1)}, \tag{1}$$

in which N is the population size, S is a selection pressure and

$$R_n = 1 + r_n + 2 \sum_{i=1}^{n-1} r_i, \tag{2}$$

where r_i is the number of solutions in rank i. Parents are then selected by stochastic remainder selection without replacement.

In addition, some of the parents for each new generation can be chosen from the archive of nondominated solutions, thus introducing multiobjective elitism to the selection process. When this is done equation (1) is modified such that:

$$p_n = \frac{N - A}{N} \left(\frac{S(N + 1 - R_n) + R_n - 2}{N(N-1)} \right), \tag{3}$$

where A is the number of parents selected from the archive.

The next section presents the results of a study investigating the algorithm's performance using various strategies for selecting from the archive and the current population.

4   Elitist Selection Strategies

A variety of selection strategies have been investigated. In each case, 10 runs of the GA were made on a representative PWR reload design problem with three objectives:

- minimization of the enrichment of the fresh fuel (the *feed enrichment*),
- maximization of the burnup of the fuel to be discharged (the *discharge burnup*), and
- minimization of the ratio of the peak to average assembly power (the *power peaking*).

In each run a population of 204 was evolved for 51 generations — the GA having been found to give satisfactory performance with these parameter settings [3]. The same random number seeds were used for each set of 10 runs.

The performance of the algorithm was measured by monitoring archiving activity. The number of solutions added to the archive, the number of solutions removed from the archive (due to being dominated by newly found solutions) and the archive size (the difference between the numbers of solutions added and removed) were all monitored. For each set of 10 runs the averages of these three tallies and their standard deviations were calculated.

The number of solutions added to the archive can be regarded as a measure of the algorithm's success in the exploring the search space, and the number of solutions removed can be regarded as a measure of the algorithm's success in advancing the pareto front between the objectives. Visual inspection of the trade-off surfaces exposed in various runs confirmed that high values of these tallies correlated with good algorithm performance.

4.1   Proportion Selected from the Archive

The first factor investigated was the proportion of parents for a new population to be selected from the archive as opposed to from the current population. In these runs a target fraction, f, of the parents to be selected from the archive was set. Early in the runs the number of solutions archived is less than fN and when this was the case just one copy of each archived solution was selected. Once the archive size exceeded fN then the fN parents were chosen randomly from the archive. The remainder of the parents were selected from the current population as described in Section 3.6 using a selection pressure, S, of 2.0.

The results shown in Table 1 reveal that the average values of the three performance measures were all observed to increase as the proportion of parents selected from the

Table 1. Algorithm performance — proportion of parents selected from the archive

Proportion drawn from archive	Solutions added Number	σ	Solutions removed Number	σ	Final archive Size	σ
0%	412.0	38.24	276.3	24.69	135.7	18.43
12.5%	527.3	30.51	366.2	24.16	161.1	32.79
25%	584.2	36.02	423.0	43.55	161.2	18.22
37.5%	629.5	61.44	458.5	67.61	171.0	16.35
50%	665.2	71.32	491.5	72.77	173.7	23.35
62.5%	681.4	81.81	503.1	74.53	178.3	23.23
75%	683.8	68.73	504.6	60.85	179.2	21.23

archive was increased up to 75%.

This is, at first sight, a rather surprising result. Conventional GA wisdom states that strongly elitist strategies result in premature convergence. The fundamental difference here is that the nature of the multiobjective search results is widely different solutions being archived, and therefore the selection of parents from the archive serves to maintain diversity in the population. It is to be expected that the heavy selection of good parents will improve algorithm performance, if problems of genetic convergence do not arise.

As there is comparatively little improvement in the measured algorithm performance in selecting more than 50% of the parents from the archive and we were reluctant to place too much emphasis on selection from the archive, we chose to conduct our further investigations using an archive selection fraction of 50%.

4.2 Number of Copies of Archive Solutions

As noted above, early in the search there may be insufficient numbers of solutions archived to fill the demand for parents. We therefore investigated the merits of making multiple copies of archived solutions to help fill this demand. When the number of solutions in the archive was less than fN up to a maximum of C copies were made. Obvi-

Table 2. Algorithm performance (after 20 generations) — copies made of archive solutions

Maximum number of copies	Solutions added Number	σ	Solutions removed Number	σ	Intermediate archive Size	σ
1	224.0	32.27	146.6	28.02	77.4	14.76
2	285.1	27.42	194.0	16.01	91.1	18.27
3	308.4	28.12	213.6	26.53	94.8	12.13
4	309.2	27.84	211.6	28.31	97.6	13.63
5	317.1	46.08	225.1	41.49	92.0	10.59

Table 3. Algorithm performance (after 51 generations) — copies made of archive solutions

Maximum number of copies	Solutions added		Solutions removed		Final archive	
	Number	σ	Number	σ	Size	σ
1	665.2	71.32	491.5	72.77	173.7	23.35
2	694.3	41.78	502.9	38.45	191.4	23.14
3	693.5	70.06	500.1	55.15	193.4	27.06
4	677.9	60.85	481.9	56.52	196.0	15.40
5	696.9	85.29	503.7	79.03	193.2	12.55

ously as the archive size increases fewer copies of each solution are made.

Table 2 shows that after 20 generations the performance of the algorithm is improved substantially by allowing up to 2 copies to be made of archive solutions and improved further (though not substantially) by allowing further copies to be made. However, Table 3 shows that by the end of the run there is no advantage in having made more than two copies — early over-selection evidently having impaired long term algorithm performance — but there is still some advantage in making two copies of archive solutions. We therefore adopted this strategy in subsequent investigations.

4.3 Selection from the Archive

Once there are more than sufficient solutions in the archive to fill the demand for parents the question then arises as to how they should be chosen. As the archived solutions are stored historically a number of options are readily available. We investigated:
- selecting them randomly (which is what had been done to this point),
- selecting the fN newest members of the archive,
- selecting the fN oldest members of the archive, and
- selecting a random 'slice' (i.e. fN consecutive members) of the archive.

The results in Table 4 show that there is little to choose between the two random selection methods. Consistently selecting the oldest solutions gives rather worse performance, while consistently selecting the newest solutions gives rather better performance. We conclude that favouring the newest archive solutions improves performance

Table 4. Algorithm performance — selection method from the archive

Selection method	Solutions added		Solutions removed		Final archive	
	Number	σ	Number	σ	Size	σ
Random	694.3	41.78	502.9	38.45	191.4	23.14
Newest members	725.4	55.12	528.4	39.91	197.0	23.11
Oldest members	651.7	49.72	461.4	37.60	190.3	22.70
Random slice	695.8	55.66	499.9	42.15	195.9	21.56

Table 5. Algorithm performance — selection pressure for the current population

Selection pressure	Solutions added		Solutions removed		Final archive	
	Number	σ	Number	σ	Size	σ
1.0	648.1	91.44	483.9	84.29	164.2	20.86
1.5	677.4	93.04	510.9	78.80	166.5	23.75
2.0	725.4	55.12	528.4	39.91	197.0	23.11
2.5	807.7	83.92	596.2	70.76	211.5	27.48
3.0	802.0	49.84	592.5	63.26	209.5	24.98
3.5	820.6	59.35	604.4	50.05	216.2	20.72
4.0	834.0	65.71	635.7	52.42	198.3	26.21
4.5	856.6	96.63	639.7	86.03	216.9	17.73
5.0	809.2	78.33	597.9	78.13	211.3	19.77

because it concentrates the search in newly found areas of promise. Favouring the oldest archive solutions conversely concentrates the search in areas which have already been well explored.

4.4 Selection from the Current Population

All our investigations thus far considered selection of parents from the archive. The remaining parents (at least 50% of the parents in most of the cases considered) are selected from the current population. We therefore examined the effect of varying the selection pressure (S in equation (1)) used in selecting parents from the current population. This was done while using our 'optimal' archive selection strategy of taking 50% of the parents from the archive, making up to 2 copies and using the newest solutions. A selection pressure S of 1.0 gives all solutions an equal probability of selection. For values of S greater than 2.0 low ranked members of the current population may have negative selection probabilities according to equation (1), in which case they are not selected at all.

The results given in Table 5 show that increasing the selection pressure to favour the selection of highly ranked members of the current population can also improve algorithm performance. It is not until S is increased to 5.0 that clear evidence of the dangers of over-selection is revealed. Again, we conclude that the diversity maintained in the population because of the nature of the multiobjective search — the population spreads out towards the pareto front rather than converging on a single optimum — enables strong selection pressures to be used to exploit good solutions without premature convergence.

To illustrate the difference achieved in algorithm performance by such 'aggressive elitism', Fig. 2 shows typical trade-off surfaces (the final archive contents plotted in two-objective space) found by (a) a very unelitist implementation selecting all its parents from the current population (none from the archive) and using a 'traditional' value of selection pressure parameter S of 2.0, and (b) an aggressively elitist implementation

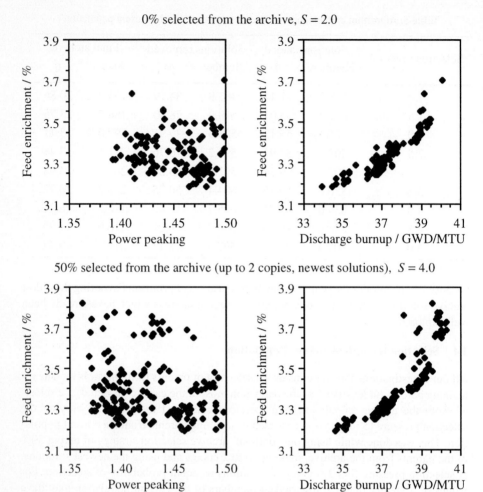

Fig. 2. Typical trade-off surfaces

selecting 50% of the parents from the archive (making up to 2 copies and using the newest solutions) and using a value of S of 4.0. It is readily apparent that the aggressively elitist implementation has exposed much more of the trade-off surface, particularly the high discharge burnup and low power peaking parts of the surface.

5   Conclusions

Although this paper has considered a single (rather specialised) application of multiobjective GA optimization, our findings should apply to other multiobjective GA applications and implementations. This study has demonstrated that, because the multiobjective optimization process naturally maintains diversity in the population and in the archive of nondominated solutions found, it is possible to improve the performance of the algorithm substantially through the use of strongly elitist selection strategies making extensive use of the archive and high selection pressures, without suffering the disadvantages of genetic convergence which such strategies would bring in single objective optimization.

There are further related topics which still require investigation such as the potential benefits of alternative selection methods, such as tournament selection, and the advantage, if any, of forms of selective pairing of parents. These are the subjects of ongoing research.

Acknowledgements

The authors gratefully acknowledge the computational resources provided in the Jesus College Computer Centre by Sun Microsystems and Electronic Data Systems and the collaborative cooperation and support of the North Carolina State University (NCSU) Electric Power Research Center.

References

1. Fonseca, C.M., Fleming, P.J.: An overview of evolutionary algorithms in multiobjective optimization. Evol. Comp. **3** (1995) 1-16
2. Downar, T.J., Sesonske, A.: Light water reactor fuel cycle optimization: theory versus practice. Adv. Nucl. Sci. Tech. **20** (1988) 71-126
3. Parks, G.T.: Multiobjective PWR reload core design by nondominated Genetic Algorithm search. Nucl. Sci. Eng. **124** (1996) 178-187
4. Poon, P.W. , Parks, G.T.: Application of Genetic Algorithms to in-core nuclear fuel management optimization. Proc. Joint Int. Conf. Mathematical Methods and Supercomputing in Nuclear Applications, Karlsruhe **1** (1993) 777-786
5. Kropaczek, D.J., Turinsky, P.J., Parks, G.T., Maldonado, G.I.: The efficiency and fidelity of the in-core nuclear fuel management code FORMOSA-P, Reactor Physics and Reactor Computations (Edited by Y. Ronen and E. Elias), Ben Gurion University of the Negev Press (1994) 572-579
6. Kropaczek, D.J., Parks, G.T., Maldonado, G.I., Turinsky, P.J.: Application of Simulated Annealing to in-core nuclear fuel management optimization. Proc. 1991 Int. Top. Mtg. Advances in Mathematics, Computations and Reactor Physics, ANS, Pittsburgh PA **5** (1991) 22.1 1.1-1.12
7. Goldberg, D.E.: Genetic Algorithms in search, optimization, and machine learning. Addison Wesley, Reading MA (1989)
8. Srinivas, N., Deb, K.: Multiobjective optimization using nondominated sorting in Genetic Algorithms. Evol. Comp. **2** (1994) 221-248
9. Baker, J.E.: Adaptive selection methods for Genetic Algorithms. Proc. Int. Conf. Genetic Algorithms and their Applications, Pittsburgh PA (Edited J.J. Grefenstette), Lawrence Erlbaum Associates, Hillsdale NJ (1985) 101-111

Niching and Elitist Models for MOGAs

Shigeru Obayashi, Shinichi Takahashi and Yukihiro Takeguchi

Department of Aeronautics and Space Engineering
Tohoku University
Sendai, Japan
s.obayashi@computer.org

Abstract. This paper examines several niching and elitist models applied to Multiple-Objective Genetic Algorithms (MOGAs). Test cases consider a simple problem as well as multidisciplinary design optimization of wing planform shape. Numerical results suggest that the combination of the fitness sharing and the best-N selection leads to the best performance.

1. Introduction

Aircraft design presents a grand challenge to numerical optimization. It is in nature multidisciplinary among aerodynamics, structure, control and propulsion. Each disciplinary model has to be accurate enough to predict aircraft performance. Especially, aerodynamic calculation is computer intensive and the resulting aerodynamic performance is very sensitive to the geometry. Therefore, a robust optimization algorithm is indispensable to this field.

Evolutionary algorithms, Genetic Algorithms (GAs) in particular, are known to be robust (Goldberg, 1989) and have been enjoying increasing popularity in the field of numerical optimization in recent years. GAs have been applied to aeronautical problems in several ways, including parametric and conceptual design of aircraft (Bramlette et al., 1989), preliminary design of turbines (Powell et al., 1989), topological design of nonplanar wings (Gage et al., 1993) and aerodynamic optimization using Computational Fluid Dynamics (CFD) (for example, Quagliarella et al., 1998).

Furthermore, GAs can search for many Pareto-optimal solutions in parallel, by maintaining a population of solutions (Goldberg, 1989). Most real world problems require the simultaneous optimization of multiple, often competing objectives. Such multiobjective (MO) problems seek to optimize components of a vector valued objective function. Unlike the single-objective optimization, the solution to MO problem is not a single point, but a family of points known as the Pareto-optimal set. Each point in this set is optimal in the sense that no improvement can be achieved in one objective component that doesn't lead to degradation in at least one of the remaining components.

GAs can be very efficient, if they can sample solutions uniformly from the Pareto-optimal set. Since GAs are inherently robust, the combination of efficiency and robustness makes them very attractive for solving MO problems. Several approaches have been proposed (Schaffer, 1985, Fonseca et al., 1993 and Horn et al., 1994) and one of them to be employed here is called Multiple Objective Genetic Algorithms (MOGAs) (Fonseca et al., 1993).

Performance of MOGAs can be measured by variety of Pareto solutions and convergence to Pareto front. To construct a better MOGA, several niching and elitist models are examined in this paper through numerical tests.

2. MOGAs

The first three sections below describe basic GA operators used here. Then the extension to multiobjective optimization problems are discussed. Finally, the niching and elitist models are introduced.

2.1. Coding

In GAs, the natural parameter set of the optimization problem is coded as a finite-length string. Traditionally, GAs use binary numbers to represent such strings: a string has a finite length and each bit of a string can be either 0 or 1. For real function optimization, it is more natural to use real numbers. The length of the real-number string corresponds to the number of design variables.

As a sample problem, let's consider the following optimization:

Maximize: $f(x, y) = x + y$

Subject to: $x^2 + y^2 \leq 1$ and $0 \leq x, y \leq 1$

Let's represent the parameter set by using the polar coordinates here as

$$(x, y) = (r \cos \theta, r \sin \theta) \tag{1}$$

since the representation of the constraints will be simplified. Each point (x, y) in the GA population is encoded by a string (r, θ).

2.2. Crossover and mutation

A simple crossover operator for real number strings is the average crossover (Davis, 1990) which computes the arithmetic average of two real numbers provided by the mated pair. In this paper, a weighted average is used as

$$\text{Child1} = ran1 \cdot \text{Parent1} + (1-ran1) \cdot \text{Parent2} \tag{2}$$
$$\text{Child2} = (1-ran1) \cdot \text{Parent1} + ran1 \cdot \text{Parent2}$$

where Child1,2 and Parent1,2 denote encoded design variables of the children (members of the new population) and parents (a mated pair of the old generation), respectively. The uniform random number $ran1$ in $[0,1]$ is regenerated for every design variable. Because of Eq. (2), the number of the initial population is assumed even.

Mutation takes place at a probability of 20% (when a random number satisfies $ran2 < 0.2$). A high mutation rate is applied due to the real number coding. Equations (2) will then be replaced by

$$Child1 = ran1 \cdot Parent1 + (1\text{-}ran1) \cdot Parent2 + m \cdot (ran3\text{-}0.5) \qquad (3)$$
$$Child2 = (1\text{-}ran1) \cdot Parent1 + ran1 \cdot Parent2 + m \cdot (ran3\text{-}0.5)$$

where $ran2$ and $ran3$ are also uniform random numbers in $[0,1]$ and m determines the range of possible mutation. In the following test cases, m was set to 0.4 for the radial coordinate r and $\pi/3$ for the angular coordinate θ.

2.3. Ranking

For a successful evolution, it is necessary to keep appropriate levels of selection pressure throughout a simulation (Goldberg, 1989). Scaling of objective function values has been used widely in practice. However, this leaves the scaling procedures to be determined. To avoid such parametric procedures, a ranking method is often used (Goldberg, 1989). In this method, the population is sorted according to objective function value. Individuals are then assigned an offspring count that is solely a function of their rank. The best individual receives rank 1, the second best receives 2, and so on. The fitness values are reassigned according to rank, for example, as an inverse of their rank values. Then the SUS method (Baker, 1987) takes over with the reassigned values. The method described so far will be hereon referred to as SOGA (Single-Objective Genetic Algorithm).

2.4. Multiobjective Pareto ranking

SOGA assumes that the optimization problem has (or can be reduced to) a single criterion (or objective). Most engineering problems, however, require the simultaneous optimization of multiple, often competing criteria. Solutions to multiobjective problems are often computed by combining multiple criteria into a single criterion according to some utility function. In many cases, however, the utility function is not well known prior to the optimization process. The whole problem should then be treated with non-commensurable objectives. Multiobjective optimization seeks to optimize the components of a vector-valued objective function. Unlike single objective optimization, the solution to this problem is not a single point, but a family of points known as the Pareto-optimal set.

By maintaining a population of solutions, GAs can search for many Pareto-optimal solutions in parallel. This characteristic makes GAs very attractive for solving MO problems. As solvers for MO problems, the following two features are desired: 1) the solutions obtained are Pareto-optimal and 2) they are uniformly sampled from the Pareto-optimal set. To achieve these with GAs, the following two techniques are successfully combined into MOGAs (Fonseca et al., 1993).

To search Pareto-optimal solutions by using MOGA, the ranking selection method described above for SOGA can be extended to identify the near-Pareto-optimal set within the population of GA. To do this, the following definitions are used: suppose

$\mathbf{x}_i$ and $\mathbf{x}_j$ are in the current population and $\mathbf{f} = (f_1, f_2, \cdots, f_q)$ is the set of objective functions to be maximized,

1. $\mathbf{x}_i$ is said to be dominated by (or inferior to) $\mathbf{x}_j$, if $\mathbf{f}(\mathbf{x}_i)$ is partially less than $\mathbf{f}(\mathbf{x}_j)$, i.e., $f_1(\mathbf{x}_i) \leq f_1(\mathbf{x}_j) \wedge f_2(\mathbf{x}_i) \leq f_2(\mathbf{x}_j) \wedge \cdots \wedge f_q(\mathbf{x}_i) \leq f_q(\mathbf{x}_j)$ and $\mathbf{f}(\mathbf{x}_i) \neq \mathbf{f}(\mathbf{x}_j)$.

2. $\mathbf{x}_i$ is said to be non-dominated if there doesn't exist any $\mathbf{x}_j$ in the population that dominates $\mathbf{x}_i$.

Non-dominated solutions within the feasible region in the objective function space give the Pareto-optimal set.

As the first test case examined later in this paper, let's consider the following optimization:

Maximize: $f_1 = x$, $f_2 = y$

Subject to: $x^2 + y^2 \leq 1$ and $0 \leq x, y \leq 1$

The Pareto front of the present test case becomes a quarter arc of the circle $x^2 + y^2 = 1$ at $0 \leq x, y \leq 1$.

Consider an individual $\mathbf{x}_i$ at generation t (Fig. 1) which is dominated by p_i' individuals in the current population. Following Fonseca et al. (1993), its current position in the individuals' rank can be given by

$$\text{rank}(\mathbf{x}_i, t) = 1 + p_i^t \tag{4}$$

All non-dominated individuals are assigned rank 1 as shown in Fig. 1. The fitness assignment according to rank can be done similar to that in SOGA.

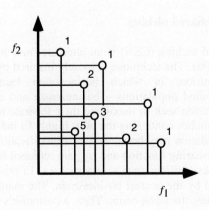

Fig. 1. Pareto ranking method.

2.5. Fitness sharing

To sample Pareto-optimal solutions from the Pareto-optimal set uniformly, it is important to maintain genetic diversity. It is known that the genetic diversity of the population can be lost due to the stochastic selection process. This phenomenon is called the random genetic drift. To avoid such phenomena, the niching method has been introduced (Goldberg, 1989). In this paper, two specific niching models are examined for MOGAs.

The first model is called fitness sharing (FS). A typical sharing function is given by Goldberg (1989). The sharing function depends on the distance between individuals. The distance can be measured with respect to a metric in either genotypic or phenotypic space. A genotypic sharing measures the interchromosomal Hamming distance. A phenotypic sharing, on the other hand, measures the distance between the designs' objective function values. In MOGAs, a phenotypic sharing is usually preferred since we seek a global tradeoff surface in the objective function space.

This scheme introduces new GA parameters, the niche size σ_{share}. The choice of σ_{share} has a significant impact on the performance of MOGAs. In our experiences, it is very difficult to determine its value on the trial-and-error basis. Fonseca et al. (1993) gave a simple estimation of σ_{share} in the objective function space as

$$N\sigma_{share}^{q-1} - \frac{\prod_{i=1}^{q}(M_i - m_i + \sigma_{share}) - \prod_{i=1}^{q}(M_i - m_i)}{\sigma_{share}} = 0 \qquad (5)$$

where N is a population size, q is a dimension of the objective vector, and M_i and m_i are maximum and minimum values of each objective, respectively. This formula has been successfully adapted here. Since this formula is applied at every generation, the resulting σ_{share} is *adaptive* to the population during the evolution process. Niche counts can be consistently incorporated into the fitness assignment according to rank by using them to scale individual fitness within each rank.

2.6. Coevolutionary shared niching

Coevolutionary shared niching (CSN) is an alternate, new niching method proposed in Goldberg et al. (1998). The technique is loosely inspired by the economic model of monopolistic competition, in which businessmen locate themselves among geographically distributed populations – businessmen and customers – where individuals in each population seek to maximize their separate interests thereby creating appropriately spaced niches containing the most highly fit individuals.

The customer population may be viewed as a modification to the original sharing scheme, in which the sharing function and σ_{share} are replaced by requiring customers to share within the closest businessman's service area. In other words, a customer is supposed to be served by the nearest businessman. The number of customers a businessman serves becomes the niche count. Then, a customer's raw fitness is divided by the niche count similar to the original sharing scheme.

The evolution of the businessman population is conducted in a way that promotes the independent establishment of the most highly fit regions or niches in the search space. The businessman population is created by an *imprint* operator that carries the best of one population over the other. Simply stated, businessmen are chosen from the best of the customer population.

This model introduces a new GA parameter d_{min} that determines the minimum distance between the businessmen. In the following test cases, this parameter d_{min} was tuned by the trial-and-error basis and kept constant during the evolution. Niche counts were incorporated into the fitness assignment according to rank similar to the fitness sharing.

2.7. Generational models

To examine effects of generational models, two elitist models are considered here. The first one is the elitist recombination (ER) model that selects two best individuals among two parents and their two offsprings. The other model is the so-called best-N (BN) model that selects the best N individuals among N parents and N children similar to CHC (Eshelman, 1991). These models are compared with the simple generational (SG) model that replaces N parents simply with N children. The population size was kept to 100 in all test cases.

3. Comparison of Niching and Elitist Models

From the techniques described above, five optimization results are shown here for the first test case to maximize $f_1 = x$ and $f_2 = y$, subject to $x^2 + y^2 \leq 1$ and $0 \leq x, y \leq 1$. Figures 2 to 4 show the results obtained from the simple generational model with the fitness sharing (SG + FS), the elitist recombination with the fitness sharing (ER + FS) and the best-N with the fitness sharing (BN + FS), respectively. The GA population is represented by dots and the Pareto front is indicated by a gray arc. When FS was used, the results were improved by the stronger elitist model. Among the three generational models examined here, the best-N selection BN was the best.

Figure 5 shows the results obtained from SG + CSN in gray dots and from BN + CSN in black dots ($d_{min} = 0.028$). The distribution of the gray dots are almost as good as that of the black dots. It also indicates that the coevolutionary shared niching CSN provides a significant improvement over FS when combined with SG. The result obtained from ER + CSN did not show any further improvement and thus it is not plotted here. Only minor improvements were obtained by using the elitist models.

The use of the adaptive σ_{share}, Eq. (5), seems to give better performance than the use of the hand-tuned, constant d_{min} when combined with BN. To confirm this observation, the results are compared in terms of average values of (r, θ) after 30 generations over five different runs as shown in Table 1. Better solutions should have r closer to 1 and θ closer to 45 deg (the uniform distribution in θ should give the average of 45 deg). For comparison, σ_{share} was also tuned by trail and error ($\sigma_{share} = 0.11$).

266

Table 1. Performance comparison of the niching parameters

	constant σ_{share}	constant d_{min}	adaptive σ_{share}
average r	0.9948	0.9914	0.9958
average θ	44.27 deg	44.78 deg	45.25 deg

This confirms that BN + FS with the adaptive σ_{share} gives the best performance. It further leads to a speculation: "adaptive σ_{share} (FS) < adaptive d_{min} (CSN) ?" CSN is very promising but further investigations will be needed, especially in the area of how to determine its parameter d_{min}.

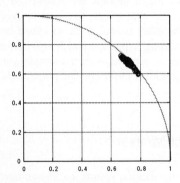

Fig. 2. Pareto solutions by SG + FS.

Fig. 3. Pareto solutions by ER + FS.

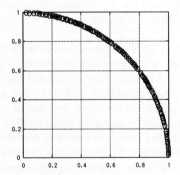

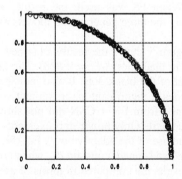

Fig. 4. Pareto solutions by BN + FS.

Fig. 5. Pareto solutions by SG + CSN (gray dots) and BN + CSN (black dots).

4. Multidisciplinary Optimization of Wing Planform Design

An application of MOGA to multidisciplinary optimization (MDO) of wing planform design (Takahashi et al., 1998) is examined in this section. The present multiobjective optimization problem is described as follows:

     1. Minimize aerodynamic drag (induced + wave drag)
     2. Minimize wing weight
     3. Maximize fuel weight (tank volume) stored in wing

under these constraints:

     1. Lift to be greater than given aircraft weight
     2. Structural strength to be greater than aerodynamic loads

Since the purpose of the present design is to examine the performance of MOGAs as a system-level optimizer, the design variables for wing geometry are greatly reduced. First, aircraft sizes were assumed as wing area of 525 ft^2 and total maximum takeoff weight of 45,000 lb at cruise Mach number of 0.75. Next, as a baseline geometry, a transonic wing was taken from a previous research (Fujii et al., 1987). The original wing has an aspect ratio of 9.42, a taper ratio of 0.246 and a sweep angle at the quarter chord line of 23.7 deg. Its airfoil sections are supercritical and their thickness and twist angle distributions are reduced toward the tip. Then, only two parameters are chosen as design variables: sweep angle and taper ratio.

The objective functions and constraints are computed as follows. First, drag is evaluated, using a potential flow solver called FLO27 (Jameson et al, 1977). The code can solve subsonic and transonic flows. From the flow field solution, lift and drag can be postprocessed. Since the flow is assumed inviscid, only a sum of the induced and wave drag is obtained. Second, wing weight is calculated, using an algebraic weight equation as described in Torenbeek (1982). Third, the fuel weight is calculated directly from the tank volume given by the wing geometry. Finally, the structural model is taken from Wakayama et al., (1995). In this research, the wing box is modeled only for calculating skin thickness. Then the wing is treated as a thin-walled, single cell monocoque beam to calculate stiffness. Flexibility of the wing is ignored. The objective function values and constraints' violations are now passed on to the system-level optimizer. MOGA is employed as the system-level optimizer here. When any constraint is violated, the rank of a particular design is lowered by adding 10.

In this section, the elitist model was frozen to BN and the results were compared between two niching models, FS and CSN. Figure 6 shows the resulting Pareto front obtained from BN + FS. BN + CSN gave a similar Pareto front and thus the result is not presented here. The major difference of the two, however, appears in the convergence history. As shown in Fig. 7, FS was able to converge the population to the Pareto front, but CSN was not. This is probably because of the adaptive σ_{share} used in FS. This result again suggests a need of an adaptive d_{min}. Figure 8 shows wing planform shapes of the resulting Pareto solutions.

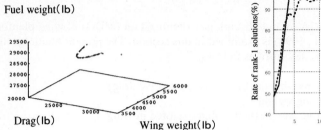

Fuel weight(lb)

Drag(lb)

Wing weight(lb)

Fig. 6. Pareto solutions in objective function space.

Fig. 7. Convergence history (average of five different runs).

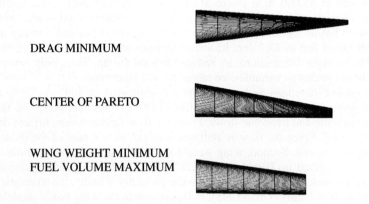

DRAG MINIMUM

CENTER OF PARETO

WING WEIGHT MINIMUM
FUEL VOLUME MAXIMUM

Fig. 8. Planform shapes of Pareto solutions.

5. Conclusion

Niching and elitist models have been examined for multiobjective Genetic Algorithms (MOGAs). The fitness sharing and coevolutionary shared niching models were considered for niching. Two elitist models, the elitist recombination and the best-N selection were compared with the simple generational model. The test cases indicate that the combination of the fitness sharing and the best-N selection provides the best performance for MOGAs so far. The results also suggest a need of an adaptive formula for d_{min} in the coevolutionary shared niching scheme.

6. Acknowledgment

This work has been supported by Bombardier Aerospace, Toronto, Canada.

References

1 Baker, J. E.: Reducing bias and inefficiency in the selection algorithm, Proceedings of the Second International Conference on Genetic Algorithms, Erlbaum, Hillsdale (1987) 14-21.
2 Bramlette, M. F. and Cusic, R.: A comparative evaluation of search methods applied to the parametric design of aircraft, Proceedings of the Third International Conference on Genetic Algorithms, Morgan Kaufmann Publishers, Inc., San Mateo (1989) 213-218.
3 Davis, L.: *Handbook of Genetic Algorithms*, Van Nostrand Reinhold (1990).
4 Fonseca C. M., and Fleming, P. J.: Genetic algorithms for multiobjective optimization: formulation, discussion and generalization, Proceedings of the 5th International Conference on Genetic Algorithms, Morgan Kaufmann Publishers, Inc., San Mateo (1993) 416-423.
5 Fujii, K. and Obayashi, S.: Navier-Stokes simulations of transonic flows over a practical wing configuration, *AIAA Journal*, 25 (3) (1987) 369-370.
6 Gage, P. and Kroo, I.: A role for genetic algorithms in a preliminary design environment, AIAA Paper 93-3933 (1993).
7 Goldberg, D. E.: *Genetic Algorithms in Search, Optimization & Machine Learning*, Addison-Wesley Publishing Company, Inc., Reading (1989).
8 Goldberg, D. E. and Wang, L.: Adaptive niching via coevolutionary sharing. In Quagliarella, D., Periaux, J., Poloni, C. and Winter, G. (Eds.), *Genetic Algorithms and Evolution Strategies in Engineering and Computer Science*, John Wiley and Sons, Chichester (1998) 21-38.
9 Horn, J., Nafplitois, N. and Goldberg, D., E.: A niched Pareto genetic algorithm for multiobjective optimization, Proceedings of the 1st IEEE Conference on Evolutionary Computation (1994) 82-87.
10 Jameson, A. and Caughey, D. A.: Numerical calculation of the transonic flow past a swept wing, COO-3077-140, New York University, July (1977) (also NASA-CR 153297).
11 Powell, D. J., Tong, S. S. and Skolnick, M. M.: EnGENEous domain independent, machine learning for design optimization, Proceedings of the Third International Conference on Genetic Algorithms, Morgan Kaufmann Publishers, Inc., San Mateo (1989) 151-159.
12 Quagliarella, D., Periaux, J., Poloni, C. and Winter, G. (Eds.): *Genetic Algorithms and Evolution Strategies in Engineering and Computer Science*, John Wiley and Sons, Chichester (1998). See Chapters 12-14.
13 Schaffer, J. D.: Multiple objective optimization with vector evaluated genetic algorithm, Proceedings of the 1st International Conference on Genetic Algorithms, Morgan Kaufmann Publishers, Inc., San Mateo (1985) 93-100.
14 Takahashi, S., Obayashi S. and Nakahashi, K.: Inverse optimization of transonic wing shape for mid-size regional aircraft, AIAA Paper 98-0601, AIAA Aerospace Sciences Meeting & Exhibit, Reno NV (January 12-15, 1998).
15 Torenbeek, E.: *Synthesis of Subsonic Airplane Design*, Kluwer Academic Publishers, Dordrecht (1982).
16 Wakayama, S. and Kroo, I.: Subsonic wing planform design using multidisciplinary optimization, *Journal of Aircraft*, 32 (4) July-August (1995) 746-753.

Parallel Evolutionary Optimisation with Constraint Propagation *

Alvaro Ruiz-Andino[1], Lourdes Araujo[1], Jose Ruz[2], and Fernando Sáenz[2]

[1] Department of Computer Science
[2] Department of Computer Architecture
Universidad Complutense de Madrid

Abstract. This paper describes a parallel model for a distributed memory architecture of a non traditional evolutionary computation method, which integrates constraint propagation and evolution programs. This integration provides a problem-independent optimisation strategy for large scale constrained combinatorial problems over finite integer domains. We have adopted a global parallelisation approach which preserves the properties, behaviour, and theoretical studies of the sequential algorithm. Moreover, high speedup is achieved since genetic operators are coarse-grained, as they perform a search in a discrete space carrying out constraint propagation. A global parallelisation implies a single population but, as we focus on distributed memory architectures, the single virtual population is physically distributed among the processors. Selection and mating consider all the individuals in the population, but the application of genetic operators is performed in parallel. The implementation of the model has been tested on a CRAY T3E multiprocessor using two complex constrained optimisation problems. Experiments have proved the efficiency of this approach since linear speedups have been obtained.

1 Introduction

In this paper we present the parallelisation, for a distributed memory architecture, of an integration of evolution programs and constraint propagation techniques. Evolution programs and constraint propagation complement each other to efficiently solve large scale constrained optimisation problems over finite integer domains [5, 6]. Evolution programs [3] are an adequate optimisation technique for large search spaces, but they do not offer a problem-independent way to handle constraints. Constraint propagation and consistency algorithms, which prune the search space before and while searching, are valid for any discrete combinatorial problem.

Evolutionary programming is inherently parallel. Moreover, in this case, task granularity is increased because of coarse-grained genetic operators, since they perform a search embedding constraint propagation.

There are three main approaches to parallelise an evolution program [2, 1]: global parallelisation, island model, and hybrid algorithms. We have adopted a global parallelisation approach because of the following reasons:

---

* Supported by project TIC95-0433.

- Properties, behaviour, and theoretical studies of the sequential algorithm are preserved.
- Crossover is coarse-grained, as it implies searching in a discrete search space performing constraint propagation.
- The higher communications rate of a global parallelisation versus other approaches does not significantly penalises speedup, since modern distributed memory multiprocessor provide fast, low-latency asynchronous read/write access to remote processors' memory, avoiding rendevouz overhead.

Our approach is based on a single virtual population physically distributed among the processors, in such a way that each processor owns a partial copy of the population. Selection of chromosomes to be replaced, to be mutated, and parents to take part in crossover, is performed in a centralised manner by a distinguished processor (*master*), but the application of genetic operators is performed in parallel. Coordination is achieved through annotations in mutual exclusion on the local memory of the master processor. Scheduling of pending operations is performed in a dynamic self-guided way, following a set of rules to minimise the number of chromosomes to fetch from remote processors.

The rest of the paper is organised as follows. Section 2 summarises the main points of the combination of constraint propagation and evolution programs presented in [6]. Section 3 presents the parallelisation model, the parallel algorithm, and the work scheduling policy. Section 4 describes the results obtained for two complex constrained optimisation problems. Finally Section 5 discusses the conclusions.

2 Constraint Propagation and Evolution Programs

Many complex search problems such as resource allocation, scheduling and hardware design [9] can be stated as constrained optimisation problems over finite integer domains. Constraint programming languages are based on a constraint propagation solver embedding an Arc-Consistency algorithm [4, 8], an efficient and general technique to solve finite domain constraint satisfaction problems. Arc-Consistency algorithms eliminate inconsistent values from the domains of the variables, reducing the size of the search space both before and while searching.

Constraint propagation techniques and evolution programs complement each other. Constraint solving techniques opens a flexible and efficient way to handle constraints in evolution programs, while evolution programs allow searching for solutions in large scale constrained optimisation problems. Other approaches to handle constraints in evolution programs require to define problem specific genetic operators, whereas constraint propagation embedded in evolution program results in a problem-independent optimisation strategy for constrained optimisation problems. This section summarises the main points of the integration.

Constraint Propagation. A constraint optimisation problem over finite integer domains may be stated as follows. Given a tuple $\langle \mathcal{V}, \mathcal{D}, \mathcal{C}, f \rangle$, where $\mathcal{V} \equiv \{v_1, \cdots, v_n\}$, is a set of domain variables; $\mathcal{D} \equiv \{d_1, \cdots, d_n\}$, is the set of an initial *finite integer domain* (finite set of integers) for each variable; $\mathcal{C} \equiv \{c_1, \cdots, c_m\}$, is a set of constraints among the variables in $\mathcal{V}$, and $f : N \times \cdots \times N \to N$ is the objective function to optimise. A constraint $c \equiv (V_c, R_c)$ is defined by a subset of variables $V_c \subseteq \mathcal{V}$, and a subset of allowed tuples of values $R_c \subseteq \bigotimes_{i \in \{j/v_j \in V_c\}} d_i$, where $\bigotimes$ denotes Cartesian product. The goal is to find an assignment for each variable $v_i \in \mathcal{V}$ of a value from each $d_i \in \mathcal{D}$ which satisfies every constraint $c_i \in \mathcal{C}$, and optimises the objective function f. A constraint $c \in \mathcal{C}$ relating variables v_i and $v_j \in \mathcal{V}$, is *arc-consistent* with respect to domains d_i, d_j iff for all $a \in d_i$ there exists $b \in d_j$ such that (a, b) satisfies the constraint c, and for all $b \in d_j$ there exists $a \in d_i$ such that (a, b) satisfies the constraint c. A constraint satisfaction problem is arc-consistent iff all $c_i \in \mathcal{C}$ are arc-consistent with respect to $\mathcal{D}$. An Arc-Consistency algorithm takes as input arguments a set of constraints to be satisfied and an initial finite integer domain for each variable. The algorithm either detects inconsistency (a variable was pruned to an empty domain), or prunes the domain of each variable in such a way that arc-consistency is achieved.

Integration of evolution programs and constraint propagation implies coming up with a solution for chromosome representation, chromosome evaluation, and genetic operators' design.

Chromosome Representation. In order to take advantage of the arc-consistency techniques embedded in the constraint solver, a chromosome is an array of finite integer domains, that is, a sub-space of the initial search space. Moreover, chromosomes are arc-consistent solutions (AC-solutions) generated by means of genetic operators based on an Arc-Consistency algorithm.

Chromosome Evaluation. Searching for a solution using an Arc-Consistency algorithm involves evaluating the AC-solution generated, since the objective function is assimilated to a domain variable whose domain is pruned while searching. The objective function f is defined by means of constraints, leading to an extended function $f' : N^* \times \cdots \times N^* \to N^*$. f' takes as arguments finite integer domains and returns a finite integer domain. A dual evaluation is used: a *fitness* value is computed from the pruned domain of the variable to optimise, but, as we are dealing with non fully determined solutions, a *feasible* value is used to take into account the probability that a feasible solution lies within the AC-solution.

Genetic operators implement stochastic heuristic arc-consistent searches, taking previous AC-solutions as an input information to guide the search for a new AC-solution. Arc-consistency is achieved at each node of the search space, removing inconsistent values from the domain of the variables. Figure 1 shows the AC-crossover function. Given two AC-solutions, the AC-crossover operator generates a new AC-solution. K (a random value between 1 and n) randomly chosen variables, $v_{perm[1]}$ through $v_{perm[K]}$, are constrained to domains from first parent. Then, Arc-Consistency algorithm is invoked, pruning the search space. Remaining variables, $v_{perm[K+1]}$ through $v_{perm[n]}$, are constrained one by one to domains from second parent, performing Arc-Consistency at each step. If inconsistency is detected at any step, variable's domain is left unchanged.

```
function AC-crossover( AC-Sol1, AC-Sol2 ) : AC-solution;
begin
   perm := random-permutation(1, n);
   K := random-int-between(1, n);
   for i = 1 to K do
      v_perm[i] := AC-Sol1[perm[i]];
   end-for;
   Perform Arc-Consistency, pruning search space
   for i = K+1 to n do
      v_perm[i] := AC-Sol2[perm[i]];
      Perform Arc-Consistency, pruning search space
      if Inconsistent then undo assigment;
   end-for;
   return generated AC-Solution
end;
```

Fig. 1. AC-Crossover

3 Parallelisation Model

A global parallelisation of the presented constrained optimisation evolution program is expected to achieve high speedups, since the constraint propagation leads to coarse-grained genetic operators. Global parallelisation implies a centralised population. Shared memory architectures support an straight implementation of this approach, whereas distributed memory architectures may suffer from communications overhead. We propose a global parallelisation model for a distributed memory architecture based on a virtual centralised population, physically distributed among the processors in order to reduce communications. Target architecture is any modern distributed memory multiprocessor that allows fast asynchronous read/write access to remote processors' memory. This feature places them in a middle point between traditional shared and distributed memory architectures.

The data distribution model, appearing in Figure 2, can be summarised as follows:

- The population is distributed among the processors in the system. Each processor owns a subset of the population and a local *localisation table* indicating a processor where non-local chromosomes can be found.
- One processor of the parallel system is distinguished as *master*. This processor behaves as any other, but it is also in charge of the sequential part of the algorithm, and keeps the shared *operation table*.
- The *master* produces the *operation table*, which reflects chromosomes selected to survive, to be mutated, and to take part in crossover (global mating). The operation table is broadcasted at the beginning of every generation, so each processor has a local copy of it.
- Genetic operations are performed in parallel. Coordination is achieved by means of atomic test&swap on the master processor's operation table. A

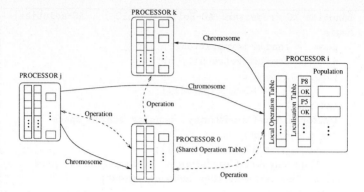

Fig. 2. Data distribution model. Solid arrows represent fetching a remote chromosome. Dotted arrows represent mutual exclusion access to the shared operation table.

processor may need to fetch (asynchronously) a chromosome from a remote processor's memory in order to perform the selected genetic operation.

At the beginning of each generation, each processor owns a subset of the population formed by:

- chromosomes generated by itself in the previous generation.
- chromosomes from the previous population fetched from a remote processor but not replaced in the current population (steady-state approach). Therefore, a chromosome may be present at many processors.

Figure 3 shows the algorithm executed in each processor. Initially a subset of the population is generated (line 1). Every time a new chromosome is generated, its evaluation (fitness and feasible values) are asynchronously written to the master's memory. Lines 2 to 14 enclose the main loop; each iteration produces a new generation. Synchronisation is needed at the beginning of each generation (line 3), in order to perform the global mating. The master establishes the genetic operations to generate the next population (line 5), filling the operation table, which is broadcasted to every processor (line 7). The loop in lines 8 to 12 performs genetic operations (crossover or mutation) until there are no more left. A processor may perform any of the pending operations (line 10), so it may need to fetch chromosomes from a remote processors' memory (line 9). The resulting offspring is kept in local memory, but the evaluation values are asynchronously written to master's memory (line 11).

Scheduling of pending operations is performed in a dynamic self-guided way, following a set of rules to minimise the number of chromosomes to be fetched from remote processors. Function Fetch_Operation() (line 8), consults the local copy of the operation table and the localisation table, choosing an operation to perform. In order to minimise the need to fetch remote chromosomes, the local operation table is scanned selecting operations in the following order:

```
    Procedure Parallel_AC-Evolution;
    begin
1       Generate a subset of the initial population;
2       while not termination() do
3           Synchronisation;
4           if I-am-the-Master then
5               Generate-Matings-and-Mutations(Operation_Table);
6           end-if;
7           Broadcasting of Operation_Table;
8           while Fetch_Operation(Operation_Table, Localisation_Table) do
9               Fetch parents, if necessary, updating Localisation_Table;
10              Perform AC-Crossover (or AC-Mutation);
11              Write fitness-feasible to Master;
12          end-while;
13          Update(Localisation_Table);
14      end-while;
    end;
```

Fig. 3. Parallel constrained evolution program.

- Crossover of two local chromosomes.
- Mutation of a local chromosome. or crossover of a local chromosome with a remote one.
- Mutation or crossover of remote chromosomes.

Once an operation is selected, the corresponding entry of the shared operation table is tested and updated in mutual exclusion. If the selected operation has already been performed by another processor, the local operation table is updated, and another operation is chosen. Otherwise, the processor writes its unique processor number in the shared operation table. Once every operation has been performed, local copies of the operation table reflect which processor has generated the new chromosomes, allowing to properly update the localisation table (line 13) for the next generation, discarding local copies of outdated chromosomes.

Figure 4 shows an example of operation fetching. Processor 1 (P1) selects in the first place the crossover operation (XV) that will replace chromosome number 3, because both parents (chromosomes 3 and 8) are in its local memory. P1 successfully test and writes its processor number in the shared operation table. P2 behaves similarly with respect to operation 2. Once P1 has finished the crossover operation, it proceeds to select operation 1, as it owns one of the involved parents, writing its number in the shared operation table. P2 also tries to fetch operation 1, but it finds that operation has been already selected by processor 1, so P2 updates its local operation tale and proceeds to select a new operation.

Figure 5 shows the time diagram for a generation. There is a sequential time fraction due to the generation and broadcast of the operation table (T_s). The

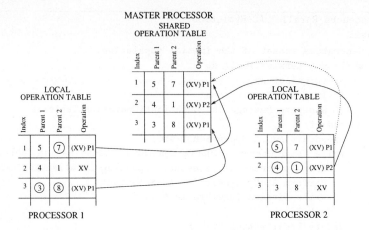

Fig. 4. Fetch Operation example. Circled numbers denote local chromosomes. Abbreviation (genetic operation to perform) in brackets denotes initial value. Solid arrows denote successful test&write operations. Dotted arrows denote unsuccessful test&write operations on the shared operation table.

time to perform a crossover in parallel (T_{xvp}) is the sequential time (T_{xvs}), increased with the time to select an operation (T_{fo}), the time to fetch the parents (T_{fp}) (only if necessary), and the time to write the evaluation values in master's memory (T_{we}). Policy to select operations favours choosing operations among local chromosomes, therefore it is expected to frequently avoid the overhead due to T_{fp}. Since genetic operators are search procedures, they can have a significantly different grain. The dynamic self-guided scheduling of the algorithm balances work load, thus reducing idle time T_{id}, introduced by the necessary synchronisation between generations.

Linear speedups will be obtained if communications overhead —T_{fo}, T_{we} and T_{fp}— is much smaller that genetic operation granularity (T_{xvs}), and when the number of genetic operations per generation is much greater than the number of processors. In this situation T_{id} and T_s are much smaller than T_p.

4   Experiments

Our system CSOS (Constrained Stochastic Optimisation System) implements the presented parallelisation model. Experiments have been carried out on a CRAY T3E multiprocessor, a distributed memory parallel system with a low latency and sustained bandwidth. Processing elements in the T3E are connected by a bi-directional 3-D torus network achieving communication rates of 480 Mbytes/s. Parallel programming capabilities are extended through the "Cray Shared Memory Library" and MPI2, which allows fast asynchronous read/write access to remote processors' memory.

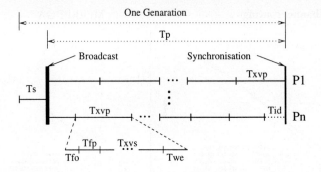

Fig. 5. Time diagram for a generation. T_s = sequential fraction (global selection for mating). T_p = parallel execution of genetic operators. T_{xvp} = parallel genetic operation. T_{xvs} = sequential genetic operation. T_{fo} = fetch an operation from master. T_{fp} = fetch remote parents. T_{we} = write evaluation values to master. T_{id} = waiting for synchronisation.

CSOS has been used to solve a number of real life constraint optimisation problems. Results obtained in two of them are reported: a VLSI signal channel routing problem, and a devices-to-FPGA mapping problem.

Channel routing consists in assigning a pair layer/track to each net from a given set of connections such that no routing segments overlap each other. The objective function to be minimised is the sum of the lengths of routing paths for a given number of tracks per layer. A chromosome is 432 words long, and average time to perform a crossover is 35 ms. Sequential execution time is 23 minutes.

A multi-FPGA (Field Programmable Gate Array) is a programmable integrated circuit that can be programmed using the hardware description language VHDL. The goal is to map the VHDL program process network into a given multi-FPGA, observing size, adjacency, and capacity constraints, minimising the maximum occupation. A chromosome is 180 words long, and average time to perform a crossover is 300 ms. Sequential execution time is 60 minutes.

Problem formulation has been programmed with a Constraint Logic Programming language over finite integer domains [7]. Therefore, problem constraints, input data, and technology-dependent parameters can be flexibly modified.

Experiments have investigated the influence of the parameters of the genetic algorithm on the speedup. A particular issue of the model affecting the speedup –the ratio of chromosomes fetched from a remote processor– is also reported. Each reported result is the average of ten executions with a different random seed.

Figure 6 shows speedup obtained for different parameter settings, all of them leading to the same number of genetic operations. The speedup is almost linear in all cases. This means that times due to communications overhead (T_{fo}, T_{fp} and T_{we}), described in Figure 5 are negligible in comparison with time to perform

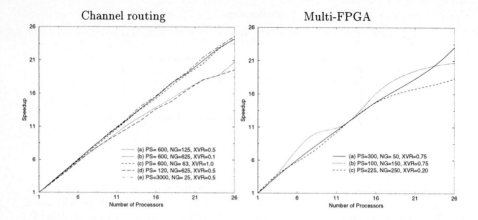

Fig. 6. Speedup obtained for different parameter settings. PS = Population size. NG = No. of generations. XVR = Ratio of population replaced with offsprings.

a crossover T_{xvs}. A lower number of crossovers per generation (small population and/or low crossover ratio) implies a higher sequential fraction and a higher idle time thus reducing speedup. Therefore, the settings scaling better, (a), (c) and (e) for the Channel routing problem and (a) for the FPGA's problem, are those with both higher population size and ratio of population replaced.

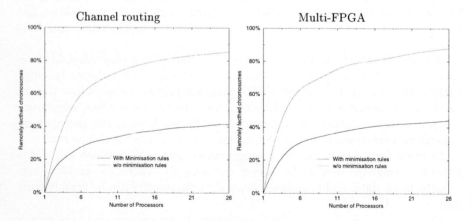

Fig. 7. Percentage of chromosomes fetched from a remote processor, with and without the minimisation policy.

Figure 7 illustrates the efficiency of the policy for selecting genetic operations, displaying the percentage of chromosomes that had to be fetched from a remote processor versus the number of processors. Solid line corresponds to the self-guided scheduling using the minimisation rules described in Section 3. Dotted line corresponds to select the first pending genetic operation. Minimisation rules halves the percentage of chromosomes fetched from a remote processor.

5 Conclusions

We have developed a parallel execution model for a non-traditional evolutionary computation method, which integrates constraint propagation techniques and evolution programs. The system, aimed to solve constrained combinatorial optimisation problems over finite integer domains, is appropriate for parallelisation due to the coarse-grain of genetic operations. The model is devoted to run on modern distributed memory platforms, which provide communications times close to those of shared memory architectures. This characteristic justifies working with a single virtual population, though distributed across the system.

The parallel version of our system CSOS, which implements the proposed model, has been ported to a CRAY T3E, a distributed memory parallel multiprocessor. Two complex constrained optimisation problems over finite integer domains, coming from the field of hardware design, have been used to test the efficiency of the parallel model. Linear speedups have been obtained when increasing the number of processors, thus proving our hypothesis that communication overhead is negligible versus genetic operation execution times. Measurements have been taken in order to check the effectiveness of genetic operations scheduling policy. Results reveal that the percentage of chromosomes fetched from remote processors diminishes by half using our policy.

References

1. Cantú-Paz, E. A survey of parallel genetic algorithms. IlliGAL Report No. 97003 (1997).
2. Grefenstette, J.J. Parallel adaptive algorithms for function optimisation. Tech. Rep. No. CS-81-19. Nashville, TN: Vanderbilt University Computer Science Department. (1981)
3. Michalewicz, Z.: Genetic algorithms + Data Structures = Evolution Programs. 2nd Edition, Springer-Verlag (1994).
4. Mohr, R., Henderson, T.C.: Arc and path consistency revisited. Artificial Intelligence 28 (1996) 225-233.
5. Paredis, J.: Genetic State-Search for constrained Optimisation Problems. 13th Int. Joint Conf. on Artificial Intelligence (1993).
6. Ruiz-Andino A., Ruz, J.J. Integration of Constraint Programming and Evolution Programs: Application to Channel Routing. 11th Int. Conf. on Industrial Applications of Artificial Intelligence. LNAI 1415, Springer-Verlag (1998) 448-459.
7. Ruiz-Andino A. CSOS User's manual. Tech. Report No. 73.98. Department of Computer Science. Universidad Complutense de Madrid, (1998).
8. Van Hentenryck P., Deville, Y., Teng C.M.: A generic Arc-consistency Algorithm and its Specialisations. Artificial Intelligence 57 (1992) 291-321.
9. Wallace, M.: Constraints in Planing, Scheduling and Placement Problems. Constraint Programming, Springer-Verlag (1994).

Methods to Evolve Legal Phenotypes

Tina Yu and Peter Bentley

Department of Computer Science, University College London,
Gower Street, London WC1E 6BT, UK.
T.Yu@cs.ucl.ac.uk P.Bentley@cs.ucl.ac.uk

Abstract. Many optimization problems require the satisfaction of constraints in addition to their objectives. When using an evolutionary algorithm to solve such problems, these constraints can be enforced in many different ways to ensure that legal solutions (phenotypes) are evolved. We have identified eleven ways to handle constraints within various stages of an evolutionary algorithm. Five of these methods are experimented on a run-time error constraint in a Genetic Programming system. The results are compared and analyzed.

1. Introduction

Constraints form an integral part of every optimization problem, and yet they are often overlooked in evolutionary algorithms (Michalewicz, 1995b). A problem with constraints has both an objective, and a set of restrictions. For example, when designing a VLSI circuit, the objective may be to maximize speed and the constraint may be to use no more than 50 logic gates. It is vital to perform constraint handling with care, for if evolutionary search is restricted inappropriately, the evolution of good solutions may be prevented.

In order to explore the relationship between constraints and evolutionary algorithms, this paper presents an evolutionary framework in which the search space and solution space are separated. In this framework, a genotype represents a point in the search space and is operated on by the genetic operators (crossover and mutation). A phenotype represents a point in solution space and is evaluated by the fitness function. The result of the evaluation gives the fitness of the phenotype, and by implication, of the underlying genotype.

In the same way that phenotypes are evaluated for fitness, not genotypes, it is the phenotypes which must satisfy the problem constraints, not the genotypes (although their enforcement may result in the restriction of some genotypes). However, unlike the fitness evaluation, constraints can be enforced at any point in the algorithm to attain legal phenotypes. As will be described later, they may be incorporated into the genotype or phenotype representations, during the seeding of the population, during reproduction, or handled at other stages.

There are two main types of constraint: the *soft constraint* and the *hard constraint*. Soft constraints are restrictions on phenotypes that should be satisfied, but will not always be. Such constraints are often enforced by using penalty values to lower fitnesses. Illegal phenotypes (which conflict with the constraints) are permitted to exist as second-class, in the hope that some portions of their genotypes will aid the search for fit phenotypes (Michalewicz, 1995b). Hard constraints, on the other hand, must always be satisfied. Illegal phenotypes are not permitted to exist (although their corresponding genotypes may be, as will be shown).

This paper identifies eleven methods to enforce constraints on phenotypes during various stages of evolutionary algorithms. Five methods are experimented on a runtime error constraint in a Genetic Programming (GP) system. The results are compared and analyzed.

The paper is structured as follows: section 2 provides related work; section 3 classifies and describes the constraint handling methods; section 4 presents the experiments; section 5 analyzes the results and section 6 concludes.

2. Related Work

Genetic Algorithms: Michalewicz and Schoenauer provide perhaps the most comprehensive reviews of implementations of constraint handling in genetic algorithms (GAs) (Michalewicz 1995b, Michalewicz & Schoenauer 1996). They identify and discuss eleven different types of system. However, upon examination it is clear that his classification is based upon differences in implementation, and perhaps because of confusion of various multiobjective techniques, it fails to group constraint handling methods which employ similar underlying concepts. Nevertheless, the work of Michalewicz and colleagues provides some of the key investigations in this area. For example, Michalewicz (1995a) describes the application of five methods (three based on penalizing illegal phenotypes) to five test functions. Michalewicz et. al. (1996) describe the use of 'behavioral memory' and other penalty-based approaches in GAs to evolve different engineering designs. Schoenauer and Michalewicz (1997) describe the use of a repair method in a GA to evolve legal phenotypes.

Evolution Strategies & Evolutionary Programming: In their original implementations, both ES and EP performed constraint handling during the creation of the initial populations. Schwefel's ES algorithm also used a 'legal mutant' constraint handling method, where the creation of an individual is simply repeated as long as the individual violates one or more constraints (Bäck, 1996). Standard EP, on the other hand, typically does not enforce constraints during the generation of new offspring. More recent research on constrained optimization problems in EP is described in (McDonnell et al., 1995) and (Fogel et al., 1996).

Genetic Programming: The traditional GP paradigm (Koza, 1992) does not distinguish genotypes from phenotypes, i.e. the search space is regarded as being the same as the solution space. An individual is represented as a program parse tree. This parse tree represents both the genotype and phenotype of an individual as it is modified by the genetic operators and it is evaluated by the fitness function. Consequently, constraints in traditional GP are perceived as being applied to phenotypes and genotypes.

For example, program parse trees in GP are restricted by syntactic constraints: they must satisfy the syntax of the underlying language. Various other forms of syntactic constraints have been proposed (Gruau, 1996; Janikow, 1996). Yu and Clack (1998) applied both syntactic constraints and type constraints in their GP system.

Banzhaf (1994) proposed an alternative paradigm for GP, where the search space is separated from the solution space. A mapping scheme is used to transform genotypes into legal phenotypes (Keller & Banzhaf, 1996).

3. Constraints in Evolutionary Algorithms

Just as evolution requires selection pressure to generate phenotypes that satisfy the objective function, evolution can have a second selection pressure placed upon it in order to generate phenotypes that do not conflict the constraints. However, using *pressure* in evolutionary search to evolve legal solutions is no guarantee that all of the solutions will always be legal (i.e., they are soft constraints).

Constraints can also be handled in two other ways: solutions that do not satisfy the constraints can be *prevented* from being created, or they can be *corrected*. Such methods can have significant drawbacks such as loss of diversity and premature convergence. Nevertheless, these two types of constraint handling ensure that all solutions are always legal (i.e., they are hard constraints). The following section identifies eleven methods which enforce 'hard constraints' or 'soft constraints'. These methods also fall within the three conceptual categories: Prevention, Correction, and Pressure, see Table 1. (Note that this categorization encompasses the Pro-Life, Pro-Choice categorization of Michalewicz and Michalewicz (1995). It is felt that the use of more neutral terminology is more appropriate for such technical classifications.)

Prevention	HARD	C1, C2, C3, C10
Correction	HARD	C4, C5
Pressure	SOFT	C6, C7, C8, C9, C11

Table 1. Classification of constraint handling methods.

3.1 Detailed Classification

Whilst previous work in classifying constraint handling methods within evolutionary search has identified implementation differences of existing systems, to date there has not been a general classification of constraint handling based on the underlying concepts of evolutionary algorithms.

Such a classification can be achieved, not only by examining the existing work of others, but also by examining the significant stages within evolutionary algorithms and identifying where it is *possible* to incorporate constraints. This allows all existing constraint handling methods to be clearly categorized and understood, and also identifies new, previously unexamined ways of tackling constraints in evolutionary search. Figure 1 shows the most significant and commonly used stages within current GAs and GP. (It should be noted that most algorithms contain a subset of these stages.)

After some careful consideration of these stages, it becomes clear that constraints can be incorporated at eleven different places within the design and execution of evolutionary algorithms (as shown on the right hand side of Figure 1). These eleven methods should not be confused with Michalewicz's (1995b) list of different researchers' implementations (which coincidentally also contains eleven elements). The methods shown in Figure 1 are categorized solely on their placement within the evolutionary algorithm, and can be used in combination or separately of each other. There follows a description of each method and its potential advantages and disadvantages:

C1: LEGAL SEARCHSPACE   *Design genotype representation.*
During the design of the evolutionary system, create a genotype representation that is only capable of representing legal solutions. Evolutionary search is then forced to

consider only the space of legal solutions, where all constraints are satisfied. This method is frequently used, although designers who use it are often unaware that they are performing constraint handling of any kind. For example, in GAs, if the range of a problem parameter must be between 0 and 255, most designers would automatically use a binary gene consisting of eight bits - and this genotype representation would then ensure that the 0-255 range constraint was always satisfied.

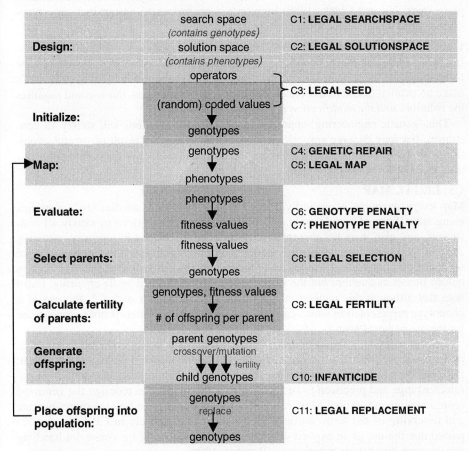

Fig. 1. Constraint placement within significant stages of evolutionary algorithms.

C2: LEGAL SOLUTIONSPACE   *Design phenotype representation.*

During the design of the evolutionary system, create a new phenotype representation, so that only legal phenotypes can be defined. All genotypes are then mapped onto these phenotypes, which by definition, must always satisfy the constraints.

Often great care can go into the design of suitable phenotypes. For example, practitioners of floor-planning problems have two important constraints: room-spaces should not overlap, and no space should be left unaccounted for. To ensure that the computer always evolves solutions that satisfy these constraints, designers of these systems use phenotype representations which define the location of rooms indirectly, by defining the location and number of dividing walls (Gero & Kazakov, 1998).

C3: LEGAL SEED *Seed with non-conflicting solutions.*

The initial population is seeded with solutions that do not conflict with the constraints and the crossover and mutation operators are designed so that they cannot generate illegal solutions. Many constraints in GP are implemented using this method. For example, Gruau (1996) uses a context-free grammar to specify syntactic constraints of parse trees. Yu and Clack (1998) employ a type system to ensure that only type-correct programs are considered during evolution.

C4: GENETIC REPAIR *Correct illegal genotypes.*

If a new individual conflicts with a constraint, correct the genes that are responsible for the conflict to make it satisfy that constraint. For algorithms such as GP which make no explicit distinction between genotypes and phenotypes, this method modifies the solution, *and the modification is inherited by its offspring.*

This 'genetic engineering' approach ensures that all solutions will satisfy all constraints, but may damage epistatic genotypes, discarding the result of careful evolution over many generations. In addition, the design of the repair procedure may be a non-trivial task for some problems.

C5: LEGAL MAP *Correct illegal phenotypes.*

Map every genotype of an individual to a phenotype that satisfies the constraints using some form of simple embryology. This forces all solutions to satisfy all constraints, and also does not disrupt or constrain the genotypes in any way, allowing evolutionary search to continue unrestricted. For algorithms such as GP which make no distinction between genotypes and phenotypes, this method modifies the solution before fitness evaluation, *but the modification is not inherited by its offspring.* (Also note that although this method is often used in combination with C2, the use of a phenotype representation which can only represent legal solutions is not a prerequisite for the use of Legal Map.)

Using a mapping stage to generate legal phenotypes is a very common approach to perform simple constraint handling. Goldberg (1989) describes perhaps the simplest: mapping the range of a gene to a specified interval. This permits constraints on parameter range and precision to be satisfied without the need to redesign the genotype representation and coding. More recently mapping stages have become more intricate and deserving of the term 'artificial embryology'. Researchers in GP have also reported that the use of an explicit genotype and mapping stage for constraint handling can increase diversity in populations (Banzhaf, 1994).

Type constraints in GP can be implemented using this method as an alternative to the Legal Seed method. A simple example is to map a value with an illegal type of 'real' into a value with legal type 'integer'. However, for other more complex types such as list or array, a proper mapping scheme may be difficult to design. This kind of type-constraint handling is called 'dynamic typing' - in contrast to the 'strong typing' approach mentioned in the Legal Seed method.

C6: GENOTYPE PENALTY *Penalize illegal genotypes.*

Identify alleles or gene fragments within genotypes that seem to increase the chances of a solution conflicting the constraints, and reduce the fitness of any individual containing these fragments of genetic code. Although the identification of 'bad genes' may discourage solutions from conflicting constraints, it will not guarantee that all solutions satisfy all constraints. In addition, with epistatic genotypes, this approach may result in the discouragement of other, epistatically linked, useful features within solutions. To date, research has investigated the automatic identification of 'good genes' during evolution to encourage the evolution of solutions with higher fitnesses (Gero & Kazakov, 1998). However, the authors of this paper are unaware of any work which identifies 'bad genes' for constraint handling.

C7: PHENOTYPE PENALTY   *Penalize illegal phenotypes.*

When a phenotype conflicts a constraint, reduce its fitness. This 'soft constraint' discourages all phenotypes that conflict the constraints, but does not force evolutionary search to generate legal solutions. In effect, the use of a penalty value becomes an additional criterion to be considered by the evolutionary algorithm, and multiobjective techniques should be used to ensure that all criteria are considered separately (otherwise one or more criteria may dominate the others) (Bentley & Wakefield, 1997). This is one of the most commonly used methods for constraint handling in evolutionary algorithms. (Indeed, it is the only one explicitly mentioned in Goldberg's book.)

C8: LEGAL SELECTION   *Select only legal parents for reproduction.*

During reproduction, only select parent solutions which satisfy the constraints. This method should be used with a fitness-based replacement method to ensure that evolution is guided to evolve fit solutions in addition to legal solutions. (If all solutions are illegal, parents which violate the fewest constraints to the least extent should be selected.) However, the exclusion of potential parents may discard beneficial genetic material and so could be harmful to evolution. Other than the work described in this paper, only one recent investigation has been made on this method (Hinterding & Michalewicz, 1998).

C9: LEGAL FERTILITY   *Increase the no. of offspring for legal parents.*

Having selected the parent genotypes (based on their fitnesses) this method allocates a larger *fertility* to parents which better satisfy the constraints. This method can be thought of as an implicit multiobjective method, allowing independent selection pressure to be exerted for high fitness and legal solutions. Being a 'soft constraint', there are no guarantees that all solutions will always satisfy the constraints. In addition, if legal parents are favoured excessively, it is possible that the diversity of the population could be reduced. To the authors' knowledge, this idea has not been previously used for constraint handling.

C10: INFANTICIDE   *Stop illegal offspring from being born.*

If a new solution conflicts a constraint, discard it, and try generating another solution using the same parents. This brute-force method, which is sometimes used in GAs (Michalewicz, 1995b), forces all solutions to satisfy the constraints, but may discard useful genetic material (and may also be prohibitively slow).

C11: ILLEGAL REPLACEMENT   *Replace illegal solutions with legal offspring.*

When replacing individuals with new offspring in the population, always replace the solutions that conflict constraints. (If all solutions satisfy the constraints, either replace randomly or replace the least fit.) This method should be used with a fitness-based selection method to ensure that evolution is guided to evolve fit solutions in addition to legal solutions. However, the replacement of potential parents discards potentially beneficial genetic material and so may be harmful to evolution. This method requires the use of a steady-state GA (Syswerda, 1989).

4. Experiments with a Run-Time Constraint in GP

This section describes experiments conducted to compare five of the constraint handling methods described above in a GP system. The experiments are focused on one particular kind of constraint in GP: the *run-time error constraint*.

GP evolves computer programs as problem solutions. Thus, in most cases the genetic material is in some sense executable. When run-time errors occur during the execution of a program, its behaviour is undefined. A fundamental constraint is therefore imposed on GP: no programs can contain run-time errors.

Unlike other types of constraint, the run-time error constraint has a special property: when it occurs the fitness cannot be calculated. (When the behaviour of the program is undefined, the evaluation of its fitness cannot be performed.) Illegal phenotypes are therefore not allowed to exist. This means that soft constraint methods (where illegal phenotypes can exist as second-class) can only be used in conjunction with a phenotype correction method - they cannot be used on their own. In the experiments, the Legal Map method is used to serve this purpose.

A constraint can be handled using many different methods, yet some are more suitable than others. For the run-time error constraint, its prevention (in methods C1, C2, C3 and C10) is extremely hard because these errors are only evident during program execution. In addition, genetic repair (method C4) requires the corrected material to follow the genotype syntax (so that it can be inherited) which is not appropriate (or easy to implement) for this constraint. Consequently, none of the hard constraint methods are suitable for this problem except for the Legal Map method (C5), which corrects illegal phenotypes (and the corrections are not inherited by offspring).

Soft constraint approaches, on the other hand, are appropriate for this problem. The experiments investigate four of these methods (C7, C8, C9, and C11). (Method C6 which penalizes illegal genotypes by identifying 'bad genes' was not investigated because of the substantial time required for its implementation).

Objective:	Find the symbolic function $x^4 - x^3 + x^2 - x$ using 9 pairs of sample points.
Terminal Set:	x
Function Set:	+, -, *, /
Fitness Cases:	9 data points (x_i, y_i) where x_i is the input value between -1.0 and 1.0 and y_i is the desired output value.
Fitness:	9/(9+*total_error*), where *total_error* is $\sum_{i=1}^{9} \lvert y_i - R_i \rvert$ and R_i is the result of phenotype execution given input x_i
Hits:	$\sum_{i=1}^{9} P_i \left(P_i = \begin{cases} 1, if \lvert y_i - R_i \rvert \le 0.01 \\ 0, otherwise \end{cases} \right)$
Parameters:	PopSize = 500, MaxTest = 25500, TreeSize = 25, Xover = 60%, Mutation = 4%, Copy = 36%, Runs = 20
Success predicate:	9 hits

Table 2. Tableau of the simple symbolic regression problem

In summary, the experiments investigate one hard constraint-handling method (Legal Map) and four soft constraint methods (Phenotype Penalty, Legal Selection, Legal Fertility, and Illegal Replacement) to enforce the zero-division run-time error constraint. The zero-division constraint was chosen as it is the most frequently observed run-time error, potentially occurring in any numerical problem tackled by GP.

The experiments use GP to solve a symbolic regression problem, which involves finding a function, in symbolic form (with numeric coefficients) that fits a given finite sample of data. It is "data-to-function" regression. The goal is to find the target function of $x^4-x^3+x^2-x$, given a data sample of nine pairs (x_i, y_i), where x_i is a value of the independent variable and y_i is the associated value of the dependent variable. Table 2 summarizes the features of this problem.

4.1 Implementation of Constraints

To allow the use of the Illegal Replacement method, the GP system uses a steady-state replacement scheme (Syswerda, 1989) where a population with a constant number of individuals is maintained. Unless otherwise stated, parents are selected using fitness proportionate selection, and offspring replace individuals with the worst fitness in the population. The five constraint handling methods were implemented as follows:

C5: Legal Map. When a run-time error occurs during the execution of a phenotype, the value '1' is returned and the execution continues. For example, if the phenotype is $5+x/x$ and $x = 0.0$, *Legal Map* changes the phenotype to: $5+1$. Corrected phenotypes are marked with a run-time error flag to allow this method to be used in conjunction with the following four.

C7 & C5: Phenotype Penalty with Legal Map. Phenotypes that have to be corrected are penalized by multiplying their *total_error* values by 2. Legal phenotypes that do not have to be corrected are not penalized.

C8 & C5: Legal Selection with Legal Map. During the selection of parents for reproduction, only programs without run-time errors are selected (randomly).

C9 & C5: Legal Fertility with Legal Map. If both parents are legal, three offspring are generated from them. If one parent is legal, two offspring are generated, and if neither of the parents is legal, only one offspring is generated from them.

C11 & C5: Illegal Replacement with Legal Map. One offspring (legal/illegal) is generated to replace a randomly selected illegal individual. If there is no illegal individual left in the population, the normal replacement scheme is used.

4.2 Results

Twenty runs were performed for each constraint handling method. Each run was terminated when a program which produced nine hits was found (i.e., when the evolved function produced output sufficiently close to the desired output for all nine data points) or when 25,500 programs had been processed. If the former occurs, the run is termed *successful*. Table 3 summarizes the experiment results.

The experiments show that Legal Map, Phenotype Penalty with Legal Map and Legal Fertility with Legal Map find a phenotype with nine hits in most of the runs (18/20 and 20/20). For the successful runs, the average number of programs tested is around 4,000. In contrast, Legal Selection with Legal Map and Illegal Replacement with Legal Map methods do not perform well. Most of the runs are unsuccessful and in the small number of successful runs, they have to test a larger number of phenotypes to find one with nine hits.

Method	Success/Runs	Average Number of Programs Processed in Successful Runs
Legal Map	18/20	3,983
Phenotype Penalty & Legal Map	18/20	4,841
Legal Selection & Legal Map	5/20	18,284
Legal Fertility & Legal Map	20/20	3,984
Legal Replacement & Legal Map	3/20	6,998

Table 3. Summary of experiment results

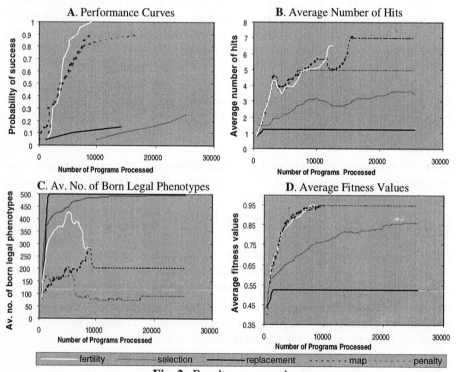

Fig. 2. Result summary charts.

Figure 2A provides the probability of success of each method based on the experiments. The Legal Map, Phenotype Penalty with Legal Map and Legal Fertility with Legal Map methods all perform comparably. Their success curves increase stability from the beginning. Most of the runs found a phenotype with nine hits before 10,000 phenotypes had been tested. However, Legal Selection with Legal Map did not achieve this. Its best success rate was 25% with a requirement of processing 25,000 phenotypes. The success probability of Illegal Replacement with Legal Map was also very low. Even when 14,000 phenotypes were processed, there was less than a 20% probability that this method would find a phenotype with nine hits.

It is clear that three of the methods provide good success rates in evolving phenotypes with nine hits, see figure 2B[1]. However, the results also show that these same methods were the worst at evolving phenotypes which satisfied the run-time error constraint. As shown in Figure 2C, the two methods with the lowest success rates: Legal Selection with Legal Map and Illegal Replacement with Legal Map were able to evolve considerably more legal phenotypes than the other methods. Only one method: Legal Fertility with Legal Map, had a high success rate and evolved larger numbers of legal phenotypes.

5. Analysis and Discussion

The experiments with the run-time error constraint demonstrate a common dilemma in all constrained optimization problems: both the objective and constraints need to be satisfied, and evolving phenotypes which fulfill one of them can sacrifice the evolution of phenotypes which fulfill the other. Using an evolutionary algorithm to find solutions for such problems is therefore difficult because evolutionary search is directed in different directions. The experiments investigated five different ways in which a GP system could be made to evolve both fit and legal programs. The results show, however, that each method exerted a different level of evolutionary pressure for the constraint and objective. It is clear that such different levels of pressure can effect the degree to which both criteria are met.

In the implementation described above, the Legal Map method (a hard constraint) is the neutral placement in the spectrum (i.e., the control method) as it *repairs* phenotypes without the addition of a second selection pressure for the constraint. The other four (soft constraint) methods use this same phenotype repair scheme with an added *pressure* to reduce the number of illegal programs evolved.

Figure 2C shows the average number of born-legal phenotypes in the population using these methods. Our control, the Legal Map method, enforces no pressure for the constraint and the average number of legal individuals remains around 200 throughout the runs. In contrast, the Illegal Replacement method shows that a very strong pressure is exerted on the GP system to evolve legal programs. After the processing of only 2,500 phenotypes, all illegal phenotypes have been replaced and the population contains only legal phenotypes. The Legal Selection method also exerts a strong pressure for the constraint. Since only legal phenotypes are selected (randomly) for reproduction, programs which satisfy the constraint are propagated quickly: after 15,000 phenotypes are processed, only legal phenotypes exist in the population. The Fertility method exerts pressure for constraints by generating more offspring for legal parents than for illegal parents. Compared to the control method, Legal Map, all twenty runs of this method show a consistent increase of legal phenotypes in the population. (The downward trend after 5,000 individuals have been processed, evident in figure 2C, is a distortion of the graph caused by a single run, and is not considered significant.)

Not all of the methods exert such consistent pressures for the constraint, however. The Penalty method generates a strong fitness-driven evolutionary process (illegal

---

[1] Note that the data shown in figure 2B were generated in separate runs.

phenotypes have their *total_error* values doubled to reduce fitness values, so pressure for the constraint drops as individuals become fitter.). As figure 2C shows, this results in the number of legal phenotypes being gradually reduced to satisfy fitness (objective) requirement. It seems likely that the use of fixed penalty values might prevent this effect.

Figure 2D shows the average fitness in the population using these methods. Driven to satisfy only the fitness (objective), the Map method raises population fitness consistently through fitness proportionate selection. Similarly, the strong fitness-oriented pressure of the Penalty method and the Fertility method raises population fitness consistently. The Selection method also raises the average fitness as it replaces the worst individuals with newly created offspring. However, the average fitness stays below 0.87 because by only selecting legal phenotypes for reproduction, the genetic diversity is dramatically reduced. (Figure 2C shows that only 15% of initial population were legal). Because of this reduced diversity, combined with the strong pressure for constraints, the population tends to converge prematurely. This is why only 5 out of the 20 runs for the Selection method were successful. The same effect is evident for the Replacement method. Again, genetic diversity is lost as a large number of illegal phenotypes are replaced. Populations converged when around 2000 phenotypes had been processed. Only 3 out of the 20 runs were successful.

In summary, the combination of pressure for the run-time error constraint and fitness directs evolutionary search to find a legal phenotype which produces nine hits. While some of the results may be due to the type of constraint tackled and the implementation of the constraint handling methods, these experiments show that the Fertility method seems to provide the best balance of evolutionary pressure on both criteria. It raises the average fitness value and at the same time reduces the number of illegal phenotypes in the population. As a result, the average number of hits in the population is raised consistently (see Fig. 2B) and successful phenotypes are found in all 20 runs.

6. Conclusions

This paper presented a framework to allow the classification of constraint handling methods within various stages of evolutionary algorithms. Such methods impose either *hard* constraints or *soft* constraints, and all use *prevention*, *correction*, or *pressure* to enforce the constraints. Eleven methods were identified, including some which had not been explored previously.

Five of these eleven methods were tested on a run-time error constraint in a GP system. The results show that depending on the problem, the methods used and their implementation, the seesaw of evolutionary pressure can either favour constraints or objectives. Of the methods examined, the Legal Fertility method provided a good balance between these two criteria, and led GP to find phenotypes which satisfied both objective and constraints.

Acknowledgements

Thanks to Bill Langdon for his Simple-GP on which our code is based and Tina's supervisor, Chris Clack, for his support. Thanks also to the anonymous reviewers.

References

1. Bäck, T., *Evolutionary Algorithms in Theory and Practice*. Oxford Uni. Press, NY (1996).
2. Banzhaf, W. Genotype-phenotype-mapping and neutral variation - a case study in genetic programming. *Parallel Problem Solving From Nature*, 3. Y. Davidor, H-P Schwefel, and R. Mnner (eds.), Springer-Verlag, (1994) 322-332.
3. Bentley, P. J. & Wakefield, J. P., Finding acceptable solutions in the pareto-optimal range using multiobjective genetic algorithms. Chawdhry, P.K., Roy, R., & Pant, R.K. (eds) *Soft Computing in Engineering Design and Manufacturing*. Springer Verlag London Limited, Part 5, (1997), 231-240.
4. Fogel, L., Angeline, P. J., Bäck, T. *Evolutionary Programming V*, Porceedings of the 5th Annual Conference on Evolutionary Programming. MIT Press, Cambridge, MA (1996).
5. Gero, J. S. and Kazakov, V. A, Evolving design genes in space layout planning problems, *Artificial Intelligence in Engineering* (1998).
6. Goldberg, D. E., *Genetic Algorithms in Search, Optimization & Machine Learning*. Addison-Wesley (1989).
7. Gruau, F., On using syntactic constraints with genetic programming. *Advances in Genetic Programming II*, P.J. Angeline & K.E. Kinnear, Jr, (eds.), MIT Press, (1996) 377-394
8. Janikow, C., A methodology for processing problem constraints in genetic programming. *Computers and Mathematics with Application*, Vol. 32 No. 8, (1996) 97-113.
9. Keller, R. and Banzhaf, W. Genetic programming using genotype-phenotype mapping from linear genomes into linear phenotypes. *Genetic Programming '96: Proc. of the 1st Annual Conf. on GP.*, MIT Press, Cambridge, MA. (1996) 116-122.
10. Koza, J. R., *Genetic Programming: On the Programming of Computers by Means of Natural Selection*. MIT Press, Cambridge, MA (1992).
11. McDonnell, J. R., Reynolds, R. G., Fogel, D. B. *Evolutionary Programming IV*, Proceedings of the 4th Annual Conference on Evolutionary Programming. MIT Press (1995).
12. Michalewicz, Z., Genetic algorithms, numerical optimization and constraints, *Proc. of the 6th Int. Conf. on Genetic Algorithms*, Pittsburgh, July 15-19, (1995a) 151--158.
13. Michalewicz, Z., A survey of constraint handling techniques in evolutionary computation methods *Proc. of the 4th Annual Conf. on Evolutionary Programming*, MIT Press, Cambridge, MA (1995b) 135--155.
14. Michalewicz, Z., Dasgupta, D., Le Riche, R.G., and Schoenauer, M., Evolutionary algorithms for constrained engineering problems, *Computers & Industrial Engineering Journal*, Vol.30, No.2, September (1996) 851--870.
15. Michalewicz, Z. and Michalewicz, M., "Pro-Life versus Pro-Choice Strategies in Evolutionary Computation Techniques", Ch. 10, *Evolutionary Computation*, IEEE Press (1995).
16. Michalewicz, Z., Schoenauer, M., Evolutionary Algorithms for Constrained Parameter Optimization Problems, *Evolutionary Computation 4* (1996) 1-32.
17. Hinterding, R. and Michalewicz, Z., Your brains and my beauty: parent matching for constrained optimisation, *Proc. of the 5th Int. Conf. on Evolutionary Computation*, Anchorage, Alaska, (1998) May, 4-9.
18. Schoenauer, M. and Michalewicz, Z., Boundary operators for constrained parameter optimization problems, *Proc. of the 7th Int. Conf. on Genetic Algorithms*, East Lansing, Michigan, July 19-23 (1997) 320-329.
19. Syswerda, G., Uniform crossover in genetic algorithms. In Schaffer, D. (ed.), *Proc. of the Third Int. Conf. on Genetic Algorithms*. Morgan Kaufmann Pub., (1989).
20. Yu, T. and Clack, C., PolyGP: A polymorphic genetic programming system in Haskell. *Genetic Programming '98: Proc. of the 3rd Annual Conf. Genetic Programming,* (1998).

Multiobjective Optimization Using Evolutionary Algorithms — A Comparative Case Study

Eckart Zitzler and Lothar Thiele

Swiss Federal Institute of Technology Zurich,
Computer Engineering and Communication Networks Laboratory (TIK),
Gloriastrasse 35, CH-8092 Zurich, Switzerland

Abstract. Since 1985 various evolutionary approaches to multiobjective optimization have been developed, capable of searching for multiple solutions concurrently in a single run. But the few comparative studies of different methods available to date are mostly qualitative and restricted to two approaches. In this paper an extensive, quantitative comparison is presented, applying four multiobjective evolutionary algorithms to an extended 0/1 knapsack problem.

1   Introduction

Many real-world problems involve simultaneous optimization of several incommensurable and often competing objectives. Usually, there is no single optimal solution, but rather a set of alternative solutions. These solutions are optimal in the wider sense that no other solutions in the search space are superior to them when *all* objectives are considered. They are known as *Pareto-optimal* solutions.

Mathematically, the concept of Pareto-optimality can be defined as follows: Let us consider, without loss of generality, a multiobjective maximization problem with m parameters (decision variables) and n objectives:

$$\text{Maximize} \quad \mathbf{y} = f(\mathbf{x}) = (f_1(\mathbf{x}), f_2(\mathbf{x}), \dots, f_n(\mathbf{x})) \tag{1}$$

where $\mathbf{x} = (x_1, x_2, \dots, x_m) \in X$ and $\mathbf{y} = (y_1, y_2, \dots, y_n) \in Y$ are tuple. A decision vector $\mathbf{a} \in X$ is said to *dominate* a decision vector $\mathbf{b} \in X$ (also written as $\mathbf{a} \succ \mathbf{b}$) iff

$$\forall i \in \{1, 2, \dots, n\} : f_i(\mathbf{a}) \geq f_i(\mathbf{b}) \quad \wedge \quad \exists j \in \{1, 2, \dots, n\} : f_j(\mathbf{a}) > f_j(\mathbf{b}) \tag{2}$$

Additionally, in this study we say $\mathbf{a}$ *covers* $\mathbf{b}$ iff $\mathbf{a} \succ \mathbf{b}$ or $\mathbf{a} = \mathbf{b}$. All decision vectors which are not dominated by any other decision vector are called *nondominated* or *Pareto-optimal*.

Often, there is a special interest in finding or approximating the Pareto-optimal set, mainly to gain deeper insight into the problem and knowledge about alternate solutions, respectively. Evolutionary algorithms (EAs) seem to be especially suited for this task, because they process a set of solutions in parallel, eventually exploiting similarities of solutions by crossover. Some researcher suggest that multiobjective search and optimization might be a problem area where EAs do better than other blind search strategies [1][12].

Since the mid-eighties various multiobjective EAs have been developed, capable of searching for multiple Pareto-optimal solutions concurrently in a single run. But up to now, no extensive, quantitative comparison of different methods has been reported in literature. The few comparisons available to date are mostly qualitative and restricted to two different methods; quite often, the test problems considered are rather simple.

In this study, however, we provide a comparison which a) uses two complementary quantitative measures to evaluate the performance of the EAs, b) bases on a NP-hard test problem (0/1 knapsack problem), which represents an important class of real-world problems, and c) includes four different multiobjective EAs as well as a pure random search algorithm. The comparison focuses on the effectiveness in finding multiple Pareto-optimal solutions, disregarding its number. Nevertheless, in the case the trade-off surface is continuous or contains many points, the distribution of the nondominated solutions achieved is also an important aspect. Although we do not consider the distribution explicitly, it indirectly influences the performance of the EA.

The paper is organized in the following way. The next section gives a brief overview of evolutionary approaches in the field of multiobjective optimization and a more detailed description of the EAs considered in this investigation. Section 3 introduces a multiobjective 0/1 knapsack problem, discusses the test data sets used in the experiments and presents the chromosome coding and decoding for the EAs. Afterwards, the experimental results are summarized in Section 4, and Section 5 comprises conclusions and future perspectives.

2 Multiobjective Evolutionary Algorithms

A comprehensive overview of EAs in multiobjective optimization was published by Fonseca and Fleming [1]. The authors categorized several evolutionary approaches regarding plain aggregating approaches, population-based non-Pareto approaches and Pareto-based approaches; moreover, approaches using niche induction techniques were considered.

Aggregation methods combine the objectives into a higher scalar function which is used for fitness calculation; they produce one single solution and require profound domain knowledge which is often not available. Population-based non-Pareto approaches, however, are able to evolve multiple nondominated solutions in parallel; thereby, the population is mostly monitored for nondominated solutions. But in contrast to the Pareto-based approaches they do not make direct use of the concept of Pareto dominance. Pareto-based EAs compare solutions according to the $\succ$ relation in order to determine the reproduction probability of each individual; this kind of fitness assignment was first proposed by Goldberg [3].

Since preservation of diversity is crucial in the field of multimodal optimization, many multiobjective EAs incorporate niching techniques, the mostly implemented of which is *fitness sharing* [2]. Fitness sharing bases on the idea that individuals in a particular niche have to share the resources available, similar to nature. Thus, the fitness value of a certain individual is the more degraded the more individuals are located in its neighborhood. Neighborhood is defined in terms of a distance measure and specified by the so-called niche radius σ_{share}. Sharing can be performed both in genotypic space and phenotypic space.

In this study we consider two population-based non-Pareto EAs and two Pareto-based EAs: the Vector Evaluated Genetic Algorithm (VEGA) [10], an EA incorporating weighted-sum aggregation [4], the Niched Pareto Genetic Algorithm [5][6], and the Nondominated Sorting Genetic Algorithm (NSGA) [11]; all but VEGA use fitness sharing to maintain a population distributed along the Pareto-optimal front. Pure aggregation methods are disregarded here because they are not designed for finding a family of solutions.

2.1 Vector Evaluated Genetic Algorithm

Probably the first who recognized EAs to be applicable in multiobjective optimization was Schaffer [10]. He presented a multimodal EA called Vector Evaluated Genetic Algorithm (VEGA) which carries out selection for each objective separately. In detail, the mating pool is divided in n parts of equal size; part i is filled with individuals that are chosen at random from the current population according to objective i. Afterwards, the mating pool is shuffled and crossover and mutation are performed as usual. Schaffer implemented this method in combination with fitness proportionate selection.

2.2 Aggregation by Variable Objective Weighting

Another approach which is based on plain aggregation was introduced by Hajela and Lin [4]. They use the weighted-sum method for fitness assignment. Thereby, each objective is assigned a weight $w_i \in]0, 1[$, such that $\sum w_i = 1$, and the scalar fitness value is calculated by summing up the weighted objective values $w_i \cdot f_i(\mathbf{x})$.[1] To search for multiple solutions in parallel, the weights are not fixed but coded in the genotype. The diversity of the weight combinations is promoted by phenotypic fitness sharing. As a consequence, the EA evolves solutions and weight combinations simultaneously. Finally, the authors emphasize mating restrictions to be necessary in order to "both speed convergence and impart stability to the genetic search" [4, p. 102].

2.3 Niched Pareto Genetic Algorithm

The Niched Pareto Genetic Algorithm proposed by Horn and Nafpliotis [5][6] combines tournament selection and the concept of Pareto dominance. Two competing individuals and a comparison set of other individuals are picked at random from the population; the size of the comparison set is given by the parameter t_{dom}. If one of the competing individuals is dominated by any member of the set, and the other is not, then the latter is chosen as winner of the tournament. If both individuals are dominated or not dominated, the result of the tournament is decided by sharing: The individual which has the least individuals in its niche (defined by σ_{share}) is selected for reproduction. Horn and Nafpliotis used phenotypic sharing on the objective values $f_1(\mathbf{x}), f_2(\mathbf{x}), \ldots, f_n(\mathbf{x})$ in their study.

[1] Normally, the objectives values have to be scaled in the case the magnitude of each objective criterion is quite different. In this study, however, scaling was not implemented due to the nature of the test problems used.

2.4   Nondominated Sorting Genetic Algorithm

Another multiobjective EA which is based on Pareto ranking is the Nondomi-nated Sorting Genetic Algorithm (NSGA) developed by Srinivas and Deb [11]. The fitness assignment is carried out in several steps. In each step, the non-dominated solutions constituting a nondominated front are assigned the same dummy fitness value. These solutions are shared with their dummy fitness values (phenotypic sharing on the parameter values $x_1, x_2, \ldots, x_n$), and ignored in the further classification process. Finally, the dummy fitness is set to a value less than the smallest shared fitness value in the current nondominated front. Then the next front is extracted. This procedure is repeated until all individuals in the population are classified. In the original study [11], this fitness assignment method was combined with a stochastic remainder selection.

3   The Knapsack Problem

A test problem for a comparative study like this has to be chosen carefully. On the one hand, the problem should be understandable and easy to formulate so that the experiments are repeatable and verifiable. On the other hand, it ideally represents a certain class of real-world problems. Both applies to the knapsack problem: the problem description is simple, yet, the problem itself is difficult to solve (NP-hard). Moreover, due to its practical relevance it has been subject to several investigations in various fields, in particular, in the domain of evolutionary computation (e.g. [8]).

3.1   Formulation as Multiobjective Optimization Problem

Generally, a 0/1 knapsack problem consists of a set of items, weights and profits associated with each item, and an upper bound for the capacity of the knapsack. The task is to find a subset of all items which maximizes the total of the profits in the subset, yet, all selected items fit into the knapsack, i.e. the total weight does not exceed the given capacity [7].

This single-objective problem can be extended straight forward for the mul-tiobjective case by allowing an arbitrary number of knapsacks. Formally, the multiobjective 0/1 knapsack problem considered here is defined in the following way: Given a set of m items and a set of n knapsacks, with

$$p_{i,j} = \text{profit of item } j \text{ according to knapsack } i$$
$$w_{i,j} = \text{weight of item } j \text{ according to knapsack } i$$
$$c_i = \text{capacity of knapsack } i,$$

find a vector $\mathbf{x} = (x_1, x_2, \ldots, x_m) \in \{0,1\}^m$, such that

$$\forall i \in \{1, 2, \ldots, n\} : \sum_{j=1}^{m} w_{i,j} \cdot x_j \leq c_i \qquad (3)$$

and for which $f(\mathbf{x}) = (f_1(\mathbf{x}), f_2(\mathbf{x}), \ldots, f_n(\mathbf{x}))$ is maximum, where

$$f_i(\mathbf{x}) = \sum_{j=1}^{m} p_{i,j} \cdot x_j \qquad (4)$$

and $x_j = 1$ iff item j is selected.

3.2 Test Data

In order to obtain reliable and sound results, we used nine different test problems, where both number of knapsacks and number of items were varied. Two, three, and four objectives were taken under consideration, in combination with 100, 250, and 500 items.

Following suggestions in [7], *uncorrelated* profits and weights were chosen, where $p_{i,j}$ and $w_{i,j}$ are random integers in the interval $[10, 100]$. The knapsack capacities were set to half the total weight regarding the corresponding knapsack: $c_i = 0.5 \sum_{j=1}^{m} w_{i,j}$. As reported in [7], about half of the items are expected to be in the optimal solution (of the single-objective problem), when this type of knapsack capacities is used.[2]

3.3 Implementation

Concerning the chromosome coding as well as the constraint handling, we draw upon results published by Michalewicz and Arabas [8]. They examined EAs with different representation mappings and constraint handling techniques on the (single) 0/1 knapsack problem. Concluding from their experiments, an approach using a vector representation and a greedy repair algorithm to correct infeasible solutions appears to be most appropriate for various kinds of knapsack capacities. We adopted this approach with a slightly modified repair mechanism.

In detail, a binary string $\mathbf{s}$ of length m is used to encode the solution $\mathbf{x} \in \{0, 1\}^m$. Since many codings lead to infeasible solutions, a simple repair method r is applied to the genotype $\mathbf{s}$: $\mathbf{x} = r(\mathbf{s})$. The repair algorithm step by step removes items from the solution coded by $\mathbf{s}$ until all capacity constraints are fulfilled. The order in which the items are deleted is determined by the maximum profit/weight ratio per item ; for item j the maximum profit/weight ratio q_j is given by the equation $q_j = \max_{i=1}^{n}\{p_{i,j}/w_{i,j}\}$.[3] The items are considered in increasing order of the q_j.

4 Experiments

4.1 Methodology

In the context of this comparative study several questions arose: What quantitative measures should be used to express the quality of the outcomes so that the EAs can be compared in a meaningful way? What is the outcome of an multiobjective EA regarding a set of runs? How can side effects caused by different selection schemes or mating restrictions be precluded, such that the comparison is not falsified? How can the parameters of the EA, particularly the niche radius, be set appropriately? In the following we deal with these problems.

---

[2] We also examined more restrictive capacities ($c_i = 200$) where the solutions contain only a few items; however, this had no significant influence on the relative performance of the EAs.

[3] This is a straight forward extension to the single-objective approach presented in [8] where $q_j = p_{1,j}/w_{1,j}$.

Two complementary measures were used in this study to evaluate the Pareto fronts produced by the various EAs. The first concerns the size of the objective value space which is covered by a set of nondominated solutions. In the two dimensional case each Pareto-optimal solution $\mathbf{x}$ covers an area, a rectangle, defined by the points $(0,0)$ and $(f_1(\mathbf{x}), f_2(\mathbf{x}))$. The union of all rectangles covered by the Pareto-optimal solutions constitutes the space totally covered, its size is used as measure. This concept may be canonically extended to multiple dimensions. An advantage of this measure is that each EA can be evaluated independent of the other EAs. On the other side, convex regions may be preferred to concave regions, possibly leading to overrating of certain solutions.[4] Therefore, we additionally compared the outcomes of the EAs directly by using the coverage relation (cf. Section 1). Given two sets of nondominated solutions, we computed for each set the fraction of the solutions which are covered by solutions in the other set.

Since in this study the focus is on finding the Pareto-optimal set rather than obtaining a uniform distribution over the trade-off surface, we did not consider the on-line performance of the EAs but the off-line performance. Thus, the Pareto-optimal set regarding all individuals generated over all generations is taken as output of an EA. In addition, to restrict the influence of random effects, the experiments were repeated ten times per test problem, always using a different randomly generated initial population (per experiment all EAs ran on the same initial population). The performance of a particular EA on a given test problem was calculated by averaging its performances over all ten experiments.

Actually, each multiobjective EA should be combined with the selection scheme originally applied. But the influence of the selection scheme on the outcome of an EA cannot be neglected, e.g., fitness proportionate selection, which is used in VEGA, is well-known to have serious disadvantages. In order to guarantee a fair comparison, all EAs considered were implemented with the same selection scheme, binary tournament selection.[5]. Unfortunately, a conventional combination of fitness sharing and tournament selection may lead to chaotic behavior of the EA, as reported by Oei, Goldberg and Chang [9]. Therefore, NSGA as well as Hajela's and Lin's approach were implemented using a slightly modified version of sharing, called *continuously updated sharing*, which was proposed by the same researchers. Thereby, not the current generation but rather the partly filled next generation is used to calculate the niche count. Horn and Nafpliotis introduced this concept in the Niched Pareto GA, too. Moreover, mating was not restricted.[6]

---

[4] In our opinion, this problem will probably always occur if the optimal Pareto front as well as the density of the search space are unknown.

[5] This selection method turned out to be superior to both stochastic remainder selection (used in [11]) and linear ranking selection on our test problems - that has been confirmed experimentally. Moreover, Srinivas and Deb themselves proposed to apply the combination of tournament selection and sharing to NSGA, which we used in this study.

[6] Hajela and Lin found it necessary to use mating restrictions in their evolutionary approach to multiobjective optimization. Therefore, all runs were also carried out

no. of knap.	no. of items	algorithm				
		Random	Weighted	Niched	VEGA	NSGA
2	100	$1.2237 \cdot 10^7$	$1.3303 \cdot 10^7$	$1.4002 \cdot 10^7$	$1.4325 \cdot 10^7$	$\mathbf{1.4559 \cdot 10^7}$
	250	$6.2888 \cdot 10^7$	$6.7418 \cdot 10^7$	$7.0643 \cdot 10^7$	$7.1992 \cdot 10^7$	$\mathbf{7.3624 \cdot 10^7}$
	500	$2.4466 \cdot 10^8$	$2.5712 \cdot 10^8$	$2.6771 \cdot 10^8$	$2.7681 \cdot 10^8$	$\mathbf{2.7831 \cdot 10^8}$
3	100	$4.0641 \cdot 10^{10}$	$4.7860 \cdot 10^{10}$	$4.7068 \cdot 10^{10}$	$4.7965 \cdot 10^{10}$	$\mathbf{4.8997 \cdot 10^{10}}$
	250	$4.9232 \cdot 10^{10}$	$5.6527 \cdot 10^{11}$	$5.5859 \cdot 10^{11}$	$5.6530 \cdot 10^{11}$	$\mathbf{5.8229 \cdot 10^{11}}$
	500	$3.6504 \cdot 10^{11}$	$4.1189 \cdot 10^{13}$	$4.0743 \cdot 10^{13}$	$4.1127 \cdot 10^{13}$	$\mathbf{4.2111 \cdot 10^{13}}$
4	100	$1.0338 \cdot 10^{14}$	$1.1897 \cdot 10^{14}$	$1.2335 \cdot 10^{14}$	$1.1871 \cdot 10^{14}$	$\mathbf{1.2464 \cdot 10^{14}}$
	250	$3.4600 \cdot 10^{15}$	$4.0347 \cdot 10^{15}$	$4.0497 \cdot 10^{15}$	$4.0464 \cdot 10^{15}$	$\mathbf{4.2122 \cdot 10^{15}}$
	500	$5.0967 \cdot 10^{16}$	$5.9123 \cdot 10^{16}$	$5.8055 \cdot 10^{16}$	$5.8651 \cdot 10^{16}$	$\mathbf{5.9959 \cdot 10^{16}}$

Table 1. Results of the experiments concerning the size of the space covered by the nondominated solutions. The numbers set in bold face give the best value achieved per test problem.

On all test problems the population size was set to 100, the probabilities of crossover and mutation were fixed (0.65 and 0.05^7, respectively), the crossover operator used was one-point crossover. Each single EA run was aborted after 500 generations.[8] The niche radii were determined experimentally, for each EA and test problem separately: First, and based on experiments, we sized the range of meaningful values for σ_{share}. Then, we chose five different niche radii and ran the EA on the test problem for each single niche radius. Afterwards, the niche radius which yielded the best result regarding the size of the space covered was selected. Finally, an analogous procedure was applied in order to find the appropriate values for t_{dom}, a parameter used by the Niched Pareto GA. On each test problem, we tried six different values $(1, 5, 10, 15, 20, 25)$ and chose the one providing the best results concerning the space covered. Thereby, the niche radii were determined in the aforementioned manner for each value separately.

4.2 Results

The results concerning the size of the space covered are shown in Table 1, where the column titled *Random* is related to the outcomes produced by a simple random search algorithm. This probabilistic algorithm, which serves as additional point of reference, randomly generates a certain number of individuals per generation, according to the rate of crossover and mutation (but neither crossover and mutation nor selection are performed). Hence, the number of fitness evaluations is the same as for the EAs. The output of the algorithm is the Pareto-optimal set of all solutions generated.

On all test problems NSGA outperformed the other approaches regarding this quality measure. Furthermore, all EAs achieved higher values than the pure

---

with mating restrictions, where we tried several mating radii σ_{mat} and niche radii σ_{share} (following the common practice of setting $\sigma_{\mathrm{mat}} = \sigma_{\mathrm{share}}$). On all test problems no improvement of the results could be observed.

[7] Michalewicz and Arabas [8] used the same values in their study.

[8] It has been experimentally verified that no significant improvement has been achieved when increasing the number of generations. This has also been observed by Michalewicz and Arabas for the single-objective 0/1 knapsack problem.

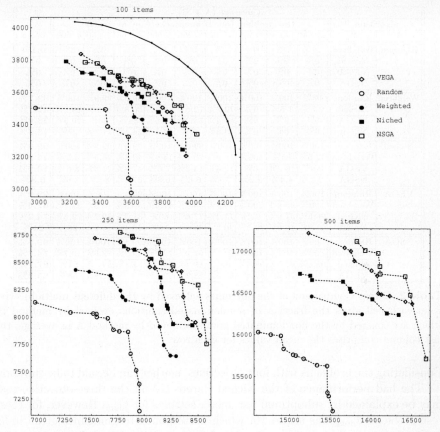

Fig. 1. Nondominated fronts for two objectives; for each method the nondominated solutions regarding all ten runs are plotted; for better visualization the points achieved by a particular method are connected by dashed lines. In the case of 100 items, the solid curve represents optimal nondominated solutions which have been calculated by integer linear programming using weighted-sum scalarization.

random search strategy. The absolute values must not be overrated, however, for the two-dimensional case the ranking of performance is very well reflected by the Pareto fronts depicted in Figure 1.

The direct comparison of the multiobjective optimization methods is given in Table 2. Again, NSGA covers the greatest fraction of the Pareto sets achieved by the other algorithms. Regarding two objectives VEGA has second best performance in this comparison, similar to the results concerning the absolute size of the space covered. On the remaining test problems, VEGA and the weighted-sum approach show almost equal performance.

Comparing the Niched Pareto GA with the weighted-sum based approach, it can be observed that the former clearly outperformed the latter in the two-objective case, while the latter performed better in the three-objective case.

		Coverage (A ≻ B)									
algorithm		test problem (no. of knapsacks / no. of items)									
A	B	2/100	2/250	2/500	3/100	3/250	3/500	4/100	4/250	4/500	mean
Random	Weighted	1,1%	0%	0%	0%	0%	0%	0%	0%	0%	**0.1%**
	Niched	0%	0%	0%	0%	0%	0%	0%	0%	0%	**0%**
	VEGA	0%	0%	0%	0%	0%	0%	0%	0%	0%	**0%**
	NSGA	0%	0%	0%	0%	0%	0%	0%	0%	0%	**0%**
Weighted	Random	98%	100%	100%	100%	100%	100%	99.3%	99.9%	100%	**99.7%**
	Niched	2.5%	1.5%	0%	72.7%	72.6%	75.7%	30.8%	49.5%	79.2%	**42.7%**
	VEGA	0%	0%	0%	41.4%	32.9%	30.6%	38%	30%	40.9%	**23.8%**
	NSGA	0%	0%	0%	23.2%	22%	14.1%	24.1%	11.7%	27%	**13.6%**
Niched	Random	100%	100%	100%	100%	99.6%	100%	99.6%	99.9%	100%	**99.9%**
	Weighted	92.5%	95%	100%	12.9%	20.1%	14.6%	40.8%	26.5%	4.5%	**45.2%**
	VEGA	0.9%	10.3%	0%	12.4%	14.2%	7.6%	47.8%	23.3%	8.6%	**13.9%**
	NSGA	0.7%	4.4%	2.2%	7.7%	5.6%	0.8%	27.1%	8.8%	3.6%	**6.8%**
VEGA	Random	100%	100%	100%	100%	100%	100%	99.4%	100%	100%	**99.9%**
	Weighted	100%	98.8%	100%	43.8%	54.6%	47.4%	34.3%	48.3%	34.7%	**62.4%**
	Niched	86.5%	87.9%	92%	73.2%	77.6%	80%	31.7%	59.7%	79.6%	**74.2%**
	NSGA	25.8%	16.9%	20.5%	20.8%	23.8%	16%	22.4%	16.9%	26%	**21%**
NSGA	Random	100%	100%	100%	100%	100%	100%	99.5%	100%	100%	**99.9%**
	Weighted	100%	100%	100%	59.7%	67.2%	72.7%	49.9%	72.8%	49.7%	**74.7%**
	Niched	93.8%	97.5%	98.8%	88%	89.7%	95.2%	51.1%	84.4%	91%	**87.7%**
	VEGA	58%	76.3%	67.4%	62.5%	58.7%	72.7%	60.5%	72.4%	58%	**65.2%**

Table 2. Direct Comparison of the outcomes achieved by the different multiobjective EAs; each cell gives the fraction of nondominated solutions evolved by method B, which are covered by the nondominated points achieved by method A in average; the last column comprises the mean values for each row.

Considering the problems with four objectives, neither can be said to be superior.

The bad performance of the Niched Pareto GA in the three-objective case may be explained by suboptimal parameter settings for t_{dom}. However, for these test problems t_{dom} was set to 10, which corresponds to guidelines given in [5] (10% of the population size); all other five t_{dom}-settings lead to worse results. As stated by Horn and Nafpliotis, the value of t_{dom} is critical to the convergence of the Niched Pareto GA, and to our experience, it seems to be rather difficult to find the optimal t_{dom}.

5 Conclusions and Future Work

In this study we compared four multiobjective EA on a multiobjective 0/1 knapsack problem with nine different problem settings. The quality of the Pareto-optimal sets achieved was measured quantitatively by the size of the space covered. Additionally, the approaches were compared directly by evaluating the outcomes regarding the concept of Pareto dominance.

All EAs clearly outperformed a pure random search strategy which randomly generates new points in the search space without exploiting similarities between solutions. Among the EAs the Nondominated Sorting Genetic Algorithm (NSGA) proposed by Srinivas and Deb [11] achieved the best evaluations on all test problems, followed by Schaffer's VEGA [10] when all nine test problems are considered. Concerning the other two approaches, the results are ambiguous: In the two-objective case, the Niched Pareto Genetic Algorithm presented by Horn and Nafpliotis [5] outperformed the weighted-sum based approach proposed by Hajela and Lin [4]. On the other side, the latter EA achieved better evaluations for three objectives. In the case of four objectives neither of them was superior.

Regarding future perspectives, the issue of distributing the population over the tradeoff surface might be subject to further examinations. In many applications, where the tradeoff surface is continuous or containing a huge number of solutions, it is essential that the EA is capable of "selecting" representative solutions. Furthermore, the influence of mating restrictions might be investigated, although restricted mating is not very widespread in the field of multiobjective EA. Finally, as stated in [1] a theory of evolutionary multiobjective optimization is much needed, examining different fitness assignment methods in combination with different selections schemes.

References

1. Carlos M. Fonseca and Peter J. Fleming. An overview of evolutionary algorithms in multiobjective optimization. *Evolutionary Computation*, 3(1):1–16, 1995.
2. D. E. Goldberg and J. Richardson. Genetic algorithms with sharing for multimodal function optimization. In *Genetic Algorithms and their Applications: Proceedings of the Second International Conference on Genetic Algorithms*, pages 41–49, Hillsdale, NJ, 1987. Lawrence Erlbaum.
3. David E. Goldberg. *Genetic Algorithms in Search, Optimization, and Machine Learning*. Addison-Wesley, Reading, Massachusetts, 1989.
4. P. Hajela and C.-Y. Lin. Genetic search strategies in multicriterion optimal design. *Structural Optimization*, 4:99–107, 1992.
5. Jeffrey Horn and Nicholas Nafpliotis. Multiobjective optimization using the niched pareto genetic algorithm. IlliGAL Report 93005, Illinois Genetic Algorithms Laboratory, University of Illinois, Urbana, Champaign, July 1993.
6. Jeffrey Horn, Nicholas Nafpliotis, and David E. Goldberg. A niched pareto genetic algorithm for multiobjective optimization. In *Proceedings of the First IEEE Conference on Evolutionary Computation, IEEE World Congress on Computational Computation*, volume 1, pages 82–87, Piscataway, NJ, 1994. IEEE Service Center.
7. Silvano Martello and Paolo Toth. *Knapsack Problems: Algorithms and Computer Implementations*. Wiley, Chichester, 1990.
8. Zbigniew Michalewicz and Jaroslaw Arabas. Genetic algorithms for the 0/1 knapsack problem. In *Methodologies for Intelligent Systems (ISMIS'94)*, pages 134–143, Berlin, 1994. Springer.
9. Christopher K. Oei, David E. Goldberg, and Shau-Jin Chang. Tournament selection, niching, and the preservation of diversity. IlliGAL Report 91011, University of Illinois at Urbana-Champaign, Urbana, IL 61801, December 1991.
10. J. David Schaffer. Multiple objective optimization with vector evaluated genetic algorithms. In John J. Grefenstette, editor, *Proceedings of an International Conference on Genetic Algorithms and Their Applications*, pages 93–100, 1985.
11. N. Srinivas and Kalyanmoy Deb. Multiobjective optimization using nondominated sorting in genetic algorithms. *Evolutionary Computation*, 2(3):221–248, 1994.
12. Manuel Valenzuela-Rendón and Eduardo Uresti-Charre. A non-generational genetic algorithm for multiobjective optimization. In *Proceedings of the Seventh International Conference on Genetic Algorithms*, pages 658–665, San Francisco, California, 1997. Morgan Kaufmann.

Representation Issues

Utilizing Dynastically Optimal Forma Recombination in Hybrid Genetic Algorithms

Carlos Cotta, Enrique Alba and José Mª Troya

Dept. of Lenguajes y Ciencias de la Computación, Univ. of Málaga
Complejo Tecnológico (2.2.A.6), Campus de Teatinos, 29071-Málaga, Spain

{ccottap, eat, troya}@lcc.uma.es

Abstract. A heuristic recombination operator is presented in this paper. This operator intelligently explores the dynastic potential (possible children) of the solutions being recombined, providing the best combination of formae (generalised schemata) that can be constructed without introducing implicit mutation. The applicability of this operator to different kind of representations (orthogonal, separable and non-separable representations) is discussed. The experimental results confirm the appropriateness of this operator to a number of widely-known hard combinatorial problems.

1. Introduction

The utilisation of recombination operators is always a controversial issue within the different families of the evolutionary-computing community. On the one hand, many evolutionary-programming practitioners consider that recombination reduces in most cases to macromutation. On the other hand, recombination is assigned a key rôle by genetic-algorithm researchers. In fact, extended recombination mechanisms have been defined in which more than two individuals contribute to create a new solution [6].

These opposed arguments have motivated a plethora of theoretical studies to determine when and how to recombine. As to the first question, the most classical answer is Goldberg's building block hypothesis [7]. This hypothesis has been notably reformulated by Radcliffe, generalising the concept of schema to abstract entities called *formae* [10] and defining representation-independent recombination operators with specific properties with respect to these formae [12]. The resulting framework (Forma Analysis) has provided very important insights on the functioning of genetic algorithms.

It is both the strength and the weakness of these representation-independent operators that their application is blind, i.e., randomly guided. The underlying idea is not to introduce any bias in the evolution of the algorithm, thus preventing premature convergence to suboptimal solutions. This intuitive idea is questionable though. First, notice that the evolution of the algorithm is in fact biased by the choice of representation and the mechanics of the particular operators. Second, there exist widely known mechanisms (e.g., spatial isolation) to promote diversity in the population, thus precluding (or at least hindering) extremely fast convergence to suboptimal solutions. Finally, it can be better to quickly obtain a suboptimal solution and restart the algorithm than using blind operators for a long time in pursuit of an asymptotically optimal behaviour.

This paper discusses the use of recombination operators that use problem knowledge to bias the generation of new solutions. To be precise, the problem knowledge is used to determine which the best possible combination of the ancestors' features is. Such operators are usually termed *heuristic* or *hybrid* operators, resulting their utilisation in a hybrid algorithm. The remainder of the paper is organised as follows: first, some background information on forma recombination is presented (Sect. 2). Second, the basis for the hybrid operator is discussed (Sect. 3). Next, the applicability of the operator is analysed on problems whose representations exhibit different features such as orthogonality (Sect. 4) or simply separability (Sect. 5). Then, experimental results are reported (Sect. 6) and, finally, conclusions are presented (Sect. 7).

2. Background on Forma Recombination

There exist some properties that can be studied when analysing the behaviour of an operator with respect to the formae it manipulates. These can be summarised in *respect*, *transmission* and *assortment* [13].

Respect represents the exploitative side of recombination. A recombination operator is said to be *respectful* if, and only if, it generates children carrying all features common to both parents. Respect becomes more important as the algorithm converges since diversity decreases and individuals are thus more likely to have similar features.

Transmission is a related property that tries to capture the classical rôle of recombination. A recombination operator is said to be *transmitting* if, and only if, all features of the children it generates are present in at least one parent. If this is not the case, the operator is said to introduce *implicit mutation*.

Finally, assortment represents the exploratory side of recombination. An operator is said to be *properly* assorting if, and only if, it can generate children carrying any combination of compatible features taken from the parents. It may be necessary to recombine the children with the parents or among themselves several times to achieve this effect. In this case, the operator is said to be *weakly* assorting.

These three properties are not always compatible. First, notice that it is always possible to define a recombination operator that respects and transmits formae, e.g., returning one of the parents as a child. However, it is obvious that such an operator has no interest. In a more general situation, it can be seen that respect does not imply transmission nor vice versa. For example, consider the following individuals representing edge-based solutions to a travelling salesrep problem:

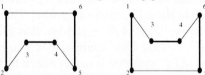

A possible recombination of these solutions is 1-3-2-5-4-6. It can be seen that all edges in this solution are present in one of the parents (i.e., this is a transmitting recombination) but no common edge occurs (i.e., the recombination is not respectful). On the other hand, 1-2-3-4-6-5 is a respectful recombination (edges 12^u, 34^u, 56^u are present) but an exogenous edge (15^u) is included[1].

---

[1] It must be noted that transmission does imply respect in *genetic* representations but, as shown in these examples, this is not the case in *allelic* [12] representations.

Likewise, assortment and respect are not always compatible. Following the above example, the undirected edges 45^u and 46^u are compatible, but combining them excludes the common edge 34^u. In such a situation, the representation is said to be *non-separable*. Not all representations have this property. For example, consider the position-based representation of permutations [7][4]. It is easy to see that common positions can be respected and then any pair of compatible position formae (i.e., assignments of different elements to different positions) can be included. Such a representation is said to be *separable*. However, notice that an arbitrary assortment of separable formae generally results in the lack of fully transmission (i.e., implicit mutation is introduced). For example, assume that 1-3-2-5-4-6 and 1-2-3-4-6-5 are recombined. Respecting 1 in the first position and assorting 6 in the sixth position (first parent) and 4 in the fourth position (second parent) forces 5 to be placed in the 2nd, 3rd or 5th position, in none of which it appears in any parent.

Finally, the three properties are fully compatible in orthogonal representations (representations in which any tuple of formae corresponding to different features are compatible). Traditional schemata are usually orthogonal. However, this is not the case for most representations. Notice that orthogonality implies separability, but the reverse is not necessarily true.

3. Random Transmission and Heuristic Recombination

As previously stated, orthogonal representations are the only ones in which the three described properties of recombination are compatible. Unfortunately, no suitable orthogonal representation can be found for most problems. In these situations, a choice has to be made to decide which of these properties should be exhibited by the recombination operator.

In this sense, there exists empirical evidence suggesting that respect is a desirable property (e.g., see [14][4]). Under the assumption of respect, the choice reduces to at most transmission or assortment in non-orthogonal separable representations. However, imposing respect in non-separable formae strongly constraints the chances for assorting, likely resulting in a trivial transmission unless implicit mutation is introduced. Such implicit mutation is usually regarded as undesirable though.

For that reason, transmission has been chosen as the central feature for the operators described in this work. This implies a trade-off between respect and assortment in non-separable representations. Moreover, this trade-off is biased towards respect since implicit mutation is always related to arbitrary assortments. Finally, notice that gene transmission implies respect in separable representations. In this context, assorting is limited but, as it will be shown, it is enhanced by the inclusion of problem-knowledge.

The proposed operator is thus a variant of Radcliffe's *Random Transmitting Recombination* (RTR). This operator is defined as follows [12]:

Definition 1 (RTR). The Random Transmitting Recombination operator is a function RTR: $S \times S \times Z \rightarrow S$ defined by RTR$(x, y, k) \equiv \gamma_{k'}(x, y)$, where $\gamma_i(x, y)$ is the ith member (under an arbitrary enumeration) of the dynastic potential $\Gamma(\{x, y\})$ of x and y, and $k'=k(mod \ |\Gamma(\{x, y\})|)$.

∎

Since the dynastic potential of two solutions is the set of all solutions that can be built using only the features of both parents, if RTR is given a random parameter k, it returns a random individual entirely composed of their parents' formae. As stated in Section 1, this random selection is unnecessary if enough problem-knowledge is available to determine which solutions in this dynastic potential are the most promising ones. The use of such knowledge is addressed in the literature in two ways:

1. *Memetic approach* [9]: after the child has been generated a local hill-climbing mechanism is applied.
2. *Patching by forma completion* [13]: a partially-specified child is generated using an operator that combines respect and assortment (e.g., the RAR_ω operator [12]). This child is then completed using either of the two following mechanisms:
   a) *Locally optimal forma completion*: the gaps are randomly filled and then a local hill-climbing procedure is applied to them.
   b) *Globally optimal forma completion*: the subspace of solutions matching the currently specified features is explored to determine the best completion of the child.

Notice that these two approaches are incompatible with the principle of forma transmission observed in this paper; the use of a local hill-climber almost surely will introduce a considerable amount of implicit mutation. Although this is not necessarily bad (in fact, memetic algorithms have been quite successful in several problem-domains, e.g., the TSP), it complicates both a general analysis and a performance prediction. This is also true for globally optimal forma completion which, additionally, can be computationally expensive.

The operator proposed in this work tries to combine the positive features of the RTR operator and the two heuristic approaches described above. Like RTR, it is a strictly transmitting operator. Like the heuristic approaches, problem-knowledge is used to select a feasible forma combination but, unlike globally optimal forma completion, only the dynastic potential is explored and hence the computational cost is considerably reduced in some cases.

Definition 2 (Dinastically Optimal Recombination). The Dinastically Optimal Recombination operator is a function DOR: $S \times S \to S$ defined by DOR $(x, y) \equiv \phi^{-1}$ [**max**$\{\phi(z) : z \in \Gamma(\{x,y\})\}$], i.e., the best member[2] of the dynastic potential of x and y. ∎

An obvious requirement for the application of DOR is the decomposability of the fitness function. This is true for most hard combinatorial problems (e.g., the TSP, scheduling problems, etc.). Notice that the choice of representation influences DOR in two ways. First, it determines which solutions are in the dynastic potential of x and y, thus conditioning which the newly created child can be. Second, a poor representation may turn DOR computationally prohibitive for two reasons:

a) Inadequate formae may define a dynastic potential whose size be comparable to the whole solution-space.

---

[2] Assume maximisation without loss of generality.

b) Even if the dynastic potential is small, inappropriate formae may carry noisy fitness information (e.g., due to epistasis). The exploration of the dynastic potential could then be reduced to exhaustive enumeration, which is undesirable.

These effects are mostly significant when non-separable formae are involved. This is confirmed by the results reported in [2] regarding the use of a hybrid operator whose functioning resembles dynastically optimal forma recombination on a non-separable edge-representation. This problem can be solved in a number of ways such as an early termination of DOR (based on the fact that the best solution can be quickly found but it may take a long time to determine its optimality) or a parallelisation of the operator. Clearly, this is a substantial topic for itself and hence we defer the study of these possibilities to a further work.

The rest of the paper will analyse the applicability of DOR to orthogonal and non-orthogonal separable representations. Notice that this simplification does not leave a trivial problem at all. As shown later, very hard problems (like SAT or flowshop scheduling) can be adequately described in terms of separable representations.

4. Dynastically Optimal Recombination of Orthogonal Formae

Non-epistatic orthogonal representations are the most adequate for any kind of hill-climbing. With such a representation, the fitness of an individual can be computed as the sum of the contribution of each basic forma, i.e.,

$$\phi(x) = \phi(\{\xi_1, \xi_2, \cdots, \xi_n\}) = \sum_{1 \le i \le n} \phi_i(\xi_i) . \tag{1}$$

It can be easily seen that a problem for which such a representation is adequate can be solved by individually optimising each contributing forma. The hardness of such an optimisation is clearly dependent on the features of each single ϕ_i.

In this context, the dynastic potential of two solutions $x = \{\eta_1, \cdots, \eta_n\}$ and $y = \{\zeta_1, \cdots, \zeta_n\}$ is the n-dimensional Cartesian product of all pairs (η_i, ζ_i). According to Equation (1), DOR is defined by DOR $(x, y) = \{\xi_1, \cdots, \xi_n\}$, where $\xi_i = \phi_i^{-1}[\mathbf{max}\{\phi_i(\eta_i), \phi_i(\zeta_i)\}]$.

Although this kind of problems is frequently used as a benchmark to assess the quality of operators and/or algorithmic models, they turn out to be trivial when problem-knowledge is included. In fact, experiments [5] realised with the Rastrigin and Schwefel functions have shown that the results of DOR are two orders of magnitude better than other operators such as Single-Point Crossover (SPX), Uniform Crossover (UX) or Random Respectful Recombination [11] for dimensionalities around 32. For that reason, this section focuses on more difficult problems. To be precise, epistatic orthogonal representations are considered.

In an epistatic representation, the contribution of each basic forma is influenced by the values of other basic formae. Thus,

$$\phi(x) = \phi(\{\xi_1, \xi_2, \cdots, \xi_n\}) = \sum_{1 \le i \le n} \phi_i(\xi_{j_{i1}}, \cdots, \xi_{j_{ik}}) . \tag{2}$$

In this more general situation, DOR cannot individually select the value of each feature. If no additional information were available about the nature of each ϕ_i, DOR could not be used since it would reduce to exhaustive enumeration. However, if an optimistic estimation can be given for $\phi_i(\cdot)$, DOR can be constructed as an embedded dynamic-programming or branch-and-bound operator, thus constituting a *weak* hybrid algorithm [3]. Notice that the more problem-knowledge available (i.e., the more accurate estimation that can be given for any partially-parameterised ϕ_i), the more efficient DOR will be.

5. Dynastically Optimal Recombination of Separable Formae

Non-orthogonal separable formae can be simultaneously respected and assorted but, unlike orthogonal formae, this may violate forma transmission since arbitrary intersections of formae taken from different solutions can be incompatible. This is usually considered a drawback of the representations since it forces the design of recombination operators to deal with this fact, adequately processing formae so as to keep feasibility in the generated solutions. However, non-orthogonality is an advantage from the point of view of the computational cost of DOR for two reasons.

First, the dynastic potential of two solutions under a non-orthogonal separable representation is smaller than under an analogous orthogonal representation. Consider that, given two solutions $x = \{\eta_1, \cdots, \eta_n\}$ and $y = \{\zeta_1, \cdots, \zeta_n\}$, their dynastic potential is composed in the latter case of all solutions $z = \{\xi_1, \cdots, \xi_n\}$, where $\xi_i \in \{\eta_i, \zeta_i\}$. Hence $|\Gamma(\{x, y\})| = 2^n$. However, if the representation is non-orthogonal, there may exist two subsets of formae Ξ and Ψ ($x \in \Xi, y \in \Psi$) such that $\Xi \cap \Psi$ is incompatible with a certain ζ_j. Such an infeasible individual must be excluded from the dynastic potential and thus $|\Gamma(\{x, y\})| < 2^n$. For example, given two permutations of n elements, 2^n strings can be generated using UX (i.e., assuming orthogonality). However, most of these strings are infeasible permutations. On the other hand, the size of the dynastic potential under a position-based representation of permutations is smaller and can be computed as 2^c, where $c \leq n/2$ is the number of non-trivial *cycles* [4] in the solutions.

Second, the granularity of each step in the computation of DOR is larger since solutions are incrementally constructed by adding sometimes more than one forma (i.e., all those formae that are implicitly forced by the formae already included in the current solution). Following the previous example, the units of construction are not single position-formae but cycles, i.e., the intersection of several basic position-formae.

These two considerations are equally valid either in the presence or the absence of epistasis although, obviously, they can be further exploited in the latter case. To be precise, consider the following definition:

Definition 3 (Compatibility Set). The compatibility set $K(\eta_i, \Xi, x, y)$ of a basic forma η_i ($x \in \eta_i$) for a partially-specified solution $\Xi \equiv \cap \xi_j$ (where $x \in \xi_j$ or $y \in \xi_j$) is the set of formae forced by the inclusion of η_i in Ξ, i.e., $K(\eta_i, \Xi, x, y) = \{\eta_{j1}, \cdots, \eta_{jk}\}$, $x \in \cap \eta_{jr}$ ($1 \leq r \leq k$) such that $\Gamma(\{x, y\}) \cap (\Xi \cap \eta_i \cap \zeta_{jr})$ is empty, $1 \leq r \leq k$.

∎

Notice that $\eta_i \in K(\eta_i, \Xi, x, y)$. Compatibility sets are the above-mentioned units of construction. In the absence of epistasis, the fitness of one of these sets can be easily computed as the sum of the contributions of each member of the set, i.e.,

$$\phi(K(\eta_i, \Xi, x, y)) = \phi(\{\eta_{j1}, \cdots, \eta_{jk}\}) = \sum_{1 \leq r \leq k} \phi(\eta_{jr}) . \qquad (3)$$

If epistasis is involved, the worst situation is that in which none of the members of the compatibility set influences the fitness calculation of the remaining members (or at least, the estimation of each fitness contribution is not improved by considering them). Nevertheless, even in this situation the number of steps for completing the best solution is reduced with respect to an analogous orthogonal representation, as previously stated.

6. Experimental Results

DOR has been evaluated on a set of benchmark problems exhibiting the different properties previously discussed. Except where otherwise noted, all experiments have been done using an elitist generational genetic algorithm (*popsize*=100, p_c=.9, p_m=1.0/n, *maxevals*=10^5) with ranking selection (η^+=2.0, η^-=.0).

The first considered problem has been the 3-SAT. This is a classical NP-hard problem for which an orthogonal representation is well-suited: a list of truth assignments. Considering the graded fitness function consisting of the number of satisfied clauses, this representation is highly epistatic: each variable occurs in many clauses whose values also depend on other variables. An optimistic estimation of ϕ_i is then provided by the number of clauses in which the *i*th variable appears minus the number of unsatisfied clauses given the current values of the variables.

The algorithm has been applied to hard random instances with a number of variables $n \in [50, 125]$, and a number of clauses $m = 4.23 \cdot n$. As indicated in [8], this value corresponds to a phase-transition in the satisfiability/unsatisfiability of the so-generated instances. Instances located within this phase-transition are the hardest to solve on average. For comparison purposes, both SPX and UX has been applied to the same instances. The results are shown in Table 1.

Table 1. Average # satisfied clauses and # times a satisfying solution is found (out of 20).

Operator	Number of variables/clauses			
	50/211	55/233	60/254	65/275
SPX	210.3 (10)	231.9 (5)	253.5 (11)	273.6 (2)
UX	210.4 (11)	232.4 (9)	253.3 (7)	274.2 (5)
DOR	210.8 (14)	232.8 (14)	254.0 (20)	274.9 (15)
	70/296	75/317	100/423	125/528
SPX	294.5 (5)	314.9 (0)	418.8 (0)	524.1 (0)
UX	294.9 (6)	315.8 (0)	418.9 (0)	524.6 (0)
DOR	296.0 (20)	316.0 (0)	421.5 (2)	526.3 (1)

As it can be seen, DOR outperforms UX and SPX, both in the average number of satisfied clauses and effectiveness in finding a satisfying solution. However, the improvement is not exceedingly good. The reason can be found in one of the already-mentioned potential drawbacks of introducing heuristic bias in the recombination operator: premature convergence. As shown in Fig.1 (left), the diversity of the population is quickly lost when using DOR if compared to UX or SPX.

To solve this problem, the experiments have been repeated with higher mutation rates. The behaviour of the algorithm is illustrated in Fig. 1 (right). While the performance of SPX and UX degrades when the mutation rate is increased, DOR remains performing well, in fact improving the results as shown in Table 2.

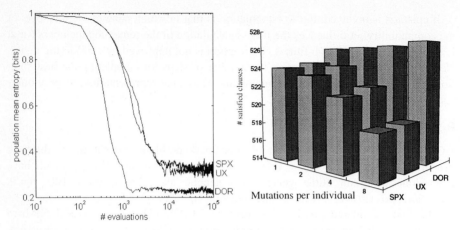

Fig. 1. Evolution of the population's entropy for the 3-SAT problem (left), and results for different mutation rates in a 125-variable instance (right).

Table 2. Results of the DOR operator for different mutation rates.

Mutations per individual	Number of variables/clauses			
	50/211	55/233	60/254	65/275
2	211.0 (20)	232.6 (12)	254.0 (20)	274.9 (19)
4	211.0 (20)	232.9 (19)	254.0 (20)	274.9 (18)
8	211.0 (20)	233.0 (20)	254.0 (20)	275.0 (20)
	70/296	75/317	100/423	125/528
2	296.0 (20)	316.0 (1)	421.5 (0)	526.4 (0)
4	296.0 (20)	316.0 (1)	421.4 (0)	526.5 (1)
8	296.0 (20)	316.5 (9)	421.4 (0)	526.9 (3)

The second test problem (*min-permutation* [5]) is a minimisation problem appropriate for non-epistatic non-orthogonal separable representations. First, a family of n bijective functions $\psi_i : [1,n] \rightarrow [1,n]$ is randomly chosen. Then, a function $\phi (x_1, \cdots, x_n)$ is defined over the space of permutations of n elements as $\Sigma \psi_i(x_i)$, $1 \leq i \leq n$.

In this situation, two possible representations can be defined for this problem: position-based and block-based. In the former, the units of construction are cycles, while in the latter these units are sequences of contiguous positions [4]. Since the fitness of a permutation is determined on the basis of individual positions, none of these two representations is a priori better, as their similar fitness variances [13] suggest (Fig. 2 - left). However, the empirical evaluation of DOR reveals that position-DOR (OCX - *Optimal Cycle Crossover*) performs better than block-DOR (OBX - *Optimal Block Crossover*). The reason can be found in the smaller size of the dynastic potential for the latter (blocks always contain one or more cycles). Nevertheless, both versions of DOR notably outperform the standard operators for permutation recombination (see [4]) as shown in Fig. 2 (right).

Finally, DOR has been applied to an epistatic non-orthogonal separable representation. To be precise, the flowshop scheduling problem has been considered. This is a well-known NP-hard problem of practical interest. As for the previous problem, two

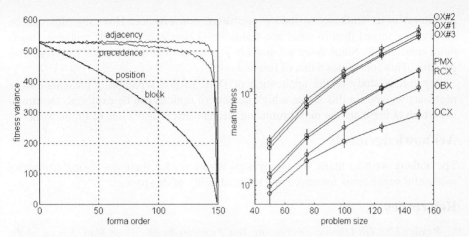

Fig. 2. Fitness variance of different representations of the *min-permutation* problem in a 150-element instance (left) and empirical results of different recombination operators (right).

Table 3. Results of different recombination operators for permutation flowshop problems.

Operator	rec19 30 × 10	rec25 30 × 15	rec31 50 × 20	rec37 75 × 10	rec39 75 × 20
OX#1	2127.8	2574.5	3146.6	5229.1	5327.1
OX#2	2123.1	2572.2	3151.1	5249.2	5299.7
OX#3	2139.3	2560.9	3127.7	5196.7	5282.7
RCX	2128.8	2571.2	3126.1	5188.8	5277.8
PMX	2120.4	2567.6	3127.3	5185.2	5279.5
OCX	2117.1	2566.5	3106.4	5166.6	5221.1
OBX	2123.5	2578.5	3117.9	5195.7	5278.9

different representations have been considered: position-based and block-based. For comparison purposes with [4], a steady-state evolution model has been used. The results for some standard instances of this problem [1] are shown in Table 3.

Again, OCX is the best overall operator and OBX performs worse due to the previously-mentioned effect. Furthermore, the epistatic nature of the representation specifically affects OBX for this reason, making its performance drop to the level of unbiased position- and block- manipulators such as PMX or RCX.

7. Conclusions

A heuristic operator has been presented in this work. This operator is characterised for not introducing any implicit mutation. On the one hand, this allows a stronger control of the algorithm since creation of new formae only takes place through explicit mutation. On the other hand, its heuristically-biased functioning makes it capable of transmitting high-order formae which would be probably disrupted by an unbiased operator, as long as they contribute to the construction of good solutions. Furthermore, the operator is capable of determining the best linkage of formae taken from different solutions, so as to create these promising macro-formae.

One of the drawbacks of the operator (in fact, an inherent drawback of all heuristic operators) is its tendency to induce premature convergence. However, this can be more easily solved than in other non-transmitting operators since the mutation rate is more controllable. Some other solutions (e.g., spatial isolation of individuals) are also possible. This constitutes a line of future work.

A rigorous study of the application of DOR to non-separable representations is necessary as well. In this sense, a high number of options can be explored. Determining which of these are the most promising mechanisms is also a line of future work.

Acknowledgements

The authors wish to thank the anonymous reviewers for their interesting comments and useful suggestions for improving the readability of this paper.

References

1. Beasley J.E.: *OR-Library: Distributing Test Problems by Electronic Mail.* Journal of the Operational Research Society 41(11):1069-1072 (1990)
2. Cotta C., Aldana J.F., Nebro A.J., Troya J.M.: *Hybridizing Genetic Algorithms with Branch & Bound Techniques for the Resolution of the TSP.* In: Artificial Neural Nets and Genetic Algorithms, Pearson D., Steele N., Albrecht R. (editors), Springer-Verlag (1995) 277-280
3. Cotta C., Troya J.M.: *On Decision-Making in Strong Hybrid Evolutionary Algorithms.* In: Tasks and Methods in Applied Artificial Intelligence, Del Pobil A.P., Mira J., Ali M. (editors), Lecture Notes in Artificial Intelligence 1415, Springer-Verlag (1998) 418-427
4. Cotta C., Troya J.M.: *Genetic Forma Recombination in Permutation Flowshop Problems.* Evolutionary Computation 6(1):25-44 (1998)
5. Cotta C., *A Study of Hybridisation Techniques and their Application to the Design of Evolutionary Algorithms*, PhD Thesis, University of Málaga (1998) - in spanish
6. Eiben A.E., Raue P.-E., Ruttkay Zs.: *Genetic Algorithms with Multi-parent Recombination.* In: Parallel Problem Solving from Nature 3, Davidor Y., Schwefel H.P., Männer R. (editors), Lecture Notes in Computer Science 866, Springer-Verlag (1994) 78-87
7. Goldberg D.E.: *Genetic Algorithms in Search, Optimization and Machine Learning.* Addison-Wesley, Reading MA (1989)
8. Mitchell D., Selman B., Levesque H.: *Hard and Easy Distributions of SAT Problems.* In: Proceedings of the 10th National Conference on Artificial Intelligence, San José CA (1992) 459-465
9. Moscató P.: *On Evolution, Search, Optimization, Genetic Algorithms and Martial Arts: Towards Memetic Algorithms.* C3P Report 826 (1989)
10. Radcliffe N.J.: *Equivalence Class Analysis of Genetic Algorithms.* Complex Systems 5:183-205 (1991)
11. Radcliffe N.J.: *Forma Analysis and Random Respectful Recombination.* In: Proceedings of the 4th International Conference on Genetic Algorithms, Belew R., Booker L. (editors), Morgan Kaufmann, San Mateo CA (1991) 222-229
12. Radcliffe N.J.: *The Algebra of Genetic Algorithms.* Annals of Mathemathics and Artificial Intelligence 10:339-384 (1994)
13. Radcliffe N.J., Surry P.D.: *Fitness Variance of Formae and Performance Prediction.* In: Foundations of Genetic Algorithms 3, Whitley L.D., Vose M.D. (editors), Morgan Kaufmann, San Mateo CA (1994) 51-72
14. Starkweather T., McDaniel S., Mathias K., Whitley D., Whitley C.: *A Comparison of Genetic Sequencing Operators*, In: Proceedings of the 4th International Conference on Genetic Algorithms, Belew R., Booker L. (editors), Morgan Kaufmann, San Mateo CA (1991) 69-76

Further Experimentations on the Scalability of the GEMGA

Hillol Kargupta[1] and Sanghamitra Bandyopadhyay[2]

[1] School of Electrical Engineering and Computer Science
Washington State University
Pullman, WA 99164-2752, USA
[2] Machine Intelligence Unit
Indian Statistical Institute, Calcutta, India

Abstract. This paper reports the recent developments of the Gene Expression Messy Genetic Algorithm (GEMGA) research. It presents extensive experimental results for large problems with massive multi-modality, non-uniform scaling, and overlapping sub-problems. All the experimental results corroborate the linear time performance of the GEMGA for a wide range of problems, that can be decomposed into smaller overlapping and non-overlapping sub-problems in the chosen representation. These results further support the scalable performance of the GEMGA.

1 Introduction

The recent past has witnessed a growing interest in designing scalable evolutionary algorithms that inductively detect the decomposable partitions (sometimes called genetic *linkage* in the Genetic Algorithm (GA) literature[8]) of the optimization problem. Messy genetic algorithms [4, 6, 5, 7, 10, 3], Dependency trees [2], distribution estimation [15, 16], are some examples. For problems that can be decomposed into smaller subproblems in the chosen representation, these algorithms are likely to work effectively by reducing the global search problem into a problem of computing and combining partial results from smaller partitions of the space. A detailed discussion on the need for addressing this class of problems on grounds of polynomial complexity search can be found elsewhere [10].

The Gene Expression Messy Genetic Algorithm (GEMGA) [10, 11, 3] offers one approach to detect decomposable partitions in terms of relations and classes. Regardless of whether or not the problem is decomposable, the GEMGA continues to look for relations that capture similarity in the fitness landscape using similarity based equivalence classes or schemata [8]. In GEMGA, the problem of associating similarities among chromosomes with similarities of their corresponding fitness values is posed as a problem of detecting approximate symmetry. Symmetry can be defined as an invariance in the pattern under observation when some transformation is applied to it. Similarities among the fitness values of the members of a schema can be viewed as a kind of symmetry, that remains invariant under any transformation that satisfies the closure property of the schema. The GEMGA exploits this observation for detecting relations among the search space members and this approach appears to be quite successful for detecting decomposable partitions of an optimization problem. This paper briefly reviews the recently proposed version (v.1.3) of the GEMGA and presents extensive results for large scale, widely reported to be difficult problems. The results clearly demonstrate linear performance of the GEMGA.

Section 2 presents a brief description of the GEMGA. Section 3 presents experimental results studying the performance of the GEMGA for a wide range of problems. Finally, Section 4 presents the conclusions and the future work.

2 A Brief Review Of The GEMGA

The GEMGA has two main strategies: (1) detect schemata that capture symmetries in the fitness landscape and (2) use these schemata to guide the future search directions. The following sections presents a short overview of the GEMGA (v.1.3) [3].

2.1 Population sizing

In order to detect a schema, the GEMGA requires that the population contains at least one instance of that schema. If we consider the population size to be a constant and randomly initialized, then this can be guaranteed only when the order (number of fixed positions) of the schema to be detected is bounded by some constant k. For a sequence representation with alphabet set Λ, a randomly generated population of size $|\Lambda|^k$ is expected to contain one instance of every order-k schema. $|\Lambda|$ denotes the size of the set Λ. The population size in GEMGA is therefore, $m = c|\Lambda|^k$, where c is a constant. Although we treat c as a constant, c is likely to depend on the variation of fitness values of the members of the schema. Note that the population size is independent of the problem size ℓ. For all the experiments reported in this paper, the population size is kept constant.

2.2 Representation

The GEMGA *chromosome* contains a sequence of *genes*. A gene is a data structure that contains the *locus*, *value*, and *capacity*. The *locus* and the *value* of a *gene* determine its position and the value respectively. The *capacity* field is used for facilitating the schema detection process in the GEMGA. The chromosome also contains a dynamic list of lists called the *linkage set*. It is a list of weighted lists. Each member of this collection of lists, called *locuslist*, defines a set of genes that are related. Each *locuslist* also contains three factors, the *weight*, *goodness* and *trials*. The weight is a measure of the number of times that the genes in *locuslist* are found to be related in the population. The *goodness* value indicates how good the linkage of the genes is in terms of its contribution to the fitness. The *trial* field indicates the number of times the linkage set has been tried.

2.3 Operators

The GEMGA has two primary operators, namely: (1) *Transcription* and (2) *RecombinationExpression*. Each of them is briefly described in the following.

Transcription The GEMGA *Transcription* operator plays an important role in detection of good schemata. It detects *local* symmetry in the fitness landscape by noting the relative invariance of the fitness values of chromosomes under transformations that changes the value of a gene, one gene at a time. It changes the current value of a gene to a different value, randomly chosen from the alphabet set and notes the change in fitness value. If the fitness deteriorates because of the change in gene value, that gene is identified as the symmetry breaking dimension and the corresponding gene capacity is set to zero, indicating that the value at that gene value cannot be changed. On the other hand, if the fitness improves or does not change at all, the corresponding capacity of the gene is set to one, indicating that this dimension offers symmetry, with respect to the pattern of improvement in fitness. Finally, the value of that gene is set to the original value and the fitness of the chromosome is set to the original fitness. This process continues for all the genes and finally all the genes whose capacities are reduced to zeroes are collected in one set, called the initial linkage set. This is stored as the first element of the linkage set associated with the chromosome. Its weight, goodness, and trial factors are initialized to 1, 0, and 0 respectively. The transcription operator does not change anything in a chromosome except the capacities and it initiates the formation of the linkage sets. Any symmetry that remains true over the whole search space also remains true within a local domain. Locally detected schemata are next observed in a population-wide global sense, as described in the following section.

RecombinationExpression The RecombinationExpression stage detects schemata that capture symmetry beyond a small local neighborhood defined by the bitwise perturbation of transcription. It consists of two phases - the PreRecombinationExpression phase and the GEMGA Recombination phase.

The PreRecombinationExpression phase determines the clusters of genes precisely defining the relations among those instances of genes. This is applied several times, specified by NoOfLinkageExpt, during the first generation for the chromosomes. First, a pair of chromosomes is selected and one of them is marked. Among the genes present in the initial linkage set of the marked chromosome (and included as the first element of its linkage set), only those that have the same value and capacities in the other are extracted and grouped as a separate set. If this set is already present in the linkage set of the marked chromosome, then the corresponding weight is incremented by a given parameter INCR_WEIGHT. Otherwise, it is included as a new linkage set.

At the end of the requisite number of experiments (NoOfLinkageExpt), an $\ell \times \ell$ conditional probability matrix is formed, whose entry i, j indicates the probability of the occurrence of gene i, when gene j is present in a linkage set.

Finally, the final linkage sets are computed using the GetFinalLinkage operator. For each row i of the Conditional matrix, its maximum value is computed, and the genes that have their probability values within an EPSILON of the maximum are included in the linkage set for i. Its weight is set to the average value of the conditional probabilities of every gene in the set.

After the PreRecombinationExpression phase, the GEMGA Recombination operator is applied iteratively on pairs of chromosomes. First, copies of a given pair is made, and one of them is marked. An element of the linkage set of the marked chromosome is selected, based on a linearly combined factor (for all the reported results it was simply the sum) of its weight and goodness, for swapping. The corresponding genes are swapped between the two chromosomes provided the goodness values of the disrupted linkage sets of the unmarked chromosome are less than that of the selected one. The linkage sets of the two chromosomes are adjusted accordingly. Depending on whether the fitness of the unmarked chromosome decreases or not, the goodness of the selected linkage set element is decreased or increased. Finally, only two of the four chromosomes (including the two original copies) are retained [3].

2.4   The algorithm

The overall structure of the GEMGA is summarized below:

1. Randomly initialize the duly sized population.
2. Execute *primordial expression* stage: Detect schemata that captures local fitness symmetry by the so called *transcription* operator. Since population size $m = c|A|^k$, this can be done in time $O(|A|^k \ell)$.
3. *PreRecombinationExpression:* Identify schemata that capture fitness symmetry over a larger domain. This only requires comparing the chromosomes with each other and no additional function evaluation is needed.
4. Execute *recombination expression* stage:
   (a) GEMGA recombination: The GEMGA uses a recombination operator, designed using motivation from cell meosis process that combines the effect of selection and crossover. Reconstruct, modify schema linkage sets and their parameters.
   (b) Mutation: Low probability mutation like simple GA. All the experiments reported in this paper used a zero mutation probability.

The primordial expression stage requires $O(|A|^k \ell)$ objective function evaluations. PreRecombinationExpression requires $O(|A|^{2k})$ pair-wise similarity computation time (no objective function evaluation). The length of the Recombination stage can be roughly estimated as follows. If t be the total number of generations in juxtapositional stage and if selection gives α copies to the best chromosome then if selection dominates the crossover, every chromosome of the population will converge to same instance when $\alpha^t = m$, i.e. $t = \log m / \log \alpha$. Substituting $m = c|A|^k$, we get, $t = \frac{\log c + k \log |A|}{\log \alpha}$. Therefore, the number of generations in recombination expression stage is $O(k)$. This result is true when

Multi-modal	GW1		
f(x) = u+2 × f'(x)	f(x) = 4	if	x = 1 # 1 # 0
where,	= 8	if	x = 1 # 0 # 0
f'(x) = 1 if odd(u)	= 10	if	x = 0 # 1 # 0
= 0 otherwise	= 0	otherwise	

Table 1. (left) Massively multimodal function and (right) GW1; u denotes the number of 1-s in the string. The symbol # denotes the don't care position.

selection is allowed to give an exponentially increasing number of copies. The overall number of function evaluations is bounded by $O(|\Lambda|^k \ell)$. This analysis assumes that the cardinality of the alphabet set of the chosen representation is bounded by a small constant (e.g. in case of binary representation it is two). The following section presents extensive test results demonstrating the linear time performance of the GEMGA.

3 Test Results

The following sections document the performance of the GEMGA for a wide range of difficult problems that can be decomposed into smaller sub-problems.

3.1 Experiment design

The performance of GEMGA is tested for five different problems, namely *i) Deceptive trap (Trap), ii) Mühlenbein (MUH), iii) Goldberg-Wang function 1 (GW1), iv) Goldberg Wang function 2 (GW2)* and *v) Massively-Multimodal function (MULTI)*. Each of the functions is constructed by concatenating order-5 subfunctions (both overlapping and non-overlapping versions are considered). These subfunctions are described below.

i) Trap: The deceptive trap [1] function is defined as, $f(x) = k$ if $u = k$; $f(x) = k - 1 - u$ otherwise; where u is the unitation variable, or the number of 1-s in the string x, and k is the length of the subfunction. If we carefully observe this trap function, we shall note that it has two peaks. One of them corresponds to the string with all 1-s and the other is the string with all 0-s. For $\ell = 200$, and $k = 5$, the overall function contains 40 subfunctions; therefore, an order-5 bounded 200-bit problem has 2^{40} local optima, and among them, only one is globally optimal. As the problem length increases the number of local optima exponentially increases.

ii) MULTI: This is a massively multimodal function of unitation where the global optima is a string of all 1's (assuming that length of the subfunction is odd). It is defined in Table 1. This function resembles a one-max function with "bumps".

iii) GW1: This function is defined in Table 1.

Mühlenbein	GW2
f(x) = 4 if x = 00000	f(x) = 10 if u=0
= 3 if x = 00001	= 8 if u=k
= 2 if x = 00011	= 7 if u=1 and odd(0)
= 1 if x = 00111	= 2 if u=1 and even(1)
= 0 if x = 01111	= 4 if u=k-1 and odd(1)
= 3.5 if x = 11111	= 3 if u=k-1 and even(1)
= 0 otherwise.	= 0 otherwise.

Table 2. Functions odd(0) and even(0) return true if the number of 0-s in x are odd and even respectively. odd(1) and even(1) are analogously defined.

iv) GW2: This function is defined in Table 2.

v) MUH: This function is defined in Table 2. The global optima is the string of all 0-s while all the strings having a number of trailing 1-s constitute the local optima. Unlike the case for *Trap*, here the building block corresponding to the global optima, has a significant amount of overlap with the local optimas.

The following section presents the test results.

3.2   Results : Uniform scaling and non-overlapping subfunctions

Figures 1—3(left) show the average number of sample evaluations from five independent runs needed to find the globally optimal solution for problem sizes ranging from 100 to 1000. For these test problems the subfunctions are uniformly scaled and non-overlapping. The population size is 200, chosen as described earlier in this paper. It is kept constant for all the problem sizes. For the *Trap*, *Mühlenbein* and *GW1* problems, the NoOfLinkageExpt, WEIGHT_THRESHOLD and EPSILON values are kept as 150, 0.7 and 0.1, while for the remaining two these are 195, 0.4 and 0.1 respectively as explained elsewhere [3]. In each case we see that the number of function evaluations required for attaining the optimal value, linearly depends on the problem size.

3.3   Results : Non-uniform scaling and non-overlapping subfunctions

Scaling offers difficulty to any BBO algorithm that uses a selection like operator for selecting better solutions from the search space. The problem is that any such sample is an instance of many different classes defined over the search space, and the contribution of different classes in the overall objective function value may be different. Some classes may contribute higher than other classes. For large problems with large degree of scaling effect, this can lead to a suboptimal convergence for the less scaled optimization variables.

The effect of scaling on the performance of GEMGA is investigated for *Trap*, *MUH* and *GW1* functions, for problem sizes of 100, 200 and 500. As earlier, each function is a concatenation of order 5 sub functions. A linearly increasing

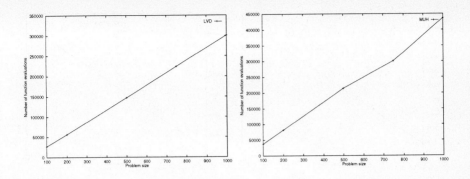

Fig. 1. Number of function evaluations vs. problem size for attaining the optimum solution in case of *uniformly scaled, non-overlapping* (left) *Trap* and (right) *MUH*.

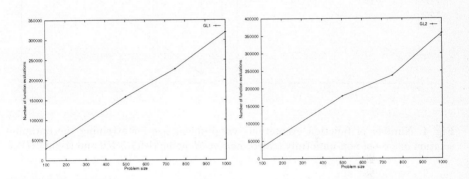

Fig. 2. Number of function evaluations vs. problem size for attaining the optimum solution in case of *uniformly scaled, non-overlapping* (left) *GW1* and (right) *GW2*.

scaling factor for each set of 5 subfunctions is taken. For example - a 500 bit problem has 100 subfunctions. The first 5 sub functions (bits 0 - 24) are scaled by 1, next 5 subfunctions (bits 25 - 49) are scaled by 2, and so on. As before, for all the problems population size, NoOfLinkageExpt, WEIGHT_THRESHOLD and EPSILON values are kept as 200, 150, 0.7 and 0.1 respectively. Figures 3(right)—4 show the results obtained for five independent runs of the algorithm for the non-uniformly scaled Trap, MUH, and the GW1 functions. The GEMGA is found to solve all the problems successfully in linear time.

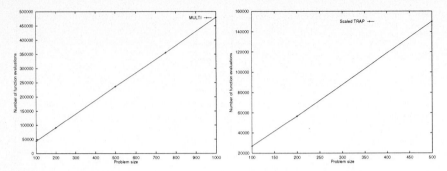

Fig. 3. Number of function evaluations vs. problem size for attaining the optimum solution in case of *non-overlapping* (left) *uniformly scaled, Massively Multimodal* and (right) non-uniformly scaled *Trap*.

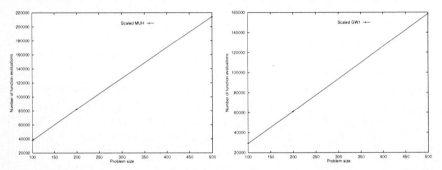

Fig. 4. Number of function evaluations vs. problem size for attaining the optimum solution in case of non-uniformly scaled, *non-overlapping* (left) *MUH* and (right) *GW1*.

3.4   Results : Uniform scaling and overlapping subfunctions

This section presents preliminary test results for two overlapping test functions Fc2 and Fc3 developed elsewhere [16]. These functions are constructed as follows:

$$Fc2(x) = \sum_{j=0}^{L-1} MUH(s_j)$$

where the s_j-s are overlapping 6-bit substrings of x. The first bit does not contribute to the fitness value. Function Fc3 is defined as follows:

$$Fc3(x) = \sum_{j=0}^{L-1} MULTI(s_j)$$

Table 3 presents the experimental results for Fc2 and Fc3. Population size is kept at 200. The results are averaged over five runs.

Function	Problem size	Number of function evaluations
Fc2	100	38417.2
	200	81350.8
Fc3	100	42900.4
	200	89872

Table 3. Average number of function evaluations to reach the optimal value for uniformly scaled problems with overlapping sub-functions.

4   Conclusions And Future Work

This paper revisits the GEMGA (v.1.3) and presents new, extensive experimental results. These results clearly demonstrate the linear time scalable performance of the GEMGA. Although the performance of the GEMGA appears to be quite scalable, it can be further enhanced as described below.

So far the GEMGA has been mainly tested against objective functions of binary variables. More work is needed for testing the performance of the GEMGA in case of problems with real valued optimization variables. Approximate representation construction is another important aspect of current GEMGA research. Currently the GEMGA work on a faithful, exact representation of this structure. However, large reduction in computational complexity may be possible by allowing a representation that may produce a bounded distortion of the actual linkage structure introduced by the optimization problem. At present, we are investigating this possibility using the theory of randomized near-isometric graph projection techniques. As reported elsewhere [12], our early experiments on embedding an n-dimensional hamming space to an $O(\log^2 n)$ dimensional Euclidean space with a distortion bounded by $O(\log n)$ looks promising.

As noted earlier, global detection of linkage structure in GEMGA requires comparing chromosomes from the population during the PreRecombinationExpression phase. This requires comparing the similarity among different chromosomes of the population. The current approach to do that requires $O(m^2)$ pair-wise similarity computation, where m is the population size. Non-expansive hash functions [14, 9] can be used for doing this in $O(1)$ time. In the recent past several mapping functions have been developed that map adjacent points in a domain (based on some distance metric) to adjacent points in the range. These functions can be used to map all the chromosomes in a population. Since the function preserves similarity, detection of linkage by checking similarities among different chromosomes will just require checking the neighborhood of every chromosome in the population table in stead of comparing it to every other chromosome in the population. This is likely to reduce the running time of the GEMGA. Application of the GEMGA to real-life applications is another dimension of our current effort. A successful data mining application of the GEMGA for feature selection from electrical power distribution network fault analysis data can be found elsewhere [13].

References

1. D. H. Ackley. *A connectionist machine for genetic hill climbing*. Kluwer Academic, Boston, 1987.
2. S. Baluja and S. Davies. Using optimal dependency-trees for combinatorial optimization: Learning the structure of the search space. Technical Report CMU-CS-97-107, Departement of Computer Science, Carnegie Mellon University, Pittsburgh, 1997.
3. S. Bandyopadhyay, H. Kargupta, and G. Wang. Revisiting the GEMGA: Scalable evolutionary optimization through linkage learning. In *Proceedings of the IEEE International Conference on Evolutionary Computation*, pages 603–608. IEEE Press, 1998.
4. K. Deb. Binary and floating-point function optimization using messy genetic algorithms. IlliGAL Report no. 91004 and doctoral dissertation, unversity of alabama, tuscaloosa, University of Illinois at Urbana-Champaign, Illinois Genetic Algorithms Laboratory, Urbana, 1991.
5. D. E. Goldberg, K. Deb, H. Kargupta, and G. Harik. Rapid, accurate optimizaiton of difficult problems using fast messy genetic algorithms. *Proceedings of the Fifth International Conference on Genetic Algorithms*, pages 56–64, 1993.
6. D. E. Goldberg, B. Korb, and K. Deb. Messy genetic algorithms: Motivation, analysis, and first results. *Complex Systems*, 3(5):493–530, 1989. (Also TCGA Report 89003).
7. G. Harik. *Learning Linkage to Efficiently Solve Problems of Bounded Difficulty Using Genetic Algorithms*. PhD thesis, Department of Computer Science, University of Michigan, Ann Arbor, 1997.
8. J. H. Holland. *Adaptation in Natural and Artificial Systems*. University of Michigan Press, Ann Arbor, 1975.
9. P. Indyk, R. Motwani, P. Raghavan, and S. Vempala. Locality-presering hashing in multidimensional spaces. In *http://www.cs.stanford.edu/ indyk*, 1997.
10. H. Kargupta. Computational processes of evolution: The SEARCH perspective. Presented in SIAM Annual Meeting, 1996 as the winner of the 1996 SIAM Annual Best Student Paper Prize, July 1996.
11. H. Kargupta. The gene expression messy genetic algorithm. In *Proceedings of the IEEE International Conference on Evolutionary Computation*, pages 814–819. IEEE Press, 1996.
12. H. Kargupta. Gene Expression: The Missing Link Of Evolutionary Computation. In C. Poloni D. Quagliarella, J. Periaux and G. Winter, editors, *Genetic Algorithms in Engineering and Computer Science.*, page Chapter 4. John Wiley & Sons Ltd., 1997.
13. H. Kargupta, E. Riva Sanseverino, E. Johnson, and S. Agrawal. The genetic algorithms, linkage learning, and scalable data mining. 1998.
14. N. Linial and O. Sasson. Non-expansive hashing. In *Journal Of ACM*, pages 509–518, 1996.
15. H. Muhlenbein and G. Paab. From recombination of genes to the estimation of distributions i. binary parameters. In *Parallel Problem Solving from Nature - PPSN IV*, pages 178–187, Berlin, 1996. Springer.
16. H. Mühlenbein and A. O. Rodriguez. Schemata, distributions and graphical models in evolutionary optimization. Personal Communication., December 1997.

Indexed Memory as a Generic Protocol for Handling Vectors of Data in Genetic Programming*

Ik Soo Lim and **Daniel Thalmann**

LIG, Department of Computer Science, Swiss Federal Institute of Technology
(EPFL), CH-1015 Lausanne, SWITZERLAND

iksoolim@iname.com, thalmann@lig.di.epfl.ch

Abstract. Indexed memory is used as a generic protocol for handling vectors of data in genetic programming. Using this simple method, a single program can generate many outputs. It eliminates the complexity of maintaining different trees for each desired parameter and avoids problem-specific function calls for handling the vectors. This allows a single set of programming language primitives applicable to wider range of problems. For a test case, the technique is applied to evolution of behavioural control programs for a simulated 2d vehicle in a corridor following problem.

1 Introduction

Ordinary computer programs use numerous well-known techniques for handling vectors of data, arrays, trees, graphs and more complex data structures. One important area for work on technique extensions for genetic programming involves developing workable and efficient ways to handle these data structures. These techniques would have immediate application to a number of problems in such fields as computer vision, biological sequence analysis, economic time series analysis, and pattern recognition where a solution to the problem involves analysing the character of an entire data structure[Koza 1997]. Recent work in this area includes that of Langdon in handling more complex data structures[Langdon 1996], Teller in recognising objects in images represented by large arrays of pixels[Teller 1996], and Handley in applying statistical zones to biological sequence data[Handley 1996].

One of genetic programming paradigm's merits is its domain-independence: it does not necessarily rely on knowledge specific on the problem to be solved. That is how it can be a general problem solver and is used for the problems of various disciplines. Then, in handling vectors of data, doing it *problem-independently* would also be important so that a single set of language primitives including

---

* This work was supported in part by Swiss National Foundation.

this genuine vector-handling primitive could be applicable for wider range of problems.

The motivation behind our work on this generic handling of vectors comes, in particular, from our interest in evolving motion controllers for animating autonomous creatures[Thalmann et al. 1997]. The motion controllers have to handle vectors of sensor readings and generate vectors of actuators' value. Depending on the creatures and the motion to be animated, different types of data (e.g. vision, touch and sound) have to be dealt with and different number of degrees of freedom in actuators need to be handled. Instead of using problem-specific function calls such as `look-for-obstacle`[Reynolds 1994], `Get-Leg-Force-2` and `Set-Leg-Force-3` [Spencer 1994] or a list of programs (one for each degree of freedoms)[Gritz and Hahn 1997], we adopt *indexed memory* technique[Teller 1994] as a generic protocol in handling vectors of data. Then, it could allow a single set of primitives such as arithmetic and logical ones with this genuine technique to continue to be used for motion control problems in various settings without any introduction of problem-specific program language primitives.

The remainder of this paper is organised as follows: after a brief introduction of both genetic programming and indexed memory, we describe the use of indexed memory for genuine handling of vector data in genetic programming. We then show how the technique is applied to evolving motion controllers of corridor-following behaviour as a preliminary test case. We conclude with a discussion and future work.

2 Genetic Programming

Genetic programming is a technique for the automatic generation of computer programs by means of natural selection[Koza 1992]. The genetic programming process starts by creating a large initial populations of elements from problem-specific functions and terminal sets. Each program in the initial population is then assessed for fitness, and the fitness values are used in producing the next generation of programs via a variety of genetic operations including reproduction, crossover and mutation. After a preestablished number of generations, or after the fitness improves to some preestablished level, the best-of-run individual is designated as the result and is produced as the output from the genetic programming system.

3 Indexed Memory

Indexed memory is a mechanism that allows programs developed by genetic programming to make use of runtime memory[Teller 1994]. The mechanism consists of a linear array of memory locations and two functions, `READ` and `WRITE`, that are added to the set of functions from which programs are created. The memory is initialised (e.g., to 0) at the start of each program execution. `READ` takes a single argument and returns the contents of the memory location indexed by that argument. WRITE takes two arguments, a memory index and a data item, and stores the data item in the memory at the specified index. WRITE returns the previous value of the specified memory location. It is shown that the indexed memory can help to evolve correct programs for certain problems, and that the combination of indexed memory and iteration allows genetic programming to produce any Turing-computable function. Others have further examined the utility of indexed memory. Andre has experimented with problems that require the use of memory, and has explored the ways in which evolved programs use indexed memory in solving these problems[Andre 1995]. Spector and Luke showed how the indexed memory can be simply modified to allow for communication between individuals within and across generations[Spector and Luke 1996].

4 A Generic Way of Handling Vectors of Data

An expression tree conventionally used in genetic programming returns only one output: the value of its node. If we need outputs more than one, one way to obtain the vector of the outputs is to simply assign one complete tree to each output: represent each program by a list of expression trees, with each tree computing one value in parallel with the other trees[Gritz and Hahn 1997]. It has two drawbacks: it is complex because it requires us to maintain many trees per program, and it prevents the trees from sharing information.

The solution we choose instead is to use indexed memory. Each population individual has not only a functional tree, but an array of elements indexed from 0 to M-1. Each of these M elements is an integer in the same range. When a program completes its evaluation, its response is considered to be the current values residing in some particular memory locations (e.g. orientation = memory[0], speed = memory[1], etc.): the value of the node is no more used.

This new use of indexed memory offers several advantages:

- A single program can generate many outputs. This eliminates the complexity of maintaining different trees for each desired parameter as in [Gritz and Hahn 1997]
- Intermediate results can be shared. For example, WRITE(1, READ(WRITE(0, ...))) assigns to speed, i.e., memory[1] the previous value of orientation, i.e., memory[0].
- It is a genuine method of handling many outputs without introducing any problem specific function calls such as Get-Leg-Force-2 and Set-Leg-Force-3 [Spencer 1994].

5 Obstacle Avoidance Problem

The goal in the obstacle avoidance problem is to find a program for controlling the movement of a 2d autonomous vehicle in a corridor-like obstacle course. The obstacle course used during the evolution consists of a right angle turn as shown Figure 2. The design of the simulated vehicle used in these experiments is similar to that of [Reynolds 1994]. In order to survive, the controllers need to determine path along a clear pathway while avoiding collision with the walls surrounding it. The vehicle has M sensors, spaced uniformly over 0.45 of a revolution across the vehicle's front: see Figure 1(b). At each simulation step, a ray-tracing operation is performed for each sensor: the distance of the closest visible obstacle is calculated from the vehicle's centre in the direction of the sensor. Then, the distance is clipped to stay between 0 and M-1 so that it is a legal memory index. When it is called, SIGNAL(X) returns the distance as seen by the Xth sensor. The control programs being evolved by genetic programming represent the vehicle's "thought process" for a single simulation step.

Sensors for vision have been widely used for the problems of obstacle avoidance and low-level navigation. Hand-crafted computer vision algorithms are used based on motion energy[Blumberg 1997], optical flow[Duchon 1996, Rabie and Terzopoulos 1996], heuristic[Renault et al. 1990]. Genetic programming automatically generates the control programs of the behaviours[Reynolds 1994 and Sims 1994]. See [Reynolds 1994] for more reference.

During fitness testing, the evolved program is run at each time step of the simulation. Using its sensors, the program inspects the environment surrounding the vehicle from its own point of view, performs some arithmetic and logical processing, and decides both the speed of the vehicle and the heading of the vehicle. The vehicle moves based on the decision. The fitness test continues until the vehicle takes the required number of steps or until it collides with one of the obstacles. The minimum speed allowed is half of its body size per simulation step while the maximum, five times of it. The maximum per-simulation-step turn is limited so that a minimum turning circle is larger than the width of the corridors of the obstacle course. As a result, the vehicle cannot spin in place, it cannot turn around in the corridor, and its only choice is to travel along the corridor.

For each fitness evaluation, two cases were tested. In case one, the vehicle starts near one end of the course while the other end for case two. This alternation and perturbations in the vehicle's initial conditions (position and orientation) were introduced to keep evolved controllers from converging prematurely towards, say, left-turners and from depending on utterly insignificant coincidental properties of the vehicle's sensors, its actuators and their interaction with the obstacle course. The raw fitness score for each fitness trial is the distance between the vehicle's final position and the corridor's end other than the one where it started.

6 The Language of GP

The terminal set consists of ephemeral random constants between 0 and M-1. All functions were constrained to return integers between 0 and M-1 so that any computed value was a legal memory index. For this experiment M was chosen to be 64, which was largely for simplicity. When a program completes its evaluation, its response is considered to be the current values residing in first two memory locations such as orientation = memory[0] and speed = memory[1].

Here is a brief summary of the language actions of non-terminals and their effects:

Algebraic Primitives: {`ADD`, `SUB`, `MULT`, `DIV`, `MAX`, `MIN`} These functions allow basic manipulation of the integers. All values are constrained to be in the range 0 to `M-1`. For example, `DIV(X,0)` results in `M-1`.

Memory Primitives: {`READ`, `WRITE`} .

Branching Primitives: {`IFLTZ`} `IFLTZ(A,B,X,Y)` replaces `X` if `A < B` or `Y` otherwise. This primitive can be used as a branch-decision function.

Signal Primitives: {`SIGNAL`, `LEAST`, `MOST`, `AVERAGE`, `VARIANCE`, `DIFF`, `DIFFERENCE`} These are the functions that can access the signals. The functions except for `SIGNAL` each takes two values. These two numbers are interpreted as (`X`,`Y`) specifying a set of sensor readings from the `X`th to `Y`th sensor. `LEAST`, `MOST`, `AVERAGE`, `VARIANCE` and `DIFFERENCE` return the respective functions applied to that set of the sensor readings. `DIFFERENCE` is the difference between the average values along the first and second half of the region.

In addition to the main genetically programmed functional tree, an automatically defined function (ADF) tree[Koza 1994] is given with two arguments. In that subexpression the terminals and non-terminals already stated are legal:

ADF: `ADF` has 2 extra terminals: `arg0` and `arg1`. These extra terminals are local variables. This `ADF` can be called as many times as desired from its main function. Like other functions, `ADF` returns an integer in the range of 0 to `M-1`.

Tournament selection was used (tournament size = 2), along with a 90% crossover rate, a 10% reproduction rate, no mutation, a population size of 500, and a maximum of 1000 generations per run.

7 Results and Discussions

Figure 2 shows the obstacle course used in the fitness testing and an assortment of typical trials. These examples were collected from several different evolved control programs. For clarity, the vehicle is redrawn every three other simulation step. Notice that the vehicle moves around rather at a constant speed though allowed to vary its speed: a reasonable solution of focusing on "steering" task to avoid any collision while keeping the speed at its minimum since there was little pressure on time cost during the evolution. To illustrate robustness of the evolved program, we introduced another obstacle course which was not encountered during the evolution. This new obstacle course consists of two opposing right angle turns followed by a U-turn and then two more right angle turns, which is more challenging than the single right angle turn: especially, its right upper part (see Figure 3). The control program still enables the vehicle to follow the new obstacle course successfully for different locations and orientations of the vehicle's initial conditions as shown in Figure 3. Though the vehicle's path is shown only for its first turn-around for clarity, the vehicle does successfully go around on and on. Figure 4 shows the change in the vehicle's internal states of retinas and indexed memory over time while it follows the corridor as in the lower left of Figure 3. Horizontal axis for indices, vertical axis for time and it begins at the upper left corner, respectively. Figure 4(a) shows the distance field in the sensors over time (black means 0 while white, 63) and Figure 4(b) shows the number of access to each sensor for its distance value (black to 0, white to 60). Notice that the sensors are not equally used: some of them are not even used at all! Figure 4(c) illustrates the state of the indexed memory (black to 63, white to 0). Among 64 memory elements, five elements change over time.

Notice how genuine the language primitives are and the bare minimum of input from the user. We could go with the same set of the primitives for other motion controllers with different types of data and different number of degree of freedom. In fact, they were also chosen as a minimal set of language primitives of PADO for image classification problems[Teller and Veloso 1996]. Though classification problems by nature require responses of *YES* or *NO*, the current value of a particular memory location was considered as its response (e.g. `response = memory[0]`). PADO being constructed as an arbitrary directed graph of nodes rather than a tree as in standard genetic programming, this was how it was ensured to give a response after a fixed time and why indexed memory was a must in PADO. If PADO is to be applied to other problems which require many, say, n outputs, nothing has to be done further: simply, `response = (memory[0], memory[1], ..., memory[n-1])` as suggested.

Input data, `SIGNAL(X)` can also be considered as another indexed memory. As a matter of fact, at each simulation step, the sensor readings are stored into read-only indexed memory and `SIGNAL(X)` only returns the value of the corresponding memory location. Input vector via *read-only* indexed memory. Output vector, *both-readable-and-writable* indexed memory.

8   Conclusions and Future Work

This paper showed how Teller's indexed memory mechanism can be used as a simple but genuine way of handling vectors of data in genetic programming. Using the technique, we evolved the robust motion controller for the corridor following problem as a test case. We are exploring scaling-up of the technique so that it is also applicable to an autonomous virtual human who has two dimensional synthetic retinas for vision sensing and dozens of degree of freedom for actuators [Thalmann et al. 1997]. Handling and integrating data of different type such as sound and touch would also be interesting.

Further experiments on the corridor following problem include one to give higher pressure on time so that the 2d vehicle has to not only follow the corridor without collision but also do it as fast as possible. Then controllers might evolve to adjust its speed adaptively such as moving fast in a straight-way and slowing down in a turn. This adaptive adjustment could be interpreted in a different but interesting way. It we consider the simulation step as one for refreshing the sensor readings rather than for time, we have an adaptive adjustment of the refreshing rate rather than the speed: a constant speed, then. Since the synthetic vision obtained by rendering the scene from its viewpoint is a main consumer of CPU resource in animating autonomous creatures[Blumberg 1997], we could save a lot of CPU time by the adaptive adjustment of the refreshing rate as suggested.

9 Appendix

Sample Program: the following is part of the program used for Figure 3. In this format, the program has 50 lines of code.

```
MAIN()    : ADD( VARIANCE( 60,32 ), VARIANCE( MAX( IFLTZ( 35,21,5,10
            ), IFLTZ( AVERAGE( DIV( 61, SUB( ADF( DIFFERENCE( SIGNAL(
            61 ),45 ), MAX( IFLTZ( 35,21,5,10 ), ...
ADF(arg0,arg1): DIV( VARIANCE( MAX( arg1, WRITE( IFLTZ( MIN( arg1,
            MIN( ADD( AVERAGE( arg1,arg0 ),arg0 ), LEAST( arg1,arg1 )
            ) ), ADD( arg0, LEAST( arg1,arg1 ) ), ...
```

References

1. [Andre 1995] D. Andre. The Evolution of Agents that Build Mental Models and Create Simple Plans Using Genetic Programming. In L. J. Eshelman (editor), *Proceedings of the Sixth International Conference on Genetic Algorithms*, pp. 248-255. San Francisco, CA: Morgan Kaufmann Publishers, Inc., 1995.
2. [Blumberg 1997] Bruce M. Blumberg. Go with the Flow: Synthetic Vision for Autonomous Animated Creatures. *1997 AAAI Conferences on Autonomous Agents*, Marina Del Ray, February, 1997.
3. [Duchon 1996] Andrew P. Duchon. Maze Navigation Using Optical Flow. In *From Animals To Animats, Proceedings of the Fourth International Conference on the Simulation of Adaptive* Behaviour, pp. 225 - 232, September 1996, MIT Press.
4. [Gritz and Hahn 1997] Larry Gritz and James K. Hahn. Genetic Programming Evolution of Controllers for 3-D Character Animation. in Koza, J.R., et al. (editors), *Genetic Programming 1997: Proceedings of the 2nd Annual Conference*, pp. 139-146. July 13-16, 1997, Stanford University. San Francisco: Morgan Kaufmann.
5. [Handley 1996] Simon G. Handley. A New Class of Function Sets for Solving Sequence Problems. In Koza, John R., Goldberg, David E., Fogel, David B., and Riolo, Rick L. (editors). *Genetic Programming 1996: Proceedings of the First Annual Conference*, July 28-31, 1996, Standford University. Cambridge, MA: MIT Press.
6. [Handley 1994] Simon G. Handley. The Automatic Generation of Plans for a Mobile Robot via Genetic Programming with Automatically Defined Functions. In Kenneth E. Kinnear, Jr. (editor) *Advances in Genetic Programming*, pp. 391 - 407. MA: MIT Press, 1994.
7. [Koza 1992] John R. Koza. *Genetic Programming: On the Programming of Computers by Means of Natural Selection*. Cambridge, MA: The MIT Press, 1992.
8. [Koza 1994] John R. Koza. *Genetic Programming II: Automatic Discovery of Reusable Programs*. Cambridge, MA: The MIT Press, 1994.

9. [Koza 1997] John R. Koza. Future Work and Practical Applications of Genetic Programming. In Baeck, T., Fogel, D. B., and Michalewicz, Z. (editors) *Handbook of Evolutionary Computation*, pp. H1.1:1-6. Bristol, UK: Institute of Physics Publishing and New York: Oxford University Press, 1997.

10. [Langdon 1996] W. B. Langdon. Using Data Structures within Genetic Programming. In Koza, John R., Goldberg, David E., Fogel, David B., and Riolo, Rick L. (editors). *Genetic Programming 1996: Proceedings of the First Annual Conference*, July 28-31, 1996, Standford University. Cambridge, MA: MIT Press.

11. [Rabie and Terzopoulos 1996] Tamer F. Rabie and Demetri Terzopoulos. Motion and Colour Analysis for Animat Perception. In *Proceedins of Thirteenth National Conf. on Artificial Intelligence (AAAI '96)*, pp. 1090 - 1097. Portland, Oregon, August 4 - 8, 1996.

12. [Reynolds 1994] Craig W. Reynolds. Evolution of Corridor Following Behaviour in a Noisy World. In *From Animals To Animats 3: Proceedings of the Third International Conference on the Simulation of Adaptive* Behaviour, pp. 402 - 410. MIT Press, 1994.

13. [Sims 1994] Karl Sims. Evolving 3D Morphology and Behaviour by Competition. *Artificial Life*, v1 n4, pp. 353-372, 1994.

14. [Spector and Luke 1996] Lee Spector and Sean Luke. Cultural Transmission of Information in Genetic Programming. In Koza, John R., Goldberg, David E., Fogel, David B., and Riolo, Rick L. (editors). *Genetic Programming 1996: Proceedings of the First Annual Conference*, pp. 209 - 214. July 28-31, 1996, Standford University. Cambridge, MA: MIT Press.

15. [Spencer 1994] Graham Spencer. Automatic Generation of Programs for Crawling and Walking. In Kenneth E. Kinnear, Jr. (editor) *Advances in Genetic Programming*, pp. 334 - 353. MA: MIT Press, 1994.

16. [Teller 1994] Astro Teller. The Evolution of Mental Models. In Kenneth E. Kinnear, Jr. (editor) *Advances in Genetic Programming*, pp. 199 - 219. MA: MIT Press, 1994.

17. [Teller and Veloso 1996] Astro Teller and Manuela Veloso. PADO: A New Learning Architecture for Object Recognition. In Ikeuchi, Katsushi and Veloso Manuela (editors). *Symbolic Visual Learning.* Oxford University Press, 1996.

18. [Thalmann et al. 1997] D. Thalmann, H. Noser and Z. Huang. Autonomous Virtual Actors based on Virtual Sensors. In R.Trappl, P.Petta (editors), *Creating Personalities, Lecture Notes in Computer Science*, pp. 25-42. Springer Verlag, 1997.

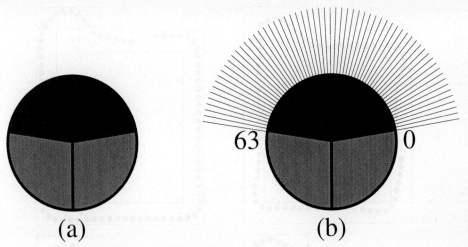

Figure 1. (a) the 2d vehicle; (b) the 60 rays for visual sensing.

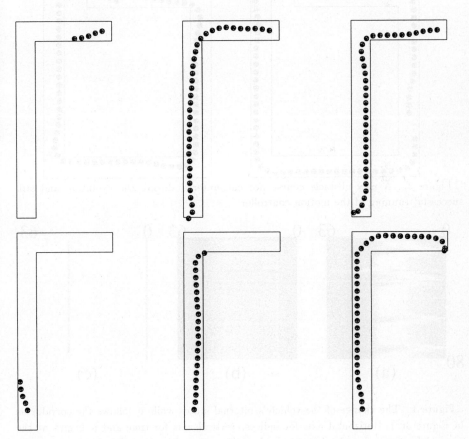

Figure 2. The obstacle course used in the fitness testing and an assortment of typical trials.

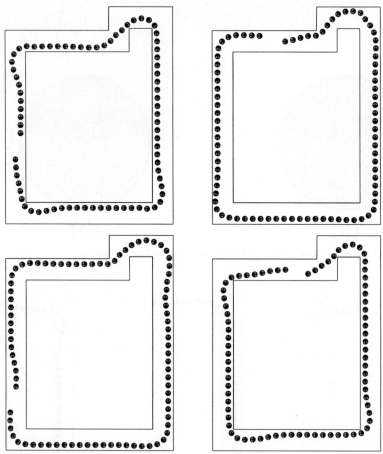

Figure 3. A new obstacle course not encountered during the evolution and still successful running of the motion controller.

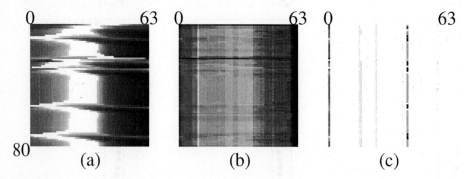

Figure 4. The change of the vehicle's internal states while it follows the corridor as in Figure 3(c). Horizontal axis for indices, vertical axis for time and it begins at the upper left corner. (a) the distance field in the sensors over time (black means 0 while white, 63); (b) the number of access to each sensor for its distance value (black to 0, white to 60); (c) the state of the indexed memory (black to 63, white to 0).

On Genetic Algorithms and Lindenmayer Systems

Gabriela Ochoa

COGS – School of Cognitive and Computing Sciences
The University of Sussex
Falmer, Brighton BN1 9QH, UK

Abstract. This paper describes a system for simulating the evolution of artificial 2D plant morphologies. Virtual plant genotypes are inspired by the
mathematical formalism known as Lindenmayer systems (L-systems). The
phenotypes are the branching structures resulting from the derivation and
graphic interpretation of the genotypes. Evolution is simulated using a genetic
algorithm with a fitness function inspired by current evolutionary hypotheses
concerning the factors that have had the greatest effect on plant evolution. The
system also provides interactive selection, allowing the user to direct simulated evolution towards preferred phenotypes. Simulation results demonstrate
many interesting structures, suggesting that artificial evolution constitutes a
powerful tool for (1) exploring the large, complex space of branching structures found in nature, and (2) generating novel ones. Finally, we emphasize
that Lindenmayer systems constitute a highly suitable encoding for artificial
evolution studies.

0. Introduction

Natural computation techniques can play a vital role in computer graphics, animation, and virtual reality. Several models have been developed that realistically
emulate a broad variety of living beings, from lower organisms all the way up the
evolutionary ladder to humans (Dawkins, 1986; Oppenheimer, 1986; Sims 1991,
1994; Reynolds 1987). In Particular, the work of Karl Sims (1991) illustrates the
potential of artificial evolution as a tool for the creation of procedurally generated
structures, textures and motions. Evolution turns out to be a method for exploring
and creating complexity that does not require human understanding of the very last
details of the process involved.

Little work has been done in computer-simulated evolution of plants. Among the
few is the work of the botanist Karl J. Niklas (1985, 1988, 1997). Niklas' model
aims to simulate the evolution of branching patterns in early land plants. Firstly, he
stated some specific hypotheses concerning plant evolution, then developed mathematical techniques for quantifying the hypothesized competitive advantages offered
by various features. To encode a plant branching pattern, three parameters or characteristics were used: (1) probability of branching, (2) branching angle and (3) rotation
angle. Using these characteristics, plant growth is simulated through several

branching cycles. For modeling evolution, a deterministic scheme for searching among the nearest neighbors in the tree-parameter space is employed. The fittest of the explored neighbors becomes the starting point for the next search cycle. This process is reiterated until the computer has identified a set of morphological characteristics that is more efficient than any immediate neighbor in the search space. Niklas' simulation model has some limitations. Clearly, the three parameters are an oversimplification of plant geometry. Many more factors may influence plant shape. Other limitations concern the way evolution is simulated. The search method proposed can easily get stuck in local minima. Furthermore, a single organism instead of a population is maintained, and sexual reproduction is not considered.

In this paper we describe a novel use of genetic algorithms and Lindenmayer systems with the aim of evolving artificial plant morphologies. The model described simulates the evolution of 2D plant morphologies. Virtual plant genotypes are inspired by the mathematical formalism known as Lindenmayer systems (L-systems). The phenotypes are the branching structures resulting from the derivation and graphic interpretation of the genotypes. The system allows for two types of artificial evolution. Interactive selection, based on human perception of the plant-like structures, allows the user to direct simulated evolution towards preferred forms. Alternatively, automated evolution is simulated using a genetic algorithm with a fitness function inspired by current evolutionary hypotheses concerning the factors that have had the greatest effect on plant evolution.

Previous work has been done in combining artificial evolution and L-systems. Jacob (1994) presents the "Genetic L-systems Programming" (GLP) paradigm, a general framework for evolutionary creation and development of parallel rewriting systems, which demonstrates that these systems can be designed by evolutionary processes. However, Jacob's example targets a somewhat simple problem: generate L-systems that form space constrained structures with a predefined number of branches. Here, we suggest a more complex fitness function with the aim of evolving structures that resemble natural plants.

Next section describes the formalism of L-systems and their graphic interpretation. Section 2 describes the proposed model: how L-systems are used as genetic encoding, the characteristics of the genetic algorithm employed, the genetic operators designed, and the fitness function's inspiration and design. Section 3 shows simulation results. Finally, section 4 discusses conclusions and suggests future work.

1. Lindenmayer Systems

L-systems are a mathematical formalism proposed by the biologist Aristid Lindenmayer in 1968 as a foundation for an axiomatic theory of biological development. More recently, L-systems have found several applications in computer graphics (Smith, 1987; Prusinkiewicz and Lindenmayer, 1990). Two principal areas include generation of fractals and realistic modeling of plants.

Central to L-systems, is the notion of rewriting, where the basic idea is to define complex objects by successively replacing parts of a simple object using a set of rewriting rules or productions. The rewriting can be carried out recursively. The most extensively studied and the best understood rewriting systems operate on character strings. Aristid Lindenmayer's work introduced a new type of string rewriting mechanism, subsequently termed L-systems. The essential difference between the most known Chomsky grammars and L-systems lies in the method of applying productions. In Chomsky grammars productions are applied sequentially, whereas in L-systems they are applied in parallel, replacing simultaneously all letters in a given word. This difference reflects the biological motivation of L-systems. Productions are intended to capture cell divisions in multicellular organisms, where many divisions may occur at the same time.

1.1. D0L-systems

In this section, we introduce the simplest class of L-systems, termed *D0L-systems* (Deterministic and context free). To provide an intuitive understanding of the main idea, let us consider the example given by Prusinkiewicz et al. (1990). See Fig. 1.

Lets us consider strings built of two letters *a* and *b* (they may occur many times in a string). For each letter we specify a rewriting rule. The rule *a → ab* means that the letter *a* is to be replaced by the string *ab*, and the rule *b → a* means that the letter *b* is to be replaced by *a*. The rewriting process starts from a distinguished string called the axiom. Let us assume that it consist of a single letter *b*. In the first derivation step (the first step of rewriting) the axiom *b* is replaced by *a* using production *b → a*. In the second step *a* is replaced by *ab* using the production *a → ab*. The word *ab* consist of two letters, both of which are simultaneously replaced in the next derivation step. Thus, *a* is replaced by *ab* , *b* is replaced by *a*, and the string *aba* results. In a similar way (by the simultaneous replacement of all letters), the string *aba* yields *abaab* which in turn yields *abaababa*, then *abaababaabaab*, and so on.

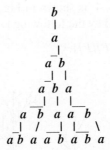

Fig. 1. Example of a derivation in a D0L-system.

1.2. Graphic interpretation of strings

Lindenmayer systems were conceived as a mathematical theory of development. Thus, geometric aspects were beyond the scope of the theory. Subsequently, several geometric interpretations of L-systems were proposed in order to turn them into a versatile tool for fractal and plant modeling. An interpretation based on turtle geometry, was proposed by Prusinkiewics et al. (1990). The basic idea of turtle interpretation is given below.

A state of the turtle is defined as a triplet *(x, y, α)*, where the Cartesian coordinates *(x, y)* represent the turtle's position, and the angle *α*, called the heading, is interpreted as the direction in which the turtle is facing. Given the step size *d* and the angle increment *δ*, the turtle can respond to the commands represented by the following symbols:

F Move forward a step of length d. The state of the turtle changes to (x', y', α), where x' = x + d cos α and y' = y + d sin α. . A line segment between points (x, y) and (x, y') is drawn.

f Move forwards a step of length d without drawing a line. The state of the turtle changes as above.

+ Turn left by angle δ. The next state of the turtle is (x, y,α +δ).

- Turn left by angle δ. The next state of the turtle is (x, y,α -δ).

To represent branching structures, the L-system alphabet is extended with two new symbols, '[' and ']', to delimit a branch. They are interpreted by the turtle as follows:

[Push the current state of the turtle onto a pushdown stack.

]   Pop a state from the stack and make it the current state of the turtle.

Given a string *v*, the initial state of the turtle $(x_o, y_o, α_o)$, and fixed parameters *d* and *δ*, the turtle interpretation of *v* is the figure (set of lines) drawn by the turtle in response to the string *v*. This description gives us a rigorous method for mapping strings to pictures, which may be applied to interpret strings generated by L-systems.

An example of a bracketed L-system and its turtle interpretation, obtained in derivations of length *n* = 1 - 4, is shown in Fig. 2. These figures were obtained by interpreting strings generated by the following L-system:

{w: F, p: F → F[-F]F[+F][F]}.

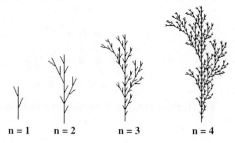

n = 1   n = 2   n = 3   n = 4

Fig. 2. Generating a plant-like structure.

2. The Model

Bracketed D0L-systems are used for encoding virtual organisms. A chromosome is constituted by a D0L-system with a single rewriting rule whose axiom (starting symbol) is always the symbol F. More precisely, the chromosome is the successor of the rule, there is no need to store the predecessor because it is always the symbol F. For example, the D0L-system showed in Fig. 2 is encoded as: $F[-F]F[+F][F]$. The phenotypes are the structures produced after deriving and interpreting the L-systems following the turtle graphic method.

2.1. Genetic Operations

When using a special genetic encoding for organisms, one must define special reproduction operations as well. These operations are often more elaborated than those in the canonical Genetic Algorithm. Our chromosomes have a well-defined syntactic structure stemming from the L-Systems formalism. To allow for a proper derivation and interpretation of genotypes, our genetic operations must produce offspring with valid syntactic structures. Three main operators were designed: crossover and two types of mutation.

- **Crossover**: The designed crossover is inspired by the Genetic Programming crossover operation (Koza, 1992). Koza's Lisp subtrees can be considered analogous to correctly bracketed substrings within an L-system. Fig. 3 shows an example of crossover. The hierarchical representation of the parents can be illustrated as:

F |+ | -FF |	F | +| -FF | | |
-FF FFF <u>-F-F</u>	+F -F-F <u>+F</u> -F F

where the underlined substrings are to be interchanged.

Parents   **Offspring**

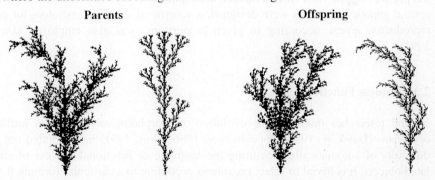

F[-FF]+[FFF]-FF[<u>-F-F</u>]   F[+F]+[-F-F]-FF[<u>+F</u>][-F][F]   F[-FF]+[FFF]-FF[+F]   F[+F]+[-F-F]-FF[-F-F][-F][F]

Fig. 3. Parents and offspring of a crossover. The underlined substrings are interchanged.

- **Mutation**: The mutation operation introduces random variations in structures of the population. Two types of mutation were designed. Each one acting on distinct parts of chromosomes (Fig. 4).

340

- **Symbol Mutation**: A randomly selected symbol of the chromosome in the set *{F, +, -}* is substituted by a random but syntactically correct string.
- **Block Mutation**: A randomly selected block in the chromosome is substituted by a random syntactically correct string.

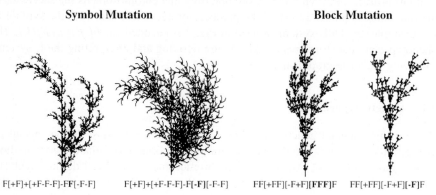

Symbol Mutation		Block Mutation	
F[+F]+[+F-F-F]-FF[-F-F]	F[+F]+[+F-F-F]-F[-F][-F-F]	FF[+FF][-F+F][FFF]F	FF[+FF][-F+F][-F]F

Fig. 4. Parent and offspring of the two types of mutation. The mutated segments are indicated in bold font.

2.2. The Genetic Algorithm

The implemented GA differs from the canonical GA (Goldberg, 1989) in several ways. Firstly, rather than binary fixed length string encoding, our genotypes are based on L-systems. They are of variable lengths and have a defined syntactic structure. Moreover, steady-state selection (Mitchell, 1996) is employed; only *1/5* of the population, the least fit individuals, are replaced in each generation. Given that several genetic operations were designed, a scheme of selecting operators for each reproductive event, according to given proportions, was also employed (Davis, 1991).

2.3. Fitness Function

Several researches modeling the evolution of morphological aspects in artificial organisms (Dawkins, 1986; Oppenheimer, 1986; Sims, 1991) have pointed out the difficulty of automatically measuring the aesthetic or functional success of simulated objects. It is trivial to select organisms according to a particular formula if you have access to all their genes. However, natural selection doesn't act directly upon genes, but rather upon their effects on organism bodies or phenotypes. The human eye is good at selecting phenotypic effects, but to construct computer programs that directly select phenotypic patterns is a difficult and sophisticated task. So, the usual practice is to rely on human perception as the selective pressure to evolve preferred forms.

Here, we pursue a higher degree of automation. So, the design of an adequate fitness function is necessary. In order to have a fitness function that indeed guides the simulated evolution towards structures resembling natural plants, we have to formulate hypotheses concerning the factors that have had the greatest effect on plant evolution. The hypotheses employed in our model are those formulated by Karl Niklas in his work (Niklas, 1985):

> [...] the majority of plants can be seen as structural solutions to constraints imposed by the biochemical process of photosynthesis. Plants with branching patterns that gather the most light can then be predicted to be the most successful. Consequently changes in the plant's shape or internal structure that increase its ability to gather light should confer competitive advantages.

> To be effective competitors for light and space, plants must perform certain other tasks. In particular they must be able to stay erect: to sustain the mechanical stresses involved in vertical growth. A second hypothesis, then, might be that evolution of plants was driven by the need to reconcile the ability to support vertical branching structures.

Thus, the designed fitness function is based on these hypotheses. To model the features there mentioned: light gathering ability, and structure stability, in an explicit analytic procedure, we constructed a function made of the following components: (a) phototropism (growth movement of plants in response to stimulus of light), (b) bilateral symmetry, (c) light gathering ability, (d) structural stability and (e) proportion of branching points. Simple algorithmic techniques have been developed for quantifying the competitive advantages offered by these features.

Selective pressures act upon phenotypes. So, before we can evaluate an organism, its encoding L-system must be derived and geometrically interpreted. Each component of the fitness function is quantified by a procedure that uses as input the geometric information produced while drawing the figure; and returns a real number between 0 and 1. A brief description of the procedures, is given below.

Let us consider a 2D Cartesian coordinate system, the origin of this system is the figure starting point. Each vertex in a figure will be represented as a pair (x, y). The five features mentioned are quantified as follows:

- **Positive phototropism (a)**: High fitness is given to structures whose maximum y coordinate is 'high'. While low fitness s given to structures whose maximum y coordinate is 'low'. This is intended to force the "growth" of structures toward light. Furthermore tall structures are supposed to be better at disseminating seeds.
- **Bilateral Symmetry (b)**: The 'weight' balance of the structure is estimated. The absolute values of vertices' x coordinates at left and at right of the vertical axis are added up. Higher fitness is given to structures whose left to right ratio is closer to one, in other words, to better balanced structures.
- **Light gathering ability (c)**: The ability to gather light is estimated by quantifying the surface area of the plant 'leaves' --- ending segments --- exposed to light. The leaves exposed to light are those that are not shadowed by other leaves when we assume that the light rays are vertical lines from top to bottom.

- **Structural stability (d)**: The branches starting from each branching point in the structure are counted. It is assumed that branching points possessing too many branches are unstable. Thus, plants possessing a high proportion of this type of nodes are rated low, while plants possessing a majority of 'stable' branching points are rated high.
- **Proportion of branching points (e)**: The total number of branching points with more than one branch leaving is calculated. This number is in direct proportion to the total number of branches in a structure. It is assumed that plants with a high number of branches are better at gathering light and disseminating seeds.

Weight parameters $(w_a, w_b, w_c, w_d, w_e)$ are then used for tuning the effect of each component on the final fitness function:

$$F(Phenotype) = \frac{aw_a + bw_b + cwc_c + dw_d + ew_e}{w_a + w_b + w_c + w_d + w_e}$$

This fitness function takes us one step further in automating the selection of phenotypic traits. However, the human participation has not been eliminated altogether. Our model maintains the user determination of the fitness function weights.

3. Simulation Results

Many experiments were carried out. A typical experiment consisted of running the GA starting from a random generated population. The values used for GA parameters are: population size = 50, number of generations = 100, generation gap = 20 %, and chromosome length range = 7-30.

Distinct plant-like morphologies were obtained depending on the selected fitness function weights. Figures 5 and 6 show some of the fittest structures for different fitness function weights.

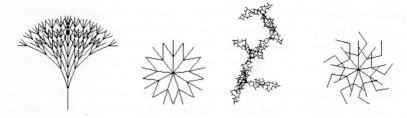

Fig. 5. Fitness function with weight values of 50 for all components

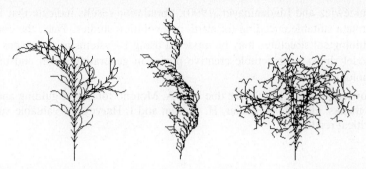

Fig. 6. Fitness function with component weights of: a = 100, b = 90, c = 40, d = 20, e = 30.

Finally, structures that resemble animals were also obtained with a fitness function favoring bilateral symmetric organisms (Fig. 7).

Fig. 7. Organisms obtained with fitness function favoring bilateral symmetric structures.

4. Discussion

A model has been described that can generate complex 2D branching structures without requiring cumbersome user specifications, design efforts, or knowledge of algorithmic details. We argue that L-Systems constitute an adequate genetic representation for studies which simulate natural morphological evolution. They allow the necessary, and very convenient, distinction between genotype and phenotype, and provide a well-defined process (*morphogenesis*) to generate the latter from the former. Moreover, they satisfy most of the important properties identified by Jefferson et al. (1991) for genetic encodings in biologically motivated studies. Among them: (a) L-systems provide a *simple, uniform model of computation*, because derivation and turtle interpretation of strings constitute a well defined way to go from genotypes to phenotypes; (b) they are *syntactically closed* under the designed genetic operations; and (c) they are *well conditioned* under genetic operators. This last requirement is not formally defined. Essentially, it requires that "small" mutational changes should (usually) cause "small" phenotypic changes, and that crossover usually produces offspring whose phenotypes are in some sense a "mixture" of the parents' phenotypes, with occasional jumps and discontinuities.

The model has employed the simplest type of L-systems (D0L-systems). Further studies may be done using complex ones, considering, for example, genotypes with several rules, context sensitive L-systems, and inclusion of 3D morphologies

(Prusinkiewicz and Lindenmayer, 1990). Simulation results indicate that L-systems constitute a suitable encoding for artificial evolution studies. Thus, the evolution of other biological structures may be modeled using L-systems as genotypes. Finally, the model shows considerable creative power in generating novel and unexpected morphologies.

Acknowledgments. Thanks are due to J. A. Moreno for useful guiding and support. Many thanks, also, to A. Meier, H. Buxton and I. Harvey for valuable suggestions and critical reading.

References

1. Davis, L.: *Handbook of Genetic Algorithms*. Van Nostrand Reinhold, (1991)
2. Dawkins, R.: *The Blind Watchmaker*. Harlow Longman, (1986)
3. Goldberg, D.: *Genetic Algorithms in Search, Optimization and Machine Learning*. Addison-Wesley, Reading (1989)
4. Jacob, C.: *Genetic L-system Programming*. Parallel Problem Solving from Nature III (PPSN'III), Lecture Notes in Computer Science, Vol. 866, Ed. Y. Davidor and P. Schwefel. Springer-Verlag, Berlin (1994) 334 - 343
5. Jefferson, D., Collins, R., Cooper, C., Dyer, M., Flowers, M., Korf, R., Taylor, C., Wang, A.: *Evolution as a Theme in Artificial Life: The Genesys / Tracker System*. In: Artificial Life II: Proceedings of the second workshop on the synthesis and simulation of living systems, Vol. X, SFI Studies in the Sciences of Complexity, Ed. C. Langton, C. Tylor, J. D. Farmer, and S. Rasmussen. Addison-Wesley, Redwood City (1991)
6. Koza, J.: *Genetic Programming: on the Programming of Computers by Means of Natural Selectio*. MIT Press, (1992)
7. Lindenmayer, A.: *Mathematical models for cellular interaction in development*. Parts I and II. Journal of Theoretical Biology, 18 (1968) 280-315.
8. Mitchell, M. 1996. *An Introduction to Genetic Algorithms*. MIT Press, (1996)
9. Niklas, K.: *Computer Simulated Plant Evolution*. Scientific American (May 1985), (1985)
10. Niklas, K.: *Biophysical limitations on plant form and evolution*. Plant Evolutionary Biology, Ed. L. D. Gottlieb and S. K. Jain. Chapman and Hall Ltd, (1988)
11. Niklas, K.: *The Evolutionary Biology of Plants*. The university of Chicago Press, Chicago (1997)
12. Oppenheimer, P.: *Real Time Design and Animation of Fractal Plants and Trees*. Proceedings of SIGGRAPH '86, in Computer Graphics. ACM SIGGRAPH, 20(4) (1986) 55-62
13. Prusinkiewics, P., Lindenmayer, A.: *The Algorithmic Beauty of Plants*. Springer-Verlag, (1990)
14. Reynolds, C.: *Flocks, Herds, and Schools: A Distributed Behavioral Model*. Proceedings of SIGGRAPH '87, in Computer Graphics. ACM SIGGRAPH, 21(4) (1987) 25-34
15. Sims, K.: *Artificial Evolution for Computer Graphics*. Proceedings of SIGGRAPH '91, in Computer Graphics. ACM SIGGRAPH, 25(4) (1991) 319-328
16. Sims, K.: *Evolving Virtual Creatures*. Proceedings of SIGGRAPH '94, in Computer Graphics. ACM SIGGRAPH, 28(4) (1994) 15-22
17. Smith, A.: *Plants, Fractals, and Formal Languages*. Proceedings of SIGGRAPH '84, in Computer Graphics. ACM SIGGRAPH, 18(4) (1984) 1-10

Genome Length as an Evolutionary Self-adaptation

Connie Loggia Ramsey[1*], Kenneth A. De Jong[2], John J. Grefenstette[3], Annie S. Wu[1], and Donald S. Burke[4],

[1] Naval Research Laboratory, Code 5514, Washington, DC 20375
[2] Computer Science Department, George Mason University, Fairfax, VA
[3] Institute for Biosciences, Bioinformatics and Biotechnology, George Mason University, Manassas, VA
[4] Center for Immunization Research, Johns Hopkins University, Baltimore, MD

Abstract. There is increasing interest in evolutionary algorithms that have variable-length genomes and/or location independent genes. However, our understanding of such algorithms both theoretically and empirically is much less well developed than the more traditional fixed-length, fixed-location ones. Recent studies with VIV (VIrtual Virus), a variable length, GA-based computational model of viral evolution, have revealed several emergent phenomena of both biological and computational interest. One interesting and somewhat surprising result is that the length of individuals in the population self-adapts in direct response to the mutation rate applied, so the GA adaptively strikes the balance it needs to successfully solve the problem. Over a broad range of mutation rates, genome length tends to increase dramatically in the early phases of evolution, and then decrease to a level based on the mutation rate. The plateau genome length (i.e., the average length of individuals in the final population) generally increases in response to an increase in the base mutation rate. Furthermore, the mutation operator rate and adapted length resulting in the best problem solving performance is about one mutation per individual. This is also the rate at which mutation generally occurs in biological systems, suggesting an optimal, or at least biologically plausible, balance of these operator rates. These results suggest that an important property of these algorithms is a considerable degree of self-adaptation.

1 Introduction

As evolutionary algorithms (EAs) are applied to new and more complex problem domains, many of the standard EAs seem artificially restrictive in a variety of ways, perhaps the most important of which is the choice of representation. There are many application areas that simply do not map well into the familiar fixed-length, fixed-position representations. However, as we move to variable-length, variable-position representations, both the theoretical and empirical foundations weaken considerably, frequently leaving the designer with little guidance.

In our case, we have been developing a GA-based computational model of viral evolution consisting of a standard GA model with a number of biologically motivated extensions, including a variable-length, variable-position representation. Initial experience with this system, called VIV (VIrtual Virus), has lead to several important insights which appear to be more general than the VIV context in which they appear, and may be of help to others attempting to extend their EA representations.

In the remainder of the paper we summarize the important features of our GA extensions, we present a series of experiments attempting to understand these extensions better, and we describe the insight gained.

2 Important Features of VIV

Early in the project it was felt that, in order to model viral evolution, a much more biologically plausible genome representation was required to reflect the fact that:

---
* Email: ramsey@aic.nrl.navy.mil

- Biological genomes are of variable lengths.
- Biological genes are independent of position.
- Biological genomes may contain non-coding regions.
- Biological genomes may contain duplicative or competing genes.
- Biological genomes have overlapping reading frames.

To achieve this in a biologically plausible manner, the genotype alphabet for VIV is the familiar set of the four bases {A,C,G,T}, triples of which are mapped into a phenotype English alphabet representing pseudo amino acid symbols and START/STOP codes.

Hence, genomes (individuals in the population) are variable-length strings whose phenotype is determined by scanning the string from left to right on each of its three reading frames, mapping the triples (codons) of bases into the phenotype alphabet, and identifying each "gene" signified by matching START/STOP codes. For each gene, its compatibility score is computed by matching it against a set of target terms representing necessary "proteins". The gene that produces the highest compatibility score for a given target term is called an "active gene". Then, the fitness of the genome is computed by taking the average of the compatibility scores for each active gene.

More details can be found in [3]. For our purposes here, we need to briefly describe how the genetic operators work on this representation. Mutation operates on the strings in the standard way, as a probability per position of changing the current symbol to a randomly selected alternative from {A,C,G,T}.

Recombination, however, is implemented as a 1-point homologous crossover operator in which a randomly chosen point on parent 1 is matched with a "homologous" crossover point on parent 2 (see [3] for more details). So, recombination takes place only when very similar regions are matched and then aligned from both parents.

The rest of the GA in VIV consists of a standard generational model using fitness proportional selection. As we began experimenting with VIV, however, we found that our intuitions gained from more traditional GAs were frequently wrong, requiring us to perform a series of careful experimental studies to understand VIV better.

3 Related Work

A number of studies have investigated one or more of the features described above in the context of GAs. An early study of variable length representation was the messy GA [7] which uses a binary representation in which both the value and position of each bit are specified. Though the number of bits used to generate a solution is constant, the number and ordering of the bits in the individuals being evolved varies. "Missing" bits are retrieved from a universal template to generate a complete solution. Harvey [10] discusses some of the issues involved with variable length representations, including the mechanics of crossover in such a system [9], and makes predictions about the evolved length of individuals in such systems. The delta-coding GA presented by Mathias and Whitley [16] uses variable length representations to control the scope of the exploration performed by the GA. SAMUEL [8] is a GA-based learning system that successfully evolves variable sized rule sets for robot navigation and control tasks. Genetic programming (GP) [13] is another class of evolutionary algorithms that evolves programs which vary in both structure and length. Studies on the evolved length of GP programs include [12, 14, 18, 23].

The investigation of non-coding regions has also gained increasing interest in recent years. Levenick [15] presented one of the first studies indicating that non-coding regions improve the performance of a GA. Several studies have investigated the effects of non-coding regions on the recombination and maintenance of building blocks in the GA [6, 21, 22]. Non-coding segments were found to reduce the disruption of building blocks but not necessarily improve the speed of finding a solution. A number of GP studies have also investigated the utility of non-coding material or "bloat" in evolved programs [11, 14, 19].

Several studies have focused on adaptive organization of information on the genome. The messy GA [7] allows the GA to adapt the composition and ordering of bits of each individual. Tests have shown that the messy GA performs better than the standard GA on a class of deceptive problems. Studies on a class of functions called the Royal Road functions [22] found that using tagged building blocks that are dynamically evolved and arranged by the GA results in a much more diverse population and significantly improved performance. Mayer [17] investigated the self-organization of information in a GA using location independent genes.

A number of studies have looked into adaptation and variation of operator rates during an EA run. Fogarty [5] investigated varying mutation rates on a time-dependent schedule during GA runs. Davis [4] studied self-adapting operators in steady-state GAs. Baeck examined the self-adaptation of mutation rates in GAs [2] and the interaction of several self-adapting features of EAs [1].

4 Initial experiences with VIV

In our initial studies with VIV, the fitness landscape was defined by a set of three target genes consisting of a total of 29 phenotype letters (Problem 1). The goal was to obtain a better understanding of how sensitive the performance of VIV was to the standard GA parameters such as population size and operator rates.

The initial results were disappointing in that no parameter setting produced particularly good problem solving performance. Although the GA quickly identifies reasonably good solutions, the performance levels were far below the optimum fitness value. What we discovered was that, without any negative selective pressure against long genomes, VIV evolved populations of individuals whose average length continued to increase without bound. The GA fairly quickly bogged down in this expanding string space, and was unable to maintain steady progress toward the optimum.

A bit of reflection provided the reason. The homologous 1-point crossover operator can produce offspring that are considerably longer than their parents. Such recombinations provide an initial selective advantage, since the additional genetic material is "free" (i.e., has no negative impact on fitness) and provides a better chance for discovering higher performance active genes.

This behavior is consistent with earlier studies with variable length GAs (e.g., [20]), and suggests the need for some sort of selective pressure against long strings. This is consistent with the biological perspective that longer genomes require more time, energy and resources to maintain and to replicate. In order to provide a simple length bias, we added a linear penalty to the fitness, based on establishing a maximum allowable genome length:

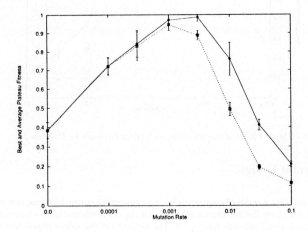

Fig. 1. Effects of mutation rate on VIV performance for Problem 1

If $Length(x) < Maxlength$, $fitness(x) = (1 - Length(x)/Maxlength) \, raw\_fitness(x)$;

otherwise, $fitness(x) = 0$.

Exploratory experiments indicated that the precise value of *Maxlength* was not particularly critical. At the same time it was clear that too severe a length bias can cause the GA to converge suboptimally, and a length bias that is too weak can result in failure to converge. In our experiments, by adding a linear length bias with $Maxlength = 7500$, genome length increased initially and then stabilized, while from a performance viewpoint VIV consistently evolved high fitness solutions.

Similar exploratory experiments suggested that VIV performance was not overly sensitive to the rate of crossover or population size. A crossover rate of 1.0 and a population size of 500 was selected and left unchanged.

However, to our surprise, the performance of VIV was quite sensitive to the mutation rate. Figure 1 illustrates the typical results we observed. The *best plateau fitness* refers to the fitness of the best individual in the final population, and the *average plateau fitness* refers to the average fitness in the final population. The maximum fitness value for our landscapes is 1.0 (a perfect match to the target words). Optimal performance for Problem 1 is achieved at mutation rates of approximately 0.001 when measuring the average fitness of the population and 0.003 for the best genome in the population, and falls off sharply if the rate is either increased or decreased.

To make sure this behavior was not an artifact of the particular properties of the fitness landscape, data was collected from a second landscape consisting of three target words totaling 49 characters to be matched (Problem 2). Optimal performance here is achieved at mutation rates of approximately 0.001. The overall results, including the shape of the curve, are strikingly similar as indicated by Figure 2.

The explanation for this sensitivity to mutation rates was not at all obvious. To understand better what was happening, we undertook a series of more carefully controlled experiments which led to some rather surprising insights. We describe these in the remainder of the paper.

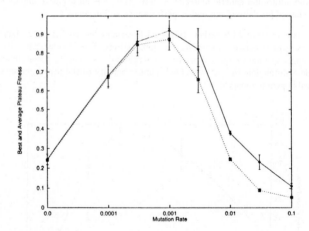

Fig. 2. Effects of mutation rate on VIV performance for Problem 2

5 Experimental Design

The next section presents a series of computational experiments that provide some new insights into the dynamics of GAs that have flexible representations. All the studies below used a population size of 500 and a 1-point homologous crossover rate of 1.0. The genomes in the initial population were generated at random, with the initial lengths set to a uniformly distributed random number between 100 and 500.

In the first set of experiments, the target phenotype is a set of three words containing a total of 29 letters. In the second set of experiments, the target phenotype is a set of three words containing a total of 49 letters. From now on, we will refer to these problems as Problem 1 and Problem 2 respectively. The set of experiments for Problem 1 was run for 2000 generations and the set for Problem 2 was run for 4000 generations. Problem 2 is more complex since it has to match 49 characters in order to derive the best solution while Problem 1 only has to match 29. The search space necessary to solve this problem is larger, and hence, the number of generations necessary to reach a plateau is also larger. For all experiments, ten independent runs were performed for each set of conditions. The graphs show the average and standard deviation of the results of the ten runs. (Error bars indicate one standard deviation over the ten runs.)

We examine the effect of different mutation rates on the VIV model. Mutation rates for all individuals were fixed over the entire run at values ranging from 0.0 (no mutation) to a fairly high rate of 0.1 (a random substitution will occur at a rate of 1 in 10 genotype base elements of an individual).

6 Results

6.1 Effects of Mutation Rate on Performance

With stochastic algorithms it is always important to verify that observed effects are statistically significant. Figures 1 and 2 present the results of the experiments on both Problem 1 and Problem 2,

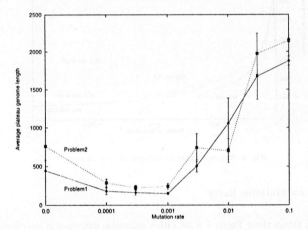

Fig. 3. Effects of mutation rate on length of individuals for Problem 1 and Problem 2

indicating the effects are significant.

6.2 Effects of Mutation Rate on Genome Length

One of the things that caught our eye was the fact that the average plateau genome length, i.e., the average genome length at which VIV stabilized, appeared to increase as we increased mutation rates. We analyzed this more closely for both problems and came up with the rather startling results presented in Figure 3.

As we increase the mutation rate from 0.0 to the observed optimal rate of approximately 0.001, the plateau genome length decreases. As we continue to increase the mutation rate beyond the observed optimal rate, the plateau genome length increases rapidly. It appears that an emergent property of VIV is that the genome length self-adapts in direct response to the mutation rate!

In order to understand this better we analyzed the time evolution of genome length under various mutation rates. The results are shown in detail in Figure 4 for Problem 1. In all cases, genome length increases significantly at the early stages of a run and then levels out at different lengths depending on mutation rate. Similar results were observed for Problem 2.

A possible explanation for these observations follows: In the early stage of evolution, there appears to be an advantage in having a long genome because it gives a better chance of discovering good genes. This advantage may outweigh the pressure toward shorter genome lengths because shorter offspring are unlikely to contain better genes early in evolution. If the mutation rate is very high (0.03 or higher), the genomes tend to remain long. This is reasonable since mutation causes so much disruption that the population fitness never improves and the genetic algorithm never converges. If the mutation rate is lower (at or below 0.01), the genome length eventually settles down to a lower plateau value. In these cases, once the population fitness improves, the selective pressure toward exploiting the building blocks already present in the shorter genomes prevails over the exploratory advantage of longer genomes.

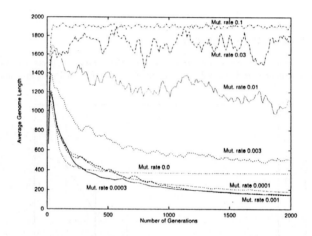

Fig. 4. Average length of individuals over 10 runs.

6.3 Effects of Low Mutation Rates

One of the striking things about Figure 3 is the rather noticeable difference in the effects that low vs. high mutation rates have on genome length. Equally as striking is the time evolution of genome length under a mutation rate of 0.0 shown in Fig. 4 in which the plateau is already reached by generation 300.

In the latter case a close examination of individuals in the population indicated that the population had prematurely converged. By generation 400, the population is approximately 98 - 99% converged. Interestingly, the few differences that exist are more often in non-coding regions of the individuals. The fact that there is no mutation means there is never any new material added in to the population. Once the existing building blocks are exploited, the individuals rapidly settle down to a homogeneous length. Furthermore, by using homologous crossover, the individuals stay at that length because they are always crossed at matching points within the individuals, never at random points.

For lower mutation rates above 0.0 (0.0001 - 0.001) the population still converges, but more slowly. With a mutation rate of 0.0001, the population is about 95% converged by generation 1700, with about half of the differences in non-coding regions. Further, all of the coding regions are lined up in the same order and almost exactly the same locations on the genome. Basically, a low mutation rate results mainly in exploitation of existing building blocks and some convergence, but there is still a low amount of mutation to allow for some exploration and therefore some improvement in performance.

6.4   Effects of High Mutation Rates

As the mutation rate rises above a threshold of 0.001 for both problems, plateau genome length also rises sharply. In other words, there appears to be some selective advantage to additional genome length as the mutation rate increases. Notice also that the curves shown in Figure 4 for higher mutations do not flatten out as the lower mutation curves do. As the mutation rate goes higher, there is more exploration occurring and much less exploitation and convergence because building blocks are constantly destroyed.

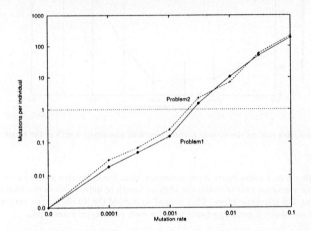

Fig. 5. Effects of mutation rate on the number of mutations per individual for Problem 1 and Problem 2

6.5   Effects of Mutation Rate on the Number of Mutations per Individual

An alternate way of understanding these results is to plot the average number of mutations per individual at steady state. As shown in Figure 5 the number of mutations per individual steadily increases as the mutation rate increases. In both problems mutation rates between 0.001 and 0.003 yield individuals in the final population whose number of mutations are about 1 per individual. This happens to be the range of mutation rates which result in the best performance as shown in Figures 1 and 2. So a good balance of all of the key elements comes about in this range of mutation rates; the genome length adapts so there is about one mutation per individual, and there is a good balance between exploitation and exploration leading to highly fit individuals in the final population. Furthermore, this is consistent with biological observations across a wide range of species of about one mutation per generation per individual, giving further reason to believe there is a nearly optimal balance of operator rates here.

This interpretation can also provide a simple explanation for why the optimal mutation rate was observed to be a little lower in Problem 2 than in Problem 1. Recall that the target word length was considerably longer in Problem 2, requiring in general longer genomes to obtain perfect matches. The combination of longer genomes and a lower mutation rate maintains the average number of mutations per individual at approximately one.

6.6   Self-adapting Scratch Space

Another interesting insight into this emergent behavior is obtained by looking at the ratio of the plateau genome lengths to the length of the target words. Since each phenotype letter is encoded by 3 genotype bases, the ratio of the length of the genome (in genotype bases) to phenotype length of the target words is expected to be at least 3 to 1. Anything greater than 3 to 1 indicates excess scratch space in the genome. Figure 6 presents the data for both problems.

For example, a mutation rate of 0.001 produces the plateau length of about 150 genotype bases in the final population for Problem 1. The target phenotype words for Problem 1 were 29 letters in

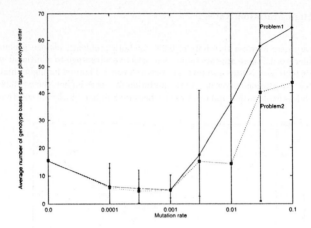

Fig. 6. Effects of mutation rate on the ratio of genome length to phenotype length of the target words for both problems

length, resulting in a 5 to 1 ratio. Since 3 are necessary, that leaves 2 extra genotype bases for scratch space. For the same mutation rate of 0.001, the plateau length of individuals in the final population for Problem 2 is about 250 genotype bases. This is used to encode the 49 phenotype target letters of the problem, so there are about 5 genotype bases used for each phenotype letter again.

This data is highly suggestive that the mutation rate determines the amount of scratch space required to solve these sorts of problems, possibly independent of the size of the problem. As the mutation rate increases, additional scratch space is needed to offset the increased disruption of mutation. At very low mutation rates, the ratios actually increase slightly as a side effect of premature convergence. Further studies are planned to investigate the amount and content of the scratch space produced.

7   Summary

With the increasing interest in evolutionary algorithms that have variable-length genomes and/or location independent genes, it is important to increase our understanding of such algorithms both theoretically and empirically. The development of VIV (VIrtual Virus), a variable length, GA-based computational model of viral evolution, has provided us with an environment to do so. Initial studies reported here have revealed several emergent phenomena of both biological and computational interest. One interesting and somewhat surprising result is that the length of individuals in the population self-adapts in direct response to the mutation rate applied, so the GA adaptively strikes the balance it needs to successfully solve the problem. Over a broad range of mutation rates, genome length tends to increase dramatically in the early phases of evolution, and then decrease to a level based on the mutation rate. The plateau genome length (i.e., the average length of individuals in the final population) generally increases in response to an increase in the base mutation rate. Furthermore, the mutation operator rate and adapted length resulting in the best problem solving performance translates to about one mutation per individual. This is also the rate at which mutation generally occurs in biological systems, suggesting an optimal, or at least biologically plausible, balance of these operator rates. These results suggest that an important property of these algorithms is a considerable degree of self-adaptation.

Acknowledgements

This work is supported by the Office of Naval Research, the National Research Council, and the Walter Reed Army Institute of Research.

References

1. T. Baeck. The interaction of mutation rate, selection, and self-adaptation within a genetic algorithm. In R. Maenner and B. Manderick, editors, *Proc. Parallel Problem Solving from Nature 2*, pages 85–94, 1992.
2. T. Baeck. Self-adaptation in genetic algorithms. In F.J. Varela and P. Bourgine, editors, *Proc. First European Conf. Artificial Life*, pages 263–271, 1992.
3. D. S. Burke, K. A. De Jong, J. J. Grefenstette, C. L. Ramsey, and A. S. Wu. Putting more genetics in genetic algorithms, 1998. To appear in *Evolutionary Computation*.
4. L. Davis. Adapting operator probabilities in genetic algorithms. In J. D. Schaffer, editor, *Proc. 3rd Int. Conf. Genetic Algorithms*, pages 61–69, 1989.
5. T. C. Fogarty. Varying the probability of mutation in the genetic algorithm. In J. D. Schaffer, editor, *Proc. 3rd Int. Conf. Genetic Algorithms*, pages 104–109, 1989.
6. S. Forrest and M. Mitchell. Relative building-block fitness and the building-block hypothesis. In *Foundations of Genetic Algorithms 2*, pages 109–126, 1992.
7. D. Goldberg, K. Deb, and B. Korb. Messy genetic algorithms: motivation, analysis, and first results. *Complex Systems*, 3:493–530, 1989.
8. J. J. Grefenstette, C. L. Ramsey, and A. C. Schultz. Learning sequential decision rules using simulation models and competition. *Machine Learning*, 5(4):355–381, 1990.
9. I. Harvey. The SAGA cross: the mechanics of crossover for variable-length genetic algorithms. In *Parallel Problem Solving from Nature 2*, pages 269–278, 1992.
10. I. Harvey. Species adaptation genetic algorithms: a basis for a continuing SAGA. In *Proc. 1st European Conference on Artificial Life*, 1992.
11. T. Haynes. Duplication of coding segments in genetic programming. In *Proc. 13th National Conference on Artificial Intelligence*, pages 344–349, 1996.
12. H. Iba, H. deGaris, and T. Sato. Genetic programming using a minimum description length principle. In *Advances in Genetic Programming*, pages 265–284, 1994.
13. J. R. Koza. *Genetic programming*. MIT Press, 1992.
14. W. B. Langdon and R. Poli. Fitness causes bloat. In *2nd On-line World Conference on Soft Computing in Engineering Design and Manufacturing*, 1997.
15. J. R. Levenick. Inserting introns improves genetic algorithm success rate: taking a cue from biology. In *Proc. 4th Int'l Conf. Gen. Alg.*, pages 123–127, 1991.
16. K. E. Mathias and L. D. Whitley. Initial performance comparisons for the delta coding algorithm. In *Proc. IEEE Conference on Evolutionary Computation*, volume 1, pages 433–438, 1994.
17. H. A. Mayer. *Genetic Algorithms Using Promoter/Terminater Sequences - Evolution of Number, Size, and Location of Parameters and Parts of the Representation*. PhD thesis, University of Salzburg, 1997.
18. P. Nordin and W. Banzhaf. Complexity compression and evolution. In *Proc. 6th International Conference on Genetic Algorithms*, pages 310–317, 1995.
19. P. Nordin, F. Francone, and W. Banzhaf. Explicitly defined introns and destructive crossover in genetic programming. In *Advances in Genetic Programming 2*, pages 111–134, 1996.
20. S. F. Smith. Flexible learning of problem solving heuristics through adaptive search. In *Proc. 8th International Joint Conference on Artificial Intelligence*, pages 422–425. Morgan Kaufmann, 1983.
21. A. S. Wu and R. K. Lindsay. Empirical studies of the genetic algorithm with non-coding segments. *Evolutionary Computation*, 3(2):121–147, 1995.
22. A. S. Wu and R. K. Lindsay. A comparison of the fixed and floating building block representation in the genetic algorithm. *Evolutionary Computation*, 4(2):169–193, 1996.
23. B. T. Zhang and H. Muhlenbein. Balancing accuracy and parsimony in genetic programming. *Evolutionary Computation*, 3(1), 1995.

Selection, Operators and Evolution Schemes

Restart Scheduling for Genetic Algorithms

Alex S. Fukunaga*

Jet Propulsion Laboratory, California Institute of Technology,
4800 Oak Grove Dr., Mail Stop 126-347, Pasadena, CA 91109-8099,
alex.fukunaga@jpl.nasa.gov

Abstract. In order to escape from local optima, it is standard practice
to periodically restart heuristic optimization algorithms such as genetic
algorithm according to some restart criteria/policy. This paper addresses
the issue of finding a good restart strategy in the context of resource-
bounded optimization scenarios, in which the goal is to generate the best
possible solution given a fixed amount of time. We propose the use of a
restart scheduling strategy which generates a static restart strategy with
optimal expected utility, based on a database of past performance of the
algorithm on a class of problem instances. We show that the performance
of static restart schedules generated by the approach can be competitive
to that of a commonly used dynamic restart strategy based on detection
of lack of progress.

It is well-known that heuristic optimization algorithms such as genetic algorithms (GAs) often converge to local optima before discovering a globally
optimal solution. Much research has focused on the problem of *preventing* premature convergence, including various niching/speciation/mating neighborhood
models (c.f. [4, 6, 3, 2, 5]). However, even when mechanisms for preventing premature convergence are implemented, extended runs of GAs still reach a point
of significantly diminishing marginal return, i.e., convergence. Furthermore, for
most real-world problems, it is not possible to know whether a GA has found
the global optimum, or whether it has become stuck at a local optimum (there
are some exceptional cases when a bound on the optimum can be computed).

Thus, it is standard practice to periodically restart GAs according to some
restart criteria/policy. However, to date, the subject of restart policies for GAs
has been neglected. A common technique is to apply some metric of progress or
convergence, and to terminate the current run and restart with a new seed when
some threshold is reached (typically when no progress has been made for a long
time, or when convergence is detected using some other metric).

In this paper, we address the issue of finding a good restart strategy in the
context of resource-bounded optimization scenarios, in which the goal is to generate the best possible solution given a fixed amount of time. We first define a
framework for resource-bounded optimization, and describe a *restart scheduling*

---

* Portions of this research was performed by the Jet Propulsion Laboratory, California
Institute of Technology, under contract with the National Aeronautics and Space
Administration. Thanks to Andre Stechert for helpful comments on a draft of this
paper.

approach which uses performance data from previous runs of the algorithm on similar problems. We experimentally evaluate the restart scheduling approach by comparing its performance to that of a restart strategy based on performance improvement probability bound on a genetic algorithm for the traveling salesperson problem (TSP). The paper concludes with a review of related work and a discussion of our results.

1 Restart Strategies for Resource-Bounded Optimization

We define the problem of *resource-bounded optimization* as follows: Let A be an optimization algorithm, and d be a problem instance (an objective function). Let T be a resource usage limit for A. In this paper, we assume that T is measured in a number of discrete "steps", or objective function evaluations – we assume that all objective function evaluations take approximately the same amount of time. Let $U(A, d, T)$, the utility of the algorithm A on d given time T, be the utility of the best solution found by the algorithm within the time bound. The task of resource-bounded optimization is to maximize U (i.e., obtain the best possible solution quality within a given time).

We assume that it does *not* matter when the maximal value of U is obtained within the time window $[0, T]$. This is a reasonable model of many real-world optimization scenarios, in which an optimization expert is given a deadline at which to present the best solution found. In this problem framework, the only thing that matters is the utility of the best solution found within the deadline. Metrics such as rate of improvement of the best-so-far solution, or convergence of the population are irrelevant with respect to how an algorithm's performance is evaluated.

In many cases, particularly if T is large enough, it is possible to start a run of A, terminate it after t_k steps, restart A and run for $t_k + 1$ steps, and repeat this process n times, where $\sum_{i=1}^{n} t_i = T$.

A *restart strategy* determines $t_1, ...t_n$, and can be either *static* or *dynamic*. Static restart strategies determine $t_1, ...t_n$ prior to running the algorithm. For example, a strategy which allocates resources equally among n restarts is a static strategy. Dynamic strategies, on the other hand, decide during runtime when a restart should take place. For example, we could repeat the following until the total number of steps taken is T: run A until a convergence criterion is met, then restart.

2 Optimizing a Restart Schedule Based on Past Performance Data

If we assume that we are applying a GA to a *class* of resource-bounded optimization problem instances where the members of the class are somewhat similar to each other with respect to how a restart strategy performs on them, then a reasonable approach to developing a restart schedule is to design a strategy which has high expected utility for the class of problems.

We define a *static restart schedule* to be the set $S = \{t_1, t_2, ...t_n\}$, where $\sum_{i=1}^{n} t_i = T$. Given an algorithm A and problem instance d, A is executed with d as the input for t_i steps, for each i, $1 \leq i \leq n$. The best solution found among all of the restarts is stored and returned as the result of the restart schedule execution. The schedule is defined as a set, rather than a sequence, since the order in which the elements are executed does not matter (we assume that the restarts are independent, and that information from previous restarts is not used in subsequent restarts).

Let $U(A, d, t)$ denote the random variable which determines the utility (best objective function value found) when algorithm A is run for time t on problem instance d. Then, $U(S, A, d, T)$ the utility of a restart schedule is also a random value related to those of the individual elements of the schedule by $U(S, A, d, T) = max(U(A, d, t_1), U(A, d, t_2), ...U(A, d, t_n))$.

In order to maximize the expected value of U, $E[U(S, A, d, T)]$, we propose an approach which uses algorithm performance data collected in previous applications of A to problems similar to d (i.e., problems drawn from the same class of problems) to determine the schedule S. We assume that "similarity" has been defined elsewhere, and that classes of problems have been previously identified prior to application of the restart scheduling algorithm.

When A is executed on an instance d, we output the quality of the best-so-far solution at every q iterations in a *performance database* entry, $DB(A, d, runID) = \{(q, u_1), (2q, u_2), (3q, u_3), ...(mq, u_m)\}$, where $runID$ is a tag which uniquely identifies the run (e.g., the random seed). By collecting a set of such entries, we collect a performance database which can serve as an empirical approximation of the distributions corresponding to the set of random variables $\mathcal{U}_{Ad} = \{U(A, d, q), U(A, d, 2q), ...U(A, d, mq)\}$. In principle, it is possible to try to approximate $U(A, d, t)$ for some arbitrary t by interpolation. However, our current scheduling algorithm (see below) only requires the random values in $\mathcal{U}_{Ad}$. It is also possible to combine data from runs on different problem instances in order to approximations for $U(A, t)$.

Figure 1 shows a sample performance database based on a set of 5 independent runs of algorithm A_1 on problem instance i_1 and 3 independent runs of A_1 on i_2. From the database, we can compute, for example, that an approximation for the expected value of $U(A_1, i_1, 30)$ is $(2 + 2 + 2 + 2 + 3)/5 = 2.2$, and $U(A_1, 20) = 22/10 = 2.2$.

We now have the infrastructure necessary to automatically synthesize a static restart strategy that maximizes the expected utility $U(A, T)$, based on a performance database.

Synthesize-restart-schedule (Figure 2) is a simple generate-and-test approach for static restart optimization. Given a *schedule increment size constant* parameter k, where $T \bmod k = 0$, our current implementation of *GenerateNextSchedule* simply enumerates all schedules $\{k, 2k, ...(T/k)k = T\}$, where all components of the problem are chunks of time which are a multiple of k. For example, if $T = 75000, k = 25000$ (i.e., total resource allocation is 75000 objective function evaluations, and the schedule elements are multiples of 25000 iterations),

$$D(A_1, i_1, 0) = \{(10, 1), (20, 2), (30, 2), (40, 3)\}$$
$$D(A_1, i_1, 1) = \{(10, 1), (20, 1), (30, 2), (40, 3)\}$$
$$D(A_1, i_1, 2) = \{(10, 1), (20, 1), (30, 2), (40, 2)\}$$
$$D(A_1, i_1, 3) = \{(10, 1), (20, 1), (30, 2), (40, 2)\}$$
$$D(A_1, i_1, 4) = \{(10, 1), (20, 3), (30, 3), (40, 4)\}$$
$$D(A_1, i_2, 0) = \{(10, 2), (20, 2), (30, 2), (40, 2)\}$$
$$D(A_1, i_2, 1) = \{(10, 2), (20, 3), (30, 3), (40, 3)\}$$
$$D(A_1, i_2, 2) = \{(10, 1), (20, 3), (30, 3), (40, 3)\}$$
$$D(A_1, i_2, 3) = \{(10, 1), (20, 3), (30, 3), (40, 3)\}$$
$$D(A_1, i_2, 4) = \{(10, 1), (20, 3), (30, 3), (40, 3)\}$$

Fig. 1. Sample performance database, based on a set of 5 independent runs of algorithm A_1 on problem instance i_1 and 5 runs of A_1 on instance i_2.

the schedules which are generated and evaluated are $S_0=\{25000,25000,25000\}$, $S_1=\{25000,50000\}$, and $S_2=\{75000\}$. Each candidate schedule is evaluated by estimating its expected utility via sampling (with replacement) from the performance database. It is important to note that evaluating a candidate schedule by sampling the performance database is typically orders of magnitude less expensive than actually executing the schedule. Thus, the meta-level search is able to evaluate thousands of candidate schedules per second on a workstation, and is much more efficient than evaluating strategies by actually executing them.

Of course, as T/k grows, the number of candidate schedules grows exponentially, so it eventually becomes infeasible to exhaustively evaluate every single candidate schedule. Future work will focus on efficient heuristic search algorithms for meta-level search. However, as shown below, the exhaustive search algorithm is more than adequate for our current empirical studies.

Note that we have discussed restart schedule optimization from a utility theoretic point of view, i.e., maximizing expected utility of a schedule. In practice, for optimization problems where the objective is to minimize an objective function (as in the following section), we simply treat the objective function as a negative utility.

3 Experiments and Results

We evaluated the restart scheduling approach using a class of symmetric Traveling Salesperson Problem (TSP) instances.

The TSP instances were generated by placing $N = 32$ cities on randomly selected (x, y) coordinates (where x and y are floating point values between 0 and 1) on a 1.0 by 1.0 rectangle. The cost of traveling between two cities c_i and c_j is the Euclidean distance between them, $d(c_i, c_j)$.

The objective is to find a tour π (a permutation of the cities) with minimal cost, $Cost_\pi = \sum_{i=1}^{n-1} d(c_{\pi(i)}, c_{\pi(i+1)}) + d(c_{\pi(n)}, c_{\pi(1)})$

```
Synthesize-restart-schedule(PerfDB,NumSamples,T,k)
bestSched = {}
bestUtility = -∞
Repeat
  S=GenerateNextSchedule(T,k)
  /* estimate expected utility of S */
  SumUtility = -∞
  for i = 1 to NumSamples
    TrialUtility = -∞
    for each element t_j in S
      DBInst = ChooseRandomDBProbIndex
      DBSeed = ChooseRandomDBSeedIndex
      U_j = DBLookUp(PerfDB,A,DBInst,DBSeed,t_j)
      if U_j > bestConfTrial
        TrialUtility = U_j
    end
    sumUtility = sumUtility + TrialUtility
  end

  U_S = sumUtility/NumSamples
  if U_S > bestUtility
    bestSched = S
    bestUtility = U_S
Until some termination condition
Return bestSched
```

Fig. 2. *Synthesize-restart-schedule:* Returns a restart schedule with highest expected utility.

The problem representation used was a Gray-coded binary genome which was interpreted as follows: The ith allele (substring) was an integer between 1 and N, representing the ordering in the TSP tour for city i. Ties were broken in left to right order. For example, the genome $(3,2,1,5,3)$ for a 4-city TSP problem means that City1 is visited third, City2 second, City3 first, City4 fifth, City5 is fourth, and the tour completes by returning to City3.

A standard, generational GA [6] was used. The crossover operator was single-point crossover, and the mutation operator was single-bit flips.

3.1 Performance Database Generation

We generated a performance database as follows:

Ten random 32-city TSP instances were generated as described above.

Sixteen different configurations of the GA were generated, by selecting values for four control parameters (population size, crossover probability, mutation probability, selection method), where: $population \in \{50, 100\}, SelectionMethod \in$

$\{roulette, tournament\}.^2$ $Pr(Crossover) \in \{0.25, 0.5\}$ (probability of a one-point crossover), and $Pr(Mutate) \in \{0.01, 0.05\}$ (probability of each bit being flipped).

For each of the TSP instances, we executed each of the GA configurations using 50 different random seeds. Each run was for 100000 iterations (objective function evaluations), i.e., the number of generations was chosen so that the $population \times NumGenerations = 100000$. Every 10000 iterations, the length of the shortest tour found so far by the current GA configuration for the current TSP instance for the current random seed was stored in a file.

3.2   The Effectiveness of Restart Schedules for Unseen Problems

Our first experiment sought to verify that the expected utilities of the restart schedules were in fact correlated with the actual performance of the restart schedules on unseen problems – otherwise, optimization of restart schedules based on the performance database is unlikely to be very useful.

Using the performance database described in the subsection above, we executed *Synthesize-restart-schedule* to generate restart schedules for the GA configuration with $population = 100$, $Pr(Cross) = 0.5$, $Pr(Mutate) = 0.05$, and $Selection = roulette$, where the resource allocation T was set to 150000 total iterations. The increment size constant used by *GenerateNextSchedule* was 10000. This was repeated for $NumSamples = 100$ and $NumSamples = 1000$. For this experiment, the algorithm was slightly modified to output **all** schedules which were enumerated as well as their expected utilities.

A new random 32 city TSP instance was generated, and for each enumerated schedule, we executed the schedule with the new TSP instance as the input 25 times, and the mean utility of the schedule on the new instance was computed. In Figure 3, we plot the expected utility of each schedule against their actual (mean) performance on the new TSP instance. The plot shows that there is indeed a high linear correlation between the expected utility of a schedule and its performance on the new instance.

3.3   Static Restart Scheduling vs. Dynamic Restart Strategies

We evaluated the relative effectiveness of the restart scheduling approach by comparing its performance on a set of test TSP problem instances with that of a dynamic restart strategy.

For each of the 16 GA configurations for which the performance database had been created (see 3.1), we ran the *Synthesize-restart-schedule* algorithm to generate a restart schedules for a resource bound of $T = 200000$ iterations. We used $NumSamples = 1000$, $k = 10000$. Executing *Synthesize-restart-schedule* only took a few seconds for each GA configuration.

---

[2] Roulette selection was implemented as in [6]. Tournament selection uses roulette selection to pick two individuals, then picks the individual with higher fitness, i.e., it applies additional sampling bias for better individuals.

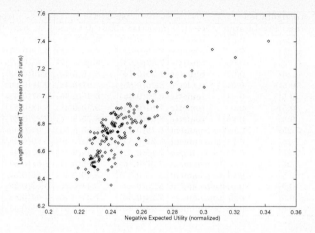

Fig. 3. Negative Expected utility of a restart schedule (smaller is better) vs. shortest tour length (mean of 25 runs), for problem instance tsp-t-32-0. The restart schedules were generated by *Synthesize-restart-schedule*, where $NumSamples = 1000$

Using these schedules, we executed each of the GA configurations on two new, randomly generated 32 city TSP instances. 25 independent trials were executed. The mean and standard deviation of the best (shortest) tour lengths for each of the configurations for each of the problems are shown in Table 1.

A commonly used dynamic restart strategy in practice is to restart a GA run after no improvement has been found after some threshold number of objective function calls, *StopThresh*. We compared static restart scheduling against this dynamic strategy.

We varied *StopThresh* between 4000 and 64000, in increments of 4000. For each value of *StopThresh*, we ran each GA configuration 25 times on each test TSP instance. The mean and standard deviation of the performances **for the value of** *StopThresh* **which performed** *best* **for each GA configuration and problem** are shown in Table 1. Thus, for each GA configuration and problem instance, we are comparing the performance of the schedule generated by *Synthesize-restart-schedule* against the dynamic strategy which performed best.

Table 1 shows that for each of the 16 GA configurations and the test problem instances, the static restart scheduling approach is able to generate schedules whose performance is competitive with the best, tuned dynamic restart strategy.

Similar results were obtained for three additional, new random TSP instances, but are not included due to space constraints.

4 Related Work

The problem of *termination criteria* for a genetic algorithm (GA) is closely related to the problem of restart policies. A stop criterion determines the termi-

Configuration				tsp-32-1		tsp-32-2	
Population	Pr(Cross)	Pr(Mutate)	Selection	best static	best dynamic	best static	best dynamic
50	0.25	0.01	roulette	6.22(0.45)	6.29(0.39)	6.48(0.46)	6.46(0.37)
100	0.25	0.01	roulette	6.19(0.52)	6.43(0.46)	6.53(0.55)	6.84(0.42)
50	0.25	0.05	roulette	7.82(0.63)	8.00(0.49)	8.35(0.47)	8.57(0.44)
100	0.25	0.05	roulette	8.23(0.74)	8.55(0.43)	8.49(0.58)	8.97(0.50)
50	0.5	0.01	roulette	6.30(0.55)	5.97(0.42)	6.41(0.60)	6.51(0.44)
100	0.5	0.01	roulette	6.25(0.46)	6.45(0.36)	6.57(0.42)	6.71(0.33)
50	0.5	0.05	roulette	7.84(0.64)	8.30(0.46)	8.48(0.54)	8.58(0.44)
100	0.5	0.05	roulette	8.31(0.57)	8.75(0.55)	8.81(0.37)	8.98(0.61)
50	0.25	0.01	tournament	5.49(0.47)	5.55(0.33)	6.03(0.40)	5.84(0.30)
100	0.25	0.01	tournament	5.22(0.43)	5.38(0.40)	5.69(0.46)	5.97(0.36)
50	0.25	0.05	tournament	7.18(0.72)	7.44(0.45)	7.82(0.48)	7.65(0.50)
100	0.25	0.05	tournament	7.36(0.46)	7.55(0.51)	8.01(0.53)	8.01(0.45)
50	0.5	0.01	tournament	5.43(0.38)	5.40(0.40)	5.76(0.32)	5.78(0.39)
100	0.5	0.01	tournament	5.23(0.44)	5.44(0.40)	5.63(0.38)	5.91(0.31)
50	0.5	0.05	tournament	7.24(0.56)	7.37(0.40)	7.64(0.64)	7.84(0.53)
100	0.5	0.05	tournament	7.24(0.45)	7.74(0.31)	7.95(0.43)	8.06(0.46)

Table 1. Shortest tour lengths found by restart schedules for problem instance tsp-32-1 and tsp-32-2. Mean and standard deviation (in parentheses) shown for 25 runs. Data for the schedule with maximal expected utility static schedule, as well as the mean and standard deviation for the dynamic schedule with the best *StopThresh* parameter value for the problem instance and GA configuration are shown.

nation condition for a GA. Intuitively, a "good" termination criterion stops an optimization algorithm run when an significant improvement can not be expected according to the observed performance behavior of the current run. Surprisingly, relatively little work has been done in the area of determining good termination criteria.

Common termination criteria used in practice include:[3]

- *Cost bound*: stop when a solution with quality at least as good as a threshold C_{thresh} was found
- *Time bound*: stop after a fixed run time or number of iterations
- *Improvement probability bound*: stop after no improvement had been found after some threshold number of generations.
- *Convergence bound*: stop after the population seems to have converged. This can be measured by phenotype-based metrics such as the standard deviation of the fitnesses of the population, or by measuring the diversity in the genomes based on sharing functions [6].

Recently, Hulin [8] proposed a *loss minimization* stop criterion which terminates the GA run when the cost of additional computation exceeds the expected gain (i.e., when the marginal utility of continuing the run is expected to be negative), and showed that the loss minimization criterion stopped significantly earlier than the improvement probability bound criteria, while obtaining virtually the same quality solutions.

---

[3] For the first three, we use the terminology used by Hulin [8]

Note that the cost bound, time bound, and improvement probability bound criteria are algorithm independent, and can be applied as a stop criterion for any iterative optimization algorithm (e.g., simulated annealing, greedy local search, etc.). In contrast, the loss minimization approach exploits algorithm structure (cost distributions in a GA population, although loss minimization criterion can be similarly derived for other optimization algorithms.

Static restart scheduling is related to *algorithm portfolios* [7], which use similar techniques to minimize the expected time to solve a satisficing (as opposed to optimization) problem by combining runs of different algorithms. The major differences between restart scheduling and algorithm portfolios arise from the fact that while restart scheduling optimizes expected utility for optimization problems, algorithm portfolios minimizes expected runtime for satisficing problems. Also, restart scheduling assumes a resource bound; algorithm portfolios are assumed to execute until a solution is found.

5 Discussion/Conclusions

This paper proposed the use of a restart scheduling strategy which generates schedules with optimal expected utility, based on a database of past performance of the algorithm on a class of problem instances. We showed that the performance of static restart schedules generated by the approach can be competitive to that of a commonly used, tuned, dynamic restart strategy.

It is somewhat counterintuitive that a restart schedule which dictates a series of algorithm restarts, completely oblivious to run-time metrics such as rate of progress, convergence, etc. can be competitive with a strategy which is explicitly designed restart when progress is not being made. We believe that one reason why the dynamic strategy does not outperform a static schedule is that restart decisions being made based only on local information about the current run, using a progress metrics which monitors whether the current run is progressing or not.

Our empirical results supports the argument that in the context of resource-bounded optimization, the control strategy should explicitly seek to maximize expected utility, instead of focusing solely on runtime progress metrics. It is important to keep in mind that the ultimate purpose of optimization strategies is to find high-quality solutions, not merely to make progress relative to (a possibly poor) previously discovered solution. An interesting direction for future work is to combine the schedule based and dynamic strategies.

When generating our static schedules, we exploit the knowledge that we are solving numerous problem instances from a class of problems, while dynamic strategies are problem class independent. It may seem that collecting the data for a performance database could be quite expensive. However, our results indicate that a relatively small database can be used to generate high quality restart schedules. The performance database used in our experiments required 50 runs each for 10 TSP instances, or 500 runs of 100000 iterations per performance database entry for a single GA configuration. *Note that this is comparable to the computational resources needed to tune a dynamic restart strategy for a single GA configuration* – for our dynamic strategy, we would need to try each candidate value of *StopThresh* several times on numerous TSP instances to find the value of *StopThresh* which yields the best average performance.

An important area for future research is scaling the approach for much larger resource bounds. As noted in Section 2, the meta-level search performed by *Synthesize-restart-schedule* becomes exponentially more expensive as T/k, the ratio of the resource bound to the schedule increment size, grows larger. Efficient, non-exhaustive algorithms for meta-level schedule optimization need to be developed in order to scale up the method significantly. In addition, evaluation of a single candidate schedule could be sped up significantly if efficient, statistical hypothesis ranking methods were used (c.f. [1]).

Our restart scheduling approach is algorithm independent, in that it can be applied to generating a restart schedule for any optimization algorithm. Furthermore, it is a straightforward extension to generate schedules which combine multiple algorithms for resource-bounded optimization, much as algorithm portfolios [7] combine multiple algorithms for satisficing algorithms. Currently, we are investigating an extension to the approach which redefines a schedule to be a set of *pairs* $S = \{(a_1, t_1), (a_2, t_2), ...(a_n, t_n)\}$, where the $a_1, ..a_n$ denote different algorithms (e.g., different GA configurations), and the $t_1, ..t_n$ denote their resource allocations (as in the restart schedules discussed in this paper).

References

1. S. Chien, J. Gratch, and M. Burl. On the efficient allocation of resources for hypothesis evaluation: A statistical approach. *IEEE Transactions on Pattern Analysis and Machine Intelligence*, 17(7):652–665, 1995.
2. R.J. Collins and D.R. Jefferson. Selection in massively parallel genetic algorithms. In *Proc. International Conf. on Genetic Algorithms (ICGA)*, pages 249–256, 1991.
3. Y. Davidor, T. Yamada, and R. Nakano. The ECOlogical Framework II: Improving GA performance at virtually zero cost. In *Proc. International Conf. on Genetic Algorithms (ICGA)*, pages 171–176, 1993.
4. K. DeJong. *An Analysis of the Behavior of a Class of Genetic Adaptive Systems*. PhD thesis, University of Michigan, Department of Computer and Communication Sciences, Ann Arbor, Michigan, 1975.
5. L.J. Eshelman and J.D. Schaffer. Preventing premature convergence in genetic algorithms by preventing incest. In *Proc. International Conf. on Genetic Algorithms (ICGA)*, pages 115–122, 1991.
6. D.E. Goldberg. *Genetic Algorithms in Search, Optimization and Machine Learning*. Addison-Wesley, 1989.
7. B.A. Huberman, R.M. Lukose, and T. Hogg. An economics approach to hard computational problems. *Science*, 275(5269):51–4, January 1997.
8. M. Hulin. An optimal stop criterion for genetic algorithms: a Bayesian approach. In *Proc. International Conf. on Genetic Algorithms (ICGA)*, pages 135–141, 1997.

A Comparative Study of Global and Local Selection in Evolution Strategies

Martina Gorges-Schleuter

Forschungszentrum Karlsruhe, Institute for Applied Computer Science
Postfach 3640, D-76021 Karlsruhe, Germany
e-mail: gorges@iai.fzk.de

Abstract. Traditionally, selection in Evolutionary Algorithms operates global on the entire population. In nature we rarely find global mating pools and thus we introduce a more-or-less geographical isolation in which individuals may interact only with individuals in the immediate locality, the local overlapping neighborhoods.

This paper studies two classes of diffusion models for Evolution Strategies (ES) where the decision for survival as well as the parent choice is performed locally only. The classes differ in that we either allow both parents to be chosen randomly from the neighborhood or one parent is chosen to be the centre individual and the other one is chosen randomly from the neighborhood. We introduce a notation for the diffusion model ES, give a theoretical analysis and present results of a numerical study.

1 Introduction

In the Evolution Strategy (ES) as introduced by Rechenberg [1] and Schwefel [2] as well as in the Genetic Algorithm (GA) as introduced by Holland [3] the evolution mechanism is imitated by using mutation and recombination to produce variation which is then subject to a selection process. Selection in GAs operates by assessing the individuals of the current population and give those with stronger fitness greater opportunities to reproduce. Selection in ES acts by generating a surplus of descendants, discarding the weakest and giving only the best the chance to reproduce, where mating chances are equal. In either case, we do have global knowledge and global rules under which the population evolves.

Promoted by the upcoming of parallel computers as well as the availability of local networks a new class of Evolutionary Algorithms (EA) had been introduced. These suggest the introduction of a continuous population structure. The model consists of a population of uniformly distributed individuals over a geographic region, which might be linear, planar or spatial. Interactions of individuals, especially the selection of partners for recombination and the selection of individuals for survival, are restricted to geographically nearby individuals, the local overlapping neighborhoods. This model is now widely referred to as diffusion model to reflect the process by which information, the characters the individuals carry, may propagate through the population structure. The essential difference to the traditional EA is the local behavior of the individuals.

Diffusion models have been introduced first for GAs [4, 5, 6]. Besides their nice properties concerning parallelization, the local selection GAs have a different behavior compared to their global selection counterparts. They promote global diversity and especially in those cases where we have a multi-modal, nonlinear environment frequently give better results [4, 5, 7, 8].

However, only little research has been done on diffusion models applied to ES. The LInear Cellular Evolution strategy (LICE) introduced by Sprave [9] seem to be the only algorithm in this category, the population structure is a ring and the parents are both selected randomly from the neighborhood.

We introduce in this paper the centric diffusion model ES where one parent is the local centre individual and the mating partner is selected randomly from the neighborhood. In addition, we allow parent choice with or without replacement and support further population structures. This paper starts in section 2 with theory. We formally introduce the various classes of diffusion model ES, outline the algorithm, describe the effects of self-mating occurring in ES whenever mother and father are chosen to be the same, and study the local and global selection methods in terms of a growth curve analysis. Section 3 is devoted to an empirical comparison of the various classes of diffusion model ES. The paper concludes in section 4 and gives an outlook on further work.

2   The Diffusion Model ES

2.1   The Notation

Schwefel and Rudolph introduced in [10] a notation for contemporary Evolution Strategies. They are now formally referenced to as

$$(\mu, \kappa, \lambda, \rho) - ES,$$

with $\mu \geq 1$ the number of parents,
$\kappa \geq 1$ the upper limit for life span,
$\lambda > \mu$, if $\kappa = 1$ the number of descendants,
$1 \leq \rho \leq \mu$ the number of ancestors for each descendant.

For $\kappa = 1$ this resembles the *comma-ES* and $\kappa = \infty$ denotes the *plus-ES*. Introducing a life span allows thus a gradual transition from either extremal form of a (μ, λ)-ES or a $(\mu + \lambda)$-ES and the number of ancestors allows the formulation of multi-parent recombination; $\rho = 2$ denotes the bisexual recombination.

We define a local selection Evolution Strategy (LES) as

$$(\mu, \kappa, \lambda/\mu, \rho, \nu) - LES,$$

with ν denoting the size of the neighborhood,
$\lambda/\mu \in I\!N$ the number of kids competing for survival,
$\rho \leq \nu$ the number of ancestors.

Let $\nu_i \in I^\nu$ denote the neighborhood induced by the population structure of any individual $a_i \in I^\mu, 1 \leq i \leq \mu$ and $I = A_x \times A_s$ is the space of individuals with

A_x denoting the set of object variables and A_s denoting the set of strategy parameters. Thus, ν_i is the set of individuals being in the reproduction community of a centre individual a_i.

In the following we assume $\kappa = 1$ and $\rho = 2$, i.e. concentrate on the comma-ES where parents of the next generation are chosen from the descendants only and use bisexual recombination. Thus, for short, we use the notation

$$(\mu, \lambda/\mu, \nu) - population\ structure$$

to denote a diffusion model ES with a given population structure.

2.2   The Algorithm

Starting from an initial population P^0 of μ individuals the generation transition from a population $P^t (t \geq 0)$ to the next population P^{t+1} is modelled as

$$P^{t+1} := \mu \times opt^\nu_{LES}(P^t)$$

where $opt^\nu_{LES} : I \to I$ defines the reproduction cycle as

$$opt^\nu_{LES} := sel_i \circ (mut \circ rec^\nu)^{\lambda/\mu} \quad (1 \leq i \leq \mu).$$

The selection operator in the traditional (μ, λ)-ES acts globally in the sense that out of λ descendants the μ best are chosen to form the next parent population. In the diffusion model ES the selection for survival act locally only and for each individual independently. Now, we have

$$sel_i : I^{\lambda/\mu} \to I \quad (1 \leq i \leq \mu)$$

which is performed independently μ times. In the following we assume still a generational approach with a distinguished parent and offspring population.

The mutation operator $mut : I \to I$ is not affected by the introduction of the concept of locality and thus is not further described here [10].

The recombination operator $rec^\nu : I^\nu \to I$ is defined as

$$rec^\nu := re \circ co_i \quad (1 \leq i \leq \mu)$$

with $co_i : I^{\nu_i} \to I^\rho$ chooses $1 \leq \rho \leq \nu$ parents, and
$re : I^\rho \to I$ creates one offspring by mixing the parent's characters.
The operator co_i acts locally only and selects ρ parents from the neighborhood ν_i for all a_i $(i = 1, \ldots, \mu)$. The operator re actually creates the descendant [10].

What remains to be described is how the parents are selected from within a neighborhood. An obvious way to adopt the parent selection method used in the traditional ES is to choose both parents randomly from a local neighborhood [9]. We call this *local parent selection* and denote it as co^l.

We propose in analogy to [6] to choose one parent to be the centre individual and to select only the second parent with uniform probability from the local neighborhood; this is denoted as co^c and called *centric parent selection*.

Now we are able to give an outline of a Diffusion Model Evolution Strategy.

Algorithm (Outline of a Diffusion Model Evolution Strategy)

initialize: $P^0 := \{a_1, a_2, \ldots, a_\mu\}$;
evaluate individuals in P^0;
$t := 0$;
terminate $:= FALSE$;
```
while (not terminate) do
    for i := 1 to i = μ do          /* for all individuals */
        for j := 1 to j = λ/μ do    /* for number of kids */
```
        select for reproduction:
            `if` (co_i^c) `then` a_i *becomes 1st parent* a_{i_1};
                `else` *choose* a_{i_1} *randomly from* ν_i;
          choose 2nd parent a_{i_2} *randomly from* ν_i;
        recombine:
           $a_i' := re(a_{i_1}, a_{i_2})$;
        mutate:
           $a_i'' := mut(a_i')$;
        evaluate a_i'';
        select for survival:
            `if` $(j = 1)$ `then` *add* a_i'' *to next population* $P^{t+1}(a_i) := a_i''$;
            `else if` $(a_i''$ *is better than* $P^{t+1}(a_i)$ $)$
                `then` *replace previous descendant* $P^{t+1}(a_i) := a_i''$;
```
        od
    od
```
    $t := t + 1$;
    `if` *(termination criterion fulfilled)* `then` *terminate* $:= TRUE$;
```
od
```

2.3 On Selfing

In the standard ES the parents are chosen from the entire population with replacement. The probability that both parents are the same increases with the decline of the pool size from which the parents are drawn. Thus, in local selection ES we expect to have an increased rate of self-mating or short selfing.

The consequence of selfing in an actual ES is, that an offspring is created from a single parent by mutation only as the recombination has no effect. If parent selection without replacement is used to exclude selfing this is denoted by a bar above the parent selection method: $\overline{co}$.

The number of different matings possible in the centric parent selection is ν with selfing and $\nu - 1$ without selfing. In the case of local parent selection we count $\nu(\nu+1)/2$ different mating possibilities if selfing is allowed and $\nu(\nu-1)/2$ otherwise. From this we can compute the rate of selfing. For the centric parent selection it is $1/\nu$ and for the local parent selection it is $\nu/\nu(\nu+1)/2 = 2/(\nu+1)$.

But, the main difference between co and $\overline{co}$ concerns the propagation of information. If selfing occurs in the centric parent selection method, then we have no propagation of information as the kid is a descendant from the centre individual itself.

2.4 Growth Curve Analysis

A standard technique to analyze selection methods is based on the examination of the growth curve of an initial single best individual over time by selection alone [11], i.e. neither recombination nor mutation are active. To extend the growth curve analysis to extinctive selection mechanisms we need to include both, the selection for reproduction and the selection for survival. This is done by selecting a pair of parents for reproduction according to co_i and define the child a_i'' to be any one of either parent. The selection for survival then selects the best offspring out of a local pool of size λ/μ to be included into the next reproduction cycle. The parent selection mechanisms differ in that the parents of each pool of competing offsprings are either a random sample taken from the local neighborhood in case of co^l or in the case of the centric parent selection co^c the pool consists of half siblings as the kids do have one parent in common.

Figure 1 shows the growth curves for a finite population of size 100 and $\lambda/\mu = 6$, a selection pressure commonly used with ES. The population structure is either a ring with $\nu = \{3, 5, 9\}$, i.e. the neighborhood includes the individual and the immediate $(\nu - 1)/2$ neighbor(s) to the right and left or a 10×10 torus with $\nu = 5$, i.e. the neighborhood includes an individual and its neighbors to the left, right, above, and below.

The legend of Figure 1 is sorted from weakest to strongest selection pressure. The strongest selection pressure is obtained when using a global selection pool. The fastest growth curve belongs to the standard (100,600)-ES which has been included as a reference. The two fastest growth curves of LES are for $\nu = \mu = 100$ being independent of the population structure, thus the name of the population structure is referenced to by *any*.

Fig. 1. Growth curves for local parent selection (l) and centric parent selection (c) without and with selfing (self) for the ring and the torus population structure.

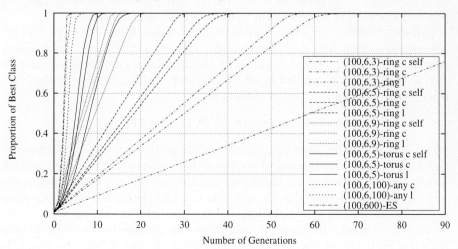

The remaining growth curves belong to local selection. For each neighborhood size and population structure there are three curves all shown in the same line type. That with the strongest selection pressure belongs to the co^l method and the middle one to co^c. The weakest pressure is achieved with the centric parent selection method without selfing $\overline{co}^c$ due to the fact that $1/\nu$ of the matings do have no propagation of the best class. The growth curve of a $(100, 6, 3) - ring$ is extremely slow taking 130 generations until the best class has overtaken the entire population.

If both parents are chosen randomly from within the neighborhood, then we have ν different possible self-matings and only a single one out of these is coupled with no propagation of the best class. We expect thus little differences in the growth curves of co^l and $\overline{co}^l$. The growth curve analysis showed that both curves are almost identical and thus have been omitted from Figure 1.

For the torus population structure the growth rate is extremely fast even though ν has been set to the smallest possible value. This is what we have expected as the propagation of the initially single best is now squarish. The ring population structure shows a much slower increase of the best class over time and the smaller the neighborhood size the slower the growth rate.

The growth curve analysis shows that the various parent selection methods in diffusion model ES introduce a wide range of selection pressure. In addition the diffusion model ES is coupled with a decrease of the loss of variability of the gene pool as discussed in [12].

3   Empirical Comparison

This section is devoted to numerical experiments for three objective functions: generalized Rastrigin function, Shekel's Foxholes, and a fractal function [13]. The implementation of our test environment is based on LICE-1.02 [9]. We added the centric parent selection method, the possibility to exclude self-mating and the support of further population structures. In this paper we focus on the ring population structure and the torus with a compact neighborhood.

All test functions are minimization problems taken from GENEsYs 1.0 [14]. The representation uses n object variables x_j ($1 \leq j \leq n$) and a single mean step size σ for all x_j as experiments with the diffusion model ES using multiple step sizes $\sigma_j, 1 \leq j \leq n$ failed in all cases. The mutation operator applied to a recombined individual a_i' is thus defined as

$$mut(a_i') = \sigma \cdot exp(\tau_0 \cdot N(0, 1) + \tau \cdot N(0, 1))$$

where $N(0, 1)$ denotes a random variable with expectation 0 and standard deviation 1. For comparison reasons we set the global mutation parameter τ_0 controlling the overall change of the mutability and the individual mutation parameter τ to the same values as used in [9]: $\tau_0 = 0.1$, $\tau = 0.3$. The recombination operator is discrete for the object variables x_j and intermediate for the step size.

For the objective functions f_5 and f_7 we run 20 experiments with 20 runs each. For each experiment we counted how often the global best was found. In the tables the average av gives the overall percentage of successful runs and gen gives the average number of generations until the global best was found. If selfing is allowed we give the average rate acc at which kids produced by self-mating are accepted to survive and become a parent.

3.1 Generalized Rastrigin Function

The generalized Rastrigin function is a multimodal and high-dimensional problem. It is known to be very difficult for ES.

$$f_7(\mathbf{x}) = n \cdot A + \sum_{i=1}^{n} x_i^2 - A \cdot \cos(2\pi x_i); \quad \mathbf{x} \in I\!\!R^n$$

$$n = 20; \quad A = 10; \quad -5.12 \le x_i \le 5.12$$

$$\mathbf{x}^* = (0, \ldots, 0); \quad f_7^* = 0$$

The individuals are initialized by setting the object variables $\forall i \; x_i = 512$ and the step size to $\sigma \in [0.5, 5]$. Table 1 summarizes the results for local and global selection ES. The columns gen reflect our results from the growth curve analysis. With an increase of the selection pressure induced by the chosen method co we observe a decrease of the number of generations until the population converges.

Table 1 shows also that the ring population structure is a better choice than the torus. In the extreme case of global parent selection, due to $\nu = \mu$, the centric method performed best. The standard ES ranks second and weakest is the method choosing both parents randomly.

Figure 2 shows the columns av for the ring. From this we see a better overall behavior of the diffusion model ES using the centric parent selection method compared to either the local parent selection or the standard ES. The higher explorative behavior of co^c and $\overline{co}^c$ give a high rate of convergence to the global optimum independently of the neighborhood size.

Table 1. Probability of finding the global optimum of f_7.

Strategy	co^l			$\overline{co}^l$		co^c			$\overline{co}^c$	
	av	gen	acc	av	gen	av	gen	acc	av	gen
(100,6,3)-ring	67.0	314	31.0	86.5	310	89.5	396	41.0	76.0	320
(100,6,5)-ring	45.0	272	18.8	61.5	270	70.5	308	18.7	70.5	290
(100,6,7)-ring	36.0	255	13.5	56.5	255	63.0	287	12.6	67.5	278
(100,6,9)-ring	34.5	244	10.4	56.5	247	65.0	276	9.6	66.5	271
(100,6,13)-ring	33.5	235	7.2	49.5	238	62.0	268	6.4	68.0	266
(100,6,25)-ring	37.5	228	3.8	45.0	229	65.0	259	3.2	69.5	259
(100,6,5)-torus	32.5	248	19.1	58.0	253	52.5	270	19.7	57.0	292
(100,6,9)-torus	34.5	235	10.5	54.5	238	65.0	264	9.6	56.5	269
(100,6,13)-torus	38.0	231	7.2	53.0	233	67.5	261	6.4	75.0	264
(100,6,100)-any	44.5	223	0.9	42.0	223	73.5	257	0.9	71.0	257
(100,600)-ES	56.5	193	1.7							

The diffusion model ES gets its highest gain from the local differentiation process when the neighborhood size is very small. In this case the centric method with selfing co^c performs best closely followed by the local method without selfing $\overline{co}^l$. On 3rd place comes $\overline{co}^c$. Local parent selection with selfing, i.e. LICE-1.02, ranks only 4th and weakest is the standard ES.

Fig. 2. Average behavior of the diffusion model ES for f_7.

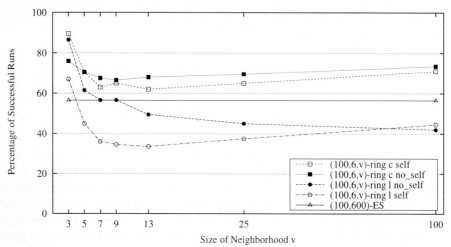

3.2 Shekel's Foxholes Function

The Shekel's Foxholes problem, widely known as the function F5 of De Jong's test suite, is known as a difficult problem for ES. The topology is an area-wide plateau with holes of different depth. With the standard ES the problem arises that once the population gets attracted from one of the holes it is almost impossible for the algorithm to leave it again. In fact in none of 200 runs of a (100,600)-ES the optimal solution was found.

$$\frac{1}{f_5(\mathbf{x})} = \frac{1}{K} + \sum_{j=1}^{25} \frac{1}{c_j + \sum_{i=1}^{2}(x_i - a_{ij})^6}; \quad \mathbf{x} \in I\!\!R^2$$

$$(a_{ij}) = \begin{pmatrix} -32 & -16 & 0 & 16 & 32 & -32 & \cdots & -32 & \cdots & 0 & 16 & 32 \\ -32 & -32 & -32 & -32 & -32 & -16 & \cdots & 16 & \cdots & 32 & 32 & 32 \end{pmatrix}$$

$$K = 500; \quad f_5(a_{1j}, a_{2j}) \approx c_j = j; \quad -65.536 \leq x_i \leq 65.536$$

$$\mathbf{x}^* = (-32, 32); \quad f_5^* \approx 1$$

The initial setting of the object variables was chosen far away from the holes $\forall i\, x_i = 500$ and the step size is $\sigma \in [1e-4, 1e4]$. From table 2 we conclude that for the function f_5 selfing is useful in combination with any parent selection method. With small ν the centric parent selection method co^c is the clear winner: the global best is found in almost all runs.

Table 2. Probability of finding the global optimum of Shekel's Foxholes problem.

Strategy	co^l			$\overline{co}^l$		co^c			$\overline{co}^c$	
	av	gen	acc	av	gen	av	gen	acc	av	gen
(100,6,3)-ring	93.5	188	35.0	26.0	230	99.0	200	51.0	74.5	261
(100,6,5)-ring	90.0	153	21.0	92.0	211	93.0	215	25.8	66.5	246
(100,6,9)-ring	90.0	156	11.8	84.5	191	77.5	232	13.2	47.5	249
(100,6,21)-ring	79.0	161	5.1	67.5	181	25.0	246	5.0	18.0	255
(100,6,100)-any	53.0	164	1.0	54.5	178	4.0	260	1.0	1.5	245

3.3 A Fractal Function

The objective function used in this section has been introduced by Bäck [13] and is a modification of the Weierstrass-Mandelbrot function. As pointed out the idea to design a fractal objective function was twofold. Firstly, the degree of complexity of a fractal function may be controlled by varying the fractal dimension $D \in [1, 2]$ and secondly, the fractal surface is likely to capture characteristics of noisy real-world problems.

$$f_{13}(\mathbf{x}) = \sum_{i=1}^{n} \left(\frac{C(x_i)}{C(1) \cdot |x_i|^{2-D}} + x_i^2 - 1 \right)$$

$$C(x) = \sum_{j=-\infty}^{\infty} \frac{1 - \cos\left(b^j x\right)}{b^{(2-D)j}}$$

$$n = 20; \quad D = 1.1; \quad b = 1.5; \quad -5.12 \le x_i \le 5.12$$

The global mutation parameter and the individual mutation parameter are set to $\tau_0 = 0.16, \tau = 0.33$ respectively, according to the suggestion of Schwefel [2]. The initial setting of the object variables is $x_i \in [-5, 5]$ and the step size is $\sigma \in [1e - 50, 1]$. The optimal solution of f_{13} is unknown. The termination criterion is a maximum of 300 generations.

Table 3. Quality of the final best solution of the fractal function f_{13}.

Strategy	co^l			co^c		
	median	best	worst	median	best	worst
(50,6,3)-ring	-0.0604	-0.0809	-0.0255	-0.0724	-0.0874	-0.0617
(50,6,3)-ring $\overline{co}$	-0.0609	-0.0853	-0.0447	-0.0701	-0.0859	0.0028
(50,6,5)-ring	-0.0580	-0.0693	-0.0345	-0.0623	-0.0746	-0.0450
(50,6,5)-ring $\overline{co}$	-0.0550	-0.0774	0.0176	-0.0556	-0.0777	0.0160
(50,300)-ES	-0.0595	-0.0682	-0.0416	-0.0595	-0.0703	-0.0415
(100,6,3)-ring	-0.0842	-0.2607	-0.0727	-0.0889	-0.6265	-0.0839
(100,6,3)-ring $\overline{co}$	-0.0819	-0.0889	-0.0703	-0.0905	-0.1719	-0.0804
(100,600)-ES	-0.0754	-0.0805	-0.0633	-0.0719	-0.0820	-0.0619

Table 3 gives the median, the best and worst final solution of 21 runs each. The population size used is either 50 or 100.

A standard (50,300)-ES using co^l (co^c) reaches a quality below 0 at generation 90 (65). The price for faster convergence of the standard ES is that at about generation 150 (190) we find only some fine tuning and at generation 200 (230) the entire population has focused to a single weaker solution. The diffusion model is different in that it needs about 110 generations to reach a quality below 0, but the variability of the gene pool is preserved for more generations and even at generation 500 we find some development in the population.

Comparing the parent selection methods we find the winner to be again the centric parent selection method with selfing co^c with the smallest neighborhood size ν, i.e. the method with the weakest selection pressure. Excluding selfing is of no help, in fact for $\mu = 50$ and $\nu = 5$ some runs even do not reach a quality below 0. The population size of 100 strengthens the results obtained for $\mu = 50$. The larger genepool yields a drastically increased quality of the final best.

4 Conclusions and Outlook

This paper introduced and compared two classes of diffusion model ES. Either of these has been varied by allowing or disallowing selfing. The growth curve analysis showed a significant weaker selective pressure of the diffusion model ES with ring population structure and small neighborhood size in comparison to either extreme global selection in diffusion model ES ($\nu = \mu$) or the standard ES. The 2-dimensional torus population structure has a significantly stronger selective pressure compared to the linear ring.

The empirical comparison showed a very strong behavior of the centric parent selection for all three test functions being superior to the local parent selection. The ability of diffusion model ES to preserve diversity in the population for longer periods of time compared to the traditional ES are the key to a very robust behavior for problems being previously resistant to ES.

The question if selfing is useful or harmful depends on the parent selection method. With the centric method decreasing the selective pressure by using selfing gives even better results. With local parent selection selfing might be harmful as it is for the Rastrigin Problem or useful as it is for Shekel's Foxholes and the fractal function.

The results presented in this paper used a diffusion model with a generational approach. An interesting open question is how the diffusion model ES will behave if a one-at-a-time generation transition is used.

Acknowledgment. The author like to thank Prof. Hans-Paul Schwefel for the discussion on the notation for diffusion model ES and Joachim Sprave for making LICE publicly available.

References

1. I. Rechenberg, *Evolutionsstrategie – Optimierung technischer Systeme nach Prinzipien der biologischen Information*, Frommann Verlag, Stuttgart (1973) in german
2. H.-P. Schwefel, *Numerical Optimization of Computer Models*, John Wiley & Sons (1981), english translation of the original edition by Birkhäuser, Basel (1977)
3. J. Holland, *Adaptation in Natural and Artificial Systems*, University of Michigan Press, Ann Arbor (1975)
4. B. Manderick, P. Spiessens, *Fine-grained Parallel Genetic Algorithm*, in Proc. of the 3rd Int. Conf. on Genetic Algorithms, Morgan Kaufmann (1989) 428–433
5. R. Collins, D. Jefferson, *Selection in Massively Parallel Genetic Algorithms*, in Proc. 4th Int. Conf. on Genetic Algorithms, Morgan Kaufmann (1991) 249–256
6. M. Gorges-Schleuter, *ASPARAGOS An Asynchronous Parallel Genetic Optimization Strategy*, in Proc. of the 3rd ICGA, Morgan Kaufmann (1989) 422–427
7. M. Gorges-Schleuter, *Explicit Parallelism of GAs through Population Structures*, Proc. of PPSN I, LNCS 496, Springer Verlag (1991) 150-159
8. M. Gorges-Schleuter, *Genetic Algorithms and Population Structures*, Doctoral dissertation, University of Dortmund (1991). Extended abstract in V. Plantamura et al (Eds.), Frontier Decision Support Concepts, Wiley, New York (1994) 261–319
9. J. Sprave, *Linear neighborhood Evolution Strategy*, Conf. on Evolutionary Programming (1994); *Software Package LICE-1.02*, both via http://ls11-www.informatik.uni-dortmund.de/people/joe
10. H.-P. Schwefel, G. Rudolph, *Contemporary Evolution Strategies*, Third Int. Conf. on Artificial Life, LNCS 929, Springer Verlag, Berlin (1995) 893–907
11. D. Goldberg, K. Deb, *A comparative analysis of selection schemes used in genetic algorithms*, in Foundations of Genetic Algorithms, Morgan Kaufmann (1991) 69–93
12. M. Gorges-Schleuter, *On Global and Local Selection in Evolution Strategies*, submitted to FOGA 5, Leiden (1998)
13. Th. Bäck, *Evolutionary Algorithms in Theory and Practice*, Oxford University Press, New York (1995)
14. Th. Bäck, *GENEsYs 1.0*, ftp://lumpi.informatik.uni-dortmund.de/pub/GA

UEGO, an Abstract Niching Technique for Global Optimization*

Márk Jelasity

Research Group on Artificial Intelligence
MTA-JATE, Szeged, Hungary
jelasity@inf.u-szeged.hu

Abstract. In this paper, UEGO, a new general technique for accelerating and/or parallelizing existing search methods is suggested. UEGO is a generalization and simplification of GAS, a genetic algorithm (GA) with subpopulation support. With these changes, the niching technique of GAS can be applied along with any kind of optimizers. Besides this, UEGO can be effectively parallelized. Empirical results are also presented which include an analysis of the effects of the user-given parameters and a comparison with a hill climber and a GA.

1 Introduction

In this section a short introduction to the history and motivation behind developing UEGO is given, but first let us state what the acronym means. UEGO stands for *Universal Evolutionary Global Optimizer*. However, it must be admitted from the start that this name is not over-informative, and the method is not even evolutionary in the usual sense. In spite of this we have kept the name for historical reasons.

1.1 Roots

The predecessor of UEGO was GAS, a steady-state genetic algorithm with subpopulation support. For more details on GAS the reader should consult [9].

GAS has several attractive features. Perhaps the most important of these is that it offers a solution to the so-called niche radius problem which is a common problem of many simple niching techniques such as *fitness sharing* ([3] or [4]), *simple iteration* or the *sequential niching* [2]. This problem is related to functions that have multiple local optima and whose optima are unevenly spread throughout the search space. With such functions the *niche radius* cannot be set correctly since if it is too small the search becomes ineffective and if it is too large those local optima that are too close to each other cannot be distinguished. The solution of GAS involves a cooling technique which enables the search to focus on the promising regions of the space, starting off with a relatively large radius that decreases as the search proceeds.

---

* This work was supported by the Hungarian Soros Fundation and FKFP 1354/1997.

However, the authors of GAS came in for a number of criticisms, one being that the algorithm was too much complex, and another that parallel implementation turned out to have many pitfalls associated with it.

1.2 Motivations

Although UEGO is based on GAS there are two major differences that were motivated by the need for a better parallel implementation and the requirement of using domain specific knowledge in an effective way.

The structure of the algorithm has been greatly simplified. As a result the parallel implementation is much easier and the basic ideas become more accessible. This is important because, as the results of the paper will show, UEGO performs similarly or better than the GA and the simple stochastic hill climber (SHC) on our test problems, and at the same time it can be parallelized better than these methods.

The new method is more abstract. The common part with GAS is the species creation mechanism and the cooling method. However, the species creation and cooling mechanism has been logically separated from the actual optimization algorithm, so it is possible to implement any kind of optimizers that work inside a species. This allows the adaptation of the method to a large number of possible search domains using existing domain specific optimizers while enjoying the advantages of the old GAS-style subpopulation approach.

In this paper an SHC is implemented as the optimizer algorithm. This choice is supported by results that show that the performance of the SHC is similar to that of the GA in many cases and sometimes may even be better (e.g. [12, 10, 13, 7]). In [5] a GA with very small population size (1) has been suggested for the graph coloring problem, which is in fact an SHC. Our results confirm that the SHC can indeed outperform the GA at least on the problems and parameter settings we considered.

1.3 Outline of the Paper

Section 2 describes UEGO; the basic concepts, the general algorithm and the theoretical tools that are used to set the parameters of the system based on a few user-given parameters. Section 3 discusses the experimental results that describe the effects of these parameters of the algorithm on the quality of the results and compares UEGO with a simple GA and an SHC. Section 4 then provides a short summary.

2 Description of UEGO

In this section the basic concepts, the algorithm, and the setting of the parameters are outlined. In UEGO, a domain specific optimizer has to be implemented. Wherever we refer to 'the optimizer' in the paper we mean this optimizer.

2.1   Basic Concepts

A key notion in UEGO is that of a *species*. A species can be thought of as a window on the whole search space. This window is defined by its *center* and a *radius*. The center is a solution, and the radius is a positive number. Of course, this definition assumes a *distance* defined over the search space. The role of this window is to localize the optimizer which is always called by a species and can see only its window, so every new sample is taken from there. This means that the largest step made by the optimizer in a given species is no larger than the radius of the given species. If the value of a new solution is better than that of the old center, the new solution becomes the center and the window is moved.

The radius of a species is not arbitrary; it is taken from a list of decreasing radii, the *radius list*. The first element of this list is always the diameter of the search space. If the radius of a species is the *i*th element of the list, then we say that the *level* of the species is *i*.

During the process of optimization, a list of species is kept by UEGO. The algorithm is in fact a method for managing this *species-list* (i.e. creating, deleting and optimizing species); it will be described in Section 2.2.

2.2   The Algorithm

Firstly, some parameters of EUGO will be very briefly mentioned more details of which can be found in Section 2.3.

As we mentioned earlier, every species has a fixed level. The maximal value for this level is given by a parameter called levels. Every valid level i (i.e. for levels from [1,levels]) has a radius value (r_i) and two fixed numbers of function evaluations. One is used when new species are created at a given level (new_i) while the other is used when optimizing individual species (n_i). To define the algorithm fully, one more parameter is needed: the maximal length of the above-mentioned species list (max_spec_num).

The basic algorithm is shown in Figure 1.

```
uego
        init_species_list()
        optimize_species( n[1] )
        for i = 2 to levels
                create_species( new[i]/length(species_list) )
                fuse_species( r[i] )
                shorten_species_list( max_spec_num )
                optimize_species( n[i]/length(species_list) )
                fuse_species( r[i] )
        rof
ogeu
```

Fig. 1. The basic algorithm of UEGO.

Now the procedures called by UEGO will be described.

Init_species_list. Create a new species list consisting of one species with a random center at level 1.

Create_species(evals). For every species in the list create random pairs of solutions in the window of the species, and for every such pair take the middle of the *section* connecting the pair. If the objective function value of the middle is worse than the pair values the members of the pair are inserted in the species list otherwise the species list remains unchanged. Every new species is assigned the actual level value (i in Figure 1).

The motivation behind this method is simple: to create species that are on different hills so ensuring that there is a valley between the new species. The parameter of this procedure is an upper bound of the function evaluations. Note that this algorithm needs a definition of section in the search space.

Fuse_species(radius). If the centers of any pair of species from the species list are closer to each other than the given radius, the two species are fused. The center of the new species will be the one with the better function value while the level is the minimum of the levels of the original species.

Shorten_species_list(max_spec_num). Deletes species to reduce the list length to the given value. Higher level species are deleted first.

Optimize_species(evals). Starts the optimizer for every species with the given evaluation number (i.e. every single species in the actual list receives the given number of evaluations). See Section 2.1.

Finally, let us make a remark about a possible parallel implementation. The most time-consuming parts of the basic algorithm is the creation and optimization of the species. Note that these two steps can be done independently for every species, so each species can be assigned a different processor. As our experimental results will clearly show, UEGO performs slightly better than the SHC and the GA even when the number of species is as high as 200.

2.3 Parameters of UEGO

The most important parameters are those that belong to the different levels: the radii and two numbers of function evaluations for species creation and optimalization (see Figure 1). In this section a method is described which sets these parameters using a few easy-to-understand parameters set by the user. In Section 3 further guidelines will be given on the meaning and setting of these remaining user-given parameters.

We will now make use of the notation introduced in Section 2.2. The user-given parameters are listed below. Short notations are also given below that will be used in equations in the subsequent sections.

evals (N): The maximal number of function evaluations the user allows for the whole optimization process. Note that the actual number of function evaluations may be less than this value.

levels (l): The maximal level value (see Figure 1).

threshold: (ν): The meaning of this parameter will be explained later.

max_spec_num: (M): The maximal length of the species list.

min_r: (r_l): The radius that is associated with the maximal level, i.e. levels.

The parameter setting algorithm to be described can use any four of the above five values while the remaining parameters are set automatically.

Speed of the optimizer. Before presenting the parameter setting method, the notion of the *speed* of the optimizer must be introduced. As explained earlier, the optimizer cannot make a larger step in the search space than the radius of the species it is working in. Given a certain number of evaluations, it is possible to measure the distance the given species moves during the optimization process. This distance can be approximated as a function of the radius and evaluations for certain optimizers using mathematical models or experimental results. This naturally leads to a notion of speed that will depend on the species radius and will be denoted by $v(r)$. As we will not give any actual approximations here, the reader should refer to [9].

The parameter-setting method is based on intuitive and reasonable *principles* which are based on personal experience with GAS. Though the parameters are still ad hoc since the principles are ad hoc as well, this method has advantages since these principles are much easier to understand, they can be expressed in human language, and the number of parameters are larger than the number of principles. These principles are now described below.

Principle of equal chance. At a level, every species moves a certain distance from its original center due to optimization. This principle ensures that every species will receive the number of evaluations that is enough to make at least a fixed distance at every level. This common distance is defined by $r_1\nu$. The meaning of threshold is now clear: it directly controls the distance a species is allowed to cover, so it actually controls the stability of the resulting species (i.e. the probability that they represent a local optimum). Recall that r_1 is always the diameter of the search space. Now the principle can be formalized:

$$\frac{v(r_i)n_i}{M} = r_1\nu \quad (i=2,\ldots,l) \tag{1}$$

Principle of exponential radius decreasing. This principle is quite straightforward; given the smallest radius and the largest one (r_l and r_1) the remaining radii are expressed by the exponential function

$$r_i = r_1(\frac{r_l}{r_1})^{\frac{i-1}{l-1}} \quad (i=2,\ldots,l). \tag{2}$$

Principle of constant species creation chance. This principle ensures that even if the length of species list is maximal, there is a chance of creating at least two more species for each old species. It also makes a strong simplification, that all the evaluations should be set to the same constant value.

$$new_i = 3M \quad (i = 2, \ldots, l) \tag{3}$$

Decomposition of N. Let us define $new_1 = 0$ for the sake of simplicity since new_1 is never used by UEGO. The decomposition of N results in the trivial equation

$$\sum_{i=1}^{l} n_i + new_i = (l-1)3M + \sum_{i=1}^{l} n_i = N \tag{4}$$

making use of (3) in the process. One more simplification is possible too; set $n_1 = 0$ whenever $l > 1$. Note that if $l = 1$ then UEGO reduces to the optimizer it uses for optimizing the species.

Expressing n_i from (1) and substituting it into (4) we can write

$$(l-1)3M + \sum_{i=2}^{l} \frac{Mr_1\nu}{v(r_i)} = N. \tag{5}$$

Using (2) as well, it is quite evident that the unknown parameters in (5) are just the user given parameters and due to the monotonity of this equation in every variable, any of the parameters can be given using effective numeric methods provided the other parameters are known. Using the above principles the remaining important parameters (n_i, new_i and r_i) can be evaluated as well. Note however that some of the configurations set by the user may be infeasible.

3   Experiments

In this section we will discuss the performance of UEGO on an NP-complete combinatorial optimization problem: the subset sum problem. A comparison with a simple GA, GENESIS [6] will be presented. As another result of the experiment the behavior of the parameters of UEGO will be illustrated.

3.1   Problem and Coding

In the case of the subset sum problem we are given a set $W = \{w_1, w_2, \ldots, w_n\}$ of n integers and a large integer M. We would like to find a $V \subseteq W$ such that the sum of the elements in V is closest to, without exceeding, M. This problem is NP-complete. Let us denote the sum of the elements in W by SW.

We created our problem instances in a similar way to the method used in [11]. The size of W was set to 50 and the elements of W were drawn randomly with a uniform distribution from the interval $[0, 10^{12}]$ instead of $[0, 10^3]$ (as was done in [11]) to obtain larger variance. According to the preliminary experiments, the larger variance of W results in harder problem instances which is important since comparing methods on almost trivial problems makes little sense. The problem instance used here turned out to be so tough that none of the methods employed could find an optimal solution. Based on the results of [8], M was set to $SW/2$. As was shown in [8], this is the most GENESIS-friendly setting, so there is no bias against GENESIS introduced by the problem instance.

We used the same coding and objective function as suggested in [11]. For a solution $(x = (x_1, x_2, \ldots, x_{50}))$,

$$f(x) = -(a(M - P(x)) + (1 - a)P(x))$$

where $P(x) = \sum_{i=1}^{50} x_i w_i$, and $a = 1$ when x is feasible (i.e. $M - P(x) \geq 0$) and $a = 0$ otherwise. Note that the problem is defined as a *maximization* problem.

3.2 The Optimizer and GA Settings

In UEGO, the optimizer was chosen to be a simple SHC as was discussed in the Introduction. In our implementation the SHC works as follows: mutate every bit of the solution with a given probability (but mutating one bit at least), evaluate the new solution and if it is better than or equal to the actual solution, it becomes the new actual solution. This type of SHC worked best in [12], as well. The mutation probability was set at $4/n$ where n is the chromosome length. This value was the same in all the experiments carried out including those with GENESIS. The other GA parameters were a population size of 50, 1-point crossover with probability 1, and elitist selection.

3.3 The Experiments

One of the two main goals of these experiments was to analyze the effects of the user-given UEGO parameters described in Section 2.3. To perform this analysis, several values were chosen for each parameter (see Table 1) then UEGO was run 50 times for every possible combination of these values. This meant that

evals	levels	max_spec_num	treshold	min_r
3000, 10000, 30000, 100000, 300000	2, 3, 5, 10	5, 10, 20, 40, 100, 200	automatically set	fixed to 1

Table 1. The values of the UEGO parameters. Experiments were performed for all combinations.

$5 \cdot 4 \cdot 6 \cdot 50 = 6000$ experiments were performed for one problem instance. Three problem instances were examined but since the results were similar in each case, only one problem instance is discussed below.

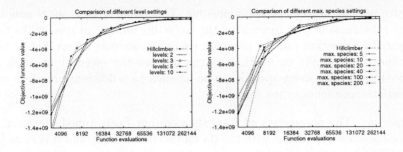

Fig. 2. With the various level settings, `max_spec_num` is 100 and for the differents max. species settings `levels` is 3.

Figure 2 shows the effects of the different parameter settings. As the plots are tipical it was inferred that the parameters of UEGO must be fairly robust for this particular problem class. Some interesting implications of this fact will be touched on in Section 3.4.

The other goal of the experiments was to make a comparision. Figure 3 shows the relevant results. Note that it was difficult to select the best and the worst

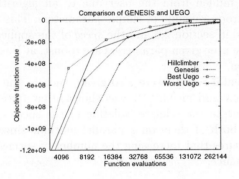

Fig. 3. The parameters for the best UEGO were `max_spec_num=20` & `levels=10`, and for the worst `max_spec_num=5` & `levels=2`.

performance because the curves cross, but the plots give a good approximation. Here SHC is simply UEGO with the setting of `levels=1`.

3.4 Discussion

UEGO *parameters.* As we saw in Figure 2, the parameters seem to be quite robust in this problem, a fact which has rather interesting implications. As was mentioned in Section 2.2, the interaction between the species is minimal so an effective parallel implemetation is possible. This point of view sheds new light on the robustness of the parameters: the larger the number of species the faster the parallel algorithm can be, provided enough processors are available. Good robustness here simply means that we can increase the speed by as much as a hundred times since every species can be handled by a different processor while the performance remains the same.

Comparison The parameters of GENESIS were not finely tuned; however, the author has some experience with the GA on this problem [8], and it is clear from Figure 3 at least that the GA is more sensitive to parameter setting. However, even if the parameter setting had been badly done, the parallel implementations of GAs cannot provide the speedup that UEGO can. So, after all, it is probably true in this case that the performance of UEGO is superior to that of a simple GA. In the case of SHC similar conclusions can be drawn: the application of the general UEGO technique to the SHC results in an increased quality of the solutions found.

4   Summary

In this paper, UEGO, a general technique for accelerating and/or parallelizing existing search methods was discussed. As was shown, most of the parameters of the system are hidden from the user due to an algorithm for calculating those parameters from a couple of simple parameters. This algorithm is based on *principles* stated in section 2.3 and the *speed* of the applied optimizer. It was also shown that the user-given parameters are robust, at least in the case of the subset sum problem.

Other experimental results were also given, such as the comparison of the technique with a GA and an SHC. It was shown, that UEGO is slightly better than both, and, due to the relative isolation of the species, UEGO should run much better than both of them on a parallel machine since the robustness of the parameters ensures that increasing the number of species does not result in decreasing performance.

5   Acknowledgements and a Note

I would like to thank my reviewers for their criticism, especially the one who — among very useful comments — clearly wrote:

The paper ... fails to show any benefit achieved by the new UEGO.

Though the situation is not that simple, there is some truth behind this statement. The coin has another side, however.

UEGO is a result of improving GAS. Every improvement made GAS less and less like a GA just like in [5]. Even the most sceptical readers have to admit that UEGO is not *worse* than the GA so they can interpret this paper as one more call for more comparisons between simple or multi-start stochastic hill climbers and GAs to find and describe the advantages of the later.

References

1. Thomas Bäck, editor. *Proceedings of the Seventh International Conference on Genetic Algorithms*, San Francisco, California, 1997. Morgan Kaufmann.
2. D. Beasley, D. R. Bull, and R. R. Martin. A sequential niche technique for multimodal function optimization. *Evolutionary Computation*, 1(2):101–125, 1993.
3. K. Deb. Genetic algorithms in multimodal function optimization. TCGA report no. 89002, The University of Alabama, Dept. of Engineering mechanics, 1989.
4. K. Deb and David E. Goldberg. An investegation of niche and species formation in genetic function optimization. In J. D. Schaffer, editor, *The Proceedings of the Third International Conference on Genetic Algorithms*. Morgan Kaufmann, 1989.
5. A. E. Eiben and J. K. van der Hauw. Graph coloring with adaptive genetic algorithms. *Journal of Heuristics*, 4(1), 1998.
6. J. J. Grefenstette. Genesis: A system for using genetic search procedures. In *Proceedings of the 1984 Conference on Intelligent Systems and Machines*, pages 161–165, 1984.
7. Hisao Ishibuchi, Tadahiko Murata, and Shigemitsu Tomioka. Effectiveness of genetic local search algorithms. In Bäck [1], pages 505–512.
8. Márk Jelasity. A wave analysis of the subset sum problem. In Bäck [1], pages 89–96.
9. Márk Jelasity and József Dombi. GAS, a concept on modeling species in genetic algorithms. *Artificial Intelligence*, 99(1):1–19, 1998.
10. A. Juels and M. Wattenberg. Stochastic hillclimbing as a baseline method for evaluating genetic algorithms. Technical report, UC Berkeley, 1994.
11. S. Khuri, T. Bäck, and J. Heitkötter. An evolutionary approach to combinatorial optimization problems. In *The Proceedings of CSC'94*, 1993.
12. M. Mitchell, J. H. Holland, and S. Forrest. When will a genetic algorithm outperform hillclimbing? In J. D. Cowan et al., editors, *Advances in Neural Information Processing Systems 6*. Morgan Kaufmann, 1994.
13. Mutsunori Yagiura and Toshihide Ibaraki. Genetic and local search algorithms as robust and simple optimization tools. In Ibrahim H. Osman and James P. Kelly, editors, *Meta-Heuristics: Theory and Application*, pages 63–82. Kluwer Academic Publishers, 1996.

Development of Problem-Specific Evolutionary Algorithms

Alexander Leonhardi[1], Wolfgang Reissenberger[1], Tim Schmelmer[2],
Karsten Weicker[3], and Nicole Weicker[1]

[1] Universität Stuttgart, Fakultät Informatik, Germany,
email: {leonhaar,reissenb,weicker}@informatik.uni-stuttgart.de
[2] University of Kansas, Department of Electrical Engineering and Computer Science,
email: tim_schmelmer@hotmail.com
[3] Universität Tübingen, Wilhelm–Schickard–Institut für Informatik, Germany,
email: weicker@informatik.uni-tuebingen.de

Abstract. It is a broadly accepted fact that evolutionary algorithms (EA) have to be developed problem–specifically. Usually this is based on experience and experiments. Though, most EA environments are not suited for such an approach. Therefore, this paper proposes a few basic concepts which should be supplied by modern EA simulators in order to serve as a toolkit for the development of such algorithms.

1 Introduction

Theoretical work as well as practical experience demonstrate the importance to progress from fixed, rigid schemes of evolutionary algorithms (EA) towards a problem–specific processing of optimization problems. Since the "No Free Lunch" theorem [WM97] proves that there is no algorithm which performs better than any other algorithm for all kinds of possible problems, it is useless to judge an algorithm irrespectively of the optimization problem. Therefore, it is necessary to find a suitable algorithm for each problem. Experience has shown that the adaptation of a problem to standard evolutionary algorithms is frequently a difficult task since a fixed representation of the search space is required (e.g. bit strings for genetic algorithms or real valued tuples for evolution strategies). Very often it is not even possible to fit the problem in the structure of the standard algorithm's search space (e.g. structural optimization [Kaw96], optimization of facility layout [AAD97], or job scheduling [FRC93]). Coding complex data structures by simple lists of bits or real values leads to the problem that there is often no one–to–one relation between these lists and the problem instances. Hence, problem knowledge is either necessary in repair operators to deal with invalid solutions or in special operators tailored to the problem.

Most existing EA simulators (e.g. [Gre90,VBT91]) offer standard algorithms like genetic algorithms or evolution strategies with invariable representations. There are only few simulation environments for evolutionary algorithms with complex high–level data structures like matrices, trees, or other combined data types (e.g. GAME [DKF93]). For instance, such data structures are used in [MHI96,BMK96].

In addition, there are numerous new flexible ideas: e.g. adaptation of evolutionary operators is presented in [SS94,Her96], the programming language RPL2 ([SR94]) uses models of structured populations, and several hybrid algorithms as combinations of standard operators from different EA are mentioned in [WGM94,IdGS94,DPT96]. Usually, those concepts are not supported by standard systems in general. Therefore, there is no possibility to test those algorithms for new applications in an uniform environment.

As a consequence, a new extensive conceptual framework for the design of evolutionary algorithms is proposed. It supports arbitrary problem representations, construction and testing of operators, and comparison of different user–defined algorithms. All well–known fields of evolutionary algorithms like genetic algorithms [Hol75,Gol89], evolution strategies [BHS91], genetic programming [Koz92], evolutionary programming [Fog92] as well as most other imaginable algorithms are possible in this framework.

The essential concepts for EA simulators are presented in Section 2. Section 3 discusses how these concepts are realized in a prototype GENOM. The ability and power of such a system is exemplified in Section 4. The paper concludes with remarks and aspects of future work in Section 5.

2 Concepts

A system for the development of problem–specific evolutionary algorithms should enable the user to find suitable algorithms for a concrete problem without restricting system constraints. Its purpose is to clarify which algorithm should be implemented efficiently.

2.1 Distinction Phenotype – Genotype

The first important concept is the strict separation of problem formulation and evolutionary method. If different methods should be tested and compared for a problem, it is indispensable to define the problem independently from the considered method in order to have a common platform for the evaluation of the methods.

Such separation results in two completely different views of an individual. On the one hand, there is the phenotypic representation for the problem in order to evaluate the individual by the fitness function. On the other hand, the algorithms only see an encoded individual – a genotype – to which the evolutionary operators are applied. Decoding – and if necessary encoding – functions switch between those views of an individual (compare Figure 1). Such a biologically oriented approach was already presented in [Ban94,TGF96].

Several advantages result from this two–sided view: First, it is possible to adapt the phenotypic representation to the problem independently from the EA, e.g. permutations may be used for a travelling salesperson problem although an

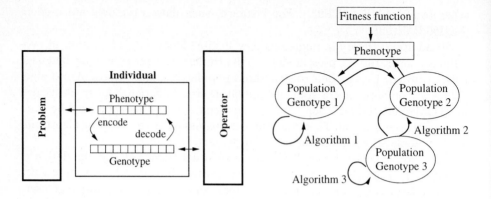

Fig. 1. Separation of problem and method (left) and interplay of populations with different genotypes in one experiment (right)

evolution strategy may be used to search for the optimum. In order to take advantage of this approach, arbitrary, universal data types for the phenotypic representation are demanded. They result in straight and simple fitness functions not restricted by method–depending representations. Second, the encapsulation of the fitness function means the fitness function needs only to be implemented once, independent of the number of methods to be tested.

On the method side, the genotypic representation should be as powerful as the phenotypic representation – they might be identical. Standard algorithms are possible with a decoding function from the standard genotypic representation to the phenotype. Finally, very sophisticated codings may be used, where e.g. the decoding function uses problem knowledge for genetic repair. An encoding function is only necessary if either existing good solutions from the problem side should be used for initialization in the method or several methods with different genotypes should be combined.

2.2 Modular operators

Another concept is the separation of operators from the representation in order to support a high re–usability and universal use of the operators. This may be reached by parameterization of the operators. Predefined standard operators should be supported as well as user–defined operators which are adjusted to specific user–defined genotypes (see Section 2.1). A modular composition allows to reuse previously defined operators. A high level of abstraction should enable the user to concentrate on the algorithms and operators and protect him from implementation details.

In addition to the toolbox character of the operators, complete evolutionary algorithms may be interpreted as operators too and used accordingly. In particular, this takes effect together with the experiment concept discussed in the next section.

2.3 Experiments

In order to combine different methods, a new concept is necessary in which the method does not represent the top instance. For that purpose, *experiments* are defined, uniting several populations with different methods and different genotypes for a problem. This enables migration between populations with identical genotype, e.g. in structural populations ([SR94]) and all parallel models of evolutionary algorithms. In addition, individuals may be exchanged among populations with different genotypes using the encoding and decoding functions. That is how methods, e.g. genetic algorithm and evolution strategy, may be combined which are incomparable otherwise (compare Figure 1). This experiment concept enables new adapted evolutionary concepts, e.g. with several operators, hybrid methods, or multiply nested loops. A system as open as possible is desired.

3 Genom

The proposed concepts have been implemented in a first prototype of a system GENOM (GENOM is an ENvironment for Optimization Methods). Altogether, GENOM is a system, which allows gradually getting into the development and design of problem–specific evolutionary algorithms. From the adaption of standard algorithms loaded from libraries to the definition of new genotypes and operators all gradations of algorithm development are possible. From that point of view, it is an open system in which great importance was attached to the fact not to exclude any conceivable adaption. In this section, the realization of the concepts in GENOM is explained.

3.1 Phenotype and Genotype

In order to obtain a maximum of flexibility, phenotype and genotype can be arbitrary data types. Both types are constructed in the same manner. They are constructed from types like real values, bits, integers, or permutations, called *atoms*, which are arranged into arbitrary structures like e.g. lists, matrices, tuples, or trees, called *cells*. On the top level, these cells are arranged into lists of arbitrary but fixed length. This enables standardization of coding and decoding. Figure 2 shows an example of an individual containing a pair cell, a matrix cell and a tree cell.

The transformation between phenotype and genotype is defined by a pair of functions: the *coding* and *decoding* function. The fixed structure of pheno- and genotype as a list of cells makes it feasible to construct the coding and decoding function according to a fixed scheme. Those schemes are based on so–called *elementary coding schemes*, which are pairs of functions describing the bidirectional transformation between tuples of cells, e.g. between a pair of real values and a list of bits. A combination of such elementary coding schemes together with a mapping of the genotype and phenotype cells to the input and output positions form the *coding schemes* (see also Figure 2). By such a mapping, the coding and decoding functions are defined simultaneously through the functions of the elementary coding schemes.

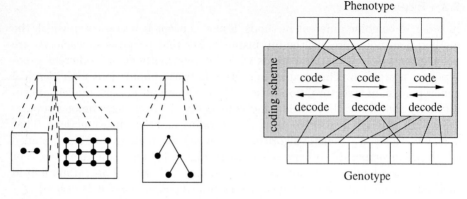

Fig. 2. Example of an individual (left) and structure of coding schemes (right)

3.2 Operators and experiments

Experimental frameworks like GENOM are intended to experiment with algorithms in order to find appropriate data structures and evolutionary algorithms to solve a given problem. Hence *experiments* contain a description of the problem (phenotype and fitness function), a collection of populations, and a top–level operator. Each population contains the genotype of its individuals and a coding scheme describing the conversion between the genotype and phenotype. Using these coding schemes, individuals can be properly migrated between populations.

Upon these populations, arbitrary methods can be defined. The methods are classified according to their scope. On the lower level, operators transform cells into cells or individuals into individuals (e.g. mutation, crossover). On the higher level, algorithms and methods work on a single population (e.g. a genetic algorithm or an evolution strategy) or even on multiple populations like a migration operator. All these methods can be parameterized and stored in libraries to achieve a maximum of flexibility and good re–usability.

Experimenting with evolutionary algorithms requires a tailored language for their definition. LEA$^+$ (Language for Evolutionary Algorithms), the definition language used in GENOM, is such a language, where experiments, individuals, coding schemes, and operators can be defined.

4 Examples

The following examples are intended to clarify how the different concepts interlock in reality. Moreover, the potential of such a system is demonstrated. The examples were realized with GENOM.

4.1 Example 1: Open–Shop Scheduling problem (OSSP)

The first example is an OSSP, which deals with the problem of generating an efficient production schedule. A number of jobs and a number of machines to process the jobs are given. Each job is composed of a set of tasks which must each be executed on a different machine for a task–specific amount of time. Neither the order of jobs, nor the order of tasks within each job are fixed and can therefore vary between two valid schedules. The phenotype is defined as a list of cells, where each cell contains the timetable for one machine.

Three experiments are based on this problem. The first experiment uses permutations to represent the schedule, the second experiment applies a genetic algorithm with a standard binary representation, while the last experiment represents the schedule by a matrix. All three experiments use the standard structure of evolutionary algorithms (recombine, mutate, select). Each experiment defines its own operators `Recombine` and `Mutate`, while all experiments use the same `Select` operator (Best Select).

This example demonstrates that the fitness function needs only to be defined once independently from the three different genotypes and algorithms. As a consequence, the results can be compared very easily since they all use the same phenotype and the same fitness function.

1. **Permutations**
   The outline for this experiment is described in [FRC93]. The genotype is a permutation of pairs (i, j), where i is the job's number and j the number of the task. It is implemented as a single cell containing the permutation. The `Recombine` operator takes two permutations, selects some random positions from the first one, and fills in the empty positions with the missing elements in consideration of the order in the second permutation. The `Mutate` operator is the 2-opt operator (e.g. [LK73]), which takes a subsequence of the permutation and reverses it. In addition, the decoding function optimizes an individual by moving elements of the permutation to the earliest possible slot. This is an example for the very powerful mechanism of coding schemes.

2. **Binary Coding**
   The coding of this experiment is based on the coding to a permutation as used in the experiment described above. Afterwards the permutation is coded into a binary string, which allows standard operators used in genetic algorithms. Hence, the genotype is a list of cells, where each cell contains one single bit.

3. **Matrix Representation**
   In this experiment, the genotype is a single cell containing a matrix. The first column of this matrix contains the job's number. The rest of each row forms a permutation, which defines the order in which the tasks for the respective job have to be executed, e.g. in the left individual of Table 1, job 4 executes its tasks in the order $1, 2, 3, 4, 5$. The order of the rows defines a priority, i.e. if there exists a conflict, which team should be granted execution first, the team from the upper row is preferred.

individual 1   individual 2   selection scheme   result

4	1	2	3	4	5
2	2	3	4	5	1
1	3	4	5	1	2
5	4	5	1	2	3
3	5	1	2	3	4

4	5	4	3	2	1
3	1	5	4	3	2
5	2	1	5	4	3
1	3	2	1	5	4
2	4	3	2	1	5

*		*	*	
	*	*		*
*	*			*
		*		

4	1	5	3	4	2
2	2	3	4	5	1
1	3	2	1	5	4
5	4	5	2	1	3
3	1	5	2	4	3

Table 1. Recombination of two matrix individuals

The recombination operator `Recombine` works similarly as the respective operator for the permutation coding. Table 1 shows a selection matrix and the result, when the operator is applied to the two individuals. The `Mutate` may switch two rows or use the 2-opt operator for permutations working on single rows, leaving the first column unmodified. This is an example for evolutionary operators tailored to the problem structure.

This example shows how the same problem can be coded into different genotypes although the same standard algorithm is used. Only the operators used in the algorithm have to be specific to the genotype.

4.2 Example 2: Travelling Salesperson Problem (TSP)

This example shows the flexibility of the experiment concept and the ability to combine different codings. Two optimization algorithms, a genetic and a threshold algorithm, are combined to form a new evolutionary algorithm. The problem to be optimized is a TSP problem and is represented by a permutation of the cities' indices. The length of the round trip through these cities is the fitness function to be minimized. Three experiments are applied to this problem.

1. **Threshold Algorithm (TA)**
   The threshold algorithm works directly on the permutation and uses the identity coding. The mutation of the individuals is done with the 2-opt operator.
2. **Genetic Algorithm (GA)**
   The second experiment is a classical genetic algorithm. Hence, the permutation has to be coded into a list of bits which is done in such a way that decoding always results in a valid permutation. A three–point–crossover is used for the recombination of individuals and a random inversion of bits for mutation. The individuals of the next generation are selected using an elitist proportional selection operator.
3. **Combined Algorithm (GA + TA)**
   This experiment contains a genetic algorithm interacting with a threshold algorithm. After every 20 generations, a few of its individuals are optimized with the threshold algorithm. Their results are migrated back and the 20

best individuals are selected for the next generation of the genetic algorithm. Here, two conceptually completely different algorithms are combined.

Figure 3 shows the fitness of the best individual displayed over the number of evaluated individuals for a typical example of the experiments described above. To show the effects more clearly, only the threshold algorithm with the best result is considered in the curve of the combined algorithm. It corresponds to the peaks in the diagram after each twentieth generation of the genetic algorithm. Although this paper is not concerned with comparing the algorithms or finding optimal parameter values, the experiments indicate that a combination of methods can do better than each of them alone.

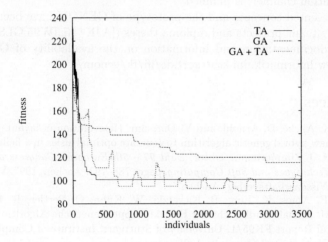

Fig. 3. The fitness of the best individual for the threshold algorithm, the genetic algorithm, and for a combination of both.

5   Remarks and Future Work

Summarizing, the proposed concepts define a very powerful tool for the design of evolutionary algorithms. All standard representations and methods (compare Chapter C1 and C3 in [BFM97]) are supported by an unifying foundation. The separation of problem formulation, coding, and algorithms has proved to be very useful. Once a problem, coding, or algorithm has been defined it can be used in various combinations and experiments (e.g. the genetic algorithm in the experiments above). Further flexibility in adapting an algorithm to a problem is facilitated by the powerful data structures for geno- and phenotype.

Nevertheless, there is still conceptual work necessary in order to integrate more general arbitrary methods to evaluate and compare experiments with different algorithms. A special topic for future work will be a general concept for the handling of constraints. So far, only repair functions are possible, e.g. as part of the decoding function ([VM97]). Finally, polymorphic and object–oriented models should be integrated into the coding concept. Furthermore, novel concepts and developments are to be expected for a general standardized EA simulation environment. This work is intended as a first step in that direction.

The purpose of GENOM is to provide a standard platform for development and evaluation of suitable and adapted representations and algorithms. For practical use, those algorithms have to be re–implemented in the application environment. A standard library of operators, codings, and algorithms is on the way to be developed. Additionally, the integration of an existing prototype for defining and running evolutionary algorithms in a distributed environment with communication channels is planned.

The presented concepts and the prototype of GENOM have been developed in student's team–projects and diploma theses ([AJK$^+$95,JW95,GLS97,Leo97]). For more documentation and information on the availability of GENOM see http://www.informatik.uni-stuttgart.de/ifi/fk/genom/ .

References

[AAD97] K. Alicke, D. Arnold, and V. Dörrsam. (R)evolution in layout–planning – a new hybrid genetic algorithm to generate optimal aisles in a ficility layout. In H.-J. Zimmermann, editor, *Eufit 97 – 5th European Congress on Intelligent Techniques and Soft Computing*, pages 788–793, Aachen, 1997. Verlag Mainz, Wissenschaftsverlag, Aachen.

[AJK$^+$95] F. Amos, K. Jung, B. Kawetzki, W. Kuhn, O. Pertler, R. Reißing, and M. Schaal. Endbericht der Projektgruppe Genetische Algorithmen. Technical Report FK95/1, University of Stuttgart, Institute of Computer Science, Dept. Formal Concepts, 1995. german.

[Ban94] W. Banzhaf. Genotype-phenotype-mapping and neutral variation — a case study in genetic programming. In Davidor et al. [DSM94].

[BB91] R.K. Belew and L.B. Booker, editors. *Proceedings of the Fourth International Conference on Genetic Algorithms – ICGA V*, San Mateo, California, 1991. Morgan Kaufmann.

[BFM97] T. Bäck, D.B. Fogel, and Z. Michalewiez, editors. *Handbook of Evolutionary Computation*. IOP Puplishing Ltd and Oxford University Press, 1997.

[BHS91] T. Bäck, F. Hoffmeister, and H.-P. Schwefel. A survey of evolution strategies. In Belew and Booker [BB91].

[BMK96] C. Bierwirth, D. Mattfeld, and H. Kopfer. On permutation representations for scheduling problems. In Voigt et al. [VERS96].

[DKF93] Laura Dekker, Jason Kingdon, and J. R. Filho. *GAME Version 2.01, User's Manual*. University College London, 1993.

[DPT96] D. Duvivier, Ph. Preux, and E.-G. Talbi. Climbing up NP–hard hills. In Voigt et al. [VERS96].

[DSM94] Y. Davidor, H.-P. Schwefel, and R. Maenner, editors. *Parallel Problem Solving from Nature – PPSN III*, volume 866 of *Lecture Notes in Computer Science*, Berlin, 1994. Springer-Verlag.

[Fog92] D.B. Fogel. An analysis of evolutionary programming. In D.B. Fogel and J. W. Atmar, editors. *Proceedings of the First annual Conference on Evolutionary Programming*, La Jolla, 1992. Evolutionary Programming Society.

[FRC93]   H.-L. Fang, P. Ross, and D. Corne. A promising genetic algorithm approach to job-shop scheduling, rescheduling and open-shop scheduling problems. In *Proceedings of the Fifth Int. Conf. on Genetic Algorithms*, pages 375–382. Morgan Kaufmann Publishers, 1993.

[GLS97]   M. Großmann, A. Leonhardi, and T. Schmidt. Abschlußbericht der Projektgruppe Evolutionäre Algorithmen. Technical Report 2, University of Stuttgart, Institute of Computer Science, 1997. german.

[Gol89]   D.E. Goldberg. *Genetic Algorithms in Search, Optimization and Machine Learning*. Addison Wesley, Reading, 1989.

[Gre90]   J.J. Grefenstette. *A User's Guide to GENESIS, Version 5.0*, 1990.

[Her96]   M. Herdy. Evolution strategies with subjective selection. In Voigt et al. [VERS96].

[Hol75]   J.H. Holland. *Adaptation in Natural and Artificial Systems*. The University of Michigan Press, Ann Arbor, 1975.

[IdGS94]   H. Iba, H. de Garis, and T. Sato. Genetic programming with local hill-climbing. In Davidor et al. [DSM94].

[JW95]   K. Jung and N. Weicker. Funktionale Spezifikation des Software–Tools EA-GLE. Technical Report FK95/2, University of Stuttgart, Institute of Computer Science, Dept. Formal Concepts, 1995. german.

[Kaw96]   B. Kawetzki. Topologieoptimierung diskreter Tragwerke mittels Evolutionsstrategien am Beispiel ebener Fachwerke. Master's thesis, University of Stuttgart, 1996. german.

[Koz92]   J.R. Koza. *Genetic Programming*. MIT Press, 1992.

[Leo97]   A. Leonhardi. Eine Beschreibungssprache für Evolutionäre Algorithmen. Master's thesis, University of Stuttgart, Institute of Computer Science, 1997. german.

[LK73]   S. Lin and B. Kernighan. An efficient heuristic procedure for the traveling salesman problem. *Operations Res.*, 21:498–516, 1973.

[MHI96]   M. McIlhagga, P. Husbands, and R. Ives. A comparison of search techniques on a wing–box optimisation problem. In Voigt et al. [VERS96].

[SR94]   P.D. Surry and N.J. Radcliffe. RPL2: A language and parallel framework for evolutionary computing. In Davidor et al. [DSM94].

[SS94]   M. Sebag and M. Schoenauer. Controlling crossover through inductive learning. In Davidor et al. [DSM94].

[TGF96]   S. Tsutsui, A. Ghosh, and Y. Fujimoto. A robust solution searching scheme in genetic search. In Voigt et al. [VERS96].

[VBT91]   H.-M. Voigt, J. Born, and J. Treptow. *The Evolution Machine, Manual, Version 2.1*. Institute for Informatics and Computing Techniques, Berlin, 1991.

[VERS96]   H.-M. Voigt, W. Ebeling, I. Rechenberg, and H.-P. Schwefel, editors. *Parallel Problem Solving from Nature – PPSN IV*, volume 1141 of *Lecture Notes in Computer Science*, Berlin, 1996. Springer-Verlag.

[VM97]   D. Vigo and V. Maniezzo. A genetic/tabu thresholding hybrid algorithm for the process allocation problem. *Journal of Heuristics*, 3(2):91–110, 1997.

[WGM94]   D. Whitley, V.S. Gordon, and K. Mathias. Lamarckian evolution, the baldwin effect and function optimization. In Davidor et al. [DSM94].

[WM97]   D.H. Wolpert and W. G. Macready. No free lunch theorems for optimization. *IEEE Transactions On Evolutionary Computation*, 1(1):67–82, April 1997.

The Effects of Control Parameters and Restarts on Search Stagnation in Evolutionary Programming

K.E. Mathias, J.D. Schaffer, L.J. Eshelman, M. Mani

Philips Research, Briarcliff Manor NY 10510, USA
kem/ds1/lje/mxm@philabs.research.philips.com

Abstract. Previous studies concluded that the best performance from an evolutionary programming (EP) algorithm was obtained by tuning the parameters for each problem. These studies used fitness at a pre-specified number of evaluations as the criterion for measuring performance. This study uses a complete factorial design for a large set of parameters on a wider array of functions and uses the mean trials to find the global optimum when practical. Our results suggest that the most critical EP control parameter is the perturbation method/rate of the strategy variables that control algorithm search potential. We found that the decline of search capacity limits the difficulty of functions that can be successfully solved with EP. Therefore, we propose a soft restart mechanism that significantly improves EP performance on more difficult problems.

1 Introduction

The conventional wisdom in Evolutionary Programming (EP)[1] indicates that no single robust parameter set exists that is suitable for a wide range of functions [7, 6, 1]. The user often needs to search for an effective parameter set for each new problem. While at some level this must be true (such as all possible problems), there is still much to be learned about how EP algorithms behave on characterizable landscapes. Furthermore, there is also the possibility that modifications to the algorithm can be invented that provide enhanced robustness for some (perhaps quite large) classes of problems.

With this general aim, we conducted a series of experiments that differ in several important aspects from those already published. During these experiments we observed that the search would often spend a very large number of trials making little or no progress. This was because the strategy variables used to perturb the problem variables became so small that the population was only capable of creeping. A soft restart mechanism, used in other evolutionary algorithms [3], was implemented as part of the EP search. We reasoned that a soft restart that retained the best individual and used it to seed the rest of the population would provide the search potential to escape attraction basins that did not contain the global optimum.

---

[1] Despite the similarities between EP and Evolutionary Strategies (ES), there are still significant differences. This work follows the traditions of EP.

2 Background

Our experiments used the basic EP algorithm as described by Fogel [5] and others[2]. Each individual is represented as a set of problem variables, $x_i, i = 1, n$, and a corresponding set of strategy variables, $\sigma_i, i = 1, n$, used to mutate the problem variables to produce offspring. All variables are usually encoded as real-valued numbers to full machine precision. After evaluating the individuals in the population, each produces a single offspring by perturbing its problem variables, adding a deviate drawn from a Gaussian distribution with zero mean and the corresponding strategy variable as the standard deviation. The strategy variables are similarly perturbed:

$x_i' = x_i + \sigma_i N_{x_i}(0, 1)$

$\sigma_i' = \sigma_i + \sigma_i \alpha N_{\sigma_i}(0, 1)$

where the primed value is the value assigned to the offspring, N(0,1) is a zero-mean unit-variance normal deviate, and α is an exogenously-set scaling parameter. An alternative perturbation method for the strategy variables is to use a lognormal [2] rather than a Gaussian distribution according to:

$\sigma_i' = \sigma_i exp(\tau N_i(0, 1) + \tau' N_j(0, 1))$

$\tau = (\sqrt{2\sqrt{n}})^{-1}$

$\tau' = (\sqrt{2n})^{-1}$

where $N_j(0, 1)$ is a normal deviate drawn once for each individual, while the other normal deviates are drawn for each x_i and σ_i. After the offspring are evaluated, survivors for the following generation are selected via a tournament. Tournament selection is accomplished by comparing the fitness of each individual (offspring and parents) against a specified number of randomly selected competitors, and a point is awarded to the individual for each competition won (i.e., a better fitness than the competitor). Those individuals with the most points form the population of the next generation.

We reviewed several papers describing work that tested the performance of EP algorithms while varying several of their parameters [7, 6, 1]. The test functions used in these works overlapped considerably as shown in Table 1, and the performance measure was the fitness of the best solution found at a pre-specified number of evaluations (trials) for multiple runs. Table 1 also lists the number of parameters used for each function in this study. Saravanan et al. [7] varied the method for perturbing the strategy variables and concluded that the lognormal method of mutation worked better for the Parabola and Ackley functions while Gaussian mutation worked better on the Rosenbrock function.

Gehlhaar et al. [6] started all initial populations in a small region quite far from the optimum, forcing the population to migrate toward the optimum. They compared σ-first/last[3] strategies, various tournament sizes and population sizes in a dependent fashion. They found that the σ-first strategy performed best

---

[2] We would like to thank N. Saravanan for providing us with experimental EP code.
[3] The σ-first strategy alters the strategy variables before generating offspring, while the σ-last strategy generates offspring from parental strategy parameters and then alters the strategy variables which the offspring inherits.

Table 1. Test functions and the number of problem variables used in previous comparisons. The † indicates that the global optimum was shifted from the origin.

Function	Saravanan et al.	Gehlhaar et al.	Angeline et al.	This Study
Parabola	3, 20, 20†	10, 20, 30	3, 30, 30†	3
Bohachevsky	2		2	2
Rosenbrock	2	10, 20, 30	2	2, 4
Ackley	20	10, 20, 30	20	20
Rastrigin		10, 20, 30		20
Schwefel				10
Griewank				10
SLE				4

and that more difficult functions required larger population sizes. They also found that increasing selection pressure by increasing tournament size improved performance. However, when applying these guidelines to a molecular docking problem they concluded that parameters tuned for analytical test functions may not provide adequate guidance for attacking more complex problems.

Angeline [1] re-examined the issue of Gaussian versus lognormal methods for perturbing the strategy parameters when noise was added to the test functions. His results led him to conclude that the Gaussian update rule performed statistically significantly better for the Parabola and Bohachevsky functions when any level of noise was added but not for the Rosenbrock and Ackley functions.

Comparisons using the average best solution found at some pre-specified number of trials are always vulnerable to tortoise and hare comparisons: an evolutionary algorithm (EA) that makes rapid progress, but exhausts the search potential in the population before discovering the global optimum (a hare) might look better than an EA that proceeds more slowly, but eventually does find the optimum. The preselected computational limit determines the result.

For our experiments we use the criterion of halting when the search discovers the global optimum. However, how close to optimum is close enough? EP typically uses machine precision whereas EAs using crossover frequently employ a coding precision for the problem variables that is considerably coarser than machine precision. If we assume that the user knows that numerical precision below the chosen coding precision is of no practical value, then it seems reasonable to halt an EP run as soon as a solution is discovered that is within the coding precision of the global optimum. So the number of trials to reach the global optimum by this criterion is the metric we have used *to a limit of 500,000 trials* (by which time the algorithm has stopped making any progress).

3 Methods

We opted for a complete factorial design in which every combination of the varied parameters was tested and analysis of variance (ANOVA) was the primary

Table 2. Search algorithm parameters used for ANOVA testing.

Factor	Levels	Nb	Functions
Sigma Strategy	σ-first, σ-last	2	
Initial Sample Distribution	Gaussian, Uniform	2	
Scale factor(α)	LgN, 0.1, 0.2, 0.3, 0.4, 0.5	6	
Tournament Rate	0.1, 0.15, 0.2, 0.25, 0.5, 0.75, 1.0, 1.5, 2.0	9	
Population	5, 10, 20, 50	4	Parabola, Bohachevsky
	10, 20, 50, 100	4	Rosenbrock-2, -4
	50, 100, 150	3	Griewank, Schwefel
	100, 150, 200, 300	4	SLE4-2
	100, 150, 200	3	SLE4-1, -4, -5
	50, 100, 150, 200	4	SLE4-3
	200, 300, 500	3	Rastrigin
	50, 100, 200, 500	4	Ackley

analytical tool. As stated above, the preferred performance metric was trials to find the global optimum. We will see that for some functions the algorithm was unable to do this consistently, and so for these cases we will examine the best performance at our ultimate termination condition which was 500,000 trials[4]. The mathematical expressions for the 13 functions tested are given in several other studies [4, 7, 6, 1] and therefore are not repeated here.[5] The factors and levels used in the experimental design for this work are shown in Table 2. All experiments were replicated 30 times for a total of 298,080 EP searches (30 * $[(6 * (2 * 2 * 6 * 9 * 3)) + ((13 - 6) * (2 * 2 * 6 * 9 * 4))]$).

Initially, we ran 13 ANOVA's (one per function) to analyze these results. Unfortunately, this approach proved to be less useful than hoped. The reason is that analysis of variance partitions the observed variance, which we soon learned comes mostly from differences among experimental conditions which work poorly. Thus, the factors that stood out in the ANOVA summary tables tended not to be those that shed light on what worked well. We then opted for a simpler approach: to identify the best cell (i.e., EP parameter set) in the design and the other cells that were statistically indistinguishable from the best cell for each function. A weak alpha test (one-tailed t-test at less than 0.90 significance level) was used as a substitute for a strong beta test. For some functions not all experiments were able to find the optimum on every replication. For these functions the best cells reported were drawn only from those that did find the

---

[4] A limit of 500,000 trials was used for all functions except Ackley. We used 250,000 trials for Ackley's function due to computational constraints.

[5] The ranges and optimality thresholds used for each function are listed in Tables 3 and 4. For the uniform initialization tests, the function variables were initialized randomly and uniformly over the corresponding range, while Gaussian initialization was performed using a standard deviation of one half the range and a mean of zero. All strategy variables were initialized randomly and uniformly between 0.0 and 5.0.

Table 3. Parameter sets yielding best performance on consistently solvable functions.

Function	σ f/l	Init u/g	Pop Size	Tourn Rate	α	Mean Evals	SEM	Signif CutOff	Param Range	Opt
Parabola	f	u	5	1.50	lgN	431.5	21.9	459.6	±5.12	e-4
Bohachevsky	f	g	10	0.50	lgN	534.0	35.4	579.4	±50.0	e-4
Rosenbrock-2	f	g	10	0.75	0.20	5,526.3	404.6		±2.048	e-5
	l	u	10	0.10	0.20	5,801.3	607.8	5,821.3		
SLE4-5	l	g	100	0.10	0.20	11,086.7	626.7		±30.0	e-1
	l	g	100	0.20	0.20	11,486.7	636.3	11,889.9		
SLE4-1	f	u	150	0.25	0.30	14,610.0	495.1		±30.0	e-1
	f	u	100	2.00	0.20	14,953.3	577.7			
	f	u	100	1.00	0.20	14,990.0	678.4			
	f	u	100	0.20	0.20	15,200.0	467.7	15,244.6		
SLE4-2	f	u	200	0.15	0.20	38,966.7	2,435.2		±30.0	e-1
	f	u	200	0.50	0.20	41,313.3	2,662.3	42,087.9		
Rosenbrock-4	f	g	20	0.15	0.10	60,250.7	5,319.8	67,069.1	±2.048	e-4
SLE4-3	l	u	100	0.15	0.10	178,973.0	11,013.9	193,089.5	±30.0	e-1

optimum every time, where such cells existed. Where no such cells existed we fall back to reporting best mean performance at termination.

4 Results

4.1 The solvable problems

Table 3 presents the results for eight of the 13 functions ranked by the mean trials to find the optimum for the best cell (i.e., parameter set). The remaining functions could not be consistently solved to optimum by any parameter set tested. The best parameter set for each function is shown in Table 3 which also lists the number of evaluations to find the optimum (Mean Evals), and the standard error of the mean (SEM). It also shows the cutoff criterion used for measuring a significant difference in performance between cells and lists those cells whose performance is indistinguishable from that of the best cell.

Considering the issue of σ-first/last, the results show that four of the 14 "best cells" used σ-last. The probability of four or fewer heads in 14 tosses of a fair coin is 9.0%. We consider this slight, but hardly compelling evidence for the superiority of the σ-first strategy. While weaker, this conclusion is consistent with previous results. Considering the distribution of the initial population (g/u), five of the 14 "best cells" used a Gaussian distribution. The probability of five or fewer heads is 21.1%. Thus, there is no evidence for the superiority of either population initialization strategy.

Tournament rate and population size should be treated together because they both influence selection pressure. Tournament rate influences the accuracy of ranking since small rates yield more ranking errors than large ones and thus, softer selection pressure. Population size influences the relative impact of selection errors. Since selection errors only occur in the vicinity of the survival boundary, these errors will be a larger fraction of all selections in a small population than a large one. Consider that in a large population even significant ranking errors among the best (worst) members are unlikely to affect their survival, while even the best performer in a population of 5 may not survive a ranking error if the tournament size is small. Note also that population size influences more than just selection pressure; it also influences the breadth of the search. It seems intuitive that success on more difficult landscapes requires broader search and that strong selection pressure rapidly focuses the search and diminishes this breadth.

To some extent these factors can be seen operating in the results above. The easiest function for EP, the Parabola, can tolerate the smallest population of 5 and a high tournament rate of 1.50. More generally, the functions which favor the smallest populations are the three easiest. On the other hand, there does not seem to be any significant correlation between tournament rate and problem difficulty, although the hardest two problems in Table 3, Rosenbrock-4 and SLE4-3, seem more sensitive to tournament rate, tolerating only low rates.

Finally, with regard to α, Gaussian mutation with an α of 0.2 works best for half of the test functions (those requiring 5,000-50,000 trials), whereas an α of 0.1 works best on the harder functions, and the lognormal strategy works best only for the easiest functions. However, the results presented in the next section do not exhibit the same trend with respect to mutation strategy.

4.2 The hardest problems

The five functions in Table 4 were never consistently solved to optimality and so must be considered the hardest functions in our test suite. Hence, we were unable to use our preferred criterion (i.e., trials to discover the optimum) to draw conclusions. Table 4 lists these functions in rough order of difficulty as assessed by the number of optima found (summed over all cells and all replications). Within each function, the cells are arranged based on the criterion of best mean performance at termination.

We find among the 27 best cells, 15 with σ-first and 12 with σ-last, a rather likely chance occurrence. But we find a preponderance of cells (22 of 27) use a uniform distribution for parameter initialization. This is statistically significant at the .99 level. All 27 cells use populations of 100 or larger indicating that broad sampling is needed on these difficult problems.

A Gaussian strategy with $\alpha = 0.1$ appears best for SLE4-4, $\alpha = 0.2$ for Ackley, and Rastrigin, whereas the lognormal strategy looks best for Griewank and Schwefel. In contrast to the results in Table 3, for the easier functions, there is no apparent correlation between the mutation strategy (including α value) and problem difficulty. However, we observe that the mutation strategy is the most critical of all EP control parameters for all functions. Considering the best 100 parameter sets, for any function where Gaussian mutation works best, at least 75% of the parameter sets have the same α value, and in all but one case

Table 4. Parameters yielding the best mean performance at termination for hardest functions. Total number of optima found (column 1) is over all replications of all cells in the design. Column 9 is the number of optima found out of 30 in the given cell.

Function	σ f/l	Init u/g	Pop Size	Tourn Rate	α	Mean Fitness	SEM	Nb Opt	Signif CutOff	Param Range	Opt
SLE4-4	f	u	200	1.00	0.10	.4161	.06845	5		±30.0	e-1
707 optima	l	u	200	0.75	0.10	.4401	.05451	2			
	f	u	150	2.00	0.10	.4656	.07916	3			
	f	u	200	0.15	0.10	.4748	.06273	3			
	l	u	100	2.00	0.10	.4908	.08662	2			
	l	u	200	1.00	0.10	.4973	.07553	5	0.5038		
Ackley	f	u	500	1.50	0.20	.1465	.07390	0		±5.0	e-5
468 optima	f	u	500	0.15	0.20	.2229	.12570	0			
	f	g	500	0.10	0.20	.2779	.09880	0	0.2412		
Griewank	f	g	150	1.00	lgN	.1889	.02661	0	0.2230	±500.0	e-3
57 optima											
Rastrigin	l	u	500	0.15	0.20	26.64	1.530	0		±5.12	e-1
0 optima	l	u	200	1.00	0.20	26.67	1.476	0			
	f	g	300	0.25	0.20	27.06	1.958	0			
	f	u	500	1.50	0.20	27.10	1.889	0			
	l	u	200	0.75	0.20	27.23	1.593	0			
	f	u	500	0.50	0.20	27.27	1.863	0			
	l	u	300	0.20	0.20	27.39	1.688	0			
	f	u	300	1.00	0.20	27.69	1.796	0			
	f	g	500	2.00	0.20	27.73	1.928	0			
	l	u	500	2.00	0.20	27.94	1.627	0			
	f	u	500	1.00	0.20	27.96	1.758	0			
	l	u	200	2.00	0.20	28.06	2.436	0			
	l	u	300	1.50	0.20	28.47	2.348	0			
	l	u	500	0.75	0.20	28.51	1.685	0			
	l	g	500	0.10	0.20	28.59	2.324	0	28.60		
Schwefel	f	u	150	2.00	lgN	-3261	54.79	0		±500.0	-4189
0 optima	f	u	150	0.50	lgN	-3198	54.03	0	-3190.8		

(SLE4-1 where 0.3 is the anomaly) this is the best α. This trend is not nearly as strong for those functions where lognormal mutation works best.

What we have observed in all our runs is a strong tendency for the σ's to simply decrease. This is due at least in part to the increasing riskiness of large mutations as the population improves. In the Gaussian strategy, a small α prevents the σ's from diminishing "too rapidly" (i.e., search stagnating before the optimum is found).

Figure 1 shows the σ_i values, averaged over the population, for the Rastrigin, Griewank and Ackley functions averaged over 30 replications using the best performing parameter set for each function (Table 4). The graphs in Figure 1 also show the fitness value of the best performer (averaged over 30 runs) as a superimposed dashed line. The fitness scale is indicated on the right-hand side

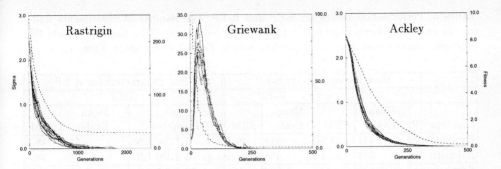

Fig. 1. Average σ values for each parameter in Rastrigin, Griewank and Ackley functions with average of best performance values.

of the graphs. Note that as the σ values become small, the progress of the search stagnates. This behavior is also observed for experiments using the lognormal strategy (Griewank), even though lognormal mutation is able to increase the *sigma*'s initially.

The problem of stagnation is compounded by an implementation detail: whenever a perturbed σ goes negative, which can happen with large α and a large negative normal deviate, then σ is set to ϵ (10^{-10}). We conjecture that once σ is driven to a small value, it is very difficult for σ to increase again to a level where significant perturbations can occur. The stagnation of search due to the decline of the σ's suggests a way to improve the EP algorithm - soft restarts.

5   Soft Restarts

A soft restart is a partial re-randomization of a stagnated population. This technique has been used successfully in other evolutionary algorithms, such as Eshelman's CHC [3]. Soft restarts in our EP experiments were executed whenever **all** chromosome σ values dropped below a defined threshold. The mechanism used to reinitialize the population was implemented as follows:

- Seed one individual with the parameters of the population's best member.
- Initialize the parameter values for the remaining individuals with values randomly chosen from a normal distribution centered around the corresponding parameter of the best individual and using randomly reinitialized σ's.
- Randomly initialize σ values for **all** members of the population as done in generation 0.

Column three of Table 5 shows the performance of the standard EP algorithm (S-EP) in terms of trials to reach the termination criterion or the average best solution after some number of maximum trials using the best parameter sets as indicated by † and ‡. Performances are averaged over 30 independent runs. The standard error of the mean (SEM) is shown in column four. Columns five and

Table 5. Performance Values for S-EP and R-EP. The number of experiments finding the optimal criteria is 30 unless indicated in parenthesis. The parameters sets for functions marked with † are from the best cell in Table 3 and ‡ are in Table 4.

| | | Best Parameters for S-EP | | | | Best Parameters for R-EP | | |
| | | S-EP | | R-EP | | | R-EP | |
Function	P	Mean Evals	SEM	Mean Evals	SEM	$Parameters^3$	Mean Evals	SEM
Parabola	†	*431	21.9	513	48.2	f u 5 1.50 LN	513	48.2
Bohachv	†	534	35.4	554	39.5	f g **5 1.00** LN	480	38.7
Rosnbrk-2	†	5,526	405	5,526	405	f u 20 **0.15** 0.2	5,052	442
SLE4-5	†	11,087	626	11,087	626	f u 100 **1.50** 0.2	10,410	759
SLE4-1	†	14,610	495	14,835	582	f u 150 0.25 0.3	14,835	582
SLE4-2	†	38,967	2,435	39,527	2,850	f u **150 0.75** 0.2	*20,285	1,293
Rosnbrk-4	†	60,251	5,320	61,760	4,938	f g 20 0.15 0.1	61,760	4,938
SLE4-3	†	178,973	11,014	178,973	11,014	f u **50 0.10** 0.1	*76,000	6,114

Function	P	Mean Evals	SEM	Mean Evals	SEM	$Parameters^3$	Mean Evals	SEM
SLE4-4	‡	(5) 0.416	0.068	(5) 0.416	0.068	f u 100 1.00 **0.2**	(11) 0.340	0.084
Ackley	‡	(0) 0.146	0.074	(0) 0.146	0.074	f u **50 0.50** 0.2	(4) *0.0040	0.0010
Griewank	‡	(0) 0.189	0.027	(4) *0.016	0.002	f u 50 1.00 **0.3**	(14) *0.0052	0.0008
Rastrigin	‡	(0) 26.60	1.53	(0) 25.90	1.34	f u 100 **0.20** 0.2	(0) *15.4	0.84
Schwefel	‡	(0) -3,261	54.8	(0) -3,330	46.5	f u 150 2.00 LN	(0) -3,330	46.5

six show the performance figures for the EP algorithm using soft restarts (R-EP) using the same parameters as S-EP. Using the parameter sets established as yielding the best performance for the S-EP algorithm, the R-EP algorithm performs statistically significantly better (indicated by *), at the 0.95 level, than the S-EP algorithm on the Griewank function and worse on the simple Parabola function, where restarting should probably be avoided. Note that restarts were never triggered in five of the functions using these parameter sets.

Realizing that the parameter sets best for R-EP might be different from those best for S-EP, we tested R-EP with other parameter sets, but still chosen from those used in the initial design (Table 2). The best parameters for R-EP are listed in column seven[6] of Table 5 followed by the corresponding performance results. The R-EP algorithm performs better than S-EP on all but three functions and statistically significantly (0.95 level) better on the SLE4-2, SLE4-3, Ackley, Griewank, and Rastrigin functions. The number of independent experiments meeting the optimum cutoff criteria also increase dramatically for the SLE4-4, Ackley, and Griewank functions. However, R-EP still performs significantly worse than S-EP on the simple Parabola (easiest function in this suite).

---

[6] Parameters are listed in the same order as in Tables 3 and 4.

The differences between the best parameter sets for S-EP and R-EP are generally in either the tournament rate or population size and are highlighted in Table 5. However, the best mutation parameters for R-EP on the Griewank and SLE4-4 functions differed from the best S-EP parameter sets while remaining the same on all other functions. In addition, wherever the best population size changed, R-EP almost always performs better with a smaller population size.

6 Conclusions

Previous studies support the general conclusion that control parameters for S-EP must be tuned for each new problem. This study, testing more functions and many more combinations of parameters, confirms that parameter tuning is critical to the performance of S-EP. However, these results show that the lognormal strategy is best on only four of the 13 functions tested, and two of these were the easiest functions. The most consistent pattern in this study is that, of all parameters tested, α is the most critical. Furthermore, using the discovery of the optimum as the cutoff criterion highlights the phenomenon of premature creep, that point where the algorithm loses its search potential because the strategy variables become too small. The addition of restarts to EP yields an algorithm capable of sustaining search longer than S-EP and results in much better performances on the difficult problems while sacrificing some performance on easy problems. The observed improvements should be considered upper bounds as the parameter sets tested were limited to those sets used in the ANOVA experiments and better performance may be possible with other parameter settings.

References

1. Peter Angeline. The Effects of Noise on Self-Adaptive Evolutionary Optimization. In L. J. Fogel, P. J. Anjeline, and T. Baeck, editors, *Evolutionary Programming V*. MIT Press, 1996.
2. T. Bäck and H.P. Schwefel. An Overview of Evolutionary Algorithms for Parameter Optimization. *Evolutionary Computation*, 1:1–23, 1993.
3. Larry Eshelman. The CHC Adaptive Search Algorithm. How to Have Safe Search When Engaging in Nontraditional Genetic Recombination. In G. Rawlins, editor, *Foundations of Genetic Algorithms*, pages 265–283. Morgan Kaufmann, 1991.
4. Larry Eshelman, Keith Mathias, and J. David Schaffer. Convergence Controlled Variation. In R. Belew and M. Vose, editors, *Foundations of Genetic Algorithms - 4*. Morgan Kaufmann, 1997.
5. David Fogel. *Evolutionary Computation: Towards a New Philosophy of Machine Intelligence*. IEEE Press, 1995.
6. Daniel K. Gehlhaar and David B. Fogel. Tuning Evolutionary Programming for Conformationally Flexible Molecular Docking. In L. J. Fogel, P. J. Anjeline, and T. Baeck, editors, *Evolutionary Programming V*. MIT Press, 1996.
7. N. Saravanan, David B. Fogel, and Kevin M. Nelson. A Comparison of Methods for Self-adaptation in Evolutionary Algorithms. *Bio Systems*, 36:157–166, 1995.

Accelerating the Evolutionary-Gradient-Search Procedure: Individual Step Sizes

Ralf Salomon

AI Lab, Department of Computer Science, University of Zurich
Winterthurerstrasse 190, 8057 Zurich, Switzerland
FAX: +41-1-363 00 35; Email: salomon@ifi.unizh.ch

Abstract. Recent research has proposed the evolutionary-gradient-search procedure that uses the evolutionary scheme to estimate a gradient direction and that performs the parameter updates in a steepest-descent form. On several test functions, the procedure has shown faster convergence than other evolutionary algorithms. However, the procedure also exhibits similar deficiencies as steepest-descent methods. This paper explores to which extent the adoption of individual step sizes, as known from evolution strategies, can be beneficially used. It turns out that they considerably accelerate convergence.

1 Introduction

Steepest-descent and evolutionary algorithms represent two very different classes of optimization techniques. For an objective function $f(x_1, \ldots, x_n) = f(\boldsymbol{x})$ with n independent variables x_i, Newton's gradient method uses the first derivatives $\partial f / \partial x_i$ along each coordinate axis to determine the n-dimensional gradient $\boldsymbol{g}$

$$\boldsymbol{g} = \nabla f(\boldsymbol{x}) = \left(\frac{\partial f}{\partial x_1}, \ldots, \frac{\partial f}{\partial x_n} \right)^T . \tag{1}$$

At any point $\boldsymbol{x}$, the gradient $\boldsymbol{g}$ always points into the direction of the maximal increase of $f(\boldsymbol{x})$, and is hence always perpendicular to the $(n\text{-}1)$-dimensional hyper surface $f(\boldsymbol{x}) = c$ with constant objective function values. Thus, by repeatedly subtracting sufficiently small fractions η of the locally calculated gradients $\boldsymbol{g}_t$

$$\boldsymbol{x}_{t+1} = \boldsymbol{x}_t - \eta \nabla f(\boldsymbol{x}_t) , \tag{2}$$

the steepest-descent method converges for sure to the next (local) optimum of any unimodal objective function $f(\boldsymbol{x})$ from any initial point $\boldsymbol{x}_0$. See [11,9] for an overview of various programming examples and acceleration methods.

Certain restrictions apply to the utility of analytical gradient methods. The problem has to be described by n real-valued parameters x_i and the objective function $f(\boldsymbol{x})$ must be both explicitly given and continuously differentiable. Especially in real-world applications, these constraints are often not fulfilled, which might be a reason why designers often resort to evolutionary algorithms. This paper focuses on problems where the gradient cannot be calculated analytically.

Evolutionary algorithms are stochastic, population-based search techniques that are highly inspired by natural evolution. They provide a framework that mainly consists of genetic algorithms [6], evolutionary programming [5,4], and evolution strategies [12,17] (see [1] for a comparison of these methods). In each generation, such algorithms generate a new population by applying variation operators, such as mutation and recombination/crossover, to the parameters x_i. By selecting population members with above-average fitness, the optimization process is guided toward regions with increasing fitness. Most recombination operators randomly exchange some parameters among only two individuals. Recent research [3,8], however, has successfully considered global recombination operators that consider *all selected* members. For example, global intermediate recombination, denoted as $(\mu/\mu_I, \lambda)$ in evolution strategies, reduces the entire population to *one* virtual parent representing the population's center of mass.

In contrast to steepest-descent methods, evolutionary algorithms discard already-gained information about the fitness functions by discarding less-fit individuals. A recently developed method [15], the evolutionary-gradient-search (EGS) procedure, has successfully fused both optimization techniques described above. It uses *all* evolutionary-generated offspring to estimate the gradient, and it then performs a steepest-descent optimization step including the self-adaptation of the step size σ_t. The procedure is briefly reviewed in Sec. 2.

It has been shown [15] that on several test functions, the EGS procedure yields considerably faster convergence than various evolution strategies and genetic algorithms. However, on objective functions with very different eigenvalues along each coordinate axis, the EGS procedure exhibits performance deficiencies well known from classical gradient methods, and the problem could not be sufficiently solved by utilizing an additional well-know acceleration method known as the momentum [13, p. 330]. Fortunately, the pertinent literature on evolution strategies [1,2,8,17,18] offers individual step sizes η_i (one for each variable x_i) and correlated mutations $x_t \leftarrow x_t + Cz$ (with C denoting the $n \times n$ correlation matrix and z denoting the mutation vector) to overcome such performance problems. Section 3 discusses the problem itself and how individual step sizes η_i including their self-adaptation can be adopted by the EGS procedure.

Section 4 describes the experimental setup, and Sec. 5 explores to which extent the EGS procedure can beneficially utilize individual step sizes. It turns out that on the cigar, individual step sizes drastically improve the procedure's performance. Particular evolution strategy variants that feature correlated mutations are approximately six times faster; however, due to the matrix multiplication, correlated mutations require at least $O(n^2)$ additional operations, whereas all other methods under considerations require only $O(n)$ operations. Section 6 finally concludes with a brief discussion.

2　The EGS Procedure

In each iteration (generation) t, the EGS procedure first estimates the direction of the gradient in an evolutionary-inspired form, and it then performs the actual

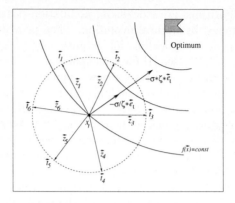

Fig. 1. The estimation of the global gradient direction and the self-adaptation of the step size σ_t of the EGS procedure. For details, see text.

iteration step in a steepest-descent fashion, which also includes a self-adaptation of the step size σ_t. At a given point $\boldsymbol{x}_t$, the EGS procedure generates λ test candidates (offspring) $\boldsymbol{t}_1 = \boldsymbol{x}_t + \boldsymbol{z}_1, \ldots, \boldsymbol{t}_\lambda = \boldsymbol{x}_t + \boldsymbol{z}_\lambda$ by applying random mutations $\boldsymbol{z}_i$ to the current point $\boldsymbol{x}_t$. All components of all mutation vectors $\boldsymbol{z}_i$ are Gaussian distributed with mean 0 and standard deviation $\sigma_t/\sqrt{n}$. For $n \gg 1$, this leads to $\|\boldsymbol{z}_i\| \approx \sigma_t$, and thus, all test points $\boldsymbol{t}_1 \ldots \boldsymbol{t}_\lambda$ are distributed on a hypersphere with radius σ_t. From Fig. 1 the following observations can be made. Some of the test candidates (e.g., $\boldsymbol{t}_1, \boldsymbol{t}_2, \boldsymbol{t}_3$) have a better fitness $f(\boldsymbol{t}_i = \boldsymbol{x}_t + \boldsymbol{z}_i)$ than the parent $\boldsymbol{x}_t$, and others have a worse fitness. The fitness difference $f(\boldsymbol{t}_i) - f(\boldsymbol{x}_t)$ depends on how close the mutation vector $\boldsymbol{z}_i$ approaches the true gradient direction. For candidates that lie on the "wrong" side, the fitness difference $f(\boldsymbol{t}_i) - f(\boldsymbol{x}_t)$ has the opposite sign. Rather than applying a global recombination operator on a set of the selected best offspring (e.g., $\boldsymbol{t}_1, \boldsymbol{t}_2, \boldsymbol{t}_3$ in Fig. 1) the procedure applies a global operator to *all* test candidates in order to calculate a unit vector $\boldsymbol{e}_t$ that points into the direction of the estimated (global) gradient $\tilde{\boldsymbol{g}}_t$:

$$\boldsymbol{e}_t = \frac{\tilde{\boldsymbol{g}}_t}{\|\tilde{\boldsymbol{g}}_t\|} \qquad \text{with} \qquad \tilde{\boldsymbol{g}}_t = \sum_{i=1}^{\lambda} \left(f(\boldsymbol{t}_i) - f(\boldsymbol{x}_t) \right) (\boldsymbol{t}_i - \boldsymbol{x}_t) \ . \tag{3}$$

It should be noted that the estimated gradient can significantly deviate from the true gradient, especially if only a few offspring $\lambda \ll n$ are generated. But it has been shown [15] that even for this case, the EGS procedure yields reasonable convergence speeds. See Appendix A for some important implementation details.

After calculating the unit vector $\boldsymbol{e}_t$, the EGS procedure performs the actual iteration step and self-adapts the step size σ_t. In its simplest form, the procedure performs a steepest-descent with two step size variations $\sigma_t \zeta$ and σ_t/ζ, with $\zeta \approx 1.8$ denoting a variation factor (see also [16]). In a more general form, several different step sizes can be tested, which may obey a logarithmic-normally distribution with mean 1. The procedure finally performs the step with the best

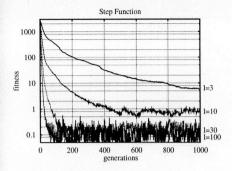

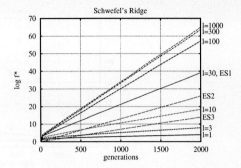

Fig. 2. EGS performance for different λ's (denoted as l) when applied to the step function f_{step}. The EGS procedure found the minimum in *all* 50 runs.

Fig. 3. Different evolution strategies and the EGS procedure with momentum and different λ's (denoted as l) at Schwefel's ridge f_{ridge}. For details, see text.

overall fitness, thus self-adapting the step size σ_{t+1} on the fly. More formally:

$$\sigma_{t+1} = \begin{cases} \sigma_t\, \zeta & \text{if} \quad f(\boldsymbol{x}_t - \sigma_t\, \zeta\, \boldsymbol{e}_t) \leq f(\boldsymbol{x}_t - (\sigma_t/\zeta)\, \boldsymbol{e}_t) \\ \sigma_t/\zeta & \text{otherwise} \end{cases}$$

$$\boldsymbol{x}_{t+1} = \boldsymbol{x}_t - \sigma_{t+1}\boldsymbol{e}_t \tag{4}$$

For analytical gradient methods, it has been shown [16] that (4) yields linear convergence and that the value of ζ is not critical; $\zeta \approx 1.839$ has been shown to be optimal [16]. Due to $\zeta \approx 1.8$, approximately 4 iterations are required to change the step size by one order of magnitude.

In extensive tests on the sphere model $f(\boldsymbol{x}) = \sum_i x_i^2$ with up to $n = 1000$ dimensions [15], the EGS procedure has shown linear convergence; with $\lambda = 30$ offspring, for example, the procedure requires approximately 2000 generations to reach a precision of $\|x_i - x_i^o\| \leq \epsilon = 10^{-5}$ for *all* 1000 parameters x_i.

In addition, the EGS procedure has adopted the *momentum term* (e.g., [13, p. 330]), which is a well-known steepest-descent acceleration method. It provides a kind of memory by incorporating previous steps as follows:

$$\boldsymbol{x}_{t+1} = \boldsymbol{x}_t + \Delta\boldsymbol{x}_{t+1} \qquad \text{with} \qquad \Delta\boldsymbol{x}_{t+1} = -\sigma_{t+1}\boldsymbol{e}_t + \alpha\Delta\boldsymbol{x}_t \tag{5}$$

with the momentum α being constrained to $0 \leq \alpha \leq 1$ and $\Delta\boldsymbol{x}_0 = \boldsymbol{0}$. With $\alpha = 0$, the update rule in (5) equals the one in (4). It is most straightforward to self-adapt α_t in the same way as the step size σ_t. In its simplest form, the procedure can test all four combinations $(\sigma_t\, \zeta, \alpha_t\, \zeta)$, $(\sigma_t\, \zeta, \alpha_t/\zeta)$, $(\sigma_t/\zeta, \alpha_t\, \zeta)$, and $(\sigma_t/\zeta, \alpha_t/\zeta)$. More generally, the procedure can test logarithmic-normally-distributed combinations of σ_t and α_t.

Figures 2 and 3 show some performance graphs, which are averages over 50 runs. In addition, $\sigma_0 = 0.1$, $\zeta = 1.8$, $\boldsymbol{x}_0 = (10, \ldots, 10)^T$, and $n = 30$ dimensions have been used. Figure 2 shows the performance of the EGS procedure *without* momentum for the step function $f_{\text{step}}(\boldsymbol{x}) = \sum_{i=1}^{30} \lfloor |x_i| + 0.5 \rfloor^2$. In all

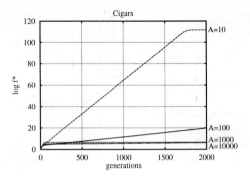

Fig. 4. Performance of the EGS procedure with $\lambda = 100$ test candidates and momentum as a function of the parameter A of the cigar function f_{cigar}. Please note that the saturation at $\log(f^*)$ for $A = 10$ is due to numerical imprecisions of the machine.

four cases $\lambda \in \{3, 10, 30, 100\}$, EGS found the optimum in *all* 50 runs. The observable oscillations are due to temporarily increases of the step size σ_t (see also Appendix A). In comparison [1], evolutionary programming and a $(30, 200)$-evolution strategy with individual step sizes require approximately 7500 and 4000 generations, respectively, whereas a canonical genetic algorithm with bit-codings and a $(30, 200)$-evolution strategy with one global step size failed on this task.

Similarly, Fig. 3 shows the normalized, logarithmic performance $\log(f^*) = \log(f(x_0)/f(x_t))$ of the EGS procedure with momentum $\alpha_0 = 0.1$ and different numbers λ of offspring when minimizing Schwefel's ridge [18] $f_{\text{ridge}}(x) = \sum_{i=1}^{30}(\sum_{j=1}^{i} x_j)^2$. The labels ES1, ES2, and ES3 refer to a $(15,100)$-evolution strategy *with* correlated mutations, a $(15,100)$-evolution strategy with individual step sizes σ_t, and a simple $(1,100)$-evolution strategy, respectively.

It should be noted here that in its current form, the EGS procedure is merely a local search procedure as most other algorithms are as well; it does not reliably locate the global optimum of multimodal functions. Similarily, existing genetic algorithms efficiently locate the global optimum only of linearly separable objective functions (see also [14]); they completely fail if applied to rotated versions of widely-used multimodal test functions.

3 EGS and Individual Step Sizes

As already mentioned in the introduction, the EGS procedure exhibits a considerable performance loss when applied to functions with very different eigenvalues along each coordinate axis. An example is given in Fig. 4, which shows the EGS performance averaged over 50 runs at the cigar $f_{\text{cigar}}(x) = x_1^2 + A \sum_{i=2}^{n} x_i^2$ with different values for $A \in \{10, 100, 1000, 10000\}$. (The saturation at $\log(f^*) \approx 112$ for $A = 10$ is due to numerical imprecisions of the machine.) Clearly, the achieved performance is but satisfying.

More generally, the performance of steepest-descent methods and evolutionary algorithms with only one global step size considerably degrades if applied to quadratic functions $f(\boldsymbol{x}) = \sum_i \omega_i x_i^2$ with very different eigenvalues $\omega_i \ll \omega_{j\neq i}$ along each coordinate axis: rather than moving along the narrow valley, the optimization path might be oscillating between both sides resulting in a very small effective progress. In such situations, the distribution of the offspring does not match the landscape of the fitness function. Figure 4 clearly shows that the momentum term is not able to sufficiently alleviate this problem.

Fortunately, the pertinent literature on evolution strategies [1, 2, 8, 17, 18] offers the utilization of individual step sizes $\boldsymbol{\eta}$ (one η_i for each variable x_i) to overcome such performance problems. In essence, individual step sizes "distort" the mutation distribution and thus the offspring distribution such that they match the topology of the fitness landscape. Evolution strategies utilize individual step sizes by implementing mutations as $\boldsymbol{\eta}_t \circ \boldsymbol{z}$ with $\circ$ denoting a component-wise multiplication operator $\boldsymbol{a} = \boldsymbol{b} \circ \boldsymbol{c}$ that is defined as $a_i = b_i \cdot c_i$. Details for the adaptation of the n individual step sizes $\boldsymbol{\eta}_t$ can be found in [1, 2, 17, 18].

The very same approach can be adopted by the EGS procedure. In this case, λ offspring are generated by $\boldsymbol{t}_i = \boldsymbol{x}_t + \boldsymbol{\eta}_t \circ \boldsymbol{z}_i$, with $\boldsymbol{\eta}_0 = (1, \ldots, 1)^T$ and with all components of the mutation vectors $\boldsymbol{z}_i$ still having standard deviation $\sigma_t / \|\boldsymbol{\eta}_t\|$ (see also Sec. 2). This variant will be denoted as EGS_{IS} throughout this paper. It should be noted that the actual optimization step (4) is still performed with the global step size σ_t; the individual step sizes $\boldsymbol{\eta}_t$ are only used for generating offspring and thus estimating the gradient.

The individual step sizes $\boldsymbol{\sigma}_t$ are adapted by the following heuristic. For each component i, the procedure compares the signs of the corresponding components of two subsequently estimated gradient directions e_i^t and e_i^{t-1}, and it adapts the step sizes according to

$$\eta_i \leftarrow \begin{cases} \eta_i\,\beta & \text{if} \quad e_i^t e_i^{t-1} > 0 \\ \eta_i & \text{if} \quad e_i^t e_i^{t-1} = 0 \\ \eta_i/\beta & \text{if} \quad e_i^t e_i^{t-1} < 0 \end{cases} \tag{6}$$

The idea behind the adaptation (6) is that for oscillating gradient components, the eigenvalue is rather large, whereas for non-oscillating components, the eigenvalue is rather small. The update rule appropriately changes the individual step sizes η_i in order to compensate the current eigenvalues. Current experience from evolution strategies [1, 7, 8, 18] *suggests* that the modification factor β should be close to 1 in order to not disturb the adaptation of the step size σ_t. With $\beta = 1.0$, the individual step sizes have no effect.

In addition to individual step sizes, the literature [1, 2, 8, 17, 18] also offers the generation of correlated mutations by means of an $n \times n$ correlation matrix C. But this is subject to future research.

4 Methods

This paper focuses on test functions with different eigenvalues; results for other functions have already been presented in [15] and partly in Sec. 2. The ellipsoid $f_{\mathrm{elli}} = \sum_{i=1}^{n} i x_i^2$ is a quadratic function with different eigenvalues $\omega_i = i$ along each axis. The cigar (see also [8]) $f_{\text{cigar}}(x) = x_1^2 + A \sum_{i=2}^{n} x_i^2$ is also an ellipses in which, however, all but one eigenvalue A is much larger than the eigenvalue of x_1. In the experiments, A was varied between 10 and 1'000'000.

Unless otherwise stated, empirical tests were done with the following parameter settings: $\sigma_0 = 0.1$, $\zeta = 1.8$, $x_0 = (10, \ldots, 10)^T$, $\eta_0 = (1, \ldots, 1)^T$, $\beta = 1.01$, $\alpha = 0.0$ (i.e., *without* momentum), $n = 30$ dimensions, and all results averaged over 50 independent trials. Shown are 1000 or 1500 generations, depending on saturation effects caused by numerical imprecisions of the machine. The initial step size σ_0 was deliberately ill-set. As has been discussed in Sec. 2, approximately 4 steps are required to change the step size by an order of magnitude. For comparison purposes, all graphs show the normalized, logarithmic performance $\log(f(x_0)/f(x_t))$, which is denoted as $\log(f^*)$ in the figures; $\log(f^*)$ measures the progress in orders of magnitude.

Comparisons with other methods are done by presenting previously published results. Evolution strategies generate offspring by using either one global step size $x_t \leftarrow x_t + \sigma_t z$, individual step sizes $x_t \leftarrow x_t + \sigma_t \circ z$ as already discussed, or correlated mutations $x_t \leftarrow x_t + Cz$. For further implementation details of the self-adaptation of σ_t and C, see [1, 2, 8, 17, 18]. It should be noted that correlated mutations C require at least $O(n^2)$ additional operations as opposed to $O(n)$ operations of all other methods.

5   Results

Experiments on the ellipses turned to out to be too simple. After a few generations, the individual step sizes were adapted and the problem was virtually identical with the sphere. Due to space requirements, this section focuses on a more interesting example, the cigar.

Figures 5-8 show the normalized, logarithmic performance of the EGS$_{IS}$ procedure when minimizing the cigar f_{cigar} with $\lambda \in \{30, 100, 200\}$ offspring. In comparison with Fig. 4, the performance has been drastically improved. It can

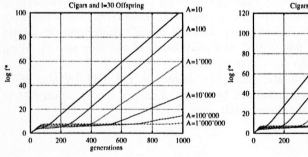
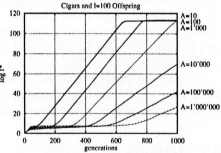
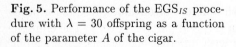

Fig. 5. Performance of the EGS$_{IS}$ procedure with $\lambda = 30$ offspring as a function of the parameter A of the cigar.

Fig. 6. Performance of the EGS$_{IS}$ procedure with $\lambda = 100$ offspring as a function of the parameter A of the cigar.

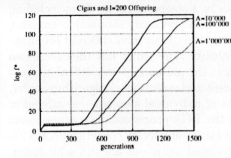
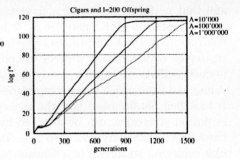

Fig. 7. Performance of the EGS$_{IS}$ procedure with $\lambda = 200$ offspring as a function of the parameter A of the cigar.

Fig. 8. Same experiment as in Fig. 7, but with the variation parameter $\beta = 1.1$ for adapting the individual step sizes η_i.

be seen that even for very large values for $A \geq 100'000$, the procedure shows high performance for $\lambda = 100$ or $\lambda = 200$ offspring.

Besides the performance, these figures also show some other interesting behaviors. As can be expected, the procedure requires some generations (about 600 for $A = 10^6$) to adjust all individual step sizes η_i. The number of generations required for adapting the individual step sizes clearly depends on the choice of β. Figure 8 presents the performance of the same experiment presented in Fig. 7, but with $\beta = 1.1$. It can be clearly seen that the number of initial generations is considerably reduced. However, the slope, i.e., the orders of magnitude per generation, is slightly reduced.

Furthermore, the performance figures also demonstrate how the number λ of offspring influence the adaptation capabilities of the individual step sizes η_i. To work properly, the adaptation heuristic of the individual step sizes requires a reasonable approximation of the gradient; otherwise the adaptation is too much influenced by statistical side effects. As could be seen in the previous figures, increasing the number λ of offspring accelerates the procedure.

In order to compare the EGS$_{IS}$ procedure with other methods, the numbers of generations required to reach a function value of $f_{\text{cigar}}(\boldsymbol{x}) \leq 10^{-10}$ have been determined. With $\boldsymbol{x}_0 = (1, \ldots, 1)^T$, $\beta = 1.1$, and $\lambda = 10n$, EGS$_{IS}$ requires 158 ($n = 5$), 214 ($n = 20$), and 332 ($n = 80$) generations, which equals 7900, 42'800, and 265'600 function evaluations, respectively. In comparison, the evolution strategy with correlated mutations presented in [8] requires approximately 2000, 9000, and 40'000, function evaluations, respectively, which is approximately six times faster. It is also reported in [8] that a simple $(\mu/\mu_I, 10)$-evolution strategy requires more than 10^8 function evaluations for the (n=5)-dimensional case.

6   Discussion

This paper has motivated and reviewed the evolutionary-gradient-search (EGS) procedure that uses the evolutionary scheme to estimate a gradient direction and that performs the parameter updates in a steepest-descent form including a self-adaptation of the step size σ_t. It has been previously shown that on many test functions, the EGS procedure performs better than three different evolution strategies with different degrees of complexity. The paper has then discussed useless oscillations that frequently appear in the presence of very different eigenvalues and from which many steepest-descent and evolutionary algorithms suffer. It has then be discussed how the concept of individual step sizes, as offered in evolution strategies, can be adopted by the EGS procedure. The experiments have shown that individual step sizes drastically accelerate convergence. Particular evolution strategies that feature correlated mutations are still a bit faster. But correlated mutations require at least $O(n^2)$ operations as opposed to $O(n)$ operations of other methods including the EGS procedure, evolutionary programming, and simple evolution strategies. Therefore, the net efficacy strongly depends on the computational costs of the objective function.

The heuristic for the step-size adaptation is very simple but requires a reasonable approximation of the gradient. For $\lambda \ll n$, the optimization path is rather erratic and goes along the gradient path only in the long term (see also [15]). Therefore, $\lambda > n$ has been used in this paper. Further research will be devoted to the question how the population size can be kept small by lazy updating the individual step sizes, i.e., updating only after several generations where significantly more than n function evaluations have been executed (see also [8]).

In addition to some performance improvements, the EGS procedure has the following advantage. Due to its hybrid nature, it features the advantages of evolutionary algorithms, i.e., maintaining populations, parallel execution, not getting stuck at plateaus, and it simultaneously offers new options for incorporating acceleration methods from classical optimization methods. In this paper, individual step sizes have been explored. The investigation of other methods, such as conjugated directions and correlated mutations, are subject to future research.

References

1. Bäck, T., Schwefel, H.-P.: An Overview of Evolutionary Algorithms for Parameter Optimization. Evolutionary Computation **1**(1) (1993) 1-23
2. Bäck, T., Kursawe, F.: Evolutionary Algorithms for Fuzzy Logic: A Brief Overview. In: Bouchon-Meunier, B., Yager, R.R., Zadeh, L.A. (eds.): *Fuzzy Logic and Soft Computing*, Vol. IV. World Scientific, Singapore (1995) 3-10
3. Beyer, H.-G.: An Alternative Explanation for the Manner in which Genetic Algorithms Operate. BioSystems **41** (1997) 1-15
4. Fogel, D.B.: *Evolutionary Computation: Toward a New Philosophy of Machine Learning Intelligence*. IEEE Press, Jersy, NJ (1995)
5. Fogel, L.J.: "Autonomous Automata". Industrial Research **4** (1962) 14-19
6. Goldberg, D.E.: Genetic Algorithms in Search, Optimization and Machine Learning. Addison-Wesley Publishing Company (1989)
7. Hansen, N., Ostermeier, A.: Adapting Arbitrary Normal Mutation Distributions in Evolution Strategies: The Covariance Matrix Adaptation. In: Proceedings of The 1996 IEEE International Conference on Evolutionary Computation (IECEC'96). IEEE (1996) 312-317

8. Hansen, N., Ostermeier, A.: Convergence Properties of Evolution Strategies with the Derandomized Covariance Matrix Adaptation: The $(\mu/\mu_I, \lambda)$-CMA-ES. In: Zimmermann, H.-J. (ed.): Proceedings of The Fifth Congress on Intelligent Techniques and Soft Computing EUFIT'97. Verlag Mainz, Achen, (1997) 650-654
9. Luenberger, D.G.: Linear and Nonlinear Programming. Addison-Wesley, Menlo Park, CA (1984)
10. Mühlenbein, H., Schlierkamp-Voosen, D.: Predictive Models for the Breeder Genetic Algorithm I. Evolutionary Computation **1**(1) (1993) 25-50.
11. Press, W.H., Teukolsky, S.A., Vetterling, W.T., Flannery, B.P.: Numerical Recipes in C. Cambridge University Press, Cambridge, UK (1994)
12. Rechenberg, I.: Evolutionsstrategie. Frommann-Holzboog, Stuttgart (1994)
13. Rumelhart *et al.* (eds.): *Parallel Distributed Processing: Explorations in the Microstructure of Cognition*, Vol. 2. The MIT Press, Cambridge, MA (1986)
14. Salomon, R.: Reevaluating Genetic Algorithm Performance under Coordinate Rotation of Benchmark Functions; A survey of some theoretical and practical aspects of genetic algorithms. BioSystems **39**(3) (1996) 263-278
15. Salomon, R.: The Evolutionary-Gradient-Search Procedure. In: Koza, J. *et al.* (eds.): Genetic Programming 1998: Proceedings of the Third Annual Conference, July 22-25, 1998. Morgan Kaufmann, San Francisco, CA (1998)
16. Salomon, R., van Hemmen, J.L.: Accelerating backpropagation through dynamic self-adaptation. Neural Networks **9**(4) (1996) 589-601
17. Schwefel, H.-P.: Evolution and Optimum Seeking. John Wiley and Sons, NY (1995)
18. Schwefel, H.-P.: Evolutionary Computation — A Study on Collective Learning. In: Callaos, N., Khoong, C.M., Cohen, E. (eds.): Proceedings of the World Multiconference on Systemics, Cybernetics and Informatics, vol. 2. Int'l Inst. of Informatics and Systemics, Orlando FL (1997) 198-205

Appendix A

When implementing the gradient estimation $\tilde{g}_t = \sum_{i=1}^{\lambda} (f(t_i) - f(x_t))(t_i - x_t)$ according to equation (3), the following details have to observed. It might be that the gradient vanishes for any reason. When the procedure is applied to the step function f_{step}, for example, it might happen that the first term always vanishes, since the step size σ_t is too small. In such cases, the unit vector $e_t = \tilde{g}_t/\|\tilde{g}_t\|$ is not defined, and unprotected calculations may result in a runtime error.

In cases where the gradient $\tilde{g}_t$ vanishes, the programmer has the following two options: (1) choose *any* of the generated test vectors, or (2) continue with generating test candidates but temporarily increase the step size σ_t until the gradient does not vanish. Both options have more or less the same effect. In the first case, the procedure would do a step along an arbitrarily chosen mutation vector z_i. If then both test steps $\sigma_t \zeta$ and σ_t/ζ yield the same fitness, e.g., in the middle of a plateau of the step function f_{step}, the procedure would increase the step size σ_t due to the selection given in (4). In the second case, the procedure would directly increase the step size σ_t until at least one test vector yields a fitness $f(x_t + z_i)$ different from the parent's fitness $f(x_t)$. As a result, it may happen that the procedure exhibits small oscillations around the optimal value of the objective function. For this paper, the second option has been implemented.

Extending
Population-Based Incremental Learning
to Continuous Search Spaces

Michèle Sebag[1,2] and Antoine Ducoulombier[2,1]

LMS, CNRS UMR 7649,	LRI, CNRS URA 410,
Ecole Polytechnique	Université d'Orsay
91128 Palaiseau Cedex	91405 Orsay Cedex
Michele.Sebag@polytechnique.fr	Antoine.Ducoulombier@lri.fr

Abstract. An alternative to Darwinian-like artificial evolution is offered by *Population-Based Incremental Learning* (PBIL): this algorithm memorizes the best past individuals and uses this memory as a distribution, to generate the next population from scratch.

This paper extends PBIL from boolean to continuous search spaces. A Gaussian model is used for the distribution of the population. The center of this model is constructed as in boolean PBIL. Several ways of defining and adjusting the variance of the model are investigated.

The approach is validated on several large-sized problems.

1 Introduction

Evolutionary algorithms (EAs) [13, 6, 5] are mostly used to find the optima of some fitness function $\mathcal{F}$ defined on a search space Ω.

$$\mathcal{F} : \Omega \to \mathbb{R}$$

From a machine learning (ML) perspective [9], evolution is similar to *learning by query*: Learning by query starts with a void hypothesis and gradually refines the current hypothesis through asking questions to some oracle.

In ML, the sought hypothesis is the description of the target concept; the system generates examples and asks the oracle (the expert) whether these examples belong to the target concept. In EA, the sought "hypothesis" is the distribution of the optima of $\mathcal{F}$; the system generates individuals and asks the oracle (a routine or the user) what their fitness is. In all cases, the system alternatively generates questions (examples or individuals) depending on its current hypothesis, and refines this hypothesis depending on the oracle's answers.

One core difference between ML and evolution is that ML, in the artificial intelligence vein, manipulates high-level, or *intensional* description of the hypothesis sought. Conversely, evolution deals with a low-level, or *extensional* description of the sought distribution: the distribution of the optima is represented by a collection of individuals (the current population).

The *Population Based Incremental Learning* (PBIL) approach bridges the gap between ML and EAs: it explicitly constructs an intensional description of the optima of $\mathcal{F}$, expressed as a distribution on Ω [2, 3]. This distribution is alternatively used to generate the current population, and updated from the best individuals of the current population. The advantage of the approach is that, as claimed throughout artificial intelligence [12], the higher level the information, the more explicit and simple the information processing can be. And indeed, PBIL involves much less parameters than even the canonical GAs [6].

PBIL was designed for binary search spaces. It actually constructs a distribution on $\Omega = \{0,1\}^N$ represented as an element of $[0,1]^N$. The basics of this scheme are first briefly recalled in order for this paper to be self contained (section 2). Our goal here is to extend this scheme to a continuous search space $\Omega \subseteq \mathbb{R}^N$. Continuous PBIL, noted $PBIL_C$, evolves a Gaussian distribution on Ω noted $\mathcal{N}(X,\sigma)$. The center X of the distribution is evolved much like in the binary case; evolving the standard deviation σ of this distribution is more critical, and several heuristics to this aim are proposed (section 3). $PBIL_C$ is finally validated and compared to evolution strategies on several large-sized problems (section 4). The paper ends with some perspectives for further research.

2   Binary PBIL

2.1   Principle

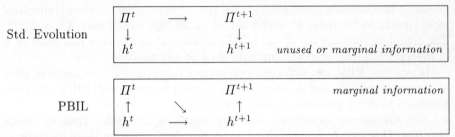

Figure 1. Comparing the generation steps in standard evolution and PBIL

Let Π denote a population of individuals in $\Omega = \{0,1\}^N$. An element h of $\mathcal{H} = [0,1]^N$ can be associated to Π, by defining h_i as the fraction of individuals in Π having their i-th bit set to 1. Conversely, an element h in $\mathcal{H}$ defines a distribution over Ω: one draws an element $X = (X_1, \ldots, X_N)$ in Ω by setting X_i to 1 with probability h_i.

PBIL relies on the following premises [2]: a) if evolution succeeds, the population Π converges toward a single[1] optimum of $\mathcal{F}$; b) the more converged the population Π, the better it is represented by h. Assuming these, PBIL discards all information in the population not contained in h: The population is simply considered as a manifestation of h. The attention is thus shifted from evolving Π by means of mutation and recombination, to evolving h (Fig. 1). To this aim, PBIL uses the information contained in the current population Π^t: h is evolved,

---

[1] This claim obviously makes no room for diversity preserving mechanisms [8].

or rather updated, by relaxation from the best individual X^{max} in Π^t:

$$h^{t+1} = (1 - \alpha) \cdot h^t + \alpha \cdot X^{max}, \qquad \alpha \ in \ ]0,1[$$

Distribution h^t can be viewed as the memory of the best individuals generated by evolution. Relaxation factor α corresponds to the fading of the memory: the higher α, the faster h^t moves toward the current local optimum.

In contrast to standard evolution, PBIL explicitly explores the space $\mathcal{H}$ of distributions on Ω. And, as noted already, this higher level representation allows for a simpler information processing: besides the population size, PBIL involves a single key parameter, α, to be compared to the various parameters controlling mutation and recombination. Further, the exploration is deterministic, in the sense that h^t is deterministically updated from the current population[2].

2.2 Discussion

Let us reformulate PBIL as a learning-by-query algorithm, by defining a partial generality order on the set of distributions $\mathcal{H}$. The generality of a distribution h is clearly related to the diversity of the population generated from h, and the diversity of the population with regard to bit i is inversely proportional to $|h_i - .5|$. Accordingly, a distribution h is more specific than h', if, for each bit i, either $0 \le h_i \le h'_i \le .5$, or $.5 \le h'_i \le h_i \le 1$.

PBIL initializes h to the most general distribution $h^0 = (.5\ldots,.5)$, and gradually specializes it along generations. Let X^h denote the (boolean) individual most similar to h^t; then, h^t is specialized on all bits i such that $X_i^h = X_i^{max}$. The complete convergence of the scheme is avoided as h_i^t never reaches 0 or 1; in theory, PBIL can generate any individual at any time.

In practice, PBIL can suffer from premature convergence. This happens when h^t gets too specific[3], and no new good individual is discovered. PBIL offers two heuristics to resist premature convergence [2]:
• Using the average of the two best individuals in Π^t, rather than the single best one. This way, h^t is generalized on all bits discriminating these individuals.
• Perturbing h^t with a Gaussian noise: with a given probability (5%), a Gaussian variable with a low standard deviation is added to h_i^t. This way, the center of the distribution is durably perturbed, which helps escaping from local minima.

A more fundamental limitation of PBIL comes from the distribution space, which implicitly assumes the linear separability of the problem (genes are considered independent). This distribution space appears too poor to fit complex fitness landscapes, such as the Long Path problem [7]. Previous experiments show that distributions used in PBIL have difficulties to overlap the narrow path [14]. Recent extensions to PBIL have considered richer distribution spaces [4].

---

[2] This raises the question of whether PBIL still pertains to the field of "Parallel problem solving from nature": is "nature" allowed to explicitly manipulate distributions? Still, a definition of "nature" is clearly beyond the scope of the paper.

[3] Parameter α partly controls the specificity of h^t, and plays the same role as selection in GAs: the diversity decreases, everything else being equal, as α goes to 1.

3 Continuous PBIL

This section first briefly discusses a previous attempt to extend PBIL to continuous search spaces, then details the proposed method and outlines $PBIL_C$.

3.1 Continuous PBIL with dichotomic distributions

To the best of our knowledge, the only extension of PBIL to continuous search spaces has been proposed in [15]. This algorithm explores the search space much like the delta-coding approach [17]. The domain of each gene is divided into two intervals ("low" and "high" values); the current distribution h (h in $[0,1]^N$) is used to determine which interval an individual belongs to:

$$X_i \in [a, b] \qquad Probability(X_i > \frac{a+b}{2}) = h_i$$

X_i is then drawn with uniform probability in the selected interval.
• At each generation, h is updated like in the boolean case, by memorizing whether the best individual takes low or high values for each gene:

$$h_i^{t+1} = (1 - \alpha) \cdot h_i^t + \alpha \cdot (X_i^{max} > \frac{a+b}{2})$$

• When h_i gets specific enough ($h_i < .1$ or $h_i > .9$), the population gets concentrated in a single interval (resp. $[a, \frac{a+b}{2}]$ or $[\frac{a+b}{2}, b]$). The search is then focused: the domain of the gene is set to the interval considered and h_i is reinitialized to .5.

In this scheme, evolution gradually focuses on the region most often containing the best individuals. One limitation is that a region which has been discarded at some point is hardly explored ever after, and this violates the ergodicity requirement. Furthermore, the search might be insufficiently focused, given the poor (uniform) distribution used within the selected interval.

3.2 Continuous PBIL with Gaussian distributions

Our approach rather explores Gaussian distributions $\mathcal{N}(X, \sigma)$ on the search space Ω, given as products of Gaussian distributions $\mathcal{N}(X_i, \sigma_i)$ on each gene domain. With no loss of generality, Ω is set to $[0, 1]^N$ in the following.

Like PBIL, $PBIL_C$ starts with a rather general distribution; then it alternatively uses this distribution to draw the population, and uses the population to update the distribution. The center of the distribution X^t is initialized to the center of the search space $(.5, \ldots, .5)$. At each generation, X^t is updated from a linear combination of the two best and the worst individuals in the current population, inspired from PBIL and Differential Evolution [16]:

$$X^{t+1} = (1 - \alpha) \cdot X^t + \alpha \cdot (X^{best, 1} + X^{best, 2} - X^{worst})$$

The diversity of the population, controlling the convergence of evolution, depends on the variance $\sigma = (\sigma_1, \ldots \sigma_N)$ of the distribution. Several heuristics have been investigated to adjust parameters σ_i.

A• The simplest possibility is to use a constant value. The trade-off between exploration and exploitation is thus settled once for all: the search cannot become too specific and it cannot be speeded up either.

B• A second possibility is to make evolution itself adjust σ. $PBIL_C$ here proceeds exactly as a self-adaptive $(1, \lambda)$-evolution strategy (ES)[4] where λ stands for the size of the population, except that the parent is replaced by the center X^t of the distribution.

C• A third possibility is to adjust σ depending on the diversity of the current best offspring; σ^t is then set to the variance of the K best current offspring:

$$\sigma_i = \sqrt{\frac{\sum_{j=1}^{K}(X_i^j - \bar{X}_i)^2}{K}}$$

where $\bar{X}$ denotes the average of the best K offspring $X^1, \ldots X^K$.

D• Last, σ can be learned in the same way as X itself, by memorizing the diversity of the K best offspring:

$$\sigma_i^{t+1} = (1 - \alpha)\sigma_i^t + \alpha\sqrt{\frac{\sum_{j=1}^{K}(X_i^j - \bar{X}_i)^2}{K}}$$

3.3 Discussion

At first sight, $PBIL_C$ is quite similar to a $(1, \lambda)$-ES, the λ offspring being generated from the single parent (X^t, σ^t). The difference is twofold.

• In $(1, \lambda)$-ES, the parent is simply replaced by the best offspring, whereas $PBIL_C$ updates X^t by relaxation. Let any offspring X^k be written $X^t + Z^k$, with Z^k being a random vector drawn according to $\mathcal{N}(0, \sigma^t)$. Then it comes:

$$X^{t+1} = (1-\alpha)X^t + \alpha(X^{best,1} + X^{best,2} - X^{worst}) = X^t + \alpha(Z^{best,1} + Z^{best,2} - Z^{worst})$$

The evolution of X^t can be viewed as a particular case of *weighted recombination* as studied by Rudolph [11]; a theoretical analysis shows that weighted recombination with optimal weights should be preferred to the simple replacement of the parents. Interestingly, the heuristic recombination used in $PBIL_C$ is intermediate between two particular cases with good theoretical properties (for $\mathcal{F}(X) = \sum X_i^2$): the half sum of the two best offspring, and the difference of the best and the worst offspring.

$PBIL_C$ uses fixed, hence non-optimal, weights; but note that α intervenes as an additional scaling factor, controlling the variance of X^t.

• Independently, the variance of X^t is also controlled from σ^t. $PBIL_C$ uses global

---

[4] In self-adaptive ES, besides the X_i an individual X carries the variance σ_i of the mutation to be applied on the X_i [13, 1]: Mutation first evolves the σ_i, then uses the new σ_i to perturb the X_i. Evolution thus hopefully adjusts the σ_i "for free", at the individual level.

mechanisms (options A, B and D) to adjust σ^t, by opposition to the local adjustment of σ achieved by self-adaptive mutation. Actually, the adjustment of σ (option D) much resembles the 1/5th rule used to globally adjust σ in early evolution strategies [10]. The difference is that the 1/5th rule criterion compares the offspring to the parents, and considers whether a sufficient fraction of offspring is more fit than the parents. In opposition, $PBIL_C$ only examines the diversity of the best fit offspring: it does not need to restrict the exploration, even if the offspring are less fit than the parent, because the center of the explored region moves more slowly than in standard ES.

To sum up, $PBIL_C$ controls the exploration-exploitation tradeoff in a way rather different from that of $(1, \lambda)$-ES. First of all, the single parent does not jump directly to a desirable location (the best offspring, or some weighted combination of the remarkable offspring), but rather makes a very small step toward this desirable location (e.g. α is set to 10^{-2} in the experiments). Variance σ is adjusted in a similarly cautious way.

It appears that ES takes instant decisions, on the basis of the instant information. On the opposite, $PBIL_C$ maintains a long-term memory, slowly updated from the instant information, and bases its cautious decisions on this long-term memory.

4 Validation

This section describes the goal of the experiments and the problems considered. We then report and discuss the results obtained.

4.1 Experiment Goals and Problems

Our goal is to study the respective advantages of evolving extensional vs intensional information about the fitness landscape. Practically, $PBIL_C$, evolving an intensional information represented as a distribution, is compared to self-adaptive evolution strategy, evolving an extensional information represented as usual as a population.

Notation	Definition		Domain Ω
F_1	$\dfrac{100}{10^{-5}+\sum_i \lvert y_i\rvert}$ with	$\begin{array}{l} y_1 = x_1 \\ y_i = x_i + y_{i-1}, i \geq 2 \end{array}$	$[-3,\ 3]^{100}$
F_2	$\dfrac{100}{10^{-5}+\sum_i \lvert y_i\rvert}$ with	$\begin{array}{l} y_1 = x_1 \\ y_i = x_i + sin\, y_{i-1},\ i \geq 2 \end{array}$	$[-3,\ 3]^{100}$
F_3	$\dfrac{100}{10^{-5}+\sum_i \lvert y_i\rvert}$ with	$y_i = .024 * (i+1) - x_i$	$[-3,\ 3]^{100}$
F_6	$\sum_i (x_i^2 - A\cos(2\pi\, x_i)) + 100A$		$[-5,\ 5]^{100}$
F_7	$\sum_i -x_i sin\sqrt{x_i}$		$[-30,\ 30]^{100}$
F_8	$\sum_i x_i^2 - \prod_i \cos(\frac{x_i}{\sqrt{i+1}})$		$[-100,\ 100]^{100}$

Table 1: Fitness functions considered. $\qquad i = 1 \ldots 100$

We deliberately consider large-sized search spaces ($N = 100$) for the following reason. In low or middle-sized spaces, populations or distributions might convey similarly accurate information about the fitness landscape. This is not true in large-sized spaces: any reasonable number of point s can only convey a very poor information about $\mathbb{R}^{100}$. Experimenting $PBIL_C$ in $\mathbb{R}^{100}$ will show how intensional evolution stands the curse of dimensionality.

Functions and search spaces considered are displayed in Table 1. Functions F_1 to F_3 have been used to evaluated binary PBIL [2]. Besides the size of the search space, F_1 and F_2 suffer from an additional difficulty, epistasis (the genes are linked via the y_i). Functions F_6 to F_8 have been extensively studied in the literature, for lower-sized search spaces ($N \leq 30$).

4.2 Experimental setting

We used two reference algorithms: boolean PBIL working on a discretization of the continuous problem (each continuous variable is coded through 9 binary variables), using either a binary or a Gray coding; and a $(10 + 50)$-ES with self adaptive mutation [1]. In the PBIL case, the size λ of the population is set to 50 and the relaxation factor α is set to .01.

$PBIL_C$ involves the same setting as PBIL ($\lambda = 50$ and $\alpha = .01$). Four options regarding the variance σ of the distributions have been considered (section 3.2):
A• Constant variance.
B• Self-adapted variance: $PBIL_C$ here behaves like a self-adaptive $(1, \lambda)$-ES, except that the parent is replaced by X^t.
C• Instant variance: σ_i is set to the variance of the best K offspring in the population. Several values of K were considered: $\lambda/2$, $\lambda/3$, $\lambda/5$.
D• Relaxed variance: σ_i is the variance of the best K offspring relaxed over the past generations; the relaxation factor is again set to $\alpha = .01$.

4.3 Results

Algorithm	σ	F1	F2	F3
(10+50)-ES		2.91 ±0.45	7.56 ±1.52	399.07 ±6.97
PBIL + binary coding		2.12	4.40	16.43
PBIL + Gray coding		2.62	5.61	366.77
	A: $\sigma_i = .02$	3.56 ±0.36	5.87 ±0.42	15.02 ±.76
	A: $\sigma_i = .05$	3.95 ±0.37	8.08 ±0.52	28.32 ±1.46
	B: σ self-adapt.	2.41 ±0.22	4.49 ±0.50	3.04 ±.34
$PBIL_C$	C: $K = \lambda/2$	2.89 ±0.36	3.52 ±0.41	5.25 ±.59
	D: $K = \lambda/2$	**4.65** ±0.49	**10.45** ±0.96	685 ±43
	D: $K = \lambda/3$	**4.40** ±0.41	**11.18** ±1.36	**2623** ±204
	D: $K = \lambda/5$	**4.76** ±0.78	**10.99** ±1	**4803** ±4986

Table 2: Best Fitness (averaged on 20 runs) for 200,000 evaluations
Best results indicated in bold   Exact optimum of F_1, F_2 and $F_3 = 10^7$

Table 2 displays the results obtained on functions F_1, F_2 and F_3. Results obtained by boolean PBIL are taken from [2]; additional results not reported here, show that boolean PBIL significantly outperforms several variants of GAs and Hill-Climbers on these functions. Note that all algorithms end rather far from the actual optimum (10^7). Still, $PBIL_C$ significantly outperforms standard ES on these problems — provided that the variance σ of the distribution is adequately set. Note also that $PBIL_C$ outperforms PBIL itself, working on a binary or Gray discretization of these continuous problems. This might be due either to the loss of information entailed by discretization, or because PBIL, as already mentioned, explores a too restricted distribution space.

The worst results of $PBIL_C$ are obtained when σ is self-adapted or set to the diversity of the current best offspring (options B and C); they are due to a fast decreasing of σ. And, in retrospect, a vicious circle occurs when σ tightly depends on the diversity of the offspring: the less diverse the offspring, the smaller σ, hence the less diverse the offspring...

Setting σ to a constant value (option A; the particular values were chosen after 10,000 evaluations preliminary runs) leads to satisfactory results, even outperforming those of standard ES. Further experiments will show whether this is rather due to the superiority of weighted recombination (replacing a parent by a combination of offspring) over replacement — or to the "long-term memory" effect, as the parent slowly moves toward the weighted combination of the offspring instead of jumping there.

The best option appears to learn the variance σ in the same way as the center of the distribution X^t (option D). Further, the fraction K of the offspring considered to update σ apparently is not a critical parameter[5].

Algorithm	σ	F6	F7	F8
(10+50)-ES		174 $\pm$29	-192.75 $\pm$18.18	489 $\pm$115
$PBIL_C$	B: σ self-adapt.	44.02 $\pm$6.44	-44.73 $\pm$32	71.62 $\pm$14
$PBIL_C$	D: $K = \lambda/2$	45.19 $\pm$4.03	-158.47 $\pm$40.87	11 10^{-6} $\pm10^{-6}$
$PBIL_C$	D: $K = \lambda/3$	44.67 $\pm$5.21	-167 $\pm$34	10^{-6} $\pm10^{-7}$
$PBIL_C$	D: $K = \lambda/5$	44.43 $\pm$4.52	-169 $\pm$27	10^{-7} $\pm10^{-8}$

Table 3: Best Fitness (averaged on 20 runs) for 200,000 evaluations
Best results indicated in bold   Exact optimum of F_6 and F_8 = 0

These trends are confirmed by preliminary experiments on F_6, F_7 and F_8 (Table 3): $PBIL_C$ significantly outperforms self-adaptive ES on two out of the three problems, the best option for adjusting σ being the relaxation from a small fraction of the best offspring.

---

[5] This holds for all problems except F_3, which is the problem with most diversity in the fitness of the offspring. This might be an indication for choosing K adaptively: e.g. retain the offspring whose fitness is greater than a given function of the average fitness and deviation of the fitness in the current population.

5   Conclusion

The main originality of PBIL is to reformulate evolution into new, higher-level, terms: rather than specifying all operations needed to transform a population into another population (selection, recombination, mutation, replacement), one only specifies how to evolve or update a distribution given the additional information supplied by the current population. At this level, many core traits of evolution (e.g. diversity, speed of changes) are explicit and can be directly controlled.

Overall, evolution shifts from the stochastic exploration of the search space Ω, to learning a distribution on Ω by reinforcement from the current population.

This paper extends PBIL from boolean to continuous search spaces, by learning Gaussian distributions $\mathcal{N}(X, \sigma)$. The resulting $PBIL_C$ algorithm can be thought of as a $(1, \lambda)$-ES, with the following differences. ES takes instant decisions, on the basis of the instant information. $PBIL_C$ maintains a long-term memory, takes its decisions on the basis of this long-term memory, and slowly updates the memory from the instant information. Practically, the parent of a $(1, \lambda)$-ES jumps toward the best offspring; in opposition, the center of the distribution in $PBIL_C$ cautiously moves toward a weighted combination of the offspring.

Similarly, self-adaptive ES locally adjusts the variance of mutation by means of instant decisions; in opposition, $PBIL_C$ cautiously updates the variance from the global diversity of the best offspring.

One argument for learning distributions is that it expectedly scales up more easily than evolving populations: a reasonable size population gives little information on large-sized search space. Experimental results on large-sized problems show that $PBIL_C$ actually outperforms standard ES on five out of six problems (with one or two orders of magnitude) and also outperforms the original PBIL working on a discretized version of the continuous problems considered.

Nevertheless, given the size of the search space, $PBIL_C$ ends rather far from the optimum on four out of six problems. Further experiments will consider other problems, and study how $PBIL_C$ behaves in the last stages of exploitation. Another perspective of research is to evolve several distributions rather than a single one. This would relax the main limitation of the PBIL scheme, that is, the fact that it can only discover a single optimum. Indeed, learning simultaneously several distributions is very comparable to evolving several species. The advantage is that comparing an individual to a few distributions might be less expensive and again more transparent, than clustering the population, adjusting the selection or the fitness function to ensure the co-evolution of species.

Acknowledgments

Many thanks to Marc Schoenauer, for many valuable comments, and to the second anonymous referee, for very insightful comments and suggestions.

References

1. T. Bäck. *Evolutionary Algorithms in theory and practice*. New-York:Oxford University Press, 1995.
2. S. Baluja. An empirical comparizon of seven iterative and evolutionary function optimization heuristics. Technical Report CMU-CS-95-193, Carnegie Mellon University, 1995.
3. S. Baluja and R. Caruana. Removing the genetics from the standard genetic algorithms. In A. Prieditis and S. Russel, editors, *Proc. of ICML95*, pages 38–46. Morgan Kaufmann, 1995.
4. S. Baluja and S. Davies. Using optimal dependency-trees for combinatorial optimization: Learning the structure of the search space. In *Proc. of ICML97*. Morgan Kaufmann, 1997.
5. D. B. Fogel. *Evolutionary Computation. Toward a New Philosophy of Machine Intelligence*. IEEE Press, Piscataway, NJ, 1995.
6. D. E. Goldberg. *Genetic algorithms in search, optimization and machine learning*. Addison Wesley, 1989.
7. J. Horn and D.E. Goldberg. Genetic algorithms difficulty and the modality of fitness landscapes. In L. D. Whitley and M. D. Vose, editors, *Foundations of Genetic Algorithms 3*, pages 243–269. Morgan Kaufmann, 1995.
8. S. W. Mahfoud. A comparison of parallel and sequential niching techniques. In L. J. Eshelman, editor, *Proc. of ICGA '95*, pages 136–143. Morgan Kaufmann, 1995.
9. T.M. Mitchell. *Machine Learning*. McGraw Hill, 1995.
10. I. Rechenberg. *Evolutionstrategie: Optimierung Technisher Systeme nach Prinzipien des Biologischen Evolution*. Fromman-Holzboog Verlag, Stuttgart, 1973.
11. G. Rudolph. *Convergence Properties of Evolutionary Algorithms*. Kovac, Hamburg, 1997.
12. S. Russell and A. Norwig. *Artificial Intelligence, a modern approach*. Prentice Hall, 1995.
13. H.-P. Schwefel. *Numerical Optimization of Computer Models*. John Wiley & Sons, New-York, 1981. 1995 – 2nd edition.
14. M. Sebag and M. Schoenauer. Mutation by imitation in boolean evolution strategies. In H.-M. Voigt, W. Ebeling, I. Rechenberg, and H.-P. Schwefel, editors, *Proc. of PPSN-IV*, pages 356–365. Springer-Verlag, LNCS 1141, 1996.
15. I. Servet, L. Trave-Massuyes, and D. Stern. Telephone network traffic overloading diagnosis and evolutionary computation technique. In *Artificial Evolution'97*, pages 137–144. Springer Verlag, LNCS 1363, 1997.
16. R. Storn and K. Price. Minimizing the real functions of the ICEC'96 contest by differential evolution. In *Proc. of ICEC96*, pages 842–844, 1996.
17. L.D. Whitley, K. Mathias, and P. Fitzhorn. Delta coding: an iterative strategy for GAs. In R. K. Belew and L. B. Booker, editors, *Proc. of ICGA '89*, pages 77–84. Morgan Kaufmann, 1989.

Multi-parent Recombination in Genetic Algorithms with Search Space Boundary Extension by Mirroring

Shigeyoshi Tsutsui

Department of Management and Information Science, Hannan University
5-4-33 Amamihigashi, Matsubara, Osaka 580-5802 Japan
tsutsui@hannan-u.ac.jp

Abstract. In previous work, we have investigated real coded genetic algorithms with several types of multi-parent recombination operators and found evidence that multi-parent recombination with *center of mass crossover* (CMX) seems a good choice for real coded GAs. But CMX does not work well on functions which have their optimum on the corner of the search space. In this paper, we propose a method named *boundary extension by mirroring* (BEM) to cope with this problem. Applying BEM to CMX, the performance of CMX on the test functions which have their optimum on the corner of the search space was much improved. Further, by applying BEM, we observed clear improvement in performance of two-parent recombination on the functions which have their optimum on the corner of the search space. Thus, we suggest that BEM is a good general technique to improve the efficiency of crossover operators in real-coded GAs for a wide range of functions.

1. Introduction

Studies on the effect of multi-parent recombination, where more than two parents are used to generate offspring, is an interesting research subject in Evolutionary Algorithms (EAs). There is of course no necessity to be restricted to two-parent recombination, as EAs allow us to emulate the ideas of natural evolution very flexibly. A few attempts to study the effect of using more than two parents for recombination in EAs are reported in the literature [1, 2, 6, 7, 8, 9, 19, 20, 23].

A brief review of multi-parent recombination in EAs has been made in [8, 9] as follows. The first attempt in this line was global recombination in Evolution Strategies (ESs) [1, 19], in which one new individual is produced, inheriting genes from more than two parents. Nevertheless, the number of parents is not fixed, thus global recombination allows for the possibility of more than two parents, but does not enforce it. The same holds for the recently introduced multi-parent Gene Pool Recombination [23] and the Gene Linkage method [20] in Genetic Algorithms (GAs). An extension of ES, the (μ/ρ, λ) multi-recombination strategy [2], does apply an adjustable operator with arity ρ, where ρ is the number of parents used.

Two generalized multi-parent recombination operators in GAs are scanning crossover and diagonal crossover, introduced in [6, 7, 8]. In [6, 7], these operators were evaluated on standard test functions with bit string representation and other types of problems and it was shown that 2-parent recombination was inferior to them. In [8], these operators were evaluated on Kauffman's NK-landscapes [15], which allow for systematic characterization and user control of the ruggedness of the fitness landscape, and it was found that sexual recombination was superior on mildly epistatic problems. In [9], a generalized version of intermediary recombination, scanning crossover, and diagonal crossover, which were all designed or modified to produce one offspring, were introduced for ESs, and it was shown that in most cases a significant improvement in performance was observed as the number of parents increased.

In recent years several real-coded GAs, for function optimization, which use real number vector representation of chromosomes, have been proposed [3, 11, 14, 16, 22] and have been shown to outperform the traditional bit string based representation. In [21], we have proposed three types of multi-parent recombination operators for real-coded GAs, namely, the *center of mass crossover operator* (CMX), *multi-parent feature-wise crossover operator* (MFX), and *seed crossover operator* (SX) . The results showed that in these three operators, performance with CMX improved as the number of parents increased on functions having multmodality and/or epistasis. Thus, we have concluded that multi-parent recombination with CMX is one good choice for real-coded GAs. But CMX had the disadvantage that it did not work well on functions which have their optimum at the corner of the search space.

In this paper, we propose a method to cope with this problem. In the method, we allow individuals to be located beyond the boundary of the search space by some extent. The fitness value of individual located beyond the boundary of the search space is set to be the same as that of the point it maps to by mirror reflection across the boundary. We call this method "boundary extension by mirroring" (BEM). With this method, the performance of CMX was improved on the test functions which have their optimum in the corner of the search space. Further, the performance improvement by BEM also holds for two-parent recombination.

In the next section we give a brief review of CMX. In Section 3, we present the BEM method. Experimental methodology and analysis of results is described in Section 4. Finally, concluding remarks are made in Section 5.

2. A Brief Review of Center of Mass Crossover Operator (CMX) [21]

CMX selects a set of real parents, then creates a set of virtual mates by mirroring each parent across a center of mass, and then, using a two-parent recombination operator called the *base operator*, crosses over each parent with its virtual mate to produce an offspring. The base operator can be any two-parent recombination operator. Thus, CMX is a natural generalization of 2-parent recombination. Possible good choices of base operator for CMX include BLX-α [10], variants of BLX-α [12] and UNDX [18]. In this paper we will use BLX-α as the base operator, since it is a simple and generalized operator for real vector recombination, and it works fairly well. Fig. 1 shows the feasible offspring space for BLX-α in the two dimensional case. Offspring are uniformly sampled from this space. When a portion of the feasible offspring space locates beyond the boundary of the search space, this portion is cut away from the feasible offspring space.

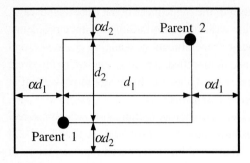

Fig. 1 BLX-α (*n* = 2)

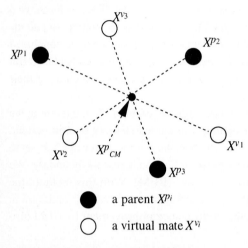

a parent X^{p_i}

a virtual mate X^{v_i}

Fig. 2 Virtual mates in CMX (*m*=3)

Fig. 2 illustrates the method of generating the virtual mates in CMX. Let $X = (x_1,....,x_n)$ represent an n dimensional real number vector representing a possible solution (chromosome). Let m ($m \geq 2$) and N ($N \geq m$) be the number of parents and population size, respectively. In this crossover (CMX), m individuals $X^{p_i} = (x_1^{p_i},...,x_n^{p_i})$, $i = 1,...,m$ are chosen at random from the parental pool $\{X_1,...,X_N\}$. Then X^p_{CM}, center of mass of the m parents, is calculated as

$$X^p_{CM} = \frac{1}{m} \sum_{i=1}^{m} X^{p_i}. \qquad (1)$$

For each $i = 1,...,m$, we generate a *virtual mate* X^{v_i}, where X^{p_i} and X^{v_i} are symmetrical with respect to X^p_{CM} as

$$X^{v_i} = 2 X^p_{CM} - X^{p_i}. \qquad (2)$$

By crossing over the real parent X^{p_i} and its virtual mate X^{v_i}, we then generate one child X^{c_i}. Thus in CMX, m children are generated from m parents. Since X^{p_i} and X^{v_i} are symmetrical with respect to X^p_{CM}, the center of the mass of m parents, CMX tends to generate offspring uniformly around the m parents. Then we choose another set of m parents (not chosen earlier) and generate m more children. This process continues until N new children are generated.

CMX did not work well on functions which have their optimum at the corner of the search space or have discontinuous fitness landscapes, but its performance improved as the number of parents increased on functions having multmodality and/or epistasis. Since real life problems normally have some degree of epistasis and multimodality, we have concluded that multi-parent recombination with CMX is one good choice for real-coded GAs although it had a disadvantage that it did not work well on functions which have their optimum on the corner of the search space. By the way, results on two other multi-parent recombination operators were as follows. The MFX operator worked well on functions which do not have epistasis. For functions having epistasis its performance degraded as the number of parents increased. The SX operator performed well on simple functions and multimodal functions with a medium number of parents, but it did not work well with a large number of parents on functions having epistasis or on multimodal functions with large number of parents.

3. Boundary Extension by Mirroring

For functions which have their optimum in the corner of the search space, the virtual individuals (see Eq. 2 and Fig. 2) may be located outside the search space. In these cases, the possibility that the base operator generates offspring around the optimum point becomes less since a portion of the feasible offspring space which locates beyond the boundary of the search space is cut away from the feasible offspring space of the base operator.

In the *boundary extension by mirroring* (BEM) method, we allow individuals to be located beyond the boundary of the search space, by some extent as shown in Fig. 3. The functional values of individuals located beyond the boundary of the search space are calculated as if they are located inside of the search space at points symmetrical with the boundary. Here we face the problem of how much we should be allowed to extend the search space beyond the boundary. If we extend too much, the efficiency of search may be degraded since the effective search space becomes large. We introduce an extension rate r_e ($0<r_e<1$) as a control parameter. The search space is centered in an extended space extended by a factor of $1+r_e$ along each dimension. The functional value of individual i with real vector $X^{(i)} = (x_1^{(i)},...,x_n^{(i)})$ is obtained as

$$f(X^{(i)}) = f(Y^{(i)}),\qquad(3)$$

where,

$$Y^{(i)} = (y_1^{(i)},\dots,y_n^{(i)}),$$

$$y_j^{(i)} = \begin{cases} 2\min_j - x_j^{(i)} : \text{if } x_j < \min_j \\ 2\max_j - x_j^{(i)} : \text{if } x_j > \max_j \\ x_j^{(i)} \qquad : \text{otherwise,} \end{cases}\qquad(4)$$

and $\min_j$ and $\max_j$ are the lower and upper limits of parameter range on the jth dimension of the search space.

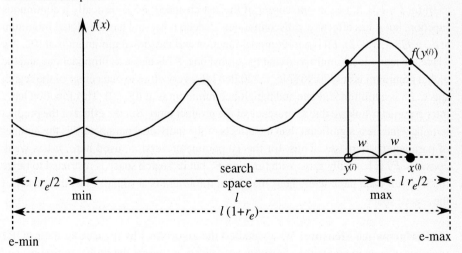

Fig. 3 Boundary extending by mirroring (BEM)

4. The Experiments

4.1 Experimental Methodology

To see the effect of the proposed BEM, we ran a real-coded GA. The experimental conditions were basically the same as in [21] as follows.

(1) Basic Evolutionary Model: The basic evolutionary model we used in these experiments is similar to that of the CHC [10] and $(\mu+\lambda)$-ES [19]. Let the population size be N, and let it, at time t, be represented by $P(t)$. The population $P(t+1)$ is produced as follows: A collection of N/m m-sets is randomly selected, and crossover is then applied to each m-set, generating N offspring which are placed in $I(t)$. The individuals are then ranked and the best N from the $2N$ in $P(t)$ and $I(t)$ are selected to form $P(t+1)$, thus the best solution obtained so far is always included in $P(t+1)$.

(2) Mutation Operator: Several mutation operators for real-coded GAs are proposed in the literature [3, 14, 16]. Since this study places its main focus on testing the effect of multi-parent crossover, we use a simple mutation operator that replaces a real number in a chromosome with another randomly selected real number.

(3) Test Functions: The test functions used here are commonly used in the literature, which includes the De Jong test suite [4] (except $F4$), and 20-parameter Rastrigin ($F6$), 10-parameter Schwefel ($F7$) and 10-paramter Griewank ($F8$) functions [17]. In addition to these functions, in this study we included a 10-paramter modified Griewank ($F9$) function which has its global minimum at the corner of the search space. These functions are summarized in Table 1. $F1$ is a simple unimodal function and has the global minimum at $(0, 0, 0)$. $F2$ has strong inter-parameter linkage (epistasis) and has the global minimum at $(1, 1)$. $F3$ is a discontinuous function with the global minimum in the rage $x_i \in [-5.12, -5.0)$ for $i = 1,...,5$, i.e., in one corner of the search space. $F5$ is basically a continuous function, but it has effectively discontinuous 25 deep holes and has the global minimum at $(-31.978, -31.978)$. $F6$ is a multimodal function and the global minimum is at $(0,...,0)$. There are many local minima around the global one. $F7$ is also a multimodal one and the global minimum is at $(420.968746,...,420.968746)$, very close to one corner of the search space. $F8$ is a multimodal one and the global minimum is at $(0,...,0)$. This function has a inter-parameter linkage due to presence of the product term. But the effect of the product term becomes less significant than the effects of the individual parameters as the number of parameters increases. Thus, for the 10 parameter version, used here, it has weak epistasis. $F9$ is basically same with function $F8$ but its search space is restricted to range $[0, 5.11]$ for each parameter. Thus the global minimum is at $(0,...,0)$, just the corner of the search space.

(4) Performance Measure: We evaluated the algorithms by measuring their #OPT (number of runs in which the algorithm succeeded in finding the global optimum) and

Table 1 Test Functions

functions	range of x_j	Δx_j	functional characteristics				
			pos.[*1]	epis.[*2]	mul.[*3]	disc.[*4]	dim.[*5]
$F1 = \sum\limits_{i=1}^{3} x_i^2$	[-5.12,5.11]	0.01	center	none	none	none	low
$F2 = 100\left(x_1^2 - x_2\right)^2 + \left(1 - x_1\right)^2$	[-2.048,2.047]	0.001	mid[*6]	strong	none	none	low
$F3 = \sum\limits_{i=1}^{5} \lfloor x_i \rfloor$	[-5.12,5.11]	0.01	corner	none	none	medium	low
$F5 = \left[0.002 + \sum\limits_{j=1}^{25} \dfrac{1}{j + \sum_{i=1}^{2}\left(x_i - a_{ij}\right)^6} \right]^{-1}$	[-65.536,65.535]	0.001	mid[*6]	none	low	strong	low
$F6 = (20 \times 10) + \left[\sum\limits_{i=1}^{20}\left(x_i^2 - 10\cos(2\pi\, x_i)\right) \right]$	[-5.12,5.11]	0.01	center	none	high	none	high
$F7 = \sum\limits_{i=1}^{10} -x_i \sin\left(\sqrt{\mid x_i \mid}\right)$	[-512,511]	1.0	corner	none	high	none	medium
$F8 = 1 + \sum\limits_{i=1}^{10} \dfrac{x_i^2}{4000} - \prod\limits_{i=1}^{10}\left(\cos(x_i / \sqrt{i})\right)$	[-512,511]	1.0	center	weak	high	none	medium
$F9 = 1 + \sum\limits_{i=1}^{10} \dfrac{x_i^2}{4000} - \prod\limits_{i=1}^{10}\left(\cos(x_i / \sqrt{i})\right)$	[0,511]	1.0	corner	weak	high	none	medium

*1: position of the optimum point, *2: epistasis, *3: multi-modality, *4: discontinuity,
*5: dimmension of the search space, *6: middle of center and corner

MNT (mean number of trials to find the global optimum in those runs where it did find the optimum). We used Δx_j value as resolution (borrowed from bit string based GAs, Table1) to determine whether the optimal solution is found. If the solution detected is within Δx_j range of the actual optimum point, we assume that the solution is detected. Let us represent the optimal solution of a function by $(o_1,...,o_n)$. Then we assume that the real coded GA is able to find the optimal solution if all parameters $(x_1,...,x_n)$ of the best individual are within the range $[(o_j - \Delta x_j/2), (o_j + \Delta x_j/2)]$ for all j.

The effect of BEM method was evaluated for extension rate $r_e = 0.1, 0.2, 0.3, 0.4$. Number of parents for CMX was changed from 2 to 16 in steps of 2. Fifty (50) runs are performed. In each run, the initial population $P(0)$ is randomly initialized in the original search space. Each run continues until the global optimum is found or a maximum of 200,000 trials is reached. A population size of 50 is used for all functions except $F8$ and $F9$. $F8$ and $F9$ required a population size of 400 for reliable performance. The α value used for the base operator BLX-α is 0.5 for all function except $F2$. $F2$ required a value of 2.0 for reasonable performance. Mutation rate is $0.2/n$ (n: number of parameters).

4.2 Empirical Analysis of Results

The results are shown in Fig. 4. In the figure, CMX with extension rate r_e is represented as CMX-r_e. For example, CMX-0.3 means CMX with extension rate of 0.2. #OPTs of all experiments except for the function $F9$ were 50 (100%). For $F9$, #OPTs were described in the figure.

The results on functions $F1$ (unimodal), $F2$ (unimodal, strong epistasis), $F6$ (highly multimodal, high dimension) and $F8$ (highly multimodal, weak epistasis) showed performance improvement as the number of parents was increased from 2. Almost no side effect of BEM was observed on functions $F1$, $F8$ and $F5$ although on function $F5$ (strong discontinuous), CMX with BEM showed performance degradation as the number of parents was increased from 2. A small amount of side effects of BEM was observed on functions $F2$ and $F6$. On these functions, extension rate of 0.4 had tendency to diminish the effect of multi-parent recombination.

As reported in [21], CMX without BEM showed clear performance degradation as the number of parents was increased from 2 on function $F3$ (corner), $F7$ (highly multimodal, corner). These two functions have the optimum at or very close to one corner of the search space and, thus, the calculation of center of mass has less meaning in the sense that it may force some of the virtual mates to be located outside of the search space. In this study, we found that applying BEM had much weakened the problem of CMX on these two functions with extension rates of 0.2-0.4. With extension rate of 0.1, the effect was not so aggressive on function $F7$. Especially, on function $F3$, CMX with BEM showed great performance improvement compared with CMX without BEM, and the effect of BEM was further more clearly observed on function $F9$ (highly multimodal, weak epistasis, and corner). On function $F9$, CMX without BEM found the global optimum only twice when the number of parents was two and the MNT for this case was 37,637.0. and could not find the global optimum when the number of parents was greater than two. On the other hand, CMX with BEM found the global optimum 50 times (100%) when the number of parents was 2, 4, 6, and 8, respectively, and MNTs for these cases were much smaller than 37,637.0, although there still remained a tendency to degrade the performance as the number of parents was increased from 2. Again, extension rates of 0.2-0.4 showed good values on function $F9$.

Although appropriate values of extension rate depends on the problem, values of [0.2, 0.3] seem good for the functions $F1$-$F9$. The BEM method was introduced to cope with the problem of CMX. But the effectiveness of BEM was also clearly observed when the number of parents was two (CMX with two parent is identical to normal two parent recombination, i.e. BLX-α in this study). This is also an important finding in this study.

5. Concluding Remarks

In previous work [21] we proposed three types of multi-parent recombination operators for real-coded GAs and showed that in each of these the performance with *center of*

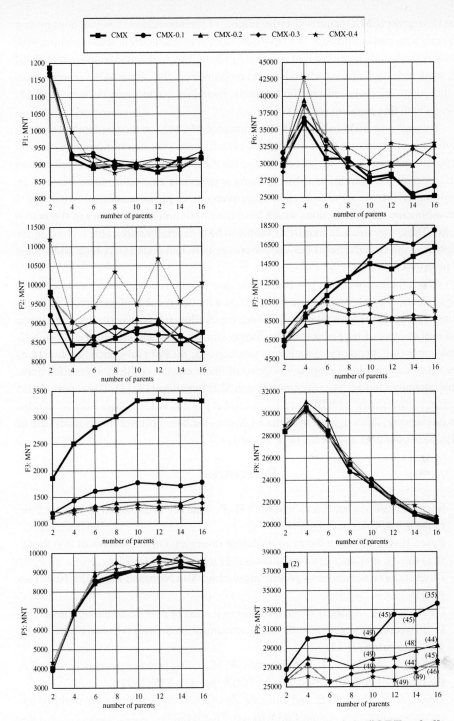

Fig. 4 The MNT plotted against the number of parents (m) (#OPTs of all experiments except for function F9 were 50 (100%))

mass crossover (CMX) improved as the number of parents increased on functions having multmodality and/or epistasis. We have concluded that multi-parent recombination with CMX is one good choice for real coded GAs. But CMX had a disadvantage that it did not work well on functions which have their optimum in the corner of the search space. In this paper, we proposed a method, namely, *boundary extension by mirroring* (BEM) to cope with this problem of CMX.

By applying BEM to CMX, the performance of CMX on the test functions which have their optimum on the corner of the search space was much improved, and the technique did not cause side effects for the functions whose optima are located around the center of the search space by choosing appropriate extension rates. Further, by applying BEM, we observed clear improvement in performance of two parents recombination on the functions which have their optimum on the corner of the search space. Thus, we conclude that BEM seems to be a generally applicable technique for improving the effectiveness of crossover operators in real-coded GAs for a wide range of functions.

Nevertheless, we must test BEM technique in a more systematic way to confirm these claims. We only tested these operators on a limited number of test functions. In bit string chromosome representation, NK-landscapes allow for systematic characterization and user control of ruggedness of the fitness landscape. Many studies try to use NK-landscapes to generate systematic test functions [5, 8]. For real-coded test functions several researchers have proposed systems of linear equations (SLE) as test functions. Inter-parameter linkage is easily controlled in SLE functions [12, 13]. To evaluate multi-parent recombination with BEM on functions having this kind of characteristic remains for future work. Although we used the BLX-α as the base operator in this study, use of other base operators also needs to be studied.

References

1. Bäck, T.,Hoffmeister, F. and Schewfel, H.-P.: A survey of evolution strategies, *Proc. of the 4th ICGA*, pp. 2-9 (1991).
2. Beyer, H.-G.: Toward a theory of evolution strategies: On the benefits of sex- the ($\mu/\mu,\lambda$) theory, *Evolutionary Computation*, $3(1)$, pp. 81-111 (1995).
3. Davis, L.: *The handbook of genetic algorithms*, Von Nostrand Reinhold, New York (1991).
4. De Jong, K. A.: *Analysis of the behavior of a class of genetic adaptive systems*. Ph. D. dissertation, Dept. Computer and Communication Sciences, University of Michigan, Ann Arbor (1975).
5. De Jong, K. A., Potter M. A. and Spears, W. M.: Using problem generators to explore the effects of epistasis, *Proc. the 7th ICGA*, pp. 338-345 (1997).
6. Eiben, A. E., Raue, P-E. and Ruttkay, Zs.: Genetic algorithms with multi-parent recombination, *Proc. of the PPSN III*, pp. 78-87(1994).

7. Eiben, A. E., van Kemenade, C. H. M. and Kok, J. N.: Orgy in the computer: Multiparent reproduction in genetic algorithms, *Proc. of the 3rd European Conference on Artificial Life*, LNAI 929, Springer-Verlag, pp. 934-945(1995).
8. Eiben, A. E. and Schippers, C. A.: Multi-parent's niche: n-ary crossover on NK-landscapes, *Proc. of the PPSN IV*, pp. 319-328 (1996).
9. Eiben, A. E, Bäck, T.: Empirical investigation of multiparent recombination operators in evolution strategies, *Evolutionary Computation, 5(3)*, pp. 347-365 (1997).
10. Eshelman, L. J.: The CHC adaptive search algorithm: how to have safe search when engaging in nontraditional genetic recombination, *Foundations of Genetic Algorithms*, Morgan Kaufmann, pp.265-283 (1991).
11. Eshelman, L. J. and Schaffer, J. D.: Real-coded genetic algorithms and interval-schemata, *Foundations of Genetic Algorithms 2*, Morgan Kaufman, pp. 187-202 (1993).
12. Eshelman, L. J., Mathias, K. E. and Schaffer, J. D.: Crossover operator biases: Exploiting the population distribution, *Proc. of the 7th ICGA*, pp. 354-361 (1997).
13. Fogel, D. B., and Atmar, J. W.: Comparing genetic operators with Gaussian mutations in simulated evolutionary processes using linear systems, *Biological Cybernetics, 66*, pp. 111-114 (1990).
14. Janikow, C. Z. and Michalewicz, Z.: An experimental comparison of binary and floating point representations in genetic algorithms, *Proc. of the Fourth ICGA*, pp. 31-36 (1991).
15. Kauffman, S. A.: Adaptation on rugged fitness landscapes, Lecture in the Science of Complexity, edited by Stein, D. Santa Fe Institute Studies in the Science of Complexity, Lect. Vol. I, Addison Wesley, pp.527-618 (1989).
16. Michalewicz, Z. : *Genetic algorithms + data structures = evolution program*, Springer-Verlag (1994).
17. Mühlenbein, H., Schomisch, M. and Born, J.: The parallel genetic algorithm as function optimizer, *Proc. of the 4th ICGA*, pp. 271-278 (1991).
18. Ono, I and Kobayashi, S: A real-coded genetic algorithm for function optimization using unimodal normal distribution crossover, *Proc. of the 7th ICGA*, pp. 246-253 (1997).
19. Schewefel, H.-P.: *Evolution and optimum seeking*, Sixth-Generation Computer Technology Series, Wiley (1995).
20. Smith, J and Fogarty, T. C.: Recombination strategy adaptation via evolution of gene linkage, *Proc. of the 1996 IEEE ICEC*, pp. 826-831, 1996.
21. Tsutsui, S and Ghosh, A.: A study on the effect of multi-parent recombination in real coded genetic algorithms, *Proc. of the 1998 IEEE ICEC*, pp. 828-833 (1998).
22. Wright, A. H.: Genetic algorithms for real parameter optimization, *Foundations of Genetic Algorithms*, Morgan Kaufman, pp. 205-218 (1991).
23. Voigt, H.-M. and Mühlenbein, H.: Gene pool recombination and utilization of covariances for the breeder genetic algorithm, *Proc. of the 1995 IEEE ICEC*, pp. 172-177 (1995).

Selective Crossover in Genetic Algorithms: An Empirical Study

Kanta Vekaria and Chris Clack

Department of Computer Science
University College London
Gower Street
London WC1E 6BT
United Kingdom
Email: {K.Vekaria, C.Clack}@cs.ucl.ac.uk

Abstract. The performance of a genetic algorithm (GA) is dependent on many factors: the type of crossover operator, the rate of crossover, the rate of mutation, population size, and the encoding used are just a few examples. Currently, GA practitioners pick and choose GA parameters empirically until they achieve adequate performance for a given problem. In this paper we have isolated one such parameter: the crossover operator. The motivation for this study is to provide an adaptive crossover operator that gives best overall performance on a large set of problems. A new adaptive crossover operator "selective crossover" is proposed and is compared with two-point and uniform crossover on a problem generator where epistasis can be varied and on trap functions where deception can be varied. We provide empirical results which show that selective crossover is more efficient than two-point and uniform crossover across a representative set of search problems containing epistasis.

1. Introduction

In the canonical genetic algorithm (GA) [Gold89], individuals are represented as fixed length binary vectors, recombination is implemented as a crossover operator, mutation is an additional operator to provide diversity in a population and the population is generational. Recombination is regarded as the driving force of a GA and is the process where segments (genes) of two individuals (parents) are exchanged to produce two new individuals (children). The number of crossover points is decided beforehand and is usually limited to 1 or 2 [Holl75].

Since Holland's work the field of GAs has grown tremendously. Along with this growth we now have a pool of genetic operators, where different permutations will yield alternative GAs (the mimicking of natural evolution is still retained). The alternative GAs have varying degrees of performance – for one kind of problem some will do extremely well but for another they will do poorly. One can argue that many factors contribute to a GA's performance such as population size, crossover/mutation rates, method of selection, representation and the recombination operator and hence this makes it difficult to pinpoint which operators to choose for optimum performance. In this research we have isolated one operator, the recombination operator.

There are now many different methods for recombination [Spea97] but one-point, two-point and uniform crossover are generally those that are commonly used. Even with just three crossover operators it has been difficult to decide a priori which form of crossover to use. Users typically pick and choose the operators in the hope that they will give optimum performance. We know from "no free lunch" theorems [WoMa95] that an operator that is suited for all problems cannot exist, but is it possible to devise a form of crossover that is suited for most practical problems?

The motivation for this paper is to present a new form of adaptive crossover "Selective Crossover" which gives better performance (i.e. the number of evaluations required to find a solution) than two-point and uniform crossover. The reason we have measured the number of evaluations is because the vast majority of the computation involved in a GA is during evaluation. The GA used in this study only re-evaluates individuals if they change (by crossover or mutation).

2. Exploration and Exploitation

An issue that is of great concern in the GA community is the balance between exploration and exploitation. An efficient optimisation algorithm is one that uses two techniques: exploration to investigate new and unknown areas in a search space and exploitation to make use of knowledge acquired by exploration to reach better positions on the search space. Pure random search is good at exploration, but has no exploitation. Hill climbing is good at exploitation but has little exploration. Genetic algorithms combine both strategies, but crossover operators have varying degrees of exploration and exploitation [EsCaSc89].

The combination of exploration and exploitation is effective but it is difficult to know where the balance lies. Many adaptive techniques [ScMo87][Davi89][WhOp94] have been introduced to provide a balance between exploration and exploitation and attempt to solve the problem of finding optimal parameters. For this study we will assume the balance lies with a strategy which gives the best overall performance across a wide range of problems (of varying epistasis; most 'real world' problems contain some epistasis). The balance is a compromise between generalisation (a crossover operator which works well with many different problems) and specialisation (a crossover operator which is optimum for a single problem). This balance can provide a good general-purpose strategy and can also be a starting point for an adaptive GA to favour specialisation.

3. Selective Crossover - Inspiration from Nature

The inspiration for our new adaptive crossover operator ("selective crossover") comes from nature, specifically Dawkin's model of evolution and dominance characteristics in nature. Dawkin's model of evolution is based on the gene [Dawk89]. He presents his theory of the gene as the fundamental unit of natural selection. Chromosomes have a life span of one generation but a genetic unit lasts for many generations, thus natural selection favours the genetic unit.

Dominance in nature is usually associated with genetic material presented using diploid chromosomes. In the diploid form a genotype carries one or more *pairs* of chromosomes, each containing information for the same functions. The genes contained in one set can be regarded as a direct alternative to the genes in the other set. When building the body the genes in one set compete with those in the other set. Genes that are dominant are expressed in the phenotype of an organism and those that are less likely to be expressed are recessive. The relationship between a dominant and recessive gene is complex: some genes that have been known to be dominant have become more recessive in successive generations and vice versa. These shifts in dominance are due to changes in fitness of an individual with respect to their environment change. Those genes that increased an individual's fitness became dominant. These dominance characteristics have evolved over generations.

Selective crossover is very much like "dominance *without* diploidy". It uses an extra vector that accompanies the chromosome to accumulate knowledge of what happened in previous generations and uses that to promote successful genes (individual bits) during crossover onto the next generation.

4. Implementation

To mimic the dominance characteristics of a gene, to bias genes during crossover, each individual (chromosome) has associated with it a real-valued vector, and thus each gene has an associated *dominance value*. Each recombination uses two parents to create two children. During recombination two parents are selected and their fitness is recorded. 'Parent 1' is considered as the *contributor*. The dominance value of each gene in both parents is compared linearly across the chromosome. The gene that has a higher dominance value contributes to 'Child 1' along with the dominance value. If both dominance values are equal then crossover does not occur at that position. Fig. 1 gives an example of selective crossover: the shaded genes have a higher dominance value than its competing gene. To keep diversity in the population 'Child 2' inherits the non-dominant genes. The need for this will become apparent later.

After crossover the two new children are evaluated. If a single child's fitness is greater than the fitness of either parent, the dominance values (of those genes that were exchanged during crossover) are increased proportionately to the fitness increase. This is done to reflect the genes' contribution to the fitness increase. Fig. 2 gives an example of the mechanism. It follows on from the selective crossover example given in Fig. 1. In Fig. 2, only 'Child 1' has an increase in fitness of 0.1 (compared with the fittest parent) hence its dominance values get updated. In Fig. 1 the bit values of 'Parent 1' and 'Parent 2' at loci 1 and 2 did not get exchanged during crossover and the bit values at loci 4 and 6 are the same. Thus, after selective crossover, the genes that effected the change in the chromosome are only those held at loci 3 and 5. Since the change of those genes at loci 3 and 5 resulted in an increase in fitness, only their dominance values get increased in 'Child 1' (shaded in Fig. 2).

Parent 1 – fitness = 0.36

0.4	0.3	0.01	0.9	0.1	0.2
1	0	0	1	0	0

Parent 2 – fitness = 0.30

0.01	0.2	0.4	0.2	0.9	0.3
0	1	1	1	1	0

Child 1

0.4	0.3	0.4	0.9	0.9	0.3
1	0	1	1	1	0

Child 2

0.01	0.2	0.01	0.2	0.1	0.2
0	1	0	1	0	0

Fig. 1. Selective Crossover

Child 1 – fitness = 0.46

0.4	0.3	0.4	0.9	0.9	0.3
1	0	1	1	1	0

Child 2 – fitness = 0.20

0.01	0.2	0.01	0.2	0.1	0.2
0	1	0	1	0	0

⇩ **Increase dominance values**

Child 1 – fitness = 0.46

0.4	0.3	0.5	0.9	1.0	0.3
1	0	1	1	1	0

Child 2 – fitness = 0.20

0.01	0.2	0.01	0.2	0.1	0.2
0	1	0	1	0	0

Fig. 2. Biasing Genes

On initialisation the dominance values are randomly generated, as is the population, but are restricted to be in the range [0,1]. By doing this we are allowing the GA to explore the search space by evolving the dominance values – to determine and promote those genes which are considered fit. 'Child 2' is needed so that important information is not lost in early generations when there is more exploration than exploitation. That way if 'Child 2' was to produce an increase in fitness to that of its parents then its genes will get promoted. Thus selection will bias the fitter individuals and lose the least fit and their dominance vectors.

The dominance values get increased when the fitness increases therefore it follows that one should decrease the dominance values when fitness decreases. We choose not to do this because we prefer not to introduce a strong bias during the early (highly explorative) generations. In our example (Fig. 2) 'Child 2' showed a fitness decrease. This child may be a prospective parent in the next generation. By not decreasing the dominance values we still allow the genes to compete with other genes (at the same locus in the population). If we were to decrease them they may never get chosen, hence introducing a strong bias in early generations: this form of bias is left for selection.

Unlike one-point or two-point crossover, selective crossover is not biased against schema with high defining length (as defined by Holland [Holl75]). Selective crossover propagates good schema regardless of their defining length – for example, if a schema consists of interacting genes at the two extremes of the chromosome, it can be propagated as easily as a schema which consists of interacting genes located adjacent to each other. Selective crossover can be considered as an extension of uniform crossover. With selective crossover the probability of crossing over at a position is dependent on what happened in previous generations whilst in uniform crossover the probability it fixed throughout (traditionally at 0.5).

5. Experiments

To determine whether a certain operator gives best overall performance we really should apply it to all problems. Since the problem domain is infinite we restrict our experiments to a small set of problems which display common and challenging characteristics: the "random L-SAT problem generator" [DePoSp97] and "deceptive trap functions" [DeGo92]. The random L-SAT problem generator allows epistasis (interaction between genes) to be varied and the deceptive trap function allows deception to be varied. Most complex problems contain some, and possibly a great degree of, epistasis and deception; these problems are thus a good representative set for practical problems.

Each experiment is averaged over 50 independent runs. In order to have a strict comparison between the operators each population is generated with the same seed (50 different seeds were used for the 50 runs). The probability of crossover (P_c) and mutation (P_m) for the GA were fixed for all runs at *0.6* and *0.001* respectively. The GA uses fitness proportionate selection (Stochastic Universal Sampling [Baker87]).

5.1. Random L-SAT Problem Generator

The random L-SAT problem generator [DePoSp97] is a boolean expression generator. It creates random problems in conjunctive normal form subject to three parameters V (number of boolean variables), C (number of disjunctive/conjunctive clauses) and L (the length of the clauses). Selecting L of the V variables uniformly randomly and negating each variable with probability 0.5 generates each clause.

The fitness function for the L-Sat Problem is:

$$f(chrom) = \frac{1}{C} \sum_{i=1}^{C} f(clause_i)$$

Where *chrom* consists of C clauses, *f(clause$_i$)* is the fitness contribution of each clause and is 1 if the clause is satisfied or 0 otherwise. Since the problem generator randomly generates problems on demand, there is no guarantee that such an assignment to the expression exists. The difficulty of the problem increases as a function of the number of boolean variables and the complexity of the boolean expression. Increasing the number of clauses increases the epistasis and complexity.

The forms of epistasis that exist in nature are pleiotropy (a gene may influence multiple traits) and polygeny (a trait maybe influenced by multiple genes). L-Sat problems are encoded as binary bit chromosomes, where each bit represents a boolean variable. Hence each clause can be regarded as a trait and thus the polygeny is of order L and the pleiotropy can be estimated because on average each variable occurs in CL/V clauses. By varying parameters V, C, and L we can vary both the type and amount of epistasis.

In our experiments we used the same parameters as De Jong, Potter and Spears. We keep V and L fixed and we vary the number of clauses C to increase or decrease the amount of pleiotropic epistasis. The number of variables V is fixed to 100 and the clause length L is set to 3. The number of clauses C is varied from 200 (low epistasis) to 1200 (medium epistasis) to 2400 (high epistasis). The chromosome length is V. The population size is 100. The GA was allowed to run for 600 generations and the number of evaluations administered was recorded at the end of each run or when a global solution was found. The results are shown in Section 6.1.

5.2. Deceptive Trap Functions

For this study we have only used a partially deceptive problem where no tight ordering exists and a single function, rather than subfunctions, is represented in the chromosome. Trap functions [Ackl87] are piecewise-linear functions of unitation [DeGo92]. A unitation u is defined as the number of 1s in a string and is considered to be the Hamming distance of the string from the local optimum. They depend only on the number of 1s in an individual and not on the positions of the 1s. A trap function divides the search space into two peaks in the Hamming Space; one leads to the global optimum and the other to a local optimum. An example of a trap function is given in Fig. 3.

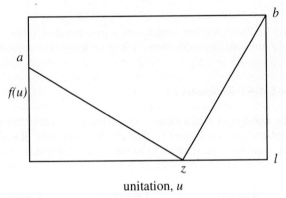

Fig. 3. A trap function with a global optimum at $u=l$.

The fitness function for a Trap Function is:

$$f(u) = \begin{cases} \frac{a}{z}(z-u), & \text{if } u \leq z; \\ \frac{b}{l-z}(u-z), & \text{otherwise;} \end{cases}$$

Where a and b are constants, l is the length of the chromosome, u is the number of 1s in the string and z is the slope change location. Deb and Goldberg [DeGo92] analysed deception in trap functions. They defined a parameter r to be the ratio of the locally to the globally optimal function values ($r = a/b$) and thus delineated boundaries between functions that are not deceptive, partially deceptive and fully deceptive. "A function is defined to be partially deceptive to an order k if all schema partitions of order less than k are deceptive" [DeGo92]. An order k trap function is one where k of the l bits in the chromosome (not necessarily situated together) are deceptive. Therefore the global optimum is when all l bits are 1s and the local optimum is when the order k schemata consists of 0's (k bits are 0s and l-k are 0s). In our experiments we use these boundaries to vary the amount of deception in a trap function.

The fitness value is scaled so that the maximum fitness is 1.0, thus $b = 1$. The parameters a and z are varied to increase or decrease deception. A fully deceptive trap function is one where all schemata with l-1 defined bits (the "order l-1" schemata) are misleading. Experiments were carried out on easy (no deception) and partially deceptive trap functions. Due to the size limitations of a conference paper we present only the results for partially deceptive trap functions with order 10, 15 and 20 misleading schemata. These show the typical behaviour as deception is increased.

The chromosome length l is 50. The population size is 1000. The results are shown in Section 6.2. For order 10, $r = a = 0.21$ and $z=30$. For order 15, $r = a = 0.35$ and $z=30$.

6. Results

For all results GA performance per evaluation is presented in tables. As mentioned earlier the GA only re-evaluates individuals if they underwent crossover or mutation.

6.1 Results for L-SAT Problems

Table 1. shows the number of evaluations (our performance measure) taken by selective, two-point and uniform crossover to find the best solution. Recall from section 5.1 that there is no guarantee such an assignment exists. The solution quality is given in square brackets and represents the average solution found in 50 runs.

	Selective	Two-point	Uniform
Low	24098 (6430) [0.997]	29206 (1064) [0.999]	29621 (5782) [0.999]
Medium	28214 (509) [0.937]	37188 (69) [0.932]	38306 (42) [0.931]
High	27573 (484) [0.916]	37275 (61) [0.911]	38310 (43) [0.911]

Table 1. Mean number of evaluations to find the best solution for low, medium and high epistasis. The standard deviation is shown in brackets. The solution quality is given in square brackets. These are averages over 50 runs.

During low epistasis all crossover operators work equally as well (selective crossover is slightly better with the least number of evaluations, Table 1). As epistasis is increased to medium and high, selective crossover finds a better solution and does this with the least number of evaluations at 28214 and 27573 respectively. The standard deviation is large with low epistasis because the GA stopped when it found a solution of 1.0 and recorded the number of evaluations. If the GA did not always find a solution of 1.0, evaluation was terminated at 600 generations.

Tests for significance were carried out, to compare the three crossover operators, on the number of evaluations yielded. Using the *t-test* with a 5% significance level, selective crossover showed a significant difference, an improvement of up to 25%. Selective crossover works well with epistatic problems because it allows exploitation of genes which are not necessarily situated together in the chromosome and it does this consistently with the least number of evaluations, thus saving online computation. These striking results led us to try selective crossover with deceptive functions, to see how it compared with the other conventional reproductive operators.

6.2   Results for Deceptive Trap Functions

Table 2 shows the mean number of evaluations taken to find the solution for order 10 and 15 trap functions. Our initial expectation was that selective crossover was too exploitative (exploration is achieved solely through the generation of Child 2 and, of course, mutation) and would always be misled by the local optimum in all experiments. In Table 2, the number of evaluations taken to reach the solution show that selective crossover took the least number of evaluations on average at 10856, but this is not a significant amount compared with uniform crossover. In an order 15 trap function selective crossover again took the least number of evaluations as well as finding a solution in early generations. Uniform crossover did not always find the solution: misleading schemata of order 15 deceived it. Selective crossover, like two-point and uniform crossover, was finally fooled by deception on an order 20 trap function.

	Selective	Two-point	Uniform
Order 10	10856 (2058) [1.0]	12735 (1372) [1.0]	11313 (1059) [1.0]
Order 15	15033 (2909) [1.0]	15168 (3286) [1.0]	15833 (5317) [0.93]

Table 2. Mean number of evaluations completed for order 10, 15 deceptive trap functions. The standard deviation is shown in brackets. The solution quality is given in square brackets. These are averages over 50 runs. Order 20 trap functions successfully deceived all three forms of crossover.

Tests for significance were carried out at the 5% level and as suspected selective crossover did not show a significant difference on the mean number of evaluations for deceptive trap functions. We can safely conclude that selective crossover did not perform poorly but did as well as two-point crossover.

7. Conclusions

We have described a new adaptive crossover operator, *selective crossover,* for use with genetic search. Its design was motivated by intuition abstracted from Dawkin's theory of natural evolution to exploit and express good characteristics.

Selective crossover uses an extra real-valued vector to bias and promote, onto the next generation, genes that have increased an individual's fitness in previous generations. It uses this vector as a means of storing knowledge about what happened in previous generations. It allows exploitation of good schemata regardless of their defining length; hence if a schema consists of interacting genes at the two extremes of the chromosome, it can be propagated as easily as a schema with interacting genes located adjacent to each other.

Experiments indicate that selective crossover performs better than, or as good as, a traditional GA, which uses two-point or uniform crossover, on a set of test problems that contain characteristics common in practical problems. The problem sets used were the L-Sat problem generator and the deceptive trap function that allowed epistasis and deception to be varied respectively. The results show that selective crossover worked exceptionally well with problems of high epistasis where it found a better solution, than the conventional operators, and did this with the least number of evaluations (~25% performance increase) which is significant at the 5% level.

Due to the generational exploitation that drives selective crossover we assumed that its performance would be poor when applied to deceptive problems. The fitness increase exploits genes and thus can easily converge at the local optimum. In the case of the trap functions, selective crossover had performance comparable with two-point and uniform crossover. Like two-point and uniform crossover, selective crossover was fooled by deception in trap functions of order 20 and above.

We conclude that the initial results of this study indicate that selective crossover may be a good candidate for a crossover operator in which practitioners can have more confidence to use as a starting point for an adaptive GA system.

8. Future Work

Currently the dominance values are increased proportionately to the fitness increase of a child. Since all genes that were changed undergo this increase we do not know which gene influenced the increase in fitness. To overcome this problem of promoting false changes the dominance values of each changed gene can be updated by sharing the fitness increase amongst these changed genes. For example, when there is an increase in fitness as a result of changing many genes, the dominance increase for each gene would be less in comparison to the fitness increase due to the change of just one gene. Further experiments will be carried out to compare selective crossover with other adaptive crossovers [WhOp94], to see how alternative ways of initialising the dominance values affects performance, and to investigate other forms of epistasis. Other experiments will include non-normalised fitness functions (i.e. Royal Road functions) and problems with a finite cardinality alphabet.

We also intend to analyse schema creation, propagation and disruption to determine exactly why and how a GA benefits from selective crossover and use those findings towards more reliable and adaptive recombination operators. Specifically, we wish to develop a recombination operator that identifies and exploits epistasis.

Acknowledgements

Our thanks to David Goldberg for his valuable comments and William Spears for the original version of GAC, on which our code is based.

References

[Ackl87] Ackley, D. H. (1987) *A connectionist machine for genetic hillclimbing*. Boston, MA:Kluwer Academic Publishers.

[Baker87] Baker, J. E. (1987) Reducing Bias and Inefficiency in the Selection Algorithm. In J.J Grefenstette, editor, *Proceedings of the 2nd International Conference on Genetic Algorithms*, 14-21. Lawrence Erlbaum Associates.

[EsCaSc89] Eshelman, L. J., Caruana, R. A. & Schaffer J. D. (1989) Biases in the Crossover Landscape. In David Schaffer (ed.), *Proceedings of the Third International Conference on Genetic Algorithms*, 10-19. Morgan Kauffman

[Davi89] Davis, L. (1989) Adapting operator probabilities in genetic algorithms. In David Schaffer (ed.), *Proceedings of the 3rd International Conference on Genetic Algorithms*, 61-69. Morgan Kauffman

[Dawk89] Dawkins, R. (1989) *The Selfish Gene - New Ed*. Oxford University Press, UK.

[DeGo93] Deb K. & Goldberg D. E. (1993). Analyzing Deception in Trap Functions. In L. D. Whitley, (ed.), *Foundations of Genetic Algorithms 2*, 93-108. CA: Morgan Kauffman.

[DePoSp97] De Jong, Kenneth A., Potter, Mitchell A. & Spears, William M. (1997) Using Problem Generators to Explore the Effects of Epistasis. In Thomas Bäck (ed.), *Proceedings of the 7th International Conference on Genetic Algorithms*, 338-345. Morgan Kauffman

[Gold89] Goldberg, D. E. (1989) *Genetic Algorithms in search, optimization and machine learning*. Addison-Wesley.

[Holl75] Holland. J. H. (1975) *Adaptation in Natural and Artificial Systems*. MIT Press.

[ScMo87] Schaffer, J. & Morishima, A. (1987) An adaptive crossover distribution mechanism for genetic algorithms. In J.J Grefenstette, (ed.), *Proceedings of the 2nd International Conference on Genetic Algorithms*, 36-40. Lawrence Erlbaum Associates.

[Spea97] Spears, W. M. (1997), Recombination Parameters. In T. Baeck, D. Fogel and Z. Michalewicz (ed.), *The Handbook of Evolutionary Computation*, Oxford University Press.

[Sysw89] Syswerda, W. (1989) Uniform Crossover in Genetic Algorithms. In J. David Schaffer, (ed.), *Proceedings of the 3rd International Conference on Genetic Algorithms*, 10-19. Morgan Kauffman.

[WhOp94] White, T. & Oppacher, F. (1994) Adaptive Crossover Using Automata. In Y. Davidor, H.-P Schwefel and R. Männer (eds.), *Proceedings of the Parallel Problem Solving from Nature Conference*, 229-238. NY:Springer Verlag.

[WoMa95] Wolpert, D. H. & Macready, W. G. (1995) No free lunch theorems for search. Technical Report 95-02-010, Santa Fe Institute.

Line-Breeding Schemes for Combinatorial Optimization

Rong Yang

Department of Computer Science
University of Bristol, Bristol, UK

Abstract. Line-breeding is an interesting mating strategy adapted to genetic algorithms. Most experiments on line-breeding have used multimodal functions as a testbed. In this work, we focus on combinatorial optimization problems. We chose the multiple constrained knapsack problem as our testbed. Several line-breeding schemes are explored, from the naive version to more advanced versions with sharing and niching. A new mechanism, dynamic mutation, is also proposed. Under this mechanism, if two individuals are very close to each other, instead of mating, a self-fertilization (i.e., a special mutation) is applied. The experiments presented in this paper show that a line-breeding scheme which uses multiple distanced champions can achieve the best performance. The paper also shows that dynamic mutation can improve not only the quality of solutions but can also identify more local optima.

1 Introduction

Line-breeding is a mating restriction practice of animal husbandry and horticulture, in which a champion individual is repeatedly bred with others. Hollstien [6] adapted it to genetic algorithms. The advantage of using line-breeding is that the population can very quickly converge to a peak. Therefore it performs well on a unimodal function. However, for a multimodal function, it performs poorly because of premature convergence. As an improved scheme, Hollstien further introduced *inbreeding with intermittent crossbreeding* where close members are repeatedly mated as long as the family fitness continues to rise and crossbreeding between different families is applied when the family fitness stops rising. This scheme performed much better than standard line-breeding for multimodal problems. Recently a group of mating restriction schemes combined with dynamic niching was studied by Miller and Shaw [8]. The work showed that, among several methods, their dynamic line-breeding scheme performed best.

Most experiments on line-breeding have used multimodal functions as a testbed. In this work, we focus on combinatorial optimization problems. Like multimodal functions, combinatorial problems also have multiple peaks. Unlike function optimization, combinatorial optimization problems are normally highly constrained. That is, the solution space is greatly discontinuous and the optima (both local and global) are most likely close to the edges.

Many practical applications of combinatorial optimization require efficiency rather than quality, i.e., to find a reasonably good solution quickly. Therefore, the line-breeding scheme is attractive. We are interested in how the line-breeding scheme can be applied to combinatorial optimization problems. More importantly, we aim to investigate how to escape from a local optimum and improve the quality of solutions.

In this paper, we explore several line-breeding schemes, from the naive version to more advanced versions with sharing or niching. We also propose a new mutation scheme, *dynamic mutation*. In this scheme, if an individual is close to the champion individual (or say, if two individuals are very close to each other), instead of mating, a self-fertilization is applied. In the next section, we will describe our schemes in detail and discuss some variations. In Section 3, we briefly present the testbed used in this work. The results of our empirical study are presented in Section 4. Finally, we draw conclusions in Section 5.

2   Line-breeding Schemes with Dynamic Mutation

2.1   Dynamic Mutation

Various mating restrictions have been studied for improving the performance of genetic algorithm. For example, to prevent low performance offspring caused by radically dissimilar parents, Deb and Goldberg [4] used a mating radius. Only if the Hamming distance between parents is within the radius is mating allowed. With a different goal, to prevent premature convergence, some other strategies restrict close individuals to mate [5, 3]. Under a line-breeding scheme, a highly fit individual which has a small Hamming distance from the champion individual can be propagated radically. This normally leads to premature convergence. Therefore, we follow the approach proposed in [5] to prevent close individuals mating with each other.

In most mating restriction schemes, when the mating condition is not met, a new individual is reselected. Here we propose an alternative method. Instead of reselecting individuals to meet the mating condition, we give up the crossover operation. A special mutation is then performed on one of the parents to produce a new offspring. This can be seen as a self-fertilization mechanism. There are two motives for introducing such a mutation. First, if parents are randomly selected, it is unlikely that an individual will be crossed over with a similar one. When this does happen, it is most likely that the population is more or less crowded with one kind of species. Therefore, it is reasonable to force the individual to reform itself towards other species. The side effect of this is that some good schemas might be disrupted. But, provided that the total number of mutating bits is not too high, the chance of losing good schemas is small. Second, if line-breeding is used, we also have a strong reason. Under line-breeding, when the mating condition is not met, it means that we are definitely dealing with a highly fit individual which is very similar to the champion. By applying a mutation to such an individual, we can efficiently maintain population diversity.

In summary, two kind of mutations are used in our algorithm: traditional static mutation and our new dynamic mutation. The static mutation is applied after every crossover with a low mutation rate (i.e., a standard mutation). The dynamic mutation is applied when a pair of parents are too similar to each other. The rate for the dynamic mutation can be much higher than the static one.

2.2 Basic Line-breeding

The simplest line-breeding scheme explored in our work is designed as follows. The individual which has the highest fitness in the initial population is the first champion. The mating pool is created by using standard binary tournament selection. The champion mates everyone in the mating pool to generate the next generation. The current champion will be replaced by a new champion of the next generation only if the new champion is fitter (i.e., using elitist rule).

In addition to the above basic mechanisms, we apply a simple intermittent cross-breeding scheme to improve the performance. That is, within a certain interval, we change the breeding fashion to a different one. Only half of the population is generated by line-breeding. The other half of the population is generated by mating between randomly selected ordinary individuals.

2.3 Line-breeding with Multiple Champions

Instead of using a single champion, this scheme uses multiple champions. The population is divided into N subpopulations. Each subpopulation is line-bred with a different champion. Here, the subpopulation is divided randomly without applying the niche sharing technique.

2.4 Line-breeding with Multiple Distanced Champions

In the above scheme, champion individuals are selected according to the fitness. Here we introduce a new criterion: to avoid selecting champions which are too close to each other. Whenever we add a new member to the champion set, we make sure that the Hamming distance between the new member and every existing member is above a certain limit. The idea is inspired by the work presented in [8], where a dynamic niching scheme is developed and peaks from each dynamic niche can be used for line-breeding within a niche.

3 Experimental Design

3.1 Test Bed – the Multiconstraint Knapsack Problem (MKP)

We choose the multiconstraint knapsack problem (MKP in short) knapsack problem to test our schemes. Mathematically, the MKP is formulated as follows:

$$maximize \left(\sum_{j=1}^{n} value_j * x_j\right), \tag{1}$$

$$subject\ to \left(\sum_{j=1}^{n} weight_{ij} * x_j \leq b_i\right), \qquad i = 1, ..., m, \tag{2}$$

$$x_j \in \{0, 1\} \tag{3}$$

That is, the objective is to maximize the total value of objects in a sack, subject to maximum weight constraints. $x_j = 1$ means the object j is in the sack, otherwise the object j is not in the sack. It is a well known NP-hard combinatorial optimization problem which has a wide range of important applications, such as capital budgeting, project selection, cutting stock problems etc.

The representation of the MKP problem in genetic algorithms is simply a n-bit binary string which corresponds to the value of variables $x_1, ... x_n$.

Note that many strings $\in \{0,1\}^n$ might not be feasible solutions, because of the weight constraints. Two distinct ways of dealing with infeasible solutions are to apply a penalty function to reduce the fitness of any infeasible solution, or to restrict the genetic algorithm to the feasible region only.

Several studies on using genetic algorithms to solve the MKP problem can be found in the literature [7, 10, 2]. In [7], the approach of penalising infeasible individuals was used. In [10], the combination of genetic algorithms with tabu search heuristic was studied. The most successful work for the MKP was done recently by Chu and Beasley [2]. They designed a heuristic operator which utilises problem-specific knowledge adopted from a surrogate duality approach [9]. By incorporating this heuristic operator into genetic algorithms, superior quality solutions were obtained, compared with other approaches.

In this work, our goal is to test the effect of mating strategies and our dynamic mutation mechanism. Therefore, instead of using the heuristic algorithm proposed in [2], we designed our own simple algorithm which does not apply any problem-specific knowledge. Our algorithm will be described in the next subsection.

3.2 A Basic Genetic Algorithm for MKP

The following operators are used in our basic algorithm:

initialization: An initial population is randomly generated.
selection: The binary tournament selection is used for creating the next generation. There are no overlapping populations.
crossover: The mating is carried out by an uniform crossover. It recombines two parents at the bit level. The offspring always inherits the bits if they are same in both parents. The rest of the bits are copied from either the first or second parent in a random fashion. If the selected parents are too close to each other, the dynamic mutation described in Section 2.1 is performed.

mutation: After each crossover, a mutation is performed that mutates a few randomly selected bits.

Apart from the dynamic mutation, the above are all standard GA operators. The only point that ought to be mentioned is how to deal with infeasible individuals. We choose the method that limits the search space to the feasible region only. Thus our genetic operators need to guarantee to generate feasible individuals. To achieve this, we use a procedure, called "`make_feasible(FreeVarList)`" It randomly selects a variable from a given `FreeVarList` and sets it to "1" if the constraints are satisfied, otherwise sets it to "0". It stops when all variables are assigned. Here, we use the term *free* variable to refer to a variable whose value is still not determined. In the initialization phase, we construct the population by calling `make_feasible(FreeVarList)` where `FreeVarList` is a full variable list. In crossover, an offspring unconditionally inherits the values if they are same in both parents. The rest of variables are treated as free variables and will be passed to the `make_feasible` procedure after mutation. In mutation, for those selected bits, we change "1" to "0" and "0" to a free variable. Note that we do not simply reverse the value because producing a value "1" might generate an infeasible offspring.

3.3 Various Algorithms

We implemented the following four different versions of the algorithm. The basic operations described in the above subsection are applied to all our algorithms. The only difference is in the mating strategy:

Algorithm 1: Selects parents randomly.
Algorithm 2: Uses the basic line-breeding scheme given in Section 2.2.
Algorithm 3: Adds the multiple champions to Algorithm 2. The size of the champion set is currently 2.
Algorithm 4: Uses the scheme given in Section 2.4. That is, champions must not be close to each other. The size of the champion set is also 2.

3.4 Examples Used

instances	No. of objects	No. of constraints	Notes
sento2	60	30	
weish26	90	5	
cb100	100	5	most correlated
cb110	100	5	medium correlated
cb120	100	5	less correlated

Fig. 1. Tested Examples

The experiments in this paper were performed using five MKP instances shown in Figure 1.

The first two are well known from the literature. The last three are from a recent work by Chu and Beasley [2]. According to [2], existing test problems presented little challenge to their heuristic algorithm. Therefore, they generated a set of larger and harder MKP instances. Apart from the sizes of the various problems, there are three groups of instances in [2]: most correlated, medium, and less correlated. In general correlated problems are more difficult to solve than uncorrelated problem. We selected one smallest instance from each group. The optimal solutions for these five instances are already known. This is ideal for testing our algorithms. All examples were obtained from the OR-Library [1].

4   Experimental Results

4.1   Comparison between Different Mating Strategies

We tested the above 5 instances under 4 different algorithms. The following configurations are used throughout the testing.

population size	100
static mutation rate	0.02
dynamic mutation rate	0.10
termination criterion	2000 consecutive generations without improvement in the best fitness
similarity criterion	Hamming distance between two individuals is less than 6

To compare the efficiency of different mating strategies, we measured the overall performance by two criteria: the quality of solution and the execution time.

The quality of solution is the result of calculating

$$(1 - \frac{best\ solution\ found}{known\ optimum}) * 100$$

This indicates by what percentage the solution is below the optimal solution. The execution time is the cpu time in seconds.

The test was carried out by using different seeds to run the same example three times. The numbers shown in Figure 2 are the average results from the three runs.

In Figure 2, the results of Algorithm 1 and 2 show that the single line-breeding scheme slightly decreased the quality of solutions compared with the standard random mating strategy, but the computation time was shortened. The multiple line-breeding scheme (i.e., Algorithm 3) achieved a better overall result than Algorithm 1 and 2. Algorithm 4 (i.e., using multiple distanced champions) achieved the best quality although the computation time was slightly increased.

problems	Algorithm 1		Algorithm 2		Algorithm 3		Algorithm 4	
	quality	time	quality	time	quality	time	quality	time
sento2	0.13	453	0.10	342	0.00	280	0.00	339
weish26	0.15	149	0.22	130	0.00	166	0.00	121
cb100	0.28	154	0.44	156	0.39	244	0.07	329
cb110	0.54	189	0.16	183	0.09	149	0.09	138
cb120	0.16	122	0.27	154	0.00	111	0.00	101
average	0.25	213	0.24	193	0.10	190	0.03	206

Fig. 2. Overall Performance of Different Algorithms

	Algorithm 1	Algorithm 2	Algorithm 3	Algorithm 4
No. of runs	3	2	10	12

Fig. 3. Number of Runs (out of 15) which Found the Optimal Solution

Figure 3 uses another kind of measure to compare the quality of different algorithms. There are five problems and three runs for each problem. Thus, we had a total of 15 runs. Figure 3 shows for each algorithm how many runs actually found the optimal solution. It shows that Algorithm 4 achieved the best result.

4.2 Effect on Dynamic Mutation

To see how dynamic mutation affects the quality of solutions, another test was carried out. We set the dynamic mutation rate to zero, to switch off dynamic mutation completely. We tested on all four algorithms (one run per problem). The results of the quality of solutions are given in Figure 4. The gap column indicates the difference from using dynamic mutation. A positive gap means worse quality while a negative gap means better quality found. It shows that in most cases without dynamic mutation the quality is poorer.

problems	Algorithm 1		Algorithm 2		Algorithm 3		Algorithm 4	
	quality	gap	quality	gap	quality	gap	quality	gap
sento2	0.11	0.00	0.00	-0.21	0.00	0.00	0.00	0.00
weish26	0.33	+0.27	0.33	0.00	0.33	+0.33	0.00	0.00
cb100	1.37	+1.10	0.95	+0.40	0.51	-0.24	0.15	+0.15
cb110	0.55	+0.37	0.27	+0.14	0.27	+0.14	0.13	+0.13
cb120	0.00	0.00	0.00	-0.33	0.22	+0.22	0.00	0.00
average	0.47	+0.35	0.31	0.00	0.27	+0.09	0.06	+0.06

Fig. 4. The Quality Obtained without Dynamic Mutation

Another important aspect is whether our final population is well distributed among different niches (i.e., not trapped under a single peak). We cannot test this precisely. Unlike optimization functions, with combinatorial optimization problems it is not easy to have a clear idea of what the solution landscape looks like. Therefore, we use the following method to get a rough approximation. We count the total number of non-duplicated *good* solutions produced in the final population. A good solution is defined as a solution whose fitness is less than 5% worse than the known optimum. It is reasonable to assume that the larger the number of good solutions found, the better the distribution achieved.

Figure 5 summarizes the results. It is clear that, using dynamic mutation, the total number of good solutions is significantly higher than without dynamic mutation. This applies to all four algorithms.

	Algorithm 1		Algorithm 2		Algorithm 3		Algorithm 4	
problems	with DM	without	with DM	without	with DM	without	with DM	without
sento2	64	13	26	15	39	20	40	36
weish26	32	20	40	26	43	25	53	43
cb100	20	9	40	7	41	15	47	38
cb110	75	66	84	40	87	51	92	85
cb120	98	94	97	59	93	77	92	77

Fig. 5. Number of Good Solutions Found

We also used another approximation to measure the population distribution. For each different run, we calculated the Hamming distance between every pair of good solutions then obtained an average Hamming distance. If the total number of good solutions found is larger and the average Hamming distance between good solutions is longer then we can estimate that a better distribution is achieved.

Figure 6 displays the average Hamming distance between good solutions. It shows much similar result as the one given in Figure 5. That is, using dynamic mutation, the average Hamming distance between good solutions is larger than without dynamic mutation.

	Algorithm 1		Algorithm 2		Algorithm 3		Algorithm 4	
problems	with DM	without	with DM	without	with DM	without	with DM	without
sento2	8	4	7	5	7	5	7	6
weish26	7	4	6	4	7	5	7	6
cb100	10	5	7	4	7	4	9	6
cb110	14	14	11	6	10	7	11	9
cb120	13	13	11	7	9	7	10	8

Fig. 6. Average Hamming Distance between Good Solutions

5 Conclusions and Discussion

5.1 Line-breeding with Multiple Distanced Champions

We have examined different line-breeding schemes for solving a representative combinatorial problem. The results show that using multiple distanced champions can achieve the best overall performance.

This conclusion is almost consistent with the study presented in [8]. One different experiment here is that we do not separate populations into niches (i.e., subpopulations). In our algorithm, a local champion mates with randomly selected individuals which are not necessarily in the same niche as the champion while, in [8], all individuals are trying to mate with their local champions. We have actually tested this idea for our problem but found that the result is not so good.

At the moment, we have only used two champions in our experimental work. As an immediate objective, we are interested in testing whether a significant improvement can be achieved by increasing the total number of champions.

5.2 Dynamic Mutation

A new mechanism, dynamic mutation, is introduced to maintain population diversity. The experiments demonstrate that better quality can be obtained by using dynamic mutation. Moreover, we believe that dynamic mutation can identify more local optima.

We view the dynamic mutation mechanism as a method of limiting the uncontrolled growth of particular niches within a population. Generally speaking, when two similar individuals are selected to mate, it is more likely that the population is more or less crowded with one kind of species. Therefore, by mutating them, we can expect to efficiently maintain population diverisity.

Acknowledgements

The work is supported by the Information-technology Promotion Agency (Japan). The author is very grateful to her sponsors in Mitsubishi Research Institute. The help from P.C. Chu for obtaining the MKP data is appreciated. Many thanks also go to Steve Gregory for his comments on the paper. Finally, the author would like to thank anonymous reviewers for the encouragement and detailed comments which are deeply appreciated.

References

1. J. E. Beasley. OR-Library: Distributing Test Problems by Electronic Mail. *Journal of the Operational Research Society*, (41):1069–1072, 1990. See also http://mscmga.ms.ic.ac.uk/info.html.

2. P. C. Chu and J. E. Beasley. A Genetic Algorithm for the Multiconstraint Knapsack Problem. Working paper, http://mscmga.ms.ic.ac.uk/pchu, The Management School, Imperial College, 1997.

3. Craighurst, R. and Martin, W. Enhancing GA Performance through Crossover Prohibitions Based on Ancestry. In *Proceedings of the Sixth International Conference on Genetic Alorithms*, pages 130–135, 1995.

4. K. Deb and D. E. Goldberg. An Investigation of Niche and Species Formation in Genetic Function Optimization. In *Proceedings of the Third International Conference on Genetic Alorithms*, pages 42–50, 1989.

5. L. J. Eshelman and J. D. Schaffer. Preventing Premature Convergence in Genetic Algorithm by Preventing Incest. In *Proceedings of the Fourth International Conference on Genetic Alorithms*, pages 115–122, 1991.

6. R. B. Hollstien. Artificial Genetic Adaptation in Computer Control System. PhD Dissertation, University of Michigan, 1971.

7. S. Khuri, T. Back, and J. Heitkotter. The Zero-one Multiple Knapsack Problem and Genetic Algorithms. In *Proceedings of The ACM Symposium of Applied Computing (SAC94)*, 1994.

8. B. L. Miller and M. J. Shaw. Genetic Algorithms with Dynamic Niche Sharing for Multimodal Function Optimization. Illigal report no. 95010, University of Illinois at Urbana-Champaign, December 1995.

9. H. Pirkul. A Heuristic Solution Procedure for the Multiconstraint Zero-one Knapsack Problem. *Naval Research Logistics*, (34):161–172, 1987.

10. J. Thiel and S. Voss. Some Experiences on Solving Multiconstraint Zero-one Knapsack Problems with Genetic Algorithms. *INFOR*, (32):226–242, 1994.

Coevolution and Learning

Finding Regions of Uncertainty in Learned Models: An Application to Face Detection

Shumeet Baluja[1,2]

[1] Justsystem Pittsburgh Research Center
4616 Henry Street
Pittsburgh, Pa. 15213
[2] School of Computer Science
Carnegie Mellon University
Pittsburgh, Pa. 15213

Abstract. After training statistical models to classify sets of data into predetermined classes, it is often difficult to interpret what the models have learned. This paper presents a novel approach for finding examples which lie on the decision boundaries of statistical models trained for classification. These examples provide insight into what the model has learned. Additionally, they can provide candidates for use as additional training data for improving the performance of the statistical models. By labeling the examples which lie on the decision boundaries, we provide information to the model in the regions in which it is most uncertain. The approaches presented in this paper are demonstrated on the real-world vision-based task of detecting faces in cluttered scenes.

1 Introduction

After training statistical models, such as artificial neural networks or decision trees, to classify a set of data into predetermined classes, it is often difficult to interpret what the models have learned. However, knowing how a model makes its decisions and which features it considers salient not only provides insights into what the model encodes, but also provides guidelines on how to improve the model's performance. In this paper, we present a novel technique to efficiently find examples which lie on the decision boundaries of learned models. We also show how these examples can be used for continuing the training of the models.

To demonstrate the techniques, we explore the task of face detection in cluttered scenes. The system used in this study is based upon the neural network-based system described in [7]. This task is chosen because (1) after the face detection networks are trained, we would like to understand what features they encode; (2) training the networks is a very slow process because finding good training examples is difficult. Both of these problems can be addressed with the methods described in this paper.

The next section describes the face detection system. Section 3 describes the techniques for finding examples on the decision boundaries. Section 4 shows how these examples can be used for continuing the model's training. Finally, Section 5 closes this paper with conclusions and directions for future research.

2 A Face Detection System

The system employed in this study is based on the neural network-based system presented in [7]. A neural network is used as a filter that receives as input a 20x20 pixel region of the image, and generates an output ranging from 1 to -1, signifying the presence or absence of a face, respectively. To detect faces anywhere in an image, the filter is applied at every location in the image. To detect faces larger than the window size, the input image is repeatedly reduced in size (by subsampling), and the filter is applied at each size. For the work presented here, we apply the filter at every pixel position in the image, and scale the image down by a factor of 1.2 for each step in the pyramid; this is the approach used in [7]

The filtering algorithm is shown in Fig. 1. First, a preprocessing step, of histogram equalization and lighting correction (see [7, 8]) is applied to each window of the image. These steps help account for lighting variation and expand the range of intensities in the window. This compensates for differences in camera input gains, in addition to improving contrast in some cases.

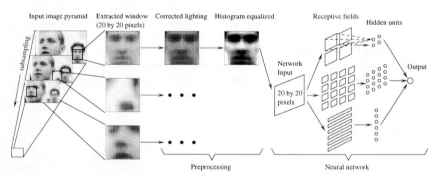

Fig. 1. The Face Detection System, based on [7]

The preprocessed window is then passed through a neural network (NN). The architecture of the NN is shown in the right half of Fig. 1. There are three types of hidden units: 4 which look at 10x10 pixel subregions, 16 which look at 5x5 pixel subregions, and 6 which look at overlapping 5x20 pixel horizontal stripes of pixels. More details about the architecture and motivations for its use can be found in [7]. The network has a single, real-valued output, which indicates whether or not the window contains a face.

To train the neural network to serve as an accurate filter, a large number of face and non-face images are needed. Nearly 1050 face examples were gathered. The images contained faces of various sizes, orientations, positions, and intensities. The eyes, tip of nose, and corners and center of the mouth of each face were labelled manually. These points were used to normalize each face to the same scale, orientation, and position [7]. Fifteen face examples are generated for the training set from each original image, by randomly rotating the images (about their center points) up to 10°, scaling between 90% and 110%, translating up to half a pixel, and mirroring. Each 20x20 window in the set is then preprocessed (by applying histogram equalization and lighting correction). A few example images are shown in Fig. 2.

Fig. 2. Example face images, randomly mirrored, rotated, translated, and scaled by small amounts.

Practically any image can serve as a non-face example because the space of non-face images is much larger than the space of face images. However, collecting a "representative" set of non-faces is difficult. Instead of collecting the images before training is started, the images are collected during training in the following manner, adapted from [8, 5]:

1. Create an initial set of non-face images by generating 1000 random images. Apply the preprocessing steps to each of these images.
2. Train a neural network to produce an output of 1 for the face examples, and -1 for the non-face examples. The training algorithm is standard error backpropagation with momentum [6]. On the first iteration of this loop, the network's weights are initially random. After the first iteration, we use the weights computed by training in the previous iteration as the starting point.
3. Run the system on an image of scenery *which contains no faces*. Collect subimages in which the network incorrectly identifies a face (an output activation ≥ 0).
4. Select up to 1000 of these subimages at random, apply the preprocessing steps, and add them into the training set as negative examples. Go to step 2.

Some examples of non-faces that are collected during training are shown in Fig. 3. Note that some of the examples resemble faces. The presence of these examples forces the neural network to learn a sharp boundary between face and non-face images. For the networks trained in this study, we used a set of 285 images of scenery for collecting negative examples in the bootstrap manner described above. A typical training run selects approximately 10,000 non-face images from the approximately 200,000,000 subimages that are available at all locations and scales in the training scenery images.

The results for the networks used in this study are comparable to those used in [7]. The networks were tested on a large set of images [3]. Two networks were trained, starting with random initial weights. The performance of these networks is given in Table 1.

---

[3] The test images are available from http://www.cs.cmu.edu/~har/faces.html

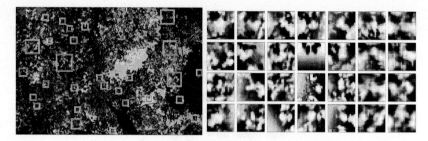

Fig. 3. During training, the partially-trained system is applied to images of scenery which do not contain faces (left). Any windows in the image detected as faces (expanded on the right) are errors, which can be added into the set of negative training examples.

Table 1. Detection and error rates for a test set which consists of 130 images and contains 507 frontal faces. It requires the system to examine a total of 83,099,211 20x20 pixel windows. Two independent networks are trained.

	Number Faces Missed	Detection Rate	False Positives	False Positive Rate
Network 1	45/507	91.1%	829	1/100240
Network 2	51/507	89.9%	693	1/136294

3 Finding Uncertain Examples

In the previous section, we described the training algorithm for the face detection networks. To find negative training examples (examples which represent "non-faces"), the network is scanned over scenery images which are known to contain no faces. Any location where the network detects a face is labeled as a negative example, and added to the training set. Although this is an effective procedure for finding negative examples, it is extremely slow. As the network is trained, the number of examples that must be seen before a single negative example is found rapidly increases. As can be seen in Fig. 4, after the network is trained from the examples from only a few of the initial scenery images, *often more than* 10^5 *examples must be seen before a single false-positive is found.*

The same method that is used to find false-positives can be used to find examples for which the network is most uncertain. Uncertainty is defined in terms of the network's output. The network's output is a real-value between -1 (indicating non-face) and $+1$ (indicating face); therefore, an input which gives an output near 0.0 indicates the network is uncertain of the classification. Finding input examples for which the network is uncertain is useful for two reasons. First, these examples provide samples on the decision boundaries; they reveal where the network does not perform well. Second, once labeled, these examples can be used for continuing training since it is known that the network is uncertain about their classification. This is a form of *active learning*, in which the learner requests information about uncertain points [1, 4].

There are at least three methods by which the uncertain examples can be found. First, similarly to the training procedure, the network can be serially

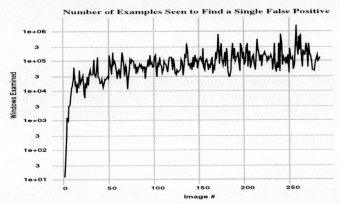

Fig. 4. The number of examples which must be examined before a single false positive (negative example) is added into the training set. X Axis: Scenery image presentation. Y Axis: Number of 20x20 windows examined.

scanned over scenery images until an input window is found for which the network outputs a value of 0.0. As described above, this method is extremely slow.

A second procedure is to use a backpropagation gradient descent procedure similar to that used for training neural networks; a cursory overview is given here. Given a 20x20 image of random pixel values as input, a forward pass of the input to the output is done (as in the standard backpropagation algorithm). If this output does not match the target (of 0.0), an error is passed back to the hidden units and then to the input layer. However, instead of using this error to update the network's weights, as would be done with the standard backpropagation algorithm, *the values of the inputs* are updated. Given a network in which the weights are frozen, this will move the inputs towards values that will reveal a network output of 0.0. This method has successfully been used to find inputs which the network maps to output of 0.0. However, the drawback to this method is that the resulting inputs can lie in a subspace that will never be encountered by the face detector network when used on real images. The reason for this is that the face detector system uses pre-processing steps, such as histogram equalization and lighting correction, which place all inputs in a limited subspace of possible inputs. Therefore, using this method to obtain inputs which the network maps to a value of 0.0 may not give a meaningful representation of the decision boundaries since the resulting inputs may violate invariants which are created by the pre-processing methods. In order to get meaningful samples, the pre-processing step must be accounted for when new inputs are found. It is difficult to account for the constraints and the non-linearities of the preprocessing steps in the backpropagation procedure.

The third approach is to use stochastic search techniques to find 20x20 images that the network maps to an output value of 0.0. However, two issues must still be resolved: the first is how to stay within the subspace of valid images, and the second is how to evaluate each image. To evaluate a new image, termed X, it is first projected into the space of valid images. This is done by applying all of the pre-processing steps used in training the face detection networks, yielding an image X'. X' is used as input into the trained network, and a forward propagation step is done, yielding the network's output, $NN(X')$. The difference between $NN(X')$ and the target output (0.0) is calculated. The larger the difference, the lower the evaluation of the image. Once an example is found for which the network outputs a value of 0.0, X' is returned. Given this evaluation procedure, which ensures that the evaluation is based on the mapping of the image to a valid subspace, we now describe the search procedures used.

3.1 An Optimization Approach to Finding Uncertain Examples

The search for an input image for which the trained network outputs a value of 0.0 is formulated as a combinatorial search problem. Three stochastic search procedures were examined: random mutation stochastic hill-climbing, population-based incremental learning (PBIL) [2], and genetic algorithms. A brief description of each is given below.

Rather than initializing the search algorithms randomly, all of the search techniques examined improved performance by being initialized with false-positives that were found through the neural-network training procedure (such as those found in Figure 3). For random mutation hill-climbing, this initialization meant that the starting point was an example selected from the set of negative examples in the training set. The hill-climbing procedure then stochastically perturbed pixels in the example (magnitude changes of up to 70% were allowed). The solution was evaluated as described previously (by performing the appropriate pre-processing, and then using it as input to the trained neural network and measuring the output). Moves to better or equal states were accepted. After 1000 consecutive non-accepted moves, the hill-climbing was restarted with another randomly selected image from the set of negative examples.

A complete description of the PBIL algorithm is beyond the scope of this paper; however, some of the basics can be found in [2]. In a manner similar to the hill-climbing procedure, a single image was used to initialize the search. A binary *modification vector* was created. The vector specified an amount to scale each pixel in the image. Each variable in this vector was represented with 5 bits. After applying the modification vector to the image, the image was pre-processed and used as input to the network. Compared to previous implementations of PBIL, the learning rate was set higher than normal (0.3), with a population size of 100. Additionally, whenever a new modification vector was created that performed better than any seen earlier, it was immediately used to update PBIL's probability vector.

Two modifications are made to the standard genetic algorithm to customize it for this domain. The first is the selection of the initial population. In many standard genetic algorithms, the initial population is selected randomly from the uniform distribution. However, using this initialization, finding even a single example which the network mapped to a value of 0.0 proved to be extremely slow. This is not surprising since the trained network already discriminates between faces and non-faces quite well (as described in Section 2). Therefore, there may be relatively few images, with respect to the possible images in the manifold spanned by images which have been appropriately pre-processed, which cause

467

a trained network to output a positive response. To alleviate this problem, the population was initialized with examples chosen from the set of 20x20 windows which were used as negative examples (these were the examples gathered as false positives during the training procedure described in Section 2). Since these images were in the training set, it is unlikely that these images will themselves cause the network to output a value of 0.0; however, the hope is that the GA will find combinations of these images that will.

The second modification to the standard GA is in the crossover operator. One-point and two-point recombination operators are designed to exploit locality in typical one-dimensional parameter encodings. We use an analogous operator for two-dimensional images. Two points, (X1,Y1) and (X2,Y2), are randomly chosen. The rectangle defined by these two points is the area that is swapped between the parents. See Fig. 3.1 for an example. [3] provides a discussion of two-dimensional crossover operators.

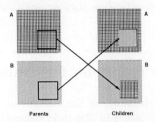

Fig. 5. 2D-Crossover.

With these two modifications, a standard steady-state genetic algorithm [9] was used with fitness proportional selection. It was empirically found that no mutation operator was required. A population size of 50 was used. By using this initialization procedure and this crossover operator, the number of evaluations required to find an image which the network mapped to an output of 0.0 was approximately 600, on average.

In the experiments performed, the genetic algorithm found the target in approximately 7-10% fewer evaluations than hill-climbing. PBIL, with the high learning rate, was able to find solutions approximately 20-30% faster than the GAs. However, due to the computational expense, only a few experiments were tried. Further experimentation should be conducted to fully understand the benefits of one method over another.

Some of the results of the search procedure are shown in Fig. 6. Note that the 60 images shown were found in a total of approximately 36,000 evaluations (forward passes through the network). In contrast, recall that when using the standard training procedure described in Section 2, by the end of training, it often took between 100,000 to 1,000,000 evaluations to find *a single* false-positive (see Fig. 4) by serially scanning over scenery images.

As can be seen from the images in Fig. 6, many of the images have dark patches where eyes would be located. The cheek, mouth, and nose areas are more variable. This indicates that the network is more sensitive to the presence of eyes than to the presence of the other features. This has been empirically

Fig. 6. 60 20x20 typical images obtained by the optimization procedures. A trained face detection neural network outputs a value close to 0.0 for each of the images, indicating that it is uncertain of their classification (face or non-face).

verified in other studies [7].

4   Using Uncertain Examples for Training

Despite the "eye-features" in some of the images in Fig. 6, when compared to the images of actual faces (see Fig. 2), it is clear that many of these images can be labeled as negative examples and then added into the training set for continued training. However, a few of the images look sufficiently close to faces that using them as examples of non-faces may confuse the network. Rather than using all of the found examples for training (as negative examples), we can select only those which are *most unlike* faces. To determine similarity to face examples, we measure the distance of each image to each of the known positive training examples (examples of which are shown in Fig. 2). Note that similarity between two examples is measured simply by the summed absolute difference between corresponding pixels. Alternatively, instead of finding images which are "far" from labeled face examples, we can find images which are "close" to labeled *non-face* examples. We can measure the distance of each image to each of the negative training examples (the type shown in Fig. 3). This last measure also has the benefit of selecting images which are similar to those that will be seen in real images, since the negative examples were selected from real images.

Both of these orderings are valid for the task. The ordering used is a combination of both. The first ordering ranks how similar each image is to the face examples; *the least similar is given the smallest rank and the most similar is given the largest rank.* The second ordering, ranks how similar the images are to the non-face examples; *here, the most similar is given the smallest rank and the least similar the largest rank.* The images with the smallest *summed* rank are used for training, see Fig. 7.

Table 2 shows the results of continuing the training of the network with the extra examples. We compare the performance to the original network by adjusting the detection threshold to give the same detection rates, and then

Fig. 7. Combined ordering of 30 20x20 images, each image was classified as a face by the network. Top-Left: smallest combined rank.

examining the number of false positives. The last column in the table shows the improvement (in terms of the reduction in the number of false positives) over the original network. For each network, 10,000 new examples were generated as described in this paper. The top $N\%$ were used for training after sorting them according to the combined metric described in the previous paragraph. The table shows the results of varying N. The same test set described in Table 1 is used.

Table 2. Results after training with found examples. Note the improvements in performance with respect to the original networks described in Table 1. Unfortunately, performance improvements do not always scale with the amount of extra training data.

	N	Faces Missed	Detect Rate	False Pos.	False Pos. Rate	% Improvement
Network 1	0.5%	45/507	91.1%	789	1/105322	4.8%
Network 1	2%	45/507	91.1%	769	1/108061	7.2%
Network 1	10%	45/507	91.1%	717	1/115898	13.5%
Network 2	0.5%	51/507	89.9%	643	1/146893	7.2%
Network 2	2%	51/507	89.9%	684	1/138088	1.2%
Network 2	10%	51/507	89.9%	640	1/147581	7.6%

5 Conclusions and Future Research

This paper has demonstrated an efficient and effective method for finding examples which lie on the decision boundaries of learned classification models. Although demonstrated with neural networks, the techniques are general, and can be used with any type of statistical model. The found examples represent the areas in which the model is uncertain; therefore, with labels, they may be used to provide useful information to the learner. In the domain of face detection, we were able to improve the performance of state-of-the-art models using the examples to continue training.

In order for this method to be successfully applied to a new domain, there must either be a procedure to search only in the space of meaningful examples, or to map all inputs into this range. For example, if it is known that all of the expected input examples span only a small range of all possible inputs, finding uncertain examples outside of this range is not useful, since they may never be encountered in practice. In the face detection domain, this problem was alleviated by beginning the search for uncertain examples from examples which had been encountered by the system, and ensuring that all of the generated inputs matched the constraints of inputs which would be seen in practice. For example, all of the images found by the search heuristics are deemed uncertain by the network *after* being pre-processed with histogram-equalization and lighting correction. Therefore, these examples meet the constraints which would be maintained in all of the false-positive images found by the system through serially scanning over the non-face training images. Further, by using the sorting metrics to select uncertain images that are most like the false positives found from the serial scanning procedure, we help to ensure that these images provide a training signal that helps the classification performance of the network when tested on real images.

There are at least two immediate directions for future research. The first is to combine the ranking procedures described in Section 4 with the evaluation function used for search. By modifying the evaluation function to include extra terms, it should be possible to search for examples which the network not only maps to a value close to 0.0, but are also dissimilar to known faces, and similar to known non-faces. One method for implementing this may be to penalize solutions which are distant from the negative examples in the training set; this will ensure that the examples found are close to those that are encountered in practice. Second, it will be interesting to determine the extent that it is possible to repeat the entire training process. For example, after training on examples for which the network is uncertain, it should be possible to find the examples which the newly trained model is uncertain, and repeat the training process.

References

1. L. Atlas, D. Cohn, and R. Ladner. Training connectionist networks with queries and selective sampling. In *Advances in Neural Information Processing Systems 2*. Morgan Kaufmann, 1989.
2. Shumeet Baluja. Genetic algorithms and explicit search statistics. In M. Mozer, M. Jordan, and T. Petsche, editors, *Advances in Neural Information Processing Systems (NIPS) 9*. MIT Press, Cambridge, MA, 1998.
3. H. M. Cartwright and S. P. Harris. The application of the genetic algorithm to two-dimensional strings: The source apportionment problem. In *Fifth International Conference on Genetic Algorithms*. Morgan Kaufmann, 1989.
4. D. Cohn, Z. Ghahramani, and M.I. Jordan. Active learning with statistical models. In *Advances in Neural Information Processing Systems 7*. MIT Press, 1995.
5. Harris Drucker, Robert Schapire, and Patrice Simard. Boosting performance in neural networks. *International Journal of Pattern Recognition and Artificial Intelligence*, 7(4):705–719, 1993.
6. John Hertz, Anders Krogh, and Richard G. Palmer. *Introduction to the Theory of Neural Computation*. Addison-Wesley, Reading, MA., 1991.
7. Henry A. Rowley, Shumeet Baluja, and Takeo Kanade. Neural network-based face detection. *IEEE Transactions on Pattern Analysis and Machine Intelligence*, 20:23–38, January 1998.
8. Kah-Kay Sung. *Learning and Example Selection for Object and Pattern Detection*. PhD thesis, MIT AI Lab, January 1996. Available as AI Technical Report 1572.
9. D. Whitley and T. Starkweather. Genitor ii: A distributed genetic algorithm. *JETAI*, 2, 1990.

On ZCS in Multi-agent Environments

Larry Bull

Intelligent Computer Systems Centre
University of the West of England
Bristol BS16 1QY, U.K.
larry@ics.uwe.ac.uk

Abstract. This paper examines the performance of the ZCS Michigan-style classifier system in multi-agent environments. Using an abstract multi-agent model the effects of varying aspects of the performance, reinforcement and discovery components are examined. It is shown that small modifications to the basic ZCS architecture can improve its performance in environments with significant inter-agent dependence. Further, it is suggested that classifier systems have characteristics which make them more suitable to such non-stationary problem domains in comparison to other forms of reinforcement learning. Results from the initial use of ZCS as an adaptive economic trading agent within an artificial double-auction market are then presented, with the findings from the abstract model shown to improve the efficiency of the traders and hence the overall market.

1 Introduction

As evolutionary computing techniques are applied to multi-agent environments, new issues arise along with new view points on traditional areas of the use of such approaches. In this paper the use of a Michigan-style [15] classifier system, Wilson's Zeroth-level classifier system (ZCS)[31], in multi-agent environments is investigated.

An abstract multi-agent model is presented and used to examine the performance of ZCS in systems of varying reward delay and inter-agent dependence. Depending on the amount of agent interdependence and the classifier system's parameters, it is found that the performance of ZCS can vary greatly in such non-stationary environments. Results indicate that with a standard roulette-wheel action selection policy ZCS can suffer from the oscillatory effects of a multi-agent system; an increase in action selection pressure is shown to be beneficial as inter-agent dependence increases. It is also found that, under most conditions, increasing the learning rate has a derogatory effect on ZCS's performance. Increasing the rate of use of the genetic algorithm (GA) [14] for rule-discovery is also found to become increasingly detrimental to the classifier system's performance as agent interdependence increases. Moving the panmictic GA of ZCS to the match set [3] is shown to be beneficial, particularly under high interdependencies, which leads to the suggestion that classifier systems are inherently appropriate for use in multi-agent environments; classifiers can form "clouds" of action strengths which provide a robustness to environmental oscillations.

Finally, the findings from the abstract model are used to improve the performance of ZCS agents in an artificial economic model of a double-auction market in which traders must learn suitable strategies to buy and sell goods effectively.

The paper is arranged as follows: the next section introduces the model. Section 3 describes the experimental set-up and Section 4 examines the effects of changes to the performance component of ZCS within the model. Section 5 presents the results of altering the reinforcement component and Section 6 examines the effects of altering the discovery component. Section 7 presents initial findings from the use of ZCS in an artificial adaptive economic agent model.

2 A Model of Multi-Agent Learning

In this paper an abstract multi-agent model is used which allows the systematic increase in complexity of the task faced by the learning system. Termed the NC model, it is based on Kauffman's NKC model [16] and shares a number of features/behaviours.

In the model an individual must solve a maze-like task represented by a (binary) tree of depth N, where reward is received at the end of N steps. On each

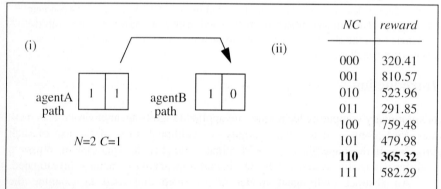

NC	$reward$
000	320.41
001	810.57
010	523.96
011	291.85
100	759.48
101	479.98
110	**365.32**
111	582.29

Fig. 1: Showing an example NC model. (i) shows how agentA's reward also depends upon the last move of the other agent. Therefore there are eight possible move configurations, each of which is assigned a random reward as shown in (ii). AgentA receives 365.32 here.

discrete time step an agent is presented with a unique input message and returns one of two output messages. The agent's N outputs are stored in a buffer representing the path taken through the maze. Thus increasing N increases the complexity of the task by increasing the delay in receiving any reward and the number of potential paths (2^N).

The reward received for taking a given route is also said to depend upon the last C moves taken by the other agent(s) with which it interacts; the moves by one agent may affect the reward received by its partner(s). Altering C, with respect to N, changes how dramatically moves by each agent deforms the reward landscape(s) of its partner(s). The model assumes all inter-agent (C) interactions are so complex that it is only appropriate to assign random values to their effects on rewards. Therefore for each of the possible pathways and interactions, a table of $2^{(N+C)}$ rewards is randomly created, with all entries in the range 0 to 1000, such that there is one reward for each combination of trails (Figure 1).

3 ZCS in Multi-Agent Systems

3.1 The Model

In this paper there are two agents (*A* and *B*) developing solutions to two different *NC* functions. Each agent is represented by a single ZCS. Initial parameters are set as in [31]: Rule base size = 400, initial rule strength = 20.0, learning rate (β) = 0.2, discount factor = 0.71, tax = 0.1, GA rate to create one rule per time step (*p*) = 0.25, crossover rate = 0.5 (one-point), and per bit mutation rate = 0.01.

All experiments are over 10 runs on each of 10 random *NC* functions, i.e. 100 runs, for 5000 iterations. All rule sets are initially equal. Inputs are coded such that at time step *t*, bit *t* of an *N*-bit string is set to 1, with all other bits set to 0. Results are shown as total system performance. The reader is referred to [31] for details of ZCS.

3.2 Classifier Systems in Multi-Agent Environments

A small number of investigators have examined the use of classifier systems in multi-agent environments. Bull et al. [e.g. 7] describe the use of Pittsburgh-style [25] classifier systems for the control of a quadrupedal robot, where each leg is represented by a separate system. Carse et al. [e.g. 8] have used fuzzy Pittsburgh-style classifier systems for routing at each node of a telecommunications network. Pittsburgh-style systems which also use reinforcement learning have been coevolved by Potter et al. [22], where an agent is represented by a number of classifier systems and a speciation-like process is included to improve performance. Multiple Michigan-style classifier systems have been used by Dorigo and Schnepf [e.g. 11] to control an autonomous robot and by Seredynski et al. [24] to examine the use of local reward sharing in a simple iterated game.

The performance of a Michigan-style classifier system, ZCS, in multi-agent environments is now examined using the *NC* model described above, with the aim of determining ways to improve its use in such environments.

4 The Performance Component

Much of the growing body of work on Machine Learning in multi-agent systems [e.g. 30] is relevant to the subject of this paper. In the closely related work of Sandholm and Crites [23] the use of Q-learning [29] within the Iterated Prisoner's Dilemma [2] is described - a multi-agent environment in which agents' pay-offs are neither totally positively nor totally negatively correlated, as in the *NC* model. They note that altering the amount of exploration of the agents, by altering the action selection pressure, causes different strategies to emerge over time; decreasing the pressure first increases the amount of cooperation seen and then decreases it.

Standard Michigan-style classifier systems use a roulette-wheel action selection policy (RW). The effects of altering the action selection pressure in ZCS within multi-agent systems have been examined. Table 1 shows how using the square of a rule's strength (Sqr), rather than just its strength, for selection in the roulette-wheel becomes increasingly beneficial as the amount of agent interdependence increases. That is, an increase in action selection pressure is found to improve performance for higher C; a reduction in exploration by the agents reduces the number of actions tried in a given situation, resulting in a more stable environment. However,

Table 1: Average performance for different action selection policies over a range of possible inter-agent epistasis (C) and task complexity (N).

C	1	4
RW	1135.98	1072.99
Sqr	1141.79	1123.42

C	1	4	8
RW	1223.14	1073.17	1150.41
Sqr	1243.07	1187.32	1213.32

C	1	4
RW	1013.00	1156.41
Det	895.55	946.54

C	1	4	8
RW	1380.19	1212.03	1166.76
Det	1165.55	972.89	922.46

C	1	4
RW	1053.32	1092.90
~Tax	906.74	1023.12

C	1	4	8
RW	1261.16	1180.59	1207.65
~Tax	1070.39	1058.81	1143.42

$N = 4$ $N = 8$

further increases in action selection pressure, e.g. deterministic selection of the strongest action set (Det), results in too much exploitation and not enough exploration. Similarly, if the taxing of match set rules not in the action set is removed (~Tax), reducing the action selection pressure and encouraging exploration, performance decreases with increasing C. Therefore findings here correspond to those of Sandholm and Crites.

Work examining the use of GAs in multi-agent systems [6] has shown that the increased (reproductive) selection pressure of standard steady state GAs [27], e.g. delete worst, results in their performing increasingly better than standard generational GAs for increasing interdependence, for similar reasons.

Unless otherwise stated, the use of the square of the rule's strengths is used throughout the rest of the paper.

5 The Reinforcement Component

The use of reinforcement learning in multi-agent environments is not a new area of investigation [e.g. 28]. However, the convergence proofs of most reinforcement algorithms do not apply in many multi-agent environments since they are usually neither stationary nor Markovian.

The effects on performance of altering the learning rate (β) in ZCS have been examined, for varying task complexity, to investigate this aspect of Michigan-style classifier systems in such environments. Here the ratio between the rate of learning

Table 2: Average performance for different learning rates (β) over a range of possible inter-agent epistasis (C) and task complexity (N).

β \ C	1	4
0.2	1133.51	1208.82
0.1	1181.41	1279.18

β \ C	1	4	8
0.2	1184.47	1138.75	1205.82
0.1	1190.51	1196.05	1243.03

β \ C	1	4
0.2	1147.94	1316.80
0.4	1024.43	1204.89

β \ C	1	4	8
0.2	1245.02	1173.92	1041.61
0.4	1125.74	996.36	1044.02

$$N = 4 \qquad\qquad N = 8$$

and the match set tax is kept the same as in Wilson's original description, i.e. 0.5; higher learning rate systems have a higher tax rate.

Table 2 shows that, in general, a lower rate of learning (e.g. $\beta = 0.1$) is most beneficial to the agents, for all C. This is not unexpected since, as noted in the previous section, adaptive multi-agent systems can perform better when sources of variance are

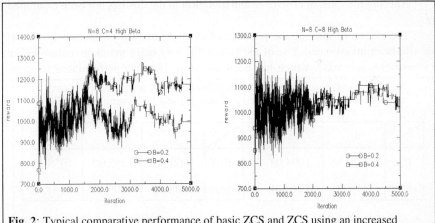

Fig. 2: Typical comparative performance of basic ZCS and ZCS using an increased learning rate on the same NC functions.

constrained. But Figure 2 shows that when both N and C are high, a higher rate of learning ($\beta = 0.4$) can perform at least as well as the standard lower rate.

With a high learning rate, each rule in a selected action set pays a high price for being chosen. If that action leads to a relatively large reward, those rules' strengths will quickly increase. Conversely, if the action leads to a relatively small pay-off, those rules' chances of being selected again quickly decreases. This can be seen to rapidly prune the possible action sets, resulting in fewer likely actions and an effective increase in action selection pressure. Changes in the environment may also be tracked more quickly; rules lose/gain strength rapidly. The results here indicate that such a process can be useful in more complex multi-agent domains. Sandholm and Crites [23] noted a similar effect, but offered no explanation.

The use of an existence tax on all rules in the classifier may be beneficial here since it would also contribute to the latter process noted above.

The effects of altering the other element in the reinforcement component, the discount factor, have not been examined here.

6 The Discovery Component

Seredynski et al. [24] have shown that the discovery component of a Michigan-style classifier system can prove beneficial in multi-agent systems. The effects of altering the rate (p) at which the genetic algorithm is used within ZCS have been investigated. It has been found that, for increasing C, higher rates (e.g. $p = 0.4$) prove increasingly detrimental and lower rates (e.g. $p = 0.1$) increasingly beneficial (not shown).

Based on these findings, the use of a triggered GA [4] may provide significant benefits in such systems.

This result is also related to findings from examining the use of the genetic operators crossover and mutation in evolving multi-agent systems [5]. It was shown that, as the amount of interdependence increases, the benefits of crossover over simple mutation can be lost and that the optimal rate of genetic search decreases; less evolutionary search than expected appears to perform better (see also [16, p250]).

Altering the rates of crossover and mutation in the GA has not been examined here.

The effects of moving the panmictic GA (Pan) of ZCS to the match sets [3] have also been investigated. Use of the GA in this way helps maintain niches within the classifier's rule base, which has been shown to improve performance in some

Table 3: Average performance for panmictic and match set GAs over a range of possible inter-agent epistasis (C) and task complexity (N).

C	1	4
Pan	1209.54	1094.08
Mat	1118.00	1161.48

$N = 4$

C	1	4	8
Pan	1060.58	1085.00	1038.15
Mat	995.89	1099.47	1161.82

$N = 8$

traditional domains. Without the use of wildcards (#), the niche GA is found to have a beneficial effect on system performance, for all values of C, where the relative increase in performance remains roughly constant (not shown).That is, ZCS without the ability to generalise is greatly helped by encouraging match set niches.

Related to this is Cedeno and Vemuri's [9] work which shows that niching in a GA population can improve its performance in non-stationary problems.

Table 3 shows results from the more general case of allowing wildcards in ZCS. For low agent interdependence, the niche GA (Mat) does not appear to provide a net benefit in terms of optima reached, but systems appear less prone to dips in performance with niching. An improvement in performance is seen for higher C however.

This can be explained by considering the constitution of match sets in ZCS. Through the existence of generalists (i.e. #'s) some, possibly all, match sets contain rules which participate in a number of match sets. In any given match set, these individuals' strengths represent an expected pay-off for their action, but with some effective noise since their strengths are also incrementing toward expected pay-offs for their action in the other match sets in which they participate. Conversely, specific rules' strengths only represent the expected pay-off for the same action in that match set. That is, there will be some variation in the predicted pay-off for an action within a given environmental state. Therefore the rules of an action set represent a "cloud" of points in the reward space of a condition/action pairing. In multi-agent environments the reward space changes due to the actions of the other agents. The results here indicate that, when the existence of match set niches is encouraged, classifier systems can perform better in such oscillating environments; the cloud of expected pay-off points provides a robustness to change.

It is noted that under the standard Bucket Brigade algorithm [15] the potential to generate this effect exists without generalisation since classifiers are chosen and rewarded individually; the strengths of identical rules can vary.

This result implies that classifier systems may be better suited to use in multi-agent environments than some other machine learning algorithms. For example, whilst a number of common features have been identified [12], standard Q-learning uses a look-up table of expected pay-off for given condition/action pairs. This means that, if there are a possible actions, the match set will consist of a individuals and each action set of just one individual. In a classifier system, a match set can be of any size from 1 (assuming covering) to r, where r is the number of rules in the rule base. Therefore the potential size of the cloud of points in reward space for a given action set is much larger in classifier systems, which may prove increasingly beneficial in more complex multi-agent environments. The ability to generalise can be added to Q-learning however [e.g. 17].

This aspect of ZCS is currently under further investigation.

The initial use of ZCS in a complex multi-agent environment is now presented.

7 ZCS as an Adaptive Economic Agent

Apart from the work described in Section 3.2, the only other known body of work examining the use of Michigan-style classifier systems in multi-agent environments exists in the field of computational economics. After [1] a number of researchers have used classifier systems to represent traders in artificial markets, e.g. [21][13][18][20]. Of these studies, only Marimon et al. [19] have made any alterations to the standard classifier system to improve its performance; they show that using a cumulative average of past rule strength speeds convergence (suggested in [1]).

Initial investigations into the use of ZCS in an artificial continuous double-auction (CDA) market have been undertaken. Briefly, a CDA consists of a number of buyers and sellers with reservation prices (known only to the agents themselves). At

478

any time buyers can make bids and sellers can make offers, with trades occurring when shouted prices are accepted. The London and New York stock exchanges use CDAs. The efficiency of such markets can be determined using Smith's [26] convergence metric, α, defined as $\alpha = 100\sigma/P_e$, where P_e is the price at which the quantity demanded is equal to the quantity supplied - the equilibrium price - and σ is the standard deviation of trade prices around P_e.

In the simulations used here, trades occur automatically when two shout prices cross and on each trading day each agent has one commodity to buy (buyer) or sell (seller), with the same reservation price as on the previous day. Agents are initially

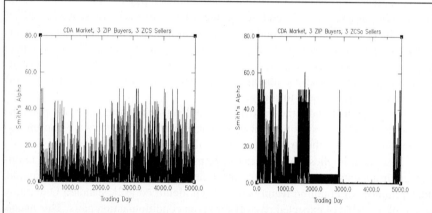

Fig. 4: Typical comparative performance of basic ZCS and ZCS using a number of altered features (ZCSa), as described in the text, in an artificial continuous double-auction.

assigned their reservation prices by dividing the price range of the market equally between the number of agents. For example, in the experiments presented here there are 3 sellers and 3 buyers, both with prices in the range 75-325 units, giving an equilibrium price of 200 units. A days trading finishes when remaining agents' reservation prices are known to not overlap.

On any discrete time step, or round, agents are told whether the last shout price was higher or lower than their current shout price, whether it was a bid or an offer, and whether it was accepted and a trade occurred. The agents also know whether they have already traded on that day; inactive agents are able to "watch" the market.

In this work (some) agents are represented by a ZCS, with the aim of learning trading rules within the CDA. On each round, an agent receives the inputs described above, coded as a binary string and returns an action to raise, lower or maintain its current shout price. Profit margins (μ) on reservation prices (λ) are initially assigned at random, though shout prices (ρ) remain within market limits, and thereafter are adjusted in steps defined by $\mu(t+1) = (\rho(t)+\Gamma(t))/\lambda - 1$, where Γ is a damping factor (see [10] for full details). Agents are rewarded only when they trade (1000μ).

The performance in the simulated CDA of 3 ZCS seller agents trading with 3 buyer agents (which use a well-known fixed strategy described in [10]) has been investigated. Runs in which the sellers had the same parameters as [31], have been compared with runs in which the results of the above work in the *NC* model were used, i.e. strengths were squared for action selection, $p = 0.1$, $\beta = 0.1$ and the GA was used in the match set.

Figure 4 shows results from typical runs, over 5000 days. The market is found to be more efficient, i.e. α is lower and for longer periods, with sellers using the altered version of ZCS (ZCSa). That is, the findings from the abstract *NC* model correspond to those of the simulated CDA. Analysis of the strategies emerging in the seller agents shows that simple rules which cause an agent to raise/lower its price if the last shout was higher/lower emerge, but no other forms of coherent strategy are noticeable during runs of this length.

8 Conclusions

In this paper it has been shown that small changes to ZCS can improve its performance in multi-agent systems and that classifier systems in general are suitable for use in such environments. Findings have been confirmed in initial investigations into the use of ZCS as an economic agent in continuous double-auction markets. Further enhancements to ZCS are currently being investigated.

Acknowledgements

This work was supported by Hewlett Packard Laboratories, Bristol. Thanks to Janet Bruten and the Agent Technology Group for the use of their software.

References

1. Arthur W B (1990), "A Learning Algorithm that Replicates Human Learning", Technical Report 90-026, Santa Fe Institute.
2. Axlerod R (1987), "The Evolution of Strategies in the Iterated Prisoner's Dilemma," in L Davis (ed.) *Genetic Algorithms and Simulated Annealing*, Pittman, pp32-42.
3. Booker L (1985), "Improving the Performance of Genetic Algorithms in Classifier Systems", in J J Grefenstette (ed.) *Proceedings of the First International Conference on Genetic Algorithms and their Applications*, Lawrence Erlbaum, pp80-93.
4. Booker L (1989), "Triggered Rule Discovery in Classifier Systems", in J D Schaffer (ed.) *Proceedings of the Third International Conference on Genetic Algorithms*, Morgan Kaufmann, pp265-275.
5. Bull L (1998), "Evolutionary Computing in Multi-Agent Environments: Operators," in V W Porto, N Saravanan, D E Waagen & A E Eiben (eds.) *Proceedings of the Seventh Annual Conference on Evolutionary Programming*, Springer Verlag, to appear.
6. Bull L (1997), "Evolutionary Computing in Multi-Agent Environments: Partners," in T Baeck (ed.) *Proceedings of the Seventh International Conference on Genetic Algorithms*, Morgan Kaufmann, pp370-377.
7. Bull L, Fogarty T C & Snaith M (1995), "Evolution in Multi-Agent Systems: Evolving Communicating Classifier Systems for Gait in a Quadrupedal Robot," in L J Eshelman (ed.) *Proceedings of the Sixth International Conference on Genetic Algorithms*, Morgan Kaufmann, pp382-388.
8. Carse B, Fogarty T C & Munro A (1995), "Adaptive Distributed Routing using Evolutionary Fuzzy Control", in L J Eshelman (ed.) *Proceedings of the Sixth International Conference on Genetic Algorithms*, Morgan Kaufmann, pp389-397.

9. Cedeno W & Vemuri V (1997), "On the Use of Niching for Dynamic Landscapes", in *Proceedings of the 1997 IEEE International Conference on Evolutionary Computation*, IEEE, pp361-366.

10. Cliff D & Bruten J (1997), "Zero is Not Enough: On the Lower Limit of Agent Intelligence for Continuous Double Auction Markets", HP Laboratories Technical Report HPL-97-141, HP Laboratories Bristol.

11. Dorigo M & Schnepf U (1992), "Genetics-based Machine Learning and Behaviour-based Robotics: A New Synthesis", *IEEE Trans. on Sys. Man and Cybernetics* 22(6):141-154.

12. Dorigo M & Bersini H (1994), "A Comparison of Q-learning and Classifier Systems", in D Cliff, P Husbands, J-A Meyer & S W Wilson (eds.) *From Animals to Animats 3*, MIT Press, pp248-255.

13. Dworman G (1994), "Games Computers Play: Simulating Characteristic Function Game Playing Agents with Classifier Systems", in *Proceedings of the 1994 IEEE Conference on Evolutionary Computing*, IEEE.

14. Holland J H (ed.)(1975), *Adaptation in Natural and Artificial Systems*, University of Michigan Press.

15. Holland J H, Holyoak K J, Nisbett R E & Thagard P R (eds.)(1986), *Induction: Processes of Inference, Learning and Discovery*, MIT Press.

16. Kauffman S A (ed.)(1993), *The Origins of Order: Self-organisation and Selection in Evolution*, Oxford University Press.

17. Lin L-J (1992), "Self-improving Reactive Agents Based on Reinforcement Learning, Planning and Teaching", *Machine Learning* 8(3):293-322.

18. Marengo L & Tordjman H (1996), "Speculation, Heterogeneity and Learning: A Model of Exchange Rate Dynamics" *KYKLOS* 49(3):407-438.

19. Marimon R, McGrattan E & Sargent T (1990), "Money as a Medium of Exchange in an Economy with Artificially Intelligent Agents", *Economic Dynamics and Control* (14):329-373.

20. Mitlohner J (1996), "Classifier Systems and Economic Modelling" *APL Quote Quad* 26(4):

21. Palmer R, Arthur W B, Holland J H, LeBaron B & Tayler P (1994), "Artificial Economic Life: A Simple Model of a Stockmarket", *Physica D* 75:264-274.

22. Potter M, De Jong K & Grefenstette J (1995), "A Coevolutionary Approach to Learning Sequential Decision Rules", in L J Eshelman (ed.) *Proceedings of the Sixth International Conference on Genetic Algorithms*, Morgan Kaufmann, pp366-372.

23. Sandholm T & Crites R H (1995), "Multiagent Reinforcement Learning in the Iterated Prisoner's Dilemma", *BioSystems* 37: 147-166.

24. Seredynski F, Cichosz P & Klebus G (1995), "Learning Classifier Systems in Multi-Agent Environments", in *Proceedings of the First IEE/IEEE Conference on Genetic Algorithms in Engineering Systems: Innovations and Applications*, IEE, pp287-292.

25. Smith S F (1980), "A Learning System Based on Genetic Adaptive Algorithms", PhD dissertation, University of Pittsburgh.

26. Smith V (ed.)(1992), *Papers in Experimental Economics*, Cambridge Press.

27. Syswerda G (1989), "Uniform Crossover in Genetic Algorithms", in J D Schaffer (ed.) *Proceedings of the Third International Conference on Genetic Algorithms*, Morgan Kaufmann, pp2-9.

28. Tsetlin M (ed.)(1973), *Automaton Theory and Modeling of Biological Systems*, Academic Press.

29. Watkins C (1989), "Learning from Delayed Rewards", PhD dissertation, University of Cambridge.

30. Weiss G (ed.)(1997), *Distributed Artificial Intelligence Meets Machine Learning*, Springer.

31. Wilson S W (1994), "ZCS: A Zeroth-level Classifier System", *Evolutionary Computation* 2(1):1-18.

Empirical Analysis of the Factors that Affect the Baldwin Effect

Kim W. C. Ku and M. W. Mak

Department of Electronic Engineering,
The Hong Kong Polytechnic University, Hong Kong

Abstract. The inclusion of learning in genetic algorithms based on the Baldwin effect is one of the popular approaches to improving the convergence of genetic algorithms. However, the expected improvement may not be easily obtained. This is mainly due to the lack of understanding of the factors that affect the Baldwin effect. This paper aims at providing sufficient evidence to confirm that the level of difficulties for genetic operations to produce the genotypic changes that match the phenotypic changes due to learning can significantly affect the Baldwin effect. The results suggest that combining genetic algorithms inattentively with any learning methods available is not a proper way to construct hybrid algorithms. Instead, the correlation between the genetic operations and the learning methods has to be carefully considered.

1 Introduction

A serious drawback of using evolutionary search to optimize the weights of recurrent neural networks (RNNs) is that many iterations are required in order to evolve into an acceptable solution. One way to speed up the convergence is to combine the efforts of local search (learning) and evolutionary search. This is because evolutionary search and local search could complement each other to yield a more efficient search algorithm.

There are two approaches to embedding learning in the evolutionary search. The first is based on Lamarckian evolution [1, 14] and the second is based on the Baldwin effect [3, 12]. We have demonstrated in our previous study [7] that Lamarckian learning is able to speed up the convergence of genetic algorithms (GAs) but Baldwinian learning fails to do so. To explain the phenomenon, we have conjectured that the more difficult it is for genetic operations to produce the changes obtained by learning, the poorer is the performance of Baldwinian learning. This paper aims at providing evidence to support this conjecture.

Different learning methods can be embedded in the evolutionary search. For examples, Montana and Davis [10] used gradient descent algorithms such as the backpropagation or its variants, and Maniezzo [8] used a learning method that flips some bits in a chromosome statistically. Researchers usually use whatever learning methods that are available without considering their appropriateness. This lack of careful consideration can lead to unsatisfactory performance. To overcome this problem, a crucial question needs to be answered: What kind of characteristics a learning method must possess so that Baldwinian learning has real benefit? This paper provides an answer through some carefully designed experiments. Our principal finding is that there should be a strong correlation between the genetic operators and the learning methods in order to get real benefit from Baldwinian learning. The desirable correlation that we have identified is that the genetic operations should easily produce the genotypic changes that match the phenotypic changes due to learning.

The rest of this paper is organized as follows. The Lamarckian evolution and the Baldwin effect are compared in Section 2. Section 3 explains how the cellular GAs and the learning methods that have been used in our previous study are modified in order to demonstrate the validity of the conjecture. In Section 4, we show how the Baldwin effect is affected. In Section 5, we identify a factor that affects the Baldwin effect. Finally, concluding remarks are given in Section 6.

2 Lamarckian Evolution versus the Baldwin Effect

Learning can be regarded as searching for better solutions in the neighborhood of the current solution. The motivation of embedding learning in evolutionary search is that it can guide the evolutionary process to find a better solution. There are two approaches to embedding learning in evolutionary search, namely the Lamarckian evolution and the evolutionary search based on the Baldwin effect.

2.1 Lamarckian evolution

In Lamarckian evolution [1, 14], the genotype and fitness of a chromosome are modified by learning. The idea is based on the assumption that an individual can genetically pass the characteristics (observed in the phenotype) acquired through learning to its offspring (encoded in the genotype). In other words, the learned behavior can directly change genotypes. As learning takes place in phenotype space, Lamarckian evolution requires an inverse mapping from the phenotype space to the genotype space, which is impossible in biological systems.

2.2 The Baldwin effect

The approach based on the Baldwin effect [3, 12] is more biological plausible. Unlike Lamarckian evolution, learning in this approach cannot modify the genotypes directly. Only the fitness is replaced by the 'learned' fitness (fitness after learning). Therefore, after learning, the selected chromosome will be associated with a 'learned' fitness which is not the same as its 'inborn' fitness (i.e. fitness before learning). Even though the characteristics to be learned in the phenotype space are not genetically specified, there is evidence [6] that the Baldwin effect is able to direct the genotypic changes.

Learning based on the Baldwin effect can be regarded as a kind of phenotypic variability; consequently, learning is able to increase the variance of the selection process (i.e. the effect of learning is to weaken selection pressure and to increase genetic polymorphism) [2]. In other words, even if a chromosome has an undesirable 'inborn' fitness, it may still have a high chance (provided that its 'learned' fitness is good) of being selected and evolved into a fitter chromosome. Another advantage of the Baldwin effect is that it can flatten out the fitness landscape around the local optima [5, 14] and enlarge the basin of attraction. This capability enables more chromosomes to be allocated around the local optima, thereby helps to find the global optimum. Because of the increase in genetic polymorphism and the enlargement of the basin of attraction, the evolutionary process can be improved. The idea that the Baldwin effect is beneficial to the evolutionary process is also supported by other researchers [11, 14].

3   Fixed-offset Mutation and Primitive Learning

Cellular GAs [4, 13] have been used to train RNNs [7]. Each weight in an RNN can be encoded as a gene in the form of floating-point numbers. A chromosome, in which the number of genes is equal to the number of weights, represents an RNN. The fitness of a chromosome is the mean squared error (MSE) between the actual and the desired outputs of the corresponding RNN.[1] In each reproduction cycle, every offspring produced by crossover is mutated before learning is applied. During mutation, some weights are changed by a positive or negative offset with exponential distribution. When learning is applied, all weights in the RNN are adjusted by gradient descent algorithms such as the real-time recurrent learning [15] or the truncated backpropagation through time [16].

Although the mutation operator and the gradient descent learning methods can be used for evolving RNNs [7], the scale of changes in the genotypes (produced by mutation) and phenotypes (produced by learning) is so large that controlling their correlation becomes very difficult. Since we aim to demonstrate how the Baldwin effect is affected by the correlation between learning methods and genetic operators, the mutation operators and the learning methods are modified. This results in a modified cellular GA which we denote it as MGA hereafter.

In the modified mutation operator, the exponentially distributed offsets are replaced by fixed offsets $\pm\delta$, where the value of δ is adjusted to the average fitness of the population after every 1000 reproduction cycles. During mutation, a processing node in the RNN (the offspring) is randomly selected, and the weights connecting to the input part of the node are changed by the fixed offsets.

The gradient descent learning methods are replaced by a primitive learning method L, where only some selected weights instead of all weights are allowed to be changed. Also, the weight changes in learning are limited to $\pm\delta$, instead of being varied according to the gradient of the error function. The learning process consists of a series of trials. In each trial, the original chromosome is changed by the above mutation procedure, and the resulting fitness is evaluated. The best fitness among the trials becomes the 'learned' fitness of the chromosome.

---

[1] In this case the better the fitness, the lower is the MSE.

With the above modifications, the correlation between the genotypic changes and the phenotypic changes becomes more controllable. The hybrid algorithms formed by the combination of the modified cellular GA and the primitive learning method are more appropriate for demonstrating the factor that affects the Baldwin effect.

4 How the Baldwin Effect is Affected

This experiment is to illustrate how the Baldwin effect is affected by the correlation between learning methods and genetic operators. RNNs with three inputs (one of them is the bias), four processing nodes (one of them is the output node) and 28 weights (i.e. $4 \times 4 + 4 \times 3 = 28$) were used to solve a temporal exclusive-OR problem. Specifically, the desired output of the RNN at time step t is the exclusive-OR of the two inputs (with values 0 or 1 generated by a random source) at time step $t - 2$.

4.1 Experiments

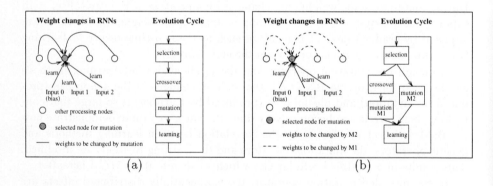

(a)   (b)

Fig. 1. Structure of (a) *MGA* and (b) *MGA-SPLIT*. The learning step is optional – it depends on whether learning is incorporated. Weights to be changed by learning are labeled with 'learn'. In the figure, only the weights connecting to a selected node are shown.

The convergence of *MGA*, with and without learning L, in training RNNs was recorded. Then, the genetic operations were modified by splitting the mutation operator into two parts, $M1$ and $M2$, to form another modified cellular GA, called *MGA-SPLIT*. The postfix 'SPLIT' emphasizes that the genetic operations are split into two sets as illustrated in Fig. 1b. The convergence of *MGA-SPLIT*, with and without learning L, was compared with that of *MGA*. The main difference between MGA-$SPLIT$ and MGA, as shown in Fig. 1, is that MGA-$SPLIT$ has two sets of genetic operators, while MGA has only one set of genetic operators. During a reproduction cycle in MGA-$SPLIT$, one set of genetic operators is selected to produce an offspring. The first set of genetic operators consists of crossover (same as MGA) and mutation $M1$, as illustrated in Fig. 1b. During mutation $M1$, a node in the RNN (the offspring) is randomly selected, and the weights connecting the selected node and other processing nodes (dash lines of Fig. 1b) are changed by fixed offsets $\pm\delta$. The second set of genetic operators consists of mutation $M2$. Unlike $M1$, however, the weight changes in $M2$ are restricted to those weights connecting the inputs to the selected node (solid lines of Fig. 1b).

In the above experimental setup, the same learning method was applied to MGA and MGA-$SPLIT$. This enables us to compare the convergence of Baldwinian learning under the influence of different genetic operations.

MGA, MGA-$SPLIT$ and their hybrid algorithms (i.e. with learning) were applied to train RNNs using a population size of 100. Two hundred simulation runs were conducted to obtain the average convergence.

4.2 Correlation Between Learning Methods and Genetic Operators

Fig. 2 compares the convergence of MGA, MGA-$SPLIT$ and their hybrid algorithms. It shows that the convergence of MGA-$SPLIT$ is better than that of MGA when learning is incorporated. The improvement in convergence is surely not due to the learning methods, since they are identical for both MGA and MGA-$SPLIT$. Nor can it be explained by arguing that MGA-$SPLIT$ is better than MGA, since the convergence of the former is in fact poorer than that of the latter, as shown in Fig. 2.

One possible explanation for the improvement in convergence is that the characteristics of MGA-$SPLIT$ make it more suitable for being combined with learning L. In other words, the correlation between the genetic operations and learning in the hybrid MGA-$SPLIT$ (MGA-$SPLIT$ with learning) results in a superior convergence. Further evidence for this claim can be found in Section 5 below.

The following summarizes the findings in the first experiment. The difference in convergence is found to be neither caused by the difference in GAs nor the difference in learning methods. Instead, the convergence is affected by the difference in the correlation between learning methods and genetic operators.

5   Factor Affecting the Baldwin Effect

Although we have demonstrated that the Baldwin effect is affected by the correlation between genetic operators and learning methods, we have not specified what kind of correlation is desirable. A clear understanding might be obtained by scrutinizing how the correlation between genetic operators and learning methods in the hybrid MGA is different from that in the hybrid MGA-$SPLIT$.

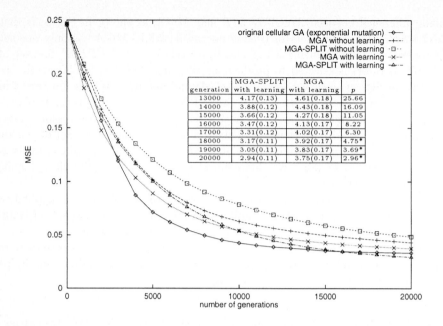

Fig. 2. Convergence of MGA, $MGA\text{-}SPLIT$, and their hybrid algorithms. The means, variances (in brackets) and significance p (calculated by Student's t-test) of the difference in means are shown in the table. Significance with value less than 0.05 is marked with an asterisk, indicating that the difference in the corresponding MSE is significant. All figures are scaled by 10^{-2}.

In $MGA\text{-}SPLIT$, the number of possible genetic changes produced by mutation $M2$ is $4 \times 2^3 = 32$ (as there are three inputs connected to four processing nodes, and each gene can be changed by $+\delta$ or $-\delta$). As a result, one of the 32 possible changes will match the phenotypic changes obtained by learning in the previous learning cycle. Therefore, the probability that mutation $M2$ produces an offspring whose genotype corresponds to the 'learned' fitness of the parent chromosome is $\frac{1}{32}$.

On the other hand, the number of possible genetic changes obtained by MGA in a reproduction cycle is much larger than 32. This is because the crossover replaces half of the genes with those of another parent chromosome, and there are $4 \times 2^7 = 512$ possible genetic changes produced by the mutation in MGA. Therefore, the genotypic changes obtained by the genetic operations in the hybrid MGA is unlikely to match the phenotypic changes obtained by learning.

The above comparisons reveal that we can consider the genotypic changes in $MGA\text{-}SPLIT$ to be confined in a similar direction to that obtained by learning method L. A desirable correlation between genetic operations and learning methods might be that the genetic operations should easily produce the genotypic changes that match the phenotypic changes due to learning. The second experiment aims to provide further evidence to support that the Baldwin effect is affected by this factor.

5.1 Experiments

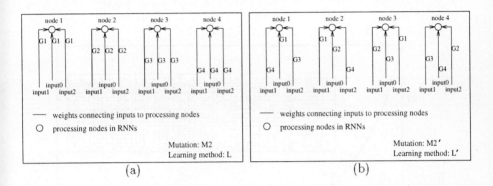

Fig. 3. Two ways of grouping the weights to form weight groups which are to be changed by (a) $M2$ or L and (b) $M2'$ or L'. There are 4 groups of weights. Weights belonging to the same group have the same label. For example, the weights connecting the three inputs to node 2 of (a) belong to the same group (G2). Only the weights connecting the inputs to the processing nodes are shown.

Here, another mutation $M2'$ and another learning method L' were used to replace $M2$ and L, respectively. In learning method L (mutation $M2$), the weights (genes) are divided into four groups as illustrated in Fig. 3a. Basically, the weights (and the genes corresponding to the weights) associated with the three inputs are grouped according to the processing node to which they are connected. The number of groups and the number of weights (genes) in each group remain the same in learning method L' (mutation $M2'$). However, the weights (genes) are grouped differently as illustrated in Fig. 3b. By combining the mutation operations ($M2$ and $M2'$) and learning methods (L and L'), four hybrid algorithms can be obtained: $M2 + L$, $M2 + L'$, $M2' + L$, $M2' + L'$.

One important characteristic of this experimental setup is that the grouping methods for mutation $M2$ and learning method L are the same; they are also identical for $M2'$ and L'. In other words, the genotypic changes obtained by mutation $M2$ are closely related to the phenotypic changes obtained by learning L; a similar correlation occurs between $M2'$ and L'. The correlation between genetic operators and learning methods is strong in $M2 + L$ and $M2' + L'$, while it is weak in $M2 + L'$ and $M2' + L$. Based on the convergence comparisons (averaged over two hundred simulation runs) of the four hybrid algorithms, we aim to illustrate that ensuring a match between the genotypic changes and the phenotypic changes due to learning can improve the convergence of Baldwinian learning.

5.2 Experimental Results

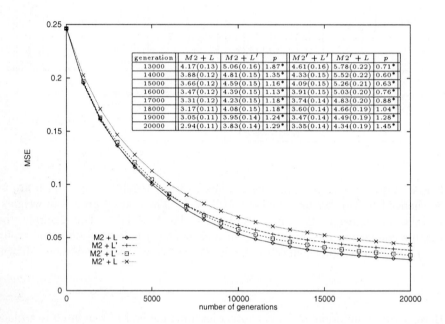

generation	$M2 + L$	$M2 + L'$	p	$M2' + L'$	$M2' + L$	p
13000	4.17(0.13)	5.06(0.16)	1.87*	4.61(0.16)	5.78(0.22)	0.71*
14000	3.88(0.12)	4.81(0.15)	1.35*	4.33(0.15)	5.52(0.22)	0.60*
15000	3.66(0.12)	4.59(0.15)	1.16*	4.09(0.15)	5.26(0.21)	0.63*
16000	3.47(0.12)	4.39(0.15)	1.13*	3.91(0.15)	5.03(0.20)	0.76*
17000	3.31(0.12)	4.23(0.15)	1.18*	3.74(0.14)	4.83(0.20)	0.88*
18000	3.17(0.11)	4.08(0.15)	1.18*	3.60(0.14)	4.66(0.19)	1.04*
19000	3.05(0.11)	3.95(0.14)	1.24*	3.47(0.14)	4.49(0.19)	1.28*
20000	2.94(0.11)	3.83(0.14)	1.29*	3.35(0.14)	4.34(0.19)	1.45*

Fig. 4. Convergence of the four hybrid algorithms. The means, variances (in brackets) and significance p (calculated by Student's t-test) of the difference in means are shown in the table. Significance with value less than 0.05 is marked with an asterisk, indicating that the difference in the corresponding MSE is significant. All figures are scaled by 10^{-2}.

The results of the second experiment, as illustrated in Fig. 4, show that the hybrid algorithm $M2 + L$ has better convergence than the hybrid algorithm $M2 + L'$. Since we used the same cellular GA (i.e. $MGA\text{-}SPLIT$), there can be two explanations to explain this result: (1) learning method L is more capable of improving the fitness than learning method L' and (2) mutation $M2$ works better with learning method L than with learning method L'. If the first explanation is correct, the hybrid algorithm $M2' + L$ should have better convergence performance than that of $M2' + L'$. However, Fig. 4 clearly shows that this is not the case. Therefore, we conclude that mutation $M2$ works better with learning method L and mutation $M2'$ works better with learning method L'. This is the only satisfactory explanation for the results in Fig. 4.

A common characteristic of the hybrid algorithms $M2 + L$ and $M2' + L'$ is that there is a strong correlation between the mutation and the learning methods (they use the same weight grouping method). As mentioned above, the probability of genotypic changes obtained by mutation $M2$ to match the phenotypic changes obtained by learning L is $\frac{1}{32}$. By means of a similar argument, the probability of genotypic-to-phenotypic matching for $M2' + L'$ is also $\frac{1}{32}$. On the other hand, the probabilities are much less than $\frac{1}{32}$ for the other two hybrid algorithms (i.e. $M2+L'$ and $M2'+L$), since the grouping of weights for learning is different from the grouping of genes for mutation. The convergence of hybrid algorithms $M2+L$ and $M2' + L'$ is superior because they make genotypic-to-phenotypic matching to be easily obtained. These results give us sufficient evidence to confirm that the level of difficulties for genetic operations to produce a match between the genotypic changes and the phenotypic changes due to learning is an important factor that affects the Baldwin effect.

Mayley [9] has made an attempt to investigate how the Baldwin effect would be affected by the correlation between genetic operations and learning methods. It has been demonstrated that the performance of the hybrid algorithms is degraded when the dimension of phenotypic changes produced by learning becomes large. However, Mayley's analysis did not consider that different learning methods might have different capabilities, which could affect the performance of the hybrid algorithms. Our results, however, clearly demonstrate that the difference in the convergence of the evolutionary search based on the Baldwin effect is neither due to the difference in GAs nor due to the difference in the learning methods being used. Instead, the level of difficulties for the genotypic changes to match the phenotypic changes is a factor that affects the Baldwin effect.

6 Conclusions

Various attempts have been made to combine genetic algorithms and learning based on the Baldwin effect. Although improvement in convergence have been made, the Baldwin effect could be detrimental in some circumstances. A guideline we have found for constructing better hybrid algorithms is that there should be a direct correlation between the genetic operations and the learning methods. Through carefully designed experiments, we have demonstrated that the level of difficulties for genetic operations to produce the genotypic changes corresponding to the 'learned' fitness can affect the Baldwin effect. However, this is not the only factor. A strong correlation does not guarantee the convergence of evolutionary search to be improved by incorporating Baldwinian learning. There could be other problems, apart from the temporal exclusive-OR problem, where the significance of the correlation factor might be overshadowed by other factors. This is to be investigated in the future.

Acknowledgments

This work was supported by the Hong Kong Polytechnic University Grant A/C No. A-PA 58.

References

1. D. H. Ackley and M. L. Littman. A case for Lamarckian evolution. In C. G. Langton, editor, *Artificial Life 3*, pages 3–10. Reading, Mass.: Addison-Wesley, 1994.
2. R. W. Anderson. Learning and evolution: A quantitative genetics approach. *Journal of Theoretical Biology*, 175:89–101, 1995.
3. J. M. Baldwin. A new factor in evolution. *American Naturalist*, 30:441–451, 1896.
4. Y. Davidor. A naturally occurring niche & species phenomenon: the model and first results. In *Proceedings of the Fourth International Conference on Genetic Algorithms*, pages 257–262, 1991.
5. W. E. Hart, T. E. Kammeyer, and R. K. Belew. The role of development in genetic algorithms. In L. D. Whitley and M. D. Vose, editors, *Foundations of Genetic Algorithms 3*, pages 315–332. San Mateo, CA: Morgan Kaufmann Pub., 1995.
6. G. E. Hinton and S. J. Nowlan. How learning can guide evolution. *Complex Systems*, 1:495–502, 1987.
7. K. W. C. Ku and M. W. Mak. Exploring the effects of Lamarckian and Baldwinian learning in evolving recurrent neural networks. In *Proceedings of the IEEE International Conference on Evolutionary Computation*, pages 617–621, 1997.
8. V. Maniezzo. Genetic evolution of the topology and weight distribution of neural networks. *IEEE Transactions on Neural Networks*, 5(1):39–53, 1994.
9. G. Mayley. Landscapes, learning costs, and genetic assimilation. *Evolutionary Computation*, 4(3):213–234, 1997.
10. D. J. Montana and L. Davis. Training feedforward neural network using genetic algorithms. In *Proceedings of the Eleventh International Joint Conference on Artifical Intelligence*, pages 762–767, 1989.
11. S. Nolfi, J. L. Elman, and D. Parisi. Learning and evolution in neural networks. *Adaptive Behavior*, 3:5–28, 1994.
12. P. Turney. Myths and legends of the Baldwin effect. In *Proceedings of the Workshop on Evolutionary Computing and Machine Learning at the 13th International Conference on Machine Learning*, pages 135–142, 1996.
13. D. Whitley. A genetic algorithm tutorial. *Statistics & Computing*, 4(2):65–85, 1994.
14. D. Whitley, V. S. Gordon, and K. Mathias. Lamarckian evolution, the Baldwin effect and function optimization. In Y. Davidor, H.-P. Schwefel, and R. Manner, editors, *Parallel Problem Solving from Nature – PPSN III*, pages 6–15. Springer-Verlag, 1994.
15. R. J. Williams and D. Zipser. Experimental analysis of the real-time recurrent learning algorithm. *Connection Science*, 1:87–111, 1989.
16. R. J. Williams and D. Zipser. Gradient-based learning algorithms for recurrent networks and their computational complexity. In Y. Chauvin and D. E Rumelhart, editors, *Backpropagation: Theory, Architectures, and Applications*, pages 433–486. Hillsdale, NJ: Lawrence Erlbaum Associates Pub., 1994.

Promoting Generalisation of Learned Behaviours in Genetic Programming

Ibrahim KUSCU

Cognitive and Computing Sciences
University of Sussex
Brighton BN1 9QH U.K.
Email: ibrahim@cogs.susx.ac.uk

Abstract. Recently, growing numbers of research concentrate on robustness of the programs evolved using Genetic Programming (GP). While some of the researchers report on the brittleness of the solutions evolved, some others proposed methods of promoting robustness. It is important that these methods are not ad hoc and specific for a certain experimental setup. In this research, brittleness of solutions found for the artificial ant problem is reported and a new method promoting generalisation of the solutions in GP is presented.
Keywords: Genetic programming, learning, robustness, generalisation.

1 Introduction

In Genetic Programming (GP) [9, 10] paradigm solutions to some learning problems are sought by means of an evolutionary process of program discovery. These learning problems, in general, can be classified into two kinds according to the way in which problems are defined: some problems use a data set such as input/output mappings of supervised learning problems and some other problems deal with real or simulated robot behaviours in an environment. Recently, growing number of researchers [12, 11, 2, 6, 15, 13] report that solutions to learning problems may result in non-robust or brittle programs. Robustness of a solution can be defined as the desired successful performance of the solution when it is applied to a similar environment (or a data set) other than it is evolved for. In [2] several approaches used by GP researchers to promote robustness are discussed and a brief review is provided in this paper. Common to the methods employed in these studies is the lack of some guidelines for the proper design and use of fitness functions, fitness cases and the evolutionary setup. This can result in ad hoc experimental setups and measures of robustness.

The concept of generalisation as used in the connectionist or symbolic learning research is similar to robustness but is much broader and requires a formal methodology for the design and evaluation of the experiments [8]. The established formalism borrowed from the generalisation oriented learning research of Artificial Intelligence (AI) can provide a useful methodology in improving research on evolving robust programs using GP. More specifically, such formalisms can be helpful in designing an evolutionary experimental setup and objectively measuring the learning performance in terms of robustness or generalisation. For example, an experiment on generalisation or robustness may be best measured if it is conducted in two distinctive stages: training and testing. Finding a solution by the help of an evolutionary process can be seen as training, and generalisation can subsequently be measured in terms of the performance of the learner during the testing process. A generalisation oriented experiment must also follow certain rules in choosing the training and testing cases such as representativeness of the training cases and degree of overlapping between the two. There are some other techniques which can help to obtain more general solutions. In [12] reducing prior knowledge about a domain and in [1] adding new features are suggested to increase generalisation performance in the applications of GP to some supervised relational learning problems.

This paper aims at providing a method for discovering general solutions for the problems simulating robot behaviours. The method is applied to the artificial ant problem [9, 7]. In [11] it is reported that analysis of the solutions found for the artificial ant problem may exhibit a high degree of brittleness. In the following sections, after briefly reviewing the research on generalisation/robustness in GP and introducing the artificial ant problem, a summary of previous research and some new results of the experiments using a method which ensures generalisation for the artificial ant problem are presented.

2 Generalisation in Genetic Programming

The problem of generalisation in genetic programming has not received the attention it actually deserves. Recently, there have been some discussions on the genetic-programming list[1] and few papers regarding the problems with generalisation. One of the major opinion is that researchers face over-fitting (i.e., memorising the training data) and brittle solutions for the problems. In this section, I will present an overview of the generalisation research in GP.

An examination of the problems in [9] has shown that almost all of the problems using a data set (i.e., input/output mappings) do *not* use a separate training and testing data sets. In these problems fitness is calculated based on a complete set of instances describing correct behaviour. The examples include the parity problems and multiplexer problem. Also in [3] test cases are used in the computation of the fitness of the individuals. As is suggested in [5] GP as being an inductive learning method must produce programs whose behaviour is applicable over all input space but not only over training instances. They further state that when training and testing phases are adapted, improving fitness function to prefer simpler expressions (i.e, smaller programs) may help to avoid over-fitting and obtain better predictive accuracy during the testing phases.

For those problems involving simulations the generality of the solutions, often, are not tested [9]. Most of the problems involve one fitness case where learning is evaluated based on the performance in one static environment. Clearly,

---

[1] The address of the list is genetic-programming@cs.stanford.edu

such an approach can easily result in a solution which only captures particular characteristics of the environment. For some simulations a random starting point is given for the agents. This can be seen as a simple form of generalisation to different starting points. However, if the environment in which an agent is evolved for a particular behavior is still static, any learning achieved may not produce a general solution but a specific solution for a given environment.

Although, the need for producing systems with generalisation ability is recently recognised in the GP community, research primarily dealing with generalisation is limited to only a few papers. For example, in a research [16] dealing with size and generality in GP, the degree of overlapping between training instances and the testing instances does not seem to be explicitly controlled. In such a case, an objective and direct comparison using a common basis between training and testing may be difficult.

Some researchers [6, 15] used noise and changed the initial conditions of the agents in order to promote robustness of the programs produced by GP to changes in the initial conditions and changes in the environmental stimuli. Use of noise can be helpful in reducing the brittleness of programs and increasing the likelihood of robustness [15]. In [6] both changing initial coordinates and the direction of the robot and introduction of noisy sensors and actuators are tried to produce robust programs for the box moving robot behaviour. Separate training and testing sets are used but no formal method of choosing training and testing cases is provided. Training and testing comparisons are done on a generation basis and the measure of robustness in testing on a different environment after the training (i.e., after evolution has stopped) is not reported. The results of the experiments were not very clear in explaining whether a robust behaviour has been reached and if so, how it is reached.

In [4] GP is used to evolve an agent who could survive in a hostile environment. Rather than using a fixed environment for a particular run, a new environment is generated randomly at the end of each generation. In this way, it is hoped that the agent can handle 'any' environment. Since the agent does not seem to be tested in a new environment after the evolution has stopped, the nature and the degree of generalisation (that might have been obtained by variable training environment during the evolution) to new environments remains unexplained.

A real time evolution of a real robot for obstacle avoidance behaviour is presented in [14]. The result of the experiments showed that the robot can exhibit a robust behaviour if it 'is lifted and placed in a completely new environment' and if the obstacles are moved around. However, the characteristics of this new environment are not specified in the paper. So, it is not very clear to see to what degree, and what kind of generalisation is obtained.

A good example of experiments attempting to reduce brittleness of the programs generated by GP is presented in [13]. The system in this paper evolves optimised maneuvers for pursuer/evader problem. The results of this study suggest that use of a fixed set of training cases may result in brittle solutions due to the fact that such fixed fitness cases may not be representative of possible situations that the agent may encounter. It is shown that use of randomly generated fitness cases at the end of each generation can reduce the brittleness of the solutions when the solution is tested against a set of large representative situations after the evolution. However, a proper selection method for training and testing cases is not provided.

One of the common aspects of most of these experiments is the lack of a formal method which can be used to determine how the training and testing processes should be conducted and how the generalisation performance should be measured.

3 How General is the Artificial Ant's Behaviour?

The artificial ant problem involves simulating navigation behavior of an ant aiming at collecting all of the food lying along an irregular trail. In [7], experiments producing an artificial ant to traverse the entire cells of a trail by collecting all of the food is presented. However, the degree of the generality of the solutions is not clear. The authors explicitly state that their system will evolve ants with features adapted to the characteristics (i.e., gaps, turns, and jumps) of that particular trail:

> 'Such efficient logic seems exquisitely adapted to the features of this particular trail, and suggest that evolution has had effect of "compiling" knowledge of this environment into structure of the organism' [7].

In [9] it is stated that a solution found for the artificial ant problem may result in a generalised behaviour for the artificial ant:

> '... We rely on the various states of the ant that actually arise along the ant's actual trajectory to be sufficiently representative of the generalised trail following problem. As we will see this one fitness case is sufficiently representative for this particular problem to allow the ant to learn to navigate this trail and reasonable generalisations of this trail' ([9], pp. 150).

The term 'reasonable generalisations' does not clearly state a degree of generalisation that can be expected from a solution of the ant problem. When we evolve an ant performing well on the Santa Fe trail, can we expect her to perform well on some variations of the same trail? According to the above statement the answer seems to be 'yes'. However, as will be shown later, the answer is most of the time 'no' and it depends highly on the nature of the variations in other trails and some specific abilities of the solutions evolved on the Santa Fe trail. A solution found for a particular environment may not be general enough to be applicable to even any minimal variations of the same environment. Even if it may be applicable, it may not be possible to know for sure which kind of variations in the environment it may be applicable for. Moreover, since any two GP solutions for a given problem may not be the same, there is a great amount of uncertainty in knowing which of the solutions will be better for what kind of variations in the environment.

4 Brittleness of Solutions Using the Santa Fe Trail

The problem definition the artificial ant problem can be found in [9]. The problem is also provided as an example problem with the lil-gp package[2]. For the initial experiment; (see below), there were no changes to the parameters provided with the lil-gp package. One parameter was added for the *testing* process. This parameter defines the number of lifetime steps of the artificial ant during the testing process for each trail. It is chosen to be 200 steps greater than the training lifetime of 400 in order to allow enough time to reveal an individual ant performing well on a test trail.

Initial experiments involved collecting perfectly performing individuals over a large number of runs. Given the parameters above, out of 1200 runs 15 individuals were found each of which can collect exactly 89 foods within the given amount of lifetime. In [11] details of experiments where the above 15 best-of-run individuals were tested on some Santa Fe-like and on some slightly different trails can be found. Very briefly, the experimental results have shown that a good performance of an artificial ant on the Santa Fe trail does not in any way guarantee a generalisation of behaviour on even very similar trails. However, it may be possible to obtain a generalised behaviour by evolving a population of artificial ants using more than one training trails.

In one of experiments [11], instead of using just one trail (i.e. the Santa Fe Trail), more than one trails were used as training cases. These trails were carefully designed to include *only* those primitives which are part of the characteristics of the Santa Fe trail. In other words, the primitives of the trails used for training were the same as Santa Fe's but had a different shape and were shorter in length. Using these trails as training trails during the evolution and testing the best solutions over all of the hand-coded test trails (presented in the previous experiments) resulted in a test performance of 100 percent for all of the trails except three very difficult ones.

One of the implications of the results found by using multiple training trails was that instead of searching for a single solution for a single environment, it may be possible to find a general solution which holds for a class of environments of which that environment is a member. Moreover, the cost of finding such a solution may not be high. However, the observations from the experiments are far from forming a basis on which one could establish some formal requirements for obtaining good generalisations. This is due to the fact that we have carefully hand-designed the training and testing trails. Next section presents a method in order to show the general applicability of the experimental findings using multiple training trails.

---

[2] Lil—gp is a C—based application development environment for Genetic programming. It is developed by Douglas Zongker at Michigan State University and available at URL: http://isl.cps.msu.edu/GA/software/lil-gp/index.html

5 Promoting Generalisation

Let X refer to the world of all possible trails and let S refer to a subset of X and in S the trails are characterised by certain attributes such as set of primitives that are allowed on a trail (i.e. a number of consecutive gap cells allowed) and the way those primitives are placed. For example, if s is defined as a set of trails with up to 3 consecutive gaps *before* corners, the Santa Fe trail is a member (instance) of s. A simplest generalisation case can be defined as follows:

> **Given a learner l's performance after it is 'trained' on a subset of S, if l exhibits a satisfactory performance on other set of instances belonging to S that do not contain instances used in the training phase, the learner l is said to have generalised over this new set of instances of S.**

The important point in the above definition is that both the training and the testing trails are chosen from the same domain of trails. The primitives and rules of placing these primitives when constructing the trails are the same for both sets of the training and testing trails. In this case, there is a common base to measure training and testing performance of an artificial ant.

The idea is tested by experimenting on a random set of trails which belong to certain class. In this case the class involved Santa Fe-like trails with up to 3 gaps when the trail is straight and just before the corners. Both training and the testing trails were randomly generated according to the following rules: (1)Each trail had no more than 35 cells (including the food and gap cells) and was placed in a 25 by 25 grid. (2)Each trail started with two consecutive food cells in either West or South direction, determined randomly. (3)The next direction is chosen randomly. (4)The number of cells in any direction is determined randomly and can be at least three and at most 8. (5)Placing food in the cells is favoured. 2/3 of the time there would be food in the cell and 1/3 of the time there would be no food (i.e. the cell represents a gap) and (6) The length and the shape of the trails were determined randomly and were variable.

In previous sections, I have summarised experimental findings [11] and stated that the solutions to the artificial ant problem found by evolving using only the Santa Fe trail do not guarantee a generalisation to similar or slightly different trails (hand-coded). In order to confirm the previous findings and see that this is not a pure coincidence, a new experiment was set up, where the 15 best solution to the Santa Fe problem were tested on a set of 100 *random* trails. This random training set is constructed according to the above procedure. None of the trails had a primitive which did not exist on the Santa Fe. In other words, the rule used to construct them was exactly the same as the rule for the Santa Fe: *a single and double gap is allowed when the trail is straight, and up to three consecutive gaps are allowed at a corner*. The results of the testing can be found in Figure 1. Each of the bar in the figure corresponds to number of trails navigated succesfully out of 100 random trails.

The results confirm the previous findings that a solution for a single environment in no way guarantees a generalised solution. Among a set of possible

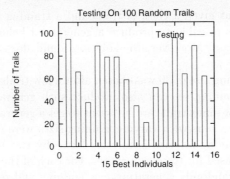

Fig. 1. The generalisation performance of individuals trained only on the Santa Fe.

solutions there might be a general one but as far as performance on this particular environment (i.e. the Santa Fe trail) is concerned one always considers these solutions as equal and has no way of knowing which one is a better generaliser.

5.1 Random Environmental Sampling for Generalisation

How can we find a general solution for a particular class of environments? As has been presented in the previous section, using multiple trails may produce some general solutions. In accordance with the above definition of generalisation, in a new experiment, 100 random trails were generated which can only have up to 3 consecutive gap cells before corners. Then this set of 100 random trails was split into two sets as a training set and a testing set. The training set contained 30 trails and the testing set contained 70 random trails plus all of the previous hand-coded (longer) trails used in testing phase of previous experiments (the choice of the number of training and testing cases were arbitrary). The aim of the experiment was to find an artificial ant with a generalised behaviour of traversing testing trails and collecting all the food.

The same parameters as provided with lil-gp were used but the lifetime steps allowed for traversing each trail during the training and testing was 150 for the shorter random trails. For the longer hand-coded trails, life-time for testing was 600 time units. A population of 300 ants was used in every GP run and after each generation the fitness was computed using the number of pieces of food collected over all of the 30 training trails. The results showed that in every run (out of 500) an artificial ant was found to be performing perfectly (i.e. collecting all the food) on the training and random testing trails. Also, when these best-of-run ants were tested on the longer test trails of the previous experiments they all showed a generalised behaviour on all of these trails but three. As in previous experiments, those three trails were the ones which had some primitives that were absent from the training trails: three gap cells making up a corner, a gap after a corner (i.e. trails 1, 4, and 6) and sharp turns. It is obvious that these primitives refer to the description of a different class of trails. Thus, it can be safely concluded that given a class of trails and a training process using trails from this class, it is possible to produce a generalised behaviour to some new trails within this class. Moreover, the solution found does not depend on the length of the trails.

Above, the training size of 30 was chosen after a few trials. It may be possible that a lower size training set can also produce such generalised behaviour. In order to find out how many trails are sufficient to get a generalised behaviour, for the same set up, new runs with varying training sizes were conducted. Starting from two trails, training set size is increased two by two up to 30 trails. 100 random trails were used for testing purposes. For each of these training sizes, 10 runs wre executed randomly generating new training and testing trails at each run. Training and testing performances per run for every different training size as well as the average performance of 10 runs were recorded.

It is found that 25 random trails would be enough to obtain a generalised behavior in every run. Although it was possible to obtain a perfect performance during the training process with smaller training sizes, generalisation was not guaranteed during the testing process. In general, the increase in the number of the training trails leads to increase in the testing performances but only after a certain level increase in the size of training data (24 to 25 training trails in this case), a perfect generalisation can be observed. The graph in Figure 2 summarizes the results by depicting the average performances of every 10 runs corresponding to a particular training size.

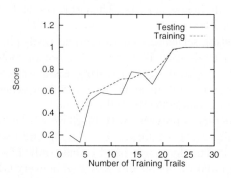

Fig. 2. Average generalisation performances of individuals trained on varying number of random trails

The results indicate that generalisation of the learned behaviours are largely influenced by the environment in which the behaviour is evolved. Single solutions for single environments are very likely to be non-general. However, if a set of features from an environment is used as a training set, it is possible to obtain a general solution with sufficient training data. Depending on the environment the training size required might be different.

6 Conclusions

It is often reported that programs discovered by GP can be brittle and non-general. In this paper after reviewing the literature on generalisation and genetic programming, it is shown that solutions to the artificial ant problem may also exhibit brittleness. A method of obtaining generalisation is proposed. It is suggested that using a set of features (i.e. multiple environments) chosen randomly from a class of environments can be used as training data. Evolving potential solutions using sufficient number of training features can result in general solutions. The method is applied to obtain general solutions for a class of the Santa Fe-like trails. By training artificial ants using a set of random trails during an evolutionary process, finding an artificial ant which is capable of traversing a wide variety of trails is shown to be possible. Another important implications is that since a small size of a training set can help to find a general solution for a given class of environments, the cost of computation is also saved.

This research mostly concentrated on environment as a factor of producing agents with relatively general behaviours. Another important factor for generalisation is the agent itself. The features of an agent such as how it is represented and what action it can perform largely determines for what class of environments the agent can produce a generalised behaviour. This is a subject of the further research.

Finally, the artificial ant problem uses a discrete environment and exhibits a discrete interaction. The findings of the experiments would be extremely useful in economising the cost of artificial evolution and in building better learning agents, if they are applicable to the simulation and real world environments with continuous interaction. This also requires some further investigation.

Acknowledgements

I would like to thank to Dr. I. Harvey for his support and guidance in developing this research. This research is funded by the Middle East Technical University, Ankara, Turkiye.

References

1. Hilan Bensusan and Ibrahim Kuscu. Constructive induction using genetic programming. In *ICML'96, Evolutionary computing and Machine Learning Workshop*, 1996.
2. Tommaso F. Bersano-Begey and Jason M. Daida. A discussion on generality and robustness and a framework for fitness set construction in genetic programming to promote robustness. In John R. Koza, editor, *Late Breaking Papers at the 1997 Genetic Programming Conference*, pages 11–18, Stanford University, CA, USA, 13–16 July 1997. Stanford Bookstore.
3. Frank D. Francone, Peter Nordin, and Wolfgang Banzhaf. Benchmarking the generalization capabilities of a compiling genetic programming system using sparse

data sets. In John R. Koza, David E. Goldberg, David B. Fogel, and Rick L. Riolo, editors, *Genetic Programming 1996: Proceedings of the First Annual Conference*, pages 72–80, Stanford University, CA, USA, July 1996. MIT Press.

4. Thomas D. Haynes and Roger L. Wainwright. A simulation of adaptive agents in hostile environment. In K. M. George, Janice H. Carroll, Ed Deaton, Dave Oppenheim, and Jim Hightower, editors, *Proceedings of the 1995 ACM Symposium on Applied Computing*, pages 318–323, Nashville, USA, 1995. ACM Press.

5. Dale Hooper and Nicholas S. Flann. Improving the accuracy and robustness of genetic programming through expression simplification. In John R. Koza, David E. Goldberg, David B. Fogel, and Rick L. Riolo, editors, *Genetic Programming 1996: Proceedings of the First Annual Conference*, page 428, Stanford University, CA, USA, 28–31 July 1996. MIT Press.

6. Takuya Ito, Hitoshi Iba, and Masayuki Kimura. Robustness of robot programs generated by genetic programming. In John R. Koza, David E. Goldberg, David B. Fogel, and Rick L. Riolo, editors, *Genetic Programming 1996: Proceedings of the First Annual Conference*, Stanford University, CA, USA, 28–31 July 1996. MIT Press. 321–326.

7. D. Jefferson, *et al.* Evolution as a theme in artificial life: The genesys/tracker system. In *Artificial Life II*. Addison-Wesley, 1991.

8. M. Kearns and U. Vazirani. *An Introduction to Computational Learning Theory.* MIT Press, Cambridge, Massachussets, USA, 1994.

9. John Koza. *Genetic Programming:On the programming of computers by means of natural selection.* MIT press, Cambridge, MA, 1992.

10. John Koza. *Genetic Programming II.* MIT press, 1994.

11. I. Kuscu. Evolving a generalised behaviour: Artificial ant problem revisited. In *The Seventh Annual Conference on Evolutionary Programming*, Forthcoming 1998.

12. Ibrahim Kuscu. Evolution of learning rules for hard learning problems. In Lawrence J. Fogel, Peter J. Angeline, and T Baeck, editors, *Evolutionary Programming V: Proceedings of the Fifth Annual Conference on Evolutionary Programming.* MIT Press, 1996.

13. F. W. Moore and O. N. Garcia. New methodology for reducing brittleness in genetic programming. In E. Pohl, editor, *Proceedings of the National Aerospace and Electronics 1997 Conference (NAECON-97).* IEEE Press, 1997.

14. Peter Nordin and Wolfgang Banzhaf. Genetic programming controlling a miniature robot. In E. V. Siegel and J. R. Koza, editors, *Working Notes for the AAAI Symposium on Genetic Programming*, pages 61–67, MIT, Cambridge, MA, USA, 10–12 November 1995. AAAI.

15. Craig W. Reynolds. An evolved, vision-based behavioral model of obstacle avoidance behaviour. In Christopher G. Langton, editor, *Artificial Life III*, volume XVII of *SFI Studies in the Sciences of Complexity*, pages 327–346. Addison-Wesley, Santa Fe Institute, New Mexico, USA, 15-19 June 1992 1994.

16. Justinian Rosca. Generality versus size in genetic programming. In John R. Koza, David E. Goldberg, David B. Fogel, and Rick L. Riolo, editors, *Genetic Programming 1996: Proceedings of the First Annual Conference*, pages 381–387, Stanford University, CA, USA, 1996. MIT Press.

Generalization in Wilson's Classifier System

Pier Luca Lanzi

Artificial Intelligence & Robotics Project
Dipartimento di Elettronica e Informazione
Politecnico di Milano
Piazza Leonardo da Vinci 32
I–20133 Milano - Italy
Voice +39-2-23993622
Fax +39-2-23993411
Lanzi@elet.polimi.it

Abstract. We analyze generalization with the XCS classifier system when the system is applied to animat problems in grid-worlds. Our aim is to give a unified view of generalization with XCS, in order to explain some of the phenomena reported in the literature. Initially, we apply XCS to two environments. Our results show that there are situations in which the generalization mechanism of XCS may prevent the system from converging to optimum. Accordingly, we study XCS's generalization mechanism analyzing the conditions under which the system may fail to evolve an optimal solution. We draw a hypothesis in order to explain the results reported so far. Our hypothesis suggests that XCS fails to learn an optimal solution when, due to the environment structure and to the exploration strategy employed, the system does not explore all the areas of the environment frequently. We thus introduce a meta exploration strategy that is used as theoretical tool to validate our hypothesis experimentally.

1 Introduction

Generalization is the most interesting feature of XCS, the classifier system introduced by Wilson [6]. XCS in fact shows to be effective in evolving near-minimal population of accurate and maximally general classifiers, as demonstrated through a number of experiments involving simple but interesting simulated environments [8]. Nevertheless, Lanzi [4] showed that there are situations in which XCS is not able to prevent overgeneral classifiers from corrupting the population. As a consequence, it may happen that the system does not converge to optimum. In order to help XCS to recover from such situations the *Specify* operator was introduced [4].

Wilson [7] observed that the phenomenon studied in [4] is related to the amount of random exploration the agent performs. Specifically, if the agent wanders around too much in between arrivals at the goal it can fail to evolve an optimal solution. Wilson in fact reports an improvement in XCS's performance when the amount of random exploration is reduced by replacing the random exploration strategy, originally employed [6], with *biased* exploration.

However, another set of experiments show that XCS with biased exploration solves the simple problem proposed in [4], but it does not guarantee the convergence to optimum in more difficult environments [2].

Results presented so far in the literature are based only on experimental evidence. Thus, even if the proposed solutions improve XCS's performance, they do not explain why such results are produced.

The purpose of this paper is to study generalization with XCS in order to get a better understanding of the phenomena reported so far, in order to explain what was observed in [4] and [7]. Initially, we extend the results previously presented in the literature comparing the Specify operator and biased exploration in two environments: Maze6 and Woods14. Our results show that Specify better adapts to both the environments while XCS with biased exploration fails to converge to good solutions. We then try to explain XCS's behavior analyzing the assumptions which underlie generalization in XCS; we thus study XCS's generalization mechanism in depth and formulate a specific hypothesis. In short, we hypothesize that XCS may not learn an optimal policy when, due to the environment structure and to the exploration strategy employed, the system does not visit all the areas of the environment frequently. We validate our hypothesis through a series of experiments. Validation is employed to derive some possible solutions for the problems previously discussed. In particular, we introduce a novel meta-exploration strategy which can be employed in order to guarantee a uniform exploration of the environment.

The strategy we propose, we call it *teletransportation*, is not presented as a *solution* to XCS problems discussed in the first part of this paper. The strategy, in fact, is not feasible for real problems, such as physical autonomous agents; teletransportation is rather a *theoretical tool* we use to validate our hypothesis.

The paper is organized as follows. Section 2 briefly overviews XCS according to [6], while Section 3 presents the design of experiments. XCS with Specify, called XCSS, and XCS with biased exploration are compared in Section 3 in Maze6 and Woods14. We then analyze the experimental results in Section 5, where we formulate a hypothesis which explains XCS's behavior. We verify our hypothesis in Section 6 by introducing teletransportation, which we use as a theoretical tool for the validation phase. Section 7 ends the paper drawing some conclusions and directions for future work.

2   Description of XCS

Classifiers in XCS have three main parameters: (i) the prediction p, which estimates the payoff that the system is expected to gain when the classifier is used; (ii) the prediction error ε, that evaluates how precise is the prediction p; finally, (iii) the fitness F, which estimates the accuracy of the payoff prediction given by p and thus is a function of ε.

At each time step, the system input is used to build a match set [M] containing the classifiers in the population whose condition part matches the sensory configuration. For each possible action a_i which appears in [M], the *system prediction* $P(a_i)$ is computed as the fitness weighted average of the classifier predictions that advocate the action a_i. $P(a_i)$ estimates the expected payoff if action a_i is performed. Action selection can be *deterministic*, the action with the highest system prediction is chosen, or *probabilistic*, the action is chosen with a certain probability among the actions with a not nil prediction. Classifiers in [M] which propose the selected action are put in the *action set* [A]. The selected action is then performed in the environment and an immediate reward r_{imm} is returned to the system together with a new sensory input configuration. The reward received from the environment is used to update the parameters of the classifiers in the action set corresponding to the previous time step $[A]_{-1}$ using a Q-learning-like technique (see [6] for details).

The genetic algorithm in XCS acts in the action set. It selects two classifiers with probability proportional to their fitnesses, copies them, and with probability χ performs crossover on the copies, while with probability μ mutates each allele.

An important innovation, introduced with XCS is the definition of *macroclassifiers*. A macroclassifier represents a set of classifiers which have the same condition and the same action using a new parameter called *numerosity*. Macroclassifiers are essentially a programming technique that speeds up the learning process reducing the number of *real*, micro, classifiers XCS has to deal with.

Specify has been introduced in [4] to help XCS to recover from those situations when the system may fail from converge to optimum. Specify acts in the action set, and replaces overgeneral classifiers with more specific offspring.

3 Design of Experiments

Discussions and experiments presented in this paper are conducted in the well-known *woods* environments. These are grid worlds in which each cell can contain a tree (a "T" symbol), a food (an "F" symbol), or otherwise can be empty. An animat placed in the environment must learn to reach food cells. The animat senses the environment by eight sensors, one for each adjacent cell, and can move in any of the adjacent cells. If the destination cell is blank then the move takes place; if the cell contains food the animat moves, eats the food, and receives a constant reward. If the destination cell contains a tree the move does not take place.

An experiment consists of a set of problems which the animat must solve. For each problem the animat is randomly placed in a blank cell of the environment; then it moves under the control of the system until it enters a food cell. The food immediately re-grows and a new problem begins.

We employed the following explore/exploit strategy: before a new problem begins the animat decide with a 50% probability whether it will solve the problem in exploration or in exploitation. We use two exploration strategies, *random* and *biased*. When in random exploration the system selects the action randomly;

when in biased exploration the system decides with a probability P_s whether to select actions randomly or to select the action corresponding the highest payoff (a typical value for P_s is 0.3). When in exploitation the animat always selects the action which predicts the highest payoff and the GA does not act. In order to evaluate the final solution, in each experiment exploration is turned off during the last 1000 problems.

XCS's performance is computed as the average number of steps to food in the last 50 exploitation problems. Every statistic presented in this paper is averaged on ten experiments.

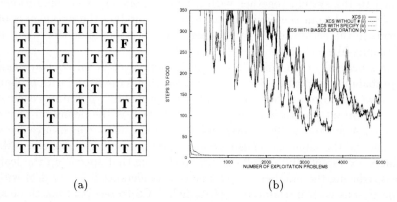

(a)   (b)

Fig. 1. (a) The Maze6 environment and (b) performance of the four versions of XCS in Maze6. Curves are averaged over ten runs.

4 Experiments with XCS

We now compare the two solutions presented in the literature to counterbalance the generalization mechanism of XCS, in two environments: Maze6 and Woods14.

Maze6 is the simple Markovian environment shown in Figure 1.a, which was introduced in [2] to study generalization within XCS. We apply four algorithms to Maze6: (i) XCS according to the original definition [6]; (ii) XCS without generalization (# are not introduced in the initial population, neither in covering or mutation); (iii) XCS with Specify [4], called XCSS; finally, (iv) XCS with biased exploration [7]. The four systems employ a population of 1600 classifiers and the same parameter settings (see [2] for details). Observe that the performances of algorithms (i) and (ii) are two important references. The former in fact indicates what the original system can do when the generalization mechanism works; while the performance of (ii) defines what are the potential capabilities of XCS, therefore it can be considered an upper limit to XCS's performance.

The results reported in Figure 1.b show that XCS (upper solid line) does not converge to an optimal solution when generalization acts, while when #

symbols are not employed (lower dashed line) the system easily reaches optimal performance. Most important, there is almost no difference between the performance of XCS with random exploration and XCS with biased exploration (upper dashed line). In contrast, as Figure 1.b shows, XCS with Specify easily converges to optimal performance. Note in fact that the performances of XCSS and XCS without generalization, at the very bottom of Figure 1, are not distinguishable.

In the second experiment, we apply different variants of XCS to the Woods14 environment shown in Figure 2. Woods14 consists of a linear path of 18 blank cells to a food cell. It was introduced by Cliff & Ross [1] in order to test the capabilities of ZCS (the classifier system introduced by Wilson [5] from which XCS originated) in building long action chains. Experimental results presented in [1] show that ZCS fails in converging to an optimal solution in Woods14, while no results have still been presented for XCS.

T	T	T	T	T	T	T	T	T	T	T	T	T
T	T				T	T	T	T		T	T	
T		T	T	T		T	T		T		T	
T		T	T	T		T		T	T	T		T
T	F	T	T	T		T	T		T	T	T	T
T	T	T	T	T	T			T	T	T	T	T

Fig. 2. The Woods14 Environment. Free cells are numbered according to their distance from the food cell.

We compare three versions of XCS in Woods14: XCS with biased exploration; XCS without generalization; XCS with Specify. As usual, all the systems have the same population size (2000 classifiers), and the same parameter settings [2]. The performance of XCS with biased exploration in Woods14, shown in Figure 3.a, evidences that although biased exploration is introduced, XCS does not converge to an optimal policy when generalization acts. On the other hand, the performance of XCS when the generalization mechanism does not act, and XCSS's performance (see Figure 3.b) confirm what observed in Maze6. XCS in fact easily solve Woods14 when generalization is off; most important, XCS is still able to evolve an optimal solution when Specify is employed.

These results for Woods14 are important because they show that XCS is successful in building long chains of actions. XCS thus performs better than ZCS not only for its generalization capabilities, as discussed in [8], but also because it proves effective in building long action chains.

The results we presented in this section evidence that, although biased exploration performs well in simple environments [2,7], it becomes ineffective in more complex environments. Specify instead confirms to be a better solution: XCSS in fact converges to optimal performance in a stable way in both environments. We believe this happens because biased exploration is a global solution to the problem of balancing the generalization mechanism, while Specify is a

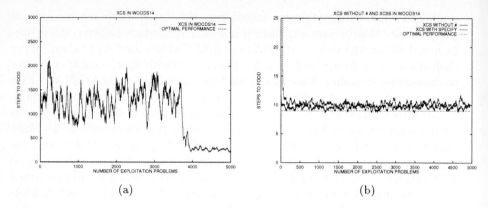

Fig. 3. (a) Performance of XCS with biased exploration in `Woods14`; (b) XCSS and XCS without generalization in `Woods14`. Observe the great difference of scale between (a) and (b).

local solution. [4] in fact observed that XCS's generalization mechanism acts in environmental niches, and these should be considered a sort of fundamental element for operators in XCS. Specify follows this principle and recovers potentially dangerous situations directly in the niches where they are detected; biased exploration instead acts on the whole population and it must take into account the structure of the entire environment.

At this point, it is worth noticing that, although our results we report for `Maze6` and `Woods14` are interesting, they cannot explain the phenomena which underlie the results observed so far in the literature. In order to understand XCS's behavior, we have to study the generalization mechanism of XCS in depth, as we do in the next section.

5   The Generalization Mechanism of XCS

We now analyze the generalization mechanism of XCS to understand which factors influence the system performance. First, we start discussing what happens when an overgeneral classifier appears in the population, in order to understand why XCS sometimes fails to converge to an optimal solution.

Overgeneral classifiers are such that, due to the presence of some don't care symbols, they match different niches with different rewards and thus they will become inaccurate. But since in XCS the GA bases the fitness upon classifiers accuracy, overgeneral classifiers, that are inaccurate, tend to reproduce less. Evolved classifiers are thus as general as possible while still being accurate.

Observe that, according to the generalization mechanism, for overgeneral classifier to be "deleted" (i.e. to reproduce less and then to be deleted) they must become inaccurate. However, this happens only if overgeneral classifiers are applied in distinct environmental niches. We thus suggest that in XCS an overgeneral classifier may still be evaluated as accurate: Due to the parameter update, in fact, a classifier becomes inaccurate only if it receives different rewards. However, this only happens when the classifier is applied in different situations that is, environmental niches. Unfortunately, there are applications in which, due to the structure of the environment and to the exploration policy, the animat does not visit all the niches with the same frequency. On the contrary, the animat tends to stay in an area of the environment for a while and then it moves to another one. When such situations occur, overgeneral classifiers, which should be evaluated as inaccurate, are still considered accurate. This phenomenon greatly influences the performance of XCS: Since in XCS fitness is based on accuracy, it may happen that overgeneral classifiers, evaluated as accurate, which should be deleted from the population, are instead reproduced.

As an example, consider an overgeneral classifier matching two niches which belong to two different areas of the environment. While the system stays in the area to which the first niche belongs, its parameters are updated accordingly to the reward it receives and thus, as long as the animat does not visit the second niche, the classifier is accurate even if it is globally overgeneral. Therefore, the overgeneral classifier is likely to be selected by the genetic algorithm; as a consequence, the system tends to allocate resources, i.e. copies, to it. When the animat moves to the other area of the environment the classifier starts becoming inaccurate, because the reward it predicts is no longer correct. At this point, two things may happen. If the classifier did not reproduce sufficiently in the first niche, the classifier is deleted because it has become inaccurate; consequently, the animat "forgets" what it learned in the previous area. If the overgeneral classifier reproduced sufficiently when in the initial niche, the (macro) classifier survives enough to adjust its parameters so that it becomes accurate with respect to the current niche. Hence, the overgeneral classifier continues to reproduce and mutate in the new niche, and it may produce even more overgeneral offspring.

The hypothesis we formulate to explain XCS's behavior observed in [4] and [7] is thus that XCS fails to learn an optimal policy in environments where the system is not very likely to explore all the environmental niches frequently.

Observe that our statement concerns the capability of the agent to explore all the environment in a uniform way, and thus is related to the environment structure and to the exploration strategy employed. Since the exploration strategies originally employed within XCS in animat problems select actions randomly, our hypothesis is directly related to the average random walk to food: The smaller it is, the more likely the animat will be able to visit all positions in the environment frequently; The larger the average random walk is, the more likely the animat is to visit more frequently a certain area of the environment.

Our hypothesis therefore explains why in certain environments XCS with biased exploration performs better than random exploration. When using biased exploration, the animat performs a random action only with a certain probability, otherwise it employs the best action. Accordingly, the animat is not likely to spend much time in a certain area of the environment but, following the best policy it has evolved, the animat moves to another area. Nevertheless, when the environmental niches are more distant, such as in `Maze6` and `Woods14`, the animat is unable to change niche as frequently as it would be necessary in order to evolve an optimal policy. This explains why XCS with biased exploration fails to converge to an optimal solution in "more complex" environments [2], while it performs well in simple environments [7].

6 Hypothesis Validation

We now empirically verify the hypothesis we outlined in the previous section. Our hypothesis suggests that XCS fails to converge to optimum in when the system is not likely to explore all the area of the environment frequently. If this hypothesis is correct, an exploration strategy which guarantees a frequent exploration of all the environmental niches should solve the problems we observed.

We thus verify our hypothesis introducing a meta-exploration strategy which guarantees a frequent exploration of all the areas of the environment. This strategy we now introduce, called *teletransportation*, must not be considered a *solution* for the problems we discussed so far. Teletransportation is instead a *tool* we use to validate our hypothesis. Accordingly, we do not discuss its relation with other exploration techniques presented in the literature.

Teletransportation works as follows. When in exploration, the animat is placed randomly in a free cell of the environment. Then it moves following one of the possible exploration strategies proposed in the literature, random or biased. If the animat reaches a food cell by a maximum number M_{es} of steps, the problem ends; otherwise, if the animat does not find food by M_{es} steps, it is *teletransported* to another empty cell and the exploration phase is restarted. This strategy guarantees, for small M_{es} values, that the animat will visits all the areas of the environment with the same frequency.

We now apply XCS with teletransportation, called XCST, to `Maze6` and `Woods14`, using the same parameters settings employed in the original experiments (see [2] for details). Figure 4.a compares the performance of XCST and XCS with biased exploration in `Maze6`, when M_{es} is set to 20 steps. Results show that, in `Maze6`, XCST converges to optimum rapidly and in a stable way, outperforming XCS with biased exploration.

Similar results are reported when XCST is applied to `Woods14`. Figure 4.b shows a typical performance of XCS with biased exploration (upper solid line) and XCST (bottom dashed line). The immediate impression is that XCST's performance is not very stable. However, to understand the results reported in Figure 4.b, we have to analyze how XCST learns. When in exploration, XCST continuously moves in the environment in order to visit all the niches frequently. Accordingly, the animat does not learn the optimal policy in the usual way, by "trajectories," that is starting in a position and exploring until a goal state is reached. On the contrary, XCST's policy *emerges* from a set of experiences of a limited number of steps the animat has collected while it was in exploration. The system therefore immediately converges to optimal policies for positions near

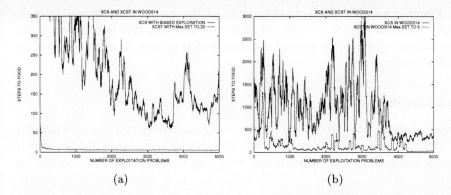

(a)   (b)

Fig. 4. (a) XCS with biased exploration and XCST in `Maze6`. M_{es} is set to 20. (b) Typical performance of XCS (solid line) and XCST (dashed line) in `Woods14`. Parameter M_{es} is set to 5 step.

the food cells, then the policy is extended during subsequent explorations in the other areas of the environments. Accordingly, in `Maze6` the policy is extended very rapidly because the environment is quite simple, while in `Woods14` the analysis of single experiments evidences that XCST rapidly learns an optimal policy for the first eight positions. Then the policy converges for the subsequent positions. At the end, the performance is only nearly optimal because for the last position of `Woods14`, the most difficult one, the optimal policy is not determined yet. The experiments in `Woods14` therefore suggest a limit of teletransportation. Since the environment is explored uniformly the positions for which is difficult to evolve an optimal solution, which would require more experience, converge very slowly to the optimum.

7   Final Discussion

We studied generalization within XCS, in order to explain some of the results previously observed in the literature. We drew a hypothesis which suggests that XCS may not converge to the optimum when the system does not visit all the areas of the environment frequently. We verified this hypothesis experimentally, by introducing a meta-exploration strategy which guarantees frequent exploration of the environment, we called it teletransportation.

Teletransportation was not proposed as a solution to the problems we observed, because it is infeasible for real applications. The strategy we introduced is rather a tool that was used to validate our hypothesis. Accordingly, teletransportation shows to be effective in reducing the effects of overgeneralization from the learning process, in order to better analyze XCS's behavior in other applications as shown in [3]. Moreover, as discussed in [2], the idea underlying teletransportation can be source on inspiration for developing a solution suitable for real applications.

Finally, we wish to point out that, although the approach we followed to study XCS's behavior regards a specific class of environments, that is grid-worlds, our conclusions appear to be general and therefore they may be extended to other environments as well.

Acknowledgments

I wish to thank Stewart Wilson for the many interesting discussions which improved my understanding of the XCS classifier system. Many thanks also to Marco Colombetti who supports my work and is always ready to discuss my doubts.

References

1. Dave Cliff and Susi Ross. Adding memory to ZCS. *Adaptive Behaviour*, 3(2):101–150, 1994.
2. Pier Luca Lanzi. A Model of the Environment to Avoid Local Learning (An Analysis of the Generalization Mechanism of XCS). Technical Report 97.46, Dipartimento di Elettronica e Informazione - Politecnico di Milano, 1997. Available at http://www.elet.polimi.it/people/lanzi/listpub.html.
3. Pier Luca Lanzi. Solving Problems in Partially Observable Environments with Classifier Systems (Experiments on Adding Memory to XCS). Technical Report 97.45, Dipartimento di Elettronica e Informazione - Politecnico di Milano, 1997. Available at http://www.elet.polimi.it/people/lanzi/listpub.html.
4. Pier Luca Lanzi. A Study on the Generalization Capabilities of XCS. In *Proceedings of the Seventh International Conference on Genetic Algorithms*. Morgan Kaufmann, 1997.
5. Stewart W. Wilson. ZCS: a zeroth level classifier system. *Evolutionary Computation*, 1(2):1–18, 1994.
6. Stewart W. Wilson. Classifier fitness based on accuracy. *Evolutionary Computation*, 3(2):149–175, 1995.
7. Stewart W. Wilson. Personal communication. 1997.
8. Stewart W. Wilson. Generalization in the XCS classifier system. In MIT Press, editor, *Proceedings of the Third Annual Genetic Programming Conference (GP-98)*, 1998.

Symbiotic Coevolution
of Artificial Neural Networks
and Training Data Sets

Helmut A. Mayer

University of Salzburg, Department of Computer Science, A–5020 Salzburg, Austria
helmut@cosy.sbg.ac.at

Abstract. Among the most important design issues to be addressed to
optimize the generalization abilities of trained artificial neural networks
(ANNs) are the specific architecture and the composition of the training
data set (TDS). Recent work has focused on investigating each of these
prerequisites separately. However, some researchers have pointed out the
interacting dependencies of ANN topology and the information contained
in the TDS. In order to generate coadapted ANNs and TDSs without
human intervention we investigate the use of symbiotic (cooperative) co-
evolution. Independent populations of ANNs and TDSs are evolved by
a genetic algorithm (GA), where the fitness of an ANN is equally credited to the TDS it has been trained with. The parallel netGEN system
generating generalized multi–layer perceptrons being trained by error–
back–propagation has been extended to coevolve TDSs. Empirical results
on a simple pattern recognition problem are presented.

1 Introduction

Dealing with real world problems we often face the problem of huge amounts
of possible training data patterns, e.g., a robot collecting sensor data from its
environment, or satellite image pixels to be classified. In order to construct
(small) TDSs the ANN can extract the most useful information – based on
certain quality measures – of, a variety of *Active Selection* methods have been
proposed in literature [Zha94] [Röb94] [Plu94]. Hereby, a small TDS is generated
iteratively by selecting the most useful patterns out of all available data. In
[MS97] we proposed *Evolutionary TDSs*, a GA–based active selection method,
where the patterns of the (sub)–optimal TDSs are selected in parallel.

With all these approaches the ANN topology remains fixed during the construction of the TDS. Evidently, the choice of the ANN architecture will influence
the training patterns selected for the TDS, hence, the overall performance of the
network. As a consequence, the work of Zhang [Zha93] and Plutowski [Plu94]
suggests to construct ANN architecture and TDS contents simultaneously. In
this paper we present an evolutionary approach to this problem by coevolving
ANN architectures and complete TDSs in independent populations. Thus, in
extension to previous work (Section 1.2) we not only search individual useful
training patterns, but a collection of cooperating patterns (TDS).

1.1 A Brief Taxonomy

With most applications of *Evolutionary Algorithms* solutions (individuals) to a problem are adapted to a static environment (fitness function). While this is certainly sufficient for a variety of real world problems having well–defined (and static) goals, certain problem domains, e.g., *Learning Robots* operating in a dynamic environment (possibly other robots), call for coevolution of individual(s) and environment(s).

The biochemist Lovelock writes in [Lov88]:

> "The evolution of a species is inseparable from the evolution of its environment. The two processes are tightly coupled as a single indivisible process."

Specifically, with the coevolution of ANNs and TDSs, the terms individual and environment can be used interchangeably, as an individual ANN (TDS) is exhibited to an environment TDS (ANN). This in mind, we will use the terms *Population I* for individuals and *Population E* for environments in the following.

Coevolution can be *Competitive (Parasitic)* or *Cooperative (Symbiotic)*, i.e., an environment (of population E) increases its fitness by decreasing or increasing the fitness of an individual in population I, respectively. The *Lifetime* of individuals in I and E can be different, e.g., E remains unchanged, while I evolves for a number of generations, or vice versa. The fitness evaluation of an individual in I can be done in a *Single* environment, m *Multiple* environments (with $m < n$, the number of environments in E), or in *All* environments n. When evaluating in multiple or all environments, the various fitness values have to be aggregated for the single individual, e.g., best or average fitness.

1.2 Related Work

Based on the pioneering work of Hillis [Hil90], Paredis [Par94] competitively coevolved the weights (evolutionary learning) of ANNs of fixed topology for a synthetic classification task. The population E consists of a fixed number of training patterns. Parasitic patterns are presented sequentially to ANNs, and the fitness of a network is based on the number of correct classifications of the last 20 examples [1]. The (parasitic) fitness of an example is given by the number of times it was incorrectly classified by ANNs it encountered most recently. In a strict sense the examples do not evolve, as they only change fitness without alteration of the patterns [Par94].

Potter and De Jong [PJ95] proposed *Cooperative Coevolutionary Algorithms* (CCGAs) for the evolution of ANNs of cascade network topology. In this approach the population I is divided into species corresponding to subtasks (ANN subnets). The quality of the ANN composed of subnets determines the fitness of

---

[1] In [Par94] this procedure is termed *Life Time Fitness Evaluation*, but it is not consistent with the definition of lifetime we gave above.

the contributing individuals of different species. Thus, cooperating individuals are rewarded inducing the evolution of collaborative species. However, with this approach the TDS never changes and represents a static environment. Coevolution occurs within population I by decomposing the problem into interacting subtasks (collaborative species).

Barbosa [Bar97] employs a competitive coevolutionary GA for structural optimization problems using a game–theoretic approach. The first player, the designer of a mechanical structure, tries to minimize the *Compliance* (a measure of the overall deformability under a specific load). The second player, nature, challenges the designer's constructions by maximizing the compliance. The choices of the two players are evolved in independent populations I (structures) and E (loads) with alternating lifetime of individuals (each population is kept "frozen" for a certain number of generations) and fitness evaluation in all environments.

2 ANN and TDS encoding

The technical platform for the coevolution of ANNs and TDSs is the netGEN system [HMS95] which has been designed for an arbitrary amount of workstations employing the *Parallel Virtual Machine (PVM)* library [GBD$^+$94] in order to train individual ANNs in parallel.

The ANN's genetic blueprint is based on a direct encoding suggested by Miller et al. [MTH89]. With this approach each connection is represented in a binary adjacency matrix called *Miller–Matrix* (MM) describing ANN architecture. Contrary to the original crossover operator exchanging rows and columns of the MM, we use standard 2–point crossover operating on a linearized MM where the triangle matrix of fixed 0s (feed–forward architecture) is not included.

The main enhancement in our *Modified–Miller–Matrix (MMM)* direct encoding scheme [HMS95] are the *Neuron Markers* which are encoded in a separate section on the ANN chromosome (the two other sections contain learning parameters and all possible connections, respectively). Technically, each neuron marker (one bit) is transferred to the main diagonal (i, i) of the MMM adjacency matrix, indicating the absence or presence of a particular neuron i and its connections (Fig. 1). As a consequence, most ANN chromosomes contain non–coding regions [2], as all connections associated with a specific neuron become obsolete, if the corresponding neuron marker is zero. The non–coding regions (*Introns*) reduce the disruptive effects of crossover [Lev91] [Wu96] [May97].

The maximum number of hidden neurons (neuron markers) has to be set in advance with this encoding scheme, hence, it could be labeled as *Evolutionary Pruning*, since the system imposes an upper bound on the complexity of the network. One of the measures to avoid overfitting is the encoding of the number of training epochs with the additional benefit of another ANN parameter being set automatically. Two learning parameters are also encoded in the genotype.

---

[2] Non–coding DNA regions or *Junk DNA* can be found in abundance in biological systems, i.e. *Eukaryotes*.

The standard back–propagation learning rate η, and a parameter δ_ϵ [3] which may also reduce overfitting, as the ANN can often be trained with substantial fewer epochs.

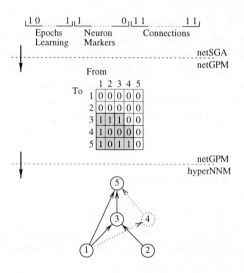

Fig. 1. ANN encoding scheme.

In addition to our modifications of the MM encoding scheme, the GA does not operate on the matrix representation, but on the concatenation of the rows of the non–zero part of the MMM's lower triangle matrix representing the possible connections. All MMM entries clamped to zero need not be processed by the GA, hence, they are not encoded in the genotype.

The TDSs are encoded as a concatenation of the desired number of training patterns (genes) which are represented as binary coded indexes to a data store file containing all available training patterns (Fig. 2). Clearly, the number of bits used to index an item in the data store is dependent on the size of the store. This encoding scheme enables the selection of one or more copies of a pattern into the TDS. A more conventional encoding for evolution of subsets [RG93] would constrain the search space which is advantageous for most set problems, however, the inclusion of multiple pattern copies might be beneficial in the case of TDSs, and should not be ruled out in advance.

Both GAs, netSGA and dataSGA, use the same basic genetic operators which are given below. For the GA selection phase we chose *Binary Tournament Selection* without replacement.

---

[3] δ_ϵ specifies an error threshold for all output neurons . If the error is below that threshold, the output neuron is considered to have zero error.

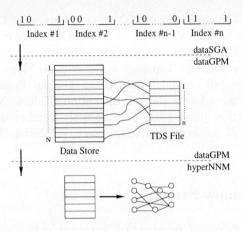

Fig. 2. TDS encoding scheme.

2.1 ANN and TDS Fitness Functions

The ANN fitness function comprises a complexity regularization term $\mathcal{E}_c$ suggested by Rumelhart [HP89]

$$\mathcal{E}_c = \sum_{i \in C_{total}} \frac{w_i^2}{1 + w_i^2}, \tag{1}$$

where w_i is the weight of a connection and C_{total} is the set of all network connections. The *Composite Fitness Function* $\mathcal{F}$ is given by a weighted sum of *Model Fitness* and *Complexity Fitness*

$$\mathcal{F} = \alpha_1(1 - \mathcal{E}_m) + \alpha_2 \frac{1}{1 + \mathcal{E}_c} \tag{2}$$

with $\alpha_1 + \alpha_2 = 1.0$, and $\mathcal{E}_m$ being the model error. Earlier work [HSM96] showed that α_2 in the range of $0.001 - 0.01$ is sufficient to guide the evolution towards ANNs of low complexity. Thus, we set $\alpha_2 = 0.01$. The model error for classification tasks is simply given by

$$\mathcal{E}_m = \frac{e_v}{n_v}, \tag{3}$$

where e_v is the number of misclassifications on the validation set, and n_v its respective size. TDS fitness is equal to the composite fitness (symbiotic coevolution).

2.2 GA and ANN Parameters

The following GA and ANN parameters have been used with all the experiments in this paper:

GA Parameters: Population Size = 50, Generations = 50, Crossover Probability p_c = 0.6, Mutation Probability p_m = 0.005, Crossover = 2–Point, Selection Method = Binary Tournament.

ANN Parameters: Network Topology = Generalized Multi–Layer Perceptron, Activation Function (all neurons) = Sigmoid, Output Function (all neurons) = Identity, Training = Error–Back–Propagation, Hidden Neurons (max 10), Learning Parameters η (max 1.0), δ_ϵ (max 0.4), Number of Training Epochs (max 1000), TDS (22 patterns) = Evolutionary, Validation/Test Set = 512 (all possible) patterns.

3 Coevolutionary Scenarios

A simple pattern recognition problem, the detection of lines and their directions, has been adopted from [HMS95]. The input to the ANN is a block of 3 × 3 black or white pixels, each corresponding to an input neuron. The output layer consists of four neurons activated depending on the line(s) contained in the input pattern. The existence of a known architecture of *minimal* complexity (minANN) (Figure 3) makes this problem amenable for analysis of experimental results.

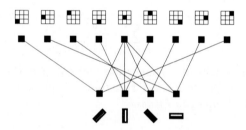

Fig. 3. The lines problem and the corresponding minimal complexity ANN.

For comparisons we define an ANN of *maximal* complexity (maxANN) by a $9 - 10 - 4$ fully connected architecture (the possible initial choice of a human designer). In order to train both networks, we use a TDS created by human intuition (provided the authors had some, Figure 4) and an evolutionary generated TDS [MS97].

The minimal and maximal complexity ANN have been trained with each of both TDSs yielding the test set accuracy given in Table 1.

The results are certainly an indicator for the significant interactions between ANN architecture and composition of the TDS. Note that none of the two architectures has been used to generate the evolved TDS, still, it is able to perfectly train the minimal network. It might be even more surprising that the human TDS is not nearly sufficient to train the minimal network, although, its architecture exactly represents the rules defining the four different lines. To further back up this observation, we evolved ANNs for the human TDS (50 generations, 25

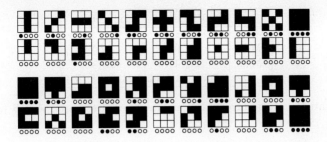

Fig. 4. Human TDS (above) and evolved TDS (below), 22 input patterns and the desired output activations.

	MinANN	MaxANN
Human TDS	0.5527	0.3594
Evolved TDS	1.0000	0.8574

Table 1. Test set accuracy for minimal and maximal ANNs trained by human and evolved TDS (1000 epochs, $\eta = 0.2$, $\delta_\epsilon = 0.1$).

runs), and none of the runs generated a network being able to classify the whole test set correctly (mean accuracy 0.6811 with a standard deviation of 0.0209).

We now look at two extreme scenarios of coevolutionary approaches to the problem at hand. With scenario A we take the maximal network, evolve a TDS for 50 generations, keep the best TDS, and use it as a static environment for the evolution of an ANN (50 generations). Thus, the lifetime of the single environment is 50 times the lifetime of the population of individuals. The scenario is extreme in the sense that it is in fact a sequential evolution of TDSs and ANNs, however, the evolution of the latter is influenced by the former.

The coevolutionary scenario B resembles two independent populations of ANNs and TDSs with equal lifetime evaluating the fitness in a single environment. A TDS is assigned randomly to each ANN, the network is trained, and the fitness of the ANN is equally credited to the TDS. Compared to scenario A this is located on the opposite side of the coevolutionary spectrum, as each individual is ultimately dependent on the single environment it is exhibited to.

In order to keep the number of fitness evaluations (ANN trainings) equal with both scenarios, we ran coevolution for 100 generations with scenario B. Experiments for both scenarios have been repeated 25 times using different random seeds. In all runs an ANN with a test set accuracy of 1.00 could be evolved. A closer look at the coevolved architectures is presented in Table 2.

Generally, both scenarios achieve similar network structures being close to the minimal (optimal) ANN. Scenario B even generates less complex networks (w. r. t. the number of connections) and evolved the best ANN of all runs having only 2 excessive connections compared to the minimal ANN. Typically, the excessive connections are trained to very small weights $(0.01 - 0.1)$, thus,

	Hidden	Connections
Mean	0.80 / 1.20	29.72 / 25.36
Min	0 / 0	17 / 14
Max	2 / 4	45 / 45
StdDev	0.7071 / 1.1902	6.2418 / 8.1949

Table 2. Statistics of coevolved ANN architectures of scenarios A / B (averaged on 25 runs).

ANN training additionally acts as a local (structural) optimization procedure. The random placement of individuals in a single environment (scenario B) is a rather brute method, as "good" ANNs might not survive a "bad" TDS (or vice versa). However, it also ensures the evolution of robust structures being able to deal with a hostile environment. This is indicated by the pattern frequency in the concatenated best TDSs evolved in scenario A and scenario B (Figure 5).

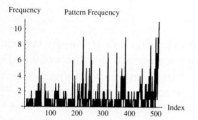 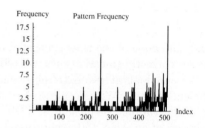

Fig. 5. Pattern frequency of concatenated best TDSs (25 runs) in scenario A (left) and scenario B (right).

While the patterns contributing to the best TDSs found in scenario A (single ANN, static environment) are widely spread, scenario B produces a more pronounced selection of (robust) patterns. Specifically, pattern 511 [4] (all black pixels), and pattern 255 (all black but upper left corner) contribute positively to TDSs for a great variety of architectures. Both patterns can also be found in the previously discussed evolved TDS (Figure 4).

Summarizing, we may say that symbiotic coevolution of ANNs and TDSs can improve the performance of ANNs utilized for classification tasks. This could be specifically useful for prediction problems (e.g., stock markets), where the available data change (increase) with time and a neural predictor could be coevolved (dynamically adapted) to new data.

---

[4] The index is the decimal representation of the binary input vector.

4 Outlook

The differences between the two extremes of coevolutionary scenarios studied in this paper are rather small suggesting similar results for scenarios in between. Nevertheless, the variation of lifetime and number of environments has to be investigated in combination with more difficult (real world) problems in the future. Among current research topics is the extraction of rules from ANNs generated by netGEN, as the low complexity architectures might enable the generation of small, consistent rule bases extracting the knowledge accumulated by evolution.

5 Acknowledgements

We wish to thank the *Austrian Center for Parallel Computation* (ACPC), Group Salzburg, for making available a cluster of DEC AXP workstations for this research. Also, we would like to thank our students Karl Fürlinger and Marc Strapetz for valuable support in data acquisition and presentation.

References

[Bar97]   Helio J. C. Barbosa. A coevolutionary genetic algorithm for a game approach to structural optimization. In Thomas Bäck, editor, *Proceedings of the Seventh International Conference on Genetic Algorithms*, pages 545–552, San Francisco, California, 1997. Morgan Kaufmann Publishers, Inc.

[GBD+94] Al Geist, Adam Beguelin, Jack Dongarra, Weicheng Jiang, Robert Manchek, and Vaidy Sunderam. *PVM 3 User's Guide and Reference Manual.* Oak Ridge National Laboratory, 1994.

[Hil90]   W. D. Hillis. Co-evolving parasites improve simulated evolution as an optimization procedure. *Physica D*, 42:228–234, 1990.

[HMS95]   Reinhold Huber, Helmut A. Mayer, and Roland Schwaiger. netGEN - A Parallel System Generating Problem-Adapted Topologies of Artificial Neural Networks by means of Genetic Algorithms. In *Beiträge zum 7. Fachgruppentreffen Maschinelles Lernen der GI-Fachgruppe 1.1.3, Forschungsbericht Nr. 580, Dortmund*, August 1995.

[HP89]   S.J. Hanson and L.Y. Pratt. Comparing biases for minimal network construction with back-propagation. In D. Touretzky, editor, *Advances in Neural Information Processing Systems, Vol. 1*, volume 1, pages 177–185. Morgan Kaufmann, 1989.

[HSM96]   Reinhold Huber, Roland Schwaiger, and Helmut A. Mayer. On the Role of Regularization Parameters in Fitness Functions for Evolutionary Designed Artificial Neural Networks. In *World Congress on Neural Networks*, pages 1063–1066. International Neural Network Society, Lawrence Erlbaum Associates, Inc., 1996.

[Lev91]   James R. Levenick. Inserting Introns Improves Genetic Algorithm Sucess Rate: Taking a Cue from Biology. In Richard K. Belew and Lashon B. Booker, editors, *Proceedings of the Fourth International Conference on Genetic Algorithms*, pages 123–127. University of California, San Diego, Morgan Kaufmann, 1991.

[Lov88]   James Lovelock. *The Ages of Gaia: A Biography of Our Living Earth*. W. W. Norton, 1988.

[May97]   Helmut A. Mayer. *ptGAs - Genetic Algorithms Using Promoter/Terminator Sequences - Evolution of Number, Size, and Location of Parameters and Parts of the Representation*. PhD thesis, University of Salzburg, 1997.

[MS97]   Helmut A. Mayer and Roland Schwaiger. Towards the Evolution of Training Data Sets for Artificial Neural Networks. In *Proceedings of the 4th IEEE International Conference on Evolutionary Computation*, pages 663–666. IEEE Press, 1997.

[MTH89]   Geoffrey F. Miller, Peter M. Todd, and Shailesh U. Hegde. Designing Neural Networks using Genetic Algorithms. In J. David Schaffer, editor, *Proceedings of the Third International Conference on Genetic Algorithms*, pages 379–384, San Mateo, California, 1989. Philips Laboratories, Morgan Kaufmann Publishers, Inc.

[Par94]   Jan Paredis. Steps towards Co–evolutionary Classification Neural Networks. In R. Brooks and P. Maes, editors, *Proceedings Artifical Life IV*, pages 545–552. MIT Press / Bradford Books, 1994.

[PJ95]   Mitchell A. Potter and Kenneth A. De Jong. Evolving Neural Networks with Collaborative Species. In *Proceedings of the 1995 Summer Computer Simulation Conference*, 1995.

[Plu94]   Mark Plutowski. *Selecting Training Examplars for Neural Network Learning*. PhD thesis, University of California, San Diego, 1994.

[RG93]   Nicholas J. Radcliffe and Felicity A. W. George. A Study in Set Recombination. In Stephanie Forrest, editor, *Proceedings of the Fifth International Conference on Genetic Algorithms*, pages 23–30. University of Illinois at Urbana-Champaign, Morgan Kaufmann, 1993.

[Röb94]   A. Röbel. The Dynamic Pattern Selection: Effective Training and Controlled Generalization of Backpropagation Neural Networks. Technical report, Technical University Berlin, 1994.

[SGE91]   Robert E. Smith, David E. Goldberg, and Jeff A. Earickson. SGA-C: A C–Language Implementation of a Simple Genetic Algorithm. TCGA Report 91002, The Clearinghouse for Genetic Algorithms, The University of Alabama, Department of Engineering Mechanics, Tuscaloosa, AL 35487, May 1991.

[Wu96]   Annie Siahung Wu. *Non–Coding DNA and Floating Building Blocks for the Genetic Algortihm*. PhD thesis, University of Michigan, 1996.

[Zha93]   Byoung-Tak Zhang. Self–development learning: Constructing optimal size neural networks via incremental data selection. Tech. Rep. No. 768, German National Research Center for Computer Science, Sankt Augustin, 1993.

[Zha94]   Byoung-Tak Zhang. Accelerated Learning by Active Example Selection. *International Journal of Neural Systems*, 5(1):67–75, 1994.

[ZMV+94] Andreas Zell, Guenter Mamier, Michael Vogt, Niels Mach, Ralf Huebner, Kai-Uwe Herrmann, Tobias Soyez, Michael Schmalzl, Tilman Sommer, Artemis Hatzigeogiou, Sven Doering, and Dietmar Posselt. *SNNS Stuttgart Neural Network Simulator, User Manual*. University of Stuttgart, 1994.

Information-Theoretic Analysis of a Mobile Agent's Learning in a Discrete State Space

Clemens Pötter

Institut für Neuroinformatik, Ruhr-Universität Bochum
D-44780 Bochum, Germany
Email: Clemens.Poetter@neuroinformatik.ruhr-uni-bochum.de

Abstract. The learning process of an agent in a discrete state space is analysed by Shannon's information measure. The agent learns the transition probabilities from one state to another. After the learning process has converged, the information is compressed by approximating the synaptic weights by the output of a symbolic program. This performs a kind of *symbolisation* of the data. Symbolisation reduces the complexity and neglects irrelevant noise. The generalisation to greater state spaces seems to work reasonably and an interpretation in the test case is given. At the level of a toy problem, the results are encouraging.

1 Introduction

Neural networks have been used for the guidance of mobile agents for several years [16,12]. Usually, the agent gets input from the environment and performs actions which are chosen by the neural net. In some sense the environment is represented in the data that the agent has collected. For the agent to be able to generate robust behaviour it is important to find a good kind of representation of the environment. We favour the representation of the *effect of actions* of the agent on the environment. In section 2, a model is presented in which the weights of a neural net can be interpreted as transition probabilities. Hebb's learning rule is used to train the network. This approach allows for information-theoretic measures to be used in order to monitor the learning process. As the number of probabilities increases with the square of the number of states and linearly with the number of actions, the estimation of the probabilities becomes more and more difficult.

This can be remedied by the fact that the environment is very redundant, and, therefore, a compression of the data in the sense of Kolmogorov complexity [1] is possible. In section 3, Mathematica^R [17] programs which reproduce the neural net are generated and the best approximation of the neural net is chosen. By extending the state space we test the generalisation capability of this approach. In section 4, we discuss the results and in the last section, after a short summary, we present some ideas of how to extend the model to more sophisticated systems.

2 Model

We take an agent with $A = 5$ possible actions

$$\mathcal{A} = \{a_1, ..., a_A\} = \{\mathrm{Id}, \mathrm{N}, \mathrm{E}, \mathrm{S}, \mathrm{W}\}$$

in a discrete state space Z of size $N = 8$, which is shown in fig. 1. It includes an obstacle and is topologically equivalent to a sphere: the states 1,2,3,4 and 5,6,7,8 form the northern and the southern hemisphere, respectively. If the agent has

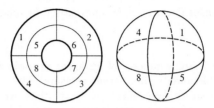

Fig. 1. Topology of the state space with $N = 8$ states. The numbers indicate the state.

an exact model of the environment and it can perform the actions in a precise manner, the next state can be calculated by a map $R_0 : \mathcal{A} \times Z \to Z$. But in real world applications, due to noise, the result of an action can differ from this map; therefore we substitute the map by

$$R : \mathcal{A} \times Z \to \mathcal{Z}$$
$$(a, i) \mapsto (p_1, ..., p_N)$$

with $\mathcal{Z}$ probability distribution over Z, and usually $\max_{1 \leq i \leq N} p_i(a, j)$ is reached for $i = R_0(a, j)$. We represent R with A matrices $W^1, ..., W^A$, which have the dimension $N \times N$. We can interpret them as synaptic weights of a neural network. The initial values are, according to the maximum entropy principle, $\frac{1}{N}$.

We assume that the agent can identify its new position after the action. If action a is chosen, only the matrix W^a is modified. According to the Hebb rule [6] the simultaneous activation of neurons increases the connecting weight, whereas the other weights decrease. In order to keep the probabilistic interpretation, the weights are normalised. The learning rate η is decreased with the learning step t: $\eta \propto 1/t$. According to [11], this ensures convergence. The Shannon entropy H [1] of $W^a(j) = (W^a_{1j}, .., W^a_{Nj})$ quantifies the uncertainty after performing action a from state j.

$$H(W^a(j)) = \sum_{i=1}^{N} W^a_{ij} \log W^a_{ij}$$

The development of the average entropy

$$\bar{H}^a = \frac{1}{N} \sum_{j=1}^{N} H(W^a(j))$$

for each action is shown in fig. 2. In all actions the uncertainty decreases, the agent gains knowledge about the structure of its environment.

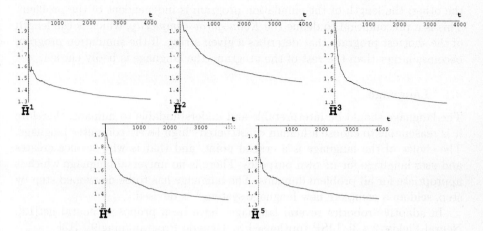

Fig. 2. The average entropies $\bar{H}^a$, $a = 1, .., 5$ depend on the learning step t, using the example with $N = 8$.

In fig. 3 the transition probabilities after 4000 learning steps are shown. Regularities can be seen, which we try to exploit in the next section.

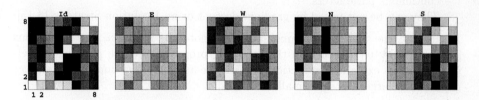

Fig. 3. Transition matrices W^a, $a = 1, .., 5$ of the example with $N = 8$: dark means low, bright means high probability.

3 Symbolisation

The process of symbolisation can be run in parallel to the development of the neural network, but due to the computational cost we apply it only once, after the learning has converged.

We know that the environment has a structure. This allows to compress the information in the neural net. We use this knowledge according to the "No free lunch"–theorem [10]. The essential of the theorem is that using previous knowledge of a problem is the only way to improve an optimisation method which is applied to this problem. So we generate a number of programs, beginning with simple ones. Due to theorem 7.2.1 [1], p.148 for every pair of complete computer languages there is a simulation program which translates from one into the other; the length of the simulation program is independent of the problem. This is a precondition to define the *Kolmogorov complexity*, which is the length of the shortest program that describes a given string. If the simulation program becomes larger than the rest of the program, the language is badly chosen.

3.1 Language

The language should be interpretable and understandable to humans; therefore it is reasonable to choose a human constructed "high level" computer language. The choice of the language is a crucial point, and that is why science creates and uses language for its own purposes. There is no universal language which is appropriate for all problem domains. The language has to be developed step by step, seldom a complete new language system [1] is devised.

In adaptive robotics several languages have been proposed: neural net[12], Neural Fields [2,4,3], LISP (optimised by Genetic Programming[9]) [13]

In Mathematica, programs can be generated and executed. In the programs two kinds of parameters are used:

- discrete structure parameters
  If the range of these variables is small, they can be tried out systematically (grid search); otherwise a Genetic Algorithm[8] or Genetic Programming can be used.
- continuous parameters
  They can be optimised by gradient descent or an Evolution Strategy[14,15].

In our case, the structure parameters were denoted by K and n_i, the continuous parameters by w_1 and w_2. In the following programs, we use previous knowledge, which is explained in section 4. With the auxiliary function m_1, where $\lfloor x \rfloor$ denotes the largest integer smaller or equal x,

$$m_1(K,i) = \begin{cases} K & \text{if } K = 0 \text{ or } K = 1 \\ \lfloor \frac{i}{4} \rfloor & \text{if } K = 2 \end{cases} \tag{1}$$

the programs created matrices

$$\tilde{W}_{ij}(K, n_i) = \begin{cases} w_1 & \text{if } 4\, m_1(K,i) + (i + n_i \bmod 4) = j \\ w_2 & \text{else} \end{cases} . \tag{2}$$

The matrices are normalised, so that the sum in each column equals one. The result is denoted by $\hat{W} = \left(\hat{W}_{ij}\right)_{1 \leq i,j \leq N}$. The optimised values for the 5 actions are $K = 2, 2, 2, 0, 1;\ n_i = 0, 1, -1, 0, 0;\ w_1 = 0.989;\ w_2 = 0.0136$.

The exact transition probabilities and the best approximation of the 5 matrices are shown in fig. 4. The error measure of the program p is defined as

---

[1] Examples for such language systems are the nomenclature of chemical elements and the New Latin names used in biology for kinds and groups of kinds of animals and plants.

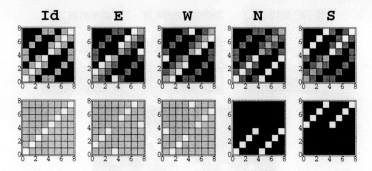

Fig. 4. Upper row: exact transition probabilities W^a; due to motoric noise the probability to reach the goal state does not equal unity, e.g. the effect of the identity action is – with a low probability – also present in all other actions. Lower row: approximations $\hat{W}^a$ of the best programs

$$\mathrm{Err}[p] = \max_{1 \le i,j \le n} |\hat{W}_{ij} - W_{ij}|.$$

For the best program the total error is 0.16263, the mean error is 0.032526, the maximum error is 0.037456

3.2 Generalisation

We examine the consequences of adding new states to the state space. As an example, a third ring is added to the state space of section 2. The new, extended state space is shown in fig. 5

Fig. 5. Topology of the extended state space with $N = 12$. The numbers indicate the state.

The best programs generated new transition matrices, but with the new number of states $N = 12$. These are shown in fig. 6.

In order to adapt the matrices to the new topology, the learning process is restarted. The resulting matrices are shown in fig. 7. More program structures are taken into account by modifying $\tilde{W}_{ij}(K, n_i)$ to

$$\tilde{W}_{ij}(K_1, K_2, K_3, n_i) = \begin{cases} w_1 & \text{if } 4K_{\lfloor i/4 \rfloor +1} + (i + n_i \bmod 4) = j \\ w_2 & \text{else} \end{cases} \tag{3}$$

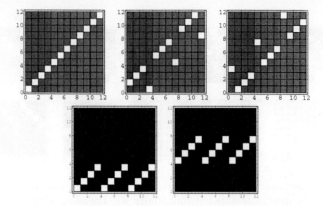

Fig. 6. generalisation of the best programs to a state space with 12 states

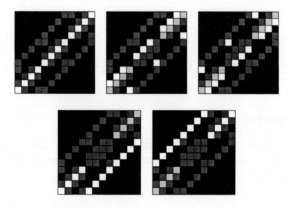

Fig. 7. transition matrices W^a in the state space with 12 states

with $K_i = 0, 1, 2$, $i = 1, 2, 3$. Out of these 81 structures, the best are shown in tab. 1. Optimising the weights we get $w_1 = 0.9908$ and $w_2 = 0.0091$; the matrices are shown in fig. 8. The total error was 0.18339, the mean error 0.036678, the maximum error 0.041658.

4 Discussion

In our model, the learned neural nets were approximated by the programs with a low error (mean errors 0.032526 and 0.036678, compared to 1 as the worst error). Whether the approximation is to be considered sufficient or not, depends on the problem. When the error threshold is low, the details of the synaptic weights are important; when the threshold is high, only the essential features matter. This question of the choice of the resolution is unavoidable due to the bias-variance dilemma [7]. If the error of the best program is higher than this

a	1 2 3 4 5
K_1	0 0 0 0 1
K_2	1 1 1 0 2
K_3	2 2 2 1 2
n_i	0 1 -1 0 0

Table 1. The best structure parameters

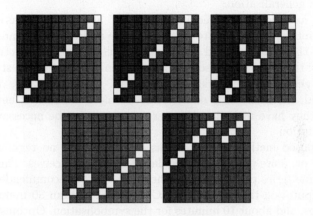

Fig. 8. approximations of the best programs

threshold, generating more programs decreases the errors. In our model the main feature of the action was found. In the framework of the program structures used, it was not possible to detect that the noise shifts the movement into a neighbour state. But this was not the aim of our model with very short programs.

According to Gell-Mann the length of the shortest description of the regularities of a system is the *effective complexity* [5]. The more complicated the obstacle configuration, the higher the effective complexity of the environment. As opposed to the Kolmogorov complexity, the effective complexity does not depend on the random events. Small changes in W_{ij}^a do not change the structure of the programs, only the continuous data (w_1, w_2) are influenced. The program consists of commands, each of which can be considered to describe a qualitative feature of an object

- the best program for the action Id ($a = 1$) is

$$\tilde{W}_{ij}(K, n_i) = \begin{cases} 0.989 & \text{if } 4\lfloor i/4 \rfloor + i \bmod 4 = j \\ 0.0136 & \text{else} \end{cases} . \tag{4}$$

where we recognise the identity of i and j, because

$$4\lfloor i/4 \rfloor + i \bmod 4 = i \text{ for all } i \in \mathbb{N}.$$

- the term "mod 4" reflects the ring structure of the environment. The numbers n_i determine whether the movement is clockwise or counterclockwise (or East-West on the sphere).
- m_2 with $(K_1, K_2, K_3) \neq (2, 1, 0)$ means that the action results in a radial movement (or North-South on the sphere).

By choosing this language we included knowledge about the environment, and therefore the model works successful.

As to the generalisation:

The identity, and the actions "moving in the ring" are generalised as expected. As there is no hint where the 4 states are added, the actions 4 and 5 are interpreted as: "Go into the first ring" and "Go into the second ring", respectively. This is without bias: the four states also could have been attached to the states 1-4. We see that the generalisation works very well here.

In general, the numbering of the states is more difficult. If new states are discovered, they have to be labeled; permutations may be necessary to keep a simple description.

The proposed method cannot be used, if there are no regularities in the environment or, more precisely, in the data the agent perceives. The application to chaotic time series prediction can, therefore, not be recommended.

The computation times on a SPARC 20 were less than 30 minutes for 4000 learning steps, and about 10 minutes for the symbolisation. Optimising the code and parallelising the algorithm, larger systems with up to 50 states are probably computationally feasible.

5 Summary and Outlook

The learning process of an agent in a discrete state space was analysed by the Shannon information. The agent represents the environment by the effect of the actions the agent can perform. We have shown that in a small model with motoric noise the knowledge of the agent increases in an information-theoretic sense.

The representations of the actions were analysed by approximating the weight matrices by programs. This method allows a *symbolisation* of distributed knowledge. The information is compressed and the results are interpretable. Furthermore it was shown that the generalisation to bigger state space works very well. The model here was quite small and previous knowledge influenced the structure of the programs.

The following extensions are possible:

- compression of the whole representation in one program:
  While in the present model the representations of the actions were analysed separately, this would reveal regularities between the actions.
- increasing number of represented states:
  beginning with a single state the agent will add a new state, if it realises that its present state is not likely to be represented. In combination with the

first extension, we think that environments with considerably more states are computationally feasible.

- Using Euclidean geometry
assigning positions $\mathbf{x}$ to the states induces a topology of the states. For positions i, j which are neighbours in this topology one of the transition probabilities W_{ij}^a is high. Exceptions to this rule indicate obstacles.
- Fuzzyfication
The states can be substituted by fuzzy sets, the transition by fuzzy rules. This way, a transition to continuous state spaces may be found.

These extensions show the flexibility of the approach, and the applicability to several research areas.

References

1. Thomas Cover and Joy A. Thomas. *Elements of Information Theory*. Wiley series in telecommunications. John Wiley and Sons, 1991.
2. CH Engels and G Schöner. Dynamic fields endow behavior-based robots with representations. *Robotics and Autonomous Systems*, 14:55–77, 1995.
3. Christof Engels. *Dynamische Neuronale Feldarchitektur zur Steuerung autonomer Systeme am Beispiel der Wegeplanung eines mobilen Roboters*. PhD thesis, Universität Dortmund, 1995.
4. C. Engels G. Schöner, M. Dose. Dynamics of behavior: Theory and applications for autonomous robot architectures. *Robotics and Autonomous Systems*, 1995.
5. Murray Gell-Mann. *The Quark and the Jaguar*. Bantam, 1994.
6. Simon Haykin. *Neural Network*, chapter Self-Organizing Systems I: Hebbian Learning. Macmillan College Publishing Company, 1994.
7. Simon Haykin. *Neural Networks*. Macmillan College Publishing Company, 1994.
8. John H. Holland. *Adaptation in Natural and Artificial Systems*. MIT Press, 1992.
9. John R. Koza. *Genetic Programming*. Complex adaptive systems. The MIT Press, 1992.
10. William G. Macready and David H. Wolpert. No free lunch theorems for search. *Santa Fe working paper*, 2(10), 1995.
11. John M. McNamara, James N. Webb, E.J. Collins, Tamás Székely, and Alasdair I. Houston. A general technique for computing evolutionarily stable strategies based on errors in decision-making. *Journal of theoretical Biology*, 189:211–225, 1997.
12. Stefano Nolfi and Domenico Parisi. Neural networks in an artificial life perspective. In *International Conference on Artificial Neural Networks*, LNCS, pages 733–737. Springer, 1997.
13. Peter Nordin and Wolfgang Banzhaf. Real time control of a khepera robot using genetic programming. *Cybernetics and Control*, 26(3), 1997.
14. Ingo Rechenberg. *Evolutionsstrategie '94*. frommann-holzboog, 1994.
15. Hans-Paul Schwefel. *Evolution and Optimum Seeking*. John Wiley, 1994.
16. Jun Tani and Naohiro Fukumura. Learning goal-directed sensory-based navigation of a mobile robot. *Neural Networks*, 7(3):553–563, 1994.
17. Stephen Wolfram. *Mathematica - A System for Doing Mathematics by Computer*. Addison-Wesley, 1988.

The Coevolution of Antibodies for Concept Learning

Mitchell A. Potter[1] and Kenneth A. De Jong[2]

[1] Navy Center for Applied Research in Artificial Intelligence,
Naval Research Laboratory, Code 5510,
Washington, DC 20375 USA
[2] Computer Science Department, George Mason University,
Fairfax, VA 22030 USA

Abstract. We present a novel approach to concept learning in which a coevolutionary genetic algorithm is applied to the construction of an immune system whose antibodies can discriminate between examples and counter-examples of a given concept. This approach is more general than traditional symbolic approaches to concept learning and can be applied in situations where preclassified training examples are not necessarily available. An experimental study is described in which a coevolutionary immune system adapts itself to one of the standard machine learning data sets. The resulting immune system concept description and a description produced by a traditional symbolic concept learner are compared and contrasted.

1 Introduction

Concept learning is a task that has been extensively studied by researchers in the field of machine learning. Much of this work has been in the area of inductive learning from examples using symbolic representation languages such as predicate calculus [5] and decision trees [9]. In most of the previous efforts to apply evolutionary computation to concept learning, binary-string representations have been evolved with a genetic algorithm and mapped into some form of symbolic representation for evaluation, such as propositional logic. For some examples of this approach, see [4, 1, 3]. In the work described here, we take a different approach by experimenting with a biologically inspired representation in which concept descriptions are evolved using a model of the immune system. For other approaches to evolving models of the immune system, see the pioneering work of Forrest et al. [2].

The motivation behind applying a model of the immune system to concept learning lies in its highly developed ability to discriminate between self and non-self. In biological immune systems, this consists of the discrimination between the vast array of molecules that are an integral part of the body of an organism and foreign molecules that left unchecked could result in disease or death. In the research described here, we apply the immune system's power of discrimination to the problem of differentiating between examples and counter-examples of a given concept. An advantage of this approach over the traditional symbolic approaches to concept learning is its generality. We believe that evolved computational models of the immune system could be successfully applied to a wide variety of discrimination problems that do not necessarily lend themselves to the supervised learning methodology typically used by symbolic concept learning systems. A controller for an autonomous vehicle, for example, may need to learn to discriminate between navigable terrain and a variety of hazards based on input from a noisy sensor array. Constructing a set of preclassified training examples that adequately covers the modalities of this task would probably not be practical. An evolutionary immune system could learn the necessary concepts by adapting instead to a simple reinforcement signal that captures the ability of the autonomous vehicle to move safely through its environment.

2   A Brief Overview of the Immune System

The purpose of an organism's immune system is to protect it against infection. This is accomplished by recognizing the molecular signature of microbes or viruses that attack its body, and once identified, eliminating the foreign molecules in a variety of ways. The immune system consists of two interrelated components: an innate defense component and an adaptive component. Here we will focus on the adaptive component, which is responsible for acquired immunity.

Molecules capable of stimulating an acquired immune response are called *antigens*. When the immune system is working properly, only foreign molecules will produce a response. There are a number of ways antigens are recognized, depending on whether the foreign molecule is inside or outside a cell boundary. It is the job of *antibodies*—protein molecules displayed on the surface of a type of white blood cell produced in the bone marrow called a B-lymphocyte or B-cell for short—to recognize antigens that are located outside a cell boundary. Recognition by a B-cell occurs when one of its antibodies comes into contact with an antigen of complementary shape. Although all the antibodies on an individual B-cell have the same three-dimensional shape, the human body, for example, has about 10 trillion of these cells and they collectively have the potential of recognizing about 100 million distinct antigens at any one time.

One should realize that the immune system is quite complex and is the focus of much current research. Although we have only provided a brief and somewhat simplistic overview of one of its processes here, this description should be sufficient for an understanding of the rest of this paper. For more details concerning the workings of the immune system, see, for example, [10].

3   Coevolving Antibodies for Concept Learning

As in previous evolutionary computation models of the vertebrate immune system (cf. [2]), our model is limited to the interaction between B-cells and antigens. This model is applied to concept learning from preclassified positive and negative

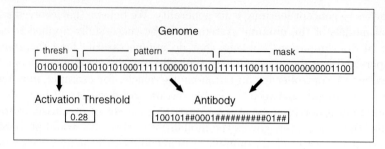

Fig. 1. Mapping from *B*-cell genome to activation threshold and antibody

examples by equating the positive examples to foreign molecules and the negative examples to self. Once the fitness of the immune system evolves to a point where all the foreign molecules and none of the self molecules are recognized, the antibodies represent a description of the concept [3]. This model can easily be generalized to learn more than one concept by simply evolving a separate family of *B*-cells for each.

The *B*-cells in our model consist of antibody and a real-valued activation threshold that represents the binding strength required to initiate an immune response. Rather than represent antibodies and antigens as three-dimensional shapes, we use a binary *schema* representation for the antibodies and represent the antigens as simple binary strings. A linear matching function that returns the percentage of matching bits in the antibodies and antigens is used to compute the binding strength. The locations at which the antibody schema contains a "don't care" are ignored. This abstraction greatly simplifies the matching process between antibodies and antigens while still exhibiting some of the key properties of the biological entities. One important property that is captured by this representation is the ability of some antibody shapes to match a wider range of antigens then others. This enables us to model a continuum of antibodies from specialists, that can only bind to a specific antigen, to more general antibodies that can bind to whole families of antigens sharing common characteristics.

The genotype to phenotype mapping of *B*-cells in our model is shown in Figure 1. We produce an antibody schema from binary pattern and mask genes. A mask bit of one generates a schema value equal to the corresponding pattern bit, while a mask bit of zero produces a "don't care" schema value. This many-to-one mapping is an abstraction of another property of real proteins—dissimilar chains of amino acids may fold into the same basic three-dimensional shape. The length of the pattern and mask genes depends on the complexity of the antigens the antibody must recognize. The real-valued activation threshold of the *B*-cell in the range $[0, 1]$ is produced from an 8-bit threshold gene.

If we were to evolve a population of *B*-cells with a standard genetic algorithm, the population would converge into a collection of very similar cells. However, it

---

[3] Given noisy examples, the immune system would be evolved until *most* of the foreign molecules and *few* of the self molecules were recognized.

is important to maintain enough diversity in the B-cells to adequately recognize many different types of foreign molecules. Earlier evolutionary immune system models solved this dilemma through the use of a diversity preserving algorithm called *emergent fitness sharing*. We take a different approach by evolving B-cells with a coevolutionary genetic algorithm in which individuals from multiple non-interbreeding species collaborate to solve the target problem [8, 7]. Each species represents only a partial solution—in this case, a collection of B-cells having similar antibodies. The fitness of a B-cell is computed by adding it to a "serum" consisting of the current best B-cells from each of the other species in the ecosystem. Foreign and self molecules are then presented to the serum. A particular B-cell is considered to have recognized an antigen if the binding strength between its antibody and the antigen exceeds its activation threshold and the antigen binds to its antibody more strongly than to any other antibody in the serum. The fitness of the B-cell is defined to be the number of foreign molecules recognized by all the antibodies in the serum, minus the number of false-positives, that is, self molecules flagged as foreign. Therefore, each B-cell is rewarded based on how well it collaborates with B-cells from each of the other species to cover only the collection of foreign molecules. The final solution consists of the best B-cell from each species.

4 The AQ Approach to Concept Learning

We will compare the solutions produced by our coevolutionary immune system with those produced by AQ15, a symbolic inductive learning system developed by Michalski et al. [6]. This system is one of the latest in a series of AQ systems that constructs conjunctive descriptions from preclassified examples using an enhanced propositional calculus representation language. Each AQ concept description consists of a disjunction of conjunctive descriptions. Once a concept description has been constructed for each class of examples the system has been presented with, the system uses a conflict resolution procedure to discriminate between unclassified examples of one concept or another based on the strength of the match with the learned descriptions and the prior probability of the concepts. See [6] for more details concerning AQ conflict resolution and its method for constructing concept descriptions.

5 Experimental Study

5.1 Congressional Voting Records Data Set

In this experimental study we evolve a political party classification system for members of the U.S. House of Representatives given their voting records. The objective, therefore, is to learn to discriminate between the concepts *Republican* and *Democrat*. This is a supervised learning task in which we are given a number of preclassified training examples. The data set from which the training examples are drawn consists of 267 Democrat and 168 Republican voting records. Each record gives the vote cast by an individual on 16 different issues. Although the actual voting records are somewhat more complex, each vote in the compiled data set has been simplified to either a yea, nay, or abstain. For compatibility with the coevolutionary immune system, the symbolic voting records were converted into 32-bit strings (antigens) using the following two-bit codes: 00 for abstain, 01 for yea, and 10 for nay. Depending on one's political orientation, the foreign molecules to be targeted by the immune system could represent either examples of Republicans or Democrats. The symbolic data set was originally used in a machine learning study by Schlimmer [11] and was compiled from actual voting records from the 98th Congress.

5.2 Experimental Setup

AQ15 is run with its default settings. Rather than simply learning a description for one of the two concepts, say Democrats, and interpreting non-conforming examples as members of the Republican party as suggested earlier in the section on coevolving antibodies, AQ learns a separate description for each concept. For example, it will first learn a description for Republicans using the Republican instances in the training set as positive examples and the Democrat instances as negative examples, and then learn a description for Democrats using the opposite orientation.

To provide a more fair comparison, our evolutionary immune system also uses this technique by coevolving two distinct classes of B-cells. One class recognizes Democrats and ignores Republicans, while the other class ignores Democrats and recognizes Republicans. As species are created, half are assigned to the Democrat class and the other half to the Republican class. Each species has a population size of 100, is initialized randomly, recombined with uniform crossover at a rate of 0.6, mutated by flipping bits at a rate of twice the reciprocal of the chromosome length, and evolved using scaled fitness-proportionate selection. Since AQ is strongly biased towards learning general solutions, the immune system is also given a generality bias by initializing approximately 90 percent of the alleles of each mask gene to zero. We begin the evolution of the system with only a single species of B-cells. New species are created and poor performing species are eliminated when evolutionary improvement stagnates.

5.3 Results

We first look at the quality of solutions produced by the immune system and AQ in terms of how well they are able to discriminate between Republicans and Democrats. Solution quality is compared using the *predictive accuracy* metric. Given the size of our data set, the tenfold cross-validation method is the recommended procedure for computing this metric [12]. One performs tenfold cross validation by randomly dividing the complete set of positive and negative examples into ten partitions of approximately equal size. Ten runs are then performed, each using a different set of nine partitions as the *training set* and the remaining partition as the *testing set*. During each run, the concept learner will use the

Table 1. Final predictive accuracy of learning methods

Learning method	Predictive accuracy
Immune System	0.964 ± 0.018
AQ System	0.956 ± 0.023

training set to construct a concept description. Once the run is complete, the concept description is applied to the testing set and the percentage of testing instances classified correctly is computed. The predictive accuracy is computed by averaging the percentage of correct classifications produced from the ten runs.

Each of the ten AQ runs was terminated when it produced a concept description capable of correctly classifying all the instances of Republican and Democrat voting records in the training set. Each run of the immune system was terminated after 100 generations of adaptation to the training set; however, learning flattened out after only a couple of generations. The predictive accuracy results are summarized in Table 1. The table includes 95-percent confidence intervals computed from the t-statistic. A t-test was also performed on these results and it was determined that there is not a statistically significant difference between the predictive accuracy of the methods.

In Table 2 we compare the number of elements in the concept descriptions produced by the two methods, specifically, the number of B-cells versus the number of conjunctive descriptions required to cover the voting record training examples. Over ten runs, the immune system consistently produced smaller descriptions than AQ. As shown in the table, on average the immune system evolved 7.0 B-cells while AQ generated 15.1 conjunctive descriptions. The table includes 95-percent confidence intervals on the mean computed from the t-statistic and a t-test was used to verify that there is a statistically significant difference between the number of cover elements produced by the methods.

To compare and contrast the roles played by these cover elements, the results from both methods were converted into a rule-based representation using a straightforward mapping by which each antibody and conjunctive description is converted into a separate rule. Specifically, to produce a rule from an antibody, the first length-two antibody schema is mapped to a test of the first vote, the second length-two schema is mapped to a test of the second vote, and so on. Table 3 gives our schemata interpretation. The table reflects that half credit is given for partial matches. Rules are activated when their match strength exceeds a rule-specific threshold as described in Section 3. In contrast, AQ normally only activates perfectly matching rules. It will use a combination of the strength of the match and the prior probability of the concepts to activate partially matching rules if no perfectly matching ones exist.

The rules for recognizing Democrats produced by the first run of the immune system and AQ are shown in Figures 2 and 3. To further visualize the roles played

Table 2. Required number of cover elements (conjunctive descriptions or antibodies)

Learning Method	Cover Elements		
	Mean	Min	Max
Immune System			
Democrat	3.80 ± 0.30	3	4
Republican	3.20 ± 0.74	1	4
Total	7.00 ± 0.67	5	8
AQ System			
Democrat	8.30 ± 0.68	6	9
Republican	6.80 ± 0.81	5	9
Total	15.10 ± 1.37	11	18

Table 3. Interpretation of antibody schema

Schema	Interpretation
00	abstain or yea (half credit) or nay (half credit)
01	yea or abstain (half credit)
10	nay or abstain (half credit)
11	yea (half credit) or nay (half credit)
0#	abstain or yea
1#	nay
#0	abstain or nay
#1	yea
##	ignore

by these rules, the number of training set examples covered and classified by each is shown in Figures 4 and 5. By *covered*, we mean that the rule was activated but not actually chosen by the conflict resolution procedure.

The first observed difference between these rule sets is that, as previously noted, significantly fewer rules were produced by the immune system than by AQ. Furthermore, the total number of tests in the immune system rule set is smaller—the AQ rule set contains 29 tests while the immune system rule set contains only 20 tests. The second difference between the rule sets is that the AQ rules are all at about the same level of generality[4] while the immune system rules vary from very general to quite specific. This is a possible explanation for the smaller number of rules produced by the immune system. By being more

---

[4] Although the first AQ rule classifies most of the examples, all of its rules are fairly general.

Rule 1
THRESH: 0.08
IF vote4: abstain or nay
vote9: yea
THEN Democrat

Rule 2
THRESH: 0.78
IF vote1: abstain or nay
vote5: abstain or nay
vote7: nay
vote8: abstain or nay
vote9: abstain or yea
vote10: nay
vote12: abstain or nay
vote15: yea
vote16: yea
THEN Democrat

Rule 3
THRESH: 0.85
IF vote2: abstain or yea
vote3: yea
vote11: abstain or yea
vote16: abstain or nay
THEN Democrat

Rule 4
THRESH: 0.77
IF vote3: abstain or yea
vote4: abstain or yea
vote5: yea (half credit) or nay (half credit)
vote7: abstain or nay
vote10: nay
THEN Democrat

Fig. 2. Rule-based interpretation of Democratic *B*-cells from immune system

Rule 1
IF vote4: abstain or nay
vote3: yea
THEN Democrat

Rule 2
IF vote4: nay
vote12: yea or nay
vote6: yea
THEN Democrat

Rule 3
IF vote15: yea
vote14: yea or nay
vote2: abstain or yea
THEN Democrat

Rule 4
IF vote3: abstain or yea
vote11: abstain or yea
vote9: yea or nay
vote7: abstain or nay
THEN Democrat

Rule 5
IF vote3: yea
vote16: abstain
vote13: yea
THEN Democrat

Rule 6
IF vote5: nay
vote15: yea
vote3: nay
THEN Democrat

Rule 7
IF vote13: nay
vote2: yea
vote3: nay
THEN Democrat

Rule 8
IF vote12: nay
vote11: abstain or yea
vote16: abstain
vote3: abstain or nay
THEN Democrat

Rule 9
IF vote11: yea
vote2: nay
vote1: nay
vote16: nay
THEN Democrat

Fig. 3. Rule-based interpretation of Democratic AQ conjunctive descriptions

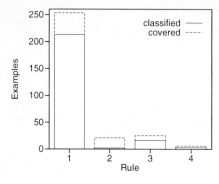
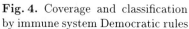
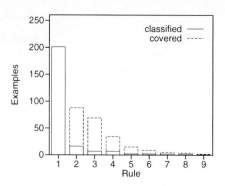

Fig. 4. Coverage and classification by immune system Democratic rules

Fig. 5. Coverage and classification by AQ Democratic rules

flexible in constructing rules with a wide range of generality, the immune system is able to learn a more concise description of the concept.

The rule sets also have a number of similar characteristics. First, the initial rules produced by both the immune system and AQ are very similar; specifically, they both consider an abstain or nay on issue number four to be strong evidence that the voting record belongs to a Democrat. This also happens to be the most general rule produced by both methods, and from Figures 4 and 5 one can see that this rule classifies most of the examples. In other words, both methods have discovered that the vote on issue number four is the most important discriminator. The second similarity is that the concept descriptions produced by both methods must rely on rules that match only a few examples to cover the training set adequately.

6 Summary and Conclusions

In summary, we have presented a novel approach to concept learning in which a coevolutionary genetic algorithm is applied to the construction of an artificial immune system whose antibodies can discriminate between examples and counter-examples of a given concept. The results from the adaptation of this immune system to one of the standard machine learning data sets is compared and contrasted with the results from AQ15—a sophisticated symbolic inductive learning system. The immune system approach produced a description of the concepts significantly more concise than that produced by AQ, while its predictive accuracy was just as high. These preliminary results suggest that the immune system approach is able to produce such a concise description by being more flexible than AQ in constructing discriminator elements with a wide range of generality.

But perhaps the most significant advantage of the coevolutionary immune system model is that it can be applied to other machine learning problems, such as acquiring task-oriented behaviors. In such cases it is necessary to recognize appropriate situations, or concepts, required to perform a task well without being explicitly trained on each. Rather, feedback is in the form of a reinforcement signal from which important concepts must be indirectly learned.

What we have described in this paper is admittedly an extremely loose model of an actual vertebrate immune system. We emphasize that the focus of this paper is to explore a new method for concept learning inspired by the immune system—not to accurately model the complex biology of immunology. It is our belief, however, that there is a potential for building more biologically faithful coevolutionary models of the immune system that may lead, not only to better machine learning systems, but also to greater insight into the workings of actual biological systems.

Acknowledgments

This work was supported by the Office of Naval Research.

References

1. K. A. De Jong, W. M. Spears, and D. F. Gordon. Using genetic algorithms for concept learning. *Machine Learning*, 13(2/3):5–188, 1993.
2. S. Forrest, B. Javornik, R. E. Smith, and A. S. Perelson. Using genetic algorithms to explore pattern recognition in the immune system. *Evolutionary Computation*, 1(3):191–211, 1993.
3. A. Giordana and F. Neri. Search-intensive concept induction. *Evolutionary Computation*, 3(4):375–416, 1995.
4. C. Z. Janikow. A knowledge-intensive genetic algorithm for supervised learning. *Machine Learning*, 13(2/3):189–228, 1993.
5. R. S. Michalski. A theory and methodology of inductive learning. In R. S. Michalski, J. G. Carbonell, and T. M. Mitchell, editors, *Machine Learning*, pages 83–134. Morgan Kaufmann, 1983.
6. R. S. Michalski, I. Mozetic, J. Hong, and N. Lavrac. The AQ15 inductive learning system: An overview and experiments. Technical Report UIUCDCS-R-86-1260, University of Illinois, Urbana-Champaign, IL, 1986.
7. M. A. Potter. *The Design and Analysis of a Computational Model of Cooperative Coevolution*. PhD thesis, George Mason University, Fairfax, VA, 1997.
8. M. A. Potter, K. A. De Jong, and J. J. Grefenstette. A coevolutionary approach to learning sequential decision rules. In L. Eshelman, editor, *Proceedings of the Sixth International Conference on Genetic Algorithms*, pages 366–372. Morgan Kaufmann, 1995.
9. J. R. Quinlan. Induction of decision trees. *Machine Learning*, 1:81–106, 1986.
10. Ivan M. Roitt. *Essential Immunology*. Blackwell Scientific Publications, eighth edition, 1994.
11. J. C. Schlimmer. *Concept Acquisition through Representational Adjustment*. PhD thesis, University of California, Irvine, CA, 1987.
12. S. M. Weiss and C. A. Kulikowski. *Computer Systems that Learn*. Morgan Kaufmann, 1991.

Does Data-Model Co-evolution Improve Generalization Performance of Evolving Learners?

J. L. Shapiro

University of Manchester, Manchester M13 9PL UK.

Abstract. In co-evolution as defined by Hillis, data which defines a problem co-evolves simultaneously with a population of models searching for solutions. Herein, one way in which this could work is explored theoretically. Co-evolution could lead to improvement by evolving the data to a set which if a model is trained on it, it will generalize better than a model trained on the initial data. It is argued here that the data will not necessarily co-evolve to such a set in general. It is then shown in an extremely simple toy example that if there is too much optimization per generation, the system oscillates between very low fitness solutions, and will perform much worse than a system with no co-evolution. If the learning parameters are scaled appropriately, the data set does evolve to one which leads to better generalization performance. The improvement can be arbitrarily better in the large population size limit, but strong finite-population effects limit this. can be achieved.

1 Introduction

Several years ago, Hillis [1] introduced a co-evolution scheme in which, while potential solutions to a problem adapt, the sample data which defines the problem co-adapts. Hillis was evolving sorting networks for sorting lists of 16 elements. The goal was to find a sorting network which sorts all lists of 16 elements with the least number of comparisons. The fitness of a network was the number of lists correctly sorted from a sample set of lists. The lists in the sample set co-evolved, where the fitness of a list was the number of sorting networks in the population which failed to sort it correctly. Using this procedure, Hillis found a sorting network which was better than that found using fixed data, and it was close to the best that was known for lists of length 16. Although there were other differences between the co-evolving and non-co-evolving experiments, Hillis argued that it was the co-evolution which led to the increase in performance.

Hillis' scheme, which I will call *data-model co-evolution* to distinguish it from other so-called co-evolutionary algorithms, has generated a great deal of recent interest, for obvious reasons. If it works in general, it could be applied to any problem which requires performance on a large number of cases, but can only be tested on a small fraction of those cases. This is a huge class of enormous importance. In addition, the approach could be applied in a wide range of algorithms.

In fact, any algorithm which can produce a population could be used to evolve the models or the data. So, in addition to evolutionary algorithms, it could be used in parallel random hill-climbing or simulated annealing in which a population is generated at each timestep via different realizations of the stochasticity. In fact, it gives a new reason to have a population of models in an algorithm; a population of models is used as a sample against which the performance of the data can be measured and improved.

There have been a number of experimental studies of this type of system. For an overview, see [2]. In this paper, a particular theoretical question will be considered. Does data-model co-evolution work by evolving the dataset to one which leads to better true or generalization performance? In the types of problems which uses a data set to define the problem, it is usually the case that the dataset contains only a tiny fraction of possible cases. The performance of a model on this data set is an estimate of the true performance, which means the performance on all possible data. Good performance on some datasets may lead to better true performance than good performance on other datasets. Is it possible that data-model co-evolution improves the performance of the models by evolving the data to such a set? A similar question was considered in [5] in the context of game playing.

2 Description of the algorithm

Data-model co-evolution is defined as follows. Let x denote a training example (data) and s denote a possible solution to the problem (model); X denotes a population of N_d data points, and S likewise to refer to a population of N_s solutions.

The fitness of a model is the sum of the fitness for each datum, $f(s, x)$. The apparent fitness or training fitness is usually taken as,

$$F_a(s) = \sum_{x \in X} f(s, x). \tag{1}$$

The true fitness or generalization fitness is given by

$$F_t(s) = \int f(s, x) P(x) dx, \tag{2}$$

where $P(x)$ is the distribution of data for the problem. The apparent fitness is a noisy and biased estimate of the true fitness, but it is the true fitness one wishes to optimize. Of course, only the apparent fitness is known.

The fitness of a datum, according to Hillis, is the number of models which gets it wrong, i.e.

$$coF_a(x) = \sum_{s \in S} [1 - f(s, x)] \tag{3}$$

The co-evolution algorithm is pair of evolutionary algorithm which alternates between the two populations. The data-set and model-set evolving algorithms can be any algorithms which produce a population of solutions: a genetic algorithm, a parallel simulated annealing algorithm, a random hill-climbing algorithm, etc.

542

3 Is data-model co-evolution a generalized query construction algorithm?

In order to find mathematical models to study how co-evolution might work, it is useful to decide how it *could* work. I suggest that there are three possibilities. First, it could work by increasing diversity in the population thereby preventing premature convergence. Second, it could work by dynamically changing the shape of the fitness function to make the problem easier. Finally, it could work by evolving the dataset to one which, if learned, gives better true (generalization) performance. Of course, it could be a combination of these.

The last hypothesis is considered here. This hypothesis puts this algorithm in the context of non-evolutionary learning algorithms for adapting a training set called *learning from examples and queries* in learning theory [6]. In this scenario, there is a "teacher" (sometimes called an oracle) which presents labeled examples of members of different classes; the learner can also present examples to the teacher to be classified. The examples which are presented to the teacher are those whose inclusion in the training set most (in some sense) improves the expected true performance. Such an algorithm can improve the performance over random examples considerably.

Query learning algorithms are always derived for a specific learning system and specific class of problem. Data-model co-evolution is completely general, however. No information about the problem or class of potential solutions is used. Instead, search is used to find the best data. This generality means it could be quite powerful if we could show that it works as a query construction algorithm. (Another difference with usual query learning is data is only added and never removed.)

We can ask the question this way, does adding a point to X which optimizes the co-fitness of equation 3 lead to an increase in the expected true fitness

$$F_t(X + x) = \int P(s|X + x)F_t(s)ds \qquad (4)$$

where the integral is over the distribution from which S is drawn (assuming the population can be expressed in this way).

In principle the answer is no. First, if there is no model which exactly solves the problem, due to noise for example or to an insufficiently complex model class, this will not lead to an increase in true performance. For this situation, the cases must remain representative of their distribution to find an optimal solution. For example, in regression, the data-set will evolve to one filled with the most extreme values, which may not give an optimal result. This point may well hold for ordinary query learning.

More generally, however, this will not lead to improvement necessarily even if perfect performance is possible. Consider the following situation. Suppose in the population there are models all with optimal *apparent* fitness. One of the models has perfect true performance. Many of the models get most of the possible data correct, but get a few wrong that are not in the current data population, and it is the same few. The remaining model gets most of the data outside current data set wrong, but not those few. Which datum should be added next. Hillis's heuristic will add a datum which eliminates the many good solutions, since it is trying to beat as many models as possible. However, to improve the expected true performance it is best is remove the one model whose true performance is bad by adding a datum which removes it (remember that the apparent fitness of all is the same, so the solution which is finally used is drawn uniformly from this population). But this will only beat one model, and so has a low fitness according to Hillis.

So this approach does not lead to improvement of generalization in all cases. It is more like an entropy heuristic; it decreases the volume of acceptable models if not their expected performance.

4 A simple example – one dimensional high-low

Although it cannot be proved to work in principle, it could still work in practice. A very simple example is now considered to see whether the data set will co-evolve to one which leads to increased true performance.

4.1 Description of the example problem

We consider Gibbs learning in the simplest toy problem from computational learning theory — the one-dimensional "high-low" problem. An instance of the problem is defined by a number $t \in (0, 1)$. In this model, a number $x \in (0, 1)$ is classified as 1 if $x > t$ and 0 otherwise. The learning problem is to make a model of the data from a set of examples $\{x_i\}$ and the classes they are in. Usually one assumes that the learning system comes from the same class as the problem. Thus, the learning system is trying to find t from a set of examples.

The optimal solution space lies between the examples which bound t ¿from either side. Let

$$x_R = \min \{x_i | x_i > t\} \qquad (5)$$
$$x_L = \max \{x_i | x_i \leq t\} . \qquad (6)$$

If learning is such that the optimal subspace is reached, true performance will be related to

$$e_g = x_R - x_L. \qquad (7)$$

It is easy to show that on average, $e_g \approx 2/N_d$, where N_d is the number of training examples. Thus, this system has the same relationship between training set size and generalization as the perceptron and other simple systems. In addition, it is easy to generate a query learning algorithm for this system. To add a new example, simple pick an x between x_R and x_L. This increases the true performance exponentially, as it is essentially binary search.

Thus, this seems a good example to test the hypothesis that co-evolution can lead to an example set which produces higher generalization, because there is such a set for the system to evolve to. This is different from the perceptron, for example, in which query learning has a much weaker effect.

4.2 The co-evolutionary learning algorithm

The dynamics of co-evolving systems is very difficult to analyze. Although the system is Markovian, the correlation between the fitness function (through the data) and the current population (through its correlation with previous generations) makes the analysis very difficult [4]. I will use a theoretical device to remove this correlation. Rather than learning for a particular number of steps, the system will learn to a particular distribution defined by a learning parameter, namely a Gibbs distribution with inverse temperature β. This is not realistic and removes the opportunity to study dynamics, but makes the problem solvable. Since we are interested in a property of the dataset which can be considered without dynamics, it is a reasonable first step. This type of learning is called Gibbs learning, and is roughly equivalent to learning via simulated annealing by annealing to the inverse temperature β. The population is generated by sampling from this distribution at each generation.

4.3 Zero temperature Gibbs co-evolutionary learning

First we will consider the following learning scenario. There is a population of models of size N_s and a population of data of size N_d. At each stage, evolution will occur sufficiently long that whichever system is evolving will evolve to the optimal subspace with regard to the other system. Thus, there will be a large number of evolution steps for each system before the other system starts to evolve. The population after the evolution will be drawn independently ¿from this optimal subspace.

For learning systems, this is called "zero temperature Gibbs learning", because the distribution from which the learners are drawn is the Gibbs distribution in the limit that the temperature goes to zero.

For the models, the optimal subspace lies between x_L and x_R as mentioned in the previous section. Thus, the population of models after evolution will be drawn uniformly between this interval. If it happens that all of the data lies on one side of t, then the missing x_L or x_R is replaced by 0 or 1, but this is very unlikely unless N_d is very small.

For the data, however, the optimal subspace is one of these intervals

$$(t, s_R) \quad \text{if more of the } s\text{'s are greater than } t; \tag{8}$$

$$(s_L, t) \quad \text{if more of the } s\text{'s are less than } t; \tag{9}$$

$$(s_L, s_R) \quad \text{there are the same number of } s\text{'s on either side of } t; \tag{10}$$

Here s_L, s_R are, as with the x's, the closest models of t on either side. Thus, the fitness for the data is maximal on side of t where most of the data is, unless there are exactly the same number of models on each side of t, which will rarely happen.

Thus, the result of the evolution is that the models move to populate the optimal subspace of the initial population. The data then moves to the side of t where more of the models are, and closer to t than they are. The models then move to the side of t where the data is not. The data then moves to where the models are, the models to where the data is not, etc. And so the system will oscillate forever. The true performance measure will oscillate between t and $(1-t)$ plus terms of order $1/N_d$. On average, the true performance after the first step will be $1/2$.

To summarize,

$$\langle F_t \rangle_{pop} = \begin{cases} \frac{2}{N_d}; & \text{without co-evolution} \\ \frac{1}{2}; & \text{with co-evolution} \end{cases} \tag{11}$$

The true fitness with co-evolution is much worse than what you get without co-evolution. It might be tempting to describe this as an example of the *Red Queen Effect* [3], where the system expends its evolutionary resources in maintaining its current fitness rather than in improving it. However, here the system actually gets much worse. This system oscillates between very low fitness states, and the reason for this is transparent. The data occupies an subspace which is optimal against the current population, but leaves other regions of space open for the models to occupy.

4.4 Finite temperature co-evolutionary learning

Obviously, it is necessary to populate sub-optimal as well as optimal subspaces. So, consider what happens if the data learns to a finite temperature Gibbs distribution with inverse temperature β_d. This parameter controls the amount of co-evolution. If β_d is 0, the Gibbs distribution is just a random distribution. The next generation of models will learn against a new batch of data, but one which will be statistically equivalent to the previous data set. As β_d is increased, it will correspond to increasing the amount of co-evolution. Of course as β_d gets increasingly large, the system will approach the oscillating system described in the previous section.

The models will continue to learn to the optimal subspace, as that did not contribute to the oscillations above, and it does make the analysis easier. Thus, the models will be uniformly distributed between x_L^0 and x_R^0, where these are the x's closest to t before the co-evolution step under consideration. Since the true fitness of the models is given by $x_R^0 - x_L^0$ before co-evolution and $x_R - x_L$ after co-evolution, we will consider how $x_R - x_L$ depends upon $x_R^0 - x_L^0$, N_d and N_s. Since learning is equivalent at each generation, this function will allow us to determine the entire sequence of intervals.

The question of interest is, will the oscillating state be preserved for less extreme amounts of co-evolution, or will the system stabilize? The answer is that it depends upon how the fitness is scaled with regard to the learning parameter β_d. An analogy that one can make is that the data population is like an ideal gas in a one-dimensional potential. Such a system cannot have a phase transition except at zero and infinite temperatures. Thus, the finite temperature behaviour must be the same as the zero temperature behaviour or as the infinite temperature behaviour. We know the zero temperature behaviour is oscillatory, so we desire that the phase transition occur at zero temperature.

We assume that the two populations are large. If we assume that the fluctuations in x are larger then the spacing between the levels,

$$\left\langle (x - \langle x \rangle_{\beta_d})^2 \right\rangle_{\beta_d} > \frac{1}{N_d} \tag{12}$$

where $< \cdot >_{\beta_d}$ denotes averaging over the Gibbs distribution, then the discreteness of the levels can be ignored. In this case, the fitness of the data can be approximated as,

$$coF_a(x) = \begin{cases} 0; & x < x_L^0 \\ N_s(x - x_L^0); & x \in (x_L^0, t) \\ N_s(x_R^0 - x); & x \in (t, x_R^0) \\ 0; & x > x_R^0. \end{cases} \tag{13}$$

We see that the gap between the two sides of t is of order N_s, because we count the number of models that the data defeats. With this scaling of the fitness, the system will always be oscillatory for large population size. (In this type of learning, β controls the trade-off between optimization and entropy, with β multiplying the cost function. The loss in fitness by populating the subspace on the other side of t is $O(N_s)$, whereas the entropy is only $\log(N_d)$. Thus the suboptimal subspace on the other side of t is only populated if β is very small, of order $N_s/\log(N_d)$.)

However, if co-fitness is divided by N_s, this system will be in the low temperature phase for finite β. This is the state we will investigate, as it is the more promising scaling. The transition to the oscillating state will only occur at $\beta_d = \infty$ for large population size.

We draw a set of x's from a Boltzmann distribution,

$$Z^{-1} \exp \left[\beta_d coF_a(x) \right] \tag{14}$$

where Z is the normalization. Then we generate the distribution of the closest value below t and above t from a set of N_d drawn from this distribution in order to compute the

$$P(x_L, x_R | x_L^0, x_R^0, N_d) \tag{15}$$

the probability distribution for the new closest values to t in terms of the old ones. Using this to average of the true fitness measure and taking the large N_d limit produces this expression,

$$\langle x_R - x_L \rangle = \tag{16}$$

$$\frac{1}{N_d \beta} \left\{ \exp \left[-\frac{e^{\beta \delta_{Rt}}}{\beta} \right] E_i \left[-\frac{e^{\beta \delta_{Rt}}}{\beta} \right] + \exp \left[-\frac{e^{\beta \delta_{tL}}}{\beta} \right] E_i \left[-\frac{e^{\beta \delta_{tL}}}{\beta} \right] - \right.$$

$$E_i \left(\frac{1}{\beta} \right) \left[\exp \left(-\frac{e^{\beta \delta_{Rt}}}{\beta} \right) + \exp \left(-\frac{e^{\beta \delta_{tL}}}{\beta} \right) \right] \right\} +$$

$$\frac{1}{N_d} \left\{ \exp \left[-\frac{e^{\beta \delta_{Rt}-1}}{\beta} \right] + \exp \left[-\frac{e^{\beta \delta_{Rt}-1}}{\beta} \right] \right\}$$

Here

$$\delta_{Rt} \equiv N_d(x_R^0 - t) \tag{17}$$

$$\delta_{tL} \equiv N_d(t - x_L^0) \tag{18}$$

$$E_i(\lambda) = \int_{-\infty}^{\lambda} \frac{e^t}{t} dt \tag{19}$$

The δ's are order 1, and the principal part of the integral is taken.

For β_d small, this goes to $2/N_d$ as expected. For large β_d, assuming the large N_d limit has been taken first, this goes to zero like $\exp(-\beta_d \delta_{max})/N_d$, where δ_{max} is the maximum of the two intervals. Thus, it is the case that the data evolves to a training set which leads to greater true performance, and with appropriately chosen parameters one can get to arbitrarily high increase in performance through co-evolution. However, it is sensitive to the scaling of the learning parameter.

Finite population effects are very important. There are two types. Finite N_d will lead to a crossover to the oscillatory behavior. This will come in when

$$\beta_d \approx \log N_d. \tag{20}$$

Thus, this will be important unless the population size is very large. Finite N_s will mean that the generalization performance due to co-evolution cannot continue to increase. There is no reason for x_L to get closer to t then the s which is closest to t. This will become important when

$$\beta_d \approx \log N_s. \tag{21}$$

Figure 1 shows a plot of theoretical results against experiments. The solid curves are theoretical curves for the true performance before co-evolution (which is independent of β) and after, according to equation 16. The experiments were done by directly sampling from the Gibbs distribution. This will not tell anything about the time to reach the distribution, since direct sampling can only be done if t is known. The diamonds show the true performance of the models before co-evolution; the asterisks are after. Also shown are the true performance with no co-evolution but with a training set twice as large (dashed curve), three times as large (dot-dashed curve), and four times as large (dotted curve). With co-evolution more data must be processed. In order for co-evolution to win over simply using a larger training set, it must either be faster or the curve must go lower than whatever line corresponds to the amount of data which must have been processed to reach this distribution. Unfortunately we cannot answer this question without putting in dynamics, and it is a crucial question.

Figure 2 shows the experimental results, averaged over t for larger values of β. The beginning of the transition to the oscillating state can be seen. If continued on for higher values of β this would go to 1/2. There is an optimal value of β which leads to an optimal true performance. Beyond this value, the oscillatory state emerges. This value grows like $\log(N_d)$.

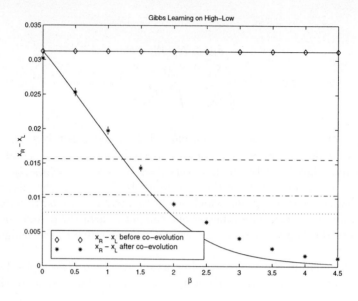

Fig. 1. The true performance of the models after a co-evolution step versus that before. The solid lines are theory; the horizontal line is before co-evolution. The line after co-evolution goes to zero showing that co-evolution can lead to arbitrary good generalization with suitably chosen parameters and infinite population size. The diamonds and asterisks are experiments using direct sampling from the Gibbs distribution. The other horizontal lines show what the true performance would without co-evolution but with the size of the data set doubled (dashed line), tripled (dot-dashed line), and quadrupled (dotted line). The parameters are: $N_s = 50$, $N_d = 64$, $t = 0.42$.

5 Conclusions

Whether data-model co-evolution can work by evolving the data to a set that leads to improved generalization was considered. It cannot be proven to be so, it was argued. A very simple toy example was solved analytically. It was shown that this system is unstable to oscillations between very low fitness states. If the learning parameter is suitably scaled, however, the data could evolve to a set leading to improved generalization performance. If continued for larger β, it would go to $1/2$.

5.1 Future work

In order to understand data-model co-evolution, much more work is required. First, we must put in dynamics, in order to estimate the time to get to this state. This is essential in calculating the efficiency of the approach. This could be done for the simulated annealer, although GA dynamics would be quite relevant. This problem is quite trivial; it would be important to find more interesting problems

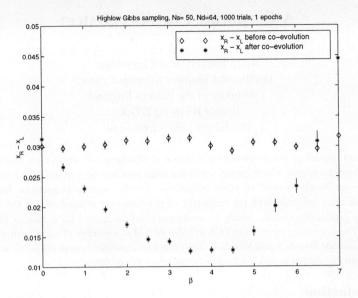

Fig. 2. The experiments of figure 1 continued for higher values of β and averaged over t. The beginning of the transition to the oscillatory behavior is seen; this is a finite population effect.

to analyze. It also might be interesting to attempt to put in interactions between the individuals.

To study the shaping hypothesis, it will be necessary to work out the dynamics in full detail, including getting the learning time. This is difficult for GAs without co-evolution, but it is clearly a very interesting problem.

References

1. Hillis, W.D. *Co-evolving Parasites Improve Simulated Evolution as an Optimization Procedure*, Physica D **42**, 228-234 (1990).
2. Paredis, Jan, *Coevolutionary Algorithms* from the Handbook of Evolutionary Computation, Bäck, T. Fogel, D. Michalewicz Z. (eds.) Oxford University Press, 1997.
3. Paredis, Jan, *Coevolving Cellular Automata: Beware of the Red Queen!*, Proceedings of the Seventh Conference on Genetic Algorithms, Bäck, T. editor, 393–399, 1997.
4. Rattray,M *Modelling the Dynamics of Genetic Algorithms Using Statistical Mechanics*, University of Manchester Ph.D. thesis, 1996.
5. Rosin, C.D., *Coevolutionary Search Among Adversaries*, University of California Ph.D. thesis, 1997.
6. Valiant, L.G. *A theory of the learnable*, Communications of the ACM, **27** no. 11, 1134 – 1142, 1984.

A Corporate Classifier System

Andy Tomlinson and Larry Bull
Intelligent Computer Systems Centre
University of the West of England
Bristol BS16 1QY, U.K.
{blob,larry} @ics.uwe.ac.uk

Abstract. Based on the proposals of Wilson and Goldberg we introduce a macro-level evolutionary operator which creates structural links between rules in the ZCS model and thus forms "corporations" of rules within the classifier system population. Rule co-dependencies influence both the behaviour of the discovery components of the system and the production system, where a corporation can take control for a number of time-steps. The system is compared to ZCS and also ZCSM in a number of maze environments which include Woods 1 and Woods 7. The corporate classifier system is shown to be the most suitable design to tackle a range of these types of problems.

1. Introduction

The idea of a "corporate" Michigan-style classifier system, as proposed by Wilson and Goldberg [13] (see also Smith[11]) is derived originally from the biological phenomenon of symbiosis. The underlying aim of the design is to encourage stronger co-operation between the rules comprising the system and thus to eliminate unwanted parasites and improve efficiency.

Here we enhance the ZCS model [15] to act as a corporate classifier system (CCS). ZCS is modified to include a "macro-level" rule-coupling operator and the operation of the GA (Genetic Algorithm [6]) is also expanded. The implementation is based on the proposals of Wilson and Goldberg.

Corporate links are formed between rules belonging to consecutive match sets and thus corporations are encouraged to encapsulate temporal chains of inference. Further, corporations are endowed with a quality referred to as "persistence" which enables them to exert a greater influence on the behaviour of the production system. It should be stated that persistence in this context is only loosely related to the characteristic introduced to SAMUEL by Cobb and Grefenstette [4]. The system is initially tested in two well known maze environments, Woods 1 and Woods 7 [15].

Finally we introduce a simple and adjustable maze environment which offers limited useful environmental stimulus and a reward only after a series of timesteps. This is used to further demonstrate the abilities of the corporate classifier system.

2. Corporations

Symbiosis, in which individuals from different species live together in close association for (possibly mutual) benefit, is known to have been a significant factor in natural evolution (e.g.[9]). A class of symbioses are known as hereditary endosymbioses in which individuals are effectively linked genetically; the association is perpetuated via synchronised reproduction.

Ikegami and Kaneko [8] were the first to use the genetic linkage mechanism in an artificial evolving system. Further work was presented by Bull, Fogarty and Pipe [2].

The possibility of a corporate classifier system (CCS) was first introduced by Wilson and Goldberg [13] as a theoretical approach to alleviating the co-operator/competitor dilemma in the Michigan-style classifier system [7], discussed in the same paper. The Pittsburgh-style classifier system [12] maintains a population not of rules, but of entire rule-bases. These are evaluated as a unit and so the rules within the rule-bases form natural co-dependencies under the GA (e.g. [5]). It was felt that a similar effect may be achievable in a Michigan-style classifier system if rules could link to form co-operative clusters for the purpose of reproduction.

The rule-base of a CCS contains not only single rules, but also clusters of classifiers or corporations. Corporations can only be reproduced or deleted as a unit, and are formed by a mutation type operator.

For reproduction, the fitness of a corporation is dependent on the strengths of its members (possibly the average strength) such that it may be advantageous for rules to link together rather than remain single.

3. Corporate Classifier Systems

3.1 Introduction

In this paper we propose an implementation of the corporate classifier system as theorised by Wilson and Goldberg. Using ZCS as a design for the basic system we then modified the structure to allow the system to perform as a corporate classifier system.

ZCS is a simplification of the basic Michigan-style classifier system architecture. Its purpose was to increase understanding of the essential mechanisms required for system functionality. In this sense it is a useful starting point from which to structure a corporate system and it also serves as a valid reference model for performance comparisons. Full details of ZCS can be found in [15].

3.2 How Are Corporations Implemented?

In ZCS, a rule consists of a condition, an action, and also a strength value. It is also reasonable to assume that it has some form of reference such as an index number. A possible implementation of a CCS has been facilitated by adding a few more parameters.

If corporations are viewed as chains of rules, a rule can at most be directly linked to only two other rules. Each rule will require two link parameters ("link forward" and "link back") that when active reference other rules within a corporation. These links will be initialised as inactive but when two rules are selected for joining, then one of each rules links ("link forward" for one rule, "link back" for the other) will be set to reference the other rule. This concept of rule-linkage is analogous to the gene-linkage employed by LEGO [10]. Here linkage between genes is used to encourage the formation and propogation of good schemata in the population of a GA. In CCS rule-linkage is used to encourage associations between rules through the formation of inter-dependent rule-chains.

In addition to this each rule also contains a "corporate size" parameter and a "corporate I.D." parameter. Initially size is set to 1 and corporate I.D. is left inactive. Within corporations, all rules will hold the same values for size and corporate I.D. and these are set during the formation of the corporation.

Coupling occurs with random probability on each time-step, in the same manner as the GA. An initial coupling probability of 0.1 (i.e. once every ten time-steps on average) was decided on but formal testing is required to determine an optimum rate.

Corporations are encouraged to encapsulate chains of inference. This is similar to the idea in [4] that some form of coupling between successively firing rules may be beneficial. Corporate links here take on a temporal connotation and imply that the rules within a corporation are placed so as to fire in succession and thus to map a proposed plan of action during the solution of a multiple time-step problem.

This is achieved by making "coupling" a niche operation, or more precisely a cross-niche operation. Coupling occurs between subsequent match sets. This means that on time-step t there is a possibility that a rule that matches the current message from the environment may link to a rule which matched the stimulus at time $t-1$. This encourages the structuring of meaningful sequences of rules.

To be selected for coupling, a rule must be in the current match set (termed [M]) and its appropriate link must be inactive. Coupling occurs over two time-steps. On the first, a rule in [M] is selected randomly from those with an inactive "link-forward", on the second, a rule in the new match set is selected again randomly from those with an inactive "link-back". Rules already in a corporation are not allowed to join to rules within their own corporation. If this precaution is not taken then there is the risk of forming "circular" corporations.

Rules are given a fitness parameter in addition to the standard strength parameter. For single rules fitness is the same as the strength value, but for corporate rules the strength and fitness values may be different. The strength parameter is used as before by the production system, however GA activity is now guided by rule fitnesses. Within a corporation all rules are given a fitness value equal to the average strength of member rules. However the rules' strengths are left unaltered.

In all environments used during testing, the system was reset after receipt of a reward from the environment on some time-step. Corporate links are not allowed to form between this reward time-step and the first one of the following trial as this "move" does not represent any form of causal transition under the control of the system.

3.3 Modifications to the discovery component

To further maintain temporal integrity amongst corporate rule-strings the GA is adjusted to operate within match sets. The idea of a niche GA operating in the match set was suggested by Booker [1] to introduce mating restrictions and thus to assist the GA in producing more meaningful offspring. Likewise in CCS the adjustment is made so that if corporations are selected for crossover then the resultant corporation should still represent a meaningful series of responses to experienced stimuli.

A roulette wheel selection policy is employed for rule replacement and this considers the reciprocals of rule fitnesses. If a corporate rule is selected for deletion then the corporation is first disbanded, then the rule is tagged for deletion.

During reproduction the crossover site is selected as usual and a single offspring rule is created from the two parent rules. This differs from the original ZCS (which produces two children from crossover) but the rate of genetic input (rule replacement rate) is consistent with ZCS. As in ZCS, when the GA is invoked, crossover is employed with a fixed probability χ. The new rule inherits 1/3 of the strength of each parent if crossover is employed (or 1/2 of the parent's strength if it is not).

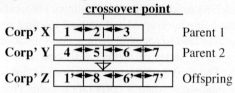

Fig.1: Corporate Crossover

The offspring rule inherits "equivalent" links to the "link back" of the first parent and the "link forward" of the second parent. These links however will have to be set not to refer to rules in the original corporations but to the equivalent rules in the new corporation.

For example, corporation X consists of rules 1, 2 and 3; corporation Y consists of rules 4,5,6 and 7 (figure 1); and rules 2 and 5 are selected for reproduction. The new offspring is termed rule 8, however rule 2 linked back to rule 1 so the new corporation (Z) will also require a copy of rule 1 from corporation X, and likewise copies of rules 6 and 7 from corporation Y. The copy of rule 1 is called rule 1', and those of rules 6 and 7 are called rules 6' and 7' respectively. Corporation Z produced by this corporate crossover operation contains the following rules: [r1', r8, r6', r7'].

Each additional rule that is reproduced in the corporation donates half of its strength to its offspring as is usual in ZCS for reproduction without crossover. Selection for rule replacement is as in ZCS (roulette wheel) but if the offspring is a corporation of size x, then the process is repeated x times. Essentially the population size is kept constant at all times. The final modification is to the mutation operator. Mutation is now extended to all members of the new corporation rather than just the new rule derived from crossover (i.e. rule 8 in the example).

3.4 Modifications to the performance component

Early testing of the system with these modifications showed that because of the dissipation of rewards and payoffs amongst action sets due to the common bucket of ZCS, although useful corporations did form they never fully established themselves within the system and exhibited lower fitness than their peers within the respective match sets. Consequently their presence made little difference to the performance of the production system and their chances of reproduction were poor (results not shown).

Therefore the production system was adjusted to respond to the presence of corporations. Action selection in the production system is determined stochastically, according to the relative strengths of the rules within the current match set. A roulette wheel policy is employed which selects a rule whose action becomes the system's action. Now, if this rule is corporate and it's link forward is active then it is tagged as being in control of the system. On the subsequent time-step, if the subsequent rule in the corporation is a member of the new match set then it automatically receives control of the system and forms an action set of size one. In this way the corporation keeps control of the production system and is solely responsible for system decisions until either a reward is received from the environment or the corporation fails to respond to some stimulus. When either of these events occur the production system returns to normal operation.

This mechanism, referred to as "persistence", allows corporations to directly prove their true worth without being interrupted and without the final reward being dissipated amongst parasitic rules that tend to accumulate in action sets close to rewards. A corporation that indicates a useful series of actions will soon achieve a fitness value that reflects its capabilities. The final modification to the production system consists of not charging tax [15] on time-steps when a corporation holds control. The system was adjusted to include these modifications and initially tested in Woods 1 and Woods 7 [15]. The next section presents the results of these tests and discusses the findings.

4 Performance in the Woods environments

The CCS model was initially tested in two standard environments, Woods 1 (Markovian with delayed reward) and Woods 7 (non-Markovian with delayed reward). Both environments are two-dimensional rectilinear grids and the system is viewed as an animat [14] traversing the grid in search of food. Full descriptions of Woods 1 and Woods 7 can be found in [15]. Figures 2 and 3 show graphs of the average steps taken to reach food over ten runs. In Woods 1 the system performed well, reaching an average of about 2.2 steps to food over 10000 runs. The optimum performance in Woods 1 is 1.7, and ZCS achieved an average of about 3 steps to food. In these tests the ZCS GA was modified to operate in the match set and the rule replacement rate was increased to 1 rule/time-step on average, to facilitate a fair comparison. The modified ZCS achieved a rate of 2.6 steps to food. In this simple Markovian environment the corporations can be seen to provide marginal benefits.

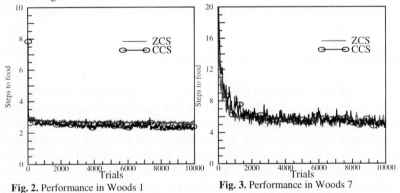

Fig. 2. Performance in Woods 1   **Fig. 3.** Performance in Woods 7

In both environments, all parameters (except ρ) are set as in Wilson's original experiments, that is:
$N = 400$, $P\# = 0.33$, $S_0 = 20.0$, $\beta = 0.2$, $\gamma = 0.71$, $\tau = 0.1$, $\chi = 0.5$, $\mu = 0.002$, $\rho = 1$, $\phi = 0.5$.
Curves are averages of 10 runs.

In Woods 1 the corporate behavioural sequences provide adequate information to attain near optimal performance. Performance in Woods 7 was not quite so impressive. There is however a possible explanation for this lack of improvement.

CCS is designed to learn and structure sequences of actions in order to encapsulate useful chains of inference while tackling multi-step tasks. If during a trial the first few steps of the task do not provide any useful information on which the system can base decisions it is unlikely that a useful corporation will have evolved which could guide the system to more certain terrain in anything like optimum time. If alternatively the system, at the beginning of a trial, is given some form of useful information with which it can to some extent discriminate about the immediate environment then it is possible that corporations may well have evolved which could steer the system through subsequent "blank" periods towards some eventual reward.

In Woods 7, at the start of a trial, the animat is positioned randomly in an unoccupied cell. From this cell it must on average, reach food having traversed 2.2 cells to match Wilson's projected optimum performance for a system equipped with arbitrary memory.

However in Woods 7 it is quite possible that the animat will not have received any information at all in the first couple of steps. When considering the initial random positioning in Woods 7 there is a 55% chance that the animat will be placed in a cell surrounded by blank cells on all 8 sides. This suggests that on over half of all trials the system is initially provided with no information at all.

This pronounced characteristic of the environment suggests that Woods 7 is not a particularly useful measure of system performance. For this reason an alternative series of test environments are presented and these are used to further gauge the performance of CCS.

5 Simple Delayed Reward Environments

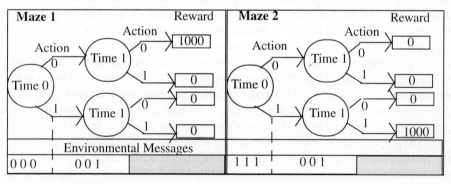

Fig. 4. Simple Delayed Reward Environment - Task 2:2

An alternative test environment is now presented which allows for a clearer differentiation between competing systems' capabilities. The new test is a simple variable multi-step environment. On each of N timesteps the system is presented with a stimulus and must select one of A actions, where A is a variable integer value which defines the breadth of a maze. N is the number of states or nodes to a reward and thus defines the maze depth. After N steps, the system receives a reward from the environment and a new task then begins. The size of the reward depends on which route the system chooses and so over time the system learns the optimum reward yielding route through the maze.

There are however more than one maze. There can be up to Mz different mazes. The system is informed which particular maze it is being presented with only on the first time-step of each trial. On all subsequent steps the stimulus is representative only of the current time-step in the trial. The maze is selected randomly at the start of each trial.

Figure 4 illustrates a simple task of this type with A set to 2, N set to 2 and Mz set to 2. The environmental stimulus at each time-step is also included. In this example, a reward of 1000 is awarded for one route on each map. All other routes receive a reward of 0.

In the example in figure 4 the message length L is set to 3. With L set to 3 there are 8 possible stimuli and so for a two map problem the maximum depth will be 7, as the first time-step (ts_0) takes two stimuli. Similarly with L set to 3 a four maze problem may have a maximum depth of 5.

Clearly ZCS will be unable to master more than a single map due to the sensory ambiguity after the first timestep, however CCS should be able to tackle multiple maze trials. In the task depicted in figure 4 some form of linkage is necessary for the system to be able to determine the appropriate move on the second timestep (ts_1). In maze one the correct action is 0 and in maze two it is 1 (the stimulus however is the same - 001).

6 Performance Comparison in Delayed Reward Environments

Wilson [15] proposed the addition of an internal "temporary memory" register to ZCS. Cliff and Ross [3] presented results showing that ZCS can exploit memory facilities in non-Markovian environments. Rules within the system (called ZCSM) have both an external and an internal condition and an external and internal action. The system is also equipped with a b-bit register, where b is a small integer value. The internal components of the rules interact with the register so as to effectively provide the system with temporary memory. Full details of system functionality can be found in [3].

ZCSM like CCS should be able to overcome the ambiguities present in the delayed reward environments. It is therefore necessary to ascertain the merits of the two systems so performances of CCS and ZCSM are now compared. ZCSM was tested twice in each environment. Once with $b = 2$ (ZCSM-02), and then again with b set to 4 (ZCSM-04). Also presented are plots of ZCS performance for further comparison. General system parameters are the same as for the tests in the Woods environments for all systems.

For the purposes of these tests the mazes are kept relatively simple. A is set to 2 for all tests so on each timestep the system merely has to make a 1-bit binary decision. L is set to 3 and the systems are tested on tasks consisting of 1, 2 and 4 mazes of depths of 2 and 3 (figures 5, 6, 7 & 8). These graphs show the average scores of ten runs for each system. In figures 4-8, task 1:2 for example represents a task consisting of a single maze of depth 2.

Again, the ZCS / ZCSM GA now operates in the match set and rule replacement rates have been increased to the effective rate in CCS based on mean corporation size for the task at hand.

Immediately it can be seen that ZCS is not really equipped to tackle these problems. If Mz is set to 1 then ZCS can operate and is able to learn a single maze but with four mazes ZCS will be intentionally correct on average about one in four times at best (i.e. when the map it has learnt is presented). It can be seen that as N is increased the system becomes increasingly unable to locate the reward.

ZCSM-02 is only just equipped to manage tasks of this complexity. A 2-bit register allows for 4 register states. With $Mz=4$ there are four optimum routes to be learned. If the system arranges its tags optimally then it can just about discriminate between good and bad moves on each timestep. In other words four rules must be discovered for each timestep and they will each need a different memory tag and of course they will each need to set the register differently to each other also. A certain amount of generalisation is possible in these mazes when A is set low and this does make the task a little easier. When N is set to 3 the system is clearly learning very little although for all depths of maze ZCSM-02 exhibits a noticable improvement over ZCS.

ZCSM-04 provides an increased memory capacity (16 states) and so should be able to tackle these tasks more comfortably than ZCSM-02. This prediction appears to be correct but the improvements are only marginal.

Of the systems that were able to even partially learn these tasks CCS seems to have performed best. At the end of a 10,000 trial run on task 2:2 (see fig. 4) the CCS rule-base was examined and below are presented two observed corporations.

Corporation 3846:
Name 349:   000 0 Strength:104.622 ID:3846 LINKS: -   134
Name 134:   0#1 0 Strength:829.912 ID:3846 LINKS: 349 -

Corporation 3846 responds to maze 1 (figure 4). At time 0 rule 349 responds to the presented stimulus (000) and proposes action 0. If rule 349 wins the auction then at time 1 rule 134 will, as it matches the new stimulus (001), automatically be in control of the production system. Rule 134 matches the stimulus and then proposes the correct action for maze 1 at time 1. This is a strong corporation and many copies of it can be seen in the rule-base.

Corporation 3931:
Name 202:   #1# 1 Strength: 63.092 ID:3931 LINKS: -   328
Name 328:   0#1 1 Strength:812.650 ID:3931 LINKS: 202 -

Corporation 3931 responds to maze 2 (figure 4). Rule 202 matches the stimulus at time 0 and proposes the correct action. On the subsequent time-step rule 328 matches the new stimulus and again proposes the correct action. This is also a strong corporation, copies of which can be seen in the rule-base. In CCS these two corporations alone are sufficient to solve task 2:2 where as ZCS is unable to tackle the ambiguity present on time-step 1.

The average number of corporations formed in CCS after 10,000 trials in task 2:2 is just under 200 and these are all of size 2. Virtually every rule in the population (size 400) has linked to a partner to form a 2-member corporation. When N is increased to 3 corporations of size 2 form initially (about 80 by trial 300) and corporations of size 3 form more slowly (50 by trial 300). By trial 2000 there are only 2 or 3 corporations of size 2, but just under 130 of size 3. Most rules in the population (about 390 of 400 rules) therefore now belong to 3-member corporations.

CCS offers a much improved performance on all tasks, however the results indicate that the discovery components of all systems found their performance impeded as N increased. Although ZCSM is equipped to solve this type of task the reason that it performs less well than CCS may be that due to the extra bits required by rules to interact with the internal register the effective search space viewed by the system has increased. This naturally makes the search proportionally more difficult.

ZCSM was also tested in Woods 1 and Woods 7. In Woods 1 it reached food in about 2.5 steps at the end of 10,000 trials which is a marginal improvement on ZCS performance. In Woods 7 results again show no improvement on ZCS performance, in fact performance is possibly slightly degraded (results not shown).

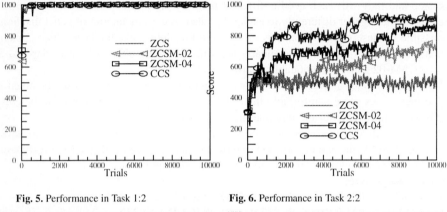

Fig. 5. Performance in Task 1:2   **Fig. 6.** Performance in Task 2:2

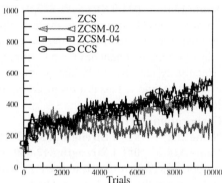

Fig. 7. Performance in Task 4:2   **Fig. 8.** Performance in Task 4:3

7 Conclusions

A rule in a Michigan-style classifier system is viewed by the GA as a binary string but is viewed by the production system as a condition/action rule. The GA interpretation can be considered as the genotype and the production system interpretation as the phenotype of the individual. The definition of corporations presented here can be said to introduce not only genotype dependencies but also phenotype dependencies to the rulebase.

This aspect of CCS has much in common with the Pittsburgh-style classifier system where rule co-dependencies are absolute. Each member (rule-base) of the Pittsburghstyle population is assessed individually and so adequate information is available to allow the GA to perform its search for good solutions.

In CCS corporations act as members of a co-operating/competing Michigan-style population. However when a corporate rule takes control of the production system the corporations behaviour becomes more analogous to that of a Pitt-style individual which must prove its utility alone. As long as the CCS corporate chain is relevant to the environment it alone controls the system. As implemented here, corporations are designed to encapsulate a chain of inference and this chain is allowed to run for its full duration. Any reward is received fully by the corporation and so its component rule-strengths, and thus its fitness, are more accurately representative of its true utility. This approach has proved reasonably beneficial for the models examined here.

In this sense the CCS design represents a significant step towards the realisation of a Michigan/Pittsburgh hybrid classifier system.

Acknowledgments

The authors would like to thank Rob Smith for a number of useful discussions during the course of this work.

References

1. Booker, L. (1985) "Improving the performance of Genetic Algorithms in Classifier Systems." Proceedings of the First International Conference on Genetic Algorithms and their Applications. (pp. 80-92). Lawrence Erlbaum Assoc.

2. Bull, L., Fogarty, T. C. & Pipe, A. G. (1995) "Artificial Endosymbiosis." In Moran, F.,Mereno, A., Merelo, J.J. and Chacon, P. (Eds.) Advances in Artificial Life - Proceedings of the Third European Conference on Artificial Life (pp.273-289), Springer Verlag.

3. Cliff, D. & Ross, S. (1994) "Adding Temporary Memory to ZCS." Adaptive Behaviour 3 (2): 101-150.

4. Cobb, H. G. & Grefenstette, J. J. (1991) "Learning the persistence of actions in reactive control rules." A.I.C.(91).

5. Grefenstette, J. J. (1987) "Multilevel credit assignment in a genetic learning system." In Grefenstette, J.J. (Ed.) Genetic Algorithms and their Applications: Proceedings of the Second International Conference on Genetic Algorithms (pp. 202-209). Lawrence Erlbaum Assoc.

6. Holland, J. H. (1975) "Adaptation in Natural and Artificial Systems." Univ. of Michigan Press, Ann Arbor.

7. Holland, J. H., Holyoak, K. J., Nisbett, R. E. & Thagard, P.R. (1986) "Induction: Processes of Inference, Learning and Discovery." MIT Press.

8. Ikegami, T. & Kaneko, K. (1990) "Genetic Fusion." Physical Review Letters, Vol 65, No. 26 (pp.3352-3355). The American Physical Society.

9. Margulis, L. (1981) "Symbiosis in Cell Evolution." Freeman.

10. Smith, J. & Fogarty, T.C. (1995) "An adaptive poly-parental recombination strategy." In Fogarty, T.C. (Ed.) Evolutionary Computing 2. (pp. 48-61), Springer Verlag.

11. Smith, R. E. (1994) "Memory Exploitation in Learning Classifier Systems." Evolutionary Computation, 2 (3):199-220.

12. Smith, S. (1980) "A learning system based on genetic algorithms." Ph.D. Dissertation (Computer Science), University of Pittsburgh.

13. Wilson, S. W. & Goldberg, D. E. (1989) "A critical review of classifier systems." In Schaffer, J. D. (Ed.) Proceedings of the Third International Conference on Genetic Algorithms, (pp.244-255), Morgan Kaufmann.

14. Wilson, S. W. (1985) "Knowledge growth in an artificial animal." In Grefenstette, J. J. (Ed). Proceedings of an International Conference on Genetic Algorithms and their Applications (pp.16-23), Lawrence Erlbaum Associates.

15. Wilson, S. W. (1994) "ZCS: A zeroth level classifier system." Evolutionary Computation, 2 (1): 1-18.

Applying Diffusion to a Cooperative Coevolutionary Model

R. Paul Wiegand

paul@tesseract.org
Computer Science Department
University of North Carolina – Charlotte, NC 28223, USA

Abstract. Perhaps one the newest and of the more interesting cooperative approaches to evolutionary computation which has been more recently explored is the area of mutualism. In mutualistic methods, the problem is subdivided into modular components where each component evolves separately, but is evaluated in terms of the other components. In this way the problem may be cooperatively solved. In an attempt to give this novel approach more adaptive ability, in this paper we explore the effects of adding varying degrees of population diffusion via a mutatable tagging scheme applied to individual chromosomes.

1. Introduction

Despite the tremendous scientific advancements of this century, and throughout history, computer science still remains inordinately inferior to nature in its ability to solve complex problems. Indeed, much advancement in the various fields of the science has come from borrowing solving techniques from nature itself. Surely there can be no mistaking this in the area of *Genetic Algorithms* (GA), arguably pioneered by John Holland (Goldberg, 1989; Holland, 1992) in 1975, as well as the more general area of *Evolutionary Computation* (EC), born as early as the late 1950's/early 1960's by a men such as Bremermann, Friedberg, Box, and Friedman (Fogel, to appear).

Borrowing from the concepts of Darwinian evolution, these early pioneers realized that the precepts of emergence and natural selection were well suited for many types of hard problems faced by computer scientists. They developed techniques for creating populations of individuals, consisting of potential solutions encoded in chromosome-like forms, and applying genetic operators (such as mutation and crossover) as these population members interbreed and are selected based on fitness values determined using varying evaluation methods.

Nature continues to be a source of inspiration for the field of EC. Concepts of cooperation and competition have since been applied in many forms, as have other forms of subpopulation and speciation techniques. Moreover, using multiple populations as a means to accomplish both coevolutionary solving as well as solving simultaneously for multiple near optimum solutions has captivated the attention of many EC researchers.

Further, recent coevolutionary advancements have included the concept of *mutualism* (Potter, 1997). Here problems are broken up such that a given subpopulation consists of individuals representing a portion of a solution. These subpopulations are evolved entirely separately, with the exception of evaluation, during which representatives are used in order to produce fitness values via cooperation.

In this study, we explore combining techniques used in studies regarding multiple subpopulation research, including mutualism. This paper discusses the use of a mutatable tagging system to allow individuals in a mutualistic model to move from subpopulation to subpopulation via a technique called *diffusion* (Spears, 1994). We will discuss this background research in more detail in section 2. In section 3, we will describe how these historic techniques were uniquely combined for our study. The results are described in section 4, and the conclusion is discussed in the final section.

2. Background

Using multiple subpopulations in a GA is a technique that has been harnessed for many purposes by many researches in the field of EC. Goldberg and Richardson's (1987) work showed how a simple GA can be used to find multiple optimum and suboptimum peaks during function optimization by using two techniques, *restricted mating* and *sharing*. Here individuals were only allowed to breed with other members of the population that were genetically similar, implicitly creating different species within the total ecology of a single GA. Sharing was then employed to prevent *crowding* of individuals on the tallest peaks by modifying fitness values of individuals in the subpopulations dynamically.

William Spears continued this research (Spears, 1994), modifying it for simplicity and performance by providing, more explicitly, the use of multiple subpopulations within the greater population. Further, individuals were restricted in mating to those individuals which were likewise a member of the same subpopulation. Membership to a given subpopulation was identified by the use of *tags*, additional bits affixed to the chromosome which specified to which species that individual belonged. Moreover, fitness sharing was implemented by taking the fitness value as formed by the evaluation process of a given individual, and dividing it by the total number of individuals which were also members of the same subpopulation. Subpopulations would thus grow and shrink dynamically from generation to generation depending on selection. We expect larger peaks to have larger subpopulation sizes, and smaller peaks to have their proportion, as the GA becomes more stable during convergence.

Although Spears performed his experiments in this study without mutation of the tag bits, he briefly discusses the concept of *diffusion*, in which the tag bits can be mutated at the same or a differing rate as the other bits in the chromosome. This rate is known as the *rate of diffusion*. In this way, parents from one generation may yield a mutated child, such that the offspring is a member of a different species.

In addition to multiple species being used in this way, it is also possible to use speciation as a means of accomplishing coevolution. Although the vast majority of such research has been primarily focussed in the area of competitive species (Schlierkamp-Voosen et al., 1994; Cohoon et al., 1987; and Tanese, 1989), there have been some significant studies of cooperative systems. Indeed, Mitchell Potter and Kenneth De Jong use this very idea in function optimization (Potter et al., 1994), yielding the concept of *mutualism*. In mutualism, a given problem is broken down into components, where each is evolved mutually, but in isolation to the other components. During evaluation of an individual from a given subpopulation, representatives are selected from the other subpopulations in order to form a complete solution, and fitness is assigned by using this cooperative structure. Potter and De Jong refer to these systems as *cooperative coevolutionary genetic algorithms* (CCGAs).

Although Potter investigates more dynamic methods of creating and eliminating species for other types of problems (Potter, 1997), such as structural construction of neural networks, what is of more significance to us is the work with function optimization, which has a more static nature in terms of component construction. When optimizing functions, Potter assigns each species to a given variable of a multi-variable function. The populations are homogeneous in the sense that they are all represented in the same bit string structure, and the same genetic operators are applied (albeit separately) to each population, though this need not be the case for all problems, as he clearly discusses (Potter, 1997).

Selecting a representative, or a *collaborator*, can be done in many ways, but most easily is accomplished by selecting the member with the highest fitness value from each of the collaborating subpopulations[1]. So each generation, all the individuals in a species under evaluation will be applied to the objective function one at a time, using the most fit individuals in the previous generation from the other species to form a complete solution. In this way these collaborators *cooperate* with the subpopulation currently being evaluated. Each species is evaluated in turn in this manner in a full *ecosystem generation*[2]. A good comparison of a standard GA to the CCGA in pseudo-code was provided by Potter (1994) and is shown below in figures 1 and 2.

```
gen = 0
Pop(gen) = randomly initialized population
evaluate fitness of each individual in Pop(gen)
while termination condition = false do begin
        gen = gen + 1
        select Pop(gen ) from Pop(gen - 1) based on fitness
        apply genetic operators to Pop(gen)
        evaluate fitness of each individual in Pop(gen)
        end
```

Fig. 1. The structure of a traditional GA

---

[1] In the case of the generation 0, we randomly select collaborators.
[2] Potter (1997) defines generation "...to be a complete pass through the select, re-combine, evaluate, and replace cycle of a single species..." and an ecosystem generation to be "...an evolutionary cycle through all species being coevolved."

```
gen = 0
for each species s do begin
        Pop_s(gen) = randomly initialized population
        evaluate fitness of each individual in Pop_s(gen)
        end
while termination condition = false do begin
        gen = gen + 1
        for each species s do begin
                select Pop_s(gen ) from Pop_s(gen - 1) based on fitness
                apply genetic operators to Pop_s(gen)
                evaluate fitness of each individual in Pop_s(gen)
                end
        end
```

Fig. 2. The structure of a Cooperative Coevolutionary GA

Notice that there will be more evaluations per ecosystem generation in the CCGA than in a traditional GA generation. In fact, the number of evaluations is $n * population\ size$, where n is the number of species (or arguments of the function). It is difficult to draw a comparison between generations in a traditional GA, and ecosystem generations in a CCGA for this reason. More appropriately, we look at the total number of evaluations performed. It is clear, however, that for the same number of function evaluations, the GA will complete more generations than the CCGA will complete ecosystem generations.

This novel approach gives us an idea how a problem can be statically sub-divided and solved in a coevolutionary, mutualistic manner. In the next section we will discuss how we were able to provide a bit more flexibility in allowing the CCGA to "tune" subpopulation sizes to a particular problem landscape, as well as providing possible future research possibilities with regards to more natural mechanisms for species to arise and become extinct.

3. Tagging and Mutualism

The application of diffusion to the CCGA model represents a very natural marriage of Potter's mutualistic model and Spear's tagging scheme. However, despite the complementary relationship of these techniques, there still remain several issues raised by the technique, which must be addressed.

Indeed, these concepts, as we have already shown, are not substantively dissimilar, as both models make use of the concept of multiple subpopulations, albeit with differing representations. As with Spears tagging, our model, here called *a diffusable cooperative coevolutionary genetic algorithm* (DCCGA), segregates individuals into specific subpopulations by means of a binary tag in the chromosome. These tags are subject to mutation at a differing rate than the other bits (the rate of diffusion), allowing parents of one generation to yield offspring that belong to a different species.

The DCCGA model, however, still subdivides the problem into cooperating populations, each representative of arguments in the function. Like Potter's model, collaborators are chosen as representatives for evaluation, and each subpopulation is evolved mutually.

The application of such a tagging scheme allows for the possibility of more species than arguments for the function; though, since the number of possible distinct species (S_o) is given as follows:

$$S_o = 2^n,$$

where n is the number of bits in the tag.

With this observation, it becomes imperative that we draw a distinction between *niche* and *species*. In the DCCGA, a *niche* is an ecological space where individuals from that space represent encoded values for a particular argument of a given function. On the other hand, a *species* is a population where the individuals of that population can interbreed, but cannot breed outside of that population. In the case of the DCCGA, there may be more than one species that fill a particular niche. Indeed, more often than not, there will be several occurrences of 2 species which representative of the same niche, i.e. two different tags represent the same parameter.

In our case, the solution is to construct a table to map each species tag to an appropriate niche. Such a mapping necessitates that there be some degree of overlap. The table is constructed sequentially, by consecutively assigning each tag to a function argument, overlapping when necessary. For example, in the case of a function which requires 5 variables, the smallest S_o which can be used is 8 (3 bits, $2^3 = 8$). As such, the following table can be constructed:

Tag	Function Argument
000	x_1
001	x_2
010	x_3
011	x_4
100	x_5
101	x_1
110	x_2
111	x_3

Tab. 1. Table illustrating the mapping of species to niche for a 5 variable function

We can see from this table that, in three cases (x_1, x_2, and x_3) there will be two different species that contain individuals representing potential values for each variable.

The next issue is that of how a single collaborator can be chosen between the two populations. In our DCCGA, this is done by simply selecting the collaborator from the subpopulation with the highest average fitness. Such a resolution is by no means the only solution to this issue, nor the most sophisticated, but should suffice for the general case.

Another issue that arises from the application of diffusion to Potter's model is that of the potential for extinction. Since the tags are subject to mutation, the population sizes are dynamic. While this is, in part the intended goal of this addition, it also serves to bring about a condition from which no evaluation is possible: extinction of all the species covering a specific niche. To resolve this, a certain degree of preservation is necessary. Here we choose to preserve the best 10% of each subpopulation. This alleviates this issue by establishing an implicit minimum population size for each species, although presents the possibility of a loss of diversity in species which have a depleted population size due to diffusion.

There are several advantages to this technique. First of all, subpopulation sizes are dynamic, consequently the search may favor one argument over another. Also, diffusion brings the gene pool of a population possible diversity benefits, in particular for asymmetric functions. In addition, the overall process is more natural, allowing for the possibility of an individual being born genetically dissimilar to its parents such that it is no longer of the same species. This indicates the possibility of future research using similar methods to provide more natural mechanisms of species creation and extinction in the dynamic CCGA approaches discussed by Potter in his dissertation (Potter, 1997). Some ideas to this end are discussed in the conclusion of this paper.

4. Experimental Results

In order to provide a thorough study, each of 12 experimental groups were used to optimize a total of 5 different functions. The groups were constructed in order to compare results of a standard GA, both with and without tagging (SSGA), CCGA, and DCCGA techniques. To get a clearer picture regarding the effect of diffusion, the diffusion rate is varied. The groups are shown below in table 2, on the following page.

With the obvious exception of those parameters listed in table 2, the parameters chosen remained consistent for all runs of all groups. These are as follows:

Representation:	binary (16 bits per function variable)
Selection:	fitness proportionate with linear scaling
Mutation:	bit-flip, $p_m=1/L$ (where L is the length of the chromosome)
Crossover:	two-point, $p_c=0.60$
Population:	100 individuals per population
Termination:	100,000 function evaluations

The functions chosen to optimize, as well as the above parameters, were chosen primarily for similarity of Potter's study. Indeed the functions optimized in this study, listed in the table 3 (also found on the following page), represent the very same functions that Potter and De Jong used in their 1994 study of CCGAs.

Experimental Group	Description of Group	Elite Preserved	Rate of diffusion
GAv1	Standard elite genetic algorithm	1	0.00
GAv2	Elite genetic algorithm	10	0.00
CCGAv1	Potter's cooperative coevolutionary genetic algorithm	1	0.00
CCGAv2	Potter's cooperative coevolutionary genetic algorithm	10	0.00
DCCGA0	Diffusable genetic algorithm	10	0.00
DCCGA2	Diffusable genetic algorithm	10	0.02
DCCGA5	Diffusable genetic algorithm	10	0.05
DCCGA10	Diffusable genetic algorithm	10	0.10
SSGA0	Simple subpopulation GA (Spears tagging)	10	0.00
SSGA2	Simple subpopulation GA (Spears tagging)	10	0.02
SSGA5	Simple subpopulation GA (Spears tagging)	10	0.05
SSGA10	Simple subpopulation GA (Spears tagging)	10	0.10

Tab. 2. Table describing the groups used in the experiment.

Definition	Range & Values
$f_1(\vec{x}) = -c_1 \cdot \exp\left(-c_2\sqrt[2]{\dfrac{1}{n}\sum_{i=1}^{n}x_i^2}\right) - \exp\left(\dfrac{1}{n}\sum_{i=1}^{n}\cos(c_3 x_i)\right) + c_1 + e$	-30.0..30.0 $n = 30$ $c_1 = 20$ $c_2 = 0.2$ $c_3 = 2\pi$
$f_2(\vec{x}) = 1 + \sum_{i=1}^{n}\dfrac{x_i^2}{4000} - \prod_{i=1}^{n}\cos\left(\dfrac{x_i}{\sqrt{i}}\right)$	-600.0..600.0 $n = 10$
$f_3(\vec{x}) = 418.9829n + \sum_{i=1}^{n} x_i \cdot \sin(\sqrt{|x_i|})$	-500.0..500.0 $n = 10$
$f_4(\vec{x}) = 3.0n + \sum_{i=1}^{n} x_i^2 - 3.0 \cdot \cos(2\pi x_i)$	-5.12..5.12 $n = 20$
$f_5(\vec{x}) = 100(x_1^2 - x_2^2)^2 + (1 - x_1^2)^2$	-2.048..2.048

Tab. 3. Table describing the functions that were optimized in the experiment.

In all cases the true global minimum of the function is zero. In all but two cases, this minimum is found at the point $\vec{x} = (0,0, \cdots)$. For the function f_3, the minimum value of zero can be found at the point $\vec{x} = (420.9687, 420.9687, \cdots)$; however, in the case of f_5, the zero value is found at point $\vec{x} = (1,1)$.

The results for solution value are shown in table 4 below. Each group was run for each function 20 times. The results reported below indicate the average of the "best-ever" values found in the 100,000 evaluations of each trial.

	f_1	f_2	f_3	f_4	f_5
GAv1	1.59E+01	8.89E+00	2.91E+01	4.16E+02	3.63E-03
GAv2	1.24E+01	8.39E-02	1.15E+01	4.23E+01	5.38E-05
CCGAv1	1.7E+00	6.05E-01	2.91E-01	3.86E-01	1.58E-04
CCGAv2	3.89E-01	2.18E-01	3.89E+00	4.47E-01	2.79E-04
DCCGA0	9.15E-01	5.21E-01	4.93E+00	3.38E-01	6.08E-04
DCCGA2	4.86E-01	5.27E-01	6.75E+00	3.74E-01	3.35E-04
DCCGA5	4.71E-01	6.11E-01	3.70E+00	2.35E-01	1.86E-04
DCCGA10	5.19E-01	6.43E-01	5.79E+00	1.41E-01	3.40E-04
SSGA0	1.99E+01	7.42E+00	3.84E+01	8.67E+02	2.13E-02
SSGA2	2.03E+01	1.05E+01	1.05E+02	1.83E+03	3.31E-02
SSGA5	2.03E+01	1.05E+01	1.25E+02	1.99E+03	3.84E-02
SSGA10	2.02E+01	2.76E+00	1.33E+02	2.08E+03	1.21E-02

Tab. 4. Table displaying the solution quality results for all 5 functions and 12 experimental groups. These values represent averages across 20 trials.

	f_1	f_2	f_3	f_4	f_5
GAv1	2.67E+00	1.54E+01	3.39E+01	5.58E+02	1.32E-02
GAv2	4.92E+00	5.09E-02	1.48E+01	9.25E+01	1.31E-04
CCGAv1	6.45E-01	2.18E-01	3.68E-01	5.90E-01	2.26E-04
CCGAv2	5.16E-01	7.90E-02	2.13E+00	1.26E+00	2.83E-04
DCCGA0	3.74E-01	2.22E-01	3.18E+00	5.90E-01	7.13E-04
DCCGA2	4.70E-01	2.05E-01	3.14E+00	7.49E-01	3.23E-04
DCCGA5	6.18E-01	1.97E-01	2.89E+00	2.43E-01	2.83E-04
DCCGA10	1.21E+00	1.74E-01	3.52E+00	1.34E-01	3.11E-04
SSGA0	1.98E-01	1.76E+01	2.47E+01	1.27E+02	4.15E-02
SSGA2	1.70E-01	2.11E+01	9.75E+00	1.30E+02	3.99E-02
SSGA5	2.20E-01	2.11E+01	1.02E+01	2.16E+02	6.05E-02
SSGA10	1.72E-01	3.64E+00	3.69E+01	6.21E+02	2.39E-02

Tab. 5. Table displaying the standard deviation of solution results across 20 trials for all 5 functions and 12 experimental groups.

5. Conclusion

Clearly, from the table above, it can be seen that the DCCGA technique was not wholly beneficial in all cases. Indeed, although the DCCGA performs quite well in most of these cases, finding the solution to each function with higher quality than the GA groups and the CCGAv1 group, still it remains obvious that the diffusive techniques were not clearly demonstrated as the reason for increased performance. For the most part, the technique that solved for the higher solution quality in these cases was the CCGAv2 group, the non-diffusive cooperative coevolutionary approach with the higher degree (10%) of elitist preservation imposed. This would seem to suggest that the primary benefit of the algorithm's method was due to its preservation policy, for these functions.

However, having stated that, there is certainly evidence that the diffusion technique *was* beneficial, albeit not the primary contributor to the increased performance. First, functions f_4 and f_5 performed better than the CCGA with 10% elite preservation applied (CCGAv2), although f_5 still did not perform as well as CCGAv1 or GAv2. Secondly, the table above clearly indicates a variation of solution quality depending on the amount of diffusion applied. Moreover, some degree of consistency can be seen in terms of the optimal diffusion rate. In three of the five cases the best diffusion rate was 5%. In the case of f_2, however, it is clear from the above results that the higher degree of elitism was most responsible for the greater solution quality. Further, in four of the five cases the standard deviation was lowest within the DCCGA groups at a rate of diffusion of 5%. In the abhorrent case, function f_2, the best rate was curiously 10%, though the better solution quality occurred with no diffusion (0%). This would seem to suggest that a diffusion rate of 5% would be a good starting point for general problems, but that it may be necessary to tune it for a given function for achieving better results.

There are several possible reasons for the mediocre performance of the DCCGA. First, there exists no real pressure for the model to tune subpopulation size. Future studies of this technique should consider providing a more competitive system for species vying for the same niche. This can be done in many ways, but one such way is to make the diffusion rate increase for a given subpopulation that was not selected to allow the contribution of a collaborator.

Alternatively, diffusion could be presenting added diversity benefits at the start of a run, but impose more disruptive effects as the algorithm converges. A possible solution to this problem might be to reduce the rate of diffusion as the system converges and stabilizes.

Another reason for the poorer than expected performance of this study's model, is the nature of the functions chosen. These functions, chosen for consistency with Potter's studies (Potter et al., 1994) are, for the most part, symmetric along all of their axes. Aside from some ancillary diversity benefit that diffusion in a coevolutionary system might bring to such a function, tuning of the subpopulation sizes may be wholly unnecessary. Future research will consider more asymmetric functions.

Also, there is room for more serious applications of the DCCGA technique in other systems. For instance, in Mitchell Potter's dissertation (Potter, 1997), he explores using a CCGA to build a neural network by constructing the hidden layers, and tuning the initial network. In this model the hidden layers are represented by individual species which are dynamic in the sense that species are created and become extinct (according to certain rules) as the model finds a solution. A variation of our technique could be used to allow diffusion to be the driving force for the creation and extinction of species. Providing a mechanism to restrict mating of an individual to a group of tags within a specified range, and evaluating by finding components based on discrete groupings of the tags could accomplish this.

The diffusable cooperative coevolutionary model offers many interesting future possibilities for study. Moreover, this study shows that there are more benefits to the DCCGA which remain largely unexplored. We intend to provide further examinations of these issues in the future.

References

1. Cohoon, J. P., Hegde, S. U., Martin, W. N., and Richards, D. "Punctuated equilibria: A parallel genetic algorithm". In: Proceedings of the Second International Conference on Genetic Algorithms. Lawrence Erlbaum Associates (1987) 148-154.
2. Goldberg, D. E. Genetic Algorithms in Search, Optimization, and Machine Learning. Addison-Wesley Reading, MA (1989)
3. Goldberg, D. E. and Richardson, J. "Genetic algorithms with sharing for multimodal function optimization. In: Proceedings of the Third International Conference on Genetic Algorithms. Morgan Kaufmann, Fairfax, VA (1987) 42-50
4. Fogel, D. B. "Unearthing a Fossil from the History of Evolutionary Computation." To appear in: Fundamenta Informaticae. IOS Press (to appear).
5. Holland, J. Adaptation in Natural and Artificial Systems. The MIT Press, Cambridge, MA (1992)
6. Potter, M. A. and De Jong, K. "A Cooperative Coevolutionary Approach to Function Optimization." In: The Third Parallel Problem Solving from Nature. Springer-Verlag, New York (1994) 249-257
7. Potter, M. A. "The Design and Analysis of a Computational Model of Cooperative Coevolution" (Doctoral dissertation, George Mason University). (1997)
8. Schlierkamp-Voosen, D. and Mühlenbein, H. "Strategy Adaptation by Compteting Subpopulations". In: Parallel Problem Solving form Nature (PPSN III). Springer, Jerusalem (1994) 199-208
9. Spears, W. "Simple subpopulation schemes". In: Proceedings of the Third conference on Evolutionary Programming. World Scientific (1994) 297-307
10.Tanese, R. "Distributed genetic algorithms. In: Proceedings of the Third International Conference on Genetic Algorithms. Morgan Kaufmann (1989) 434-439.

Cellular Automata, Fuzzy Systems and Neural Networks

Studying Parallel Evolutionary Algorithms: The Cellular Programming Case

Mathieu Capcarrère,[1] Andrea Tettamanzi,[2] Marco Tomassini,[3] and Moshe Sipper[1]

[1] Logic Systems Laboratory, Swiss Federal Institute of Technology, 1015 Lausanne, Switzerland. E-mail: name.surname@di.epfl.ch, Web: lslwww.epfl.ch.
[2] Department of Computer Science, University of Milano, Via Comelico 39/41, 20135 Milano, Italy. E-mail: tettaman@dsi.unimi.it, Web: eolo.usr.dsi.unimi.it/~tettaman/.
[3] Institute of Computer Science, University of Lausanne, 1015 Lausanne, Switzerland. E-mail: Marco.Tomassini@iismail.unil.ch, Web: www-iis.unil.ch.

Abstract. Parallel evolutionary algorithms, studied to some extent over the past few years, have proven empirically worthwhile—though there seems to be lacking a better understanding of their workings. In this paper we concentrate on cellular (fine-grained) models, presenting a number of statistical measures, both at the genotypic and phenotypic levels. We demonstrate the application and utility of these measures on a specific example, that of the cellular programming evolutionary algorithm, when used to evolve solutions to a hard problem in the cellular-automata domain, known as synchronization.

1 Introduction

Parallel evolutionary algorithms have been studied to some extent over the past few years. A basic tenet of such parallel algorithms is that the population has a spatial structure. A number of models based on this observation have been proposed, the two most important being the *island* model and the *grid* model. The coarse-grained island model features geographically separated subpopulations of relatively large size. Subpopulations exchange information by having some individuals migrate from one subpopulation to another with a given frequency and according to various migrational patterns. This can work to offset premature convergence, by periodically reinjecting diversity into otherwise converging subpopulations. In the fine-grained grid model individuals are placed on a d-dimensional grid (where $d = 1, 2, 3$ is used in practice), one individual per grid location (this location is often referred to as a *cell*, and hence the fine-grained approach is also known as *cellular*). Fitness evaluation is done simultaneously for all individuals, with genetic operators (selection, crossover, mutation) taking place locally within a small neighborhood. From an implementation point of view, coarse-grained island models, where the ratio of computation to communication is high, are more adapted to multiprocessor systems or workstation clusters, whereas fine-grained cellular models are better suited for massively parallel machines or specialized hardware. Hybrid models are also possible, e.g., one might consider an island model in which each island is structured as a grid of locally interacting individuals. For a recent review of parallel evolutionary algorithms (including several references) the reader is referred to [16].

Though such parallel models have proven empirically worthwhile [1, 4, 7, 8, 10, 15, 17], there seems to be lacking a better understanding of their workings. Gaining insight into the mechanisms of parallel evolutionary algorithms calls for the introduction of statistical measures of analysis. This is the underlying motivation of our paper. Specifically, concentrating on cellular models, our objectives are: (1) to introduce several statistical measures of interest, both at the genotypic and phenotypic levels, that are useful for analyzing the workings of fine-grained parallel evolutionary algorithms, and (2) to demonstrate the application and utility of these measures on a specific example, that of the cellular programming evolutionary algorithm [12]. Among the few theoretical works carried out to date, one can cite Mühlenbein [9], Cantú-Paz and Goldberg [2], and Rudolph and Sprave [11]. The latter treated a special case of fine-grained cellular algorithms, studying its convergence properties; however, they did not present statistical measures as done herein.

We begin in Section 2 by describing the cellular programming evolutionary algorithm and the synchronization task. Section 3 introduces basic formal definitions, and various statistical measures used in the analysis of cellular evolutionary algorithms. In Section 4, we apply the statistics of Section 3 to analyze the cellular programming algorithm when used to evolve solutions to the synchronization problem. Finally, we conclude in Section 5.

2 Evolving Cellular Automata

2.1 Cellular automata

Our evolving machines are based on the cellular automata model. Cellular automata (CA) are dynamical systems in which space and time are discrete. A cellular automaton consists of an array of cells, each of which can be in one of a finite number of possible states, updated synchronously in discrete time steps, according to a local, identical interaction rule. The state of a cell at the next time step is determined by the previous states of a surrounding neighborhood of cells. This transition is usually specified in the form of a *rule table*, delineating the cell's next state for each possible neighborhood configuration [12]. The cellular array (grid) is d-dimensional, where $d = 1, 2, 3$ is used in practice; in this paper we shall concentrate on $d = 1$. For such one-dimensional CAs, a cell is connected to r local neighbors (cells) on either side, where r is a parameter referred to as the radius (thus, each cell has $2r + 1$ neighbors, including itself).

The model investigated in this paper is an extension of the CA model, termed *non-uniform cellular automata* [12, 14]. Such automata function in the same way as uniform ones, the only difference being in the cellular rules that need not be identical for all cells. Our main focus is on the *evolution* of non-uniform CAs to perform computational tasks, using the cellular programming approach. Thus, rather than seek a *single* rule that must be universally applied to all cells in the grid, each cell is allowed to "choose" its own rule through evolution.

2.2 The cellular programming algorithm

Each cell of the non-uniform, $r = 1$ CA contains an 8-bit genome, which defines its rule table. Our interest is in evolving these initially random genomes so that the CA as a whole comes to perform a given task. The CA is presented with a random initial configuration and runs for a fixed number of time steps. Observing the final steps, cells that exhibit good performance on the task at hand are assigned a fitness score of 1, while the other cells are assigned a score of 0. This is repeated for several hundred random configurations, thus allowing each cell to accumulate fitness points. Low-fitness cells then replace their genomes with the crossed-over and mutated genomes of their higher-fitness neighbors. The evolutionary process continually alternates between a series of random initial configurations (fitness runs) and the application of genetic operators (in a local manner). For details see [12, 13].

2.3 The synchronization task

The one-dimensional synchronization task was introduced by Das *et al.* [5], and studied by Hordijk [6] and Sipper [12, 13], the latter using non-uniform CAs. In this task the CA, given any initial configuration, must reach a final configuration, within M time steps, that oscillates between all 0s and all 1s on successive time steps. The synchronization task comprises a non-trivial computation for a small-radius CA. Using cellular programming we evolved non-uniform CAs that successfully solve this task. Fitness was computed by considering the last four time steps for a given initial configuration, with each cell in the largest block of cells oscillating in the correct manner receiving a fitness score of one.

3 Statistical Measures

3.1 Basic definitions and notation

In this section we formally define the basic elements used in this paper. A *population* is a collection of individuals (cells), each represented by a genotype. A genotype is not necessarily unique—it may occur several times in the population. In addition, as the population considered has a topology, the spatial distribution of the genotypes is of interest. Let n be the number of individuals in the system. Let R_i, $1 \leq i \leq n$ be the genome of the ith individual. Let Γ be the space of genotypes and $G(\Gamma)$ be the space of all possible populations. Let $f(\gamma)$ be the fitness of an individual having genotype $\gamma \in \Gamma$. When the cells are arranged in a row, as is the case in the example of Section 2, a population can be defined as a vector of n genotypes $x = (R_1, \ldots, R_n)$.

For all populations $x \in G(\Gamma)$, an occupancy function $n_x \colon \Gamma \to N$ is defined, such that, for all $\gamma \in \Gamma$, $n_x(\gamma)$ is the number of individuals in x sharing the same genotype γ, i.e., the occupancy number of γ in x. The size of population x, $\|x\|$, is defined as $\|x\| \equiv \sum_{\gamma \in \Gamma} n_x(\gamma)$.

We can now define a share function $q_x: \Gamma \to [0,1]$ giving the fraction $q_x(\gamma)$ of individuals in x that have genotype γ, i.e., $q_x(\gamma) = n_x(\gamma)/\|x\|$.

Consider the probability space $(\Gamma, 2^\Gamma, \mu)$, where 2^Γ is the algebra of the parts of Γ and μ is any probability measure on Γ. Let us denote by $\tilde{\mu}$ the probability of generating a population $x \in G(\Gamma)$ by extracting n genotypes from Γ according to measure μ. It can be shown that it is sufficient to know either of the two measures—μ (over the genotypes) or $\tilde{\mu}$ (over the populations)—in order to reconstruct the other.

The fitness function establishes a morphism from genotypes into real numbers. If genotypes are distributed over Γ according to a given probability measure μ, then their fitness will be distributed over the reals according to a probability measure ϕ obtained from μ by applying the same morphism. This can be summarized by the following diagram:

$$
\begin{array}{ccc}
\Gamma & \xrightarrow{\ f\ } & \mathbb{R} \\[2pt]
\wr & & \wr \\[2pt]
\mu & & \phi
\end{array}
\tag{1}
$$

The probability $\phi(v)$ of a given fitness value $v \in [0, +\infty)$ is defined as the probability that an individual extracted from Γ according to measure μ has fitness v (or, if we think of fitness values as a continuous space, the probability density of fitness v): for all $v \in [0, +\infty)$, $\phi(v) = \mu(f^{-1}(v))$, where $f^{-1}(v) \equiv \{\gamma \in \Gamma : f(\gamma) = v\}$.

An evolutionary algorithm can be regarded as a time-discrete stochastic process

$$
\{X_t(\omega)\}_{t=0,1,2,\ldots},
\tag{2}
$$

having the probability space $(\Omega, \mathcal{F}, P)$ as its base space, $(G(\Gamma), 2^{G(\Gamma)})$ as its state space, and the natural numbers as the set of times, here called *generations*. Ω might be thought of as the set of all the evolutionary trajectories, $\mathcal{F}$ is a σ-algebra on Ω, and P is a probability measure over $\mathcal{F}$.

The transition function of the evolutionary process, in turn based on the definition of the genetic operators, defines a sequence of probability measures over the generations.

Let $\tilde{\mu}_t$ denote the probability measure on the state space at time t; for all populations $x \in G(\Gamma)$,

$$
\tilde{\mu}_t(x) = P\{\omega \in \Omega : X_t(\omega) = x\}.
\tag{3}
$$

In the same way, let μ_t denote the probability measure on space $(\Gamma, 2^\Gamma)$ at time t; for all $\gamma \in \Gamma$,

$$
\mu_t(\gamma) = P[\kappa = \gamma \,|\, \kappa \in X_t(\omega)].
\tag{4}
$$

Similarly, we define the sequence of probability functions $\phi_t(\cdot)$ as follows: for all $v \in [0, +\infty)$ and $t \in N$,

$$
\phi_t(v) = \mu_t(f^{-1}(v)).
\tag{5}
$$

In the next two subsections we introduce several statistics pertaining to cellular evolutionary algorithms: genotypic statistics, which embody aspects related to the genotypes of individuals in a population, and phenotypic statistics, which concern properties of individual performance (fitness) for the problem at hand. Keeping in mind the synchronization problem studied herein, we concentrate on a one-dimensional spatial structure. We present a more complete set of measures as well as detailed proofs of the propositions given below in [3].

3.2 Genotypic statistics

One important class of statistics consists of various genotypic diversity indices (within the population) whose definitions are based on the occupancy and share functions delineated below.

Occupancy and share functions. At any time $t \in N$, for all $\gamma \in \Gamma$, $n_{X_t}(\gamma)$ is a discrete random variable with binomial distribution

$$P[n_{X_t}(\gamma) = k] = \binom{n}{k} \mu_t(\gamma)^k [1 - \mu_t(\gamma)]^{n-k}; \tag{6}$$

thus, $E[n_{X_t}(\gamma)] = n\mu_t(\gamma)$ and $\text{Var}[n_{X_t}(\gamma)] = n\mu_t(\gamma)[1 - \mu_t(\gamma)]$. The share function $q_{X_t}(\gamma)$ is perhaps more interesting, because it is an estimator of the probability measure $\mu_t(\gamma)$; its mean and variance can be calculated from those of $n_{X_t}(\gamma)$, yielding

$$E[q_{X_t}(\gamma)] = \mu_t(\gamma) \quad \text{and} \quad \text{Var}[q_{X_t}(\gamma)] = \frac{\mu_t(\gamma)[1 - \mu_t(\gamma)]}{n}. \tag{7}$$

Structure. Statistics in this category measure properties of the population structure, that is, how individuals are spatially distributed.

Frequency of transitions. The frequency of transitions $\nu(x)$ of a population x of n individuals (cells) is defined as the number of borders between homogeneous blocks of cells having the same genotype, divided by the number of distinct couples of adjacent cells. Another way of putting it is that $\nu(x)$ is the probability that two adjacent individuals (cells) have different genotypes, i.e., belong to two different blocks.

Formally, the frequency of transitions $\nu(x)$ for a one-dimensional grid structure can be expressed as

$$\nu(x) = \frac{1}{n} \sum_{i=1}^{n} \left[R_i \neq R_{(i \bmod n)+1} \right], \tag{8}$$

where $[P]$ denotes the indicator function of proposition P.

Diversity. There are a number of concievable ways to measure genotypic diversity, two of which we define below: population entropy, and the probability that two individuals in the population have different genotypes.

Entropy. The entropy of a population x of size n is defined as

$$H(x) = \sum_{\gamma \in \Gamma} q_x(\gamma) \log \frac{1}{q_x(\gamma)}. \tag{9}$$

Entropy takes on values in the interval $[0, \log n]$ and attains its maximum, $H(x) = \log n$, when x comprises n different genotypes.

Diversity indices. The probability that two individuals randomly chosen from x have different genotypes is denoted by $D(x)$.

Index $D(X_t)$ is an estimator of quantity

$$\sum_{\gamma \in \Gamma} \mu_t(\gamma) \left(1 - \mu_t(\gamma)\right) = 1 - \sum_{\gamma \in \Gamma} \mu_t(\gamma)^2, \tag{10}$$

which relates to the "breadth" of measure μ_t.

Proposition 1 *Let x be a population of n individuals with genotypes in Γ. Then,*

$$D(x) = \frac{n}{n-1} \sum_{\gamma \in \Gamma} q_x(\gamma)(1 - q_x(\gamma)). \tag{11}$$

Proof. See [3].

We observe that for all populations $x \in G(\Gamma)$,

$$D(x) \geq \frac{H(x)}{\log n}. \tag{12}$$

One can observe that $D(x)$ rises more steeply than entropy as diversity increases.

An interesting relationship between D and ν is given by the following proposition.

Proposition 2 *Given a random one-dimensional linear population x of size n, the expected frequency of transitions will be given by*

$$E[\nu(x)] = D(x). \tag{13}$$

Proof. See [3].

3.3 Phenotypic statistics

Phenotypic statistics deal with properties of phenotypes, which means, primarily, fitness. Associated with a population x of individuals, there is a fitness distribution. We will denote by ϕ_x its (discrete) probability function.

Performance. The performance of population x is defined as its average fitness, or the expected fitness of an individual randomly extracted from x, $E[\phi_x]$.

Diversity. The most straightforward measure of phenotypic diversity of a population x is the variance of its fitness distribution, $\sigma^2(x) = \text{Var}[\phi_x]$.

Structure. Statistics in this category measure how fitness is spatially distributed across the individuals in a population.

Ruggedness. Ruggedness measures the dependency of an individual's fitness on its neighbors' fitnesses. For a one-dimensional population, x, of size n, $x \in G(\Gamma)$, ruggedness can be defined as follows:

$$\rho^2(x) = \frac{1}{n} \sum_{i=1}^{n} \left[1 - \frac{1 + 2f(R_i)}{1 + f(R_{(i \bmod n)+1}) + f(R_{(i-2 \bmod n)+1})} \right]^2. \tag{14}$$

Notice that $\rho^2(x)$ is independent of the fitness magnitude in population x, i.e., of performance $E[\phi_x]$.

4   Results and Analysis

Using the different measures presented in the previous section we analyzed the processes taking place during the execution of the cellular programming algorithm presented in Section 2. This was carried out for the synchronization task for CAs of size 150. The results are based on 75 runs. (Additional tasks are studied in [3].)

The evolutionary dynamics of the synchronization task were found to exhibit at most three fitness phases: a low-fitness phase, followed by a rapid-increase phase, ending with a high-fitness phase. Note that for this task a successful run is considered to be one where a perfect fitness value of 1.0 is attained. The evolutionary runs can be classified into four distinct classes, two of which represent successful runs (Figures 1a and 1b), the other two representing unsuccessful runs (Figures 1c and 1d). The classification is based on the number of phases exhibited during evolution. We first present some general trends, followed by detailed results of our experiments according to these three fitness phases.

In all runs the entropy (H) falls from a high of approximately 0.8 to a low of approximately 0.7 within the first 20 generations, and from then on generally tends to decline. Though this decline is not monotonic, the entropy always ends up below 0.4. This fall in entropy is due to two factors. First, we observed in all runs a steep drop in the transition frequency (ν) in the first few generations, followed by an almost continuous drop in the subsequent generations. Though it may be intuitive that, given the possibility of rule replication between neighboring cells after each generation, blocks will tend to form, our measures now provide us with quantitative evidence. We noted that the transition frequency

(ν) progresses towards an oscillatory state about values below 0.3. The second factor involved in the lower entropy is the number of rules. One can see directly that low ν implies few rules. This is corroborated by the diversity (D) measure's decreasing trend.

For the the task studied herein the objective is to reach a high average fitness over the entire population, rather than consider just the highest-fitness individual cell. Thus, intuitively we can expect that the phenotypic variance will tend to be minimized, and we can factually check that both the fitness variance (σ^2) and ruggedness (ρ^2) are always very low towards the end of an evolutionary run. Usually the evolved CA had less than 10 different rules out of the 256 possible ones. We now detail the fitness phases.

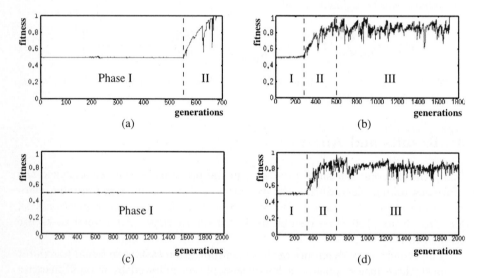

Fig. 1. The evolutionary runs for the synchronization task can be classified into four distinct classes, based on the three observed fitness phases: phase I (low fitness), phase II (rapid fitness increase), and phase III (high fitness). (a) Successful run, exhibiting but the first two phases. The solution is found at the end of phase II. (b) Successful run, exhibiting all three phases. The solution is found at the end of phase III. (c) Unsuccessful run, "stuck" in phase I. (d) Unsuccessful run, exhibiting all three phases. Phase III does not give rise to a perfect solution.

Phase I: Low fitness. This phase is characterized by an average fitness of 0.5, with an extremely low fitness variance. However, while exhibiting phenotypic (fitness) "calmness," this phase is marked by high underlying genotypic activity: the entropy (H) steadily decreases, and the number of rules strongly diminishes. An unsuccessful type-c run (Figure 1c) results from "genotypic failure" in this phase. To explain this, let us first note that for the synchronization task, only rules with neighborhoods 111 mapped to 0 and 000 mapped to 1 may appear in a successful solution. This is the "good" quadrant of the rule space, whereas the "bad" quadrant is the one that comprises rules mapping 111 to 1 and 000 to 0. The low fitness variance, indicating a weak selection pressure, may explain why, in type-c runs, the grid evolves towards the bad quadrant. Only the mutation operator can possibly hoist the evolutionary process out of this trap. However, it is usually insufficient in itself, at least with the mutation rate used herein (0.001). Thus, in such a case the algorithm is stuck in a local minimum, and fitness never ascends beyond 0.53 (Figure 1c).

Phase II: Rapid fitness increase. A rapid increase of fitness characterizes this phase, its onset marked by the attainment of a 0.54 fitness value (at least). This comes about when a sufficiently large block of rules from the good quadrant emerges through the evolutionary process. In a relatively short time after this emergence (less than 100 generations), evolved rules over the entire grid all end up in the good quadrant of the rule space; this is coupled with a high fitness variance (σ^2). This variance then drops sharply, while the average fitness steadily increases, reaching a value of 0.8 at the end of this phase. Another characteristic of this phase is the sharp drop in entropy. On certain runs a perfect CA was found directly at the end of this stage, thus bringing the evolutionary process to a successful conclusion (Figure 1a).

Phase III: High fitness. The transition from phase II to phase III is not clear cut, but we observed that when a fitness of approximately 0.82 is reached, the fitness average then begins to oscillate between 0.65 and 0.99. During this phase the fitness variance also oscillates between approximately 0 and 0.3. While low, this variance is still higher than that of phase I. Whereas in phases I and II we observed a clear decreasing trend for entropy (H), in this phase entropy exhibits an oscillatory pattern between values of approximately 0.3 and 0.5. We conclude that when order (low entropy) is too high, disorder is reinjected into the evolutionary process, while remaining in the good quadrant of the rule space; hence the oscillatory behavior. On certain runs it took several hundred generations in this phase to evolve a perfect CA—this is a success of type b (Figure 1b). Finally, on other runs no perfect CA was found, though phase III was reached and very high fitness was attained. This is a type-d unsuccessful run (Figure 1d) which does not differ significantly from type-b successful runs.

5 Concluding Remarks

In this paper we introduced several statistical measures of interest, both at the genotypic and phenotypic levels, that are useful for analyzing the workings of fine-grained parallel evolutionary algorithms in general. We then demonstrated their application and utility on a specific example, that of the cellular programming evolutionary algorithm, which we employed to evolve solutions to the synchronization problem.

We observed the notable difference between activity at the genotypic level and at the phenotypic level, which we were able to study quantitatively. The synchronization task was seen to undergo (at most) three fitness phases, the nature of which (or the absence of which) served to distinguish between four types of evolutionary runs.

Parallel evolutionary algorithms have been receiving increased attention in recent years. Gaining a better understanding of their workings and of their underlying mechanisms thus presents an important research challenge. We hope that the work presented herein represents a small step in this direction.

References

1. D. Andre and J. R. Koza. Parallel genetic programming: A scalable implementation using the transputer network architecture. In P. Angeline and K. Kinnear, editors, *Advances in Genetic Programming 2*, Cambridge, MA, 1996. The MIT Press.
2. E. Cantú-Paz and D. E. Goldberg. Modeling idealized bounding cases of parallel genetic algorithms. In J. R. Koza, K. Deb, M. Dorigo, D. B. Fogel, M. Garzon, H. Iba, and R. L. Riolo, editors, *Genetic Programming 1997: Proceedings of the Second Annual Conference*, pages 353–361, San Francisco, 1997. Morgan Kaufmann Publishers.
3. M. Capcarrère, A. Tettamanzi, M. Tomassini, and M. Sipper. A statistical study of a class of cellular evolutionary algorithms. *Submitted*, 1998.
4. J. P. Cohoon, S. U. Hedge, W. N. Martin, and D. Richards. Punctuated equilibria: A parallel genetic algorithm. In J. J. Grefenstette, editor, *Proceedings of the Second International Conference on Genetic Algorithms*, page 148. Lawrence Erlbaum Associates, 1987.
5. R. Das, J. P. Crutchfield, M. Mitchell, and J. E. Hanson. Evolving globally synchronized cellular automata. In L. J. Eshelman, editor, *Proceedings of the Sixth International Conference on Genetic Algorithms*, pages 336–343, San Francisco, CA, 1995. Morgan Kaufmann.
6. W. Hordijk. The structure of the synchonizing-ca landscape. Technical Report 96-10-078, Santa Fe Institute, Santa Fe, NM (USA), 1996.
7. A. Loraschi, A. Tettamanzi, M. Tomassini, and P. Verda. Distributed genetic algorithms with an application to portfolio selection problems. In *Proceedings of the International Conference on Artificial Neural Networks and Genetic Algorithms*, pages 384–387. Springer-Verlag, New-York, 1995.
8. B. Manderick and P. Spiessens. Fine-grained parallel genetic algorithms. In J. D. Schaffer, editor, *Proceedings of the Third International Conference on Genetic Algorithms*, page 428. Morgan Kaufmann, 1989.
9. H. Mühlenbein. Evolution in time and space–the parallel genetic algorithm. In Gregory J. E. Rawlins, editor, *Foundations Of Genetic Algorithms I*. Morgann Kaufmann Publishers, 1991.
10. M. Oussaidene, B. Chopard, O. Pictet, and M. Tomassini. Parallel genetic programming and its application to trading model induction. *Parallel Computing*, 23:1183–1198, 1997.
11. G. Rudolph and J. Sprave. A cellular genetic algorithm with self-adjusting acceptance threshold. In *First IEE/IEEE International Conference on Genetic Algorithms in Engineering Systems: Innovations and Applications*, pages 365–372, London, 1995. IEE.
12. M. Sipper. *Evolution of Parallel Cellular Machines: The Cellular Programming Approach*. Springer-Verlag, Heidelberg, 1997.
13. M. Sipper. The evolution of parallel cellular machines: Toward evolware. *BioSystems*, 42:29–43, 1997.
14. M. Sipper. Computing with cellular automata: Three cases for nonuniformity. *Physical Review E*, 57(3):3589–3592, March 1998.
15. T. Starkweather, D. Whitley, and K. Mathias. Optimization using distributed genetic algorithms. In H.-P. Schwefel and R. Männer, editors, *Parallel Problem Solving from Nature*, volume 496 of *Lecture Notes in Computer Science*, page 176, Heidelberg, 1991. Springer-Verlag.
16. A. Tettamanzi and M. Tomassini. Evolutionary algorithms and their applications. In D. Mange and M. Tomassini, editors, *Bio-Inspired Computing Machines: Toward Novel Computational Architectures*, pages 59–98. Presses Polytechniques et Universitaires Romandes, Lausanne, Switzerland, 1998.
17. M. Tomassini. The parallel genetic cellular automata: Application to global function optimization. In R. F. Albrecht, C. R. Reeves, and N. C. Steele, editors, *Proceedings of the International Conference on Artificial Neural Networks and Genetic Algorithms*, pages 385–391. Springer-Verlag, 1993.

Learning to Avoid Moving Obstacles Optimally for Mobile Robots Using a Genetic-Fuzzy Approach

Kalyanmoy Deb, Dilip Kumar Pratihar, and Amitabha Ghosh

Kanpur Genetic Algorithms Laboratory (KanGAL)
Department of Mechanical Engineering
Indian Institute of Technology, Kanpur
Kanpur, Pin 208 016, India
E-mail: {deb, dkpra, amitabha}@iitk.ernet.in

Abstract. The task in a motion planning problem for a mobile robot is to find an obstacle-free path between a starting and a destination point, which will require the minimum possible time of travel. Although there exists many studies involving classical methods and using fuzzy logic controllers (FLCs), they are either computationally extensive or they do not attempt to find optimal controllers. The proposed genetic-fuzzy approach optimizes the travel time of a robot off-line by simultanously finding an optimal fuzzy rule base and optimal membership function distributions describing various values of condition and action variables of fuzzy rules. A mobile robot can then use this optimal FLC on-line to navigate in the presence of moving obstacles. The results of this study on a number of problems show that the proposed genetic-fuzzy approach can produce efficient rules and membership functions of an FLC for controlling the motion of a robot among moving obstacles.

1 Introduction

Building autonomous robots, which can plan its own motion during navigation through two-dimensional or three-dimensional terrains, has been one of the major areas of research in robotics [11,6,8]. Latombe [11] provides an extensive survey of different classical approaches of motion planning, particularly in the presence of stationary obstacles. Both graphical as well as analytical methods have been developed by several investigators to solve the mobile robot navigation problems among moving obstacles, known as dynamic motion planning problems. These methods include path velocity decomposition [6,8], accessibility graph technique [7], incremental planning [12], probabilistic approach [17], potential field approach [15,16,1], and others. Moreover, different learning techniques have also been used by researchers to improve the performance of conventional controllers [4,5].

Each of these methods has its own inherent limitations and is capable of solving only a particular type of problems. Canny and Reif [3] studied the computational complexity of some of these methods and showed that motion planning for a point robot in a two-dimensional plane with a bounded velocity is an

NP-hard problem, even when the moving obstacles are convex polygons moving at a constant linear velocity without rotation. Potential field method [15, 16, 1], in which a robot moves under the action of combined attractive and repulsive potentials created artificially, is the most widely used technique for solving dynamic motion planning problems. Since at every time step a new potential field must be created to find an obstacle-free direction, the method is local in nature and often has the chance of converging to a sub-optimal solution. Moreover, it is intuitive that many computation of such local travel directions using artificial potential field method may be computationally expensive.

To reduce the computational complexity, some heuristics have also been developed by several researchers. Fuzzy logic controllers (FLCs) have been used by several investigators in the recent past [2, 18, 14] to solve the dynamic motion planning problem. However, in all such studies, no effort is spent to find optimal FLCs (instead an FLC is designed based on a particular user-defined membership function and rules). With the availability of a versatile yet efficient optimization method (GA), optimal FLCs for dynamic motion planning problems can be developed, like they have been used in other applications of FLCs, such as the cart-pole balancing [10], cart centering [19], and others [9, 13].

In the present study, we concentrate on dynamic motion planning (DMP) problem, where the objective is to find an obstacle-free path between a starting point and a destination point, requiring the minimum possible time of travel. Since the DMP problem is unrealistic to solve on-line for every new scenario a robot faces, we convert the problem into a similar yet an approximate off-line optimization problem. The optimiation problem involves finding an optimal fuzzy rule base that the robot should use for navigation, when left in a number of author-defined scenarios of moving obstacles. Once the optimal rule base is obtained off-line, the robot can then use it on-line to navigate in other scenarios of moving obstacles.

In the remainder of this paper, we describe the genetic-fuzzy approach by drawing a simile of the motion planning problem with a natural learning process. The proposed approach incorporates some practical considerations, which, along with the use of a fuzzy logic controller, makes the overall approach easier to be used in practice. The efficacy of the proposed approach is demonstrated by solving a number of motion planning problems.

2 Proposed Genetic-Fuzzy Approach

We describe the genetic-fuzzy approach by drawing a connection between the motion planning problem with a natural learning process. The purpose of the DMP problem of a robot is to find an obstacle-free path which takes a robot from a point A to a point B with minimum time. There are essentially two parts of the problem:

1. Learn to find *any* obstacle-free path from point A to B, and
2. Learn to choose that obstacle-free path which takes the robot in a minimum possible time.

Both these problems are somewhat similar to the learning phases a child would go through while solving a similar obstacle-avoidance problem. If a child is kept in a similar (albeit hypothetical) situation (that is, a child has to go from one corner of a room to another by avoiding a few moving objects), the child learns to avoid an incoming obstacle by taking detour from its path. It is interesting that while taking the detour, it never calculates the precise angle of deviation form its path. This process of avoiding an object can be thought as if the child is using a rule of the following sort:

If an object is very near and is approaching, then turn right to the original path.

Because of the imprecise definition of the deviation in this problem, it seems natural to use a fuzzy logic technique in our study, instead of an exact representation of the deviation angle.

The second task of finding an optimal obstacle-free path arises from a simile of solving the same problem by an experienced versus an inexperienced child. An inexperienced child may take avoidance of *each* obstacle too seriously and deviate by a large angle each time it faces an obstacle. This way, this child may lead away from the target and take a long winding distance to reach the target. Whereas, an experienced child may deviate barely from each obstacle, thereby taking the quickest route to the target point. If we think about how the experienced child has learned this trick, the answer is through experience of solving many such similar problems in the past. Previous efforts helped the child find a set of good rules to do the task efficiently. This is precisely the task of an optimizer which needs to discover an optimal set of rules needed to avoid obstacles and to reach the target point in a minimum possible time. This is where the GA comes as a natural choice.

Thus, the use of fuzzy logic technique helps in quickly determining imprecise yet obstacle-free paths and the use of a GA helps in learning an optimal set of rules that a robot should use while navigating in presence of moving obstacles. This process is illustrated in Figure 1.

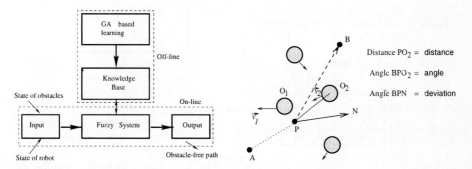

Fig. 1. Genetic-fuzzy approach

Fig. 2. A schematic showing condition and action variables

A GA is used to create the knowledge base (fuzzy rule base) of a robot off-line. For on-line application, the robot uses its optimal fuzzy rule base to find an obstacle-free path for a given input of parameters depicting the state of moving obstacles and the state of the robot.

2.1 Representation of a Solution

A solution to the DMP problem is represented by a set of rules which a robot will use to navigate from point A to point B (Figure 2). Each rule has three conditions: distance, angle, and relative velocity. The distance is the distance of the nearest obstacle forward from the robot. Four fuzzy values of distance is chosen: very near (VN), near (N), far (F), and very far (VF). The angle is the relative angle between the path joining the robot and the target point and the path to the nearest obstacle forward. The corresponding fuzzy values are left (L), ahead left (AL), ahead (A), ahead right (AR), and right (R). The relative velocity is the relative velocity vector of the nearest obstacle forward with respect to the robot. In our approach, we do not use this variable explicitly, instead follow a practical incremental procedure. Since, a robot can sense the position and velocity of each obstacle at any instant of time, the critical obstacle ahead of the robot can always be identified. In such a case (Figure 2), although an obstacle O_1 is nearer compared to another obstacle O_2, the relative velocity v_1 of O_1 directs away from robot's path towards the target point B and the relative velocity v_2 of O_2 directs towards the robot (Position P). Thus, the obstacle O_2 is assumed to be the critical obstacle forward.

The action variable is deviation of the robot from its path towards the target (Figure 2). This variable is considered to have five fuzzy values: L, AL, A, AR, and R. Triangular membership functions are considered for each membership function (Figure 3). Using this rule base, a typical rule will look like the following:

If distance is VN and angle is A, then deviation is AL.

With four choices for distance and five choices for angle, there could be a total of 4×5 or 20 valid rules possible. For each combination of condition variables, a suitable action value (author-defined) is associated, as shown in Table 1.

Table 1. All possible rules are shown

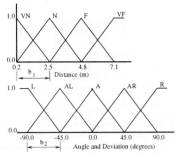

	angle				
distance	L	AL	A	AR	R
VN	A	AR	AL	AL	A
N	A	A	AL	A	A
F	A	A	AR	A	A
VF	A	A	A	A	A

Fig. 3. Author-defined membership functions

The task of GAs is to find which rules (out of 20) should be present in the optimal rule base. We represent the presence of a rule by a 1 and the absence by a 0. Thus, a complete solution will have a 20-bit length string of 1 and 0. The value of i-th position along the string marks the presence or absence of the i-th rule in the rule base.

2.2 Evaluating a Solution

A rule base (represented by a 20-bit binary string) is evaluated by simulating a robot's performance on a number of scenarios (say S) and by keeping track of the travel time T in each scenario. Since a robot may not reach the destination using an arbitrary rule base, the robot is allowed a maximum travel time. In this case, a penalty proportional to a time needed to cover the Euclidean distance from the final position to the target point is added to the allowed maximum travel time. An average of travel times in all S scenarios is used as the *fitness* of the solution.

The robot's complete path is a collection of a number of small straight line paths traveled for a constant time ΔT in each step. To make the matter as practical as possible, we have assumed that the robot starts from zero velocity and accelerates during the first quarter of the time ΔT and then maintains a constant velocity for the next one-half of ΔT and decelerates to zero velocity during the remaining quarter of the total time ΔT. For constant acceleration and deceleration rates (say a), the total distance covered during the small time step ΔT is $3a\Delta T^2/16$. At the end of the constant velocity travel, the robot senses the position and velocity of each obstacle and decides whether to continue moving in the same direction or to deviate from its path. This is achieved by first determining the predicted position of each obstacle, as follows:

$$P_{\text{predicted}} = P_{\text{present}} + (P_{\text{present}} - P_{\text{previous}}). \tag{1}$$

The predicted position is the linearly extrapolated position of an obstacle from its current position P_{present} along the path formed by joining the previous P_{previous} and present position. Thereafter, the nearest obstacle forward is determined based on $P_{\text{predicted}}$ values of all obstacles and fuzzy logic technique is applied to find the obstacle-free direction using the rule base dictated by the corresponding 20-bit string. If the robot has to change its path, its velocity is reduced to zero at the end of the time step; otherwise the robot does not decelerate and continues in the same direction with the same velocity $a\Delta T/4$. It is interesting to note that when the latter case happens (the robot does not change its course) in two consecutive time steps, there is a saving of $\Delta T/4$ second in travel time per such occasion. Overall time of travel (T) is then calculated by summing all intermediate time steps needed for the robot to reach its destination. This approach of robot navigation can be easily incorporated in a real-world scenario[1].

---

[1] In all the simulations here, we have chosen $\Delta T = 4$ sec and $a = 1$ m/s^2. These values make the velocity of the robot in the middle portion of each time step equal to 1 m/sec.

588

3 Results

We consider four different approaches:

Approach 1: Author-defined fuzzy-logic controller. A fixed set of 20 rules (Table 1) and author-defined membership functions (Figure 3) are used. No optimization method is used to find optimal rule base or to find the optimal membership function distributions.

Approach 2: Optimizing membership functions alone. Only the membership function distributions of condition and action variables are optimized. All 20 rules (Table 1) are used. The bases b_1 and b_2 (refer Figure 3) are coded in 10 bit substrings each. The parameters b_1 and b_2 are decoded in the ranges (1.0, 4.0) cm and (25.0, 60.0) degrees, respectively. Symmetry is maintained in constructing other membership function distributions. In all simulations here, the membership function distribution for deviation is kept the same as that in angle.

Approach 3: Optimizing rule base alone. Only the rule base is optimized in this approach. Author-defined membership functions (Figure 3) are used.

Approach 4: Optimizing membership functions and rule base simultaneously. Membership functions and the rule base are optimized. Here, a GA string is a 40-bit string with first 20 bits denoting the presence or absence of 20 possible rules, next 10 bits are used to represent the base b_1 and the final 10 bits are used to represent the base b_2.

In all runs of the proposed approach, we use binary tournament selection (with replacement), the single-point crossover operator with a probability p_c of 0.9 and the bit-wise mutation operator with a probability p_m of 0.02. A maximum number of generations equal to 100 is used. In every case, a population size of 60 is used. In all cases, $S = 10$ different author-defined scenarios are used to evaluate a solution.

We now apply all four approaches to eight-obstacle problems (in a grid of 25×20 m^2). The optimized travel distance and time for all approaches are presented in Table 2. The first three rows in the table show the performance of

Table 2. Travel distance D (in meter) and time T (in sec) obtained by four approaches

Scenario	Approach 1		Approach 2		Approach 3		Approach 4	
	D	T	D	T	D	T	D	T
1	27.203	28.901	26.077	27.769	26.154	27.872	26.154	27.872
2	26.957	28.943	25.966	27.622	26.026	26.546	26.026	26.546
3	29.848	36.798	28.623	35.164	26.660	34.547	27.139	35.000
4	33.465	43.365	26.396	27.907	26.243	27.512	26.243	27.512
5	32.836	41.781	27.129	33.000	26.543	32.390	27.041	33.000
6	33.464	43.363	28.001	31.335	27.164	31.000	27.164	31.000

all approaches on three scenarios that were used during the optimization process and the last three rows show their performance on new test (unseen) scenarios. The table shows that in all cases, Approaches 2, 3 and 4 have performed better than Approach 1 (no optimization).

Paths obtained using all four approaches for scenario 4 (unseen) are shown in Figure 4. It is clear that the paths obtained by Approaches 3 and 4 (travel

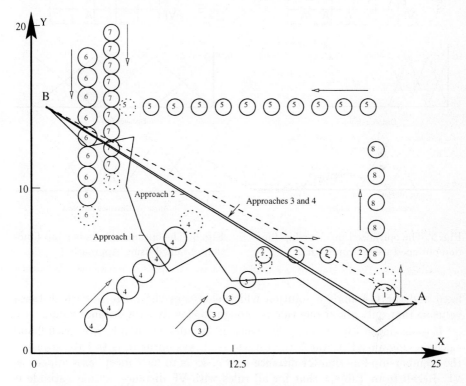

Fig. 4. Optimized paths found by all four approaches for the eight-obstacle problem are shown. The dashed circles mark the critical positions of obstacles found by the FLC.

time 27.512 sec) are shorter and quicker than that obtained by Approaches 1 (travel time 43.365 sec) and 2 (travel time 27.907 sec).

The optimized rule bases obtained using Approaches 3 and 4 are shown in Tables 3 and 4. The optimized membership functions obtained using Approaches 2 and 4 are shown in Figures 5 and 6, respectively. Here, Approach 4 (simultaneous optimization of rules and membership functions) has elongated the membership function distributions so that classification of relative angle is uniform in the range of $(-90, 90)$ degrees. In Approach 3, since membership functions are specified, the GA-optimized solution needed many rules specifying an appropriate action for each value of distance. In Approach 4, membership functions are not

Table 3. Optimized rule base (nine rules) obtained using Approach 3.

Table 4. Optimized rule base (five rules) obtained using Approach 4.

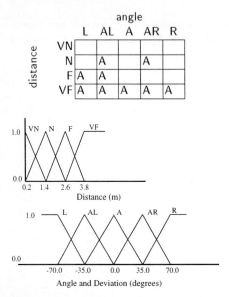

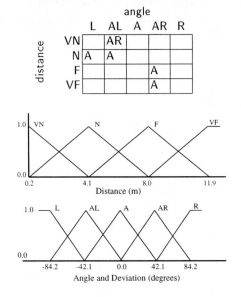

Fig. 5. The optimized membership function obtained using Approach 2.

Fig. 6. The optimized membership function obtained using Approach 4.

fixed and the GA finds a solution which elongates the range of each **distance** value so that only about one rule is enough to classify each **distance** value.

It is also interesting to note that since all 20 rules are used in Approach 2 and since moving ahead (towards the target) is always optimal, GAs have adjusted the membership function for **distance** in way so as to have most cases appear as VF. Recall from Table 1 that for all rules with VF distance, action variable is always ahead.

Both Tables 3 and 4 show that there are more rules for L and AL angles than for R and AR angles. This is merely because only 10 scenarios are considered during the optimization process and it could have been that in most cases the critical obstacles come in the left of the robot, thereby causing more rules specifying L or AL to appear in the optimized rule base. By considering more scenarios during the optimization process, such bias can be avoided and equal number of rules specifying left and right considerations can be obtained.

From Table 2, it can be observed that Approach 3 (optimization of rule base only) has resulted in a much quicker path than Approach 2 (optimization of membership function only). This is because finding a good set of rules is more important for the robot than finding a good set of membership functions. Thus, it may be argued that the optimization of rule base is a rough-tuning process and the optimization of the membership function distributions is a fine-tuning process. In most scenarios, the optimized solutions are already obtained during the optimization of rule-base only and optimization of membership function has a marginal effect to improve the solution any further.

Although the performance of Approaches 3 and 4 are more-or-less similar, we would like to highlight that Approach 4 is more flexible and a more practical approach. Since the membership functions used in Approach 3 are well-chosen by the authors, the performance of Approach 3 is good. However, for more complicated problems, we recommend using Approach 4, since it optimizes both the rule base and membership functions needed in a problem.

4 Conclusions

In this study, learning capability of a genetic-fuzzy approach has been demonstrated by finding optimal/near-optimal FLCs for solving motion planning problem of a mobile robot. In the genetic-fuzzy approach, obstacle-free paths have been found locally by using fuzzy logic technique, where optimal membership functions for condition and action variables and an optimal rule base have been found using genetic algorithms. Based on this basic approach, three different approaches have been developed and compared with an author-defined (non-optimized) fuzzy-logic controller (FLC).

The genetic-fuzzy approach developed here is also practical to be used in a real-world situation. One of the major advantages of the proposed method is that the optimization is performed off-line and an optimal rule base is obtained before-hand. Robots can then use this optimal rule base to navigate in presence of unseen scenarios in an optimal or a near-optimal manner. This paper shows how such a rule base can be achieved.

This study can be extended in a number of ways. Since the optimized travel time depends on the chosen incremental time step ΔT, this parameter can also be kept as an action variable. This way, a robot can make a longer leap in a particular obstacle-free direction or make shorter leap if there are a crowd of obstacles in the course of path. In this connection, controlling speed of the robot to allow passing of moving obsctacles may also be considered.

In this study, we have used an author-defined set of 20 rules (Table 1), all of which may not have the optimal combination of condition and action variables. GAs can be used to eliminate this bias by using a different representation scheme, as follows:

$$201500130\ldots4$$

The above string has 20 positions (representing each combination of action and condition variables) and each position can take one of six values: 0 for absence of the rule, 1 for first option of action variables (say, L), 2 for the second option, and so on. This way every solution represented by a 20-position vector represents a valid rule base. Nevertheless, the results of this study show that the proposed GA-fuzzy approach is efficient and a natural choice to the robot navigation problem, which should get more attention in applications of robotics in the coming years.

References

1. Barraquand J., Langlois B. and Latombe J.C., Numerical potential field techniques for robot path planning, *IEEE Trans. Syst., Man and Cybern.*, 22, 224-241, 1992.
2. Beaufrere. B. and Zeghloul, S. "A mobile robot navigation method using a fuzzy logic approach", *Robotica* 13, 437-448 (1995).
3. Canny J. and Reif J., New lower bound techniques for robot motion planning problems, *Proc. 27-th IEEE Symp. on Foundations of Computer Science*, Los Angeles, CA, 49-60, 1987.
4. Donnart J.Y. and Meyer J.A., Learning reactive and planning rules in a motivationally autonomous animat, *IEEE Trans. on Systems, Man and Cybernetics -Part B: Cybernetics*, 26(3), 381-395, 1996
5. Floreano D. and Mondada F., Evolution of Homing Navigation in a Real Mobile Robot, *IEEE Trans. on Systems, Man and Cybernetics -Part B: Cybernetics*, 26(3), 396-407, 1996.
6. Fujimura K. and Samet H., A hierarchical strategy for path planning among moving obstacles, *IEEE Trans. on Robotics and Automation*, 5(1), 61-69, 1989.
7. Fujimura K. and Samet H., Accessibility : a new approach to path planning among moving obstacles, *Proc. of IEEE Conf. on Computer Vision and Pattern Recognition*, Ann Arbor, MI, 803-807, 1988.
8. Griswold N.C. and Eem J., Control for mobile robots in the presence of moving objects, *IEEE Trans. on Robotics and Automation*, 6(2), 263-268, 1990.
9. Herrera F., Herrera-Viedma E., Lozano M. and Verdegay J.L., Fuzzy tools to improve genetic algorithms, *Proc. of the Second European Congress on Intelligent Techniques and Soft Computing*, 1532-1539, 1994.
10. Karr C., Design of an adaptive fuzzy logic controller using a genetic algorithm, *Proc. of the Fourth Int. Conf. on Genetic Algorithms*, Morgan Kaufmann, San Mateo CA, 450-457, 1991.
11. Latombe J.C., *Robot Motion Planning*, Kluwer Academic Publishing, Norwell, MA, 1991.
12. Lamadrid J.G., Avoidance of obstacles with unknown trajectories: Locally optimal paths and periodic sensor readings, *The Int. Jl. of Robotics Research*, 496-507, 1994.
13. Lee M. and Takagi H., Integrating design stages of fuzzy systems using genetic algorithms, *Proc. of the Second IEEE Int. Conf. on Fuzzy Systems*, 612-617, 1993
14. Martinez A. et al, Fuzzy logic based collision avoidance for a mobile robot, *Robotica*, 12, 521-527, 1994.
15. Okutomi M. and Mori M., Decision of robot movement by means of a potential field, *Advanced Robotics*, 1(2), 131-141, 1986.
16. Newman W.S. and Hogan N., High speed robot control and obstacle avoidance using dynamic potential functions, *Proc. IEEE Int. Conf. on Robotics and Automation*, 14-24, 1987.
17. Sharma R., A probabilistic framework for dynamic motion planning in partially known environments, *Proc. of IEEE Int. Conf. on Robotics and Automation*, Nice, France, 2459-2464, 1992.
18. Takeuchi T., Nagai Y. and Enomoto Y., Fuzzy Control of a Mobile Robot for Obstacle Avoidance, *Information Sciences*, 45(2), 231-248, 1988.
19. Thrift P., Fuzzy logic synthesis with genetic algorithms, *Proc. of the Fourth Int. Conf. on Genetic Algorithms*, Morgan Kaufmann, San Mateo CA, 509-513, 1991.

Evolutionary Neural Networks for Nonlinear Dynamics Modeling

I. De Falco, A. Iazzetta, P. Natale and E. Tarantino

Research Institute on Parallel Information Systems (IRSIP)
National Research Council of Italy (CNR)
Via P. Castellino, 111
80131 Naples - Italy

Abstract. In this paper the evolutionary design of a neural network model for predicting nonlinear systems behavior is discussed. In particular, the Breeder Genetic Algorithms are considered to provide the optimal set of synaptic weights of the network. The feasibility of the neural model proposed is demonstrated by predicting the Mackey–Glass time series. A comparison with Genetic Algorithms and Back Propagation learning technique is performed.

Keywords: Time Series Prediction, Artificial Neural Networks, Genetic Algorithms, Breeder Genetic Algorithms.

1 Introduction

Artificial Neural Networks (ANNs) have been widely utilized in many application areas over the years. Nonetheless their drawback is that the design of an efficient architecture and the choice of the synaptic weights require high processing time. In particular, learning neural network weights can be considered a hard optimization problem for which the learning time scales exponentially becoming prohibitive as the problem size grows [1]. Many researchers working in the field of Genetic Algorithms(GAs) [2, 3] have tried to use these to optimize neural networks [4, 5]. A typical approach followed by them is to use a GA to evolve the optimal topology of an appropriate network and then utilize Back Propagation (BP) [1] to train the weights. BP is the most common method used to find the set of weights. Unfortunately, this method is based on gradient, so it gets stuck in the first local optimum it finds. Evolutionary Algorithms have also been utilized to try to overcome these BP limitations in the training process. The usage of these algorithms might yield several advantages with respect to the BP technique. In fact, firstly, they can be used even for non-continuous problem since they do not require gradient information. Secondly, they reduce the possibility to get stuck in local optima. Thirdly they provide the user with more possible neural network configurations among which he can choose the most appropriate to his needs.

The first evolutionary approaches for the learning phase have been performed by using GAs. This genetic approach allows to attain good results but to do this it has the disadvantage to have extremely high costs in speed of the evolutive search process. This makes GAs impractical for large network design [6, 7].

Recently, other evolutionary systems, based on a real representation of the variables and on real–valued operators, have been revealed to be effective with respect to GAs for optimizing both ANN structures [8] and ANN weights [9, 10]. In [10], among other problems, time series prediction is considered. This problem represents a sound test to investigate the effectiveness of forecasting techniques. The problems are faced in [10] by using Evolutionary Programming [11].

We have found that for many real–valued problems Breeder Genetic Algorithms (BGAs)[12, 13, 14] have outperformed GAs. Therefore, our idea is to implement a hybrid system, based both on ANNs ability to understand nonlinearities present in the time series and on BGAs capability to search a solution in the massively multi-modal landscape of the synaptic weight space. Of course this procedure does not guarantee to find the optimal configuration, anyway it allows to attain a configuration close to optimal performance. We wish to examine the performance of the resulting system with respect to both the classical GA driving ANNs and to the BP on its own.

A standard benchmark for prediction models, the Mackey–Glass (MG) time series [15], is considered. The results obtained are compared against those achieved by the other above mentioned techniques in order to establish their degrees of effectiveness.

In order to preserve the features of GAs and BGAs we have decided to make nothing to reduce the detrimental effect of the permutation problem [7]. In fact, our aim is to compare the techniques on the test problem, rather then to attempt to achieve the best possible solution.

The paper is organized as follows. In section 2 a description of the aforementioned benchmark problem is reported. In section 3 some implementation details are outlined. In section 4 the experimental results are presented and discussed. Section 5 contains final remarks and prospects of future work.

2 The Mackey–Glass Series

We can attempt to predict the behavior of a time series generated by a chaotic dynamical system as shown in [16]: the time series is transformed into a reconstructed state space using a delay space embedding [17]. In this latter space, each point in the state space is a vector $\mathbf{x}$ composed of time series values corresponding to a sequence of n delay lags:

$$x(t), x(t - \delta), x(t - 2\delta), \ldots , x(t - (n - 1)\delta) \tag{1}$$

The next step is to assume a functional relationship between the current state $\mathbf{x}(t)$ and the future state $\mathbf{x}(t + P)$,

$$\mathbf{x}(t + P) = f_P(\mathbf{x}(t)). \tag{2}$$

The aim is to find a predictor $\hat{f}_P$ which approximates f_P, so that we can predict $x(t + P)$ based on n previous values. If the data are chaotic, the f_P is necessarily nonlinear. P represents the number of time steps ahead we wish to perform our prediction.

Based on Takens' theorem [18], an estimate of the dimension D of the manifold from which the time series originated can be used to construct an ANN model using at least $2D + 1$ external inputs [19]. For a noise–free system of dimension D, it is sufficient to choose $n = 2D + 1$. It is obvious that for a D–dimensional attractor, n must be at least as large as D [16].

The time series used in our experiments is generated by the chaotic Mackey–Glass differential delay equation [15] defined below:

$$\frac{dx}{dt} = a\frac{x(t - \tau)}{1 + x^c(t - \tau)} - bx(t) \tag{3}$$

where a, b, c and τ are costants. The value of τ is very important, because it determines the system behavior. In fact, for initial values of x in the time interval $[0,\tau]$, the system approaches a stable equilibrium point for $\tau < 4.53$, a limit cycle for $4.53 < \tau < 13.3$, and after a series of period doublings for $13.3 \leq \tau \leq 16.8$ the system becomes chaotic. From the value 16.8 on, τ controls how chaotic the series is. The larger τ, the larger the dimensionality of the attractor. For example, for $\tau = 17$ D is 2.1, while for $\tau = 23$ D is 2.4, for $\tau = 30$ D is 3.5, and for $\tau = 100$ D is 7.5.

For our experiments we have decided to set the above values as it follows: $\tau = 17$, $a = 0.2$, $b = -0.1$, $c = 10$. As regards P, we have performed a set of experiments, with $P = 6$.

3 The Evolutionary Prediction System

Following the recipe by Lapedes and Farber [20] for the Mackey–Glass, we have decided to consider a family of MLPs with the following features: the input layer consists of four nodes, two hidden layers, ten neurons per hidden layer, hyperbolic tangent as activation function in the hidden layers, semi–linear activation in the output node. Our aim is to provide an automatic procedure to optimize the learning phase of these neural networks for time series prediction. The hybrid system we have designed and implemented consists in a BGA which evolves a population of individuals or chromosomes which represent potential candidate solutions. Being the network topology totally fixed (4–10–10–1), the number of connection weights to be determined is 171 (actually, 150 are the real connections between neurons and 21 are the bias values for the nodes belonging to the two hidden layers and the output layer). We have decided to let these values vary within the range [-0.6, 0.6]. Thus, each individual is constituted by an array of 171 real values. Each of these chromosomes is a "genetic encoding" in which the genotype codes for the different sets of connection weights of each MLP. Such encodings are transformable into the corresponding neural networks (phenotypes). The evaluation of the phenotypes determines the fitness of the related genotype.

The parameter we have chosen to evaluate the goodness of an individual is the normalized mean square error on the training set, E_t. We define E_t as:

$$E_t = \frac{\left(\frac{1}{N-1}\sum_{i=1}^{N}(x_i - o_i)^2\right)^{\frac{1}{2}}}{\left(\frac{1}{N-1}\sum_{i=1}^{N}(x_i - \bar{x})^2\right)^{\frac{1}{2}}} \tag{4}$$

where x_i is the i–th input value, o_i is the i–th predicted value.

Specifically the fitness function we use is the following:

$$\mathcal{F}(\mathbf{y}) = E_t \tag{5}$$

In the evolutionary algorithm μ genotypes of the population are individually evaluated to determine the genotypes that code for high fitness phenotypes. A selection process allows to establish the survivors. Appropriate genetic operators are used to introduce variety into the population and to sample variants of candidate solutions of the next generation. Thus, over several generations, the population gradually evolves toward genotypes that correspond to high fitness phenotypes. The process is repeated until an adequate network is achieved or a stopping criterion is fulfilled.

Let $\mathrm{MLP}(\mathbf{y}_i)$ with $i \in \{1, \dots, \mu\}$ be the algorithm for training the MLP related to the individual $\mathbf{y}_i$ representing a neural network configuration. The general scheme for the BGA is the following:

Given a training set T_s;
Procedure *Breeder Genetic Algorithm*
begin
    randomly initialize a population of μ sets of connection weights;
    while (termination criterion not fulfilled) **do**
        transform the genotypes into the corresponding phenotypes $\mathbf{y}_i$;
        train $\mathbf{y}_i$ by means of $\mathrm{MLP}(\mathbf{y}_i)$ on T_s;
        evaluate the trained network $\mathbf{y}_i$;
        save the genotype of the best trained network in the new population;
        select the best λ sets of synaptic weights;
        for $i = 1$ **to** $\mu - 1$ **do**
          randomly select two structures among the λ;
          recombine them so as to obtain one offspring;
          perform mutation on the offspring;
        od
        update variables for termination;
    od
end

4   Experimental results

The data of the time series have been divided into two sets: the training data set T_s used to train the prediction system, and the verifying set V_s to evaluate the performance of the trained system. The former consists of 1200 samples, while the latter is made of 300 values.

The population size for all the experiments has been set to 100. Preliminary runs have been made to determine the best operators for the BGA. As far as the recombination operator is concerned, we have taken into account the Discrete Recombination (DR), the Extended Intermediate Recombination (EIR), the Extended Line Recombination (ELR), the Fuzzy Recombination (FR) [21] and the BGA Line Recombination (BGALR) [22]. This latter operator works as follows: let $\mathbf{x} = (x_1, \dots, x_n)$ and $\mathbf{y} = (y_1, \dots, y_n)$ be the parent strings with $\mathbf{x}$ being the one with better fitness, then the offspring $\mathbf{z} = (z_1, \dots, z_n)$ is computed by

$$z_i = x_i \pm range_i \cdot 2^{-k \cdot \sigma} \cdot \frac{y_i - x_i}{\|\mathbf{x} - \mathbf{y}\|} \qquad \sigma \in [0, 1]$$

As regards ELR, EIR and FR, on the basis of their definitions in [21], several values for the typical parameter d have been used, the best ones resulting in all cases $d = 0.5$. For the mutation operator, the Discrete Mutation (DM) and the Continuous Mutation (CM) have been investigated, with different values for their parameters k and $range_i$. The best values for them have been set as $k = 16$ and $range_i = 0.75$. The DR and the ELR have turned out to be the worst ones. DR allows to obtain a very fast decrease in the best fitness during first generations, but it loses power as the number of generations increases. BGALR and EIR have been very close as regards performance, the former being slightly better. Furthermore, it has allowed to achieve runs showing average values much closer to the best values than EIR. So, the BGALR has been chosen as recombination operator. Due to its structure, it does not require to apply a further mutation operator. In Table 1 we report the best final values and the average final values achieved by using the different recombination operators. The latter values are averaged over 10 runs. The mutation operator for all of the runs has been the CM (where needed, of course).

Table 1. The best final (*best*) and the average final (*av_ge*) values obtained (averaged over 10 runs)

	best	av_ge
DR	0.4042	0.4249
ELR	0.4591	0.4656
FR	0.3768	0.3849
EIR	0.3165	0.3412
BGALR	0.2617	0.3136

Some trial runs have also been made to find a good value for the truncation

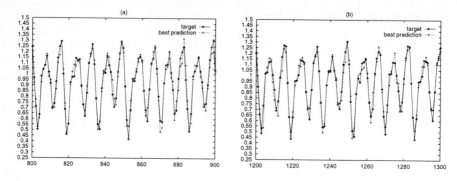

Fig. 1. The results of the BGA on the training set (a) and on the verifying set (b)

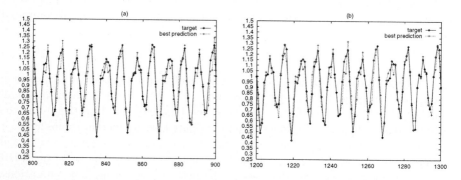

Fig. 2. The results of the GA on the training set (a) and on the verifying set (b)

rate, resulting in $T = 20\%$. The maximum number of generations allowed is 1000. In all runs, however, most of the evolution takes place during the first 500–600 generations.

All of the runs performed with BGALR show quite similar behavior. In Fig. 1 we report the results obtained in the best run. In this case we have obtained an error of 0.2617 on the training set (E_t) and of 0.2832 on the verifying set (E_v). Fig. 1(a) shows the target curve and the obtained one for a slice of the training set, namely the slice [800-900], for clarity's sake. Fig. 1(b) reports the target and the output for the verifying set, in the slice [1200–1300].

It is interesting to compare these results against those achieved by us when using binary GAs to drive evolution. In this case we have decided to employ one-point crossover with probability $P_c = 0.8$ and bit-flip mutation with probability $P_m = 0.005$. Each variable has been encoded with 10 bits. The population size is 100, and the maximum number of generations is 1000. Several runs with different selection methods have been performed, resulting in truncation with threshold $T = 20\%$ being the best. The best final value over 10 runs has been 0.4878 for the training set, resulting in $E_v = 0.4880$. Fig 2 reports the results on the training set (a) and the results on the verifying set (b).

We report also the results achieved by the BP on the problem under account.

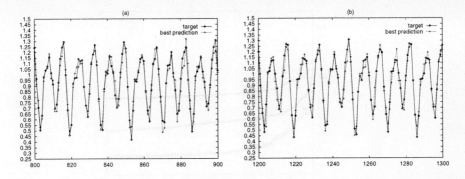

Fig. 3. The results of the BP on the training set (a) and on the verifying set (b)

We have used values for the learning of $\alpha = 0.5$ and $\eta = 0.05$. This latter has been used throughout all the previously described experiments as well. We have used both a simple BP (SPB) which stops in the first local optimum it meets, and a more sophisticated one (BP), which has been provided with a mechanism allowing to escape local optima. Namely, training is performed and the final weight set is saved. Then, learning is repeated and if a new weight set leading to E_t decrease is found, it is saved. This mechanism is iterated. The saved weight set is restored every time the search leads to solutions which are worse than the saved one. When the new solution is worse than the saved one by more than 20% the learning ends. We have carried out several experiments with different number of training epochs, resulting in a number of 400 being the most suitable for both techniques. Fig. 3 reports the results on the training set (a) and the results on the verifying set (b) for the best BP run. This run has $E_t = 0.1049$ and $E_v = 0.1468$.

Table 2 summarizes the best final results and the average final results with the different techniques.

Table 2. E_t and E_v for the best runs with the different techniques

	E_t	E_v
GA	0.4878	0.4880
BGA	0.2617	0.2832
SBP	0.1194	0.1573
BP	0.1049	0.1468

In Fig. 4 the evolutions of the three techniques employed are shown. Each training phase for the BP is plotted as one generation, to keep the figure congruent. As it can be seen the performance of the BGA is always better than that of GAs at parity of number of generations. MLP trained with the cycling BP technique is the best during all evolution.

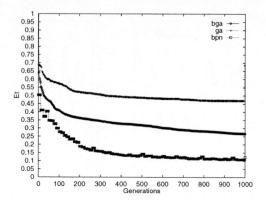

Fig. 4. The evolution of the different techniques utilized

5 Conclusions and Future Works

In this paper an evolutionary approach for automating the design of a neural network model for time series prediction has been investigated. The BGAs have been used in facing the optimization of the search in the large connection weights space. The approach has been tested on a standard benchmark for prediction techniques, the Mackey–Glass series. We have focused our attention on the prediction for $t + 6$. The experimental results have proved the effectiveness of the BGA proposed for the Mackey–Glass time series prediction with respect to GAs. In particular, the BGALR recombination operator has turned out to be the most suitable for the problem at hand. We are trying to draw some hypothesis on why this happens. It has been reported by Whitley [7] that the problem of training an MLP may represent an application that is inherently not a good match for GAs that rely heavily on recombination. Some researchers do not use recombination, while other have used small populations and high mutation rates in conjunction with recombination. The basic feature of the BGALR operator is that in order to create each new component of an offspring it performs, apart from recombination, also some kind of mutation. This might be seen as an extremely high mutation probability, and seems to be in accordance with Whitley's assumption. Though the automatic procedure here provided has allowed to achieve a network architecture with good performance, the results of BGAs are worse than those obtained by BP techniques. However, it is to point out that we have considered naive implementations of the GAs and the BGAs to perform their comparison. More sophisticated evolutionary algorithms, which do not use recombination operators [10], allow to attain performance comparable with that achieved by BP techniques.

Future work will be focused both on the investigation of the relative importance of recombination and mutation and on the search of an appropriate fitness function. In fact, it is not clear the dependence of the results on the specific fitness function chosen. In this paper we have used to evaluate individuals the classical error on the training set, typical of MLPs. In [23] it is suggested to take into account the fact that the search performed by a GA is holistic, and not local as is usually the case when perceptrons are trained by traditional methods. We aim to find new fitness functions which can take advantage of this idea. Of course, in order to ascertain the effectiveness of the evolutionary approach in facing a learning process, different time series prediction problems have to be analyzed.

Furthermore, since the BGA method can also be easily distributed among several processors, we intend to perform the implementation of a parallel version of the evolutionary approach proposed with the aim at improving the performance and the quality of neural networks, while decreasing the search time.

References

1. D. E. Rumelhart, J. L. McLelland, *Parallel Distributed Processing*,**I-II**, MIT Press, 1986.
2. J. H. Holland, *Adaptation in Natural and Artificial Systems*, University of Michigan Press, Ann Arbor, 1975.
3. D. E. Goldberg, *Genetic Algorithms in Search, Optimization and Machine Learning*, Addison-Wesley, Reading, Massachussetts, 1989.
4. J. D. Shaffer, D. Whitley and L. J. Eshelman, Combination of Genetic Algorithms and Neural Networks: A Survey of the State of the Art, in *Combination of Genetic Algorithms and Neural Networks*, J. D. Shaffer, L. D. Whitley eds., pp. 1–37, 1992.
5. X. Yao, A Review of Evolutionary Artificial Networks, *Int. J. Intelligent Systems*, **8** (4), pp. 539–567, 1993.
6. D. J. Montana and L. Davis, Training Feedforward Neural Networks using Genetic Algorithms, *Proceedings of the Eleventh International Joint Conference on Artificial Intelligence*, Morgan Kaufmann, pp. 762–767, 1989.
7. D. Whitley, Genetic Algorithms and Neural Networks, in *Genetic Algorithms in Engineering and Computer Science*, J. Periaux, M. Galan and P. Cuesta eds., John Wiley, pp. 203–216, 1995.
8. I. De Falco, A. Della Cioppa, P. Natale and E. Tarantino, Artificial Neural Networks Optimization by means of Evolutionary Algorithms, in *Soft Computing in Engineering Design and Manufacturing*, Springer–Verlag, London, 1997.
9. A. Imada and K. Araki, Evolution of a Hopfield Associative Memory by the Breeder Genetic Algorithm, *Proceedings of the Seventh International Conference on Genetic Algorithms*, Morgan Kaufmann, pp. 784–791, 1997.
10. X. Yao and Y. Liu, A New Evolutionary Systems for Evolving Artificial Neural Networks, *IEEE Trans. on Neural Networks*, **8** (3), pp. 694–713, 1997.
11. D. B. Fogel, *Evolutionary Computation: Towards a New Philosophy of Machine Intelligence*, New York, NY 10017-2394: IEEE Press, 1995.
12. H. Mühlenbein and D. Schlierkamp–Voosen, Analysis of Selection, Mutation and Recombination in Genetic Algorithms, *Neural Network World*, **3**, pp. 907–933, 1993.
13. H. Mühlenbein and D. Schlierkamp–Voosen, Predictive Models for the Breeder Genetic Algorithm I. Continuous Parameter Optimization, *Evolutionary Computation*, **1**(1), pp. 25–49, 1993.

14. H. Mühlenbein and D. Schlierkamp–Voosen, The Science of Breeding and its Application to the Breeder Genetic Algorithm, *Evolutionary Computation*, **1**, pp. 335–360, 1994.

15. M. Mackey and L. Glass, Oscillation and Chaos in Physiological Control System, *Science*, pp. 197–287, 1977.

16. D. Farmer and J. Sidorowich, Predicting Chaotic Time Series, *Physical Review Letter* **59**, pp. 845–848, 1987.

17. N. H. Packard, J. D. Crutchfield, J. D. Farmer and R. S. Shaw, Geometry from a Time Series, *Physical Review Letters*, **45**, pp. 712–716, 1980.

18. F. Takens, Detecting Strange Attractors in Turbulence, in *Lecture Notes in Mathematics*, Springer–Verlag, Berlin, 1981.

19. M. Casdagli, S. Eubank, J. D. Farmer and J. Gibson, State Space Reconstruction in the Presence of Noise, *Physica D*, **51**, pp. 52–98, 1991.

20. A. Lapedes and R. Farber, Nonlinear Signal Processing using Neural Networks: Prediction and System Modeling, Los Alamos National Laboratory Technical Report LA-UR-87-2662, 1987.

21. H. M. Voigt, H. Mühlenbein and D. Cvetković, Fuzzy Recombination for the Continuous Breeder Genetic Algorithm, *Proceedings of the Sixth International Conference on Genetic Algorithms*, Morgan Kaufmann, 1995.

22. D. Schlierkamp–Voosen and H. Mühlenbein , Strategy Adaptation by Competing Subpopulations, *Proceedings of Parallel Problem Solving from Nature (PPSNIII)*, Morgan Kaufmann, pp. 199–208, 1994.

23. P.G. Korning, Training of neural networks by means of genetic algorithm working on very long chromosomes, Technical Report, Computer Science Department, Aarhus, Denmark, 1994.

Hybrid Distributed Real-Coded Genetic Algorithms*

Francisco Herrera[1], Manuel Lozano[1] and Claudio Moraga[2]

[1]Department of Computer Science and Artificial Intelligence
University of Granada, 18071 - Granada, Spain
[2]Dept. of Computer Science
University of Dortmund, 44221 - Dortmund, Germany

Abstract. Distributed genetic algorithms keep, in parallel, several subpopulations that are processed by genetic algorithms, with each one being independent from the others. A migration mechanism produces a chromosome exchange between the subpopulations. These algorithms may be categorized as homogeneous or heterogeneous ones when all the subpopulations apply genetic algorithms with the same configuration, or not, respectively.

In this paper, we present the hybrid distributed real-coded genetic algorithms. In these algorithms the connection of homogeneous distributed genetic algorithms, which apply different crossover operators and selective pressure degrees, forms a higher level heterogeneous distributed genetic algorithm. Experimental results show that the proposal consistently outperforms equivalent heterogeneous and homogeneous distributed genetic algorithms.

1   Introduction

Distributed genetic algorithms (DGAs) are one of the most important representatives of methods based on spatial separation ([4, 16, 21]). Their basic idea lies in the partition of the population into several subpopulations (whose sizes are relatively small), each one of them being processed by a genetic algorithm (GA), independently from the others. A *migration* mechanism produces a chromosome exchange between the subpopulations.

These algorithms show two determinant advantages:

- The preservation of the diversity due to the semi-isolation of the subpopulations, which may stand up to the premature convergence problem, and
- They may be easily implemented on parallel hardware, obtaining, in this way, substantial improvements on computational time.

DGAs may be assigned to the following two categories with regards to the subpopulation homogeneity ([14]):

---

* This research has been partially supported by CICYT TIC96-0778 and DGICYT SAB95-0473.

- **Homogeneous DGAs.** Every subpopulation uses the same genetic operators, control parameter values, fitness function, coding schema, etc. Their principal advantage is that they are easily implemented, which explains that most DGAs proposed in the literature are members of this type ([4, 16, 21]).
- **Heterogeneous DGAs.** The subpopulations are processed using GAs with either different control parameter values, or genetic operators, or coding schema, etc ([10, 9, 14, 17, 19]). These algorithms have been considered as suitable tools for avoiding the premature convergence problem and for maximizing the exploration and exploitation on the search space ([10, 17, 21]).

Some distributed models have been proposed that combine the advantages of DGAs with the ones of other spatial separation based methods, reporting good results. This is the case of mixed parallel GAs ([7]), structured DGAs ([22]) and DGAs based on the ECO framework ([15]). In general, these approaches involve a hierarchy where a DGA constitutes the upper level. In [3], it is suggested that DGAs may be used at low levels as well.

In this paper, we present a type of DGAs based on real coding (see [13]), the *Hybrid Distributed Real-Coded GAs*, that introduce the previous idea in order to allow the features of both homogeneous and heterogeneous DGAs to be combined. It involves a hierarchical structure where a higher level heterogeneous DGA joins homogeneous DGAs that are connected with each other. The homogeneous DGAs are differentiated according to the exploration and exploitation properties of the crossover operators applied to their subpopulations along with the selective pressure associated with the selection mechanism used. Furthermore, we build an instance of this type of DGAs based on the FCB-crossover operators ([12]), which allow different exploration or exploitation degrees to be introduced.

The paper is set out as follows: in Section 2, we present the Hybrid Distributed Real-coded GAs, in Section 3, we build the instance based on FCB-crossover operators, in Section 4, the experiments carried out for determining the efficacy of the instance are described, and finally, some concluding remarks are dealt with in Section 5.

2   Hybrid Distributed RCGAs

In this Section, we present the Hybrid Distributed Real-coded GAs (HD-RCGAs). They are an extension of the Gradual Distributed Real-coded GAs (GD-RCGAs) ([10]). GD-RCGAs are a class of heterogeneous DGAs in which subpopulations are distinguished by applying crossover operators with different degrees of exploration or exploitation and by using different selective pressure degrees. This framework allows a spread search (*reliability*) along with an effective local tuning (*accuracy*) to be simultaneously achieved ([10]).

HD-RCGAs are built by assigning to every node of a GD-RCGA a homogeneous DGA whose subpopulations use the same crossover operator and selective pressure degree than the corresponding node in the GD-RCGA. In this way, HD-RCGAs introduce a hierarchical structure where lower level homogeneous DGAs (denoted as lower-DGAs) are connected with each other, forming a higher level heterogeneous DGA (denoted as higher-DGA).

Next, in Subsection 2.1, we introduce the structure of the higher-DGA, explaining its topology and the features associated with the crossover operators applied to every lower-DGA, in Subsection 2.2., we deal with the selection scheme chosen for the lower-DGAs, and finally in Subsection 2.3., we discuss about the migration scheme used by the HD-RCGAs.

2.1 Structure of the Higher-DGA

Figure 1 shows the structure of the higher-DGA. It is based on a hypercube topology with three dimensions, that has two important sides to be differentiated:

- The **Front Side** is devoted to the exploration. It is made up of four lower-DGAs, $DGA1$, ..., $DGA4$, which apply a different exploratory crossover operator to their subpopulations. The exploration degree of the crossover operators increases clockwise, starting at the lowest, the one applied by $DGA1$, and ending at the highest, the one associated with $DGA4$.
- The **Rear Side** is for exploitation. It is composed of four lower-DGAs, $dga1$, ..., $dga4$, which undergo different exploitative crossover operators. The exploitation degree of the crossover operators increases clockwise, starting at the lowest, the one for $dga1$, and finishing at the highest, the one employed by $dga4$.

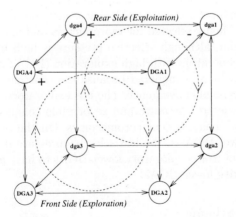

Fig. 1. Structure of the higher-DGA

With this structure a suitable effect may be achieved: *parallel multiresolution* with regard to the crossover operator's action. This implies that the distances of the elements generated by crossover from their parents are gradually different from one lower-DGA to other. Furthermore, lower-DGAs are adequately connected for exploiting this multiresolution in a gradual way, offering the refinement or the expansion of the best zones emerging. The migrations between them produce these final effects.

2.2 Selection Scheme

The selection scheme is made up by *linear ranking* ([1]) for the selection probability calculation, and *stochastic universal sampling* ([2]) as sampling algorithm. The elitist strategy ([5]) is assumed as well. The selective pressure of linear ranking is determined by a parameter, $\eta_{min} \in [0, 1]$. If η_{min} is low, high pressure is achieved, whereas if it is high, the pressure is low. Different η_{min} values are assigned to the lower-DGAs, DGA1, ...,DGA4 and dga1, ...,dga4, such as is shown in Table 1.

Table 1. η_{min} values for the lower-DGAs

Exploitation				Exploration			
+	$\longleftarrow$		−	−	$\longrightarrow$		+
dga4	dga3	dga2	dga1	DGA1	DGA2	DGA3	DGA4
0.9	0.7	0.5	0.1	0.9	0.7	0.5	0.1

These assignments are chosen in order to overcome two possible problems that may appear in an HD-RCGA due to the lower-DGAs are likely to converge at different rates (the exploitative ones shall converge faster than the exploratory ones): 1) the *conquest* problem: an individual from an exploitative lower-DGA that is sent to an exploratory one may be immediately selected more often, hence it may conquer this lower-DGA, and 2) the *non-effect* problem, an individual belonging to an exploratory lower-DGA that is inserted into an exploitative one has little chance of being selected for reproduction and may be wasted.

On the one hand, although selective pressure is high in those lower-DGAs that use crossover operators with high exploration (DGA3 and DGA4), they do not run the risk of being conquered because the constant generation of diversity prevents any type of convergence. The less exploratory lower-DGAs (DGA1 and DGA2) lose selective pressure and so possible conquerors have not many advantages against their resident chromosomes. On the other hand, the more exploitative an lower-DGA is, the less selective pressure it shall undergo. This allows migrants sent from exploratory lower-DGAs to have a chance of surviving in higher exploitative lower-DGAs.

2.3 Migration Scheme

There are two types of migrations in an HD-RCGA:

1. **Local migrations.** They are produced between subpopulations in the same lower-DGA. They will set depending on their topology, which will be more

simple (less dense) than the topology of the higher-DGA, such as is suggested in [3].

2. **Global migrations.** They are produced between subpopulations belonging to different lower-DGAs. They occur every 10 generations in the sequence of application that is shown in Figure 2, i.e., first, the refinement migrations, second, the refinement/expansion migrations, third, the expansion migrations, and then, the sequence starts again.

   Global migrations follow the migration strategy *emigration*: the best individuals leave their subpopulation and migrate to the corresponding neighboring subpopulation. In this way, the best elements (emigrants) do not affect the same lower-DGA for a long time, which would probably occur using the elitist strategy, and therefore the conquest is more difficult for them. Furthermore, these good elements may undergo refinement or expansion after being included in the destination lower-DGA.

Fig. 2. Global migrations between lower-DGAs

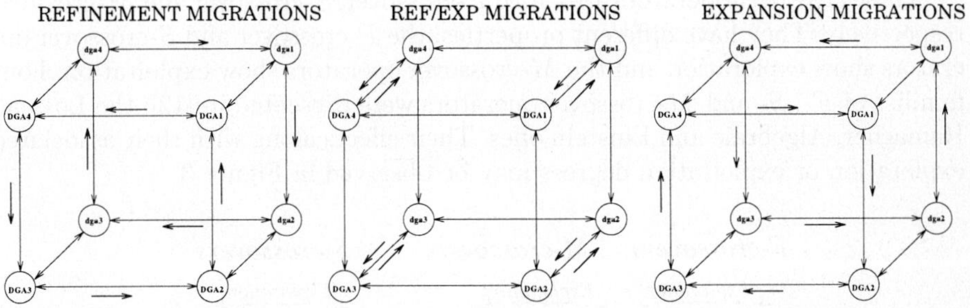

REFINEMENT MIGRATIONS   REF/EXP MIGRATIONS   EXPANSION MIGRATIONS

3 An HD-RCGA Based on FBC-crossovers

In this Section, we implement an instance of HD-RCGA using the FCB-crossover operators ([12]), called HD-RCGA-FCB. These operators are suitable for this purpose since they allow different exploration or exploitation degrees to be obtained.

Next, in Subsection 3.1., we present the FCB-crossover operators, and in Subsection 3.2, we propose HD-RCGA-FCB, explaining its topology and how the FCB-crossover operators are assigned to each lower-DGA in order to allow the higher-DGA to obtain the gradual effects shown in Figure 1.

3.1 FCB-crossover Operators

Let us assume that $X = (x_1 \ldots x_n)$ and $Y = (y_1 \ldots y_n)$ $(x_i, y_i \in [a_i, b_i] \subset \Re,$ $i = 1 \ldots n)$ are two real-coded chromosomes that have been selected to apply the crossover operator to them. In short, the action interval of the genes x_i and y_i, $[a_i, b_i]$, may be divided into three intervals, $[a_i, x_i]$, $[x_i, y_i]$ and $[y_i, b_i]$, that bound three regions to which the resultant genes of some combination of x_i and

y_i may belong. These intervals may be classified as exploration or exploitation zones. The interval with both genes being the extremes is an exploitation zone, the two remaining intervals are exploration zones.

With regards to these intervals, in [12], three monotone and non-decreasing functions are proposed: F, S and M, defined from $[a,b] \times [a,b]$ into $[a,b]$, $a,b \in \Re$, which fulfill: $\forall c, c' \in [a,b]$,

$$F(c,c') \leq \min\{c,c'\}, \ S(c,c') \geq \max\{c,c'\} \text{ and } \min\{c,c'\} \leq M(c,c') \leq \max\{c,c'\}.$$

Each one of these functions allows us to combine two genes giving results belonging to each one of the aforementioned intervals. Now, if $Q \in \{F,S,M\}$, we may generate the offspring $Z = (z_1 \ldots z_n)$ as

$$z_i = Q(x_i, y_i), \quad i = 1 \ldots n.$$

These crossover operators are called F-crossover, S-crossover and M-crossover, respectively. They have different properties: the F-crossover and S-crossover operators show exploration and the M-crossover operators show exploitation. Four families of F-, S- and M-crossover operators were presented in [12]: the Logical, Hamacher, Algebraic and Einstein ones. Their effects along with their associated exploration or exploitation degrees may be observed in Figure 3.

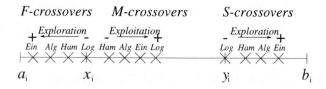

Fig. 3. FCB-crossover Operators

Two extensions of these operators were proposed: the Heuristic FBC-crossover operators ([8]) and the Dynamic FCB-crossover operators ([11]).

3.2 General Features of HD-RCGA-FCB

We propose to use the *Cube-Connected Cycles* structure ([18]) as topology for HD-RCGA-FCB (Figure 4).

In HD-RCGA-FCB, the lower-DGAs are rings with six subpopulations. Each lower-DGA is connected to other three by means of three subpopulations in the ring. With regard to the local migrations (between the subpopulations in each ring), they are produced 5 generations after each global migration. Each subpopulation sends its best element to a neighboring subpopulation following the directions shown in Figure 4. The migration scheme emigration is assumed as well for these migrations.

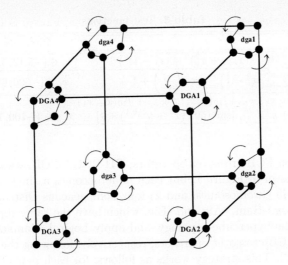

Fig. 4. Topology for HD-RCGA-FCB

Subpopulations in the lower-DGAs of the rear side undergo M-crossover operators, whereas the ones in the lower-DGAs of the front side use F- and S-crossover operators. Table 2 shows the FCB-crossover operators that are applied by every lower-DGA.

Table 2. Crossover configuration for HD-RCGA-FCB

Read Side	M-crossover	Front Side	F- and S-crossover
$dga1$	Hamacher	$DGA1$	Logical
$dga2$	Algebraic	$DGA2$	Hamacher
$dga3$	Einstein	$DGA3$	Algebraic
$dga4$	Logical	$DGA4$	Einstein

These assignments between lower-DGAs and FCB-crossover operators allow the higher-DGA to produce the gradual effects shown in Figure 1, thanks to the properties of these operators (Figure 3).

4 Experiments

Minimization experiments were carried out in order to study the behavior of HD-RCGA-FCB. The test functions used were: *Generalized Rosenbrock's* function (f_{Ros}) ([5, 20]), *Griewangk's* function (f_{Gri}) ([6]) and *Expansion of f_{10}* (ef_{10}) ([23]). They are shown in Table 3. We considered $n = 25$. These functions have been considered as very complex ones ([16, 19, 23])

We have executed HD-RCGA-FCB with a subpopulation size of 8 chromosomes. Its results have been compared with the ones of: 1) a Gradual Distributed

Table 3. Test functions

Definition	Intervals	Optimum
$f_{Ros}(\mathbf{x}) = \sum_{i=1}^{n-1}\left(100\cdot(x_{i+1}-x_i^2)^2 + (x_i-1)^2\right)$	$x_i \in [-5.12, 5.12]$	$f^*_{Ros} = 0$
$f_{Gri}(\mathbf{x}) = \frac{1}{4000}\sum_{i=1}^{n} x_i^2 - \prod_{i=1}^{n}\cos\left(\frac{x_i}{\sqrt{i}}\right) + 1$	$x_i \in [-600, 600]$	$f^*_{Gri} = 0$
$ef_{10}(\mathbf{x}) = f_{10}(x_1, x_2) + \ldots f_{10}(x_{i-1}, x_i)\ldots + f_{10}(x_n, x_1)$ $f_{10}(x, y) = (x^2+y^2)^{0.25}\cdot[\sin^2(50\cdot(x^2+y^2)^{0.1}) + 1]$	$x, y \in (-100, 100]$	$f^*_{ef_{10}} = 0$

RCGA based on FCB-crossover operators, GD-RCGA-FCB, whose structure is like the one shown in Figure 1, but each node becomes a single subpopulation with a size of 48 chromosomes, and 2) four homogeneous Distributed RCGAs, D-RCGA-S4-Log, -Ham, -Alg and -Ein, which have the same topology as HD-RCGA-FCB, the hypercube topology, and apply Logical, Hamacher, Algebraic and Einstein FCB-crossover operators, respectively, following the strategy $ST4$ proposed in [12]. This strategy works as follows: for each pair of chromosomes from a total of $\frac{1}{2}\cdot p_c \cdot N_S$, four offspring are generated, the result of applying two exploratory crossover operators, an exploitative one and an operator with "relaxed" exploitation, which put together the two properties. All four offspring will form part of the population. The algorithms were executed 15 times, each one with 5,000 generations.

Table 4 shows the results obtained. For each function, we introduce the average of the *Best* fitness values found at the end of the runs, the final average *Online* measure ([5]) (the average of the fitness of all the elements appearing throughout the GA's execution), and the percentage of *Success* with respect to a threshold of 0.1 for f_{Ros}, 0.01 for f_{Gri} and 0.1 for $f_{ef_{10}}$. Online is considered here as a population diversity measure.

Table 4. Results

Algorithms	f_{Ros}			f_{Gri}			ef_{10}		
	Best	Online	Success	Best	Online	Success	Best	Online	Success
HD-RCGA-FCB	1.4e+00	7.9e+04	93.3	6.1e-03	2.3e+02	80.0	7.2e-02	1.1e+02	86.7
GD-RCGA-FCB	8.7e+00	1.4e+05	60.0	6.4e-03	3.2e+02	80.0	4.0e-01	1.3e+02	0.0
D-RCGA-S4-Log	2.2e+01	9.0e+02	0.0	7.9e-03	4.2e+00	80.0	2.3e-01	2.3e+01	0.0
D-RCGA-S4-Ham	2.2e+01	1.3e+04	0.0	1.7e-02	7.5e+01	60.0	1.8e+00	1.6e+02	0.0
D-RCGA-S4-Alg	2.3e+01	2.4e+04	0.0	1.1e-02	1.1e+02	66.7	2.3e+00	1.7e+02	0.0
D-RCGA-S4-Ein	2.3e+01	3.4e+04	0.0	8.6e-03	1.4e+02	73.3	1.7e+00	1.8e+02	0.0

Next, we point out some important considerations about the results obtained.

- In general, HD-RCGA-FCB improves the *Best* and *Success* performance measures of GD-RCGA-FCB and the ones of the Distributed RCGAs for all functions.
- In particular, we should underline its very accurate results for f_{Ros} and ef_{10}. It obtains the best *Success* and *Best* measures for f_{Ros}, 93.3% and 1.4, respectively, and for ef_{10}, 86.7% and 7.2e-2, respectively.

- This algorithm produces high levels of diversity (see its high *Online* values) and a suitable final local refinement. In this way, reliability and accuracy were simultaneously improved and so the better results are obtained.

We may conclude that the combination of heterogeneous and the homogeneous features improves the behavior of each one of them separately, in such a way that both, reliability and accuracy, are carried through to a suitable conclusion. So, this combination is a promising way for empowering DGAs to have a great measure of success on complex problems.

5 Concluding Remarks

In this paper, we have presented the HD-RCGAs. In these algorithms a higher level heterogeneous DGA joins homogeneous DGAs that use crossover operators with different exploration and exploitation degrees and different selective pressure degrees. An instance was proposed based on FCB-crossover operators. The results of the experiments carried out on three complex test functions have shown that in general the proposal outperforms equivalent heterogeneous and homogeneous DGAs, offering two main advantages simultaneously, better reliability and accuracy.

Hence, we may conclude that the combination of homogeneous and heterogeneous DGAs is a promising way for increasing the efficacy of DGAs. This paper is a first investigation on a basic implementation of this idea, the connection of different homogeneous DGAs establishing a higher level heterogeneous DGA. Finally, we should point out that future research needs to be done in the following topics related to HD-RCGAs: 1) Study other topologies for the lower-DGAs and the ones that connect them (higher-DGA topology), considering the most suitable types of local and global migrations associated with these topologies, 2) Study the impact of the control parameters that affect the behavior of the lower-DGAs and the higher-DGA, such as migration rates, migration intervals, subpopulation sizes, etc., and 3) Design higher level homogeneous DGAs based on lower level heterogeneous DGAs.

References

1. Baker J.E.: Adaptive Selection Methods for Genetic Algorithms. Proc. of the First Int. Conf. on Genetic Algorithms and their Applications, J.J. Grefenstette (Ed.) (L. Erlbaum Associates, Hillsdale, MA, 1985) 101-111.
2. Baker, J.E.: Reducing Bias and Inefficiency in the Selection Algorithm. Proc. Second Int. Conf. on Genetic Algorithms, , J.J. Grefenstette (Ed.) (L. Erlbaum Associates, Hillsdale, MA, 1987) 14-21.
3. Cantú-Paz E.: A Survey of Parallel Genetic Algorithms. IlliGAL Report 97003, Illinois Genetic Algorithms Laboratory, University of Illinois at Urbana-Champaign, IL (1997).
4. Cohoon J.P., Martin W.N., Richards D.S.: Genetic Algorithms and Punctuated Equilibria in VLSI. Parallel Problem Solving from Nature 1, H.-P. Schwefel, R. Männer (Eds.) (Berlin, Germany, Springer-Verlag, 1990) 134-144.

5. De Jong K.A.: An Analysis of the Behavior of a Class of Genetic Adaptive Systems. Doctoral Dissertation, University of Michigan (1975).
6. Griewangk A.O.: Generalized Descent of Global Optimization. JOTA 34 (1981) 11-39.
7. Gruau F.: The Mixed Genetic Algorithm. Parallel Computing: Trends and Application, G.R. Joubert, D. Trystram, F.J. Peters, D.J. Evans (Eds), Elsevier, 1994.
8. Herrera F., Lozano M.: Heuristic Crossovers for Real-coded Genetic Algorithms Based on Fuzzy Connectives. 4th International Conference on Parallel Problem Solving from Nature (Springer, Berlin, 1996), 336-345.
9. Herrera F., Lozano M.: Heterogeneous Distributed Genetic Algorithms Based on the Crossover Operator. Second IEE/IEEE Int. Conf. on Genetic Algorithms in Engineering Systems: Innovations and Applications, 1997, 203-208.
10. Herrera F., Lozano M.: Gradual Distributed Genetic Algorithms. Technical Report #DECSAI-97-01-03, Dept. of Computer Science and Artificial Intelligence, University of Granada, Spain (1997).
11. Herrera F., Lozano M., Verdegay J.L.: Dynamic and Heuristic Fuzzy Connectives-Based Crossover Operators for Controlling the Diversity and Convergence of Real-Coded Genetic Algorithms. Int. Journal of Intelligent 11 (1996) 1013-1041.
12. Herrera F., Lozano M., Verdegay J.L.: Fuzzy Connectives Based Crossover Operators to Model Genetic Algorithms Population Diversity. Fuzzy Sets and Systems 92(1) (1997) 21-30.
13. Herrera F., Lozano M., Verdegay J.L.: Tackling Real-Coded Genetic Algorithms: Operators and Tools for Behavioural Analysis. Artificial Intelligent Review 12(4) (1998).
14. Lin S-C., Punch III W.F., Goodman E.D.: Coarse-Grain Genetic Algorithms: Categorization and New Approach. Proc. Sixth IEEE Parallel and Distributed Processing (1994) 28-37.
15. Maresky J.: On Efficient Communication in Distributed Genetic Algorithms. M.S. Dissertation, Institute of Computer Science, The Hebrew University of Jerusalem (1994).
16. Mühlenbein H., Schomisch M., Born J.: The Parallel Genetic Algorithm as Function Optimizer. Fourth Int. Conf. on Genetic Algorithms, R. Belew, L.B. Booker (Eds.) (Morgan Kaufmmann, San Mateo, 1991) 271-278.
17. Potts J.C., Giddens T.D., Yadav S.B.: The Development and Evaluation of an Improved Genetic Algorithm Based on Migration and Artificial Selection. IEEE Trans. on Systems, Man, and Cybernetics 24 (1994) 73-86.
18. Preparata J.F., Vuillemin J.E.: The Cube-Connected Cycles: A Versatile Network for Parallel Computation. Communications of the ACM 24(5), (1981) 300-309.
19. Schlierkamp-Voosen D., Mühlenbein H.: Strategy Adaptation by Competing Subpopulations. Parallel Problem Solving from Nature 3, Y. Davidor, H.-P. Schwefel, R. Männer (Eds.) (Berlin, Germany, Springer-Verlag, 1994) 199-208.
20. Schwefel H-P.: Numerical Optimization of Computer Models, Wiley, Chichester (1981).
21. Tanese R.: Distributed Genetic Algorithms. Proc. of the Third Int. Conf. on Genetic Algorithms, J. David Schaffer (Ed.) (Morgan Kaufmann Publishers, San Mateo, 1989) 434-439.
22. Voigt H.M., Born J.: A Structured Distributed Genetic Algorithm for Function Optimization. Parallel Problem Solving from Nature 2, R. Männer, B. Manderick (Eds.) (Elsevier Science Publishers, Amsterdam, 1992) 199-208.
23. Whitley D., Beveridge R., Graves C., Mathias K.: Test Driving Three 1995 Genetic Algorithms: New Test Functions and Geometric Matching. Journal of Heuristics 1 (1995) 77-104.

Mechanisms of Emergent Computation in Cellular Automata

Wim Hordijk, James P. Crutchfield, Melanie Mitchell

Santa Fe Institute, 1399 Hyde Park Road, Santa Fe, NM 87501, USA
email: {wim,chaos,mm}@santafe.edu

Abstract. We introduce a class of embedded-particle models for describing the emergent computational strategies observed in cellular automata (CAs) that were evolved for performing certain computational tasks. The models are evaluated by comparing their estimated performances with the actual performances of the CAs they model. The results show, via a close quantitative agreement, that the embedded-particle framework captures the main information processing mechanisms of the emergent computation that arise in these evolved CAs.

1 Introduction

In previous work we have used genetic algorithms (GAs) to evolve cellular automata (CAs) to perform computational tasks that require global coordination. The evolving cellular automata framework has provided a direct approach to studying how evolution (natural or artificial) can create dynamical systems that perform *emergent computation*; that is, how it can find dynamical systems in which the interaction of simple components with local information storage and communication gives rise to coordinated global information processing [3].

In [5, 6], we analyzed the evolutionary search process by which a genetic algorithm designed CAs to perform various tasks. References to other work relating to evolving cellular automata can be found in [3, 5, 6]. In this paper we focus on how the behavior of evolved CAs implements the emergent computational strategies for performing these tasks. We develop a class of "embedded-particle" models to describe the computational strategies. To do this, we use the computational mechanics framework of Crutchfield and Hanson [2, 7], in which a CA's information processing is described in terms of regular domains, embedded particles, and particle interactions. We then evaluate this class of models by comparing their computational performance to that of the CAs they model. The results demonstrate, via a close quantitative agreement between the CAs and their respective models, that the embedded particle framework captures the functional features that emerge in the CAs' space-time behavior and that underlie the CAs' computational capability and evolutionary fitness.

2 CAs and Computation

This paper concerns one-dimensional binary-state CAs with spatially periodic boundary conditions. Such a CA consists of a one-dimensional lattice of N two-state machines ("cells"), each of which changes its state as a function, denoted ϕ, of the current states in a local neighborhood. In a one-dimensional CA, a neighborhood consists of a cell and its *radius* r neighbors on either side.

The lattice starts out with an initial configuration (IC) of cell states (0s and 1s) and this configuration changes at discrete time steps during which all cells are updated simultaneously according to the CA's rule ϕ. The rule ϕ can be expressed as a look-up table that lists, for each local neighborhood, the state which is taken by the neighborhood's central cell at the next time step.

One-dimensional binary-state cellular automata are perhaps the simplest examples of decentralized, spatially extended systems in which emergent computation can be observed. In our studies, a CA performing a computation means that the input to the computation is encoded as the IC, the output is decoded from the configuration reached at some later time step, and the intermediate steps that transform the input to the output are taken as the steps in the computation.

To date we have used a genetic algorithm (GA) to evolve one-dimensional, binary-state $r = 3$ CAs to perform a density-classification task [3, 5] and a synchronization task [6].

For the density classification task, the goal is to find a CA that decides whether or not the IC contains a majority of 1s (i.e., has high density). Let ρ_0 denote the density of 1s in the IC. If $\rho_0 > 1/2$, then within M time steps the CA should reach the fixed-point configuration of all 1s (i.e., all cells in state 1 for all subsequent iterations); otherwise, within M time steps it should reach the fixed-point configuration of all 0s. M is a parameter of the task that depends on the lattice size N. As an example, figure 1(a) shows a space-time diagram of a GA-evolved CA ϕ_{dens5} for the density classification task, starting with a randomly generated IC (in this case with $\rho_0 < 1/2$). Cells in state 1 are colored black, cells in state 0 are colored white. Time increases down the page.

For the synchronization task, the goal is to find a CA that, from any IC, settles down within M time steps to a periodic oscillation between an all-0s configuration and an all-1s configuration. Again, M is a parameter of the task that depends on N. Figure 1(c) shows a space-time diagram of a GA-evolved CA, denoted ϕ_{sync5}, for the synchronization task, again starting with a randomly generated IC.

Since a CA uses only local interactions, and thus has to propagate information across the lattice to achieve global coordination, both tasks require nontrivial computation. For example, in the synchronization task, the *entire* lattice has to be synchronized, which means the CA must resolve, using only local interactions, separate regions of the lattice that are locally synchronized but are out of phase with respect to one another.

We define the performance $\mathcal{P}_{N,I}(\phi)$ of a CA ϕ on a given task as the fraction of I randomly generated ICs on which ϕ reaches the desired behavior within M time steps on a lattice of length N. Here, we use $N = 149$, $M = 2N$ and $I = 10^4$.

3   Analysis of Evolved CAs

Due to the local nature of a CA's operations, it is typically very hard, if not impossible, to understand the CA's global behavior—in our case, the strategy for performing a computational task—by directly examining either the bits in the look-up table or the temporal sequence of 0-1 spatial configurations of the lattice.

Crutchfield and Hanson developed a method for detecting and analyzing the "intrinsic" computational components in the CA's space-time behavior in terms of regular domains, embedded particles, and particle interactions [2, 7]. This method is part of their *computational mechanics* framework for understanding information processing embedded in physical systems [1].

Briefly, a *regular domain* is a homogeneous region of space-time in which the same "pattern" appears. More formally, the spatial patterns in a regular domain can be described by a regular language that is mapped onto itself by the CA rule ϕ. An *embedded particle* is a spatially localized, temporally recurrent structure found at *domain boundaries*, i.e., where the domain pattern breaks down. When two or more particles "collide" they can produce an interaction result—e.g., another set of particles or a mutual annihilation.

In the space-time diagram of ϕ_{dens5} in figure 1(a), some of the domains, particles, and interactions are labeled. Three regular domains are readily apparent in ϕ_{dens5}'s space-time behavior: the all-white domain, the all-black domain, and a checkerboard domain (alternating white and black cells). The boundaries between these domains form the embedded particles, which can collide and interact with each other, creating other particles or simply annihilating.

Using computational mechanics, we can analyze the space-time behavior of evolved CAs in terms of these domains, particles, and interactions. In particular, the particles and their interactions can be made more explicit by suppressing the domains. Figure 1 shows examples for both ϕ_{dens5} and ϕ_{sync5}. For example, in ϕ_{sync5}'s space-time behavior (figure 1(c)), there are two regular domains: the "synchronized" domain (the parts of the lattice which display the desired oscillation) and a second domain which has a zigzag pattern. Having identified these domains, we can build a filter based on the regular languages that represent the domains. Using this filter, the domains can be detected and then suppressed, revealing the domain boundaries. The filtered space-time diagram for ϕ_{sync5} is shown in figure 1(d), where the regular domains are mapped to 0s (white) and the domain boundaries are mapped to 1s (black). A similar procedure for ϕ_{dens5} leads to the filtered space-time diagram in figure 1(b).

Briefly, the domain filter can be constructed in the following way. First, the (minimal) finite automata representing the regular languages of the domains need to be constructed. A series of transitions between states within each one of these finite automata represents an allowed sequence of site values in the domain configuration. That is, following these transitions is equivalent to remaining within a specific regular domain. Next, a finite-state transducer is built by connecting the separate finite automata of the regular domains by "wall" transitions. The latter represent transitions from one domain to another and so correspond to domain boundaries. Output symbols can be added to the wall transitions to give distinct labelings to the boundaries, if desired. As this transducer scans a CA configuration from left to right (say), it reads the consecutive cell states (0 or 1) and outputs a 0 or a 1 depending on whether it made an intradomain or a wall transition, respectively. In this way, a new, filtered configuration of "domain" and "wall" values is generated based on the presence of regular domains in the original configuration. Doing this for the configuration at each time step results in a filtered space-time diagram as shown in figures 1(b) and 1(d). (See [2] for details of transducer construction and use.)

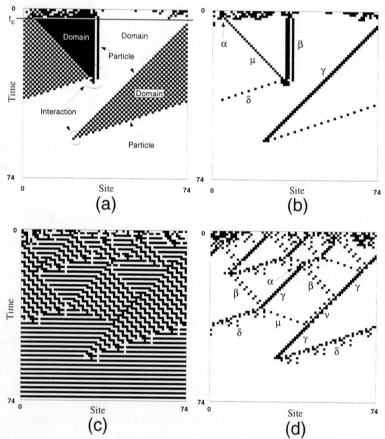

Fig. 1. (a) Space-time diagram of a GA-evolved CA ϕ_{dens5} that classifies high or low density of 1s in the initial configuration. Different regular domains, embedded particles, and particle interactions can be observed. (b) Filtered version of the space-time diagram in (a). Domains are mapped to white, domain boundaries to black. The different particles are labeled with Greek letters. (c) Space-time diagram of GA-evolved CA ϕ_{sync5} that, starting from a random IC, comes to global synchronization. (d) Filtered version of (c). Note that the same Greek letters in figures (b) and (d) do not denote the same particles.

The regular domains of ϕ_{dens5} and ϕ_{sync5} are readily apparent in their space-time diagrams, being easily identified by eye. The identification and construction of domain minimal automata are not always so straightforward. Computational mechanics provides an algorithm, called ϵ-*machine reconstruction*, for the recognition and identification of regular domains, including construction of their corresponding finite automaton representations, in spatio-temporal data [2, 4, 7].

Using computational mechanics, we can extract the relevant information about the domains, particles, and their interactions from the space-time diagrams of a given CA. A catalog of ϕ_{sync5}'s observed domains, particles, and their temporal periodicities and velocities, and all possible particle interactions, is given in table 3. The *temporal periodicity* p of a particle is the number of time steps after which its spatial configuration repeats. The *velocity* v of a particle is the *displacement* d (the number of sites the particle has shifted in space after exactly one temporal period), divided by the temporal periodicity: $v = d/p$. For example, the particle μ in figure 1(d) has a temporal periodicity of $p = 2$, after which it has shifted $d = 6$ sites, so its velocity is $v = 6/2 = 3$.

Table 1. A catalog of ϕ_{sync5}'s domains, particles and their properties, and interactions, some of which can be observed in the filtered space-time diagram of figure 1(c). An interaction result denoted by $\emptyset$ means that the two particles annihilate. The probabilities associated with the interaction results are also provided. If no explicit probability is given for an interaction result, it occurs with probability 1. These interaction result probabilities are explained in section 4.

ϕ_{sync5} **Particle Catalog**						
Domains Λ			**Particles P**			
Label	Regular language		Label	Wall	p	d	v
Λ^s	$\Lambda_0^s = 0^4 0^*,\ \Lambda_1^s = 1^4 1^*$		α	$\Lambda_1^s \Lambda_0^s$	-	-	-
Λ^z	$\Lambda_0^z = (0001)^*,\ \Lambda_1^z = (1110)^*$		β	$\Lambda_0^z \Lambda_0^s,\ \Lambda_1^z \Lambda_1^s$	2	2	1
Interactions I			γ	$\Lambda_0^s \Lambda_1^z,\ \Lambda_1^s \Lambda_0^z$	2	-2	-1
Type	Interaction	Interaction	δ	$\Lambda_0^z \Lambda_1^s,\ \Lambda_1^z \Lambda_0^s$	4	-12	-3
decay	$\alpha \rightarrow \gamma + \beta$		μ	$\Lambda_0^s \Lambda_0^z,\ \Lambda_1^s \Lambda_1^z$	2	6	3
react	$\beta + \gamma \xrightarrow{0.84} \delta + \mu$	$\beta + \gamma \xrightarrow{0.16} \nu$	ν	$\Lambda_0^z \Lambda_1^z,\ \Lambda_1^z \Lambda_0^z$	2	-2	-1
	$\mu + \delta \rightarrow \gamma + \beta$	$\nu + \delta \rightarrow \beta$					
	$\mu + \nu \rightarrow \gamma$						
annihilate	$\mu + \beta \rightarrow \emptyset$	$\gamma + \delta \rightarrow \emptyset$					

Particles transfer information about properties of local regions across the lattice to distant sites. Particle collisions are the loci of information processing and result in either the creation of new information in the form of other particles or in annihilation. The computational mechanics analysis provides us with this particle-level description, which we claim captures the main mechanisms by which the CA transfers and processes local information to accomplish the emergent computation required by the task.

4 A Formal Model of Computational Strategies

To formalize the notion of computational strategy in a CA, and the resulting emergent computation, we model the CA's behavior using only the notions of domains, particles, and interactions, moving away from the underlying individual cells in a configuration to a higher level description. The resulting embedded-particle model employs a number of simplifying assumptions.

Before the assumptions are stated, we first define the *condensation time* t_c as the *first* time step at which the lattice can be completely described in terms of domains and particles. To identify this condensation time in a CA's space-time diagram, we can extend the transducer that is used to filter out domains to also recognize particles. In terms of the transitions in the transducer, particles are specific sequences of wall transitions that lead from states in one domain to those in another. Including these transition paths in the set of allowed transitions, the transducer can recognize both regular domains *and* the particles. (A more detailed example of how to extend the transducer to incorporate the particles can be found in [8].) Using this extended transducer, the condensation time t_c is then defined as the first time step at which filtering the lattice does not generate any disallowed transitions.

The occurrence of the condensation time is illustrated in figure 1(a) for ϕ_{dens5}. The condensation time ($t_c = 4$ in this particular case) is marked by the solid line. It is the time step at which the non-domain/particle structures at the first few time steps have died out and there remain only domains and particles. The particular value of t_c for a given CA depends on the IC, but we can estimate the average condensation time $\overline{t_c}$ for a given rule by sampling t_c over a large set of random ICs. The measured value of $\overline{t_c}$ for various rules will be used later when we evaluate the particle models. For ϕ_{dens5} on a lattice size of 149, $\overline{t_c} \approx 12$.

As a first simplifying assumption of the model, we ignore the details of the space-time dynamics up to t_c and assume that the net effect of this behavior is to generate some distribution of particles of various types, probabilistically located in the configuration at time t_c. In other words, we assume that beyond generating this distribution at t_c, the initial "pre-condensation" dynamics are not relevant to predicting the performance of the CA.

To estimate this particle probability distribution at t_c, we again employ the extended transducer that is used for determining t_c. Using a large set of random ICs (in our case 10^4), the CA is run on each one up to the actual condensation time, i.e., up to the first time step at which the extended transducer only goes through domain and wall transitions while scanning the configuration. Next, the number of times each of these transitions are taken is counted and this is averaged over the set of 10^4 condensation-time configurations. From these counts, a *transition probability* for each allowed transition can be calculated. The extended transducer, together with the estimated transition probabilities, provides an approximation of the actual particle probability distribution at $\overline{t_c}$.

As a second simplifying step, we assume that all particles have zero width, even though, as can be seen in figure 1, particles actually have varying widths.

As a third simplification, we allow interactions only between pairs of particles. No interactions involving more than two particles are included in the model.

A fourth simplifying assumption we make is that particle interactions are instantaneous. As can be seen in figure 1, when two particles collide and interact with each other, typically the interaction takes time to occur—for some number of time steps the configuration cannot be completely decomposed into domains and particles. In the embedded-particle model when two particles collide they are immediately replaced by the interaction result.

The interaction result of a particle collision is determined by the phases that both particles are in at the time of their collision. As a fifth simplifying assumption, we approximate this relative phase dependence by a stochastic choice of interaction result. To determine an interaction result, the model uses a particle catalog (e.g., as shown in table 3 for ϕ_{sync5}) that contains interaction-result probabilities. For each possible pair of particle types, this catalog lists all the interaction results that these two particles can produce, together with the probability that each particular result occurs. These probabilities can be estimated empirically by simply counting, over a set of 10^4 random ICs, how often each interaction result occurs in the space-time diagram. In the model, when two particles collide, the catalog is consulted and an interaction result is determined at random according to these probabilities. For example, in table 3, the $\beta + \gamma$ interaction has two possible outcomes. Each is given with its estimated probability of occurrence.

In summary, the embedded-particle model of a CA's computational strategy consists of: (1) A catalog of possible domains, particle types, and pairwise particle interactions and results, along with the interaction-result probabilities for each; and (2) An approximate particle probability distribution at $\overline{t_c}$, represented by the domain-particle transducer with estimated transition probabilities.

5 Evaluating the Embedded-Particle Model

One way to evaluate an embedded-particle model is to compare its task performance to that of the CA it models. A close agreement would support our claim that the embedded-particle model is a good description of the CA's computational strategy. This is a quantitative complement to the computational mechanics analysis which establishes the structural roles of domains, particles, and interactions.

To run the model, we start by generating an initial particle configuration at $\overline{t_c}$, according to the particle probability distribution in the model (i.e., we ignore the "pre-condensation" phase). Since this probability distribution is represented by the transducer with estimated transition probabilities, we now use this transducer as a domain-particle *generator* instead of a recognizer. Starting in a randomly chosen state (according to an empirically determined probability distribution), the transducer traverses N lattice sites, and at each site it chooses a transition according to the estimated probabilities and then outputs either a domain or a particle symbol, according to which transition was chosen.

This process creates an initial particle configuration by placing a number of particles of various types in the configuration at random locations according to the approximated particle probability distribution. The result is that we know for each particle in the initial particle configuration (at $t = \overline{t_c}$) its type and also its velocity and spatial location. It is then straightforward to calculate geometrically at what time step t_i the first interaction between two particles will occur. The particle catalog is then consulted and the result of this particular interaction is determined. The two interacting particles are replaced by the interaction result, yielding a new particle configuration at time step t_i.

This process of calculating the next interaction time and replacing the interacting particles with their interaction result is iterated either until there are no particles left (i.e., they have all annihilated one another) or until a given maximum number $(M - \overline{t_c})$ of time steps is reached, whichever occurs first.

Since the embedded-particle model contains information about which domains are associated with which particles, we can keep track of the domains between the particles at each time step while the model is run. Thus, if all particles eventually annihilate one another, we know which domain is left occupying the entire lattice. This way, we can check whether running the model resulted in the correct final behavior for the given task.

6 Results

We can now evaluate the performance of an embedded-particle model by running it on a large number I of initial particle configurations at $\overline{t_c}$ and calculating the fraction over which it displays the correct behavior; i.e., that it settles down to the correct domain within the maximum number of allowed time steps. This performance estimate is then compared to the actual performance of the CA from which the model was built. Here we used $N = 149$, $M = 2N$, and $I = 10^4$.

Figure 2(a) shows the results of comparing the average performance of five evolved CAs for density classification with the performance predicted by their respective models. In all cases the average performance is calculated over 10 sets of 10^4 random ICs (in case of the actual CAs) or initial particle configurations (in case of the models). The five CAs appeared at different generations during one particular run of the GA on the density classification task. Each successive CA implemented an improved computational strategy for performing the task, reflected in the successive increases in performance. The evolutionary process that gave rise to these CAs is discussed in more detail in [5].

Figure 2(b) shows similar results for five CAs that appeared during a GA run on the synchronization task (note that the first one, ϕ_{sync1}, had a performance of 0). These CAs were qualitatively described in [6]. Table 2 shows the performance data for all ten CAs, including the standard deviations of the measured average performances. Recall that typical space-time behavior of ϕ_{dens5} and ϕ_{sync5} was shown in figures 1(a) and 1(c), respectively.

Generally, there is very good agreement between the CA and embedded-particle model performances. Furthermore, most of the discrepancies can be

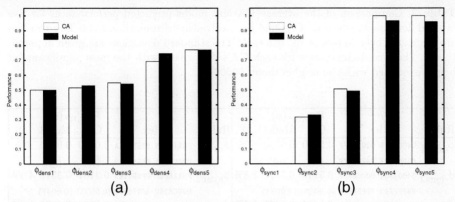

Fig. 2. Comparison of the average CA performances (labeled "CA") and the model-estimated average performances (labeled "Model") for (a) five evolved density classification CAs and (b) five evolved synchronization CAs.

traced back directly to the simplifying assumptions underlying the particle models. For example, the discrepancies for ϕ_{sync4} and ϕ_{sync5} are partly caused by the "zigzag" domain having a spatial periodicity of four (see figure 1(c)). Due to the periodic boundary conditions on a lattice of size 149, a CA can never settle down to a configuration containing only the zigzag domain, since 149 is not divisible by 4. However, this can happen in the embedded-particle model, since it ignores the spatial periodicity of domains. Such configurations are counted as incorrect behavior in the models and this results in slightly lower predicted versus actual performances. The observed discrepancies, which will be explained in more detail elsewhere, demonstrate where our simplifying assumptions fail. We can improve on the model's agreement with these and other CAs by incorporating additional features, such as taking particle phases into account.

7 Conclusions

Emergent computation in decentralized spatially extended systems, such as in CAs, is still not well understood. In previous work we have used an evolutionary approach to search for CAs that are capable of performing computations that require global coordination. We have also qualitatively analyzed the emergent "computational strategies" of the evolved CAs in terms of domains, particles, and particle interactions. The embedded-particle models described here provide a means to more rigorously formalize the notion of "emergent computational strategy" in spatially extended systems and to make quantitative predictions about the computational behavior and evolutionary fitness of the evolved CAs. This is an essential, quantitative part of our overall research program—to understand how natural spatially extended systems can perform globally coordinated computations and how evolutionary processes can give rise to systems with sophisticated emergent computational abilities.

Table 2. Comparison of the average CA and model-predicted performances for five evolved density-classification CAs and five evolved synchronization CAs. The averages are calculated over 10 sets of 10^4 ICs each. The standard deviations are given in parentheses. The hexadecimal code for each CA's ϕ is given, with the most significant bit being associated with the neighborhood 0000000.

Rule	Hex	$\mathcal{P}_{149,10^4}(\phi)$ CA	Model	Δ	Rule	Hex	$\mathcal{P}_{149,10^4}(\phi)$ CA	Model	Δ
ϕ_{dens1}	04004489 020107FF	0.5000	0.5000	0%	ϕ_{sync1}	F8A19CE6 B65848EA	0.0000	0.0000	0%
	6B9F7793 F9FFBF7F	(0)	(0)			D26CB24A EB51C4A0	(0)	(0)	
ϕ_{dens2}	04004581 00000FFF	0.5145	0.5291	2.8%	ϕ_{sync2}	F8A1AE2F CF6BC1E2	0.3161	0.3316	4.9%
	6B9F7793 7DFFFF7F	(0.0026)	(0.0034)			D26CB24C 3C266E20	(0.0033)	(0.0047)	
ϕ_{dens3}	05004581 00000FFF	0.5487	0.5405	1.5%	ϕ_{sync3}	F8A1AE2F CE6BC1E2	0.5063	0.4923	1.4%
	6B9F7793 7FBFFF5F	(0.0027)	(0.0055)			C26CB24E 3C226CA0	(0.0059)	(0.0037)	
ϕ_{dens4}	05004581 00000FBF	0.6923	0.7447	7.6%	ϕ_{sync4}	F8A1CDAA B6D84C98	0.9991	0.9655	3.4%
	6B9F7593 7FBDF77F	(0.0055)	(0.0070)			5668B64A EF10C4A0	(0.0002)	(0.0019)	
ϕ_{dens5}	05040587 05000F77	0.7702	0.7689	0.2%	ϕ_{sync5}	FEB1C6EA B8E0C4DA	1.0000	0.9596	4.0%
	03775583 7BFFB77F	(0.0036)	(0.0052)			6484A5AA F410C8A0	(0)	(0.0021)	

Acknowledgments

This research was supported by the Santa Fe Institute under ONR grant N00014-95-1-0975, NSF grants IRI-9320200 and IRI-9705853, DOE grant DE-FG03-94ER25231, and Sandia National Laboratory contract AU-4978.

References

1. Crutchfield, J. P.: The calculi of emergence: Computation, dynamics, and induction. Physica D **75** (1994) 11–54.
2. Crutchfield, J. P., Hanson, J. E.: Turbulent pattern bases for cellular automata. Physica D **69** (1993) 279–301.
3. Crutchfield, J. P., Mitchell, M.: The evolution of emergent computation. Proceedings of the National Academy of Sciences, USA 92 **23** (1995) 10742–10746.
4. Crutchfield, J. P., Young, K.: Inferring statistical complexity. Physical Review Letters **63** (1989) 105–108.
5. Das, R., Mitchell, M., Crutchfield, J. P.: A genetic algorithm discovers particle-based computation in cellular automata. Parallel Problem Solving from Nature—PPSN III, Davidor, Y., Schwefel, H.-P., Männer, R., eds. (1994) 244–353.
6. Das, R., Crutchfield, J. P., Mitchell, M., Hanson, J. E.: Evolving globally synchronized cellular automata. Proceedings of the Sixth International Conference on Genetic Algorithms, Eshelman, L. ed., (1995) 336–343.
7. Hanson, J. E., Crutchfield, J. P.: The attractor-basin portrait of a cellular automaton. Journal of Statistical Physics **66** (5/6) (1992) 1415–1462.
8. Hanson, J. E., Crutchfield, J. P.: Computational Mechanics of Cellular Automata: An Example. Physica D **103** (1997) 169–189.
9. Wolfram, S.: Cellular Automata and Complexity. Addison-Wesley, 1994.

Towards Designing Neural Network Ensembles by Evolution

Yong Liu and Xin Yao

Computational Intelligence Group, School of Computer Science
University College, The University of New South Wales
Australian Defence Force Academy, Canberra, ACT, Australia 2600
Email: {liuy,xin}@cs.adfa.oz.au

Abstract. This paper proposes a co-evolutionary learning system, i.e., CELS, to design neural network (NN) ensembles. CELS addresses the issue of automatic determination of the number of individual NNs in an ensemble and the exploitation of the interaction between individual NN design and combination. The idea of CELS is to encourage different individual NNs in the ensemble to learn different parts or aspects of the training data so that the ensemble can learn the whole training data better. The cooperation and specialisation among different individual NNs are considered during the individual NN design. This provides an opportunity for different NNs to interact with each other and to specialise. Experiments on two real-world problems demonstrate that CELS can produce NN ensembles with good generalisation ability.

1 Introduction

Many real-world problems are too large and too complex for a single monolithic system to solve alone. There are many examples from both natural and artificial systems which show that a composite system consisting of several subsystems can reduce the total complexity of the system while solving a difficult problem satisfactorily. The success of neural network (NN) ensembles in improving classifier's generalisation is a typical example[1].

Given the advantages of NN ensembles and the complexity of the problems that are beginning to be investigated, it is clear that NN ensemble processing is and will be an important and pervasive problem-solving technique. NN ensemble design in engineering, however, has relied on human expertise (often a committee) to manually divide a system into specialised parts, often in an *ad hoc* manner. While manual design may be appropriate when there are experienced human experts with sufficient prior knowledge of the problem to be solved, it is certainly not the case for those real-world problems where we do not have much prior knowledge. Tedious trial-and-error processes are often involved in designing NN ensembles in practice.

This paper proposes a co-evolutionary learning system, i.e., CELS, to design NN ensembles automatically without human intervention based on negative correlation learning[2, 3] and speciation[4]. Evolutionary learning is population-based learning method[5]. Combining individual NNs in a population into a NN ensemble has a close relationship to modular design of NN ensembles. Each individual NN in the population can be regarded as a module. The evolutionary process can be regarded as a natural and automatic way to produce different modules.

CELS is different from previous work in designing NN ensembles in three major aspects. First, most previous work did not acknowledge or exploit the negative correlation among individual NNs as a driving force in the control of problem-solving activity. The individual NNs are often trained independently. There is no consideration of whether what one individual NN learns has already been learned by other individuals. CELS emphasises specialisation and cooperation among individual NNs in the ensemble. In CELS, an evolutionary algorithm (EA)[6] have been used to search for a population of diverse individual NNs that together solve a problem (e.g., classify examples). To maintain a diverse population while applying EA's selection operator, EA approach must incorporate some kind of speciation technique by which individuals in a population can form several species automatically through evolution. Negative correlation learning and a fitness sharing have been used to encourage the formation of different species. The idea of negative correlation learning is that each individual NN in an ensemble attempts to not only minimise the error between the target and its output, but also to decorrelate its error from the rest NNs in the ensemble. The fitness sharing[4] refers to one type of speciation techniques in evolutionary computation by which individuals in a population can form several species automatically through evolution.

Second, most previous work often separated individual NNs design from average procedures, and followed the two-stage design process; first generating the individual NNs, and then combining them. The possible interactions among them cannot be exploited until the combination stage. There is no feedback from the combination stage to the individual design stage. It is possible that some of the independently designed individual NNs do not make much contribution to the whole system. CELS learns and combines individual NNs in the same evolution process. This provides an opportunity for different NNs to interact with each other and to specialise. There has been an attempt in learning and combining in the same learning process in design the mixtures-of-experts architectures[7]. However, both the architectures and the learning algorithms of the mixtures-of-experts architectures are quite distinct from CELS. CELS is more flexible than the mixtures-of-experts architectures. In CELS, the individual NNs are not necessarily homogeneous and each individual NN can be trained by different learning algorithms. Furthermore, CELS is not limited to NNs. It can be applied to virtually any learning system.

Third, the number of NNs in the ensemble is often prefined and fixed in most previous work. The design of NN ensembles is usually done manually through a trial-and-error process. In CELS, all the NNs are evolved, not manually crafted. The number of NNs needs not be pre-fixed by human designers, who may or may not have sufficient a priori knowledge to do so.

The rest of this paper is organised as follows: Section 2 describes CELS in detail and gives motivations and ideas behind various design choices; Section 3 presents experimental results on CELS and some discussions; and finally Section 4 concludes with a summary of the paper and a few remarks.

2 Evolving Neural Network Ensembles

In its current implementation, CELS is used to evolve NN ensembles, while each NN is a feedforward NN with sigmoid transfer functions. However, this is not an inherent constraint. In fact, CELS has minimal constraint on the type of learning systems which may be evolved. The major steps of CELS are given as follows:

1. Generate an initial population of M NNs, and set $k = 1$. The number of hidden nodes for each NN, n_h, is specified by the user. The random initial weights are uniformly distributed inside a small range.
2. Train each NN in the population on the training set for a certain number of epochs using the negative correlation learning. The number of epochs, n_e, is specified by the user.
3. Randomly choose a block of n_b NNs as parents to creat n_b offspring NNs by Gaussian mutation.
4. Add the n_b offspring NNs to the population and train the offspring NNs using the negative correlation learning while the rest NNs' weights are frozen.
5. Calculate the fitness of each NN in the population and prune the population to the M fittest NNs.
6. If the maximum number of generations has been reached, stop the evolutionary process and go to Step 7. Otherwise, $k = k + 1$ and go to Step 3.
7. After the evolutionary process, cluster the NNs in the population into a prescribed minimum number to a prescribed maximum number of cluster sets. These cluster sets are then used to construct NN ensembles. The optimal number of cluster sets is determined by evaluating all ensembles that can be constructed in this way.

There are two-level adaptations in CELS: the local learning based on negative correlation learning at the individual level and the evolutionary learning based on evolutionary programming (EP)[6] at the population level. Details about each component of CELS are given in the following sections.

2.1 Negative Correlation Learning

In CELS, the local learning carried out by each NN is performed by a negative correlation learning. The negative correlation learning has been successfully applied to NN ensembles[2, 3]. It introduces a correlation penalty term into the error function of each individual NN so that the individual NN can be trained cooperatively. Specially, the error function E_i for individual i is defined by

$$E_i = \frac{1}{N}\Sigma_{n=1}^{N}E_i(n)$$

$$= \frac{1}{N}\Sigma_{n=1}^{N}\left[\frac{1}{2}\left(d(n) - F_i(n)\right)^2 + \lambda p_i(n)\right] \tag{1}$$

where N is the number of training patterns, $E_i(n)$ is the value of the error of individual NN i at presentation of the nth training pattern, $F_i(n)$ is the output of individual NN i on the nth training pattern, and p_i is a correlation penalty function. The purpose of minimising p_i is to negatively correlate each individual's error with errors for the rest of the ensemble. The parameter $\lambda > 0$ is used to adjust the strength of the penalty. The function p_i can be chosen as

$$p_i(n) = (F_i(n) - F(n)) \, \Sigma_{j \neq i} \, (F_j(n) - F(n)) \tag{2}$$

where $F(n)$ is a simple averaging of the output of individual NNs in the ensemble on the nth training pattern

$$F(n) = \frac{1}{M} \Sigma_{i=1}^{M} F_i(n) \tag{3}$$

The partial derivative of E_i with respect to the output of individual i on nth training pattern is

$$\frac{\partial E_i(n)}{\partial F_i(n)} = F_i(n) - d(n) - \lambda(F_i(n) - F(n)) \tag{4}$$

The standard back-propagation (BP) algorithm with pattern-by-pattern updating [8] has been used for weight adjustments in our ensembles. Weight updating of NNs is performed using Eq.(4) after the presentation of each training case. One complete presentation of the entire training set during the learning process is called an *epoch*.

The sum of $E_i(n)$ over all i is

$$
\begin{aligned}
E(n) &= \Sigma_{i=1}^{M} E_i(n) \\
&= \left(\frac{1}{2} - \lambda \right) \Sigma_{i=1}^{M} (d(n) - F_i(n))^2 + \lambda M (F(n) - d(n))^2
\end{aligned} \tag{5}
$$

From Eqs.(1), (4) and (5), the following observations can be made:

1. During the training process, all the individual NNs interact each other through their penalty functions, i.e., Eq.(2).
2. For $\lambda = 0.0$, there is no correlation penalty term in the the error functions of the individual NNs, and the individual NNs are trained independently using BP. That is, independent learning using BP for the individual NNs is a special case of our algorithm.
3. For $\lambda = \frac{1}{2}$, Eq.(5) can be re-written as

$$E(n) = \frac{M}{2} (F(n) - d(n))^2 \tag{6}$$

The term $(F(n) - d(n))^2$ in Eq.(6) is the error function of the ensemble. From this point of view, negative correlation learning provides a novel way to decompose the learning task of the ensemble into a number of subtasks for each individual.

2.2 Mutation and Fitness Evaluation

The n_b offspring are generated as follows:

$$\mathbf{w}_i' = \mathbf{w}_i + \mathbf{N}(0,1) \tag{7}$$

where $\mathbf{w}_i'$ and $\mathbf{w}_i$ denote the weights of offspring i and parent i, respectively, $i = 1, \cdots, n_b$. $\mathbf{N}(0,1)$ denotes a Gaussian variable with mean zero and standard deviation one. The n_b offspring NNs are added to the population, and further trained by the negative correlation learning.

Many fitness sharing schemes have been proposed in recent years. Explicit and implicit fitness sharing are two most popular ones[9]. However, most fitness sharing schemes were first proposed for multi-objective function optimisation. They might not be suitable for CELS. An implicit fitness sharing is used in CELS based on the idea of "covering" the same training case by shared individuals. The procedure of calculating shared fitness is carried out case-by-case over the training set. For each training case, if there are $p > 0$ individuals that correctly classify it, then each of these p individuals receives $1/p$ fitness reward, and the rest individuals in the population receive zero fitness reward. Otherwise, all the individuals in the population receive zero fitness reward. The fitness reward is summed over all training cases. The division of each fitness reward by the number of individuals acts as a primitive form of fitness sharing. This method is expected to generate a smoother shared fitness landscape and thus more efficient for CELS to search.

2.3 Combination Methods

Two methods for constructing the NN ensembles were tested. One used all the individual NNs in the last generation and the other selected one representative from each species in the last generation. The species in the population is determined by clustering the individuals in the population using the *k-means algorithm*[10]. The resulting clusters will correspond to different species. The representative for each species is the fittest individual in the species.

Three combination methods for determining the output of the ensemble have been investigated in CELS. The first is simple averaging. The output of the ensemble is formed by a simple averaging of output of individual NNs in the ensemble. The second is majority voting. The output of the most number of individual NNs will be the output of the ensemble. The third is winner-takes-all. For each case of the testing set, the output of the ensemble is only decided by the individual NN whose output has the highest activation.

3 Experimental Studies

We have applied CELS to two benchmark problems, including the Australian credit card data set and the diabetes data set. Both data sets were obtained from the UCI machine learning benchmark repository. They are available by anonymous ftp at ics.uci.edu (128.195.1.1) in directory /pub/machine-learning-databases.

The Australian credit card data set is to assess applications for credit cards based on a number of attributes. There are 690 cases in total. The output has two classes. The 14 attributes include 6 numeric values and 8 discrete ones, the latter having from 2 to 14 possible values.

The diabetes data set is a two class problem which has 500 examples of class 1 and 268 of class 2. There are 8 attributes for each example. The data set is rather difficult to classify. The so-called "class" value is really a binarised form of another attribute which is itself highly indicative of certain types of diabetes but does not have a one to one correspondence with the medical condition of being diabetic.

Because a single train-and-test experiment may generate misleading performance estimates when the sample size is relatively small. CELS has been tested using m-fold cross-validation technique, in which the data is randomly divided into m mutually exclusive data groups of equal size. In each train-and-test process, one data group is selected as the testing set, and the other $(m-1)$ groups become the training set. The estimated error rate is the average error rate from these m groups. In this way, the error rate is estimated efficiently and in an unbiased way. The parameter m was set to be 10 for the Australian credit card data set, and 12 for the diabetes data set, respectively.

The parameters used in CELS were set to be the same for both problems: the population size M (25), the number of generations (200), the number of hidden nodes n_h (5), the reproduction block size n_b (2), the strength parameter λ (0.75), the number of training epochs n_e (5), the minimum number of cluster sets (3), and the maximum number of cluster sets (25). These parameters were selected after some preliminary experiments. They were not meant to be optimal.

3.1 Experimental Results

A Population as an Ensemble Tables 1–2 show CELS's results for the two data sets, where the ensemble consists of the whole population in the last generation. The *accuracy rate* refers to the percentage of correct classifications produced by CELS. In comparison with the accuracy rates obtained by three combination methods, winner-takes-all outperformed simple averaging and majority voting on both problems. In simple averaging and majority voting, all individuals have the same combination weights and are treated equally. However, not all individuals are equally important. Because different individuals created by CELS were able to specialise to different parts of the testing set, only the outputs of these specialists should be considered to make the final decision of the ensemble for this part of the testing set. The winner-takes-all combination method performed better because there are good and poor individuals for each case in the testing set and winner-takes-all selects the best individual.

A Subset of the Population as an Ensemble For the previous implementation of CELS, all the individuals in the last generation were used in the en-

	Simple Averaging		Majority Voting		Winner-Takes-All	
	Training	Testing	Training	Testing	Training	Testing
Mean	0.910	0.855	0.917	0.857	0.887	0.865
SD	0.010	0.039	0.010	0.039	0.007	0.028
Min	0.897	0.797	0.900	0.812	0.874	0.812
Max	0.924	0.913	0.928	0.913	0.895	0.913

Table 1. Accuracy rates of CELS for the Australian credit card data set. The results are averaged on 10-fold cross-validation. *Mean, SD, Min* and *Max* indicate the mean value, standard deviation, minimum and maximum value respectively.

	Simple Averaging		Majority Voting		Winner-Takes-All	
	Training	Testing	Training	Testing	Training	Testing
Mean	0.795	0.766	0.802	0.764	0.783	0.779
SD	0.007	0.039	0.007	0.042	0.007	0.045
Min	0.783	0.703	0.786	0.688	0.774	0.703
Max	0.805	0.828	0.810	0.828	0.794	0.844

Table 2. Accuracy rates of CELS for the diabetes data set. The results are averaged on 12-fold cross-validation. *Mean, SD, Min* and *Max* indicate the mean value, standard deviation, minimum and maximum value respectively.

sembles. It is interesting to investigate whether we can reduce the size of the ensembles by selecting one representative from each species for combination. Such investigation can provide some hints on whether all the individuals in the last generation will contain some useful information and shed some lights on the importance of a population in evolutionary learning.

We used the k-means algorithm to divide the individuals in the population into different species. These species are then used to construct NN ensembles, in which one representative from each species was selected for combination. The number of species starts from 3 to 25 (i.e., the population size). The optimal number of species was determined by measuring the performance of these constructed ensembles on the training set. The accuracy rate was chosen as the measure of performance. The results of the ensemble formed by the representatives from species are given in Table 3. The combination method used is winner-takes-all. The t-test values comparing the accuracies of the ensembles using the representatives from species to the ensembles using the whole population are 0.80 for the Australian credit card data set, and -0.36 for the diabetes data set. No statistically significance difference was observed between them for both data sets, which implies that the ensemble does not have to use the whole population to achieve good performance. The size of the ensemble can be substantially smaller than the population size. The reduction in the size of the ensembles can be seen from Table 4 which gives the sizes of the ensembles using the representatives from species.

	Card		Diabetes	
	Training	Testing	Training	Testing
Mean	0.887	0.868	0.783	0.777
SD	0.004	0.030	0.009	0.042
Min	0.881	0.812	0.770	0.719
Max	0.890	0.913	0.798	0.844

Table 3. Accuracy rates of the ensemble formed by the representatives from species. The results are averaged on 10-fold cross-validation for the Australian credit card data set, and 12-fold cross-validation for the diabetes data set. *Mean, SD, Min* and *Max* indicate the mean value, standard deviation, minimum and maximum value respectively.

	Mean	SD	Min	Max
Card	13.2	7.8	5	25
Diabetes	16.3	6.4	5	25

Table 4. Tizes of the ensembles using the representatives from species. The results are averaged on 10-fold cross-validation for the Australian credit card data set, and 12-fold cross-validation for the diabetes data set. *Mean, SD, Min* and *Max* indicate the mean value, standard deviation, minimum and maximum value respectively.

Comparisons with Other Work Direct comparison with other evolutionary approaches to designing ensembles is very difficult due to the lack of such results. Instead, the best and latest results available in the literature, regardless of whether the algorithm used was an evolutionary, a BP or a statistical one, were used in the comparison.

Tables 5–6 compare CELS's results, including the results of the ensembles using the whole population and the ensembles using the representatives from species, with those produced by a number of other algorithms[11]. The *error rate* refers to the percentage of wrong classifications on the testing set. As demonstrated by the results, CELS has been able to achieve the generalisation performance comparable to or better than the best ones of 22 algorithms tested[11].

Algorithm	Error Rate	Algorithm	Error Rate	Algorithm	Error Rate
CELS	0.135, 0.132	CART	0.145	ITrule	0.137
Discrim	0.141	IndCART	0.152	Cal5	0.131
Quadisc	0.207	NewID	0.181	Kohonen	FD
Logdisc	0.141	AC^2	0.181	DIPOL92	0.141
SMART	0.158	Baytree	0.171	Backprop	0.154
ALLOC80	0.201	NaiveBay	0.151	RBF	0.145
k-NN	0.181	CN2	0.204	LVQ	0.197
CASTLE	0.148	C4.5	0.155		

Table 5. Comparison among CELS and others [11] in terms of the average testing error rate for the Australian credit card data set. The results are averaged on 10-fold cross-validation. "FD" indicates Kohonen algorithm failed on that data set.

Algorithm	Error Rate	Algorithm	Error Rate	Algorithm	Error Rate
CELS	0.221, 0.223	CART	0.255	ITrule	0.245
Discrim	0.225	IndCART	0.271	Cal5	0.250
Quadisc	0.262	NewID	0.289	Kohonen	0.273
Logdisc	0.223	AC^2	0.276	DIPOL92	0.224
SMART	0.232	Baytree	0.271	Backprop	0.248
ALLOC80	0.301	NaiveBay	0.262	RBF	0.243
k-NN	0.324	CN2	0.289	LVQ	0.272
CASTLE	0.258	C4.5	0.270		

Table 6. Comparison among CELS and others [11] in terms of the average testing error rate for the diabetes data set. The results are averaged on 12-fold cross-validation.

4   Conclusion

CELS provides an automatic way of designing NN ensembles, where each NN is an individual or a representative from each species in the population. The negative correlation learning and fitness sharing were adopted to encourage the formation of species in the population. Both the number of species and function of each species are evolved automatically. However, the architectures of NNs in the ensemble are predefined at the moment. One way to vary the architectures is by EPNet[5].

CELS was tested on the Australian credit card and the diabetes problems. Very competitive results have been produced by CELS in comparison with other algorithms[11].

The three combination methods have also been investigated in this paper. Compared with simple averaging and majority voting, the winner-takes-all fits CELS well because only the best individual rather than all individuals for each case is considered to make the final decision of the ensemble.

References

1. X. Yao and Y. Liu, "Making use of population information in evolutionary artificial neural networks," *IEEE Transactions on Systems, Man and Cybernetics*, **28B**(3),pp.417–425, June 1998.
2. Y. Liu and X. Yao, "Negatively correlated neural networks can produce best ensembles," *Australian Journal of Intelligent Information Processing Systems*, **4**(3/4), pp.176–185, 1997.
3. Y. Liu and X. Yao, "A cooperative ensemble learning system," *Proc. of the 1998 IEEE International Joint Conference on Neural Networks (IJCNN'98)*, Anchorage, USA, 4-9 May 1998, pp.2202–2207.
4. X. Yao, Y. Liu and P. Darwen, "How to make best use of evolutionary learning," *Complex Systems — From Local Interactions to Global Phenomena*, IOS Press, Amsterdam, pp.229–242, 1996.
5. X. Yao and Y. Liu, "A new evolutionary system for evolving artificial neural networks," *IEEE Transactions on Neural Networks*, Vol.8, no.3, pp.694–713, May 1997.
6. D. B. Fogel, *Evolutionary Computation: Towards a New Philosophy of Machine Intelligence*, IEEE Press, New York, 1995.
7. R. A. Jacobs, M. I. Jordan, S. J. Nowlan, and G. E. Hinton, "Adaptive mixtures of local experts," *Neural Computation*, Vol.3, pp.79–87, 1991.
8. S. Haykin, *Neural Networks: A Comprehensive Foundation*, Macmillan College Publishing Company, Inc., pp.151–152, 1994.
9. P. Darwen and X. Yao, "Every niching method has its niche: fitness sharing and implicit sharing compared," *Parallel Problem Solving from Nature (PPSN) IV* (H.-M. Voigt, W. Ebeling, I. Rechenberg, and H.-P. Schwefel, eds.), Vol. 1141 of *Lecture Notes in Computer Science*, (Berlin), pp. 398–407, Springer-Verlag, 1996.
10. J. MacQueen, "Some methods for classification and analysis of multivariate observation," *Proceedings of the 5th Berkely Symposium on Mathematical Statistics and Probability*, Berkely: University of California Press, Vol.1, pp.281–297, 1967.
11. D. Michie and D. J. Spiegelhalter and C. C. Taylor, *Machine Learning, Neural and Statistical Classification*, Ellis Horwood Limited, London, 1994.

Selection of Training Data for Neural Networks by a Genetic Algorithm

Colin R Reeves and Stewart J Taylor

School of Mathematical and Information Sciences
Coventry University
Priory Street
Coventry, CV1 5FB
UK

Abstract. In applications of artificial neural networks (ANNs), it is common to partition the available data into (at least) two sets. One is then used to train the net, while the other is used as a 'test set' to measure the generalization capability of the trained net.

The partition is generally almost completely arbitrary, and little research has been done on the question of what constitutes a good training set, or on how it could be achieved. In this paper, we use a genetic algorithm (GA) to identify a training set for fitting radial basis function (RBF) networks, and test the methodology on two classification problems—one an artificial problem, and the other using real-world data on credit applications for mortgage loans.

In the process, we also exhibit an interesting application of Radcliffe's *RAR* operator, and present results that suggest the methodology tested here is a viable means of increasing ANN performance.

1   Introduction

One of the problems in training an artificial neural networks (ANN) is to ensure that the final network model is able to generalize well—that is, to achieve high performance on unseen data drawn from the same statistical population as the training data. This problem also arises in conventional statistics, but there it is possible to use theoretical analysis of the model to provide unbiased estimators. The complications of using non-linear models means that this route is not open. It is therefore customary to partition the available data into (at least) two sets, one of which is used to train the net, while the other is used as a 'test set' to measure the generalization capability of the trained net. It is not so commonly realized that this partition may influence the performance of the trained net quite significantly. In some earlier experiments [1] we found that different partitions of a given data set gave substantial differences in error rates for classification problems.

The question thus arises as to whether it is possible to select training data in a way that can enhance the performance of an ANN.

2 Training Set Selection

It is intuitively obvious that some points in a given set of data will have a greater effect on the network weights than others. Thus, in modern statistics it is now common to investigate the 'influence' of each data point on the coefficients obtained in a linear model. Methods of detecting points with special influence are comprehensively surveyed by Cook and Weisberg [2]. In the case of linear least squares problems, the identification of influential points can be done with very little extra effort in terms of computational requirements.

The concept of influence is also related to the question of identifying *outliers*— points that appear not to fit the general pattern of the data. The assumption is that such points belong to a different population. Of course, we can never be sure whether this is the case, but often such points are rejected in order to obtain what is hoped to be a better or more 'robust' fit to the unknown 'true' model. There is a considerable statistical literature on this subject also—a good review is that given by Barnett and Lewis [3].

The related subject of 'data editing' has also been investigated in the application of k-nearest neighbour methods for classification, as in the collection of papers by Dasarathy [4], where again it is acknowledged that not all points are of equal worth in determining the classification of a 'new' point. For instance, points near to the inter-class boundaries will have more influence than those which are in the 'interior'. Points with little influence can therefore be deleted, provided that a sufficient number of near-boundary points are retained as a set of exemplars. Here the motivation has often been primarily computational—to avoid the need of calculating the k nearest neighbours using every point in the training set—but as with the case of robust regression, it has also been recognized that exclusion of some points can enhance the reliability of the estimates made from the data.

In some neural network applications, a similar situation also applies. For example, there may be situations where there is too much data (as in [5] for example), and in such cases a similar argument can be made for deleting points that are far from the boundary on the grounds of computational expense. However, it is not just in such cases that the principle applies. In [5], an approach was described that used an initial crude estimate of the decision boundaries to select appropriate training data, followed by a phased addition of points to the training set, as shown in Fig. 1. This procedure required the specification of a parameter θ and a test for the potential boundary status of a point at step 2, and at step 3 a definition of convergence. It was also necessary to decide on the size of the initial training set in step 1. All of these proved somewhat sensitive and problem-specific.

There were other problems with this approach. Not only was the computational burden high, since multiple re-optimizations with back-propagation were used, but there was also the somewhat arbitrary nature and size of the resulting training set.

In this research we adopted a different approach. First, we used radial basis function (RBF) nets, since training is significantly quicker than for nets that

1. Take a random sample $\mathcal{T}$ from the data set $\mathcal{S}$.
2. If the proportion of potential boundary points (PBPs) in $\mathcal{T}$ is less than θ, draw further points from $\mathcal{S}\backslash\mathcal{T}$; if they are PBPs, update $\mathcal{T}$ by exchanging them with non-PBPs; stop when the criterion is satisfied.
3. Train the net using $\mathcal{T}$ until convergence.
4. Test the trained net on $\mathcal{S}\backslash\mathcal{T}$; add any mis-classified points to $\mathcal{T}$.
5. Repeat steps 3 and 4 until no further improvement.

Fig. 1. Selection strategy used in reference 5

use back-propagation. Secondly, instead of an *ad hoc* approach to training set selection, we used a genetic algorithm (GA) that attempted to select a training set with the objective of minimizing some error criterion.

Before proceeding to describe the GA approach, some other recent pieces of related research should be mentioned. Plutowski has completed a very comprehensive study [6] into the general question of training set selection in the context of function approximation (i.e. regression problems). A similar approach has also been reported by Röbel [7], and Tambouratzis [8] has described an approach based on Smolensky's harmony theory. However, these approaches are based on a selection criterion that relates to the training data only. It would surely be better to allow the data points to be included on the basis of the *generalization* performance observed. This paper will describe how a genetic algorithm (GA) can be used for such a purpose.

3 The Application of Genetic Algorithms

In a conference such as this, knowledge of the basic principles of GAs can almost certainly be assumed. However, the application of GAs to the problem of selecting training subsets raises an interesting question of implementation. An 'obvious' encoding would seem to consist of a binary string of length N (where there are N points from which to choose), with the presence or absence of each point in the subset being signified by a 1 or a zero respectively, but this actually causes several problems. Radcliffe [9] has forcibly pointed out the problematic aspects of binary representation and simple crossover in such cases, and in Radcliffe and George [10], a better approach to subset selection problems is proposed. This uses a different recombination operator, which is called $RAR(w)$. The basic principle is to allow points that are in *both* parents to be passed on to the child ('respect'), while also permitting a mixture of both parents to be inherited—in the sense that the child subset may consist of points that belong to one parent but not both ('assortment').

The parameter w is capable of tuning the effect of this crossover-like operator either in the direction of complete respect as $w \to \infty$, or towards complete assortment as $w \to 0$. Choosing $w = 3$ was found to be a good compromise, as in [10], which contains a complete description of this operator.

4   Experiments

All the experiments reported here used RBF nets: mathematically, the distance between each input vector $\mathbf{x}$ and each of k *centres* $\mathbf{c}_i$ is calculated. These distances are then passed through a non-linearity, and a weighted sum of these values is used to predict the output y. In effect, it fits a non-linear model

$$\rho(\mathbf{x}) = \lambda_0 + \sum_{i=1}^{k} \lambda_i \phi(||\mathbf{x} - \mathbf{c}_i||/\sigma_i^2).$$

These nets have the advantage that non-linearities can be incorporated into the first-order question of how many RBF 'centres' there should be, where they should be located, and what scaling parameter(s) σ should be used. The choice of architecture and parameters for this problem was as follows: the k-means clustering algorithm was used to find k centres, the σ values estimated as in Moody and Darken [11], and the function ϕ was a Gaussian. The problem then reduces to a second-order one of solving a system of linear equations, which can be accomplished in a number of ways—for example, singular value decomposition (SVD), as was used in the research reported here.

The usual Euclidean distance metric was used, which involves the square of the difference between each input variable and the corresponding centre. In cases where one of the input variables has a much smaller range than the other variables, the activation of the unit will be relatively insensitive to this variable. In such cases a simple transformation of the input data is usually recommended. Here we found the mean and variance of each input variable in the complete data set, and re-scaled the inputs to have zero mean and unit variance.

4.1   Continuous XOR Problem

The method was initially tested on an artificial classification problem—a continuous analogue of the well-known XOR problem. In this 2-class problem points in the opposite quadrants of a square come from the same class. Formally, for inputs $x_i \in [-1, 1]$,

$$x_1 x_2 < 0 \to C_1$$

$$x_1 x_2 > 0 \to C_2.$$

In this case we created a training set of 200 data points, generated randomly in the square $[-1, 1]^2$. The approach was to use a GA to select an 'exemplar set' of $n < 200$ from the first set; the fitness of this subset could be assessed accurately by plotting the decision boundary and computing the error from the difference in area between the true and fitted decision classes.

The first step was to ascertain the appropriate network architecture. In this case it is intuitively clear that four RBF centres at the centre of each quadrant would provide the best model. Some preliminary experiments were carried out to investigate the effect of different numbers of centres using the full training set, and they confirmed this expectation. The output y was a 2-dimensional vector where $(1, 0)$ represented C_1 and $(0, 1)$ represented C_2. In 'decoding' a fitted y value, the class was indicated by the largest value (e.g. $(0.2, 0.7)$ represents C_2).

We then applied a GA with a population of size $\min(2n, 100)$, a mutation rate of $1/n$, a crossover probability of 1 and an incremental reproduction strategy (i.e. one offspring is generated and immediately inserted into the population in place of one of the currently below average strings). Selection was by means of linear ranking. To determine a stopping criterion, we ran the GA for an initial epoch of 200 offspring generations and recorded the best exemplar set found. For subsequent epochs of 50 offspring generations, the best solution is compared, and if no improvement has been made over the previous epoch the algorithm terminates. The GA was run for values of n running from 5 to 195 in steps of 5. Whether all these choices and parameter settings for the GA are in any sense 'optimal' is of course unknown (and unlikely), so for comparison, the effect of using a randomly selected subset was also investigated at each value of n. In this way, we can at least check if the GA is doing better than a random search.

The whole procedure was run 30 times with different groups of training and validation sets. Fig. 2 compares the performance of the selected subset (averaged over 30 replications) at different subset sizes with that of a randomly selected subset of the same size. The error rate using the full training set is also shown for comparison. It is clear that while choosing smaller subsets in general degrades the performance achieved on the full set, selecting them using the GA considerably reduces the error rate.

Another interesting feature is shown in Fig. 3. Here, an 'incorrect' architecture has deliberately been chosen: only 2 centres were used instead of 4. Although the performance of the network is much worse than in Fig. 2, it is interesting to see that subset selection can at least partially compensate for the poor choice of architecture if the exemplar sets are relatively small.

The procedure is open to the obvious objection that in this problem we know what the answer should be. In practice, the decision boundaries are unknown, and some sort of regularization [12] should be employed to avoid the problem of overfitting. A common approach would be to evaluate fitness on an additional 'validation set' of a further 200 randomly generated points, and to evaluate the final network on a previously unseen 'test set'. The GA selection process was repeated using this approach, with the results shown in Fig. 4.

This has several interesting features. Firstly, randomly-chosen subsets appear to give very erratic performance. No explanation could be found for this. Secondly, the measured error rate on the test set was generally smaller than when computing the real error accurately. This suggests the test set approach is underestimating the true error. However, calculations confirmed that the *relative* positions of the lines on the graph were not affected, and it thus appears that the selected subset needs to be substantially larger ($n > 50$) before any improvement is obtained, and that the improvement is somewhat smaller. Nevertheless, there is still an improvement.

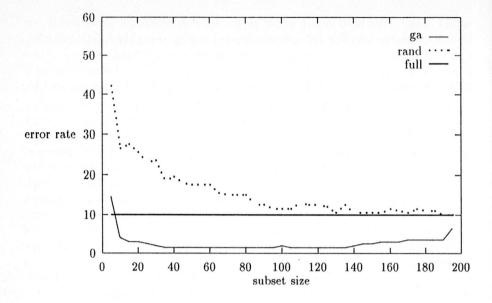

Fig. 2. Error rates for different sizes of subset using 4 centres. Note that the error rates here are those obtained by exact calculation.

4.2 A Real-World Classification Problem

The results of the above tests were sufficiently encouraging for a more interesting application to be investigated. In this case, we used data on 2403 customers of a major UK supplier of mortgage loans. Data were available on 28 variables for each customer, recorded at the time the loan was granted, and customers had subsequently been classified into two classes according to their tendency to fall into arrears.

As a first step, a principal components analysis was carried out, which showed that nearly all of the variation in the data could be explained by the first 18 principal components, thus reducing the dimensionality of the problem. The customers were then divided into 3 equal-sized groups of 801, taking some care to ensure that the proportion of customers in different classes was roughly the same in each group, since there were substantially more 'good' customers than 'bad' ones overall. The first set was used as a training set, from which the exemplar set was to be chosen; the 2nd was a validation set, used to determine when to stop training, and the performance of the final network was measured on the 3rd (test) set.

The RBF nets in this case all had 6 centres—preliminary experiments using the full training set showed little by increasing the number of centres further, as can be seen in Fig. 5.

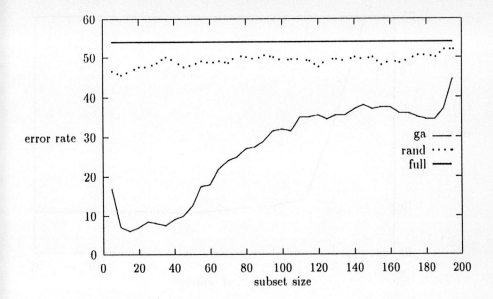

Fig. 3. Error rates for different sizes of subset using 2 centres. Note that the error rates here are those obtained by exact calculation.

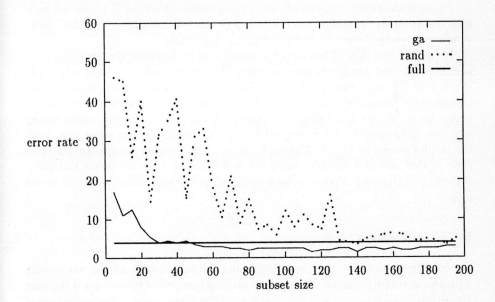

Fig. 4. Error rates for different sizes of subset using 4 centres. Note that the error rates here are those obtained on the unseen test sets.

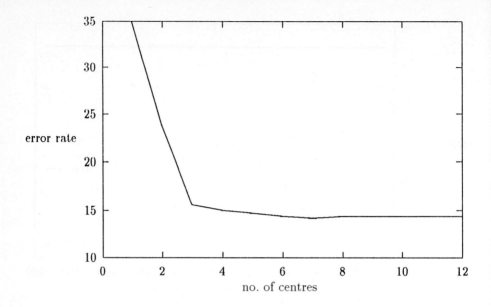

Fig. 5. Error rates for different numbers of centres using the full training set.

Figure 6 shows the mis-classification rates observed on the GA-selected subsets, compared to a random selection and to the full training set. Again, these values are averaged over 30 independent random trials.

It can be seen that GA-selected training sets do improve the generalization performance over randomly-selected ones. The improvement is not very large (from a 14.3% error rate to about 12.7%), but in practice, when dealing with thousands of customers every year, it is large enough to make a real impact on losses due to arrears and bad debts. Once more, the effect of using a poor model was also investigated—a 1-centre RBF net was trained in the same way, with the results shown in Fig. 7. Although the net has a higher generalization error than in the case of 6 centres, using selected training data has again mitigated the effect of choosing a poor architecture, especially with fairly small exemplar sets.

5 Conclusions

Genetic algorithms have been used before in conjunction with ANNs, but usually with the aim of finding an appropriate architecture, or of improving a training algorithm, or of selecting suitable features of the input space. (The collection of papers found in [13] provides several examples of these approaches.) This paper has shown that using a GA to select training sets for RBF neural networks is also a viable and potentially useful technique. In the case of the artificial problem, it reduced the generalization error to a very small value, even when an exact

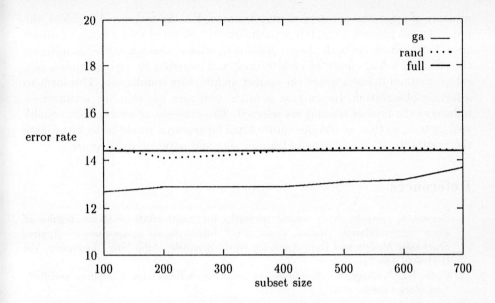

Fig. 6. Error rates for different sizes of subset with the home loans data using 6 centres.

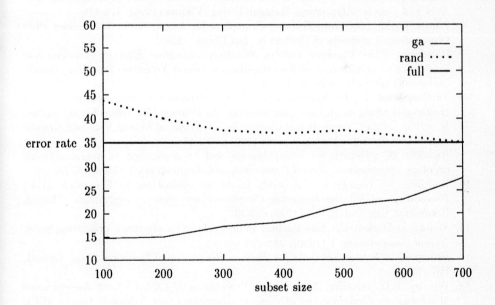

Fig. 7. Error rates for different sizes of subset with the home loans data using 1 centre.

measure of error was not used to stop training. For the real-world problem, the improvement was not large, but was consistently observed over a range of subset sizes. Furthermore, in both cases it appears that using this approach can mitigate the effect of a bad choice of architecture, and can thus be recommended as a robust method in cases where the correct architecture is unknown. This leads to a further observation. In practice, it might well turn out that the architecture influences the type of training set selected. The converse, of course, may equally well be true, so that an obvious future topic for research would be to investigate the possibility of co-evolution of training sets and network architecture.

References

1. Reeves, C., Steele, N. : Neural networks for multivariate analysis: results of some cross-validation studies. *Proc. of 6th International Symposium on Applied Stochastic Models and Data Analysis*, World Scientific Publishing, Singapore, Vol II (1993), 780-791.
2. Cook, R., Weisberg, S. : *Residuals and Influence in Regression*. Chapman and Hall, New York (1982).
3. Barnett, V., Lewis, T. : *Outliers in Statistical Data*. Wiley, Chichester (1978).
4. Dasarathy, B. : *Nearest Neighbor (NN) Norms: NN Pattern Classification Techniques*. IEEE Computer Society Press, Los Alamitos, CA (1991).
5. Reeves, C. : Training set selection in neural network applications. In Pearson, D., Albrecht, R., Steele, N. : *Proc. of 2nd International Conference on Artificial Neural Nets and Genetic Algorithms*. Springer-Verlag, Vienna (1995), 476-478.
6. Plutowski, M. : *Selecting Training Exemplars for Neural Network Learning*. PhD Dissertation, University of California, San Diego (1994).
7. Röbel, A. : *The Dynamic Pattern Selection Algorithm: Effective Training and Controlled Generalization of Backpropagation Neural Networks*. Technical Report, Technical University of Berlin (1994).
8. Tambouratzis, T., Tambouratzis, D. : Optimal training pattern selection using a cluster-generating artificial neural network. In Pearson, D., Albrecht, R., Steele, N. : *Proc. of 2nd International Conference on Artificial Neural Nets and Genetic Algorithms*. Springer-Verlag, Vienna (1995), 472-475.
9. Radcliffe, N. : Genetic set recombination and its application to neural network topology optimisation. *Neural Computing and Applications*, 1 (1993), 67-90.
10. Radcliffe, N., George, F. : A study in set recombination. In Forrest, S. (Ed.) *Proceedings of 5th International Conference on Genetic Algorithms*. Morgan Kaufmann, San Mateo, CA (1993), 23-30.
11. Moody, J., Darken, C. : Fast learning in networks of locally-tuned processing units. *Neural Computation*, 1 (1990), 281-294.
12. Bishop, C. : *Neural Networks for Pattern Recognition*. Clarendon Press, Oxford, UK (1995).
13. Whitley, L.D., Schaffer, J.D. (Eds.) : *Proceedings of COGANN-92: International Workshop on Combinations of Genetic Algorithms and Neural Networks*. IEEE Computer Society Press, Los Alamitos, CA (1992).

Discovery with Genetic Algorithm Scheduling Strategies for Cellular Automata

Franciszek Seredyński *

Institute of Computer Science, Polish Academy of Sciences
Ordona 21, 01-237 Warsaw, Poland
sered@ipipan.waw.pl

Abstract. In this paper genetic algorithms (GA) are used to evolve cellular automata (CA) structures suitable to perform scheduling tasks of a parallel program in two-processor systems. For this purpose a program graph is considered as CA with elementary automata changing their states according to local rules. Changing states of CA can be interpreted in terms of migration of tasks in a multiprocessor system. To design rules of CA two neighborhoods are considered and studied. There are two phases of the proposed CA-based scheduling algorithm. In the first phase effective rules for CA are discovered by GA. In the second phase CA works as a distributed scheduler. In this phase, for any initial allocation of tasks in a system, CA-based scheduler is able to find an allocation which minimizes the total execution time of the program in the system.

1 Introduction

The problem of multiprocessor scheduling [1] belongs, due to its NP-completeness, to one of unsolved issues in parallel computing. Current works concerning a scheduling problem are oriented either on selection problems for which *exact* solutions can be constructed or designing *heuristic* algorithms to find near-optimal solutions for more general cases. To this stream of research belong in particular scheduling algorithms based on applying techniques derived from nature such as simulated annealing, genetic algorithms or neural networks.

In this paper we study recently proposed [8] technique for scheduling based on applying CA. CA presents a distributed system of single, locally interacting units which are able to produce a global behavior. Recent results [2, 3, 9] show that CA combined with evolutionary techniques can be effectively used to solve complex classification and synchronization problems.

The remainder of the paper is organized as follows. The next section discusses accepted models of a parallel program and a parallel system in the context of a scheduling problem. Section 3 provides a background on CA. Section 4 contains a description of a proposed CA-based scheduling algorithm with genetic algorithm-based engine for discovering scheduling rules. Results of experimental study of the scheduler are presented in Section 5. Last section contains conclusions.

---

* Currently at Dep. of Math and CS, CCB319, UMSL, St. Louis, MO 63121, USA

2 Multiprocessor Scheduling

A multiprocessor system is represented by an undirected unweighted graph $G_s = (V_s, E_s)$ called a *system graph*. V_s is the set of N_s nodes of the graph representing processors and E_s is the set of edges representing bidirectional channels between processors. A parallel program is represented by a weighted directed acyclic graph $G_p = < V_p, E_p >$, called a *precedence task graph* or a *program graph*. V_p is the set of N_p nodes of the graph representing elementary tasks. Weights b_k of the nodes describe the processing time needed to execute a given task on any processor of a system. E_p is the set of edges of the precedence task graph describing the communication pattern between the tasks. Weights a_{kl} of the edges describe a communication time between pairs of tasks k and l, when they are located in neighbor processors. Figure 1 (upper) shows examples of a program graph and a system graph representing a multiprocessor system consisting on two processors *P0* and *P1*.

The purpose of *scheduling* is to distribute the tasks among the processors in such a way that the precedence constraints are preserved, and the *response time* T (the total execution time) is minimized. The response time for a given allocation of tasks in multiprocessor topology depends on a *scheduling policy* applied in a given processor. We assume that a scheduling policy is defined for a given run of a scheduling algorithm, and is the same for all processors.

We assume that for each node k of a precedence task graph sets of *predecessors(k)*, *brothers(k)* (i.e. nodes having at least one common predecessor), and *successors(k)* are defined. We also assume that for each node k of a precedence task graph such parameters as *static* and *dynamic level* and *co-level* can be defined.

3 Cellular Automata

One dimensional CA [10] is a collection of two-states elementary automata arranged in a lattice of the length N, and locally interacted in a discrete time t. For each cell i called a central cell, a neighborhood of a radius r is defined, consisting of $n_i = 2r + 1$ cells, including the cell i.

It is assumed that a state q_i^{t+1} of a cell i at the time $t + 1$ depends only on states of its neighborhood at the time t, i.e. $q_i^{t+1} = f(q_i^t, q_{i1}^t, q_{i2}^t, ..., q_{ni}^t)$, and a transition function f_g, called a *general rule*, which defines a rule of updating a cell i. A length L_g of a general rule and a number of neighborhood states for a binary uniform CA is $L_q = 2^n$, where $n = n_i$ is a number of cells of a given neighborhood, and a number of such rules can be expressed as 2^{L_q}. For CA with e.g. $r = 2$ the length of a rule is equal to $L_q = 32$, and a number of such rules is 2^{32} and grows very fast with L_q. For this reason some other types of rules are used to make them shorter and decrease their total number.

Such a possibility gives e.g. defining a transition function f_t on the base of the sum of cells' states in a neighborhood, i.e. $q_i^{t+1} = f_t(q_{i-r}^t + ... + q_{i-1}^t + q_i^t + q_{i+1}^t + ... + q_{i+r}^t)$. For CA with $r = 2$ the length of a rule (called a totalistic rule) is reduced now to $L_t = 6$, and the total number of rules is equal to 2^6.

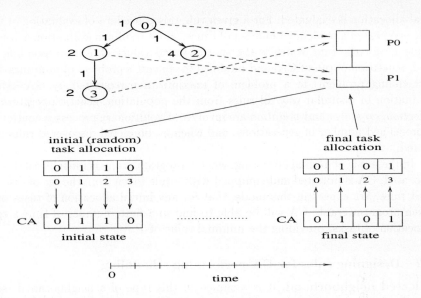

Fig. 1. An idea of CA-based scheduler: an example of a program graph and a system graph (upper), corresponding CA-based scheduler (lower)

4 Cellular Automata-based Scheduler

4.1 A concept of CA-based scheduler

It is assumed that with each task of a program graph an elementary automaton is associated. A topology of a program graph defines a structure of CA. The structure of the proposed CA is not regular, however, we still assume that CA is a binary automaton. It results in considering the scheduling problem only for the 2-processor topology: the state 0 or 1 of a cell means that a corresponding task is allocated either in the processor $P0$ or $P1$, respectively.

An idea of CA-based scheduler is presented in Figure 1. For a program graph (Figure 1 (upper)) a CA is created. An initial state of CA corresponds to an initial allocation of tasks in the two-processor system (Figure 1 (lower-left)). Next, the CA starts to evolve in time according to some rule. Changing states of evolving CA corresponds to changing the allocation of tasks in the system graph, what results in changing the response time T. A final state of the CA corresponds to a final allocation of tasks in the system (Figure 1 (lower-right)).

The scheduler operates in two modes: a mode of learning of CA rules and a mode of normal operating [8]. The purpose of the learning mode is to discover effective rules for scheduling. Searching rules is conducted with use of genetic algorithm (GA) [5, 6]. For this purpose an initial random population of rules is created. For a given random allocation of a program graph into a system graph CA is initialized, and equipped with a rule from the population of rules. CA starts to evolve its states during predefined number of time steps, what results in changing an allocation of task of a program graph. The response time T for a final allocation is evaluated. For a given rule this procedure of evaluation of the rule is repeated a predefined number of times, and it results in evaluation a fitness value T^* for the rule, which is the sum of found values of T corresponding to each repetition of run of CA, and modified to convert a problem of minimization (scheduling problem) to a problem of maximization requested by GA. After evaluation in a similar way all rules from the population, genetic operators of *selection, crossover* and *mutation* are involved. Evolutionary process is continued a predefined number of generations, and when is completed discovered rules are stored.

In the mode of normal operating, when a program graph is initially randomly allocated, CA is initiated and equipped with a rule taken from the set of discovered rules. We expect in this mode, that for any initial allocation of tasks of a given program graph, CA will be able to find in a finite number of time steps, allocation of tasks, providing the minimal value of T.

4.2 Designing rules for CA performing scheduling

Selected neighborhood. It is assumed in this type of a neighborhood (see, [8]) that only two selected representatives of each set of predecessors, brothers and successors will create a neighborhood of a cell associated with a task k. A state of a neighborhood is defined on the base of states of corresponding parts of the neighborhood. A total number of states of a neighborhood can be calculated as $2*5*5*5$ and is equal to 250. A length of a rule (a transition function) is 250 bits. A space of solutions of the problem is defined by a number 2^{250} of possible transition functions. GA with a population of rules is used to discover an appropriate rule for CA to solve a scheduling problem.

Full neighborhood with totalistic rules. To reduce a number of states of CA another definition of a neighborhood and a transition function was considered. It is assumed under this approach that a neighborhood of a given cell k is constituted of single cells, each representing a corresponding set of predecessors, brothers and successors. A state of a cell representing a given set will be defined in a way similar to that how totalistic rules are defined. A state of a central cell will be defined as previously by an order number of a processor where the task is allocated. A neighborhood will consists of 4 cells.

As previously we will consider the same set of attributes of each task from corresponding sets of neighbors of a given task. Let $\mathcal{P}_{P0}^k$ and $\mathcal{P}_{P1}^k$ are sets of predecessors of a task k, allocated in processors $P0$ and $P1$, respectively; $\mathcal{B}_{P0}^k$ and $\mathcal{B}_{P1}^k$ are sets of brothers allocated in $P0$ and $P1$, respectively; $\mathcal{S}_{P0}^k$ and $\mathcal{S}_{P1}^k$ are sets of successors allocated in $P0$ and $P1$, respectively. Let us assume as previously that selected attributes for sets of predecessors, brothers and successors are co-level, a computational time and a communication time respectively.

Let us calculate for sets $\mathcal{S}_{P0}^k$ and $\mathcal{S}_{P1}^k$ values of some totalistic measure concerning the accepted attribute co-level, selected for these sets. This totalistic measure can be $\sum_{i \in \mathcal{P}_{P0}^k} d_i$, and $\sum_{j \in \mathcal{P}_{P1}^k} d_j$, respectively. In a similar way values for this measure corresponding to selected attributes are defined for sets $\mathcal{B}_{P0}^k$ and $\mathcal{B}_{P1}^k$, $\mathcal{S}_{P0}^k$ and $\mathcal{S}_{P1}^k$.

A state of a given cell being a part of a neighborhood, and representing e.g. a set of predecessors will be defined in the following way:

- state 0: if $\sum_{i \in \mathcal{P}^k_{P_0}} d_i > \sum_{j \in \mathcal{P}^k_{P_1}} d_j$
- state 1: if $\sum_{i \in \mathcal{P}^k_{P_0}} d_i < \sum_{j \in \mathcal{P}^k_{P_1}} d_j$
- state 2: if $\sum_{i \in \mathcal{P}^k_{P_0}} d_i = \sum_{j \in \mathcal{P}^k_{P_1}} d_j$
- state 3: there is no predecessors corresponding to a task k.

States of remaining cells representing sets of brothers and successors are defined in a similar way. A total number of neighborhood states, taking into account states of defined above parts at the neighborhood, can be calculated as $2*4*4*4$, and is equal to 128. A length of a rule now is 128 bits, and a total number of rules for the problem is 2^{128}.

5   Experiments

In experiments reported in this section it is assumed that CA works sequentially, i.e. at a given moment of time only one cell updates its state. An order of updating states by cells is defined by their order number corresponding to tasks in a precedence task graph. A single run (step) of CA is completed in N_p (N_p - a number of tasks of a program graph) moments of time. A run of CA consists of a predefined number G of steps.

A number of experiments with program graphs available in the literature has been conducted. The first program graph refered as $gauss18$ is shown in Figure 2a. It represents the parallel Gaussian elimination algorithm consisting of 18 tasks. The next program graph ($g18$) is shown in Figure 2b [4]. Figure 2c presents a program graph $g40$ [7] with computational and communication costs equal to 4 and 1, respectively. Figure 2d shows a binary out-tree program graph. We refer to it as $tree15$. We also use a binary out-tree $tree127$. Computation and communication weights of out-trees are equal to 1.

Experiment #1: program graph $gauss18$
In the learning mode of this experiment a population of rules of GA was equal to 100. Figure 3a shows a fitness function $fitt = T^*$ of GA, changing during evolutionary process and Figure 3b presentss a response time T corresponding to the initial and final tasks' allocations (corresponding to maximal value of the $fitt$).

For each generation of GA a set of four test- problems was created. Each problem is a random task allocation in the system graph. Each rule from a given population is evaluated on a test problem. For this purpose, CA with a given rule and an initial state corresponding to a given initial allocation is allowed to run a some number of steps. An efficiency of a given rule is evaluated as the average value of response times found for each test-problem. To calculate T for a given final allocation of tasks a scheduling policy of the type: a task with the highest value of a dynamic level-first, was applied.

648

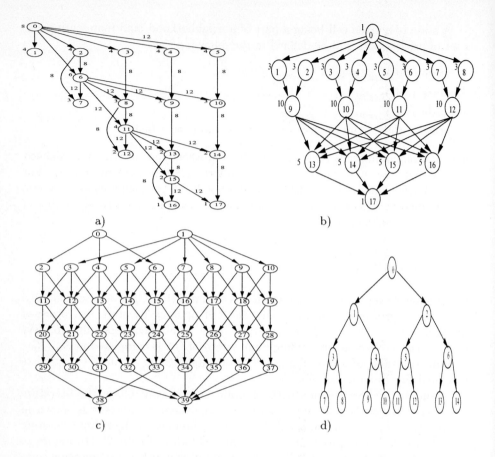

a)

b)

c)

d)

Fig. 2. Program graphs: *gauss*18 (a), *g*18 (b), *g*40 (c), and *tree*15 (d)

After evaluation of all rules from a population, GA operators are applied. A proportional selection with elitist strategy was used. A crossover with a probability $p_c = 0.95$, a bit-flip mutations with $p_m = 0.001$ and hillclimbing were applied. CA neighborhood was created using the idea of the selected neighborhood. Rules of CA providing an optimal scheduling with $T = 44$ were found (see, Figure 3b) during about 50 generations.

After run of GA its population contains rules suitable for CA-based scheduling. Quality of these rules we can find out in the normal operating mode. We generate some number of test problems, and use them to test each of found rules. Figure 3c shows results of the test conducted with 100 random initial allocation of the *gauss*18. For each found rule the average value of T (avr T) found by CA in the test problem is shown. One can see that 29 rules are able to find an optimal scheduling for each representative of the test. Figure 3d shows a frequency of finding an optimal solution by each rule.

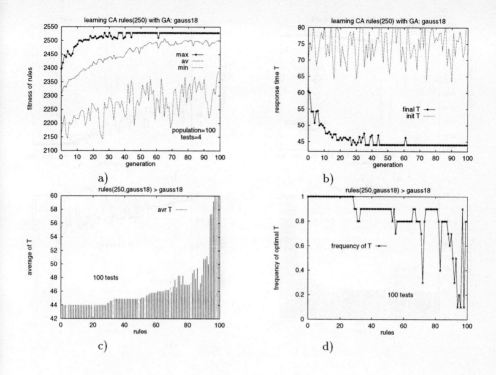

Fig. 3. CA-based scheduler for *gauss*18. Learning mode: (a) and (b). Normal operating: (c) and (d)

Experiment #2: program graph $g40$

A population of rules of a size 200 was used in the learning mode of the experiment. For each generations of GA a set of five test problems was created. Figures 4a,b show that rules of CA providing an optimal scheduling with a response time $T = 80$ was found after 160 generations.

Figure 5 shows a run of CA-based scheduler with the best found rule. Left part of the figure presents a space-time diagram of CA consisting of 40 cells, and the right part shows graphically a value of T corresponding to an allocation found in a given step. One can see that CA finds a steady-state corresponding to an allocation providing an optimal response time $T = 80$ in the step 14.

Experiment #3: program graph $g18$

CA neighborhood with totalistic rules and a scheduling policy of the type: the highest value of a static level- first, were used in the experiment. GA needs about 20 generations (see, Figure 6b) to discover in a learning process a CA rule providing an optimal solution with $T = 46$.

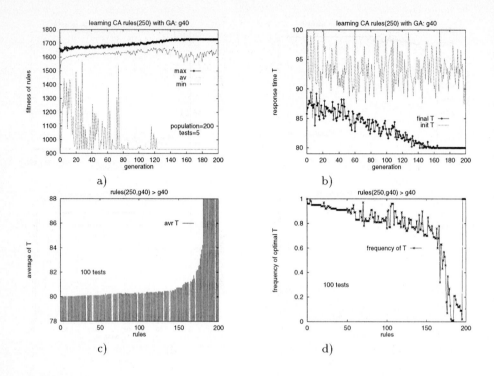

Fig. 4. CA-based scheduler for $g40$. Learning mode: (a) and (b). Normal operating: (c) and (d)

Experiment #4: program graphs $tree15$ and $tree127$
GA needs not more than 5 generations to discover a CA rule for the program graph $tree15$ providing an optimal response time $T = 9$. The experiment was conducted with CA neighborhood with totalistic rules and a scheduling policy of the type: the lowest order number of a task-first. CA rules discovered for a small size of a binary out-tree can be effectively used to schedule binary out-trees of much greatest sizes. Figure 7 shows a space-time diagram of CA working with the rule($tree15$) and solving the problem with the binary out-tree $tree127$ consisting of 127 tasks.

6 Conclusions

Results concerning ongoing research on development of CA-based distributed algorithms of scheduling tasks of parallel programs in parallel computers have been presented. They show that GA is able to discover for a given instance of a problem effective rules for CA-based scheduler, and next to perform scheduling in a fully distributed way. While discovered rules perfectly work for a given instance of a problem, several new questions arise. How the proposed method-

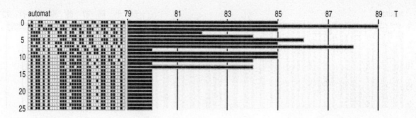

Fig. 5. Space-time diagram of CA-based scheduler for $g40$

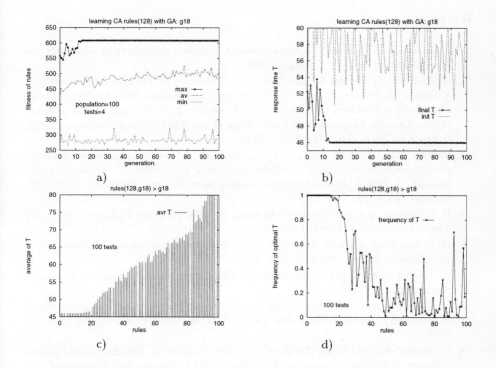

Fig. 6. CA-based scheduler for $g18$. Learning mode: (a) and (b). Normal operating: (c) and (d).

ology can be extended on the case when a number of processors is greater than two. How general are these rules ? Are they suitable for another instances of the scheduling problem ? These questions are the subject of our current research.

Acknowledgement

The work has been partially supported by the State Committee for Scientific Research (KBN) under Grant N8 T11A 009 13.

Fig. 7. Space-time diagram of CA-based scheduler using rules(*tree*15) for *tree*127

References

1. J. Błażewicz, K.H. Ecker, G. Schmidt and J. Węglarz, *Scheduling in Computer and Manufacturing Systems*, Springer, 1994

2. D. Andre, F. H. Bennet III and J. R. Koza, Discovery by Genetic Programming of a Cellular Automata Rule that is Better than any Known Rule for the Majority Classification Problem, in J. R. Koza, D. E. Goldberg, D. B. Fogel, and R. L. Riolo (Eds.), *Genetic Programming*, Proceedings of the First Annual Conference 1996, A Bradford Book, The MIT Press, 1996

3. R. Das, M. Mitchell, and J. P. Crutchfield, A genetic algorithm discovers particle-based computation in cellular automata, in Davidor, Y., Schwefel, H.-P., Männer, R. (Eds.), *Parallel Problem Solving from Nature – PPSN III*, LNCS 866, Springer, 1994, pp. 344-353

4. H. El-Rewini, and T. G. Lewis, Scheduling Parallel Program Tasks onto Arbitrary Target Machines, *J. Parallel Distrib. Comput.* 9, 1990, pp. 138-153

5. D. E. Goldberg, *Genetic Algorithms in Search, Optimization and Machine Learning*. Addison-Wesley, Reading, MA, 1989

6. Z. Michalewicz, *Genetic Algorithms + Data Structures = Evolution Programs*, Springer, 1992

7. M. Schwehm and T. Walter, Mapping and Scheduling by Genetic Algorithms, in B. Buchberger and J. Volkert (Eds.), CONPAR 94 - VAPPVI, LNCS 854, Springer, 1994

8. F. Seredynski, Scheduling Tasks of a Parallel Program in Two-Processor Systems with use of Cellular Automata, in J. Rolim (Ed.), *Parallel and Distributed Processing*, LNCS 1388, Springer, 1998, pp. 261-269

9. M. Sipper, *Evolution of Parallel Cellular Machines*. The Cellular Programming Approach, LNCS 1194, Springer, 1997

10. S. Wolfram, Universality and Complexity in Cellular Automata, *Physica D* 10, 1984, pp. 1-35

Simple + Parallel + Local = Cellular Computing

Moshe Sipper

Logic Systems Laboratory, Swiss Federal Institute of Technology, CH-1015 Lausanne, Switzerland. E-mail: Moshe.Sipper@di.epfl.ch, Web: lslwww.epfl.ch/~moshes.

Abstract. In recent years we are witness to a growing number of researchers who are interested in novel computational systems based on principles that are entirely different than those of classical computers. Though coming from disparate domains, their work shares a common computational philosophy, which I call *cellular computing*. Basically, cellular computing is a vastly parallel, highly local computational paradigm, with simple cells as the basic units of computation. It aims at providing new means for doing computation in a more efficient manner than other approaches (in terms of speed, cost, power dissipation, information storage, quality of solutions), while potentially addressing much larger problem instances than was possible before—at least for some application domains. This paper provides a qualitative exposition of the cellular computing paradigm, including sample applications and a discussion of some of the research issues involved.

1   What is cellular computing?

The reigning computing technology of the past fifty years, often referred to as the von Neumann architecture, is all but ubiquitous nowadays. Having proliferated into every aspect of our daily lives, the basic principle can be summed up as follows: one complex processor that sequentially performs a single complex task (at a given moment). In recent years we are witness to a growing number of researchers who are interested in novel computational systems based on entirely different principles. Though coming from disparate domains, their work shares a common computational philosophy, which I call *cellular computing*.

At the heart of this paradigm lie three principles:

1. Simple processors, referred to as cells.
2. A vast number of cells operating in parallel.
3. Local connections between cells.

Cellular computing is thus a vastly parallel, highly local computational paradigm, with simple cells as the basic units of computation.

Let us take a closer look at what is meant by these three principles. Firstly, the basic processor used as the fundamental unit of cellular computing—the cell—is simple. By this I mean that while a current-day, general-purpose processor is capable of performing quite complicated tasks, the cell can do very little in and of itself. Formally, this notion can be captured, say, by the difference between a universal Turing machine and a finite state machine. In practice, our experience of fifty years in building computing machines has left us with a good notion of what is meant by "simple."

The second principle is vast parallelism. Though parallel computers have been built and operated, they usually contain no more than a few dozen processors. In the parallel computing domain, "massively parallel" is a term usually reserved for those few machines that comprise a few thousand (or at most tens of thousands) processors. Cellular computing involves parallelism on a whole different scale, with the number of cells measured at times by evoking the exponential notation, 10^x. To distinguish this huge number of processors from that involved in classical parallel computing, I shall use the term *vast* parallelism (as opposed to "mere" massive parallelism). This quantitative difference leads, as I shall argue, to novel qualitative properties, as nicely captured by the title of a 1972 paper by Philip Anderson "More is Different" [2]. (Note that while not all works presented to date necessarily involve vast parallelism, partly due to current technological limitations, this underlying principle still stands firm).

The third and final distinguishing property of cellular computing concerns the local connectivity pattern between cells. This means that any interactions taking place are on a purely local basis—a cell can only communicate with a small number of other cells, most of which (if not all) are physically close by. Furthermore, the connection lines usually carry only a small amount of information. One implication of this principle is that no one cell has a global view of the entire system—there is no central controller.

Combining these three principles results in the equation *cellular computing = simplicity + vast parallelism + locality*. It is important to note that changing any single one of these terms in the equation results in a totally different paradigm; thus, these three axioms represent necessary conditions of cellular computing (Figure 1).

Cellular computing is at heart a paradigm that aims at providing new means for doing computation in a more efficient manner than other approaches (in terms of speed, cost, power dissipation, information storage, quality of solutions), while potentially addressing much larger problem instances than was possible before—at least for some application domains. This paper describes the essence of cellular computing; I provide a *qualitative* exposition, my goal being to convince the reader of the viability of this emerging paradigm. Toward this end I first present in the next section four representative examples of cellular computing, noting that in spite of their differences they all share in common the above three principles. Then, in Section 3 I shall discuss some general issues, followed by concluding remarks in Section 4. (In the full version, I expound upon many of the issues underlying cellular computing, such as properties of the different models, system characteristics, and more [23].)

2 Four examples of cellular computing

To get an idea of what is meant by cellular computing I shall set forth four examples in this section. Though differing in many ways, e.g., the underlying

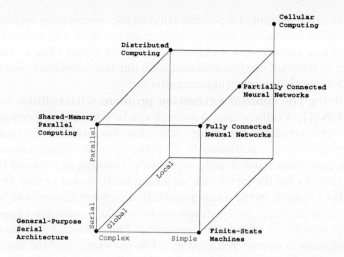

Fig. 1. *Simple + Parallel + Local = Cellular Computing.* Changing any single one of these terms in the equation results in a totally different paradigm, as shown by the above "computing cube." Notes: (1) Cellular computing has been placed further along the parallelism axis to emphasize the "vastness" aspect (see text). (2) Artificial neural networks can be divided into two classes (for our purposes): fully connected architectures, where no connectivity constraints are enforced (e.g., Hopfield networks, Boltzmann machines), and partially connected networks (e.g., the Kohonen network, which exhibits local connectivity between the neurons in the feature map, though each of these is still connected to all input neurons).

model, the problems addressed, input and output encoding, and more, I argue that they all sprout from the common cellular-computing trunk. (To facilitate their referencing each example is given a three-letter mnemonic.)

1. A cellular adder (ADD). Cellular automata are perhaps the quintessential example of cellular computing, as well as the first to historically appear on the scene. Conceived in the late 1940s by Ulam and von Neumann, the model is that of a dynamical system in which space and time are discrete [28, 29]. A cellular automaton consists of an array of cells, each of which can be in one of a finite number of possible states, updated synchronously in discrete time steps, according to a local, identical interaction rule. The state of a cell at the next time step is determined by the current states of a surrounding neighborhood of cells. This transition is usually specified in the form of a rule table, delineating the cell's next state for each possible neighborhood configuration. The cellular array (grid) is n-dimensional, where $n = 1, 2, 3$ is used in practice.

In a recent work, Benjamin and Johnson [3] presented a cellular automaton that can perform binary addition: given two binary numbers encoded as the initial configuration of cellular states, the grid converges in time towards a final configuration which is their sum. The interesting point concerning this work is the outline given therein of a possible wireless nanometer-scale realization of the adding cellular automaton using coupled quantum dots. (As pointed out in [3], the device is a nanometer-scale classical computer rather than a true quantum computer. It does not need to maintain wave function coherence, and is therefore far less delicate than a quantum computer).

2. Solving the contour extraction problem with cellular neural networks (CNN). A cellular neural network can be regarded as a cellular automaton where cellular states are analog rather than discrete, and the time dynamics are either discrete or continuous [5–7]. Since their inception, almost a decade ago, they have been studied quite extensively, resulting in a lore of both theory and practice. As for the latter, one major application area is that of image processing. For example, in the contour extraction problem the network is presented with a gray-scale image and extracts contours which resemble edges (resulting from large changes in gray-level intensities). This operation, oft-used as a preprocessing stage in pattern recognition, is but one example of the many problems in the domain of image processing solved by cellular neural networks.

3. Solving the directed Hamiltonian path problem by DNA computing (DNA). The idea of using natural or artificial molecules as basic computational elements (i.e., cells) has been around for quite some time now (e.g., [9, 10]). The decisive proof-of-concept was recently given by Adleman [1] who used molecular biology tools to solve an instance of the directed Hamiltonian path problem: given an arbitrary directed graph the object is to find whether there exists a path between two given vertices that passes through each vertex exactly once. Adleman used the following (nondeterministic) algorithm to solve this hard (NP-complete) problem:

Step 1: Generate random paths through the graph.
Step 2: Keep only those paths that begin with the start vertex and terminate with the end vertex.
Step 3: If the graph has n vertices, then keep only those paths that enter exactly n vertices.
Step 4: Keep only those paths that enter all of the vertices of the graph at least once.
Step 5: If any paths remain, say "Yes"; otherwise, say "No."

The key point about Adleman's work is the use of DNA material along with molecular biology tools to implement the above algorithm. Vertices and edges of the graph were encoded by oligonucleotides (short chains of usually up to 20 nucleotides). In the test tube these would then randomly link up with each other, forming paths through the graph (step 1), to be then subjected to a series of molecular "sieves" that essentially carried out the remaining steps. The extremely small cell size in this form of cellular computing (a DNA molecule) gives rise to vast parallelism on an entirely new scale. Adleman estimated that such molecular computers could be exceedingly faster, more energy efficient, and able to store much more information than current-day supercomputers (at least with respect to certain classes of problems).

It could be argued that DNA molecules violate the simplicity-of-cells principle. However, while such molecules may exhibit complex behavior from the biologist's standpoint, they can be treated as simple elements from the computational point of view. As put forward by Lipton [17]: "Our model of how DNA behaves is simple and idealized. It ignores many complex known effects but is an excellent first-order approximation." Indeed, it seems that in DNA computing the basic cell (DNA molecule) is typically treated as a simple elemental unit, on which a small number of basic operations can be performed in the test tube [17]. This is similar to several other instances in computer science where irrelevant low-level details are abstracted away; for example, the transistor is usually regarded as a simple switch, with the complex physical phenomena taking place at the atomic and sub-atomic levels being immaterial.

4. Solving the satisfiability problem with self-replicating loops (SAT).

In his seminal work, von Neumann showed that self-replication, previously thought to exist only in nature, can be obtained by machines [28]. Toward this end he embedded within a two-dimensional cellular-automaton "universe" a machine known as a universal constructor-computer, able both to construct any other machine upon given its blueprint (universal construction) and also to compute any computable function (universal computation). Here, the term "machine" refers to a configuration of cellular-automaton states; indeed, the ability to formally describe such structures served as a major motivation for von Neumann's choice of the cellular-automaton model. Self-replication is obtained as a special case of universal construction, when the machine is given its own blueprint, i.e., instructions to build a universal constructor. This latter's complexity prohibited its implementation, and only partial simulations have been carried out to date. Langton [16] showed that if one renounces universal construction, stipulating but self-replication, a much simpler, and entirely realizable structure can be obtained. His so-called self-replicating loop does nothing but replicate. More recently, researchers have shown that one can embed a program within the loop, thus having the structure replicate as well as execute a program [20, 27]. The motivation for such programmed replicators is the possibility of obtaining a vastly parallel, cellular computing environment.

Chou and Reggia [4] have recently shown that self-replicating loops can be used to solve the NP-complete problem known as satisfiability (SAT). Given a Boolean predicate like $(x_1 \lor x_2 \lor \neg x_3) \land (\neg x_1 \lor \neg x_2 \lor x_3)$, the problem is to find the assignment of Boolean values to the binary variables x_1, x_2, and x_3 that satisfies the predicate, i.e., makes it evaluate to True (if such an assignment exists). In [20, 27] the program embedded in each loop is copied unchanged from parent to child so that all replicated loops carry out the same program. Chou and Reggia took a different approach in which each replicant receives a distinct partial solution that is modified during replication. Under a form of artificial selection, replicants with promising solutions proliferate while those with failed solutions are lost. The process is demonstrated in Figure 2. This work is interesting in that it can be considered a form of DNA computing in a cellular automaton, using self-replicating loops in a vastly parallel fashion. A molecular implementation of this approach might be had by using synthetic self-replicators, like those described, e.g., by Rebek, Jr. [21]. Lipton [17] presented a DNA-computing solution to the SAT problem, similar to Adleman's method discussed above. He noted that "biological computations could potentially have vastly more parallelism than conventional ones." [17]

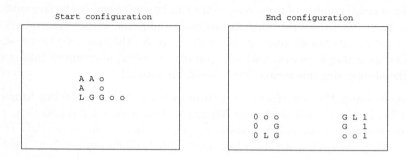

Fig. 2. Solving the satisfiability (SAT) problem with self-replicating loops. Shown above for a three-variable problem: $(\neg x_1 \vee x_3) \wedge (x_1 \vee \neg x_2) \wedge (x_2 \vee \neg x_3)$. The initial configuration of the two-dimensional cellular automaton contains a single loop with three embedded binary bits (marked by As). This loop self-replicates in the cellular space, with each daughter loop differing by one bit from the parent, thus resulting in a parallel enumeration process. This is coupled with artificial selection that culls unfit solutions, by eliminating the loops that represent them (each loop represents one possible SAT solution). In the end only two loops remain, containing the two truth assignments for the predicate in question: $x_1, x_2, x_3 = 0, 0, 0$ or $1, 1, 1$.

3 Discussion

In this section I shall discuss a number of issues related to cellular computing, ending with a presentation of some possible avenues for future research.

Cellular computing and parallel computing. It could be claimed that the concept of cellular computing is not new at all, but is simply a synonym for the longstanding domain of parallel computing. In fact, the two domains are quite disparate in terms of the models and the issues studied. Parallel computing traditionally dealt with a small number of powerful processors, studying issues such as scheduling, concurrency, message passing, synchronization, and more. This clearly differs from cellular computing, whose underlying philosophy is quite distinct from that of parallel computing (Figure 1). The only area of intersection may be the few so-called "massively parallel machines" that have been built and studied by parallel computing practitioners (e.g., [14]). As noted in Section 1, cellular computing has the potential of exhibiting vastly parallel computation, giving rise to an entirely new phenomenology. (Interestingly, models such as cellular automata were usually regarded by hard-core parallel computing practitioners as being "embarrassingly parallel" and therefore uninteresting.)

Considering the domain of parallel computing one can observe that decades of research have not produced the expected results—parallel machines are not ubiquitous and most programmers continue to use sequential programming languages. I believe that one of the major problems involves the domain's ambitious goal (at least at the outset) of supplanting the serial computing paradigm. The parallel computing lesson for cellular computing practitioners might thus be that they should not aim for an all-encompassing, general-purpose paradigm, which will replace the sequential one (at least not at present...); rather, one should find those niches where such models could excel. There are already a number of clear proofs-of-concept, demonstrating that cellular computing can efficiently solve difficult problems.

Next, I wish to discuss what I call the *slow fast train*. Consider a 300-kmh fast train arriving at its destination, with passengers allowed to disembark through but a single port. This is clearly a waste of the train's parallel exit system, consisting of multiple ports dispersed throughout the train. This metaphor, dubbed the slow fast train, illustrates an important point about parallel systems, namely, their potential (ill-)use in a highly sequential manner. Note that for most cellular computing models, it is not too difficult to prove computation universality by embedding some form of serial universal machine. This proves that, *in theory*, the model is at least as powerful as any other universal system. However, *in practice*, such a construction defeats the purpose of cellular computing by completely degenerating the parallelism aspect. Thus, on the whole, one wants to avoid slowing the fast train.

Cellular computing and complex systems. In recent years there is a rapidly growing interest in the field of complex systems [11, 15, 19]. While there are evident links between complex systems and cellular computing it should be noted that the two are not identical, the former being a scientific discipline, the latter primarily an engineering domain. As is the time-honored tradition of science and engineering, fruitful cross-fertilization between the two is manifest.

Research themes. Finally, I wish to outline a number of themes that present several possible avenues for future research.

- As noted in Section 1, cellular computing is a computational paradigm that underlies a number of somewhat disparate domains. In this respect, we wish to gain a deeper understanding of the commonalities and differences between the different approaches. Among the important questions are: What classes of computational tasks are most suitable for cellular computing? Can these be formally defined? Can informal guidelines be given? Can we relate specific properties and behaviors of a certain model with the class of problems it is most suitable for? And, vice versa, for a given problem (or class of problems), how do we choose the most appropriate cellular model?
- Adaptive programming methodologies for cellular computing, including evolutionary algorithms [13, 22] and neural-network learning [8].
- Most real-world problems involve some degree of global computation. Thus,

understanding how local interactions give rise to global ("emergent") computational capabilities is a central research theme [12]. Furthermore, it is important to explore the application of adaptive methods to the programming of such behavior [18,22].

- What are the major application areas of cellular computing? Research to date has raised a number of possibilities, including: image processing, fast solutions to some NP-complete problems, generating long sequences of high-quality random numbers [24,25]—an important application in many domains (e.g., computational physics and computational chemistry), and, finally, the ability to perform arithmetic operations (e.g., ADD example) raises the possibility of implementing rapid calculating machines on a very small (nano) scale.

- The scalability issue. Cellular computing potentially offers a paradigm that is more scalable than classical ones. This has to do with the fact that connectivity is local, and there is no central processor that must communicate with every single cell; furthermore, these latter are simple. Thus, adding cells should not pose any major problem, on the surface. However, in reality this issue is not trivial both at the model as well as the implementation level. As noted by Sipper [22], *simple* scaling, involving a straightforward augmentation of resources (e.g., cells, connections), does not necessarily bring about *task* scaling, i.e., maintaining of (at least) the same performance level. Thus, more research is needed on the issue of scalability.

- Fault tolerance. Lipton [17] noted that: "The main open question is, of course, if one can actually build DNA computers based on the methods described here. The key issue is errors. The operations are not perfect." This motivated, e.g., Deaton *et al.* [13] to apply evolutionary techniques to search for better DNA encodings, thus reducing the errors during the DNA computation. Sipper, Tomassini, and Beuret [26] studied the effects of random faults on the behavior of some evolved cellular automata, showing that they exhibit graceful degradation in performance, able to tolerate a certain level of faults (see also references therein to other works on faults and damage in cellular models).

- Novel implementation platforms, such as reconfigurable processors (digital and analog), molecular devices, and nanomachines.

4 Concluding remarks

Cellular computing is a vastly parallel, highly local computational paradigm, with simple cells as the basic units of computation. This computational paradigm has been attracting a growing number of researchers in the past few years, producing exciting results that hold prospects for a bright future. Though several open questions yet remain, it is always encouraging to consider the ultimate proof-of-concept: nature.

Acknowledgments

I am grateful to Mathieu Capcarrere, Daniel Mange, Eduardo Sanchez, and Marco Tomassini for helpful discussions.

References

1. L. M. Adleman. Molecular computation of solutions to combinatorial problems. *Science*, 266:1021–1024, November 1994.
2. P. W. Anderson. More is different. *Science*, 177(4047):393–396, August 1972.
3. S. C. Benjamin and N. F. Johnson. A possible nanometer-scale computing device based on an adding cellular automaton. *Applied Physics Letters*, 70(17):2321–2323, April 1997.
4. H.-H. Chou and J. A. Reggia. Problem solving during artificial selection of self-replicating loops. *Physica D*, 115(3-4):293–312, May 1998.
5. L. O. Chua and T. Roska. The CNN paradigm. *IEEE Transactions on Circuits and Systems*, 40(3):147–156, March 1993.
6. L. O. Chua and L. Yang. Cellular neural networks: Applications. *IEEE Transactions on Circuits and Systems*, 35(10):1272–1290, October 1988.
7. L. O. Chua and L. Yang. Cellular neural networks: Theory. *IEEE Transactions on Circuits and Systems*, 35(10):1257–1271, October 1988.
8. V. Cimagalli and M. Balsi. Cellular neural networks: A review. In E. Caianiello, editor, *Proceedings of Sixth Italian Workshop on Parallel Architectures and Neural Networks*, Singapore, 1994. World Scientific.
9. M. Conrad. On design principles for a molecular computer. *Communications of the ACM*, 28(5):464–480, May 1985.
10. M. Conrad and E. A. Liberman. Molecular computing as a link between biological and physical theory. *Journal of Theoretical Biology*, 98:239–252, 1982.
11. P. Coveney and R. Highfield. *Frontiers of Complexity: The Search for Order in a Chaotic World*. Faber and Faber, London, 1995.
12. J. P. Crutchfield and M. Mitchell. The evolution of emergent computation. *Proceedings of the National Academy of Sciences USA*, 92(23):10742–10746, 1995.
13. R. Deaton, R. C. Murphy, J. A. Rose, M. Garzon, D. R. Franceschetti, and S. E. Stevens, Jr. A DNA based implementation of an evolutionary search for good encodings for DNA computation. In *Proceedings of 1997 IEEE International Conference on Evolutionary Computation (ICEC'97)*, pages 267–271, 1997.
14. W. D. Hillis. *The Connection Machine*. The MIT Press, Cambridge, Massachusetts, 1985.
15. K. Kaneko, I. Tsuda, and T. Ikegami, editors. *Constructive Complexity and Artificial Reality, Proceedings of the Oji International Seminar on Complex Systems-from Complex Dynamical Systems to Sciences of Artificial Reality*, volume 75, Nos. 1-3 of *Physica D*, August 1994.
16. C. G. Langton. Self-reproduction in cellular automata. *Physica D*, 10:135–144, 1984.
17. R. J. Lipton. DNA solution of hard computational problems. *Science*, 268:542–545, April 1995.
18. M. Mitchell, J. P. Crutchfield, and P. T. Hraber. Evolving cellular automata to perform computations: Mechanisms and impediments. *Physica D*, 75:361–391, 1994.

19. H. R. Pagels. *The Dreams of Reason: The Computer and the Rise of the Sciences of Complexity*. Bantam Books, New York, 1989.

20. J.-Y. Perrier, M. Sipper, and J. Zahnd. Toward a viable, self-reproducing universal computer. *Physica D*, 97:335–352, 1996.

21. J. Rebek, Jr. Synthetic self-replicating molecules. *Scientific American*, 271(1):48–55, July 1994.

22. M. Sipper. *Evolution of Parallel Cellular Machines: The Cellular Programming Approach*. Springer-Verlag, Heidelberg, 1997.

23. M. Sipper. Cellular computing. 1998. (Submitted).

24. M. Sipper and M. Tomassini. Co-evolving parallel random number generators. In H.-M. Voigt, W. Ebeling, I. Rechenberg, and H.-P. Schwefel, editors, *Parallel Problem Solving from Nature - PPSN IV*, volume 1141 of *Lecture Notes in Computer Science*, pages 950–959. Springer-Verlag, Heidelberg, 1996.

25. M. Sipper and M. Tomassini. Generating parallel random number generators by cellular programming. *International Journal of Modern Physics C*, 7(2):181–190, 1996.

26. M. Sipper, M. Tomassini, and O. Beuret. Studying probabilistic faults in evolved non-uniform cellular automata. *International Journal of Modern Physics C*, 7(6):923–939, 1996.

27. G. Tempesti. A new self-reproducing cellular automaton capable of construction and computation. In F. Morán, A. Moreno, J. J. Merelo, and P. Chacón, editors, *ECAL'95: Third European Conference on Artificial Life*, volume 929 of *Lecture Notes in Computer Science*, pages 555–563, Heidelberg, 1995. Springer-Verlag.

28. J. von Neumann. *Theory of Self-Reproducing Automata*. University of Illinois Press, Illinois, 1966. Edited and completed by A. W. Burks.

29. S. Wolfram. *Cellular Automata and Complexity*. Addison-Wesley, Reading, MA, 1994.

Evolution, Learning and Speech Recognition in Changing Acoustic Environments

Anne Spalanzani and Harouna Kabré

CLIPS-IMAG Laboratory
Joseph Fourier University, BP 53
38041 Grenoble cedex 9, France
{Anne.Spalanzani, Harouna.Kabre}@imag.fr

Abstract. In this paper, we apply Evolutionary Algorithms (EA) to evolve Automatic Speech Recognition Systems (ASRSs) in order to adapt them to acoustic environment changes. The general framework relates to the Evolutionary paradigm and it addresses the problem of robustness of speech recognition as a two level process. First, some initial ASRSs based on feed-forward Artificial Neural Networks (ANNs) are designed and trained with an initial speech corpus. Second, the ASRSs are tested in Virtual Acoustic Environments (VAEs) in which we playback some speech test data. By using Evolutionary Operators as mutation, crossover and selection, the adaptation of initial ASRSs to a new VAE is achieved. The VAE includes different real world noises and are physical models of real rooms (1 floor, 1 ceiling and 4 walls) thanks to image methods of sound propagation in small rooms.

0. Introduction

This paper presents the combination of learning and evolution methods applied to speech recognition in changing in Virtual Acoustic Environments (VAE). This research was motivated by the problems encountered by Automatic Speech Recognition Systems (ASRSs) to adapt to new acoustic environments as it is known that mismatches between training and testing data are the main factor degrading the performance of ASRSs. Different strategies have been proposed in literature for solving this problem in the case of slight environment changes (see Section 1). However, many problems remain for the adaptation to unknown acoustic environments or dramatic acoustic condition changes and a fundamental research is needed. In this paper, we suggest to combine EA with ANNs (see Spears et al. 1993 for a overview of these hybrid methods and their applications). Applied to speech recognition, we propose to work not only with one ASRS but with a population of ASRSs able to evolve in a changing VAE.

Section 1 presents the main techniques used for the robustness of automatic speech recognition systems. Section 2 describes our model and results obtained are presented in Section 3.

1. Background

It is known that the performances of Automatic Speech Recognition Systems (ASRSs) decrease when their training and testing conditions are different. Therefore, this problem represents a great challenge for speech researchers as far as the deployment of speech technology in real world (which includes noisy, reverberant, wire noise, etc. conditions) is concerned. Indeed, it is not possible for a designer to foresee all the circumstances which might be involved in the use of those different systems.

To overcome this problem of mismatch between a training environment and an unknown testing environment, many speech researchers have proposed different strategies which we classify in four classes:

- *Structure modification* approaches (Das et al. 1994, Gong 1995);
- *Stimuli modification* approaches (Bateman et al. 1992, Mansour and Juang 1988);
- *Integration of multiple sources* of information approaches (Yuhas 1989, McGurk and MacDonald 1976);
- *Hybrid* approaches (Junqua and Haton 1996).

In the first group, the adaptation to a new environment is achieved by changing the parameters of a speech recognition model. E.g. for a Hidden Markov Model (HMM) this implies the modification of the number of states, of gaussians, etc. Equivalently for a neural network, the number of units and the number of layers would be adjusted.

The second group focuses on a richer pre-processing of the input speech signal before presenting to the model; e.g. by trying to suppress environment noises or by modifying acoustic parameters before the classification level.

Those two groups are extensively analyzed in (Gong 1995).

The third group is increasingly addressed and corresponds to the combination of at least two sources of information to improve the robustness. For example, speaker's lips movements and their corresponding acoustic signals are processed and integrated to improve the robustness of the ASRSs.

The fourth group is based on the idea that hybridization should improve robustness of ASRSs by compensating the drawbacks of a given method with the advantages of the other. For example many contributions have focused on the combination of HMMs and ANNs to take advantage of the discrimination power of ANNs while preserving the time alignment feature of HMMs. Unfortunately, as far as the robustness problem is concerned, very few studies have used EA as a second level on ANNs and HMMs in order to achieve auto-adaptation of ASRSs to some new acoustic environments (e.g. for environment selection, etc.).

Section 2 presents a way to adapt ASRSs to new environments by introducing evolutionary algorithm techniques.

2. Method

The method is based on evolutionary algorithms (Spears and et al. 1993). The general overview of the model follows the algorithm shown in Figure 1.

A population of ASRSs is built in an initial VAE. In our study, we chose to focus on ASRSs built with feedforward Artificial Neural Network. The creation of the initial population resorts to make a desired number of copies of a pre-trained ANN while making a random change of its weights. The environment is changed by either taking a new VAE, a different speech database or a different noise. (We considered different noises such as door closing, alarm, radio, etc.). The change is such that the ASRSs are no longer well-suited to this environment. At this moment, after a period of training, an adaptation cycle starts thanks to genetic operators.

---

1. **Init** a population of ASRSs.
2. **If** duration of simulation not elapsed **change** the VAE **else goto** 6.
3. **Train** ASRSs.
4. **Evaluate, Select** and **Reproduce** ASRSs.
5. **If** duration of adaptation elapsed **then goto** 2 **else goto** 3.
6. end.

Fig. 1. Algorithm for evolving ASRSs so that they adapt to new VAEs.

Our simulations take place in EVERA (Environnement d'Etude de la Robustesse des Apprentis), our speech Artificial Life simulator which has been described in (Kabré and Spalanzani 1997). The main purpose of EVERA is to provide a test-bed for the evaluation and improvement of the robustness of ASRSs. Two models are proposed in EVERA, a model of environment and a model of organisms (i.e. ASRSs) which evolve in it. In our study, the environment is a VAE and the organisms are modeled as Artificial Neural Networks. The VAE allows the simulation of the transfer function between acoustic sources (e.g. speaker and noise) and a microphone position. Thanks to Allen model of sound propagation in small rooms (Allen and Berkley 1979), by varying the reflection coefficient of walls, floor and ceiling, it is possible to control the reverberation time. This latter measures the time needed for the sound emitted in a VAE to extinct. The difficulty of recognition increases with the reverberation time. The convolution between a speech signal taken from any database and the VAE impulse response gives the speech signal for training the ANNs.

3. Experiments

3.1. Environment

For the experiments, we use a database of the 10 French vowels. Each presented environment consists of 20 sounds of vowels where noises (radio, alarm, fire, door) have been added. Each vowel is uttered 100 times and half the corpus is used to pre-train the ASRSs.

The different vowel sounds are firstly recorded during a session for which a male speaker pronounces all the vowels. Each of them is convoluted to the VAE impulse response (depending on reverberation), then added to noises. Finally, each vowel sound is preprocessed by the Perceptual Linear Predictive analysis (Hermansky

1990), which is at the moment one of the best speech pre-processing methods. The result is a 7-dimension vector characterizing the spectral information of reverberated and noisy vowel sounds. Associated to targets (output demanded for the ANNs), these vectors are presented as inputs.

3.2. Population

The population consists of fully connected feedforward neural networks composed of 7 input, 15 hidden and 10 output units. The structure has been empirically designed for the vowel recognition task. The backpropagation algorithm is applied for training the different ANNs.

3.3. Genetic Operators

The population was first tested in a sole environment change to tune the parameters of the simulation, i.e. type of selection, mutation rate, number of organisms.

We first simulate a population of 20 ASRSs trained in an environment with low noise of "door closing" and put in an environment with a loud noise of "radio". Figure 2 shows the comparison of two types of selection with four different mutation rates. The first selection is a classical roulette wheel selection (Goldberg 1989). The second one, selects the best ASRS to generate the new population. By multiplying a few ANN's weights (depending on mutation rate) by a random variable uniformly distributed over an interval, mutation generates 20 new ASRSs.

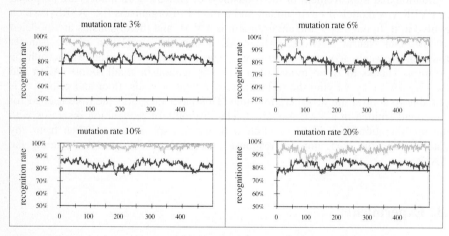

Fig. 2. Influence of selection for 4 different mutation rates during 500 generations. Simulation of a population of 20 ASRSs. The black line shows the performances (average of the recognition rate) of a population selected with a roulette wheel selection, crossing rate is 60%. The grey curve shows the performances of a population where the best ASRS is selected. The straight line shows the performances of ANNs without evolution.

As Figure 2 shows, speech recognition is performed better by the population selected with a drastic method. For example, selecting the best ASRS to reproduce and mutate enhances the recognition rate by 20% so that it can reach almost 100% when mutation rate is 10%.

Furthermore, it can be noticed that the superiority of the results with selection of the best ASRS compared to roulette wheel selection does not depend on the mutation rate.

However, the mutation rate seems to have an importance on the stability of the results. Low mutation rate does not give enough diversity whereas high mutation rate is too disturbing. This can be verified in Figure 3 considering the performance of the best ASRS of the population. That can be an important point of our simulation as our goal is to find an efficient speech recognition system.

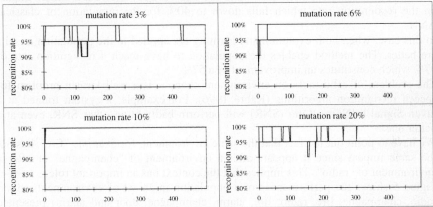

Fig. 3. Influence of the mutation rate on the recognition rate of the best ASRS. Selection of the best ASRS is performed during 500 generations.

The population size we chose seems to be a good compromise to have quite stable results and not too long simulations. Figure 4 shows the influence of the population size on the stability of the results during the 500 generations.

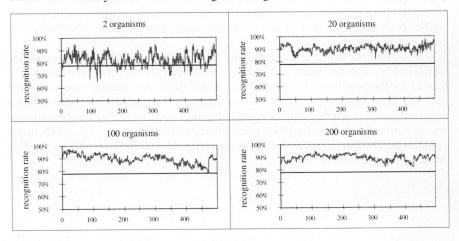

Fig. 4. Influence of the population size on the average of the recognition rate. Selection of the best ASRS, mutation rate is 10%. 500 generations.

3.4 Changing Environments

The environment is composed of 5 different noises (door, radio, fire, alarm and champagne) which have more or less influence on vowels discrimination because of their signal to noise ratio and because of the reverberation of the VAE.

Figure 5 shows the results for a population of 20 ASRSs in a changing VAE. For each environment, the population has 500 generations to adapt.

The first thing to notice is the effect of the environment changes. The transition between the environment of "radio" and the one of "fire" shows a dramatic impact on the recognition rate which falls down to 40% for the population of classical ANNs.

In this case, when both evolution and learning are applied to the population, results are better. The method enables the population to have reach a recognition rate of 97% which constitutes an improvement of a 57%.

The problem of robustness on environment changes is a well known problem for speech recognition algorithms (Kabré 1996). For example, a system trained at a given Signal to Noise Ratio (SNR) will perform badly at an other SNR, even at a better one.

We have to point out the fact that the same environment, for example "fire", has not the same impact since it appears after a environment of "champagne" or after a environment of "radio". This implies that the context has an important role.

Figure 5 shows the performances of a population in an set of environments (door, radio, champagne, fire, radio, fire, alarm, champagne, door and alarm) presented three times. It can be noticed that the performances of the population of ANNs decrease more and more during the simulation and will continue in the same way if the number of environments increases. This can be interpreted as a relearning problem. It is known that the initialization of connection weights can lead to local minima and bad performances (F.A. Lodewyk and E. Barnard 1992). The problem encountered here is that ANNs have already converged with a previous set of data and are not able to converge with good performances on other very different data. That is what evolution by genetic operators avoid. The performances are stable. Moreover, performances of population selected by classical roulette are better than ANNs' performances. That is not what we noticed in Figure2 when only one environment change occurs.

It is interesting to notice that the number of generations to adapt to a new VAE, which is 500, does not seem to be necessary. Actually, only a few generations are needed for the population to adapt, that is about 10 for the roulette wheel selection and only 2 or 3 when the best ASRS is selected. Stopping the evolution when a certain criterion is reached should be an interesting point to approach. This criterion would not be difficult to find as we are interested in finding a good ASRS in the population. The only choice to make is an acceptable recognition rate for the best ASRS of the population.

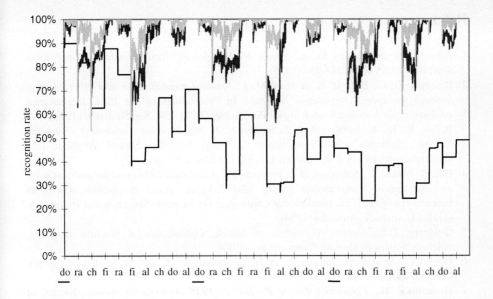

Fig. 5. Performances (average of the recognition rate) of a population of 20 ASRSs in a changing VAE. The black line shows the performances of a population selected with a roulette wheel selection, crossing rate is 60%. The grey curve shows the performances of a population where the best ASRS is selected. The straight lines show the performances of ANNs without evolution. each VAE is defined by a triplet (noise, reverberation time, SNR). The environment changes occur by passing from a triplet to another.

4. Conclusion

In this study, EA are applied to adapt a population of ASRSs to different noisy and reverberant acoustic environments. The following results have been obtained :
(1) We have succeeded in building adaptive ASRSs which gave encouraging results. For example, an 30% improvement in average is achieved by using evolution in the changing environments (Figure 5).
(2) The selection of the best individual for the creation of the next generation is interesting to obtain a rapid adaptation to a new environment.
(3) The nature of the environment changes need to be taken into account. The kind of disturbance has an importance also. This result confirms what we have observed in another study (Kabré, 1996) and shows the importance in our future studies to take care of the spectral information selection at the sensor level.
Although exploratory, the results obtained encourage us in the search of a new algorithm for auto-adaptive speech systems. It would permits the population to gather the VAE dynamically and adapt by itself to the changing environments, thus "perceiving" their acoustic environments.

References

1. Allen J., B. & Berkley D. A.: *Image Method for efficiently simulating small-room acoustics.* JASA 65(4):943-950 (1979).
2. Bateman, D. C., Bye, D. K. & Hunt M. J.: *Spectral normalization and other spectral technics for speech recognition in noise.* In Proceedings of the IEEE International conference. on Acoustic Speech Signal Processing, (1)241-244. San Francisco (1992).
3. Belew, R. K., McInerney, J. & Schraudolph, N. N.: *Evolving Networks : Using the Genetic Algorithm with Connectionist Learning.* In Proc. Second Artificial Life Conference, pages 511-547, New York, (1991). Addison-Wesley
4. Das, S., Nadas, A., Nahamoo, D. & Picheny, M.: *Adaptation techniques for ambient noise and microphone compensation in the IBM Tangora speech recognition system.* In Proceedings of the IEEE International Conference On Acoustic Speech Signal Processing. (1)21-23. Adelaide, Australia (1994).
5. Goldberg, D.E.: *Genetic Algorithms in Search, Optimization & Machine Learning.* Addison-Wesley Publishing Company, Inc (1989).
6. Gong, Y.: *Speech recognition in noisy environments: A survey,* Journal of Speech Communication (1995), 16 : 261-291.
7. Hermansky, H.: *Perceptual Linear Predictive (PLP) Analysis of Speech,* Journal of Acoustic Society Am (1990), 87(4) 1738-1752.
8. Holland, H.: *Adaptation in Natural and Artificial Systems.* The University of Michigan Press (1975).
9. Junqua, J. C. & Haton, H.: *Robustness in Automatic Speech Recognition,* Ed Kluwer Academic Publisher (1996).
10. Kabré, H. & Spalanzani A.: *EVERA: A system for the Modeling and Simulation of Complex Systems.* In Proceedings of the First International Workshop on Frontiers in Evolutionary Algorithms, FEA'97, 184-188. North Carolina (1997).
11. Kabré, H.: *On the Active Perception of Speech by Robots.* IEEE RJ/MFI (Multi-sensor Fusion and Integration for Intelligent Systems), 775-785. Washington D.C (1996).
12. Wessels, L and Barnard, E. *Avoiding False Local Minima by Proper Initialization of Connections.* IEEE Transactions on Neural Networks, vol. 3, No 6, (Nov. 1992).
13. Mansour, D. & Juang, B. H.: *A family of distortion measures based upon projection operation for robust speech recognition.* IEEE International Acoustic Speech Signal Process, 36-39. New York (1988).
14. McGurk, H., MacDonald, J.: *Hearing Voices and Seeing Eyes,* Nature, 264:746-748 (1976).
15. Mühlenbein, H. & Schlierkamp-Voosen, D.: Evolution as a Computational Process. Lecture Notes in Computer Science, 188-214, Springer, Berlin (1995).
16. Spears, W.M., De Jong, K.A., Bäck, T., Fogel, D. and De Garis, H.: *An Overview of Evolutionary Computation.* In Proceedings of the European Conference on Machine Learning (1993), (667) 442-459.
17. Yuhas, B.P., Goldstein, M.H. & Sejnowski, T.J.: *Interpretation of Acoustic and Visual Speech Signal using Neural Networks.* IEEE Common Magazine (1989).

Ant Colonies, Immune Systems, and Other Paradigms

Ant Colonies for Adaptive Routing in Packet-Switched Communications Networks

Gianni Di Caro and Marco Dorigo

IRIDIA – Université Libre de Bruxelles – Belgium
{gdicaro, mdorigo}@ulb.ac.be

Abstract. In this paper we present AntNet, a novel adaptive approach to routing tables learning in packet-switched communications networks. AntNet is inspired by the stigmergy model of communication observed in ant colonies. We present compelling evidence that AntNet, when measuring performance by standard measures such as network throughput and average packet delay, outperforms the current Internet routing algorithm (OSPF), some old Internet routing algorithms (SPF and distributed adaptive Bellman-Ford), and recently proposed forms of asynchronous online Bellman-Ford (Q-routing and Predictive Q-routing).

1. Introduction

In this paper we consider the problem of adaptive routing in communications networks: we focus on routing for wide area datagram networks with irregular topology, the most remarkable example of such networks being the Internet.

The routing algorithm that we propose in this paper was inspired by previous works on ant colonies and, more generally, by the notion of *stigmergy* [15], that is, the indirect communication taking place among individuals through modifications induced in their environment. Real ants have been shown to be able to find shortest paths using as only information the pheromone trail deposited by other ants [2]. Algorithms that take inspiration from ants' behavior in finding shortest paths have recently been successfully applied to discrete optimization [4, 7, 11, 12, 13, 14, 18].

In ant colony optimization a set of artificial ants collectively solve a combinatorial problem by a cooperative effort. This effort is mediated by indirect communication of information on the problem structure they collect while building solutions. Similarly, in AntNet, the algorithm we propose in this paper, artificial ants collectively solve the routing problem by a cooperative effort in which stigmergy plays a prominent role. Ants adaptively build routing tables and local models of the network status using indirect and non-coordinated communication of information they concurrently collect while exploring the network.

We report on the behavior of AntNet as compared to the following routing algorithms: Open Shortest Path First (OSPF) [17], Shortest Path First (SPF) [16], distributed adaptive Bellman-Ford (BF) [20], Q-routing [5], and PQ-routing [6]. We considered a variety of realistic experimental conditions. In all cases AntNet showed the best performance and the most stable behavior, while among the competitors there was no clear winner.

This work was supported by a Madame Curie Fellowship awarded to Gianni Di Caro (CEC TMR Contract N. ERBFMBICT-961153). Marco Dorigo is a Research Associate with the FNRS.

2. Problem Characteristics

The goal of every routing algorithm is to direct traffic from sources to destinations maximizing network performance. The performance measures that usually are taken into account are *throughput* (correctly delivered bits per time unit) and *average packet delay*. The former measures the quantity of service that the network has been able to offer in a certain amount of time, while the latter defines the quality of service produced at the same time.

The general problem of determining an optimal routing algorithm can be stated as a multi-objective optimization problem in a non-stationary stochastic environment. Information propagation delays, and the difficulty to completely characterize the network dynamics under arbitrary traffic patterns, make the general routing problem intrinsically distributed. Routing decisions can only be made on the basis of local and approximate information about the current and the future network states. Additional constraints are posed by the network switching and transmission technology.

3. The Communication Network Model

In the following, a brief description of the features of the considered communication network model is given. In this paper we focus on irregular topology datagram networks with an IP-like (Internet Protocol) network layer and a very simple transport layer. We developed a complete network simulator (in C++) where the instance of the communication network is mapped on a directed weighted graph with N nodes. All the links are viewed as bit pipes characterized by a bandwidth (bits/sec) and a transmission delay (sec), and are accessed following a statistical multiplexing scheme. For this purpose, every routing node holds a buffer space where the incoming and the outgoing packets are stored. All the traveling packets are subdivided in two classes: data and routing packets. All the packets in the same class have the same priority, so they are queued and served only on the basis of a first-in-first-out policy, but routing packets have a higher priority than data packets.

Data packets are fed into the network by applications (i.e., processes sending data packets from origin nodes to destination nodes) whose arrival rate is dictated by a selected probabilistic model. The number of packets to send, their sizes and the intervals between them are assigned according to some defined stochastic process.

At each node, packets are forwarded towards their destination nodes by the local routing component. Decisions about which outgoing link has to be used are made by using the information stored in the node routing table. When link resources are available, they are reserved and the transfer is set up. The time it takes to a packet to move from one node to a neighboring one depends on its size and on the link transmission characteristics. If on a packet's arrival there is not enough buffer space to hold it, the packet is discarded. Packets are also discarded because of expired time to live. No arrival acknowledgment or error notification packets are generated back to the source.

After transmission, a stochastic process generates service times for the newly arrived data packet, that is, the delay between its arrival time and the time when it will be ready to be put in the buffer queue of the selected outgoing link.

We have not implemented a "real" transport layer. That is, we have not implemented mechanisms for a proper management of error, flow, and congestion control. The reason is that we want to check the behavior of our algorithm and of its competitors in conditions which minimize the number of interacting components. Note that the dynamics of adaptive routing and of flow and congestion control components are tightly coupled and that they should therefore be designed to match each other.

4. AntNet: Adaptive Agent-based Routing

As remarked before, the routing problem is a stochastic distributed multi-objective problem. These features make the problem well suited for a multi-agent approach like our AntNet system, composed of two sets of *homogeneous mobile agents* [21], called in the following *forward* and *backward* ants. Agents in each set possess the same structure, but they are differently situated in the environment; that is, they can sense different inputs and they can produce different, independent outputs. In AntNet we retain the core ideas of the ant colony optimization paradigm, but we have translated them to match a distributed, dynamic context, different from combinatorial optimization. Ants communicate in an undirected way according to the stigmergy paradigm, through the information they concurrently read and write in two data structures stored in each network node k:

(i) an array $M_k(\mu_d, \sigma_d^2)$ of data structures defining a simple parametric statistical model of the traffic distribution for all destinations d, as seen by the local node k,

(ii) a routing table, organized as in distance-vector algorithms [20]; the table stores for each pair (d,n) a probability value P_{dn}

$$\sum_{n \in N_k} P_{dn} = 1, \ d \in [1, N], \ N_k = \{neighbors(k)\}$$

which expresses the goodness of choosing n as next node when the destination node is d.

The AntNet algorithm can be informally described as follows.

• At regular intervals, from every network node s, a forward ant $F_{s \to d}$, is launched, with a randomly selected destination node d. Destinations are chosen to match the current traffic patterns.

• Each forward ant selects the next hop node using the information stored in the routing table. The next node is selected, following a random scheme, proportionally to the goodness (probability) of each not still visited neighbor node and to the local queues status. If all neighbors have been already visited a uniform random selection is applied considering all the neighbors.

• The identifier of every visited node k and the time elapsed since its launching time to arrive at this k-th node are pushed onto a memory stack $S_{s \to d}(k)$ carried by the forward ant.

• If a cycle is detected, that is, if an ant is forced to return to an already visited node, the cycle's nodes are popped from the ant's stack and all the memory about them is destroyed.

• When the ant $F_{s \to d}$ reaches the destination node d, it generates a backward ant $B_{d \to s}$, transfers to it all of its memory, and then dies.

• The backward ant makes the same path as that of its corresponding forward ant, but in the opposite direction. At each node k along the path it pops its stack $S_{s \to d}(k)$ to know the next hop node.

• Arriving in a node k coming from a neighbor node f, the backward ant updates M_k and the routing table for all the entries corresponding to every node i on the path $k \to d$, that is the path followed by ant $F_{k \to d}$ starting from the current node k.

- The sample means and variances of the model $M_k(\mu_i, \sigma_i^2)$ are updated with the trip times $T_{k \to i}$ stored in the stack memory $S_{s \to d}(k)$.
- The routing table is changed by incrementing the probabilities P_{if} associated with node f and the nodes i, and decreasing (by normalization) the probabilities P_{in} associated with the other neighbor nodes n. Trip times $T_{k \to i}$ experienced by the forward ant $F_{s \to d}$ are used to assign the probability increments.

$T_{k \to d}$ is the only explicit feedback signal we have: it gives an indication about the goodness r of the followed route because it is proportional to its length from a physical point of view (number of hops, transmission capacity of the used links, processing speed of the crossed nodes) and from a traffic congestion point of view[1]. The problem is that $T_{k \to d}$ can only be used as a reinforcement signal. In fact, it cannot be associated with an exact error measure, given that we do not know the optimal trip times, which depend on the net load status. The values stored in the model M_k are used to score the trip times by assigning a goodness measure $r \equiv r(T_{k \to d}, M_k)$, $r \in]0,1]$ (r is such that the smaller $T_{k \to d}$, the higher r). This dimensionless value takes into account an average of the observed values and of their dispersion: $r \propto (1 - W_{k \to d}/T_{k \to d}) + \Delta(\sigma, W)$, where $W_{k \to d}$ is the best trip time experienced over an adaptive time window, and $\Delta(\sigma, W)$ is a correcting term (the rationale behind this choice for r is discussed in [8]); r is used by the current node k as a positive reinforcement for the node f the backward ant $B_{d \to s}$ comes from. The probability P_{df} is increased by the computed reinforcement value r: $P_{df} \leftarrow P_{df} + (1 - P_{df}) \cdot r = P_{df} \cdot (1 - r) + r$. In this way, the probability P_{df} will be increased by a value proportional to the reinforcement received and to the previous value of the node probability (that is, given a same reinforcement, small probability values are increased proportionally more than big probability values).

Probabilities P_{dn} for destination d of the other neighboring nodes n implicitly receive a negative reinforcement by normalization. That is, their values are reduced so that the sum of probabilities will still be 1: $P_{dn} \leftarrow P_{dn} \cdot (1 - r)$.

The transformation from the raw value $T_{k \to d}$ to the definition of the more refined reinforcement r is similar to what happens in Actor-Critic systems [1]: the raw reinforcement signal ($T_{k \to d}$, in our case) is processed by a critic module which is learning a model of the underlying process, and then is fed to the learning system.

It is important to remark that every discovered path receives a positive reinforcement in its selection probability. In this way, not only the (explicit) assigned value r plays a role, but also the (implicit) ant's arrival rate.

An important aspect of the AntNet algorithm is that the routing tables are used in a probabilistic way not only by the ants, but also by the packets. This mechanism allows an efficient distribution of the data packets over all the good paths and has been observed to significantly improve AntNet performance. A node-dependent threshold value avoids the choice of low probability links.

As a last consideration, note the critical role played by ant communication. In fact, each ant is complex enough to solve a single sub-problem but the global routing optimization problem cannot be solved efficiently by a single ant. It is the interaction between ants that determines the emergence of a global effective behavior from the network performance point of view. The key concept in the cooperative aspect lies in

---

[1] This last aspect is extremely important: forward ants share the same queues as data packets (backward ants do not, they have priority over data to faster propagate the accumulated information), so if they cross a congested area, they will be delayed. This has a double effect: (i) the trip time will grow and then back-propagated probability increments will be small, and (ii) at the same time these increments will be assigned with a bigger delay.

the indirect and non-coordinated way communication among ants happens (stigmergy, [15]). We used stigmergy as a way of recursively transmitting, through the nodes' structures, the information associated with every "experiment" made by each ant.

5. Routing Algorithms Used for Comparison

The following algorithms, belonging to the various possible combinations of static and adaptive, distance vector and link state classes [20], have been implemented and used to run comparisons. **OSPF** (static, link state) is our implementation of the official Internet routing algorithm [17] (since we did not consider failure conditions the algorithm reduces to static shortest path routing). **SPF** (adaptive, link state) is the prototype of link-state algorithms with dynamic metric for link costs evaluations. A similar algorithm was implemented in the second version of ARPANET [16]. We implemented it with state-of-the-art flooding algorithms and link cost metrics [19]. Link costs are evaluated over moving windows using a link usage metric based on the fraction of time the link has been used during the last observation window. This metric was the most effective among the several we considered. **BF** (adaptive, distance-vector) is an adaptive implementation of the distributed Bellman-Ford algorithm with dynamic metrics [3]. Link costs are evaluated as in SPF above. **Q-R** (adaptive, distance-vector) is the Q-routing algorithm as proposed in [5]. This is an online asynchronous version of the Bellman-Ford algorithm. **PQ-R** (adaptive, distance-vector) is the Predictive Q-routing algorithm [6], an extension of Q-routing.

6. Experimental Settings

We have selected a limited set of classes of tunable components and for each of them we have made realistic choices.

Topology and physical properties of the net. In our experiments we used two networks: NSFNET and an irregular 6 x 6 grid. NSFNET is a real net, that is, the old (1987) T1 US backbone, while the 6 x 6 grid was proposed in [5]. NSFNET is composed of 14 nodes and 21 bi-directional links, and the 6 x 6 grid has 36 nodes and 50 bi-directional links. The topology and the propagation delays of NSFNET are those used in [8], while for the 6 x 6 grid see [5]. Links have a bandwidth of 1.5 Mbit/s in NSFNET, and 10 Mbit/s in the 6 x 6 grid net. All nets have null link and node fault probabilities, local buffers of 1 Gbit, and packets maximum time to live set to 15 sec.

Traffic patterns. Traffic is defined in terms of open sessions between a pair of active applications situated on different nodes. We considered three basic spatial and temporal traffic pattern distributions:

- Uniform Poisson (UP): for each node is defined an identical Poisson process for sessions arrival, that is, inter arrival times are negative exponential distributed.
- Hot Spots (HS): some nodes behave as hot spots, concentrating a high rate of input/output traffic. Sessions are opened from the hot spots to all the other nodes.
- Temporary Hot Spot (TMPHS): a temporary sudden increase in traffic load is generated switching on some hot spots for a limited period of time.

All the experiments have been realized considering various compositions of the above main patterns. For all the session types, packets sizes, packets inter arrival times and the total number of generated bits follow a negative exponential distribution.

Metrics for performance evaluation. We used two standard performance metrics: *throughput* (delivered bits/sec), and *data packets delay* (sec). For data packets delay we use either the average value over a moving time window, or the empirical distribution that takes into account the intrinsic variability of packet delays.

Routing algorithms parameters. For each algorithm the routing packets size and elaboration time are reported in Table 1. The other main parameters are the following. In AntNet, the generation interval of ants is set to 0.3 (sec), the exploration probability is set to 0.05, and the ant processing time is set to 3 ms. In OSPF, SPF, and BF, the length of the time interval between consecutive routing information broadcasting and the length of the time window to average link costs are the same, and they are set to 0.8 or 3 seconds, depending on the experiment. In Q-R and PQ-R the transmission of routing information is data-driven.

Table 1. Routing packets characteristics for the implemented algorithms. N_h is the incremental number of hops done by the forward ant, N_n is the number of neighbors of node n, and N is the number of network nodes.

	Ant Net	SPF & OSPF	BF	Q-R & PQ-R
packet size (byte)	$24+8 \cdot N_h$	$64+8 \cdot N_n$	$24+12 \cdot N$	12
packet elaboration time (msec)	3	6	2	3

7. Results

The goal of a routing algorithm is to route all the generated traffic, without losses, while keeping packets delay as low as possible (i.e., it should operate the network far from saturation conditions). Moreover, packet losses would require retransmission (this is managed by the congestion control layer, which is not implemented in our simulator) with a further increase in traffic. Therefore, when observing the results presented in the following of this section, the first performance comparison will be done on throughput, and a fair comparison on packet delays can only be done for those algorithms which have a similar throughput.

Experiments reported in this section compare AntNet with the previously described routing algorithms. All experiments are averaged over 10 trials. Parameters values for traffic characteristics are given in the figures' captions with the following meaning: NHS is the number of hot spot nodes, MSIA is the mean of the sessions inter arrival time distribution, MPIA-UP and MPIA-HS are the means of the packet inter arrival time distributions for the UP and HS sessions respectively. In all the experiments the mean of the packet size distribution is set to 4096 bit, and the mean of the total number of bits produced by each session is set to 2 Mb.

The results obtained on the NSFNET for (i) a uniform Poisson traffic load (UP) distribution, (ii) hot spots superimposed to a uniform Poisson traffic load (UPHS), and (iii) temporary hot spots superimposed to a light UP load, are shown respectively in figures 1, 2, and 3. The uniform Poisson traffic was chosen to be "heavy", that is, we set the values of the traffic patterns parameters to values that caused the network to reach a state very close to saturation. The reason to do this is that it is only under heavy load conditions that differences among competing algorithms can be appreciated in a meaningful way. In fact, when the traffic load is low, almost all the algorithms perform similarly. On the other hand, if the traffic load is too high, then a reasonable assumption is that it is a temporary situation. If it is not, structural changes to the network characteristics, like adding new and faster connection lines, rather than improvements of the routing algorithm, are in order. In both figures 1 and 2, the bigger, outer graph shows the throughput, while the smaller, inner graph shows the empirical distribution of packet delays. From these two figures we can extract the following information: (i) all the algorithms, with the exception of OSPF and PQ-R, can successfully route the totality of the generated throughput, and (ii) AntNet is the only algorithm capable of maintaining the packet delay of more than 90% of the packets below 0.5 sec.

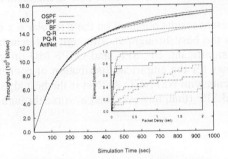

Fig. 1. NSFNET: A comparison of AntNet with five competing algorithms for a heavy uniform Poisson traffic (UP). Average over 10 trials. MSIA=1.5, MPIA-UP=0.2.

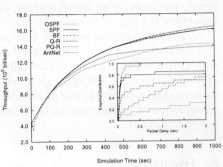

Fig. 2. NSFNET: A comparison of AntNet with five competing algorithms for hot spots superimposed to a heavy uniform Poisson traffic (UPHS). Average over 10 trials. NHS=4, MSIA=2.0, MPIA-UP=0.3, MPIA-HS=0.05.

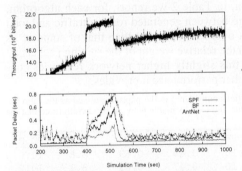

Fig. 3. NSFNET: A comparison of AntNet with SPF and BF (the behavior of the other algorithms was much worse): after 400 sec some hot spots are superimposed to a light UP load for 120 sec (TMPHS-UP). Reported throughput and packet delay values are averages over a moving time window of 0.5 sec. Average over 10 trials. NHS=4, MSIA=1.5, MPIA-UP=0.5, MPIA-HS=0.05.

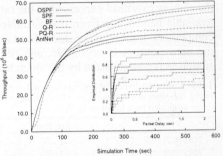

Fig. 4. 6 x 6 irregular grid net: A comparison of AntNet with five competing algorithms for a heavy uniform Poisson traffic (UP). Average over 10 trials. MSIA=1.0, MPIA-UP=0.1.

In Fig. 3 we investigate the answer of the algorithms to a sudden increase of traffic load. During the whole simulation the network is given a light UP load distribution; at simulation time $t=400$ the hot spots are switched on, to be subsequently switched off at time $t=520$. The figure shows only AntNet, SPF, and BF since the other algorithms' performance was so much worse that their graphs were out of scale. The upper graph in Fig. 3 shows the instantaneous throughput averaged over a window of 0.5 sec. It is clear that there are no significant differences among AntNet, SPF, and BF: their graphs are practically superimposed on the whole simulation time. The three algorithms increase their throughput when the hot spots are switched on, and, once the hot spots are switched off, they quickly forget the transitory situation. The lower graph (Fig. 3) shows the instantaneous packet delay averaged over a window of 0.5 sec. Here we chose not to report the empirical distribution because we wanted to highlight the answer in time of algorithms. The graph confirms the superiority of AntNet over the other algorithms also in this case: after time t=400 the average packet delay greatly increases for all the algorithms, except for AntNet which is able to maintain it well below 0.4 sec.

As a last experiment, in Figure 4 we present results obtained on the irregular 6 x 6 grid network. Once again, AntNet offers the best throughput, although differences with Q-R and PQ-R are not statistically significant. BF, SPF, and OSPF lose up to 20% of the packets. The inner graph shows for the empirical distribution of packet delays a similar pattern to that of experiments with NSFNET: AntNet is the best algorithm, followed, in this case, by OSPF and SPF (that, however, had a worse throughput performance).

8. Discussion

The results presented are rather sharp: AntNet performs better, both in terms of throughput and of average delay, than both classic and recently proposed algorithms[2]. Among the competitors there is not a clear winner.

Concerning network resources utilization, in Table 2 we report, for each algorithm, the routing overhead expressed as the ratio between generated routing traffic and total available bandwidth. Even if the AntNet overhead is higher than that of some of its competitors, it must be considered that (i) the relative weight of the routing packets on the net resources is negligible, and (ii) this slightly higher network resources consumption is compensated by the much higher performance it provides.

Table 2. Routing overhead for experimental conditions considered in the paper expressed as the ratio between the generated routing traffic by each algorithm and total available network bandwidth (note that the ratios are scaled by a factor of 10^{-3}).

	AntNet	OSPF	SPF	BF	Q-R	PQ-R
NSFNET UP (10^{-3})	1.70	<0.10	0.40	0.69	8.6	10.0
NSFNET UPHS (10^{-3})	1.70	<0.10	0.47	0.69	8.1	10.0
6x6 (10^{-3})	2.30	<0.10	0.16	0.24	8.0	9.4

Differences among algorithms performances can be understood on the basis of the different degree of adaptivity and of speed with which the different algorithms respond to changing traffic conditions. The very low performance of OSPF can be explained by both the lack of use of an adaptive metric (which all the other methods use), and by the fact that we set link costs only on the basis of a shortest path computation. Differently, on real networks (on the Internet, for example) these are set by network administrators who use additional heuristic knowledge about traffic patterns. To explain why AntNet performs better than the others is slightly more tricky. We identified the following main reasons: (i) the use of local versus global information, and (ii) the different routing table update frequencies, which are discussed in the following.

---

[2] Experiments similar to those presented in this paper have been run on other network topologies with increasing number of nodes and different traffic patterns obtaining similar results (see [8, 9, 10]).

The use of local versus global information. BF, Q-R and PQ-R work with local estimates of distances to destinations. These estimates are updated by using strictly local information: the traffic situation on outgoing links and the distance estimates maintained by neighbor nodes. Differently, AntNet samples the network and redistributes the global information ants collect: backward ants redistribute the global information relative to the paths sampled by the corresponding forward ants to all the nodes they visited. SPF maintains a global representation of the whole network in each node, which is updated by periodic flooding of local link costs information. If one of this cost information is badly estimated (as it is often the case when dynamic metrics are used), the wrong estimate propagates to all the local representations of the network. Here it is used to calculate shortest paths to build the new routing tables. The result is that a single erroneous estimate will negatively affect all the routing tables. From this point of view, AntNet is more robust: an incorrect update will affect only entries relative to the ant destination in those routing tables belonging to the ant path.

Routing table update frequency. In BF and SPF the broadcast frequency of routing information plays a critical role, particularly so for BF which has only a local representation of the network status. This frequency is unfortunately problem dependent, and there is no easy way to make it adaptive, while, at the same time, avoiding large oscillations. In Q-R and PQ-R, routing tables updating is data driven: only those Q-values belonging to pairs (i,j) of nodes visited by packets are updated. Although this is a reasonable strategy, given that the exploration of new routes could cause undesired delays to data packets, this causes delays in discovering new good routes, and is a great handicap in a domain where good routes change all the time. In AntNet, we experimentally observed the robustness to changes in the ants' generation rate. For a wide range of values of the generation rate, the more the ants generated, the better the algorithm works, until the traffic induced by ants ceases to be negligible with respect to the data traffic.

9. Related Work

AntNet is not the only algorithm based on the ant colony metaphor that has been applied to routing. Schoonderwoerd et al. [18] have considered the routing problem in connection-oriented communications networks. Their approach is different from ours in many respects. First, their communication network was modeled after a very specific type of telephone network: (i) they considered links carrying an infinite number of full-duplex, fixed bandwidth channels, (ii) their nodes are just reconfigurable switches with limited connectivity (that is, there is no necessity for queue management in the nodes). Second, their ants did not share transmission channels with data packets (i.e., they used a "virtual" network). These assumptions are strongly reflected in their algorithm structure: since we use a realistic communications network simulator which models a general data network, it is impossible to re-implement and compare their algorithm with ours.

10. Conclusions

In this paper we proposed AntNet, a novel algorithm for routing in communications networks inspired by previous work on artificial ants colonies in combinatorial optimization. We compared AntNet to a set of state-of-the-art algorithms using a realistic network simulator using the T1-NSFNET network and an irregular 6 x 6 grid network as benchmark problems. In all the experiments we ran, AntNet had the best distribution of packet delays, and was among the best algorithms as far as throughput was concerned. More, AntNet showed a robust behavior under the different traffic conditions and the ability to reach a stable behavior very quickly. AntNet had also, as well as OSPF, SPF and BF, a negligible impact on the use of network bandwidth.

References

1. Barto A.G., Sutton R.S., & Anderson C.W. 1983. Neuronlike Adaptive Elements that Can Solve Difficult Learning Control Problems. *IEEE Tr. on Syst., Man, and Cyb.* 13: 834–846.
2. Beckers R., Deneubourg J.L., & Goss S. 1992. Trails and U-turns in the Selection of the Shortest Path by the Ant Lasius Niger. *J. of Theor. Biology* 159:397–415.
3. Bertsekas D. & Gallager R. 1992. *Data Networks.* Englewood Cliffs, NJ: Prentice-Hall.
4. Bonabeau E., Dorigo M., & Theraulaz T. (in press). *From Natural to Artificial Swarm Intelligence.* Oxford University Press.
5. Boyan J. A. & Littman M. L. 1994. Packet Routing in Dynamically Changing Networks: A Reinforcement Learning Approach. In *Proc. of NIPS-6,* San Francisco, CA: Morgan Kaufmann, 671–678.
6. Choi S. P. M. & Yeung D.-Y. 1996. Predictive Q-Routing: A Memory-based Reinforcement Learning Approach to Adaptive Traffic Control. In *Proc. of NIPS-8*, Cambridge, MA: The MIT Press, 945–910.
7. Costa D. &, Hertz A. 1997. Ants Can Colour Graphs. *J. of the Oper. Res. Soc.* 48:295-305.
8. Di Caro G. & Dorigo M. 1998. AntNet: Distributed Stigmergetic Control for Communications Networks. *Tech.Rep. IRIDIA/98-01*, Université Libre de Bruxelles, Belgium. To appear in *Journal of Artificial Intelligence Research (JAIR).*
9. Di Caro G. & M. Dorigo 1998. An adaptive multi-agent routing algorithm inspired by ants behavior. *Proceedings of PART98 – Fifth Annual Australasian Conference on Parallel and Real-Time Systems*, September 28–29, 1998, University of Adelaide, Australia, in press.
10. Di Caro G. & M. Dorigo 1998. Distributed Adaptive Routing by Artificial Ant Colonies. *PDCS'98 – 1998 International Conference on Parallel and Distributed Computing and Systems,* October 28–31, 1998, Las Vegas, Nevada.
11. Dorigo M. 1992. *Ottimizzazione, Apprendimento Automatico, ed Algoritmi Basati su Metafora Naturale* (Optimization, Learning and Natural Algorithms). Ph.D.Thesis, Politecnico di Milano, Italy (in Italian), pp.140.
12. Dorigo M. & Gambardella L. M. 1997. Ant Colony System: A Cooperative Learning Approach to the Traveling Salesman Problem. *IEEE Trans. on Evol. Comp.* 1(1): 53–66.
13. Dorigo M., Maniezzo V., & Colorni A. 1991. Positive Feedback as a Search Strategy. *Tech. Rep. No. 91-016*, Dip. di Elettronica, Politecnico di Milano, Italy.
14. Dorigo M., Maniezzo V., & Colorni A. 1996. The Ant System: Optimization by a Colony of Cooperating Agents. *IEEE Trans. on Syst., Man, and Cybern.–Part B* 26(2): 29–41.
15. Grassé P. P. 1959. La reconstruction du nid et les coordinations inter-individuelles chez *Bellicositermes natalensis et Cubitermes sp.* La théorie de la stigmergie: Essai d'interprétation des termites constructeurs. *Insect Sociaux* 6: 41–83.
16. McQuillan J. M., Richer I., & Rosen E. C. 1980. The New Routing Algorithm for the ARPANET. *IEEE Trans. on Commuications* 28:711–719.
17. Moy J. 1994. OSPF Version 2. Request for Comments (RFC) 1583, Network Work Group.
18. Schoonderwoerd R., Holland O., Bruten J., & Rothkrantz L. 1996. Ant-based Load Balancing in Telecommunications Networks. *Adaptive Behavior* 5(2):169–207.
19. Shankar A. U., Alaettinoglu C., Dussa-Zieger K., & Matta I. 1992. Performance Comparison of Routing Protocols under Dynamic and Static File Transfer Connections. *ACM SIGCOMM Computer Communication Review* 22(5): 39–52.
20. Steenstrup M. E. (ed.) 1995. *Routing in Communications Networks.* Prentice-Hall.
21. Stone P. & Veloso M. 1996. Multiagent Systems: A Survey from a Machine Learning Perspective. *Tech. Rep. CMU-CS-97-193*, Carnegie Mellon University, PA.

The Stud GA: A Mini Revolution?

Wael Khatib   Peter J Fleming

Department of Automatic Control and Systems Engineering
University of Sheffield – Sheffield - UK

Abstract. This paper presents a new approach to function optimisation using a new variant of GAs. This algorithm is called the Stud GA. Instead of stochastic selection, the fittest individual, the Stud, shares its genetic information with all others using simple GA operators. The standard Gray coding is maintained. Simple techniques are added to maintain diversity of the population and help achieve the global optima in difficult multimodal search spaces. The benefits of this approach are an improved performance in terms of accuracy, efficiency and reliability. This approach appears to be able to deal with a wide array of functions and to give consistent repeatability of optimisation performance. A variety of test functions is used to illustrate this approach. Results presented suggest a viable and attractive addition to the portfolio of evolutionary computing techniques.

0. Introduction

The various approaches within evolutionary computing can be grouped as follows:

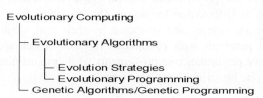

Figure 1. Evolutionary Computing Approaches

There are many advocates of all the various techniques above. Fogel (1995) sheds light on the various merits and weaknesses of each of the algorithms and their derivatives. Although there are many applications of evolutionary computing, the work in this paper is concerned with search and optimisation using genetic based techniques.

Most genetic algorithms (GAs) use selection and crossover as the two main operators along with mutation as a secondary or background operator. Most work in GAs is concerned with the mechanisms used in these operators. Another area of research is representation. The standard GA uses chromosome strings with discrete bit representation. Other implementations of GAs use integer strings especially for combinatorial optimisation. The Breeder GA (Muhlenbein et al., 1991) uses real numbers directly for continuous function optimisation. Using bit representation makes the GA suitable for encoding any type of function with mixing of various data types possible within the same string. The choice of encoding technique for problem representation has implications for the possible types of crossover operators. Bit representations give more flexibility for crossover using simple bit swapping between individuals. Real number strings employ weighted differences to perform crossover. The combination of selection and crossover tends to eventually reduce the diversity of the population which can stop a GA from making further progress in optimisation terms. Mutation is used to reduce this effect although it is not guaranteed that mutation can prevent entrapment in regions of local optima. Other methods such as fitness sharing, mating restriction and dynamic parameter encoding (DPE) attempt to do the same.

Benchmarking the various algorithms, one is looking to establish some or all of the following (**A.R.E.A.S**):

- **A**ccuracy: Ability of the algorithms to arrive at the global optimum.
- **R**eliability: The ability of the algorithm to repeat the performance.
- **E**fficiency: Cost of the optimisation (number of function evaluations).
- **A**pplicability: Ability of the algorithm to deal with different problem types.
- **S**tability: A minimal set of control parameters with limited ranges.

1. Objectives

The main objective of this work is to provide a new approach to genetic algorithms that can improve the performance criteria (AREAS). BGAs and other emerging algorithms such as Differential Evolution, (Storn, 1996), give some improvement. However, these algorithms are restricted by their real number representation to optimisation of problems with continuous function search spaces. This work attempts to achieve performance improvements while maintaining the simplicity and power of a discrete bit-string based algorithm.

2. Motivation

The field of multidisciplinary optimisation (MDO) is mainly found in the aero-structural design industry. MDO problems are concerned with optimisation of an objective(s) the attribute of which are dependent on contributions from various disciplines. There is usually strong coupling between the disciplines. The nature of these problems presents the optimiser with two main challenges:

- Computational cost: The unit cost per function evaluation is usually high. Coupling increases the optimisation cost.

- Organisational complexity: Interactions between the various disciplines are needed to arrive at a viable overall design. These interactions complicate the process further.

In trying to apply evolutionary computing techniques to MDO problems, issues of performance become very important. This work is motivated, in part, by the need for an effective algorithm that can deal with practical MDO problems (Khatib and Fleming, 1997). The improvement in performance will make the new algorithm suitable for application as an attractive alternative not only to MDO problems, but also to other search and optimisation scenarios.

3. The Stud GA

The basic idea behind the Stud GA is to use the best individual in the population to mate with all others to produce the new offspring. No stochastic selection is used here. The following describes the Stud GA:

```
1. Initialise a random population
2. Choose the fittest individual for mating (the Stud).
3. Perform crossover between the Stud and the remaining
   elements.
4. Repeat until stopping criteria met.
```

The crossover operation is the heart of this algorithm. The current implementation of the Stud GA performs the following:

- `Shuffle two stud elements (chosen randomly).`
- `Check the diversity in terms of the hamming distance`
  `between the shuffled stud and the current mate:`
  - ➢ `If diversity is above a set threshold, perform`
    `crossover to produce one child,`
  - ➢ `Else, mutate the current mate to produce the`
    `child.`
- `Repeat for all other mates.`

The mutation used here is the standard bit mutation with a low probability of (0.001-0.003). Inverting one bit also proved useful as an alternative. Two crossover types were tried; the standard two point crossover and a reduced surrogate uniform crossover. The latter type is performed such that only different bits are exchanged randomly between two parents to produce one child. In the case of the two-point crossover, one child is chosen randomly from the two produced. The hamming distance is used as the diversity measure. This is simply the number of different bits divided by the length of each string. The ex-or logic gate is used to find the bits that are different. The threshold is chosen to be 10% throughout. The diversity comparison and crossover are done per decision variable.

3.1. The Extended Chromosome

A potential weakness that was observed for this kind of approach is the likelihood of entrapment in regions of local optima when the function is multimodal and small in size, typically 2 decision variables. This can be attributed to the lack of diversity that is naturally present in a high dimensional space. To avoid this problem, a new extended chromosome structure is used. For a two dimensional problem, say, the chromosome is allowed to have multiple entries for each variable, 5 pairs say. The crossover operation is done on this extended chromosome. Once the chromosome is decoded into the phenotypic domain, the required number of decision variables is chosen randomly from the available pool. Experiments with this approach appear to justify its use. Note that Gray coding is used throughout this work.

This implementation of the Stud GA uses an elitist strategy by carrying through the best individual.

4. The Test Functions

In order to test the performance of the Stud GA, a wide selection of test functions was used. The functions were chosen from three previous studies that looked at various aspects of optimisation using evolutionary computing techniques.

- **Group A:** De Falco et al. (1996) studied the performance of BGAs against 9 various GAs which were tested by Scott Gordon and Whitley (1993). De Jong's functions along with Rastrigin's, Schwefel's and Griewangk's were used in these studies as the test bed. From De Jong's test functions, we use the first and second. We also use the latter three functions. De Jong's first is an easy unimodal function. The second is a harder multimodal function. Rastrigin's function is rather difficult with a large search space characterised by many local optima. Schwefel's function is slightly easier than Rastrigin's but has a second-best optimum which is quite distant from the global optimum. Griewangk's function has a product term which presents a GA with added difficulty due to strong coupling between the decision variables.

DJ F1: $f(x) = \sum_{i=1}^{3} x_i^2, x_i \in [-5.12, 5.11]$

DJ F2: $f(x) = 100(x_1^2 - x_2)^2 + (1 - x_1)^2, x_i \in [-2.048, 2.047]$

Rastrigin's: $f(x) = 200 + \sum_{i=1}^{20} x_i^2 - 10\cos(2\pi x_i), x_i \in [-512, 511]$

Schwefel's: $f(x) = 4189.8291 + \sum_{i=1}^{10} -x_i \cdot \sin(\sqrt{|x_i|}), x_i \in [-512,511]$

Griewangk's: $f(x) = \sum_{i=1}^{10} \frac{x_i^2}{4000} - \prod_{i=1}^{10} \cos(\frac{x_i}{\sqrt{i}}) + 1, x_i \in [-512,511]$

- **Group B:** Fogel (1995, pp. 170) presents three 2-d functions taken from Bohachevsky et al. (1986) . All of these functions are multimodal. These functions are optimised using an evolutionary programming algorithm (EP), a standard GA and another one using DPE.

Fog1: $f(x,y) = x^2 + 2y^2 - 0.3\cos(3\pi x) - 0.4\cos(4\pi y) + 0.7$

Fog2: $f(x,y) = x^2 + 2y^2 - 0.3[\cos(3\pi x)\cos(4\pi y)] + 0.3$

Fog3: $f(x,y) = x^2 + 2y^2 - 0.3[\cos(3\pi x) + \cos(4\pi y)] + 0.6 *$

$x, y \in [-50,50]$ *(note that the constant term in the third function should be + 0.6 if the optimum is to be zero).*

- **Group C:** Keane (1996) conducted a study into various optimisation algorithms using a difficult constrained multimodal function called 'Bump':

maximise $f(x_i) = \left\{ abs\left(\sum_{i=1}^{m} \cos^4(x_i) - 2\prod_{i=1}^{m}\cos^2(x_i) \right) \right\} / \sqrt{\sum_{i=1}^{m} ix_i^2}$

subject to $\prod_{i=1}^{m} x_i \rangle 0.75, \ \sum_{i=1}^{m} \frac{x_i}{m} \langle 7.5., \ 0 < x_i < 10, i = 1, ..., m$

This function produces a number of peaks that get smaller with distance from the origin, and which are nearly symmetrical about $x_i = x_j, i, j = 1, ..., m$. (see Figure 2)

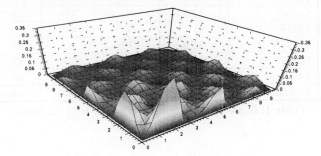

Figure 2: 'Bump' function for $m = 2$**.**

5. Results

For the sake of comparison, the performance measures are similar to those used by the previous researchers. Each set of functions presents different challenges and are thus addressed in different ways.

5.1. Group A Functions

The optimisation of the two De Jong functions, DJ F1 and DJ F2, is benchmarked using two parameters: the average number of generations to achieve convergence (Gen), and the standard deviation of that quantity (StdG). Convergence is achieved for values falling below 0.01. This is the same for Rastrigin's and Schwefel's functions. A tighter value of 0.0001 is chosen for Griewangk's function. The GA is allowed to run for a maximum of 1000 generations using 400 individuals. It suffices to say that this method does not really require this high number of individuals to function properly. The latter three functions are more difficult. Their optimisation process is assessed using the number of times out of a total of 30 runs that the GA achieves the optimum. The Average final value (AvV) is also used.

Results in Table 1 show that the Stud GA is competitive with the BGA and far outperforms all the other GAs. This is more profound in the results for the three more difficult multimodal problems (Table 2). The Stud GA can also achieve high precision in the final results if a suitable resolution is chosen for the bit representation. Typically, resolution values between 14 and 50 bits might be used here.

Algorithm	DJ F1		DJ F2	
	Gen	StdG	Gen	StdG
Stud GA	2.3	0.6	5.1	3.7
BGA	3.1	0.3	10.9	8.6
SGA	30.7	7.4	284	198
ESGA	28.9	6.8	83	55
pCHC	28.4	6.5	153	139
Genitor	17.0	4.1	190	160
I-SGA	41.3	11.2	417	253
I-ESGA	32.3	7.6	81	40
I-pCHC	33.2	7.4	78	57
I-Genitor	23.2	5.3	112	94
Cellular	32.5	8.0	105	94

Table 1: Convergence results for the De Jong functions

Algorithm	Rastrigin		Schwefel		Griewangk	
	NR	AvV	NR	AvV	NR	AvV
Stud GA	30	0	30	0	30	0
BGA	30	0	30	0	30	0
SGA	0	6.8	0	17.4	0	0.161
ESGA	2	1.5	16	17.3	1	0.107
pCHC	23	0.3	15	5.9	0	0.072
Genitor	0	7.9	20	13.2	3	0.053
I-SGA	0	3.8	9	6.5	7	0.050
I-ESGA	13	0.6	13	2.6	3	0.066
I-pCHC	10	0.9	28	0.2	3	0.047
I-Genitor	23	0.2	24	0.9	6	0.035
Cellular	24	0.2	26	0.7	1	0.106

Table 2: Convergence results for the Ras/Sch/Grie

5.2. Group B Functions

Using the extended chromosome structure, the Stud GA is able to give results comparable with those in Fogel (1995). Results in Table 3 show that the performance of the GA using DPE, which allows the GA to zoom in on promising regions as the search progresses (Schraudolph and Belew, 1992), gives answers with better precision using the same resolution of 14 bits. Using a higher resolution of 50 bits, the Stud GA performs better than the GA with DPE. The Stud GA outperforms the standard GA even with 14 bit resolution.

Algorithm	Fog1	Fog2	Fog3
Stud GA 14 bits	4.462×10^{-4}	3.726×10^{-4}	3.726×10^{-4}
Stud GA 50 bits	7.105×10^{-15}	5.609×10^{-10}	6.079×10^{-7}
EP	5.193×10^{-96}	8.332×10^{-101}	1.366×10^{-105}
DPE 14 bits	1.479×10^{-9}	2.084×10^{-9}	1.215×10^{-5}
GA 14 bits	2.629×10^{-3}	4.781×10^{-3}	2.444×10^{-3}

Table 3: Results for the Fogel functions (average best of 10 runs).

Fogel lists data for the average best value achieved for 10 runs with 10080 evaluations each. Another measure, the average mean of all the population at the end of the run, does not give any useful information about the performance of the Stud GA. This is because the mechanisms of this method allow more diversity to be maintained throughout. This means such a value will tend to be less competitive compared with standard GAs. The latter tend to lead to final populations with fit individuals throughout. There is emphasis by Fogel and others especially users of BGA about the ability of algorithms to achieve a very high precision in the final answer. For example, values of order 10^{-100} are quoted. Using higher resolutions, the

Stud GA was able to give better answers in terms of precision but not quite the same level as those attained by EP. A simple DPE-like implementation with the Stud GA gave results of even higher precision than those quoted for EP. Although the subject of variable resolution bit representations is a fresh research issue, we do not, however, see any real benefit in achieving this level of precision in practical applications.

5.3. The Bump Function

In a previous study, Keane (1996) used the Bump function to test a variety of evolutionary and adaptive optimisation algorithms. In his study, Keane found a multi-population (5*50) GA to be best for optimising this function when compared to an evolutionary strategy, evolutionary programming and simulated annealing. A total of 150000 function evaluations were used and the best GA (and overall) result was 0.779. The implementation used a simple penalty function to address the constraints and that is what is used with the Stud GA. Keane used elaborate techniques to prevent premature convergence of the GA.

The Stud GA implementation for the Bump function uses a 14-bit Gray-coded chromosome structure for a 50-dimensional case (m=50). 50 individuals were used. The standard two point crossover gave slightly better results. Other parameters are as before (minimum diversity = 10% per variable, mutation rate = 0.001, crossover rate = 0.9). Note that mutation is only performed on any two variables that are nearly identical.

The Stud GA gave an astonishing result. An optimum value of 0.82 is achieved consistently within 15000 function evaluations. This means the steady state result is better, and the cost in terms of the number of evaluations is 10 times cheaper. Figure 3 shows the convergence for a typical run of the Stud GA.

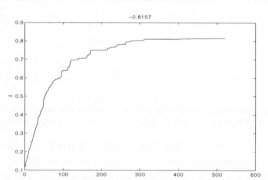

Figure 3. Convergence for Stud GA on Bump

6. Conclusions

This paper presented a new and fresh approach to GAs for function search and optimisation. The motivation behind this method is to achieve improvements in various performance metrics. Recent emerging methods such as BGAs attempt to do the same. These methods are only suitable for continuous function spaces since they rely on real number encoding. The Stud GA maintains the traditional discrete bit representation and makes no use of stochastic selection. The approach is simple, yet it appears to be a powerful tool for dealing with difficult multimodal spaces.

There are many more tests to be conducted to establish the true potential of this approach. Work is already under way to apply this method to complex high-dimensional multidisciplinary optimisation problems. Initial application and extension of the stud GA to the field of multiobjective optimisation appears to indicate more promising applications for this method.

Acknowledgement

The work of the first author is supported by an industrial CASE award of the Engineering and Physical Sciences Research Council (EPSRC,UK) and British Aerospace PLC, Sowerby Research Centre. We would like to acknowledge the support of Dr Phil Greenway (Sowerby).

References

1. Bohachevsky, I. O., Johnson, M. E., and Stein, M. L.: *Generalised Simulated Annealing for Function Optimization*. Technometrics,Vol 28:3, pp. 209-218. [in 3]
2. De Falco, I., Del Balio, R., Della Cioppa, A, Tarantino, E.,.: *A comparative Study of Evolutionary Algorithms for Function Optimisation*. Proceedings of the Second (WWW) Workshop on Evolutionary Computing (WEC2), Nagoya, Japan (1996)
3. Fogel, D.: *Evolutionary Computing, Toward a New Philosophy of Machine Intelligence*. IEEE Press, Piscataway, NJ (1995)
4. Keane, A.,.: Experiences with Optimizers. In: Proceedings of the IMechE/IEE Symposium on Genetic Algorithms in Design Optimisation. London, UK (January 31, 1996).
5. Khatib W. and Fleming P.J., *Evolutionary computing for multidisciplinary optimisation, Proc 2nd IEE/IEEE International Conference on Genetic Algorithms in Engineering Systems: Innovations and Applications GALESIA 97*, Glasgow, 1997, pp. 7-12.
6. Muhlenbein, H., and Schilierkamp-Voosen, D.: *Predictive Models for The Breeder Genetic Algorithm I. Continuous Parameter Optimization*. Evolutionary Computation, Vol 1, No. 1, pp. 25-49 (1993).[in 2]
7. Scott Gordon, V., and Whitley, D.: *Serial and Parallel Genetic Algorithms as Function Optimizers*. In: Proceedings of the 5th International Conference on Genetic Algorithms, (Forrest, S. Ed.), pp. 177-183, Morgan-Kaufmann (1993).
8. Schraudolph, N.N., and Belew, R.K.: *Dynamic Parameter Encoding for Genetic Algorithms*. In Machine Learning, Vol. 9, Iss. 1, pp. 9-21, The Netherlands (June 1992).
9. Storn, R., and Price, K.: *Minimizing the Real Function of the ICEC'96 Contest by Differential Evolution*. Int. Conference on evolutionary Computation, Nagoya, Japan (1996).

An Island Model Based Ant System with Lookahead for the Shortest Supersequence Problem

René Michel and Martin Middendorf

Institute for Applied Computer Science and Formal Description Methods,
University of Karlsruhe, D-76128-Karlsruhe, Germany

Abstract. In this paper we introduce an Ant Colony Optimisation (ACO) algorithm for the Shortest Common Supersequence (SCS) problem, which has applications in production system planning, mechanical engineering and molecular biology. The ACO algorithm is used to find good parameters for a heuristic for the SCS problem. An island model with several populations of ants is used for the ACO algorithm. Besides we introduce a lookahead function which makes the decisions of the ants dependent on the state arrived after the decision.

1 Introduction

The Shortest Common Supersequence (SCS) problem is a problem with applications in areas like production system planning, mechanical engineering and computational molecular biology (see e.g. [7, 14]). Formally, the problem is: Given a set L of strings over an alphabet Σ, find a string of minimal length that is a *supersequence* of each string in L. A string S is a supersequence of a string T if S can be obtained from T by inserting zero or more characters. As an example consider the set $L = \{abba, acca, cbbc, abca\}$ for which the string $acbbca$ is a shortest supersequence.

The SCS problem is NP-complete even for quite restricted problem instances over an alphabet of size 2 ([13, 12]). Dynamic programming algorithms as well as Branch-and-Bound algorithms for SCS have been studied by Fraser [8]. However, the dynamic programming algorithms are successful only for a very small number of strings, because otherwise, their space requirement is too large. Branch-and-Bound algorithms need to much time to be practical, except for strings over very small alphabets. Several heuristics have also been investigated for SCS [1, 7, 8, 9, 10]. A genetic algorithm for SCS was proposed in [1].

In this paper we propose an *Ant Colony Optimisation (ACO)* approach for the SCS problem. ACO is a population based approach for finding good solutions to combinatorial optimisation problems. The idea of ACO was initiated by Dorigo, Maniezzo, and Colorni in [4, 6] and has already been applied to several problems like the *Travelling Salesman* (TSP) problem [6], the *Vehicle Routing* problem [2], and the *Quadratic Assignment* problem [5].

ACO imitates the behaviour of real ants searching for food. Initially, ants search their environment for food in a random manner. As soon as an ant detects a source of food, it evaluates the quality and quantity of the food and carries some of it back to the nest. On its return trip it lays a chemical pheromone trail on the ground. The quantity of that pheromone trail depends on the ants evaluation of the food source and is meant to guide other ants to the discovered source of food and back to the nest. Since other ants will be attracted by the pheromone and also lay their pheromone onto the trail it will become stronger the more ants use it. This has the effect that the closer a source of food is to the nest the stronger the pheromone trail to that source will grow because this trail is frequented more often. Due to the evaporation of the pheromone the trails will not overload. Evaporation is also necessary to keep that system adaptive to changes of the environment and the detection of new food sources. When talking about an algorithmic framework for this mechanism, the set of feasible solutions to the combinatorial problem corresponds to the real ants search area, the objective function corresponds to the amount/quality of the found food, and the pheromone trail has its analogy in an adaptive memory.

A more detailed explanation on how to put these analogies to work in the case of the TSP and some other problems can be found in [6]. To apply ACO to a combinatorial problem Dorigo, Maniezzo, and Colorni propose the following steps (see [6] for detailes): 1. Defining an appropriate graph representation of the problem which ants can search, 2. Defining the autocatalytic feedback process, 3. Defining a constructive heuristic for the problem which works on the graph representation, 4. Defining a constraint satisfaction method.

Here we propose a different approach which was inspired by the way Branke, Middendorf, and Schneider [1] put a genetic algorithm for the SCS problem to work: Instead of looking for a graph representation we directly use the string representation of our problem. To each character of a string we associate a parameter and its value guides a fast constructive heuristic that is used by the ants to build up a supersequence. Thus, the parameter values function as trail information. Not depending on a special graph representation one can hope that this approach can also be applied to other problems. But the advantage of not having to find an appropriate graph representation and a heuristic working on it may lead to problems later: It can be difficult to find an appropriate way of updating the trail information such that ants are guided to good solutions.

In our ant system we use an island model, i.e. different populations of ants work on the same problem. Every population lays its own pheromone trail which is not accessible to ants of other populations. The populations work not totally independently but exchange trail information after every certain number of iterations.

We also introduce a lookahead function to our ant system. This makes the choice of which symbol to append next to the supersequence not only dependent on the heuristic values of the current iteration but also takes into consideration the influence of that choice on the next iteration. Therefore when deciding whether or not to append some symbol s we do not only have to calculate the probability according to the chosen heuristic but also have to simulate this possible choice and evaluate the resulting state in some way.

2 Heuristics for the SCS Problem

A well known greedy heuristic for SCS is the Majority Merge (MM) heuristic [7]. Given a set L of strings MM builds a supersequence starting from the empty string as follows: It looks at the first characters of every string in L (i.e. the front), appends the most frequent symbol, say a to the supersequence and then removes a from the front of the strings. This process is repeated until all strings are exhausted.

One problem with the MM heuristic, especially when applied to random strings, is that MM does not take into account the possibly different lengths of the strings. Clearly, it makes sense to focus on the long strings when deciding which symbol in the front is chosen next. In [1] a weighted variant LM of MM was proposed that takes these lengths into account. For each character of a string a weight is assigned which is the length of the remaining string (length of the shortest suffix which contains that character). Formally, for a character s_i of a string $S = s_1 s_2 \ldots s_n$, $i \in [1 : n]$ its weight w_i is $n - i$. The heuristic LM works similar to MM but always chooses that symbol of the front whose sum of the weights of all its occurrences in the front is maximal. For ease of description we consider MM in the following as a heuristic that uses a weight of 1 for every character of a string.

To make the heuristics MM and LM parameter dependent we use an idea from [1]. To each character s_i of a string $S = s_1 s_2 \ldots s_n$, $i \in [1 : n]$ we assign a parameter value τ_i. The heuristics now choose always that symbol s from the front of the strings for which the sum of the products of the weight and the parameter value of each occurrence of s is maximal.

Example. Consider the strings in Figure 2 where each character has an associated parameter value. MM would choose an a as the next symbol to append to the supersequence. This is because the sum of the parameter values (times 1) of the a's in the front is 0.25 while the parameter value of the b in the front is 0.2. LM would choose b as the next symbol because the sum of the products of parameter value times weight is $4 \cdot 0.20 = 0.8$ for b and $3 \cdot 0.05 + 2 \cdot 0.20 = 0.55$ for the a's.

$$
\begin{array}{cccc}
\text{b} \!\!-\!\! & \text{a} \!\!-\!\! & \text{b} \!\!-\!\! & \text{c} \\
0.20 & 0.08 & 0.11 & 0.04
\end{array}
$$

$$
\begin{array}{ccc}
\text{a} \!\!-\!\! & \text{b} \!\!-\!\! & \text{c} \\
0.05 & 0.18 & 0.06
\end{array}
$$

$$
\begin{array}{cc}
\text{a} \!\!-\!\! & \text{c} \\
0.20 & 0.06
\end{array}
$$

Fig. 1. Example parameter assignment

3 ACO for the SCS Problem

In this section we describe our ACO algorithms AS-SCS-MM and AS-SCS-LM which are based on the heuristics MM and LM, respectively. Besides, several improvements of the basic ACO algorithms are proposed. For a better understanding here is a very rough outline of a basic ACO:

1. Initialise the pheromone trail (the parameter values)
2. For I^{max} iterations repeat:
   (a) For each ant $k \in \{1, 2, \ldots, m\}$ build a new solution
       (a supersequence) using the pheromone trail
       and the given heuristic.
   (b) Keep track of the best solution found so far.
   (c) Update the trail information.

3.1 AS-SCS-MM

This section provides a more detailed description of AS-SCS-MM, an ACO algorithm which makes use of the MM heuristic described above.

Let $S_1, S_2, \ldots, S_n$ denote the n given input strings over an alphabet Σ and $s_{ij} \in \Sigma$ the character at position j of string i. Each character s_{ij} has an associated parameter value τ_{ij} which has the function of the pheromone trail. During initialisation each τ_{ij} is set to 1. Let there be m ants searching the solution space. At a given iteration ant $k \in \{1, 2, \ldots, m\}$ uses its state vector $\mathbf{v}_k = (v_{k1}, v_{k2}, \ldots, v_{kn})$ to keep track of the progress of the computation of its supersequence $\mathcal{S}_k$. $\mathbf{v}_k$ describes the front of the strings as introduced in chapter 2. For example in a 2-string problem a vector $(3, 5)$ would describe a state where the 2 leading characters of the first string and the 4 leading characters of the second string are already embedded in $\mathcal{S}_k$, whereas the third character of string 1 and the fifth character of string 2 are still waiting for a suitable extension of $\mathcal{S}_k$ before they can be embedded.

At the beginning of each iteration these vectors are set to $\mathbf{1}$. The computation of a supersequence $\mathcal{S}_k$ is finished when $\mathbf{v}_k = \mathbf{v}_{fin}$ where $\mathbf{v}_{fin} = (|S_1|+1, |S_2|+1, \ldots, |S_n|+1)$. The candidate-set $\mathcal{C}_k = \{s \in \Sigma \mid \exists i : s = s_{iv_{ki}}\}$ denotes the set of symbols which are occurring in the actual front of the strings and therefore are possible candidates to be appended to $\mathcal{S}_k$ next.

In the following we describe one iteration of the algorithm from the point of view of some arbitrary ant k. Initially, state vector $\mathbf{v}_k$ is set to $(1, 1, \ldots, 1)$, $\mathcal{S}_k$ is the empty string, and $\mathcal{C}_k$ contains exactly those symbols occurring at the beginning of the input strings. As long as the state vector $\mathbf{v}_k$ is different from $\mathbf{v}_{fin}$ the following steps are repeated:

1. Our ant chooses a symbol $s \in \mathcal{C}_k$ according to the following probability distribution:

$$p(s, \mathbf{v}_k) = \frac{\left[\displaystyle\sum_{i \in \mathcal{I}_k \,:\, s_{iv_{ki}} = s} \tau_{iv_{ki}} \right]^{\alpha}}{\displaystyle\sum_{s' \in \mathcal{C}_k} \left[\displaystyle\sum_{i \in \mathcal{I}_k \,:\, s_{iv_{ki}} = s'} \tau_{iv_{ki}} \right]^{\alpha}} \tag{1}$$

where $\mathcal{I}_k$ denotes the set of indices for which $v_{ki} \neq |S_i| + 1$. The parameter α is a mean to control the variance of the distribution.

2. The symbol s is appended to the supersequence:

$$\mathcal{S}_k = \mathcal{S}_k s \tag{2}$$

3. The new state vector $\mathbf{v}_k$ has to be calculated. Let $\mathcal{M}_k(|\mathcal{S}_k|)$ be the set of characters $s_{iv_{ki}}$ in the front for which $s_{iv_{ki}} = s$ holds. $\forall i \in \{1, \ldots, n\}$ set

$$v_{ki} = \begin{cases} v_{ki} + 1 & ; \quad if \; s_{iv_{ki}} \in \mathcal{M}_k(|\mathcal{S}_k|) \\ v_{ki} & ; \quad else \end{cases} \tag{3}$$

Now $\mathcal{S}_k$ is a valid supersequence of the given input strings and our ant has to calculate the values $\Delta \tau_{ij}^k$ to contribute to the update of the pheromone trail:

1. It calculates the value $\Theta = \frac{1}{|\mathcal{S}_k|}$ which is a measure of quality of the found supersequence.

2. Now it can calculate its contribution to the update of the trail. The idea is that the total amount of pheromone added for the characters in a set $\mathcal{M}_k(l)$, $l \in [1 : |\mathcal{S}_k|]$ depends on l - the smaller l is the more pheromone is added because for small l the characters in $\mathcal{M}_k(l)$ should be chosen early. To each character in one set $\mathcal{M}_k(l)$ the same amount of pheromone is added. Formally, for all $l \in \{1, 2, \ldots, |\mathcal{S}_k|\}$ and each character $s_{iv_{ki}} \in \mathcal{M}_k(l)$:

$$\Delta \tau_{iv_{ki}} = \frac{\Theta}{|\mathcal{M}_k(l)|} \cdot \frac{|\mathcal{S}_k| - l + 1}{|\mathcal{S}_k|} \tag{4}$$

At the end of the iteration when all ants have performed the steps described above the overall amount of new trail can be calculated as follows:

$$\Delta \tau_{ij} = \sum_{k=1}^{m} \Delta \tau_{ij}^k \tag{5}$$

The update of the trail values τ_{ij} is done according to the following formula:

$$\tau_{ij} = \rho \cdot \tau_{ij} + \gamma \Delta \tau_{ij} \tag{6}$$

where γ is a parameter which allows to scale the amount of pheromone put onto the trail and $\rho \in [0, 1]$ is a value with determines the *persistence* of the trail information. Low values of ρ mean only a short time of influence of the pheromone due to *evaporation*.

3.2 AS-SCS-LM

Instead of the MM heuristic we can also use the LM heuristic to guide the ants on their way to good solutions. All we have to do is to change formula (1) to:

$$p(s, \mathbf{v}_k) = \frac{\left[\sum_{i \in \mathcal{I}_k \, : \, s_{iv_{ki}} = s} \tau_{iv_{ki}}(|S_i| - v_{ki} + 1) \right]^{\alpha}}{\sum_{s' \in \mathcal{C}_k} \left[\sum_{i \in \mathcal{I}_k \, : \, s_{iv_{ki}} = s'} \tau_{iv_{ki}}(|S_i| - v_{ki} + 1) \right]^{\alpha}} \tag{7}$$

3.3 Lookahead Function

To improve the solution quality we propose to use a *lookahead function* which takes into account the influence of the choice of the next symbol to append on the next iteration. Therefore when deciding whether or not to append some symbol s we do not only calculate the probability according to the chosen heuristic but also simulate this possible choice and evaluate the resulting state in some way. In this work we compute the maximum of the sum of products of parameter values and weight for the occurrences of the characters in the resulting state:

$$\mu(\mathbf{v}_k, s) = \max_{s' \in \tilde{\mathcal{C}}_k} \left(\sum_{i \in \tilde{\mathcal{I}}_k \, : \, s_{i\tilde{v}_{ki}} = s'} \tau_{i\tilde{v}_{ki}} \right) \tag{8}$$

where $\tilde{\mathbf{v}}_k$ ($\tilde{\mathcal{C}}_k$, $\tilde{\mathcal{I}}_k$) denotes the state vector (candidate-set, index set) that would derive from the vector $\mathbf{v}_k$ ($\mathcal{C}_k$, $\mathcal{I}_k$) if symbol s was chosen.

To make use of this lookahead function μ the calculation of the transition probabilities is changed accordingly. In the case of AS-SCS-MM formula (1) is changed to (the parameter β controls the influence μ):

$$p(s, \mathbf{v}_k) = \frac{\left[\sum_{i \in \mathcal{I} \, : \, s_{iv_{ki}} = s} \tau_{iv_{ki}} \right]^{\alpha} \cdot [\mu(\mathbf{v}, s)]^{\beta}}{\sum_{s' \in \mathcal{C}_k} \left(\left[\sum_{i \in \mathcal{I} \, : \, s_{iv_{ki}} = s'} \tau_{iv_{ki}} \right]^{\alpha} \cdot [\mu(\mathbf{v}, s')]^{\beta} \right)} \tag{9}$$

In the case of AS-SCS-LM formula (7) has to be changed analogously.

3.4 The Pseudo-Random-Proportional Action Choice Rule

As a possibility to improve the solution quality we used the *pseudo-random-proportional* action choice rule as introduced by Dorigo and Gambardella [3]. The way an ant determines the next symbol to append to its supersequence now depends on a value q chosen randomly with uniform distribution in $[0, 1]$ and a threshold parameter $q_0 \in [0, 1]$: If $q \leq q_0$ the symbol s for which $p(s, \mathbf{v}_k) = \max_{s' \in C_k} p(s', \mathbf{v}_k)$ is chosen to be appended next and otherwise s is chosen according to the probability distribution p. The parameter q_0 has the effect that the higher q_0 is the smaller is the probability to make a random choice.

3.5 Elitist Strategy

An idea taken from genetic algorithms is the *elitist strategy*, i.e. to let the best solution found so far contribute to the trail update in every iteration. So the ants search more in the neighbourhood of that solution, in hope of further improving it. For a more detailed explanation of elitist strategy in ACO see [6].

3.6 Island Model

In this paper we introduce an *island model approach* for ACO. The island model is a concept that is often used for genetic algorithms. In our ACO we have different populations of ants working on the same problem instance independently. This means every population lays its own pheromone trail which is not accessible to ants of other populations. After a certain number of iterations some exchange of best solutions between the populations is done so the populations influence each other via an elitist strategy. In our ACO algorithm every population receives the overall best solution found so far.

4 Results

The ACO algorithm was tested on problem instances of different alphabet sizes, different number of strings and also different types of strings. We compare the results with the heuristic LM and with the GA of [1] that is based on the parameterised version of LM. The used parameter settings are: $\alpha = 9$ and trail persistence $\rho = 0.5$, in the case of enabled lookahead function $\beta = 9$, threshold value $q_0 = 0.9$, number of populations was 8 with 2 ants plus two elitist ants in each population, and information exchange took place every 4 iterations. For each test run the ACO algorithms were allowed to perform 150 iterations. The tests were done on a dual-board machine with two Pentium-II 300MHz processors. The running times of the test runs were up to 20 minutes for larger problem instances (16 strings of length 160 over an alphabet of size 16). In the following tables AS-SCS-LM$^+$ (AS-SCS-MM$^+$) denotes AS-SCS-LM (resp. AS-SCS-MM) with lookahead function described in 3.3. Each value is averaged over 5 instances (the same as have been used in [1]) and 5 runs per instance.

Table 1 shows the results for sets of 16 random strings of length 160 over alphabets of sizes 2, 4, and 16. For all instances AS-SCS-LM$^+$ gave better results than AS-SCS-MM$^+$, AS-SCS-LM, GA, and LM. Heuristic LM showed always the worst performance. While the difference in performance are not large for smaller alphabets of size 2 or 4, AS-SCS-LM$^+$ clearly outperforms the other algorithms for the alphabet of size 16. Although heuristic MM alone is worse than LM (see [1]) AS-SCS-MM$^+$ with lookahead function performs better than AS-SCS-LM without lookahead function.

Table 1. Best string length found: 16 random strings of length 160

$|\Sigma|$	LM	GA	AS-SCS-LM	AS-SCS-MM$^+$	AS-SCS-LM$^+$
2	246.6	241.8	242.2	242.1	**241.4**
4	387.6	377.2	377.1	373.6	**371.0**
16	985.2	965.5	943.4	885.4	**876.2**

The results for sets of random strings with different lengths are shown in Table 2. The results are similar to the results for random strings of equal lengths. Again AS-SCS-LM$^+$ outperforms AS-SCS-LM and GA for strings over an alphabet of size 16. Since MM is not a good heuristic for strings of different lengths and in contrast to the result for equal length strings, AS-SCS-LM, and the GA perform better than AS-SCS-MM$^+$.

Table 2. Best string length found: 4 random strings of length 80, 4 of length 40

$|\Sigma|$	LM	GA	AS-SCS-LM	AS-SCS-MM$^+$	AS-SCS-LM$^+$
2	112.6	**107.9**	109.8	111.4	109.4
4	159.4	**145.5**	149.4	152.5	145.6
16	296.8	260.2	259.5	263.5	**247.6**

Since in many applications the strings to be merged are often interdependent and quite similar we also tested the algorithms on sets of similar strings. These strings were generated as randomly chosen subsequences (of length 80 or 90) of a random string of length 100 over an alphabet of size 4. Observe that it is quite likely that the original supersequence of length 100 is a shortest supersequence.

Table 3 shows that on the "easier" instances of length 90 AS-SCS-LM$^+$, AS-SCS-LM, and the GA could nearly always find a supersequence of length 100 which supposedly is optimal. Heuristic LA performs slightly worse in this case and is much worse for the similar strings of length 80. But also AS-SCS-LM$^+$ and especially AS-SCS-LM and AS-SCS-MM$^+$ are worse than the GA which could even in this case always find a supersequence of length 100.

Figure 2 shows the influence of the islands, the Pseudo-Random-Proportional action choice rule, and the trail information on the quality of the solution. In the figure "*random proportional*" means that the parameter q_0 was set to 0, "*no is-*

Table 3. Best string length found:16 similar strings

Length	LM	GA	AS-SCS-LM	AS-SCS-MM+	AS-SCS-LM+
90	105.2	**100.0**	100.6	**100.0**	**100.0**
80	166.8	**100.0**	130.0	121.6	116.3

lands" runs were done with only one population containing 16 ants and 16 elitist ants, and the "*no trail*" curve shows how solution quality developed when ants ignored the trail values. The figure shows clearly that trail information is quite important for finding a good solution. Also the Pseudo-Random-Proportional action choice rule can improve solution quality significantly. For a few number of iterations (< 20) the island model performs slightly worse than the ACO algorithm while it was slightly better for a larger number of iterations (≥ 20). These results fit well to those obtained in [11] for a genetic algorithm with an island model on several test problems. Since the differences in solution quality between the island model ACO and the "no islands" ACO are quite small, to decide whether the island model is a real advantage over the "no islands" model deserves further investigation.

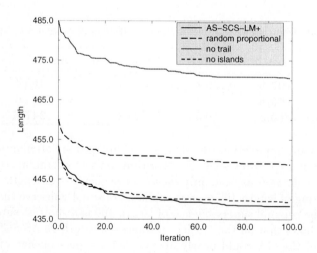

Fig. 2. Best string length found: 16 random strings of length 80 over an alphabet of size 16, averaged over 15 runs.

5   Conclusion

In this paper we presented an Ant Colony Optimisation (ACO) algorithm for the Shortest Common Supersequence (SCS) problem. Instead of using a graph representation of the problem we directly used the string representation of the problem and assigned a pheromone value to each character of the strings. These values guide the ants when applying a heuristic to find a short supersequence. A lookahead function which evaluates the quality of next possible states also influences the decision of the ants. The ACO algorithm was based on an island model where several populations of ants work on the same problem instance independently but exchange their best solution after every certain number of iterations. Our test results show that the ACO algorithm improves the bare heuristic and compares favorably with a genetic algorithm for the SCS problem.

References

1. J. Branke, M. Middendorf, and F. Schneider. Improved heuristics and a genetic algorithm for finding short supersequences. *OR-Spektrum*, 20:39–46, 1998.
2. B. Bullnheimer, R.F. Hartl, and C. Strauß. Applying the ant system to the vehicle routing problem. In *2nd Int. Conference on Metaheuristics – MIC97*, 1997.
3. M. Dorigo and L.M. Gambardella. Ant-Q: A reinforcement learning approach to the traveling salesman problem. In *Proceedings of ML-95, Twelfth Intern. Conf. on Machine Learning*, pages 252–260. Morgan Kaufmann, 1995.
4. M. Dorigo, V. Maniezzo, and A. Colorni. An autocatalytic optimizing process. Technical Report No. 91-016, Politecnico di Milano, Italy, 1991.
5. M. Dorigo, V. Maniezzo, and A. Colorni. The ant system applied to the quadratic assignment problem. Technical Report No. IRIDIA/94-28, Universite Libre de Bruxelles, Belguim, 1994.
6. M. Dorigo, V. Maniezzo, and A. Colorni. The ant system: Optimization by a colony of cooperating agents. *IEEE Trans. Systems, Man, and Cybernetics – Part B*, 26(1):29–41, 1996.
7. D.E. Foulser, M. Li, and Q. Yang. Theory and algorithms for plan merging. *Artificial Intelligence*, 57:143–181, 1992.
8. C.B. Fraser. *Subsequences and Supersequences of Strings*. PhD thesis, Dept. of Computer Science, University of Glasgow, 1995.
9. C.B. Fraser and R.W. Irving. Approximation algorithms for the shortest common supersequence. *Nordic Journal of Computing*, 2:303–325, 1995.
10. T. Jiang and M. Li. On the approximation of shortest common supersequences and longest common subsequences. *SIAM J. Comput.*, 24:1122–1139, 1995.
11. U. Kohlmorgen, H. Schmeck, and K. Haase. Experiences with fine-grained parallel algorithms. to appear in *Annals of Operations Research*, 1997.
12. M. Middendorf. More on the complexity of common superstring and supersequence problems. *Theoret. Comput. Sci.*, 124:205–228, 1994.
13. K.-J. Räihä and E. Ukkonen. The shortest common supersequence problem over binary alphabet is NP-complete. *Theoret. Comput. Sci.*, 16:187–198, 1981.
14. V. G. Timkovsky. Complexity of common subsequence and supersequence problems and related problems. *Cybernetics*, 25:565–580, 1990.

Parameter-Free Genetic Algorithm Inspired by "Disparity Theory of Evolution"

Hidefumi Sawai[1] and Sachio Kizu[2]

[1] Kansai Advanced Research Center, CRL, MPT, Kobe,
651-2401 Japan, e-mail: sawai@crl.go.jp
[2] Toshiba R & D Center, Kawasaki, 210 Japan
e-mail: skizu@isl.rdc.toshiba.co.jp

Abstract. We propose a novel Genetic Algorithm which we call a Parameter-free Genetic Algorithm ($PfGA$) inspired by the "disparity theory of evolution". The idea of the theory is based on different mutation rates in double strands of DNA. Furthermore, its idea is extended to a very compact and fast adaptive search algorithm accelerating its evolution based on the variable-size of population taking a dynamic but delicate balance between exploration (i.e., global search) and exploitation (i.e., local search). The PfGA is not only simple and robust, but also does not need to set almost all genetic parameters in advance that need to be set up in other Genetic Algorithms. To verify the effectiveness of the PfGA, we compared its results with those on the first Internatinal Contenst on Evolutionary Optimization at ICEC'96 using some recent function optimization problems. A parallel and distributed PfGA architecture is being investigated as an extension of this work, some preliminary results of which are shown.

1 Introduction

The Genetic Algorithm (GA)[2] is an evolutionary computation paradigm inspired by biological evolution. GAs have been successfully applied to many practical applications such as functional optimization problems, combinatorial optimization problems, and optimal design of parameters in machines[3]. However, the design of genetic parameters in a GA has to be determined by trial and error, making optimization by GA *ad hoc*. One of the most important research areas in Evolutionary Computation is to adapt genetic parameters and operators in a *self-adaptive* manner because such adaptation can tune an algorithm during solving a given problem. In [12], a classification of adaptation is developed, which covers different levels (such as environment, population, individual and component) and types (such as static and dynamic ones).

However, it is a very time-consuming task to design an optimal evolutionary strategy in an adaptive way because we have to perform the evolutionary algorithm many times by trial and error. To relieve the user of this kind of adaptive parameter-setting problem, we propose a Parameter-free Genetic Algorithm ($PfGA$)[17][18] [19] where no control parameters for genetic operations need to be set as constants in advance. It merely uses arbitrarily random values or

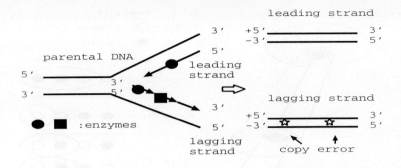

Fig. 1. A hypothesis in the *disparity theory of evolution*

probabilities for setting almost all genetic parameters. The PfGA is inspired by the "disparity theory of evolution" which was proposed by Furusawa et al.[5][6]. The idea is based on the disparity of copy error rates in the *leading* and *lagging* strands of DNA when each strand makes its copy. The error rate in the lagging strand is much higher than that of the leading strand. So the error rate accumulates more in the lagging strand than in the leading strands as generations proceed. The offsprings from the leading strands rarely suffer from the copy error (we call it a *wild type*). On the other hand, the offsprings from the lagging strand accumulate more copy error than the leading strand.

Consequently, asymmetry or disparity occurs in the two kinds of offsprings. This leads to *diversity* in a biological ecosystem. Inspired by the idea of the "disparity theory of evolution," we proposed a Parameter-free Genetic Algorithm (PfGA) where almost none of the genetic parameters, such as initial population size, crossover rate, and mutation rate, need to be set up by a user in advance. All that is needed is a random number generator. The search strategy in the PfGA is based on a dynamic change of subpopulation size extracted from the population which enables an adaptive search to take a delicate balance between global and local search methods. This two kinds of search methods correspond to exploration and exploitation, respectively, and maintain diversity in GAs.

2　Disparity Theory of Evolution

As Charles Darwin claimed in the "Origin of Species" in 1859[1], a major factor contributing to evolution is mutation, which can be caused by spontaneous misreading of bases during DNA synthesis. Semiconservative replication of double-stranded DNA is an asymmetric process, in which there is a leading and a lagging strand. Furusawa et al. proposed a "disparity theory of evolution"[5] based on a difference in frequency of strand-specific base misreading between the leading and lagging DNA strands (i.e., disparity model). Fig.1 shows a hypothesis in the disparity theory of evolution. In the figure, the leading strand is copied smoothly, whereas in the lagging strand a copy error can occur because

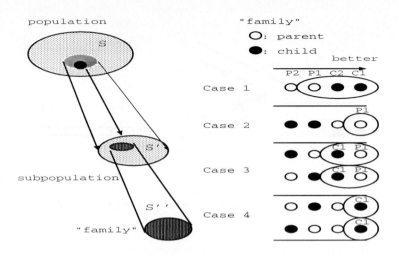

Fig. 2. Population S, subpopulation S', family S" (left) and selection rules (right) in Parameter-free GA

plural enzymes are necessary to produce its copy. This disparity or asymmetry in producing each strand occurs because of the different mutation rates in the leading and lagging strands. Thus "diversity" of DNAs is maintained in a population as generations proceed. The disparity model guarantees that the mutation rate of some leading strands is zero or very small. When circumstances change, for example when the original wild type can not survive, selected mutants might adapt under the new circumstances as a new wild type. In their study, the disparity model was compared with a parity model in which there was no statistical difference in the frequency of base misreading between strands as in the generally accepted model. The disparity model outperformed the parity model in a knapsack optimization problem. They clearly showed that the advantageous situation for the disparity model happened in the cases of a small population, strong pressure, a high mutation rate, sexual reproduction with diploidy, and strong competition. On the other hand, survival conditions for the parity model are a large population, weak selection pressure, a low mutation rate, asexual reproduction with haploidy, and weak competition.[6]

3 Parameter-free Genetic Algorithm

The PfGA is inspired by the *disparity theory of evolution*, described in the previous section. The population of the PfGA is considered as a whole set S of individuals which corresponds to all possible solutions. From this whole set S, a subset S' is introduced. All genetic operations such as selection, crossover, and mutation are conducted for S', thus evolving the subpopulation S'. From the subpopulation S', we introduce a *family* which contains two parents and two children generated from the two parents (see Fig.2 (left)).

Table 1. Test functions

$F1 : Sphere Model :$
$$f(x_i) = \sum_{i=1}^{n} (x_i - 1)^2 \qquad\qquad -5 \le x_i \le 5$$

$F2 : Griewank's\ Funtion :$
$$f(x_i) = \frac{1}{d} \sum_{i=1}^{n} (x_i - 100)^2 - \prod_{i=1}^{n} cos(\frac{x_i - 100}{\sqrt{i}}) + 1,$$
$$d = 4000, -600 \le x_i \le 600$$

$F3 : Shekel's\ foxholes :$
$$f(x_i) = -\sum_{i=1}^{m} \frac{1}{\sum_{j=1}^{n} (x_j - a_{ij})^2 + c_i}, \qquad m = 30, 0 \le x_i \le 10$$

$F4 : Michalewicz'\ Function :$
$$f(x_i) = -\sum_{i=1}^{n} sin(x_i) sin^{2m}(\frac{ix_i^2}{\pi}), \qquad m = 10, 0 \le x_i \le \pi$$

$F5 : Generalized\ Langerman's\ Function :$
$$f(x_i) = -\sum_{i=1}^{m} c_i [exp(-\frac{1}{\pi} \sum_{j=1}^{n} (x_j - a_{ij})^2) cos(\pi \sum_{j=1}^{n} (x_j - a_{ij})^2)]$$
$$m = 5, 0 \le x_i \le 10$$

The PfGA procedure is as follows:

Step 1. Select one individual randomly from the whole population S, and add this individual to the subpopulation S'.

Step 2. Select one individual randomly from the whole population S, and again add this individual to the subpopulation S'.

Step 3. Select two individuals randomly from the subpopulation S' and perform crossover between these individuals as "parent 1 (P_1)" and "parent 2 (P_2)".

Step 4. For one randomly chosen child of the two children generated from the crossover, perform mutation at random.

Step 5. Among the parents $(P_1$ and $P_2)$ and the two generated children $(C_1$ and $C_2)$ select one to three individuals depending on the following cases (i.e., case 1 to 4 to follow), and feed them back to the subpopulation S'.

Step 6. If the number of individuals in subpopulation S' is greater than one, go to Step 3; otherwise, go to Step 2.

For the crossover operation of PfGA, we use multiple-point crossover in which n crossover points (n is a random number, $0 < n < gene\ length$, which always changes every time when the crossover takes place) are randomly selected and genes are replaced between two parents' chromosomes. For the mutation operation, one child is randomly chosen from the two offsprings. Then a randomly chosen portion of the child's chromosome is inverted (i.e., bit-flipped). For the selection operation, we compare the fitness values of all individuals (C_1, C_2, P_1, P_2) in the family. Selection rules shown in Figure 2 are used for four different cases depending on the fitness values f of the parents and children.

Case 1: If the fitness values of the two children are better than those of the parents, then C_1, C_2 and $arg\ max_{P_i}(f(P_1), f(P_2))$ are left in S', thus increasing the size of S' by one.

Case 2: If the fitness values of C_1 and C_2 are worse than those of P_1 and P_2, then only $arg\ max_{P_i}(f(P_1), f(P_2))$ is left in S', thus decreasing the size of S' by one.

Case 3: If the fitness value of either P_1 or P_2 is better than that of the children, $arg\ max_{C_i}(f(C_1), f(C_2))$ and $arg\ max_{P_i}(f(P_1), f(P_2))$ are left in S', thus maintaining the size of S'.

Case 4: In all other situations, $arg\ max_{C_i}(C_1, C_2)$ is preserved and then one individual randomly chosen from S is added to S', thus maintaining the size of S'.

Considering the relationship between the PfGA and the *disparity theory of evolution*, the chromosome of best individual in *family* corresponds to a *wild-type* at present which is a *leading strand* in the "disparity theory of evolution." Offsprings generated by the crossover and mutation from two parents correspond to *lagging strands*. In selection the best individual (P_1) in the cases 2 and 3 is regarded as a current wild-type whereas the best individual (C_1) in the cases 1 and 4 is regarded as a *new* wild-type because P_1 is replaced with C_1. In other words, C_1 (i.e., a new wild-type) is produced by "pivoting" on P_1 (i.e., a current wild-type) exploring the neighborhood of P_1, thus resulting in the better location in the search space. The reason why only one offspring is mutated while preserving another offspring is to maintain the characteristic (chromosome) inherited from two parents.

4 Experiment

Experiments were performed on the function optimization (minimization) problems shown in Table 1. The dimension n for all problems was set to five. These functions have their own upper and lower bounds defined by their range of variables x_i [7]. $F1$, the Sphere model which takes its minimum 0 at $x_i = 1$, is separable and is a shifted function of De Jong's Sphere model: $f(x) = \sum_{i=1}^{n} x_i^2$ [4]. $F2$ is the Griewank's function which takes its minimum 0 at $x_i = 100$. $F3$ represents the Shekel's foxholes[4], with n*m local minima. Its global minimum is approximately -10.40. $F4$ is the Michalewicz' function which takes its global minimum -4.688. The last but most difficult function $F5$, the Generalized Langerman's function, has a global minimum of -1.4 or below, which is very difficult to find by conventional optimization methods such as neural networks or simulated annealing. The defined variables were encoded using 22 to 24 bits in Gray coding, depending on each function.

To evaluate the performance of the PfGA with other evolutionary algorithms, we compared it with the results of the first ICEO (International Contest on Evolutionary Optimization)[8]. Bersini et al. held the first ICEO at the 1996 ICEC (Int. Conf. on Evolutionary Computation) where eight different algorithms took part in it. In the functional optimization problems, the following three performance indexes were introduced; the Expected Number of Evaluations per Success (ENES), the best value reached (BV) and the Relative Time (RT). These indexes were measured on every problems of the test bed for the 5 dimensional version. The ENES index represents the mean number of function evaluations needed to reach a certain fitness value, Value To Reach (VTR), given with each problem. The ENES is computed by running 20 independent runs of the algorithm until the VTR is reached. RT is defined by (CT-ET)/ET, where CT is the total CPU time to perform the algorithm with 10,000 iterations, and ET the CPU time to perform 10,000 fitness function evaluations. Consequently, the less RT, the more compact the algorithm becomes.

5 Comparison of results with the 1st ICEO

Table 2. Results of PfGA for test functions in the 1st ICEO (5 dimensions)

Function	ENES	BV	RT	VTR	#iteration	%success
F1: Sphere model	4,067	0.0	0.91	1.0e-6	1.0e4	100
F2: Griewank's function	8,673	4.49e-5	0.90	1.0e-4	1.0e4	15
F3: Shekel's foxholes	1,619	-10.40	0.33	-9	1.0e4	15
F4: Michalewicz' function	5,131	-4.688	0.90	-4.687	1.0e4	50
F5: Langerman's function	5,274	-1.50	0.43	-1.4	1.0e4	25
Average	4,632	-	0.70	-	1.0e4	41

Table 2 shows the results of PfGA performance on five test functions in the first ICEO. In the case of 5 dimensions, all five test functions converged with 10,000 evaluations, exceeding the VTR at an average success rate of 41%. We compared the performance of PfGA with the results of eight other algorithms that participated in the first ICEO[8]. The smaller the ENES index is, the better the algorithm is regarded in the ICEO. According to this criterion, the PfGA reaches the second place among the nine algorithms including PfGA. The smaller the RT index is, the more compact the algorithm is. The PfGA has the third place among them with respect to this criterion. Therefore, the PfGA is relatively better with respect to the ENES index, even though it is quite compact. The first place algorithm in the ICEO was "inductive search[9]," the RT index of which is 2 and it uses *a priori* knowledge that the test functions take their minimal values by the same values of x_i ($i = 1, \ldots, n$) because of the separability of functions. This algorithm works well for any separable functions taking their minimal values by the same values of x_i. Since these kind of situations never happen for generally multi-dimensional functions, it is an *ad hoc* algorithm[10].

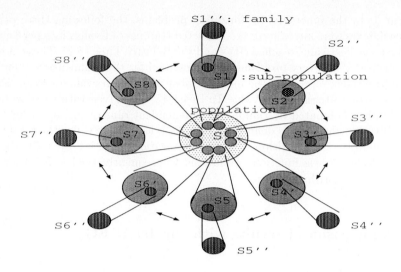

Fig. 3. A parallel and distributed architecture of the PfGA

6 Distributed Parallel Processing of PfGA

Generally speaking, parallel processing aims at accelerating the speed of processing. In the case of GA, it aims at reaching better solutions faster than sequential processing by extending the search space. Parallel and distributed processing of GA has been extensively studied[13][14][15][16], the granularity ranging from fine- to coarse-grained, and the mode of processing covering both synchronous and asynchronous processing. The *granularity* concerns the size of a process assigned to a processor. In the case of a fine-grained parallel GA model, the (overlapping) neighborhoods of the individuals constitute the units of processing. On the other hand, coarse-grained parallel GA assigns a subpopulation as a unit of processing, and some few individuals are migrated among subpopulations at an appropriate rate. The latter model is called an "island model", and one island (subpopulation) consists of one "deme" which is a minimum recombinational unit of biological species. In this paper we use the latter model.

Fig. 3 shows an architecture of parallel PfGA which is now being investigated. This architecture is based on that of Fig. 2. The whole population S is located at the center from which M subpopulations $\{S'_i | i = 1, \ldots, M\}$ are extracted (M=8, in this case). Of course if the number of processors increases, the number of subpopulations could also increase. Each "family" shown as S''_i is extracted from each subpopulation S'_i. If better individuals produced in some subpopulation S'_i, the individuals are copied and migrated among the subpopulations (the bilateral arrows indicate this situation). One possible migration method is as follows: if case 1 or 4 happens in some family, the individual C_1 that is better than its two parents can be copied to other subpopulations as an emigrant. In case 1, as two children are better than its two parents, it might be possible for the two children to emigrate to other subpopulations, but this might cause a premature convergence decreasing the diversity of the population (in fact, however, case 1 rarely happens). When other subpopulations receive the immigrant, they have to decide to accept it or not because the number of individuals will increase and lead to an explosion of diversity if any immigrants are unconditionaly accepted. To avoid such a situation, one possible method is to eliminate the worst individual among all individuals in the subpopulation and adding the "candidate" immigrant. This maintains the sizes of subpopulations. If the immigrant is eliminated, the immigration can not be substantially realized. This architecture is being implemented using several workstations connected with local-area networks (LAN). PVM (Parallel Virtual Machine)[11] software is used to evolve the subpopulations in parallel and asynchronously. PVM is network software that uses dynamic load balancing between assigned processors.

Table 3 shows the experimental results on the paralllel distributed PfGA using five subpopulations for five processors. This does not necessarily mean that each subpopulation evolves on the corresponding single processor, because two subpopulations sometimes simultaneously evolve in one processor if its load is lighter than others. As compared to the results in Table 2, the success rate increased from 41% to 65%. The ENES indexes in Table 3 decrease approximately to a rate of 59% in Table 2, Also, the BV index for Griewank's function becomes better than that in Table 2.

Table 3. Results of Parallel Distributed PfGA for test functions in the 1st ICEO.

Function	ENES	BV	VTR	#iteration	%success
F1: Sphere model	985	0.0	1.0e-6	1.0e4	100
F2: Griewank's function	3,845	3.34e-10	1.0e-4	1.0e4	85
F3: Shekel's foxholes	3,325	-10.404	-9	1.0e4	15
F4: Michalewicz' function	3,236	-4.688	-4.687	1.0e4	80
F5: Langerman's function	3,529	-1.500	-1.4	1.0e4	45
Average	2,747	-	-	1.0e4	65

7 Discussion

The PfGA is an algorithm inspired by the disparity theory of evolution. The leading strand with a small mutation rate is in a sense "conservative" to the change of environment, whereas the lagging strand is "revolutionary" or innovative. These features in the two kinds of strands produce "diversity" of population where the leading strand contributes to stability of population, and the lagging strand contributes to flexibility of population. In terms of the PfGA, these strands correspond to the best individual in subpopulation S' and offsprings produced by crossover and mutation, respectively. Furthermore, the diversity of individuals maintains a delicate balance of search processes between exploitation and exploration in the PfGA.

We also performed a parallel distributed processing of PfGA, where some subpopulations evolved asynchronously using multiple processors (workstations controlled by PVM network software). This caused a significant improvement on the success rates as well as the performance indexes such as the ENES and BV. In the current stage, we can simulate an asexual ecological system. Furthermore, if we introduce gender (i.e., male and female) into each individual, we can simulate a sexual ecological system where sexual reproduction will be realized.

8   Conclusion

The proposed PfGA is inspired by the "disparity theory of evolution" in which there is a difference in frequency of strand-specific base misreading between the lagging and leading DNA strands. It shows a rapid evolutionary behavior, does not require the setting of genetic parameters, and is easy to construct. Its ease of construction and the fact that it does not need parameter tuning are particularly important in all practical applications. This scheme of PfGA is easily applied to combinatorial optimization problems such as TSP (Traveling Salesman Problem) and JSP (Job-shop Scheduling Problem). Moreover, the PfGA is well-suited to distributed and parallel processing in which many subpopulations can be evolved either synchronously or asynchronously using parallel processors with some migration between subpopulations. This is a possible extension of the current PfGA being investigated. We demonstrated an asynchronously coarse-grained (island) architecture for the PfGA using plural workstations, which showed some encouraging results. The compactness of this algorithm may effectively resolve dynamically changing problems and problems in a noisy enviroment. Therefore, it may possibly be used as a powerful engine for solving such difficult real-world problems and studying ecosystems.

Acknowledgement

The authors would like to express their gratitude to Dr. Jon Shapiro at Manchester University in U.K., and Dr.Ferdinand Peper at AVIS, KARC, CRL for proof-reading and helpful suggestions for this manuscript, and to Mr. S.Adachi for his valuable help to perform the simulations on the PfGA.

References

1. Charles Darwin, "On the Origin of Species by Means of Natural Selection or the Preservation of Favoured Races in the Struggle for Life,"London, John Murray, 1859.
2. J.H.Holland, "Adaptation in Natural and Artificial System," The University of Michigan Press, 1975.

3. D.E. Goldberg, "Genetic Algorithm in Search, Optimization, and Machine Learning," Addison Wesley, 1989.

4. De Jong, "An Analysis of the Behavior: a Class of Genetic Adaptive Systems," Doctoral dissertation, University of Michigan, 1975.

5. M. Furusawa and H. Doi, "Promotion of Evolution: Disparity in the Frequency of Strand-specific Misreading Between the Lagging and Leading DNA Strands Enhances Disproportionate Accumulation of Mutations," J. theor. Biol., vol. 157, pp 127-133, 1992.

6. K. Wada, H. Doi, S. Tanaka, Y. Wada, and M. Furusawa, "A Neo-Darwinian Algorithm: Asymmetrical Mutations due to Semiconservative DNA-type replication Promote Evolution," Proc. Natl. Acad. Sci., USA, vol. 90, pp 11934-11938, Dec. 1993.

7. T.Baeck, D.Fogel and Z.Michalewicz (Eds.), "Handbook of evolutionary computation," New York: Oxford University Press, 1997.

8. The Organising Committee: H.Bersini, M.Doringo, S.Langerman, G.Seront, L.Gambardella, "Results of the First International Contest on Evolutionary Optimization (1st ICEO)," 1996 IEEE Int. Conf. on Evolutionary Computation (ICEC'96), pp611-615, 1996.

9. G. Bilchev and I. Parmee, "Inductive Search," 1996 IEEE Int. Conf. on Evolutionary Computation (ICEC'96), pp832-836, 1996.

10. D.Whitley, K.Mathias, S.Rana and J.Dzubera, "Building Better Test Functions," Proc. of the Sixth Int. Conf. on Genetic Algorithms, pp 239-246, Morgan Kaufmann, 1995.

11. Al Geist, Adam Beguelin, Jack Dongarra, Weicheng Jiang, Robert Manchek and Vaidy Sunderam, "PVM UER'S GUIDE AND REFERENCE MANUAL," 1993.5.

12. R.Hinterding, Z.Michalewicz and A.E.Eiben, "Adaptation in Evolutionary Computation: A Survey," Proc. of the 1997 IEEE Int. Conf. on Evolutionary Computation, pp65-69, 1997.

13. T.C.Belding, "The Distributed Genetic Algorithm Revisited," Proc. of the Sixth Int. Conf. on Genetic Algorithms, pp114-121, Morgan Kaufmann, 1995.

14. E.C-Paz and D.E.Goldberg, "Predicting Speedups of Idealized Bounding Cases of Parallel Genetic Algorithms," Proc. of the Seventh Int. Conf. on Genetic Algorithms, pp113-126, Morgan Kaufmann, 1997.

15. I.K.Evans, "Embracing Premature Convergence: The Hypergamous Parallel Genetic Algorithm," Proc. of the Int. Conf. on Evolutionary Computation '98, pp621-626, 1998.

16. T.Maruyama, T.Hirose and A.Konagaya, "A Fine-Grained Parallel Genetic Algorithm for Distributed Parallel System," Proc. of the Fifth Int. Conf. on Genetic Algorithms, pp184-190, Morgan Kaufmann, 1993.

17. S.Kizu, H.Sawai, and T.Endo, "Parameter-free Genetic Algorithm: GA without Setting Genetic Parameters," Proc. of the 1997 Int. Symp. on Nonlinear Theory and its Applications, vol.2 of 2, pp1273-1276, Dec.1997.

18. H.Sawai, S.Kizu, and T.Endo, "Parameter-free Genetic Algorithm (PfGA)", Trans. IEICE, Japan, vol. J81-D-II, No.2, pp450-452, Feb. 1998 (in Japanese).

19. H.Sawai, S.Kizu, and T.Endo, "Performance Comparison of the Parameter-free Genetic Algorithm (PfGA) with Steady-state GA", Trans. IEICE, Japan, vol. J81-D-II, No.6, pp1455-1459, June. 1998 (in Japanese).

Immune Network Dynamics for Inductive Problem Solving

Vanio Slavov[1] and Nikolay I. Nikolaev[2]

[1] Information Technologies Lab, New Bulgarian University,
Sofia 1113, Bulgaria, e-mail: vslavov@inf.nbu.acad.bg

[2] Department of Computer Science, American University in Bulgaria,
Blagoevgrad 2700, Bulgaria, e-mail: nikolaev@nws.aubg.bg

Abstract. This paper develops an inductive computation algorithm upon biological mechanisms discovered by the immunology. We build an evolutionary search algorithm based on a model of the immune network dynamics. According to it, the concentration of lymphocyte clone-like solutions is determined by the degree of recognition of antigens, as well as the extent of behavioral interaction with other members of the population. The antigen-like examples also change their concentration to gear up solutions matching slightly covered examples. These dynamic features are incorporated in the fitness function of the immune algorithm in order to achieve high diversity and efficient search navigation. Empirical evidence for the superiority of this immune version before the simple genetic algorithm on automata induction tasks are presented.

1 Introduction

Recent research investigates evolutionary search algorithms designed in analogy with models of the biological immune system [Farmer et. *al.*, 1986; Bersini and Varela, 1991; Smith et. *al.*, 1993; Forrest et. *al.*, 1993]. These studies are motivated by the strong similarities between their immanent mechanisms and functionalities: 1) they both perform adaptive learning of recognized patterns; 2) they learn by fitness proportional selection and mutation. The hypothesis is that the immune system could be envisioned as a parallel search algorithm whose dynamics is useful for addressing inductive, NP-hard combinatorial problems.

These arguments inspire us to employ immune system microscopic mechanisms in an evolutionary algorithm in order to achieve macroscopic properties suitable for solving inductive problems. We use an idiotypic network model of the immune system from the theoretical biology [De Boer and Hogeweg, 1989], and develop an immune version of the genetic algorithm. Since the network learns by search for lymphocytes that detect foreign antigens, a fitness function that incorporates the complex dynamics of the network model is elaborated. This dynamics has two aspects: 1) a model stimulating involvement of the lymphocyte clones in adaptive responses to antigens, and encouraging self-regulating interactions between the lymphocytes that make up the network; 2) a model prescribing concentration increase of an antigen when it is slightly recognized. The dynamics of the antigens guides the network adaptation by gearing up lymphocytes that match antigens having highest concentration.

The immune algorithm is applied for solving an instance of the intractable finite-state automata induction problem [Gold, 1978]. In the implementation individual automata are associated with lymphocyte clones, and the examples are assumed antigens. The proliferation of an automaton depends on two factors: 1) the degree of recognized examples; and 2) the extent of its behavioral complementarity with other automata, in sense of capacity to recognize a subset of examples different from these matched by the remaining automata. The network dynamics promotes diversity. This is a macroscopic property influenced by the changes in the examples' power, which provoke perturbations of the network connectivity. Such perturbations are useful for navigating the population flow on the fitness landscape since they allow to escape from local optima, and contribute for achieving efficient search. Computer experiments demonstrate that the immune version outperforms the simple genetic algorithm [Goldberg, 1989].

This paper is organized as follows. We offer the biological idiotypic network model in section two. Section three describes the immune algorithm. Empirical evidence for its search characteristics, acquired during automata induction, are given in section four. Finally, a discussion is made and conclusions are derived.

2 Biological Immune Networks

A biological immune network of *lymphocyte clones*[3] adaptively learns to discriminate self genes from non-self, or foreign *antigens*. According to the idiotypic network theory [Jerne, 1974], lymphocyte cells make protective *antibody* molecules which recognize antigens, and also recognize other antibodies. The antibodies detect antigens with receptor regions on their structures, called *idiotypes*. Pattern recognition occurs at molecular level and is based on complementarity in shape between: 1) the binding idiotype site on a lymphocyte surface, and a portion of an antigen; and 2) an idiotype and an anti-idiotype attached on two interacting lymphocyte cells.

2.1 Clonal Selection and Hypermutation

The acquisition of an immune response includes the following phases: 1) generation of diverse antibody types from the gene segments in the bone marrow; 2) secretion of antibodies from the lymphocytes with high affinity for the antigens; 3) *somatic hypermutation* of the lymphocytes; and 4) *clonal selection* and elimination of lymphocyte clones proportional to their degree of matching antigens.

The efficiency of pattern matching depends on the diversity of available receptor shapes, which determine the antibody types. A complex process chooses shapes at random from gene segments. A large repertoire of receptors with specific shapes implies high potential to produce useful receptors that detect and bind structurally related antigens. Lymphocyte cells that carry such useful receptors are activated to secrete them as antibodies, grow into clones and replicate. Thus, the lymphocytes that perfectly recognize antigens are strongly stimulated to proliferate in the clonal selection. Besides, cells with high recognition potential arise by hypermutation and are also subject to selection.

---

[3] Clone is a pair of a lymphocyte cell and one type of antibody produced by it.

2.2 Idiotypic Network Dynamics

The clonal selection process is driven by antibody interactions, and it is influenced by the concentrations of the antigens. Lymphocyte clones participate in idiotypic interactions, by means of which they self-regulate their abilities to learn patterns. The evolution of the network topology leads to maturation of the immune response, which features itself by increased average match of antigens.

The model of lymphocyte dynamics in the *idyotypic network* involves two components [Perelson, 1989]. First, it describes to what degree antibodies recognize non-self antigens, and the level of mutual recognition with other antibody types. Second, it shows the production of new clones, as well as the elimination of inviable lymphocytes. The *concentration* of a clone in the next population is proportional to the initial concentration, without the dying suppressed clones, plus the proliferation of stimulated clones evoked by excitatory interactions.

3 The Immune Algorithm

We develop an immune algorithm with counterparts of the biological immune micromechanisms using a discrete version of the above idiotypic network model. This is an immune version of the genetic algorithm tailored to identify a benchmark automaton with no more than a given number of states from provided examples.

3.1 Automata Induction

The finite-state automata (FSA) induction is a highly intractable search problem. It is proven that the identification of a deterministic finite k-state automaton, compatible with given input-output behavior, is NP-complete [Gold, 1978]. We study the problem of finding an FSA with no more than M states that best matches a sample of strings. Strings can be positive or negative depending on whether they belong to the language defined by the automaton.

A deterministic FSA is defined with the tuple $FSA = (\Sigma, Q, \delta, q_0, F)$, where: Σ is a finite alphabet of input symbols, Q is a finite set of states, $\delta(q, a)$: $Q \times \Sigma \to Q$ is the transition function, $q_0 \in Q$ is the initial state, and $F \subseteq Q$ is the set of accepting states. We encode such automaton by its state-transition table. Automaton with no more than M states of L input letters is coded by an integer array of length $(L + 1)M$. The first $L.M$ cells represent the transition table δ. The last M cells encode the final states F. The state q is interpreted as final if the cell with number $LM + q$ contains a non-zero value.

3.2 Automata Identification by Immune Dynamics

The computational mechanisms analogous to these in the biological immune system are as follows: a lymphocyte clone corresponds to a finite-state automaton; the concentration of a clone is the fitness of the automaton; the structural binding abilities of the clone are associated with the recognizing capacity of the automaton; the interaction between two lymphocytes is the complementarity in the behavior of the automata; the power of an example is conceived as antigen concentration. The network comprises all automata in the population.

The *fitness function* for control of the immune algorithm is elaborated to adapt the automata concentration changes in response to the mutual interactions as follows [De Boer and Hogeweg, 1989]:

$$F_i^{n+1} = S_i - d.F_i^n + p.F_i^n.\text{Prol}(Ag_i^n, \text{Id}_i^n)$$

where: F_i^{n+1} is the fitness of the i-th automaton at generation $n+1$;
S_i is a free influx, d is turnover, and p is proliferation constant;
Ag_i^n is the antigen score of the i-th automaton;
Id_i^n is the total anti-idiotype excitation of automaton i;
Prol is the rate of proliferation.

This differential equation describes somatic evolution of clonal selection. The learning continues till the network converges to a stable state governed by the following *proliferation function* Prol:

$$\text{Prol}(Ag_i^n, \text{Id}_i^n) = \frac{Ag_i^n + \text{Id}_i^n}{p_1 + Ag_i^n + \text{Id}_i^n}$$

The activating proliferation function has a threshold effect. The original is bell-shaped [De Boer and Hogeweg, 1989], but here we deliberately use only the exciting part of the curve. So, fit and interacting individuals receive a greater stimulation to proliferate, while suppression from other automata is neglected.

The antigen score of an automaton should reflect how many antigens it is driven by, so it is reasonable to depend on the power of its eliciting strings. We define the *antigen score* Ag_i^n of automaton i as linearly proportional to the power X_j^n of the example strings $1 \leq j \leq R$ which it recognizes:

$$Ag_i^n = \sum_{j=1, i \neq j}^{R} B_{ij}.X_j^n$$

where the *binding* B_{ij} of an automaton i as 1 if the automaton i recognizes the example j and 0 otherwise.

This antigen score depends on the examples' power X_j^n changes. The more the automata that recognize an example, the less its power. When a small number of powerful examples remains they are supposed to increase the importance of the automata that match it, and thus to provoke perturbation of the search. The *power* X_k^n of an example k is defined as the number of automata that correctly recognize it plus a term for constant recruitment γ_k:

$$X_k^{n+1} = Y_k^n.(\alpha - \sum_{j=1}^{N} B_{jk}.F_j^n / \sum_{i=1}^{N} F_j^n) + \gamma_k$$

The amount of *anti-idiotype excitation* Id_n^i of automaton i by other automata depends on the degree of its interaction A_{ij} with the other $1 \leq j \leq N$ automata:

$$\text{Id}_i^n = 1/(E.N) \sum_{j=1, i \neq j}^{N} A_{ij}.F_j^n$$

On this basis, we hypothesize that the algorithm will exhibit different dynamical behavior: 1) initially the global excitation should be large; 2) in the phases of global search it should fluctuate and be relatively high; and, 3) in the phases of local search it should decrease rapidly because of the convergence to a locally optimal solution. A distinguishing characteristic feature of this excitation function is that it prescribes the behavior of an automaton to be regulated by all other automata in the population. The automata compete for attaining higher learning accuracy and taking over the population.

The strength of idiotypic interactions between automata A_{ij} should be considered in sense of automata behavior in order to contribute for the diversity. Two automata are assumed complementary when the strings recognized by them are from disjoint sets. We quantify the *affinity* A_{ij} between two automata i and j as the number of examples which i recognizes correctly and on which j fails:

$$A_{ij} = |E_i^n - E_j^n|$$

where E_i^n is the subset of examples correctly recognized by automaton i at generation n from all provided examples E, $E_i^n \subseteq E$, and $E_j^n \subseteq E$. We assume that the network is symmetric $A_{ij} = A_{ji}$ for $1 \leq i, j \leq N$, as well as $A_{ii} = 0$.

The strength of these affinity interactions determines the idiotypic network topology, and hence the ability of the algorithm to learn. Our formulation of A_{ij} above implies that the fit automata may be expected to navigate the search well as they are stimulated to: 1) detect correctly more examples; and 2) cover slightly overlapping sets of examples, which favors the distinct, non-similar automata. Such a fitness function makes the individuals distributed, or the complementary automata co-existent in the population.

3.3 Selection and Mutation

The evolutionary behavior of this immune version of the genetic algorithm is governed by *fitness proportional selection*. The selected automata are altered by an *uniform replacement mutation* operator. Each allele in the genome representation of the automata transition table was modified with probability $P\mu \leq 0.2$.

4 Performance Dynamics

An investigation of the immune algorithm dynamics was carried out. We considered a finite-state automaton (Figure 1), which is a very difficult benchmark instance for learning. The sample consisted of 34 boolean strings, distributed as 16 positive and 18 negative. The population included 50 automata. The reported results were derived with reference values for the free parameters in the fitness function as follows: $S_i = 0.1$, $d = 1$, $p = 1.85$, $p_1 = 0.5$, $\gamma_k = 0.001$ and $\alpha = 1.5$. The initial concentration of the automata was calculated by solving the differential equation at steady state for $F^0 = F^{n+1}$, which gives: $F^0 = S_i.(p_1 + 1)/(p_1 + 1 + d + d.p_1 - p)$.

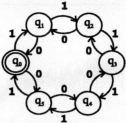

Figure 1. The deterministic finite-state automaton subject of learning

4.1 Learning Accuracy

The *learning accuracy* of the immune algorithm was studied with the maximal number of recognized strings by the best automaton. We see on Figure 2 that the algorithm converges to the global solution despite the degradation.

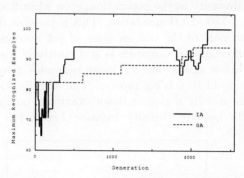

Figure 2. Maximal percentage of recognized strings by the best automaton taken from typical runs with the immune and the simple genetic algorithm [Goldberg, 1989]

The immune algorithm self-regulates and escapes trapping in a local optimum (approximately 95% recognized strings) due to the interactions among the automata. Self-regulation is the intrinsic ability of the immune network to discover wired automata which improve each other's fitness. The claim is that the immune network connectivity is a source of high population diversity, which is a potential for robust search navigation.

4.2 Immune Network Connectivity

The learning activity of the immune network depends on its *connectivity* [DeBoer and Hogeweg, 1989; Stewart and Varela, 1989; Farmer, 1990]. The computational network remembers examples by switching between different combinations of automata, driven by their behavioral links.

The connectivity of the network, maintained by the immune algorithm, can be measured by the strength of the *idiotype excitation* and by the *population diameter*. The affinity between two automata is a criterion for the strength of their interaction as it accounts for their mutual behavioral binding (Figure 3). When the automata cover different subsets of examples, they arouse each other and the algorithm conducts distributed search. This means that the immune algorithm sustains a high variety of hypothetical problem solutions.

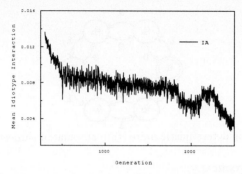

Figure 3. Mean idiotype excitation among all automata in the population recorded during the typical run illustrated on Figure 1

On the above plot one may observe that while the algorithm conducts search it supports a high diversity in the population, even when it exploits local landscape areas between 1800-2200 generation. This is possible due to the exciting role of the unsolved part of the task in sense of yet uncovered examples. The concentration of unrecognized examples is still relatively high (Figure 4). The plot on the figure below shows that the mean examples' power very slowly decreases during the problem solving process. The identification of the globally best automaton features by a sloping down examples' power, after generation 2200, that eventually leads to diversity decrease (Figure 3).

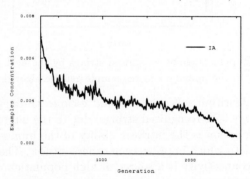

Figure 4. Mean power (concentration) of the examples calculated till the global automaton solution takes over the population

The population diameter can serve as another estimate of the network connectivity. Figure 5 depicts the changes of the population diameter, measured as the mean Hamming distance among all the automata in the population. The changes of the population diameter suggest reshaping of the network topology. From a global perspective there is a waving tendency, which points states of sparse and dense networks. The capture of powerful examples evokes perturbations of the network. These connectivity perturbations are essentially search perturbations that indicate progressive search and potential of the algorithm to escape from local optima. From a local perspective the connectivity decreases and finally the algorithm converges on similar individuals.

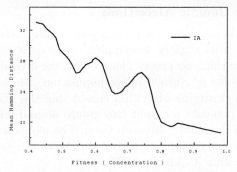

Figure 5. Relation between the syntactic population diameter and the automata
fitness obtained from a particular run

The memorization of more and more examples by the automata in the population is a consequence forced by the adapting interactions between them.

4.3 Examples Influence

It is interesting to understand how these changes of the examples' power influence the ability of the immune algorithm to escape from local extrema. A local optima is such a state in which most, almost all examples are covered by the individuals in the population but despite this the algorithm cannot improve since the acquired structure of the individuals is incorrect. Figure 6 demonstrates that the immune algorithm can cope with such states. We display the inverse relation between the concentration of a particular important example, and the number of automata that recognize it.

When more automata tend to recognize the important example, its concentration decreases (near generation 900). After that, the automata begin to avoid this example as its power is low, which leads again to increase of its power since less automata are inclined to match it (at generation 1300). This leads to excitation of the automata that recognize this example, and moves the whole population away from this local landscape area. The complex dynamics of the interdependence between the power of an example and the number of individuals that match it enables occasional search perturbations.

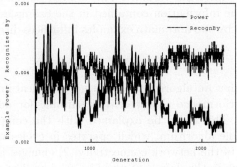

Figure 6. Interplay between the power of a selected powerful example and the number
of automata that recognize it

720

4.4 Immune vs. Genetic Algorithms

The diversity in inductive problem solving can be interpreted as the ability to recognize examples from slightly overlapping subsets, because this contributes for increasing the learning accuracy. That is why, the diversity may also be analyzed with the *number of clusters* in the population. We compute the clusters using the K-means clustering algorithm considering the affinity as a distance characteristic. The population is split into groups around selected seed individuals by maximizing the affinity between them. The plots on Figure 7 point out that the immune version supports higher variety in the population than the simple genetic algorithm [Goldberg, 1989].

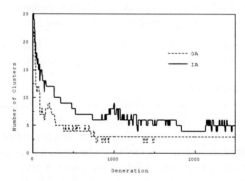

Figure 7. Population clustering measured by the K-means clustering algorithm with the immune version and the simple genetic algorithm

A greater number of clusters means a greater number of antigen-antibody complexes in the population. These plots help us understand that the immune algorithm accommodates more individuals with different qualities. The ensemble of distinct automata features by dynamics, which causes qualitatively specific manners of behavior during the evolutionary search process: 1) in the phase of global search the diversity is high; 2) in the phase of local search the population is arranged in the vicinity of the approached peak, and the diversity slowly diminishes between generations 1800-2200; and 3) when the search improves, the population diversity increases variably. This is because the distinct individuals are fostered with the information contained in the examples, or the number of different recognized by two automata examples influences directly their fitnesses.

5 Discussion

We demonstrated that an algorithm simulating biological immune network dynamics exhibits performance characteristics suitable for addressing inductive computation tasks. This could be explained with the complex dynamical behavior of the immune algorithm, which operates in cycles with three features: 1) transformations of the network connectivity; 2) changes in the search mode; and 3) modifications in the degree of problem solving. The network connectivity influences the search mode, while the search mode determines the problem solving quality as to whether or not there are reachable fit solutions.

Initially the network is highly wired, and the search mode is oscillatory. This indicates global search during which the problem solving entropy is high. After that, the immune algorithm evolves the network topology which makes transition to asymptotic search. During the asymptotic search the algorithm exploits the local region of problem solutions. The unsolved part of the problem, however, may attempt to cause changes in the search regime toward chaotic. Cycles of such three search phases from oscillatory through asymptotic to chaotic alternate continuously, and the system self-regulates. That is how the immune algorithm dynamics provokes adaptive search.

6 Conclusion

This paper proposed an evolutionary algorithm navigated by a fitness function defined in analogy with a connectionist model of the biological immune system. Viewing the learning as immunity phenomena, it is an original attempt to employ the immune networks as computational mechanisms. We demonstrated that their dynamics can be applied for solving a classical NP-complete search problem, the induction of finite-state automata. The empirical findings suggest that it can also solve efficiently other instances of such intractable search problems.

Further research should be oriented toward deeper understanding of the computational properties and principles of this connectionist immune algorithm.

References

1. Bersini, H. and Varela, F. Hints for Adaptive Problem Solving Gleaned from Immune Networks. In H.P.Schwefel and H.Mühlenbein (eds.), *Proc. First Int. Conf. Parallel Problem Solving from Nature, PPSN I*, Springer, Berlin, 343-354, 1991.
2. De Boer, R. J. and Hogeweg, P. Idiotypic Networks Incorporating T-B Cell Cooperation. The Condition for Percolation. *J. Theoretical Biology*, **139**, 17-38, 1989.
3. Farmer, J. D., Packard, N. H. and Perelson, A. S. The Immune System, Adaptation and Machine Learning. *Physica*, **22**D, 187-204, 1986.
4. Farmer, J. D., A Rosetta Stone for Connectionism. *Physica*, **42**D, 153-187, 1990.
5. Forrest, S., Javornik, B., Smith, R. E. and Perelson, A. S. Using Genetic Algorithms to Explore Pattern Recognition in the Immune System, *Evolutionary Computation*, 1: 3, 191-211, 1993.
6. Gold, E. M. Complexity of Automaton Identification from given Data. *Information and Control*, **37**, 302-320, 1978.
7. Goldberg, D. *Genetic Algorithms in Search, Optimization, and Machine Learning*, Addison-Wesley Publ., Reading, MA, 1989.
8. Jerne, N.K. Towards a Network Theory of the Immune System. *Annual Immunology (Institute Pasteur)*, 125 C, 373-389, 1974.
9. Perelson, A. S. Immune Network Theory. *Immunological Reviews*, **110**, 5-36, 1989.
10. Smith, R.E., Forrest, S. and Perelson, A. Searching for Diverse, Cooperative Populations with Genetic Algorithms. *Evolutionary Computation*,1:2, 127-149, 1993.
11. Stewart, J. and Varela, F.J. Exploring the Meaning of Connectivity in the Immune Network. *Immunological Reviews*, **110**, 37-61, 1989.
12. Varela, F., Coutinho, A., Dupire B. and Vaz, N. M. Cognitive Networks: Immune, Neural, and Otherwise. In: *Theoretical Immunology*, Perelson, A. D. (ed.), Addison-Wesley, New York, vol. II, 359-374, 1988.

Parallelization Strategies for Ant Colony Optimization

Thomas Stützle

FB Informatik, FG Intellektik, TU Darmstadt
Alexanderstr. 10, D-64283 Darmstadt, Germany
stuetzle@informatik.th-darmstadt.de

Abstract. Ant Colony Optimization (ACO) is a new population oriented search metaphor that has been successfully applied to $\mathcal{NP}$-hard combinatorial optimization problems. In this paper we discuss parallelization strategies for Ant Colony Optimization algorithms. We empirically test the most simple strategy, that of executing parallel independent runs of an algorithm. The empirical tests are performed applying $\mathcal{MAX}$–$\mathcal{MIN}$ Ant System, one of the most efficient ACO algorithms, to the Traveling Salesman Problem and show that using parallel independent runs is very effective.

1 Introduction

Ant Colony Optimization (ACO) is a new population based search metaphor inspired by the foraging behavior of real ants. Among the basic ideas underlying ACO is to use an algorithmic counterpart to the *pheromone trail*, used by real ants, as a medium for communication among a colony of artificial ants. The seminal work on ACO is Ant System [9, 11] which was first proposed for solving the Traveling Salesman Problem (TSP). In Ant System, the ants are simple agents that are used to construct tours, guided by the pheromone trail and heuristic information based on intercity distances. Since the work on Ant System, several improvements of the basic algorithm have been proposed including Ant Colony System [10], $\mathcal{MAX}$–$\mathcal{MIN}$ Ant System [24] and the rank-based version of Ant System [4]. Additionally, the performance of ACO algorithms can be significantly enhanced by adding a local search phase in which solutions are improved by a local search procedure [10, 23, 16]. Thus, the most efficient ACO algorithms are actually hybrid algorithms consisting of a solution construction mechanism and a subsequent local search phase.

Ant Colony Optimization approaches are population based, i.e., a population of agents is used to find a desired goal. Population based approaches are naturally suited for parallel processing. Yet, for population oriented search procedures several possibilities of exploiting parallelism exist and their applicability depends strongly on the particular problem they are applied to and on the hardware available. In this article we discuss possibilities of parallel processing for the most efficient ACO algorithms on MIMD architectures. In particular, we motivate and investigate the execution of parallel independent runs of ACO algorithms. We show that high quality solutions can be achieved by such an approach presenting computational results for one of the currently most efficient ACO algorithm for the TSP, $\mathcal{MAX}$–$\mathcal{MIN}$ Ant System.

The paper is organized as follows. To make the paper self-contained, we first introduce Ant Colony Optimization and the application of $\mathcal{MM}$AS to the TSP. In Section 3 we motivate the use of parallel independent runs and discuss other possibilities of parallel processing for ACO algorithms. The computational results are presented and discussed in Section 4. The paper ends discussing related work and outlining future work.

2 Ant Colony Optimization

2.1 Ant Colony Optimization applied to the TSP

The TSP is the problem of finding a shortest closed tour through a set of n cities traversing every city exactly once. A symmetric TSP can be represented by a complete weighted graph G with n nodes, the weights being the intercity distances $d_{ij} = d_{ji}$ between cities i and j. The TSP is a $\mathcal{NP}$-hard optimization problem and is used as a standard benchmark for many heuristic algorithms [13]. Like many other general purpose approaches, Ant System, which is the seminal work on Ant Colony Optimization, has been motivated presenting its application to the TSP.

$\mathcal{MAX}$–$\mathcal{MIN}$ Ant System is one of the enhancements of Ant System and shares important features like the tour construction mechanism with Ant System. It is a population based approach using m ants. To solve TSPs each edge of the graph has associated a pheromone level τ_{ij} that is updated by the ants during algorithm execution. The pheromone level is a desirability measure, the higher is the pheromone level of an edge the higher should be the probability an ant uses this specific edge. Additionally, the ants may also use heuristic information that in case of the TSP is chosen as $\eta_{ij} = 1/d_{ij}$, giving preference to short intercity connections. To construct a tour, each ant is initially set on a randomly chosen city. Then, in each step an ant selects from its current city i one of the cities it has not yet visited according to the following probability distribution:

$$
p_{ij} = \begin{cases} \dfrac{\tau_{ij}^{\alpha} \cdot \eta_{ij}^{\beta}}{\sum_{k \ not \ visited} \tau_{ik}^{\alpha} \cdot \eta_{ik}^{\beta}} & if \text{ city } j \text{ is not yet visited} \\ 0 & otherwise \end{cases}
\tag{1}
$$

The probability distribution for the selection of the next city is biased by parameters α and β which determine the relative influence of the trail strength and the heuristic information. To keep track of the cities already visited, every ant maintains a list, that is used to store its partial tour. After all ants have constructed a complete tour and have calculated the tour length, the trails are updated. Similar to ACS, in $\mathcal{MMAS}$ only one ant (corresponding to the ant with the iteration best tour or the ant with the best tour found during the run of the algorithm) is allowed to update the trails whereas in Ant System all ants lay down some pheromone. The trail intensities are updated according to:

$$
\tau_{ij}^{new} = \rho \cdot \tau_{ij}^{old} + \Delta\tau_{ij}
\tag{2}
$$

where ρ, with $0 < \rho < 1$, is the persistence of the trail, thus $1 - \rho$ models the trail evaporation. The lower ρ, the faster the information gathered in previous iterations is forgotten. The amount $\Delta\tau_{ij}$ is equal to $1/L_{\text{best}}$, if edge $[i, j]$ is used by the updating ant on its tour, otherwise zero. L_{best} is the tour length of the trail updating ant. Thus, frequently used edges receive a higher amount of pheromone and will be selected more often in future cycles of the algorithm. The two basic steps *tour construction* according to (1) and *trail update* according to (2) are then repeated for a given number of iterations or for some maximally allowed computation time. We refer to the complete cycle of tour construction and trail update as one iteration.

The main differences between $\mathcal{MMAS}$ and Ant System are that in $\mathcal{MMAS}$ only one ant is allowed to provide a feedback mechanism by updating the trails and that the trails are limited to an interval between some maximum and minimum possible values τ_{max} and τ_{min}. A minor difference is that in $\mathcal{MMAS}$ the trails are initialized to their maximum value τ_{max}. Minimum and maximum trail limits are used to keep the exploration of new tours on a sufficiently high level. In particular, the trail limits are used to counteract premature stagnation of the search. Stagnation may occur if the differences between the trail intensities on the edges get so high that the same tours are constructed again and again. On the other side, the trail limits should not be too tight to allow exploitation of the search experience accumulated by the pheromone trails.

2.2 Adding Local Search

The nowadays most efficient ACO algorithms use local search algorithms to improve the solutions constructed by the ants, i.e., they are hybrid algorithms. The performance of hybrid algorithms often depends crucially on the kind of local search procedure that is used to improve solutions. For example, when applying genetic local search algorithms to the TSP, it has been shown that the best performance is obtained using the sophisticated Lin-Kernighan local search algorithm [28]. Yet, an efficient implementation of the Lin-Kernighan heuristic is rather involved, thus, for simplicity we use 3-opt as a local search procedure [15]. Our implementation of 3-opt is sped up using standard techniques as described in [2, 13]. In particular, we perform a fixed-radius nearest neighbor search and use *don't look bits* for the outer loop optimization, see [2] for details on these techniques.

In Table 1 we present results for the sequential version of $\mathcal{MMAS}$ on some TSP instances taken from TSPLIB [20]. All ants are allowed to improve their solution after every iteration. As parameter setting we used $\alpha = 1, \beta = 2, \tau_{max} = L_{best}/(1 - \rho)$, $\tau_{min} = \tau_{max}/2n$. For instances with $n < 500$ we use 10 ants, for larger instances 25. The runs are performed on a Sun UltraSparc II Workstation with two UltraSparc I 167MHz processors with 0.5MB external cache. Due to the sequential implementation of the algorithm only one processor is used. The computational results are one of the best obtained so far with an ACO approach applied to the TSP. Compared to other algorithms, the genetic algorithm of [19] and those using the sophisticated Lin-Kernighan algorithm [17, 13, 18] perform better.

Table 1. Performance of the sequential implementation of $\mathcal{MMAS}$ on several symmetric TSP instances. Averages over 10 runs. Given are the best solution found, the average solution quality and the worst solution found. The number in the instance descriptor is the number of cities in each instance, see text for more details. Additionally we give the average time to find the best solution, the maximally allowed computation time and the average number of iterations to find the best solution in a run.

Instance	Optimum	Best	Average	Worst	avg.time	max.time	avg.iterations
d198	15780	15780	15780.3	15781	43.4	300	236.1
lin318	42029	42029	42029	42029	132.7	450	494.2
pcb442	50778	50785	50886.5	50912	288.7	900	1164.5
att532	27686	27703	27707.4	27728	429.0	1800	561.2
rat783	8806	8806	8811.5	8821	935.2	2100	878.2
pcb1173	56892	56892	56960.3	57091	3728.7	4500	1837.4
d1291	50801	50801	50845.8	50909	2482.5	4500	1054.1

3 Parallelization Strategies

Ant Colony Optimization as a population-based search metaphor is as such inherently parallel. Yet, there is no golden rule for how to parallelize ACO algorithms. How to parallelize ACO algorithms efficiently, depends strongly on the available computing platform and the problem to which the algorithm is applied. Today a very common way to parallelization is given by MIMD architectures like, e.g., a cluster of workstations. In our discussion we concentrate on parallelization possibilities in such an environment.

3.1 Parallel runs of one algorithm

The most simple way to obtain a parallel version of an algorithm is the parallel independent execution on k processors of the sequential algorithm. Using parallel independent runs is appealing as basically no communication overhead is involved and nearly no additional implementation effort is necessary. Of course, using independent runs of an algorithm in parallel is only useful if the underlying algorithm is randomized, i.e., if the search process relies on random decisions. ACO algorithms and $\mathcal{MMAS}$, in particular, are such algorithms as, for example, the tour construction process is highly random. To describe the performance of a randomized heuristic algorithm, we may adopt one of the following two points of view. On the one hand, we can describe the solution quality obtained after executing an algorithm for time t by a random variable C_t with associated distribution function $F_t(c)$. Alternatively, if we fix a required solution quality, say, $q\%$ above a lower bound or a known optimal solution, we can view the algorithm dependent run-time needed to find such a solution as a random-variable T_q with distribution $G_q(t)$.[1] Knowledge of both distributions can give very helpful indication on the effectiveness of parallel independent runs.

In case of parallel independent runs the best solution of the k runs is taken as the final solution. In such a situation we are interested in the solution quality distribution of *best-of-k* runs. Given the distribution $F_t(c)$, the distribution function of $C_t^{\prime k}$, the random variable corresponding to the final solution quality of best-of-k runs, can easily be calculated as $F_t^k(c) = 1 - (1 - F_t(c))^k$ in case of minimization problems. Alternatively, if we require the algorithm to reach a given bound on the solution quality, the runs are stopped as soon one process reaches such a bound. Again, the run-time distribution $G_q^{\prime k}(t)$ for executing k runs in parallel can be calculated as $G_q^k(t) = 1 - (1 - G_q(t))^k$. Performing parallel independent runs is efficient if the run-time is exponentially distributed, as in this case optimal speed-up is obtained. The main effect of performing multiple independent runs is that the solution quality distributions and the run-time distribution will get more peaked and be shifted to the left.

To judge the effectiveness of using parallel independent runs, the sequential version and the parallel version should be given the same CPU-time. Thus, one should compare the solution quality distribution $F_t^k(c)$ running k times the algorithms for time t with the distribution $F_{t \cdot k}(c)$ of executing a single run of the algorithm for time $t \cdot k$. Results can more easily be compared, for example, using the expected solution quality $E[C_t^k]$ and $E[C_{kt}]$. In case $E[C_t^k] = E[C_{kt}]$, and the variances of C_t^k and C_{kt} are similar, we could talk of an "optimal" speed-up, as the time needed to reach a specific solution quality in time t with k runs is the same as the average solution quality obtained with 1 run of time

---

[1] Actually, we should speak of a two-dimensional random variable (T, Q). $G_q(t)$ and $F_t(c)$ are simply the marginal distributions of (T, Q).

$k \cdot t.^2$ In case of $E[C_t^k] < E[C_{kt}]$ the resulting "speed-up" could even be regarded as "super-optimal". Similar arguments apply to run-time distributions. For a discussion of how to calculate speed-up in this case we refer to [27].

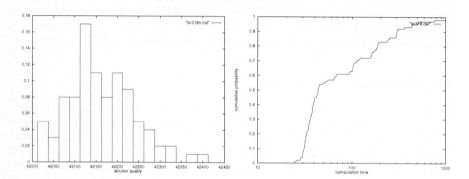

Fig. 1. On the left side histogram of the solution quality for $\mathcal{MMAS}$ on lin318 after $t = 20$sec. On the right side the cumulative run-time distribution is given for obtaining the optimal solution value of 42029. Based on 100 independent runs of $\mathcal{MMAS}$.

To give an idea on the shape of the distributions, we present in Figure 1 a histogram of the solution quality (left side) and the run-time distribution (right side) for the application of $\mathcal{MMAS}$ to TSPLIB instance lin318. As can be observed, the histogram of the solution quality is multimodal. In this case, repeated execution of the algorithm for the given time bound will significantly increase the probability of finding high quality solutions. The run-time distribution on the right of Figure 1 indicates that, with a high probability, the optimal solution is found fast ($G(60) = 0.57$). Yet, for longer run-times the distribution is much less inclined. In such a situation parallel independent runs may be effective. For example, the probability that 5 parallel independent runs find the optimal solution within 60 sec is $1 - (1 - G(60))^5 = 0.985$. For the sequential algorithm, using the same overall run-time, we get $G(300) = 0.88$, lower than for running the algorithm five times for 60 secs.[3] Looking at the curve again, it is noteworthy that a certain time t_{init} is needed by $\mathcal{MMAS}$ until an optimal solution can be found with a probability larger than zero. This effect will limit the obtainable speed-up by performing parallel independent runs. In case only very short computation times are allowed, parallelization has to be used to speed up the execution of a single run to get a reasonable solution quality, see next section for a short discussion of this issue.

Instead of running one algorithm with *one* particular parameter setting independently on k processors, it may also prove advantageous to run one algorithm with different search strategies or different parameter settings. Such an approach is specially appealing in case an algorithm's performance on different problem instances depends on the algorithm's parameter settings. In case of the application of $\mathcal{MMAS}$ to the TSP, we did not notice significant dependencies of the algorithm's parameter settings on particular problem instances, one fixed setting appeared to perform generally well. Yet, such a strategy

---

[2] Usually, speed-up is defined w.r.t. an optimal sequential algorithm. Here we use speed-up to compare a parallel version of an algorithm with its sequential version.

[3] In this case the run-time distribution is below an exponential distribution, thus, even "super-optimal" speed-ups may be obtained for a low number of independent runs.

using different local search procedures should prove successful when applying $\mathcal{MMAS}$ or other nature-inspired algorithms to the Quadratic Assignment Problem, as in this case the algorithms performance depends strongly on the instance type [22, 26].

Still, more improvement over using parallel independent runs may be gained by cooperation in form of solution exchanges among the search processes. Similar to parallel approaches for genetic algorithms like the island-model, communication among the ant colonies solving a particular problem could take place by exchanging of ants with very good solutions among the single ant colonies. These ants then may modify the pheromone trails of other ant colonies. Other possibilities would be to exchange or combine whole pheromone matrices among the ant colonies to influence the search direction of the others. A study of these possibilities is intended for future research, for the experimental investigation we concentrate on parallel independent runs.

3.2 Speeding up a single run

In case that only very low computation time is available, another possibility of parallel processing is to speed up a single run of an algorithm. A first implementation of Ant System on a transputer and a connection machine has been presented in [3]. In [5] parallelization strategies for Ant System have been discussed, presenting synchronous and asynchronous master-slave schemes for Ant System. Here, we extend the work of [5] by considering alternative schemes of speeding up runs of ACO algorithms like Ant Colony System [10] or $\mathcal{MAX}$–$\mathcal{MIN}$ Ant System [23] that rely strongly on local search applications.

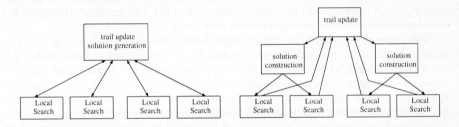

Fig. 2. Parallelization by Master–Slave approach, see text for details.

In case local search algorithms are used to improve solutions, one possibility of parallel processing consists in a master-slave approach. One master processor is used to update the main data structures for the ACO algorithm, constructs initial solutions for the local search algorithms, and sends the solutions to other processors which improve them by local search. The master collects these locally optimal solutions and in case a sufficient number of such solutions have arrived, it updates the trail matrix before constructing more solutions. This situation, also implementable in asynchronous mode, is depicted in Figure 2 on the left side. Such a parallelization scheme is particularly interesting if the update of the trails and the construction of solutions consumes much less time than the local search. This, for example, is the case when applying ACO algorithms to the Quadratic Assignment Problem [16, 22, 14]. In this case the construction of solutions and the update of the trail matrix is of complexity $O(n^2)$, whereas the local search is of complexity $O(n^3)$. Profiler data for the sequential algorithm $\mathcal{MMAS}$ show that roughly 99% of the time is spent improving the solutions by local search. Yet, for the application of $\mathcal{MMAS}$ or ACS to the TSP the situation is completely different. For the TSP the local search runs very fast using the implementation tricks described in [2]. In general, only roughly 70 - 80% of the time is spent by the local search, roughly 10 - 15% of the time is spent constructing tours and 5-10% of the time is needed for updating the trail matrix.[4] In this case, for a parallel implementation on several processors, a situation like that depicted in Figure 2 on the right side might be preferable. One processor keeps the main data structures for the trail matrix and updates it. One or several other processors can use the trail matrix to construct solutions and send those to the processors that local search to these solutions. The improved solutions are sent back to the main processor. Again, communication can be done in asynchronous mode. A major disadvantage of these approaches is that communication has to take place frequently. In general, the obtainable speed-up by such an architecture will be less than optimal due to the communication overhead.

4 Experimental Results

In this section we present computational results for the execution of parallel independent runs of $\mathcal{MMAS}$ with up to 10 processes. It is difficult to calculate the exact speed-up for parallel independent runs, because the solutions quality has to be taken into account. To circumvent this problem we concentrate on the following experimental setting. We compare the average solution quality of $\mathcal{MMAS}$ running k times for time limit t_{max}/k to that of a single run of time t_{max}. Like noted in Section 3.1, for very short run-times the solution quality for $\mathcal{MMAS}$ will be rather poor, as the algorithm needs some initialization time t_{init} to have a reasonably high chance to find high quality solutions.[5] Also, t_{init} will increase with increasing dimension of the TSP instance. Therefore, the computation times were chosen roughly in such a way that $t_{max}/k \geq t_{init}$.

The experimental results are presented in Table 2 for several values of k. The two smallest instances are regularly solved to optimality, for d198 only in few runs the optimal solution has not been found. The effect of using parallel independent runs for these two instances can be noted in the reduction of the average time needed until the optimal solution is found. For example, for lin318 with 6 independent runs, the mean time to find the optimal solution is 22.0 sec as opposed to 132.7 for the sequential version. Thus, the obtained speed-up would be $t_1/t_6 = 6.03$, for 10 independent runs the speed-up would be 6.7. For larger problem instances, the best average results are always obtained with $k \geq 2$ runs of the algorithm. Due to the increased number of executions of the algorithm, the probability to get stuck at a rather bad solution is low, therefore the average solution quality increases.

Note, that this way to investigate the effect of parallelization is strongly related to an often posed question for Simulated Annealing algorithms: Is it preferable to execute one long Simulated Annealing run of time t_{max} or is it better to execute k short runs of time t_{max}/k [8]? The experimental results presented here suggest, as it was the case with Simulated Annealing, that an increased solution quality with $\mathcal{MMAS}$ can be obtained by restarting the sequential algorithm after some given time bound. We are convinced

---

[4] This situation is worse, in case 2-opt is used as local search procedure. Then roughly 50% of the time is spent for the trail update and the tour construction. Nevertheless, the situation would be better if the Lin-Kernighan heuristic is used for the local search, as it is usually more time consuming.

[5] This is not a particular problem of $\mathcal{MMAS}$, but any optimization algorithm will need some time t_{init} to find very high quality solutions for the TSP.

Table 2. Performance of parallel independent runs for $\mathcal{MMAS}$ on symmetric TSP instances. Averages over 10 runs (except for d1291, 5 runs), for 1 (sequential case) to 10 parallel independent runs. Given are the average solution quality reached, the best average solution quality is indicated in bold face. The parameter settings for $\mathcal{MMAS}$ are those presented in Section 2. t_{max} is the maximally allowed time for the sequential algorithm, computation times refer to a UltraSparc I processor (167MHz).

Instance	t_{max}	1	2	4	6	8	10
d198	300	15780.3	15780	15780.1	15780	15780	15780
lin318	450	42029	42029	42029	42029	42029	42029
pcb442	900	50886.5	50873.0	50875.3	**50852.7**	50862.9	50860.6
att532	1800	27707.4	27702.5	27702.1	27703.5	27702.3	**27699.0**
rat783	2100	8811.5	8810.8	**8809.5**	8810.6	8810.8	8813.1
pcb1173	4500	56960.3	56960.9	56922.4	**56912.6**	56929.7	56969.1
d1291	4500	50845.8	**50809.0**	50821.8	50825.2	50826.6	50830.0

that this observation also holds for a variety of other regularly used search metaphors like Genetic Algorithms.

5   Related Work

Parallelization strategies are widely investigated in the area of Evolutionary Algorithms, see [6] for an overview. In [21] the performance of parallel independent runs of genetic algorithms has been investigated theoretically and on some test problem "superlinear" speed-up could be observed. Most parallelization strategies can be classified into *fine-grained* and *coarse-grained* approaches. Characteristic of fine-grained approaches is that very few, often only one, individuals are assigned to one processors and individuals are connected by a *population-structure*. An example of an implementation of such an approach for the TSP is ASPARAGOS [12] that was able to find very good solutions to the TSP instance att532. A typical example of a coarse grained approach is the *island*-genetic algorithm in which the population of a genetic algorithm is divided into several subpopulations. Communication takes place by exchanging individuals at certain time-points among the subpopulations.

Using independent runs is also studied for Simulated Annealing. The question to answer is whether it is profitable to execute one long run or in the same time several short runs [8]. For an introduction to concepts of parallel Simulated Annealing see [1]. Similarly, parallel, independent runs are also investigated for Tabu Search. In [25] it is argued that in case the run-time to find an optimal solution to QAPs is exponentially distributed, optimal speed-up using independent runs of the algorithm can be obtained. In fact, empirical evidence is given that the run-time distribution is very close to an exponential distribution. In [27] parallel independent runs of Tabu Search are investigated for the Job-Shop problem. A classification of parallel Tabu Search metaheuristics is presented in [7].

6 Conclusions

For many modern randomized algorithmic approaches to combinatorial optimization, parallelization strategies have been examined. We start the discussion of parallelization possibilities of the most efficient Ant Colony Optimization algorithms. The parallelization strategy to be used depends on the particular problem one has to solve and the available hardware. Of special appeal to randomized algorithms like Ant Colony Optimization approaches is the use of parallel independent runs. Our experimental investigation of this strategy for one particular ACO algorithm, $\mathcal{MAX}$–$\mathcal{MIN}$ Ant System, on the Traveling Salesman Problem has shown that such a simple parallelization scheme can be highly efficient. More elaborate mechanisms are only justified if they give better performance than the execution of independent runs.

One line of future research is to investigate the effectiveness of parallel ACO algorithms on other problems like the QAP. Of even larger interest is the investigation of the benefit of using cooperation among the single runs of the algorithm. Here, previous investigations on fine-grained parallelization of genetic algorithms and the island-model seem to suggest that still some performance improvement can be obtained by cooperation among parallel processes.

References

1. E. Aarts and J. Korst. *Simulated Annealing and Boltzman Machines – A Stochastic Apporach to Combinatorial Optimization and Neural Computation.* John Wiley & Sons, 1989.
2. J.J. Bentley. Fast Algorithms for Geometric Traveling Salesman Problems. *ORSA Journal on Computing*, 4(4):387–411, 1992.
3. M. Bolondi and M. Bondanza. Parallelizzazione di un Algoritmo per la Risoluzione del Problema del Commesso Viaggiatore. Master's thesis, Politecnico di Milano, 1993.
4. B. Bullnheimer, R.F. Hartl, and C. Strauss. A New Rank Based Version of the Ant System — A Computational Study. Technical report, University of Viena, 1997.
5. B. Bullnheimer, G. Kotsis, and C. Strauss. Parallelization Strategies for the Ant System. Technical Report POM 9/97, University of Vienna, 1997.
6. E. Cantú-Paz. A Survey of Parallel Genetic Algorithms. Technical Report IlliGAL 97003, University of Illinois at Urbana-Champaign, 1997.
7. T.G. Crainic, M. Toulouse, and M. Gendreau. Toward a Taxonomy of Parallel Tabu Search Heuristics. *INFORMS Journal on Computing*, 9(1):61–72, 1997.
8. N. Dodd. Slow Annealing Versus Multiple Fast Annealing Runs – An Empirical Investigation. *Parallel Computing*, 16:269–272, 1990.
9. M. Dorigo. *Optimization, Learning, and Natural Algorithms.* PhD thesis, Politecnico di Milano, 1992.
10. M. Dorigo and L.M. Gambardella. Ant Colony System: A Cooperative Learning Approach to the Traveling Salesman Problem. *IEEE Transactions on Evolutionary Computation*, 1(1):53–66, 1997.
11. M. Dorigo, V. Maniezzo, and A. Colorni. The Ant System: Optimization by a Colony of Cooperating Agents. *IEEE Transactions on Systems, Man, and Cybernetics – Part B*, 26(1):29–41, 1996.
12. M. Gorges-Schleuter. Comparison of Local Mating Strategies in Massively Parallel Genetic Algorithms. In *PPSN-II*, pages 553–562, 1992.
13. D.S. Johnson and L.A. McGeoch. The Traveling Salesman Problem: A Case Study in Local Optimization. In E.H.L. Aarts and J.K. Lenstra, editors, *Local Search in Combinatorial Optimization.* John-Wiley and Sons, Ltd., 1997.
14. E.D. Taillard L. Gambardella and M. Dorigo. Ant Colonies for the QAP. Technical Report IDSIA-4-97, IDSIA, 1997.

15. S. Lin. Computer Solutions of the Traveling Salesman Problem. *Bell Systems Technology Journal*, 44:2245–2269, 1965.
16. V. Maniezzo, M. Dorigo, and A. Colorni. The Ant System Applied to the Quadratic Assignment Problem. Technical Report IRIDIA/94-28, Université Libre de Bruxelles, Belgium, 1994.
17. Olivier C. Martin and Steve W. Otto. Combining Simulated Annealing with Local Search Heuristics. *Annals of Operations Research*, 63:57–75, 1996.
18. P. Merz and B. Freisleben. Genetic Local Search for the TSP: New Results. In *Proc. of the IEEE Conf. on Evol. Comp. (ICEC'97)*, pages 159–164, 1997.
19. Y. Nagata and S. Kobayashi. Edge Assembly Crossover: A High-power Genetic Algorithm for the Traveling Salesman Problem. In *Proc. of ICGA'97*, pages 450–457, 1997.
20. G. Reinelt. TSPLIB — A Traveling Salesman Problem Library. *ORSA Journal On Computing*, 3:376–384, 1991.
21. R. Shonkwiler. Parallel Genetic Algorithms. In *Proceedings of ICGA'93*, 1993.
22. T. Stützle. $\mathcal{MAX}$-$\mathcal{MIN}$ Ant System for the Quadratic Assignment Problem. Technical Report AIDA–97–4, TH Darmstadt, July 1997.
23. T. Stützle and H. Hoos. The $\mathcal{MAX}$-$\mathcal{MIN}$ Ant System and Local Search for the Traveling Salesman Problem. In *IEEE Conf. on Evol. Comp. (ICEC'97)*, pages 309–314, 1997.
24. T. Stützle and H. Hoos. Improvements on the Ant System: Introducing $\mathcal{MAX}$-$\mathcal{MIN}$ Ant System. In *Proceedings of ICANNGA'97*. Springer Verlag, Wien, 1997.
25. É.D. Taillard. Robust Taboo Search for the Quadratic Assignment Problem. *Parallel Computing*, 17:443–455, 1991.
26. É.D. Taillard. Comparison of Iterative Searches for the Quadratic Assignment Problem. *Location Science*, pages 87–105, 1995.
27. H.M.M. ten Eikelder, B.J.M. Aarts, M.G.A. Verhoeven, and E.H.L. Aarts. Sequential and Parallel Local Search Algorithms for Job Shop Scheduling. Paper presented at the Metaheuristics conference 1997, 1997.
28. N.L.J. Ulder, E.H.L. Aarts, H.-J. Bandelt, P.J.M. van Laarhoven, and E.Pesch. Genetic Local Search Algorithms for the Traveling Salesman Problem. In *Proceedings PPSN-I*, number 496 in LNCS, pages 109–116. Springer Verlag, 1991.

Self-Organising Pattern Formation: Fruit Flies and Cell Phones

Richard Tateson

BT Laboratories, Martlesham Heath, Ipswich IP5 3RE, UK

Abstract. The bristles of the fruit fly, *Drosophila*, form part of the peripheral nervous system of the animal. The pattern of these bristles in the adult is produced by self-organisation of cell types during embryonic and larval development. The mechanism of bristle differentiation has been the inspiration for the optimisation algorithm presented here. The algorithm is used to produce a dynamic channel plan for a cell phone network. Radio channels are a scarce resource and minimising interference is a significant problem for mobile network operators.

1. Introduction

1.1 Growing A Channel Allocation Plan

The purpose of the work presented here is to show how the mechanisms of bristle differentiation in the fruit fly can be used as an inspiration for an online dynamic channel allocation algorithm. The self-organising nature of the fruit fly developmental process is preserved and with it the advantages of robustness and flexibility. The mechanisms used so effectively by nature to ensure that two adjacent fruit fly cells do not both make bristles can be adapted to ensure that two nearby cell phone cells do not use the same channel.

Producing an efficient channel allocation plan is not only an important part of running an efficient mobile network, it is a formidable abstract mathematical problem. In a network of j base stations with k available channels the number of different ways of allocating l channels to each cell is:

$$\left(\frac{k!}{((k-l)!)(l!)} \right)^{j}$$

For example there are 6×10^{253} different ways of assigning 4 channels out of 29 to each base station in a 58 base station network. Clearly an exhaustive search of solution space is not an appropriate method for optimising such a problem. Various algorithms have been applied to this problem including 'subspace approach' (Lochtie and Mehler 1995), simulated annealing (Aarts and Korst 1989) and neural networks (Kunz 1991). Lochtie et al (1997) compare various methods.

1.2 Bristle Differentiation

The developing fruitfly, in common with most multicellular organisms, accomplishes the task of creating and positioning different cell types with exquisite precision. This is achieved not by a central controller dictating a grand plan but by a combination of short and medium range interactions among the cells themselves.

One example of this is the development of the sensory bristles on the back of the adult fly (Figure 1). Each bristle arises from a single cell and is separated from its neighbouring bristles by several epidermal cells (Stern 1954). How is the correct pattern of these two different cell types, bristle and epidermal, produced?

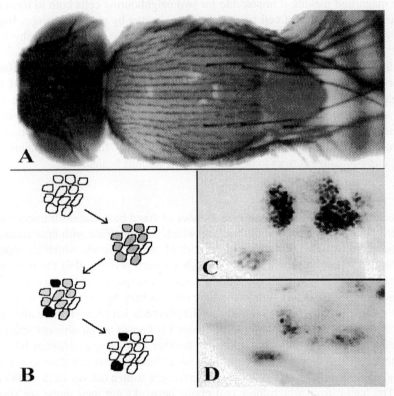

Figure 1 Neural differentiation in *Drosophila*. (A) The adult fly showing the evenly spaced bristles on the back. (B) A schematic of the process of selecting the cells which will make bristles. All cells are initially equivalent, some acquire bristle potential and some of these realise that potential by inhibiting their neighbours. (C and D) Tissue from the developing fly stained to reveal cells with bristle potential. Many cells initially stain (C) but eventually only a few cells retain bristle potential (D)   (A, C and D taken from Tateson 1998)

The crucial events take place during late larval life in a layer of cells just one cell thick. Large groups of cells have already acquired the potential to make bristles (Cubas et al 1991, Ruiz-Gomez and Ghysen 1993). A small number of well spaced bristle-forming cells must be selected from these groups of cells. The rest of the cells form the cuticle of the fly instead

The mechanisms involved are well characterised (reviewed by Artavanis et al 1995): the essence of the process is a mutually inhibitory interaction among all the cells; each cell tries to assert its own ability to form a bristle and in so doing dissuade its neighbours from forming bristles (Heitzler and Simpson 1991).

At the molecular level inhibition is achieved by the production of a ligand which binds to a receptor on the surface of neighbouring cells (Fehon et al 1990). Binding inhibits the neighbouring cells from forming bristles and acts to reduce their own production of inhibitory ligand. Thus small initial differences in ligand production are magnified making it impossible for two neighbouring cells both to form bristles. The required pattern of cell types (bristles separated by cuticle) emerges from short range interactions among equivalent cells without any control hierarchy or externally imposed design. In other words it is a self-organising process.

Self-organisation is a good strategy for the development of a multicellular organism because it allows a precise outcome to be reached without the need for very high precision in the mechanism. If the form of the adult fruitfly had to be achieved by 'dumb' cells merely carrying out the explicit instructions of a distant controller then damage to the embryo or a tiny error in interpreting the instructions of the controller would be magnified into a catastrophic flaw in the adult. Self-organisation allows errors to be corrected and wounds healed.

1.3 Cell Phone Channel Planning

A cell phone network consists of a number of fixed base station transceivers and a much larger number of mobile handsets which communicate with base stations via a radio channel. There is a limited number of radio channels which the operator is permitted to use and there are not enough for each phone call in the network to be carried on a different channel. Thus a central principle of such networks is channel reuse (Lee 1989): at any time many base stations may be transceiving on each channel. This introduces the possibility of interference between phone calls. Interference from other calls using the same channel is known as 'co-channel interference'. 'Adjacent channel' interference, due to another call using a different but 'nearby' channel, is also a problem: a call made on a channel corresponding to a frequency band of 4000 - 4025 kHz is liable to interference from a call on 4025 - 4050 kHz.

The 'cells' from which these cell phone networks get their name are simply the coverage areas of base stations (Figure 2). The problem facing the network operator is to allocate channels to base stations such that demand for channels across the network is met while keeping interference below acceptable levels. These aims are clearly in conflict: the more channels allocated to each base station the harder it is to plan the channel reuse to avoid unacceptable interference.

An added difficulty is that the demand across the network is neither uniform nor static. Some cells will experience high demand at particular times of the day but lower than average demand for the rest of the day, for example cells containing major arteries of commuter traffic. Even worse, for efficient channel allocation, are the unpredictable fluctuations in demand resulting from a road accident for example.

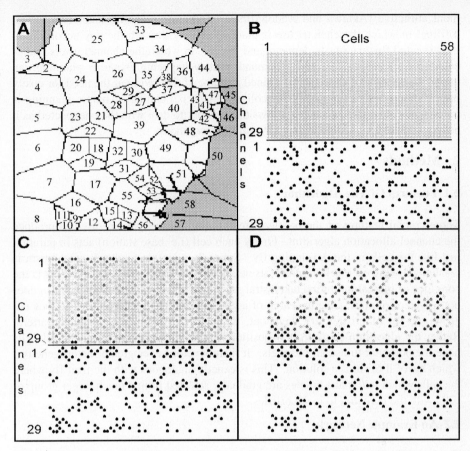

Figure 2 Panel A is a map of a 58 cell mobile phone network in East Anglia, UK (redrawn from Lochtie and Mehler 1995). Panels B to D show channel usage and corresponding solutions at progressively later stages of optimisation. In each case the upper half of the panel shows the simulated, partial usage of each of 29 channels in each of the 58 cells of the network (the darker the dot, the higher the usage). The lower panel shows the solution which is extracted from this simulated usage. The solution is 'black and white' - a channel is either used (black) or not (white). Initially simulated usage is homogeneous and the solution is random (B). As time goes on the simulated usage becomes more heterogeneous and the extracted solution can be seen to be drawn from the simulated usage with few ambiguities (D).

It is currently common practice for operators to use a fixed channel allocation plan. The channels used by any particular base station do not change over the course of a day, or even a week. Changes to the plan, as well as the construction of new base stations, will be undertaken every few months if necessary to meet quality of service criteria. New base station technology, allowing speedy changes in channel use by base stations, is making the idea of dynamic channel allocation planning more attractive (Akaiwa and Andoh 1993). Dynamic planning takes two forms: 'offline' in which the channel use is planned to vary through the day according to the expected fluctuations in demand, and 'online' in which the channel use is reallocated in response to changes in demand as they happen. Dynamic planning can allow quality of service to be maintained as demand rises without the need for costly base station construction (Delli Priscoli et al 1997). 'Online' dynamic planning is particularly attractive because it allows the network to deal with the unexpected as it happens. Fixed, or offline, plans may fail in emergencies.

2. Methods

2.1 Features Of The Algorithm

Three crucial features of the bristle differentiation mechanism are used to produce the channel allocation algorithm. Firstly each cell (i.e. base station) acts in parallel, just like the cells in the developing fly. Secondly a simple feedback mechanism is created allowing each cell to inhibit its neighbours from using a channel. This is the core idea of mutual inhibition taken straight from the fly. Finally the algorithm does not traverse solution space in search of a good solution just as the fruit fly does not grow one set of bristles, try them out, then grow a new set in a better pattern. Rather the algorithm starts from a position of near homogeneity in which all cells have the potential to use all channels. It then develops ever greater heterogeneities which move it towards a solution. This is exactly analogous with the fruit fly where the cells which *will* make bristles are gradually selected from a much larger group of cells with the *potential* to make bristles.

2.2 An Example Network

The example cell phone network to which the algorithm is applied is taken from Lochtie and Mehler (1995). It is a network in the East Anglian region of the UK with 58 base stations (figure 2) and 29 radio channels available to be allocated to those base stations.

Lochtie and Mehler (1995) report a subspace approach technique which allows a fixed, uniform demand for 4 channels in each cell to be successfully met without breaching their interference criteria. I have used the same interference criteria for the simulations reported below. These criteria are certainly an over-simplification. More subtle interference criteria could be incorporated into the simulation without increasing the computation time if the data were available.

2.3 Details Of The Algorithm

The process of producing a channel allocation plan begins with an initialisation phase of assembling the necessary information. This is followed by an iterative progression from homogeneity towards a solution. A solution can be extracted at any time but the quality of that solution improves as time goes on.

Initialisation: Firstly a co-channel interference table must be provided. This is a 58 x 58 table which gives a value to the strength with which each cell can cause interference in each other cell. Next a 58 x 58 adjacent channel interference table is needed. In both cases the full 58 x 58 table is used. Thus if better data is available concerning the interference values between two cells it can be incorporated into the relevant table without changing the number of computations per iteration

The next step is to obtain the demand for channels (i.e. the maximum number of simultaneous phone calls) which is to be met in each cell. This information can be changed as the algorithm runs allowing new solutions to be produced in response to unforeseen changes in demand.

A value for the noise parameter is also needed. This is the size of the uniform random distribution from which the initial differences between cells and the perturbations to which cells are subjected in every iteration are taken. For the simulations reported here, noise is 1% of the initial usage values unless otherwise stated.

Lastly the 'initial usage' of each channel in each cell must be determined. The idea of 'usage' is important and needs a bit of explanation. Each cell is imagined, for the purposes of the algorithm, to be partially using all 29 channels. At the start of the simulation all cells have almost equal 'usage' of all channels but as time goes on cells 'use' some channels more than others, depending on the inhibition they experience from their neighbours and from adjacent channels in the same cell. This idea of partial usage is purely a mechanism by which the algorithm moves *towards* a solution - it would never itself be a valid solution to the channel allocation problem. The job of producing a valid solution from the current usage values falls to the 'solution extractor' (see below).

Iteration: The iterative step simply involves calculating the new 'usage' of each channel in each cell based on the current 'usage' and the inhibition perceived by that cell on the channel in question. Inhibition is the sum of all the usages of that channel, or adjacent channels, by all the other cells multiplied by the appropriate interference table value. New Usage can then be calculated using the formula:

$$U_{jkt} = \frac{U_{jk(t-1)}}{(1+I_{jk})} + N$$

Where: U_{jkt} is usage of channel k in cell j at time t
I_{jk} is inhibition calculated for channel k in cell j
N is the noise parameter

Finally time t increments and the next iteration begins. This simulates synchronous update of cells. In effect the 58 cells work in parallel to solve the problem.

Solution Extraction: At any time a simple filter program can be used to produce a valid real solution from the current usage values (figure 2). Channels are allocated to a cell in descending order of their simulated usage in that cell until demand is met. Satisfying demand for channels is thus treated as a hard constraint.

3. Results

3.1 Uniform Demand

Lochtie and Mehler (1995) use subspace approach to produce a channel allocation plan with uniform demand for 4 channels. The plan gives zero interference according to their interference criteria which I have adopted. It was therefore of interest to see if the algorithm described here can eliminate interference when all cells demand 4 channels. Figure 3 shows the total interference in the network for various uniform levels of demand. In effect a solution has been extracted from the algorithm after every iteration and the interference corresponding to that solution is plotted.

In the case where uniform demand is 4 the algorithm rapidly finds a zero interference solution. Indeed the algorithm reproducibly finds zero interference solutions even when every cell demands 7 channels.

At demands of greater than 7 no zero interference solutions are expected and none is found. However, the algorithm still produces a marked downward trend in the interference.

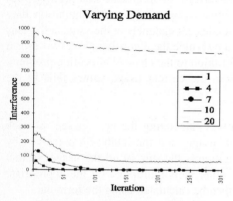

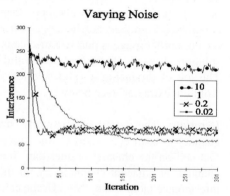

Figure 3 Optimisation to different levels of uniform demand across the network. Total network interference for the solution extracted at each iteration is shown   The key shows the number of channels used by each cell in the five simulations.

Figure 4   Optimisation to a uniform demand of 10 in every cell with different values chosen for the noise parameter. Once again total network interference for the solution extracted at each iteration is shown. The key shows noise values as percentage of initial usage.

The algorithm was applied to another channel allocation problem (Lochtie et al 1997) to allow comparison with simulated annealing as well as subspace approach. The search space was smaller in this example but the ratio of demand to available channels was higher. The quality of solutions produced was the same as subspace approach but lower than simulated annealing. This suggests that the strength of the algorithm may not be in finding the best solution but in its ability to move smoothly and dynamically from one good solution to another (see 3.4 below).

3.2 The Effect Of Noise

The influence of the noise parameter on the behaviour of the algorithm was tested by varying it in successive optimisation runs. In each case demand was 10 in all cells to ensure that no zero interference solutions exist and thereby making this a meaningful test of optimisation behaviour.

The results (figure 4) illustrate the dangers of low values for the noise parameter. When noise is set to 0.02 the algorithm reaches its asymptote within 40 iterations but this asymptote is not the global minimum. With a noise value of 1 the algorithm approaches its asymptote more slowly but finds a lower interference solution after 150 iterations. A noise value of 10 is sufficient to almost completely destroy the downward trend achieved by the mutually inhibitory mechanism. It results instead in a random search (and shows, in the process, the futility of such a search method).

3.3 Spreading The Load

The results so far have been presented as total interference in the network. This is a good measure of the performance of the algorithm because it shows to what degree the short range inhibition acting between cells, without any knowledge of the total interference for the whole network, is able to drive down the overall interference value. The success of the algorithm in finding low interference plans arises from the purely selfish, shortsighted response of each cell to inhibition.

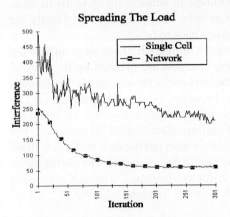

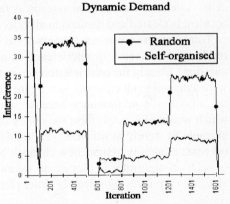

Figure 5 Comparing the trend in total network interference with the trend in highest interference in any single cell. Single cell interference has been multiplied by 58 for ease of direct comparison.

Figure 6 Simulated dynamic demand. Initially demand is uniformly 6 across the network and interference is successfully eliminated. At iteration 100 'rush hour' is simulated. At iteration 600 a road accident is simulated and traffic queues form in surrounding cells at iterations 800 and 1200.

However it is also important to measure the behaviour of the algorithm at the level of individual cells. It is possible that a channel planning algorithm could achieve an overall low network interference by making interference zero in most cells but high in one cell. Figure 5 shows results from a test designed to highlight such 'sacrificing'. A plot of the highest interference in any single cell is shown with the single cell value multiplied by 58 for comparison with total interference.

The interference in individual cells falls as the overall interference in the network falls. Interference is spread across many cells rather than concentrated in a few.

3.4 Dynamic Response

Testing the algorithm under conditions of uniform demand is useful in allowing comparison with earlier work and evaluation of basic behaviour of the algorithm. It does not, however, address the issue of dynamic, responsive channel allocation. A simulation of dynamic demand was created to see how well the algorithm deals with non-uniform, changing patterns of demand (figure 6).

The simulation begins with uniform demand of 6 and a zero interference solution is found. Rush hour then begins in three of the large towns covered by the network: Ipswich (cells 52, 53 and 54 in figure 2), Great Yarmouth (cells 41, 42, 43, 45, 46), and Norwich (cells 35, 36, 37 and 38). Demand in these cells rises abruptly to 10. A little later rush hour ends and demand returns to 6. An accident then occurs on the road to Norwich, cell 39. Demand in this cell rises to 10, traffic queues begin to form and spread to cells 27, 30 and 31 resulting in demand rising to 10 in those cells. Eventually congestion spreads as far as cells 37, 38, 32 and 34. Finally the accident is cleared and demand in all cells drops back to 6.

Total interference across the network is shown in figure 6. Each surge in demand results in an increase in interference as new channels are grabbed by the cells in question. Clearly the total interference in the network is far less than if 10 channels were assigned to all channels (see figure 4). However, this is not a good measure of the algorithm's performance because some trivial algorithms could be imagined which would also outperform the policy of uniform allocation of 10 channels. For example an algorithm which, having established a zero interference uniform 6 channel plan, randomly assigns new channels to meet rising demand. The performance of such an algorithm is plotted on figure 6 for comparison. The self-organising algorithm produces significantly better plans than this 'random' algorithm.

4. Discussion

The algorithm described in this paper is successful in producing good solutions to a difficult and industrially important problem. The algorithm rapidly finds better quality solutions than could be found by random search and compares well with another published technique (Lochtie and Mehler 1995).

The core of the analogy with bristle differentiation in *Drosophila* has been adhered to. The algorithm arrives at progressively better solutions by a process of mutual inhibition between cells. The cells have no global information and each acts only on the basis of the inhibition it perceives from its neighbours. The algorithm, just like the developing fruit fly, does not search solution space but instead moves through shades of grey towards a black and white solution (figure 2).

The method reported here also benefits from being well suited to online dynamic channel allocation. Changing demand for channels can be readily accommodated and the channel allocation plan already in use is altered to minimise the increase in interference resulting from use of the new channels.

The next step in testing the algorithm is to confront it with more realistic interference data. It would be interesting to see how the algorithm would perform in dealing with calls in a real mobile network, dynamically updating the plan in real time. Only access to genuine call records will make this type of simulation possible.

Finally there is the possibility of applying the basics of the self-organising algorithm to other problems which might be represented in a suitable way.

5. References

1. Aarts, E. and Korst, J.: *Simulated Annealing and Boltzmann Machines.* Wiley (1989)
2. Akaiwa, Y. and Andoh, H.: *Channel Segregation-A Self-Organized Dynamic Channel Allocation Method: Application To TDMA/FDMA Microcellular System.* . IEEE Journal On Selected Areas In Communications 11 (6) (1993) 949-954
3. Artavanis Tsakonas, S., Matsuno, K. and Fortini, M. E.: *Notch signalling.* Science 268 (1995) 225-232
4. Cubas, P., De Celis, J. F., Campuzano, S. and Modolell, J.: *Proneural clusters of achaete-scute expression and the generation of sensory organs in the Drosophila imaginal disc.* Genes and Development 5 (6) (1991) 996-1008
5. Delli Priscoli, F., Magnani, N. P., Palestini, V. and Sestini, F.: *Application Of Dynamic Channel Allocation To The GSM Cellular Network.* IEEE Journal On Selected Areas In Communications 15 (8) (1997) 1558-1566
6. Fehon, R. G., Kooh, P. J., Rebay, I., Regan, C. L., Xu, T., Muskavitch, M. and Artavanis Tsakonas, S.: *Molecular-interactions between the protein products of the neurogenic loci Notch and Delta, two EGF-homologous genes in Drosophila.* Cell 61 (1990) 523-534
7. Heitzler, P. and Simpson, P.: The choice of cell fate in the epidermis of Drosophila. Cell 64 (1991) 1083-1092
8. Kunz, D.: *Channel Assignment For Cellular Radio Using Neural Networks.* IEEE Transactions on Vehicular Technology 40 (1) (1991) 188-193
9. Lee, W. C. Y. : *Mobile Cellular Telecommunications Systems.* McGraw-Hill Book Company, New York (1989)
10. Lochtie, G. D. and Mehler, M. J.: *Subspace Approach To Channel Assignment In Mobile Communications.* IEE Proceedings Communications 142 (3) (1995) 179-185
11. Lochtie, G. D., van Eijl, C. A. and Mehler, M.J.: *Comparison Of Energy Minimising Algorithms For Channel Assignment In Mobile Radio Networks.* In: Proceedings of the 8th IEEE International Symposium on Personal Indoor and Mobile Radio Communications (PIMRC'97) 3 (1997) 786-790
12. Ruiz Gomez, M. and Ghysen, A.: *The expression and role of a proneural gene, achaete, in the development of the larval nervous-system of Drosophila.* EMBO Journal 12 (1993) 1121-1130
13. Stern, C.: *Two or three bristles.* Am. Scientist 42 (1954) 213-247
14. Tateson, R. E.: *Studies of the roles of wingless and Notch during the development of the adult peripheral nervous system of Drosophila.* PhD Thesis, Cambridge University 1998

Applications:
TSP, Graphs and
Satisfiability

A New Genetic Local Search Algorithm for Graph Coloring

Raphaël Dorne and Jin-Kao Hao

LGI2P/EMA-EERIE
Parc Scientifique Georges Besse
F-30000 Nîmes-France
email: {dorne,hao}@eerie.fr

Abstract. This paper presents a new genetic local search algorithm for the graph coloring problem. The algorithm combines an original crossover based on the notion of union of independent sets and a powerful local search operator (tabu search). This new hybrid algorithm allows us to improve on the best known results of some large instances of the famous Dimacs benchmarks.

1 Introduction

The graph coloring problem is one of the most studied NP-hard problems and can be defined informally as follows. Given an undirected graph, one wishes to color with a minimal number of colors the nodes of the graph in such a way that two colors assigned to two adjacent nodes must be different. Graph coloring has many practical applications such as timetabling and resource assignment. Given the NP-completeness of the coloring problem, it becomes natural to design heuristic methods. Indeed many heuristic methods have been developed, constructive methods in the 60's and 70's [1, 12], local search meta-heuristics [10, 11, 2] and hybrid algorithms [6, 14, 3] in the 80's and 90's.

In the field of combinatorial optimization, the best solutions are often obtained by specialized local search algorithms or population-based algorithms without crossover. However, there are cases where hybrid evolutionary algorithms have produced very competitive results, for example for the traveling salesman problem [7], the quadratic assignment problem [13] and the bin-packing problem [5]. In general, these hybrid algorithms rely on a "meaningful" specialized crossover which combines high quality solutions produced by an "efficient" local search method. It should be clear that random crossovers are hardly meaningful for any combinatorial optimization problem, therefore are little helpful to producing high quality solutions. The main point here is that the crossover must be specialized to, and meaningful for the problem.

In this paper, we present an original crossover tailored to the coloring problem. This crossover, that we call UIS, is based on the notion of Union of Independent Sets. The UIS crossover, combined with a tabu search method leads to a simple, yet very powerful algorithm. Indeed, this new algorithm allows us to improve on the best known results of some large benchmarks.

2 Graph coloring

Definition: Given an undirected graph $G=(V,E)$ with $V=\{v_1,...,v_n\}$ being the set of nodes and $E=\{e_{ij}|$ $\exists$ an edge between v_i and $v_j\}$ the set of edges. The graph coloring problem is the following optimization problem: to determine a partition of V in a *minimum* number (the *chromatic number*) of color classes $C_1, C_2, ..., C_k$ such that for each edge $e_{ij} \in E$, v_i and v_j are not in the same color class [15]. Such a color class is called an *independent set*.

Let $c(v_i)$ be the color (represented by a positive integer) assigned to the node v_i, a *proper coloring* must verify the following *constraint*:

$$\forall e_{ij} \in E, \quad c(v_i) \neq c(v_j) \tag{1}$$

Benchmarks: In this paper, we use well known benchmarks (random graphs) from the 2nd Dimacs Challenge[1]. A random graph is denoted by $G_{n,d}$ where n represents the number of nodes and $d \in [0,1]$ the density of edges defined on the graph, which means that the number of edges of the graph is about to be $d.(n.(n-1)/2)$. Random graphs are difficult to color. It is believed that none of today's algorithms is able to color optimally such graphs having more than 100 nodes with a 0.5 density [11]. In this study, we are interested in some large and hard graphs (500 or 1000 nodes).

Johnson et al. : a set of 6 instances of 500 and 1000 nodes with edge densities of 0.1, 0.5 and 0.9, denoted by DSJC500.1.col, DSJC500.5.col, DSJC500.9.col, DSJC1000.1.col, DSJC1000.5.col, DSJC1000.9.col.

Hertz & De Werra : a set of 7 instances of 500 and 1000 nodes with edge density of 0.5, denoted by ggg1, ..., ggg5, gggg1 and gggg2.

3 Related work

Hertz and De Werra are the first who have applied tabu search to the coloring problem [10]. They proposed a simple coding for solutions and a natural 1-change neighborhood. In addition, to color large graphs ($\geq$300 nodes), they introduced a pre-processing technique which removes some independent sets from a graph leading to a reduced residual graph. Their algorithm, combined with this pre-processing, has produced excellent results on random graphs. Similarly, a simulated annealing algorithm is reported in [2].

Johnson et al. gave the first systematic investigation about the performance of simulated annealing, *Dsatur* [1] and *RLF* [12] on random graphs. A new algorithm called *XRLF* was also proposed. Extensive tests of these algorithms on various random graphs have led to mixed results: no clear dominance of a single algorithm was observed over all the tested instances.

Fleurent and Ferland investigated a tabu algorithm and in particular a hybrid algorithm combining genetic algorithm and tabu search [6]. They replaced random

---

[1] Available via ftp: dimacs.rutgers.edu/pub/challenge/graph/benchmarks/.

mutation by tabu search and developed a specialized crossover operator based on conflicting nodes (adjacent nodes having the same color). They employed the pre-processing technique of *Hertz and De Werra* to remove independent sets. Their hybrid algorithm has produced excellent results on the 2nd Dimacs challenge benchmarks. However, the computing times to obtain these results were very high for some large instances. *Costa* presented a similar hybrid algorithm called *EDM* and obtained comparable results [3].

Morgenstern proposed a distributed, population based and multi-strategy method [14]. He introduced a special neighborhood which is different from all the other previous studies. This highly specialized method has produced the best results for a large number of Dimacs challenge benchmarks.

4 A genetic local search algorithm

4.1 General algorithm

First, recall that the graph coloring problem consists in minimizing the number of colors k used. Before we present our algorithm, let us explain first the minimization process used. Following [10], we fix k, the number of available colors, to a given value and use our hybrid algorithm to search for a proper k-coloring. This is done by minimizing the number of violated constraints to 0 ($f^* = 0$) according to Eq.(1). If such a coloring is found, we decrease k and repeat the above search process until no more possible proper k-coloring is found within the allowed iterations. Therefore, the goal of our hybrid algorithm is to find a proper k-coloring for a fixed k. The general algorithm is given as follows.

Algorithm 1: Genetic local search algorithm for coloring
Data: G, a graph
Result: the number of conflicts with k fixed colors
% f, f^* : fitness function and its best value encountered so far
% s^* : best individual encountered so far
% $i, MaxIter$: the current and maximum number of iterations allowed
% $best(P)$: returns the best individual of the population P
begin
    $i = 0$
    generate(P_0)
    $s^* = best(P_0)$
    $f^* = f(s^*)$
    while ($f^* > 0$ **and** $i < MaxIter$) **do**
        $P_i' = $ crossing(P_i, T_x); /*using UIS crossover */
        $P_{i+1} = $ mutation(P_i'), /*using tabu search */
        if ($f(best(P_{i+1})) < f^*$) **then**
            $s^* = best(P_{i+1})$
            $f^* = f(s^*)$
        $i = i + 1$
    return f^*
end

As we can see, the algorithm follows a simple evolution cycle. It crosses two individuals from time to time and then it mutates the individuals of the population. More precisely, at each generation, the UIS crossover (Section 4.4) is applied with probability T_x to each possible pair (Ind_1, Ind_2) (determined randomly) of individuals of the population: p/2 pairs for a population of p individuals. If a crossover takes place on (Ind_1, Ind_2), the offsprings e_1 and e_2 replace Ind_1 and Ind_2 regardless of their fitness. Otherwise, Ind_1 and Ind_2 remain unchanged. Each individual of the population is then improved using a tabu algorithm (Section 4.3).

Different values of T_x lead to different application rates of the crossover operator. Setting T_x to 0 will give n independent executions of the tabu algorithm. Changing T_x allows one to determine the importance of the crossover.

The individuals in the initial population may be generated randomly, or using an existing coloring algorithms. We use the *RLF - Recursive Largest First* algorithm [12]. The *RLF* algorithm has poor performance, however, it gives naturally an initial value for k, the number of colors to be used in a coloring.

4.2 Encoding and fitness function

Given a graph $G=(V, E)$ with n nodes and k the number of available colors (numbered from 1 to k), an individual (or a configuration in a local search terminology) $s = <c(v_1), c(v_2), ..., c(v_n)>$ corresponds to a complete assignment of the k colors to the nodes of the graph. The size of the search space S, is equal to $|S|=k^n$, and becomes very large as soon as the graph has more than 100 nodes.

For each individual s, the fitness $f(s)$ is simply the number of unsatisfied color constraints (Eq. (1)).

$$f(s) = \sum_{(v_i, v_j) \in E} q(v_i, v_j) \quad \text{where } q(v_i, v_j) = \begin{cases} 1 \text{ if } c(v_i) = c(v_j) \\ 0 \text{ elsewhere} \end{cases}$$

The goal of the optimization process here is to minimize $f(s)$ until $f(s)=0$ for the fixed k, which corresponds to a proper k-coloring.

4.3 Mutation by tabu search

The mutation used in this hybrid algorithm is ensured by a tabu search (TS) algorithm. For a complete presentation of TS, the reader is invited to consult the recent book by Glover and Laguna [9].

Tabu search is an advanced local search meta-heuristic. A TS algorithm visits iteratively a series of locally best configurations according to a neighborhood. In order to avoid a possible cycling. TS uses a special short term memory called *tabu list*, that maintains last l encountered configurations or more generally pertinent attributes of these configurations (l is called *tabu tenure*). At each iteration, TS chooses one best neighboring configuration among those not forbidden by tabu list, even if the chosen configuration is no better than the current one.

The TS algorithm used in our hybrid algorithm for the coloring problem is the one presented in [4] augmented with a random-walk option (see below). The main characteristics of this TS algorithm is the following.

Neighborhood function N: $S \to 2^S$, $\forall s$ and $s' \in S$, $s' \in N(s)$ if and only if s and s' are different at the value of a single "conflicting" node (i.e. it has the same color as some adjacent nodes.). Thus, a neighbor of s can be obtained by changing the color of a conflicting node. A move is then characterized by a couple $< i, c >$, i and c being respectively a node and a color.

Configuration evaluation: Special data structures and techniques are used to evaluate rapidly the fitness of each neighboring configuration. This is done by maintaining incrementally in a matrix δ the *move value* or *fitness variation* for each possible move from the current solution s.

Tabu list and tabu tenure: When a node v_i in a configuration s is assigned a new color (i.e. when a move is carried out), the pair $< v_i, old\_color >$ is classified tabu for l (tabu tenure) iterations. That is, the old color will not be allowed to be re-assigned to v_i during this period. The tabu tenure l is dynamically adjusted by a function defined over the number of conflicting nodes. More precisely, let CV be the set of conflicting nodes in s, then $l = \alpha * |CV| + random(g)$ where α and g are empirically determined.

Mixed move strategy: At each iteration, a neighboring configuration s' must be chosen to replace the current one s. The choice is realized with the following strategy: according to a probability p_{rw}, carry out a "random-walk", i.e. to pick randomly a neighbor among all the neighbors in $N(s)$; according to $1 - p_{rw}$, carry out a normal tabu iteration, i.e. to pick a best (non-tabu) neighbor in $N(s)$.

4.4 The UIS crossover

The UIS crossover follows the definition of the coloring problem with independent sets (cf. Section 2): a proper k-coloring is a collection of k independent sets. With this point of view, an individual corresponds to k color classes of n nodes: some classes are conflict-free (independent sets) and the others are not. According to this interpretation, if we try to maximize the size of each independent set by a combination mechanism, we will reduce the sizes of non-independent sets, which in turn helps to push these sets into independent sets. The UIS crossover is based on this idea.

UIS tries to unify pairs of independent sets (I_{p_1}, I_{p_2}) taken respectively from two parent-colorings p_1 and p_2. Two children-colorings e_1 and e_2 are the result of a set of unions. The pair of independent sets (I_{p_1}, I_{p_2}) to be unified are those which have the largest number of nodes in common. Let us see how to generate e_1 from p_1 and p_2.

Let $I_{p_1,c}$ be the largest conflict-free subset (an independent set) of the class having the color c in p_1, we seek, among the k color classes of p_2, the independent set $I_{p_2,c'}$ (a conflict-free subset of a color class) such that $I_{p_2,c'}$ has the largest number of nodes in common with $I_{p_1,c}$ ($\forall c' \in [1..k]$, $| I_{p_1,c} \cap I_{p_2,c'} |$ is maximal).

If there are more than one possible $I_{p_2,c'}$, one is taken randomly. This operation is repeated for each color of p_1 to obtain the set of unions U_{c_1} corresponding to the pairs of independent sets for e_1:

$$U_{c_1} = \{ (I_{p_1,1}, I_{p_2,j_1}), ..., (I_{p_1,i}, I_{p_2,j_i}), ..., (I_{p_1,k}, I_{p_2,j_k}) \}$$

where $(I_{p_1,i}, I_{p_2,j_i})$ is the union of $I_{p_1,i}$ and I_{p_2,j_i} with j_i representing the color of the independent set of p_2 which is unified with the one of p_1 which has the color i (See Fig.1).

Once this set is obtained, we generate the child e_1 by assigning the color of $I_{p_1,i}$ to the nodes of $(I_{p_1,i}, I_{p_2,j_i})$. Note that U_{c_1} does not necessarily contains all the nodes of the graph. For each node $v \in V\text{-}U_{c_1}$, it keeps the color of p_1. To generate e_2, we carry out the same operation while exchanging p_1 with p_2 (cf. Fig. 1).

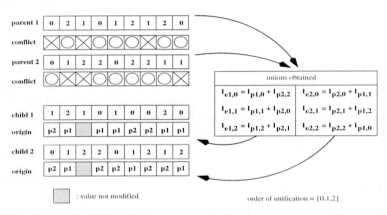

Fig. 1. UIS crossover

In terms of complexity, for each color of a parent p_1, we visit all the nodes of p_2 to find the best union. When all the unions are identified, we just have to assign the nodes of the children according to these unions. Thus the complexity of the UIS is in $O(k \times n)$ in the worst case.

Let us mention that using the notion of independent sets, other crossover operators are equally possible. For example, parallel to the current study, [8] investigates several such operators as well as other hybrid evolutionary algorithms.

Finally, note that the UIS crossover is completely different from conflict-based crossovers for the coloring problem [6]. There the coloring problem is considered as an assignment problem: an individual is an assignment of values to variables. Using this interpretation, an offspring will try to copy conflict-free colors from their parents. Previous work showed that combined with a local search algorithm, this crossover may give interesting results for some graphs. However, the search power of such a crossover is limited compared with the UIS operator.

5 Experiments and results

Our tests were carried out on an UltraSparc1 station with a 143 MHz processor and a memory of 128 Megabytes. The maximum number of moves (iterations) for our hybrid algorithm is fixed to be 10 000 000 moves for an attempt of finding a proper k-coloring. For very hard instances, this number is fixed to be 200 000 000 moves. Let us note that a crossover are also countered as a move.

Experiments are carried out on benchmarks described in Section 2. Results are compared with the best ones published in the literature:

1. *Fleurent and Ferland*, a tabu search algorithm (denoted by 1a in the tables) and a genetic tabu algorithm (denoted by 1b) [6]. These algorithms use the pre-processing technique of [10] for graphs larger than 300 nodes.
2. *Costa*, an evolutionary hybrid algorithm *EDM* (denoted by 2) with the above pre-processing technique [3].
3. *Morgenstern*, two local search algorithms S_0 and S_1 (denoted by 3a and 3b) based on a particular neighborhood. Two distributed algorithms based on a population of configurations called M_0 and M_1 (denoted by 3c and 3d). Finally a hybrid algorithm called $M_0 \backslash dXRLF$ (denoted by 3e) using a population of individuals initialized by a parallelized version of *Johnson et al's XRLF* algorithm [14].

Our genetic local search algorithm is defined by four parameters (P_1, P_2, P_3, P_4):

P_1 the number of individuals of the population.
P_2 the crossover rate T_x for UIS.
P_3 the random-walk rate p_{rw}.
P_4 the value of α for the tabu tenure (g being always fixed to 10).

For example, the setting (10,0.2,0.1,2) corresponds to a hybrid algorithm with 10 individuals using the crossover UIS with a rate of 0.2 %, the random walk mutation with a rate of 0.1 % (a rate of tabu mutation equal to 99.9 %) and a tabu tenure equal to $2 \times |CV|$+random(10).

Tables 1 to 4 compare our results (denoted by CISM - Crossover by Independent Sets and Mutation) with those of the best existing algorithms described above. The best known results are summarized in columns 2-4: the smallest known number of colors, the algorithms which produced such a coloring and the best computing time necessary to obtain this result. When an algorithm does not appear for an instance, it means either the algorithm was not tested on this instance or it did not find the indicated coloring. For example, the first line of Table 1 indicates that two algorithms (1b and 2) find a coloring with 49 colors for the ggg1.col-ggg5.col graphs and the most effective algorithm (cited first) needs more than 6 hours to obtain this result.

The last five columns give the results obtained by our algorithm (denoted by CISM). We give the total number of runs with the number of failures between brackets (5th column), the smallest number of colors obtained (6th column), the number of moves and average time on the successful runs (7th and 8th columns), and the values of parameters used by the algorithm (last column). Improved results *w.r.t* the best known ones are highlighted in bold. Note that computing times are given only for indicative purpose because the best known results have been obtained on different machines and each algorithm uses very different data structures. The most important criterion for a comparison is the quality of colorings found.

problem	Best known			CISM				
	k^*	method	time	runs	k^*	moves	time	param.
ggg1-ggg5	49	1b,2	20 376	3(0)	**48**	10 656 000	16 410	10,0.05,0.5,2
gggg1-gggg2	84	1b	147 600	1(0)	**83**	143 580 000	304 654	20,0.03,0.3,2

Table 1. Random Graphs from *Hertz and De Werra*

Table 1 gives a comparison on random instances between our algorithm CISM and the algorithms (1a), (1b) and (2) on large instances from *Hertz and De Werra* (5 graphs of 500 nodes and 2 graphs of 1000 nodes). k^* corresponds to the smallest number of colors obtained for all the instances of a same class.

We notice that our algorithm CISM obtains respectively 48- and 83-colorings and outperforms thus the best known results for these two classes of graphs. Let us recall that without a pre-processing (described above), none of 1a, 1b, 2 and our tabu algorithm is able to find colorings respectively with a number of colors smaller than 50 and 88 colors. This implies that the UIS operator contributes largely to the search power of our hybrid algorithm.

To further confirm this result, Table 2 shows the results on the random instances of *Johnson et al.* with 10, 50, and 90 % edge densities.

problem	Best known			CISM				
	k	method	time	runs	k	moves	time	param.
DSJC500.1.col	12	3d	5 452	5(0)	12	5 970 000	1 250	10,0.2,1,2
DSJC500.5.col	48	3e	49 000	5(3)	48	19 693 000	12 283	10,0.2,1,2
DSJC500.9.col	126	3e	158 400	10(8)	126	3 812 000	9 110	10,0.1,1,5
DSJC1000.1.col	21	3c	210	5(0)	**20**	16 757 000	8 768	10,0.2,1,2
DSJC1000.5.col	84	3e,1b	118 000	2(1)	**83**	120 522 000	270 159	20,0.03,0.3,2
DSJC1000.9.col	226	3c	65 774	1(0)	**224**	13 282 000	67 907	10,0.03,0.3,4

Table 2. Random Graphs from *Johnson et al.*

On these graphs smaller than 500 nodes, there are several local search methods which can find good colorings. For larger instances, few methods are able to obtain interesting results even with a powerful pre-processing. The best results are obtained by *Morgenstern* using the most complex versions of his population-based algorithms (3c, 3d and 3e). We notice from Table 2 that for graphs of 500 nodes, our algorithm finds consistently the best known colorings with shorter solving times on average. For the graphs of 1000 nodes, our results improves on the best known colorings for each instance whatever the edge density. In particular, for the largest instance DSJC1000.9.col, the number of colors needed is reduced from 226 to 224.

Tables 3 and 4 give more detailed comparisons between our algorithm and the best algorithm $M_0 \backslash dXRLF$ (3e) on the two largest instances: DSJC1000.5.col and DSJC1000.9.col.

For DSJC1000.5.col, *Morgenstern* noticed that without the help of *XRLF* his algorithms 3c and 3d occasionally find 88-colorings. Only an initial generation with *XRLF* allows his algorithm $M_0 \backslash dXRLF$ (3e) to find 84-colorings. It is also important to note that *XRLF* finds already 86-colorings and consequently its contribution in the algorithm 3e seems considerable.

Let us note that 84-colorings were also obtained by *Fleurent and Ferland* with their hybrid algorithm (1b) and our tabu algorithm. However 84-colorings are only possible with the help of *Hertz and de Werra's* pre-processing technique. Without this pre-processing, neither *Fleurent and Ferland's* nor our tabu algorithm is able to find colorings better than 89-colorings.

k	Best known method	runs	time	CISM runs	moves	time	param.
85	3e	10(0)	$\simeq$ 40 000	4(0)	36 750 000	104 500	10,0.03,0.3,2
84	3e	10(0)	118 000	4(0)	54 210 000	144 650	10,0.03,0.3,2
83	-	-	-	2(1)	120 522 000	270 159	20,0.03,0.3,2

Table 3. Coloring DSJC1000.5.col

Our hybrid algorithm CISM finds not only consistently best known 84-colorings and provides also a 83-coloring never found before. Note that initial configurations generated by *RLF* require about 105 colors for this graph and that such colorings can be easily obtained by any good local search algorithm. For example, our tabu algorithm finds 91-colorings with random initial configurations. Therefore, it is the UIS crossover that contributes to the above results.

In terms of computing time, our algorithm is slower than $M_0 \backslash dXRLF$ (3e) for finding 84 and 85-colorings. However, a fair comparison remains difficult due to the mixture of 3e. Let us simply mention that the method 3e without *XRLF* (i.e. 3c) needs 91 000 seconds to find 89-colorings.

k	Best known method	runs	time	CISM runs	moves	time	param.
226	3c	10(0)	75 800	10(0)	11 660 000	62 673	10,0.03,0.3,4
225	-	-	-	3(0)	12 938 000	67 245	10,0.03,0.3,4
224	-	-	-	4(3)	13 266 000	67 907	10,0.03,0.3,4

Table 4. Coloring DSJC1000.9.col

For DSJC1000.9.col, our algorithm finds the best known result with 226 colors and goes on to find colorings with 225 and even a 224 coloring. For this graph, the previous comparative remarks about DSJC500.9.col remain valid.

6 Conclusion

In this paper, we introduced a new crossover called UIS for the graph coloring problem. This crossover is based on the notion of unions of independent sets. The UIS operator, combined with a tabu search algorithm leads to a simple, yet very powerful hybrid algorithm. Experiments of this algorithm on well-known benchmarks have produced excellent results. Indeed, it finds the best known results for random graphs of 500 nodes (densities 10%, 50% and 90%). More importantly, it improves on the best known results for random graphs of 1000 nodes (densities 10%, 50% and 90%). (Improved results have also been obtained on other classes of graphs, but not reported here).

The algorithm should be improved both in terms of search power and computing time. First, variants of UIS and other hybridizing schema are worthy of investigation. Second, the presented algorithm can be easily parallelized, thus the computing time can be expected to be largely reduced.

References

1. D. Brélaz. New methods to color vertices of a graph. *Communications of ACM*, 22: 251-256, 1979.
2. M. Chams, A. Hertz, and D. De Werra. Some experiments with simulated annealing for coloring graphs. *European Journal of Operational Research*, 32: 260-266, 1987.
3. D. Costa, A. Hertz, and O. Dubuis. Embedding of a sequential procedure within an evolutionary algorithms for coloring problems in graphs. *Journal of Heuristics*, 1(1): 105–128, 1995.
4. R. Dorne and J.K. Hao Tabu search for graph coloring, T-coloring and set T-colorings. *Presented at the 2nd Intl. Conf. on Metaheuristics*, Sophia-Antopollis, France, July, 1997, Under review for publication.
5. E. Falkenauer A hybrid grouping genetic algorithm for bin-packing. *Journal of Heuristics*, 2(1): 5-30, 1996.
6. C. Fleurent and J.A. Ferland. Genetic and hybrid algorithms for graph coloring. *Annals of Operations Research*, 63: 437–463, 1995.
7. B. Freisleben and P. Merz. New genetic local search operators for the traveling salesman problem. *Proc. of PPSN-96, Lecture Notes in Computer Science 1141*, pp890-899, Springer-Verlag, 1996.
8. P. Galinier and J.K. Hao New crossover operators for graph coloring. Research Report, April 1998.
9. F. Glover and M. Laguna. *Tabu Search*. Kluwer Academic Publishers, 1997.
10. A. Hertz and D. De Werra. Using tabu search techniques for graph coloring. *Computing*, 39: 345–351, 1987.
11. D.S. Johnson, C.R. Aragon, L.A. McGeoch, and C. Schevon. Optimization by simulated annealing: an experimental evaluation; part ii, graph coloring and number partitioning. *Operations Research*, 39(3): 378–406, 1991.
12. F.T. Leighton. A graph coloring algorithm for large scheduling problems. *Journal of Research of the National Bureau Standard*, 84: 79–100, 1979.
13. P. Merz and B. Freisleben. A genetic local search approach to the quadratic assignment problem. *In Proc. of ICGA-97*, pp 465-472, Morgan Kaufmann Publishers, 1997.
14. C. Morgenstern. Distributed coloration neighborhood search. *Discrete Mathematics and Theoretical Computer Science*, 26: 335-358. American Mathematical Society, 1996.
15. C.H. Papadimitriou and K. Steiglitz. *Combinatorial Optimization - Algorithms and Complexity*. Prentice Hall, 1982.

Improving the Performance of Evolutionary Algorithms for the Satisfiability Problem by Refining Functions

Jens Gottlieb and Nico Voss

Technische Universität Clausthal, Institut für Informatik,
Julius-Albert-Straße 4, 38678 Clausthal-Zellerfeld, Germany.
{gottlieb,nvoss}@informatik.tu-clausthal.de

Abstract. The performance of evolutionary algorithms (EAs) for the satisfiability problem (SAT) can be improved by an adaptive change of the traditional fitness landscape. We present two adaptive refining functions containing additional heuristic information about solution candidates: One of them is applicable to any constraint satisfaction problem with bit string representation, while the other is tailored to SAT. The influence of the refining functions is controlled by adaptive mechanisms. A comparison of the resulting EA with other approaches from literature indicates the suitability of our approach for SAT.

1 Introduction

The satisfiability problem (SAT) is the first problem proved to be NP-complete [GJ79] and can be stated as follows. For a given function $b : \mathbb{B}^n \to \mathbb{B}$, $\mathbb{B} = \{0,1\}$, the question is: Does there exist an $x = (x_1, \ldots, x_n) \in \mathbb{B}^n$ with $b(x) = 1$? Without loss of generality, we assume conjunctive normal form for b, i.e. $b = c_1 \wedge \cdots \wedge c_m$ with each clause c_i being a disjunction of literals. In the following, $D(c_i) \subseteq \{1, \ldots, n\}$ denotes the set of the indices of all variables contained in c_i.

All known exact methods for SAT, e.g. the Davis-Putnam procedure [DP60], have an exponential worst case complexity. Many heuristics for SAT have been proposed, including local search [SLM92, Fra96] and evolutionary algorithms (EAs) [DJS89, EvdH97, FF96]. We propose an EA for SAT employing a problem specific mutation operator and refined fitness functions. Some static refining functions have been presented in a previous study [GV98], but they seemed to have no influence on the performance of the EA. We guessed that the reason for this could be the static nature of the considered functions and that adaptive functions could be more appropriate. This hypothesis is confirmed in this paper.

We proceed as follows: After a presentation of details concerning EAs for SAT in Sect. 2, the concept of refining functions is introduced together with two specific adaptive refining functions in Sect. 3. We propose some mechanisms to control the influence of refining functions in Sect. 4. Section 5 presents the results for the different approaches, including a comparison with other algorithms for SAT. Finally, we summarize our results and give ideas for further research in Sect. 6.

2 Representation and Operators

Some representation schemes like the clausal representation [Hao95], the path representation [GV98] and the float representation [BEV98] have been introduced for SAT, but the reported results indicate inferior performance when compared to the "natural" bit string representation. Therefore we select this representation, according to [BEV98, DJS89, EvdH97, FF96, Fra94, GV98, Par95].

The standard bit mutation has been used frequently in EAs for SAT [DJS89, Par95], but is clearly outperformed by the mutation operator from [GV98]. Therefore we employ this operator, which relies on the fact that in the current solution candidate x at least one of the bits associated with $D(c_i)$ for each unsatisfied clause c_i must be changed to obtain an optimal solution. Hence, all unsatisfied clauses are traversed in random order and the corresponding bits are changed with probability $p_M \cdot f(x)/m$. This probability increases with higher fitness values $f(x)$ to ensure roughly the same bit flip probability even for near-optimal solution candidates. Futhermore, at most one flip per bit is allowed.

We have tested the crossover from [GV98], which has outperformed 1-point, 2-point and uniform crossover. For the SAT instances we consider in this paper, this crossover has – roughly speaking – no influence on the overall performance, an observation that has been made for other instances and crossovers, too [EvdH97, Par95]. Hence, we decided to discard the crossover from our EA.

3 Refining Functions

An appropriate fitness function is essential for an EA to work well. It is convenient to take $f : \mathbb{B}^n \to \{0, \dots, m\}$ as fitness function for a SAT instance with m clauses, with $f(x)$ denoting the number of satisfied clauses for solution candidate $x \in \mathbb{B}^n$, see e.g. [FF96, Fra94, Par95]. Hence, the goal is to find an x with maximum $f(x)$. We call f the *basic fitness function* as it forms the basis for all other fitness functions which are proposed in this paper.

There exist many solution candidates having the same basic fitness value but not really the same "distance" from an optimum, because the fitness is just an estimation of the real quality. We want to capture these differences by another heuristic quality measure, which we assume to have the form $r : \mathbb{B}^n \to [0, 1)$. By simply adding r to f, or more generally taking $f + \alpha r$, $\alpha > 0$, as fitness function, it is possible to distinguish between solution candidates having the same basic fitness value. The resulting function $f + \alpha r : \mathbb{B}^n \to [0, m + \alpha)$ has a more diversified range, filling gaps in the range $\{0, \dots, m\}$ of f. Therefore, we call r a *refining function*, and $f + \alpha r$ a *refined fitness function*. A refining function is called *adaptive*, if it depends on the progress of the evolutionary search (including the generation count and the current population); otherwise it is called *static*. (See [HME97] for a detailed survey of types and levels of adaptation.) We call a refining function *problem dependent*, if it makes use of the problem structure; it is called *problem independent*, if it is based only on the representation scheme.

Two remarks should be made with respect to fitness functions proposed in literature. The simplest approach of taking $b : \mathbb{B}^n \to \mathbb{B}$ as fitness function has the main drawback that unless the EA has found a solution, all individuals have the same fitness value 0, forcing the EA to act like pure random search. Thus, many authors have used f as fitness function [Fra94, FF96, Par95]. By normalizing f to $g : \mathbb{B}^n \to [0, 1)$, this function is indeed the refined fitness function $b + \alpha g$ with $\alpha = 1$, basic fitness function b and refining function g, which is static and problem dependent. This indicates that refining functions have implicitly already been used. Our approach of refining g can be interpreted as a second refining step to b.

The best EAs for SAT use a stepwise adaptation of weights (SAW) [BEV98, EvdH97]: Each clause is assigned a weight which is initialized with 1, and in some stages of the evolutionary process some weights are increased in order to identify "difficult" clauses. Hence, the EA starts with f and proceeds with a series of modified fitness functions. Each of these functions has a discrete range with cardinality bounded by $m + 1$ and 2^m, with most of them having a larger cardinality than f. Thus, one aspect of SAW is the greater variety of different fitness values. This principle is also essential for our refining functions.

3.1 Two Static Refining Functions

Let p_j and n_j be the numbers of positive and negative literals in the clauses of b which correspond with variable j. If $p_j > n_j$, it might be promising to set $x_j = 1$: This could cause a higher number of satisfied clauses and more alternatives for other variables in these clauses. Together with the corresponding argument for the case $p_j < n_j$, this idea leads to the refining function

$$r_1(x) = \frac{1}{n} \sum_{j=1}^{n} \frac{x_j p_j + (1 - x_j) n_j}{1 + p_j + n_j}$$

which originates from [GV98]. For demonstration purposes, we also consider

$$r_2(x) = \frac{1}{n} \sum_{j=1}^{n} \frac{(1 - x_j) p_j + x_j n_j}{1 + p_j + n_j}$$

obtained from r_1 by replacing x_j by $1 - x_j$. This function is somehow complementary to r_1 and therefore its behaviour could be expected to differ significantly from r_1. Both r_1 and r_2 are problem dependent as they are based on the distribution of the positive and negative literals in b. Futhermore, these functions are static as they do not exploit any information from the evolutionary process.

3.2 An Adaptive Refining Function for Bit Strings

Suppose an individual which violates at least one clause and has the best fitness in the current population. If this individual is locally optimal, the selection phase could drive the EA into premature convergence. Such situation prevents the EA with high probability from continuing its search in other promising regions. Hence, a mechanism which facilitates to escape from such local optima could be very helpful. The more generations one individual has the highest fitness in the population, the higher we expect the probability that this individual is a local optimum. Thus, we propose a refining function that favours solution candidates which drive the EA search away from such individuals. This refining function implicitly considers the length of time this individual has dominated the population. (Note that the age of indiviuals has already been used explicitly by other EA variants [AMM94].)

In the following, we use the function $K : \mathbb{B} \to \{-1, 1\}$ defined by $K(1) = 1$ and $K(0) = -1$ to simplify some formulas. The refining function

$$r_3(x) = \frac{1}{2} \left(1 + \frac{\sum_{j=1}^{n} K(x_j) w_j}{1 + \sum_{j=1}^{n} |w_j|} \right)$$

is based on weights w_j for each bit, which are initialized to 0 and adapted during the evolutionary process. Positive weights w_j indicate that the corresponding bits are favoured to be 1, while negative weights express a preference to 0. High absolute weights indicate high preferences, hence the weights can be interpreted as parameters determining the search direction of the EA. The weight adaptation is involved after each generation and depends on the best individual x' in the current population. The adaptation is defined by

$$w_j = w_j - K(x'_j) \quad \text{for } j \in \{1, \ldots, n\},$$

yielding a moderate adjustment of the weights towards the complement of the best individual. It is clear that r_3 is adaptive. Furthermore, r_3 is problem independent, because its definition and the weight adaptation are only based on the representation and not on the problem structure.

We remark that the weights can be conceived as a simple memory which saves information about the evolutionary process and helps to escape from local optima. The idea of using adaptive memory structures to leave local optima is not new and has been successfully used by tabu search, see [GL97]. The main difference is that tabu search uses its memory explicitly to determine the next solution candidate and our approach applies the weights only implicitly to exercise a stochastic influence on the search direction.

3.3 An Adaptive Refining Function Utilizing the Structure of SAT

Given a bit string x, we define $S(x)$ and $U(x)$ to be the sets of the indices of those clauses which are satisfied and unsatisfied by x, respectively. Futhermore, let $C_j = \{i \in \{1, \ldots, m\} \mid j \in D(c_i)\}$ be the set of clause indices which are associated with bit x_j. The refining function r_4 considers weights w_j for each bit to influence the search direction of the EA, but the adaptation process and the function itself are based on the structural properties $S(x)$, $U(x)$ and C_j of b, therefore r_4 is problem dependent.

The weights are interpreted in the same way as described for r_3. Responsible for the quality of a solution candidate x are mainly those bits that are involved in the satisfied clauses. Many bits contained in unsatisfied clauses must be changed anyway to obtain better solution candidates. Hence, it is reasonable to use

$$r_4(x) = \frac{1}{2}\left(1 + \frac{\sum_{j=1}^{n} w_j K(x_j) \cdot |C_j \cap S(x)|}{1 + \sum_{j=1}^{n} |w_j| \cdot |C_j|}\right),$$

which emphasizes the accordance between the weights and the bits contained in satisfied clauses. Suppose x' to be the best individual in the current population. For a further improvement of x', it is necessary to flip some bits contained in unsatisfied clauses. The adaptation

$$w_j = w_j - K(x'_j) \cdot |C_j \cap U(x')| \quad \text{for } j \in \{1, \ldots, n\}$$

directs the search towards solutions satisfying yet unsatisfied clauses. This process is involved after each generation to focus the search on "difficult" clauses.

4 Constructing Refined Fitness Functions

To make use of refining functions, we need a mechanism to control their influence on the EA. The impact of a refining function r in the refined fitness function $f + \alpha r$ depends on the parameter $\alpha > 0$, which we call *influence level (of the refining function)*. For $\alpha \to \infty$ and $\alpha \to 0$, the EA ignores information from f and r, respectively. Hence, we need a value for α which yields a good trade-off between the influences of f and r during the EA search.

The easiest way to construct a refined fitness function is to take a constant value for α. As our EA employs tournament selection, the smallest reasonable value is $\alpha = 1$, which we have used in our previous study [GV98]. For this value, the overall influence of r is relatively small, as it becomes only influential if individuals with same basic fitness values compete in a tournament. Higher values for α increase the influence of the refining function, enabling the selection of individuals with smaller basic fitness, due to their higher refining function value. A disadvantage of a constant α is that a reasonable value must be determined before the EA run, which could be very time-consuming.

These considerations motivate an adaptive mechanism to control the value of α during the EA run, hoping that the adaptation determines good α values. This would also enable the EA to search at different influence levels, which makes sense in particular if the effectiveness of α depends on the progress of the EA search. We initialize α with a constant δ and adapt α after each generation by

$$\alpha = \begin{cases} \alpha + \delta & \text{if } \Delta(f + \alpha r) < \delta \\ \delta & \text{if } \Delta(f + \alpha r) \geq \delta \end{cases}, \tag{1}$$

where $\Delta(f + \alpha r)$ denotes the fitness increase from the best individual of the last generation to its counterpart in the current generation. If no improvements were found over subsequent generations, the probability of being trapped in a local optimum with respect to f is high. Hence α is increased, enabling r to guide the EA away from the current region of the search space. Roughly speaking, the adaptation lets the EA work with a low α to find a local optimum of f, and then increases α to escape from this local optimum in a direction determined by r.

The adaptation allows different influence levels in subsequent generations, but the EA is always focused on one influence level when the next generation is determined. To make the EA even more flexible, we maintain two influence levels α_1 and α_2 which are used simultaneously: One half of the population is selected according to $f + \alpha_1 r$, while the selection of the other half is based on $f + \alpha_2 r$. Both influence levels are adapted independently by (1) with parameters δ_1 and δ_2 to control the search focus. Usually, we use a small δ_1 to concentrate on f by a moderate increase of α_1, and a higher δ_2 to allow a fast increase of α_2 to leave local optima very fast (in direction determined by r).

5 Results

We use the problem generator mkcnf.c written by Allen van Gelder[1] and restrict our investigations to satisfiable 3-SAT instances with ratio $m/n \approx 4.3$, which have been reported by Mitchell et al. [MSL92] to be the hardest instances. We apply our EA to a set of 50 randomly generated instances with $n = 50$ and $m = 215$, and consider 10 independent runs for each instance. We use an EA with elitism, population size $P = 20$ and tournament selection with tournament size $t = 2$. All individuals are mutated using the mutation parameter $p_M = 0.3$, and the EA run is stopped after $T = 100\,000$ fitness evaluations. According to [BEV98, EvdH97], we measure the performance of our EA primarily by the success rate (SR), denoting the percentage of all runs where a solution was found, and the average number of fitness evaluations (AES) needed to find a solution.

5.1 Comparison of the Refined Fitness Functions

First, we compare the refined fitness functions based on the static refining functions r_1 and r_2 for different constant α values. Figure 1 (left) shows that the SR for r_1 and r_2 is inferior to the basic fitness function. Furthermore, both refining functions yield a similar SR, contradicting the expectation mentioned in Sect. 3.1. This made us look closer at the results for the 50 instances. We recognized that the instances which were easy for r_1 were more difficult for r_2, and vice versa. The reason for this is the complementary definition of r_1 and r_2. We guess that the performance of a static refining function depends strongly on the conformity with the structure of the considered instance. Static refining functions guide the search into an a priori determined region of the search space, hence the EA could easily be mislead if this region does not contain a solution.

Figure 1 (left) also shows the results for the adaptive refining functions r_3 and r_4, which exhibit a significant SR increase in comparison with the basic fitness function. This can be explained by the adaptation to the structure of the instance at hand. The SR of r_3 and r_4 for an adaptively controlled α is shown

---

[1] ftp://dimacs.rutgers.edu/pub/challenge/satisfiability/contributed/UCSC/instances

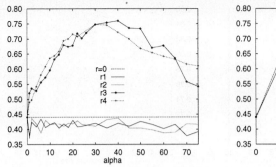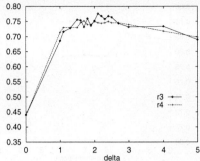

Fig. 1. SR for the basic fitness function $(r = 0)$ and refined fitness functions $f + \alpha r_1$, $f + \alpha r_2$, $f + \alpha r_3$, $f + \alpha r_4$ for different constant α values (left); SR for $f + \alpha r_3$ and $f + \alpha r_4$ with adaptive α (right)

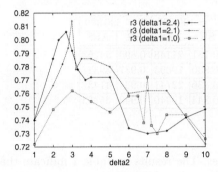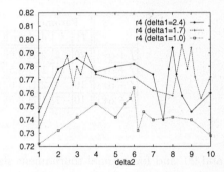

Fig. 2. SR for $f + \alpha r_3$ (left) and $f + \alpha r_4$ (right) controlled by different α_1 and α_2

in Fig. 1 (right). The best SR for r_3 and r_4 is slightly higher than for constant α, which could be caused by the ability to search at different influence levels.

The mechanism employing α_1 and α_2 to allow a more flexible search yields another improvement with respect to SR, see Fig. 2. It is important to use different values for δ_1 and δ_2, and δ_1 must not be too small. Once again, the problem independent refining function r_3 performs slightly better than r_4. When designing the adaptive refining functions, we have expected r_4 to perform better than r_3. Therefore, we checked whether the performance is influenced by other EA parameters. We tested different population sizes and investigated the effect of selection pressure; δ_1 and δ_2 were chosen according to the best combinations observed in Fig. 2. The (surprising) results are shown in Fig. 3. For both population sizes, the problem dependent refining function r_4 needs higher tournament sizes t to achieve the best performance, while the SR for r_3 deteriorates with increasing t. Therefore care must be taken when interpreting the previous figures with respect to the relation between r_3 and r_4, because $t = 2$ is a very good choice for r_3 but the worst for r_4. Finally, we compared r_3 and r_4 for population sizes 10

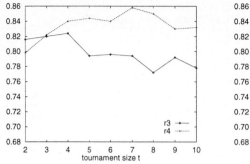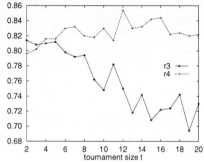

Fig. 3. SR for different tournament sizes t and population sizes 10 (left) and 20 (right)

Table 1. SR for 50 independent runs with optimal tournament size

	Parameters				$T = 100\,000$		$T = 300\,000$	
	P	t	δ_1	δ_2	SR	AES	SR	AES
$f + \alpha r_3$	20	2	2.1	3.0	0.781	21148	0.890	54263
$f + \alpha r_4$	20	12	1.7	8.5	0.830	19095	0.937	39317
$f + \alpha r_3$	10	4	2.1	3.0	0.836	22741	0.934	41437
$f + \alpha r_4$	10	7	1.7	8.5	0.844	19340	0.943	35323

and 20, and for optimal tournament sizes. The results in Table 1 indicate that r_4 outperforms r_3 for the considered parameters of T and P.

5.2 Comparison with Other Algorithms

Whether our EA is well suited for SAT or not, can be verified by a comparison with other algorithms which have been reported to be successful in solving hard SAT instances. Table 2 shows the results for our EAs (with the same parameters as in Table 1) on a set of satisfiable instances generated by `mkcnf.c`, which have been investigated by Bäck et al. [BEV98], and the reported results for their best EA and a version of WGSAT. The EA from [BEV98] employs the $(1, \lambda^*)$ selection strategy, a mutation operator (M1) changing exactly one bit, and the SAW mechanism to adapt the fitness function. Note that parameter λ^* has been fine tuned for each problem size n. WGSAT is a local search algorithm proposed by Frank [Fra96] and based on adaptive clause weights to decide the next bit flip. Bäck et al. have experimented with some WGSAT versions, and found a version with an optimized number of restarts (ONR) to be most effective [BEV98].

The problem specific refined fitness functions yield a slightly better SR than the $(1, \lambda^*)$ EA and dominate WGSAT, while the problem independent refined fitness functions reach a comparable SR as the $(1, \lambda^*)$ EA. With respect to AES, our EAs outperform the other algorithms. Note that our algorithms are tuned

Table 2. Results for 50 independent runs ($T = 300\,000$) on the instances from [BEV98]

No	n	$f + \alpha r_3$ ($P = 20$)		$f + \alpha r_4$ ($P = 20$)		$f + \alpha r_3$ ($P = 10$)		$f + \alpha r_4$ ($P = 10$)		$(1, \lambda^*)$ EA (SAW, M1)		WGSAT (ONR)	
		SR	AES	SR	AES	SR	AES	SR	AES	SR	AES	SR	AES
1	30	1	338	1	430	1	411	1	253	1	754	1	6063
2	30	1	34586	1	14370	1	27182	1	18236	1	88776	0.96	78985
3	30	1	6577	1	6807	1	7194	1	6494	1	12516	1	31526
4	40	1	825	1	689	1	1048	1	549	1	3668	1	13328
5	40	1	407	1	473	1	418	1	316	1	1609	1	2899
6	40	0.90	95674	1	47197	1	61073	1	24684	0.78	154590	0.94	82031
7	50	1	485	1	752	1	485	1	480	1	2837	1	28026
8	50	1	3390	1	8991	1	20238	1	11634	1	8728	1	60160
9	50	0.42	112503	0.78	121090	0.56	102515	0.92	85005	0.54	170664	0.32	147718
10	100	0.16	163097	0.54	127885	0.14	76038	0.22	142058	0.16	178520	0.06	192403
11	100	1	19262	0.98	6302	0.98	21758	1	18324	1	43767	0.44	136152
12	100	1	19833	1	26512	0.94	46693	1	15816	1	37605	0.58	109091

for instances with $n = 50$, hence we expect that an increase in performance can be achieved for $n = 100$ by more parameter tuning.

6 Conclusions

We have presented an approach to combine the usual fitness function for SAT with other heuristics. The best results are obtained with adaptive refining functions and adaptive mechanisms to control their influence. The obtained results are promising and indicate the suitability of the approach for SAT.

We expect that the ideas of this paper can also be successfully applied to other constraint satisfaction problems (CSPs). It would be interesting to generalize the problem independent refining function to CSPs over domains with higher cardinality. Other important aspects of the presented ideas need to be examined in greater detail, e.g. the effect of selection pressure, the behaviour for larger problem instances or other possibilities to apply simultaneously two different influence levels. Moreover, alternative control mechanisms for the influence level and other adaptive refining functions should be developed and analyzed.

References

[AMM94] J. Arabas, Z. Michalewicz and J. Mulawka, GAVaPS – a Genetic Algorithm with Varying Population Size, In *Proceedings of the 1st IEEE International Conference on Evolutionary Computation*, 73 – 78, IEEE Service Center, Piscataway, NJ, 1994

[BEV98]   T. Bäck, A. E. Eiben and M. E. Vink. A Superior Evolutionary Algorithm for 3-SAT. In *Proceedings of the 7th Annual Conference on Evolutionary Programming*, Lecture Notes in Computer Science, Springer, 1998 (in press)

[DJS89]   K. A. De Jong and W. M. Spears. Using Genetic Algorithms to Solve NP-Complete Problems. In J. D. Schaffer (ed.), *Proceedings of the Third International Conference on Genetic Algorithms*, 124 – 132, Morgan Kaufmann Publishers, San Mateo, CA, 1989

[DP60]   M. Davis and H. Putnam. A Computing Procedure for Quantification Theory. *Journal of the ACM*, Volume 7, 201 – 215, 1960

[EvdH97]   A. E. Eiben and J. K. van der Hauw. Solving 3-SAT with Adaptive Genetic Algorithms. In *Proceedings of the 4th IEEE International Conference on Evolutionary Computation*, 81 – 86, IEEE Service Center, Piscataway, NJ, 1997

[FF96]   C. Fleurent and J. A. Ferland. Object-oriented Implementation of Heuristic Search Methods for Graph Coloring, Maximum Clique and Satisfiability. In D. S. Johnson and M. A. Trick (eds.), *Cliques, Coloring and Satisfiability: 2nd DIMACS Implementation Challenge*, DIMACS Series in Discrete Mathematics and Theoretical Computer Science, Volume 26, 619 – 652, 1996

[Fra94]   J. Frank. A Study of Genetic Algorithms to Find Approximate Solutions to Hard 3CNF Problems. Golden West International Conference on Artificial Intelligence, 1994

[Fra96]   J. Frank. Weighting for Godot: Learning Heuristics for GSAT. In *Proceedings of the 13th National Conference on Artificial Intelligence and the 8th Innovative Applications of Artificial Intelligence Conference*, 338 – 343, 1996

[GJ79]   M. R. Garey and D. S. Johnson. *Computers and Intractability: A Guide to the Theory of NP-Completeness*. W. H. Freeman, San Francisco, CA, 1979

[GL97]   F. Glover and M. Laguna. *Tabu Search*. Kluwer Academic Publishers, 1997

[GV98]   J. Gottlieb and N. Voss. Representations, Fitness Functions and Genetic Operators for the Satisfiability Problem. In J.-K. Hao, E. Lutton, E. Ronald, M. Schoenauer and D. Snyers (eds.), *Artificial Evolution*, Lecture Notes in Computer Science, Volume 1363, 55 – 68, Springer, 1998

[Hao95]   J.-K. Hao. A Clausal Genetic Representation and its Evolutionary Procedures for Satisfiability Problems. In D. W. Pearson, N. C. Steele, and R. F. Albrecht (eds.), *Proceedings of the International Conference on Artificial Neural Nets and Genetic Algorithms*, 289 – 292, Springer, Wien, 1995

[HME97]   R. Hinterding, Z. Michalewicz and A. E. Eiben. Adaptation in Evolutionary Computation: a Survey. In *Proceedings of the 4th IEEE International Conference on Evolutionary Computation*, 65 – 69, IEEE Service Center, Piscataway, 1997

[MSL92]   D. Mitchell, B. Selman, and H. Levesque. Hard and Easy Distributions of SAT Problems. In *Proceedings of the 10th National Conference on Artificial Intelligence*, 459 – 465, 1992

[Par95]   K. Park. A Comparative Study of Genetic Search. In L. J. Eshelman (ed.), *Proceedings of the Sixth International Conference on Genetic Algorithms*, 512 – 519, Morgan Kaufmann, San Mateo, CA, 1995

[SLM92]   B. Selman, H. Levesque, and D. Mitchell. A New Method for Solving Hard Satisfiability Problems. In *Proceedings of the 10th National Conference on Artificial Intelligence*, 440 – 446, 1992

Memetic Algorithms and the Fitness Landscape of the Graph Bi–Partitioning Problem

Peter Merz and Bernd Freisleben

Department of Electrical Engineering and Computer Science (FB 12),
University of Siegen, Hölderlinstr. 3, D–57068 Siegen, Germany
E-Mail: {pmerz,freisleb}@informatik.uni-siegen.de

Abstract. In this paper, two types of fitness landscapes of the graph bi-partitioning problem are analyzed, and a memetic algorithm – a genetic algorithm incorporating local search – that finds near-optimum solutions efficiently is presented. A search space analysis reveals that the fitness landscapes of geometric and non-geometric random graphs differ significantly, and within each type of graph there are also differences with respect to the epistasis of the problem instances. As suggested by the analysis, the performance of the proposed memetic algorithm based on Kernighan-Lin local search is better on problem instances with high epistasis than with low epistasis. Further analytical results indicate that a combination of a recently proposed greedy heuristic and Kernighan-Lin local search is likely to perform well on geometric graphs. The experimental results obtained for non-geometric graphs show that the proposed memetic algorithm (MA) is superior to any other heuristic known to us. For the geometric graphs considered, only the initialization phase of the MA is required to find (near) optimum solutions.

1   Introduction

The *graph partitioning problem* is an $\mathcal{NP}$-hard combinatorial optimization problem [11] that arises in many applications such as parallel and distributed computing, VLSI circuit design and simulation, transportation management, and data mining. In this paper, we consider a special case, the *graph bi-partitioning problem (GBP)*, which can be stated as follows. Given a undirected Graph $G = (V, E)$, the GBP is to find a partition of the nodes in two equally sized sets such that the number of edges between nodes in the different sets is minimized. More formally, the problem is to minimize $c(V_1, V_2) = |\{(i,j) \in E : i \in V_1 \land j \in V_2\}|$, where $c(V_1, V_2)$ is referred to as the cut size of the partition.

Several exact solution approaches to graph partitioning have been proposed, but since the problem is NP-hard, the practical usefulness of these approaches is limited to fairly small problem instances. To find partitions of larger graphs, several heuristics have been developed that are able to produce (near) optimum solutions in reasonable time. Among these are (a) heuristics especially developed for graph bi-partititioning, such as the Kernighan-Lin algorithm [16] and greedy algorithms [1], and (b) general-purpose heuristic optimization approaches, such as simulated annealing [12], tabu search [2] and genetic algorithms [4, 22].

In this paper, we first analyze the fitness landscape of the GBP and then present a memetic algorithm that is able to produce near-optimum solutions for several GBP instances efficiently. The fitness landscapes of geometric and non-geometric random graphs are investigated by performing a fitness distance analysis (FDA) based on the Kernighan-Lin local search heuristic [16] and a recently proposed differential greedy heuristic [1].

The proposed memetic algorithm [20, 21] is a genetic local search algorithm similar to the ones we previously used for other combinatorial optimization problems [9, 10, 17, 18, 19]. It incorporates local search as well as the mentioned greedy heuristic for initialization, and operates on a population of local minima rather than arbitrary candidate solutions.

2 The GBP Fitness Landscape

The analysis of fitness landscapes of combinatorial optimization problems is a promising path to performance prediction as well as for developing new theories for designing effective search strategies. A technique used by several researchers [3, 13, 14] is *fitness distance analysis* (FDA), which is performed by producing N individuals (solutions) and plotting their fitness (solution quality) against their distance to an optimum solution (where an appropriate distance measure between solutions is assumed to exist).

2.1 A distance measure for the GBP

A solution of the GBP can be coded in a bit string of length N, where N is the number of nodes of the graph: A 0 at locus i indicates that node i belongs to set 1 (V_1) while a 1 indicates that the node belongs to set 2 (V_2). In binary coded problems, the hamming distance is (often) used as a distance measure between solutions: two solutions have distance d if they differ at d bit locations. However, in case of the GBP not all bit combinations of length N represent feasible solutions. Because both vertex sets have to be equally sized, it is required that a genome contains as many 1s as 0s. Since flipping of a single bit would lead to an infeasible solution, the smallest possible change in a solution that maintains feasibility is to flip two bits simultaneously, a 1 to a 0 and a 0 to a 1. Thus, the distance between two feasible GBP solutions A and B can be defined as the minimum size of the subsets to exchange between the two sets of A to obtain solution B from A.

2.2 Local search for the GBP

A local search procedure tries to find a fitter solution in the neighborhood of the current solution. If a better solution is found, the new solution is accepted as the current solution, and the neighborhood search restarts. If no better solution is found in the neighborhood, a local optimum has been reached. The simplest neighborhood for the GBP is the *1-opt* neighborhood. It is defined as the set of solutions that can be reached from the current one by exchanging one node from set 1 with one node from set 2. The *k-opt* neighborhood is defined as $\mathcal{N}_k(s) = \{s' \in S : D(s, s') \leq k\}$, where S is the set of all possible solutions. Since the neighborhood size grows rapidly with k ($|\mathcal{N}_{k\text{-}opt}| = O(n^{2k})$), local search procedures for large k become impractical. Kernighan and Lin [16] proposed a local search heuristic that efficiently searches a small subset of the *k-opt* neighborhood, which is still one of the best heuristics for the GBP and therefore used in our investigation.

2.3 The test instances

The test instances studied in our experiments are taken from Johnson et al. [12], since they have used by several researchers to test their algorithms and thus are a good basis for comparing the results presented in this paper. Two types of randomly generated instances were considered in [12]:

The first type is denoted by G*n.p*, where n represents the number of nodes and p the probability that any given pair of vertices in the graph constitutes an edge; the expected average degree is thus $p(n-1)$. The second type is a geometric graph denoted by U*n.d*, where n is the number of nodes and d the expected average vertex degree.

The number of edges emanating from the vertices determines the amount of epistasis in a given problem instance. This becomes obvious when the objective function $f(x) = c(V_1, V_2)$ is rewritten as a sum of fitness contributions of each site of the genome $x \in \{0,1\}^n$ representing the partition (V_1, V_2):

$$f(x) = \sum_{i=1}^{n} \sum_{j=1}^{n} \frac{1}{2} w_{ij} |x_i - x_j| = \sum_{i=1}^{n} f_i(x_i, x_{i_1}, \ldots, x_{i_{k(i)}}) \tag{1}$$

with $V = \{1, \ldots, n\}$ and $w_{ij} = 1$, if $(i, j) \in E$, 0 otherwise. Similar to the NK-landscapes defined in [15], the fitness contribution f_i of a site i depends on the gene value x_i and of $k(i)$ other genes $x_{i_1}, \ldots, x_{i_{k(i)}}$, where $k(i)$ denotes the degree of vertex i. While for NK-landscapes $k(i) = K$ is constant for all i, in the GBP instances introduced above $k(i)$ varies. The results of our FDA described in the following are based on considering four test instances with different average vertex degrees for both types of graph.

2.4 FDA for selected GBP instances

Instead of using the actual fitness values in the FDA plots, we decided to "normalize" them by subtracting the optimum fitness, such that differences in the fitness distributions become more obvious. Since optimum solutions for the instances described above are not known, we use the best known solutions for the instances instead. These solutions are likely to be the optimum solutions but their optimality has not been proven yet.

Two sets of FDAs for each type of the GBP instances considered were performed. In the first of these, 10000 local optima were generated with the

Kernighan-Lin heuristic applied to randomly generated partitions. In the second set, 10000 solutions produced by a recently proposed constructive heuristic for the GBP, called *Differential Greedy* (Diff-Greedy) [1], were used. Diff-Greedy randomly builds partitions from scratch by alternately adding vertices to one of the sets until each vertex is included in either the first or the second set. Performing a FDA for Diff-Greedy is motivated by the fact that in [1] Battiti and Bertossi have shown that this approach is very effective especially for geometric problem instances. The results of both sets of FDAs are summarized in Table 1, where the average distance to the optimum (D_{opt}), the average distance to the other solutions (D_{other}), the number of distinct solutions N, and the correlation coefficient $\rho(f, D) = \frac{cov(f,D)}{\sigma(f)\sigma(D)}$ are displayed.

Table 1. Average distances and fitness distance coefficients

Instance	Kernighan-Lin				Diff-Greedy			
	D_{opt}	D_{other}	N_{KL}	ρ	D_{opt}	D_{other}	N_{DG}	ρ
G1000.0025	212.89	225.20	10000	0.37	209.03	220.68	10000	0.34
G1000.005	221.80	227.78	10000	0.20	220.30	223.47	10000	0.16
G1000.01	218.09	226.00	10000	0.29	215.25	222.13	10000	0.23
G1000.02	212.44	224.70	10000	0.47	208.29	222.07	10000	0.40
U1000.05	217.09	224.68	10000	0.26	113.19	144.59	9995	0.61
U1000.10	192.80	206.61	9997	0.36	127.96	153.74	9363	0.58
U1000.20	128.85	157.33	4511	0.65	134.13	149.43	8037	0.58
U1000.40	94.06	129.62	613	0.83	104.35	135.66	5129	0.66

Surprisingly, the results for the Kernighan-Lin heuristic are totally different for the two types of instances. As shown in more detail by the plots in Fig. 1, for the G$n.p$ graphs (left column of Fig. 1), the number different fitness values increases with increasing vertex degree. For example, for instance G1000.0025 the produced local optima have 56 different fitness values and for G1000.02 this number is 163. This can be explained by the fact that with a relatively high average vertex degree the fitness values f_i per site are higher than for a low average degree. The distances of the generated local optima are relatively far away from each other, they are distributed over the whole search space, and some of them have maximum distance to each other. However, the optimal partition is closer to near optimum partitions than are the near optimum partitions to themselves. This indicates that the optimum lies more or less central among the other local optima, which suggests that a crossover based memetic algorithm might be beneficial.

For the U$n.d$ graphs, the plots are totally different (right column of Fig. 1). Here, with increasing average node degree, the number of distinct local minima decreases. Furthermore, the average distance to the other local optima is much smaller than for the G$n.p$ instances. However, for instance U1000.05 the optimum lies far away from the other generated minima, indicating that the likelihood of being able to solve this type of instance easily by local search based algorithms increases with higher epistasis.

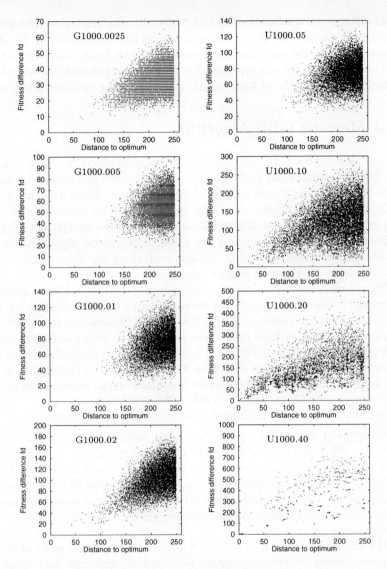

Fig. 1. G1000.*d* (left) and U1000.*p* (right) fitness-distance plots KL

In the FDA for solutions generated by Diff-Greedy (Table 1 (right)), the results are again completely different for the both types of instances. Although the fitness distance plots are omitted due to space limitations, it is obvious that fitness and distance are more correlated in the U*n.d* instances. For U1000.05, the average distance to the optimum is higher than for U1000.10 and U1000.20, indicating that Diff-Greedy performs well on geometric instances with low average vertex degree. For the high average degree (U1000.20 and U1000.40), the fitness distance correlation coefficient is lower than for Kernighan-Lin generated solutions. In case of the $Gn.p$ instances, the solutions produced by Diff-Greedy lie far away from the optimum with respect to both fitness and distance. Since Diff-Greedy is superior to Kernighan-Lin for low epistasis and vice versa for high epistasis, a combination of both seems to be promising for geometric graphs.

3 A Memetic GBP Algorithm

Memetic algorithms (MA) [20, 21] are population-based heuristic search approaches for optimization problems. They are inspired by Dawkins' notion of a *meme* [5], defined as a unit of information that reproduces itself while people exchange ideas. The difference between genes and memes is that memes are typically adapted by the persons who transmit them. In the context of evolutionary computation, memetic algorithms are thought of genetic algorithms in which individuals can be refined during lifetime, and where the altered information is then transferred to the next generation.

Our general genetic local search approach proposed in [9, 10] is a special case of a memetic algorithm, which has been shown to be very effective for several combinatorial optimization problems [18, 19, 17]. Opposed to hybrid evolutionary algorithms that use local refinement techniques as additional operators, MAs are designed to search in the space of locally optimal solutions instead of searching the space of all candidate solutions. This is achieved by applying local search after application of each of the genetic operators. Thus, in any generation, the population of individuals consists solely of local optima.

The MA for the GBP is based on the following components:

Initialization and local search: There are two obvious possibilities for generating the initial population: either producing completely random solutions, or using a randomized constructive heuristic such as Diff-Greedy. For local improvement after initialization and after application of the genetic operators, we use the Kernighan-Lin heuristic with a refined data structure based on the ideas of Fiduccia and Mattheyses [8].

The genetic operators:
The crossover operator is the HUX [6], a variant of the uniform crossover (several other crossover operators were investigated, but their results were inferior to HUX). In order to maintain feasibility, HUX must be adapted for application to the GBP. HUX can be performed by first copying all 0s and 1s that are found at the same locations in both parents. The remaining entries are filled with ones in random order from alternating parents until $\frac{n}{2}$ 1s are included. Those entries that are still undefined will be filled with 0s. Thus, HUX is biased so that nearly as much 1s are taken from the first as from the second parent.

Before recombination is performed one of the parents is inverted if the Hamming distance between the parents is greater than $\frac{n}{2}$.

Selection and diversification: Mate selection is performed on a purely random basis without bias to fitter individuals. Selection for survival is done by selecting the best individuals from the pool of parents and children by taking care that each phenotype exists only once in the new population. If the GA converges (no change in the population for 30 generations), the search is restarted by mutating all members of the population except the best one, followed by local searches to obtain locally optimal solutions. The mutation is performed by creating new solutions with distance D to the old ones, where D is set to the average distance in the population after initialization. The restart technique is borrowed from the CHC algorithm by Eshelman [7].

4 Experimental Results

We conducted several experiments by applying our algorithms to 16 different instances, 8 graphs of the first type and 8 graphs of the second type described in section 2.3.

The memetic algorithm described above, including the Kernighan-Lin heuristic and differential greedy, has been implemented in $C++$. All experiments were performed on a Pentium II PC (300 MHz) with the operating system Linux 2.0. In order to compare the performance of the algorithms, the two types of instances were considered separately. For the $Gn.p$ graphs we performed experiments with our MA using Diff-Greedy initialization, a population size of 40, and a crossover rate of 0.5 for HUX.

Table 2 shows the best cut sizes found by our algorithm compared to the best cut sizes found by Bui and Moon (GBA)[4], and Johnson et al. (SA)[12].

Table 2. Best cut sizes found by 3 different algorithms

Instance	MA	GBA	SA	Instance	MA	GBA	SA
G500.005	49	49	52	U500.05	2	2	4
G500.01	218	218	219	U500.10	26	26	26
G500.02	626	626	628	U500.20	178	178	178
G500.04	1744	1744	1744	U500.40	412	412	412
G1000.0025	93	95	102	U1000.05	1	1	3
G1000.005	445	445	451	U1000.10	39	39	39
G1000.01	1362	1362	1367	U1000.20	222	222	222
G1000.02	3382	3382	3389	U1000.40	737	737	737

The average cut sizes and running times (in seconds) for the $Gn.p$ graphs obtained from 30 runs are displayed in Table 3 for three different algorithms. After 30 generations (30g), our results are always better than the results obtained by two alternative approaches, CE-GA[22] and BFS-GBA [4], which have been shown to be the currently best algorithms for bi-partitioning [22]. Running the MA up to a predefined time limit (TL), even better average values could be achieved. The CPU-times given in the table should be taken with care since they refer to different hardware platforms: CE-GA was run on a SGI-O2 workstation (R5000, 180 MHz) and BFS-GBA on a Sun Sparcstation IPX.

Table 3. Average cut sizes and CPU times for non-geometric graphs

Instance	MA (30g) cut	time	MA (TL) cut	time	CE-GA cut	time	BFS-GBA cut	time
G500.005	51.3	2	50.3	60	54.1	24.9	54.0	6
G500.01	218.4	2	218.1	60	221.8	23.7	222.1	8.1
G500.02	628.2	4	627.2	60	631.1	27.5	631.5	11.7
G500.04	1746.3	9	1745.3	60	1750.3	33.4	1752.5	21.6
G1000.0025	97.5	6	95.9	120	104.5	79.2	103.6	16.8
G1000.005	451.9	8	448.6	120	458.5	79.9	458.6	23.7
G1000.01	1368.0	14	1364.2	120	1374.6	79.5	1376.4	37.1
G1000.02	3385.6	22	3384.2	120	3396.8	85.8	3401.7	62.3

The fitness distance analysis for the $Gn.p$ graphs suggests that searching landscapes of problems with low epistasis is harder than searching graphs with a high average vertex degree and thus high epistasis. The selection pressure is much lower for graphs with low average degree since the fitness values of the local optima lie very close together. This is reflected by the results obtained from our experiments. The deviation from the optimum is higher for the instances with inherent low epistasis. A new best solution for G1000.0025 could be found, indicating that previous heuristics have even more difficulties to find near optimum solutions for graphs with low average vertex degree.

Table 4. Average cut sizes and CPU times for geometric graphs

Instance	DG+KL cut	time	CE-GA cut	time	BFS-GBA cut	time
U500.05	2.0	0.10	2.2	13.4	3.7	7.5
U500.10	26.0	0.79	26.0	10.5	32.7	9.6
U500.20	178.0	0.37	178.0	26.3	197.6	11.5
U500.40	412.0	0.07	412.0	9.2	412.2	9.9
U1000.05	1.0	0.04	3.2	43.3	1.8	17.6
U1000.10	39.0	1.64	39.0	20.1	55.8	30.9
U1000.20	222.0	0.56	225.9	37.1	231.6	33.0
U1000.40	737.0	0.22	738.2	38.1	738.1	37.0

The fitness distance analysis for the $Un.d$ graphs has indicated that the combination of Diff-Greedy and Kernighan-Lin local search is likely to be beneficial for solving geometric instances. While the former is effective for problems with low epistasis, the latter is effective in the presence of high epistasis. The results of our experiments for Multi–Start Diff Greedy + Kernighan Lin (DG+KL) are displayed in Table 4. The CPU times to find the best known solutions is provided in seconds. Again, for the different approaches different hardware platforms have been used.

The results demonstrate the effectiveness of the DG+KL combination: BFS-

GA and CE-GA are clearly outperformed by DG+KL. Thus, by using Diff-Greedy for initialization in the MA, all two types of graphs considered in this paper can be solved effectively with the proposed MA. However, in case of the geometric graphs studied, genetic operators are not required for solving the considered instances; the DG+KL combination alone is sufficient to arrive at near-optimum solutions.

5 Conclusions

In this paper, we have analyzed selected fitness landscapes of the graph bi-partitioning problem and have presented a memetic algorithm that is able to find near optimum solutions very efficiently. For the instances studied, a search space analysis based on Kernighan-Lin local search revealed that the fitness landscapes of geometric and non-geometric random graphs are significantly different, and instances with high epistasis are easier to solve by local search based heuristics than instances with low inherent epistasis. This result is surprising, since for NK-landscapes the opposite is true: here, the number of local optima increases with increasing K and hence with higher epistasis. Furthermore, an analysis based on a recently proposed greedy heuristic indicated that the combination of this heuristic with Kernighan-Lin local search works very well for geometric graphs.

The performed experiments have shown that the memetic algorithm proposed in this paper is highly effective on the instances studied. For the non-geometric graphs, it produced equal or better solutions than all other heuristics known to us; even a new best solution could be found for one instance. Incorporating the greedy heuristic in the initialization phase of the memetic algorithm yielded an approach that produced similarly good results for the geometric graphs; in this case, however, the mere combination of the greedy heuristic and Kernighan-Lin local search is sufficient. Thus, for both types of graph, our memetic algorithm appears to be superior to any other algorithm we are aware of.

References

1. R. Battiti and A. Bertossi. Differential Greedy for the 0–1 Equicut Problem. In D.Z. Du and P.M. Pardalos, editors, *Proceedings of the DIMACS Workshop on Network Design: Connectivity and Facilities Location*. Amer. Math. Soc., 1997.
2. R. Battiti and A. Bertossi. Greedy, Prohibition, and Reactive Heuristics for Graph-Partitioning. *IEEE Transactions on Computers*, 1997, to appear.
3. K.D. Boese. Cost versus Distance in the Traveling Salesman Problem. Technical Report TR-950018, UCLA CS Department, 1995.
4. T. N. Bui and B. R. Moon. Genetic Algorithm and Graph Partitioning. *IEEE Transactions on Computers*, 45(7):841–855, 1996.
5. R. Dawkins. *The Selfish Gene*. Oxford University Press, Oxford, 1976.
6. L. J. Eshelman and J. D. Schaffer. Preventing Premature Convergence in Genetic Algorithms by Preventing Incest. In *Proceedings of the 4th Int. Conference on Genetic Algorithms*, pages 115–122. Morgan Kaufmann, 1991.

7. L.J. Eshelman. The CHC Adaptive Search Algorithm: How to Have Safe Search When Engaging in Nontraditional Genetic Recombination. In G. J. E. Rawlings, editor, *Foundations of Genetic Algorithms*, pages 265–283. Kaufmann, 1991.

8. C. M. Fiduccia and R. M. Mattheyses. A Liner-Time Heuristic for Improving Network Partitions. In *Proceedings of the 19th ACM/IEEE Design Automation Conference DAC 82*, pages 175–181, 1982.

9. B. Freisleben and P. Merz. A Genetic Local Search Algorithm for Solving Symmetric and Asymmetric Traveling Salesman Problems. In *Proceedings of the 1996 IEEE International Conference on Evolutionary Computation*, pages 616–621. IEEE Press, 1996.

10. B. Freisleben and P. Merz. New Genetic Local Search Operators for the Traveling Salesman Problem. In H.-M. Voigt, W. Ebeling, I. Rechenberg, and H.-P. Schwefel, editors, *Proceedings of the 4th Conference on Parallel Problem Solving from Nature - PPSN IV*, pages 890–900. Springer, 1996.

11. M. R. Garey and D. S. Johnson. *Computers and Intractability: A Guide to the Theory of NP-Completeness*. Freeman, New York, 1979.

12. D. S. Johnson, C. R. Aragon, L. A. McGeoch, and C. Schevon. Optimization by Simulated Annealing; Part I, Graph Partitioning. *Operations Research*, 37:865–892, 1989.

13. T. Jones and S. Forrest. Fitness Distance Correlation as a Measure of Problem Difficulty for Genetic Algorithms. In L. J. Eshelman, editor, *Proceedings of the 6th Int. Conference on Genetic Algorithms*, pages 184–192, Kaufman, 1995.

14. S. A. Kauffman. *The Origins of Order: Self-Organization and Selection in Evolution*. Oxford University Press, 1993.

15. S. A. Kauffman and S. Levin. Towards a General Theory of Adaptive Walks on Rugged Landscapes. *Journal of Theoretical Biology*, 128:11–45, 1987.

16. B. Kernighan and S. Lin. An Efficient Heuristic Procedure for Partitioning Graphs. *Bell Systems Journal*, 49:291–307, 1972.

17. P. Merz and B. Freisleben. On the Effectiveness of Evolutionary Search in High-Dimensional NK-Landscapes. In *Proceedings of the 1998 IEEE International Conference on Evolutionary Computation*, pages 741–745, IEEE Press, 1998.

18. P. Merz and B. Freisleben. A Genetic Local Search Approach to the Quadratic Assignment Problem. In T. Bäck, editor, *Proceedings of the 7th International Conference on Genetic Algorithms*, pages 465–472, Morgan Kaufmann, 1997.

19. P. Merz and B. Freisleben. Genetic Local Search for the TSP: New Results. In *Proceedings of the 1997 IEEE International Conference on Evolutionary Computation*, pages 159–164, IEEE Press, 1997.

20. P. Moscato. On Evolution, Search, Optimization, Genetic Algorithms and Martial Arts: Towards Memetic Algorithms. Technical Report No. 790, Caltech Concurrent Computation Program, California Institue of Technology, USA, 1989.

21. P. Moscato and M. G. Norman. A Memetic Approach for the Traveling Salesman Problem Implementation of a Computational Ecology for Combinatorial Optimization on Message-Passing Systems. In M. Valero, E. Onate, M. Jane, J. L. Larriba, and B. Suarez, editors, *Parallel Computing and Transputer Applications*, pages 177–186, IOS Press, 1992.

22. A. G. Steenbeek, E. Marchiori, and A. E. Eiben. Finding Balanced Graph Bi-Partitions Using a Hybrid Genetic Algorithm. In *Proceedings of the IEEE International Conference on Evolutionary Computation ICEC'98*, pages 90–95, IEEE press, 1998.

Investigating Evolutionary Approaches to Adaptive Database Management Against Various Quality of Service Metrics

Martin J Oates, David Corne

Dept of Computer Science, University of Reading, Reading, RG6 6AY, UK, E-mail:
moates@srd.bt.co.uk, D.W.Corne@reading.ac.uk

Abstract. The management of large distributed databases is becoming more complex as user demand grows. Further, global access causes points of geographic contention to 'follow the sun' during the day giving rise to a dynamic optimisation problem where the goal is to constantly maximise the quality of service seen by the database users. A key quality criterion is to optimise the quality of service perceived by the worst-served user by finding a choice of client-server mapping which best balances issues such as exploitation of fast servers and communications links, and the degradation in response-time due to over-use of such servers/links. Any approach to solving the problem must be fast (so that results remain applicable) and successful over a variety of different database usage scenarios and quality of service metrics. This paper investigates the effectiveness of several local and evolutionary search approaches to this problem, focusing on the variations in performance across a range of QoS metrics.

1. Introduction

Traditional site mirroring has been shown to be effective at distributing high loads on internet servers where demand is simultaneously generated over a wide area. However, where access is global, demand will tend to originate in localised regions at different times of the day, for example shifting from Europe to the Americas and then to the Asia Pacific region in a 24 hour cycle. Whilst there will always be overlap, peak demand is unlikely to coincide, except during the release of eagerly awaited software or news. Localised mirroring in one region only, will simply shift the contention onto the global communications networks when demand shifts to other regions. Mirroring in each region is not only costly, but also leads to over-duplication of data and greater problems with integrity and multiple updates.

The authors are engaged in a long term research activity, sponsored by British Telecommunications Plc, investigating the practicalities of autonomous management of access to distributed databases using Evolutionary Computing techniques (Oates et al, 1998). Such a system will dynamically balance demand across the available servers based on optimising a quality of service metric which takes into account both the load on each server, and the load on the links of the interconnecting communications network. The current access configuration takes into account how the pattern of both retrieval and update operations changes from each point of demand as time passes.

Work has already been published on applying Evolutionary techniques to distributed database design by Rho and March (1994), March and Rho (1995) and Cedano and Vemuri (1997), but this has focused on static design based on aggregate loading patterns or has not considered communication costs. Bilchev and Olafsson (1998) have approached the problem based on high levels of duplication, whilst Edwards (1997) has suggested a binary combinatorial allocation algorithm to reduce the search space. Previous publications by the authors have built on Edwards' model comparing the performance of EC techniques on the basic system model and an enhanced form of it (Oates, Corne and Loader, 1998), and investigating parameter selection by a quality of service metric for Genetic Algorithm based solutions (Oates and Corne, 1998). So far this work has been based on a single database usage scenario (that is, a fixed underlying communications network, with a given snapshot of database usage in terms of retrieval rates and update rates for each client), and has looked at just two quality of service metrics. For the eventual applicability of this research, it is critical that the optimisation methods tested are robust across a range of distinct database usage scenarios, and also across a wide range of different quality of service performance metrics which may be applied. This paper describes investigations into the relative performance of several optimisation methods on seven distinct quality of service metrics, and two distinct database usage scenarios.

2. Model and Method

Using a model of the distributed information system, covering performance of both database servers and communications networks, the performance of the system as seen by individual client applications, can be estimated for current load conditions over a range of different access and server configurations. The choice of configuration is determined by an optimisation algorithm whilst the system model is based on work at BT Labs by Edwards (1997), and is based on assumptions that the performance of both servers and communications links degrade under load according to Little's Law and the principles of MM1 queues. The model has been described in (Oates Corne, 1998), and full details and an implementation in C are being placed on the ECTELNET website (http://www.dcs.napier.ac.uk/evonet/). ECTELNET is the Telecommunications subgroup of the European Network of Excellence in Evolutionary Computation.

The model characterises the non-congested performance of each server, the degree of 'parallelism' that each server can exploit, the non-congested performance of each client/server communication link, and the usage profile, or load, of each client in terms of the data retrieval rate, update rate and degree of overlap between these two modes of access. Given a 'solution vector' by the optimiser, which defines for each client which server it should currently connect to, the basic model calculates the load on each server and link, taking into account any required multiple updates. It then calculates the degraded performance of each server and link, and returns the worst performance as defined by transaction time seen by any client. (Enhanced versions of the model bias this result as will be discussed later). This result is then seen as an inverse measure of the 'Quality of Service' for the underlying information system. The optimisation algorithm seeks to minimise the returned value by finding a suitable configuration of client accesses. This is a classic 'minimax' scenario.

The 'solution vector' has one entry per client, the value of each entry specifying which server that client should access. Hence we use a k-ary representation, where the alleles of a 'client' gene range over the number of servers available within the system. Each node is considered capable of being both a client and server. This effectively creates an n^n search space, where n equals the number of client/server nodes in the system. We will look at two distinct database usage scenarios, A and B, each with 10 nodes. Scenario A considers a network of servers of similar capabilities all within a factor of 2 from least to best raw performance capability. The performance of each link in the underlying network covers a similar range. An arbitrary loading pattern is applied covering both retrievals and updates from each node. With this scenario, and the basic model, the optimiser can find many different 'least worst' solution vectors. By contrast, 'Scenario B' splits the nodes into 2 regions. Within each region communications costs are low, but access across regions incurs a high penalty. Each region has a 'super node' with raw performance of a factor of 10 greater than other nodes in the same region. Individual node loading is fairly arbitrary however updates originate more frequently from the 'super nodes'. This scenario, with the basic model, has only one globally optimal solution, with all nodes in a region accessing their region's supernode.

Potential Solution Vector :

Client Node >	1	2	3	4	5	6	7	8	9	10
Which Server to Use >	1	4	3	4	3	2	2	3	4	1

The 'basic model' as described has also been used in a variety of modified forms to produce different measures of 'quality of service'. As will be seen, these can significantly alter the landscape of the search space making it far harder to find global optima. In the basic model, the fitness of a solution vector is the worst response time seen from any server; all servers take part in the calculation, since even if a server is currently not being accessed by a client, it is still receiving regular updates, which affect its quality as a 'standby' if another server fails. The first variant, however, only considers the performance of servers which are currently 'used' in the solution vector. This variant is referred to as 'just used'. The second variant adds 10% of the access time for all servers to the 'least worst' server time returned. This strikes a balance between minimising worst performance and aggregate server performance and is referred to as 'plus avg'. The third variant adds 10% of the comms access time seen by all clients on the worst server, divided by the number of servers used. This adds a bias based on aggregate user perception but with weighting in favour of over-duplication of data. This was argued for on the basis of enhanced resilience and is referred to as 'plus used'. Fourth, the 'plus servers' variant adds 10% of the average performance of all used servers to the 'least worst' result. Fifth, the 'plus 10%' variant adds 10% of the average of all client accesses weighted by their usage rate to all used servers, whilst finally, 'plus all' adds all (100%) of this, rather than just 10%.

This last variant is seen as probably the most realistic in terms of representing user perception of Quality of Service.

Earlier work by the authors (Oates et al, 1998) clearly showed how just one of these variants on one scenario complicated the search space landscape significantly enough as to lose hill-climbing algorithms in the 'hanging valleys' it created. Five techniques have been investigated and are reported on here. Firstly a simple 'hill-climbing' optimiser (HC), using only single gene mutation, was tried. This algorithm only ever has 2 solutions to choose from, the 'parent' solution or its mutated 'child'. If the 'child' delivers a result better or equal to the parent, then it replaces the parent, otherwise the parent remains as the 'current' solution. Second, Simulated Annealing (SA) was also used, with a geometric cooling schedule, with starting and final temperatures chosen after a preliminary tuning session.

Third, a breeder-style (Mühlenbein et al, 1994) Genetic Algorithm was used, employing 50% elitism, whereby a random population of solutions are initially generated, evaluated and ranked. The worst performing half of the population are then deleted, to be replaced by children generated by random selection of two parents from the 'best' half of population, using uniform crossover followed by uniformly distributed allele replacement mutation. This is subsequently referred to as 'BDR'. Fourth, a tournament-style Genetic Algorithm was used, again with a randomly generated initial population, but this time three members of the population are chosen at random. These 3 are ranked and the best and second are used as parents to produce a child which replaces the 'worst' performing member of the three way tournament. The same crossover and mutation methods are used as in the 'Breeder' GA described above. This is subsequently referred to as 'TNT'.

Finally, for some model variants, Edwards' original search algorithm is used for comparison. This algorithm considers in turn every possible combination of nodes as potential servers and then considers, for each client, which of these available servers would give the fastest response (regardless of load from other nodes at this stage). This is then used to construct a solution vector which is evaluated taking into consideration contention and comms network performance. It can be considered to be a 'greedy heuristic' algorithm and reduces the search space to considering 2^n solution vectors, each requiring a time roughly proportional to 'n' to derive them. As such, when successful, it can prove effective for low values of 'n', however cannot be deemed scaleable for values of 'n' much in excess of 15.

3. Results

For each of the first 4 optimisation methods described above, 1000 trial runs were performed, each starting with a different, randomly generated solution or population of solutions. For each of these 4000 runs, each method was allowed first 1000 and then 5000 evaluations, reporting the fitness value of the best found solution in each case. Of these 8000 runs, the 'best known fitness' value was noted. For the Simulated

Annealer, the temperature gradient was adjusted between the 1000 and 5000 evaluation runs to maintain comparable start and end temperatures.

Model	Alg	Evals	Scenario A			Scenario B		
			On Tgt	< 5%	> 30%	On Tgt	< 5%	> 30%
Basic	HC	1K	865	984	0	666	666	310
		5K	997	1000	0	683	683	317
	SA	1K	764	917	0	398	398	528
		5K	993	1000	0	976	976	24
	BDR	1K	614	875	0	159	159	569
		5K	979	998	0	950	950	44
	TNT	1K	731	918	0	344	344	525
		5K	982	1000	0	931	931	64
+ avg	HC	1K	26	514	47	110	112	888
		5K	21	525	46	90	90	910
	SA	1K	27	793	1	608	936	64
		5K	54	993	0	1000	1000	0
	BDR	1K	0	874	0	21	616	48
		5K	157	993	0	997	999	1
	TNT	1K	20	768	1	327	634	344
		5K	132	913	0	772	785	209
+ used	HC	1K	498	762	6	0	0	1000
		5K	610	755	5	0	0	1000
	SA	1K	482	785	0	6	6	991
		5K	857	990	0	224	224	776
	BDR	1K	442	787	0	0	0	998
		5K	935	1000	0	51	51	744
	TNT	1K	402	748	0	0	0	1000
		5K	925	999	0	88	88	672

Table 1- Results for Scenario A and B

The tests were run on both the 'A' and 'B' scenarios against the 'basic', 'plus avg', and 'plus used' models and the results are summarised in Table 1. This shows the number of 'best found solutions', out of the 1000 runs per optimiser/evaluation limit combination, which matched the 'best known fitness' value for that model/scenario combination. This is referred to as 'On Target'. In an industrial application it may not be necessary to find exactly the best solution, and so the number of solutions found with values within 5% of the 'best known fitness value' is also given. However solutions worse than 30% 'off target' are deemed to be unacceptable and the number of solutions falling into this category is shown also.

As can clearly be seen, on Scenario A, with the basic model, all methods, even at only 1000 evaluations, deliver good results. No solution was found at worse than 30% off the 'best known fitness value'. At 5000 evaluations there is little to choose between algorithms, with HC marginally best, but all methods show improved performance given more evaluations The 'plus avg' metric however, completely fools HC, with no significant improvement between 1000 and 5000 evaluations. SA, BDR and TNT give similar performances to each other, all requiring 5000 evals to get respectable results, with BDR arguably the best based on 'on target' results. 'Plus used' gives similar results to 'plus avg' on Scenario A, with BDR a slightly clearer winner. Scenario B completely throws the hillclimber, even on the 'basic' model there is little difference between 1000 and 5000 evaluations, both giving appalling results. SA, BDR and TNT give similar results to each other on the 'basic' model, with SA the superior in almost all cases, however what is of interest is the difference in results between 'plus avg' and 'plus used'. The latter is clearly a difficult search space to operate in, and it is debatable whether SA, with 22.4% on target versus BDR with only 5.1%, is better than BDR with only 74.4 % worse than 30% off target versus SA with 77.6%, at 5000 evaluations. Neither are respectable results.

What is of particular interest here is that starting from the 'plus avg' model on 'Scenario A', the move to either the 'plus used' model or to 'Scenario B' individually does not present a challenge to either BDR or SA at 5000 evaluations, however the combination of 'Scenario B' and the 'plus used' model introduces a highly difficult search space. This will be explored later in this paper, together with the effect on GA parameter choice.

| | | Scenario A | | | Scenario B | | |
Model	# Evals	On Tgt	< 5%	> 30%	On Tgt	< 5%	> 30%
just used	1K	769	936	0	80	80	824
	5K	983	1000	0	829	829	171
+ servers	1K	305	822	3	843	843	57
	5K	511	988	0	1000	1000	0
+10% all	1K	70	916	0	104	104	886
	5K	166	999	0	820	820	180
+ all	1K	81	852	0	24	24	975
	5K	152	996	0	402	402	598

Table 2 Extended Model Results for Scenarios A & B

By way of comparison on Scenario A, Edwards' algorithm delivers 'best found' solutions of between 81% and 88% worse than the 'best known fitness value' over the range of models, and this is disappointing particularly with respect to the basic model. This algorithm executes 1023 'evaluations' preceded by approximately 10K pre-evaluation checks. On Scenario B, Edwards' algorithm consistently finds the 'best known fitness value'. This performance is in high contrast to the performance of the other methods, and clearly shows that for some types of solution, a greedy combinatorial algorithm can out perform an evolutionary one, and vice versa. The performance of a hybrid 'greedy/GA' algorithm has yet to be investigated. Similar tests were run at 1000 and 5000 evaluations, again repeated 1000 times, for the remaining models : 'just used', 'plus servers', 'plus 10% of all' and 'plus all', against both 'A' and 'B' scenarios, table 2 gives the results for Simulated Annealing.

Using Simulated Annealing as the benchmark, combinations of model and scenario

Model	Scenario A	Scenario B
'Edwards'	Hard	Easy
basic	Very Easy	Moderate
just used	Very Easy	Hard
plus avg	Easy	Very Easy
plus used	Very Easy	Very Hard
plus servers	Easy	Easy
plus 10% of all	Easy	Hard
plus all	Easy	Very Hard

Table 3 - Summary of search space difficulty

were then categorised as on a scale from 'very easy' through to 'very hard' dependent on how many 'on target' or near hits were achieved and how few were '>30% off'. This is summarised in table 3. Of particular interest here is the sudden transition from 'Very Easy' to 'Very Hard' going from Scenario A to B using the 'plus used' model (and similar effect with 'plus all').

To see if better results could be obtained from the Genetic Algorithms if different population sizes and mutation rates were used, an extensive series of tests was run using population sizes varying from 2 to 100 members, in increments of 2, with mutation rates varying from 2% to 50% probability per gene in increments of 2%. For each combination of the above, the tuned Breeder GA was allowed 5000 evaluations, delivering the 'best found fitness value' and the evaluation number at which this was first found. These were combined into a single value taking the number of evaluations needed, and biasing it by an offset dependent on the square of the difference between the 'best found fitness value' of the particular run and the 'best known fitness value. This was then rerun 50 times, each with a different randomly generated initial population, and the value of the 50 runs averaged into a single measure of the quality of performance for each 'tuning combination'. This technique is explained in more detail in (Oates et al, 1998) and (Oates and Corne, 1998). Low values therefore represent good solutions consistently found in a minimum number of evaluations.

The results for the 'plus avg' model on Scenario A are shown in Fig 1. Here it can be seen that there is a trough feature running from regions of low population size with medium levels of mutation (circa 14 to 24%) through to high populations with lower mutation rates (circa 4 to 8%). This 'trade-off' is of no surprise as both increased population size and increased mutation rate provide sources of genetic diversity. Clearly there is an ideal balance to be struck between these two, with either too much or too little genetic diversity being detrimental to performance. The plateau feature at higher mutation rates (>24%) and the apparent dip at around 48% mutation are crossover features produced as the ever high level of mutation causes an increase in error penalty whilst the number of raw evaluations that the GA is able to exploit reduces. This later effect is soon swamped by the former, and this phenomenon is explained in (Oates and Corne, 1998). Fig 1 also suggests that combinations of even lower mutation rates (< 2%) with higher population sizes (> 100) should also give good results, and this will be discussed in a forthcoming publication.

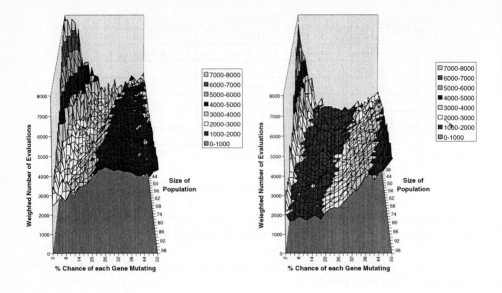

Fig 1 Scenario A with 'plus avg' Model   Fig 2 Scenario A with 'plus used' Model

Interestingly Fig 2, showing the performance for the Breeder GA with the 'plus used' model on Scenario A, shows a much wider region of stable performance. The trough feature is again apparent, but with a much wider (and lower) base which supports the earlier categorisation for Scenario A with 'plus used' as actually being easier that with 'plus avg', when trying to consistently find good solutions. What is not totally apparent from Fig 2 however, but is clear from the raw data, is that the lowest points of this trough occur at population sizes below 40 with mutation rates in the range of 14 to 24%. The base of the trough rises from this point with increased population size, as the increased range of breeding partners slows the GA down.

Fig 3 shows the 'plus avg' results for Scenario B. Here we can still see the trough and plateau features, however the 'cliff edge' feature that is apparent once either mutation rate or population size fall below certain levels, shows that where there is insufficient genetic diversity, the high frequency of having to apply high error penalties completely swamps the results leading to totally unacceptable performance. Again, whilst Fig 3 may suggest even better results could be achieved at population sizes > 100 with mutation rates < 10%, the lowest point of the trough is actually at a population size of around 40, with mutation at 12%. The floor of the trough again rises from this point with increased population size. Fig 4 shows the results for Scenario B with the 'plus used' model. Note the scale of the 'Evaluations' axis is nearly three orders of magnitude greater, showing that the 'error squared penalty' is dominant and that there must be a high rate of inability to find 'best known fitness value' solutions in less than 5000 evaluations among the 50

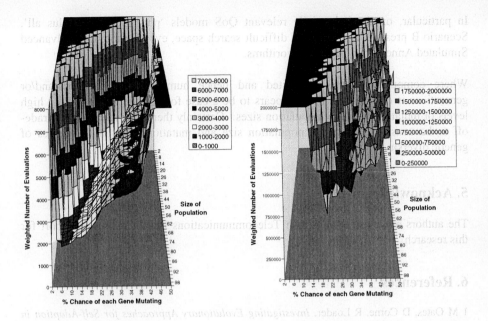

Fig 3 Scenario B with 'plus avg' Model   Fig 4 Scenario B with 'plus used Model

runs, even under 'ideally tuned' conditions. These results suggest that areas of much higher population or much higher mutation should be explored, however mutation > 50% is most unlikely to yield good results, as discussed in (Oates and Corne, 1998).

Mutation rates used here could be described as uncommonly high, however these have been used because of their apparent success with relatively low population sizes. The overall computation time for the Breeder GA significantly increases with higher populations due to the ranking of the entire population each generation. Also, given the fixed number of evaluations, large populations restrict the number of generations allowed by the Breeder GA. Despite these features, it is still clearly true that with well chosen tuning parameters, consistently good performance can still be achieved in both these variant cases. A study comparing performance when very high/low mutation rates are applied to this problem is currently underway.

4. Conclusions

The choice of specific QoS model used as the evaluation function can have a dramatic effect on the complexity of the search space and hence on how easy it is to find global optima. This in turn can lead to the requirement for more complex optimisers. Basic Hillclimber is shown to be quite ineffective on any 'realistic' model of this problem.

The dynamic nature of the problem, here demonstrated in two contrasting scenarios, implies that no single algorithmic approach is likely to be efficient in all circumstances. Instances have been shown here, where a greedy / combinatorial approach can out-perform an evolutionary one and vice-versa.

In particular, on the industrially relevant QoS models 'plus used' and 'plus all', Scenario B presents a particularly difficult search space, even for the more advanced Simulated Annealer or Genetic Algorithms.

Where computation time is limited and hence number of evaluations and/or generations is constrained, there appears to be a case for considering unusually high levels of mutation with low population sizes. Certainly there is evidence for a trade-off to be considered between population size and mutation rate - both sources of genetic diversity.

5. Acknowledgements

The authors are grateful to British Telecommunications Plc for ongoing support for this research.

6. References

1 M Oates, D Corne, R Loader, *Investigating Evolutionary Approaches for Self-Adaption in Large Distributed Databases*, in Proceedings of the 1998 IEEE International Conference on Evolutionary Computation pp. 452-457

2 S Rho and S.T. March, *A Nested Genetic Algorithm for Database Design*, in Proceedings of the 27th Hawaii International Conference on System Sciences, 1994, pp.33-42.

3 S.T. March and S Rho, *Allocating Data and Operations to Nodes in Distributed Database Design*. IEEE Transactions on Knowledge and Data Engineering 7(2), April 1995, pp.305-317.

4 W Cedeno and V.R. Vemuri, Database Design with Genetic Algorithms, in D. Dasgupta and Z. Michalewicz (eds.), *Evolutionary Algorithms in Engineering Applications*, Springer-Verlag, 1997, pp. 189-206.

5 G Bilchev and S Olafsson, *Comparing Evolutionary Algorithms and Greedy Heuristics for Adaption Problems*, in Proceedings of the 1998 IEEE International Conference on Evolutionary Computation pp. 458-463

6 D Edwards, *Performance Adaption Algorithm (draft 4x4c)* , British Telecommunications Advanced Networks and Systems Project Document, 1997.

7 M Oates and D Corne, *QoS based GA Parameter Selection for Autonomously Managed Distributed Information Systems*, in Proceedings of 1998 European Conference on Artificial Intelligence pp. 670-674

8 H. M hlenbein and D. Schlierkamp-Voosen, *The Science of Breeding and its application to the Breeder Genetic Algorithm*, Evolutionary Computation 1, pp. 335-360, 1994.

Genetic Algorithm Behavior in the MAXSAT Domain

Soraya Rana and Darrell Whitley

Colorado State University, Fort Collins CO. 80523, USA
{rana, whitley}@cs.colostate.edu

Abstract. Random Boolean Satisfiability function generators have recently been proposed as tools for studying genetic algorithm behavior. Yet MAXSAT problems exhibit extremely limited epistasis. Furthermore, all nonzero Walsh coefficients can be computed *exactly* for MAXSAT problems in polynomial time using only the clause information. This means the low order schema averages can be computed quickly and exactly for very large MAXSAT problems. But unless P=NP, this low order information cannot reliably lead to the global optimum, thus nontrivial MAXSAT problems must be deceptive.

1 Introduction

A common assumption is that a simple genetic algorithm assembles a solution using low-order schema information. When an optimization problem has low-order schema information that leads away from the global optimum, it is considered **deceptive**. In this paper we examine MAXSAT as an example of a problem domain that can be proven to contain misleading low order schema information. Furthermore, MAXSAT search spaces tend to result in similar schema fitness averages. These two attributes of MAXSAT problems make them an unsuitable application for traditional genetic algorithms.

Genetic algorithms are typically applied to black-box optimization problems; however, MAXSAT problems are not black-box optimization problems. As it turns out, the problem description for arbitrary random MAXSAT problems can be used to compute low order schema information **exactly** and in a linear amount of time with respect to the number of clauses. If $P \neq NP$, then this low order information cannot reliably lead to a global optimum. We will empirically illustrate that a genetic algorithm converges to many distant points and that those points are only partially consistent with the low order schema information.

2 A Walsh Analysis of Satisfiability Problems

A method for studying the epistasis in a binary function is to use Walsh analysis [5,6,9]. All binary functions can be represented as a weighted sum of **Walsh functions** denoted by ψ_j, where $0 \leq j \leq 2^L - 1$ with each Walsh function being $\psi_j : \mathcal{B}^L \rightarrow \{-1, 1\}$. The real-valued weights are called **Walsh coefficients**.

Walsh functions are defined using a bitwise-AND of the function index and its argument. Note that operations on indices such as j act on the binary representation of j. Let $bc(j)$ be a count of the number of 1 bits in string j. The 2^L Walsh coefficients for function $f(i)$ can be computed by a Walsh transform:

$$w_j = \frac{1}{2^L} \sum_{i=0}^{2^L-1} f(i)\psi_j(i) \quad \text{where} \quad \psi_j(x) = (-1)^{bc(j \wedge x)}$$

So, if $bc(j \wedge x)$ is odd, then $\psi_j(x) = -1$ and if $bc(j \wedge x)$ is even, then $\psi_j(x) = 1$. Note these equations require that the enumeration and evaluation of all 2^L strings to compute a single coefficient. Thus, Walsh analysis generally requires exponential time with respect to L.

The Boolean Satisfiability problem (SAT) is to determine whether or not there is some setting of variables such that a Boolean expression can be made TRUE. SAT problems are generally presented in conjunctive normal form using clauses of a particular length, K. When KSAT problems are solved using optimization algorithms rather than backtracking algorithms, all variables are given a setting and evaluated. However, black box optimizers cannot effectively optimize a function that returns nothing but a 0 or 1. Rather than combining the clauses using the AND operator, the numeric truth value for each individual clause, 0 for FALSE or 1 for TRUE, are summed together. This form of the evaluation function is called MAXSAT. An L-bit MAXSAT problem can be represented as a sum of C disjunctive clauses, f_i:

$$f(x) = \sum_{i=1}^{C} f_i(x)$$

where $f, f_1, f_2, ... f_C : \mathcal{B}^L \to \mathcal{R}$. Each clause evaluation, f_i, takes an L-bit string as input but extracts and uses only K-bits in the calculation, where K is the length of the clause. This constraint means that each clause contributes to only 2^K Walsh coefficients [8].

Since the Walsh transform can be performed by a simple linear transformation, the Walsh transform of a MAXSAT problem can be treated as a sum of the Walsh transforms of the individual clauses.

$$W(f(x)) = \sum_{i=1}^{C} W(f_i(x))$$

Consider a 3-bit single clause problem using $f(x) = \neg x_2 \vee x_1 \vee x_0$. We construct the Walsh matrix to compute the Walsh coefficient vector, w, using matrix multiplication.

$$w = \frac{1}{8} \begin{bmatrix} 1 \\ 1 \\ 1 \\ 1 \\ 0 \\ 1 \\ 1 \\ 1 \end{bmatrix}^T \begin{bmatrix} 1 & 1 & 1 & 1 & 1 & 1 & 1 & 1 \\ 1 & -1 & 1 & -1 & 1 & -1 & 1 & -1 \\ 1 & 1 & -1 & -1 & 1 & 1 & -1 & -1 \\ 1 & -1 & -1 & 1 & 1 & -1 & -1 & 1 \\ 1 & 1 & 1 & 1 & -1 & -1 & -1 & -1 \\ 1 & -1 & 1 & -1 & -1 & 1 & -1 & 1 \\ 1 & 1 & -1 & -1 & -1 & -1 & 1 & 1 \\ 1 & -1 & -1 & 1 & -1 & 1 & 1 & -1 \end{bmatrix} = \begin{bmatrix} 0.875 \\ -0.125 \\ -0.125 \\ -0.125 \\ 0.125 \\ 0.125 \\ 0.125 \\ 0.125 \end{bmatrix} \quad (1)$$

The fitness vector for any disjunctive clause must be 1 everywhere except for a single 0 where the clause is FALSE. Since ψ_0 is the average fitness, $w_0 = \frac{2^K - 1}{2^K}$. The remaining Walsh functions evaluate to -1 exactly as often as 1. All but one value will cancel and this value depends on where the fitness is zero. Since the clause is disjunctive, the only time the fitness is zero is when all literals are simultaneously FALSE. Define the function $z = negvec(c, L)$ to take a clause description as input and return an L-bit string that makes the clause false. Variables included in the vector that are unused in the clause will be filled with 0's in z. The remaining Walsh coefficients can be written as:

$$w_j = -\frac{1}{2^K}\psi_j(negvec(c, L)) \qquad \forall j \neq 0$$

3 Observations about the Walsh Analysis of MAXSAT

The number of Walsh coefficients is exponential with respect to K; however, $K << L$ and is typically a bounded constant. The most commonly used value for K is 3 which will be adopted for the remainder of the paper. There are only $7C$ calculations required to enumerate the set of nonzero Walsh coefficients for arbitrary MAX3SAT expressions. Normally the value of C is linear with respect to L; therefore, the set of nonzero Walsh coefficients is sparse and enumerable in polynomial time. Furthermore, the set of all nonzero Walsh coefficients represent nothing but simple counts of variable uses over the set of clauses.

Consider a small MAXSAT function $f : \mathcal{B}^4 \to \mathcal{R}$ with $f(x) = f_1 + f_2 + f_3$ and

$$f_1 = (\neg x_2 \vee x_1 \vee x_0) \qquad f_2 = (\neg x_3 \vee x_2 \vee x_1) \qquad f_3 = (x_3 \vee \neg x_1 \vee \neg x_0).$$

The Walsh coefficient w_2 is computed for f as follows:

$$w_2 = -\frac{1}{8}\psi_2(negvec(f_1, 4)) - \frac{1}{8}\psi_2(negvec(f_2, 4)) - \frac{1}{8}\psi_2(negvec(f_3, 4))$$

The w_2 coefficient is a measure of the linear contribution of the Boolean variable x_1. All three clauses use the variable x_1 so they are all included in the calculation.

The Walsh function indices are masks that isolate variables or combinations of variables. The $negvec()$ function produces a mask corresponding to negated variables. When this vector and the Walsh function index are merged together by the bitwise-AND, the information that is extracted is the parity of the negation information for a particular subset of variables.

Thus, the Walsh coefficients for MAXSAT problems are nothing more than a constant $-\frac{1}{2^K}$ multiplied by a count over the uses of subsets of variables across the set of all clauses. The following method shows how to compute a simple count that can be used to calculate the nonzero Walsh coefficients for arbitrary MAXSAT problems.

Define $T(x, c)$ for variable x and clause c as follows:

$$T(x, c) = \begin{cases} 1 \text{ if } x \text{ is present} \\ -1 \text{ if } \neg x \text{ is present} \\ 0 \text{ otherwise} \end{cases}$$

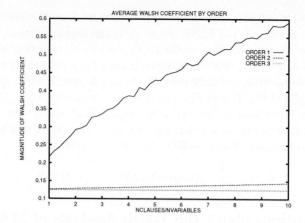

Fig. 1. Average magnitudes of nonzero Walsh coefficients (excluding w_0).

Define $use(c)$ to return a subset of all variables used by a clause c. Let $S_{v,c}$ be a sign (± 1) determined for a clause c and a subset of variables v as follows:

$$S_{v,c} = \prod_{x \in v} T(x,c) \quad \text{where} \quad v \in \bigcup_{c \in f} (\mathcal{P}(use(c)))$$

Then the Walsh term associated with a particular variable combination v is

$$w_v = \frac{-1}{2^K} count_v \quad \text{where} \quad count_v = \sum_c S_{v,c}$$

For order-1 Walsh coefficients, these counts simply compute the difference between the number of times a variable is used positively and the number of times a variable is used negatively.

Schema averages are sometimes used to try to understand the behavior of genetic algorithms. Order-1 schema are computed using Walsh coefficients w_0 and w_i, where w_i measures the contribution of a single bit [5]. The order-1 schema averages are only a constant offset of the order-1 Walsh coefficients. Thus, all order-1 schema competitions are *decided* by the following heuristic:

If a variable occurs positively more often than negatively, the variable should be set to TRUE otherwise set the variable FALSE.

It follows that if the order-1 schema are not misleading, then this heuristic *decides* the MAXSAT problem. In practice, all non-trivial MAXSAT problems are *deceptive:* the schema information is inherently misleading. We might also ask if there is useful order-2 or order-3 schema information. Figure 1 shows the average magnitude of *nonzero* Walsh coefficients for a large set of randomly generated 100 variable MAX3SAT problems. The horizontal axis represents the ratio of clauses to variables; steps were taken in increments of 0.2. Each point in the graph is the average of 30 problem instances. Each line tracks the average magnitude of all nonzero Walsh coefficients for order-1, order-2, and order-3 interactions.

The plot indicates that the order-1 terms are relatively large compared to the order-2 and order-3 Walsh coefficients. Since order-2 and order-3 schema averages include order-1 Walsh coefficients, it follows that these schema averages will also tend to be consistent with the order-1 schema averages. Furthermore, since all of this information can be computed in polynomial time and it is fairly consistent, this information cannot lead to the global optimum if $P \neq NP$. Therefore, MAXSAT problems must be deceptive to a genetic algorithm. Also notice that many of the Walsh coefficients are the same (either 0 or 0.125), and thus many schema averages will be identical. Not only is the MAXSAT landscape misleading, it is also relatively flat.

4   Empirical Verification

We have provided theoretical evidence to support the claim that genetic algorithms should not perform well in the MAXSAT domain. To verify this, we ran a Simple Genetic Algorithm (SGA) with tournament selection on a small set of random MAXSAT problem instances. Our SGA implementation used tournament selection with a tournament size of 4, population size of 500, mutation rate 0.1, and probability of crossover of 0.6. The purpose of this experiment is to analyze the convergence points of the genetic algorithm. We ran two other algorithms to illustrate that our example problems are reasonable MAXSAT problems. The first algorithm is the Davis-Putnam (DP) algorithm [2], a well known complete algorithm for solving SAT problems. The second algorithm is a stochastic greedy hill-climbing search algorithm known as GSAT [10].

All three algorithms were designed using different notions of work. For Davis-Putnam, work is measured by the number of recursive calls (i.e. size of the search tree). The measure of work for GSAT is the number of flips taken (i.e. path length). Since the genetic algorithm is a black box optimizer, the measure of work for the SGA is the number of evaluations. Although the measures of work differ, we gave all three algorithms a fair chance to solve the problem. The DP algorithm is deterministic so it was run only once on each of the test problems. Since GSAT and the SGA will converge to potentially different locations, we ran both algorithms 20 times on each example problem. For each run, GSAT was given a rather stringent cutoff of 10 tries per run and 500 flips per try. The genetic algorithm was allowed to run for 200 generations, which was sufficient for the population to converge for every run.

As the ratio of clauses to variables is varied in MAX3SAT problems, a phase transition occurs where random problem instances transition from being generally SAT to generally UNSAT. The problem difficulty has an easy-hard-easy pattern with the hard problems falling in the phase transition. This transition occurs when the number of clauses is approximately 4.3 times the number of variables [1, 7]. We randomly generated three 100-variable MAX3SAT problems for this small experiment. The problems were generated with respect to a tar-

Prob.	SGA		DP	GSAT			
	Solved	Evals	Calls	Solved	Flips	Side	Down
Underconstrained	19	22250.9	32	20	160.2	136.5	23.7
Hard	2	39246.5	147	15	1762.73	2406.2	165.85
Overconstrained	8	32545.9	92	20	1001.2	898.7	102.5

Table 1. Results of running SGA, Davis-Putnam, GSAT and SGA on three MAX3SAT problem instances of varying levels of difficulty.

get string so they were guaranteed to be satisfiable. The three example problems were randomly generated using 300 clauses (underconstrained), 430 clauses (hard) and 600 clauses (overconstrained).

Table 1 lists the results of running all three algorithms on the example problems. The genetic algorithm located solutions to all three problems but solved the hard problem very infrequently. When an incomplete search algorithm such as a genetic algorithm is run on SAT problems, if it is unable to locate a solution reliably, then it will mistakenly indicate that the problem is UNSAT. The genetic algorithm also ran several orders of magnitude slower than either DP or GSAT. Davis-Putnam solved all three problems very quickly with relatively few recursive calls. GSAT also solved all three problems, although it was unable to locate an optimum on all 20 runs on the hard problem. The average number of flips (steps) taken by GSAT for the solved problem instances is also given. The behavior of all of the algorithms corresponds to the familiar easy-hard-easy pattern for the three problems.

The GSAT experiment provides some very useful information about the structure of the MAXSAT search space. The MAXSAT search space is known to be made up of many flat plateaus [4]. The GSAT experiments illustrate the amount of time spent wandering through flat regions. Two extra columns are listed in the table for GSAT, *Side* and *Down*. GSAT is a steepest descent bit-climber that randomly chooses between the set of best available moves. GSAT will always take moves until it has reached the designated *max flips*. The first column *Side* lists the average number of sideways moves (i.e. where the best available move does not change the evaluation) taken on a single run. The second column, *Down*, corresponds to improving moves since our evaluation function tracks the number of UNSAT clauses. No uphill (worse) moves were needed to solve these problems. Clearly, GSAT spends the vast majority of time wandering across flat plateaus. Without some mechanism for moving across plateaus, any search algorithm would be at a serious disadvantage.

The analog to plateaus in the context of schemata are schema averages that are similar (or identical). Considering the limited set of Walsh coefficients, it would appear that many schemata should share identical fitnesses. In other words, just as the space appears flat to GSAT, the space will also appear flat to a genetic algorithm. However, a traditional genetic algorithm has no way to deal with this problem.

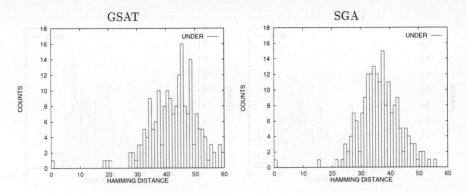

Fig. 2. Distance between convergence points on the underconstrained problem.

4.1 Distances between Convergence Points

A set of convergence points for SGA and GSAT was generated from the 20 different runs on each example problem. SGA would often converge to a set of slightly different points that shared the same best fitness. When there were ties, the convergence point was created using votes for each bit value by the best individuals. The distances between convergence points can indicate whether or not there are large regions of the space that SGA and GSAT find particularly attractive. If there are specific regions that are good, then the convergence points should be close together. Otherwise, the convergence points will be far apart. For each test problem, we computed the Hamming distances between all pairs of convergence points and created a histogram to indicate how those distances were distributed. There were 20 convergence points and thus 190 pairings of convergence points.

Figure 2 shows the distribution of distances between the set of convergence points for GSAT and SGA on the underconstrained problem. Recall that SGA solved this problem 19 times and GSAT solved this problem 20 times. Thus, most of the convergence points represent a satisfying solution. The Hamming distance between solutions, however, is very large. The distances are, in fact, consistent with randomly generated pairs of strings. Thus, there are many attractive regions that contain global optima. In some sense, this problem is easy because there are solutions scattered throughout the search space.

The histograms in Figure 3 present the Hamming distances between the convergence points for the hard problems. The distribution of Hamming distances for GSAT tend to be flatter than the SGA. The GSAT histogram also appears to be multimodal. This indicates that many solutions were clustered together but the clusters were relatively distant. This is indicative of there being a few distinct regions that contain global optima. However, given the amount of exploration done by GSAT and the poor performance of the genetic algorithm, it also appears that there are many highly fit regions that do not contain global optima.

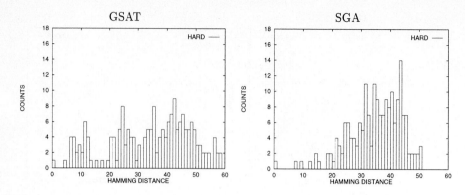

Fig. 3. Distance between convergence points on the hard problem.

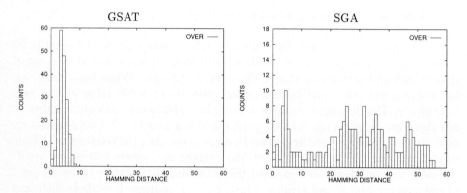

Fig. 4. Distance between convergence points on the overconstrained problem.

The last figure, Figure 4 presents the distributions of Hamming distances between convergence points on the overconstrained problem. Notice that the histogram for GSAT required a larger range than all other histograms along the y-axis. It is clear that the convergence points for GSAT were all clustered together in one large region. The SGA Hamming distance distribution is multimodal. The peak that occurs in the low range of Hamming distances corresponds to the differences between convergence points that were global optima. The local optima form the second set of larger Hamming distances.

The Hamming distances between convergence points indicates that the SGA and GSAT were converging to points that were very different from one another. This behavior is consistent with the argument that the MAXSAT landscape is very flat. Essentially, there is little information to guide the search in any predictable way. The next question to ask is whether or not the SGA convergence points were consistent with the low order schema information.

		L-String			Global Target		
		All	Global	Local	All	Global	Local
UNDER	GSAT	36.45	36.45	–	45.25	45.25	–
	SGA	29.95	30.32	23.00	44.85	44.95	43.00
HARD	GSAT	36.45	37.13	34.40	35.45	36.80	31.40
	SGA	32.70	35.00	32.44	40.50	34.00	41.22
OVER	GSAT	33.30	33.30	–	4.1	4.1	–
	SGA	32.40	32.75	32.17	20.60	4.75	31.17

Table 2. Distances between the convergence points and the low order string and a known optimum.

4.2 Where the Low Order Schemata Lead ...

Deception occurs when low order schema information does not lead to a global optimum. To examine whether or not this occurs in MAXSAT, we defined the **L-string** to indicate the string that is most consistent with the low order schema information. To construct this string, we enumerated all possible order-3 partitions and ranked the schemata. All top ranked schemata contributed votes for its fixed bit positions. The order-1 information was not used to generate the **L-String** because approximately $10 - 15$ bit positions had Walsh coefficients of 0 and would result in a partially specified string. The remaining positions that were specified by order-1 schema information were identical to the corresponding values in the **L-String**. In all cases, the **L-String** was not a global optimum.

The **L-String** and a second string, the **Global Target**, were compared to each of the convergence points. The **Global Target** strings were the strings used to create each of the random problem instances. Table 2 lists the average distances distances between the convergence points and the **L-String** and **Global Target**. The column **All** lists the difference between the L-String and Global Target compared to the set of all convergence points. The two other columns, **Global** and **Local** represent averages over the subsets of convergence points that were global optima and local optima respectively. The purpose for partitioning the set of convergence points is to determine whether or not the global optima tend to be clustered together. The L-Strings tend to differ from all convergence points by more than 30 bits indicating inconsistencies between low order and high order schema information. The Global Target string is also far from the convergence points for the underconstrained and the hard problems. However, it is obvious that the global optima are tightly clustered into one region in the overconstrained problem.

5 Conclusions

This paper has reviewed theoretical observations about the MAXSAT domain and the inevitability of deception in this domain. We have supported the theory by studying the convergence points of a Simple Genetic Algorithm. For three MAXSAT examples of varying difficulty, the low order information differed by more than 30% from the convergence points. Furthermore, the convergence points were not localized. The convergence points also tended to differ from one another by 30%. This behavior indicates that the problems are not only deceptive, but there are also many equally good regions for a genetic algorithm to explore. If there were biases in the schemata, the genetic algorithm would have converged consistently to specific regions of the search space for the same problem. Yet the convergence behavior appears to be almost random.

Larger empirical studies of genetic algorithms for optimization of MAXSAT problems have illustrated that a traditional genetic algorithm does not perform well [3]. The theoretical results and this small set of results illustrate that algorithms that solely use schema information to search will be at a disadvantage in the MAXSAT domain.

References

1. P. Cheeseman, B. Kanefsky, and W. M. Taylor. Where the *really* hard problems are. In *Proc. Twelfth International Joint Conference on Artificial Intelligence*, 1991.
2. M. Davis and H Putnam. A computing procedure for quantification theory. *Journal of the ACM*, 7:201–215, 1960.
3. J. Frank. A Study of Genetic Algorithms to Find Approximate Solutions to Hard 3CNF Problems. *Golden West International Conference on Artificial Intelligence*, 1994.
4. J. Frank, P. Cheeseman, and J. Stutz. When gravity fails: Local search topology. *Journal of Artificial Intelligence Research*, 7:249–281, 1997.
5. D. Goldberg. Genetic algorithms and walsh functions: Part I, a gentle introduction. *Complex Systems*, 3:129–152, 1989.
6. D. Goldberg. Genetic algorithms and walsh functions: Part II, deception and its analysis. *Complex Systems*, 3:153–171, 1989.
7. D. Mitchell, B. Selman, and H. Levesque. Hard and easy distribution of sat problems. In *Proc. Tenth National Conference on Artificial Intelligence*, San Jose, CA, 1992.
8. S. Rana, R. Heckendorn, and D. Whitley. A tractable walsh analysis of Sat and its implications for genetic algorithms. In *Proc. Fifteenth National Conference on Artificial Intelligence*, 1998.
9. C. Reeves and C. Wright. Epistasis in genetic algorithms: An experimental design perspective. In Larry Eshelman, editor, *Proceedings of the Sixth International Conference on Genetic Algorithms*, pages 217–224. Morgan Kaufmann, 1995.
10. B. Selman, H. Levesque, and D. Mitchell. A new method for solving hard satisfiability problems. In *Proc. Tenth National Conference on Artificial Intelligence*, pages 440–446, San Jose, CA, 1992.

An Adaptive Mutation Scheme for a Penalty-Based Graph-Colouring GA

Peter Ross and Emma Hart

Dept. of AI, University of Edinburgh,
5 Forrest Hill, Edinburgh EH1 2QL
{peter,emmah}@dai.ed.ac.uk

Abstract. The folklore of evolutionary algorithms still seems to contain some gross over-generalistions, such as that direct encodings are inferior to indirect ones, that penalty-function methods are often poor, and that observed performance on a few instances can be extrapolated to a whole class. In the interests of exploring the status of such folklore we have continued to investigate in depth the use of a simple representation for graph-colouring problems. In this paper we demonstrate that good performance on a variety of medium-sized problems can be obtained with a simple adaptive mutation scheme. The scheme was originally motivated by considering an artificial counter-example to an earlier approach that had seemed very successful, because it had been used to solve some large real-world exam timetabling problems for certain universities. Those solutions were used in practice, and it would have been tempting to assert that the method was a practical success. This paper represents part of a continuing effort to map out the strengths and weaknesses of using a simple direct encoding and penalty functions for graph colouring.

Keywords: adaptive mutation, penalty functions, graph colouring

1 Introduction

In the simple graph-colouring problem there are n nodes, and some or all pairs are joined by edges; there are e edges in all. The task is to colour each node, using no more than C colours, such that no two nodes joined by an edge have the same colour. Finding such a colouring is in general an NP-complete problem, but it is known (for example) that for a given graph and a given C the number of ways of colouring the graph is given by a graph-dependent polynomial whose leading terms are $C^n - eC^{n-1} + (e(e-1)/2 - t)C^{n-2} \cdots$ where t is the number of triangles in the graph.

Graph-colouring methods are of considerable practical value, for example in solving basic exam timetabling problems. Each node represents an exam, each edge represents the fact that there exists some student who has to be present at both the exams joined by the edge, and colours represent time-slots. In practice there are other constraints too, such as temporal orderings imposed on certain subsets, exclusions of certain exams from certain slots, and of course exam hall capacities, besides soft constraints such as the wish to space out every student's exams as far as possible.

In other papers (eg [5, 4, 10, 11]) we have investigated the use of a very simple representation for such problems, consisting of n integers each of which lies in the range $1 \cdots C$ inclusive. If the i-th integer has value s_i then exam/node i has time-slot/colour s_i. Fitness is penalty-based: $1/(1 + \sum \text{penalties})$, and for simple graph-colouring the penalty is merely 1 per violated edge. Among other things, that earlier work showed that the standard random mutation scheme, in which either a single allele or each allele was mutated to some other randomly-chosen value, did not work well for such problems. A memetic scheme in which a single gene was chosen, whether randomly or acording to the violations it caused, and was changed to the value which *most* reduced the penalty score, also did not work well. A hand analysis of the populations during a run in a very few cases suggested that the problem was this: early in the run, some such change caused a useful penalty reduction. Another such change caused a further useful reduction, even though the two changes together also caused some new violation. However, the overall improvement outweighed the damage at that stage, and the GA proceeded to spread those allele choices throughout the population. Close to the end of the run, only those violations caused by the earlier improvements remained to be cured; but by then every member of the population contained them and no single mutation step could fix them. Indeed, it might take more than a few serendipitous mutations to undo the problem. What did seem to work well were forms of mutation that produced a gentle pressure towards improvement; for example, choose a gene at uniform random, and conduct a tournament of small size (such as 2) to find a better value for it. This seemed to help prevent the GA from falling into the kind of deadlock trap just mentioned. Software that implements a number of such schemes is freely available from our site mentioned at the end of this paper.

GAs using such methods (in particular, in which only a single gene gets mutated at each step) have been used to construct solutions on request for large problems sent in by certain universities, who have then used those solutions. This would usually be taken to indicate that the method was a significant success. However, in recent work [12] we reported that our GA failed to solve some lightly-constrained small artificial problems. In particular, the construction process could produce nested sets of problems; every possible edge in the graph-colouring problem had a random real number between 0 and 1 associated with it, and the edge was included if and only if its real number was less than the user-specified probability parameter p. Thus, for a given seed, increasing p merely caused *extra* edges to be added. It tuned out that for any fixed seed, the GA could relaibly solve problems for small and large p but not for some range of values in between; in particular it could solve highly-constrained problems but not some sub-problems of them. Interestingly, various non-evolutionary algorithms also failed on precisely those troublesome problems, even though all the problems had solutions. Such a phase transition is in the spirit of considerable work done on constraint satisfaction problems by Smith, Prosser and others (see eg [13, 9]), although much of that work has focussed on random problems whose solvability is unknown; the interest there lies in algorithms capable of either solving a problem or proving it unsolvable and the majority of awkward problems lie in the region where neither task is particularly easy.

It is worth mentioning that many other encoding methods have been used both for graph-colouring and for exam timetabling problems. Space limits prevent us from surveying them; but for graph-colouring Falkenauer's Grouping GA [7] has been well received, and for exam timetabling the interested reader might consult two recent proceedings [2, 3] that include many GA papers. It is, however, regrettably rare for such work to conduct a systematic investigation of the performance and sensitivity of the recommended approach; usually such work at most reports results on benchmark collections such as Carter's set available from http://ie.utoronto.edu/~mwc/testprob

2 An artificial counter-example

The restriction, in some of our past work, to mutating at most one gene at each step is not very strong. After all, many GAs that do genewise mutation use a low rate, such that the expected number of mutated genes is 1 or even lower at each step. One way to explore the limits of any method is to try to construct specific counter-examples that reveal some weakness clearly. We show such an example here.

Consider the graph shown in figure 1. The 'diamond' shapes each contain

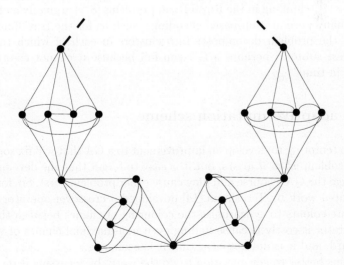

Fig. 1. A counter-example

two cliques of size $S = 5$; a clique in a graph is a subset such that ever member of the subset is connected to very other one. The two cliques in any one diamond overlap by $S - 1$. The diamonds can be arranged in a ring, although this is not a necessary feature. The task is to colour the graph using S colours.

It should be clear that the S members of each clique must each be a different colour, and therefore the nodes which link successive diamonds must all have exactly the same colour. The types of GA mentioned above cannot spot this in time. Fitness rises as each clique gets solved, but the need to co-ordinate how each clique is solved does not become apparent until too late; these GAs are not capable of doing sufficient 'backtracking' of any kind to get out of such trouble. Even for small S, say $S = 5$ and 6 or even fewer diamonds, such GAs fail. Yet for $S = 5$, each clique has a chance of just under 1 in 26 of being solved by a random assignment of colours, so an initial population of (say) 50 chromosomes is extremely likely to contain some solved cliques. Moreover, consider a random assignment of colours to the nodes in any diamond. The expected number of violated constraints will be 4. In the subset of random assignments in which the two linking nodes have the same colour, the expected number is also 4; so there is no bias in the initial population towards making the linking nodes have the same colour or towards them having different colours.

The problem for the GAs does stem from the need to co-ordinate the linking nodes rather than from solving cliques. Many practical problems solved efficiently by the GA contain much larger cliques; for example, the King Fahd University problem in Carter's benchmark set contains two distinct cliques of size 19 each. It seems reasonable to conjecture that the phenomenon is more widespread; that although a representation may contain good, short, high-quality building blocks and a GA may be able to find them, it may still fail because it needs to co-ordinate them but cannot do so in time because drift or selection pressure limits its options. Hitchhiking in the Royal Road problems [8] is arguably an instance of this. In many permutation-based encodings, such as for the travelling-salesman problem, the problem decomposes into clusters in each of which there is one clearly best subtour; perhaps a GA can fail because it cannot co-ordinate the subtours in time?

3 An adaptive mutation scheme

It is often tempting to develop an improvement to a GA that will fix some specific type of problem *when it arises*, but it is easy to forget that the development will also change the GA's course and may cause other problems first. So, for example, some related work by Terashima [14] developed a crossover operator that tried to permute colours to synchronise the colouring of cliques between the parents. This operator is costly because finding even non-maximal cliques of worthwhile size is hard, and it is not yet clear that it is economic.

It seems better to get mutation to do the work, by focussing it on where the difficulties lie. The following mutation scheme therefore arose fairly naturally. For each gene g, count the number of violations it is involved in; call this v_g.

Then mutate each gene with probability $(0.1 + v_g)m / \sum_g v_g$, where m is a user-settable basic rate of mutation. The 0.1 ensures that every gene has at least a small chance of being mutated, but genes that cause no problems at all even when there are large numbers of violations will have a suitably low chance. When there are few violations left, mutation is concentrated on the offenders, and more heavily as their numbers drop. Unlike other adaptive schemes reported in the literature, this scheme seems to work best when $m = 1.0$. It will easily handle the case of 6 diamonds in the above counter-example, although it still has difficulty with significantly larger versions of the same problem.

4 Tests

The following tests used a steady-state GA with a population size of 50. Rank-based selection was used, with a bias of 1.5. Crossover was one-point; tests suggested this was slightly better than (say) two-point or uniform. The adaptive mutation scheme outlined above was used with a base rate of $m = 1.0$; if a gene was mutated, a search was conducted to find any better allele and if one was found it was used; otherwise a random allele was used. This proved to be a little better than (say) using a small-sized tournament to pick a new allele and for all the problems conducted here the difference in wall-clock time was trivial.

A standard limit of 50000 evaluations was used, on the grounds that using very much more than this would not be considered impressive by anybody!

4.1 Large clique problems

In these tests the problem consisted of a maximally-connected graph of size 25, 50 or 75 nodes; such cliques are appreciably larger than seem to occur even in large real-world exam timetabling problems. For each size, the GA was run 50 times. Table 1 summarise the results. The GA solved the problem swiftly every time, and the number of evaluations seems to be almost linear in the problem size. It

Size	Average evals	Std. dev. evals
25	197	46.41
50	431	65.83
75	683	116.72

Table 1. Performance on large cliques

is worth noting that a nonadaptive mutation scheme, which mutates each gene with a fixed probability to a new value found in the same way, takes over three times as long even with an optimally-tuned mutation rate. The above results are merely a reassurance that a GA can handle large cliques; Brelaz's algorithm [1] would of course handle them without trouble. Moreover, the chance of correctly colouring some clique of size k that is contained within a clique of size n, when n colours are available, is $n!/(n^k(n-k)!)$. This means that if the task is to solve a large clique of size 75, then there is approximately an even chance that an initial random population of 50 chromosomes will include a correctly-coloured clique of size 24.

4.2 Equipartite graphs

In the interests of comparison with Eiben et al's study [6], tests were conducted on equipartite graphs produced with Culberson's generator (see section 6). Each problem had 200 nodes. The generator first creates a solution by dividin the nodes into three classes as nearly equally as it can (67, 67 and 66 in this case); members of a class will all have the same colour in a solution. Any pair of nodes from different classes are then joined by an edge with user-specified probability p; the expected number of edges is $(67 \times 66 + 67 \times 66 + 67 \times 67)p = 13333p$. Such solvable equipartite problems are reputedly very hard to solve. Eiben et al developed a 'stepwise adaptation of weights' (SAW) scheme using a permutation-based encoding of nodes to consider. Fitness was the weighted sum of nodes that proved impossible to colour; hard nodes had their weights increased systematically during a run. They found that this scheme significantly outperformed Falkenauer's grouping GA and Brelaz's DSatur algorithm [1] on 200, 500 and 1000-node problems.

Eiben at al, in [6], present their results through a series of graphs; space limits prevent us doing the same here. Anyway the data is inherently multi-dimensional; 2-d or 3-d graphs would not properly capture the overall trends. We tried a range of values of p: from 0.010 to 0.065 in steps of 0.005 and from 0.1 to 0.25 in steps of 0.05. The first of these to ranges is significant because it contains the phase transition for these problems – around $p = 0.05$ performance is bad and neither our scheme nor theirs manages to solve the problems. For $p = 0.1$ and above performance is excellent; indeed, for $p = 0.2$ and above the GA solves each problem every time in an average of less than 8000 evaluations. For example, for $p = 0.85$ (around 11,333 edges) it took under 4500 evaluations to solve the problem, with perfect reliability.

For each of the sixteen values of p in the two ranges mentioned above, ten problems were generated; for each problem, 10 GA runs were done with the same configuration as in the previous section. Details of these 1600 runs can be obtained over the Internet, see section 6. In brief: at $p = 0.010$ performance is perfect on every problem, taking 600-800 evaluations perproblem. By $p = 0.025$ performance is falling seriously, with only 1 or 2 runs per 10 solving each problem, at close to the 50000 evaluations limit (allowing a larger limit increases the success rate). Around $p = 0.050$ performance is terrible, and the GA typically does not solve the problem even if allowed very much more than 50000 evaluations. By $p = 0.065$ performance is recovering, and is comparable to $p = 0.025$.

It is worth noting that Eiben et al used a limit very much higher than 50000 evaluations, although it is hard to tell from their graphs how many evaluations were typically needed away from the phase transition region. It is also worth noting that they used a $(1+1)$ scheme without recombination, arguing that this still counted as an evolutionary algorithm. In our case it is necessary to have a significant population, and performance is better with one-point crossover than without any crossover.

5 Conclusions

Performance on large-clique problems, and on 200-node problems when not near the phase-transition region, is excellent: fast and highly reliable. We have tried some of the same sets of problems as studied in [6], with comparable results to their SAW scheme which they report as outperforming a grouping GA. As yet we have not had time to test a set of 1000-node problems. However, we would predict equivocal performance; we would expect the kind of reasoning outlined at the end of section 2 to apply, given that we are using such a simple encoding. Nevertheless the results reported here are very encouraging, and suggest that such an adaptive mutation scheme may be worth trying on other problems that use some simple direct encoding and penalty-based fitness.

6 Software (etc) availability

Some of our software is freely available from `ftp://ftp.dai.ed.ac.uk/pub`. These include *gatt*, a timetabling-specific GA, and *pga*, a GA package useful for teaching and basic research in GAs. *Pga* offers a large number of command-line configuration options, such as island and cellular models, steady-state, generational and breeder GAs and the ability to vary chromosome length for those problems for which it is meaningful to do so. In particular it includes the adaptive-mutation scheme described above, as an option in the exam-timetabling-specific parts. Other software available at the site include a version of Brelaz's famous DSatur algorithm for graph-colouring; a program that will exhaustively enumerate all the cliques in a graph; and a bug-fixed version of the very-long-period Berkeley random number generator, seriously buggy versions of which are provided with at least certain recent versions of Solaris, HPUX, Linux etc as the *random()* and *srandom()* system calls. Buggy versions can be recognised by the fact that using *random()&01* repeatedly will produce a sequence of bits that passes standard tests of pseudo-randomness; but the actual sequence is entirely determined by the value of the random number seed modulo 4! Since this is a natural way to generate an initial population in any bit-encoded GA, it is entirely possible that many published empirical GA studies have only sampled four different initial populations.

The data summarising the major batch of 1600 GA runs described above can be found in `ftp://ftp.dai.ed.ac.uk/pub/peter/gcadaptm.txt`

Joe Culberson's graph generator package and some related material is at `http://www.cs.ualberta.ca/~joe/Coloring/index.html`

7   Acknowledgements

Emma Hart is supported by EPSRC grant GR/L22232.

References

1. D. Brelaz. New methods to color the vertices of a graph. *Communications of the ACM*, 22:251–256, 1979.
2. E. Burke and P.M. Ross. *The Practice and Theory of Automated Timetabling*. LNCS 1153. Springer-Verlag, Heidelberg, October 1996.
3. E.K. Burke and M. Carter. *The practice and Theory of Automated Timetabling: Proccedings of the 2nd International Conference*. LNCS (to appear). Springer-Verlag, Hedielberg, 1998.
4. Dave Corne and Peter Ross. Some combinatorial landscapes on which a genetic algorithm outperforms other stochastic iterative methods. In T. Fogarty, editor, *Evolutionary Computing: AISB Workshop, Sheffield 1995, Selected Papers*, LNCS 993. Springer-Verlag, 1995.
5. Dave Corne, Peter Ross, and Hsiao-Lan Fang. Fast practical evolutionary time-tabling. In Terry C. Fogarty, editor, *Selected Papers: AISB Workshop on Evolutionary Computing, Lecture Notes in Computer Science No 865*, pages 250–263. Springer Verlag, 1994.
6. A.E. Eiben, J.K. van der Hauw, and J.I. van Henert. Graph colouring with daptive evolutionary algorithms. *Journal of Heuristics*, 4(1), 1998.
7. E. Falkenauer. A new representation and operators for genetic algorithms applied to grouping problems. *Evolutionary Computation*, 2(2):123–144, 1994.
8. Stephanie Forrest and Melanie Mitchell. Relative building block fitness and the building block hypothesis. In L. Darrell Whitely, editor, *Foundations of Genetic Algorithms 2*. San Mateo: Morgan Kaufmann, 1993.
9. Patrick Prosser. Binary constraint satisfaction problems: Some are harder than others. In A. Cohn, editor, *Proceedings of the 11th European Conferenc e on Artificial Intelligence*, pages 95–99. John Wiley & Sons, Ltd., 1994.
10. Peter Ross and Dave Corne. Comparing genetic algorithms, simulated annealing, and stochastic hillclimbing on timetabling problems. In T. Fogarty, editor, *Evolutionary Computing: AISB Workshop, Sheffield 1995, Selected Papers*, LNCS 993. Springer-Verlag, 1995.
11. Peter Ross and Dave Corne. The phase transition niche for evolutionary algorithms in timetabling. [2], pages 309–324.
12. P.M. Ross, E. Hart, and D. Corne. Some observations on g-based exam timetabling. pages –.
13. Barbara Smith. Phase transition and the mushy region in constraint satisfaction problems. In A. Cohn, editor, *Proceedings of the 11th European Conference on Artificial Intelligence*, pages 100–104. John Wiley & Sons, Ltd., 1994.
14. H. Terashima-Marin. personal communication.

Inver-over Operator for the TSP

Guo Tao[1] and Zbigniew Michalewicz[2]

[1]State Key Labortory of Software Engineering,
Wuhan University,
Wuhan, Hubei, 430072
P.R. China
gt@rjgc.whu.edu.cn

[2]Department of Computer Science,
University of North Carolina,
Charlotte, NC 28223, USA
zbyszek@uncc.edu

Abstract. In this paper we investigate the usefulness of a new operator, inver-over, for an evolutionary algorithm for the TSP. Inver-over is
based on simple inversion, however, knowledge taken from other individuals in the population influences its action. Thus, on one hand, the
proposed operator is unary, since the inversion is applied to a segment
of a single individual, however, the selection of a segment to be inverted
is population driven, thus the operator displays some characterictics of
recombination.

This operator outperforms all other 'genetic' operators, whether unary or
binary, which have been proposed in the past for the TSP in connection
with evolutionary systems and the resulting evolutionary algorithm is
very fast. For test cases, where the number of cities is around 100, the
algorithm reaches the optimum in every execution in a couple of seconds.
For larger instances (e.g., 10,000 cities) the results stay within 3% from
the estimated optimum.

1 Introduction

The traveling salesman problem (TSP) is one of the most widely studied NP-
hard combinatorial optimization problems. Its statement is deceptively simple,
and yet it remains one of the most challenging problems in Operational Research.

Let $G = (V, E)$ be a graph where V is a set of vertices and E is a set of
edges. Let $C = (c_{ij})$ be a distance (or cost) matrix associated with E. The TSP
requires determination of a minimum distance circuit (Hamiltonian circuit or
cycle) passing through each vertex once and only once. C is said to satisfy the
triangle inequality if and only if $c_{ij} + c_{jk} \geq c_{ik}$ for all $i, j, k \in V$ (in such a case
we talk about $\triangle$TSP). Euclidean TSP problems (ETSP), i.e., problems where V
is a set of points in R^2 and c_{ij} is an Euclidean (straight-line) distance between
i and j, are, of course, special cases of $\triangle$TSP.

A lot of algorithms have been proposed to solve TSP. Some of them (based
on dynamic programming or branch and bound methods) provide the global
optimum solution (the largest nontrivial instance of the TSP solved to optimality
is of 7397 cities [1], however, it required almost 4 years of CPU time on network of
machines). Other algorithms are heuristic ones, which are much faster, but they
do not guarantee the optimal solutions. There are well known algorithms based

on 2-opt or 3-opt change operators, Lin-Kerninghan algorithm (variable change) as well algorithms based on greedy principles (nearest neighbor, spanning tree, etc). The TSP was also approached by various "modern heuristic" methods, like simulated annealing, evolutionary algorithms, tabu search, even neural networks. However, these techniques were mainly applied to test cases with relatively small number of cities (usually less than 1000), whereas such problems are now solved routinely within a few hours [10].

In this paper we investigate a new evolutionary algorithm based on a new operator *inver-over*,[1] which incorporates the knowledge taken from other individuals in the population. One can view this operator as a mixture of inversion and recombination: on one hand, the inversion is applied to a part of a single individual, however, the selection of a segment to be inverted depends on other individuals in the population.

It seems that the proposed algorithm still can't compete (at least as far as computational time is concerned) with efficient approaches based on local search [10], however, it has a few adventages. First of all, it is extremely simple and easy to implement (less than 100 lines of C code). Additionally, experimental results indicate that this operator outperforms all other evolutionary operators (whether unary or binary), which have been proposed in the past for the TSP (PMX, OX, CX, ER, Edge-2, Edge-3, MPX, RAR, GNX, 2-repair, simple inversion, swap, remove and reinsert, and many others). Moreover, the evolutionary algorithm based on the proposed operator is quite fast (in comparison with other evolutionary techniques) and the quality of results are very high. For test cases, where the number of cities is around 100, the algorithm reaches the optimum in every execution. For larger instances (10,000 cities) the results stay within 3% from the estimated optimum.

The paper is organized as follows. The next section provides a brief background information on evolutionary algorithms which have been developed for the TSP. Section 3 provides a description of the proposed algorithm with a new adaptive inversion operator. Section 4 reports on experimental results and section 5 concludes the paper.

2   TSP and evolutionary approach

Initially, main effort of researchers was directed at discovery of an appropriate recombination operator, which would produce an offspring by preserving partial tours from the parents. For example, partially matched crossover (PMX) builds an offspring by choosing a subsequence of a tour from one parent and preserving the order and position of as many cities as possible from the other parent. A subsequence of a tour is selected by choosing two random cut points, which serve as boundaries for swapping operations. Order crossover (OX) builds offspring by choosing a subsequence of a tour from one parent and preserving the relative order of cities from the other parent. Cycle crossover (CX) builds offspring in

---

[1] The name for this operator was invented by Bob Reynolds during the EP'98 conference.

such a way that each city (and its position) comes from one of the parents. Of course, many other binary operators (and variants of the above operators) for the path representation have been defined. On the other hand, unary operators were usually defined as a swap (of two cities) or as inversion of a segment of cities. Simple inversion selects two points along the length of the chromosome, which is cut at these points, and the substring between these points is reversed. Such simple inversion guarantees that the resulting offspring is a legal tour. It is reported [27] that in a 50-city TSP, a system with inversion outperformed a system with a "cross and correct" operator. However, an increase in the number of cut points decreases the performance of the system.

The operators listed above take into account cities (i.e., their positions and order) as opposed to edges — links between cities. Clearly, the linkage of this city with other cities might be more important than the particular position of a city in a tour. Consequently, Grefenstette [8] developed a class of heuristic operators that emphasizes edges. However, as reported in [8], such operators transfer around 60% of the edges from parents — which means that 40% of edges are selected randomly. Whitley, Starkweather, and Fuquay [27] have developed a new crossover operator: the edge recombination crossover (ER), which transfers more than 95% of the edges from the parents to the single offspring. Later, the edge recombination crossover was further enhanced [23, 16]. In [17] a new local search operator was developed, which makes a use of both crossover and mutation. In [15] a new selection method was introduced as well as new crossovers (edge exchange crossover EEX and subtour exchange crossover SXX). Similarly, a new crossover (edge assembly crossover EAX) was investigated in [20]. However, these new operators were tested on relatively small instances of TSP; in many cases the reported computational time was not encouraging (few minutes for 100 city problems).

Several researchers investigated the combination of local search heuristics and evolutionary systems. Probably this is the most popular trend and the state-of-the-art in the evolutionary field: most researchers believe that the efficient implementation of quality local optimizer is crucial for the efficiency of any evolutionary algorithm. Many researchers have been applying various crossover operators (e.g., MPX operator [19]) to locally optimal individuals [2, 7, 19, 16, 25, 5], i.e., individuals after improvement made by a local search.[2] Evolutionary techniques, extended by a local search algorithm, perform very well (better then multistart local search algorithm by itself); in many experiments such systems returned a near-optimum solution (for many test cases with e.g., 442, 532, 666 cities, the deviation from the optimal tour length was less than 1%).

There were attempts to solve the TSP by evolutionary algorithms based on paradigm of evolution strategies [9, 21] or evolutionary programming [6]; there

---

[2] A term *memetic algorithm* refers to an evolutionary algorithm where local optimization is applied to all solutions before evaluation. This can be thought of as evolutionary algorithm is applied in the subspace of local optima, with local optimization acting as a repair mechanism for children luing outside this subspace (i.e., not being locally optimal).

were also attempts to build evolutionary systems based on non-standard representations (e.g., matrix representations). In [26] an evolutionary system is used to improve a simple heuristic algorithms for the TSP by perturbing city coordinates; results for problem sizes up to 500 cities were reported.

Very few reports provide the computational time required for solving some instances of TSP; rather the number of function evaluations are reported. Thus it is quite hard to compare different approaches, as various proposed operators have different time complexity. Eshelman reports [5] 2.5 hours (single processor Sun SPARKstation), for a 532 city problem; Gorges-Schleuter [7]: between 1 and 2 hours on the same problem (parallel implementation, 64 T800 transputers); Braun [2]: around half an hour for a 431 city problem (SUN woirkstation). All these times indicate that evolutionary algorithm might be too slow for solving larger instances (say, 10,000 cities) of the TSP.

3 Evolutionary algorithm with the inver-over operator

Most evolutionary algorithms developed so far for the TSP (not extended by a local search routine) can not compete with other heuristic methods (e.g., Lin-Kerninghan algorithm) neither in precision of results nor in computational time. Evolutionary algorithms based on crossover operator usually are quite espensive (in terms of computational time), whereas algorithms based on mutation only (whether simple inversions or swaps) do not escape efficiently local optima. It is why, as indicated in the Introduction, most recent effort aimed at combining evolutionary engine with a local search method.

What characteristic should a 'pure' evolutionary algorithm have for the TSP to compete with local search methods? It seems that the TSP problem requires a relatively strong selection pressure, which would move the search to a promising area of the search space, and an *efficient* operator, which produces an offspring without a burden of many additional calculations and allows the algorithm to escape local optima. Clearly, unary operators require much less time (in comparison with binary operators), however, they have not produced satisfactory results. Thus it might be worthwhile to experiment with an operator which combines adventages of unary and binary operators.

A new evolutionary algorithm developed for the TSP has the following characteristics:

- each individual competes with its offspring only,
- there is only one operator used; however, this inver-over operator is adaptive: it takes a clue from the current population,
- the number of times the operator is applied to an individual during a single generation, is variable.

Such an algorithm can be perceived as a set of parallel hill-climbing procedures, which preserve the spirit of Lin-Kerninghan algorithm (each hill-climber performs a variable number of edge-swaps). However, the inver-over operator has

adaptive components: (1) the number of inversions applied to a single indiu-
vidual and (2) the segment to be inverted is determined by another (randomly
selected) individual. So it is possible to view this algorithm as an evolutionary
one with a strong selective pressure and with an adaptive operator.

```
random initialization of the population P
while (not satified termination-condition) do
{
    for each individual S_i ∈ P do
    {
        S' = S_i
        select (randomly) a city c from S'
        repeat
        {
            if (rand() ≤ p)
                select the city c' from the remaining cities in S'
            else
            {
                select (randomly) an individual from P
                assign to c' the 'next' city to the city c in the selected individual
            }
            if (the next city or the previous city of city c in S' is c')
                exit from repeat loop
            inverse the section from the next city of city c to the city c' in S'
            c = c'
        }
        if (eval(S') ≤ eval(S_i))
            S_i = S'
    }
}
```

Fig. 1. The outline of the algorithm

Figure 1 provides a more detailed description of the whole algorithm in general and of the proposed operator in particular. With a low probability[3] p the
second city for inversion is selected randomly. This is necessary: without a possibility to generate new connections, the algorithm would search only among
connections between cities present in the initial population. If $rand() > p$, a
randomly selected mate provides a clue for the second marker for inversion. In
that case the inversion operator resembles crossover, as part of the pattern (at
least 2 cities) of the second individual appears in the offspring.

Let's illustrate a single iteration of this operator on the following example.
Assume that the current individual S' is

---

[3] Interestingly, experimental results indicated that the value of this parameter was
independent of the number of cities in a test case. Note also, that the function
$rand()$ (Figure 1) generates a random float from the range [0..1].

$$S' = (2, 3, 9, 4, 1, 5, 8, 6, 7),$$

and the current city c is 3. If the generated random number $rand()$ does not exceed p, another city c' from the same individual S' is selected (say, c' is 8), and appropriate segment is inverted, producing the following offspring

$$S' \leftarrow (2, 3, 8, 5, 1, 4, 9, 6, 7)$$

(note the position of the cutting points for the selected segment, which are after cities 3 and 8). Otherwise (i.e., $rand() > p$), another individual is (randomly) selected from the population; assume, it is $(1, 6, 4, 3, 5, 7, 9, 2, 8)$. This individual is searched for the city c' "next" to city 3 (which is 5), thus the segment for inversion in S' starts after city 3 and terminates after city 5; consequently, the new offspring is

$$S' \leftarrow (2, 3, 5, 1, 4, 9, 8, 6, 7).$$

Note again, that a substring 3 – 5 arrived from the "second parent". Note also, that in either case the resulting string is intermediate in the sense that the above inversion operator is applied several times before an offspring is evaluated. This process terminates when the next city c' (to the current city c) in randomly selected individual is also "next city" in the original individual. For example, assume that after a few inversions, the current individual S' is

$$S' = (9, 3, 6, 8, 5, 1, 4, 2, 7),$$

and the current city c is 6. If $rand() > p$, a city 'next' to city 6 is recovered from a (randomly) selected individual from the population; assume, it is city 8 (if $rand() \leq p$, a random city is selected, so it may also happen that city 8 was chosen). Since city 8 already follow city 3, the sequence of inversions terminates.

4 Experiments and results

In this section we present the experimental results of the proposed algorithm. All experiments are performed on a Pentium Pro 180 machine. The unit of the time listed in the result tables is one second. The two paramaters of the algorithm had the following values: population size $m = 100$ and probability of random inversion $p = 0.02$. The termination-condition is satisfied when the best solution of the population remains unchanged for the last 10 iterations (of the while loop).

Almost all test cases (except CHN144[4]) were chosen from TSPLIB [22]. The optimal solution of each test case is known. The size of these test cases vary from 30 cities to 2,392 cities. We have also created one (random) instance (RAN10000) of 10,000 cities, and relied on the formula [11] for the expected ratio k of the Held-Karp bound to $\sqrt{n}$ for n-city random ETSP; for $n \geq 100$ it is:

$$k = 0.70805 + \frac{0.52229}{\sqrt{n}} + \frac{1.31572}{n} - \frac{3.07474}{n\sqrt{n}}.$$

---

[4] See http://www.iwr.uni-heidelberg.de/iwr/comopt/soft/TSPLIB95/TSPLIB.html.

So, the length of the optimal tour is estimated as $L^* = k\sqrt{n \cdot R}$, where n is the number of cities and R is the area of the square box within which the cities were randomly placed. For our instance, the number of cities is $n = 10,000$ and the edge length (of the square box) is 400, so the approximate length of the optimum solution is 28536.3.

We list the test cases and their optimal solutions in table 1. Note that in calculating the optimal solution, each distance is rounded to integer value (except, of course, the last test case, RAN10000, where the exact distances are calculated). There were ten runs of the algorithm performed for each test case. The results (listed also in table 1) represent average scores of these ten runs. For each test case, the table provides the value of the optimum solution, the *average* value found by the algorithm, average computational time (seconds), average total number of inversions and the average total number of iterations (while loop) performed during a run.

Instance	Optimum	Result	Time	Inversions	Iterations
EIL30	420	420	0.31	46505	129
EIL51	426	426	1.09	147972	399
EIL76	538	538	2.11	257613	651
EIL101	629	629.2	7.52	787792	2447
ST70	675	675	1.98	239152	643
KROA100	21282	21282	2.94	319182	785
KROC100	20749	20749	3.23	344272	874
KROD100	21294	21294	4.13	432336	1221
LIN105	14379	14379	3.34	350943	876
CHN144	30347	30359.2	16.81	1432780	4839
PCB442	50778	51097.5	172.21	6961960	23265
PR2392	378032	388095	5366.23	38341600	126846
RAN10000	28536.3	29551.4	167501	207775822	676840

Table 1. Results of the algorithm with adaptive inversion

The above results demonstrate clearly the efficiency of the algorithm. Note that for the first nine test cases the optimum was found in all ten runs (except the test case EIL101, where the algorithm failed only once in ten runs). The number of cities in these test cases varies from 30 to 105. For the test case with 144 cities the average solution was only 0.04% above the optimum, for the test case with 442 cities—0.63% above the optimum, and for the test case with 2392 cities—2.66%. Moreover, for a random test case with 10,000 cities the average solution stayed within 3.56% from the Held-Karp lower bound (whereas the best solution found in these ten runs was less than 3% above this lower bound).

Note also, that the running time of the algorithm was reasonable: few seconds for problems with up to 105 cities, below 3 minutes for the test case of 442 cities,

below 90 minutes for the test case with 2392 cities. These represent fraction of
time needed by other evolutionary algorithms based on crossover operators.

It is also interesting to compare the proposed algorithm to two other algorithms. This first one is based on simple inversion and the second one is based
on Lin-Kerninghan algorithm.[5] The comparison with the first algorithm provides information on the significance of the proposed adaptive inversion operator
versus blind inversion, whereas the other one—on relative merits of the tested
algorithms.

Instances	Optimum	Simple Inversion			Lin-Kerninghan	
		Result	Time	Iterations	Results	Time
EIL30	420	432.6	58.326	74.71	421.8	0.013
EIL51	426	451.7	77.755	93.79	427.4	0.012
EIL76	538	580.9	138.763	149.66	549.7	0.026
EIL101	629	680.6	339.364	325.06	640	0.0.39
ST70	675	720.7	104.756	116.27	684.6	0.034
KROA100	21282	23136.8	253.823	241.18	21380.9	0.04
KROC100	20749	23175.5	319.7	296.88	20961	0.034
KROD100	21294	23746.8	282.806	264.17	21417.3	0.045
LIN105	14379	15627.8	350.96	311.85	14566.5	0.039
CHN144	30347	33156.7	707.033	537.80	30602.1	0.054
PCB442	50778	—	—	—	51776.5	0.137
PR2392	378032	—	—	—	389413	0.719

Table 2. Results of the Simple Inversion and Lin-Kerninghan algorithms

Table 2 give the results of such comparisons. The results of the algorithm
based on random inversion were provided by our algorithm with parameter p
set to 1.0. Note that for test cases with around 100 cities, the error (percentage
above the optimum) was much higher (more than 10%). Time of the run increased in a significant way, in some cases more than 100 times (the termination
condition was left without a change). Because of this increase in time, we do
not report the results of this algorithm for the largest test cases. On the other
hand, the Lin-Kerninghan algorithm takes a fraction of time necessary for our
algorithm (e.g., below 1 second for the test case with 2,392 cities). However,
the precision of results is much lower. Table 2 provides averages of ten runs of
the Lin-Kerninghan algorithm: note, that none of the test cases resulted with
the optimum solution in all ten runs. So, the proposed evolutionary algorithm
has much better consistency than the Lin-Kerninghan algorithm. On the other
hand, if Lin-Kerninghan algorithm was run for the same *time* as our evolutionary
system (as opposed just to the same number of runs), probably it would win the
competition easily.

[5] We have experimented with the implementation provided by Bill Cook, available
from ftp.caam.rice.edu/pub/people/bico/970827/.

5 Conclusions

There are a few interesting observations which can be made on the basis of the experiments:

- the proposed system is probably the quickest evolutionary algorithm for the TSP developed so far. All other algorithms based on crossover operators provide much worse results in a much longer time (the exact comparison between various methods will be given in the full version of the paper [24]);
- the proposed system has only three parameters: population size, the probability p of generating random inversion, and the number of iterations in the termination condition; most of the other evolutionary systems have many additional parameters;
- it is worthwhile to emphasise the precision and stability of the system for relatively small test cases (almost 100% accuracy for all considered test cases up to 105 cities); the computational time was also acceptable (3-4 seconds);
- the system introduces a new, interesting operator, which combines features of inversion (or mutation) and crossover. Results of experiments reported in the previous section indicate clearly that the inver-over operator is significantly better than random inversion. The probability parameter p (in all experiments kept constant at 0.02) determines a proportion of blind inversions and guided (adaptive) inversions.

Further research will concentrate on (1) the significance of the selection method in connection with the inver-over operator (e.g., it would be interesting to experiment with (μ, λ)-selection and compare it with the current one, which allows competition between parent and offspring only), (2) adaptive (or self-adaptive) change of the parameter p (if successful, the system will have only one parameter: population size, apart from termination condition), (3) the significance of the population size and the termination condition (the current version of the system has fixed population size of 100 and terminates if there is no improvement in 10 iterations of the while loop), (4) full comparison of the proposed technique with other algorithms (including other evolutionary systems, tabu search, simulated annealing, and other heuristic methods), (5) experiments with larger instances of TSP (up to 1,000,000 cities).

References

1. Applegate, D. Bixby, R.E., Chvatal, V., and Cook, W., Finding cuts in the TSP: a preliminary report. Report 95-05, DIMACS, Rutgers University, NJ.
2. Braun, H., On solving traveling salesman problems by genetic algorithms. In Proc. PPSN'90, pp.129–133.
3. Davis, L., (Editor), *Genetic Algorithms and Simulated Annealing*, Morgan Kaufmann Publishers, San Mateo, CA, 1987.
4. Davis, L., *Handbook of Genetic Algorithms*, Van Nostrand Reinhold, NY, 1991.
5. Eshelman, L., The CHC adaptive search algorithm: How to have safe search when engaging in nontraditional genetic recombination. In Proc. FOGA'90, pp.265–283.

6. Fogel, D.B., An evolutionay approach to the traveling salesman problem. Biol. Cybern., Vol.60, pp.139–144, 1988.
7. Gorges-Schleuter, M., ASPARAGOS: An asynchronous parallel genetic optimization strategy. In Proc. ICGA'91, pp.422–427.
8. Grefenstette, J.J., Incorporating Problem Specific Knowledge into Genetic Algorithms. In [3], pp.42–60.
9. Herdy, M., Application of the Evolution Strategy to Discrete Optimization Problems. In Proc. PPSN'90, pp.188–192.
10. Johnson, D.S., The Traveling Salesman Problem: A Case Study. In *Local Search in Combinatorial Optimization*, E. Aarts and J.K. Lenstra (Editors), John Wiley, 1996, pp.215–310.
11. Johnson, D.S., McGeoch, L.A., and Rothberg, E.E., Asymptotic experimental analysis for the Held-Karp traveling salesman bound. Proc. Seventh Annual ACM–SIAM Symposium on Discrete Algorithms, ACM, New York, and SIAM, Philadelphia, PA, pp. 341–350.
12. Karp, R.M., Probabilistic Analysis of Partitioning Algorithm for the Traveling Salesman Problem in the Plane. Mathematics of Operations Research, Vol.2, No.3, 1977, pp.209–224.
13. Lidd, M.L., Traveling Salesman Problem Domain Application of a Fundamentally New Approach to Utilizing Genetic Algorithms. Tech. Rep., MITRE Corp., 1991.
14. Lin, S. and Kerninghan, B.W., An Effective Heuristic Algorithm for the Traveling Salesman Problem. Operations Research, pp.498–516, 1972.
15. Maekawa, K., Mori, N.,Tamaki, H., Kita, H. and Nishikawa, Y., A genetic solution for the traveling salesman problem by means of a thermodynamical selection rule. Proc. IEEE ICEC '96.
16. Matias, K. and D. Whitley, Genetic operators, the fitness landscape and the traveling salesman problem. In Proc. PPSN'92, pp.219–228.
17. Merz, P.and B. Freisleben, Genetic local search for the TSP: New results. Proc. IEEE ICEC '97.
18. Michalewicz, Z., *Genetic Algorithms + Data Structures = Evolution Programs*, Springer-Verlag, 3rd edition, 1996.
19. Mühlenbein, H., Evolution in time and space – The parallel genetic algorithm. In Proc. FOGA'90, pp.316–337.
20. Nagata, Y. and Kobayashi, S., Edge assembly crossover: A high-power genetic algorithm for the traveling salesman problem. Proc. ICGA '97.
21. Nurnber, H.-T. and Beyer, H.-G., The dynamics of Evolution Strategies in the optimization of traveling salesman problem, Proc. of EP'97.
22. Reinelt, G., TSPLIB – A Traveling Salesman Problem Library. ORSA Journal on Computing, Vol.3, No.4, pp.376–384, 1991.
23. Starkweather, T., McDaniel, S., Mathias, K., Whitley, C., and Whitley, D., A Comparison of Genetic Sequencing Operators. In Proc. ICGA'91, pp.69–76.
24. Tao, G. and Michalewicz, Z., Evolutionary Algorithms for the TSP. In preparation.
25. Ulder, N.L.J., Aarts, E.H.L., Bandelt, H.-J., van Laarhoven, P.J.M., Pesch, E., Genetic Local Search Algorithms for the Traveling Salesman Problem. In Proc. PPSN'90, pp.109–116.
26. Valenzuela, Ch.L. and Williams, L.P., Improving Simple Heuristic Algorithms for the Travelling Salesman Problem using a Genetic Algorithm. In Proc. ICGA'97, pp.458–464.
27. Whitley, D., Starkweather, T., and Fuquay, D'A., Scheduling Problems and Traveling Salesman: The Genetic Edge Recombination Operator. In Proc. ICGA'89, pp.133–140.

Repair and Brood Selection in the Traveling Salesman Problem

Tim Walters
Redwood City, California
t.walters@computer.org

Abstract. The traveling salesman problem (TSP) has been a popular subject for genetic algorithm research. The heavy constraints of the problem make the results of a standard crossover operation invalid. This paper investigates a technique of chromosome repair called Directed Edge Repair (DER) that compensates for invalid edges from crossover or mutation. The algorithm is combined with the technique of brood selection from genetic programming and with the 3-opt local search technique. Tests on several problems from TSPLIB are reported. The algorithm was able to find optimal solutions to problems up to 1577 cities. On many of the problems, brood selection improved the accuracy of solutions without adding additional computation time.

1. Introduction

The *traveling salesman problem* (TSP) may be stated very simply: given a set of n cities with distances D_{ij} between each pair of cities c_i and c_j, find a path that visits all cities exactly once and has the minimum total distance ΣD_{ij} of the cities visited. If $D_{ij}=D_{ji}$ then the problem is said to be a *symmetric* TSP (STSP), otherwise it is considered an *asymmetric* TSP (ATSP).

The problem has been studied frequently in the GA community. Because a random list of city numbers usually fails to represent a valid tour, standard recombination techniques like one point crossover are unusable. Instead several techniques have been developed to maintain a valid tour during crossover. The Edge Crossover operators (Dzubera and Whitley 1994) and MPX (Gorges-Schleuter 1997) attempt to preserve as much information as possible, while a strategy like DPX (Freisleben and Merz 1996) is intentionally disruptive. Mutation, if applied, is designed to convert a valid tour to another valid tour by swapping edges connecting two or more cities.

Genetic algorithms have been applied to several other constraint problems using a repair algorithm (Michalewicz 1997). In this technique, no special care is taken to avoid generating invalid individuals during crossover or mutation. Instead, a constraint violation is handled by modifying the chromosome before evaluation to make a valid individual. In many problems, a repair procedure following crossover is easier to implement than special crossover or mutation operators that preserve a valid representation. It would thus be interesting to discover whether there are any restrictions on repair techniques that prevent them from solving a benchmark problem like the TSP.

A chromosome may also be modified before evaluation by the addition of a local search heuristic. In the case of the TSP, the well-known 2-opt heuristic examines all pairs of edges and exchanges the endpoints when this will reduce the length of the tour. Further improvements may be gained by examining all triples in an improvement called 3-opt. The Lin-Kernighan optimization (Lin and Kernighan 1973) further improves this by looking for k-opt improvements. Some of the best results with a GA on the TSP have been obtained with fast versions of 1-pass 3-opt (Gorges-Schleuter 1997) and with Lin-Kernighan (Merz and Freisleben 1997). Good results were also reported for the Edge Assembly Crossover (EAX) (Nagata and Kobayashi 1997). In this approach edges from the two parents are combined into subtours, which are then converted into a legal tour using a minimum spanning tree algorithm. An interesting crossover technique used in EAX is the generation of up to 100 offspring until an improvement is seen.

A similar crossover technique has been studied in genetic programming under the name *soft brood selection*. Soft brood selection was first proposed by Altenberg (1994) to improve the evolvability of genetic programs. In brood selection, a pair of parents will generate several children (a brood) and only the best one or two children will be selected as offspring for the rest of the genetic algorithm. ("Soft" selection refers to the fact that children are selected based on their fitness values relative to each other, as opposed to the "hard" selection by global fitness criteria). Tackett (1994) analyzes this as a recombination operator under the name *greedy recombination*, and argues that brood selection is a greedy local search for the best subexpression insertion and donation sites. This technique is easily adaptable to the TSP, where we are searching for optimal subtour insertion sites.

This paper studies a repair approach to the TSP, using a notation based on nearest neighbor proximity. The search for an optimal solution is assisted by brood selection and by a fast 3-opt optimization process. Section 2 describes the chromosome representation, repair and evaluation of chromosomes, and operators on the chromosomes. Section 3 gives implementation details of a GA that uses the representation and its operators. Section 4 gives the results of tests of the GA on several TSP instances and observations based on the tests' results. Section 5 gives conclusions and suggestions for further work.

2. The Genetic Algorithm

2.1 Nearest Neighbor Indexing

The chromosome representation used in this study is a vector of n integers for a problem with n cities. For each city i the gene g_i represents the directed edge from city i to the next city visited in the tour. It is worth noting in the case of the STSP that a directed edge representation contains some redundancy. A tour in one direction $A \to B \to C \to D$ is equivalent to the reverse tour $D \to C \to B \to A$, but has a completely different notation. This will cause some duplication of the search effort.

The actual number used is not the city number but the relative proximity of the next city in the tour, i.e. its nearest neighbor index from city i. In this notation, the nearest neighbor to a city is represented by 1, the next nearest by 2, and so on.

The nearest neighbor index values are illustrated in Tables 1 and 2. Table 1 shows the distance matrix for an STSP with 8 cities, A through H. In Table 2, the nearest neighbor index values are shown for each city. The nearest neighbor to city A is city H, with a distance of 3. For city F, four cities have distance 4. In the case of ties like

	A	B	C	D	E	F	G	H
A	0	6	8	9	5	4	7	3
B	6	0	5	3	5	4	2	4
C	8	5	0	4	3	9	7	5
D	9	3	4	0	6	8	4	6
E	5	5	3	6	0	7	7	3
F	4	4	9	8	7	0	4	4
G	7	2	7	4	7	4	0	5
H	3	4	5	6	3	4	5	0

Table 1. Distance matrix for an 8 city tour.

	A	B	C	D	E	F	G	H
1	H	G	E	B	C	A	B	A
2	F	D	D	C	H	B	D	E
3	E	F	B	G	A	G	F	B
4	B	H	H	E	B	H	H	F
5	G	C	G	H	D	E	A	C
6	C	E	A	F	F	D	C	G
7	D	A	F	A	G	C	E	D

Table 2. Nearest neighbor index values for the 8 city tour

this, the nearest neighbor is chosen as the first in the list of cities (here, first in alphabetical order).

This nearest neighbor notation has the advantage of normalizing the edge numbers to a standard value. Since we are trying to minimize the total distance for the tour, we expect that many edges in an optimal tour will connect cities that are close together. For example, since the nearest neighbor always has the value 1, an initialization heuristic that is trying to connect all cities to their nearest neighbors would start with index values of 1 for each city.

Not only is the nearest neighbor used in initialization methods to obtain a low valued tour, but as noted in (Reinelt 1994) and (Lin and Kernighan 1973) most cities in good or optimal solutions are connected to near neighbors. Examination of several optimal tours during this study found at least 40% of the edges connected to the nearest neighbor, 80% connected to the first three neighbors, and 95% connected to the first ten. By limiting search to cities within this range of neighbor indices, the search space can be reduced dramatically.

2.2 Repair

Evaluation of a chromosome is based on repair. Although it is true that any given tour in a given direction has a single representation, most chromosomes with arbitrary values do not represent a legal tour. Usually, several gene values will need to be changed before a legal tour can be constructed. The approach taken in this paper assigns as many edges as possible from the original chromosome. If an edge from a particular city cannot be assigned to the tour, a new directed edge from the same city is found, with a distance as close as possible to the one specified in the original gene value. By attempting to assign edges that are close in distance to the original values specified in the chromosome, it is hoped that the final tour is close to the one originally described in the genes. We call this algorithm Directed Edge Repair (DER).

The first step in constructing the tour is to construct an ordered list of edges to allocate. For each gene value the corresponding city and distance value for the edge are determined and placed into a list of edges. This working list is then sorted by length, so that shorter edges will be processed first. To prevent domination of the solutions by specific short edges, the sort key used for each sort is recomputed from the edge length plus a small random noise P_{lnoise} (typically 20%). Starting with the shortest edge in the list, we assign each edge to the tour in order, unless the edge would connect to a city that is already visited, or if the connection would create a closed cycle with fewer than *n* edges. If an edge cannot be assigned, the neighbor index value is adjusted to a new value that represents a city whose distance is as close as possible to the length of the failed edge. After all possible edges in the working list have been assigned, the list of failed edges is moved to the working list. Another pass is made through the working list, and assignment continues as before, with new index values for failed edges chosen to be the untried edge with distance as close as possible to the original value.

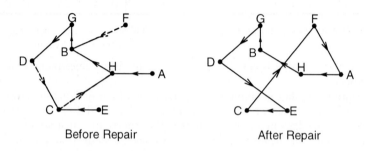

Before Repair   After Repair

	First				Working List									Last	
Pass	B		E		A		H		G		F		D		C	
1	1	G	1	C	1	H	3	B	2	D	2	B	2	C	4	H
2											1	A	1	B	3	B
3													3	G	2	D
4													4	E	1	E
5															5	G
6															6	A
7															7	F

Figure 1. Example of directed edges and the working list during repair. Graphs of the initial edges in the chromosome are shown before repair and after the final tour is constructed. Each column in the working list represents the starting city of the directed edge. Table entries represent nearest neighbor index and ending city for each pass.

Figure 1 shows an example of the DER process, using the same 8 city tour data shown earlier. After sorting the edges by length, the first working list is constructed and is shown in the row for Pass 1, with shortest edges on the left. For each edge the nearest neighbor index is shown along with the city it represents. The first edges in the list are assigned without conflicts, from B→G, E→C, A→H, H→B, and G→D. The remaining edges, F→B, D→C, and C→H, connect to cities which are already visited and must be adjusted. The adjusted values for each edge are shown in the row for Pass 2. Since the ordering of the starting cities for each edge does not change from pass to pass, the edge from city F will be the next one tested. For city F, the nearest neighbor index is changed from 2 to 1, corresponding to city A, and in pass 2 the edge F→A is found to be legal and is assigned. The edges from the remaining two cities are adjusted through several subsequent passes until the final edge values of D→E and C→F are discovered.

When used, local search in DER is treated as an extension to the repair technique and is applied immediately after a valid tour is constructed. After local search a fitness value may be computed, and the constructed tour may be used to generate a replacement for the original chromosome (a "Lamarckian" replacement). Some researchers have reported improved results with a partial replacement rate (notably, Orvosh and Davis (1993) found best results when replacing only 5% of the time). However, no significant improvement from partial replacement was seen in this study. All results here are reported with a 100% replacement rate.

2.3 Crossover and Mutation

With a repair procedure built into the evaluation, it is no longer required that crossover and mutation preserve valid tours. This allows standard crossover and mutation operators can be used. This study uses a modified two-point crossover, which was found to perform somewhat better than uniform crossover. Crossover proceeds by identifying two parents and alternately designating one parent a donor and the other a recipient. For STSP tours, one half of the time the order of all edges in the donor parent will be reversed, to avoid any bias due to the redundant directed edge representation. A crossover size is selected as a fraction of the number of unique edges. A starting edge is then selected randomly from the unique edges in the two tours. This edge is copied from the donor to the recipient, and the successor to the starting edge in the donor tour becomes the next edge to be copied. This process continues until the required number of differing edges is copied over to the recipient. By following the tour order of the donor tour we hope to preserve subtour information. After a child is generated, the roles of donor and recipient are swapped and another child is generated, using the same crossover point and size. Since the edges copied will follow a different tour order, the two children will generally have different sets of edges exchanged.

Mutation is somewhat simpler, and is accomplished by simply modifying the gene values for randomly chosen cities. Mutation is applied with a fixed probability to children immediately after they are generated.

Brood selection (or greedy recombination) consists of a simple wrapper around the normal crossover and mutation operators. Using the notation of (Tackett 1994), the *brood size factor* $R_B(n)$ denotes that each 2 parents produce $2 \times n$ offspring from which 2 children are selected. In this implementation, two broods of n offspring are created, one for each parent in its role as crossover recipient. (We will refer to this factor of n simply as the brood size.) In each brood, all children that are duplicates of other members of the global population are culled, and the best remaining child is selected as an offspring. In the case that no child remains in the brood, crossover fails and no child is generated. Crossover thus may return 0, 1, or 2 children.

3. Implementation Details

This study was implemented in C on a 300MHz Pentium II. The work was based on the SUGAL 2.1 Genetic Algorithm package, written by Dr. Andrew Hunter at the

University of Sunderland, England. All studies used the 70% "ranked unconditional" replacement method, in which the best 30% of the population is maintained, and the remaining 70% is always replaced. Roulette selection was used with a bias of 1.8, based on a linear scaling of the tour length. To improve diversity, individuals generating duplicate tours were rejected.

As mentioned earlier, almost all of the neighbor index values in optimal tours are very small. In this study genes are initialized with a probability of .45, .25, and .15 for the first 3 nearest neighbors, respectively, with the remainder distributed uniformly between neighbors 4 through 10. Mutation is applied with a probability of .20, with each mutation consisting of a change of from 4 to 7 genes to new values using the same neighbor index distribution as initialization. Crossover sizes were varied randomly for each crossover from 2 edges to 70% of the total edges.

All studies used a sort noise factor P_{lnoise} of 0.2, with a standard quicksort routine used to sort the initial working list.

Local optimization was performed using a 3-opt routine coded to restrict searches to 40 nearest neighbors and to recently changed edges using "don't look bits" as described in (Bentley 1990). Note that some other researchers have extended the use of don't look bits to limit the starting points for optimization to edges changed by mutation or crossover (for example, Iterated Lin-Kernighan (Johnson 1990) and the GLS algorithm described in (Merz and Freisleben 1997)). This technique was not found to be effective with the 3-opt optimization used in this study.

All distance metrics are computed at the start of the problem and stored in memory along with a full sorted neighbor list for each city. This increased computation speed, but limited the size of the problems to about 2000 cities.

Test problems were obtained from the TSPLIB library (Reinelt 1991). In general the problems chosen have been examined in several other studies. However, one problem, kroB100, is reported because of the difficulty DER had in solving it.

4. Experimental Results

4.1 Brood Selection

Brood selection is a computationally intensive technique that attempts to maximize the outcome of each crossover. It seems reasonable to test not only the improvement in solution quality, but the amount of computer time required as well. To measure this tradeoff, a series of experiments were performed with the att532 problem. Each test consisted of 100 runs using the same initial population. The brood size was varied from 1 to 20, with the number of evaluations limited to a constant. The first run was set to 500 generations with a brood size of 1, the second was run with a brood size of 2 and was limited to 250 generations, and so on. Note that since mutation is applied with a constant probability per individual, the total number of mutations per run will also be approximately the same.

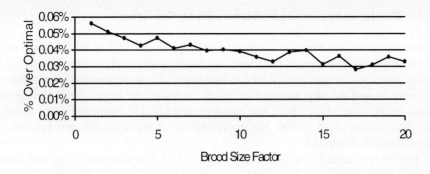

Figure 2. Average solution quality of att532 as a function of brood size

The results, in Figure 2, show the effectiveness of larger brood sizes. Even though the number of evaluations is held constant, large brood sizes consistently find better solutions than a brood size of 1. The effectiveness of brood selection in finding improved individuals during crossover is also apparent: with a brood size of 20, solutions are found within a limit of 25 generations. (Increasing the brood size beyond 20 causes the average quality to get worse as the number of generations becomes insufficient to find an optimal solution.) To see if a similar effect appears in other problems, we next examine several more problems using brood sizes of 1 and 10.

4.2 Results on Symmetric Problems without Optimization

Table 3 summarizes the performance of DER on STSP problems without optimization. Results are the average of 20 runs, with a population of 500. As before, the number of evaluations is kept the same, so that 1000 generations are computed for a brood size of 1 and 100 generations for a brood size of 10. The frequency an optimal solution was found is given in the column fOpt, and the average solution quality is reported as the percent above optimal. Time is reported in seconds.

The performance of DER on kroA100 and lin105 is quite similar, finding the optimal solution frequently without brood selection and with even better performance with brood selection. Performance is not nearly as good on kroB100, where no run was able to get better than 0.27% above optimal. Also, a brood size of 10 is significantly faster, apparently due to the reduced number of generations required.

Problem	Pop	$R_B(n)$	Gen	f Opt	Ave.	Time
kroA100	500	1	1000	65%	0.068	134
		10	100	80%	0.039	112
kroB100	500	1	1000	0%	1.004	132
		10	100	0%	0.474	112
lin105	500	1	1000	85%	0.187	141
		10	40	100%	0.000	48

Table 3. Results of symmetric problems without optimization.

4.3 Results on Symmetric Problems with Optimization

Table 4 presents the results of adding a fast 3-opt local search to the DER algorithm. 3-opt substantially improves the speed and accuracy of the algorithm. In some of the experiments all 20 runs were solved to optimality. For these problems the number of generations and the time reported are for the run with the largest number of generations. In the case of f11577, the initial population was optimized using a nearest neighbor search depth of 200, but the remainder of the algorithm was run with the normal search depth of 40.

For the two smallest problems, d198 and lin318, it was possible to find optimal values 100% of the time both with and without brood selection. For these two problems brood selection does not seem to merit the extra computation time. It is interesting to note, however, that in both cases a brood size of 10 is able to reduce the number of generations required by a factor of 3. For the other problems, DER was able to find optimal solutions in all cases, and with higher accuracy with a brood size of 10 than with a brood size of 1.

Problem	Pop	$R_B(n)$	Gen	f Opt	Ave.	Time
d198	100	1	15	100%	0.000	4.6
		10	4	100%	0.000	10.6
lin318	100	1	38	100%	0.000	9.2
		10	11	100%	0.000	23
pcb442	100	1	500	85%	0.028	116
		10	39	100%	0.000	91
att532	100	1	500	25%	0.049	162
		10	50	40%	0.038	157
rat783	100	1	500	75%	0.022	210
		10	50	80%	0.010	212
f11577	200	1	500	40%	0.013	1703
		10	50	55%	0.007	1667

Table 4. Results of symmetric problems with optimization.

4.4 Results on Asymmetric Problems

In Table 5 the results on several asymmetric problems are displayed. For ATSP experiments it is important to restrict the actions of 3-opt to the single move which does not change a subtour direction. This weakens the action of the optimizer somewhat but does not otherwise cause any changes in the DER algorithm. For the three smallest problems a population of 20 proved adequate to find optimal solutions 100% of the time, but for problem ftv170 a population of 50 was required. In the two problems ry48p and kro124p a brood size of 1 was adequate to always find an optimal solution. Again we see that a brood size of 10 is able to reduce the number of generations required, but not enough to improve the total computation time required. In the more difficult problems `ft70` and `ftv170`, brood selection is able to increase the accuracy to 100%.

Problem	Pop	$R_B(n)$	Gen	f Opt	Ave.	Time
ry48p	20	1	49	100%	0.000	0.3
		10	8	100%	0.000	0.4
ft70	20	1	500	60%	0.035	3.6
		10	30	100%	0.000	2
kro124p	20	1	35	100%	0.000	0.4
		10	19	100%	0.000	1.6
ftv170	50	1	500	50%	0.163	16.4
		10	21	100%	0.000	7.3

Table 5. Results of asymmetric problems with optimization.

5. Conclusions and Future Work

This paper has presented a repair based DER algorithm for the traveling salesman problem. Without optimization techniques it is able to find optimal solutions in some small problems, while with optimization it has found optimal solutions in symmetric and asymmetric problems as large as 1577 cities. This demonstrates that repair can produce viable solutions in this combinatorial problem.

The results with brood selection are particularly interesting for several reasons. As a computational technique it is relatively easy to add to an existing GA, and certainly seems to offer one more setting to try during a run. In this study the easier problems were only slowed down by the addition of the extra search in the large broods, but in the more difficult problems it was possible to increase accuracy with no extra overhead. Further work will be required to determine the optimal brood size for a particular problem. As with any GA setting, the exact value used for brood size need not be constant over an entire run but could be chosen adaptively, perhaps responding to conditions of the problem, the relative progress in convergence, or the parents of the brood. Computation time could be reduced by using an inexpensive function for initial testing of the brood, as described in (Tackett 1994). A final interesting observation is the uniform reduction in the number of generations in all studies with a large brood size. Clearly the convergence speed is aided by finding crossovers of high quality. A heuristic or adaptive strategy that improves the success of finding successful crossovers could also improve the results shown here.

Acknowledgements

The author would like to thank J. David Schaffer for introducing him to the literature on brood selection. This paper benefited greatly from reading of an early draft by Peter Merz, and from additional comments by Bryant Julstrom. Portions of the optimization code were derived from code originally written by Ken Boese.

References

1. Altenberg, L. The Evolution of Evolvability in Genetic Programming. In Kinnear, K. E., Jr.(ed.):*Advances in Genetic Programming*. MIT Press(1994) 47-74
2. Bentley, J. L.: Experiments on Traveling Salesman Heuristics. In: Proceedings of the 1st Annual ACM-SIAM Symposium on Discrete Algorithms (SODA '90), San Francisco, CA, USA. SIAM (1990) 91-99
3. Dzubera, J., and Whitley, D.: Advanced Correlation Analysis of Operators for the Traveling Salesman Problem. In: Parallel Problem Solving From Nature - PPSN III, Jerusalem (October, 1994). Springer Verlag (1994) 68-77
4. Freisleben, B., and Merz, P.: New Genetic Local Search Operators for the Traveling Salesman Problem. In: Parallel Problem Solving From Nature - PPSN IV, Berlin, Germany (September 22-26, 1996). Springer-Verlag, Heidelberg (1996) 890-899
5. Gorges-Schleuter, M.: Asparagos96 and the Traveling Salesman Problem. In: Proceedings of the 1997 IEEE International Conference on Evolutionary Computation, Indianapolis, Indiana (April 13-16, 1997). IEEE Press (1997) 171-174
6. Johnson, D. S.: Local Optimization and the Traveling Salesman Problem. In: Automata, Languages and Programming, 17th International Colloquium, Warwick University, England. Springer-Verlag, Berlin (1990) 446-461
7. Lin, S., and Kernighan, B. W.: *An Effective Heuristic Algorithm for the Traveling-Salesman Problem*. Operations Research, 21 (1973) 498-516
8. Merz, P., and Freisleben, B.: Genetic Local Search for the TSP: New Results. In: Proceedings of the 1997 IEEE International Conference on Evolutionary Computation, Indianapolis, Indiana (April 13-16, 1997). IEEE Press (1997) 159-164
9. Michalewicz, Z. Repair Algorithms. In Bäck, T., Fogel, D. B. and Michalewicz, Z.(eds.):*Handbook of Evolutionary Computation*. Institute of Physics Publishing and Oxford University Press(1997) C5.4:1-5
10. Nagata, Y., and Kobayashi, S.: Edge Assembly Crossover: A High-power Genetic Algorithm for the Traveling Salesman Problem. In: Proceedings of the Seventh International Conference on Genetic Algorithms, East Lansing, Michigan (July 19-23, 1997). Morgan Kaufmann, San Francisco (1997) 450-457
11. Orvosh, D., and Davis, L.: Shall We Repair? Genetic Algorithms, Combinatorial Optimization, and Feasibility Constraints. In: Proceedings of the Fifth International Conference on Genetic Algorithms (ICGA'93), San Mateo, California. Morgan Kaufmann, San Mateo (1993) 650
12. Reinelt, G.: *TSPLIB-- A Traveling Salesman Problem Library*. ORSA Journal on Computing, 3 (4) (1991) 376-384
13. Reinelt, G.: *The Traveling Salesman: Computational Solutions for TSP Applications*. Lecture Notes in Computer Science, Vol. 840. Springer-Verlag, Heidelberg (1994)
14. Tackett, W. A.: Greedy Recombination and Genetic Search on the Space of Computer Programs. In: Foundations of Genetic Algorithms 3, Estes Park, Colorado. Morgan Kaufmann, San Francisco (1994) 271-297

The Traveling Salesrep Problem, Edge Assembly Crossover, and 2-opt

J. Watson, C. Ross, V. Eisele, J. Denton, J. Bins, C. Guerra,
D. Whitley, A. Howe

Computer Science Department, Colorado State University, Fort Collins, CO 80523
{watsonj, rossc, eisele, bins, denton, guerra, whitley, howe}@cs.colostate.edu

Abstract. Optimal results for the Traveling Salesrep Problem have been reported on problems with up to 3038 cities using a GA with *Edge Assembly Crossover* (EAX). This paper first attempts to independently replicate these results on Padberg's 532 city problem. We then evaluate the performance contribution of the various algorithm components. The incorporation of 2-opt into the EAX GA is also explored. Finally, comparative results are presented for a population-based form of 2-opt that uses partial restarts.

1   Introduction

Nagata and Kobayashi [7] report optimal solutions on Traveling Salesrep Problems (TSPs) ranging in size from 101 to 3038 cities. They also report modest computations times on a 200MHz Pentium, ranging from approximately 13 minutes for the well known Padberg 532 city problem [8], to 2.5 hours for a 3038 city problem. These results are an important break-through for two reasons. First, they represent a dramatic improvement over previous evolutionary-based optimization methods for the Traveling Salesrep Problem; other researchers have reported good results for the Padberg 532 city problem, but rarely optimal solutions on problems of this size and larger. Second, these results are close enough to the state-of-the-art that evolutionary-based optimization methods could have a very real potential to provide the basis for new state-of-the-art approaches to the Traveling Salesrep Problem.

Although not explored in this paper, Freisleben and Merz [3] also report impressive performance on problems of similar complexity. Their algorithm, Genetic Local Search (GLS), exploits the 'big-valley' structure of TSP fitness landscapes documented in [1]. To exploit this structure, crossover in GLS is implemented using a computationally intensive search algorithm. Furthermore, GLS maintain an extremely small (≤ 40) population of individuals. In contrast, the EAX GA uses relatively weak search operators and a large population to obtain similar performance results.

This paper explores three questions. Two of these questions relate directly to the work of Nagata and Kobayashi. First, can the results be independently replicated from their description of the algorithm? We can answer this question in the affirmative; our implementation replicates the original results to within, on average, 0.054% of the optimal tour cost; we document our implementation of their algorithm in Section 2 to enable resolution of the remaining discrepancies. Given this success, we then ask the question 'What components of the Nagata and Kobayashi algorithm are critical to performance?' We cannot definitively answer this question, but we provide some partial answers by testing the effects of removing or replacing various components of their algorithm and measuring the resulting performance impact.

The third question relates to the use of 2-opt. For the past ten years, researchers have reported near-optimal results on Padberg's 532 city problem using evolutionary algorithms [2] [5] [6]. Yet all of these approaches have used 2-opt as a local search algorithm within the genetic algorithm. Given this observation, we ask: 'To what degree does the success of these algorithms depend on the use of 2-opt and to what degree do the "evolution-based" features in the various algorithms contribute to producing good results?'

A distinguishing characteristic of the Nagata and Kobayashi algorithm is that it does not use 2-opt. Their recombination operator, *Edge Assembly Crossover* (EAX), uses the edges from the two parents to construct disjoint subtours. Then, using a construction analogous to a minimal spanning tree, the subtours are connected in a greedy fashion to produce the child tour. Thus, the EAX operator is not "blind;" local information is exploited in determining which edges to use to connect subtours. Thus, there would seem to be no reason not to also use 2-opt in conjunction with the algorithm.

Another important trait of the EAX operator is that it will introduce new edges into the child when connecting subtours. Edges not in the parents, or perhaps not even in the population, are introduced into offspring. We are now convinced that a good operator for the TSP must be able to introduce new edges into the offspring. This is contrary to the tenets put forward by Radcliffe [9] [10] and contrary to the goals behind the construction of operators such as Edge-3 [12] [5] which attempt to inherit as many edges from parents as possible.

The argument as to why good new edges must be introduced during recombination (or by mutation, or local search) is simple. Mathias and Whitley [5] point out that the complete graph of all possible edges for a symmetric TSP has $(N^2 - N)/2$ edges, where N is the number of cities. Each tour samples N of these edges, so a population must be of size at least $(N-1)/2$ in order to sample each edge exactly once. Assume population size is proportional to the number of the cities (as in the Nagata and Kobayashi algorithm and the algorithms presented here). Then each edge occurs twice in expectation in an initial random population. Selection can therefore quickly eliminate edges from the population. Good edges can also be lost if they occur in poor tours. Thus it is important for operators to intelligently introduce new good edges. Unlike other crossover operators, EAX makes the introduction of new edges an integral part of recombination–which may contribute to its effectiveness.

The next section describes our implementation of the Nagata and Kobayashi algorithm. Section three describes our comparative experiments. Our study focuses exclusively on Padberg's symmetric 532 city problem for several reasons.

First, it has been widely studied and is notoriously difficult to solve to optimality. Seocnd, Nagata and Kobayashi also found this problem to be harder than any of the larger problems they investigated. Finally, Section four discusses the role of 2-opt in hybrid evolutionary algorithms.

2 Nagata and Kobayashi's Algorithm

Once two parents have been selected for crossover, the EAX operator merges these two individuals into a single graph denoted by R. The two parents are denoted by A and B, respectively. Each edge in R is annotated with the parent to which it belongs. R may contain two instances of the same edge, if both parents contain the edge. R is next divided into a set of disjoint subtours.

2.1 Edge Assembly Crossover (EAX): AB-Cycles

Let v_i represent a vertex from R and let $(v_i, v_j), i \neq j$, represent an edge. Suppose (v_i, v_j) represents an edge randomly chosen from parent A. (Note that A and B are just randomly assigned labels; the choice of A is arbitrary.) Choose one vertex (either v_i or v_j) as the origin. If v_i is the origin, then choose an edge which leads from the second vertex, v_j, to any other vertex in R. However, this edge must come from parent B. If more than one such edge exists, a random selection is made. The algorithm continues to traverse R, at each step alternately picking edges from parent A and parent B.

After each edge is traversed, the algorithm checks to see if adding this new edge to the set of previously selected edges will result in what Nagata and Kobayashi term an *AB-cycle*. An AB-cycle is a even-length sub-cycle of R with edges that alternately come from A and B. An AB-cycle may repeat cities, but not edges. While there can be two edges between a pair of cities, they are uniquely identified as an A or B edge, and thus distinct.

Once an AB-cycle has been found it is stored and the edges making up that cycle are removed from R. The algorithm repeats this procedure until R contains no more edges, having been completely decomposed into a set of AB-cycles.

The first several edges used in the construction of the AB-cycle may not appear in the final AB-cycle. This occurs when the final edge connects back onto the subgraph at some city x other than the origin city, and the induced subcycle is an AB-cycle. In this case the 'extraneous' edges are left in the R graph, to eventually be used in forming another cycle. In this situation Nagata and Kobayashi choose an edge incident with x from R to begin construction of the next AB-cycle. As we can find no reason to prefer this method over random selection, our algorithm always selects the starting location of a new AB-cycle at random from R.

When R is undirected, as is the case for the symmetric TSP, the set of AB-cycles is not uniquely determined by the algorithm. Furthermore, a number of "ineffective" AB-cycles may be formed by the algorithm. Such cycles consist solely of two edges between the same pair of cities. Any ineffective AB-cycles are removed from consideration by the remaining phases of the algorithm.

2.2 Edge Assembly Crossover (EAX): E-set to Offspring

After construction of the set of AB-cycles, a subset of AB-cycles is chosen to be used in the generation of an intermediate child. This subset is called an *E-set*. Two methods for selecting AB-cycles for inclusion into the E-set are defined by Nagata and Kobayashi. The first, denoted by $EAX(rand)$, simply selects each AB-cycle for inclusion into the E-set with a probability of 0.5. The second method, denoted by $EAX(heuristic)$, makes use of a heuristic metric to determine the inclusion of an AB-cycle into the E-set. The metric balances the need for maintaining population diversity against the need to reduce overall tour cost. We implemented the heuristic metric as described in [7]. As described in the next subsection, the EAX GA uses these two methods in different contexts.

Construction of an intermediate child, C, begins with a copy of parent A. Then each edge of each subtour in the E-set is examined, with the following actions taken on C. If the edge from the E-set is a member of parent A, the edge is deleted from C. If the edge is a member of parent B, the edge is added to C. The result is a set of disjoint subtours which comprise the intermediate child.

The last stage of the EAX operator involves transformation of the intermediate child into a single legal tour. The subtours are merged into a single tour using a greedy construction procedure. The smallest tour, in terms of number of edges, is selected from the set of subtours. A pair of edges, one from the smallest subtour and one from another distinct subtour, is then selected such that merging of the two subtours at those edges minimizes the change in overall tour cost. Let (v_q, v_{q+1}) be an edge in one subtour, and (v'_r, v'_{r+1}) be an edge in the other. The location of the verticies is arbitrary and addition on the indices for edges in v and v' is $mod(|v|)$ and $mod(|v'|)$. A greedy algorithm for connecting subtours uses the following metrics:

$$Cut(q,r) = (\$(v_q, v_{q+1}) + \$(v'_r, v'_{r+1}))$$

$$Link(q,r) = MIN \left((\$(v_q, v'_r) + \$(v_{q+1}, v'_{r+1})), (\$(v_q, v'_{r+1}) + \$(v_{q+1}, v'_r)) \right)$$

where $\$(v_i, v_j)$ is the cost of edge (v_i, v_j). Then we seek:

$$MIN \left[Link(q,r) - Cut(q,r) \right] \quad \forall r, q$$

This process of merging subtours is repeated until a single tour remains. Nagata and Kobayashi use a heuristic method to reduce the number of edge pairs considered. We use an exhaustive enumerative of all edge pairs, since the procedure did not contribute significantly to the overall runtime.

2.3 The EAX Genetic Algorithm

Nagata and Kobayashi introduce a variation on a traditional generational GA which employs a form of elitist tournament selection. Two parents are randomly selected, without replacement, from the population and recombined using crossover. The two parents and the resulting child are then compared, and the individual with the best fitness is passed to the next generation. This procedure is repeated to produce all N members of the next generation. Nagata and Kobayahsi claim that the EAX GA is better able to maintain population diversity by giving a large number of parents the ability to pass children into the next generaton.

Finally, the EAX GA defines recombination as an iterative procedure. First, a child is produced using the $EAX(heuristic)$ E-set construction method. Should this fail to produce a child with better fitness than both parents, the $EAX(rand)$ E-set construction method is used to produce more children until either such an improved child is found or 100 children are produced. We refer to this method as *iterative child generation*, or ICG.

3   Empirical Results

In this section, we investigate the performance contribution of the various components of the Nagata and Kobayahsi algorithm. For convenience we will refer to their GA as the *EAX GA*, while *EAX operator* will refer to the actual recombination operator.

We first compared the EAX GA with GENITOR [1] [11], with both using the EAX operator. GENITOR is a steady-state GA, with a child always replacing the worst member of the population. Linear ranked selection was employed, with a bias of 1.25.

Next, we focused on the use of "offspring improving" operators such as ICG and 2-opt. ICG, in conjunction with the ability of the EAX operator to produce a variety of children (depending on the composition of the E-set), increases the probability of creating a child with higher fitness than either parent. Local search mechanisms such as 2-opt [5] also increase this probability. One of the issues we explore is the use of 2-opt in place of ICG.

Lastly, the performance of another crossover operator, Edge-3 [5], is explored in the context of both the 2-opt and ICG search operators.

As noted, the test problem is Padberg's 532 city problem. TSPLIB [2] reports 27686 as the optimal tour cost for this instance. A population size of 500 was used in both the EAX and GENITOR GA's; the sizing is identical to that reported in [7]. A GA population was considered converged when the best individual fitness equaled the average individual fitness; all runs were allowed to fully converge. The code was implemented in C on a SUN Ultrasparc-30. We used the UNIX rand48 family of random number generators.

Each experimental trial consisted of 30 runs of a particular combination of GA, crossover operator, and search operator. The final tour cost and number of evaluations required for convergence was recorded for each run. For purposes of comparison with GENITOR results, the number of evaluations required by

---

[1] GENITOR can be found at http://www.cs.colostate.edu/ genitor

[2] TSPLIB: www.iwr.uni-heidelberg.de/iwr/comopt/soft/TSPLIB95/TSPLIB.html

ALG	X-over Operator	Search Op	Mean	Percent Abv. Opt.	Best	Percent Abv. Opt.	Worst	Percent Abv. Opt.	Std. Dev.
EAX	EAX	None	27840	0.56	27713	0.09	28010	1.17	86.91
EAX	EAX	ICG	27709	0.08	27693	0.03	27739	0.19	9.32
EAX	EAX	2-opt	27742	0.20	27708	0.08	27838	0.55	29.12
GEN	EAX	None	28379	2.50	28065	1.37	28720	3.73	181.75
GEN	EAX	ICG	27830	0.52	27739	0.19	28004	1.15	77.40
GEN	EAX	2-opt	27861	0.63	27759	0.26	28002	1.14	70.80
GEN	EDGE-3	NONE	74049	167.46	69890	152.44	78966	185.22	2615.70
GEN	EDGE-3	2-OPT	27878	0.70	27781	0.34	27999	1.13	54.00

Table 1. Final tour costs.

ALG	X-over Operator	Search Op	Mean	Best	Worst	Std. Dev.
EAX	EAX	None	72367	60500	85500	5755
EAX	EAX	ICG	51433	45500	56000	2605.5
EAX	EAX	2-opt	36317	31000	43500	2978.3
GEN	EAX	None	19883	15737	22664	1812.3
GEN	EAX	ICG	14680	12359	16734	1145.7
GEN	EAX	2-opt	10525	7981	12251	1088.6
GEN	Edge-3	None	288187.10	242744	333388	20151.41
GEN	Edge-3	2-opt	145369.83	109216	243464	23955.66

Table 2. Number of evaluations required for convergence.

the EAX GA is taken as the product of the population size and number of generations required for convergence.

Tables 1 and 2 summarize the results from all experimental trials. Table 1 reports tour costs; Table 2 reports the number of evaluations required for convergence. The number of evaluations represents the number of times a single pair of parents was used to produce a child. This number does not include any additional tour evaluations required by the search operators. The first three columns of each table represent the algorithm components used in a given trial. The remaining columns report summary statistics for the various trials.

3.1 Influence of Genetic Algorithm on Performance

A substitution experiment was used to determine the relative contribution of the EAX GA and GENITOR to search performance. We performed two one-tailed T-tests (GA as the independent variable, final tour cost and number of evaluations as the dependent variables) on the data from all experimental trials using the EAX crossover operator. The T-test with tour cost as the dependent variable indicated a significant difference ($t(178) = 3.42, p < 0.01$), with the EAX GA outperforming GENITOR. Similarly, the T-test with number of evaluations as the dependent variable indicated a significant difference $(t(178) = 12.12, p <$ 0.01), with GENITOR converging faster on average than the EAX GA.

The reduction in tour cost obtained by the EAX GA comes at the expense of roughly tripling the number of tour evaluations in comparison to GENITOR. However, the reduction is significant, and enables the EAX GA to find solutions within a fraction of the optimal tour cost. Furthermore, as shown in Table 1, the EAX GA also offers the benefit of lower variance in final tour cost than that provided by GENITOR.

3.2 Influence of Iterative Child Generation on Performance

As described in Section 2, ICG enables the EAX operator to generate multiple potential offspring from the same set of parents, increasing the probability of finding an improved child. In constrast, previous work on the TSP [4] [2] [5] [6] has focused on using variants of 2-opt to increase the fitness of a child produced by some crossover operator. In either case, the goal is equivalent: to find offspring similar to or superior to the parents in fitness. Thus, we analyze which method has the higher payoff. Finally, we also evaluated the performance of the EAX operator without ICG or 2-opt.

For completeness, we evaluated the performance of the EAX operator both with and without ICG. We performed two one-tailed T-tests (selection of ICG as the independent variable, final tour cost and number of evaluations as the dependent variables) on the data from experimental trials using both GA's.

Both T-tests indicated significant differences in both tour cost $(t(118) =$ $3.42, p < 0.01)$ and number of evaluations $(t(118) = 2.51, p < 0.01)$, with ICG substantially decreasing final tour costs. ICG has the additional apparent benefit of decreasing the number of evaluations required for convergence, a side-effect of improving the probability of finding a child better than both parents. However, this benefit is actually detrimental to run-time; the number of evaluations does not count the considerable number of tour evaluations consumed in the search for a better child.

To determine whether various offspring improvement operators (none, 2-opt, or ICG) led to different performance, we ran a pair of two-way ANOVA's (GA and search operator as the independent variables, final tour cost and number of evaluations as the dependent variables) on data from experimental trials using the EAX operator and both GA's.

The ANOVA's with tour cost as the dependent variable indicated significant main effects in both the GA $(F(1) = 346.5, p < 0.01)$ and the search operator $(F(2) = 241.3, p < 0.01)$. Similarly, a significant interaction effect between the GA and search operator was detected $(F(2) = 100.4, p < 0.01)$. The ANOVA's with number of evaluations as the dependent variable provided nearly identical results, with main and interaction effects detected at $p < 0.01$.

A final two-tailed T-test used tour cost as the dependent variable and the choice of either the ICG or 2-opt as the independent variable indicated no significant difference $(t(118) = 0.93, p < 0.0325)$ in mean tour cost. Given roughly equal mean tour costs, 2-opt offers significant advantages over the ICG search operator. First, each additional tour evaluation performed by 2-opt can be done in constant time, in contrast to the full linear-time evaluation required by ICG. Second, inspection of Table 1 indicates 2-opt converges nearly twice as fast as ICG (verified by a one-tailed t-test, $p < 0.01$).

3.3 Influence of ICG and 2-opt on Edge-3 recombination

The previous section focused on the impact of various search operators on performance. Both the 2-opt and ICG substantially enhanced the performance of the 'plain' EAX operator. However, the complexity of the EAX operator is high in comparison to other operators such as Edge-3 [5] and MPX [6]. In this section, we examine the performance impact of the 2-opt and ICG on the Edge-3 crossover operator. In addition, the performance is compared with that obtained using the EAX operator.

We performed a simple experiment to measure the performance of the hybridization of the Edge-3 crossover and ICG search operators. Under Edge-3, children inherit a high (95-99%) fraction of tour edges directly from their parents. The remaining edges are chosen at random such that a legal tour is constructed. The hybridization of Edge-3 and ICG was implemented simply by iterating the Edge-3 operator on identical parents until either 100 iterations were performed or a child better than both parents was found.

The Edge-3/ICG hybridization was used in conjunction with the GENITOR GA. Thirty runs were performed, resulting in an average tour cost of 46818.49, which is substantially worse than any of the results obtained using the EAX operator. In spite of the poor relative performance, the ICG search operator substantially improved the performance obtained by the Edge-3 operator when used in isolation; as shown in Table 1, the mean tour cost obtained using Edge-3 in isolation was 74049.67.

Finally, we compared the performance of the GENITOR/Edge-3/2-opt hybrid with that of the EAX/EAX/2-opt hybrid using two one-tailed T-tests. Both T-tests indicated significant differences in both tour cost ($t(29) = 3.02, p < 0.01$) and number of evaluations ($t(29) = 33.16, p < 0.01$). In both cases, the EAX/EAX/2-opt hybrid outperformed the GENITOR/Edge-3/2-opt hybrid.

It should be noted that the difference in mean tour cost between the two variants is only 136; the statistical significance stems primarily from the low variance in tour cost obtained with 2-opt. In spite of a significant increase in evaluations, the 2-opt operator was able to reduce differences in tour costs between the EAX and Edge-3 operators to nearly identical levels. This 'performance leveling' prompted us to investigate the performance of 2-opt when used in relative isolation.

4 The Impact of 2-opt

As shown in the previous section, 2-opt is extremely effective at improving the performance of the EAX and GENITOR GA's for the TSP. This lead us to ask

ALG	X-over Operator	Search Op	Mean	Percent Abv. Opt.	Best	Percent Abv. Opt.	Worst	Percent Abv. Opt.	Std. Dev.
EAX	EAX	ICG	27709	0.08	27693	0.03	27739	0.19	9.32
EAX	EAX	2-opt	27742	0.20	27708	0.08	27838	0.55	29.12
GEN	EDGE-3	2-opt	27878	0.70	27781	0.34	27999	1.13	54.00
2-opt	N.A.	N.A.	27985	1.08	27841	0.55	28211	1.89	90.11

Table 3. A comparison of the best algorithms with 2-opt using partial restarts.

the question 'What if 2-opt were the only operator?' Of course, 2-opt must be applied to distinct starting tours to produce different results. So to create different starting points, we used an idea which has connections to both evolutionary algorithms and local search.

A small population of solutions is used (30 in this case). 2-opt is applied to each solution in the population until all of the solutions are locally optimal. The best solution in the population is then used to re-seed the entire population.

Starting at a random city, the best solution is broken into segments composed of two adjacent edges. These fragments are then randomly reconnected. The entire population is regenerated in this way and then 2-opt is applied to all of the new solutions. The idea is that this both provides a type of partial restart to local search, and also preserves good "building blocks" from the previous best solution.

There are many variations on this idea that could be explored: the best two or three solutions could be used to reseed the population and the best solutions could be broken into fragments that preserve segments composed of three or four edges. However, we wished to keep this search strategy simple.

Table 3 presents results for the 2-opt with partial restarts algorithm. The other results in the table are those previously reported in this paper for the EAX GA using ICG and 2-opt, as well as the GENITOR/Edge-3/2-opt hybrid algorithm. A pair of one-tailed T-tests indicate that there is a significant difference in final tour costs between the 2-opt with partial restarts algorithm and both the original Nagata and Kobayahsi algorithm ($(t(58) = 3.57, p < 0.01)$) and the EAX GA/EAX operator/2-opt hybrid algorithm ($(t(58) = 2.93, p < 0.01)$). In spite of the poor relative performance, it is surprising how well a simple algorithm based on 2-opt works in this domain.

5 Conclusions

We replicated the results of Nagata and Kobayahsi with only a very slight error margin. We document our interpretation of their algorithm description in an effort to resolve the remaining discrepancies. More importantly, we provide results that raise important issues concerning what components of their algorithm are critical to performance. Our results suggest that 2-opt might be used as an effective replacement for ICG. Since the EAX operator uses local information anyway, there is no reason not to use 2-opt to improve the resulting child.

The effectiveness of the selection mechanism in the EAX GA in comparison to the selection mechanism in GENITOR was also surprising. Allowing an improved offspring to replace one of the parents instead of the worst member of the population may have two important effects. It clearly results in lower selective pressure; but it is also likely that when children replace parents the children still retain some of the "genetic material" of the parents. Thus, this selection scheme may result in the population maintaining diversity for a longer period of time. This point of view is supported by the data which shows that the EAX GA converges much slower than GENITOR.

References

1. K. Boese. Cost versus distance in the traveling salesman problem. Technical report, Computer Science Department, Univeristy of California, Los Angeles, 1995.
2. Larry Eshelman. The CHC Adaptive Search Algorithm. How to Have Safe Search When Engaging in Nontraditional Genetic Recombination. In G. Rawlins, editor, *FOGA -1*, pages 265–283. Morgan Kaufmann, 1991.
3. Bernd Freisleben and Peter Merz. New genetic local search operators for the traveling salesman problem. In H.M. Voigt, W. Ebeling, Ingo Rechenberg, and H.P. Schwefel, editors, *Parallel Problem Solving from Nature, 4*, pages 890–899. Springer/Verlag, 1996.
4. Martina Gorges-Schleuter. ASPARAGOS An Asynchronous Parallel Genetic Optimization Strategy. In J.D. Schaffer, editor, *Proc. of the 3rd Int'l. Conf. on GAs*, pages 422–433. Morgan Kaufmann, 1989.
5. Keith E. Mathias and L. Darrell Whitley. Genetic Operators, the Fitness Landscape and the Traveling Salesman Problem. In R. Männer and B. Manderick, editors, *Parallel Problem Solving from Nature, 2*, pages 219–228. Elsevier Science Publishers, 1992.
6. H. Mühlenbein. Evolution in Time and Space: The Parallel Genetic Algorithm. In G. Rawlins, editor, *FOGA -1*, pages 316–337. Morgan Kaufmann, 1991.
7. Yuichi Nagata and Shigenobu Kobayashi. Edge assembly crossover: A high-power genetic algorithm for the traveling salesman problem. In T. Bäck, editor, *Proc. of the 7th Int'l. Conf. on GAs*, pages 450–457. Morgan Kaufmann, 1997.
8. W. Padberg and G. Rinaldi. Optimization of a 532 City Symmetric TSP. *Optimization Research Letters*, 6(1):1–7, 1987.
9. Nicholas J. Radcliffe. The algebra of genetic algorithms. *Annals of Maths and Artificial Intelligence*, 10:339–384, 1994.
10. N.J. Radcliffe and P.D. Surry. Fitness variance of formae and performance predictions. In D. Whitley and M. Vose, editors, *FOGA - 3*, pages 51–72. Morgan Kaufmann, 1995.
11. Darrell Whitley and Joan Kauth. GENITOR: A Different Genetic Algorithm. In *Proceedings of the 1988 Rocky Mountain Conference on Artificial Intelligence*, 1988.
12. Darrell Whitley, Timothy Starkweather, and D'ann Fuquay. Scheduling Problems and Traveling Salesmen: The Genetic Edge Recombination Operator. In J. D. Schaffer, editor, *Proc. of the 3rd Int'l. Conf. on GAs*. Morgan Kaufmann, 1989.

Scheduling, Partitioning
and Packing

Load Balancing in Parallel Circuit Testing with Annealing-Based and Genetic Algorithms

C.Gil[1], J. Ortega[2], A.F. Díaz[2], M.G. Montoya[1], A.Prieto[2]

[1]Dept. de Arquitectura de Computadores y Electrónica
Univ. Almería- Spain
[2]Dept. de Arquitectura y Tecnología de Computadores
Univ. Granada-Spain

Abstract. A new combination of Simulated Annealing and Tabu Search is presented for load balancing in a parallel circuit testing procedure. The testing procedure requires a circuit partitioning algorithm to distribute the workload among the processors in such a way that similar sized parts of the circuit are assigned to each processor while communications are minimised. The hybrid algorithm for circuit partitioning is compared with pure tabu search and simulated annealing algorithms, and also with a genetic algorithm. The solutions obtained are evaluated for the circuits of a frequently used benchmark set.

0. Introduction

The test problem consists of searching for the set of assignments to the circuit inputs that allows us to distinguish between a faulty and a fault-free circuit (Klenke et al., 1992). The most frequently used model of fault is the single stuck-at fault that fixes the faulty line to the logical value 0 (stuck-at 0 fault) or 1 (stuck-at 1 fault). Whereas in a combinational logic circuit only one test pattern is required to test a given stuck-at fault, a sequential circuit requires a series of test vectors to detect a fault. Nevertheless, by using Design For Testability (DFT) techniques the problem can be reduced to the generation of tests for combinational circuits (Klenke et al., 1992). Moreover, most algorithms for testing sequential circuits translate the generation of test sequences into iterative combinational methods. Therefore, it is important to possess efficient procedures to solve the problem of testing combinational circuits, which despite being considered a subproblem of the sequential test problem, is in fact an NP-complete problem (Klenke et al., 1993; Patil et al., 1990). As the increase in the size and complexity of the circuits has been faster than the improvements achieved with the new serial procedures, it would very useful to speed up test generation by using parallel computers (Gil et al., 1997, 1998; Klenke et al., 1992, 1993; Patil et al., 1990).

The strategies that can be used to parallelize a test algorithm can be classified as:
a) *Fault partitioning*, where the set of faults is divided among the processors that

generate the patterns for each fault in their corresponding fault list; b) *Search-Space partitioning*, where the space of assignments to the inputs, the space of assignments to the lines, or both, is divided among the processors which work together in the search for a pattern for each fault; and c) *Circuit partitioning* where the circuit is distributed among the processors that apply the corresponding test algorithm to each subcircuit. An important drawback to strategies (a) and (b) when they are implemented in multicomputers is that every processor must have fast access to the whole structure of the circuit. It implies that the circuit needs to be stored in the local memories of the processors used to speed up the test pattern generation process, thus requiring a lot of memory resources. This is an important limitation for highly complex circuits, because the memory requirements can be excessive. Moreover, the load of the circuit in the multicomputer would require a lot of time, thus limiting the speedup achieved by the parallel program. One solution to this problem could be the partition of the circuit into disjoint subcircuits which are assigned to different processors (strategy (c)). This technique allows each processor to work with a smaller part of the circuit in local memory, thus speeding up the test pattern generation for the complete circuit. Very little has been published describing parallel test generators using circuit partitioning. A Parallel ATPG (Automatic Test Pattern Generator) which uses circuit partitioning combined with the PODEM algorithm is provided by Klenke et al. (1993). Nevertheless, the experimental results obtained show higher runtimes for the parallel test generator with respect to the execution in only one processor. As the authors of the paper indicate, this increase in the execution time is due to the overhead resulting from the implementation of the PODEM algorithm across the circuit partitioning because the number of elemental operations required by the PODEM algorithm is not decreased by the parallelization.

A new parallel procedure called PARALSUB has been recently proposed (Gil et al., 1998) It is based on a new test generation algorithm (Gil et al., 1998) which combines the Boolean difference and the properties of the Reed-Muller spectrum (Green, 1991; Ortega et al., 1993) to obtain the test equation for each node, and to determine one of its solutions, i.e. a test pattern. The procedure starts with a partition algorithm that determines subcircuits with similar sizes to balance the workload of the processors (considered as proportional to the number of nodes), and minimizes the number of cuts. Once each processor receives its corresponding subcircuit, it is possible for all the processors to apply the test generation algorithm concurrently in order to determine the local test equation at the nodes in each subcircuit. Then, to determine the absolute test equations whose solutions are the test patterns, each processor has to communicate with those processors having parts of the circuit connected to its own part. PARALSUB presents good figures for communication/computation rates, thus providing good values for the efficiency obtained when the it is applied to the circuits used as benchmarks.

Section 1 gives a more precise definition of the circuit partitioning problem and presents the cost function associated with it. The description of the meta-heuristics implemented to solve the circuit partitioning problem is given in Sections 2 and 3.

Finally, the experimental results provided are compared in Section 4, and Section 5 gives the conclusions of the paper.

1. Circuit Partitioning and Load Balancing

The circuit partitioning problem arises in many VLSI applications (Kumar et al., 1994). Due to the increasing complexity of VLSI circuits, the NP-complete (Garey et al, 1979) character of many VLSI CAD problems makes a "divide and conquer" approach more attractive to solve these problems in reasonable periods of time, and so circuit partitioning has become an important process to first carry out in these applications. Furthermore, the circuit partitioning problem appears when trying exploit the concurrency in the target circuit (*data parallelism*) instead of exploiting the concurrency of the algorithm (*functional parallelism*) (Kumar et al., 1994). As the data structure of the algorithm is defined by the corresponding netlist, it is relatively easy to describe the program by a graph. The volume of processing associated with each node is that corresponding to the application of the algorithm to the elements of the circuit allocated to a given processor, and the communication cost results from transferring data between processors with interconnected subcircuits allocated. Due to these characteristics, it is very useful to possess efficient algorithms for circuit partitioning because these would allow a balanced distribution of the workload among processors.

As our goal is to use all the available processors in the multicomputer to process the circuit in parallel while trying to keep all the processors working during the whole run time, the number of subcircuits is fixed to be equal to the number of available processors in the machine, and the objectives correspond to obtain subcircuits with similar sizes to balance the workload of the processor (considered as proportional to the number of nodes), and minimizing the number of cuts. In the following, a formulation of the problem is provided.

Let $G = (X, A)$ be the directed acyclic graph associated with a combinational circuit C, where X denotes the set of components (inputs, logical gates, and outputs) and A the set of lines used for signal propagation. The nodes of X can be classified as inputs, logical gates and outputs of circuit C. Thus X is the union of three disjoint sets, the set of inputs E, the set of logical gates P (nodes), and the set of outputs S. The problem is to find a partition of X into a fixed number of K subsets X_k, $(k=1,...,K)$ such that each induced subgraph $G_k=(X_k, A_k)$ satisfies:

1. $X = \bigcup_{k=1}^{K} X_k$ and $X_k \cap X_h = \varnothing, \forall k \neq h, (k,h) \in \{1,...,K\}^2$

2. $p_k = |X_k \cap P| \neq \varnothing \quad \forall k = 1,...,K$

3. $L_i \leq p_k \leq L_u$, with $L_i = \lfloor n/K \rfloor - \lfloor n/K \rfloor \cdot \theta$ and $L_u = \lfloor n/K \rfloor + \lfloor n/K \rfloor \cdot \theta$, $k=1,...,K$; where $n=|P|$; $\lfloor n/K \rfloor$ represents the number of gates that should be included in each subcircuit to obtain a partition of similar sized subcircuits; and θ is the parameter representing the proportion of gates that is tolerated as a deviation with respect to $\lfloor n/K \rfloor$. In this work, θ has been set to values between 0.2 and 0.3.

838

4. $G_k(X_k, A_k)$ is a connected graph, $k = 1,...,K$.

In this way, given a circuit graph $G=(X,A)$, the problem is formulated as a combinatorial optimization problem in which the cost function $c(s)$ to minimize is defined as:

$$c(s) = \alpha \cdot n\_cuts(s) + \beta \cdot \sum_{k=1}^{K} 2^{deviation(k)} \qquad (1)$$

where $deviation(k)$ is the amount by which the number of gates in the subcircuit G_k varies from the bounds L_u or L_i; $n\_cuts(s)$ is the number of cuts of the solution; and s is any solution to the circuit partitioning problem, feasible or otherwise, i.e. verifying the above condition 3 or not. Thus, whenever for all $k=1,..,K$, in a given partition s, the deviation in the number of gates of G_k with respect to $\lfloor n/K \rfloor$ is less than $\theta \cdot \lfloor n/K \rfloor$, the solution is feasible and the cost is $c(s) = \alpha \cdot n\_cuts(s) + \beta K$, since $deviation(k) = 0$ $(k=1,..,K)$.

The *neighborhood N(s)* of the current solution s contains all solutions $\bar{s}$ which may be obtained from s by transferring only one gate from one subcircuit (*source subcircuit*) to another circuit (*destination subcircuit*). The gate that is transferred must belong to the *boundary* of the corresponding subcircuit, which contains all the gates connected to at least one gate belonging to a different subcircuit. These gates are called *boundary gates*. Moreover, the destination subcircuit must be one of the subcircuits connected to the transferred gate. In this way, the previously described condition 4 is verified during the process. Fig. 1 shows an example of boundary gate movements. The algorithm begins with gates p1 and p2 (Fig. 1.a). As these gates are not boundary gates, they are not selected, and the algorithm proceeds with gate p3. Gate p3 is a boundary gate, but it cannot be moved because a move of gate p3 will leave only one gate in subcircuit 2 and each subcircuit must have at least 2 gates. The same happens with gate p4. Gate p5 is a boundary gate that can be moved and this is allocated to subcircuit 2. In this case, the number of cuts remains the same because one cut appears and another disappears. Like p3 and p4, gate p6 cannot be moved, and finally p7 is not a boundary gate.

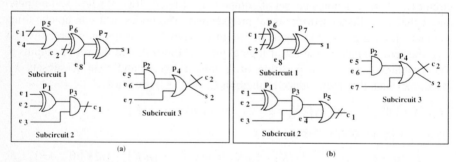

(a)   (b)

Fig. 1. An example of moving the boundary gate p5 in subcircuit 1 (a) to the subcircuit 2 (b).

Several approaches for circuit partitioning have been reported (Alpert et al., 1995). The move-based procedures build the solution iteratively by applying a move or transformation to the current solution. The set of possible transformations that can be applied to a given solution defines the neighbourhood structure of the solution space, which is explored repeatedly by moving from the current solution to a neighbouring one. These procedures include stochastic meta-heuristics, such as Simulated Annealing (SA) (Aarst et al., 1990), Tabu Search (TS) (Glover et al.,1993), and Genetic Algorithms (GA) (Reeves, 1993), which allow movements towards solutions worse than the current one in order to escape from local minima. In the next section, we present a hybrid algorithm that inserts elements of a Tabu Search into a Simulated Annealing algorithm, the Mixed Simulated Annealing and Tabu Search (MSATS) algorithm.

2. The MSATS algorithm

MSATS is a hybrid method that uses the best features of the two meta-heuristics, SA and TS, to outperform the results provided by each. At each iteration of MSATS, admissible moves are applied to the current solution, allowing transitions that increase the cost function as in SA. When a move increasing the cost function is accepted, the reverse move is forbidden during some iterations in order to avoid cycling, as in TS. The restrictions in the admissible moves are implemented by using a short term memory function which determines how long a tabu restriction will be enforced and the admissible moves at each iteration. In MSATS, the temperature t is used as a parameter to control the probability of accepting a new solution and changes by multiplying it by *tfactor* ($0<tfactor<1$), as in SA. At a given temperature, only the solutions which are selected by the SA cooling schedule are considered as candidates to produce a transition. Thus, a certain randomness is introduced into a pure TS, in order to explore zones of the solution space that do not appear very promising at first. As the algorithm also has the characteristics of a Tabu Search, it avoids the cycles around local minima, allowing a more efficient exploration of the solution space without revisiting solutions, as may occur in a pure SA.

At high temperatures, MSATS behaves almost like a pure SA because most of the transitions are accepted, and it is very unlikely to select one of the transitions included in the tabu list. On the other hand, at low temperatures the solutions that increase the cost are rarely selected in a pure SA and the effect of Tabu Search is also small. Thus, the difference in the behaviour of MSATS with respect to a pure SA due to the use of tabu moves is more important at intermediate temperatures.

MSATS stops when one of the following conditions is verified: (*i*) the temperature is equal to a final value, (*ii*) the number of moves applied without improving the best solution found so far reaches a maximum bound of consecutive iterations, *Max_failures*, and (*iii*) the number of iterations reaches *max_iterations*.

3. The Genetic Algorithm

The Genetic Algorithm (GA) implemented begins with an encoding and initialization phase during which each string in the population is assigned a uniformly distributed random point in the solution space. Each iteration of the genetic algorithm begins by evaluating the fitness of the current generation of strings. A new generation of offspring is created by applying crossover and mutation to pairs of parents who have been selected according to their fitness. The specific characteristics of the GA implemented are described below.

Solution Representation: Let K be the number of subcircuits into which the circuit with graph G is divided, and let n ($n=|P|$) be the number of logic gates of the original circuit; then each solution is represented by an array S of n elements as $S=A_1, A_2, A_3,...,A_n$ with $A_i \in [1,...,K]$, where the A_i element in array S represents the subcircuit to which the logic gate i belongs.

Fitness function: The fitness function is obtained directly from the cost function described in (1).

Reproduction or selection: The fitness value c_i of the best string i of generation T is compared with the fitness value c_j of the worst string j of generation $T+1$. If $c_i < c_j$, then string j is replaced by string i. This is an elitist strategy (Goldberg et al., 1989) that ensures that the maximum fitness value of the population does not decrease as the process of evolution continues.

Crossover: The crossover operator should generate feasible solutions when applied to a given population in order to implement an efficient search in the solution space. It begins by randomly choosing a cut point b where $1 \leq b \leq n$, where n is the string length; an interval $[b, b+rank]$ is then generated. The elements of the string that correspond to boundary gates in the two selected solutions, *mate1* and *mate2* respectively, will be exchanged. To do this, a procedure called *subcircuit()* determines the subcircuits to which the boundary gate selected belongs in *mate1* and *mate2*, respectively *subcircuit1* and *subcircuit2*. Then, other procedure, called *change_part()*, uses the selected gate and *subcircuit2* to transform the solution *mate1*, and the selected gate and *subcircuit1* to transform *mate2*.

Mutation: The operation of mutation involves the perturbation of a string position which has been randomly chosen. The perturbation involves changing the string position to one of its possible positions taking into account the inputs and outputs of the subcircuit.

Stop condition: The algorithm terminates either (i) when convergence is reached, i.e., all the strings in the population have nearly equal values for their fitness function, or (ii) when a previously specified number of generations is reached.

4. Experimental results

In this section we summarize the results obtained by using the algorithms MSATS, SA, TS and GA for circuit partitioning. The benchmark circuits used to evaluate the performances are those included in the ISCAS´85 (Brglez et al., 1995), which is the set of circuits usually considered to evaluate test-pattern generation procedures. Each circuit in the set is noted as cXXX where XXX is the number of lines.

The parameters are set to their best experimental values. These values for the MSATS, SA and TS algorithms are the following. *Max_failures* is set to 0.25*(*max_iterations*), and *tfactor* to 0.99. The value of *max_iterations* is usually taken as 1000, and the initial temperature, t_0 as 100. For these values, the cost function reaches a stable final value at the end of the 1000 iterations. An increase in the number of iterations does not allow us to get better solutions unless the value of *tfactor* is increased. This, however, implies an increase in the run time and, except for extremely large circuits, the new solution does not imply a great improvement. The parameters that produced the best experimental results in the GA algorithm are the following:

Population size: Choosing the population size for GAs is an important decision. If it is too small, then the algorithm converges quickly without enough processing. On the other hand, if the population size is too large, then the rate at which the fitness value climbs is slow. Among the population sizes checked, the value producing best experimental results was 100.

Probability of crossover: The probability of crossover has to be selected carefully. If the probability of crossover is very low, strings are operated upon less often, increasing the expected time between two operations on the strings. On the other hand, if the probability of crossover is very high, the rate at which strings are operated upon increases. Good performance is associated with a crossover probability from 0.8 to 0.9.

Probability of mutation: The probability of mutation, like the probability of crossover, has to be selected carefully. The probability of mutation varies from 0.01 to 0.09.

Table 1 presents the best results obtained by SA, TS, GA, and MSATS compared with the solutions s1 for partitions of K=4, 8, 16 and 32 subcircuits. The row *cuts reduction* indicates the average of the reduction in the number of cuts obtained by MSATS with respect to the best solution of those provided by SA, TS, and GA, in each case. The solutions s1 in Table 1 are obtained by an algorithm named Input Partitioning, in which the circuit graph is traversed in a depth-first way, starting from the inputs. This fast partitioning algorithm has been applied to circuit partitioning in parallel logic simulations (Patil et al., 1989), and takes $O(n)$ time to obtain partitions in which strongly connected components of the graph are assigned to the same partition.

As can be seen, the results (*cuts*) obtained by MSATS outperform those obtained with TS, SA, and GA in most cases. As the circuit size increases, the neighbourhood of a given solution also grows, and the effect of considering tabu transitions is more important in MSATS. The computing times (*secs.*) for MSATS are similar to those of Simulated Annealing and lower than those of TS.

The Genetic Algorithm provides good solutions. They usually outperform those provided by TS and SA, and in some cases are similar to, or even better than those provided by MSATS. Nevertheless, the times required to obtain such solutions are greater than those required by MSATS.

Table 1. A summary of results with the best obtained solutions and the times for the algorithms: solution s1, SA, TS, GA, and MSATS.

circuit	algorithm	K=4		K=8		K=16		K=32	
		cuts	sec.	cuts	sec.	cuts	sec.	cuts	sec.
c499	s1	94	0,3	143	0,5	205	0,6	225	0,7
	SA	58	2,3	86	3,2	132	4,1	172	7,5
	TS	51	11,4	79	15,2	132	17,1	175	19,5
	GA	**43**	17.6	87	24.6	**104**	31.4	**154**	39.7
	MSATS	54	2,4	**78**	3,1	119	3,9	168	7,2
	cuts reduc(%)	-20		2		10		-12	
c1355	s1	137	0,5	240	0,7	351	0,9	394	1,1
	SA	**45**	6,0	97	8,1	**98**	11,2	156	16,4
	TS	46	34,6	94	39,4	**98**	47,8	148	61,9
	GA	46	38,7	80	45,5	106	53.5	148	70,8
	MSATS	**45**	6,1	**70**	7,9	**98**	10,2	**128**	15,7
	cuts reduc(%)	0		13		0		14	
c1908	s1	210	0,7	298	0,9	450	1,2	629	1,4
	SA	74	9,5	125	11,5	168	12,9	234	20,2
	TS	76	60,2	120	68,5	156	78,5	225	84,9
	GA	**70**	72,4	**108**	81,8	143	89,1	215	97,6
	MSATS	71	9,5	**108**	10,9	**125**	12,1	**205**	19,0
	cuts reduc(%)	-2		0		13		5	
c3540	s1	333	0,9	535	1,2	771	1,5	1023	1,9
	SA	156	16,2	250	20,9	375	26,5	478	42,8
	TS	179	83,2	259	76,4	377	90,7	498	124,6
	GA	149	91,6	225	99,8	295	106,3	525	143,7
	MSATS	**132**	16,9	**221**	20,1	**298**	25,4	**455**	40,6
	cuts reduc(%)	12		2		2		5	
c6288	s1	155	1,8	334	2,3	671	2,9	947	3,8
	SA	135	30,8	315	35,1	450	44,8	745	70,5
	TS	157	145,7	320	168,5	550	211,8	774	290,6
	GA	112	187,4	**243**	234,3	470	254,6	674	304,6
	MSATS	**102**	30,6	301	34,2	**355**	42,6	**524**	66,9
	cuts reduc(%)	9		-20		22		17	

Thus, if a GA is used for circuit partitioning before applying the parallel test procedure, the efficiency of the parallel procedure will decrease by an important factor, with respect to using MSATS.

The MSATS algorithm is used as a first step in the parallel test-pattern generator PARALSUB (Gil et al., 1998). The communication between processors is needed to complete the determination of the test equation in each node, and it grows with the number of cuts among subcircuits. Thus, one way to demonstrate the performance of MSATS is to consider the increase in the speedup provided by the parallel test-generator when the number of processors grows. If the speedup grows proportionally to the number of processors or, in other words, if the efficiency is more or less constant, the performance of MSATS is adequate according to the conditions given in Section 1. Speedup results for the ISCAS´85 circuits are provided in Table 2. The speedups obtained with K processors are given in the columns labeled S_K and the number of cuts produced when the circuit is partitioned into K subcircuits are given in the columns C_K in Table 2.

Table 2. Speedups, number of cuts and fault coverages obtained with the parallel test-pattern-generator executed in an Intel Paragon.

Circuit	faults	S_4	C_4	S_8	C_8	S_16	C_16	Coverage
c432	864	3.70	40	6.23	61	10.34	85	98%
c499	998	3.85	54	6.34	78	11.43	119	99%
c880	1760	3.87	37	7.05	80	12.56	129	100%
c1355	2710	2.93	45	6.25	70	11.65	98	98%
c1908	3816	2.50	71	6.86	108	10.26	125	98%
c3540	7080	3.67	132	6.40	221	10.20	298	98%
c6288	12570	2.75	102	6.53	301	10.45	355	97%

5. Conclusions

The use of circuit partitioning in a parallel test pattern generator has been presented and formulated as a combinatorial optimization problem by using a cost function comprising the contribution of the number of cuts and the deviation with respect to a balanced distribution of the gates among the different subcircuits. Some general-purpose optimization algorithms such us Simulated Annealing and Genetic Algorithms, which are physically and biologically-based heuristics, respectively, and Tabu Search have been applied to solve the optimization problem considered. We have also developed a new algorithm, called MSATS, which reduces the possibility of cycles in the search process by applying the Tabu Search characteristics to a Simulated Annealing algorithm. In a shorter time, MSATS not only provides a lower number of cuts, but also a more balanced distribution of gates among subcircuits than TS and SA. Compared with a Genetic Algorithm, MSATS is able to provide solutions with similar qualities in most cases, and better solutions, but requires less time. Indeed, obtaining sufficiently good solutions in a short time is very important in order to achieve good efficiencies in the parallel test pattern generator.

Acknowledgements. Paper supported by project TIC97-1149 (CICYT, Spain).

References

1. Aarts, E., Korst, J.: *Simulated Annealing and Boltzmann Machines. A stochastic Approach to Combinatorial Optimization and Neural Computing*. John Wiley & Sons, 1990.
2. Alpert, C.J., Kahng, A.: *Recent Developments in Netlist Partitioning: A survey*. Integration: the VLSI Journal, 19 (2) (1995) 1-81.
3. Brglez, F., Fujiwara, H.: *Neural Netlist of Ten Combinational Benchmark Circuts and a Target Translator in FORTRAN*. In: Proceedings of IEEE Int. Symp. Circuits Syst., Special Session ATPG, (1985).
4. Garey, M.R., Johnson, D.S: *Computers and Interactibility: A Guide to the Theory of NP-Completeness*. W.H. Freeman & Company, San Francisco (1979).
5. Gil, C.,Ortega, J.: *A Parallel Test Pattern Generator based on Spectral Techniques*. In: Proceedings of the 5th Euromicro on PDP, London, UK (January 22-24, 1997). IEEE Computer Society, (1997) 199-204.
6. Gil, C., Ortega, J.: *Parallel Test Generation using circuit partitioning and spectral techniques*. In: Proceedings of the 6th Euromicro Workshop on PDP, Madrid, Spain (January 21-23, 1998). IEEE Computer Society (1998) 264-270.
7. Gil, C., Ortega, J.: *Algebraic Test-Pattern Generation based on the Reed-Muller Spectrum*. IEE Proc. Computer and Digital Techniques (accepted for publication July 1998).
8. Glover, F., Laguna, M.: *Tabu Search*. In: Modern Heuristic Techniques for Combinatorial Problems. C.R. Reeves (Eds.). Blackwell, London (1993) 70-150.
9. Goldberg, D.E.: *Genetic Algorithms in Search , Optimization, and Machine Learning*, Addison-Wesley (1989).
10. Green, D.H.: *Families of Reed-Muller forms*. Int. J. Electronics. 70 (2) (1991) 259-280.
11. Klenke, R.H., Williams R.D., Aylor, J.H.: *Parallel-Processing Techniques for Automatic Test Pattern Generation*. IEEE Computer, (January 1992), 71-84.
12. Klenke, R. H., Williams, R. D., Aylor, J. H.: *Parallelization Methods for Circuit Partitioning Based Parallel Automatic Test Pattern Generation*. IEEE VLSI Test Symposium, (1993) 71-78.
13. Kumar, V., Grama, A., Gupta, A., Karypis, G.: *Introduction to Parallel Computing. Design and analysis of algorithms*. The Benjamin/Cummings Publishing company (1994).
14. Goldberg, D.E.: *Genetic Algorithms in Search , Optimization, and Machine Learning*. Addison-Wesley (1989).
15. Patil, S., Banerjee, P.: *A Parallel Branch and Bound Algorithm for Test Generation*. IEEE Trans. on CAD. (March 1990) 9 (3) (1990) 313-322.
16. Patil, S., Banerjee, P., Polychronopoulos, C.D.: *Efficient circuit partitioning algorithms for parallel logic simulation*. In: Proceeding of the Supercomputing Conference (1989).
17. Reeves, C.R.: *Genetic Algorithms*. In: Modern Heuristic Techniques for Combinatorial Problems. C.R. Reeves (Eds.) Blackwell (1993) 151-196.

A Heuristic Combination Method for Solving Job-Shop Scheduling Problems

Emma Hart, Peter Ross

Department of Artificial Intelligence, University of Edinburgh,
Edinburgh EH1 2QL, Scotland

Abstract. This paper describes a heuristic combination based genetic algorithm, (GA), for tackling dynamic job-shop scheduling problems. Our approach is novel in that the genome encodes a choice of algorithm to be used to produce a set of schedulable operations, alongside a choice of heuristic which is used to choose an operation from the resulting set. We test the approach on 12 instances of dynamic problems, using 4 different objectives to judge schedule quality. We find that our approach outperforms other heuristic combination methods, and also performs well compared to the most recently published results on a number of benchmark problems.

1 Introduction

Job-Shop scheduling problems are known to be NP-hard, and cannot be solved in polynomial time. Many approximate and heuristic-based methods have been proposed to attempt to find near-optimal solutions to large problems in realistic time-scales, a large number of which include the use of genetic algorithms. A wide variety of GA techniques have been proposed, using many different representations and operators, and relating to a broad spectrum of problems, e.g. [2].

A common problem encountered in using a GA for scheduling problems is how to represent a problem on a chromosome. Early work in the field yielded two 'extreme' approaches to representing schedules. Nakano and Yamada, [9], used a binary representation to encode schedules for benchmark job-shop problems. A complex effort was required to design such an encoding, and its use in a GA context needed specialised repair operators to retain the ability to decode chromosomes as feasible schedules. The other 'extreme', for example [1], is a 'direct encoding' of a schedule, in which an encoded schedule was a direct representation of the schedule itself, with data structures and attributes designed to simply mimic the real schedule. Hence no decoding of a chromosome was necessary, but the genetic operators needed to use much domain and constraint knowledge to appropriately mutate schedules, and to maintain feasible schedules. A somewhat in-between approach uses an 'indirect' encoding in which a schedule building algorithm is combined with genetic search through the space of potential inputs to the schedule builder, for example [5].

An interesting subclass of representations are those loosely defined as 'Heuristic Combination Methods', (HCM), varieties of which have been reported by

Dorndorf, [3], Fang, [5], and Norenkov, [10]. These methods all use an implicit representation of a schedule in which each gene in the chromosome represents a heuristic to be used at each step of generating a schedule. We present a new version of an HCM, and compare its performance to several other representations on a number of problems. In particular, we concentrate on dynamic job shop problems, as these have most relevance to the nature of most real-world problems. Several different schedule quality measures are considered for each problem, in order to evaluate the robustness of the algorithm.

2 Schedule Generation

The general job shop problem assumes J jobs have to be processed on M machines, in a pre-defined order. Each operation of job j on machine m is denoted by (j_i, m_i), and has a processing time of p_{jm}. The total processing time of a job is given by P_j. In a dynamic job-shop problem, each job has a release date r_j, and a due-date d_j by which time it must complete. The importance of each job is given by a weight w_j. A machine can only process one machine at a time, and preemption of any operation on a machine is not allowed. Feasible schedules fall into four classes; inadmissible, semi-active, active and non-delay. Figure 1,[4], illustrates the relationship between each type of schedule. There are an infinite number of *inadmissible* schedules, which contain excess idle time, and therefore are of no interest. *Semi-Active* schedules contain no excess idle time. *Active* schedules contain no idle time, and furthermore, have no operations which can be completed earlier without delaying other operations. The optimal schedule is guaranteed to fall within the set of active schedules. *Non-Delay* schedules are a subset of active schedules, in which operations are placed into the schedule such that no machine is ever kept idle if some operation is able to be processed on it.

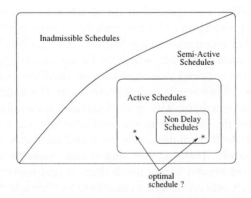

Fig. 1. Types of feasible schedule

Active schedules can be generated using the Giffler and Thompson algorithm

[6], (G&T), which is given in figure 2. Non-delay schedules are generated by a modification of this algorithm shown in figure 3, in which the operation chosen to be scheduled is always the one that can start earliest. Both methods result in a conflict set of operations, G, from which an operation must be chosen to be scheduled.

Dorndorf and Pesch [3] proposed a 'priority-rule based' genetic algorithm, incorporating the G&T algorithm. This used a chromosome $(p_1, p_2....p_{j*m})$, where gene p_i encoded a dispatch rule to be used to resolve the conflicts produced as the i_{th} iteration of the G&T algorithm. They tested this algorithm on a number of static job-shop benchmark problems, using makespan as the objective, obtaining results which have since been superseded by other methods, for example see [11]. Our approach extends this by noticing from figure 1 that as non-delay schedules are a subset of all active schedules, in some cases it may be sufficient to search the space of *non-delay* schedules rather than all *active* schedules. As we do not know *a priori* what type of schedule is optimal, as well as encoding a heuristic rule, our approach also encodes on the chromosome the *methodology*, (i.e G&T or Non-Delay), to use to construct the conflict set each time an operation needs to be scheduled.

---

1. Calculate the set C of all operations that can be scheduled next

2. Calculate the completion time of all operations in C, and let m^* equal the machine on which the minimum completion time t is achieved.

3. Let G denote the conflict set of operations on machine m^* - this is the set of operations in C which take place on m^*, and whose start time is less than t.

4. Select an operation from G to schedule

5. Delete the chosen operation from C and return to step 1.

Fig. 2. Giffler and Thompson Algorithm

Thus, each gene in the chromosome encodes a pair $(Method, Heuristic)$, which denotes the method that should be used to calculate the conflicting set of schedulable operations at iteration t, and the heuristic to be used to select an operation from the set. The representation guarantees a feasible solution, and straightforward recombination operators can be used which always produce feasible offspring. We refer to this method as *HGA – heuristically-guided GA*.

> 1. Calculate the set C of all operations that can be scheduled next
>
> 2. Calculate the starting time of each operation in C and let G equal the subset of operations that can start earliest
>
> 3. Select an operation from G to schedule
>
> 4. Delete the chosen operation from C and return to step 1.

Fig. 3. Non Delay Algorithm

3 Test Problems and Heuristics

We test our approach on 12 different dynamic job-shop scheduling problems taken from Morton & Pentico,[8], using four normalised weighted objective functions; Weighted Earliness plus Tardiness (ETwt), Weighted Flowtime (Fwt), Weighted Tardiness (Twt) and Weighted Lateness (Lwt). If we define the completion time of job j as C_j, then the lateness, L_j, of a job j can be defined as $C_j - d_j$, the earliness, E_j, as $max(-L_j, 0)$, and the tardiness, T_j, as $max(L_j, 0)$. The definitions of the objective functions are given in table 1. 12 heuristics are defined to select between operations in the conflict set. These are shown in table 2. With the exception of the RND heuristic, all of these heuristics take account of the weighting attached to each job. RND is included to ensure that every job in the conflict set can be chosen by at least one heuristic, as it is not possible to guarantee this otherwise.

Objective Function	Objective	Normalised Definition
ETwt	Minimize	$\left(\sum_j w_j(E_j + T_j)\right) / \left(\sum_j w_j P_j\right)$
Fwt	Minimize	$\left(\sum_j w_j(C_j - r_j)\right) / \left(\sum_j w_j P_j\right)$
Twt	Minimize	$\left(\sum_j w_j T_j\right) / \left(\sum_j w_j P_j\right)$
Lwt	Minimize	$\left(\sum_j w_j L_j\right) / \left(\sum_j w_j P_j\right)$

Table 1. Objective Function Definitions

4 GA Parameters

We use a parallel GA, with 5 sub-populations of size 50 arranged in a ring, with migration of one chromosome from one population to the next occurring every

Rule	Description
WSPT	Weighted shortest processing time
WLWKR	Weighted Least Work Remaining
WTWORK	Weighted Total Work
EGD	Earliest Global Due Date
EOD	Earliest Operational Due Date
EMOD	Earliest Modified Operational Due Date
MST	Modified Slack Time
SOP	Slack per Operation
POPNR	Lowest ratio of processing time of imminent operation to weighted value of remaining operations
PSOP	Weighted smallest sum of (next processing time + SOP)
PWKR	Weighted smallest ratio of processing time to work remaining
RND	Choose a Random operation from those operations that can't be chosen by another heuristic

Table 2. Heuristics Used for Dynamic Job-Shop Problems

5 generations. The length of a chromosome is equal to the number of operations to be scheduled. Uniform crossover is used, and crossover always takes place between gene pairs, so that an (M, H) schema is never destroyed by crossover. A mutation operator mutates each heuristic in the genome to another randomly chosen heuristic with probability $p = 0.01$. For each heuristic mutated, the corresponding method allele is mutated with probability 0.5. We use a generational reproduction strategy, with rank selection. All experiments are run for 1000 generations, to allow a fair comparison with the experiments of [7] and [4].

5 Experiments

The results for the dynamic problems are compared to those obtained using Priority Rules, to those of Fang, [4], and those most recently reported by Lin *et al*, [7] using a parallel GA they refer to as *PGA*. In each case we report the best result found in 10 repeated experiments, (as did both [7] and [4]). We also compare the results using *HGA* to experiments using the heuristic representation, but in which the choice of algorithm was restricted to either completely G&T or completely Non-Delay, to gauge the effectiveness of evolving choice of algorithm alongside the choice of heuristic. These experiments are referred to as *HGA*(G&T) and *HGA*(ND). respectively.

The final series of experiments investigated the effect of not including the RND heuristic in the set of alleles, *HGA*(NR). Inclusion of this heuristic has the undesirable effect that repeated evaluations of the same chromosome may result in different schedules, depending on the interpretation of the RND heuristic, and hence a chromosome that was fit in one generation may suddenly become unfit in the next. This obviously has undesirable consequences for the stability of a GA population, as good solutions from one generation may be eliminated entirely at the next generation.

	Size	Fang	Pri.	PGA	HGA	HGA (ND)	HGA(G&T)	HGA (NR)
jb1	10x3	0.475	0.529	0.474	0.474	0.527	0.474	0.474
jb2	10x3	0.758	0.758	0.499	0.753	0.905	0.753	0.753
jb4	10x5	0.620	0.622	0.621	0.619	0.620	0.619	0.619
jb9	15x3	0.384	0.395	0.369	0.370	0.379	0.381	0.374
jb11	15x5	0.263	0.415	0.262	0.271	0.403	0.271	0.271
jb12	15x5	0.247	0.494	0.246	0.247	0.488	0.247	0.247
ljb1	30x3	0.322	0.654	0.279	0.280	0.653	0.280	0.280
ljb2	30x3	0.632	0.868	0.601	0.602	0.751	0.612	0.598
ljb7	50x5	0.374	0.515	0.254	0.284	0.449	0.287	0.269
ljb9	50x5	1.178	0.935	0.739	0.832	0.854	0.967	0.797
ljb10	50x8	0.621	0.882	0.598	0.566	0.691	0.548	0.567
ljb12	50x8	0.607	0.667	0.461	0.522	0.469	0.473	0.466

Table 3. Weighted Earliest + Tardiness (ETwt)

	Size	Fang	Pri.	PGA	HGA	HGA (ND)	HGA (G&T)	HGA (NR)
jb1	10x3	1.237	1.231	1.231	1.236	1.236	1.236	1.236
jb2	10x3	1.778	1.772	1.768	1.766	1.771	1.766	1.766
jb4	10x5	1.109	1.111	1.108	1.107	1.112	1.107	1.107
jb9	15x3	1.768	1.947	1.754	1.754	1.759	1.760	1.754
jb11	15x5	1.794	1.795	1.706	1.706	1.716	1.834	1.706
jb12	15x5	1.259	1.257	1.256	1.256	1.258	1.256	1.256
ljb1	30x3	1.431	1.494	1.391	1.389	1.487	1.389	1.389
ljb2	30x3	1.826	1.924	1.777	1.777	1.804	1.837	1.782
ljb7	50x5	1.669	1.692	1.557	1.548	1.563	1.709	1.542
ljb9	50x5	2.659	2.490	2.324	2.349	2.394	2.626	2.337
ljb10	50x8	1.728	1.776	1.697	1.673	1.680	1.761	1.675
ljb12	50x8	2.138	2.207	2.080	2.070	2.058	2.237	2.068

Table 4. Weighted FlowTime (Fwt)

6   Results

The results are shown in tables 3,4,5, and 6. *HGA* outperforms the GA reported by Fang in 40 out of 48 cases, produces equal results for 5 cases, and is only

	Size	Fang	Pri.	PGA	HGA	HGA (ND)	HGA (G&T))	HGA (NR)
jb1	10x3	0.164	0.178	0.162	0.163	0.180	0.163	0.163
jb2	10x3	0.087	0.086	0.086	0.086	0.086	0.086	0.086
jb4	10x5	0.556	0.560	0.559	0.556	0.557	0.556	0.556
jb9	15x3	0.177	1.185	0.169	0.170	0.170	0.181	0.170
jb11	15x5	0.000	0.000	0.000	0.000	0.000	0.000	0.000
jb12	15x5	0.139	0.218	0.139	0.139	0.219	0.139	0.139
ljb1	30x3	0.215	0.276	0.190	0.194	0.279	0.192	0.194
ljb2	30x3	0.459	0.460	0.395	0.407	0.419	0.437	0.407
ljb7	50x5	0.110	0.109	0.060	0.056	0.069	0.091	0.055
ljb9	50x5	0.982	0.796	0.651	0.652	0.674	0.917	0.630
ljb10	50x8	0.455	0.479	0.438	0.418	0.442	0.438	0.418
ljb12	50x8	0.478	0.489	0.399	0.392	0.397	0.424	0.399

Table 5. Weighted Tardiness (Twt)

	Size	Fang	Pri.	PGA	HGA	HGA (ND)	HGA (G&T)	HGA (NR)
jb1	10x3	-0.168	-0.173	-0.173	-0.167	-0.167	-0.167	-0.167
jb2	10x3	-0.824	0.812	-0.839	-0.819	-0.814	-0.816	-0.819
jb4	10x5	0.490	0.497	0.493	0.489	0.494	0.489	0.489
jb9	15x3	-0.073	-0.047	-0.078	-0.079	-0.073	-0.072	-0.079
jb11	15x5	-0.607	-0.607	-0.751	-0.643	-0.702	-0.580	-0.636
jb12	15x5	-0.102	-0.082	-0.103	-0.102	-0.101	-0.102	-0.102
ljb1	30x3	-0.195	-0.112	-0.214	-0.224	-0.126	-0.224	-0.224
ljb2	30x3	-0.043	0.013	-0.078	-0.078	-0.051	-0.022	-0.051
ljb7	50x5	-0.414	-0.411	-0.507	-0.514	-0.501	-0.399	-0.523
ljb9	50x5	0.702	0.622	0.354	0.389	0.423	0.595	0.388
ljb10	50x8	-0.096	-0.038	-0.108	-0.139	-0.136	-0.041	-0.134
ljb12	50x8	0.256	0.256	0.113	0.158	0.121	0.310	0.136

Table 6. Weighted Lateness (Lwt)

beaten in 3 cases. Comparison to the results obtained using Priority Rules shows that HGA outperforms them in 44 out of 48 cases, equals the results in 2 cases, and is beaten in 2 cases. The performance of HGA is less robust when compared to those results recently published by Lin. However, it outperforms Lin's PGA in 18 cases, equals the results in a further 9 cases, and it is beaten in the remaining 21 cases. HGA(NR) beats Lin's results in an additional 2 cases. The objective for which HGA produces the poorest results is ETwt, and the best results are found for objective Fwt.

For all objectives, evolving the choice of scheduling method is beneficial. Comparison of HGA to G&T only shows that in only 3 cases does the evolution of method hinder the search and decrease performance. For the remaining cases, HGA produces better results than $HGA(G\&T)$ in 25 cases, and equivalent results for the other 20 cases. Comparison to Non-Delay shows 4 cases where better results are achieved using Non-Delay only. HGA produces better results than $HGA(ND)$ on 40 cases, and equivalent results on the remaining 4 cases.

The decision as to whether or not to include the RND heuristic is less clear. Comparison of the results obtained by HGA and HGA(NR) shows that in just over half the cases (28) no difference between results is observed. From the remaining 20 cases, better results are obtained in 9 cases by including the RND allele, and worse results on 11 cases. Hence, although not including the RND allele may prevent some operations from being chosen at some points in the schedule, this appears to slightly outweigh the possible disadvantages of including it, i.e. that the population may be unstable from one generation to the next.

7 Analysis and Discussion

Both G&T and Non-Delay algorithms result in a conflict set of operations at each iteration, of size ≥ 1. If the conflict set has only one operation, then any of the available h heuristics will obviously select this operation. If we denote the number of conflict sets of size > 1 by d, then the size of the search space is equal to d^h.

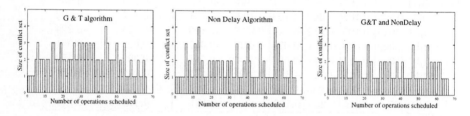

Fig. 4. Size of conflict set vs number of operations

We investigate the variation on conflict set size as operations are scheduled using the best chromosome evolved by HGA for problem $ljb1$, objective Fwt. The result is shown in figure 4, which also contrasts the effect of setting the *method* genes to denote G&T only and to Non-Delay only, leaving the *heuristic* genes fixed.

Use of G&T only leads to a high value of d, and hence a large search space. On the other hand, Non-Delay schedule generation results in a low value of d, but may exclude the optimal schedule from consideration. By evolving the algorithmic choice, we reach a compromise between the two schemes. These diagrams also give us a clue as to why HGA is able to perform successfully — in each chromosome there are a large number of redundant *heuristic* alleles, which can effectively have any value. Thus many *different* chromosomes may evaluate to the *same* schedule.

It also seems reasonably intuitive that the crucial stages in the scheduling process lie in constructing the early part of the schedule, where the knock-on effect on making some decision can have serious consequences on the remainder of the schedule. This implies that some of the decisions made in the latter part of the schedule are of little importance. This points to a possible alternative method of reducing the search space; that is concentrate on evolving some crucial partial schedule, then generate the remainder by other means. Consider the following experiment; take the best chromosome output by HGA for problem $ljb1$, and replace the final i heuristic genes with heuristics chosen at random. Repeat the experiment, with i ranging from 1 to l, where l is the length of the chromosome. For each value of i, 250 chromosomes were generated and evaluated. Figure 5 shows the best objective found at each value, with the best objective found by Lin, Fang, and Priority rules also shown for comparison. The diagram shows that placement of the first 34 of the total 67 operations in the schedule is critical, after which random generation of the remainder produces satisfactory results.

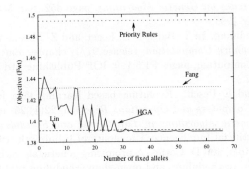

Fig. 5. Best Fwt objective obtained for ljb1 vs number of alleles fixed

8   Conclusion

This paper presented a new GA which evolves a combination of scheduling algorithm and heuristic choice to be used at each stage of the scheduling process. In particular, evolving the choice of scheduling algorithm is shown to be highly beneficial. The representation is straightforward, and can be used with standard recombination operators, which always produce feasible solutions. The results are promising across a range of problems and objectives when compared to those most recently published. The GA could perhaps be tuned further with respect to individual objectives by using a specialised set of heuristics for the objective in question, rather than the general set used here.

Furthermore, analysis of the behaviour of the algorithm suggests several ways in which it may be improved. The diagrams presented in section 7 suggest that it may be feasible to concentrate on evolving a *partial* schedule, with an obvious reduction in search space size, and then rapidly produce the remainder of the schedule via another more efficient means, perhaps by hybridisation with a hill-climber. Similarly, more efficient search maybe produced by directing mutation and crossover operators to those areas of the chromosome where the conflict set produced as a result of applying the scheduling algorithm is largest. However, the results found so far using "off-the-shelf" operators are extremely encouraging.

Acknowledgements

Emma Hart is supported by EPSRC grant GR/L22232.

References

1. R. Bruns. Direct chromosome representation and advanced genetic algorithms for production scheduling. In S. Forrest, editor, *Proceedings of the Fifth International Conference on Genetic Algorithms*, page 352. San Mateo: Morgan Kaufmann, February 1993.
2. R. Bruns. Scheduling. In T. Bäck, D.B. Fogel, and Z. Michalewicz, editors, *Handbook of Evolutionary Computation*, release 97/1, chapter Part F: Applications of Evolutionary Computing, pages F1.5:1–9. IOP Publishing Ltd and Oxford University Press, 1997.
3. U. Dorndorf and E. Pesch. Evolution based learning in a job shop scheduling environment. *Computers and Operations Research*, 22(1):25–40, 1995.
4. H-L. Fang. *Genetic Algorithms in Timetabling and Scheduling*. PhD thesis, Department of Artificial Intelligence, University of Edinburgh, 1994.
5. H-L. Fang, P. Ross, and D. Corne. A promising genetic algorithm approach to job-shop scheduling, rescheduling, and open-shop scheduling problems. In S. Forrest, editor, *Proceedings of the Fifth International Conference on Genetic Algorithms*, pages 375–382. San Mateo: Morgan Kaufmann, 1993.
6. B. Giffler and G.L. Thompson. Algorithm for solving production scheduling problems. *Operations Research*, 8(4):487–503, 1960.
7. S-C. Lin, E.D. Goodman, and W.F. Punch. A genetic algorithm approach to dynamic job-shop scheduling problems. In Thomas Bäck, editor, *Proceedings of the Seventh International Conference on Genetic Algorithms*, pages 481–489. Morgan-Kaufmann, 1997.
8. T.E. Morton and D.W. Pentico. *Heuristic Scheduling Systems*. John Wiley, 1993.
9. R. Nakano and T. Yamada. Conventional genetic algorithms for job shop problems. In R.K. Belew and L.B. Booker, editors, *Proceedings of the Fourth International Conference on Genetic Algorithms*, pages 474–479. San Mateo: Morgan Kaufmann, 1991.
10. I.P. Norenkov and E.D. Goodman. Solving scheduling problems via evolutionary methods for rule sequence optimization. Second World Conference on Soft Computing, 1997.
11. R.J.M. Vaessens, E.H.L. Aarts, and J.K. Lenstra. Job shop scheduling by local search. *INFORMS Journal of Computing*, 8:302–317, 1996.

Reduction of Air Traffic Congestion
by Genetic Algorithms

Sofiane Oussedik[1] and Daniel Delahaye[2]

[1] CMAP / Eurocontrol ***
[2] LOG / CENA †
{oussedik, delahaye}@cmapx.polytechnique.fr
Centre de Mathématiques Appliquées
Ecole Polytechnique
91128 Palaiseau Cedex, France

Abstract. The annual number of flights in Western Europe has increased from about 2.6 million in 1982 to about 4.5 million in 1992,
an increase of 73%. Acute congestion of the Air Traffic Control system
has been the result. One way to reduce this congestion is to modify the
flight plans (slot of departure and route) in order to adapt the demand
to the available capacity. This paper addresses the general time-route assignment problem. A state of the art of the existing methods shows that
this problem is usually partially treated and the whole problem remains
unsolved due to the complexity induced.
We perform our research on the application of stochastic methods on
real traffic data, and without using the flow network concept, but by
simulating the flight of each aircraft. The first results shows that our
Genetic Algorithms based method is able to reduce congestion of the
french airspace by a factor 2. Special coding techniques and operators
are used to improve the quality of the genetic search.

1 Introduction

As there are many aircraft simultaneously present in the sky, pilots must be
helped by an air traffic controller on the ground who has a global view of the
current traffic distribution in the airspace and can give orders to the pilots to
avoid collisions. A single controller is not able to manage all the aircraft, that's
why the airspace is partitioned into different sectors, each of them being assigned
to a controller.

As any human being, a controller has working limits, and when the number
of aircraft increases, some parts of the airspace reach this limit and become
congested. In the past, the first way to reduce these congestions was to modify
the structure of the airspace in a way that increases the capacity (increasing
the number of runways, increasing the number of sectors by reducing their size).
This has a limit due to the cost involved by new runways and the way to manage

---

*** Eurocontrol Experimental Center
† Laboratoire d'Optimisation Globale / Centre d'Etudes de la Navigation Aérienne

traffic in too small sectors (a controller needs a minimum amount of airspace to be able to solve conflicts). The other way to reduce congestion is to modify the flight plans in a way to adapt the demand to the available capacity. Then congestion is expected to be reduced by moving (in a limited domain) the time of departure of aircraft (in the past and in the future) and by changing the current flight paths (without too much extradistance).

This paper shows how well stochastic optimization is able to manage this kind of problem.

2 Previous Related Works

Traffic assignment techniques have been developed in order to reduce congestion in transportation networks by spreading the traffic demand in time and in space. Dafermos and Sparrow [5] coined the terms *user-optimized* and *system-optimized* transportation networks to distinguish between two distinct situations in which users act unilaterally, in their own self-interest, in selecting their routes, and in which users select routes according to what is optimal from the societal point of view, in that the total costs in the system are minimized. Classical approaches are applied to static traffic demand and are mainly used to optimize traffic on a long time period and can only capture the macroscopic events.

When a more precise matching between traffic demand and capacity has to be found, microscopic events have to be taken into account, and dynamic traffic assignment techniques have to be used, ([12] gives a good description of those techniques). The main ones are the following : Space-time network [14], Variational Inequality [7], Optimal Control [8], Simulation [3] and Dynamic Programming [11, 13, 2].

All the previous approaches are not able to manage the whole problem due to its complexity.

A first attempt of resolution of the whole problem can be found in [6]. This paper present a flow modeling of the air traffic network and give a resolution principle of the route-time bi-allocation problem based on stochastic optimization with very good results. The present approach is the following of this work. The major difference between these two approches relies on the air network modeling. In the following, a model is proposed and a method is developed that yield "very good" solutions for realistic instances of the whole problem. In this model, which is more realistic for air traffic, the concept of route flow is no more valid and this induce a control workload spreading over the space and a stronger complexity.

3 A Simplified Model

3.1 Introduction

Congestion in the airspace is due to aircraft which have close positions in a four-dimensional space (one time dimension and three space dimensions). It is then relevant to investigate ways to separate those aircraft in this four-dimensional space by changing their slot of departure (time separation) or by changing their route (spatial separation) or both. Those changes must be done in a way that takes into account the objectives of the airlines. That's why the moving of the *slot of departure* must be done in a limited domain and the *possible routes* must not generate too large additional distances.

According to the controllers themselves, the workload induced in a control sector is a function of the three main following criteria :

- the conflict workload that results from the different actions of the controller to solve conflicts.
- the coordination workload corresponds to the information exchanges between a controller and the controller in charge of the bordering sector or between a controller and the pilots when an aircraft crosses a sector boundary.
- the monitoring aims at checking the different trajectories of the aircraft in a sector and induces a workload.

We can now define our goals more precisely in the following way :

one considers a fleet of aircraft with their associated route and slot of departure. For each flight a set of alternative routes and a set of possible slots of departure are defined. One must find "optimal" route and slot allocation for each aircraft in a way that significantly reduces the peak of workload in the most congested sectors and in the most congested airports, during one day of traffic.

The workload computing is based on the aircraft trajectories discretization (time step dt) produced by off-line simulation. The workload indicator used is the summation of the coordination and monitoring workloads regarding to critical capacities of the controller's workload. The conflict workload has been omited in order to match the operational capacity.

3.2 Mathematical formulation

A pair of decision variable (δ_i, r_i) is associated with each flight in which δ_i is the advance or the delay from the original slot of departure and r_i is the new route. With this notation $(0, r_0)$ will be considered as the most preferred choice from the user point of view. Those two decision variables (δ_i, r_i) will be chosen from two finite-discrete sets : Δ for the slots and R for the routes. The routes are ordered according to cost induced to the associated flight.

As it has been previously said, workload in a sector S_k at time t can be expressed by the summation of two terms :

$$W_{S_k}^t = Wmo_{S_k}(t) + Wco_{S_k}(t) \ ;$$

Where $Wmo_{S_k}(t)$ is the monitoring workload (quadratic term related to the number of aircraft overloading a sector monitoring critical capacity C_m),

$Wcos_{S_k}(t)$ the coordination workload (quadratic term of the number of aircraft overloading a critical coordination capacity C_c).

As there are some uncertainties on the aircraft position, control workload has been smoothed in order to improve the robustness of the produced solution. This smoothing is done by averaging the control workload over a time window :

$$\widetilde{W}^t_{S_k} = \frac{1}{2.D+1} \sum_{x=t-D}^{x=t+D} W^x_{S_k}$$

where :
$\widetilde{W}^t_{S_k}$ represent the sector S_k smoothed workload during t and D is the length of the smoothing window.

Formulation of the objective function

The objective is defined in the following way : " one must try to reduce congestion in the most overloaded sectors" ; this will spread the congestion over several sectors. So, we have :

$$obj = \min \sum_{k=1}^{k=P} \left((\sum_{t\in T} \widetilde{W}^t_{S_k})^\phi \times (\max_{t\in T} \widetilde{W}^t_{S_k})^\varphi \right)$$

where :

- $\sum_{t\in T} \widetilde{W}^t_{S_k}$: is the sector S_k congestion surface computed during the day.
- $\max_{t\in T} \widetilde{W}^t_{S_k}$: is the maximum sector congestion reported during the day.
- P is the number of elementary sectors.

The parameters $\phi \in [0,1]$ et $\varphi \in [0,1]$ gives more or less importance to congestion *maximum* or to congestion *surface*.

3.3 Problem complexity

Before investigating an optimization method, the associated complexity of our problem must be studied. The model previously developed is discrete and induces a high combinatoric search space. As a mater of fact, if R_n, Δ_n are the route set and the slot moving set associated with flight n, the number of points in the state domain is given by :

$$|State| = \prod_{n=1}^{n=N} (|R_n|.|\Delta_n|)$$

where $|S|$ denotes the cardinality of the set S.

For instance, for 20000 flights with 10 route choices and 10 possible slot movings, : $|State| = 100^{20000}$. Moreover, those decision variables are not independent due to the connection induced by the control workload and the airport congestions, so, decomposition methods cannot be applied. It must be noticed that the objective function is not continuous (then it is not convex) and may have several equivalent optima. This problem has been proved to be a strong NP-hard[1] problem with non-separable state variables which can be well addressed by stochastic optimization.

4 Genetic Algorithms

Genetic Algorithms (GAs) are probabilistic search algorithms. Given an optimization problem they try to find an optimal solution. GAs start by initializing a set (population) containing a selection of encoded points of the search space (individuals). By decoding the individual and determining its cost the fitness of an individual can be determined, which is used to distinguish between better and worse individuals. A GA iteratively tries to improve the average fitness of a population by construction of new populations. A new population consists of individual (children) constructed from individuals of the old population (parents) by the use of re-combination operators. Better (above average) individuals have higher probability to be selected for re-combination than other individuals (survival of the fittest). After some criterion is met, the algorithm returns the best individuals of the population.

In contrast to the theorical foundations [9, 4], GAs have to deal with limited population sizes and a limited number of generations. This limitation can lead to premature convergence, which means that the algorithm gets stuck at local optima. A lot of research has been undertaken to overcome premature convergence (for an overview see [10]). Also, experiments have shown that incorporation of problem specific knowledge generally improve GAs. In this paper attention will be paid how to incorporate Air Traffic specific information into a Genetic Algorithm.

5 Application to Airspace Congestion

5.1 Introduction

The way this specific genetic algorithm works is the following. A set of flight plans is generated from each chromosome candidate and the whole associated day of traffic is generated. Sector congestion are registered and the associated fitness is computed. The problem specific features of the Genetic Algorithm are now described.

5.2 Data Coding and biased initial population

For each flight, the possible new path and new slot moving have been supposed to be chosen in two discrete-finite sets associated with each flight. In this case a straight forward coding has been used in the sense that each chromosome is built as a matrix (see fig. 1-(a)) which gather the new slot moving (for the time of departure) and the new route number (for the flight path). With this coding, a population of individuals can be created by choosing a new slot moving number

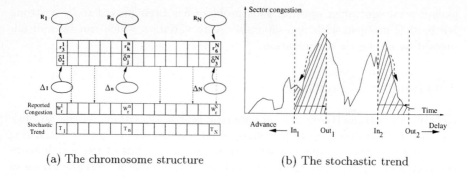

(a) The chromosome structure   (b) The stochastic trend

Fig. 1. Special coding and stochastic problem specific knowledge

and a new route number from individual sets associated with each flight with a positive probability to move the flights which are involved in the congestion peaks (to each flight we associate the reported congestion during the flight and the stochastic trend, these two indicators are explained explained below - see also, fig. 1–(a) and (b)) and a very small probability for the others.

5.3 Fitness Evaluation

The fitness of each individual is defined by the ration of the congestion associated with the initial distribution of the flight plans (ref) and the distribution given by the chromosome $(chrom)$:

$$fitness(chrom) = \frac{W(ref)}{W(chrom)}$$

where :

$$W(X) = \sum_{k=1}^{k=P} \left((\sum_{t\in T} \widetilde{W}^t_{S_k,X})^\phi \times (\max_{t\in T} \widetilde{W}^t_{S_k,X})^\varphi \right)$$

So, when $fitness(chrom) > 1$, it means that the induced congestion is lower than the reference one.

5.4 Recombination Operators

To be able to recognize the aircraft involved in the biggest sector congestion new information must be added to the chromosome which indicates for each gene, the maximum level of sector congestion encountered during a flight.

Crossover
The successive steps of this new crossover operator are the following :

- two parents are first selected according to their fitness ;
- the summation of the sector congestion levels is computed for each flight in both parents. For a flight n, total congestion level in the parent p will be noted W_n^p ;
- an order relationship is then constructed with the total congestion level in the following way :
  - flight planing n in parent 1 is said to be "much better" than flight planing n in parent 2 if $W_n^1 < \delta.W_n^2$; where $\delta \in [0.7, 0.95]$;
  - flight planing n in parent 2 is said to be "much better" than flight planing n in parent 1 if $W_n^2 < \delta.W_n^1$;
  - flight planing n in parent 1 and in parent 2 are said to be "equivalent" if none of the previous relations matches;
- if a flight planning "is much better" in the first parent than in the second then it is copied in the second ;
- if a flight planning "is much better" in the second parent than in the first then it is copied in the first ;
- if the two flight plannings "are equivalent" they are randomly exchanged with a constant probability (0.5) ;

Mutation

As already noted, this operator only affect the flights involved in the highest peaks of congestion, and also determine wether it is "more suitable" to delay or advance a flight (see fig.1–(b)). So to compute the *stochastic trend* over all the sectors, we compute the signed indicator $T_n \in [-1, 1]$ which is a sort of bias to advance or delay each flight. T_n is a signed pondered (by the encountered flight congestion) summation over sectors. The sign indicates the sector state during the entree and the left of the flight (congestion increase or decrease).

The mutation operator works in the following way :

- a threshold congestion level (Th) is randomly chosen ;
- then for each flight n in the chromosome the following are applied :
- if $(W_n > Th)$ then the associated flight plan is modified :
  - if $T_n > rand(1)$ then we randomly assign a futur slot to the flight.
  - if $T_n < -rand(1)$ then we randomly assign a past slot to the flight.
  - otherwise we randomly affect the flight slot with no preference for the advance or the delay.
- else the flight planing is unchanged;

$rand(x)$ represent a random float between the $[0, x]$ range.

6 Results on a real day of traffic

6.1 Introduction

The computations were based on a whole real day traffic data which corresponds to 6381 flights that cross the french airspace on the $21th$ of *June* 1996. The number of elementary sectors was 89. We consider also that the congestion of an elementary sector S_k at time period t is equal to the congestion of the sectors grouping R_{S_K} to whom it belongs ($\widetilde{W}^t_{S_k} = \widetilde{W}^t_{R_{S_k}}$) during the same period. By this, we take into acount the changes in the critical capacities values during the day. Also, the critical capacity of the prohibited sectors (as military sectors) is set equal to 0.

To test the improvements of our new-recombinators (OGA), the results of a simple genetic algorithm (SGA) are reported.

The presented tests are performed with the elitism principle and have been processed on a Pentium Pro 200Mhz Computer

The results below are obtained by using slots moving only in order to do some comparisons with classical methods which investigate the time-allocation problem only.

6.2 The results

The tests parameters for both algorithms are : the smoothing window $D = 5min$; the population length $pop_{length} = 50$; $dt = 1min$ so, $T = 1440$ minutes for the day ; $\phi = 0.9$ and $\varphi = 0.1$. The last two parameters are chosen to give more importance to the decrease of the maximum congestion peaks.

The number of generations : 300 ; and the maximum slots moving in the futur or in the past : 45 minutes.

- For the **OGA**, we have, $P_c = 0.3$: the probability to undergo a crossover and $P_m = 0.4$: the chromosome mutation probability.
- For the **SGA** : The initial population is created by giving random slot numbers to the flights with a probability 0.5 of not moving the slot ; $P_c = 0.3$ for each chromosome and $P_m = 0.02$ for each flight in the population.

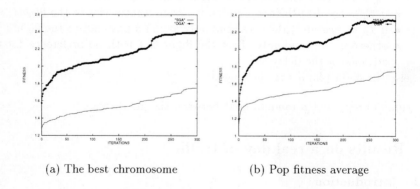

(a) The best chromosome   (b) Pop fitness average

Fig. 2. Evolution of the population best and fitness average

The fig.2 shows that the original congestion, in the sense given by the optimization criterion, could be respectively divided by 1.74 with the SGA and by 2.40 by using the OGA. Even with the small population size used, the results given by the genetic algorithm are very encouraging.

On the figure 3, it can be noticed that the max workload on one of the most overloaded sectors has been divided by 3.07 by using the OGA and by 1.78 with the SGA. The figure fig.3-(b) represent the fig.3-(a) zoomed on the greatest congestion peaks range. As expected, the workload is spread around the peak as in a smoothing process.

The computation times (OGA : 14 hours, SGA : (5 : 30) hours) are the weak point of this GAs based method, but when using GAs as pre-tactial method taking place during the two days preceeding the day of operations, the computations can be done on night. Also, a parallel GA will be helpfull to decrease the processing time.

To make a more precise comparison of the OGA and the SGA, the SGA was used for 1000 generations which is equivalent to 16 processing hours. The best chromosome fitness was equal to 2.02 which still always less than the OGA one. The number of delayed flights of the SGA was 4120 against 3510 for the OGA and the total slots moving minutes was 126508 for the SGA against 107782 for the OGA. This is due to the fact that the crossover and the mutation of the SGA are irrelivant regarding to their total random choices. When they are applied, they somethimes affect aircraft involved in the underloaded sectors.

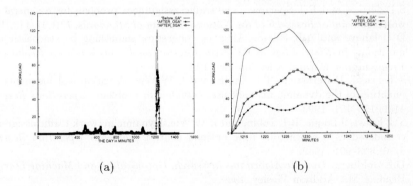

(a)   (b)

Fig. 3. Spreading the sectors congestion

7 Conclusion

Our objectif was the reduction of the Air Traffic Congestion by reaching a system equilibrium. To that end, Genetic Algorithms have been used and new recombinators have been presented and show that the incorporation of Air Traffic specific knowledge improves the results of the GA. Also, the strength of this model is its ability to manage the constraints of the airlines companies in a microscopic way by using individual sets of decision variables associated with each flight. The next steps of our research are : - the introduction of new alternative routes ; - the introduction of new stochastic operators including more ATM specific knowledge ; - the hybridation of the GA with other heuristic and deterministic methods ; - and, developing a sector complexity indicator more efficient then the only monitoring and coordination ones, by taking into acount the sectors microscopic events as the aircrafts separation.

8 Acknowledgements

We would like to thank Marc Schoenauer for his remarks and suggestions which were very helpful during our work.

References

1. M Ben-Akiva, A DePalma, and I Kaysi. Dynamic network models and driver information systems. *Transportation Research*, 25A(5):251–266, 1991.
2. D.J Bertsimas and S Stock. The air traffic flow management problem with en-route capacities. Technical report, A.P Sloan School of Management. M.I.T, 1994.
3. E Cascetta and G.E Cantarella. A day-to-day and within-day dynamic stochastic assignment model. *Transportation Research*, 25A(5):277–291, 1991.
4. R Cerf. *Une Théorie Asymptotique des Algorithmes Génétiques*. PhD thesis, Université Montpellier II (France), 1994.
5. S Dafermos and F.T Sparrow. The traffic assignment problem for a general network. *Journal of Research of the National Bureau of Standards*, 73B:91–118, 1969.
6. D Delahaye and A.R Odoni. Airspace congestion smoothing by stochastic optimization. In *Proceedings of the Sixth International Conference on Evolutionary Programming*. Natural Selection inc., 1997.
7. T.L Friesz, D Bernstein, T.E Smith, and B.W Wie. A variational inequality formulation of the dynamic network user equilibrium problem. *Operations Research*, 41(1):179–191, 1993.
8. T.L Friesz, J Luque, R.L Tobin, and B.W Wie. Dynamic network traffic assignment considered as a continuous time optimal control problem. *Operation Research*, 37(6):893–901, 1989.
9. D.E Goldberg. *Genetic Algorithms in Search, Optimization and Machine Learning*. Reading MA Addison Wesley, 1989.
10. Z Michalewicz. *Genetic algorithms + Data Structures = Evolution Programs*. Springer-verlag, 1992.
11. A.R Odoni. The flow management problem in air traffic control. In A.R Odoni et al, editor, *Flow Control of Congested Networks*, volume F38 of *ASI Series*, pages 269–288. NATO, 1987.
12. M. Papageorgiou. *Concise encyclopedia of traffic and transportation systems*. Pergamon Press, 1991.
13. P Vranas, D Bertsimas, and A.R Odoni. The multi-airport ground-holding problem in air traffic control. *Operation Research*, 42(2):249–261, 1994.
14. D.J Zawack and G.L Thompson. A dynamic space-time network flow model for city traffic congestion. *Transportation Science*, 21(3):153–162, 1987.

Timetabling the Classes of an Entire University with an Evolutionary Algorithm

Ben Paechter, R. C. Rankin, Andrew Cumming and Terence C. Fogarty

Napier University, Edinburgh, Scotland
benp@dcs.napier.ac.uk

Abstract. This paper describes extensions to an evolutionary algorithm that timetables classes for an entire University. A new method of dealing with multi-objectives is described along with a user interface designed for it. New results are given concerning repair of poor recombination choices during local search. New methods are described and evaluated that allow timetables to be produced which have minimal changes compared to a full or partial reference timetable. The paper concludes with a discussion of scale-up issues, and gives some initial results that are very encouraging.

1. Introduction

Napier University uses a timetable that was produced by an evolutionary algorithm incorporating a local search. The system timetables 100% of classes and optimises them according to twelve competing objectives.

Timetabling the classes of a University involves finding timeslots for the events such that each event can have the resources (rooms, students, and lecturers) that it requires, and so that constraints on the relative timing of events are maintained. This process produces feasible timetables. In addition to producing feasible timetables, we want to produce timetables that are 'good' measured against some criteria. The production of feasible timetables involves satisfying the hard constraints of the problem. The production of good timetables involves satisfying as many of the soft constraints as possible.

The Napier University problem involves placing 2000 events into 45 timeslots and 183 rooms, and optimising the timetables of 700 lecturers and 1000 student groups. The number of ways to put 2000 events into 45 timeslots is 45^{2000}. Clearly, the vast majority of these timetables are infeasible, because some hard constraint is broken. The problem then becomes how to find good timetables in a search space that contains very few feasible timetables.

There have been several attempts to solve this type of problem with evolutionary algorithms; some examples of these can be found in [1], [2], [4], [5], [6], [7], [8], [10] and [18]. The method used here is distinguished by its use of local search to deal mainly with hard constraints and genetic operators to solve mainly soft constraints. Others have used evolutionary algorithms combined with local search in other ways.

For example, in [3] Burke et al. describe a system that timetables examinations using a local search, in this case the local search is used mainly to solve soft constraints.

2. Summary of Previous Work

The algorithm described here was originally presented in [11] where the principle of using an indirect representation was established. Refinements were made in [12]. In [13] the idea of timeslot suggestion lists was first presented and suitable recombination operators were defined. Directed and targeted mutation were addressed in [14]. In [15] the advantages of local search and Lamarckian writeback were clearly shown, and results for a large real problem were shown to give a considerable improvement over manual methods.

In order to solve the feasibility problem, a local search is employed which searches from a point in the search space specified by each new chromosome to a point with greater feasibility. The result of this is that the evolutionary algorithm can now search through the smaller space of feasible and nearly feasible timetables for timetables that are good.

An indirect representation is used which codes for how a timetable will be produced by the local search engine. The representation is split into two parts.

The first is a permutation that specifies the order in which the events should be considered when trying to fit them in to the timetable. When building an unseeded population the permutation is initialised using a heuristic which ensures that the more difficult-to-place events are considered first.

The second part of the representation specifies a number of suggested timeslots for each event (normally there are two suggestions, one coming from each parent). When building an unseeded population, the suggested timeslots for an event are assigned randomly from the list of possible timeslots for that event (those times when the event could take place if there were no other events to consider).

The search proceeds as follows: events are considered in the order specified by the permutation. For each event an attempt is made to place the event in the primary suggested timeslot. If this fails (because some hard constraint would be broken by doing so) then the other suggested timeslots are tried in order. If none of the suggested timeslots is possible, then other timeslots are tried according to a problem specific heuristic that examines the timeslots which do not incur a penalty first.

If at the end of this process the event has not been placed, it is considered unplaced (which attracts a fitness penalty) and the next event in the permutation is considered.

If an event is placed then the timeslot used is written back into the chromosome as the primary suggested timeslot. The timeslot that was occupying this position (if different) is moved into the second position (and any others are shuffled down). This writing back of the local search results makes the algorithm Lamarckian.

For each event a child inherits its primary timeslot suggestion from one parent and its secondary timeslot suggestion (if more than one suggestion is stored) from the other. The operator is based on multi-point recombination, and as the chromosome is traversed there is an equal chance at every point that the parent contributing the primary suggestion will be switched. When using more than two suggested timeslots, the subsequent suggestions are taken alternately from each parent. This operator conforms with the concepts from Forma Theory of *respect* and *assortment* [16]. The permutation is inherited from one parent only.

Three mutation operators are used; all work on the primary suggested timeslot for one event. The first operator is a blind mutation that randomly reassigns the primary suggested timeslot to some other possible timeslot. This mutation operator ensures that all parts of the search space are reachable.

The other two mutation operators make use of problem specific knowledge to direct the mutation in a way that may be useful. The first is *selfish mutation* which involves an event "stealing" the timeslot used by another event. The second is *co-operative mutation* which involves an event finding another event with which it can swap primary timeslot suggestions, to the possible advantage of both. The directed mutation operators also make changes to the permutation to ensure that during the local search the events end up getting the timeslots they expect. These operators are very useful, particularly in the later stages of a run and when used in conjunction with *targeted mutation*.

Targeted mutation allows mutations of the chromosome to be targeted at those parts of the chromosome that code for parts of the phenotype that attract penalties on evaluation. During evaluation, a score is kept for each event of the extent to which that event detracts from the fitness of the whole timetable. When calculating the chance that the genetic material for an event will mutate, each event has a base chance of mutating, an amount is then added to this which is directly proportional to the degree to which this event detracts from the fitness of the whole timetable. Targeted mutation has little effect, if any, when used with blind mutation alone, but a significant effect when used with directed mutation operators, particularly in the early stages of a run.

Ross et al. in [17] have described other mutation operators for timetabling that use problem specific knowledge. There they are used mainly to solve hard constraints in an algorithm that does not employ a local search. Mutation operators which use problem specific knowledge were described earlier by Eiben et al. in [9].

After recombination and mutation a child may be less feasible than either of its parents. This decrease in feasibility will often be repaired by the local search mechanism undergone by all new chromosomes.

3. User Interface for the Evaluation of Multi-Objectives

During the local search hard constraints are never broken. This means that the resulting timetables never have broken hard constraints, but that some events may remain unplaced. The number of unplaced events can then be reduced by treating the constraint *all events must be placed* as a soft constraint. This soft constraint is then considered along with the other soft constraints. The breaking of soft constraints is measured using *problem measures*. Each problem measure counts the number of occurrences of some problem with the timetable, so we want to reduce the values of the problem measures.

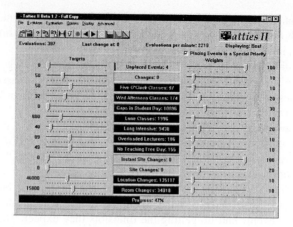

Fig. 1. The User Interface

The way in which the quality of a timetable is measured reflects the fact that users have targets for individual problem measures. Once the target for a problem measure has been met the user does not wish the algorithm to waste more effort reducing the value further. Users also care more about reaching the targets for some problem measures than they do for others. If users are only allowed to specify weights then they tend to change these as the run progresses when certain problem measures reach acceptable levels or levels beyond which they know no improvement is possible. If a run is going to take more than a few minutes then the user either has to sit and watch the evolution in case a weight needs to be changed, or has to accept that the algorithm may waste time optimising something that cannot or need not be optimised further.

In order to take account of this, a user interface has been designed that allows the user to specify (and change during the course of a run) a target t and a weight w, for each of the twelve problem measures: see Figure 1. Targeted mutation rates are then calculated so as not to try to improve problem measures beyond the target and the evaluation function is then constructed so as to give no extra benefit to a chromosome that reduces a problem measure below the target.

In order to evaluate a chromosome we need to know how much progress it has made towards each of the problem measure targets. In order to measure the progress towards a target we have to define the start point s. This is approximated by examining 200 random chromosomes and taking the worst score that occurs on that problem measure (users can provide other values for s if so required). If a problem measure has the value v then the progress on that problem measure p can then normally be calculated by: $p = \max(0, (v - t) / (s - t))$. If p has the value 0 then the target has been met. The progress of the algorithm over all problem measures P can be calculated as the weighted average over all values of p.

The user can also specify that placing events is a special priority. If this is the case then the comparison of two timetables is done sequentially. First the number of unplaced events is considered. If one timetable has fewer unplaced events then it is considered the better timetable. Only if the number of unplaced events is the same (or both timetables have reached the target for unplaced events) is the progress on the other problem measures considered.

4. Experiments with Timeslot Suggestion Lists

Experiments have been conducted to measure the effect of having different numbers of timeslot suggestions within the chromosome. With one suggestion, only one parent contributes to the placing of that event. With two suggestions there is a back-up timeslot from the other parent. When we have three or four suggestions then information from grandparents is stored (as a result of the recombination operator).

Two experiments were conducted. In the first the value of P that could be achieved in a set elapsed time was measured, given targets of zero on all problem measures. In the second the time taken for P to reach 0.05 (within 95% of the overall target) was measured for targets reflecting those commonly used by users. For each experiment real data for a single large department was used with 10 problem measures. Results were averaged over 50 runs. The same initial 50 populations were used for each set of runs. The results can be seen in figures 2 and 3. The chart in figure 2 is truncated at a point thought to be around the optimum value of P.

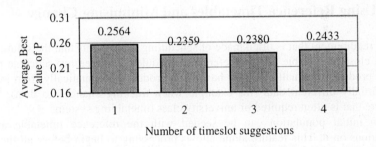

Fig. 2. Progress Achieved Over Given Time

Elapsed time is used as a measure in these experiments since the time taken to perform an evaluation depends on the chromosome being evaluated and the method being used. Hence, measuring against the number of evaluations would produce erroneous results. All experiments in this paper were carried out on a dedicated 200MHz Pentium Pro computer.

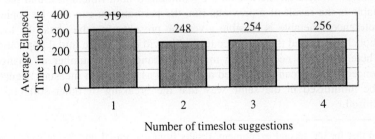

Fig. 3. Time Taken for Given Progress

For each experiment a paired Student's T-test shows a very highly significant (probability greater than 99.99%) improvement using suggestions from both parents, and no significant difference using suggestions from grandparents. For the first experiment we can say with 99% confidence that the average value of P with one suggested timeslot is 0.2564 ± 0.0069 and with two suggested timeslots is 0.2359 ± 0.0087. For the second experiment we can say with 99% confidence that the average time with one suggested timeslot is 319 ± 28 and with two suggested timeslots is 248 ± 23.[1]

These results are as we might expect, as storing suggestions from both parents is equivalent to repairing "mistakes" made by the recombination operator. If the "wrong" parent was chosen to contribute a particular timeslot, then this is rectified by the search mechanism. The lack of significant difference for increasing numbers of suggested timeslots is probably because any benefit from storing the timeslots suggested by grandparents is counteracted by the extra processing overhead required.

5. Using Reference Timetables and Minimising Change

A requirement that is often made of scheduling problems is that the solution should be as close as possible to some reference schedule. The reference schedule may have been produced manually, or may have been produced automatically from incomplete or partially different data (for example when tracking changes to data). This is a feature that is often required of university class timetabling systems.

An initial population can be seeded with the reference timetable and small variations on it. This feature alone allows processing to begin before all the data has been collected as runs with new data can be seeded with the results of previous runs. Of course there is a danger here that what was a global optimum may become a local optimum of the new data, so care is needed in deciding when is it better to start a run from scratch.

The seeding is done by first finding all the events that are common to both the present timetable data and the reference timetable. The primary timeslot suggestion for each of these events is then copied from the reference timetable. All but one of the chromosomes then undergoes a mutation in order to add some variety to the population. Where all the events are common to both timetables, and the reference timetable is the result of a previous run, the permutation can also be copied. Where the reference timetable is feasible given the present timetable data, the local search will not change it and the reference timetable will exist in the initial population.

Where it is also necessary to minimise changes, the number of changes to the reference timetable can be counted and treated as a problem measure. Hence changes can be minimised in the same way that the breaking of other soft constraints is minimised.

---

[1] Note that for the second experiment, results from one initial population were ignored. This was because the result for using one suggested timeslot was over 6000 seconds. The algorithm had become trapped in a local minimum at $P=0.06$. It was considered that this value was such an outlier that we could safely conclude that this was a very "unlucky" run and that more could be learned by not considering it.

When minimising changes a modified search algorithm is used: events are considered in the order specified by the permutation. For each event an attempt is made to place the event in the primary suggested timeslot. If this fails (because some hard constraint would be broken by doing so) then the event is considered unplaced and the next event in the permutation is considered. When all events have been considered a further attempt is then made to place the unplaced events. First, the secondary suggested timeslot is tried, then the other timeslots according to the heuristic that examines the timeslots which do not incur a penalty first.

This type of search is designed to minimise the "domino" effect of changing an event's timeslot when conducting the search. The difference between this method and the standard method is that with this method all events get to try their primary suggested timeslot before any gets to try other timeslots. There is no chance that an event unable to use its slot will cause an avalanche of changes by "stealing" another event's timeslot.

Table 1. Comparisons of Methods to Minimise Change

% Change	Standard Search	Modified Search
Number of Changes is not a Problem Measure	54.5±1.8	48.3±1.1
Number of Changes is a Problem Measure	47.6±1.3	43.9±0.9

The following experiment was designed to test the modified search algorithm and the effect of treating changes to the reference as a problem measure. A real timetable data set was optimised to produce a reference timetable. The data set was then changed in a number of ways so that about 18% of the events could no longer be placed in the timeslots specified by the reference timetable. These events now had to find new slots and in doing so some would have to displace other events. The new data set was then optimised and changes to the reference were counted. The system was allowed to run until all the events had been placed. The results, over 50 runs, can be seen in Table 1. The figures are percentage change from the reference timetable and are given with 99% confidence intervals.

The results clearly show that each of the two methods gives an improvement, both individually and together. A Student's paired T-test shows an extremely high significance in the improvements (greater than 99.9999% for each comparison pair).

While the modified search keeps the number of changes to a reference timetable lower, it makes the algorithm less effective when it is not necessary to stay close to a reference. The *Progress Achieved Over Given Time* experiment produced a result of $P=0.2656±0.008$ for the modified search compared with $P=0.2359±0.0087$ for the standard search – clearly a worse result (99% confidence intervals). The *Time Taken for Given Progress* experiments produced a result of 646±550 seconds for the modified search compared with 248±23 for the standard search – over twice the average time for the same result and a much increased spread. This is partly surprising since reducing the "domino" effect of changes to the chromosome reduces epistasis. The reduction in performance may be due to the fact that since an unplaced event does not have the chance to "steal" another event's timeslot, the unplaced events tend to stay the same with each evaluation and the search is restricted to a smaller part of the search space. It may be possible to rectify this by increasing the amount of directed mutation. Further work is required to investigate this area.

6. Issues of Scale-Up

One of the crucial questions asked by researchers looking at search algorithms is "Will my algorithm scale up from test problems to large real world problems?". A solution that does not scale up to solve problems in the real world is of little practical use. Our experience has been that our algorithm has scaled up well from initial test data, to data for a whole department, and finally to data for a whole institution. However, the way the solution scales up is something that requires further investigation, in order that general rules can be learned.

Providing real data for scale-up experiments is difficult. The first problem is how to provide data sets of different sizes but similar nature. The second is how to measure the relative performance on data sets that have different ranges of problem measures. The extent to which the algorithm approaches the optimum might be an appropriate measure, but unfortunately, for real world data, the optimum is not known.

Table 2. Scale-Up Results

Number of Events	Elapsed Time (seconds)
74	47±5
155	270±109
307	591±205
587	926±149

The following experiment is not perfect but can give us at least an idea of how the algorithm scales up as the search space grows exponentially. A real data set was used and smaller subsets of this were produced. For each data set the room availability was adjusted so that 91% utilisation of rooms was required for each. Each of the data sets was given a target for each problem measure that was 80% of the approximated worst case value s. The time taken for all events to be placed and for P to reach 0.05 was then measured over 25 runs. The results and 95% confidence intervals are shown in Table 2 and Figure 4.

Because of the difficulty in constructing reliable experiments we are careful not to make strong claims about the results, but the results are very encouraging. Further experiments are required to confirm them. Some of the factors that may contribute to the favourable scale-up figures observed are discussed below:

Firstly, increasing the size of the problem increases the number of rooms available. The heuristic which initialises the ordering permutation ensures that difficult to place events are considered first, at least in the early stages of a run. This means that these events have a greater choice of accommodation in larger runs.

Secondly, timetabling problems partially partition into departments, programmes and levels. There is not a total partition since all partitions are connected by conflicting requirements for resources. However, the algorithm can still make good use of implicit parallelism to work on several partial partitions at once. In the test data (and most real world timetabling problems) larger problems have a larger number of partial partitions and so the degree of implicit parallelism employed increases as the problem grows.

Finally, Ross et al. have shown in [19] that phase transitions exist for evolutionary algorithms applied to timetabling problems. They showed that for some problems that were not completely partitioned, as the number of constraints increased the problem got harder to solve until a particular point when it started to get easier. This work is not completely relevant because it examined an evolutionary algorithm without local search and artificial rather than real data. It also examined increases in constraints rather than increases in events. It is possible however that phase transitions may be playing a part in the results observed. Further work is required in this area.

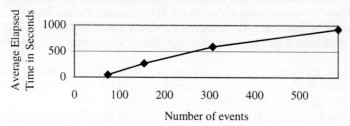

Fig. 4. Scale-Up Graph

7. Conclusions

We have described a new method for treating the optimisation of multi-objectives that fits with the way the user works, and we have described a user interface which facilitates it. We have shown that using back-up timeslots from the other parent can allow the search mechanism to repair "mistakes" made during recombination, and that this gives a significant improvement in results. We have defined two methods for dealing with optimisation relative to a reference timetable, and have shown that each of these gives a significant improvement. Finally we have shown that initial studies on the scalability of our approach to this problem are very encouraging.

References

1. Burke, E. K., Elliman D., and Weare, R., "A Genetic Algorithm for University Timetabling" AISB Workshop on Evolutionary Computing, Leeds, 1994.
2. Burke, E. K., Elliman, D. and Weare, R., "Specialised Recombinative Operators for Timetabling Problems", Proceedings of the AISB Workshop in Evolutionary Computing, Springer-Verlag Lecture Notes in Computer Science Series No 993, Heidleberg, 1995.
3. Burke, E. K., Newall, J. P. and Weare, R. F. "A Memetic Algorithm for University Exam Timetabling", Practice and Theory of Automated Timetabling, Burke and Ross Eds. Springer Verlag, 1996.

4. Caldeira, J. P., and Agostinho, C. R., "School Timetabling Using Genetic Search", Practice and Theory of Automated Timetabling, Toronto, 1997.
5. Carter, M. and Laporte, G. "Recent Developments in Practical Course Timetabling", Practice and Theory of Automated Timetabling, Toronto, 1997.
6. Colorni, A., Dorigo M., Maniezzo, V. "Genetic Algorithms and Highly Constrained Problems: The Time-Table Case". Parallel Problem Solving from Nature I, Goos and Hartmanis (eds.) Springer-Verlag, Heidelberg, 1990.
7. Corne, D., Ross, P. and Fang, H., "Fast Practical Evolutionary Timetabling" Proceedings of the AISB Workshop on Evolutionary Computing, Springer-Verlag Lecture Notes in Computer Science Series No. 865, Heidelberg, 1994.
8. Corne, D., and Ogden, Rev. J., "Evolutionary Optimisation of Methodist Preaching Timetables", Practice and Theory of Automated Timetabling, Toronto, 1997.
9. Eiben, A.E., Raue, P. E. and Ruttkay, Z. "Heuristic Genetic Algorithms for Constrained Problems". Working Papers for the Dutch AI Conference, Twente, 1993.
10. Mamede, N. and Renta, T, "Repairing University Timetables Using Genetic Algorithms and Simulated Annealing", Practice and Theory of Automated Timetabling, Toronto, 1997.
11. Paechter, B., Luchian, H., and Cumming, A., "An Evolutionary Approach to the General Timetable Problem", The Scientific Annals of the "Al. I. Cuza" University of Iasi, special issue for the ROSYCS symposium 1993.
12. Paechter B., Luchian H., Cumming A., and Petriuc M., "Two Solutions to the General Timetable Problem Using Evolutionary Methods", The Proceedings of the IEEE Conference of Evolutionary Computation, 1994.
13. Paechter, B., Cumming, A., Luchian, H., "The Use of Local Search Suggestion Lists for Improving the Solution of Timetable Problems with Evolutionary Algorithms.", Proceedings of the AISB Workshop in Evolutionary Computing, Springer-Verlag Lecture Notes in Computer Science Series No 993, Heidleberg, 1995.
14. Paechter, B., Cumming, A., Norman, M., and Luchian, H., "Extensions to a Memetic Timetabling System", Practice and Theory of Automated Timetabling, Burke and Ross Eds. Springer Verlag, 1996.
15. Paechter, B., Rankin, R. C. and Cumming A, "Improving a Lecture Timetabling System for University Wide Use", Practice and Theory of Automated Timetabling, Toronto, 1997.
16. Radcliffe, N. J. "Forma Analysis and Random Respectful Recombination" Proceedings of the Fourth International Conference on Genetic Algorithms", Morgan-Kaufmann, 1991.
17. Ross, P., Corne, D., and Fang, H., "Improving Evolutionary Timetabling with Delta Evaluation and Directed Mutation", Parallel Problem Solving from Nature III, Springer-Verlag, Heidelberg, 1994.
18. Ross, P. and Corne, D. "Comparing Genetic Algorithms, Simulated Annealing, and Stochastic Hillclimbing on Several Real Timetable Problems", Proceedings of the AISB Workshop in Evolutionary Computing, Springer-Verlag Lecture Notes in Computer Science Series No 993, Heidleberg, 1995.
19. Ross, P., Corne D. and Terashima H., "The Phase Transition Niche for Evolutionary Algorithms in Timetabling" Practice and Theory of Automated Timetabling, Burke and Ross Eds. Springer Verlag, 1996.

Genetic Algorithms for the Multiple Container Packing Problem

Günther R. Raidl, Gabriele Kodydek

Department of Computer Graphics
Vienna University of Technology
Karlsplatz 13/1861, 1040 Vienna, Austria
e-mail: {raidl,kodydek}@eiunix.tuwien.ac.at

Abstract. This paper presents two variants of Genetic Algorithms (GAs) for solving the Multiple Container Packing Problem (MCPP), which is a combinatorial optimization problem comprising similarities to the Knapsack Problem and the Bin Packing Problem. Two different representation schemes are suggested, namely direct encoding and order based encoding. While order based encoded solutions are always feasible, a repair algorithm is used in case of direct encoding to ensure feasibility. Additionally, local improvement operators have been applied to both GA variants. The proposed algorithms were empirically compared by using various sets of differently sized test data. Order based encoding performed better for problems with fewer items, whereas direct encoding exhibited advantages when dealing with larger problems. The local improvement operators lead in many cases not only to better final results but also to shorter running times because of higher convergence rates.

1 Introduction

The *Multiple Container Packing Problem* (MCPP) is a combinatorial optimization problem which involves finding the most remunerative assignment of n items with given weights and values to C containers such that each item is assigned to one container or remains unassigned, and the total weight of each container does not exceed a given maximum. This problem has applications in various fields as e.g. in air baggage handling and many other important sectors of a modern economy. In detail, it can be formulated as follows:

$$\text{maximize } f = \sum_{i=1}^{C}\sum_{j=1}^{n} v_j x_{i,j}, \tag{1}$$

$$\text{subject to } \sum_{i=1}^{C} x_{i,j} \le 1, \quad j = 1, \ldots, n, \tag{2}$$

$$\sum_{j=1}^{n} w_j x_{i,j} \le W_{\max}, \quad i = 1, \ldots, C, \tag{3}$$

$$x_{i,j} \in \{0,1\}, \quad i = 1, \ldots, C, \ j = 1, \ldots, n,$$

$$\text{with } w_j > 0, \ v_j > 0, \ W_{\max} > 0.$$

Let w_j be the weight and v_j be the value of item j. The variables searched for are $x_{i,j}$ ($i = 1, \ldots C$, $j = 1, \ldots, n$): If item j is assigned to container i, $x_{i,j}$ is set to 1, otherwise to 0. The goal is to maximize the total value of all assigned items (1). The n constraints in (2) ensure that each item is assigned to one container at maximum. According to (3), each of the C containers has a total maximum weight $W_{\max}$ which must not be exceeded by the sum of the weights of all items assigned to this container.

The next section gives a short survey of combinatorial problems related to the MCPP and of *Genetic Algorithms* (GAs) for solving them. In Sect. 3, two GA variants differing in their solution encoding techniques are presented, and specific local improvement operators are introduced. An empirical comparison of the new GAs using various test problem sets follows in Sect. 4. Finally, some conclusions are drawn in Sect. 5.

2 Related Problems

There are some other combinatorial optimization problems which are closely related to the MCPP. The well-known *Knapsack Problem* (KP) can be seen as the variant of the MCPP with only one container ($C = 1$): Which items should be selected for packing into a single knapsack to get the highest possible total value while not exceeding a given total weight? The KP is not strongly NP-hard [8], and efficient approximation algorithms have been developed for obtaining near optimal solutions, see e.g. [13]. The more general and strongly NP-hard *Multiconstrained Knapsack Problem* (MKP) involves more than one ($m > 1$) limited resources leading to m constraints. E.g. additionally to the weight, the volume might be a second constrained resource. Various exact algorithms and heuristics for the MKP can be found in [13]. A comprehensive review is given in [3, 5].

Another combinatorial optimization problem related to the MCPP is the *Bin Packing Problem* (BPP): In this problem, the goal is to minimize the number of containers necessary to pack all n items while not violating any weight constraint. The values of items do not play a role. Like the MKP, the BPP in its general form is NP-hard, see [6]. Note that the MCPP can also be seen as a complex combination of the KP and the BPP, since the MCPP can be divided into two strongly depending parts which must be solved simultaneously: (a) Select items for packing, and (b) distribute chosen items over the available containers.

One more related problem, which can be seen as a more general form of the BPP, is known under the term *General Assignment Problem* (GAP), see [3, 4]: A set of jobs ($\hat{=}$ items) must be assigned to a set of agents ($\hat{=}$ containers). Each possible assignment has its individual capacity requirements and costs, and each agent has its individual capacity limits. The goal is to distribute all jobs in a way to pay minimal costs while satisfying all constraints.

In the last years, Genetic Algorithms [1, 2, 7, 10, 14] have proven to be very well suited for finding nearly optimal solutions to difficult instances of the (M)KP, BPP, GAP, and similar combinatorial problems. Olsen presented in

[15] a GA for the KP using a bit string representation for solutions. Infeasible solutions containing constraint violations are penalized by adding a suitable term to the objective function. Difficulties lie in the selection of the penalty function and its coefficients to prevent premature convergence and infeasible final solutions. Olsen compared various penalty functions for such a GA. In a similar GA of Khuri et al. [12], a graded penalty term was used; only moderate results were reported on a small number of standard test problems. Rudolph and Sprave [17] presented a GA in which parent selection is restricted to happen between "neighboring" solutions. Infeasible solutions were penalized as in [12].

Another approach to handle infeasible solutions is to incorporate a repair algorithm which transforms each infeasible solution into a feasible one (see [10, 14] for a general introduction). In the (M)KP, this can be done by setting some genes to 0. Chu describes such a GA in his PhD thesis [3] and together with Beasley in [5]. This GA uses a heuristic algorithm based on the shadow prices of the LP-relaxed solution[1] for selecting the genes which are set to 0 in case of unsatisfied constraints. Additionally, the GA includes a local optimization operator for improving each newly generated solution by setting previously unset genes to 1 as long as no constraints are violated. Empirical comparisons of the GA to other approaches using various standard test problems are documented in [3, 5]. The results show that Chu's GA performs superior to the other methods concerning the quality of the final solutions. In [16], we presented another GA for the MKP also including a heuristic repair algorithm and local improvement. The starting population is generated by using a greedy heuristic, which speeds up the convergence to high quality solutions essentially. For the same test data, this improved GA finds much faster slightly better solutions than that of Chu.

A different technique for representing solutions of the (M)KP is to use an order based encoding scheme, which is well known from GAs for the *Traveling Salesman Problem* (TSP), see [14]. A first fit algorithm is used as a decoder to get the selected items. This approach guarantees that only feasible solutions are generated. Hinterding presented in [11] a GA with such a representation for the KP. He used *uniform order based crossover* (see [2, 10, 14]) as recombination operator and realized that disallowing duplicates in the population significantly improves results. Sun and Wang [18] proposed a very similar order based GA for the more general *0-1 integer programming problem* in which the weights w_j may also be negative. Owing to this property, a more complex decoding function is necessary to guarantee feasibility.

For the BPP, an efficient hybrid GA is presented in [6]. A GA for the GAP is discussed in [3, 4]. This approach uses a repair algorithm for improving infeasible solutions, but reaching feasibility cannot be guaranteed for all cases. Furthermore, a greedy heuristic is used to locally improve solutions by reassigning jobs to different agents involving lower costs. Regarding the quality of final solutions, the GA outperformed several other optimization techniques for most test problems.

---

[1] The solution of the *Linear Programming* relaxation of the original problem, where discrete parameters are substituted by continuous ones.

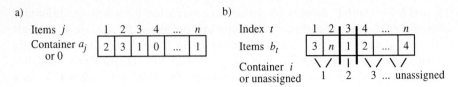

Fig. 1. (a) Direct encoding versus (b) order based encoding

3 GAs for the MCPP

Inspired by [3, 4, 5, 16], a steady-state GA with tournament selection and a replacement scheme which eliminates the worst solution or the last one generated in case of duplicates is used as a basis instead of the traditional generational GA.

According to the experiences from the previous GAs for the (M)KP, BPP, and GAP, two different solution encoding schemes seemed suitable for the MCPP: *Direct encoding* (DE), similar to [4, 5, 12, 15, 16, 17], and *order based encoding* (OBE), compare [11, 18]. These two techniques are described in detail in the following.

3.1 Direct Encoding

A solution is encoded as a vector **a** consisting of n genes a_j $(j = 1, \ldots, n)$. Each a_j represents the number i $(i = 1, \ldots, C)$ of the container to which item j is supposed to be assigned or the special value 0 if no assignment to any container should be done, see Fig. 1a.

With this representation it is easily possible that solutions are generated which violate constraints (2) concerning the maximum total weight $W_{\max}$ of containers. Results of the mentioned GAs for related problems suggest the usage of a repair mechanism within the chromosome decoding function rather than penalizing such infeasible solutions.

The algorithm for decoding and possibly repairing a chromosome **a** is shown in Fig. 2a. First, the current weights of all containers (vector **s**) are initialized with 0. Then, all items are processed in a random, always different order so that not the same items are favored every time. Each item j is checked if it fits into the container possibly specified in a_j, in which case the item is actually assigned and the current weight of the container s_{a_i} is increased accordingly. If adding item j would result in exceeding the total maximum weight $W_{\max}$, the value of the corresponding gene a_j is set to 0 meaning that the item is not assigned to any container.

Note that this encoding scheme allows the usage of the standard recombination and mutation operators as uniform crossover and flip mutation, which behaved best in performed experiments.

a)
```
procedure DecodeDE (a);
s ← 0;
for all items j in random order do
    if a_j ≠ 0 then
        if s_{a_j} + w_j ≤ W_max then
            s_{a_j} ← s_{a_j} + w_j;
            assign item j to container a_j;
        else
            a_j ← 0;
done;
```

b)
```
procedure ImproveDE (a);
for all unassigned items j
        in random order do
    for all containers i
            in random order do
        if s_i + w_j ≤ W_max then
            s_i ← s_i + w_j;
            a_j ← i;
            assign item j to container a_j;
            skip remaining containers;
done;
```

Fig. 2. Direct encoding: (a) chromosome decoding including repair mechanism and (b) heuristic improvement

a)
```
procedure DecodeOBE (b);
i ← 1; s ← 0; t ← 1;
while i ≤ C do
    if s_i + w_{b_t} ≤ W_max then
        s_i ← s_i + w_{b_t};
        assign item b_t to container i;
    else
        e_i ← t;
        i ← i + 1;
        if i ≤ C then
            s_i ← w_{b_t};
            assign item b_t to container i;
    t ← t + 1;
done;
```

b)
```
procedure ImproveOBE (b);
for t ← e_C to n do
    for all containers i
            in random order do
        if s_i + w_{b_t} ≤ W_max then
            s_i ← s_i + w_{b_t};
            j ← b_t;
            for k ← t - 1 downto e_i do
                b_{k+1} ← b_k;
            b_{e_i} ← j;
            for r ← i to C do
                e_r ← e_r + 1;
            assign item j to container i;
            skip remaining containers;
done;
```

Fig. 3. Order based encoding: (a) chromosome decoding and (b) local improvement

3.2 Order Based Encoding

A solution is represented by a permutation of all items $j = 1, \ldots, n$ stored in a chromosome $\mathbf{b} = (b_1, \ldots, b_n)$, see Fig. 1b. The first fit algorithm shown in Fig. 3a is used as a decoder to get the item/container assignments: All available containers i $(i = 1, \ldots, C)$ are consecutively filled with the items in the order given by permutation $\mathbf{b}$. If an item b_t does not fit into the current container i, the algorithm will proceed with the next container, and the index t of this first item not fitting into container i is stored in e_i for later usage during local improvement. If all containers are packed in this way, the remaining items are treated as unassigned. This method ensures that only feasible solutions are created, and no repair mechanism is necessary.

When using order based encoding, special recombination and mutation operators are needed to prevent solutions with duplicate or missing items. Various recombination methods known from the TSP such as order crossover, partially matched crossover, uniform order based crossover, and cycle crossover satisfy those requirements, see [14]. Preliminary experiments indicated a slightly better performance for the MCPP when order crossover was used. As mutation operator the exchange of two randomly chosen items performed better than insertion or inversion.

3.3 Local Improvement Algorithms

As already mentioned, many GAs benefit from the inclusion of local or heuristic improvement techniques applied to some or all newly generated solutions, see e.g. [3, 4, 5, 16]. Such a hybridization should therefore also be considered for the MCPP. The basic idea is to improve each newly generated solution by trying to assign its unassigned items to a container that has not reached its maximum total weight yet.

Figure 2b shows the algorithm when using direct encoding in detail: All previously unassigned items j ($a_j = 0$) are processed in random order, and each container is checked in random order if enough space is available to hold item j. In this case, the item is assigned to the found container and the algorithm proceeds with the next unassigned item.

When using order based encoding, the local improvement gets a little more complicated, see Fig. 3b: Again, the algorithm processes all unassigned items, now starting with the first one at position e_C in $\mathbf{b}$. Each container is checked in random order if there is enough space left for putting item b_t into it. In this case, the item is moved from its current position to position e_i and is now considered the last element of container i. For this purpose all items between these two positions need to be moved one gene up, and the container border indexes e_i to e_C must be incremented.

4 Implementation and Experimental Results

Miscellaneous randomly generated test data sets were used to practically examine a GA using direct encoding with and without local improvement (DEI, DE) and order based encoding with and without local improvement (OBEI, OBE). These four GA variants have been implemented on a Pentium-II PC (266 MHz) using Linux, the GNU C++ compiler and the publicly available Genetic Algorithms Library GAlib by M. Wall [19].

Various characteristics and parameters of the steady-state GA, which were determined by preliminary experiments and found to be robust and well suited for the MCPP in general, are summarized in Table 1. It is essential that duplicate solutions are disallowed in the population (by using the replacement scheme already described in Sect. 3) because otherwise the GA converges too fast to only poor solutions. For the KP a similiar behavior has already been observed by

Table 1. Characteristics of the GA with the two solution encoding variants

GA:	steady state, no duplicate solutions
Goal:	maximize total value of assigned items (f)
Selection:	tournament ($k = 2$)
Recombination:	DE: uniform crossover ($p_c = 0.5$), OBE: order crossover ($p_c = 0.5$)
Mutation:	DE: flip mutation ($p_m = 1/n$), OBE: swap mutation ($p_m = 1/n$)
Population size:	100
Termination:	200,000 solutions evaluated without finding a new best solution

Table 2. Gaps of best-of-run solutions with needed numbers of evaluations *evals* and CPU-times t for problems with different numbers of containers C and fixed total container weights $W_{\max} = 100$ (average values from 10 runs/problem)

$W_{\max} = 100$	$n = 30$				$n = 50$				$n = 200$			
	C	%-gap	evals	t[sec]	C	%-gap	evals	t[sec]	C	%-gap	evals	t[sec]
DE	3	2.74	11140	0.9	5	2.60	270720	37.7	20	1.91	377300	162.9
	6	2.69	139260	12.0	10	1.43	379180	53.2	40	1.94	675140	295.2
	9	3.31	98860	9.2	15	2.53	162220	23.7	60	1.99	730200	322.7
	12	2.48	92640	8.2	20	2.58	244820	36.3	80	2.89	644500	295.6
DEI	3	2.74	5620	0.5	5	2.58	119620	17.4	20	1.65	711080	336.0
	6	2.45	38900	3.5	10	1.10	408280	62.2	40	1.64	755220	356.5
	9	3.01	19260	1.8	15	1.99	262800	42.5	60	1.48	935840	452.4
	12	1.58	81680	8.0	20	1.50	305340	48.7	80	2.09	823100	401.5
OBE	3	3.16	61200	4.9	5	2.96	194300	25.6	20	2.84	706000	383.9
	6	2.82	183560	13.1	10	1.73	352680	44.9	40	2.52	1371840	723.9
	9	3.25	140780	9.8	15	2.35	397320	48.8	60	2.10	1431300	698.8
	12	1.42	167120	12.4	20	2.03	358880	43.7	80	2.36	1431560	621.4
OBEI	3	2.74	78400	9.0	5	2.28	193980	37.1	20	2.57	717940	713.9
	6	2.32	72000	7.4	10	1.58	299900	52.4	40	2.49	778920	860.9
	9	2.90	32520	3.2	15	2.00	231300	39.0	60	2.28	1262140	1274.7
	12	1.05	184500	15.9	20	1.67	231660	33.4	80	2.62	1009600	833.5

Hinterding [11]. Note that each GA run was terminated when no improvements were encountered within the last 200,000 evaluations. This condition ensures that the GA has enough time to converge. In general, we were primarily interested in finding high-quality solutions and only secondary in the needed CPU-time.

Test problems were generated in three different sizes, namely with n=30, 50, and 200 items. Item weights w_j were randomly chosen out of the interval $[5, 95]$ giving an average item weight of $\overline{w} = 50$. The item values v_j were generated by multiplying the weight w_j of each item by a relative item value randomly taken from $[0.8, 1.2]$. In a first set of test problems, the total container weight $W_{\max}$ was set to 100 allowing two items of average weight to be packed in a single

Table 3. Gaps of best-of-run solutions with needed numbers of evaluations *evals* and CPU-times t for problems with different total container weights W_{max} and fixed numbers of containers C (average values from 10 runs/problem)

	W_{max}	$n = 30, C = 3$			$n = 50, C = 5$			$n = 200, C = 20$		
		%-gap	*evals*	*t*[sec]	*%-gap*	*evals*	*t*[sec]	*%-gap*	*evals*	*t*[sec]
DE	100	2.74	11140	0.9	2.60	270720	37.7	1.91	377300	162.9
	200	0.68	80180	6.8	0.42	573420	80.7	0.71	1045960	455.3
	300	0.50	64400	5.5	0.51	454560	64.4	0.45	933200	407.1
	400	0.39	208120	17.7	0.40	240400	34.2	0.32	1105640	484.7
DEI	100	2.74	5620	0.5	2.58	119620	17.4	1.65	711080	336.0
	200	0.66	33360	3.0	0.35	331180	49.2	0.51	760720	371.8
	300	0.47	17040	1.5	0.30	230960	35.2	0.27	1021280	474.6
	400	0.37	160660	14.7	0.39	315820	47.8	0.25	1028240	476.7
OBE	100	3.16	61200	4.9	2.96	194300	25.6	2.84	706000	383.9
	200	0.96	129980	9.8	0.88	368880	47.5	1.26	742280	408.9
	300	0.53	84100	6.0	0.48	434700	54.0	0.76	773060	393.1
	400	0.45	99400	7.2	0.53	286480	35.5	0.41	744180	314.6
OBEI	100	2.74	78400	9.0	2.28	193980	37.1	2.57	717940	713.9
	200	0.68	113240	11.7	0.60	299620	48.3	2.49	558300	462.7
	300	0.44	131040	12.0	0.70	243020	37.8	1.64	514560	341.7
	400	0.33	199720	16.7	0.53	505960	70.2	0.64	565960	291.3

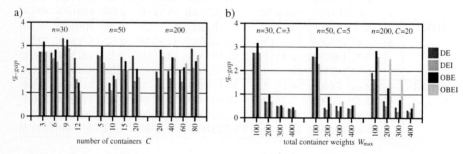

Fig. 4. Average gaps for problems with (a) varying number of containers C and (b) varying total container weights W_{max}

container, and the number of containers C was varied in a way that roughly 20, 40, 60, and 80 percent of the n items could be packed in total: $n = 30$: $C \in \{3, 6, 9, 12\}$, $n = 50$: $C \in \{5, 10, 15, 20\}$, $n = 200$: $C \in \{20, 40, 60, 80\}$. This test series includes therefore 12 problems, and the four GA variants were run 10 times for each problem.

Since the optimal solution values for most of these problems are not known, the quality of a final solution is measured by the percentage gap of the GA's solution value f with respect to the optimal value of the LP-relaxed problem

$f_{\max}^{\mathrm{LP}}$. This upper bound can easily be determined for any MCPP by sorting all items according to their relative values v_j/w_j and summing up the item values v_j starting with the best item until a total weight of $CW_{\max}$ is reached. The last item is counted proportionately. Knowing the LP optimum, the gap is determined by $\%\text{-}gap = 100(f - f_{\max}^{\mathrm{LP}})/f_{\max}^{\mathrm{LP}}$. Table 2 shows average results derived from 10 runs per problem instance. Beside the gaps of the best-of-run solutions, the numbers of evaluated solutions *evals* and CPU-times t in seconds until these best-of-run solutions were found are presented. The average gaps are also depicted in Fig. 4a.

In a second test series the number of containers was fixed ($n = 30$: $C = 3$, $n = 50$: $C = 5$, $n = 200$: $C = 20$), and the total container weight $W_{\max}$ was varied from 100 to 400 in steps of 100. Table 3 and Fig. 4b show average results for these 12 problem instances.

In general, direct encoding did always benefit from local improvement, order based encoding in case of small or medium sized problems. Clearly, local improvement increases the CPU-time needed for a single evaluation. Nevertheless entire runs using DEI and OBEI were most of the time only slightly slower and sometimes even faster than runs with DE and OBE because the locally improved GAs usually needed fewer evaluations to converge.

For small-sized problems ($n = 30$), OBEI lead nearly always to the smallest gaps (best results), while OBE gave the worst final solutions. For large-scale problems ($n = 200$), the results are surprisingly different: Generally, the direct encoding GA variants were better than the order based ones. Especially DEI outperformed all other approaches by far. The results of OBEI are in this case often even worse than those of OBE. Furthermore, the execution times were significantly higher for OBEI and OBE (except for the problems with larger $W_{\max}$).

A reason for the different behaviors of the two encoding schemes seems to be that the order based approach with its order crossover is more disruptive and introduces therefore more diversity into the population. Smaller problems with fewer items benefit from this property because the GA can easier escape from local optima. For larger problems this property turns into a disadvantage because the GA converges slower.

5 Conclusions

Two GA variants using different encoding schemes and recombination and mutation operators were introduced for the MCPP. While infeasible solutions never appear in OBE(I), a repair algorithm has been incorporated into the decoding function of DE(I). Both encoding approaches performed generally well, but the order based method, which seems to be more disruptive, exhibited advantages for problems with fewer items. Direct encoding performed better for larger problems. The introduction of the local improvement operators lead in many cases not only to better results, but also to shorter total running times because of higher convergence rates.

References

1. Bäck T.: Evolutionary Algorithms in Theory and Practice, Oxford University Press, New York (1996)
2. Bäck T., Fogel D. B., Michalewicz Z.: Handbook of Evolutionary Computation, Oxford University Press (1997)
3. Chu P. C.: A Genetic Algorithm Approach for Combinatorial Optimization Problems, Ph.D. thesis at The Management School, Imperial College of Science, London (1997)
4. Chu P. C., Beasley J. E.: A Genetic Algorithm for the Generalized Assignment Problem, Computers & Operations Research **24**(1) (1997) 17–23
5. Chu P. C., Beasley J. E.: A Genetic Algorithm for the Multidimensional Knapsack Problem, working paper at The Management School, Imperial College of Science, London (1997)
6. Falkenauer E.: A Hybrid Grouping Genetic Algorithm for Bin Packing, working paper at CRIF Industrial Management and Automation, CP 106-P4, 50 av. F. D. Roosevelt, Brussels, Belgium (1994)
7. Fogel D. B.: Evolutionary Computation – Toward a New Philosophy of Machine Intelligence, IEEE Press, Piscataway, NJ (1995)
8. Garey M. D., Johnson D. S.: Computers and Intractability: A Guide to the Theory of NP-Completeness, Freeman, San Francisco (1979)
9. Gavish B., Pirkul H.: Efficient Algorithms for Solving Multiconstraint Zero-One Knapsack Problems to Optimality, Mathematical Programming **31** (1985) 78–105
10. Goldberg D. E.: Genetic Algorithms in Search, Optimization and Machine Learning, Addison–Wesley (1989)
11. Hinterding R.: Mapping, Order-independent Genes and the Knapsack Problem, in Proc. of the 1st IEEE Int. Conference on Evolutionary Computation 1994, Orlando, FL (1994) 13–17
12. Khuri S., Bäck T., Heitkötter J.: The Zero/One Multiple Knapsack Problem and Genetic Algorithms, in Proc. of the 1994 ACM Symposium on Applied Computing, ACM Press (1994) 188–193
13. Martello S., Toth P.: Knapsack Problems: Algorithms and Computer Implementations, J. Wiley & Sons (1990)
14. Michalewicz Z.: Genetic Algorithms + Data Structures = Evolution Programs, Springer, Berlin (1992)
15. Olsen A. L.: Penalty Functions and the Knapsack Problem, in Proc. of the 1st International Conference on Evolutionary Computation 1994, Orlando, FL (1994) 559–564
16. Raidl G. R.: An Improved Genetic Algorithm for the Multiconstrained 0–1 Knapsack Problem, in Proc. of the 1998 IEEE International Conference on Evolutionary Computation, Anchorage, Alaska (1998) (to appear)
17. Rudolph G., Sprave J.: Significance of Locality and Selection Pressure in the Grand Deluge Evolutionary Algorithm, in Proc. of the International Conference on Parallel Problem Solving from Nature IV (1996) 686–694
18. Sun Y., Wang Z.: The Genetic Algorithm for 0–1 Programming with Linear Constraints, in Proc. of the 1st ICEC'94, Orlando, FL (1994) 559–564
19. Wall M.: GAlib – A C++ Genetic Algorithms Library, Version 2.4, Massachusetts Institute of Technology, http://lancet.mit.edu/ga (1996)

Buffer Memory Optimization in DSP Applications: An Evolutionary Approach

Jürgen Teich and Eckart Zitzler[1] and Shuvra Bhattacharyya[2]

[1] Institute TIK, Swiss Federal Institute of Technology,
CH-8092 Zurich, Switzerland
[2] EE Dept. and UMIACS, University of Maryland,
College Park MD 20742, U.S.A.

Abstract. In the context of digital signal processing, synchronous data flow (SDF) graphs [12] are widely used for specification. For these, so called single appearance schedules provide program memory-optimal uniprocessor implementations. Here, buffer memory minimized schedules are explored among these using an *Evolutionary Algorithm* (EA). Whereas for a restricted class of graphs, there exist optimal polynomial algorithms, these are not exact and may provide poor results when applied to arbitrary, i.e., randomly generated graphs. We show that a careful EA implementation may outperform these algorithms by sometimes orders of magnitude.

1 Introduction

Dataflow specifications are widespread in areas of digital signal and image processing. In dataflow, a specification consists of a directed graph in which the nodes represent computations and the arcs specify the flow of data. Synchronous dataflow [12] is a restricted form of dataflow in which the nodes, called *actors* have a simple firing rule: The number of data values (*tokens, samples*) produced and consumed by each actor is fixed and known at compile-time.

The SDF model is used in many industrial DSP design tools, e.g., SPW by Cadence, COSSAP by Synopsys, as well as in research-oriented environments, e.g., [3, 11, 14]. Typically, code is generated from a given schedule by instantiating inline actor code in the final program. Hence, the size of the required program memory depends on the number of times an actor appears in a schedule, and so called *single appearance schedules*, where each actor appears only once in a schedule, are evidently program memory optimal. Results on the existence of such schedules have been published for general SDF graphs [1].

In this paper, we treat the problem of exploring single appearance schedules that minimize the amount of required buffer memory for the class of acyclic SDF graphs. Such a methodology may be considered as part of a general framework that considers general SDF graphs and generates schedules for acyclic subgraphs using our approach [2].

1.1 Motivation

Given is an acyclic SDF graph in the following. The number of single appearance schedules that must be investigated is at least equal to (and often much greater than) the number of topological sorts of actors in the graph. This number is not polynomially bounded; e.g., a complete bipartite graph with $2n$ nodes has $(n!)^2$ possible topological sorts. This complexity prevents techniques based on enumeration from being applied sucessfully. In [2], a heuristic called APGAN (for algorithm for pairwise grouping of adjacent nodes (acyclic version)) has been developed that constructs a schedule with the objective to minimize buffer memory. This procedure of low polynomial time complexity has been shown to give optimal results for a certain class of graphs having a regular structure. Also, a complementary procedure called RPMC (for recursive partitioning by minimum cuts) has been proposed that works well on more irregular (e.g., randomly generated) graph structures. Experiments show that, although being computationally efficient, these heuristics sometimes produce results that are far from optimal. Even simple test cases may be constructed where the performance (buffer cost) obtained by applying these heuristics differs from the global minimum by more than 2000%, see Example 1.

Example 1. We consider two test graphs and compare different buffer optimization algorithms (see Table 1). The 1st graph with 10 nodes is shown in Fig. 1b). For this simple graph, already 362 880 different topological sorts (actor firing orders) may be constructed with buffer requirements ranging between 3003 and 15 705 memory units. The 2nd graph is randomly generated with 50 nodes. The 1st method in Table 1 uses an Evolutionary Algorithm (EA) that performs 3000 fitness calculations, the 2nd is the APGAN heuristic, the 3rd is a *Monte Carlo* simulation (3000 random tries), and the 4th an exhaustive search procedure which did not terminate in the second case.

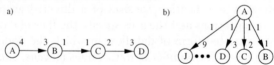

Fig. 1. Simple SDF graphs.

The motivation of the following work was to develop a methodology that is

method	Graph 1 best cost (units)	Graph 1 runtime (s)	Graph 2 best cost (units)	Graph 2 runtime (s)
EA	3003	4.57	669 380	527.87
APGAN	3015	0.02	15 063 956	1.88
RPMC	3151	0.03	1 378 112	2.03
Monte Carlo	3014	3.3	2 600 349	340.66
Exhaust. Search	3003	373	?	?

Table 1. Analysis of existing heuristics on simple test graphs. The run-times were measured on a SUN SPARC 20.

- *Cost-competitive:* the optimization procedure should provide solutions with equal or lower buffering costs as the heuristics APGAN and RPMC in most investigated test cases.
- *Run-time tolerable:* in embedded DSP applications, compilers are allowed to spend more time for optimization of code as in general-purpose compilers, because code-optimality is critical [13].

1.2 Proposed Approach

Here, we use a unique two-step approach to find buffer-minimal schedules:
(1) An Evolutionary Algorithm (EA) is used to efficiently explore the space of topological sorts of actors given an SDF graph using a population of N individuals each of which encodes a topological sort.
(2) For each topological sort, a buffer optimal schedule is constructed based on a well-known dynamic programming post optimization step [2] that determines a loop nest by parenthesization (see Fig. 2) that is buffer cost optimal (for the given topological order of actors). The run-time of this optimization step is $\mathcal{O}(N^3)$. The overall picture of the scheduling framework is depicted in Fig. 2.

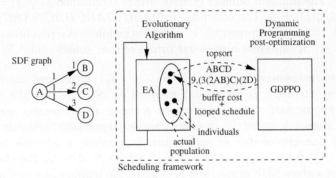

Fig. 2. Overview of the scheduling framework using Evolutionary Algorithms and Dynamic Programming (GDPPO: generalized dynamic programming post optimization for optimally parenthesizing actor orderings [2]) for constructing buffer memory optimal schedules.

Details on the optimization procedure and the cost function will be explained in the following. The total run-time of the algorithm is $\mathcal{O}(Z\,N^3)$ where Z is the number of evocations of the dynamic program post-optimizer.

2 An Evolutionary Approach for Memory Optimization

2.1 The SDF-scheduling framework

Definition 1 SDF graph. An SDF graph [12] G denotes a 5-tuple $G = (V, A, produced, consumed, delay)$ where
- V is the set of nodes (*actors*) ($V = \{v_1, v_2, \cdots, v_K\}$).
- A is the set of directed arcs. With $source(\alpha)$ ($sink(\alpha)$), we denote the source node (target node) of an arc $\alpha \in A$.

888

- *produced* : $A \to \mathbf{N}$ denotes a function that assigns to each directed arc $\alpha \in A$ the number of produced tokens *produced*(α) per invocation of actor *source*(α).
- *consumed* : $A \to \mathbf{N}$ denotes a function that assigns to each directed arc $\alpha \in A$ the number of consumed tokens per invocation of actor *sink*(α).
- *delay* : $A \to \mathbf{N}_0$ denotes the function that assigns to each arc $\alpha \in A$ the number of initial tokens *delay*(α).

A *schedule* is a sequence of actor firings. A properly-constructed SDF graph is compiled by first constructing a finite schedule S that fires each actor at least once, does not deadlock, and produces no net change in the number of tokens queues associated with each arc. When such a schedule is repeated infinitely, we call the resulting infinite sequence of actor firings a *valid periodic schedule*, or simply *valid schedule*. Graphs with this property are called *consistent*. For such a graph, the minimum number of times each actor must execute may be computed efficiently [12] and captured by a function $q : V \to \mathbf{N}$.

Example 2. Figure 1a) shows an SDF graph with nodes labeled A, B, C, D, respectively. The minimal number of actor firings is obtained as $q(A) = 9$, $q(B) = 9$, $q(C) = 12$, $q(D) = 8$. The schedule $(\infty(2ABC)DABCDBC(2ABCD)A(2BC)$ $(2ABC)A(2BCD))$ represents a valid schedule. A parenthesized term $(n\ S_1\ S_2\ \cdots, S_k)$ specifies n sucessive firings of the "subschedule" $S_1\ S_2\ \cdots\ S_k$.

Each parenthesized term $(n\ S_1\ S_2\ \cdots\ S_k)$ is referred to as *schedule loop* having *iteration count* n and *iterands* $S_1, S_2,\ \cdots, S_k$. We say that a schedule for an SDF graph is a *looped schedule* if it contains zero or more schedule loops. A schedule is called *single appearance schedule* if it contains only one appearance of each actor. In general, a schedule of the form $(\infty\ (q(N_1)N_1)\ (q(N_2)N_2)\ \cdots\ (q(N_K)N_K))$ where N_i denotes the (label of the) ith node of a given SDF graph, and K denotes the number of nodes of the given graph, is called *flat single appearance schedule*.

2.2 Code generation and buffer cost model
Given an SDF graph, we consider code generation by inlining an actor code block for each actor appearance in the schedule. The resulting sequence of code blocks is encapsulated within an infinite loop to generate a software implementation. Each schedule loop thereby is translated into a loop in the target code.

The memory requirement is determined by the cost function

$$buffer\_memory(S) = \sum_{\alpha \in A} max\_tokens(\alpha, S), \qquad (1)$$

where $max\_tokens(\alpha, S)$ denotes the maximum number of tokens that accumulate on arc α during the execution of schedule S.[3]

---
[3] Note that this model of buffering – maintaining a separate memory buffer for each data flow edge – is convenient and natural for code generation. More technical advantages of this model are elaborated in [2].

Example 3. Consider the flat schedule $(\infty(9A)(12B)(12C)(8D))$ for the graph in Fig. 1a). This schedule has a buffer memory requirement of $36 + 12 + 24 = 72$. Similarly, the buffer memory requirement of the schedule $(\infty(3(3A)(4B))(4(3C)(2D)))$ is $12 + 12 + 6 = 30$.

2.3 Related Work

The interacion between instruction scheduling and register allocation in procedural language compilers has been studied extensively [9], and optimal management of this interaction has been shown to be intractable [8]. More recently, the issue of optimal storage allocation has been examined in the context of high-level synthesis for iterative DSP programs [5], and code generation for embedded processors that have highly irregular instruction formats and register sets [13, 10]. These efforts do not address the challenges of keeping code size costs manageable in general SDF graphs, in which actor production and consumption parameters may be arbitrary. Fabri [6] and others have examined the problem of managing pools of logical buffers that have varying sizes, given a set of buffer lifetimes, but such efforts are also in isolation of the scheduling problems that we face in the context of general SDF graphs.

From Example 1, it became clear that there exist simple graphs for which there is a big gap between the quality of solution obtained using heuristics such as APGAN and an Evolutionary Algorithm (EA). If the run-time of such an iterative approach is still affordable, a performance gap of several orders of magnitude may be avoided.

Exploration of topological sorts using the EA Given an acyclic SDF graph, one major difficulty consists in finding a coding of feasible topological sorts. Details on the coding scheme are given in the next section that deals with all implementation issues of the evolutionary search procedure.

Dynamic programming post optimization In [2], it has been shown that given a topological sort of actors of a consistent, delayless and acyclic SDF graph G, a single-appearance schedule can be computed that minimizes buffer memory over all single-appearance schedules for G that have the given lexical ordering. Such a minimum buffer memory schedule can be computed using a dynamic programming technique called GDPPO.

Example 4. Consider again the SDF graph in Fig. 1a). With $q(A) = 9$, $q(B) = q(C) = 12$, and $q(D) = 8$, an optimal schedule is $(\infty(3(3A)(4B))(4(3C)(2D)))$ with a buffer cost of 30. Given the topological order of nodes A, B, C, D as imposed by the arcs of G, this schedule is obtained by parenthesization of the string. Note that this optimal schedule contains a break in the chain at some actor k, $1 \leq k \leq K - 1$. Because the parenthesization is optimal, the chains to the left of k and to the right of k must also be parenthesized optimally. This structure of the optimization problem is essential for dynamic programming.

3 Parameterization of the Evolutionary Algorithm

The initial population of individuals, the *phenotype* of which represents a topological sort, is randomly generated. Then, the population iteratively undergoes fitness evaluation (Eq. 1), *selection*, *recombination*, and *mutation*.

3.1 Coding and Repair Mechanism

The optimization problem suggests to use an order-based representation. Each individual encodes a permutation over the set of nodes. As only topological sorts represent legal schedules, a simple repair mechanism transforms a permutation into a topological sort as follows: Iteratively, a node with an indegree equal to zero is chosen and removed from the graph (together with the incident edges). The order in which the nodes appear determines the topological sort. The tie between several nodes with no ingoing edges is normally broken by random. Our algorithm, however, always selects the node at the leftmost position within the permutation. This ensures on the one hand, that each individual is mapped unambiguously to one topological sort, and, on the other hand, that every topological sort has at least one encoding.

Example 5. Recall the SDF graph depicted in Figure 1b), and suppose, the repair algorithm is working on the permutation BCDEFAGHIJ. Since the node A has no ingoing edges but is predecessor of all other nodes, it has to be placed first in any topological sort. The order of the remaining nodes is unchanged. Therefore, the resulting topological sort after the repair procedure is ABCDEFGHIJ.

3.2 Genetic Operators

The selection scheme chosen is *tournament selection*. Additionally, an *elitist strategy* has been implemented: the best individual per generation is preserved by simply copying it to the population of the next generation. Since individuals encode permutations, we applied uniform order-based crossover [4][7], which preserves the permutation property. Mutation is done by permuting the elements between two selected positions, whereas both the positions and the subpermutation are chosen by random (*scramble sublist mutation* [4]).

3.3 Crossover Probability and Mutation Probability

We tested several different combinations of crossover probability p_c and mutation probability p_m on a few random graphs containing 50 nodes.[4]

Based on experimental results, we have chosen a population size of 30 individuals. The crossover rates we tested are 0, 0.2, 0.4, 0.6, and 0.8, while the mutation rates cover the range from 0 to 0.4 by a step size of 0.1. Altogether, the EA ran with 24 various p_c-p_m-settings on every test graph. It stopped after 3000 fitness evaluations. For each combination we took the average fitness (buffer cost) over ten independent runs. Exemplary, the results for a particular graph are visualized by the 3D plot in Figure 3; the results for the other random test graphs look similar.

Obviously, mutation is essential to this problem. Setting p_m to 0 leads to the worst results of all probabilty combinations. If p_m is greater than 0, the obtained average buffer costs are significantly smaller—almost independently of the choice of p_c. As can be seen in Figure 4 this is due to premature convergence. The curve

---

[4] Graphs consisting of less nodes are not very well suited to obtain reliable values for p_c and p_m, because the optimum is yet reached after a few generations, in most cases.

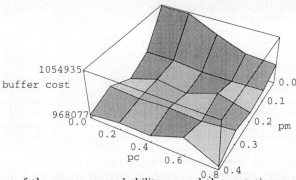

Fig. 3. Influence of the crossover probability p_c and the mutation probability p_m on the average fitness for a particular test graph (3000 fitness evaluations).

representing the performance for $p_c = 0.2$ and $p_m = 0$ goes horizontally after about 100 fitness evaluations. No new points in the search space are explored. As a consequence, the Monte Carlo optimization method, that simply generates random points in the search space and memorizes the best solution, might be a better approach to this problem. We investigate this issue in the next section.

On the other hand, the impact of the crossover operator on the overall performance is not as great as that of the mutation operator. With no mutation at all, increasing p_c yields decreased average buffer cost. But this is not the same to cases where $p_m > 0$. The curve for $p_c = 0.6$ and $p_m = 0.2$ in Figure 4 bears out this observation. Beyond it, for this particular test graph a mutation probability of $p_m = 0.2$ and a crossover probability of $p_c = 0$ leads to best performance. This might be interpreted as hint that *Hill Climbing* is also suitable in this domain. The Hill Climbing approach generates new points in the search space by applying a neighborhood function to the best point found so far. Therefore, we also compared the Evolutionary Algorithm to Hill Climbing.

Nevertheless, with respect to the results on other test graphs, we found a crossover rate of $p_c = 0.2$ and a mutation rate of $p_m = 0.4$ to be most appropriate for this problem.

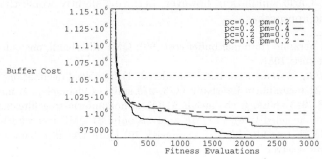

Fig. 4. Performance of the Evolutionary Algorithm according to four different p_c-p_m-combinations; each graph represents the average of ten runs.

System	BMLB	APGAN	RPMC	MC	HC	EA	EA + APGAN
1	47	47	52	47	47	47	47
2	95	99	99	99	99	99	99
3	85	137	128	143	126	126	126
4	224	756	589	807	570	570	570
5	154	160	171	165	160	160	159
6	102	108	110	110	108	108	108
7	35	35	35	35	35	35	35
8	46	46	55	46	47	46	46
9	78	78	87	78	80	80	78
10	166	166	200	188	190	197	166
11	1540	1542	2480	1542	1542	1542	1542

Table 2. Comparison of performance on practical examples; the probabilistic algorithms stopped after 3000 fitness evaluations. BMLB stands for a lower buffer limit: buffer memory lower bound.[6]

4 Experiments

To evaluate the performance of the Evolutionary Algorithm we tested it on several practical examples of acyclic, multirate SDF graphs as well as on 200 acyclic random graphs, each containing 50 nodes and having 100 edges in average. The obtained results were compaired against the outcomes produced by APGAN, RPMC, Monte Carlo (MC), and Hill Climbing (HC). We also tried a slightly modified version of the Evolutionary Algorithm which first runs APGAN and then inserts the computed topological sort into the initial population.

Table 2 shows the results of applying GDPPO to the schedules generated by the various heuristics on several practical SDF graphs; the satellite receiver example is taken from [15], whereas the other examples are the same as considered in [2]. The probabilistic algorithms ran once on each graph and were aborted after 3000 fitness evaluations. Additionally, an exhaustive search with a maximum run-time of 1 hour was carried out; as it only completed in two cases[5], the search spaces of these problems seem to be rather complex.

In all of the practical benchmark examples that make up Table 2 the results achieved by the Evolutionary Algorithm equal or surpass the ones generated by RPMC. Compared to APGAN on these practical examples, the Evolutionary Algorithm is neither inferior nor superior; it shows both better and worse performance in two cases each. Furthermore, the performance of the Hill Climbing approach is almost identical to performance of the Evolutionary Algorithm. The Monte Carlo simulation, however, performs slightly worse than the other probabilistic approaches.

---

[5] Laplacian pyramid (minimal buffer cost: 99); QMF filterbank, one-sided tree (minimal buffer cost: 108).

[6] The following systems have been considered: 1) fractional decimation; 2) Laplacian pyramid; 3) nonuniform filterbank (1/3, 2/3 splits, 4 channels); 4) nuniform filterbank (1/3, 2/3 splits, 6 channels); 5) QMF nonuniform-tree filterbank; 6) QMF filterbank (one-sided tree); 7) QMF analysis only; 8) QMF tree filterbank (4 channels); 9) QMF tree filterbank (8 channels); 10) QMF tree filterbank (16 channels); 11) satellite receiver.

<	APGAN	RPMC	MC	HC	EA	EA + APGAN
APGAN	0%	34.5%	15%	0%	1%	0%
RPMC	65.5%	0%	29.5%	3.5%	4.5%	2.5%
MC	85%	70.5%	0%	0.5%	0.5%	1%
HC	100%	96.5%	99.5%	0%	70%	57%
EA	99%	95.5%	99.5%	22%	0%	39%
EA + APGAN	100%	97.5%	99%	32.5%	53.5%	0%

Table 3. Comparison of performance on 200 50-actor SDF graphs (3000 fitness evaluations); for each row the numbers represent the fraction of random graphs on which the correspondig heuristic outperforms the other approaches.

Although the results are nearly the same when considering only 1500 fitness evaluations, the Evolutionary Algorithm (as well as Monte Carlo and Hill Climbing) cannot compete with APGAN or RPMC concerning run-time performance. E.g., APGAN needs less than 2.3 second for all graphs on a SUN SPARC 20, while the run-time of the Evolutionary Algorithm varies from 0.1 seconds up to 5 minutes (3000 fitness evaluations).

The results concerning the random graphs are summarized in Table 3; again, the stochastic approaches were aborted after 3000 fitness evaluations.[7] Interestingly, for these graphs APGAN only in 15% of all cases is better than Monte Carlo and only on in two cases better than the Evolutionary Algorithm. On the other hand, it is outperformed by the Evolutionary Algorithm 99% of the time.[8] This is almost identical to the comparison between Hill Climbing and APGAN. As RPMC is known to be better suited for irregular graphs than APGAN [2], its better performance (65.5%) is not surprising when directly compared to APGAN. Although, it is beaten by the Evolutionary Algorithm as well as Hill Climbing in 95.5% and 96.5% of the time, respectively.

The obtained results are very promising, but have to be considered in association with their quality, i.e., the magnitude of the buffer costs achieved. In [16], this issue is investigated in detail. In average the buffer costs achieved by the Evolutionary Algorithm are half the costs computed by APGAN and only a fraction of 63% of the RPMC outcomes. Moreover, an improvement by a factor 28 can be observed on a particular random graph with respect to APGAN (factor 10 regarding RPMC). Compared to Monte Carlo, it is the same, although the margin is smaller (in average the results of the Evolutionary Algorithm are a fraction of 0.84% of the costs achieved by the Monte Carlo simulation). Hill Climbing, however, might be an alternative to the evolutionary approach; the results shown in Table 3 might suggest a superiority of Hill Climbing, but regarding the absolute buffer costs this hypothesis could not be confirmed (the costs achieved by the Evolutionary Algorithm deviate from the costs produced by Hill Climbing by a factor of 0.19% in average).

---

[7] The Evolutionary Algorithm ran about 9 minutes on each graph, the time for running APGAN was constantly less than 3 seconds.

[8] Considering 1500 fitness calculations, this percentage decreases only minimally to 97.5%.

5 Conclusions

In summary, it may be said that the Evolutionary Algorithm is superior to both APGAN and RMPC on random graphs. However, both might also be randomized, and thus provide other candidates for comparison, a topic of future research. A comparison with simulated annealing might also be interesting. However, this general optimization method offers many implementation trade-offs such that a qualitative comparison is not possible except under many restricted assumptions.

References

1. S. Bhattacharyya. Compiling data flow programs for digital signal processing. Technical Report UCB/ERL M94/52, Electronics Research Laboratory, UC Berkeley, July 1994.
2. S. S. Bhattacharyya, P. K. Murthy, and E. A. Lee. *Software Synthesis from Dataflow Graphs.* Kluwer Academic Publishers, Norwell, MA, 1996.
3. J. Buck, S. Ha, E.A. Lee, and D.G. Messerschmitt. Ptolemy: A framework for simulating and prototyping heterogeneous systems. *International Journal on Computer Simulation*, 4:155–182, 1991.
4. Lawrence Davis. *Handbook of Genetic Algorithms*, chapter 6, pages 72–90. Van Nostrand Reinhold, New York, 1991.
5. T. C. Denk and K. K. Parhi. Lower bounds on memory requirements for statically scheduled dsp programs. *J. of VLSI Signal Processing*, pages 247–264, 1996.
6. J. Fabri. *Automatic Storage Optimization.* UMI Research Press, 1982.
7. B. R. Fox and M. B. McMahon. Genetic operators for sequencing problems. In Gregory J. E. Rawlins, editor, *Foundations of Genetic Algorithms*, pages 284–300. Morgan Kaufmann, San Mateo, California, 1991.
8. M.R. Garey and D.S. Johnson. *Computers and Intractability: A Guide to the Theory of NP-Completeness.* Freeman, New York, 1979.
9. W.-C. Hsu. Register allocation and code scheduling for load/store architectures. Technical report, Department of Computer Science, University of Wisconsin at Madison, 1987.
10. D. J. Kolson, A. N. Nicolau, N. Dutt, and K. Kennedy. Optimal register assignment to loops for embedded code generation. *ACM Trans. on Design Automation of Electronic Systems*, 1(2):251–279, 1996.
11. R. Lauwereins, M. Engels, J. A. Peperstraete, E. Steegmans, and J. Van Ginderdeuren. Grape: A CASE tool for digital signal parallel processing. *IEEE ASSP Magazine*, 7(2):32–43, April 1990.
12. E.A. Lee and D.G. Messerschmitt. Synchronous dataflow. *Proceedings of the IEEE*, 75(9):1235–1245, 1987.
13. P. Marwedel and G. Goossens (eds.). *Code generation for embedded processors.* Kluwer Academic Publishers, Norwell, MA, 1995.
14. S. Ritz, M. Pankert, and H. Meyr. High level software synthesis for signal processing systems. In *Proc. Int. Conf. on Application-Specific Array Processors*, pages 679–693, Berkeley, CA, 1992.
15. S. Ritz, M. Willems, and H. Meyr. Scheduling for optimum data memory compaction in block diagram oriented software synthesis. In *Proceedings of the International Conference on Acoustics, Speech and Signal Processing*, volume 4, pages 2651–2654, May 1995.
16. J. Teich, E. Zitzler, and S. S. Bhattacharyya. Optimized software synthesis for digital signal processing algorithms - an evolutionary approach. Technical Report 32, TIK, ETH Zurich, Gloriastr. 35, CH-8092 Zurich, January 1998.

Design and
Telecommunications

The Breeder Genetic Algorithm for Frequency Assignment

Christine Crisan* and Heinz Mühlenbein**

GMD - German National Research Center for Information Technology
D - 53754 Sankt Augustin
Germany

Abstract. The Frequency Assignment Problem is an NP-complete problem which occurs during the design of a cellular telecommunication network. In this paper we describe a real-world frequency assignment scenario. We designed a Breeder Genetic Algorithm (BGA) capable of dealing with up to 5500 carriers which have to be assigned frequencies. The total number of available frequencies is about 50. The optimization goal is twofold: to assign as many frequencies as possible and to minimize the interference costs which are caused by the assignment.

1   Introduction

With the perennial increase of the demand of mobile telephone services and the restricted frequency spectrum dedicated to these services, the problem of optimal usage of frequencies has become a major step in planning and operating a digital *mobile telecommunication network (MTN)*. Two main steps can be identified in the process of designing a *MTN*. The first step is often refered to as the *Site Positioning Problem (SPP)*. This step involves the positioning of antennae within the area which has to be covered by the *MTN*. The positioning not only consists of choosing the sites where the antennae will be installed, but also defining their parameters. The main goal of the *SPP* is to position as few antennae as possible while ensuring a complete coverage of the area. By covering an area we mean that for every point within the area there has to exist an antenna from which the point receives a signal of sufficient field strength. The second step consists of assigning frequencies to the antennae. This step is known by the name of *Frequency Assignment Problem (FAP)*. Each antenna introduced by the *SPP* defines a cell, which is the area of the network which will be served by the corresponding antenna. The number of frequencies required by an antenna is given by the expected amount of traffic in the corresponding cell and defines the *traffic constraint*. Depending on the distance between and the strength of two antennae, there are also *interference constraints* which the frequencies assigned to these antennae have to fulfill: the *co-channel, adjacent-channel* and *co-site* constraint. The first two constraints refer to identical or,

---

*   email: Christine.Crisan@gmd.de
**   email: Heinz.Muehlenbein@gmd.de

regarding the frequency spectrum, adjacent frequencies which may be used only by base stations which cannot interfere with one another. The *co-site* constraint implies that frequencies used at a certain base station must be at a predefined minimum distance with regard to the frequency spectrum.

Up to now many methods have been already proposed for the FAP [2, 4, 5, 9]. Unfortunately, all these methods deal with FAP models which stem from the *analog* cellular design, which do not reflect exactly the interference situation in a real world *digital* cellular network. Furthermore many of those benchmarks have been too simple [3]. In this paper we deal with a new FAP model as introduced in [12].

The paper is structured as follows. First we describe the FAP and give a mathematical description of the optimization problem. Then the implemented Breeder Genetic Algorithm (BGA) with its genetic operators is presented. Results using real world data with up to 5500 frequency requirements, $3.9 \cdot 10^5$ interference constraints and only 50 frequencies are presented in Section 5.

To our knowledge, the use of an Evolutionary Algorithm with this FAP model as well as reporting results for such high dimensional frequency assignments are both new.

2 Problem Description

Given are

1. A set $B = (bs_1, \ldots, bs_n)$ of n base stations and for each base station bs_i
   - The *frequency demand*, which defines the number of required frequencies by each base station. The frequency demands are also referred to as *carriers*. Let c_i be the frequency demand of the base station bs_i. The total frequency demand is then $N := \sum_{i=1}^{n} c_i$.
   - The set of *forbidden frequencies*, E_i, which concerns frequencies which must not be assigned at certain locations, i.e. base stations. Such constraints can occur, for example, at the borders of the network.
2. A set of *valid frequencies*, $\mathcal{D}$, which is the set of all the available frequencies.
3. An $(n \times n)$ *interference probability matrix* $\mathcal{P}(B) = (p_{ij})_{i,j=1,\ldots,n}$. A value p_{ij}, $i \neq j$ indicates how a frequency used at base station i will be perturbed, if the same frequency or an adjacent frequency is used at the same time by base station j. Note that this matrix is not a symmetric.
4. A set of optimization goals:
   - No base station should be assigned a frequency from its corresponding set of forbidden frequencies.
   - *Co-site* constraints have to be fulfilled: no identical or adjacent frequencies may be assigned at the same base station.
   - *Co-channel* and *adjacent-channel* constraints have to be fulfilled: identical or adjacent frequencies must not be assigned at the same time at certain locations. The co-site, co-channel and adjacent-channel constraints are also referred to as *interference constraints*.

- The interference costs (which are defined with help of the matrix $\mathcal{P}(\mathcal{B})$) must be minimized.
- The *traffic* constraint has to be fulfilled, i.e. each base station should be assigned the necessary number of frequencies. Sometimes, due to the results of the *SPP*, there exists no solution which satisfies all the constraints described above. In that case, each base station should be assigned as many frequencies as possible, so that all constraints are still satisfied.

We now give a description of the FAP as a combinatorial optimization problem. We define first a frequency assignment instance, then a frequency assignment plan and finally the frequency assignment problem, as described in this paper.

Definition 1 (Frequency Assignment Instance) *A frequency assignment instance is described by a five tuple*

$$I = (BS_I, TRX_I, \mathcal{D}_I, d_I, p_I) \tag{1}$$

with

1. $BS_I = \{bs_1, \ldots, bs_n\}$ *a set of base stations,*
2. $TRX_I : BS_I \longrightarrow \mathbb{N}$ *the carrier demand for each base station,*
3. $\mathcal{D}_I = \bigcup_{i=1}^{n} D_i$ *the set of all available frequencies,*
4. $d_I : BS_I \times BS_I \longrightarrow \{0, 1, 2\}$ *the frequency separation function and*
5. $p_I : BS_I \times BS_I \longrightarrow [0, 1]$ *the interference probability function.*

TRX_I defines the number of carriers which must be assigned to each base station. Each set D_i defines the set of frequencies which may be assigned to the base stations. d_I models the interference constraints. $d_I(bs_i, bs_j)$ gives the minimal distance between frequencies which may be assigned to the base stations bs_i and bs_j. p_I defines the interference probability matrix, $\mathcal{P}(\mathcal{B})$.

Definition 2 (Frequency Assignment Plan) *A frequency assignment plan for an instance I is a function*

$$\sigma(I) : BS_I \longrightarrow \wp(\mathcal{D}_I) \tag{2}$$

which assigns each base station bs_i a set of frequencies for which the following holds

$$\sigma(I)(bs_i) \subseteq D_i \tag{3}$$

and

$$|\sigma(I)(bs_i)| = TRX_I(bs_i) \tag{4}$$

Definition 3 (Frequency Assignment Problem) *A frequency assignment problem is an optimization problem defined by*

1. *a frequency assignment instance I,*
2. *a set of solutions $S_{FAP}(I)$ which consists of all the possible frequency assignment plans $\sigma(I)$ and*

3. *a cost function*

$$C_{FAP} : S_{FAP}(I) \longrightarrow \mathbb{R} \qquad (5)$$

which assigns each solution $\sigma_i(I) \in S_{FAP}(I)$ a real number $c(\sigma_i(I))$, which defines the quality of the solution.

The cost function depends on the number of violated constraints and the interference defined by the interference probability function p_I.

The aim of the optimization problem is to find a frequency assignment plan $\sigma^*(I) \in S_{FAP}$ so that

$$\forall \sigma_i(I) \in S_{FAP} \qquad c(\sigma^*(I)) \leq c(\sigma_i(I)). \qquad (6)$$

The use of an Evolutionary Algorithm with this FAP model is new. This model is more powerful [12] than those presented for example in [4, 9, 6]. The FAP as described in Definition 3 is a multi objective optimization problem: both the interference constraints and the global interference have to be minimized. From the point of view of an *MTN* provider though, a good frequency assignment plan must not violate at all the interference constraints. Thus we extend the optimization problem and define a feasible frequency assignment plan to be one for which the interference constraints are fulfilled.

Definition 4 (Feasible Frequency Assignment Plan) *A feasible frequency assignment plan is a frequency assignment plan*

$$\sigma(I) : BS_I \longrightarrow \wp(D_I \cup \{NOT\_ASSIGNED\}) \qquad (7)$$

for which for each two base stations bs_i and bs_j and frequencies $f_k \in \sigma(I)(bs_i)$ and $f_l \in \sigma(I)(bs_j)$, $f_k, f_l \in D_I$, $|f_k - f_l| \geq d_I(bs_i, bs_j)$ holds.

Note that the domain of the *feasible* frequency assignment plan is extended by the value $NOT\_ASSIGNED$, which indicates that also incomplete frequency assignment plans may be considered. In this case the cost function will also contain a penalty term to penalize incomplete assignments.

The FAP then consists of finding a feasible assignment with minimal interference costs and minimal number of unassigned frequencies. The interference costs of a frequency assignment plan are defined as in [12] by the *price of interference*.

The problem of finding a feasible solution for a FAP has been shown to be NP-complete since, in its simplest form, the FAP can be reduced to the graph coloring problem. [8].

3   Optimization Approach

In the past we have solved some of the CALMA benchmark problems [13]. Those problems have proved to be easy for our algorithm [3]. The results obtained there can be interpreted as follows: good mutation operators are vital for the optimum search while a crossover operator makes the search more robust. Solution evaluations after a crossover step are much more costly than evaluations after just a mutation step ($O(n^2)$ vs. $O(n)$). Therefore, the usage of crossover can be justified only if it produces better solutions. The FAP considered in this paper is a superset of the problems considered in [3], considering both the problem complexity and the problem dimension and number of constraints. In this paper we adopt the best mutation operator which we presented in [3] and introduce a new crossover operator which regards problem specific information. The operators are presented in the next section.

The problem considered in this paper consists of finding a feasible frequency assignment plan with minimal interference costs. As stated in the previous section, finding a feasible solution for the FAP is an NP-complete problem already. From an optimization point of view, the question arises on how to define a solution of the FAP. The first option would be to consider both feasible and infeasible solutions. In this case infeasible solutions must be penalized in some way, so that they are discarded by the optimization algorithm. The second approach would be to consider only feasible solutions.

In this paper we consider a mixture of both approaches. We apply a two step optimization. The first optimization step is concerned with finding a feasible solution by minimizing the number of violated interference constraints. The second optimization step then tries to find a solution with minimal interference costs, while keeping the solution feasible. If within the first optimization step the algorithm is not able to find a feasible solution, then the variables (or carriers) which still violate some constraints are marked and not considered in the next optimization step. The second step minimizes the interference costs and tries to reinsert some or all of the variables which were eliminated after the first optimization step. At the end of the optimization the user is presented with a feasible solution with minimal costs. Note that the solution may be a partial solution, i.e. there may still be some variables which are not assigned frequencies.

4   Genetic Approach

Now we define the ingredients of the BGA. First, a genetic encoding of the problem and a fitness function, i.e. a solution evaluation function are defined. Then the Mutation and Crossover operators are presented.

4.1   Encoding

Based upon the definition of the FAP we now define a genetic encoding of the problem. A gene corresponds to one frequency assignment of a base station and a chromosome corresponds to a solution of the FAP. Each individual is made up of one chromosome. An individual is represented by an N-dimensional vector $\sigma(I) = (f_1, \ldots, f_N)$ with N the total number of frequency requirements and f_i the assignment of the i-th requirement. See also Figure 1.

In [3] we defined the Hamming Distance between two individuals to be the total number of different frequency assignments. Locally optimal solutions showed to be very different from each other. In view of the crossover operator which

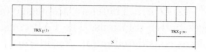

Fig. 1. Encoding of a solution

we introduce in this paper we define now a new Hamming Distance (HD). Let $V : \sigma(I) \longrightarrow \{0,1\}$ be defined by

$$V(\sigma(I)(i)) = v_i = \begin{cases} 0 \text{ if variable } i \text{ does not violate any interference constraints} \\ 1 \text{ otherwise} \end{cases}$$

(8)

The normalized Hamming Distance between two individual $\sigma(I) = (f_1, \ldots, f_N)$ and $\sigma'(I) = (f'_1, \ldots, f'_N)$ is then defined by

$$h_d(\sigma(I), \sigma'(I)) = \frac{1}{N} \sum_{i=1}^{N} sgn|v_i - v'_i| \qquad (9)$$

with sgn the signum function. h_d is 0 if the solutions are similar regarding their quality and structure. We define the *genetic variance* δ of a population to be the normalized distance of the best individual to the rest of the population. As long as δ is high the genetic search should be promising. When δ tends to zero, the parents will become more and more similar.

4.2 Fitness Function

Within the first optimization step the fitness of an individual $s = (f_1, \ldots, f_N)$ is defined by

$$\mathcal{F}(\sigma(I)) = tNOV(s) + \sum_{i=1}^{n} \sqrt{bsNOV(i)} \qquad (10)$$

with $tNOV$ the total number of interference constraint violations of the solution s and $bsNOV(i)$ the number of constraint violations of the base station i.

The fitness function of the second optimization step is defined by the price of interference [12] of an individual, i.e. solution.

4.3 Initialization

For the first optimization step individuals are randomly generated. We just take care that the assignment of a base station is always feasible. This means, that the minimal distance between the frequencies assigned to a base station is always greater than or equal to $d(bs_i, bs_i)$. The initial individuals of the second optimization step are the feasible solutions computed by the first optimization step.

4.4 Mutation

Several mutation operators have already been implemented in order to study their effects on the FAP. Here we just present the operator which showed to be the most successful one [3].

Extended Interference Mutation (EIM) This mutation operator first builds up a candidate list of variables which, by changing their assignment, might lead to a better solution. One variable from the candidate list is randomly chosen for mutation and assigned a new frequency. The candidate list contains the variables which violate at least one constraint and all other variables which are involved with the first ones in a constraint. Note that the newly assigned frequency is chosen so that the assignment of the base station to whom the variable belongs to remains feasible.

4.5 Crossover

It has been shown that well known crossover operators such as 1Point-, 2Point- or Uniform-Crossover do not perform well on the FAP [5]. We present a new operator which takes into account problem specific information. First we define the neighborhood of a station.

Definition 5 (Neighborhood of a base station) *We define the neighborhood of a base station bs_i, $N(bs_i)$ to be the set of all the base stations bs_j for which there is a constraint which involves the base station bs_i on the one hand and each of the base station bs_j on the other hand:*

$$N(bs_i) = \{bs_j | d_I(bs_i, bs_j) \neq 0\}$$

Subgraph Crossover (SGC) Let $\sigma_1(I)$ and $\sigma_2(I)$ be two individuals chosen for the crossover and $\sigma_o(I)$ be the offspring. Then the offspring is generated as follows:

- Find all base stations bs_i which do not violate any constraint.
- Choose randomly one of these base station. Let this base station be bs_i and let it belong to $\sigma_1(I)$.
- Compute the neighborhood $N(bs_i)$.
- Compute the offspring $\forall k = 1, \ldots, N$ by the scheme

$$\sigma_o(I)(bs_k) = \begin{cases} \sigma_1(I)(bs_k) \text{ if } bs_k \in N(bs_i) \\ \sigma_2(I)(bs_k) \text{ otherwise} \end{cases}$$

- Repair the worst damages caused by the crossover between the two parents.

The rationale behind this operator can be explained as follows. Two individuals denote two different solutions of the FAP. Each of the two solutions defines an assignment which is better in some area of the mobile network. By applying the crossover operator we try to substitute a bad area from one individual by a better area from the other individual. Repair operations are needed between the border of the considered area to the rest of the network.

5 Experiments with the BGA

5.1 Considered Problems

We considered six different real world examples to test the implemented operators. The examples differ in the dimension (N) and the number of constraints (Ctr). The examples are described in Table 1.

Table 1. Parameters of the problem instances

Instance	N	Ctr
1	670	$1.6 \cdot 10^4$
2	670	$1.0 \cdot 10^4$
3	1340	$6.7 \cdot 10^4$
4	2256	$1.2 \cdot 10^5$
5	2256	$1.0 \cdot 10^5$
6	5500	$3.9 \cdot 10^5$

5.2 Results

The FAP is implemented within the framework of a Breeder Genetic Algorithm as described in [10]. The Response to Selection Equation [11] gives a means to judge the performance of the breeding process. Here, we just summarize the derivation of the equation. For a deeper understanding the reader is referred to [11].

Let $M(t)$ denote the mean fitness of the population at time t. The change in fitness caused by the selection is given by

$$R(t) = M(t) - M(t-1) \tag{11}$$

and is called *response to selection*. $R(t)$ measures the expected progress of the population. The *selection differential* $S(t)$ is defined by the difference between the mean fitness of the selected individuals, $M_s(t)$ and the population mean:

$$S(t) = M_s(t) - M(t). \tag{12}$$

In the process of artificial breeding, both $R(t)$ and $S(t)$, can be easily computed. The connection between $R(t)$ and $S(t)$ is given by the equation

$$R(t) = b_t \cdot S(t). \tag{13}$$

In quantitative genetics b_t is called the *realized heritability*. It is normally assumed that b_t is constant for a number of generations. This leads to

$$R(t) = b \cdot S(t). \tag{14}$$

In general, the progress is due to a genetic search as long as the ratio $R(T)/S(t)$ is greater than 0.1. If it is approaching zero or is even less than zero, then mutation is the driving force behind the search. In Figure 2 the curves show $R(t)/S(t)$ and δ for the first problem instance. For approximately 200 generations $R(t)/S(t)$ has positive values. At this stage of the optimization the best individual is already close to the best found solution.

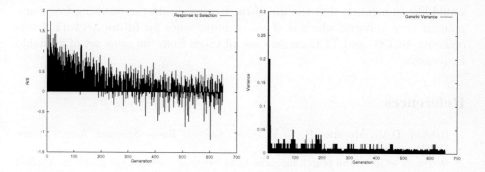

Fig. 2. Response to Selection $R(t)/S(t)$ (left) and Normalized Distance δ (right)

Table 2 shows the obtained results. For each population size (PopSize) 10 runs were performed. For each experiment the number of unassigned frequencies, NA, (see Section 2) and the interference costs (Interf) of the solution are given. Experiments with larger population yield better results. This is a strong

Table 2. Experimental results

Instance	PopSize					
	32		64		128	
	NA	Interf	NA	Interf	NA	Interf
1	29.36	$7.4 \cdot 10^{-1}$	33.46	$6.8 \cdot 10^{-1}$	28.9	$7.1 \cdot 10^{-1}$
2	2.86	3.38	2.2	3.37	3.86	3.29
3	109.2	1.92	106.7	1.89	102.6	1.78
4	0	$2.8 \cdot 10^{-1}$	0	$1.7 \cdot 10^{-1}$	0	$9.8 \cdot 10^{-2}$
5	0	$8.5 \cdot 10^{-1}$	0	$7.6 \cdot 10^{-1}$	0	$7.0 \cdot 10^{-1}$
6	41	3.78	41	3.97	39	3.75

indication for a good exploration of the fitness landscape by the crossover operator. For an *MTN* even small improvements in the global interference costs (Interf) are very important for a high quality network. Benchmarks with a mobile telecommunication provider showed that our algorithm gets very good solutions.

6 Conclusions and Future Work

We have applied a custom tailored genetic algorithm to a high dimensional frequency assignment problem. We have shown that the algorithm is able to produce high quality results on the test problems. Real world benchmarks have shown that our algorithm produces competitive results.

For those familiar with the GSM standard for mobile telecommunications we would like to mention that the use of the frequencies in the resulting frequency plans is very uniform, which is of major importance for future network developments. BCCH- and TCH-carriers are all taken from the same set of available frequencies.

References

1. Balston, D.M., Macario, R. C. V. (Eds): Cellular Radio Systems. Artech House (1993)
2. Bouju, A. et al.: Tabu search for radio links frequency assignment problem. Applied Decision Technologies, London. UNICOM Conf. (1995).
3. Crisan, C., Mühlenbein, H.: The Frequency Assignment Problem: A Look at the Performance of Evolutionary Search. Artificial Evolution, LNCS 1363. (1998) 263–273.
4. Crompton, W., Hurley, S., Stephens, N.M.: A Parallel Genetic Algorithm for Frequency Assignment Problems. Proc. of IMACS SPRANN. (1994) 81–84.
5. Dorne, R., Hao, J.-K.: An Evolutionary Approach for Frequency Assignment in Cellular Radio Networks. Proc. of IEEE Intl. Conf. on Evolutionary Computation. (1995) 539–544.
6. Duque-Anton, M. et al.: Channel Assignment for Cellular Radio Using Simulated Annealing. IEEE Trans. on Veh. Tech. 42. (1993) 14–21.
7. Funabiki N., Takefuji, Y.: A Neural Network Parallel Algorithm for Channel Assignment Problems in Cellular Radio Networks. IEEE Trans. on Veh. Tech. 41. (1992) 430–437.
8. Gamst, A., Rave, W.: On the frequency assignment in mobile automatic telephone systems. GLOBECOM 82. (1982) 309–315.
9. Hao, J.-K., Dorne, R.: Study of Genetic Search for the Frequency Assignment Problem. Artificial Evolution, LNCS 1063. (1996) 333-344.
10. Mühlenbein, H., Schlierkamp-Voosen D.: Predictive Models for the Breeder Genetic Algorithm. Evolutionary Computation. (1993) 25–49.
11. Mühlenbein, H., Schlierkamp-Voosen D.: The science of breeding and its application to the breeder genetic algorithm. Evolutionary Computation 1(4). (1994) 335–360.
12. Plehn, J.: Applied Frequency Assignment. Proc. of the IEEE Veh. Tech. Conference. (1994).
13. Description of the CALMA Benchmark Problems. http://dutiosd.twi.tudelft.nl/~rlfap/

A Permutation Based Genetic Algorithm for Minimum Span Frequency Assignment

Christine Valenzuela[1], Steve Hurley[2] and Derek Smith[3]

[1] School of Computing and Mathematics, University of Teesside, TS1 3BA.[†]
[2] Department of Computer Science, Cardiff University, CF2 3XF, UK.
[3] Division of Mathematics and Computing, University of Glamorgan, CF37 1DL, UK.

Abstract. We describe a Genetic Algorithm (GA) for solving the minimum span frequency assignment problem (MSFAP).The MSFAP involves assigning frequencies to each transmitter in a region, subject to a number of constraints being satisfied, such that the span, i.e. the range of frequencies used, is minimized. The technique involves finding an ordering of the transmitters for use in a sequential (greedy) assignment process. Results are given which show that our GA produces optimal solutions to several practical problem instances, and compares favourably to simulated annealing and tabu search algorithms.

1 Introduction

The frequency assignment problem is a difficult, NP-hard, problem of considerable importance. The radio spectrum is a limited natural resource that is used in a variety of civil and military services. The most well known example would be in cellular mobile phone networks. Third generation mobile systems will achieve a world-wide mass market giving enhancements in the areas of quality and security, incorporating broad-band and multi-media services, and offering higher capacity based on bandwidth on demand. These features will be supported by means of integrated terrestrial and satellite modes of delivery to provide comprehensive coverage - ranging from the office environment, through street and urban areas, to complete coverage of rural and remote regions throughout the world.

To facilitate this expansion the radio spectrum allocated to a particular service provider needs to be assigned as efficiently and effectively as possible. The minimum span frequency assignment problem (MSFAP) is one in which it is required to assign frequencies to a set of transmitters such that certain compatibility constraints, which model potential interference between pairs of transmitters, are satisfied. In addition to satisfying the constraints the objective is to minimise the *span* of the assignment i.e. the difference between the largest frequency used and the smallest frequency used.

The purpose of this paper is to explore the possibility of combining a Genetic Algorithm (GA) with sequential (greedy) assignment methods. Traditionally,

---

[†] *Current address:* Department of Computer Science, George Mason University, Virginia, USA.

GAs and other meta-heuristics have been applied to an initial solution consisting of an assignment of frequencies to transmitters, the techniques operating on the problem directly using local search to perturb the allocation of frequencies in an attempt to minimise the number of constraint violations [3, 11, 17]. In [11] a sequential method is used to find an initial assignment, which is then improved by simulated annealing or tabu search. With the GA described here the iterative transformations are applied to permutations of transmitters. A simple sequential assignment algorithm is then applied to each of these permutations to produce an allocation of frequencies that does not violate any constraints. Thus the permutations of transmitters output by the GA are interpreted by the sequential algorithm to produce candidate solutions to the MSFAP.

1.1   Interference and Constraints

Interference can occur between a pair of transmitters if the interfering signal strength is sufficiently high. Whether a transmitter pair has the potential to interfere depends on many factors, e.g. distance, terrain, power, antenna design. The higher the potential for interference between a transmitter pair the larger the *frequency separation* that is required. For example, if two transmitters are sufficently geographically separated then a frequency can be re-used i.e. the same frequency assigned. At the other extreme if two transmitters are located at the same site then they may require, say, five frequencies separation (this is called the *co-site* constraint).

To model this interference a *constraint graph* is constructed which gives the separations needed between each transmitter pair. This graph is usually represented by a $N \times N$ matrix, A, (N is the number of transmitters in the network) where each element a_{ij} defines the frequency separation between transmitters i and j i.e. if f_i and f_j are the frequencies assigned to transmitter i and j respectively then

$$|f_i - f_j| > a_{ij}$$

The MSFAP is to find a frequency assignment that satisfies all the constraints and such that the span of the assignment is minimised.

1.2   Sequential Assignment Algorithms

Sequential assignment methods mimic the way the problem might be solved manually. They are fast enough for large problems but tend to give results which are well short of the best possible. The transmitters are simply considered one at a time, successively assigning allowable frequencies as we proceed, until either we have assigned all transmitters or run out of frequencies. An important factor affecting the quality of solutions generated by this method is how the next transmitter is chosen. We may therefore generate a series of assignment methods based on three components:

- initial ordering,
- choice of next transmitter,
- assignment of frequency.

The simplest way to choose the next transmitter is sequentially, simply picking the next one on the list produced by the initial ordering. A more complicated method, which has proved more effective than sequential selection with the various initial ordering methods, is called general saturation degree. In this method the choice of the next transmitter is influenced by the constraints imposed by all those transmitters that have already been chosen. One could view the more complicated process as a method for correcting those mistakes that have already been made by the initial ordering technique.

The simplest assignment technique is to assign the smallest acceptable channel i.e. the lowest numbered channel to which it can be assigned without violating any constraints. Variations upon this technique attempt to assign transmitters to channels that are already used in favour of those that are not. A detailed description of sequential assignment methods can be found in [11].

In this paper we use our GA to search a state-space of initial orderings. The choice of the next transmitter is made sequentially using the ordering obtained, with the smallest acceptable frequency assigned to each transmitter.

2   The Search Space Generated by Permutations of Transmitters

It is important to establish that the state-space of initial orderings contains permutations capable of producing good (or even optimal) solutions following the application to the orderings of the chosen method for allocating frequencies to the transmitters. Some experiments on small problems are documented below. We allocate frequency channels to the initial orderings in the following way: the choice of the next transmitter is made sequentially and the smallest acceptable channel is assigned to each transmitter. All possible permutations of a simple 12 transmitter problem are generated (479,001,600 in total) allowing the examination of the entire state-space, and 1000 permutations are produced at random for a problem containing 95 transmitters. Graphs indicating the frequency of occurrence of the spans evaluated for the permutations, using the simple frequency assignment algorithm outlined above, are plotted in Figure 1 and Figure 2.

The graphs show a range of spans for both of the problems. The exhaustive search of the permutation space for the 12 transmitter problem locates the optimum span of 22, whilst the random search carried out in the case of the 95 transmitter problem locates a best span of 52, which is 4 channels above the optimum solution of 48 [17]. In both cases, however, these values represent improvements over the best produced by combining together the various sequential assignment methods (initial ordering, selecting the next transmitter and selecting a frequency), where best solutions of 24 and 54 are obtained respectively for the 12 and 95 transmitter problem. The above experiments demonstrate clearly that "good" permutations of transmitters can be converted into excellent solutions

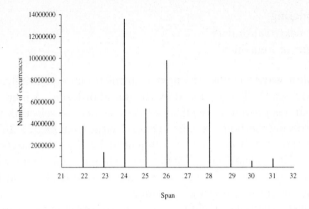

Fig. 1. Spans evaluated from all permutations of a 12 transmitter problem

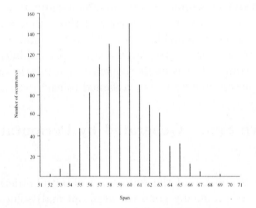

Fig. 2. Spans evaluated from 1000 permutations of a 95 transmitter problem

to the MSFAP, at least in the case of small problem instances, thus providing the motivation to try a genetic search on larger problem instances.

3 The Genetic Algorithm

The simple genetic algorithm (GA) used here is based on that which has appeared in [20]. It is derived from the model of Holland in [9] and is an example of a 'steady state' GA (based on the classification of Syswerda in [18]). It uses the 'weaker parent replacement strategy' first described by Cavicchio in [2]. The GA, outlined in Figure 3, applies the genetic operators to permutations of transmitters. The fitness values are based on the spans produced when the simple sequential assignment algorithm is applied to each permutation list produced by the GA. In Algorithm 1 the first parent is selected deterministically in sequence, but the second parent is selected in a roulette wheel fashion, the

```
Procedure GA1
BEGIN
    Generate N_pop random permutations (N_pop is the population size).
    Apply the Generalised Saturation Degree (GSD) algorithm to each
    individual to produce N_pop frequency assignments and store each one.
    Store best-so-far.
    REPEAT
       FOR each member of the population
          this individual becomes the first parent;
          select a second parent using roulette wheel selection on ranks;
          apply cycle crossover to produce one offspring;
          apply mutation to offspring;
          evaluate span produced by offspring;
          if offspring better than weaker parent then it replaces it in
           population;
          if offspring better than best-so-far then it replaces best-so-far;
       ENDFOR
    UNTIL stopping condition satisfied.
Print best-so-far.
END
```

Fig. 3. Algorithm 1 - The Genetic Algorithm

selection probabilities for each genotype being calculated using the following formula:

$$genotype\ selection\ probability = \frac{(population\ size + 1 - Rank\ of\ geneotype)}{\sum Ranks}$$

where the genotypes are ranked according to the values of the spans that they have produced, with the best ranked 1, the second best 2 etc.

The GA breeds permutations of transmitters and frequencies are assigned to the resulting lists of transmitters by a simple sequential assignment technique (see section 1.2 above).

Experiments have demonstrated that better results are obtained if the Generalized Saturation Degree (GSD) algorithm is applied to the initial permutation lists produced by a pseudo-random number generator, prior to invoking the Genetic Algorithm. (These experiments will be documented elsewhere.) The GSD algorithm used in the second step of Algorithm 1 is described next.

3.1   Generalized Saturation Degree (GSD)

Let V be a set of transmitters and V_c be the transmitters of V already assigned frequencies. Frequency n is said to be denied to the unassigned transmitter v if there is a transmitter u in V_c assigned to frequency n such that transmitter

u and v would interfere i.e. assuming an edge exists between u and v in the constraint graph then there is insufficient frequency separation between them. If frequency n is denied to transmitter v, the influence of frequency n, denoted by I_{nv} , is the largest weight of any edge connecting v to a transmitter assigned to frequency n. The number

$$\sum I_{nv}$$

(where the sum is taken over all frequencies n denied to v) is called the generalized saturation degree of v. The technique for selecting the next transmitter is as follows: Select a transmitter with maximal generalized saturation degree (break ties by selecting the transmitter occurring first in the initial ordering).

3.2   Mutation

The mutation chosen was to select two transmitters at random from a permutation list, and swap them.

3.3   Cycle Crossover

Permutation crossovers were originally developed primarily for the travelling salesman problem (TSP), where the genotypes consist of lists of cities which are converted to TSP tours. Because TSP tours are circuits, it is irrelevant which city is represented first on the list. The permutation lists represent cycles and an edge in a TSP tour always joins the last city on the list to the first. Thus for the TSP it is the relative sequence of cities that is important, rather than the absolute sequence. In the frequency assignment problem, however, the permutation lists making up the genotypes represent lists of transmitters, and intuitively it would seem likely that absolute sequences are important in this case.

The best known permutation operators from an historical standpoint (which are also amongst the simplest to implement) are *Partially Matched Crossover* (PMX) [8], *Order Crossover* (OX) [4, 5] and *Cycle Crossover* (CX) [13]. In test experiments if was found that CX produced better results on the MSFAP than either PMX or OX, thus it is the chosen operator here. (For a description of the three crossovers, PMX, OX and CX see [8]).

In the next subsection we examine the ability of the cycle crossover to pass characteristics of parents onto their offspring. In order to do this Pearson's Correlation Coefficient has been calculated between the spans of 1000 offspring versus and the corresponding mid-parent values.

3.4   Offspring versus Mid-parent Correlation

From an initial population of 1000 individuals, 1000 pairs of parents are selected using the selection mechanism defined in Figure 3, and from them 1000 offspring are generated using CX and one mutation. It is important to establish that offspring resemble their parents and produce solutions with similar values for the span. If this turns out not to be the case, then the GA is at best equivalent to a random search.

Table 1 shows the values of Pearson's Correlation Coefficient, r_{xy}, for a range of problems using CX for offspring versus mid-parent values of the span for 1000 samples. Results are shown for six representative problem instances.

Table 1. Examples of offspring versus mid-parent correlation

Problem	r_{xy}
P1	0.2703
P2	0.2405
P3	0.2419
P4	0.2767
P5	0.2061
P6	0.2098

The values for the correlation coefficient in the table are all highly significant at the 0.0001% level, showing that parental features that contribute to their span values are indeed passed on to their offspring.

4 Results

For the GA the population size is 500. One mutation per offspring is used, and cycle crossover is the recombination operator. The GA terminates after 200 generations have elapsed with no improvement to the best-so-far. The population is initially seeded with 500 random permutations. These are then subject to the Generalized Saturation Degree algorithm, and it is the new orderings produced by the application of this algorithm which form the starting population for the GA.

The examples are based on the so-called Philadelphia problem which originally appeared in [1], and was subsequently used by several authors [6, 7, 12, 14, 21]. The problem is based on a cellular phone network consisting of 21 cells. The demands in each cell define the number of frequenices that need to be assigned to each of the cells. The distance between cell centres is taken to be 1. The hexagonal geometry is given in Figure 4 Constraints between transmitters are generated by considering the distance between the transmitters.

Additional variations on the Philadelphia problem can be also be defined to further test the performance of the GA. Table 2 defines the Philadelphia variations used for the test problems (d_k denotes the smallest distance between transmitters which can use a separation of k channels, N denotes the total number of frequencies that need to be assigned i.e. the number of transmitters and C denotes the total number of compatability constraints that need to be satisfied. Problem P8, described in [19], contains the same number of transmitters and

Fig. 4. The Cellular Geometry of the Philadelphia Problems

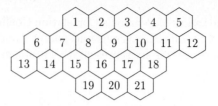

constraints as P1, the difference being some of the constraints require a higher separation (since the d_1 distance is smaller). The following cell demand vectors are used:

$$
\begin{aligned}
\mathbf{m} &= (8,25,8,8,8,15,18,52,77,28,13,15,31,15,36,57,28,8,10,13,8) \\
\mathbf{m_2} &= (5,5,5,8,12,25,30,25,30,40,40,45,20,30,25,15,15,30,20,20,25) \\
\mathbf{m_3} &= (20,20,20,20,20,20,20,20,20,20,20,20,20,20,20,20,20,20,20,20,20) \\
\mathbf{m_4} &= (16,50,16,16,16,30,36,104,154,56,26,30,62,30,72,114,56,16,20,26,16)
\end{aligned}
$$

Table 2. Philadelphia problem variations

Problem	d_0	d_1	d_2	d_3	d_4	d_5	Cell demands	N	C
P1	$\sqrt{12}$	$\sqrt{3}$	1	1	1	0	m	481	97,835
P2	$\sqrt{7}$	$\sqrt{3}$	1	1	1	0	m	481	76,979
P3	$\sqrt{12}$	$\sqrt{3}$	1	1	1	0	m_2	470	78,635
P4	$\sqrt{7}$	$\sqrt{3}$	1	1	1	0	m_2	470	56,940
P5	$\sqrt{12}$	$\sqrt{3}$	1	1	1	0	m_3	420	65,590
P6	$\sqrt{7}$	$\sqrt{3}$	1	1	1	0	m_3	420	44,790
P7	$\sqrt{12}$	$\sqrt{3}$	1	1	1	0	m_4	962	391,821
P8	$\sqrt{12}$	2	1	1	1	0	m	481	97,835

The GA results are given in Table 3. Comparisons are given with Tabu Search (TS) and Simulated Annealing (SA) algorithms which are detailed in [11]. The TS and SA algorithms do not operate by generating a good permutaion of transmitters (as in the GA) but instead attempt to iteratively improve a complete assignment. The value in parentheses indicates the number of assignments processed by the SA, TS, and GA algorithms. The"Best seq" column gives the best span obtained from using a standard sequential (greedy) assignment method, details can be found in [11]. Lower bounds on the minimum span have been calculated in [16, 17, 15]. It can be seen that for the problems considered here the GA always equals or outperforms the SA algorithm and only fails to improve on the results of TS algorithm in one case (P6). The number of assignments

Table 3. Genetic algorithm results (* denotes one run)

Problem	Lower bound	Best seq.	TS	SA	GA	GA (mean 4 runs)
P1	426	447	428 (76,902,785)	428 (8,973,775)	426 (147,500)	426.25
P2	426	475	429 (76,843,178)	438 (81,066,945)	426 (186,000)	426*
P3	257	284	269 (74,920,399)	260 (103,073,177)	258 (225,500)	259.25
P4	252	268	257 (81,215,422)	259 (9,057,107)	253 (186,000)	253.75
P5	239	250	240 (66,941,918)	239 (9,494,007)	239 (275.500)	239.5
P6	178	230	188 (70,277,837)	200 (9,052,191)	198 (119,000)	198
P7	855	894	858 (9,617,414)	858 (162,899,774)	856 (212,000)	856*
P8	524	592	535 (190,046,283)	546 (410,198,288)	527 (650,000)	527*

tested is considerably lower for the GA, although the time to generate a new assignment is much higher than TS or SA.

It should be mentioned that the TS algorithm can outperform the GA in examples P3, P4, P6 and P8 (finding optimal solutions for P1,P2,P3,P4,P5,P7 and P8) if a *critical subgraph* of the original constraint graph is identified and a minimum span assignment for this subgraph initially found and this assignment is used as the starting (partial) assignment for the complete problem. However, generating assignments using this subgraph approach remains exploratory and no firm foundation exists for its general applicability. Full details of the subgraph approach can be found in [10, 17, 15].

5 Conclusions

A genetic algorithm which computes minimum span frequency assignments has been presented. Results of using the GA on a set of standard benchmark problems show that the GA performs well against SA and TS algorithms that have appeared previously in the literature. It has been noted that the TS algorithm when used in conjuction with the assignment of critical subgraphs improves on the assignments generated by the GA. However, it is important to note that the the critical subgraph approach is exploratory. Consequently, algorithms are needed which compute frequency assignments from the constraint graph of the complete problem. However, future work will involve testing the performance of the GA on the critical subgraph approach.

References

1. L.G. Anderson. A simulation study of some dynamic channel assignment algorithms in a high capacity mobile telecommunications system. *IEEE Transactions on Communications*, COM-21:1294–1301, 1973.
2. D.J. Cavicchio. *Adaptive search using simulated evolution*. PhD thesis, University of Michigan, 1970.

3. W. Crompton, S. Hurley, and N.M. Stephens. A parallel genetic algorithm for frequency assignment problems. In *Proc. IMACS/IEEE Conference on Signal Processing, Robotics and Neural Networks*, pages 81–84, Lille, France, 1994.

4. L. Davis. Applying adaptive algorithms to epistatic domains. In *Proceedings 9th International Joint Conference on Artificial Intelligence*, pages 162–164, 1985.

5. L. Davis. Job shop scheduling with genetic algorithms. In J. Grefenstette, editor, *Proceedings International Conference on Genetic Algorithms and their Applications*, pages 136–140. Lawrence Erlbaum Associates, 1985.

6. N. Funabiki and Y. Takefuji. A neural network parallel algorithm for channel assignment problems in cellular radio networks. *IEEE Transactions on Vehicular Technology*, 41(4):430–437, 1992.

7. A. Gamst. Some lower bounds for a class of frequency assignment problems. *IEEE Transactions on Vehicular Technology*, 35:8–14, 1986.

8. D.E. Goldberg. *Genetic Algorithms in Search, Optimization and Machine Learning*. Addison Wesley, 1989.

9. J.H. Holland. *Adaption in natural and artificial systems*. University of Michigan Press, Ann Arbor, 1975.

10. S. Hurley and D.H. Smith. Meta-heuristics and channel assignment. In R.A. Leese, editor, *Methods and algorithms for channel assignment*. Oxford University Press, to appear 1998.

11. S. Hurley, D.H. Smith, and S.U. Thiel. FASoft: A system for discrete channel frequency assignment. *Radio Science*, 32:1921–1939, 1997.

12. R. Leese. Tiling methods for channel assignment in radio communication networks. In *3rd ICIAM Congress*, 1996.

13. I.M. Oliver, D.J. Smith, and J.R.C. Holland. A study of permutation operators on the travelling salesman problem. In *Proceedings 2nd International Conference on Genetic Algorithms*, pages 224–230, 1987.

14. K.N. Sivarajan, R.J. McEliece, and J.W. Ketchum. Channel assignment in cellular radio. In *Proceedings of 39th Conference, IEEE Vehicular Technolgy Society*, pages 846–850, 1989.

15. D.H. Smith, S.M. Allen, and S. Hurley. Lower bounds for channel assignment. In R.A. Leese, editor, *Methods and algorithms for channel assignment*. Oxford University Press, to appear 1998.

16. D.H. Smith and S. Hurley. Bounds for the frequency assignment problem. *Discrete Mathematics*, 167/168:571–582, 1997.

17. D.H. Smith, S. Hurley, and S.U. Thiel. Improving heuristics for the frequency assignment problem. *European Journal of Operational Research*, to appear 1998.

18. G. Syswerda. Uniform crossover in genetic algorithms. In J.D. Schaffer, editor, *Proceedings 3rd International Conference on Genetic Algorithms*, pages 2–9. Lawrence Erlbaum Associates, 1989.

19. D. Tcha, Y. Chung, and T. Choi. A new lower bound for the frequency assignment problem. *IEEE/ACM Transactions on Networking*, 5(1):34–39, 1997.

20. C.L. Valenzuela. *Evolutionary divide and conquer: A novel genetic approach to the TSP*. PhD thesis, Imperial College, University of London, 1995.

21. W. Wang and C. Rushforth. An adaptive local search algorithm for the channel assignment problem (cap). *IEEE Transactions on Vehicular Technology*, 45(3):459–466, 1996.

Comparison of Evolutionary Algorithms for Design Optimization

Wilfried Jakob, Martina Gorges-Schleuter, Ingo Sieber

Forschungszentrum Karlsruhe, Institut für Angewandte Informatik
Postfach 3640, D-76021 Karlsruhe, Germany
e-mail: jakob@iai.fzk.de

Abstract. The production of specimen for microsystems or microcomponents is both, time and material-consuming. In a traditional design process the number of possible variations which can be considered is very limited. Thus, in micro-system technology computer-based design techniques become more and more important - similar to the development of microelectronics.
In this paper we compare Evolutionary Algorithms based on Evolution Strategies and the extended Genetic Algorithm GLEAM for solving the design optimization problem. The reference problem is the design optimization of a 2-lens-system being part of a heterodyne receiver, a microoptical communication module. As this is a real world problem, the design must be as insensitive to fabrication tolerances as possible. The results obtained are compared to a more complex task: the robot path planning problem.

1   Introduction

To achieve both, the improvement of the quality of a design of microsystems or micro-components and the reduction of the time and material-consuming production of specimen, advanced simulation and optimization techniques are required. The computer aided development is based on simulation models which must be computable sufficiently fast and need to be parameterizable. In addition they need to be accurate enough, as the quality of an optimization depends highly on the quality of the simulation model; for details we refer to [1]. This paper focuses on the optimization process itself. As the time required for a single evaluation varies from a couple of seconds to some minutes depending on the problem on hand the reduction of the number of fitness calculations is essential for the applicability of evolutionary search techniques to the design optimization task. On the other hand the search technique must be general enough in order to produce reliable results for different applications. We compare the results of the Evolutionary Algorithm GLEAM [2,3,4] and the concept of foreruns with those obtained by standard Evolution Strategies [5] and an extension of ES to spatial structured populations and local selection [6] as well as with a traditional hill climbing method.

Our **SIM**ulation and **O**ptimization **T**ool Environment **SIMOT** [7] will on one hand support the designer to develop and optimize simulation models and on the other hand to optimize complex (micro-)systems or components. It includes optimization tools and simulators. The optimization tools GAMA (Genetic Algorithm for Model Adaptation) and GADO (Genetic Algorithm for Design Optimization) are based on GLEAM and are developments of our institute [8, 9]. The simulators are commercial tools: an FEM simulator, an analog network simulator and Mathematica[1]. The optimizer and the simulator are loosely coupled and may be chosen depending on the problem to be solved. For the optical system described further on we used Mathematica for the simulation and GADO as optimizer. The optimization of the design of a collimation system under realistic production conditions shows how SIMOT is successfully used on a multiple objectives problem with conflicting criteria. The search space of the application is of complex nature although there are only few variables to be considered.

To confirm the forerun approach we use a more complex but nevertheless fast to simulate task, the robot path planning problem.

2 Evolutionary Design Optimization

During the design process the engineer is faced with a large search space of possible design solutions and parameterizations. Building models is limited to a few only. The situation becomes better by creating a computer model which might be evaluated by a simulator. During an optimization process many simulations with various parameter settings have to be done. The complexity of the search space is in general high so that a manual exploration is limited and mainly influenced by personal knowledge, previous experiments, intuition of the engineer and good luck. An optimal system design might not be expected under these conditions.

Assuming that we are able to build a simulation model being accurate enough and parameterizable, then the engineer's optimization task can be supported by evolutionary search techniques explorating and exploitating the search space. The engineer's task is now the specification of the optimization parameters and restrictions and the formulation of the criteria of optimization. In case of multiple objectives being not mutually independent we cannot optimize for the quality goals separately. The formulation of grading functions and priorities as described below gives the engineer the possibility to provide the optimizer with a suitable way of making its decisions.

3 Optimization Algorithms

In this section we give a brief description of the optimization algorithms included in our comparison.

3.1 GLEAM

GLEAM uses a list-like hierarchical data structure. The elements of the data structure depend on the actual application. The hierarchy may be used to treat parts of the data structure as a unit, termed section, and thus prevent them from being separated by the crossover operators or to hide them completely thus prevent them from being modified by any of the genetic operators.

---

1. Mathematica is a registered trademark of Wolfram Research, Inc.

The mutation operator is inspired from its counterpart in evolution strategies in the sense that small variations of genetic values are more likely than larger ones. GLEAM allows the usage of any arbitrary alphabet for the internal representation being mostly naturally induced by the application considered. Assuming that the elements of the underlying alphabet (i.e. the values a certain gene can take) are sorted by some criteria, we create before applying the mutation operator a division of the range of values into classes. By mutation a change of the current gene value to a random value within the nearby classes is very likely and this probability shortens with the distance of a class as defined by a prespecified step function. There are various crossover operators implementing traditional n-point crossover and uniform crossover as used in genetic algorithms and crossover operators respecting the creation and existence of sections, which itself underlay the evolutionary process.

Each genetic operator may be independently activated on a percentage basis. Whenever an operator is chosen, a new offspring is generated. Thus if several genetic operators have a percentage of choice greater than zero, there is a chance that more than one offspring will be generated. The resulting set of full siblings will be evaluated and only the best will be considered to be included into the population as described by the survival rule. Thus there is a surplus of descendants and only the best may reproduce again.

3.2 Concept of Foreruns

Two different types of experiments were performed: the first type consists of a single more-or-less "large" population while the second one is split into a forerun and a main run. The forerun consists of small sized pre-populations performing only a small number of generations. The final best individuals obtained from the foreruns are used to initialize the main population. The idea of combining foreruns followed by a main run is inspired by the promising results of using previous knowledge for the initial population reported in [3] and shall hopefully reduce the number of required evaluations.

3.3 Spatially Structured Populations

The population used in GLEAM consists of uniformly distributed individuals over a geographic region. Interaction of the individuals, i.e. the selection process acting through both, mate selection for reproduction and the selection of descendants for survival, is limited to geographically nearby individuals, the locally overlapping neighborhoods.

In the following experiments with GADO a closed ring structure has been chosen and the size of the neighborhood of any individual is set to 9, thus including the centre individual and its immediate four neighbors to the right and left, respectively. Each centre individual and its partner being chosen within the neighborhood by linear ranking produce offsprings by means of mutation and / or crossover. The descendants are evaluated and the best of them is compared with the centre individual and replaces it immediately, but only if the offspring is better than the weakest in its neighborhood (survival rule better local least) and with the exception of those centre individuals being the best within their neighborhood, then the offspring must be better than the individual itself (local elitism) [4]. This process is continued until a termination criterion is reached, for example a maximum number of evaluations has been done or a prespecified quality is reached.

920

3.4 Standard and Diffusion Model Evolution Strategies

Evolution Strategies are especially powerful algorithms for numerical optimization. Their representation use n object variables x_i ($1 \le i \le n$) and a set of strategy parameters. We use a comma-ES with step size parameters only. The recombination of the object parameters is discrete and for the step size intermediate. There exist multi-modal problems being very difficult for the standard ES with global selection.

Now we use an ES with a diffusion model to clarify the influence of the population structure. As described above we have a spatially structured population with individuals limited to local interaction. Both, the selection of partners for recombination and the selection of descendants for survival are restricted to geographically nearby individuals.

The local parent selection method chooses both parents randomly with replacement from a neighborhood [10], the centric parent selection method takes the centre individual of a neighborhood as first parent and chooses only the second parent randomly from within the neighborhood [6]. In the runs reported we generated 6 descendants on each site at generation t. From this local pool of descendants only the best is chosen to survive and it replaces the centre individual in the next generation t+1. Thus, the local interaction ES, named LES, uses a generational approach whereas GLEAM uses a one-at-a-time transition. A notation, a growth curve analysis and an empirical comparison of the various classes of LES is presented in [6].

3.5 Local Hill Climbing Algorithm

Our simple derivation free hillclimber (Gauss-Seidel-Strategy with fixed step size for the line search and multiple restart) starts from a random initial setting of the parameters. One of them is chosen and optimized until no further improvement of this parameter is possible, then the next one is chosen and optimized and this is repeated until no further improvement is possible.

4 Optimization of a Microoptical Collimation System

The design of systems incorporating a laser beam, as microoptical applications do, mostly requires the modification of the "raw" beam. The beam must be expanded, refocused and collimated. This modification can be performed by using lenses, mirrors or prisms [11]. For our application, the collimation system, we will use two microoptical ball lenses. The geometry of the 2-lens system is shown in Fig. 1.

The beam as it comes out of a single mode fiber is refocused by the first lens and then collimated by the second one in order to position the collimated beam waist at the location of the photodiode. In an ideal case of geometric optics it is possible under some restrictions to derive for each lens with refractive value n1 a second lens with refractive value n2 so that an arbitrary irradiation is yielded. In reality, we need to place the elements into prefabricated LIGA structures [12] and this can only be done with some tolerances. These tolerance values of insertion are given in the top row of Fig. 1.

The variations of the placement influence the position of the beam waist and the diameter of the beam at the photodiode. The optimization task is to determine a collimation system being as insensitive as possible with respect to the variances of insertion.

Fig. 1. Geometry of the collimation system. The bottom box shows the definition of the optimization criteria and the range of success values.

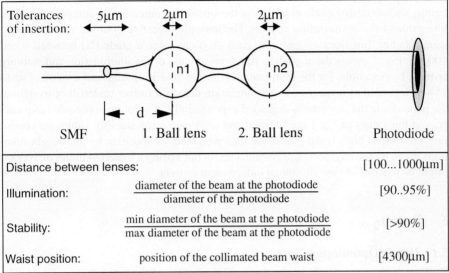

Distance between lenses:			[100...1000µm]
Illumination:	$\dfrac{\text{diameter of the beam at the photodiode}}{\text{diameter of the photodiode}}$		[90..95%]
Stability:	$\dfrac{\text{min diameter of the beam at the photodiode}}{\text{max diameter of the beam at the photodiode}}$		[>90%]
Waist position:	position of the collimated beam waist		[4300µm]

The optimization parameters are the refractive values n1 and n2 of the ball lenses in the range of 1.4 to 2.0 and a value z in the range of 1.0 to 2.0. Using z and the focus of the first ball lens we compute the distance of the fiber to the first lens as

$$d = \frac{z \cdot n1 \cdot R}{2 \times (n1 - 1)}$$

where n1 is the refractive value of the first lens and R=450µm is the radius of this ball lens.

The optimization criteria are stability, illumination, waist position and distance between the two lenses. The definition of these values as well as the range of valid values is given in Fig. 1. The optimum values are 100% for stability, 90% for illumination, 4300µm for the beam waist position and the distance between the lenses should be preferably be above 100µm and below 1000µm.

Fig. 2. Grading functions for illumination (left) and stability (right) .

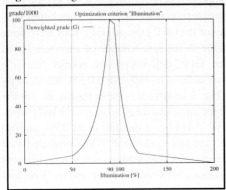
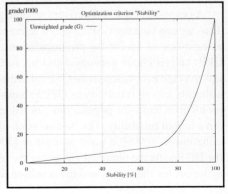

The collimation system is simulated with Mathematica, where the extreme values of the displacement are used to determine the number of necessary Mathematica simulations for one design evaluation. Using the simulation outcome we compute the absolute value of the optimization criteria. The multiple objective optimization is done by using grading functions assigning to each absolute value a grade (N) between 0 and 100000. Fig. 2 shows these grading functions at hand of the illumination and stability criteria. For example, for the illumination criterion 90% is optimal and a value of up to 95% is regarded as a success; if the simulation detects a further underfill or overfill at the photodiode the outcome is degraded exponentially. A solution is regarded as a success, if the values of Fig.1 are fulfilled and with increasing stability values successful runs are ranked higher. All grades are then weighted, as specified by the weight functions given by the engineer, and summed up. In our setting a total maximum of 100000 might be reached in case of mutual independent criteria.

5   Results

5.1   Design Optimization Task

First we present the results of the design optimization of the heterodyne receiver. The hillclimber produced widely differing solutions. Especially, the demands on stability were hard to fulfil. This indicates the highly multimodal nature of the problem. The number of evaluations needed until this strategy converges differs in a wide range of 2000 to 42000 yielding in a range of quality grade values between 72340 and 79068. The best solution found has a stability of 90.3%, an illumination with small overfill of 90.7% and a waist position at 4294.3μm.

For reasons of comparability the runs using GLEAM and the ES were limited to an upper limit of about 36000 evaluations. For each setting (job) 40 runs were done and the quality threshold was set to a grade of 80500, which is not the best we could achieve (the best solution found has a quality of 81031), but a pretty good design quality. We recorded how many runs meet this requirements and how many evaluations were used by the "good" runs. The results are shown in Table 1.

As none of the HC runs meet the target grade the figures for the number of evaluations are calculated on the base of all runs and not of only the "good" ones as with the rest of the table. It is obviously that the HC approach is not sufficient to tackle the task.

As expected GLEAM delivers reliable good results with increasing population size. Thus we can take the GSP7 job as a reference for the GPP jobs. All GPP jobs were done using a size of 16 for the pre-populations. Due to the low number of successful runs GPP1 and GPP4 are not considered any further. GPP2 delivers reliable results with 21% less average evaluations than GSP7. Further reductions to 46% can only be achieved by a slightly loss of reliability as GPP3 shows. Fig. 3 summarizes these results. So for the problem on hand pre-populations can reduce the computational load significantly without a loss of reliability. The best solution of GLEAM has a stability of 91.22%, an illumination of 90.00%, a waist position at 4300.1μm and a grade of 81031.Compared with the HC results the obtained values for the refractive indices lead to completely different materials for the lenses and the resulting distances between the fiber and the first lens

Table 1. Results from hillclimber (HC), GLEAM with single (GSP) and pre-populations (GPP) and Evolution Strategy (ES) and local interaction ES (LES) for the 2 lens problem.

Job	Pre Populations Number	Gen.	Main Population Size	# of Successfull Runs	Speed-up wrt GSP7 [%]	Evaluations of Pre and Main Pops. Median	Average	Variance
HC				1		6483	10986	15354
GSP1			60	28		2570	3844	3765
GSP2			90	28		4472	5845	6782
GSP3			120	36		4295	4802	3905
GSP4			150	39		4231	5252	4799
GSP5			180	39		5825	6276	3989
GSP6			210	39		5858	6644	4020
GSP7			240	40		7674	7743	4282
GPP1	10	10	60	33	41	4082	4601	3433
GPP2	20	10	60	40	21	5719	6113	4291
GPP3	10	20	60	39	46	3407	4147	3168
GPP4	10	10	90	37	33	5343	5195	3301
GPP5	10	20	90	39	30	3193	5448	4792
ES			60	18	53	3600	3600	1819
ES			120	28	7	6480	7200	3285
LES-l			60	33	56	3960	3442	1457
LES-l			90	35	33	4860	5164	2502
LES-c			60	37	45	4380	4287	1667
LES-c			90	40	30	4860	5439	2549

characterize two different optical systems ($n1_{HC} = 2.0$, $n1_G = 1.60$; $n2_{HC} = 1.58$, $n2_G = 1.55$; $d_{HC} = 495\mu m$, $d_G = 791.6\mu m$).

The rows labelled ES in Table 1 give the results for a (60,360)-ES and a (120,720)-ES, respectively. A population size of 60 (120) in the ES corresponds in terms of descendants generated in a single generation to a population size of 120 (240) in GLEAM. The standard ES with global selection has problems to find good solutions reliable for our multi-modal problem of fractal nature.

The rows labelled LES in Table 1 give the results for the local interaction ES with a ring population structure. Due to the results from [6] the neighborhood size is set to 3, the smallest possible. The LES uses only a single step size parameter for all object variables as experiments with a LES using multiple step sizes failed in all cases.

The LES with local parent selection (LES-l) is much more reliable than the global rule ES. The population size 60 found in 80% a solution better than the threshold 80500 and the larger population of size 90 in 88% of the runs.

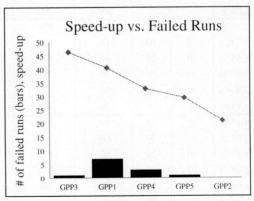

Fig. 3. Speed-up of the GPP runs from Table 1 with respect to GSP7 vs. number of failed runs

The best choice for a local interaction ES is one using the centric parent selection method (LES-c). Due to the soft selection pressure of this local strategy, balancing well exploitation and exploration, all runs for the larger population size converged to a quality above 80500. In addition the number of evaluations needed is comparable low to the GPP3 job of GLEAM.

5.2 Robot Path Planning Task

The question arises how general are these results or are they specific to the problem on hand? Unfortunately it is not possible to conduct such an amount of runs with our previous problem of optimizing a micropump [1] because of the long time of some minutes for each simulation. Thus we decided to fall back to a more complex but very fast to simulate problem, the collision free path planning of a robot movement. The difference to the numerical design optimization problem is that the nature of this task is closer to genetic programming as commands for the robot control are evolved.

The task is to move the end effector of an industrial robot from a given to a target position which is located behind an obstacle on a line as straight and smooth as possible. To do this the robot must turn around 135 degrees avoiding collision with two further obstacles. Beside collision avoidance the deviation from the target, the quality of the path, and the required time for the move are the most important optimization criteria. The robot is controlled on axis level and the sequence and parameters of control commands are subject to evolution. Details of this task and earlier investigations can be found in [3] and results of industrial applications of this approach in [13].

Table 2. Results from GLEAM with single (GSP) and pre-populations (GPP) for the path planning problem using small deme sizes of 5 for the pre-populations and 7 for the main populations.

Job	Pre Populations		Main Popu-lation Size	# of Success-full Runs	Speed-up wrt GSP4 [%]	Evaluations of Pre and Main Pops.		
	Number	Gen.				Median	Average	Variance
GSP1			60	181		40564	79418	110413
GSP2			90	197		42891	72161	107893
GSP3			120	200		48325	73853	109271
GSP4			180	200		65467	77624	59479
GSP5			240	200		77550	93107	84347
GPP1a	10	10	60	189	22	34199	60227	74277
GPP2a	20	10	60	198	19	45550	62543	50927
GPP3a	10	20	60	197	31	43382	53792	38634
GPP4a	10	10	90	198	31	43948	53416	33375
GPP5a	20	10	90	199	9	55375	70995	53907
GPP6a	10	20	90	199	17	48880	64499	49883
GPP1b	10	10	60	197	21	40318	61069	70152
GPP2b	20	10	60	198	13	55687	67849	49867
GPP3b	10	20	60	197	16	53823	65578	46968
GPP4b	10	10	90	200	20	49972	62233	48588
GPP5b	20	10	90	198	14	60893	67160	22477
GPP6b	10	20	90	200	6	61417	72851	50514

Due to the short simulation times of about 1 msec we performed 200 runs for each setting. A run is regarded as successful if the resulting path is collision free, the target deviation is less than 4 mm and the path is "acceptable smooth and straight". The two groups of GPP jobs in Table 2 differ in the population size of 16 (a) and 24 (b) for the pre-populations. As with the design optimization increasing population sizes stabilize the results of GLEAM as the GSP runs show. From a population size of 120 onwards all runs are successful. Despite of the success of GSP3 we choose GSP4 as the reference because the maximum total number of evaluations is with 716000 much lower than the 1.26 million offsprings of GPP3. Thus 716000 is used as upper limit for the number of calculated offsprings for the GPP jobs which must undergo the average value of 77624 evaluations to be better than the single population approach. The first sequence of jobs were made with a deme size of 9 for both, the pre- and the main populations. Most of the jobs delivered 196 or more successful runs but 3 were significantly worse: those with the settings of GPP1a, GPP1b and GPP4a of Table 2. This indicates that settings based on 10 populations with a maximum of 10 generations are fairly small for this problem using this comparable large deme size.

Inspired from the results described in [6] we reduced the deme size of the pre-population to 5 and for the main population to 7. Table 2 shows the results. Now only the GPP1a job must be rejected. All others deliver a greater or the same number of successful runs as with the larger deme sizes. Thus the results from [6] are confirmed by applying it to the GLEAM algorithm on a complete different problem. The jobs with a setting of 10 populations with a maximum of 10 generations each have the greatest potential for improvement due to the low number of evaluations needed in the pre-populations. Now, with the smaller deme sizes they are no longer too instable and deliver the best results, when they are combined with a main population size of 90, as GPP4a and GPP4b show.

GPP1b and GPP3a deliver good improvements too, but as 3 runs failed and we have comparable improvements with lower or no failed runs we do not consider these settings any further. Fig. 4 summarises these results. On the other hand the improvement of 31% or 20% resp. is not as promising as with the 2-lens-problem. Thus we can state that pre-populations can lower the computational load for the

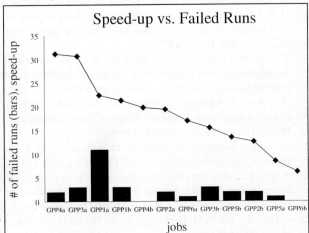

Fig. 4. Speed-up with respect to GSP4 vs. number of failed runs.

robot task too but not in the same magnitude as with the design optimization problem.

So in general the concept of foreruns seem to be able to reduce the amount of evaluations while maintaining the quality of the search.

6   Conclusions

As a result of the investigation in this paper we can state that the Evolutionary Algorithm GLEAM as well as the extension of ES to spatially structured populations are able to solve the multi-modal problem of the 2-lens-system presented. The standard ES with global selection is not able to solve this problem with a sufficiently high convergence reliability. The theoretical investigation as well as the empirical findings using test-bed functions from literature presented in [6] are confirmed by the real-world problem of design optimization taking restrictions of the fabrication process into account.

The concept of foreruns for initialization of the main population of GLEAM as motivated in [3] proved its superiority to a single population concept. A halving of the computational load could be achieved with the design optimization problem at hand. The tendency of these results could be approved for a more complicated application, the collision free robot path planning problem.

Acknowledgements. We like to thank Prof. Christian Blume for the kind permission to use the robot simulator for the work outlined in section 5.2.

References

1.   W. Süß, S. Meinzer, A. Quinte, W. Jakob, H. Eggert: *Simulation and Design Optimization of a Micropump*. Proceedings of MICROSIM'97, Lausanne, Sept. 1997, 127-135
2.   C. Blume: *GLEAM - A System for "Intuitive Learning"*. Proc. of the 1st Int. Workshop on Parallel Problem Solving from Nature. LNCS 496, Springer-Verlag (1991)
3.   W. Jakob, M. Gorges-Schleuter, C. Blume: *Application of Genetic Algorithms to Task Planning and Learning*. Proc. 2nd Int. Conf. PPSN, North-Holland (1992) 291-300
4.   M. Gorges-Schleuter: *Parallel Evolutionary Algorithms and the Concept of Pop. Structures* In: V. Plantamura et al. (Eds): Frontier Decision Support Concepts. Wiley (1994) 261-319
5.   H.-P. Schwefel: *Evolution and Optimum Seeking*. Wiley &Sons, New York (1995)
6.   M. Gorges-Schleuter: *A Comparative Study of Global and Local Selection in Evolution Strategies*. This Proc. on PPSN V.
7.   W. Süß, W. Jakob, M. Gorges-Schleuter et al.: *Design Optimization of Microsystems based on Adaptive Search Techniques*. Computer Aided Optimium Design of Structures V, Computer Mechanics Publications, Southampton (1997) 121-130
8.   W. Jakob, S. Meinzer, A. Quinte, M. Gorges-Schleuter, H. Eggert: *Partial Automated Design optimization Based on Adaptive Search Techniques*. Proceedings of ACEDC 96, PEDC, University of Plymouth (1996)
9.   M. Gorges-Schleuter, W. Jakob, S. Meinzer et al.: *An Evolutionary Algorithm for Design Optimization of Microsystems*. Proc. PPSN IV, LNCS 1141, Springer (1996) 1022-1032
10. J. Sprave: *Linear Neighborhood Evolution Strategy,* Proc. 3rd Ann. Conf. on Evolutionary Programming, World Scientific, River Edge, NJ (1994) 42-51
11. D. C. O'Shea: *Elements of Modern Optical Design*. Wiley & Sons (1985)
12. P. Bley, J. Göttert, M. Harmening et al.: *The LIGA Process for the Fabrication of Micromechanical and Microoptical Components*. Micro System Technologies 91, VDE Verlag, Berlin (1991)
13. C. Blume: *Planning of Collision-free Movements for Industrial Robots Using Evolutionary Algorithms (in german)*. Automatisierungstechnische Praxis (atp) 12/97, Oldenburg Verlag. 58-67 (1997)

Aspects of Digital Evolution: Evolvability and Architecture

Julian F. Miller[1] and Peter Thomson[1]

[1]Department of Computing, Napier University, 219 Colinton Road,
Edinburgh, EH14 1DJ, UK. Email: j.miller@dcs.napier.ac.uk,
p.thomson@dcs.napier.ac.uk
Telephone: +44 (0)131 455 4305

Abstract. This paper describes experiments to determine how the architecture *vis-a-vis* routing and functional resources affect the ease with which combinational logic designs may be evolved on a field-programmable gate array (FPGA). We compare two chromosome representations with differing levels of connectivity, and show that the amount of routing and functional resource have a marked effect on the success of the evolutionary process.

0. Introduction

There is, at the current time, a growing interest in designing electronic circuits using evolutionary techniques [11]. Koza [8] showed how simple digital circuits could be evolved using Genetic Programming, and Iba et. al. [5] showed how it was possible to design circuits by evolving the functionality and connectivity of interconnected AND, OR, and NOT gates for intended use on a programmable logic array device (PLA). The group at EPFL developed a cellular automaton in hardware using Xilinx XC6216 Field Programmable Gate Arrays (FPGAs) which was able to carry out global synchronisation tasks despite the fact that the cells behaviour was determined locally [2]. Thompson [12] used a genetic algorithm to directly evolve configuring bit strings for the Xilinx 6216 chip to create a circuit which would carry out a frequency discrimination task. Other workers have evolved digital circuits with a variety of representations [3, 4, 7]

Our own early work evolving digital electronic circuits using genetic algorithms has concentrated on arithmetic circuits [1][10]. Although we showed that it was possible to evolve novel designs for small circuits (e.g. the two-bit multiplier) we recognised how much more difficult it became to evolve circuits with just a modest increase in function complexity, e.g. the three-bit multiplier.

In this paper our motivation is the understanding of the design factors which influence the ease with which we can evolve 100% functionally correct digital combinational circuits. We contend that the issue of the circuit *architecture* is of primary importance here. The circuit architecture means essentially how the digital logic is implemented using logical sub-blocks, how complex is the logic within the sub-blocks, and how the sub-blocks may be connected together. The particular model of the architecture we are concerned with here is known as *fine-grained*. In this architecture the circuit is implemented using an array of simple cells, each of which may become any two-input logic gate or single control multiplexer. Also the cells have a regular connection pattern. Such an architecture is provided on the Xilinx XC6216 FPGA. Here we are concerned with the relative importance of the amount of functional cells and the connectivity (routing) of those cells in the *evolvability* of combinational logic circuits.

We have already devised two different chromosome representations A and B for feed-forward logic circuits [1][9][10]. Type A chromosome was a netlist - a set of interconnections and gate level functionality for a rectangular array of cells which form the connections between the primary inputs and outputs. The inputs of cells in a particular column could be connected to the outputs of cells in previous columns (or indeed the primary inputs) according to a *levels-back* connectivity parameter. The type B chromosome was again a netlist, however it simulated exactly the architecture of the Xilinx 6216 FPGA. Here we compare the performance of the two representations and then go on to examine in some detail how varying the connectivity and functionality of the array of cells affects the evolvability of a two-bit binary multiplier circuit.

1. Two Chromosome Representations of a cellular array

1.1 Chromosome A

Consider a 3 x 3 array of logic cells between two required primary inputs and two required outputs using a chromosome of type A. The inputs 0 and 1 represent fixed values, logic '0' and logic '1' respectively.

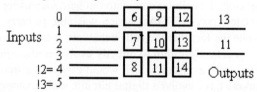

Fig. 1. A 3 x 3 geometry of uncommitted logic cells with inputs, outputs and netlist numbering.

The inputs (two in this case) are numbered 2 and 3, with 2 being the most significant. The lines 4 and 5 represent the inverted inputs 2 and 3 respectively. The logic cells which form the array are numbered column-wise from 6 to 14. The outputs are numbered 13 and 11, meaning that the most significant output is connected to the output of cell 13 and the least significant output is connected to the output of cell 11. These integer values, while denoting the physical location of each input, cell or output within the structure, now also represent connections or *routes* between the various points. Each of the logic cells is capable of assuming the functionality of any two-input logic gate, or, alternatively a 2-1 *multiplexer* (MUX) with single control input. A sample chromosome is shown below:

$$0\ 2\ -1 \quad 1\ 3\ -5 \quad 2\ 4\ 3 \quad 2\ 6\ 7 \quad 0\ 8\ -10 \quad 7\ 8\ -4 \quad 6\ 11\ 9 \quad 6\ 4\ -9 \quad 2\ 11\ 7 \quad 13 \quad 11$$

Fig. 2 A type A chromosome for the 3 x 3 geometry of Figure 1

In this arrangement the chromosome is split into groups of three integers. The first two values represent points to which the first and second inputs of the gate are connected. The third value may either be positive - in which case it is taken to represent the control input of a MUX - or negative - where it is taken to represent a two-input gate. The inputs are labeled A and B for convenience. The following notation is used: (i) & = AND, (ii) | = OR, (iii) ^ = exclusive-OR, and (iv) ! = NOT. For the chromosome, the allowed functions are listed in Table 1, where -1 indicates A&B, -2 indicates A&!B and so on through to -12.

1.2 Chromosome B

The Xilinx 6216 FPGA internal cell architecture is an arrangement of 64 x 64 simple cells. Each cell can be either a two-input logic gate or a 2-1 line MUX.

Since we are considering only combinational designs it is vital to allow only *feed-forward* circuits. To achieve this we chose a cell connection scheme in which inputs are fed into a cell which are *East-going* or *North-going* only. If the cell is a MUX then we allow the control input of the MUX to arrive from the North (indicated by 'S'). In Figure 3 the cells are numbered according to their column and row position with the origin at the bottom left hand corner of the array. All arrows pointing towards (outwards from) a cell represent inputs (outputs). The primary inputs connect to cells on the leftmost column and lowest row. The primary outputs exit the cells which are located on the topmost row and the rightmost column (in this case cells in column and row two).

The cells are allowed to be one of the types shown in Table 1. A and B represent 'E' and 'N' inputs and C represents 'S' input. If a cell at position (col, row) is a MUX then the 'S' input is assumed to the 'E' output of the cell located at position (col-1, row+1). If the MUX cell is located at column zero then we take the control input of the MUX from the primary input located at position (-1, row+1). In such a scheme cells in the top row are not allowed to be MUXs.

The chromosome has four parts; functional, routing, input, and output. The functional chromosome is a set of integers representing the possible cell types as indicated by gate type in Table 1.

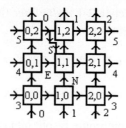

Fig. 3. Cell connections for Chromosome B

For N cells in the rectangular array there are N pairs (i,j), i ,j ε {0,1,2}, of routing genes which make up the routing chromosome, where the first (second) element of the pair represents the North (East) output. If i or j equals 0 then the North (East) output is connected to the East (North) input, and if i or j equals 1 then the North (East) output is connected to the North (East) input. If a routing gene is 2 then the corresponding cell output is a function of the cell inputs. Thus, the routing chromosome ignores the corresponding gene in the functional chromosome if its value is set to 0 or 1. The input chromosome has #rows + #columns elements. Each element can take any integer from 0 to #primary_inputs - 1. The output chromosome has #primary_outputs elements which represent the places in the cellular array from which the primary outputs are to be taken. To illustrate the interpretation of the chromosome consider the chromosome example (Table 2), which represents a chromosome for a 2x3 array of cells. For the sake of argument imagine that the target function is a 1-bit adder with carry. This has three inputs A, B, Cin and two outputs S and Cout.

Table 1. Allowed functionalities of cells

Gate Type	Function	Gate Type	Function
-4	!A & !C + !B & C	6	A ^ B
-3	A & !C + !B & C	7	A | B
-2	!A & !C + B & C	8	!A & !B
-1	A & !C + B & C	9	!A ^ B
1	0	10	!B
2	1	11	A | !B
3	A & B	12	!A
4	A & !B	13	!A | B
5	!A & B	14	!A | !B

We read the chromosome in the cell order (0,0) - (2,0) and (0,1) - (2,1) following from Figure 3. The inputs and outputs are also read in as shown in Figure 1. Thus the cell at (1,1) is a MUX of type - 1 (see Table 1). Its outputs as indicated by (2,2), in the routing part, are routed out to North and East. The inputs on the bottom row are Cin, A, A, and along the left edge, Cin and B. The Outputs S and Cout are connected to the top row middle cell and bottom right hand corner cell (east output) respectively.

In the genetic algorithm we used uniform crossover with tournament selection (size 2). Winners of tournaments are accepted with a probability of 0.7. The routing chromosomes are all initialised to 2; 0 and 1 are only introduced by mutation, this is found to be more effective than random initialisation., this allows initially the circuit to use the maximum number of functional cells. Figure 4 demonstrates that this is advantageous. We use a fixed mutation rate which can be expressed as the percentage of all genes in the population to be randomly altered. The breeding rate represents the percentage of all chromosomes in the population which will be replaced by their offspring.

Table 2. Example chromosome for 2x3 array

Functional Part	Routing Part	Input part	Output part
2,9,11,12,-1,6	0,1,2,1,1,2,2,2,2,2,0,0	2,0,0,2,1	3,1

2. Functional and Routing Cell Resource Allocation

In considering new architectures for digital circuit evolution, there are two key issues: (a) *functionality of cells* - where evolution selects the logical functionality of a particular cell, and determines whether or not that cell should possess functionality, and (b) *routing* - where the routes that provide the interconnect between functional cells are evolved into non-functional cells (or functional cells which are partially used as routes).

The routeability of circuits is an important practical issue which is aptly demonstrated by a combinational design problem known as SBOX. This is a circuit used in data encryption. Traditional synthesis techniques are not able to produce a design which will place and route on to the Xilinx 6216 within the geometric bounding-box currently desired by engineers. This shows the importance of designing in such a way as to incorporate both issues of functionality of circuits *and* also the manner in which they route on target devices.

We conducted four sets of experiments. The first contrasted the relative effectiveness of evolution using type A and type B chromosomes. The second looked at the effectiveness of allocating functional and routing cells in particular patterns. The third compared the performance obtained using a differentiated cellular structure with that of an undifferentiated structure for a fixed maximum available functional resource. The fourth was to allocate increasingly more routing resource for a fixed average number of functional cells. The purpose being an assessment of the dependence of the evolvability of circuits with relative amounts of functionality and routing.

3. Results

In all experiments the average fitness was calculated over 10 iterations of the GA. The population size was 50, the breeding rate was 100% and the mutation rate 1%. Elitism was always used as it improves the performance markedly [9]. In the first set of experiments we compared the performance of chromosome A (levels-back = 2) with chromosome B. Figure 4 below shows the result of this. Figure 4(a) shows the numbers of instances of 100% functionally correct circuits for the two approaches, while Figure 4(b) shows the performance in terms of average fitness achieved.

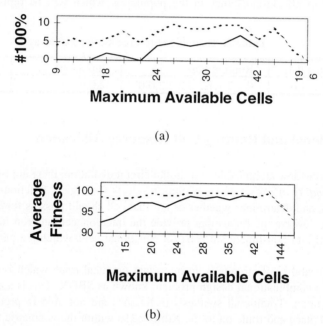

(a)

(b)

Fig. 4. Comparison of Cell Structure A (broken) with Cell Structure B

Clearly, the chromosome representation A is able to evolve the circuit more easily (shown as a broken line). This is not entirely surprising because of the much greater freedom that A has in its choice of inter-cell routing. However, it does show that routing is important. Note that when the number of available cells reaches a value of around 40 the two approaches have approximately the same effectiveness. This may be because the amount of function and routing resource is so great that the second more constrained representation has become rich enough in resource to achieve a similar level of performance. One other noteworthy feature of Figure 4 is the almost constant level of performance of the representation A. This is surprising because the search-space is growing enormously over this interval. However, the solution space may be growing at the same rate. It may be that in these problems the *navigability* of the fitness landscape is more important than it overall size.

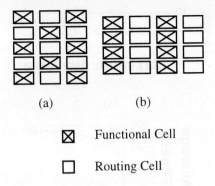

(a)   (b)

☒   Functional Cell

☐   Routing Cell

Fig. 5. The chequerboard and stacked pattern of functional cells

In the second set of experiments we deliberately *differentiated* functional and routing cells in particular patterns - chequerboard or stacked. This is shown in Figure 5.

These patterns were preserved throughout the run using directed mutation. We found the two schemes made very little difference to the success of evolution - as measured by the average fitnesses that were obtainable. This is an interesting result because it shows that when the same proportion of routing resource is available to two different internal structures, they produce comparable results. Therefore, it may be that it is not so much the structure of functional and routing resources that is so important, but rather the ability for each functional cell to find many *alternative* routes to neighbouring cells. This freedom was the essential difference between approaches A and B. This conclusion does not mean that differentiation of cells is ineffective. Many more experiments need to be carried out to assess the actual way in which differentiation should take place.

In our third set of experiments we compared the effectiveness of a differentiated cell approach with an undifferentiated scheme. In the differentiated strategy, cells are forced to be either functional or routing - although some of the functional cells can through mutation and crossover incorporate internal routes. In order to compare a differentiated scheme with an undifferentiated one, we have to double the number of cells. This is so that the maximum number of available functional cell outputs was the same for the two methods. The results are shown in Figure 6.

Clearly, the differentiated approach (shown as a broken line) is the more effective of the two up to approximately 25 available functional cells. Thus it appears that a differentiated scheme eases the evolutionary process, and must be taken into account in the design of an architecture suitable for evolution. It is also interesting to note the very similar average fitness growth with increasing number of available cells. This suggests that the number of functional cells is the dominant factor. This is probably because there are many different ways in logic of building the same circuit functionality, and the increasing availability of cells which provide these options leads to a greater chance that the evolutionary path through the space of all possible circuits will be successful.

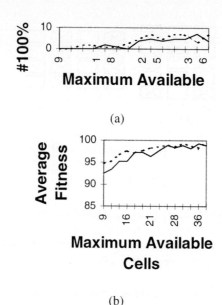

(a)

(b)

Fig. 6. Comparison of Differentiated and Undifferentiated Cell Structures

In the fourth set of experiments we allocated functional cells with different probabilities. A geometry of cells is selected, then functional cells are introduced with a
chosen probability. This means that for a probability of, say, 0.1, and a geometry of
16 cells, then 3.2 cell outputs (each cell possesses 2 actual outputs) on average will be
allocated as functional. The remainder become routing cells. Clearly, as the geometry
is increased, the total amount of available routing resource is increased for the same
probability. Therefore, we obtain a set of results which have similar numbers of functional cells but different amounts of routing. This enables us to compare how this
eases the evolutionary process. The results of these experiments are detailed in Figure
7.

The graph of Figure 7 demonstrates that routing, whilst not dominant, is a vitally
important consideration in the success of evolution as applied to circuit design. The
graph shows that even when a structure has a more than adequate functional resource,
it is still extremely difficult to evolve 100% correct designs if it is starved of routing
options. The average fitness is unable to achieve the level that is mandatory (>96% on
average) in order for 100% correct designs to emerge. This is very clear in the case
where the number of cell outputs which are devoted to routing is between 0 and 5
(see routing allocation legend) on average. In this particular set of results, there are
simply too few routing options for evolution to find any 100% correct solutions except perhaps where functional options dominate (at the higher end).

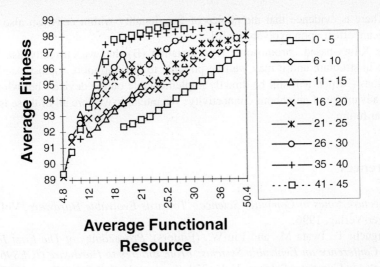

Average Functional Resource

Fig. 7. Results for Functional against Fitness for Different Routing Resource

4. Conclusions

This paper has discussed the importance of the architecture to digital evolution. We show that the selection of the amount of functional and routing resource is important for the evolvability of circuits.

This is particularly highlighted in the case where the amount of functional resource is kept constant and the amount of routing resource is steadily increased. We saw that in the functionally starved domain (< 10 in Figure 7) the amount of routing resources provided is less important, whereas in the functionally enriched domain (>18), the availability of routing has a much more pronounced effect upon the success of evolution. The success of chromosome A relative to B leads us to conclude that one of the most important factors in designing an architecture specifically for evolution is the average number of neighbouring cells to which any particular cell may connect. We defined two differentiated cell structures and found a similarity of performance which may be explained by the fact that the average cell neighbourhood size was approximately the same. We intend to examine other differentiated schemes in which this neighbourhood size is varied more markedly.

Therefore, these two points should be taken into account when attempting to create any new architecture for evolution: (i) that adequate functional resources should be supplied, closely followed by adequate routing resources, and (ii) that these should be arranged in structures whereby full advantage can be taken of inter-function connectivity.

Another aspect which may affect the evolvability of circuits is the type of functional cell resource supplied (what gates are provided, in terms of type and complexity). There is evidence that the choice of functionality within cells can also have a significant effect upon evolvability [6].

The Xilinx-based chromosome representation (B) that we currently use is very simple in structure and it may well be possible to develop more sophisticated representations - which will still be directly implementable on the device - but which take better advantage of neighbour connectivity. We intend to explore all of these issues in the near future.

References

[A] *Lecture Notes in Computer Science - Towards Evolvable Hardware*, Vol. 1062, Springer-Verlag, 1996.
[B] Higuchi T., Iwata M., and Liu W., (Editors), *Proceedings of The First International Conference on Evolvable Systems: From Biology to Hardware (ICES96)*, Lecture Notes in Computer Science, Vol. 1259, Springer-Verlag, Heidelberg, 1997.
1. Fogarty T. C., Miller J. F., and Thomson P.: *Evolving Digital Logic Circuits on Xilinx 6000 Family FPGAs*, in Soft Computing in Engineering Design and Manufacturing, P.K. Chawdhry,R. Roy and R.K.Pant (eds), Springer-Verlag, London, pages 299-305,1998.
2. Goeke M., Sipper M., Mange D., Stauffer A., Sanchez E., and Tomassini M., "Online Autonomous Evolware", in [B], pp. 96 -106
3. Higuchi T., Iwata M., Kajitani I., Iba H., Hirao Y., Furuya T., and Manderick B., "Evolvable Hardware and Its Applications to Pattern Recognition and Fault-Tolerant Systems", in [A], pp. 118-135.
4. Hemmi H., Mizoguchi J., and Shimonara K., " Development and Evolution of Hardware Behaviours", in [A], pp. 250 - 265.
5. Iba H., Iwata M., and Higuchi T., Machine Learning Approach to Gate-Level Evolvable Hardware, in [B], pp. 327 - 343.
6. Kalganova T., Miller J. F.: *Some Aspects of an Evolvable Hardware Approach for Multiple-Valued Combinational Circuit Design*, submitted to ICES'98, March 1998.
7. Kitano H., "Morphogenesis of Evolvable Systems", in [A], pp. 99-107.
8. Koza J. R., *Genetic Programming*, The MIT Press, Cambridge, Mass., 1992.
9. Miller J. F., Thomson, P.: *Aspects of Digital Evolution: Geometry and Learning*, submitted to ICES'98, March 1998.
10. Miller J. F., Thomson P., and Fogarty T. C.: *Designing Electronic Circuits Using Evolutionary Algorithms. Arithmetic Circuits: A Case Study*, in Genetic Algorithms and Evolution Strategies in Engineering and Computer Science: D. Quagliarella, J. Periaux, C. Poloni and G. Winter (eds), Wiley, 1997.
11. Sipper M., Sanchez E., Mange D., Tomassini M., Perez-Uribe A., and Stauffer A.: *A Phylogenetic, Ontogenetic, and Epigenetic View of Bio-Inspired Hardware Systems*, IEEE Transactions on Evolutionary Computation, Vol. 1, No 1., pp. 83-97.
12. Thompson A: *An Evolved Circuit, Intrinsic in Silicon, Entwined with Physics*, in [B], pp.390-405.

Integrated Facility Design Using an Evolutionary Approach with a Subordinate Network Algorithm

Bryan A. Norman, Alice E. Smith and Rifat Aykut Arapoglu

Department of Industrial Engineering
University of Pittsburgh
Pittsburgh, PA 15261 USA
banorman@engrng.pitt.edu or aesmith@engrng.pitt.edu

Abstract. The facility design problem is a common one in manufacturing and service industries and has been studied extensively in the literature. However, restrictions on the scope of the design problem have been imposed by the limitations of the optimization techniques employed. This paper uses an evolutionary approach with a subordinate network optimization algorithm to produce integrated designs that have better translations into physical plant designs. A new distance metric to consider material travel along the perimeter of the departments to and from input/output locations is devised. This perimeter distance metric is used in the objective function to produce facility designs that simultaneously optimize design of department shapes, department placement and location of the department input/output points.

1. Introduction

Facility design problems are a family of design problems involving the partitioning of a planar region into departments or work centers of given area, so as to minimize the costs associated with projected interactions between departments. These costs usually reflect material handling costs among departments. Such problems occur in many organizations, including manufacturing cell design, hospital design, and service center design. By any monetary measure, facilities design is an important problem and one that has assumed even greater importance as manufacturers strive to become more agile and responsive (Tompkins, 1997). For U.S. manufacturers, between 20% to 50% of total operating expenses are spent on material handling and an appropriate facilities design can reduce these costs by at least 10% to 30% (Meller and Gau, 1996). Dr. James A. Tompkins, one of the seminal researchers in the field, recently wrote, "Since 1955, approximately 8 percent of the U.S. GNP has been spent annually on new facilities. In addition, existing facilities must be continually modified...These issues represent more than $250 billion per year attributed to the design of facility systems, layouts, handling systems, and facilities locations..." (Tompkins, 1997). Altering facility designs due to incorrect decisions, forecasts or assumptions usually involves considerable cost, time and disruption of activities. On the other hand, good designs can reap economic and operational benefits for a long time period. Therefore, computational time is not an important issue for these design decisions, instead the critical aspect is layouts that translate readily into physical reality and minimize material handling costs. The problem primarily studied in the literature has been "block layout" which only specifies the placement of the departments, without regard for aisle structure and material handling system, machine placement within departments or input/output (I/O) locations. Block layout is usually a precursor to these subsequent design steps, termed "detailed layout." Two recent survey articles on the facility design problem are Kusiak and Heragu (1987) and Meller and Gau (1996).

The problem was originally formalized by Armour and Buffa (1963) as follows. There is a rectangular region, R, with fixed dimensions H and W, and a collection of n required departments, each of specified area a_j and dimensions of h_j and w_j, whose total area, $\sum_j a_j = A = H \times W$. There is a material flow F(j,k) associated with each pair

of departments (j,k) which generally includes a traffic volume in addition to a unit cost to transport that volume. There may also be fixed costs between departments j and k. F(j,k) might also include inter-floor costs. The objective is to partition R into n subregions representing each of the n departments, of appropriate area, in order to:

$$\min \quad Z = \sum_{\substack{j=1 \\ j \neq k}}^{n} \sum_{k=1}^{n} F(j,k) d(j,k,\Pi) \tag{1}$$

where d(j,k,Π) is the distance between the centroid of department j and the centroid of department k in the partition Π. This centroidal distance is easy to calculate and it is intuitive in that the mass of material is considered to move between the centers of departments along the shortest rectilinear (Manhattan) or Euclidean distance. However, the centroid distance metric is not realistic in that it ignores the aisle structure that is present in all facilities, where the aisles are normally located along the departmental perimeters and connect I/O points in each department.

Because of the computational complexities in optimizing multiple and non-linear objectives and constraints, only limited work has been done to improve upon the centroid to centroid distance metric; distance along aisles (Benson and Foote, 1997 and Tretheway and Foote, 1994) and expected distance using integration (Bozer and Meller, 1997). The recent work of Benson and Foote (1997) in particular, considers the placement of aisles and I/O points *after* the relative location of the departments and the general aisle structure have been selected. Related work on integrated facility layout that considers machine placement includes papers by Nagi and others (Harhalakis, et al., 1996 and Kane and Nagi, 1997). This work uses predefined departmental shapes set on a grid covering the facility space. In Harhalakis et al. (1996), Dijkstra's shortest path algorithm is used to calculate the rectilinear distance to and from pre-specified I/O points. In Kane and Nagi (1997), I/O points are placed during the optimization and a constraint is imposed to encourage aisles that are straight. Both papers use a simulated annealing heuristic to alter departmental placement. Another related work is by Banerjee et al. (1997) where a genetic algorithm finds a "rough" layout that is then fully defined using a subordinate mathematical programming routine. The number of I/O's per department is pre-specified and then they are optimally located with the department placement. Rectilinear distance (but not along departmental perimeters) is calculated between I/O points.

This paper seeks to improve upon these attempts at integrated facility design by using a perimeter distance metric. If aisles have negligible area compared to the plant area and aisle capacity and direction of flow are not considered (i.e., two way flow through each aisle is allowed), I/O points can be placed concurrently with block layout, producing a one stage optimization procedure that considers material flow from I/O to I/O along departmental perimeters. This still does not achieve the ideal situation where a true aisle structure will also be optimally designed concurrently. This simplification, instead, assumes that all department perimeters are legitimate aisles.

2. Formulation and Solution Methodology

The basic assumption is that the departments must be rectangular, of specified area, and fit within a rectangular bounding facility that is equal to, or larger than, the sum of the departmental areas. The formulation used is "flexbay" of Tate and Smith (1993, 1995) that is a more restrictive version of a slicing tree formulation (Tam, 1992a and 1992b) (see Figure 1). Flexbay makes cuts in a single direction to establish a set of bays that can vary in area. The bays are then subdivided into departments. The flexbay encoding can enforce both departmental areas and departmental shapes, through use of a maximum aspect ratio constraint[1] or a minimum departmental side length constraint for a stated department area. The flexbay approach can only design departments that are rectangular; therefore any irregular departments would have to somehow be cast as rectangular components.

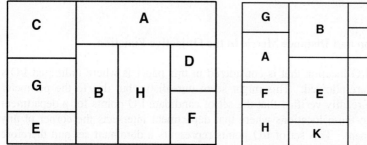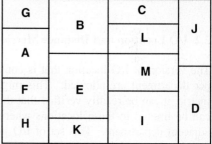

Fig. 1. Typical slicing tree (left) and flexbay (right) layouts

2.1 The Evolutionary Approach

To find the optimal or near-optimal block layout, a genetic algorithm (GA) is used

---

[1] Aspect ratio is the ratio of the longer side to the shorter side of a department.

with the flexbay formulation. The genetic algorithm works with a variable length encoding of the layout where there is a one to one correspondence between each encoding and each layout, excepting mirror image layouts. The encoding is a permutation of departments that specifies their order within the layout, with a concatenated string indicating where the bay breaks within the permutation occur. For example, the flexbay layout of Figure 1 would be represented with the following encoding:

G A F H B E K C L M I J D H K I

where the last three characters indicate bay breaks after departments H, K and I. While the number of departments in the string is fixed, the number of bay breaks is not, and may assume any value from zero (no bay breaks) to n (the number of departments).

Crossover is accomplished through a variant of uniform crossover, where two parents create one offspring. The department sequence is subject to uniform crossover with repair to ensure feasible permutations. The bay structure is taken directly from one parent or the other with equal probability. Mutation consists of permutation altering (50%), or adding (25%) or deleting (25%) a bay break. The permutation mutation is inversion between two randomly selected departments in the permutation. Crossover and mutation are performed independently of each other, with all solutions (parents and offspring) currently available equally likely to be mutated. This independence strategy was noted by Reeves (1997) to hold potential as a general GA strategy. Solutions are selected for crossover using a rank-based quadratic method and a constant population size is maintained. Tate and Smith (1995) includes the details of these.

2.2 I/O Location and Distance Metric in the Objective Function

The version of I/O location that is considered in this paper is where unlimited I/O's per department are allowed. This might seem unrealistic, but due to the perimeter metric, it can be readily verified that the set of candidate I/O points for a department can be limited to those locations where that department intersects the corner of any adjacent department. This set of I/O points represents a dominant set and therefore the algorithm can be limited to consider only these points as potential I/O locations. Because of the flexible bay construct, the number of I/O points can be further bounded to $2n$-2 and does not depend on bay structure (Norman et al., in review). Using the example of Figure 1, the candidate I/O points would be as shown in Figure 2 on the left. To clarify the perimeter distance metric, if the I/O's used were as shown in Figure 2 on the right, the material will traverse over the perimeters shown in the dashed lines.

If each department can have an unconstrained number of I/O stations then the interdepartmental aisle travel distances can be found by formulating this problem as one of finding the shortest path on a network. The flexbay representation facilitates the development of this model due to the inherent bay structure imposed on the layout. All of the arc lengths in the resulting shortest path problem will be positive since they represent physical distances. The shortest path problem with positive arc lengths has been well studied in the network optimization literature and efficient algorithms exist for solving this problem exactly (Ahuja et al., 1993). This makes it possible to quickly evaluate the actual aisle travel distance for each layout that is generated during the search process as a subordinate call from the GA.

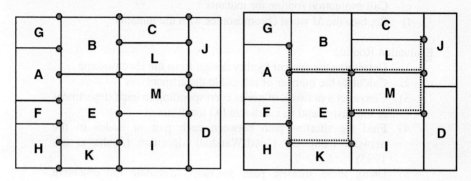

Fig. 2. Possible I/O points on a flexbay layout (left) and material flow (right)

The objective function of the GA is:

$$Z(\Pi) = \sum_{\substack{j=1 \\ j \neq k}}^{n} \sum_{k=1}^{n} F_{j,k} d_{j,k} + m^3 \left(Z_{feas} - Z_{all} \right) \qquad (2)$$

where m is the number of departments in layout Π which violate the aspect ratio or minimum side length constraint, Z_{feas} is the objective function value for the best feasible solution found so far, and Z_{all} is the unpenalized objective function value for the best solution found so far. In this case $d_{j,k}$ is defined as the shortest rectilinear distance along departmental perimeters between the I/O stations of departments j and k as found by the subordinate network optimization. The penalty function is a variation of the adaptive one proposed by Smith and others (Coit et al., 1996, Smith and Coit, 1997, Smith and Tate, 1993). It has the property of self-scaling by using feedback during the search on the relative difference between the best feasible and infeasible solutions, and includes a distance metric to feasibility (in this case, the number of infeasible departments in the layout). Of course when $m = 0$ (no departments violate the aspect ratio constraint) the objective function is simply the summed rectilinear distances between I/Os along department perimeters times the flow quantities between each pair of departments.

The flow of the algorithm is shown below in pseudocode:

1. Randomly initialize the population of chromosomes
2. For $j = 1$ to the maximum number of generations
   a) Select two parent chromosomes based on ranked fitness and perform uniform crossover with repair to produce one offspring

b) Call evaluation routine for offspring
c) Replace the worst chromosome in the current population with the offspring
d) Randomly select M chromosomes[2] for mutation using the mutation rate and perform mutation
e) Call evaluation routine for mutants
f) Replace the M worst chromosomes with the mutants

Evaluation Routine
1) Determine the current facility design from the chromosome
2) Calculate the number of infeasible departments, m
3) Construct a network of nodes corresponding to each department in the design and its candidate I/O locations
4) Find the shortest path between each pair of nodes in the network using the Floyd-Warshall algorithm (Ajuha et al., 1993)
5) Using these shortest path distances, calculate the objective value using equation 2

3. Test Problems and Results

Several problems from the literature were solved in the manner described in Section 2. While the material flows, departmental areas and constraints are identical to those previously studied, results cannot be compared directly as the distance metric used previously was the centroid to centroid. The problems are from Bazaraa (Bazaraa, 1975 and Hassan et al., 1986) (14 departments) and Armour and Buffa (1963) (20 departments). The GA settings were the same as in Tate and Smith (1995): population size of 10, mutation rate of 50% and number of solutions (offspring and mutants) generated = 600,000. While the small population size and large mutation rate are nonstandard in the GA literature, for this implementation, larger population sizes and / or reduced mutation rates were not superior. A variety of GA parameter settings were explored, and while the search was not particularly sensitive to alterations in the parameters, the combination used in the research herein was the most effective. The number of solutions generated that is needed to adequately explore the search space is dependent strongly on the number of departments, n. The 600,000 value was appropriate for the larger Armour and Buffa problem while the smaller Bazaraa problem converged in much fewer number of solutions searched.

Objective function values from the perimeter metric are in Table 1, where the best, median, worst and standard deviation over ten random seeds are shown. The twenty department Armour and Buffa (A&B) problem was studied with maximum aspect ratios of 10, 7, 5, 4, 3 and 2, which represent problems ranging from lightly constrained to extremely constrained. The Bazaraa problem used a maximum side

---

[2] M is upper bounded by at least one less than the population size, creating an elitist GA.

length of one as the shape constraint as done by previous authors. For comparison using the Bazaraa 14 problem, the best design using the perimeter metric is shown compared to the best layout from Tate and Smith (1995) using the rectilinear centroid to centroid distance metric in Figure 3. Also shown are the I/O points and the material flow paths inherent in each formulation. Note that department 14 (shaded) is a "dummy" department with no flows, hence the lack of an I/O. It appears that the perimeter metric with I/O location on the boundaries of the departments is a better reflection of the physical movement of material for most manufacturing and service scenarios. The centroid method not only traverses through the interior of intervening departments, it assumes the minimum rectilinear distance between pairs of departments, creating nearby parallel paths as seen in departments 5 and 6. Designs where the centroids are not located along the same line (as they are in departments 1 through 4) would create even more paths. This is shown in Figure 4, the Armour & Buffa problem with aspect ratio constraint of 3, for the best Tate and Smith (1995) layout and the best of this research. As a further comparison of the merit of concurrently optimizing both department layout and I/O placement, the objective function (equation 2) was calculated for the best layouts from Tate and Smith (1995) (Figures 3 and 4 top, respectively). I/Os were placed on these layouts using the shortest path algorithm. The values of equation 2 were 2847.1 and 997.8 (Bazaraa and Armour and Buffa, respectively), which compares with the values of 1343.2 and 942.6 for the concurrent approach of this paper. Therefore, performing the optimization separately (first, the block layout, then the I/O and routing) results in designs that are generally inferior to those found by combining the steps during optimization.

Table 1. Comparisons of results over ten seeds

Problem	Best	Median	Worst	Standard Deviation
Bazaraa 14	1343.2	1459.2	1607.9	92.8
A&B 20/10	757.1	862.9	1221.0	147.2
A&B 20/7	785.8	1079.9	1267.4	155.2
A&B 20/5	949.4	1319.6	2176.4	343.0
A&B 20/4	1025.7	1189.2	1758.1	236.3
A&B 20/3	942.6	1478.1	2298.5	354.0
A&B 20/2*	1244.1	1873.6	3359.8	787.2

* For the six of the ten runs that found feasible layouts.

4. Conclusions

Using the flexible GA meta-heuristic with the very efficient subordinate exact network optimization algorithm enables effective and efficient optimization of facility designs that correspond well to physical designs. A new distance metric that more accurately reflects material handling costs than does the popular departmental centroid to centroid distance metric was developed. The perimeter distance metric is coupled with the location of the input and output locations of each department. This makes it possible to *concurrently* optimize four facets of the facility design problem:

department locations within the facility, department shapes within certain constraints, I/O placement and travel paths along the department perimeters. Since facility design has significant monetary ramifications, improved optimization approaches to more realistic, albeit more complex, formulations will result in tangible benefits over a long time horizon.

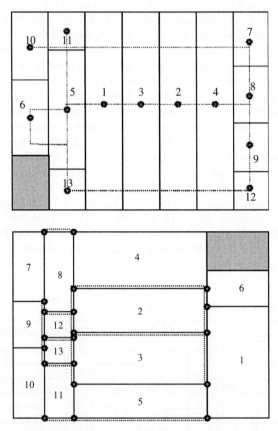

Fig. 3. I/O points and flow paths (dashed) for the centroid distance metric (top) and the perimeter distance metric (bottom) for the Bazaraa 14 problem

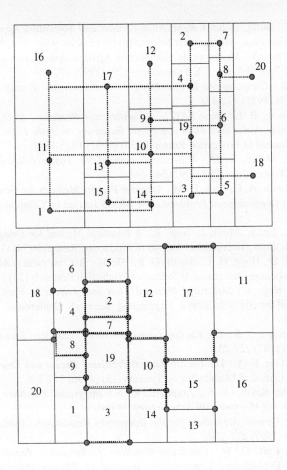

Fig. 4. I/O points and flow paths (dashed) for the centroid distance metric (top) and the perimeter distance metric (bottom) for the Armour and Buffa problem with aspect ratio constraint of 3

Acknowledgment

Alice E. Smith gratefully acknowledges the support of the U.S. National Science Foundation CAREER grant DMI 95-02134.

References

1. Ahuja, R. K., Magnanti, T. L., Orlin, J. B.: *Network Flows: Theory, Algorithms, and Applications*, Prentice-Hall, Upper Saddle, NJ (1993)

2. Armour, G. C., Buffa, E. S.: *A Heuristic Algorithm and Simulation Approach to Relative Allocation of Facilities.* Management Science (9) (1963) 294-309
3. Banerjee, P., Zhou, Y., Montreuil, B.: *Genetically Assisted Optimization of Cell Layout and Material Flow Path Skeleton.* IIE Transactions (29) (1997) 277-291
4. Bazaraa, M. S.: *Computerized Layout Design: A Branch and Bound Approach.* AIIE Transactions (7) (1975) 432-438
5. Benson, B., Foote, B. L.: *Door FAST: A Constructive Procedure to Optimally Layout a Facility Including Aisles and Door Locations Based on an Aisle Flow Distance Metric.* International Journal of Production Research (35) (1997) 1825-1842.
6. Bozer, Y. A., Meller, R. D.: *A Reexamination of the Distance-based Facility Layout Problem.* IIE Transactions (29) (1997) 549-560
7. Coit, D. W., Smith, A. E., Tate, D. M.: *Adaptive Penalty Methods for Genetic Optimization of Constrained Combinatorial Problems.* INFORMS Journal on Computing (8) (1996) 173-182
8. Harhalakis, G., Lu, T., Minis, I., Nagi, R.: *A Practical Method for Design of Hybrid-type Production Facilities.* International Journal of Production Research (34) (1996) 897-918
9. Hassan, M. M. D., Hogg, G. L., Smith, D. R.: *Shape: A Construction Algorithm for Area Placement Evaluation.* International Journal of Production Research (24) (1986) 1283-1295
10. Kane, M. C., Nagi, R.: *Integrated Material Flow and Layout in Facilities Design.* In Proceedings of the Sixth Industrial Engineering Research Conference, Miami FL (May 1997) 919-924
11. Kusiak, A., Heragu, S. S.: *The Facility Layout Problem.* European Journal of Operational Research (29) (1987) 229-251
12. Meller, R. D., Gau, K.-Y.: *The Facility Layout Problem: Recent and Emerging Trends and Perspectives.* Journal of Manufacturing Systems (15) (1996) 351-366
13. Norman, B. A., Smith, A. E., Arapoglu, R. A.: *Integrated Facilities Layout Using a Perimeter Distance Measure.* IIE Transactions, in review
14. Reeves, C. R.: *Genetic Algorithms for the Operations Researcher.* INFORMS Journal on Computing (9) (1997) 231-250.
15. Smith, A. E., Coit, D. W.: *Constraint-Handling Techniques - Penalty Functions.* In Handbook of Evolutionary Computation, Institute of Physics Publishing and Oxford University Press, Bristol, U.K. (1997) Chapter C5.2
16. Smith, A. E, Tate, D. M.: *Genetic Optimization using a Penalty Function.* In Proceedings of the Fifth International Conference on Genetic Algorithms, Urbana, IL (July 1993) 499-505
17. Tam, K. Y.: *Genetic Algorithms, Function Optimization, and Facility Layout Design.* European Journal of Operational Research (63) (1992a) 322-346
18. Tam, K. Y.: *A Simulated Annealing Algorithm for Allocating Space to Manufacturing Cells.* International Journal of Production Research (30) (1992b) 63-87
19. Tate, D. M., Smith, A. E.: *Genetic Algorithm Optimization Applied to Variations of the Unequal Area Facilities Layout Problem.* In Proceedings of the Second Industrial Engineering Research Conference, Los Angeles (May 1993). IIE, Atlanta (1993) 335-339
20. Tate, D. M., Smith, A. E.: *Unequal-area Facility Layout by Genetic Search.* IIE Transactions (27) (1995) 465-472
21. Tompkins, J. A.: *Facilities Planning: A Vision for the 21st Century.* IIE Solutions (August 1997) 18-19
22. Tretheway, S. J., Foote, B. L.: *Automatic Computation and Drawing of Facility Layouts with Logical Aisle Structures.* International Journal of Production Research (32) (1994) 1545-1556

An Evolutionary Algorithm for Synthesizing Optical Thin-Film Designs

Jinn-Moon Yang and Cheng-Yan Kao

Department of Computer Science and Information Engineering,
National Taiwan University, Taipei, Taiwan
E-mail: {moon,cykao}@solab.csie.ntu.edu.tw

Abstract. This paper presents an evolutionary approach, called Family Competition Evolutionary Algorithm (FCEA), to design optical thin-film multilayer systems. FCEA integrates self-adaptive mutations, decreasing-based mutations, and four-layer selections to balance exploration and exploitation. One antireflection coating and one narrow-band rejection filter are presented to demonstrate that our approach is a powerful technique. Our approach consistently performs better than other evolutionary algorithms and other published results on these two problems. From experimental results of antireflection coating, our optimal solutions exhibit a pronounced semiperiodic clustering of layers and these solutions also confirm the theoretical prediction between the optical thickness and the best achievable reflectance.

1. Introduction

The optical thin film coating is importance to all modern optics and is stated as follows [15] broadly: any device or material is deliberately used to change the spectral intensity distribution or the state of polarization of the electromagnetic radiation incident on it in order to satisfy performance specification and some constraints. The thickness of thin films is the order of the wavelength of light and is infinite small as it compares to extent of films. Thin-film multilayer systems can be widely used to in the infrared, visible and ultraviolet regions of spectrum. Optical thin-film coatings have numerous remarkable applications in many branches of science and technology, such as scientific instrument manufacturing, spectroscope, medicine, and astronomy. They also have used in architecture, the automotive industry, energy conversion, computer and display devices, and communication [6]. In recent year, thin-film optical coatings are applied to optoelectronic devices, for instance, fiber communication, liquid crystal display, laser diodes, and light-emitting.

To design an optical coating problem can be formulated as an global minimization problem and this approach becomes the most widely used technique for designing optical thin-film coatings. Nevertheless, the formulated problem is extremely difficult because of the large number of local minimum in the merit function, and so it is hard to find feasible solutions efficiently no matter what methods are applied. Whichever of these approach is used, the objective is to find the thickness, refractive indices, and layers of a thin film system whose performance closely matches the specified performance. These numerical approaches can be classified into refinement methods [1, 4] and synthesis methods [14, 5, 18].

Refinement methods [1, 4], such as damped least square, modified gradient, golden section, Hook and Jeeves search, and simplex method, normally require a starting design that is closed to the desired performance. Then, a desired solution is achieved by gradually modifying the staring design. Unfortunately, to choose a starting design is time-consuming and difficult tasks in complexity system and the performance of refinement methods is very sensitive to start points. On the other hand, synthesis method [14], such as gradient evolution, flip-flop method, inverse Fourier transform [8, 15], and simulated annealing [19], can generate their own starting designs. Unfortunately, the quality of many synthesis approaches are not enough well so that they need a refinement method to refine their obtained solutions. Many above approaches require the determination of first and second derivation of the merit function or require other limitations. Therefore, to develop a good synthesis method is an important research topic.

In recent years, there has been a growing effort on applying evolutionary algorithms, including Genetic Algorithms (GAs) [8, 16], Evolution Strategies (ESs) [3, 12, 17] and Evolutionary Programming (EP), to synthesize multilayer thin-film systems. These articles demonstrate that evolutionary algorithms are robust and obtain competitive results with others synthesis methods. A bit-string genetic algorithm [8] was used simple five-layer structures to solve the silver-based heat problem and a standard evolution strategies[12] was applied to design a filter used in colorimetry. In [16], authors apply gradient method to improve the results obtained by real-coded genetic algorithm. The mixed-integer ES optimization techniques [3, 17] were applied to anti-reflection problems. However, these standard evolutionary algorithms have disadvantages in specific domain [21, 22] or they focused on some simple or specific multilayer system.

The main focus of this article is to develop a new evolutionary algorithm, called Family Competition Evolutionary Algorithm (FCEA), to synthesize multilayer thin-film systems. The approach integrates self-adaptive Gaussian mutation, self-adaptive Cauchy mutation, decreasing-based Gaussian mutation, and family competition. In order to illustrate the power of our approach, we considered two different thin-film design problems that were widely used as benchmarks for various optimizing approaches. These experimental results indicate that FCEA is a powerful and robust optimization technique.

2. Optical Multilayer Thin-Film Systems

To consider the thin-film system consists of M layers shown in Fig. 1. The spectral reflectance profile depends on the wavelength λ, the number of layers M, and the refractive indices vector $\vec{n}$ and the thickness vector. The number of element for each vector $\vec{n}$ and $\vec{d}$ is M. Let the spectral reflectance of M-layer layer system be denoted as $R(\vec{n},\vec{d},\lambda)$ where λ is the interesting wavelength. The desired spectral reflectance profile are fitted by minimizing a suitable merit function [15] which composes of an appropriate function of $R(\vec{n},\vec{d},\lambda)$ defined within the wavelength range of interesting: $[\lambda_u, \lambda_1]$ where λ_1 and λ_u are is low bound and high bound of interesting spectrum region. Then, a widely working merit function [15] can be defined in the following equation:

$$f(\vec{n},\vec{d}) = \int_{\lambda_u}^{\lambda_1} \{[R(\vec{n},\vec{d},\lambda) - \hat{R}(\lambda)]^2\}^{1/2} d\lambda, \tag{1}$$

where $\hat{R}(\lambda)$ is the target reflectance. In computer practice, this integral is approximated by a summation over a discrete number W of wavelength value λ_k and can be represented as:

$$f(\vec{n},\vec{d}) = \sum_{k=1}^{W} \{[R(\vec{n},\vec{d},\lambda_k) - \hat{R}(\lambda_k)]^2\}^{1/2}. \tag{2}$$

The most general method of calculating $R(\vec{n},\vec{d},\lambda_k)$ is based on a matrix formulation [15] which is useful especially when the number of optimizing parameters is large. According to the matrix method, the reflectance $R(\vec{n},\vec{d},\lambda_k)$ of a multilayer system at wavelength λ_k is given by

$$R(\vec{n},\vec{d},\lambda_k) = \left| \frac{\eta_a E_k - H_k}{\eta_a E_k + H_k} \right|^2 \tag{3}$$

where η_a is refractive index of incident medium. E_k and H_k, the electric and magnetic vector, respectively, are obtained in the following:

$$\begin{bmatrix} E_k \\ H_k \end{bmatrix} = (\prod_{j=M}^{1} \begin{bmatrix} \cos\phi_j & i\eta_j^{-1}\sin\phi_j \\ i\eta_j\sin\phi_j & \cos\phi_j \end{bmatrix}) \begin{bmatrix} 1 \\ \eta_s \end{bmatrix}, \tag{4}$$

where $\phi_j = \frac{2\pi}{\lambda_k}(n_j d_j \cos\theta_j)$, $\tag{5}$

and η_s refractive index of substrate medium. n_j, d_j and θ_j are the refractive indices, thickness, and angle of incidence of the jth layer, respectively.

949

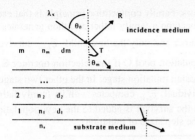

Fig. 1. Construction parameters of an optical multilayer system: n_j and d_j are the refractive indices and thickness of the jth layer, θ_0 and θ_j are the incidence angle of incident medium and of the jth layer, M is the number of layers, R is reflectance, and T is transmittance. n_a and n_s are the refractive indices of the incidence and substrate medium.

Before you design a multilayer coating system, it is necessary to define the requirements. Most often this is defined by specifying the transmittance T or reflectance R at a number of wavelengths in the interesting spectral region. The target of designing a thin-film system is to find the number of layers M, the refractive indices n_j, and the thickness d_j of the jth layer, in order to match closely the specified performance. A coating system is called normal-incidence coating if the incident angle θ_0 shown in Fig. 1 is zero, otherwise it is called oblique-incidence coating.

There are some basic conclusions to design an optical multilayer thin-film system: (1) At normal light incidence, it is no advantage to use more than two materials that have the lowest n_l and highest n_h refractive indices according to the maximum principle [18]. In this case, the most general structure of multilayer system is $(n_l n_h)^M$ or $(n_h n_l)^M$. (2) Refractive indices must fall within a lower and upper bound or must limit to some available materials. If the refractive value is allowed continuous then the problem is called inhomogeneous coating, otherwise called homogeneous coating which is much easier to construct experimentally. To convert inhomogeneous layers to equivalent two-material system is easy. (3)The number of layers may be limited because the cost of coatings increase with number of layers. (4) Thickness cannot be negative and very thin layers are difficult controled for some deposition processes. In this paper, a layer be eliminated if its thickness is lower 0.001 μm.

3. Family Competition Evolutionary Algorithm (FCEA)

The FCEA starts with generating a population of N solutions, actually chosen from the search space. Each solution is represented as a quadratic real vector, $(\bar{x}_i, \bar{\sigma}_i, \bar{v}_i, \bar{\psi}_i), \forall i \in \{1,...,N\}$. $\bar{x}$ is the desired optimizing variable vector, i.e., the vector of refractive indices and thickness of a solutions. $\bar{\sigma}$, $\bar{v}$, and $\bar{\psi}$ are the step-size vectors of decreasing-based Gussian mutation, self-adaptive Gaussian mutation, and self-adaptive Cauchy mutation, respectively. The outline of FCEA is given in Fig. 2. Each solution is evaluated according to the merit function $f(\bar{x}_i)$ defined as Equation (2). Then, FCEA enters evolutionary stages that consisted of three kinds family competition: decreasing-based Gaussian mutation stage, self-adaptive Cauchy mutation stage, and self-adaptive Gaussian mutation stage. Each stage applied different operators, including crossover operators, mutation operators, and selection operators to generated a new population called quasi-population: P',P'', and P'''. In decreasing-based Gaussian mutation stage, FCEA employed population selection to select best N solutions from the union set of parent pool P and children pool C. Replacement selection is applied in others two self-adaptive mutation stages.

The FamilyCompetition procedure uses five parameters to generate a new quasi-population which becomes the population pool of next stage. Each family competition stage uses two kind of operators, selections and mutation operators, and two parameters, the family competition length [21] and recombination rate, as the parameters of the FamilyCompetition procedure. The family competition is the procedure that consists of four steps from line 5 to line 8 in Fig. 2(b). In the repeat loop, each individual $\bar{a}$ in the population P generates L offspring via recombination and mutation operators, where L is the family competition length. The L offspring competes with each other and then the individual $\bar{c}_{best}$ with the best fitness survives. We call the child with the best fitness as the "best child" hereafter. The individual $\bar{a}$ will be referred as the "family father" who is the essential parent to participate the genetic operators. Family competition principle is that each individual in the population has equal probability to become a family father and then generates L children who are genetically similar to their family father and only the best child $\vec{c}_{best}$ survives.

The best child $\vec{c}_{best}$ is directly added to the new population pool C if the selection operator S is population selection, i.e., in the decreasing-based Gaussian mutation stage. In the other two stages, replacement selection is used. In these cases, the individual $\vec{c}_{best}$ competes with its family father and the one with the better fitness survives, and then the survival is added to the new population pool C. The adaptive rules are then applied to adjust the step sizes of mutations.

---

g←0 /* g is the generation number. P(g) is original pool. P'(g), P''(g), and P'''(g) are quasi-pool */

Initialize population P(g) ($(\vec{x}_i,\vec{\sigma}_i,\vec{v}_i,\vec{\psi}_i), i \in \{1,...,N\}$, N is population size.)

Evaluate fitness score of each individual $f(\vec{x}_i,\vec{\sigma}_i,\vec{v}_i,\vec{\psi}_i)$

while termination criteria is not satisfied do

  1.   C ←FamilyCompetition(P(g),PopulationSelection,DecreasingGaussianMutation, L_d, p_{cd})

  2.   P'(g) ←select the best N candidates from { $P(g) \cup C$ } /* population selection */

  3.   P''(g) ←FamilyCompetition(P'(g),ReplaceSelection,Self-adaptiveCauchyMutation, L_s, p_{cs})

  4.   P'''(g) ←FamilyCompetition(P''(g),ReplaceSelection,Self-adaptiveGaussianMutation, L_s, p_{cs})

  5.   P(g+1)←P'''(g)

  6.   g←g+1

endwhile

(a)

FamilyCompetition(P,S,M,L, p_c)

  / P denotes a population pool; S denotes replacement S_R or population selection S_P; M denotes a mutation operator; L is the family competition length; p_c denotes the crossover rate. */*

1.   C ← ∅ /* set children pool C to empty */

2.   **for** each individual $\vec{a}$ in P

3. $\vec{c}_{best}$ ← +∞ /* the objective is minimization */

4.   **Repeat** L times / *family selection* */

5.   a. Randomly select another individual $\vec{b}$ from P /* *crossover selection* */

6.   b. $\vec{a}'$ ←**recombination**($\vec{a},\vec{b}$) with probability p_c

7.   c. $\vec{a}''$ ←M ($\vec{a}'$)

8.   d. **If** $f(\vec{a}'') \leq \vec{c}_{best}$ **then** $\vec{c}_{best} \leftarrow \vec{a}''$

9.   **if** S is ReplacementSelection **then** /: *replacement selection* */

10.   **if** $f(\vec{c}_{best}) \leq f(\vec{a})$ **then**   a. add $\vec{c}_{best}$ to C

11.   b. apply growing rule of decreasing-based mutation

12.   **else**   a. add $\vec{a}$ to C

13.   b. apply decreasing rule of self-adaptive mutation

14.   **else**   Add $\vec{c}_{best}$ to C.

15.   endfor

16.   return(C)

(b)

Fig. 2. The outline of family competition evolutionary algorithm.

In order to illustrate the genetic operators, let us denote family parent $\vec{a} = (\vec{x}_a,\vec{\sigma}_a,\vec{v}_a,\vec{\psi}_a)$, the other parent $\vec{b} = (\vec{x}_b,\vec{\sigma}_b,\vec{v}_b,\vec{\psi}_b)$, and the generated offspring $\vec{c} = (\vec{x}_c,\vec{\sigma}_c,\vec{v}_c,\vec{\psi}_c)$. In the following subsections, the symbol x_j^d denotes j^{th} element of the individual $\vec{d}$, $\forall j \in \{1,...,K\}$. K equals M when the system is two-material periodic multilayers; otherwise, K equals 2*M. M is the layer number of a thin-film system.

3.1 Genetic Operators

1). **Self-adaptive Mutation**: Self-adaptive Gaussian mutation [2], i.e. Equation (6) and (7), has been widely applied to numeric optimization problems successfully. Self-adaptive Cauchy [23], that is, Equation (8) and (9), can improve the performance of Gaussian mutation for some rugged functions [23]. These two mutations generate a child by first mutating step size, stated in equation (6) and (8), and then mutate the object variables $\bar{x}$ according to the probability distribution function, shown in equation (7) and equation (9), for each dimension.

$$v_j^c = v_j^a * \exp(\tau^{\cdot} * N(0,1) + \tau * N_j(0,1)), \tag{6}$$

$$x_j^c = x_j^a + v_j^c * N(0,1), \tag{7}$$

$$\psi_j^c = \psi_j^a * \exp(\tau^{\cdot} * N(0,1) + \tau * N_j(0,1)), \tag{8}$$

$$x_j^c = x_j^a + \psi_j^c * C(t), \tag{9}$$

where $N(0,1)$ is a normal distribution with mean 0 and standard derivation 1. $N_j(0,1)$ indicates that a new normal random value for each dimension. C(t) is a Cauchy random number with parameter t = 1.0. The factors of τ and τ' are set to $(\sqrt{K})^{-1}$ and $(\sqrt{2\sqrt{K}})^{-1}$ which are proposed by Schwefel.

2). **Decreasing-based Gaussian Mutation:** Decreasing-based Gaussian mutation uses an annealing-like concept to decrease the step size of Gaussian distribution. This mutation applied the same decreasing rate for each dimension in order to achieve unbiased search in feasible space and it works as follows:

$$\sigma_j^c = \gamma * \sigma_j^a, \tag{10}$$

$$x_j^c = x_j^a + \sigma_j^c * N(0,1), \tag{11}$$

where r is the decreasing rate and set to 0.95 in our experiments.

3) **Modified Discrete Recombination:** Discrete recombination generates a child that inherits genes from two parents with equal probability. We modify discrete recombination so that the child inherits genes from the family parent $\bar{a}$ with probabilities 0.8 and another parent $\bar{b}$ with probability 0.2. That is, a child inherits genes from the family parent with high higher probability. a child inherits genes from the family parent with high higher probability and this operator works as follows:

$$x_j^c = \begin{cases} x_j^a & \text{with probabilty } 0.8 \\ x_j^b & \text{with probabilty } 0.2 \end{cases} \tag{12}$$

4) **BLX-0.5 and Intermediate Recombination:** The BLX-0.5 is used successfully in GAs and is stated as follows:

$$\varpi_j^c = \varpi_j^a + \beta(\varpi_j^b - \varpi_j^a), \tag{13}$$

where β is chosen from uniform distribution in [-0.5, 1.5]. BLX-0.5 is called as intermediate recombination if β is equal to 0.5. FCEA employed the intermediate recombination in strategy variables, i.e. $\bar{\sigma}$, $\bar{v}$, and $\bar{\psi}$. In contrast to strategy variables, FCEA applied discrete recombination, BLX-0.5, and intermediate recombination to desired vector $\bar{x}$ with different probabilities that are p_{dc}, p_{hc}, and p_{ic}, respectively. In this paper, p_{dc}, p_{hc}, and p_{ic} are set to 0.7, 0.1 and 0.2, respectively.

3.2 Selection Operators

FCEA applies four-level selection operators. First, recombination selection selects two individuals, one is family parent $\bar{a}$ and another one is randomly selected from the population, for crossover operators described in Section 3.1. FCEA uses recombination operators with recombination selection and mutation operators to generate L offspring (L is the length of family competition) in order to explore fairly the search space for each individual $\bar{a}$. These L offspring, generated from the same family parent $\bar{a}$, are called a family. The members of a family may be similar to each other because they inherit more genes from the family parent $\bar{a}$ via recombination selection and modified discrete crossover operator. This operator, selects the best member of a family and discard the others, is called family competition. Third, replacement selection is to select a better one from a family parent and its best child. In two self-adaptive mutation stages, FCEA employs lower recombination rate and self-adaptive mutations in order to tune the solutions. Obviously, replacement selection may slow down the convergence speed but it can keep the diversity of the population. Finally, population selection is exactly similar to $(\mu+\mu)$-ES that selects the best N individuals from the union set of parent set and offspring set.

3.3 Step-Size Control

The performance of Gaussian mutation and Cauchy is completely influenced by their step size. FCEA combines self-adaptive and adaptive techniques to control the step size of Gaussian and Cauchy mutations. We summarize two rules: A-rules for self-adaptive mutations and D-rules for decreasing-based mutation as follows:

A-rules

    A-rule-a (an adaptive rule of self-adaptive mutations)

        v is adjusted according to Equation (6) and Equation (8)

    A-rule-d (and decreasing rule of self-adaptive mutation):

$$v_j^a = \gamma * v_j^a \ \forall j \in \{1,...,n\} \text{ if } \bar{a} \text{ better than its best offspring . (line 13 of Fig. 2(b))}$$

D-rules

    D-rule-d (a decreasing rule of decreasing-based mutation):

        σ_i is adjusted according to Equation (10)

    D-rule-g (a growing rule of decreasing-based mutation):

$$\sigma_j^c = \alpha * v_j^c \text{ if } \sigma_{mean}^c < \beta * v_{mean}^c \text{ and } c_{best} \text{ is better } \bar{a} . \text{ (line 11 of Fig. 2(b))}$$

where v is the step size of self-adaptive mutations, σ is the step size of decreasing mutation, v_{mean} and σ_{mean} denote the mean value of the step-size vector of self-adaptive mutations and decreasing mutation, respectively. The values of α and β are set to 0.1 and 0.1 in our experiments, respectively.

4. Experimental Results

In this section, we synthesized two different thin-film problems in order to demonstrate that FCEA is a powerful technique. The first problem is a well-known infrared antireflection coating problem [1] because antireflection coatings are more produced than any other type filters. This problem is a two-material periodic multilayer system. The second problem is a narrow-band rejection filter and its available refractive indices are continuous. These two problems have been widely discussed in some research; thus, FCEA can compare the performance with other approaches to demonstrate that our approach is a robust and powerful approach. Table 1 indicates the setting values of FCEA strategy variables shown in Fig. 2 for these two problems. We obtained these parameter settings by testing over 100 runs on the first problem. The initial values of step size, thickness and refractive indices of each layer will be stated in Section 4.1 and 4.2.

Table 1. The parameter settings of FCEA strategy variables for these two problems. These values are obtained by testing over 100 runs on the infrared antireflection coating problem.

parameter name	the value of parameter
population	population size is 50
family competition length	$L_d = 3$ (length in decreasing-based stage), $L_s = 6$ (length in two adaptive stages)
recombination rate	p_{cD}=0.8 (crossover rate in decreasing-based stage), p_{cA}=0.2 (crossover rate in two adaptive stages)
rate of three kinds recombination operator	p_{cd}=0.7 (discrete recombination), p_{cb}=0.2 (BLX-0.5), and p_{ch}=0.1 (intermediate recombination).
decreasing rate	γ=0.95

4.1 Infrared Antireflection Coating: two-material periodic coating problem

This problem was first proposed by Aguilera et al. [1] and its interesting wavelength is in infrared region. The goal is to reduce the reflectance to zero at 0.1 μm wavelength increments between 7.7 and 12.3 μm; therefore, W defined in equation (2) is 47. The incident medium is air and the substrate refractive index is $n_s = 4.0$. The only used coating materials are Ge ($n_h = 4.2$) and ZnS ($n_l = 2.2$). At least 57 different solutions, obtained from over 20 non-evolutionary approaches [1, 4-7] and from over three evolutionary approaches [3, 16, 17], have been published for this problem since 1988. Above all, many predicated solutions and theoretical approaches on this coating problem have been published. Any application of an evolutionary approach should focus on a comparison to solutions obtained by well-known approaches; therefore, this problem is a good benchmark problem. We used the two-materials periodic structure, i.e. $(n_l n_h)^M$ or $(n_h n_l)^M$ where M is the number of layer, to synthesize this problem. Initially, the step sizes of $\bar{\sigma}$, $\bar{v}$, and $\bar{\psi}$ are set to 0.08, 0.02, and 0.02, respectively. The initial thickness of each layer was uniformly selected from the region between 0.2 and 1.0.

FCEA was totally executed 100 times for various total optical thickness and various layer numbers. Fig. 3(a) shows spectral profile of typical evolutionary intermediate solutions obtained by FCEA and Fig. 3(b) presents refractive-index profile of the last solution. The merit function (MF) value is 61.07% while function evaluations is 100. MF is promoted to 1.01%, 0.7%, and 0.63% while function evaluations are 50,000, 150,000 and 300,000, respectively. After FCEA executes 650,000 function evaluations, the last solution quality is 0.60 whose layer number 23 and thickness is 38.61 μm. From our experimental results, we observed that the solution quality was improved quickly in the early search time. Table 2 shows several optimal solutions obtained our FCEA approach based on different total optical thickness. Table 2 and Fig. 4(a) indicate that the solution quality become better while the total thickness is thicker.

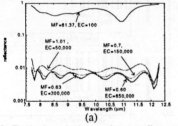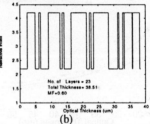

(a)   (b)

Fig. 3. Typical evolutionary intermediate solutions obtained by our FCEA in the synthesis of the infrared antireflection problem. (a) is the spectral reflection profiles of solutions where EC denotes function evolutionary times and MF represents the merit function value .(b) is the refractive-index profile of the last solution whose MF is 0.60% and thickness is 38.61 μm.

Table 2. Some optimal solutions obtained by our FCEA for the infrared antireflection problem.

	S-20	S-27	S-33	S-40	S-44	S-51	S-54	S-61	S-70
Number of Layers	15	17	23	23	27	26	35	34	36
Total Thickness (•m)	20.34	27.04	33.96	40.17	44.98	50.99	54.13	61.7	71.15
Merit Function (%)	0.855	0.697	0.614	0.577	0.553	0.523	0.517	0.509	0.494

FCEA can obtain very closed to optimal solutions and can compete with the performance of other approach based on Fig. 4(a) and Table 2. Fig. 4(a) presents the solutions obtained in this paper, other solutions [1, 3-7, 16], and some approximated predicated solutions [5, 17, 20]. FCEA outperformed other approaches [1, 3-4, 7, 16-17] and was competitive with needle method [5] which is very powerful approach. Because almost published results whose total thickness were between 20 μm and 35 μm, FCEA was executed 50 runs on this problem via limiting the total thickness between 20 μm and 35 μm and setting EC to 150,000 times in order to compare with these approaches. The average performance was 0.85%, the average total thickness was 32.23 μm, and the best solution was 0.656% by our FCEA. FCEA performs much better than non-evolutionary approaches [1, 3-4] based on these results. The average performance of mixed-integer ES [3] was in the range 0.94-1.63% when EC was set to 150,000. This approach obtain the best performance was 0.709% whose optical thickness was 34.60 μm when EC was set to 1,250,000 times. Obviously, FCEA is better than mixed-integer ES according to the results of Table 2. FCEA competes with the results that obtained by combining real-coded genetic algorithm with gradient approach [16] on several different total optical thickness, and FCEA had better performance than real-coded genetic algorithm when gradient method is not applied to refine its solutions.

FCEA obtained two observed results that consisted with parallel ES [17] according to Fig 4(a). First, Willey's predicated optimal values [20] were overestimated as the total thickness is lower than 30 μm. Second, we also observed the "Bermuda triangle" when the optical thickness range 11and 17 μm. However, Fig 4(a) shows that FCEA outperformed parallel ES [17] as the optical thickness is beyond 30 μm. We considered that the RMS predicated optimum [5] may be the best approximated solutions when the optical thickness is over 30 μm. This result was non-consisted with [17].

Fig. 4(b) shows that a serial of layers clusters could be observed in the refractive-index profiles of the obtained optimal solutions in this paper. Such clusters have been previously stated in wide-band antireflection coating [5]. The dash line indicated that the first cluster of the three solutions consisted of 10 layers with an optical thickness about 22 μm. Hence, it is possible to generate antireflection coatings with lower reflection simple by adding clusters and then numerically refining all the layers.

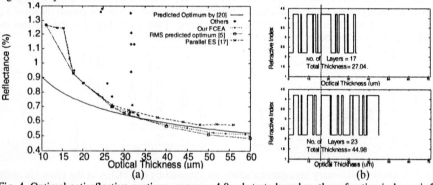

Fig. 4. Optimal antireflective coatings on a n_s = 4.0 substrate based on the refractive index pair 2.2 and 4.2 for different overall optical thickness of the system. (a) optimal solutions obtained in this paper shown in Table 2 and results obtained by others for the same problem, including several approximations of the best achievable reflectance based on a given optical thickness. (b) shows two refractive-index profiles of some best solutions obtained by our FCEA.

4.2 Narrow-Band Rejection Filter: Inhomogeneous coating problem

This problem is a narrow-band rejection filter [24, 16]. The target is that the reflectance value is 90% between 0.58 and 0.62 μm and zero outside this band in the visible region between 0.5 and 0.7 μm. The incident medium is air and the substrate is glass (n_s=1.52). The merit function was calculated at 48 wavelengths which are 16 equidistant wavelengths for three wavelength range: 0.5-0575 μm, 0.585-0.61 μm, and 0.625-0.70 μm. The feasible refractive indices region is between 1.35 and 2.20 μm, so this problem is an inhomogeneous optical coating problem. This problem was first solved by inverse Fourier transform methods [24]. FCEA set step sizes of $\bar{\sigma}$, $\bar{v}$, and $\bar{\psi}$ to 0.04, 0.01, and 0.01, respectively. The initial thickness of each layer was uniformly set the region between 0.05 and 0.5 and the refractive indices are randomly selected from the feasible region between 1.35 to 2.20. The unit is μm. Initial layer numbers are randomly selected between 31 and 40.

FCEA was executed 50 runs on this problem with the maximum total thickness 20 μm and maximum EC is 250,000 to fairer compare performance with other approaches. The average performance was 1.72% and the average thickness was 17.9 μm. We extended the EC to 850,000 and we obtained best solution was 0.541% with thickness 18.54 μm. The required time was about 1.5 hour when our program ran on Intel-pentium 166 Mhz. Fig. 5 shows the spectral reflection profile and refractive-index profile of the best solution obtained by our FCEA.

Here we compared our performance with inverse Fourier transform method [24] and hybrid approach that combined genetic algorithm and gradient method [16]. The average reflectance of hybrid method [16] was 0.3% for 0.5-0.575 μm, 90.07% for 0.585-0.615 μm, and 0.26% for 0.625-0.700 μm. The hybrid method must assign the total thickness to 20 μm and the layer number to 40. This hybrid approach needed about 6-10 hour (on Hewlett-Packard 700 workstation) to obtain solutions. On the other hand, the average reflectance of our best solution whose layer number is 31 and thickness is 18.54 μm in this paper, was 0.3% for 0.5-0.575 μm, 90.02% for 0.585-0.615 μm, and 0.30% for 0.625-0.700 μm. Our approach can optimize the merit function value and the layer number at the same time. They [16] stated that their results were competitive with inverse Fourier transform method. Therefore, our approach was competitive with these two methods and our approach was more flexible.

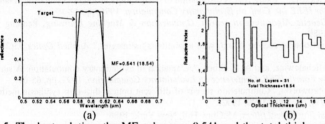

(a)   (b)

Fig. 5. The best solution, the MF value was 0.541 and the total thickness is 18.54, of rejection filter found by FCEA: (a). Spectral reflections profile of the best rejection filter. (b) refractive-index profile of the best solution.

5. Conclusions

Our approach uses multiple mutation operators and four-level selections to balance exploitation and exploration. Results from two thin-film coating problems confirm the flexibility and robustness of our approach. FCEA integrates decreasing-based Gaussian mutation with self-adaptive Gaussian mutation and Cauchy mutation to compensate for the shortcoming of each other. For instance, decreasing-based mutations are able to help self-adaptive mutations to jump out local optimal in the whole search time. On the other hand, self-adaptive mutations can adapt step sizes of decreasing-based mutations to improve their efficient in the later search time. FCEA is able to adapt the step sizes of mutation operators via monitoring progress to improve performance and efficiency.

FCEA has four selection strategies, including recombination selection, family competition, replacement selection, and population selection, to balance the global and local search. To combine together recombination selection, family competition and replacement selection to make a local search well and to keep the population diversity. Population selection was designed as a global competition to discard some worse individuals and to speed up the convergence.

From the experimental results of two multilayer thin-film problems, we demonstrate that our approach is better than over ten refinement methods and over six synthesizing methods. Also, FCEA outperformed mixed-integer ES and hybrid method, combining the real-code genetic algorithm with gradient method, based on experimental results. From experimental results of antireflection coating, the optimal solutions of FCEA exhibit semiperiodic clustering of layers and can be used to confirm the theoretical prediction between the optical thickness and the best achievable reflectance. Our primary conclusion, based on the results form our experiments, is that our approach is a powerful synthesis method to design optical multilayer systems.

References

1. J. A. Aguilera, et al., "Antireflection coatings for germanium IR optics: a comparison of numerical design methods," *Applied Optics 27(14)*, pp. 2832-2840, 1988.
2. T. Bäck and H. P. Schwefel, "An overview of evolution algorithms for Parameter Optimization," *Evolutionary Computation*, vol. 1, no. 1, pp. 1-23, 1993.
3. T. Bäck and M. Schutz, "Evolution strategies for mix-integer optimization of optical multilayer systems," *in Proc. of Fourth Ann. Conf. on Evolutionary Programming*, 1995, pp. 33-51.
4. J. A. Dobrowolski and R. A. Kemp, "Refinement of optical multilayer systems with different optimization procedures," *Applied Optics 29(19)*, pp. 2876-2893, 1990.
5. J. A. Dobrowolski, et al., "Optimal single-band normal-incidence antireflection coatings," *Applied Optics 35(4)*, pp. 644-658, 1996.
6. J. A. Dobrowolski, "Numerical methods for optical thin films," *Optics and Photonics News 8(6)*, pp. 24-33, Jun, 1997.
7. J. Druessel and J. Grantham, "Optimal phase modulation for gradient-index optical filters," *Optics Letters 18(19)*, pp. 1583-1585, 1993.
8. T. Eisenhammer, et al., " Optimization of interference filters with genetic algorithms applied to silver-based heat mirrors," *Applied Optics 32(31)*, pp. 6310-6315, 1993.
9. D. B. Fogel and J. W. Atmar, "Comparing Genetic Operators with Gaussian Mutations in Simulated Evolutionary Processes Using linear Systems," *Biological Cybernetic*, vol. 63, pp. 111-114, 1993.
10. D. B. Fogel and A. Ghozeil, "Using fitness distribution to design more efficient evolutionary computations," *in Proc. of the IEEE Int. Conf. on Evolutionary Computation*, 1996, pp. 11-19.
11. D. E. Goldberg, *Genetic Algorithms in search, Optimization & Machine Learning*, Reading. MA: Addison-Welsley,1989.
12. H. Greniner, "Robust optical coating design with evolutionary strategies," *Applied Optics 35(28)*, pp. 5477-5482, 1996.
13. R. Hinterding, Z. Michalewicz, and A. E. Eiben, "Adaptation in evolutionary computation: A survey," *In Proceeding of the Fourth IEEE. Conference on Evolutionary Computation*, 1997, pp. 65-69.
14. L. Li and J. A. Dobrowolski, "Computation speeds of different optical thin-film synthesis methods," *Applied Optics 31(19)*, pp. 3790-3799, 1992.
15. H. A. Macleod, *Thin film optical filters*, McGraw-Hill, New York, 1986.
16. S. Martin, J. Rivory, and M. Schoeanauer, "Synthesis of optical multilayer systems using genetic algorithms," *Applied Optics 34(13)*, pp. 2247-2254, 1995.
17. M. Schutz and J. Sprave, "Application of parallel mixed-integer evolutionary strategies with mutation rate pooling," *in Proc. of Fifth Ann. Conf. on Evolutionary Programming*, 1996, pp. 345-354.
18. A. V. Tikhonravov, "Some theoretical aspects of thin-film optics and their applications," *Applied Optics 32(28)*, pp. 5417-5426, 1993.
19. W. J. Wild and H. Buhay, "Thin film multilayer design optimization using Monte Carlo approach," *Optics Letters 11(1)*, pp. 745-747, 1986
20. R. A. Willy, "Predicting achievable design performance of broadband antireflective coating," *Applied Optics 32(28)*, pp. 5447-5451, 1993.
21. J. M. Yang, Y. P. Chen, J. T. Horng, and C. Y. Kao, "Applying family competition to evolution strategies for constrained optimization," in the Lecture Notes in Computer Science, 1213, P. J. Angline et al.(Eds), Evolutionary Programming VI, 201-211, 1997.
22. J. M. Yang, C. Y. Kao and J. T. Horng, "A continuous genetic algorithm for global optimization." In *Proceeding of the Seventh Intl. Conference on Genetic Algorithm* 1997, 230-237.
23. X. Yao and Y. Liu, "Fast evolutionary programming," *in the Fifth Annual Conf. on Evolutionary Programming*, 1996, pp. 451-460.
24. G. Bovard, "Derivation of a matrix describing a rugate dielectric thin film," *Applied Optics 27(10)*, pp. 1998-2005, 1988.

Model Estimations and Layout Problems

Implementing Genetic Algorithms with Sterical Constraints for Protein Structure Prediction

Eckart Bindewald, Jürgen Hesser, Reinhard Männer

Lehrstuhl für Informatik V, Universität Mannheim 68131 Mannheim, Germany

Abstract. In this paper we present new kinds of genetic operators for protein structure prediction. These operators solve the problem of atom collisions during the conformational search. They restrict the search space to collision-free conformations by enforcing sterical constraints on the protein at each optimization step.

The results are compared to a standard genetic algorithm. The sterical constraint operators improve the results of the genetic algorithm by many orders of magnitude.

1 Introduction

Ab initio protein structure prediction is still an unsolved problem [2]. A program that is able to compute the conformation of a protein only from its sequence would be very important for the biosciences [1].

The structure prediction problem can be formulated as an optimization problem, because it leads to the problem of finding the energy minimum in the conformational space of the protein.

Extensively used approaches to this search problem are molecular dynamics, simulated annealing and also genetic algorithms [5] [6] [7] . In our work we found that a standard genetic algorithm suffers from the following problem: The standard genetic algorithm starts with a population of proteins with random conformations. A conformation of a protein with random torsion angles is very likely to contain collisions between its atoms. These collisions correspond to high energies in the used energy model. Hence the initial population of a standard genetic algorithm consists of protein conformations with extremely high energy ("bad" individuals). Standard genetic algorithms may need many thousand function evaluations to find protein conformations which have no atomic collisions.

In this paper we show how to solve this problem by applying constraints to the conformational space being searched by the genetic algorithm. The problem specific constraints ("sterical constraints") are such that only collision free conformations are allowed, while conformations with collisions are forbidden.

To fulfill the constraints we developed operators for initialization, mutation and crossover, that have as output only individuals which conform to the sterical constraints.

We present the developed operators and compare their performance to a standard genetic algorithm.

2   Problem setting

2.1   Protein models

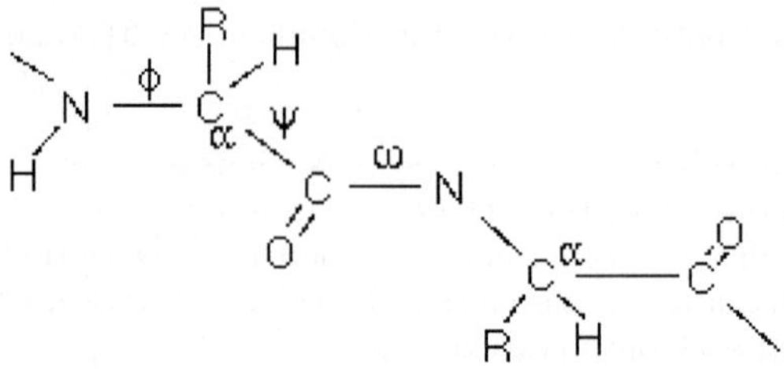

Fig. 1. Structural formula of a piece of a protein backbone.

Proteins are chains of amino acids. Figure 1 shows the structural formula of a short piece of the backbone of a protein. The only degrees of freedom of the protein backbone are essentially the φ and ψ angles. The ω angle of the so called peptide bond is not freely rotatable. The bond lengths and bond angles are also quite rigid and are held fixed in our simulation. In our simulation all ω angles of the protein were held fixed at 180 degrees. The side chains of the protein (denoted as "R" in figure 1) add more degrees of freedom, because they may contain free rotatable bonds.

2.2   The Ecepp/2 protein model

To model a protein with a computer program, we used the Ecepp/2 energy model to compute protein conformations and energies [8]. The energy according to this model is a sum of an electrostatic energy term, a non-bonded interaction term, a torsion angle energy term and a sulphur-bridge interaction term. In this model the conformation and the energy of a protein is a function of its torsion angles. The bond lengths and the bond angles are set to fixed values. We search for the conformation of the protein with the lowest energy. Hence the optimization problem is to find the global minimum of the energy of the protein as a function of its torsion angles.

2.3   Genetic algorithms and the program package Genetic

A genetic algorithm mimics the process of selection, mutation and crossover that occurs in nature. A genetic algorithm tries to optimize a population of individuals. In a standard genetic algorithm, the information of the characteristics is coded in a bitstring, the "chromosome". In our case an individual represents a protein conformation. This is done by interpreting the bitstring as the torsion angles of the protein.

The genetic algorithm iteratively applies the operations selection, crossover and mutation to the population of individuals. The algorithm tries in this way to find individuals with the highest objective function. The objective function of an individual is in our case the negative energy of its corresponding protein conformation. Hence the genetic algorithm will optimize toward low energy protein conformations.

We chose the program package Genetic for running our genetic algorithm [4]. It proved to be a flexible framework, for which it is straightforward to implement new genetic operators.

2.4   The test proteins

For testing our genetic algorithm, we chose the Abl-SH3 domain of the protein tyrosine kinase [9]. We chose this protein, because it is a globular protein of moderate size (57 amino acids) whose structure is known [10]. Another reason for choosing it, is that it is a relatively small protein, which has a defined structure without having sulphur bridges.

We also chose the polypeptide met-enkephalin for comparing our genetic operators. Met-enkephalin is a very short polypeptide (only 5 amino acids), for which a substantial amount of computational analysis has been done [11] .

3   Genetic operators for sterical constraints

3.1   Definition of sterical constraints

Atoms of a molecule cannot be located arbitrarily close to each other. In the case of a covalent bond between two atoms, their distance is approximately given by characteristic bond distances. In the Ecepp/2 model we used, the bond distances are fixed.

The minimum distance between non-covalently bonded atoms is approximately the sum of the van der Waals radii of the individual atoms. [3]

Hence the coordinates of the atoms of the molecule cannot have arbitrary values: They are constrained, such that all atoms of the molecule maintain a minimum distance from each other. We used that knowledge about molecules in order to define constraints, which we call in this paper sterical constraints. These sterical constraints devide the search space into disjunct regions: conformations, in which at least one pair of atoms is closer to each other than its defined minimum distance are disallowed conformations. The sterical constraints are said to be violated in this case. In the other case, when none of the atoms are too close to each other, the conformation is "allowed", the sterical constraints are fulfilled.

The van der Waals radii of the different atom types where taken from [3]. They were multiplied with an empirical reduction factor $a = 0.58$. This value for

a was chosen because it turned out to be the highest value for which the carbon atoms in the benzene rings of the aromatic amino acids where not counted as colliding.

3.2 Sterical constraint initialization

The initialization routine should produce protein conformations, which fulfill the sterical constraints. It turned out, that for Abl-SH3 it is very unlikely, that a conformation with random torsion angles fulfills the sterical constraints. Of 10000 random conformations not one of them was consistent with the constraints. In other words, the space of collision-free conformations is more than 4 orders of magnitudes smaller than the original search space!

We wanted our initialization routine to produce collision-free conformations.

We solved this problem by implementing a build-up process, which has collision-free protein conformations as an output.

Starting with a collision-free amino acid, the routine gradually adds amino acids with random φ/ψ angles to the main chain. The distribution of the φ/ψ angles is modeled according to the φ/ψ angle distribution of natural proteins, which is described in Ramachandran plots [12]. The angle distribution of the Ramachandran plots was approximated with Gaussian functions. It would have been possible, to just pick φ/ψ angle pairs of natural proteins from a database instead.

The ω angles of the protein are set to 180 degrees. We chose sidechain angle combinations from a self made sidechain conformation library.

If the new amino acid leads to no collision, the next amino acid is added, until the protein is complete. The result is a collision-free protein.

If the additional amino acid leads to a collision, the last n amino acids are taken away, and a new build up is tried again. The value n is computed in the following way: Let r be a random number according to a Gaussian distribution centered at zero and with a deviation of 1.5. The value n was chosen to be the absolute value of r rounded to its next integer value. Those n amino acids taken away, a new build up is tried again until the protein is complete.

3.3 Sterical constraint mutation

The mutation operator in genetic algorithms typically applies small random changes to an individual. In our approach, we designed the mutation operator such that it operates in the subspace of the sterically allowed protein conformations. It takes a collision-free conformation as input. The operator picks randomly one or several φ/ψ angle pairs. To the selected backbone angle pairs a two-dimensional Gaussian distributed random offset is added. With a different probability all sidechain angles of randomly chosen amino acids are replaced by a different entry from our sidechain conformation library. The operator then checks, if the resulting conformation violates the sterical constraints. If the constraints are violated, the mutation operator is applied again to the original conformation, until a collision-free conformation is obtained.

This way the resulting individual is guaranteed to fulfill the sterical constraints.

3.4   Sterical constraint crossover

The crossover operator takes as input two protein conformations, which obey the sterical constraints. Two random peptide bonds (ω angle, see figure 1) are then picked, where the conformations are "cut" into three pieces per individual. The resulting pieces are then exchanged according to a twopoint crossover.

The resulting individuals are then checked, if they both obey the sterical constraints. If not, the operator takes again the original individuals and chooses another random peptide angle as a cutting point, until the resulting individuals fulfill the sterical constraints. If after a certain number of trials no collision-free offspring was obtained, the crossover operator merely copies the original individuals.

This way the resulting individuals are guaranteed to fulfill the sterical constraints.

3.5   Standard genetic algorithm

The genetic algorithm with the sterical constraint operators were compared to a "standard" genetic algorithm. The initialization was a random bit initialization of each chromosome. The crossover operator was a standard twopoint crossover. The mutation operator was a simple bit-flip mutation operator. The selection method chosen for the standard genetic algorithm and for the sterical constraint genetic algorithm was deterministic crowding.

4   Results

4.1   Initialization

The initialization histograms (fig. 2) were generated with a population size of 250 individuals (250 initialized protein conformations). The energies of the randomly initialized conformations of Abl-SH3 varied between $10^{11} kcal/mol$ and $10^{24} kcal/mol$. The protein conformations generated with the sterical constraint initialization procedure had energies between 400 and $3000 kcal/mol$ (see also table 4.1). The results of the initialization of met-enkephalin are shown in table 3.

4.2   Optimization

The optimization runs (figure 4) were done with a population size of 200 individuals and 200 generations. Figure 4 left shows the optimization with a standard genetic algorithm, figure 4 right shows the optimization with the specialized sterical constraint operators. Both diagrams show an average of the best individual

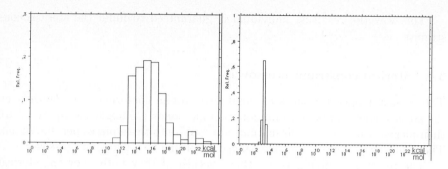

Fig. 2. Histogram of energies of 250 initialized conformations of Abl-SH3. left: random initialization. right: Initialization with sterical constraints.

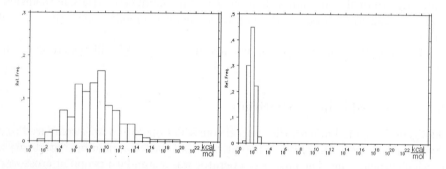

Fig. 3. Histogram of energies of 250 initialized conformations of met-enkephalin. left: random initialization. right: Initialization with sterical constraints.

	minimum	maximum	mean
Abl-SH3 random initialization	$4.39 * 10^{11}$	$2.17 * 10^{23}$	$1.33 * 10^{21}$
Abl-SH3 steric constraint init.	449.24	2900.45	1470.75
met-enkephalin random init.	93.3	$2.18 * 10^{19}$	$1.04 * 10^{17}$
met-enkephalin steric constraint init.	8.68	413.0	79.26

Table 1. Results of random and sterical constraint initialization 250 conformations of Abl-SH3 and met-enkephalin. (in kcal/mol)

of the population over 5 optimization runs. The distribution of the different energies was not assumed to be symmetrical, so above and below the graph of the mean of the optimization runs is the partial deviation plotted. As shown in the table 2, the result of the standard genetic algorithm applied to Abl-SH3 after 200 generation is $(7.7 \pm 2.5) * 10^5 kcal/mol$. The result of the genetic algorithm using the sterical constraint operators is $-101.9 \pm 2.3 kcal/mol$. In the case of met-enkephalin, the optimization results of the standard genetic algorithm and the sterical constraint genetic algorithm do not differ much (see table 2).

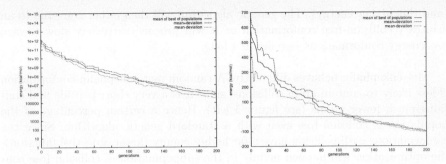

Fig. 4. Optimization of Abl-SH3. Left: standard genetic algorithm. Right: genetic algorithm with sterical constraint genetic operators.

	result(kcal/mol)
Abl-SH3 with standard ga	$(7.71 \pm 2.48) * 10^5$
Abl-SH3 with sterical constraint ga	-101.92 ± 2.32
met-enkephalin with standard ga	-3.17 ± 0.37
met-enkephalin with sterical constraint ga	-2.35 ± 0.33

Table 2. Results of optimization of Abl-SH3 and met-enkephalin with standard genetic algorithm and with sterical constraint operators. An average of 5 optimization runs is taken.

5 Discussion

The results show that genetic operators, which enforce sterical constraints dramatically improve the optimization results of the protein Abl-SH3. With the standard genetic algorithm the lowest energies of the populations of Abl-SH3 are initially at about $10^{12}kcal/mol$ in the first generation. No individual had an energy below $10^7kcal/mol$ at the 200th generation. Using the sterical constraint operators, the lowest energies of the populations of Abl-SH3 are initially at about $500kcal/mol$ in the first generation and at about $-100kcal/mol$ at the 200th generation.

The optimization results for the polypeptide met-enkephalin are disappointing. Obviously the sterical constraints do not play an important role in optimizing this short oligopeptide.

We interpret the different behavior of the two proteins in the following way: As can be seen in figure 2, it is very unlikely for a completely random conformation of the protein Abl-SH3 to be collision-free. That means that the space of collision-free conformations is much smaller than the overall conformational space. Hence a standard genetic algorithm needs a long time to find collision-free conformations. Once collision-free conformations are found, the standard mutation and crossover operators are likely to produce conformations with collision (and this higher energy). The genetic algorithm will then either converge to an arbitrary collision-free conformation or it will proceed extremely slow toward low energy conformations (see figure 4 left).

Met-enkephalin behaves differently: A random met-enkephalin conformation is less likely to contain atom collisions, since it is a very short peptide and contains much fewer atoms (see figure 3 left). Hence a certain percentage of the population is collision-free even with a standard genetic algorithm. Since the conformations with collision have a far higher energy (lower objective function), the optimization will happen mainly in the subpopulation of collision free conformations. If that subpopulation is big enough the genetic algorithm does not need the sterical constraint genetic operators in order to find low energy conformations.

6 Conclusion

New genetic operators tailored for conformational search were presented. They are designed to restrict the search space of the genetic algorithm to protein conformations without atom collisions (sterical constraints).

The optimization results are dramatically improved with these genetic operators in the case of the Abl-SH3 domain of tyrosine kinase.

In the case of the oligopeptide met-enkephalin the sterical constraint genetic operators did not improve the optimization. The reason for is, that for the very short oligopeptide met-enkephalin atomic collision are far less likely than for the longer protein Abl-SH3.

The sterical constraint genetic operators improve the optimization results of protein conformational search and they can be a useful tool in combination with other techniques in order to reduce the search space in protein conformational search especially for long proteins.

References

1. Merz K.M., Le Grand S.M.; The Protein Folding Problem and Tertiary Structure Prediction. Birkhäuser (1994).
2. Jones D.: Progress in protein structure prediction. Current Opinion in Structural Biology. 7 : 377-387 (1997).
3. Stryer L.: Biochemistry. Freeman & Co. (1995).
4. Battle D.L.: Implementing Genetic Algorithms; Masters Thesis, University of Tennessee, Knoxville, (1991).
5. Finkelstein A.: Protein structure: what is possible to predict now? Current Opinion in Structural Biology. 7 : 60-71 (1997).
6. Unger R., Moult J.: Genetic algorithms for protein folding simulations. J.Mol.Biol. 231 , S.75-81 (1993).
7. Pederson J., Moult J.: Ab initio structure prediction for small polypeptides and protein fragments using genetic algorithms. Proteins 23 : 454-460 (1995).

8. Scheraga H.A., Browman J., Carruthers L.M., Kashuba K.L., Momamy F.A., Pottle M.S., Rosen S.P., Rumsey S.M.: Ecepp/2: Empirical Conformational Energy Program for Peptides. Cornell University, Ithaca, New York, QCPE 454.
9. see entry "1ABL" of protein database at http://www.pdb.bnl.gov
10. Pisabarro MT, Ortiz AR, Serrano L, Wade RC : Homology modeling of the Abl-SH3 domain. Proteins 20(3): 203-215 (1994).
11. Beiersdörfer S., Schmitt J., Sauer M., Schulz A., Siebert S., Hesser J., Männer R., Wolfrum J.: Finding the Conformation of Organic Molecules with Genetic Algorithms. Lecture Notes in Comp.Sci., 1141, S. 972-981, Springer Verlag (1996).
12. Ramachandran G.N., Ramakrishnan C., Sasisekharan V.: Stereochemistry of polypeptide chain configurations. J.Mol.Biol. 7 , 95-99, (1963).

Optimal Placements of Flexible Objects: An Adaptive Simulated Annealing Approach

S.K. Cheung, K.S. Leung, A. Albrecht * and C.K. Wong **

Department of Computer Science and Engineering,
The Chinese University of Hong Kong, Shatin, Hong Kong
email: {skcheung, ksleung, andreas, wongck}@cse.cuhk.edu.hk

Abstract. This paper deals with the computation of equilibrium states for the placement of flexible objects within a rigid boundary. The equilibrium states have to be calculated from uniformly distributed random initial placements. The final placements must ensure that any particular object is deformed only within the limit of elasticity of the material. A simulated annealing approach has been proposed and implemented in [2] to solve the problem. In this study, an adaptive simulated annealing algorithm is proposed with time complexity upper bounded by $O(n \cdot ln^2 n)$. The general approach is to determine at a given temperature and a given grid size whether the optimization has achieved a stable state, which will be defined later. The temperature and the grid size are then decreased adaptively. In terms of both run-time and final force of the placement, better results are obtained when compared with those obtained in [2].

1 Introduction

We consider optimal placements of two-dimensional flexible objects within a rigid boundary. The objects are disks of equal size and of the same material. The placements must be admissible, i.e., we must ensure that any flexible object is deformed only within the elasticity limit of the material.

In [1] and [2], various optimization problems were analyzed for placements of flexible objects and simulated annealing algorithms (SAAs) were proposed as algorithmic solutions. Two specifically tailored cooling schedules were designed with time complexity $O(n^{3/2} \cdot \ln^{5/2} n)$ and $O(n \cdot \ln^2 n)$, respectively. Based on the previous approach, we propose an adaptive approach of simulated annealing by determining whether a stable state is achieved and we then adjust the temperature and grid size adaptively. The time complexity of the algorithm is upper bounded by $O(n \cdot ln^2 n)$.

The potential applications of our approach are in the design of new amorphous polymeric and related materials [6, 7, 9] as well as in the design of package cushioning systems [5]. Indeed, our approach was extended and applied to real

---

* On leave from BerCom Ltd., Bruno-Taut-Straße 4 - 6, D-12527 Berlin, Germany
** On leave from IBM T.J. Watson Research Center, P.O.Box 218, Yorktown Heights, N.Y., U.S.A.

applications: simulation of two-dimensional composite packings [4] and calculation of the elastic moduli of two-dimensional random networks [3].

In Section 2, we introduce our physical model, including the derivation of an approximate deformation/force relationship and also the definition of the objective function. We present the adaptive SAAs in Section 3. Finally, the experimental results and concluding remarks are presented in Sections 4 and 5, respectively.

2   Problem Formulation

We consider the placement of flexible disks within a rigid rectangular boundary. The disks are of equal size with diameter d and built from the same material. By L and H we denote the length and the height of the boundary, respectively. For the $L \times H$ placement region a subdivision by a grid of step size w is performed in both directions, and it is assumed that L and H are both multiples of the elementary grid unit w. We denote $h := h_w := \frac{H}{w}$ and $l := l_w := \frac{L}{w}$. The center Z of a single unit can be placed only into one of the $K := (h-1) \cdot (l-1)$ grid nodes, excluding the nodes on the boundary.

2.1   Physical Model

Intersection of Two Disks The intersection of two disks with the centers Z_1 and Z_2 is interpreted for both disks as a *deformation* of depth Δ. The value Δ is the distance measured on the line connecting the centers from the intersecting point on the original border (the arc) to the chord halving the distance between the centers (see Fig. 1). The length of the chord between the two points P_1 and P_2, where the borders are crossing, is denoted by s and called the *deformation length*. We use the notation *deformation triangle* for the triangle defined by P_1, Z_1, and P_2. A part of a disk, as formed, e.g., by Q_1, Z_2, and Q_2, that is enclosed by two radii and the smaller arc between Q_1 and Q_2, is called a *circular sector*. By $R = R(Z_1, Z_2)$ we denote the Euclidean distance between the centers of disks. The maximal deformations of a disk are bounded by the limit of elasticity of the material. Let Δ_{max} denote this upper bound for deformations, which is a constant depending on the material and the size of disks. For any placement P one has to ensure that the limit of elasticity is not violated, i.e., the centers of the disks have to be separated by a distance of at least $R \geq d - 2 \cdot \Delta_{max}$.

Resultant Force of a Disk With any deformation Δ a force $\mathbf{F}$ can be associated which tries to recover the original shape. If a disk is intersecting with several other disks, the vector sum of the forces acting in the opposite directions can be calculated. The origin of the resultant force can be considered as acting from the center of the disk (see Fig. 2). This vector sum of forces $-\mathbf{F}_{res}$ determines the strength and the direction of a move that the disk is trying to perform.

From the viewpoint of a particular disk, the resultant force $\mathbf{F}_{res}(u)$ tries to move the disk u into its direction. If for any placed unit this resulting force is

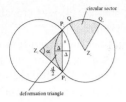 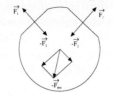 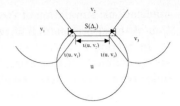

Fig. 1. Intersection   **Fig. 2.** Resultant Force   **Fig. 3.** Length $l(u, v)$

equal to zero, the arrangement is said to represent an *equilibrium state*. If for all disks $\mathbf{F}_{res}(u) < \varepsilon$ for a small ε, the packing is said to represent a near-equilibrium state. To establish a relationship between deformations and resulting forces is a difficult task, in particular for large deformations. The following formula is assumed to reflect approximately the relationship between a single deformation Δ and the resulting force $\mathbf{F}$ for a relatively large range of deformations :

$$\Delta = C_1 \cdot |\mathbf{F}| - C_2 \cdot |\mathbf{F}| \cdot \left(\frac{\alpha}{2} + \sin \frac{\alpha}{2}\right). \tag{1}$$

This formula is the result of numerical computations which were performed on several flexible materials and objects of different size. The constants C_1 and C_2 depend on the material. The angle α is related to the deformation triangle (see Fig. 1). The ratio $\frac{\alpha}{2}$ was chosen in order to ensure monotonicity also for large values $\alpha \leq \pi$, and we assume that $C_1 - C_2 \cdot \left(\frac{\pi}{2} + 1\right) > 0$ is satisfied. The force $|\mathbf{F}|$ is calculated from Δ by

$$|\mathbf{F}| = \frac{\Delta}{C_1 - C_2 \cdot \left(\frac{\alpha}{2} + \sin \frac{\alpha}{2}\right)}. \tag{2}$$

If Δ is replaced by $\frac{d}{2} \cdot \left(1 - \cos \frac{\alpha}{2}\right)$ (see Fig. 1), one obtains

$$|\mathbf{F}| = \frac{d}{2} \cdot \frac{1 - \cos \frac{\alpha}{2}}{C_1 - C_2 \cdot \left(\frac{\alpha}{2} + \sin \frac{\alpha}{2}\right)}. \tag{3}$$

The force $\mathbf{F}$ represents the force acting at the center of the deformation, where the deformation depth is equal to Δ. In order to estimate the total force, one should define the forces for all other points of the deformation line of length $s(\Delta)$. But since we are interested in the computation of equilibrium states, rather than in the concrete values of acting forces, we take $\mathbf{F}$ as a representative for the forces resulting from the deformation Δ. In general, one can expect for relatively dense packings of units that a particular unit is built only by deformation triangles, without circular sectors (see Fig. 1). In this case there is an additional problem: If a single unit is "intersecting" with several other units, the intersection line, in general, is not equal to $s(\Delta)$. As shown in Fig. 3, $l(u, v)$ is the actual deformation length instead of $s(\Delta)$. In order to take into account only the actual force associated with the length $l(u, v)$ of the intersection line between two units, the following modification of formula (2) is introduced : The force $\mathbf{F}$ is divided by the deformation length $s(\Delta)$ and then multiplied by $l(u, v)$:

$$|\mathbf{F}_{norm}| = \frac{l(u, v)}{C_1 - C_2 \cdot \left(\frac{\alpha}{2} + \sin\frac{\alpha}{2}\right)} \cdot \frac{\Delta}{s(\Delta)}. \tag{4}$$

Since we employ in the following only (4), we will use, in general, the notation $\mathbf{F}$ instead of $\mathbf{F}_{norm}$.

2.2 Objective Function

Configuration Space and Neighborhood Relation The corresponding set of placements is denoted by $\mathcal{C}_n$ and is called the configuration space. The transitions between placements are defined as a subset $\mathcal{N}$ of the Cartesian product $\mathcal{C}_n \times \mathcal{C}_n$, i.e., it is not allowed to place more than one center of an object into a single grid node. The ordered pair $[P, P'] \in \mathcal{C}_n \times \mathcal{C}_n$ is included into $\mathcal{N}$, iff P and P' differ at most in the position of a single object and the center of this object is located in neighboring grid nodes. The definition of $\mathcal{N}$ includes $[P, P] \in \mathcal{N}$, and we denote $\mathcal{N}_P$ for the neighbors of P. Because a grid node, except for the nodes on the boundary, has eight neighbors, the number of P' in $\mathcal{N}_P$ is upper bounded by $8 \cdot n + 1$, if P consists of n objects. The lower bound is $|\mathcal{N}_P| \geq 12 \cdot \lfloor \sqrt{n} \rfloor - 3$ for a dense square packing P of all n objects.

Subdivisions of Placement Region For each unit u_j, $j = 1, 2, ..., n$, we define the set $S(u_j)$ of surrounding units that may cause a deformation of u_j. The set $S(u_j)$ can be calculated by searching in a distance smaller than d from the center of u_j. In order to avoid the test for all of the remanding $(n - 1)$ units u_i, whether or not a unit u_i has a center distance $R(u_i, u_j) < d$, the placement region is subdivided into equal-sized subareas $\mathcal{D}$, e.g., in the rectangular case into an array-like structure. The subdivisions $\mathcal{D}$ are characterized by the coordinates of their boundary. The size of the subareas is related to the diameter d. Hence, from the center of u_j and d, the neighboring subdivisions and a particular element of $S(u_j)$ can be calculated in time $O(d \cdot \ln K)^{O(1)}$: By [2], (22) and (27), $\ln K$ is related to the representation length of the number of a unit, and $O(\ln K)$ digits are sufficient for the representation of coordinates. If u_j is moved during the computation, the subdivision $\mathcal{D}$ to which u_j belongs can be determined in the same way.

Force Calculation Let m denote the number of forces $\mathbf{F}^{(i)}$ applied from different sides to the unit u_j, $i = 1, 2, ..., m$. For regular placements, like in the hexagonal or square case, m is less than or equal to six. We suppose that the forces $\mathbf{F}^{(i)}$ are ordered, e.g., counterclockwise with respect to their appearance at the border of u_j. If $R(u_i, u_j) < d$, i.e., $u_i \in S(u_j)$, the resulting deformation $\Delta_{ij} > 0$ is calculated by $\Delta_{ij} := \frac{1}{2} \cdot (d - R(u_i, u_j))$, where $R(u_i, u_j) = \sqrt{(x_i - x_j)^2 + (y_i - y_j)^2}$ for the centers (x_i, y_i) and (x_j, y_j) of the units u_i and u_j, respectively. Furthermore, the length $l(u_j, u_i)$ of the intersection line is calculated from the centers (x_i, y_i), (x_j, y_j), and the diameter d. With any pair $[\Delta_{ij}, l(u_i, u_j)]$, a force $\mathbf{F}$ is associated in accordance with the approximate formula (4). The forces $\mathbf{F}$ assigned to a single unit are used for the calculation of the objective function. In a similar way the interactions with the boundary are considered, where $\Delta_j := \left(\frac{d}{2} - R(u_j)\right)$ and $R(u_j)$ is the distance between the unit u_j and the boundary for a single intersection.

We then have to define the direction of the force $\mathbf{F^{(i)}}$. This direction is determined by the counterclockwise angle α_{ij} between the x axis and the line connecting the centers of u_i and u_j. The calculation of α_{ij} is given by [2], (149) in Appendix B. The force $\mathbf{F^{(i)}}$ can be interpreted as a vector of length $|\mathbf{F^{(i)}}|$ being located in the center of u_j, where the direction is defined by the angle α_{ij} to the x axis. As the next step, the resulting force of a single unit is calculated which "tries to move" this unit. This is done recursively, building pairwise the vector sum of two forces. The corresponding formulas are presented in [2], Appendix B by (150). The complexity of these local computations depends on m and d, but m is upper bounded by a value which is related to d and Δ^{max}. Thus, a particular local force $\mathbf{F}(u)$ can be calculated in time $(d \cdot \log K)^{O(1)}$.

Given an arbitrary placement $P \in \mathcal{C}_n$, the objective function is derived from the local forces $|\mathbf{F_j}|$. In order to take into account all local forces, but also to avoid large values of the objective function, we define

$$\mathcal{Z}(P) := \frac{1}{n} \cdot \sum_{j=1}^{n} |\mathbf{F_j}| \tag{5}$$

to be the *objective function* assigned to P.

Definition 1 *A placement P is said to be in an equilibrium state, iff $\mathcal{Z}(P) = 0$.*

Since in our case the placements are depending on a grid structure, it cannot be expected, in general, that there exist placements in an equilibrium state. However, the main goal is to find admissible placements P minimizing the objective function $\mathcal{Z}(P)$. It is important to note that based on the specific structure of $\mathcal{N}$, the computation of placement parameters, such as mentioned in the previous points, must be performed only *locally*. That means, once the distances of units $R(u, v)$ and the assigned forces have been calculated for the initial placement P_{init}, the distances and forces may change only for the unit that is "moved" during a single transition $P \to P'$ and for the units surrounding this "moved" disc. The calculation of neighboring units requires a search procedure, but this search can be performed efficiently by using the above-mentioned subdivisions of the placement region.

3 Adaptive Simulated Annealing Algorithms

The application of SAAs was introduced in [8] as a new stochastic approach for solving optimization problems. SAAs are acting within a configuration space $\mathcal{C}$

in accordance with a certain neighborhood structure $\mathcal{N}$, where the particular steps are controlled by the value of an objective function $\mathcal{Z}$.

3.1 Convergence of Markov Chains

First we have to define how the transitions between placements are depending on $\mathcal{Z}$. This is realized by the following stochastic procedure which is at first considered for a single transition between configurations: Given a pair of placements $[P, P'] \in \mathcal{N}$, we denote by $G[P, P']$ the probability of generating P' from P and by $A[P, P']$ the probability of accepting P' once it has been generated from P. Since we consider a single step of transitions, the value of $G[P, P']$ depends on the set $\mathcal{N}_P := \{ P' : [P, P'] \in \mathcal{N} \}$. In most cases, a uniform probability with respect to P is taken by setting

$$G[P, P'] := \begin{cases} \frac{1}{|\mathcal{N}_P|}, & \text{if } P' \in \mathcal{N}_P, \\ 0, & \text{otherwise.} \end{cases} \tag{6}$$

Based on the already mentioned upper and lower bounds for $\mathcal{N}_P$, one obtains for n objects and $P' \in \mathcal{N}_P$,

$$\frac{1}{8 \cdot n + 1} \leq G[P, P'] \leq \frac{1}{12 \cdot \lfloor \sqrt{n} \rfloor - 3}. \tag{7}$$

As for $G[P, P']$ there are different possibilities for the choice of acceptance probabilities $A[P, P']$. A straightforward definition related to the underlying analogy to thermodynamical systems is the following:

$$A[P, P'] := \begin{cases} 1, & \text{if } \mathcal{Z}(P') - \mathcal{Z}(P) \leq 0, \\ e^{-\frac{\mathcal{Z}(P') - \mathcal{Z}(P)}{c}}, & \text{otherwise,} \end{cases} \tag{8}$$

where c is a control parameter having the interpretation of a *temperature* in annealing procedures. In [2], Section 5.1, the following theorem is proved:

Theorem 1 *The stochastic simulated annealing procedure minimizing $\mathcal{Z}$ for placements of flexible objects, which is based on (6) and (8), tends to the global minimum for $c \to 0$.*

3.2 Simulated Annealing Heuristics

For implementations of simulated annealing algorithms one has to define the concrete values or the computation rules for the following parameters: (i) starting value $c(0)$, i.e., the initial "temperature;"; (ii) length L_c of Markov chains for a fixed "temperature" c; (iii) cooling schedule; and (iv) stopping criterion.

Adaptive Length of Markov Chains With respect to the procedure described in the previous section, a modification is introduced: an adaptive grid size. In general, one can expect that in equilibrium states the centers of units are not located in grid nodes. In order to improve the final results calculated on the grid structure, an adaptive grid size is introduced which reduces the grid size during the optimization.

For a given temperature and grid size (gs), we determine whether the optimization has achieved a stable state. One has to define the term "stable state", and in our case, the state is achieved when force-increasing and force-decreasing transitions are equally likely to happen. The details are now discussed. For a given gs, we count the number of the force-increasing and force-decreasing transitions and represent them by as f_{gs}^+ and f_{gs}^-, respectively and define $r_{gs} := \frac{|f_{gs}^+ - f_{gs}^-|}{f_{gs}^+ + f_{gs}^-}$. We use $|f_{gs}^+ - f_{gs}^-|$ to measure whether the force-decreasing and force-increasing transitions are equally likely to happen, i.e., the smaller the value, the closer the values of f_{gs}^+ and f_{gs}^-. Then we use r_{gs} to measure the relative difference. Let $L_{gs(n)} = f_{gs(n)}^+ + f_{gs(n)}^-$ denote the length of the nth Markov chain where $gs(n)$ is the nth chosen grid size and we constrain the length by $L_{min} \leq L_{gs(n)} \leq L_{max}$, $\forall n > 0$. We set $L_{min} = (8 \cdot n + 1)$ and $L_{max} = 10 \cdot L_{min}$ for all experiments. We define a threshold value δ and if $r_{gs(n)} < \delta$, the optimization is considered as stable at $gs(n)$. The first time when $r_{gs} < \delta$, the current system force is called the first stable force $\mathcal{Z}(P)_f$, where $gs = gs(0) = gs_{max}$ and gs_{max} is the initial (maximal) grid size. $\forall n > 0$, if $r_{gs(n)} < \delta$ or $L_{gs(n)} \geq L_{max}$, the grid size may be reduced and the new grid size $gs(n+1)$ will be calculated by:

$$gs(n+1) := \begin{cases} gs(n) - 1, & \text{if } gs(n) \leq gs_m \text{ and } L_{gs(n)} \geq L_{max}, \\ gs(n), & \text{if } gs(n) \leq gs_m, \\ gs_m - \frac{(gs(n) - gs_m)}{2}, & \text{otherwise}, \end{cases} \tag{9}$$

where $gs_m := \frac{\mathcal{Z}(P) \cdot gs_{max}}{\mathcal{Z}(P)_f}$ and $\mathcal{Z}(P)$ is the current system force. The temperature will be reduced as described in the next section. The values of f_{gs}^+ and f_{gs}^- is reset to zero and then the above procedure is repeated.

By using the above procedure, at different temperatures and grid sizes, the lengths of Markov chains are different in values but within the bounds L_{min} and L_{max}. Each value depends on the current progress of the optimization.

Cooling Schedule The cooling schedule is based on the "Cooling Schedule II" as described in [2], Section 5.3. The initial temperature is defined as $c(0) = -\frac{\Delta \mathbf{Z}^{max}(p_1)}{\ln(1 - p_2)}$, where p_1 is the maximal deformation, p_2 is a small positive value and a parameter of our approach, and $\Delta \mathbf{Z}^{max}(p_1)$ is the upper bound for the maximal difference of the objective function (see [2], Section 5.1). The decrementing rule is given by the simple relation $c(t+1) := p_3 \cdot c(t)$, where p_3 is close to but smaller than one. The stopping criterion is derived from $c(t_{fin}) \leq \frac{\Delta \mathbf{Z}^{max}(p_1)}{\ln\left[l \cdot \left(8 \cdot n + 1\right)\right]}$.

One obtains $t_{fin} \leq \lceil \frac{1}{\ln p_3} \cdot \ln\left(-\frac{\ln(1-p_2)}{\ln[l \cdot (8 \cdot n + 1)]}\right) \rceil$. If the grid size is lowered to $gs(n)$, we calculate $t = \lfloor (1 - \frac{gs(n)}{gs_{max}}) \cdot t_{fin} \rfloor$ and $c(t) = c(0) \cdot (p_3)^t$. Once $gs(n) = gs_{min}$, where gs_{min} is the minimal grid size, then $t = t_{fin}$ (i.e., the final temperature is reached). At the final temperature, the $2 \cdot L_{max}$ transitions will be performed before the algorithm terminates.

We will now derive an upper bound for the expected run-time. Let T_{loc} denote an upper bound for the time needed to perform the local computation for a transition. T_{loc} is estimated to be $O(\ln^2 n)$ (see [2], Section 5.2). Since we are forcing the grid size to be decreased by one when $L_{gs(n)} \geq L_{max}$, the expected run-time of computing equilibrium placements for n flexible objects is upper bounded by $T \lesssim (gs_{max} - gs_{min} + 2) \cdot L_{max} \cdot T_{loc}$. In this case, we have a run-time upper bounded by $O(n \cdot ln^2 n)$ as $L_{max} = 10 \cdot (8 \cdot n + 1) = O(n)$.

4   Experimental Results

In our experiments, the generation probabilities were modified in the following way: For any of the n units, one calculates the magnitude and direction of the resulting force and denote them by F_{res} and α_{res}, respectively. Among the eight surrounding grid nodes of the center of a unit, the node $k(\alpha_{res})$ located in the direction of α_{res} is chosen, according to a subdivision into sectors with an angle $\frac{\pi}{4}$. To placements P', representing the move to a grid node $k_j(\alpha_{res})$, a higher probability is assigned:

$$G[P, P'] := \begin{cases} \frac{1-\rho}{n} \cdot min(1, \frac{F_{res}^j}{\overline{F_{res}}}), & P' \text{ corresponds to the move to} \\ & k_j(\alpha_{res}), \\ \frac{\rho}{|\mathcal{N}_P|-n} \cdot min(1, \frac{F_{res}^j}{\overline{F_{res}}}), & \text{otherwise,} \end{cases} \quad (10)$$

where $j = 1, 2, ..., n$, F_{res}^j is the magnitude of the resultant force of unit j, $\overline{F_{res}}$ is the mean magnitude of resultant forces of all units, and $\rho > 0$ by assuming that $F_{res}^j > 0$. Since $G[P, P'] > 0$ is still satisfied for any $P' \in \mathcal{N}_P$, the general convergence properties remain unchanged. This modification allows us to speed-up the process of filling out free space of placements, especially in initial random placements, because the units can move into the free space without enhancing the local force. It also allows us to move the units with relatively greater resultant forces more frequently.

We will present the results of $30, 40, 50, 60, 150$ and 325 units. The parameters were defined as follows: disk diameter $d = 50$ mm; $gs_{max} = 1$ mm; $gs_{min} = 0.0001$ mm; material: low-density polyethylenes ($C_1 = 1.21 \cdot 10^{-2}$ mm/N, $C_2 = 4.69 \cdot 10^{-3}$ mm/N); $p_2 = 0.1$, $p_3 = 0.9$, $\rho = 0.3$, $\delta = 0.05$. For 150 and 325 units, $H = L = 500$ mm, and for the other, $H = L = 250$ mm.

In order to show the robustness of our adaptive algorithm, for each number of units, five runs on different initial random configurations are performed. Table 1 shows the mean and standard deviation of the values of $tran$, $\mathcal{Z}$ and t respectively, for the five runs together with the results obtained in [2]. From

Figures 4 to 9, the final placements of different numbers of units are shown. In the figures two values are assigned to each unit: The upper value indicates the label of unit, while the lower one represents the residue force of this unit.

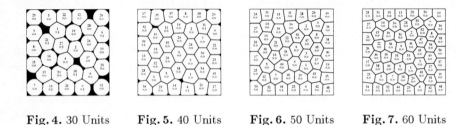

Fig. 4. 30 Units   **Fig. 5.** 40 Units   **Fig. 6.** 50 Units   **Fig. 7.** 60 Units

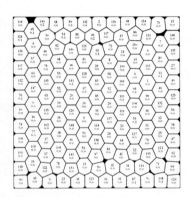

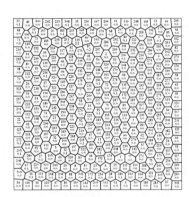

Fig. 8. 150 Units   **Fig. 9.** 325 Units

5 Concluding Remarks

Based on the previous simulated annealing approach, we have designed an adaptive simulated annealing algorithm computing equilibrium placements of flexible objects. The adaptive algorithms determine at a given temperature and grid size whether the optimization has achieved a stable state. The temperature and grid size are then decreased adaptively. The expected run-time of computing equilibrium placements of n objects is upper bounded by $O(n \cdot ln^2 n)$. In terms of the final sum of forces and run-time, the adaptive approach performs significantly better than the previous SA approach for our problem. Further research will be directed on further improvements of run-time by parallelization schemes.

Table 1. Results of Adaptive Simulated Annealing

	ASA						SA^2		
n	$\overline{tran}$	$tran_{\sigma_n}$	$\overline{\mathcal{Z}}$	$\mathcal{Z}_{\sigma_n}$	$\overline{t}$	t_{σ_n}	$tran$	$\mathcal{Z}$	t
30	22444	3372.73	0.98	0.01	112.20 s	9.65 s	94381	0.99	383 s
40	32939	5408.83	0.98	0.00	215.40 s	35.08 s	135418	4.67	1015 s
50	54810	4343.60	0.99	0.00	414.20 s	26.59 s	165488	1.00	1211 s
60	58553	9641.75	0.99	0.01	475.40 s	83.42 s	202921	6.12	1522 s
150	231482	69044.76	2.96	0.75	1906.60 s	589.87 s	511857	12.10	4020 s
325	677722	129785.01	12.36	5.74	11366.60 s	2729.76 s	1144484	31.90	16850 s

SA^2 - Cooling Schedule II was chosen [2], n - Number of units, $tran$ - Number of transitions
$\mathcal{Z}$ - Final force value, t - Run-time of SUN Sparc machine with 50MHz CPU

Acknowledgment

Research partially supported by the Strategic Research Program at the Chinese University of Hong Kong under Grant No. SRP 9505 and two Hong Kong Government RGC Earmarked Grant, Ref. No. CUHK 333/96E and CUHK 352/96E.

References

1. A. Albrecht, S. K. Cheung, K. C. Hui, K. S. Leung, and C. K. Wong. Optimal placements of flexible objects: Part I: Analytical results for the unbounded case. *IEEE Transactions on Computers*, 46:890–904, August 1997.
2. A. Albrecht, S. K. Cheung, K. C. Hui, K. S. Leung, and C. K. Wong. Optimal placements of flexible objects: Part II: A simulated annealing approach for the bounded case. *IEEE Transactions on Computers*, 46:905–929, August 1997.
3. A. Albrecht, S. K. Cheung, K. S. Leung, and C. K. Wong. Computing elastic moduli of two-dimensional random networks of rigid and nonrigid bonds by simulated annealing. *Mathematics and Computers in Simulation*, 44(2):187–215, 1997.
4. A. Albrecht, S. K. Cheung, K. S. Leung, and C. K. Wong. Stochastic simulations of two-dimensional composite packings. *Journal of Computational Physics*, 136(2):559–579, 1997.
5. D. C. Allen. Package cushioning systems. In F. A. Paine, editor, *The Packaging Media*, pages 5.44–5.64. Blackie & Son Ltd, 1977.
6. A. Jagota and G. W. Scherer. Viscosities and sintering rates of a two-dimensional granular composite. *Journal of the American Ceramic Society*, 76(12):3123–3135, December 1993.
7. V. B. Kashirin and E. V. Kozlov. New approach to the dense random packing of soft spheres. *Journal of Non-Crystalline Solids*, 163(1):24–28, October 1993.
8. S. Kirkpatrick, C. D. Gelatt Jr., and M. P. Vecchi. Optimization by simulated annealing. *Science*, 220:671–680, May 1983.
9. A. Z. Zinchenko. Algorithms for random close packing of spheres with periodic boundary conditions. *Journal of Computational Physics*, 114:298–307, 1994.

Encapsulated Evolution Strategies for the Determination of Group Contribution Model Parameters in Order to Predict Thermodynamic Properties

Hannes Geyer, Peter Ulbig, and Siegfried Schulz

Institute for Thermodynamics, 44221 Dortmund (Germany)
Department of Chemical Engineering, University of Dortmund
Member of the Collaborative Research Center SFB 531

Abstract. The computation of parameters for group contribution models in order to predict thermodynamic properties usually leads to a multiparameter optimization problem. The model parameters are calculated using a regression method and applying certain error criteria. A complex objective function occurs for which an optimization algorithm has to find the global minimum. For simple increment or group contribution models it is often sufficient to use deterministically working optimization algorithms. However, if the model contains parameters in complex terms such as sums of exponential expressions, the optimization problem will be a non-linear regression problem and the search of the global optimum becomes rather difficult. In this paper we report, that conventional multimembered (μ,λ)- and $(\mu+\lambda)$-Evolution Strategies could not cope with such non-linear regression problems without further ado, whereas multimembered encapsulated Evolution Strategies with multi-dimensional step length control are better suited for the optimization problem considered here.

1. Introduction

In chemical engineering the simulation of chemical plants is an important task. Millions of chemical compounds are known yet and experimental data are often not available. For this reason there is a need for calculation methods which are able to predict thermodynamic properties. Group contribution methods are useful tools in chemical engineering and serve for the prediction of a wide range of thermophysical properties such as activity coefficients, excess enthalpies or enthalpies of vaporization. Up to now, more than 100 increment and group contribution methods are known which differ to a great extent in mathematical complexity. In many modern methods such as UNIFAC [2], the model parameters appear in sums of exponential terms, especially if a temperature dependence is to be described. The optimization of model parameters of such complex group contribution methods usually leads to a nonlinear regression problem, which is often characterized by a multimodal objective function (see figure 1). The group contribution model EBGCM [8], which is competitive to the UNIFAC-models [2,12], can be used in order to predict various thermodynamic properties. The property being considered in this work is the excess enthalpy h^E.

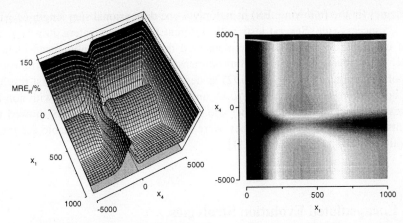

Fig. 1. Adaptive surface of a mod. UNIFAC Group contribution model [12]
$MRE_R = f(x_1, x_4)$ where x_2, x_3, x_5, $x_6 =$ const.

The destination function here is not the model equation in which the model parameters occur but an error criterion which establishes the relation between the group contribution model (h^E_{calc}) [3,8] and the respective experimental data (h^E_{exp}). The error criterion used here is a mean relative range related error (MRE_R), where N is the number of data sets – consisting of n data points –, which have to be fitted. One data set corresponds to an excess enthalpy isotherm, which is dependent of the molefraction x_{ji} of a considered binary mixture of organic liquids (see figure 4). The range $\Delta h^E_{exp,R}$ is defined as the difference between the largest and the smallest h^E value on the isotherm being considered, in order to do not underrate small excess enthalpy isotherms during the optimization of the model parameters.

$$MRE_R = \frac{1}{Nn} \cdot \sum_{j=1}^{N} \sum_{i=1}^{n} \left| \frac{h^E_{calc}(x_{ji}) - h^E_{exp}(x_{ji})}{\Delta h^E_{exp,R}} \right| \overset{!}{=} 0 \qquad (1)$$

2. Motivation

In order to optimize the parameters of different group contribution models only local search algorithms like the simplex-algorithm of Nelder and Mead [5], Gauß-Newton, Levenberg etc. could be used so far. Because of the multimodal character of the non-linear regression problem which is to be treated here they are not suitable because of their deterministic way of action. Only after the development of a Genetic Algorithm [3] substantial results which could be interpreted could be delivered [3,8,9]. As, however, the optimization problem which is to be solved has a real valued character it was the obvious thing to implement a similar but purely real valued acting algorithm. According to the theories of Rechenberg [6] it was tried to optimize parameters of group contribution models with the help of encapsulated Evolution

Strategies (in the following: ES) using only a one dimensional step length (n_σ=1) and the 1/5 success rule. Several tests with different tuning parameters, however, delivered unacceptable results only. Implemented multimembered non-encapsulated ES, which were developed next, use multi-dimensional and, if necessary, correlated control of step length (n_σ=n, n_α=(n^2-n)/2) as described by Bäck [1]. The first result was, that conventional multimembered (μ,λ)- and ($\mu+\lambda$)-ES could not cope with non-linear regression problems without further ado. Especially because (μ,λ)-ES showed worse results than ($\mu+\lambda$)-ES although they were thought to be more suitable for the self-adaption of the strategic variables [1].

3. Encapsulated Evolution Strategies

Finally only the combination of the theories of Rechenberg [6] and Schwefel [10,11] lead to useful results. Here multimembered (μ,λ)- and ($\mu+\lambda$)-ES with multi-dimensional (correlated) step length control were used in an encapsulated version and should deliver better results than the already used Genetic Algorithm and some Multistart-Simplex-Algorithms. Here a sequential isolated optimum seeking process is carried out in several planes (mostly two):

$$\left[r_1^{\vec{x}} r_1^{\vec{\sigma}} r_1^{\vec{\alpha}} \ \mu_1[s_1]\lambda_1 \left(r_2^{\vec{x}} r_2^{\vec{\sigma}} r_2^{\vec{\alpha}} \ \mu_2[s_2]\lambda_2 \right)^{\gamma_2} \right]^{\gamma_1} - \text{ES} \tag{2}$$

The 3-number letter code used in the strategy notation marks the used recombination mechanism for each plane in the following order: objective variables $\vec{x}$, standard deviations $\vec{\sigma}$, and rotation angles $\vec{\alpha}$, if necessary. The recombination operators can be chosen as $r_i^{\vec{x}}, r_i^{\vec{\sigma}}, r_i^{\vec{\alpha}} \in \{-,d,D,i,I,g,G\}$[1]. A 2-number letter code indicates a renunciation of a correlated step length control. The selection mechanism s_i [1] can be chosen as plus [+] or as comma [,] for each plane independently.

Every offspring λ_1 is the founder of a new sub-population for γ_2 new generations during the main iteration steps γ_1. This sub-population can act totally independently of the population on the first level. The offspring λ_1 coming from the first level is duplicated μ_2 times for every parent in the second plane. The offspring then works as a starting value for the iteration on level two. This encapsulated iteration always starts using newly initialized strategic variables (standard deviations $\vec{\sigma}$ and rotation angles $\vec{\alpha}$). After γ_2 generations usually the best individual which was found is then returned to the bottom level. The returned individuals when using an encapsulated ES are not assigned with the original set of variables which they got during the recombination-mutation-procedure in the course of the ($\mu_1[s_1]\lambda_1$)- ES on the bottom level, but the returned individuals are exposed to the selection procedure on the bottom level in the usual way.

4. Results of the numerical experiments

In order to analyze the used ES more exactly and to obtain more useful statements it was necessary to generate a test system where the global optimum was exactly known at $MRE_R = f(\vec{x}) = 0.0$ % (table 1).

parameter	global optimum	definition area
x_1	0.6139137	[-200, +200]
x_2	4066.7201283	[-20000,+20000]
x_3	68.7611711	[-6000, +6000]
x_4	-1.9259706	[-200, +200]
x_5	2271.8324498	[-20000,+20000]
x_6	-28.8807056	[-6000, +6000]

Table 1. Optimum parameters and definition area of the analyzed test system

Virtual values for the excess enthalpy with already fitted model parameters were predicted by the EBGC-model equation [3,8] to ensure that those can be theoretically reproduced inevitably during the optimization. The system mainly used for the examination of the algorithms was the system acetone-water consisting of 3*9=27 data points, that means nine data points for three different temperatures, respectively (figure 4). The curve of the excess enthalpy versus the mole fraction here is sigmoid and therefore it is a very demanding system concerning the group contribution model EBGCM used to predict the curve of the isotherms and concerning the algorithm used for the optimization of the group contribuation model parameters.

Figure 2 and 3 show two plots of the considered EBGCM-test system, where 4 of the 6 parameters were fixed to their optimum value given in table 1. The objective function is been punished out of the definition area of each parameter, namely by an exponentially increasing penalty function returning extremly high MRE_R-values. Parameters beyond their definition areas cause fitting-curves between missing data-points within an isotherm, which make no sense from a thermodynamic point of view. The plots emphasize the complexity and the multimodality of the considered restricted optimization problem already in a lower dimension space of variables ($n=2$).

Versions of different ES were tested on the basis of this 6-parametric test system in order to determine the optimum tuning parameters of an Evolution Strategy for the optimization of EBGC-model parameters. Since Evolution Strategies are stochastic optimization algorithms every type of strategy was tested in 50 independent runs. The criterion serving for the comparison was the arithmetic mean of all 50 results. For a better comparison between different variants of tested ES and some Multistart-Simplex-Algorithms (table 2) a similar amount of function calls ($\approx$ 300.000 per run) were mostly made for every type of strategy. A work station of the type SUN Ultra 1 (167 MHz) needs about 20 minutes per run and about 17 hours per strategy type

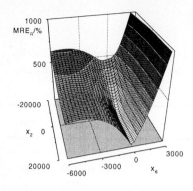

Fig. 2. Adaptive surface of the test system
$MRE_R = f(x_2, x_6)$ (x_1, x_3, x_4, x_5=const.)

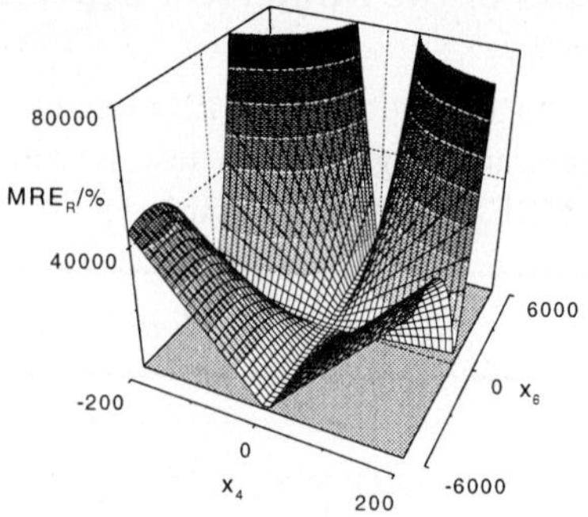

Fig. 3. Adaptive surface of the test system
$MRE_R = f(x_4, x_6)$ (x_1, x_2, x_3, x_5=const.)

when using an ES. Real EBGCM-isotherms are to be fitted to 200-4000 data points so that the search for a type of ES with a minimum need of function calls is inevitable.

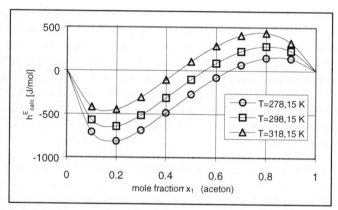

Fig. 4. Test system (acetone-water) at 3 temperatures; n=6 objective variables

The results in table 2 show the inefficiency of the exclusive use of purely deterministically working optimization algorithms (here simplex-algorithm by Nelder and Mead [5]) for the determination of parameters of group contribution models by nonlinear regression. An improvement which, however, is not satisfying can be achieved only sufficiently by high frequency of repeating the algorithm (multistart strategy). The purely deterministically working algorithm achieves better results by a stochastic part resulting from repeated starts from different starting points chosen by random. A `10*SNM^7000`-strategy is a simplex-algorithm with 7000 iteration steps, which is repeated 9 times. It is rather useful to improve the optimization results determined by stochastically working algorithms (Evolutionary Algorithms) by deterministically working algorithms. This can be achieved by arranging the algorithms serially.

Multistart Algorithm	$\overline{MRE_R}$ / %	$\overline{f\ calls}$	best / %	worst / %	$\sigma_{(50)}$/%
`10*SNM^7000`	15.18	305003	2.802	30.006	5.52
`35*SNM^3000`	11.62	298179	3.897	19.299	3.70
`150*SNM^1000`	8.41	264046	2.529	13.327	2.52
`340*SNM^500`	6.78	284100	1.482	10.688	2.62
`700*SNM^250`	7.34	294575	2.255	10.766	2.53

Table 2. Optimization results of a Simplex-Nelder-Mead algorithm tested on the 6-dimensional test system (MRE_R- and *f-calls*-values are an average of 50 runs per strategy type)

Table 3 shows an extract of all on the basis of the 6-parametric test system (figures 2,3,4) tested ES. Besides the notation of the analyzed ES the arithmetic mean of all 50 MRE_R-results in per cent are shown. The start step length was either defined absolutely (e.g.: 25) for every parameter the same or was defined in per cent (e.g.: 20%) of each total definition area (absolute values) divided by $\sqrt{n}$ (n=number of objective variables), in order to make the standard deviations independent from n and from different definition areas of the parameters. The rotation angles – if used – were initialized by random between $[-\pi,+\pi]$ as suggested in [1,11]. Besides that the number of the needed function calls per run is listed as well as the best and the worst determined error of the 50 runs and finally the found out standard deviation for all runs is shown to characterize the reliability and ability of reproduction of every used ES. The symbol N marks a standardization of the definition areas of the parameters which were to be fitted. The parent individuals (objective variables) are always chosen by random during their initialization. When using an encapsulated ES, the parent individuals on the second (higher) level are created by duplicating the parent individuals on the first (lower) level.

The obtained results clearly show that conventional multimembered non-encapsulated ES even at high population values only deliver very unsatisfying results. The results being presented in the first part of table 3 show that [+]-strategies can obviously act better within the solution space of the given optimi zation problem than [,]-strategies. This in all probability has the reason that the adaptive surface at the n-dimensional space of variables is characterized by narrow long and bent valleys [3,8]. This seems to lead to a more difficult self-adaption of the strategic variables when using [,]-ES than [+]-ES. Evidently ES show difficulties following narrow ridge-like search paths (especially at rising number of dimensions). Considering that it can be understood why repeated non-encapsulated ES – started from new randomly generated starting points by keeping the fittest during the optimum seeking process (e.g. `160*(GG 7+19)^100`) – lead to better optimization results: by the repetition of the search for the optimum an isolation in the solution space occurs which has the consequence that the probability of finding the global or a very good local optimum is increased. The difficulties of the given optimization problem can already be seen

Evolution Strategy	$\overline{MRE_R}$ / %	start $\bar{\sigma}$	f calls	best / %	worst / %	$\sigma_{(50)}$ /%
(dI 120,800)^380	10.61	25	304000	10.302	10.825	0.09
(dI 120+800)^380	10.16	25	304000	5.534	10.704	1.18
15*(dI 15,100)^200	7.75	25	300000	0.252	10.136	1.95
15*(dI 15+100)^200	5.85	25	300000	0.195	10.025	2.57
160*(GG 7,19)^100	1.39	2%	304000	0.063	3.725	0.82
160*(GG 7+19)^100	0.99	2%	304000	0.063	3.339	0.80
160*(GGG 7+19)^100 N	4.06	2%	304000	0.924	7.248	1.70
[GG 4,8(GG 7,19)^200]^10	5.05	20%\4%	304080	0.221	9.611	2.06
[GG 4+8(GG 7,19)^200]^10	4.39	20%\4%	304080	0.110	9.043	2.02
[GG 4,8(GG 7+19)^200]^10	2.91	20%\4%	304080	0.034	9.053	2.37
[GG 4+8(GG 7+19)^200]^10	1.19	20%\4%	304080	0.023	8.250	1.99
[-- 4+8(-- 7+19)^200]^10	3.61	20%\4%	304080	0.004	8.928	2.55
[dI 4+8(dI 7+19)^200]^10	2.31	20%\4%	304080	0.012	5.556	2.28
[dG 4+8(dG 7+19)^200]^10	1.92	20%\4%	304080	0.024	8.691	2.38
[GG 4+8(GG 7+19)^200]^10	1.40	15%\4%	304080	0.005	5.652	2.05
[GG 4+8(GG 7+19)^200]^10	0.81	10%\4%	304080	0.005	5.950	1.59
[GG 4+8(GG 7+19)^200]^10	0.47	5%\4%	304080	0.001	5.389	1.25
[GG 4+8(GG 7+19)^200]^10	3.14	20%\8%	304080	0.211	8.923	2.30
[GG 4+8(GG 7+19)^200]^10	0.77	20%\2%	304080	0.003	5.532	1.48
[GG 4+8(GG 7+19)^200]^10	1.33	20%\1%	304080	0.000	5.534	1.92
[GG 4+8(GG 7+19)^200]^5	3.46	20%\4%	152040	0.027	9.204	2.55
[GG 4+8(GG 7+19)^200]^20	0.50	20%\4%	608160	0.000	5.510	1.33
[GG 4+8(GG 7+19)^200]^30	0.04	20%\4%	912240	0.001	0.402	0.06
[GG 2+8(GG 7+19)^200]^10	1.16	20%\4%	304080	0.007	7.838	1.77
[GG 6+8(GG 7+19)^200]^10	1.49	20%\4%	304080	0.002	7.228	1.96
[GG 4+8(GG 4+19)^200]^10	1.50	20%\4%	304080	0.010	5.797	1.95
[GG 4+8(GG 10+19)^200]^10	1.73	20%\4%	304080	0.003	7.048	2.24
[GG 4+8(GGG 7+19)^200 N]^10 N	5.15	20%\4%	304080	0.235	9.728	2.13
[GGG 4+8(GGG 7+19)^200 N]^10 N	4.65	20%\4%	304080	0.107	9.237	2.41
[GGG 4+8(GG 7+19)^200 N]^10 N	1.77	20%\4%	304080	0.004	5.530	2.30
[GGG 4+8(GGG 7+19)^200]^10	11.27	20%\4%	304080	2.579	26.649	6.09
[GG 4+8(GG 7+19)^300]^7	1.73	20%\4%	319256	0.011	5.521	2.19
[GG 4+8(GG 7+19)^100]^20	1.22	20%\4%	304160	0.016	5.501	1.70
[GG 4+8(GG 7+19)^ 50]^40	2.64	20%\4%	304320	0.426	5.590	1.99
[GG 3+8(GG 7+19)^100]^40	0.02	5%/2%	608320	0.003	0.204	0.03

Table 3. Optimization results of different Evolution Strategies tested on the 6-dimensional EBGCM test system (MRE_R-values are an average of 50 runs per strategy type) [4]

when looking at the results of repeatedly starting ES,– the adaptive surface is so complicated that it is crucial to find convenient starting points which is guaranteed by a continuously repeated start of the algorithm.

The last result in the first paragraph shows the influence of the correlated step length control when using non-encapsulated ES for the parameter optimization of the used test system. Obviously the correlation has no positive influence on the course of optimization of this problem (also see discussion of part 8).

The second part of table 3 shows an improvement of encapsulated ES in contrast to (repeatedly started) non-encapsulated ES. Whereas on the encapsulated (upper) level several sub populations act independently, i.e. they are isolated, and search for a local minimum, their initialization points on the lower level seem to be lead to more successful directions within the solution space because of the selection process during the optimization. Another result which could be observed was again that [+]-variants of encapsulated ES proved to be the most effective as well as on the upper as on the lower level.

The third part of table 3 shows the influence of the recombination on the efficiency of the used algorithm. The use of a panmictic generalized intermediate recombination (Code: "G") has proven to be effective for the objective variables as well as for the standard deviations, and rotation angles – if necessary –, especially because this type of recombination offers the most number of possible recombination results for the following mutation.

The choice of a suitable start step length is very important as it can be seen in the fourth and fifth part of table 3. Apparently start step lengths chosen too large do not harmonize with a relatively low chosen iteration time on both levels and vice versa. This cannot only be observed on the basis of the found MRE_R-results but also on the decrease of the standard deviation $\sigma_{(50)}$ of all determined MRE_R-results of all 50 runs.

The sixth paragraph shows clearly that a sufficient number of main iteration steps on the lower level is decisive. A total number of 300.000 function calls at 10 main iteration steps (see last result in the second part of table 3) is not sufficient to obtain qualitatively good reproducible results. It is obvious that the ability of producing reproducible results rises strictly monotonously with an increasing number of main iteration steps on the lower level. The global optimum of each of the 50 runs is not found until a number of almost one million function calls is reached.

Investigations on the most suitable selective pressure on every level of iteration of encapsulated ES have shown that an increase of the selective pressure of λ/μ has a positive influence on the course of optimization (see paragraph seven in table 3). The best optimization results could be obtained using a selective pressure of about $\lambda/\mu \approx 2.7$ on both levels.

Paragraph eight shows the influence of the correlated control of step length when using encapsulated ES on the course of optimization at the adaptation of the parameters of the used test system. The results show that for this test system a correlated step length control do not always improve the results determined without the use of correlation, but it was obvious, that a correlated step length control on the lowest level only leads to better results than on the highest level only or on both levels at the same time. It seems to be absolutely necessary for the use of the correlated step length control that all parameters are standardized on an identical interval as the result shows in the one but last paragraph in table 3. However, this effect cannot be described reliably because the theory of the self adaptation of the strategic variables with correlated step length control has not been investigated sufficiently. First general theoretical investigations on the correlated step length control are carried out by Rudolph [7]. It can be assumed that by the coordinate transformation an exchange of information between the parameters occurs which means that the self adaptation of the strategic variables can be disturbed if the definition intervals of the parameters differ too much and if they are not standardized.

The last but one paragraph nine in table 3 shows the effects of a different number of iteration steps on the second (higher) level of ES if a similar number of function calls is kept. It can be clearly seen that a decrease of the duration of the iteration on the first (lower) level has a highly positive influence even if the duration of the iteration is decreased on the second (higher) level.

The last paragraph of table 3 finally shows the result of an ES based on the determined optimum tuning parameters concluded from all results shown by way of extract in table 3. The optimum tuning parameters can only be transferred partly to the parameter optimization of different group contribution models or optimization problems of different types of non-linear regression. The optimum tuning parameters which were found are to be understood as indicatory values which can be used for different optimization problems of similar type.

The different optimization progress for encapsulated and non-encapsulated ES is shown in figure 5. The lowest determined error reached at the respective number of function calls is plotted. It becomes clear that encapsulated ES are superior for the discussed optimization problem.

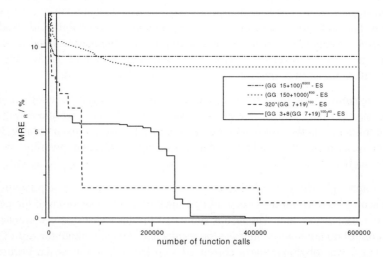

Fig. 5.   Convergence-Speed diagram of encapsulated, non-encapsulated, and repeatedly started Evolution Strategies [4]

The analyses carried out deal only with the optimization of 6 interaction parameters of the EBGC-model in the form of a test system. These however are characteristic for the interaction parameters between 2 maingroups (similar to functional groups of molecules) [3,8] within a binary mixture. However, as there are more than 2 maingroups involved, parameters between 3 and more maingroups must be determined simultaneously which leads to an optimization in higher dimensional spaces ($n=18$, 36, 60 ...). In order to reduce optimization in higher dimensional spaces interaction parameters can be determined successively by keeping already determined parameters constant. By this however thermodynamic information during the optimization is lost. For adaptations in higher dimensional spaces other tuning options for applied ES must be found which require a much greater deal of computing power.

Acknowledgements The work presented is a result of the Collaborative Research Center SFB 531 sponsored by the Deutsche Forschungsgemeinschaft (DFG).

References

1. Bäck, Th., *Evolutionary Algorithms in Theory and Practice*, Informatik Centrum Dortmund, Oxford University Press, New York/Oxford (1996)
2. Fredenslund, A., Jones, R. L. and Prausnitz, J. M., *Group-contribution estimation of activity coefficients in nonideal liquid mixtures*. AIChE Journal, 21, (1975) 1086-1099
3. Friese, T., Ulbig, P., and Schulz, S., *Use of Evolutionary Algorithms for the Calculation of Group Contribution Parameters in order to Predict Thermodynamic Properties. Part 1: Genetic Algorithms*, Computers & Chemical Engineering (1998) (in press)
4. Geyer, H., Ulbig, P., and Schulz, S., *Use of Evolutionary Algorithms for the Calculation of Group Contribution Parameters in order to Predict Thermodynamic Properties. Part 2: Evolution Strategies*, Computers & Chemical Engineering (1998) (submitted)
5. Nelder, J. A., Mead, R., *A simplex method for function minimization*, In: Computer Journal, 7 (1965)
6. Rechenberg, I., *Evolutionsstrategie '94*, Werkstatt Bionik und Evolutionstechnik, Band 1, Friedrich Frommann, Stuttgart (1994)
7. Rudolph, G., *On correlated mutations in evolution strategies*. In R. Männer and B. Manderick, Parallel Problem Solving from Nature, 2, Elsevier, Amsterdam (1992) 105-114
8. Ulbig, P., *Entwicklung der Gruppenbeitragsmodelle UNIVAP & EBGCM zur Vorhersage thermodynamischer Größen sowie Bestimmung der Modellparameter unter Verwendung evolutionärer Algorithmen*, PhD Thesis, Institute for Thermodynamics, University of Dortmund (1996)
9. Ulbig, P., Friese, T., Geyer, H., Kracht, C., and Schulz, S., *Prediction of thermodynamic properties for chemical engineering with the aid of Computational Intelligence*. In: Progress in Connectionist-Based Information Systems - Proceedings of the 1997 International Conference on Neural Information Processing and Intelligent Information Systems, Vol. 2, Springer, New York (1997) 1259-1262
10. Schwefel, H.-P., *Numerical Optimization of Computer Models*, Wiley, Chichester (1981)
11. Schwefel, H.-P., *Evolution and Optimum Seeking*, Wiley, New York (1995)
12. Weidlich, U., Gmehling, J.: *A modified UNIFAC model*. Ind. Eng. Chem. Res., Vol. 26. (1987) 1372

Recombination Operators for Evolutionary Graph Drawing

Daniel Kobler[1] and Andrea G. B. Tettamanzi[2]

[1] Department of Mathematics, Swiss Federal Institute of Technology,
EPFL, CH - 1015 Lausanne, Switzerland
E-mail: Daniel.Kobler@epfl.ch
[2] Università degli Studi di Milano, Dipartimento di Scienze dell'Informazione
Via Comelico 39, I-20135 Milano, Italy
E-mail: tettaman@dsi.unimi.it

Abstract. This paper illustrates an evolutionary algorithm for drawing graphs according to a number of esthetic criteria. Tests are carried out on three graphs of increasing difficulty and the performance of four different recombination operators are compared. The results are then briefly discussed and compared to those obtained with a tabu search.

1 Introduction

A number of data presentation problems involve the drawing of a graph on a two-dimensional surface, like a sheet of paper or a computer screen. Examples include circuit schematics, communication and public transportation networks, social relationships and software engineering diagrams. In almost all data presentation applications, the usefulness of a graph drawing depends on its readability, i.e. the capability of conveying the meaning of the diagram quickly and clearly. Readability issues are expressed by means of *esthetics,* which can be formulated as optimization criteria for the drawing algorithm [2].

An account of esthetic criteria that have been proposed and various heuristic methods for satisfying them can be found in [15]. An extensive annotated bibliography on algorithms for drawing graphs is given in [4] and [2]. The methods proposed vary according to the class of graphs for which they are intended and the esthetic criteria they take into account. For most reasonable esthetic requirements, however, it turns out that solving this problem exactly is prohibitively expensive for large graphs.

Evolutionary algorithms are a class of optimization methods inspired by Biology. It is assumed that the reader is already familiar with the main concepts and issues relevant to these algorithms; good reference books are [13, 8, 12, 1].

2 The Problem

Given an unoriented graph $G = (V, E)$, we want to determine the coordinates for all vertices in V on a plane so as to satisfy a certain number of esthetic requirements.

The esthetic criteria employed in this work are the following:

- there should be as few edge crossings as possible, ideally none;
- the length of each edge should be as close as possible to a parameter L;
- the angles between edges incident to the same vertex should be as uniform as possible (ideally the same).

A usually considered criterion requiring the vertices to be evenly distributed on the available space is in fact entailed by the second and third criteria stated above.

In general, the optimization problems associated with most esthetics are NP-hard [10, 11]. For instance, it has been proven that even just minimizing the number of edge crossings is an NP-hard problem [6]. Therefore the problem described above is also NP-hard, thus providing a valid motivation for resorting to an evolutionary approach.

The use of evolutionary algorithms for drawing *directed* graphs, a problem of great practical importance, already began to be explored by Michalewicz [12]. Surprisingly, however, that application disappeared from subsequent editions of his book. Michalewicz's work considers only two criteria, namely that arcs pointing upward should be avoided and there should be as few arc crossings as possible. Direction of edges is not addressed here. Rather, we deal with other types of graphs arising, for example, when representing on paper telecommunication networks, where links are always bidirectional.

3 The Algorithm

The algorithm whose elements are illustrated below is a generational replacement island-based evolutionary algorithm. In such an algorithm, there may be several populations, the *islands*, each of them undergoing evolution according to a generational replacement evolutionary algorithm, and from time to time good individuals migrate from an island to another.

3.1 Encoding and initialization

How a graph is drawn on a plane, i.e. a candidate solution to our problem, is completely determined by the (x, y) coordinates assigned to each vertex. Therefore, a genotype consists in a vector $((x_1, y_1), \ldots, (x_{|V|}, y_{|V|}))$, where (x_i, y_i) are the coordinates of the i-th vertex of the graph, encoded as two integers in $\{-4096, \ldots, 4095\}$, which can be considered as the basic *genes* of an individual. It is worth noticing that this is not a bit-string representation and thus genetic operators always act on pairs of coordinates (or vertex positions) according to their meaning.

Initial vertex positions for each individual are independently randomly generated and according to the same uniform probability over the whole drawing page. Generation of initial graphs could also be carried out with the help of greedy algorithms, which indeed have been tried, although they are not discussed in this paper.

3.2 Fitness

Three factors contribute to determining an individual's fitness, one for each esthetic criterion:

- the number of edge crossings, χ;
- the mean relative square error σ of edge lengths defined as

$$\sigma = \frac{1}{|E|} \sum_{e \in E} \left(\frac{\|e\| - L}{L} \right)^2, \tag{1}$$

  where $\|e\|$ is the length of edge e;
- the cumulative square deviation Δ of edge angles from their ideal values, defined as

$$\Delta = \sum_{v \in V} \sum_{k=1}^{N_v} \left(\psi_k(v) - \frac{2\pi}{N_v} \right)^2, \tag{2}$$

  where N_v is the number of edges incident into vertex v and the $\psi_k(v)$, $k = 1, \ldots, N_v$, are the angles between adjacent vertices.

Multi-objective techniques can be used for this problem, but in our approach, we decided to combine the objectives in one function. An individual's fitness, f, to be maximized, is then calculated as follows:

$$f = a \frac{1}{\sigma + 1} + b \frac{1}{\chi + 1} + c \frac{1}{\Delta + 1}, \tag{3}$$

where a, b and c are constants that control the relative importance of the three criteria and compensate for their different numerical magnitudes. Their values have been empirically determined as $a = 0.1$, $b = 0.8$ and $c = 0.1$ for the experiments described below; however, the reader should be aware that by modifying these constants the drawings produced by the algorithm can widely vary.

Since the three criteria employed conflict with each other and cannot in general be all completely satisfied at the same time, the fitness defined in (3) can only take the theoretical maximum of 1 in very few special cases.

3.3 Selection and crossover

Two selection strategies have been used: elitist fitness proportionate selection with a simple fitness scaling and ranking selection as described in [16].

Four different types of crossover, each needing two parents to create one or two offsprings, have been experimented. Crossover is applied with a given probability p_{cross} to each couple of selected individuals. In the first two crossovers, the two parents are equivalent:

- the *uniform* crossover, where the vertex positions that make up an individual's genotype have the same probability of being inherited from either parent;

- the *convex hull* crossover, where the coordinates of each vertex in the off-spring are a linear combination of the coordinates of the same vertex in its parents: suppose that (x_1, y_1) and (x_2, y_2) are the coordinates of a vertex in the two parents, then the same vertex in the offspring will have coordinates (X, Y), where X and Y are two independent, normally distributed random variables with mean respectively $\frac{x_1+x_2}{2}$ and $\frac{y_1+y_2}{2}$ and with the same variance σ_{cross}^2, which is a parameter of the algorithm.

We also introduce two new crossovers, in which the first parent plays a more important role. In both cases, a subset V' of vertices is created and the offsprings are created as follows: the first offspring inherits the coordinates of a vertex v from the first (resp. second) parent if $v \in V'$ (resp. $v \notin V'$). The opposite holds for the second offspring. The two crossovers differ in their construction of V':

- the *plane cut* crossover, similar to one-point crossover, but applied to the grid on which the drawing is done. The line joining two randomly generated points splits the grid in two parts, say A and B. Then V' is the set of vertices that are in part A of the grid in the first parent.
- the *neighborhood* crossover, which tries to take advantage of good parts of a drawing. A set V' of given cardinality n' (parameter of the algorithm) is obtained by doing Breadth-First Scanning of the graph, starting from an arbitrary vertex (that is, take its neighbors, and then their neighbors, ...). In the case of a graph with several connected components, several starting vertices may have to be used in order to bring the cardinality of V' up to n'.

Overall, the algorithm is elitist, in the sense that the best individual in the population is always passed on unchanged to the next generation, without undergoing crossover or mutation.

3.4 Mutation and migration

Mutation perturbs individuals by adding to each of their vertices independent centered Gaussian noise, whose variance σ_{mut}^2 is a parameter of the algorithm. This mutation operator is very similar to the convex hull crossover described above, the main difference being that in the case of crossover both parents participate in setting the mean of the new vertex position distribution.

If there are several islands, some migration occurs on a regular basis, defined by the user. Each island i sends to island $i + 1$ (where the successor of the last island is island 1) a copy of its best individual currently available. This new individual replaces the worst individual in island $i + 1$.

4 Experimental Results

The algorithm described above (denoted by EA) was implemented and run on several Pentium 120 and 200 workstations, under the Windows 95/NT operating systems and on Silicon Graphics workstations (200 MHz).

4.1 The Test Suite

The experiments were performed using three test graphs, that will be denoted H, D and N.

- H is the hypercube in 4 dimensions and contains $|V_H| = 16$ vertices and $|E_H| = 32$ edges.
- D represents the divisibility links of the integers from 2 to 30: the vertices corresponding to two numbers are linked if and only if one of these numbers divides the other. By removing the isolated vertices, this graph has $|V_D| = 25$ vertices and $|E_D| = 51$ edges.
- N is a piece of Internet. This graph is much bigger than the other two, having $|V_N| = 325$ vertices and $|E_N| = 327$ edges. It has several connected components.

The desired length for edges was set to $L = 8192/\sqrt{|V|}$, i.e. the average distance between closest vertices when they are uniformly distributed over the whole drawing plane.

4.2 Test Runs

A set of test runs was defined with the aim of understanding which combinations of parameter settings and operators work better. For each of the two graphs H and D, all combinations of the following alternatives were tried (between parentheses are given short codes for all alternatives):

- one island of 100 individuals ($\langle\text{popSize}\rangle = $ C), two islands of 50 individuals ($\langle\text{popSize}\rangle = $ 2L) or four islands of 25 individuals ($\langle\text{popSize}\rangle = $ 4I);
- fitness proportionate selection or ranking selection ($\langle\text{selection}\rangle = $ f or r);
- $p_{\text{mut}} = 0.1$ ($\langle\text{mutRate}\rangle = $ X) or $p_{\text{mut}} = 0.01$ ($\langle\text{mutRize}\rangle = $ C);
- convex hull crossover with variance $\sigma^2_{\text{cross}} = L$ ($\langle\text{crossover}\rangle = $ cl), neighborhood crossover with cardinality $n' = \lfloor|V|/2\rfloor$ ($\langle\text{crossover}\rangle = $ nn'), plane cut crossover ($\langle\text{crossover}\rangle = $ p) or uniform crossover ($\langle\text{crossover}\rangle = $ u);
- $p_{\text{cross}} = 0.5$ ($\langle\text{crossRate}\rangle = $ H) or $p_{\text{cross}} = 0.2$ ($\langle\text{crossRate}\rangle = $ V).

The mutation variance was always set to $\sigma^2_{\text{mut}} = L$. Furthermore, convex-hull crossover was always used without mutation, since it already carries a kind of mutation with it.

Experiment were code-named according to the following convention:

$$\langle\text{graph}\rangle\langle\text{popSize}\rangle\langle\text{selection}\rangle\text{ul}\langle\text{mutRate}\rangle\langle\text{crossover}\rangle\langle\text{crossRate}\rangle.$$

For graph N, which is considerably more demanding, only a few runs with one island, using the combinations that worked best on the other two graphs, were performed.

All runs were carried on for 10,000 generations, corresponding to an average execution time of about one hour for the two "simpler" graphs and of several hours for the "tougher" graph.

4.3 Results

Overall, 168 experimental runs were performed on both graphs H and D, whose results are given in Table 1. The best solution of every column is in bold. The results for graph N are summarized in Table 2 and Fig. 1 shows the best results, in terms of fitness, obtained by the EA applied to graphs D and N. Because of the large number of the possible parameter settings, these experiments do not allow robust assessments, but they give some tendencies.

A quick inspection of the results shows that, on average, runs with more islands tend to give better results, even though the difference with the single-island runs is not dramatic.

$\langle pS \rangle = c$	$\langle pS \rangle = 2L$	$\langle pS \rangle = 4I$	Run description	$\langle pS \rangle = c$	$\langle pS \rangle = 2L$	$\langle pS \rangle = 4I$
0.110	0.104	0.107	$\langle pS \rangle$ful0clH	0.086	0.085	0.087
0.109	0.104	0.110	$\langle pS \rangle$ful0clV	0.086	0.085	0.081
0.187	0.187	0.145	$\langle pS \rangle$fulCn8H	0.144	0.208	0.173
0.187	0.187	0.179	$\langle pS \rangle$fulCn8V	0.206	0.171	0.191
0.148	0.169	0.146	$\langle pS \rangle$fulCpH	0.170	0.151	0.168
0.174	0.167	0.163	$\langle pS \rangle$fulCpV	0.160	0.167	0.148
0.186	0.186	**0.187**	$\langle pS \rangle$fulCuH	**0.225**	0.225	0.173
0.166	0.166	**0.187**	$\langle pS \rangle$fulCuV	0.204	**0.226**	0.224
0.179	0.179	0.145	$\langle pS \rangle$fulXn8H	0.224	0.166	0.204
0.165	0.165	0.178	$\langle pS \rangle$fulXn8V	0.131	0.207	0.205
0.138	0.141	0.184	$\langle pS \rangle$fulXpH	0.158	0.154	**0.226**
0.141	0.164	0.162	$\langle pS \rangle$fulXpV	0.156	0.166	0.224
0.188	**0.188**	0.165	$\langle pS \rangle$fulXuH	0.139	0.207	0.159
0.144	0.144	0.186	$\langle pS \rangle$fulXuV	0.165	0.208	0.159
0.106	0.106	0.109	$\langle pS \rangle$rul0clH	0.083	0.085	0.085
0.103	0.106	0.107	$\langle pS \rangle$rul0clV	0.085	0.085	0.087
0.145	0.145	0.184	$\langle pS \rangle$rulCn8H	0.167	0.156	0.207
0.181	0.181	0.140	$\langle pS \rangle$rulCn8V	0.208	0.164	0.205
0.189	0.167	0.158	$\langle pS \rangle$rulCpH	0.167	0.193	0.207
0.166	0.168	0.186	$\langle pS \rangle$rulCpV	0.219	0.137	0.156
0.143	0.143	0.168	$\langle pS \rangle$rulCuH	0.219	0.206	0.171
0.164	0.164	0.183	$\langle pS \rangle$rulCuV	0.173	0.153	0.174
0.145	0.145	0.163	$\langle pS \rangle$rulXn8H	0.127	0.151	0.221
0.180	0.180	0.145	$\langle pS \rangle$rulXn8V	0.145	0.177	0.220
0.140	0.162	0.146	$\langle pS \rangle$rulXpH	0.157	0.145	0.156
0.161	0.178	0.153	$\langle pS \rangle$rulXpV	0.178	0.169	0.168
0.157	0.157	0.162	$\langle pS \rangle$rulXuH	0.127	0.127	0.142
0.161	0.161	0.166	$\langle pS \rangle$rulXuV	0.111	0.140	0.205
0.156	0.158	0.158	average	0.158	0.161	0.172

Table 1. Summary of results for graph H (on the left) and graph D (on the right) after 10,000 generations.

Run description	NCfulCn162H	NCfulCpH	NCfulCuH	NCfulCuV	NCfulXuH	NCfulXpH
f	0.091	**0.097**	0.089	0.088	0.020	0.047

Table 2. Summary of results for graph N after 10,000 generations.

A comparison of the effectiveness of the four proposed recombination operators can be carried out by calculating the average fitness reached by runs using each one of them:

Recombination	uniform	convex hull	plane cut	neighborhood
avg. f on H	**0.167**	0.107	0.161	**0.167**
avg. f on D	0.179	0.085	0.171	**0.182**

There is a clear indication that convex hull crossover is the worst of the four, and that uniform and neighborhood crossovers are the best, with a slight advantage for the latter. It is interesting to notice that these two recombination

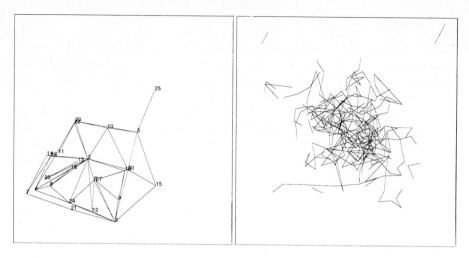

Fig. 1. Layouts of graph D (on the left) having fitness 0.226 ($\chi = 5$, $\sigma = 0.084$ and $\Delta = 168.204$) and of graph N (on the right) having fitness 0.097 ($\chi = 886$, $\sigma = 0.059$ and $\Delta = 1173.7$). Solutions found by the EA after 10,000 generations.

operators are the ones that, respectively, use the least and the most topological information about the graph. The higher crossover rate appears to be more advisable, although not by far.

As for mutation, runs with the lower mutation rate consistently gave better results. Of the two selection strategies employed, fitness-proportionate selection with scaling fares a little better than ranking selection, but this might change for different settings of the selection pressure in the latter.

4.4 Tests with a tabu search

In order to allow some comparisons with other results, a tabu search has also been designed to solve this problem. Tabu search (TS) will not be detailled here: the interested reader can refer to [7, 9]. A solution s' is said to be a neighbor solution of s if s' can be obtained by applying a movement to s. Here a movement consists in adding a centered Gaussian noise to a random vertex v with variance σ_{TS}^2. Movements that bring v back in a square of side $\frac{\text{size of grid}}{500}$ centered on a previous position of v are forbidden during a certain number of iterations. This last number is regularly changed to a new value, randomly chosen within some bounds that depend on the mean length of the tabu list B_{length} as suggested in [5]. Such dynamic tabu lists have shown to be quite robust [5, 14]. The number of (randomly selected) movements M tested at each iteration of the TS is also given by the user.

A relatively small set of test runs has been defined for the tabu search, applied to graphs H and D. Similarly to Sect. 4.2, the experiments were code-named according to the following convention:

$$\langle\text{graph}\rangle\langle\sigma_{TS}^2\rangle\langle\text{basicLength}\rangle\langle\text{mvtNb}\rangle$$

Run description	f
H500DC	**0.189**
H500CC	**0.189**
H500CL	0.188
H1000DC	0.187
H1000CC	0.188
H1000CL	0.188
HLDC	0.186
HLCC	0.185
HLCL	0.180
H3000DC	0.181
H3000CC	0.181
H3000CL	0.176
H5000DC	0.176
H5000CC	0.176
H5000CL	0.172

Run description	f
D400DC	0.163
D400CC	0.149
D400CL	0.118
D800DC	0.158
D800CC	0.175
D800CL	0.155
DLDC	0.227
DLCC	0.227
DLCL	0.221
D2500DC	0.207
D2500CC	0.206
D2500CL	0.219
D4000DC	0.248
D4000CC	**0.249**
D4000CL	0.180

Run description	f
N110CC	0.102
NLDC	**0.105**
NLCC	0.104
N1150CC	0.103

Table 3. Summary of results for graphs H, D and N with tabu search.

where

- $\langle \sigma^2_{\mathrm{TS}} \rangle$ is a number or the length L;
- $\langle \mathrm{basicLength} \rangle$ is D (if $B_{\mathrm{length}} = 500$) or C (if $B_{\mathrm{length}} = 100$);
- $\langle \mathrm{mvtNb} \rangle$ is C (if $M = 100$) or L (if $M = 50$).

The number of iterations is such that the number of solutions evaluated by the TS is equal to the number of individuals generated by the EA. Since evaluating a neighbor solution in the TS can be done faster than calculating the fitness of an individual, the execution time is divided by a factor of 2 or 3 for graphs H and D (even more for graph N).

The results are given in Table 3, the best solution for each graph being shown in bold. The values of σ^2_{TS} taken for graphs H and D are different, in order to have in both cases (approximately) the values $L/4$, $L/2$, L, $1.5 \cdot L$ and $2.5 \cdot L$. We notice that, as expected, the exact value of B_{length} is not important. Also, it is better to visit 100 neighbor solutions at each of the 10,000 iterations than 50 neighbor solutions during 20,000 iterations. But the value of M must not be increased too much, since otherwise the number of iterations would be too small for the algorithm to "have time" to find a good solution.

Using the best solutions obtained by the EA and the TS as initial solution for a tabu search with a small value of σ^2_{TS} (and less iterations), as a kind of "post-optimisation", did not provide significant improvements.

5 Discussion

If we compare the results obtained by the EA and the TS, we notice that the latter gave better values for f. Moreover, even if both algorithms evaluate the same number of solutions, the TS needs less time to do so. The definition of a movement used in the TS was chosen to make a more meaningful comparison with the EA, but other definitions may be considered as well.

The performance of the EA can be increased by using a directed mutation operator. One which has been tried with good results moves a vertex in a new position which is normally distributed around the center of the positions of neighbor vertices, with a variance inversely proportional to the number of these

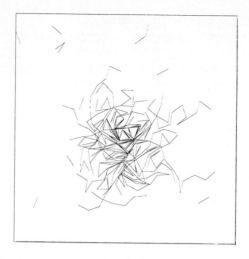

Fig. 2. A layout of graph N found by the tabu search after 10,000 iterations, having fitness 0.105 ($\chi = 138$, $\sigma = 0.008$ and $\Delta = 1364.58$).

neighbors. This operator has not been included in this paper for lack of space and time, but it will be experimented within a future work. Its use in the TS has not yet been tried.

The drawings obtained for the graph N by both algorithms (see Fig. 1 and 2) show that the quality of the solution can easily be improved by moving some vertices. But these improvements (easily detected by a human observer) do mainly concern the angles between edges and would therefore, because of the high value of Δ, have only a small effect on the value of f.

Even though one might think that using evolutionary algorithms for graph drawing represents a departure from classical algorithmic strategies found in computational geometry literature, a number of implicit similarities with well-known classical heuristics can be found. For instance, including a term inversely proportional to σ as defined in (1) in the fitness function recalls the so-called *spring embedder* force-directed method [3], whereby the drawing process is to simulate a mechanical system, where vertices are replaced by rings and edges are replaced by springs: the springs attract the rings if they are too far apart and repel them if they are too close.

Since the settings of the parameters controlling the relative weights of the esthetic criteria are very arbitrary and the quality of a drawing is inherently subjective, an idea for further work would be to allow the algorithm to interact with a human operator, using its responses to optimally tune the parameters relevant to the fitness function.

Acknowledgments

The research of the first author was supported by a Swiss National Fund for Scientific Research project under grant 21-45070.95. The research of the second author was partially supported by M.U.R.S.T. 60% funds. These supports are gratefully acknowledged. The authors thank Prof. Gianni Degli Antoni for his support and useful discussions and Genetica—Advanced Software Architectures S.r.l. in Milan for the extensive use of their computing equipment.

References

1. T. Bäck. *Evolutionary algorithms in theory and practice*. Oxford University Press, Oxford, 1996.
2. G. Di Battista, P. Eades, R. Tamassia, and I. G. Tollis. Algorithms for drawing graphs: An annotated bibliography. Technical report, Available on the Internet, URL: `ftp://wilma.cs.brown.edu/pub/papers/compgeo/gdbiblio.ps.Z`, 1989.
3. P. Eades. A heuristics for graph drawing. *Congressus Numerantium*, 42:149–160, 1984.
4. P. Eades and R. Tamassia. Algorithms for drawing graphs: An annotated bibliography. Technical Report CS-89-09, Department of Computer Science, Brown University, 1989.
5. C. Fleurent and J.A. Ferland. Genetic and hybrid algorithms for graph coloring. *Annals of Operations Research*, 63, 1996.
6. M. R. Garey and D. S. Johnson. Crossing number is NP-complete. *SIAM Journal on Algebraic and Discrete Methods*, 4(3):312–316, 1983.
7. F. Glover and M. Laguna. *Tabu Search*. Kluwer Academic Publ., 1997.
8. D. E. Goldberg. *Genetic Algorithms in Search, Optimization & Machine Learning*. Addison-Wesley, Reading, MA, 1989.
9. A. Hertz, E. Taillard, and D. de Werra. Tabu search. In J. K. Lenstra, editor, *Local Search in Combinatorial Optimization*. Wiley, 1995.
10. D. S. Johnson. The NP-completeness column: An ongoing guide. *Journal of Algorithms*, 3(1):89–99, 1982.
11. D. S. Johnson. The NP-completeness column: An ongoing guide. *Journal of Algorithms*, 5(2):147–160, 1984.
12. Z. Michalewicz. *Genetic Algorithms + Data Structures = Evolution Programs*. Springer-Verlag, Berlin, 1992.
13. H.-P. Schwefel. *Numerical optimization of computer models*. Wiley, Chichester; New York, 1981.
14. E. Taillard. *Recherches itératives dirigées parallèles*. PhD thesis, Ecole Polytechnique Fédérale de Lausanne, 1993.
15. R. Tamassia, G. Di Battista, and C. Batini. Automatic graph drawing and readability of diagrams. *IEEE Transactions on Systems, Man and Cybernetics*, 18(1):61–79, 1988.
16. D. Whitley. The GENITOR Algorithm and Selection Pressure: Why Rank-Based Allocation of Reproductive Trials is Best. In J. D. Schaffer, editor, *Proceedings of the Third International Conference on Genetic Algorithms*, pages 116–121, San Mateo, CA, 1989. Morgan Kaufmann.

Optimisation of Density Estimation Models with Evolutionary Algorithms[*]

Martin Kreutz[1][**], Anja M. Reimetz[2], Bernhard Sendhoff[1],
Claus Weihs[2], and Werner von Seelen[1]

[1] Institut für Neuroinformatik, Ruhr-Universität Bochum, Germany
[2] Fachbereich Statistik, Universität Dortmund, Germany

Abstract. We propose a new optimisation method for estimating both the parameters and the structure, i.e. the number of components, of a finite mixture model for density estimation. We employ a hybrid method consisting of an evolutionary algorithm for structure optimisation in conjunction with a gradient-based method for evaluating each candidate model architecture. For structure modification we propose specific, problem dependent evolutionary operators. The introduction of a regularisation term prevents the models from over-fitting the data. Experiments show good generalisation abilities of the optimised structures.

1 Introduction

The estimation of the probability density function (pdf) of a data generating process is one of the primary tools in the analysis and modeling of stochastic or partially stochastic systems. If a complete *a priori* model of the system is lacking and no parametric model can be assumed, the density estimation has to be based completely on the available data. Mixture densities have been considered as general semi-parametric models for density estimation:

$$p(\boldsymbol{x}|\boldsymbol{\theta}) = \sum_{i=1}^{m} \alpha_i \, \phi_i(\boldsymbol{x}|\theta_i) \;, \quad \boldsymbol{x} \in \mathbb{R}^n \;, \quad \boldsymbol{\theta} = (\alpha_i, \ldots, \alpha_m, \theta_i, \ldots, \theta_m) \tag{1}$$

$$\sum_{i=1}^{m} \alpha_i = 1 \;, \quad \alpha_i \geq 0 \; \forall \, i = \{1, \ldots, m\} \tag{2}$$

Finite mixture models have several appealing properties: they are universal in the sense that they can approximate any continuous probability distribution, they can cope with multimodal distributions and their complexity can be easily adjusted by the number of components. In this article we employ mixtures of normal densities:

$$\phi_i(\boldsymbol{x}|\theta_i) = \frac{1}{\sqrt{2\pi}^n \prod_{k=1}^{n} \sigma_{ik}} \exp\left(-\frac{1}{2} \sum_{k=1}^{n} \left(\frac{x_k - \mu_{ik}}{\sigma_{ik}}\right)^2\right) \tag{3}$$

$$\theta_i = (\mu_{i1}, \ldots, \mu_{in}, \sigma_{i1}^2, \ldots, \sigma_{in}^2) \in \mathbb{R}^{2n} \tag{4}$$

[*] Supported by the BMBF under Grant No. 01IB701A0 (*SONN II*).
[**] email: Martin.Kreutz@neuroinformatik.ruhr-uni-bochum.de

When constructing statistical models using a limited quantity of data, the issue of model selection is very crucial. We address this problem in an evolutionary framework. The determination of the size of the model and the arrangement of its components can be regarded as a structure optimization problem for which we employ an evolutionary algorithm with specific, problem dependent operators. For the optimisation of the model parameters we use the maximum penalised likelihood approach. This optimisation task has been carried out in [8] with evolution strategies, in this paper we employ the EM algorithm [7]. The remainder of this article is organised as follows. In Section 2 we address the issue of regularisation. The evolutionary algorithm is described in Section 3. Section 4 presents the experimental results and conclusions are drawn in Section 5.

2 Regularisation

The method of maximum likelihood is widely used in statistical inference. The likelihood is the probability for the occurrence of sample $X = \{x_1, \ldots, x_N\}$ for the chosen probability density model (characterised by its parameters $\boldsymbol{\theta}$). Assuming the x_i to be iid. sampled with pdf $p(x|\boldsymbol{\theta})$ the log-likelihood function reads

$$L(\boldsymbol{\theta}) = \log \prod_{k=1}^{N} p(\boldsymbol{x}_k|\boldsymbol{\theta}) = \sum_{k=1}^{N} \log \, p(\boldsymbol{x}_k|\boldsymbol{\theta}). \tag{5}$$

However, if infinite-dimensional objects such as functions of one or more continuous variables are involved, the principle of maximum likelihood is usually inadequate. Attempting to maximise the likelihood in such contexts usually results in an infinite value for the likelihood and degeneracy of the model. In the context of normal mixtures, eq. (3), we observe that the likelihood will be infinite, if one of the density functions $\phi_i(x|\theta_i)$ approaches a delta function placed on one data point. In structure optimisation of normal mixtures, methods solely based on the likelihood, therefore, tend to increase the number of kernel functions, place their centres on the data points and minimise their widths. A general approach to transform this ill-posed optimisation problem into a well-posed problem is the introduction of regularisation terms which reflect specific assumptions about the density model. The aim is the simultaneous minimisation of bias and variance of the model which is possible in the case of infinite data sets but leads to the *bias-variance dilemma* [2] in practical applications. A sensible choice for regularisation is to demand a smooth density model. A common choice of a *smoothness* functional $J(\boldsymbol{\theta})$ is the integral of the squared second derivative

$$J(\boldsymbol{\theta}) = \int_{-\infty}^{+\infty} p''(x|\boldsymbol{\theta})^2 \, \mathrm{d}x \tag{6}$$

which has an appealing interpretation as the global measure of curvature of p. Hence, the complete objective function reads

$$F(\boldsymbol{\theta}) = L(\boldsymbol{\theta}) - \lambda \, J(\boldsymbol{\theta}). \tag{7}$$

The *smoothing* parameter λ controls the relative influence of the two criteria. There are several possibilities to extend this function to multivariate functions. In the multivariate case the second derivative is described by the Hessian:

$$H = (h_{rs}) \quad ; \quad h_{rs} = \begin{cases} \dfrac{\partial^2 p(\boldsymbol{x}|\boldsymbol{\theta})}{\partial x_r^2} \,, & r = s \\[2ex] \dfrac{\partial^2 p(\boldsymbol{x}|\boldsymbol{\theta})}{\partial x_r\,\partial x_s} \,, & r \neq s \end{cases} \tag{8}$$

The squared second derivative C and the matrix of integrals D is defined by

$$C = (c_{rs}) = H^{\mathsf{T}} H \quad ; \quad c_{rs} = \sum_{r=1}^{n} h_{rt}\, h_{ts} \tag{9}$$

$$D = (d_{rs}) \quad ; \quad d_{rs} = \int_{-\infty}^{+\infty} c_{rs}\, \mathrm{d}\boldsymbol{x}. \tag{10}$$

In order to yield a scalar measure of smoothness of p either the determinant or the trace of D can be taken. These measures correspond to the product and the sum of eigenvalues of D, respectively, and both are invariant under a linear non-singular transformation. We use the trace of D for simplicity:

$$J(\boldsymbol{\theta}) = \mathrm{tr}\, D = \sum_{r=1}^{n} d_{rr}. \tag{11}$$

The derivation of the diagonal elements d_{rr} is given in appendix A.

3   Evolution of density models

The structure or architecture of a model has a direct impact on training time, convergence, generalisation ability, robustness, etc. of the model. Therefore, the choice of at least a near optimal architecture is a key issue in model building. The optimisation of the structure of a model represents a difficult problem for search algorithms since the search space is in general non-differentiable and multimodal. Furthermore, the mapping from architecture to performance is indirect, strongly epistatic, and dependent on initial conditions. Evolutionary algorithms (EA) have been considered as a promising method for dealing with these problems especially in the area of neural networks [11]. Less attention has been paid to the artificial evolution of mixture models for density estimation. From approximation theory we know that they are universal approximators [5] and their local nature permits to learn faster than global models (like NN) [4]. Furthermore, with regard to EAs, the local interaction between the components in mixture models leads to a lower epistasis. This justifies the usage of a simple direct encoding. The advantages of locality, however, are obtained at the expense of a potentially large number of components required to cover the data space. This leads to the severe problem of over-fitting the data and under-fitting the noise level, respectively.

In our method this problem is handled by an appropriate regularisation (see Section 2). For the evolution of structures we use a variant of the *steady-state* evolutionary algorithm. In each generation two parents are randomly selected from the population and the operators crossover and mutation are applied with the probabilities P_c and P_m, respectively. The two offsprings are evaluated by training them with the EM algorithm and replace the two worst individuals in the population. This is repeated for a predefined number of generations.

3.1   Genome representation

All parameters of the mixture density are encoded directly in the genome, which are comprised of a variable length string of composite *genes*. Each gene encodes the parameters (centre and width) of a single density function as well as the corresponding mixing coefficient:

$$\mathcal{G}_i = (\alpha_i, \mu_{i1}, \ldots, \mu_{in}, \sigma_{i1}^2, \ldots, \sigma_{in}^2), \tag{12}$$

where n denotes the dimension of the input space. The length of the genome varies with the number m of kernel density functions:

$$\mathcal{C} = (\mathcal{G}_1, \ldots, \mathcal{G}_m). \tag{13}$$

All parameters are encoded as floating point values.

3.2   Recombination

One additional difficulty which arises in the context of recombination is referred to as the problem of *competing conventions*: Due to the invariance to permutation of the kernel functions distinct genomes map to phenotypes which are functionally equivalent. For that reason the recombination of two successful parents employing different conventions is unlikely to produce successful offspring. In [1] this problem was circumvented by a special 2-point crossover operator which is based on crosspoints in the input variable space (and therefore the space of possible centres for the Gaussian) rather than on the position in the genome. We employ a modified version of this operator. The two crosspoints $\boldsymbol{\mu}^{(1)}$ and $\boldsymbol{\mu}^{(2)}$ are sampled randomly with uniform distribution in the space which is spanned by all centres $\boldsymbol{\mu}_j$:

$$\boldsymbol{\mu}^{(1,2)} = (\mu_1^{(1,2)}, \ldots, \mu_n^{(1,2)}) \text{ with } \mu_i^{(1,2)} \sim R\left[\min_{i=1,\ldots,m} \mu_{ij}, \max_{i=1,\ldots,m} \mu_{ij}\right] \tag{14}$$

These two points define a *hypervolume* in the space of centres. All centres of the two selected parents lying inside this hypercube are exchanged by the crossover operator. After crossover, the first offspring contains those genes $\mathcal{G}i$ (kernel functions) from the second parent which satisfy:

$$\left(\mu_j^{(1)} \le \mu_{ij} \le \mu_j^{(2)}\right) \vee \left(\mu_j^{(2)} \le \mu_{ij} \le \mu_j^{(1)}\right) \quad \forall\, j = \{1, \ldots, n\} \tag{15}$$

together with those genes from the first parent which do not satisfy this condition. The second offspring contains all remaining genes from both parents. This crossover operator treats functionally equivalent phenotypes using different *conventions* as identical.

3.3 Mutation

Several mutation operators for structure modification of the model were considered. A very straightforward choice are simple insertion and deletion operators. The component insertion operator introduces a new kernel function with random centre and width, whereas the component deletion operator simply deletes a randomly selected kernel function. However, the insertion and deletion of kernels in the structure optimisation of the model can be very disruptive and violate the principle of a strong causal mapping between the genotype and phenotype or fitness space [9]. In order to minimise these effects and to better control the impact of mutation we employ special *merge* and *split* operators. We optimise the parameters of the kernel(s) for the case of merging (two kernels are replaced by one) and splitting (one kernel is replaced by two). In both cases an appropriate distance measure between the three Gaussian functions (according to eq. (3)) is given by

$$d_{\phi\tilde{\phi}\hat{\phi}} = \int\limits_{-\infty}^{\infty} \left(\phi(\boldsymbol{x}, \boldsymbol{\mu}, \boldsymbol{\sigma}^2) - \left(\tilde{\phi}(\boldsymbol{x}, \tilde{\boldsymbol{\mu}}, \tilde{\boldsymbol{\sigma}}^2) + \hat{\phi}(\boldsymbol{x}, \hat{\boldsymbol{\mu}}, \hat{\boldsymbol{\sigma}}^2) \right) \right)^2 d\boldsymbol{x}. \tag{16}$$

All integrands in eq. (16) are of the general form $\int \phi \overline{\phi} \, d\boldsymbol{x}$ which can be solved analytically

$$\int\limits_{-\infty}^{\infty} \phi \overline{\phi} \, d\boldsymbol{x} = \frac{1}{\sqrt{2\pi}^n \prod\limits_{i=1}^{n} \sqrt{\sigma_i^2 + \overline{\sigma}_i^2}} \exp\left(-\frac{1}{2} \sum\limits_{i=1}^{n} \frac{(\mu_i - \overline{\mu}_i)^2}{\sigma_i^2 + \overline{\sigma}_i^2} \right) \tag{17}$$

We therefore get an analytical solution for $d_{\phi\tilde{\phi}\hat{\phi}}$, eq. (16). Since we want to minimise the disruptive effect of the operators *merge* and *split*, we minimise $d_{\phi\tilde{\phi}\hat{\phi}}$ with respect to the parameters which have to be chosen. In the case of the *merge* operator, we have to choose the centre $\boldsymbol{\mu}$ and the variance $\boldsymbol{\sigma}^2$ of the replacement function. For the *split* operator, we fix the centre values of the two new functions $\tilde{\boldsymbol{\mu}}$ and $\hat{\boldsymbol{\mu}}$ as a function of the centre vector $\boldsymbol{\mu}$ and optimise the variances $\tilde{\boldsymbol{\sigma}}^2$ and $\hat{\boldsymbol{\sigma}}^2$. A possible choice of the centre values would be to select the coordinate with the largest σ^2 component, (let us assume this is k) and use

$$\tilde{\mu}_i = \mu_i \;\wedge\; \hat{\mu}_i = \mu_i \;\forall i \neq k \;, \quad \tilde{\mu}_k = \mu_i + \gamma \sigma_k \;\wedge\; \hat{\mu}_k = \mu_i - \gamma \sigma_k. \tag{18}$$

In our experiments we set $\gamma = 1$. The remaining parameters are optimised using a modified Newton method. In Figure 1 we show two examples one for the *merge* operator (a) and one for the *split* operator (b).

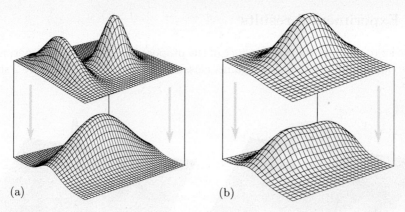

Fig. 1. Application of the *merge* operator (a) and the *split* operator (b).

3.4   Fitness evaluation

Each candidate model structure is evaluated by adapting its parameters to the given data. This can be seen as a missing data estimation problem for which we employ an Expectation-Maximization (EM) algorithm [7]. In this context the EM algorithm is used for maximum penalised likelihood or *a posteriori* estimation, that is the maximisation of $F(\boldsymbol{\theta})$ according to eq. (7). Unfortunately, the EM algorithm applied to this function involves a nonlinear optimisation problem in the M-step. Alternatives like the *one-step-late* algorithm [3] or the smoothed EM algorithm [10] avoid this problem and usually converge to the same solution when the amount of penalty required is small. However, in our context both methods turned out to be numerically unstable and did not converge. In the simulations reported here, the nonlinear optimisation in the M-step is performed through an iterative second order method, the Broyden-Fletcher-Goldfarb-Shanno algorithm [6]. Since the iterations in the M-step are computationally expensive in contrast to the re-estimation of the expectations in the E-step we perform only a few iterations in the inner loop. Due to the monotonic increase of the objective function in each EM-step the convergence to the next local optimum is guaranteed. The expectation step of the EM algorithm involves the construction of an auxiliary function (see [7] for details)

$$Q(\boldsymbol{\theta}|\boldsymbol{\theta}') = \sum_{i=1}^{m}\sum_{k=1}^{N} \log(\alpha_i\,\phi_i(\boldsymbol{x}_k|\theta_i))\pi_i(\boldsymbol{x}_k,\boldsymbol{\theta}') \quad \text{with} \quad \pi_i(\boldsymbol{x},\boldsymbol{\theta}') = \frac{\alpha_i'\,\phi_i(\boldsymbol{x}|\theta_i')}{p(\boldsymbol{x}|\boldsymbol{\theta}')}. \tag{19}$$

In the estimation with no penalty $Q(\boldsymbol{\theta}|\boldsymbol{\theta}')$ is maximised with respect to the parameters $\boldsymbol{\theta}$ in each maximisation step. In the penalised case, however, we have to maximise

$$Q(\boldsymbol{\theta}|\boldsymbol{\theta}') - \lambda\,J(\boldsymbol{\theta}). \tag{20}$$

The derivatives of $Q(\boldsymbol{\theta}|\boldsymbol{\theta}')$ and $J(\boldsymbol{\theta})$ with respect to β_i, μ_{ij} and σ_{ij} which are required for the optimisation of eq. (20) are given in Appendix A and B.

4 Experimental results

In order to evaluate the performance of the proposed method several experiments were carried out to compare it against classical methods like EM. Figure 2 shows

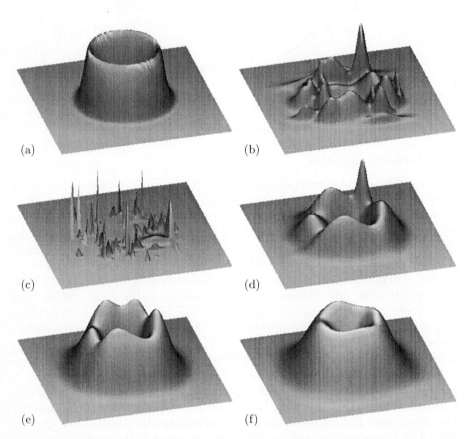

Fig. 2. Plots of density estimates. (a) True density. (b) Maximum likelihood estimate using EM (20 kernels). (c) Unregularised maximum likelihood estimate using EA and structure optimisation (484 kernels). (d) Regularised estimate with $\lambda = 0.001$ (229 kernels). (e) Regularised estimate with $\lambda = 1$ (47 kernels). (f) Regularised estimate with $\lambda = 10$ (5 kernels).

the results of different density estimations. Figure 2 (a) shows the true density which has to be estimated. We sampled 500 points for the training set and left 500 points out for the test set. The conventional maximum likelihood estimation using the EM algorithm and a fixed number of kernels, see Figure 2 (b), leads to severe over-fitting of the training set. In Figure 3 (a) the out-of-sample performance on the test set decreases with increasing over-fitting on the training set. Figure 2 (c) shows the results of a maximum likelihood estimation with the EA

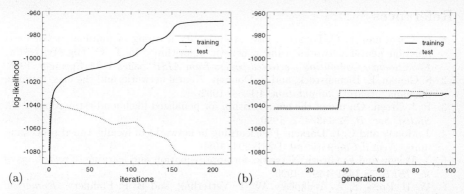

Fig. 3. (a) Maximum likelihood estimation using EM (20 kernels). (b) Maximum penalised likelihood estimation ($\lambda = 1$) using EA and structure optimisation (47 kernels).

and no regularisation. If no penalty is imposed the structure optimisation process tends to place one Gaussian function with infinitely small width at each point of the training set. In Figure 2 (d) – (f) the results of the maximum penalised likelihood estimation combined with structure optimisation are shown for different values of the penalty factor λ. Even for rather small values of λ the effect of over-fitting is drastically reduced. Furthermore, the results obtained with different values of λ varying over several orders of magnitude suggest that the choice of λ is fairly robust. Figure 3 (b) shows that in a regularised density estimation ($\lambda = 1$) the out-of-sample performance behaves nearly like the performance on the training set. This allows for accurate predictions of the generalisation ability of the optimised models. In all experiments we set the population size to 20, the number of generations to 100 and the probabilities for crossover and mutation to $P_c = 0.5$ and $P_m = 0.1$.

5 Conclusion and further work

A new method has been proposed for the construction of mixture models using an evolutionary algorithm. Experiments in estimating a simple density have been presented which show that evolutionary algorithms combined with the EM algorithm can produce models with good generalisation abilities. The objective function favours models which are smooth and have a low tendency to over-fit the data. However, the number of components is only indirectly controlled by the smoothness criterion. A *parsimony* requirement – the famous Occam's razor – calls for an objective function which focuses on the minimum number m of components in a mixture. Depending on the context, it may be appropriate to replace the second order derivative in defining $J(\boldsymbol{\theta})$ by some higher order derivatives. This corresponds to a different assumption about what we exactly mean by *smooth*. We have used Lamarckian evolution in our experiments, for the case of time-varying distributions, however, it might be sensible not to pass the optimised parameters back. Finally, it would be interesting to evaluate the proposed hybrid method on larger problems with higher dimensional input spaces.

References

1. B. Carse and T. C. Fogarty. Fast evolutionary learning of minimal radial basis function neural networks using a genetic algorithm. In T. C. Fogarty, editor, *Evolutionary Computing – selected papers from AISB*, pages 1–22. Springer, 1996.
2. S. Geman, E. Bienenstock, and R. Doursat. Neural networks and the bias/variance dilemma. *Neural Computation*, 4:1–58, 1992.
3. P. J. Green. On use of the em algorithm for penalized likelihood estimation. *J. R. Statist. Soc. B*, 52:443–452, 1990.
4. J. Moody and C. L. Darken. Fast learning in networks of locally–tuned processing units. *Neural Computation*, 1:281–294, 1989.
5. T. Poggio and F. Girosi. Networks for approximation and learning. *Proceedings of the IEEE*, 78:1481–1497, 1990.
6. W. H. Press, S. A. Teukolsky, W. T. Vetterling, and B. P. Flannery. *Numerical Recipes in C: The Art of Scientific Computing*. Cambridge University Press, 1992.
7. R. A. Redner and H. F. Walker. Mixture densities, maximum likelihood and the EM algorithm. *SIAM Review*, 26:195–239, 1984.
8. A. M. Reimetz. Strukturbestimmung von probabilistischen neuronalen Netzen mit Hilfe von Evolutionären Algorithmen. Master's thesis (Diplomarbeit), Fachbereich Statistik, Universität Dortmund, 1998.
9. B. Sendhoff, M. Kreutz, and W. von Seelen. A condition for the genotype–phenotype mapping: Causality. In T. Bäck, editor, *Proc. International Conference on Genetic Algorithms*, pages 73–80. Morgan Kaufman, 1997.
10. B. W. Silverman, M. C. Jones, J. D. Wilson, and D. W. Nychka. A smoothed em approach to indirect estimation problems, with particular reference to stereology and emission tomography. *J. R. Statist. Soc. B*, 52:271–324, 1990.
11. L. D. Whitley. Genetic algorithms and neural networks. In J. Periaux and G. Winter, editors, *Genetic Algorithms in Engineering and Computer Science*. Wiley, 1995.

A Derivation of the diagonal elements of D

For the calculation of the trace only the diagonal elements of D are required:

$$d_{rr} = \sum_{t=1}^{n} \int_{-\infty}^{+\infty} h_{rt}^2 \, dx = A_r + \sum_{t=1,t\neq r}^{n} B_{rt} \tag{21}$$

The symbols A_r and B_{rt} which stand for the partial second derivatives are introduced for convenience. After some straightforward but tedious calculations we get:

$$A_r = \int_{-\infty}^{+\infty} \left(\frac{\partial^2 p(x|\boldsymbol{\theta})}{\partial x_r^2} \right)^2 dx = \sum_{i=1}^{m} \sum_{j=1}^{m} \alpha_i \alpha_j E_{ij} U_{ijr} \tag{22}$$

$$B_{rt} = \int_{-\infty}^{+\infty} \left(\frac{\partial^2 p(x|\boldsymbol{\theta})}{\partial x_r \, \partial x_t} \right)^2 dx = \sum_{i=1}^{m} \sum_{j=1}^{m} \alpha_i \alpha_j E_{ij} V_{ijrt} \tag{23}$$

$$E_{ij} = \frac{1}{\sqrt{2\pi}^n \prod_{k=1}^{n} (\sigma_{ik}^2 + \sigma_{jk}^2)^{\frac{1}{2}}} \exp\left(-\frac{1}{2} \sum_{k=1}^{n} \frac{(\mu_{ik} - \mu_{jk})^2}{\sigma_{ik}^2 + \sigma_{jk}^2} \right) \tag{24}$$

$$U_{ijr} = \frac{3(\sigma_{ir}^2 + \sigma_{jr}^2)^2 - 6(\sigma_{ir}^2 + \sigma_{jr}^2)(\mu_{ir} - \mu_{jr})^2 + (\mu_{ir} - \mu_{jr})^4}{(\sigma_{ir}^2 + \sigma_{jr}^2)^4} \tag{25}$$

$$V_{ijrt} = \frac{(\sigma_{ir}^2 + \sigma_{jr}^2 - (\mu_{ir} - \mu_{jr})^2)(\sigma_{it}^2 + \sigma_{jt}^2 - (\mu_{it} - \mu_{jt})^2)}{(\sigma_{ir}^2 + \sigma_{jr}^2)^2 (\sigma_{it}^2 + \sigma_{jt}^2)^2}. \tag{26}$$

For the maximisation of the objective function we need the gradient of $J(\boldsymbol{\theta})$ and therefore the gradients of A_r and B_{rt}. Since we have to guarantee condition (2) on α_i we use the following transformation:

$$\alpha_i = \exp(\beta_i) \Big/ \sum_{j=1}^{m} \exp(\beta_j). \tag{27}$$

Symbolic derivation of A_r and B_{rt} with respect to β_i, μ_{ij}, and σ_{ij} yields:

$$\frac{\partial A_r}{\partial \beta_s} = 2\,\alpha_s \left[\sum_{j=1}^{m} \alpha_j \, E_{sj} \, U_{sjr} - A_r \right] \tag{28}$$

$$\frac{\partial A_r}{\partial \mu_{sq}} = 2\,\alpha_s \sum_{j=1}^{m} \alpha_j \, E_{sj} \frac{\mu_{jq} - \mu_{sq}}{\sigma_{jq}^2 + \sigma_{sq}^2} \left[U_{sjr} + \delta_{qr}\, \Delta_{sjq}^{(1)} \right] \tag{29}$$

$$\frac{\partial A_r}{\partial \sigma_{sq}} = 2\,\alpha_s \sum_{j=1}^{m} \alpha_j \, E_{sj} \frac{\sigma_{sq}}{\sigma_{jq}^2 + \sigma_{sq}^2} \left[U_{sjr} \left(\frac{(\mu_{jq} - \mu_{sq})^2}{\sigma_{jq}^2 + \sigma_{sq}^2} - 1 \right) + \delta_{qr}\, \Delta_{sjq}^{(2)} \right] \tag{30}$$

$$\frac{\partial B_{rt}}{\partial \beta_s} = 2\,\alpha_s \left[\sum_{j=1}^{m} \alpha_j \, E_{sj} \, V_{sjrt} - B_{rt} \right] \tag{31}$$

$$\frac{\partial B_{rt}}{\partial \mu_{sq}} = 2\,\alpha_s \sum_{j=1}^{m} \alpha_j \, E_{sj} \frac{\mu_{jq} - \mu_{sq}}{\sigma_{jq}^2 + \sigma_{sq}^2} \left[V_{sjrt} + \delta_{qr}\, \Delta_{sjq}^{(3)}(t) + \delta_{qt}\, \Delta_{sjq}^{(3)}(r) \right] \tag{32}$$

$$\frac{\partial B_{rt}}{\partial \sigma_{sq}} = 2\,\alpha_s \sum_{j=1}^{m} \alpha_j \, E_{sj} \frac{\sigma_{sq}}{\sigma_{jq}^2 + \sigma_{sq}^2} \left[V_{sjrt} \left(\frac{(\mu_{jq} - \mu_{sq})^2}{\sigma_{jq}^2 + \sigma_{sq}^2} - 1 \right) \right.$$
$$\left. + \delta_{qr}\, \Delta_{sjq}^{(4)}(t) + \delta_{qt}\, \Delta_{sjq}^{(4)}(r) \right] \tag{33}$$

$$\Delta_{sjq}^{(1)} = \frac{12(\sigma_{jq}^2 + \sigma_{sq}^2) - 4(\mu_{jq} - \mu_{sq})^2}{(\sigma_{jq}^2 + \sigma_{sq}^2)^3} \tag{34}$$

$$\Delta_{sjq}^{(2)} = \frac{36(\sigma_{jq}^2 + \sigma_{sq}^2)(\mu_{jq} - \mu_{sq})^2 - 12(\sigma_{jq}^2 + \sigma_{sq}^2)^2 - 8(\mu_{jq} - \mu_{sq})^4}{(\sigma_{jq}^2 + \sigma_{sq}^2)^4} \tag{35}$$

$$\Delta_{sjq}^{(3)}(k) = \frac{2(\sigma_{jk}^2 + \sigma_{sk}^2 - (\mu_{jk} - \mu_{sk})^2)}{(\sigma_{jq}^2 + \sigma_{sq}^2)(\sigma_{jk}^2 + \sigma_{sk}^2)^2} \tag{36}$$

$$\Delta_{sjq}^{(4)}(k) = \Delta_{sjq}^{(3)}(k) \left(\frac{2(\mu_{jq} - \mu_{sq})^2}{\sigma_{jq}^2 + \sigma_{sq}^2} - 1 \right) \tag{37}$$

B Derivatives of $Q(\boldsymbol{\theta}|\boldsymbol{\theta}')$ with respect to β_i, μ_{ij} and σ_{ij}

$$\frac{\partial Q(\boldsymbol{\theta}|\boldsymbol{\theta}')}{\partial \beta_i} = \sum_{k=1}^{N} \left(\pi_i(\boldsymbol{x}_k, \boldsymbol{\theta}') - \alpha_i \right) \qquad (\beta_i \text{ according to eq. (27)}) \tag{38}$$

$$\frac{\partial Q(\boldsymbol{\theta}|\boldsymbol{\theta}')}{\partial \mu_{ij}} = \sum_{k=1}^{N} \frac{x_{kj} - \mu_{ij}}{\sigma_{ij}^2} \pi_i(\boldsymbol{x}, \boldsymbol{\theta}') \tag{39}$$

$$\frac{\partial Q(\boldsymbol{\theta}|\boldsymbol{\theta}')}{\partial \sigma_{ij}} = \sum_{k=1}^{N} \left(\frac{(x_{kj} - \mu_{ij})^2}{\sigma_{ij}^3} - \frac{1}{\sigma_{ij}} \right) \pi_i(\boldsymbol{x}, \boldsymbol{\theta}'). \tag{40}$$

Genetic Algorithm in Parameter Estimation of Nonlinear Dynamic Systems

E. Paterakis   V. Petridis   A. Kehagias

Department of Electrical and Computer Engineering
Aristotle University– Thessaloniki - Greece

Abstract. We introduce a multi-model parameter estimation method for non-linear dynamic systems. The method employs a genetic search with a recursive probability selection mechanism for parameter estimation. The method is applied to nonlinear systems with known structure and unknown parameters. A new technique is used to determine the selection probabilities. First, a population of models with random parameter vectors is produced. Second, a probability is recursively assigned to each member of a generation of models. The probabilities reflect the closeness of each model output to the true system output. The probabilities have to satisfy an entropy criterion so as to enable the genetic algorithm to avoid poor solutions. This is a new feature that enhances the performance of the GA on the parameter estimation problem. Finally, the probabilities are used to create a new generation of models by the genetic algorithm. Numerical simulations are given concerning the parameter estimation of a planar robotic manipulator.

0. Introduction

Several designs of evolutionary algorithms, which include genetic algorithms (GA), evolution strategies (ES), evolutionary programming (EP), etc., have been used in static optimization problems. A static parameter optimization problem can be stated as an estimation of the vector ϑ_0 of d parameters which minimize/maximize the cost function $\Im(\cdot)$. When GA is used for parameter estimation of dynamic nonlinear systems, the parameter estimation problem can be described as follows. Assuming that a parametric mathematical model $\mathcal{Y}(\vartheta_0)$ of the system and a set of input/output measurements are known, find a parameter vector ϑ that minimizes the cost function $\Im(\vartheta)$. The cost function $\Im(\vartheta)$ measures the similarity of the model with parameter vector ϑ with the actual system is $\mathcal{Y}(\vartheta_0)$. The parameters are varied over some set of feasible values and their range determines the parameter space. According to the mathematical model $\mathcal{Y}$ of the system a model set $\mathcal{M}$ is constructed that is indexed by the parameter vector ϑ. In practice the $\mathcal{M}$ can have vast number of members hence exhaustive search of the parameter space has to be precluded. We have to remark that proper selection of the input data and input/output ports is important (Walter & Pronzato '90), (Söderström and Stoica '89). Identifiability issues are discussed in (Walter & Pronzato '90), (Lecourtier & Walter '81), (Vajda & Rabitz '89). In the following, we will assume that the system is identifiable.

In this paper we use a GA to solve to parameter estimation problem. Two new features enhance the GA: a recursive selection probability mechanism and an entropy criterion. The recursive scheme gives the ability for on-line estimation while the role of entropy criterion is twofold. First, it maintains sufficient diversity within the GA population, which guarantees high probability of finding the global optimum. Second, it reduces the number of evaluation steps for each generation. These two characteristics of the entropy criterion with the contribution of the recursive probability selection mechanism provide us with a new approach to the parameter estimation problem of nonlinear dynamical systems.

We applied our method to parameter estimation of the MIT serial Link Direct Drive Arm with four (4) parameters. The experiment configuration provides no system states measurements and only the initial conditions are known. We also applied a classical approach to the parameter estimation problem with probability selection proportional to the inverse of mean square error without the use of the entropy criterion. A large number of numerical simulations have shown that the presented method is more efficient even in case of noisy data. Note that, we do not validate the solutions according to output response as in (Kim et al,'96) but we check a posteriori the closeness of the solutions to the actual parameter vector. We have previously used this method for parameter estimation of nonlinear models in (Petridis et al,'98).

The paper is organized as follows. In Section 1 the parameter estimation problem is stated. In Section 2 the proposed production mechanism of selection probabilities is explained. In Section 3 the entropy criterion is presented and its contribution to the parameter estimation method is discussed. The use of the GA in parameter estimation problem is illustrated in Section 4. In Section 5 the method is applied to parameter estimation of a two joint robot manipulator. Finally conclusions are presented in Section 6.

1. Parameter Estimation Problem

The estimation problem consists in determining the member of the set that best describes the data according to a given criterion. The purpose of the estimation has to be outlined. If the final goal is a control strategy for a particular system the accuracy of estimation should be judged on the basis of the time response. However, if the final goal is to analyze the properties of a system the accuracy of estimation should be judged on the basis of deviations in the model parameters. Such problems can be found in engineering problems and also in biology, economy, medicine etc.

The data are produced by the actual system $\mathcal{S}$ when it operates under a given experimental condition. The output of the system at time t will be denoted by $y(t)$ (where $y(t) \in \Re^q$), and a sequence of outputs $y(0), \dots, y(t)$ will be denoted by y_t. The vectors $u(t)$ (where $u(t) \in \Re^m$), u_t denote the input at time t and the sequence of applied inputs, respectively. Similarly $\varphi(t)$ (where $\varphi(t) \in \Re^n$), φ_t denote the system states at time t and the sequence of system states, respectively. The vector ϑ

(where $\vartheta \in \Re^d$) denotes the parameter vector. Consider now the following family of discrete time dynamic systems $\mathcal{G}(f,g,t,y,\varphi,u,\vartheta_0)$:

$$\varphi(t) = f(\varphi(t-1),u(t);\vartheta_0), \quad y(t) = g(\varphi(t),u(t);\vartheta_0) \qquad (1)$$

In the system of type (1) the functions $f(\cdot)$ and $g(\cdot)$ are known. The input u_t and the r initial conditions are also known. The output y_t is measurable and only the parameter vector ϑ_0 is unknown. All the possible ϑ that can be applied to $\mathcal{G}$ construct a model set which will be denoted by $\mathcal{M}$. The model set is indexed by the finite dimensional parameter vector ϑ, so that a particular model in the model set will be denoted by $\mathcal{M}(\vartheta)$. The vector ϑ ranges over a set denoted by $\mathcal{D}_{\mathcal{M}}$ (where $\mathcal{D}_{\mathcal{M}} \subseteq \Re^d$), which generally will be assumed to be compact. It is also assumed that $\vartheta_0 \in \mathcal{D}_{\mathcal{M}}$. Taking into account noisy measurements, as in real world problems, the $\mathcal{G}$ changes to:

$$\varphi(t) = f(\varphi(t-1),...,\varphi(t-r),u(t);\vartheta_0), \quad \tilde{y}(t) = y(t) + w(t) \qquad (2)$$

Now $\hat{y}_t$ is the measurable output and $w(t)$ is white, zero mean output noise. Sampling the noisy system output $\tilde{y}(t)$ for T time steps, a data record C can be constructed, where $\dim C = q \cdot T$ and q is the number of outputs. Note that the dynamic system requires that a sufficient number of output are measured otherwise the system may be unidentifiable. An exhaustive search of $\mathcal{M}$ has to be precluded in realistic situations where $\mathcal{M}$ has a vast number of members. On the other hand GA is a global search scheme taking into account only a small part of $\mathcal{M}$. The need for a global optimum search scheme arises from the fact that the fitness function may have local minima, either inherent or due to noisy measurements (Ljung, '87), (Söderström and Stoica '89). Also, GA has not the drawbacks of the standard estimation techniques in case of discontinuous objective functions. Hence, the use of this evolutionary scheme is very attractive for parameter estimation of nonlinear dynamical systems. In the GA, an evolvable population P of potential solutions has to be defined taking values over the $\mathcal{D}_{\mathcal{M}}$ Hence as P (where $P \subseteq \mathcal{D}_{\mathcal{M}}$) is denoted a set of distinct values of $\vartheta \in \mathcal{D}_{\mathcal{M}}$. The set P is finite dimensional, namely $P = \{\vartheta_1,\vartheta_2,...,\vartheta_K\}$, where K is a fixed number. The set P^j includes the potential solutions at the generation j. The output $y_i^j(t)$ corresponds to the parameter vector $\vartheta_i^j \in \Theta^j$ where $1 \le i \le K$ is the index of the model and j is the generation index. The model validation is achieved through the discrepancy between the noisy measured output $\tilde{y}(t)$ and the model output $y_i^j(t)$ at time step t and it is given by $E_i^j(t)$, where $\|\cdot\|$ denotes Euclidean norm:

$$E_i^j(t) = \left\| y_i^j(t) - \tilde{y}(t) \right\|^2 \qquad (3)$$

The sum of $E_i^j(t)$ for every time step t, where $0 \le t \le T$, defines the mean square error (MSE) function $w_i^j(T)$ for the particular model with parameter vector ϑ_i^j at the j generation:

$$w_i^j(T) = \sum_{t=0}^{T} E_i^j(t) \qquad (4)$$

The function $w_i^j(T)$ is positive so it can stand as a fitness function. The estimate of ϑ_0 at the j-th generation is ϑ_i^{j*}:

$$\vartheta_i^{j*} = \arg\min_{s=1,2,\dots K} w_i^j(T) \qquad (5)$$

Therefore the parameter estimation problem can be stated as a static optimization problem of finding the value ϑ^* that minimizes the fitness function $w(T)$.

2. Production of Selection Probabilities

So far, we have described the parameter estimation problem and we referred to its solution through a number of populations of potential solutions P. We do not mention anything about how the transition from P^j to P^{j+1} occurs. Based on the fitness function of (4), a probability is assigned to each member of P^j. This probability expresses the similarity of the model output to system output and it is relative to the performance of each other member of P^j. Several production schemes of selection probabilities have been proposed in literature. One of them is the following:

$$p_i^j(T) = \frac{1/w_i^j(T)}{\sum_{m=1}^{K} 1/w_m^j(T)} \qquad (6)$$

The trial solutions with parameter vectors $\vartheta_i^j \in P^j$ where $1 \le i \le K$ have to be evaluated over the whole measurement data record C in order to calculate these selection probabilities. Another selection probability scheme is the following:

$$p_i^j(T) = \frac{e^{-w_i^j(T)}}{\sum_{s=1}^{K} e^{-w_s^j(T)}} \qquad (7)$$

Substituting $w_i^j(T)$ from (4) we have the Boltzmann selection probability mechanism where σ is the temperature parameter, which is usually constant.

$$p_i^j(T) = \frac{e^{-\sum_{t=1}^{T} \frac{E_i^j(t)}{\sigma}}}{\sum_{s=1}^{K} e^{-\sum_{t=1}^{T} \frac{E_s^j(t)}{\sigma}}} \qquad (8)$$

Here, we propose a new method of production of the selection probabilities. The method is based on the selection scheme (8), although it has two differences. First, the probabilities are calculated recursively and second, there is no need to take into account all the measurement record C in order to evaluate the trial solutions. The probability update rule for the time step t is defined as:

$$p_i^j(t) = \frac{p_i^j(t-1) \cdot e^{-\frac{E_i^j(t-1)}{\sigma(j)}}}{\sum_{s=1}^{K} p_s^j(t-1) \cdot e^{-\frac{E_s^j(t-1)}{\sigma(j)}}} \qquad (9)$$

Where $p_s^j(0) = 1/K \ \forall \ j$ and $s = 1 \dots K$ is the prior probability distribution. Having no prior information about the parameters, a uniform prior probability distribution is a reasonable choice (Peterka, '81). The algorithm parameter σ is now dynamically adjusted at every generation, in order to prevent degeneration of GA. Degeneration of the GA occurs when one selection probability is near to one or all the selection probabilities are equal.

The main point that makes this method different from the others is that the evaluation of each model selection probability is performed for a total of $T^j \leq T$ time steps. The number of T^j time steps are defined by the entropy criterion, which is explained in Section 2. The role of the entropy criterion is twofold. First, it prevents premature convergence of the algorithm retaining thus the required population diversity. Second, it makes the algorithm able to use fewer output measurements than it would otherwise be necessary $(T^j \leq T)$. Repeating for times $t = 0, t = 1, \ldots, t = T^j$ finally one can obtain:

$$p_i^j(T^j) = \frac{p_i^j(0) \cdot e^{-\sum_{t=0}^{T_i} \frac{E_i^j(t)}{\sigma(j)}}}{\sum_{s=1}^{K} p_s^j(0) \cdot e^{-\sum_{t=0}^{T_i} \frac{E_i^j(t)}{\sigma(j)}}} \tag{10}$$

In conclusion, the proposed method has the following advantages. The probabilities are updated when new information becomes available. Hence, it can be used in on-line applications. The exponential function accentuates differences between models and allows a multiplicative formulation of the update rule. The use of entropy criterion improves the performance of the algorithm. The trial solutions are evaluated for $T^j \leq T$ time steps and GA is prevented from degeneration. The main idea is that we can take a decision whenever enough information is available. The results of the proposed production method of selection probabilities are illustrated in Section 5 where it is compared with a method, which uses the MSE mechanism of (6).

3. Entropy Criterion

Genetic algorithm requires each generation to contain a sufficient variety of models. If one of the selection probabilities is allowed to tend to one and the others near zero, the next generation of models will only contain the best model of the previous generation. Thus, the genetic algorithm may get stuck with a poor model, which provides only a local minimum of estimation error. On the other hand, it is clear that if the selection probabilities do not concentrate sufficiently on the most promising models, then the search of the parameter space will be essentially random search. To avoid either of the above situations we introduce a novel criterion based on the entropy of the probabilities $p_1^j(t), p_2^j(t), \ldots, p_K^j(t)$. The entropy $H^j(t)$ of $p_1^j(t), p_2^j(t), \ldots, p_K^j(t)$ at time step t is defined by

$$H^j(t) = -\sum_{s=1}^{K} p_s^j(t) \cdot \log(p_s^j(t)) \tag{11}$$

The maximum value of $H^j(t)$ is $\log(K)$, and is achieved when $p_1^j(t) = p_2^j(t) = .. = p_K^j(t) = 1/K$. The minimum value of $H^j(t)$ is zero, and is achieved for $p_i^j(t)=1$, $p_s^j(t)=0$, $s\neq i$, i.e. when all probability is concentrated on one model. Now consider the following dynamic threshold $\overline{H}^j(t)$ such as

$$\overline{H}(t) = \log(K)\frac{t}{T} \qquad (12)$$

where $1\leq t\leq T$ in time steps. This is simply an increasing function with respect to t. It is clear that the inequality

$$H^j(t) < \overline{H}(t) \qquad (13)$$

will be satisfied for some $t\leq T$. The above inequality express the *entropy criterion*; when the entropy of $p_1^j(t), p_2^j(t),.., p_K^j(t)$ falls bellow $\overline{H}(t)$, then probability update stops and the next generation of models is produced. Termination will take place at some value of entropy between 0 and $\log(K)$, ensuring that the selection probabilities are neither too concentrated, nor too diffuse. This means that probability update is performed for a variable number of time steps determined by the entropy criterion.

4. Genetic Algorithm in Parameter Estimation Problem

Having the population P^j and the selection probabilities $p_1^j(t), p_2^j(t),.., p_K^j(t)$ we are ready to make the final step in order to pass to the next generation (j+1). First of all, the trial solutions in P^j have to be encoded by strings of bits. Note that in the initial generation the models $\vartheta_i^0 \in P^0$ have arbitrary parameter values but always in $\mathcal{D}_{\mathcal{M}}$ Each parameter vector $\vartheta_i^j \in P^j$ is translated as a chromosome and each parameter into it as a gene. Specifically, a mapping is taking place from $\mathcal{D}_{\mathcal{M}}$ to a discrete set of bit strings. Assume that a gene is represented by n bits the chromosome occupies $n*d$ bits. Thus, there are 2^{n*d} parameter combinations resulting in 2^{n*d} models. What is important here is the change of the model set $\mathcal{M}$ to a discrete model set. The discretization has to be done taking into account the trade off between slowness of the algorithm and desirable accuracy of solution.

All the chromosomes are potential parents with a selection probability for mating. A steepest ascent hill-climbing operator is applied to the chromosome with the maximum selection probability and a elitism operator is applied. A roulette wheel is used to select the pair of parents. Genetic operators such as crossover and mutation are applied to selected parents. The whole genetic process is stopped when K individuals have been produced. Then a re-mapping is made from the discrete set of bit strings to $\mathcal{D}_{\mathcal{M}}$ and a new set of solutions P^{j+1} is ready to be evaluated.

Schematically the flow of the parameter estimation algorithm is the following.

- Create a population with K members from a model set with arbitrary parameter vectors.
- Assign an initial probability to each model

- START the parameter estimation loop.
  - START the production of selection probabilities loop.
    - Update recursively the selection probabilities.
    - IF the entropy criterion is not satisfied then CONTINUE in the loop
    - ELSE EXIT from loop.
  - START the production of the next generation
    - The steepest ascent hill-climbing operator is applied to the parameter vector with the maximum selection probability and the elitism operator is applied.
    - Selection of parents and application to them genetic operators such as crossover and mutation
  - REPEAT the production loop until K individuals have been produced.
- IF the algorithm converges to a solution or the maximum number of generations is exceeded STOP ELSE CONTINUE in the parameter estimation loop.

5. Results

Our algorithm is now applied to the problem of estimating the parameters of the MIT Serial Link Direct Drive Arm. This is configured as a two-link horizontal manipulator by locking the azimuth angle at 180^0 (Atkeson et al,'86). The input to the manipulator is the angle sequence $\overline{\omega}_t = (\overline{\omega}_{1t}, \overline{\omega}_{2t})$. A PD controller controls the manipulator so joint angles ω_{1t}, ω_{2t} track the reference input $\overline{\omega}_t$. Therefore the problem is parameter estimation under closed loop conditions. Ignoring gravity forces, the equations describing the manipulator and controller are the following

$$\begin{bmatrix} K_{p1} & 0 \\ 0 & K_{p2} \end{bmatrix} \cdot \begin{bmatrix} \omega_1(t) - \overline{\omega}_1(t) \\ \omega_2(t) - \overline{\omega}_2(t) \end{bmatrix} + \begin{bmatrix} K_{u1} & 0 \\ 0 & K_{u2} \end{bmatrix} \cdot \begin{bmatrix} \dot{\omega}_1(t) - \dot{\overline{\omega}}_1(t) \\ \dot{\omega}_2(t) - \dot{\overline{\omega}}_2(t) \end{bmatrix} =$$

$$\begin{bmatrix} I_1 + I_2 + m_2 l_1 l_2 \cos(\omega_2) + \frac{1}{4}(m_1 l_1^2 + m_2 l_2^2) + m_2 l_1^2 & I_2 + \frac{1}{2} m_2 l_1 l_2 \cos(\omega_2) + \frac{1}{4} m_2 l_2^2 \\ I_2 + \frac{1}{2} m_2 l_1 l_2 \cos(\omega_2) + \frac{1}{4} m_2 l_2^2 & I_2 + \frac{1}{4} m_2 l_2^2 \end{bmatrix} \cdot \begin{bmatrix} \ddot{\omega}_1(t) \\ \ddot{\omega}_2(t) \end{bmatrix} +$$

$$\begin{bmatrix} F & -m_2 l_1 l_2 \sin(\omega_2) \\ m_2 l_1 l_2 \sin(\omega_2) & F \end{bmatrix} \cdot \begin{bmatrix} \dot{\omega}_1(t) \\ \dot{\omega}_2(t) \end{bmatrix} + \begin{bmatrix} -2m_2 l_1 l_2 \sin(\omega_2) \\ 0 \end{bmatrix} \cdot \dot{\omega}_1(t) \dot{\omega}_2(t)$$

The inertial parameters are $I_1 = 8.095 \text{Nt} \cdot \text{m} \cdot \text{s}^2/\text{rad}$, $I_2 = 0.253 \text{Nt} \cdot \text{m} \cdot \text{s}^2/\text{rad}$. The coefficient of friction is $F = 0.0005 \text{Nt} \cdot \text{m} \cdot \text{s}/\text{rad}$. The gain parameters of the PD controller are $K_{p1} = 2500$, $K_{u1} = 300$ for the first joint, and $K_{p2} = 400$, $K_{u2} = 30$ for the second joint. The mass and the length parameters, namely $m_1 = 120.1 \text{Kgr}$, $m_2 = 2.1 \text{Kgr}$, $l_1 = 0.462 \text{m}$, $l_2 = 0.445 \text{m}$, are considered unknown for the purposes of this example.

The system equations are discretized in time (with a discretization step $dt = 0.01\sec$) to obtain equations of the form $\phi(t) = f\big(\phi(t-1), u(t); \vartheta_0\big)$, $y(t) = g\big(\varphi(t); \vartheta_0\big)$:

$$\varphi(t) = \begin{bmatrix} \omega_1(t) \\ \omega_2(t) \\ \omega_1(t-1) \\ \omega_2(t-1) \end{bmatrix}, \quad y(t) = \begin{bmatrix} \omega_1(t-1) \\ \omega_2(t-1) \\ l_1 \cos\big(\omega_1(t-1)\big) + l_2 \cos\big(\omega_1(t-1) - \omega_2(t-1)\big) \\ l_1 \sin\big(\omega_1(t-1)\big) + l_2 \sin\big(\omega_1(t-1) - \omega_2(t-1)\big) \end{bmatrix}, \quad u(t) = \begin{bmatrix} \overline{\omega}_1(t) \\ \overline{\omega}_2(t) \end{bmatrix}, \quad \vartheta = \begin{bmatrix} m_1 \\ m_2 \\ l_1 \\ l_2 \end{bmatrix}$$

where $\varphi(t)$, $y(t)$, $u(t)$ and ϑ are the state, output, input and parameter vector, respectively; the last two terms in $y(t)$ are the coordinates of the manipulator end point. This completes the description of the system.

The parameter estimation algorithm is applied using genetic algorithm parameters as follows: number of bits per parameter n=13, crossover probability q=0.8, population size K=50, number of crossover and mutation points p=4, number of generations $I_{max} = 5000$. The vector ϑ ranges over the set $\mathcal{D}_M$. The lower bound of $\mathcal{D}_M$ at the each direction chosen to be 30% of the true value of the corresponding parameter, and the upper bound chosen to be 200% of the true value of the corresponding parameter.

Several experiments are run with the above setup, varying the level of the noise present in the measurements (noise free, $\pm 0.25^0$, $\pm 0.50^0$, $\pm 1^0$, $\pm 2^0$, $\pm 3^0$ and $\pm 5^0$); noise is white, zero-mean and uniformly distributed. For every choice of the model type and noise level one hundred experiments are run; the accuracy of the parameter estimates for every experiment is expressed by the following quantity:

$$S = \frac{\dfrac{|\delta m_1|}{m_1} + \dfrac{|\delta m_2|}{m_2} + \dfrac{|\delta l_1|}{l_1} + \dfrac{|\delta l_2|}{l_2}}{4}$$

where δm_1 is the error in the estimate of m_1 and similarly for the remaining parameters. In other words, S is the average relative error in the parameter estimates.

The results using recursive selection probabilities are presented in Fig1. Each curve is the cumulative histogram of S for one hundred experiments at a given noise level. We also applied a genetic algorithm with selection probability mechanism of (6). The cumulative results of MSE selection probabilities are presented in Fig2. As can be seen, these results are significantly worse than the results of recursive selection probability mechanism.

Cumulative Histogram

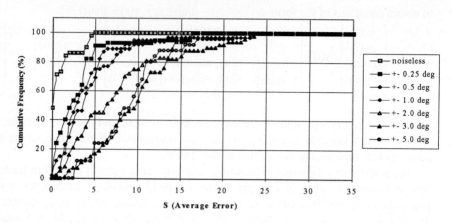

Fig. 1. Results with Recursive Selection Probability

Cumulative Histogram

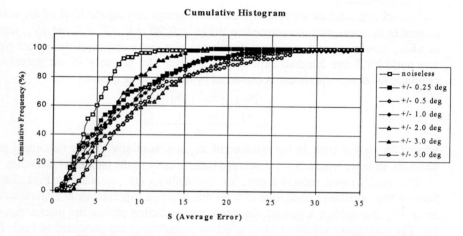

Fig. 2. Results with Mean Square Error Selection Probability

Finally, it must be mentioned that the average duration of one run of the recursive parameter estimation method is 7 minutes on HP Apollo 735 workstation. Runs involving models with recursive selection probability require around 500 generations, each generation requiring around 150 input/output measurements, while runs involving MSE selection probability require around 1200 generations, each generation requiring exactly 300 input/output measurements.

6. Conclusions

We have applied a GA on parameter estimation problem and tested its performance on the MIT Serial Link Direct Drive Arm. The test problem is hard because of the strong nonlinearities of the system, the insensitivity to mass values, the presence of noise in the data and the existence of the PD controller. The performance of the algorithm is quite good, even for high noise levels. At low noise levels, the number of models that are close to the true system with accuracy better than 2% is quite high.

The success of our method is attributed to the following features. First is the probability selection mechanism. The use of an exponential error function, and the resulting use of a competitive and multiplicative scheme, accentuate the competition between rival models and facilitates the selection of the best model in a search subset. Second is the entropy criterion which ensures an appropriate balance between extreme and insufficient diversity, such that the algorithm is not trapped at local minima. The recursive nature of the probability selection mechanism and the use of the entropy criterion reduce the computation required for the algorithm to obtain parameter estimates within the specified accuracy.

An additional attractive feature of our algorithm is its generality; no particular assumptions have been made about the form of the system equations (1), nor about the probability distribution function of the noise on the measurements. In particular, $f(\cdot)$ and $g(\cdot)$ need not be continuous.

References

1. Atkeson A., Ch. H. An and J. N. Hollerbach, "Estimation of inertial parameters of manipulator links and loads", Int. J. of Robotics Res., Vol.5, pp.101-119, (1986).
2. Kim Jong-Hwan, Chae Hong-Kook, Jeon Jeong-Yul and Lee Seon-Woo, "Identification and Control of Systems with Friction Using Accelerated Evolutionary Programming", IEEE Control Systems, pp 38-47 (August 1996).
3. Lecourtier. Y. and E. Walter, "Comments on "On parameter and structural identifiability: nonunique observability/reconstructibility for identifiable systems, and other ambiguities and new definitions. ", IEEE Trans. on Automatic Control, vol.26, pp. 800-801, (1981).
4. Ljung L., System Identification: Theory for the User, Englewood Cliffs, NJ, Prentice Hall, (1987).
5. Peterka V., " Baysian System Identification", Automatica, vol.17, No 1, pp.41-53, (1981).
6. Petridis V., Paterakis E. and Kehagias A. "A hybrid Neural Genetic Multi-Model Parameter Estimation Algorithm", to appear in IEEE Trans. on Neural Networks (1998).
7. Söderström T. and Stoica P., System Identification, Englewood Cliffs, NJ, Prentice Hall, (1989).
8. Vajda S.and Rabitz H., "State Isomorphism Approach to Global Identifiability of Nonlinear Systems", IEEE Trans. on Automatic Control, vol. 34, No 2, pp.220-223, (1989).
9. Walter E and Pronzato L., "Qualitative and Quantitative Experiment Design for Phenomelogical Models - A Survey", Automatica, vol.26, No 2, pp.195-213, (1990).

Optimizing Web Page Layout Using an Annealed Genetic Algorithm as Client-Side Script

J. González Peñalver, J. J. Merelo

Department of Architecture and Computer Technology
University of Granada (Spain)
{jesus|jmerelo}@kal-el.ugr.es, http://kal-el.ugr.es/geneura

Abstract. The high volume of information available on the Internet makes it necessary to use search and organization tools to filter and display it. This presentation must make efficient use of the surface the browser leaves; this is even more true in the case of personalized newspapers, in which all the news and publicity must be presented in only one "coup d'oeil", to make them as effective as possible. In this paper, a system to automatically paginate web newspapers on the browser is presented. The system uses a genetic algorithm with integer representation and variable mutation amplitude, fine-tuned by a greedy algorithm. This combination proves to be much better than the genetic algorithm alone. The algorithm is proved to be able to lay out the web page in real time, that is, a time insignificant with respect to the time it takes to load an average page. The system will be embedded in several personalized news sites that are being developed at Granada University.

1 Introduction

In these days of information overload, one of the few resources that are in short supply is screen real estate. When a request is made to an Internet search engine, answers are dumped out onto the user´s browser, with the user having to scroll down or check several pages to find what she wants.

If the search engine is specialized on news, the ideal answer should look as much as possible as the original newspaper, that is, all news headers should appear on screen, with short paragraphs describing them more in depth. The same applies to a personalized web newspaper: if a person describes the kind of news she is interested in, and these news fall in several categories, all categories should be presented at the same time when the web page is loaded. Real estate occupation must be minimized, and at the same time empty screen spaces should be avoided, since the more the screen surface is used, the better. Furthermore, when *push* technologies start to be more fashionable (and standard), laying out all user windows *and* channels on the screen will be a challenge, and it will have to be done in real time.

The problem of laying out text rectangles in a limited surface minimizing empty space in it is not really new, only the medium is new. It is the same problem that, for instance, yellow pages typesetters faced: if they had to typeset by hand thousands of pages, it would take also thousands of man-hours; that is why it has been tackled using automated procedures by several firms, one of them in Finland, using the so-called $V.I.P^E$ system [12], and another one in Germany, with the YPSS++ system (which is quoted, but not presented in Graf´s web page [4]). A similar problem appears in *fax newspapers*, in which news were clipped and sent by fax to customers. Both problems were treated in Lagus et al.'s paper [12]. In a general context, it also occurs in multimedia and hypermedia systems, as it is reviewed in Hower et al.'s paper [8]. Besides, automatically laying out a personalized newspaper in a personalized news context has been dealt with in the Krakatoa project [10].

In general, laying out the different articles that form a newspaper can be considered a two-dimensional bin-packing problem (if the content is fixed, and the space can be varied) or a two-dimensional multiple-knapsack problem (if the space is fixed and the contents can be selected). These problems are in general NP-hard, but in the case of a newspaper that is going to be laid out in a grid of a fixed number of columns and rows, it becomes linear in time [12]. The newspaper layout or pagination problem can be then formulated as the problem of laying out a fixed set of news contained in rectangular boxes, with no overlapping, putting all of them within the limits of the browser, in a minimum surface and in a minimum amount of time. Since a web page can have an *a priori* infinite length, but a finite width, all available articles can be put on a page (with, of course, a *weight* limit, but if articles have no graphics, that is not really a problem), which means that laying out a web page is a fixed-content, variable-space problem, that is, a two-dimensional bin-packing problem. This problem has been widely studied and solved using genetic algorithms before in [2].

The approach presented in this paper will be to combine a genetic algorithm with variable mutation amplitude and a greedy algorithm to solve that problem, and do it using a program that is delivered to the web client program along with the content. There are two ways of paginating a web page that is going to be delivered to a client: do it on the web server, or do it on the client, that is, the user´s own computer. Since a personalized news site is expected to be a high-volume site, many requests could pile up at any one time; if each delivered page is going to be laid out on the server, it will most probably result in server overload, and in an overall slowdown of server operation; on the other hand, if a lean chunk of code can be delivered along with the information, and that code can carry out pagination with enough speed in the client, no server resources are consumed (other than those used to process the query and send the content), and the whole process can have a much higher throughput, being able to process many more requests per time unit.

In this paper, we will describe how the layout of a web page served by a personalized news site is optimized, on the client, using a Genetic Algorithm implemented in JavaScript. The layout of this paper is as follows: the state of the art in layout optimization, especially page layout optimization, will be described in section 2; the genetic algorithm used will be presented in section

3, to proceed to results in section 4 and a discussion and presentation of future lines of work in section 5.

2 State of the art

Some of the results obtained in facility layout [7, 6, 3, 11] can be applied to automatic pagination, although the formulation of a space layout problem is slightly different, since relations among the different objects are assumed. Different news in a page can be related by their content, but the page layout algorithm is not concerned with it, at least not in this stage of research. In any case, since it is a NP-hard problem which starts to be intractable for a number of objects bigger than 10, genetic algorithms have been used to find suboptimal solutions by Kochhar et al [11] and Gero et al. [3]. In facility layout problems, objects placed can have shapes other than rectangular, they are usually placed in a fixed grid, and the restrictions are that, besides not overlapping, machines that work in sequence must be close to one another, paths that lead from one machine to another should not overlap, and so on. These requirements are different from what we find in page layout optimization. Besides, usually facilities are divided as a grid, and objects within those facility occupy a small number of cells, which allows the problem to be treated as a combinatorial optimization problem, instead of a function optimization problem: minimization of the surface occupied by the articles.

Some papers have also focused in automatic layout of multimedia presentations [8], but with an emphasis on a correct presentation of information more than on cramming the maximum amount of information in available screen space. Automatic generation of presentations is treated as a constrained optimization problem by some researchers like Graf et al.[5], whose approach is to take into account constraints such as semantic and pragmatic relations specified by a presentation planner. The problem is much more complex than page layout, but some of its results could be used when applying automatic layout to real newspapers; for instance, placing related articles together, or the most important articles in the top.

Personalized newspaper layout, as such, has been treated in several papers. The *Krakatoa project* [10], which is a personalized newspaper that, presented in a Java applet form, customizes the layout for each user. The newspaper layout does not depend on the size of each article, but on the user and community preferences; thus, it does not really optimize layout: it typesets the newspaper in two columns, with available space partaked among articles depending on the user and user community profile.

Another group of workers in the Finnish Research Institute VTT applied simulated annealing optimization of page layout for paginating fax newspapers and the yellow pages of several countries [12]. In this paper, a heuristic and two simulated annealing methods are presented. The best simulated annealing algorithm (SA2) selects which articles are going to be included, and situates them on the page at the same time. Overlapping is allowed, and sometimes a slight overlap of articles is observed in the final result. They present two different SA algorithms:

- In algorithm **SA1**, the articles used are fixed, they can be changed in shape, and placed in different positions. Total surface and overlap is minimized. Results mentioned in the paper indicate that the method is not too good, taking too much time and resulting in bad layouts
- In algorithm **SA2**, the articles are chosen from the pool and placed using a best-fit situation. The operators that move the SA algorithm from one configuration to another are insert and remove article. This method is the best of all, and it takes only 30 seconds in a Sun Microsystem's SPARC20 workstation. This delay is probably too much for setting a web page, but most of today's machines are faster than that, so it can be considered acceptable.

The method presented in this paper tries to solve a problem very similar to SA1, but using a finetuned genetic algorithm instead of simulated annealing. GAs are usually slower than SA, but manage to find better solutions. That is one of the reasons why GA is used in this paper. Besides, the time requirement is also important: layout should be around one order of magnitude faster than what is achieved by both SA algorithms, The object of this paper is to present a method that is, at the same time, faster and more accurate than SA.

3 Method

The surface of the window is divided in columns and rows, for instance, 4 columns and a row every 50 pixels, this has the effect of reducing the search space and, at the same time, making the result more similar to real newspapers. Article boxes have a fixed width (multiple of columns width) and fixed height (multiple of rows height), but position of their upper left corner is variable. The chromosome will include the representation of an (x, y) pair for each article where x represents the column and y the row where its upper left corner lays.

In principle, bitstring representation could have been used; but JavaScript does not feature packed bitstrings as a native data type, and besides, a representation adequate for the data type that is going to be evolved was chosen, as is proposed by Michalewicz [13] and other authors. Thus, each box position is represented by a pair of integers: the genetic representation includes the coordinates of each box as such, it does not have to be decoded to compute fitness; each *chromosome* is an array of 2*(number of article boxes) integers. We don't know of anybody using this representation for this problem, but perhaps it has been used before.

Once the genetic representation has been chosen, the genetic operators should be able to act on it. Obviously, classical bit-flip is not an option, since binary representation is not used; gene-disrupting crossover either; but a diversity-generation mutation-like operator will be needed, as well as a feature-combination operator like crossover.

In this case, *mutation* will change the x or y coordinate so that the article box moves an integer number of columns or an integer amount of rows. The amplitude of this change decreases with time using an hyperbolic function (that is why this algorithm is denominated *annealed*); at the beginning, positions change widely, while only small changes allowed by the end of training.

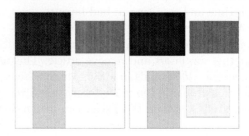

Fig. 1. How mutation operator works: it moves one of the article boxes, in one direction, by an integer amount of rows or columns; in this case,the article box in the lower right corner has moved several rows down the page.

The *crossover* operator will interchange the *genes* of two chromosomes that are situated between two randomly chosen points. It is quite similar to normal 2-point crossover, except that coordinates are fully transferred to the offspring. Two-point crossover is considered more efficient than single-point crossover in normal genetic algorithms; the same stands for integer-representation algorithms. Besides, this crossover operator combined with the integer representations avoids the gene-disrupting actions of normal binary crossover, and makes it act as a pure crossover operator, without mutating any gene at the same time, as it happens when binary crossover operator splits some genes.

Selection, reproduction and elimination procedures correspond to an steady state algorithm : a part of the population is eliminated and substituted by the offspring of the remaining ones. The proportion of the population that is eliminated is the sum of the proportion that undergoes mutation (P_m) and the one that undergo crossover (P_x), $P_x + P_m < 1$.

The genetic algorithm is run for a prefixed number of generations, usually 20, before being applied a greedy algorithm for finetuning. If there is overlapping after the prefixed number of generations, the GA continues until there is no more overlapping.

A population is always composed of 50 tentative layouts, which have been found to be enough for the problem, and fit well within the memory constraints of a JavaScript script, which cannot use more than 30Ks.

The JavaScript GA source code is delivered together with the page, is public domain, and is available from the demo web page
`http://gargamel.ugr.es/~jesus/layout`.

3.1 Fitness function

The function to be minimized in this problem is the total area, taking into account the restrictions of no overlapping and using only available width. The former is taken into account already in the fitness function (that is, minimal surface already means minimal width), but the latter must be also included in the fitness function.

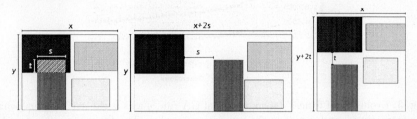

Fig. 2. Overlapping article boxes. t is the vertical dimension of the overlapped rectangle, s the horizontal one. The pictures at the right hand side estimate the two posible layouts without overlapping as far from the best one as the first one.

Taking that into account, the fitness function F calculates the surface of the smaller rectangle that can contain the layout stored inside a chromosome. Once this rectangle is computed, for each couple of boxes that are overlapping, a penalty is applied. As shown in figure 2, the function estimates the two layouts without overlapping as far from the optimal one as the original one and chooses the one with bigger surface. This function can be defined as follows:

$$F = (x + \sum_{i}^{n} x_i)(y + \sum_{i}^{n} y_i)$$ (1)

$$x_i = 2s_i \,,\, y_i = 0 \quad \text{if } (x+2s_i)y > x(y+2t_i)$$
$$x_i = 0 \,,\, y_i = 2t_i \qquad \text{otherwise}$$

where n is the number of overlappings in a layout, x_i and y_i are the horizontal and vertical penalty terms and t_i and s_i measure the extent of the horizontal and vertical overlap for each overlapping i; that is, the fitness function takes into account a penalty term that varies with the amount of overlapping; that way, good solutions with no overlapping can evolve from solutions with a lot of overlapping, through solutions with less overlapping. Using a penalty function usually obtains better results than simply eliminating invalid solutions, as has already been pointed out by some researchers [1].

Almost in every optimization problem, the optimal solution is close to a lot of bad solutions. If these bad solutions are eliminated in the search process, it will be nearly impossible to find the optimal one because the search process will look for solutions far from it [9]. That is why the fitness function estimates the distance from a solution with overlapping to the best one and adds the double

Cost Evolution

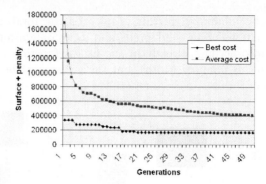

Fig. 3. Evolution of fitness during a typical GA run. y axis is the surface plus penalty, in square pixels, and x axis is the generation number. The fitness usually goes down steeply at the beginning of training, with a slow decrease towards the end of training.

of this distance as shown in figure 2, to get the surface of a solution as far from the best one as the original but without overlapping.

Fitness, which is equivalent to area plus penalty, is minimized. The usual evolution of a GA run is shown in figure 3, with the average and minimum cost plotted against the number of generations. The cost or fitness after the greedy algorithm is not plotted. The algorithm starts usually by eliminating solutions with overlap, and then minimizes the surface that all boxes occupy.

This fitness function has the main problem that empty space within the rectangle that surrounds all article boxes is not minimized by the GA, this is usually taken care of by the greedy algorithm; this fact will be taken into account in further versions of the algorithm. For instance in figure 2, the rectangle in the lower right corner could move freely withouth overlapping with anyone else, and without its right hand side corner being bigger than x, and still have the same fitness, but the layout is not optimal, is not exactly the same: it is much better if it is as close as possible to the boxes on the left and top.

3.2   Improving the solution by means of a greedy algorithm

Since genetic algorithms are not gradient descent algorithms, it usually takes them a long time to reach the best solution; and even in this case, finding the best solution is not guaranteed. In this application, real-time operation is a must, that is why a greedy surface-size gradient-descent algorithm is applied at the end of the genetic algorithm to reach the best solution. Using only a greedy algorithm would not always find the best solution from the initial values, and a genetic algorithm would take a long time to reach the global solution: using a genetic algorithm followed by a greedy one takes the best of both worlds.

There could be other ways of combining stochastic optimization algorithms like GAs with gradient-descent algorithms like a greedy algorithm: for instance, a greedy algorithm could have been applied to every solution each generation; but this would make the genetic algorithm much slower.

The greedy algorithm applied after the genetic serarch just moves each article box to the left and to the top while it doesn't overlap with others, eliminating the gaps between boxes.

4   Results

The first result is that the GA+greedy algorithm combination finds web pages with an optimal layout; a demo is running at
http://gargamel.ugr.es/~jesus/layout (not integrated yet in a personalized news site). An example of the web page after the algorithm is run is shown on figure 4.

Second, we wanted to check how good is the algorithm depending on how crowded is the page; it should be more difficult, or at least it should take longer, when the surface occupied by the articles in relation to the total Web page surface is higher. We used the same set of articles, reducing the web page surface, so that articles occupied 50% to 90% of available surface in 10% increments. Results are shown in table 1.

Surface %	T $\pm\sigma$	F $\pm\sigma$
50%	6500 ± 180	280000 ± 26000
60%	6700 ± 100	279000 ± 24000
70%	6730 ± 121	279000 ± 24000
80%	6666 ± 233	330000 ± 70000
90%	6664 ± 175	318000 ± 43000

In this table, T is the mean and standard deviation of execution times measured in milliseconds in a Intel Pentium II 233MHz with 64MB of main memory, and F is the mean and standard deviation of the fitness during 10 executions. The time needed to find the solution is virtually the same in all cases, but the surfaces of the solutions found are slightly bigger for more crowded environments, with a higher standard deviation too. However, solutions are good enough; it should be taken into account that the default surface in most Web browsers (without resizing) is 640x480 = 307200 pixels; that size is lately being substituted by the bigger 800x600 = 480000 pixels.

Another set of tests was made to prove the need of the greedy algorithm applied to the best chromosome found by the genetic search. A pure genetic algorithm without greedy fine-tuning was run 5 times, obtaining an average of 200 generations with a range of (24, 695); in average, it would take around 5 times more for a genetic algorithm alone than for a genetic+greedy algorithm to find a solution. It could take up to 10 times as much, in the worst case.

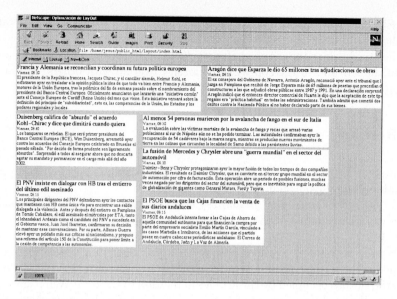

Fig. 4. Final looks, after the GA and the greedy algorithm of a simulated newspaper page with 7 articles.

5 Discussion

The Internet has opened a wide field of applications in the last few years, but few evolutionary algorithms have been applied to it so far. In particular, this paper opens the possibility of sending a genetic algorithm along with web pages so that it might perform many duties within it, from layout optimization, through any tutorial application we might come up with, to functional optimization.

In particular, the JavaScript genetic algorithm *script* presented in this paper is able to perform the layout of a news web page in real time in a Pentium machine, that is, in a time significantly less than the typical load time for a web page (which could be placed around one minute). The algorithm's speed is in the same order of magnitude or faster than the simulated annealing algorithms presented in Lagus et al.'s paper [12], and performance seems a bit better, but this is difficult to compare. This might be due to using a faster computer basically.

The JavaScript implementation of a genetic algorithm is available from the authors, and besides, the script will be integrated in several personalized news sites that are already working in Granada University, like for instance, the Spanish newspaper search engine at http://www-etsi2.ugr.es/hermes.

In the future, the fitness function will be improved to take into account the empty spaces between the articles, so that the greedy algorithm can be eliminated. Other applications will also be investigated: for instance, application to interactive chat web pages, and layout of personal ads pages.

It would be also interesting to implement simulated annealing in the same web page, and compare time and performance for the same setup: same language, same computer.

6 Acknowledgements

This work has been supported in part by CICYT's project Proyecto BIO96-0895 (Spain) and DGICYT's project PB-95-0502.

References

1. D. M. Tate A. E. Smith. Genetic optimization using a penalty function. In Stephanie Forrest, editor, *Proceedings of the 5th International Conference on Genetic Algorithms*, pages 499–505. University of Illinois at Urbana - Champaign, Morgan Kaufmann, July, 17-21 1993.
2. G. Bilchev. Evolutionary metamorphs for the bin packing problem. In *Proceedings of the Fifth Annual Conference on Evolutionary Computing*, 1996.
3. J. S. Gero and V. A. Kazakov. Evolving design genes in space layout planning problems. Technical report, Dept. of Architectural and Design Science, University of Sydney, 1997.
4. W. H. Graf. Graf's home page. Web adress: http://www.dfki.de/~graf/.
5. W. H. Graf. Constraint-based graphical layout of multimodal presentations. In Lefvialdi Catarci, Costabile, editor, *Advanced Visual Interfaces, Procs. of the Int. Workshop AVI92*, World Scientific Series in Computer Science. World Scientific Press, 1992.
6. S. S. Heragu. Recent models and techniques for solving the layout problem. *European Journal of Operations Research*, (57):136–144, 1992.
7. S. S. Heragu and A. S. Alfa. Experimental analysis of simulated annealing based algorithms for the layout problem. *European Journal of Operations Research*, (57):190–202, 1992.
8. W. Hower and W. H. Graf. Research in constraint-based layout, visualization, cad, and related topics: A bibliographical survey. Technical report, Deutsches Forschungzentrum für Küntsliche Intelligenz GmbH, 1995. Research Report RR-95-12.
9. M. Hilliard J. T. Richrardson, M. R. Palmerm G. Liepins. Some guidelines for genetic algorithms with penalty functions. In J. David Schaffer, editor, *Proceedings of the Third International Conference on Genetic Algorithms*, pages 191–197, San Mateo, California, June 4-7 1989. George Mason University, Morgan Kaufmann.
10. Omonari Kamba, Krishna Bharat, and Michael C. Albers. The Krakatoa chronicle - an interactive, personalized newspaper on the web. Technical Report Number 95-25, Technical Report, Graphics, Visualisation and Usability Center, Georgia Institute of Technology, USA, 1995.
11. J. S. Kochhar, B. T. Foster, and S. S. Heragu. Hope: A genetic algorithm for the unequal area facility layout problem. *Computers and Operations Research*, 1997.
12. K. Lagus, I. Karanta, and J. Yläa-Jääski. Paginating the generalized newspapes - a comparison of simulated annealing and a heuristic method. In Hans-Michael Voigt, Werner Ebeling, Ingo Rechenberg, and Hans-Paul Schwefel, editors, *Parallel Problem Solving From Nature – PPSN IV*, volume 1141 of *Lecture Notes in Computer Science*, pages 595–603, Dortmund, Germany, September 1996. Springer-Verlag.
13. Zbigniew Michalewicz. *Genetic Algorithms + Data Structures = Evolution programs*. Springer-Verlag, 2nd edition edition, 1994.

Solving the Capacitor Placement Problem in a Radial Distribution System Using an Adaptive Genetic Algorithm

Koichi Hatta, Masashige Suzuki, Shin'ichi Wakabayashi, and Tetsushi Koide

Faculty of Engineering, Hiroshima University
4-1 Kagamiyama 1 chome, Higashi-Hiroshima 739-8527 JAPAN

Abstract. In this paper, an adaptive genetic algorithm for the capacitor placement problem in a radial distribution system is presented. Based on the measure of the superiority of an individual called elite degree, the adaptive GA dynamically tunes GA parameters such as crossover and mutation during the GA run. The proposed GA is applied to test distribution systems including IEEE 69 with successful results.

1 Introduction

Capacitors are widely used to compensate the reactive power in an electric power distribution system. The capacitor placement problem(CPP) is the determination of location, type and size of capacitors to be placed in a distribution system at different load levels. The objective is to minimize the total cost which is the amount of energy losses of whole system and investment and maintenance cost of installed capacitors while the voltage constraints of each node of the system hold.

Many methods have been proposed to solve the CPP. Stochastic algorithm approach is recently focused on finding a global optimum solution. The simulated annealing method and tabu search method [7] can provide a nearly global optimal solution, but the associated computational burden is heavy. The genetic algorithm approach has been proposed to determine the optimal placement of capacitors [10]. However, setting GA parameters to appropriate values is difficult to enhance the GA performance.

An adaptive GA is the GA which dynamically tunes parameter values during the GA execution. Many adaptive strategies of tuning GA parameters have been proposed [3][6][9]. In [5], we proposed a measure called *elite degree* which estimates the potential superiority of an individual and proposed an adaptive GA which adaptively selects the crossover operator and the mutation rate based on elite degree. In this paper, we present new crossover and mutation operators for CPP and propose an adaptive GA based on elite degree. The proposed GA is applied to 3 test distribution systems and the simulation result shows the effectiveness of the proposed method.

This paper is organized as follows. First, we describe the capacitor placement problem CPP. After explaining our adaptive approach briefly, we propose an adaptive GA for CPP. Finally, experimental results of the proposed method applying to 3 distribution systems are shown to compare with the simulated annealing method.

2   Capacitor Placement Problem

For the capacitor placement problem (CPP) in this paper, the load data is represented as a sequence of load level i $(i = 0, 1, \cdots, nt)$. The load level i has the magnitude L_i of the load and each level has interval time T_i, during which it continues. Load levels are assumed to be given in the decreasing order, i.e., $L_i \geq L_{i+1}$.

Two different types of capacitors are considered to install in the distribution system.

(1) **Fixed capacitor:** A fixed capacitor has a constant size of capacity at all load levels.

$$u_k^0 = u_k^1 = \cdots = u_k^{nt}$$

(2) **Switched capacitor:** A switched capacitor can change its capacity at each load level. We assume that the capacitor size u_k at L_0, denoted u_k^0, is the maximal, and the switched capacitor at ith load level has the following size.

$$0 \leq u_k^i \leq u_k^0$$

The objective function f_0 is formulated as the sum of the power loss of whole system at all load levels and the cost of installing capacitors.

$$f_0 = k_e \sum_{i=0}^{nt} T_i p_i(\boldsymbol{x}^i) + \sum_{k=1}^{nc} (r_{ck} u_k^0 + c_k) e_k$$

In the above formulation, $\boldsymbol{x}^i$ is the state vector of all nodes at load level i. The state vector represents the states of all nodes, and the state of a node consists of real power, reactive power and voltage at that node. Let $p_i(\boldsymbol{x}^i)$ be the power loss of whole system per hour at load level i. The power loss of load level i is represented as $k_e T_i p_i(\boldsymbol{x}^i)$, where k_e is a constant, which means the energy cost per unit power. The power loss of whole system is the sum of $k_e T_i p_i(\boldsymbol{x}^i)$ at all load levels.

The capacitor cost is the investment and maintenance cost of installing capacitors. The maintenance cost depends on the size of capacitor u_k^0. Contrarily, the investment cost is constant c. Using the decision variable $e \in \{0, 1\}$ to show whether the capacitor is installed or not, the cost of capacitor k is represented as $(r_{ck} u_k^0 + c_k) e_k$, $(k = 1, 2, \cdots, nc)$, where r is the cost coefficient per unit size and nc is the number of candidate locations to install capacitors.

The CPP is the minimization problem of f_0. Constraints of the CPP are as follows. Let C_1 and C_2 be the sets of switched capacitors and fixed capacitors, respectively.

$$G^i(\boldsymbol{x}^i, \boldsymbol{u}^i) = 0 \quad i = 0, 1, \cdots, nt \quad \text{(power flow constrains)}$$
$$H^i(\boldsymbol{x}^i, \boldsymbol{u}^i) \leq 0 \quad i = 0, 1, \cdots, nt \quad \text{(voltage constraints)}$$
$$\boldsymbol{o} \leq \boldsymbol{u}^o \leq \boldsymbol{u}^{max} \cdot \boldsymbol{e}$$
$$k \in C_1 \Rightarrow 0 \leq u_k^i \leq u_k^0 \quad i = 0, 1, \cdots, nt$$
$$k \in C_2 \Rightarrow u_k^i = u_k^0 \quad i = 0, 1, \cdots, nt$$

We use the the power flow constraints [7] to obtain the state of each node. Voltage constraints specify the upper and lower bounds on node j as follows.

$$V_{min} \leq V_j \leq V_{max}$$

3 Adaptive GA based on Elite Degree (EAGA)

The adaptive GA *EAGA* proposed in this paper uses a measure called elite degree [5]. Elite degree is defined by using the history of an individual, which makes it possible to estimate the potential goodness of an individual.

3.1 Elite degree

Let the generation of initial population be the generation 0, and $\tau(> 0)$ be the current generation. Let the ith individual of the population in the generation τ be individual d_i^τ ($0 \leq i \leq Popsize - 1$, where $Popsize$ represents the population size), and Anc_i^τ (j) be the set of ancestors in $\tau - j$ generation of individual d_i^τ.

In case of the maximization problem, assuming that the distribution of fitness values of individuals is a normal distribution, where μ and σ are the mean and the standard deviation of fitness values of individuals, respectively, we regard an individual as an elite if the individual has a fitness value greater than or equal to $\mu + \alpha \times \sigma$, where α is a real number and satisfied with $0 \leq \alpha$. Then, elite degree $E(\tau, i)$ of individual d_i^τ is defined by the following equation.

$$Elite_i^\tau(j) = \{ d_k^{\tau-j} | d_k^{\tau-j} \in Anc_i^\tau(j),$$
$$\mu_{\tau-j} + \alpha \times \sigma_{\tau-j} \leq f(d_k^{\tau-j}) \}$$

$$E(\tau, i) = \frac{\displaystyle\sum_{j=0}^{level\_max} \left\{ \left| Elite_i^\tau(j) \right| \times \beta^j \right\}}{\displaystyle\sum_{j=0}^{level\_max} \left\{ \left| Anc_i^\tau(j) \right| \times \beta^j \right\}}$$

Where, $Elite_i^\tau(j)$ is the set of elite ancestors of d_i^τ on level $\tau - j$, $f(d_k^{\tau-j})$ is the fitness value of k-th individual on level $\tau - j$. We call α the *elite decision factor* and β ($0 \leq \beta \leq 1$) the *elite influence factor*. For the minimization problem, we can define elite degree in a similar manner.

3.2 Adaptive parameter tuning

There have been proposed many crossover operators [8] [11] which have various characteristics from the viewpoint of preserving good schemata in parents. For example, it is known that 2 point crossover is less disruptive for schema than uniform crossover. Thereby, 2 point crossover is considered to be more appropriate for local improvement of an individual than uniform crossover. From this property, we choose crossover operators adaptively depending on the state of an individual. First, we divide the population into two subsets according to elite degrees of individuals. Next, for high elite degree individuals, the schema preserving crossover is applied. Otherwise, the search space exploring crossover is applied.

For two individuals d_i^τ, d_j^τ chosen randomly for the crossover, the crossover operator is selected by the following algorithm.

[Adaptive crossover selection based on $E(\tau, i)$]

> **if** $(E(\tau, i) + E(\tau, j)) \geq D)$
> $\quad$ *Schema preserving crossover*;
> **else**
> $\quad$ *Search space exploring crossover*;

where D is the constant value specified by the user, and ranging of $0 \leq D \leq 2$. The adaptive tuning of mutation rate is similarly performed, but its explanation is omitted in this paper due to lack of space.

4 EAGA for Capacitor Placement Problem

4.1 Representation

For each load level, a solution of CPP is represented as the chromosome d which is composed of nc genes. A gene has three elements of location l_k, type t_k and size z_k of capacitor. That is, $Gene_k = < l_k, t_k, z_k >, (k = 1, 2, \cdots, nc)$. The location of capacitor is coded as an index of the node, at which the capacitor is installed. This coding makes it possible to treat a large number of nodes when only a small number of capacitors is allowed to be installed. In general, many capacitors may not be installed whereas the number of nodes is relatively large, because the installing cost of one capacitor is considered to be expensive. When the number of installed capacitors is less than nc, remaining locations in a chromosome are set to 0. The type of capacitor has the length of just 1 bit since one of two types of capacitor is selected. The size of capacitor is coded as a discrete value, which is calculated by dividing the real capacitor size by the base capacitor size. If the switched capacitor is selected, the actual size (capacity) of the capacitor at each load level is set to a value which is proportional to the value of the current load level.

4.2 Crossover

We propose two crossover operators performing on chromosomes. One is the linear crossover, which is similar to linear recombination in evolution strategies (ES) [2]. This is designed to improve solutions represented by parents. The other is the discrete crossover, which is designed for exploring the search space globally. In both crossovers, two genes at the same locus of parents are operated in turn. First, we describe the linear crossover for CPP.

Location If the location of either parent is 0, no operation is performed. If the location of both parents are not 0, the distance between two nodes is calculated along the path between two nodes in the distribution system, where the distance means the path length between two nodes. Next, the offset is calculated by multiplying weight w ($0 < w < 0.5$) to the distance. Then, the locations of the offspring are set to the nodes moved by the offset from the locations of their parents along the path between two parents.

Type Type of capacitor is not changed.

Size Let V_1, V_2 be the sizes of parent 1 and parent 2. The sizes of offsprings 1 and 2, denoted Z_1 and Z_2, are given as follows.

$$Z_1 = (1 - w)V_1 + wV_2$$
$$Z_2 = (1 - w)V_2 + wV_1$$

Next, we describe the discrete crossover for CPP. The discrete crossover uses a 0-1 mask generated randomly. The mask has the same number of elements as the number of elements (genes) in individuals. For each gene on the parents, the mask indicates which parent will pass its gene to offspring 1. Offspring 2 receives the gene in that position from the other parent.

4.3 Mutation

The mutation maintains the diversity of the population. In the proposed GA, based on the elite degree, we adaptively change not only the mutation rate but also the mutation operator. We introduce two types of the mutation, the mutation dedicated for elite individuals, and the mutation for non elite individuals. The former is intended to the local improvement of the solution, and the latter maintains the diversity of the population. In this strategy, if an individual is elite, the mutation for elite is applied. Otherwise, mutation for non elite is applied. First, we describe the mutation for elite as follows.

Location If the capacitor is not located in a parent, the location is not changed. If the capacitor is already located in a parent, the decision whether to relocate the capacitor or not is made by a binary number generated at random. In case that the capacitor is to be relocated, the new location of offspring is set to the neighbor of the location specified by the parent.

Type The type of capacitor is not changed.

Size The decision whether to change the size or not is made by a binary number generated at random. If the size is to be changed, the size of offspring is calculated from the size specified by the parent with adding or subtracting 2 unit capacities.

In the mutation for non-elite, all locations, types and sizes in chromosome are changed randomly.

4.4 Handling constraints and fitness

Several methods have been proposed to handle violations of constrains. In the proposed GA, the penalty function is applied to the fitness value by adding a large value to the cost. The penalty function is calculated from the amount of violations of voltage constraints of nodes. In each generation, the fitness values of all individuals are evaluated by using the following equation.

$$Fitness = cost + \omega \cdot V_{err}$$
$$cost \ : \ \text{objective function } f_o$$
$$V_{err} \ : \ \text{sum of violations in the voltage constraint}$$
$$\omega \ : \ \text{weight coefficient}$$

4.5 Outline of proposed algorithm EAGA-CPP

We show the outline of the proposed algorithm for the capacitor placement problem EAGA-CPP in Figure 1. First, we generate an initial population randomly. Next, the fitness value and elite degrees of individuals are calculated. Referring the fitness value of individual, individuals are selected by the roulette selection. Then, mutation is applied to the survived individuals. If an individual is elite, mutation for elite is applied. Otherwise, mutation for non elite is applied. Next, crossover is performed. If the sum of elite degrees of individuals is greater than threshold D, linear crossover is applied to those individuals. Otherwise, discrete crossover is applied. After that, generation is incremented to repeat until the terminal condition is satisfied.

5 Experiments

5.1 Test systems and parameters

The proposed adaptive GA for CPP has been implemented using C language based on public domain GA software GENESIS 5.0 [4] and executed on the Ultra COMP Station Model 170. The part of fitness calculation in GA is programmed using the power flow code [12] written in FORTRAN. Test systems are 3 distribution systems shown in Tables 1 and 2. S1 and S2 are 19 and 29 node systems generated by hand. S3 is a 69 node system, and load data for all

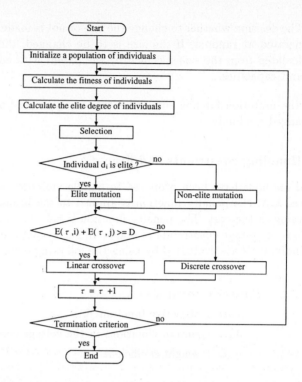

Fig. 1. Flowchart of the EAGA Algorithm.

test cases are obtained from [1]. In this experiment, each chromosome consists of 5 genes. That is, 5 capacitors are allowed to install in a given distribution system in maximum. Each gene consists of 19 bits. The bit lengths of location, type and size of a gene are 10, 1 and 8 bits, respectively. For the linear crossover, the weight for offset is set to 0.2. For the mutation, the mutation rate for high elite degree individuals is set to 0.01 and for low elite degree individuals 0.1. The penalty function is set to a large constant. Other GA parameters used in this experiment are shown in Table 3.

To analyze the feature of the proposed adaptive GA for CPP, we are concerned with the following 3 points.

Effect of adaptive crossover selection We examine the influence of parameter value of adaptive GA upon the GA performance. We change the threshold D of adaptive crossover selection from 0 to 2 by 0.5. The cases of $D = 0$ and $D = 2$ correspond to non adaptive crossover methods in which all individuals are reproduced by linear crossover and discrete crossover, respectively. On the other hand, $0 < D < 2$ means the cases that individuals are reproduced **with adaptive selection of crossover operators.**

Table 1. System data.

Test system	S_1	S_2	S_3
Nodes	19	29	69
Loads	11	17	48

Table 2. Load data.

Load level	L_0	L_1	L_2
Value	1.8	1	0.5

Time interval	T_0	T_1	T_2
Value	1000	6760	1000

Table 3. GA Parameters.

GA parameters	Value	GA parameters	Value
Total experiments	10	Scaling window	5
Population	50	*level_max*	5
Crossover rate	0.6	Elite decision factor α	0.2
Selection strategy	Elitist	Elite influence factor β	0.5
Generation gap	1.0	Total evaluations	10000

Effect of mutation We compared the proposed adaptive mutation with the non adaptive mutation, in which all individuals are mutated with the conventional non adaptive method (i.e., random mutation).

Comparison of the solution We compare the results obtained with EAGA-CPP to the existing SA approach from the viewpoint of the total system cost and computation time.

5.2 Experimental results

Table 4 shows the best results of EAGA-CPP with changing threshold D. The solutions in the table were the average of 10 runs and the terminal condition is 10000 evaluations. The row of "cost" shows the best solution which has been found until the end of GA run. "imp. rate" means the improvement rate of the cost between the best solution and the cost before the installment of capacitors. "eval. rate" shows the percentage of the fitness calculation time in the total CPU time. The values with the bold font in the table shows the best result for each test system. From the table, the proposed adaptive method with $D = 0.5$ shows the best results. The computation time is nearly equal to the time of non adaptive method, and the cost is better than the one of non adaptive method.

Table 5 shows the results when random mutation was applied. In this experiment, other parameters besides mutation are the same values as shown in Table 3. Best solutions were found when $D = 0.5$ for system 1, $D = 1$ for system 2, and $D = 2$ for system 3. Adaptive crossover selection produces the best solutions for systems 1 and 2 even if the mutation is non adaptive. For system 3, adaptive mutation selection is considered to be more important than adaptive crossover selection to improve the solution. We consider that, if the number of nodes and branches increases like system3, the mutation for elite will contribute the GA performance more than linear crossover, which was designed for local improvement.

Table 5 also shows the results of SA. The terminal condition of SA is set to 50000 evaluations because SA temperature should decrease slowly. The results of SA are worse than the results of GA concerning with both the solution and the computation time. We consider that SA was trapped into a local optimum.

Table 4. Results of EAGA-CPP.

	Linear Crossover			EAGA-CPP ($D = 0.5$)			Discrete Crossover		
	S_1	S_2	S_3	S_1	S_2	S_3	S_1	S_2	S_3
Cost	1432	2702	2417	**1422**	**2696**	**2410**	1433	2734	2428
Generation	283	212	260	**265**	**249**	**265**	443	352	401
Imp. rate (%)	27.15	30.80	31.96	**27.28**	**30.91**	**32.18**	26.72	29.65	31.54
CPU time (sec.)	264	498	964	260	495	975	266	496	988
Eval rate(%)	89.4	94.1	96.3	89.1	93.4	96.5	89.2	94.5	96.3

Table 5. Results of random mutation and SA.

	Random mutation			Simulated Annealing		
	$S_1(D = 0.5)$	$S_2(D = 1)$	$S_3(D = 2)$	S_1	S_2	S_3
Cost	1426	2722	2451	1464	2800	2467
Generation	215	229	260	—	—	—
Imp. rate (%)	27.08	30.25	31.04	25.13	28.25	30.59
CPU time (sec.)	263	507	982	1577	2987	5911

6 Conclusion

In this paper, we proposed the adaptive genetic algorithm for the capacitor placement problem. The proposed algorithm is based on the measure of superiority of individual called elite degree, which is used to adaptively select GA parameters such as crossover and mutation during the GA execution. The simulation results demonstrated that the proposed adaptive strategy of crossover and mutation for the capacitor placement problem have performed better than the standard GA and SA.

Future works are the application of the proposed GA to large sized distribution systems and real distribution systems. For the large systems, it is necessary for the algorithm to reduce the computation time. Since it takes much time to solve the power flow equation in total computation time, reducing the computation time of power flow equation program is also important.

Acknowledgment The authors would like to appreciate Yoshifumi Zoka for his helpful comments and suggestions.

References

1. Baran, M. E., Wu, F. F.: Optimal Capacitor Placement on Radial Distribution System. IEEE Transactions on Power Delivery, Vol. 4, No. 1 (1989) 725–734
2. Bäck, T., Hammel, U., Schwefel, H. P.: Evolutionary Computation: Comments on the History and Current State. IEEE Transaction on Evolutionary Computation, Vol.1, No. 1 (1997) 3–17
3. Cao, Y. J., Wu, Q. H.: Optimal Reactive Power Dispatch Using an Adaptive Genetic Algorithm. Proc. IEE/IEEE Genetic Algorithms in Engineering Systems: Innovations and Applications (1997) 117–122
4. Grefenstette, J. J.: Optimization of Control Parameters for Genetic Algorithms. IEEE Transaction on Systems, Man, and Cybernetics, Vol. SMC-16, No. 1 (1986) 122–128
5. Hatta, K., Matsuda, K., Wakabayashi, S., Koide, T.: On-the-fly Crossover Adaptation of Genetic Algorithms. Proc. IEE/IEEE Genetic Algorithms in Engineering Systems: Innovations and Applications (1997) 197–202
6. Hinterding, R., Michalewicz, Z., Eiben, A. E.: Adaptation in Evolutionary Computation: A Survey. Proc. IEEE International Conference on Evolutionary Computation (1997) 65–69
7. Huang, Y. C., Yang, H. T., Huang, C. L.: Solving the Capacitor Placement Problem in a Radial Distribution System Using Tabu Search Approach. IEEE Transactions on Power Systems, Vol. 11, No. 4 (1996) 1868–1873
8. Spears, W. M.: Adapting Crossover in Evolutionary Algorithms. Proc. Evolutionary Programming Conference (1995) 367–384
9. Srinivas, M., Patnaik, L. M.: Adaptive Probabilities of Crossover and Mutation in Genetic Algorithms. IEEE Transaction on Systems, Man, and Cybernetics, Vol. 24, No. 4 (1994) 656–667
10. Sundhararajan, S., Pahwa, A.: Optimal Selection of Capacitors for Radial Distribution Systems Using Genetic Algorithms. IEEE PES Summer Meeting, paper no. 93 SM 499-4 (1993)
11. White, T., Oppacher, F.: Adaptive Crossover Using Automata. Proc. Parallel Problem Solving from Nature - PPSN III (1994) 229–238
12. Zoka, Y., Sasaki, H., Kubokawa, J., Yokoyama, R., Tanaka, H.: An Optimal Deployment of Fuel Cells in Distribution Systems by Using Genetic Algorithms. Proc. IEEE International Conference on Evolutionary Computation (1995) 479–484

Author Index

Agapie, A.   3
Alba, E.   305
Albrecht, A.   968
Arapoglu, R.A.   937
Araujo, L.   270

Baluja, S.   461
Bandyopadhyay, S.   315
Bentley, P.   280
Beyer, H.-G.   34, 109
Bhattacharyya, S.   885
Bindewald, E.   959
Bins, J.   823
Branke, J.   119
Bull, L.   471, 550
Burke, D.S.   345

Capcarrère, M.   573
Chakraborty, S.   129
Cheung, S.K.   968
Clack, C.   438
Collins, J.J.   178
Corne, D.   775
Cotta, C.   305
Crisan, C.   897
Crutchfield, J.P.   613
Cumming, A.   865

De Falco, I.   593
De Jong, K.A.   345, 530
Deb, K.   129, 583
Delahaye, D.   855
Denton, J.   823
Di Caro, G.   673
Díaz, A.F.   835
Dorigo, M.   673
Dorne, R.   745
Droste, S.   13
Ducoulombier, A.   418

Eiben, A.E.   201
Eisele, V.   823
Eshelman, L.J.   398

Fleming, P.J.   683
Fogarty, T.C.   865
Fonlupt, C.   47
Freisleben, B.   765
Fukunaga, A.S.   357

Geyer, H.   978
Ghosh, A.   583
Gil, C.   835
González Peñalver, J.   1018
Goldberg, D.E.   23
Gorges-Schleuter, M.   367, 917
Gottlieb, J.   755
Grefenstette, J.J.   345
Guerra, C.   823

Hao, J.-K.   745
Hart, E.   139, 795, 845
Hatta, K.   1028
Hemert, J.I. van   201
Herrera, F.   603
Hesser, J.   959
Hordijk, W.   613
Horn, J.   23
Hornby, G.S.   97
Howe, A.   823
Hurley, S.   907
Husbands, P.   221

Iazzetta, A.   593

Jakob, W.   917
Jansen, Th.   13
Jelasity, M.   378

Kabré, H.   663
Kallel, L.   57
Kao, C.-Y.   947
Kargupta, H.   315
Kazarlis, S.   211
Kehagias, A.   1008
Khatib, W.   683
Kim, D.G.   221
Kita, H.   149
Kizu, S.   702
Kobler, D.   988
Kodydek, G.   875
Koide, T.   1028
Kozieł, S.   231
Kreutz, M.   998
Ku, K.W.C.   481
Kuscu, I.   491

Lanzi, P.L.   501
Laumanns, M.   241
Leonhardi, A.   388
Leung, K.S.   968
Lewis, J.   139
Lim, I.S.   325
Liu, Y.   623
Lozano, M.   603

Männer, R.   959
Mak, M.W.   481
Mani, M.   398
Marchiori, E.   201
Mathias, K.E.   398
Mayer, H.A.   511
Merelo, J.J.   1018
Merz, P.   765
Michalewicz, Z.   231, 803
Michel, R.   692
Middendorf, M.   692
Miller, I.   250
Miller, J.F.   927
Mitchell, M.   613
Montoya, M.G.   835
Moraga, C.   603
Mori, N.   149

Mühlenbein, H.   897

Natale, P.   593
Naudts, B.   67
Naudts, J.   67
Nikolaev, N.I.   712
Nishikawa, Y.   149
Nissen, V.   159
Norman, B.A.   937

Oates, M.J.   775
Obayashi, S.   260
Ochoa, G.   335
Ortega, J.   835
Oussedik, S.   855
Oyman, A.I.   34

Paechter, B.   865
Parks, G.T.   250
Paterakis, E.   1008
Petridis, V.   211, 1008
Pötter, C.   521
Pollack, J.B.   97
Potter, M.A.   530
Pratihar, D.K.   583
Preux, P.   47
Prieto, A.   835
Propach, J.   159

Quick, R.J.   77

Raidl, G.R.   875
Ramsey, C.L.   345
Rana, S.   785
Rankin, R.C.   865
Ratle, A.   87
Rayward-Smith, V.J.   77
Reeves, C.R.   633
Reimetz, A.M.   998
Reissenberger, W.   388
Ritchie, G.   139
Robilliard, D.   47
Ross, C.   823
Ross, P.   795, 845
Rudolph, G.   169, 241

Ruiz-Andino, A.   270
Ruz, J.   270
Ryan, C.   178

Sáenz, F.   270
Salomon, R.   408
Sawai, H.   702
Schaffer, J.D.   398
Schmelmer, T.   388
Schulz, S.   978
Schwefel, H.-P.   34, 241
Sebag, M.   418
Seelen, W. von   998
Sendhoff, B.   998
Seredyński, F.   643
Shapiro, J.L.   540
Sieber, I.   917
Sipper, M.   573, 653
Slavov, V.   712
Smith, A.E.   937
Smith, D.   907
Smith, G.D.   77
Spalanzani, A.   663
Stagge, P.   188
Steenbeek, A.G.   201
Stützle, Th.   722
Suzuki, M.   1028

Takahashi, S.   260
Takeguchi, Y.   260
Tao, G.   803
Tarantino, E.   593
Tateson, R.   732
Taylor, S.J.   633
Teich, J.   885

Tettamanzi, A.G.B.   573, 988
Thalmann, D.   325
Thiele, L.   292
Thomson, P.   927
Tomassini, M.   573
Tomlinson, A.   550
Troya, J.M.   305
Tsutsui, S.   428

Ulbig, P.   978

Valenzuela, C.   907
Vekaria, K.   438
Voss, N.   755

Wakabayashi, S.   1028
Walters, T.   813
Watson, J.-P.   823
Watson, R.A.   97
Wegener, I.   13
Weicker, K.   388
Weicker, N.   388
Weihs, C.   998
Whitley, D.   785, 823
Wiegand, R.P.   560
Wong, C.K.   968
Wu, A.S.   345

Yang, J.-M.   947
Yang, R.   448
Yao, X.   623
Yu, T.   280

Zitzler, E.   292, 885

Springer
and the
environment

 Springer

Lecture Notes in Computer Science

For information about Vols. 1–1415

please contact your bookseller or Springer-Verlag

Vol. 1416: A.P. del Pobil, J. Mira, M.Ali (Eds.), Tasks and Methods in Applied Artificial Intelligence. Vol.II. Proceedings, 1998. XXIII, 943 pages. 1998. (Subseries LNAI).

Vol. 1417: S. Yalamanchili, J. Duato (Eds.), Parallel Computer Routing and Communication. Proceedings, 1997. XII, 309 pages. 1998.

Vol. 1418: R. Mercer, E. Neufeld (Eds.), Advances in Artificial Intelligence. Proceedings, 1998. XII, 467 pages. 1998. (Subseries LNAI).

Vol. 1419: G. Vigna (Ed.), Mobile Agents and Security. XII, 257 pages. 1998.

Vol. 1420: J. Desel, M. Silva (Eds.), Application and Theory of Petri Nets 1998. Proceedings, 1998. VIII, 385 pages. 1998.

Vol. 1421: C. Kirchner, H. Kirchner (Eds.), Automated Deduction – CADE-15. Proceedings, 1998. XIV, 443 pages. 1998. (Subseries LNAI).

Vol. 1422: J. Jeuring (Ed.), Mathematics of Program Construction. Proceedings, 1998. X, 383 pages. 1998.

Vol. 1423: J.P. Buhler (Ed.), Algorithmic Number Theory. Proceedings, 1998. X, 640 pages. 1998.

Vol. 1424: L. Polkowski, A. Skowron (Eds.), Rough Sets and Current Trends in Computing. Proceedings, 1998. XIII, 626 pages. 1998. (Subseries LNAI).

Vol. 1425: D. Hutchison, R. Schäfer (Eds.), Multimedia Applications, Services and Techniques – ECMAST'98. Proceedings, 1998. XVI, 532 pages. 1998.

Vol. 1427: A.J. Hu, M.Y. Vardi (Eds.), Computer Aided Verification. Proceedings, 1998. IX, 552 pages. 1998.

Vol. 1429: F. van der Linden (Ed.), Development and Evolution of Software Architectures for Product Families. Proceedings, 1998. IX, 258 pages. 1998.

Vol. 1430: S. Trigila, A. Mullery, M. Campolargo, H. Vanderstraeten, M. Mampaey (Eds.), Intelligence in Services and Networks: Technology for Ubiquitous Telecom Services. Proceedings, 1998. XII, 550 pages. 1998.

Vol. 1431: H. Imai, Y. Zheng (Eds.), Public Key Cryptography. Proceedings, 1998. XI, 263 pages. 1998.

Vol. 1432: S. Arnborg, L. Ivansson (Eds.), Algorithm Theory – SWAT '98. Proceedings, 1998. IX, 347 pages. 1998.

Vol. 1433: V. Honavar, G. Slutzki (Eds.), Grammatical Inference. Proceedings, 1998. X, 271 pages. 1998. (Subseries LNAI).

Vol. 1434: J.-C. Heudin (Ed.), Virtual Worlds. Proceedings, 1998. XII, 412 pages. 1998. (Subseries LNAI).

Vol. 1435: M. Klusch, G. Weiß (Eds.), Cooperative Information Agents II. Proceedings, 1998. IX, 307 pages. 1998. (Subseries LNAI).

Vol. 1436: D. Wood, S. Yu (Eds.), Automata Implementation. Proceedings, 1997. VIII, 253 pages. 1998.

Vol. 1437: S. Albayrak, F.J. Garijo (Eds.), Intelligent Agents for Telecommunication Applications. Proceedings, 1998. XII, 251 pages. 1998. (Subseries LNAI).

Vol. 1438: C. Boyd, E. Dawson (Eds.), Information Security and Privacy. Proceedings, 1998. XI, 423 pages. 1998.

Vol. 1439: B. Magnusson (Ed.), System Configuration Management. Proceedings, 1998. X, 207 pages. 1998.

Vol. 1440: K.S. McCurley, C.D. Ziegler (Eds.), Advances in Cryptology 1981 – 1997. Proceedings. Approx. XII, 260 pages. 1998.

Vol. 1441: W. Wobcke, M. Pagnucco, C. Zhang (Eds.), Agents and Multi-Agent Systems. Proceedings, 1997. XII, 241 pages. 1998. (Subseries LNAI).

Vol. 1442: A. Fiat. G.J. Woeginger (Eds.), Online Algorithms. XVIII, 436 pages. 1998.

Vol. 1443: K.G. Larsen, S. Skyum, G. Winskel (Eds.), Automata, Languages and Programming. Proceedings, 1998. XVI, 932 pages. 1998.

Vol. 1444: K. Jansen, J. Rolim (Eds.), Approximation Algorithms for Combinatorial Optimization. Proceedings, 1998. VIII, 201 pages. 1998.

Vol. 1445: E. Jul (Ed.), ECOOP'98 – Object-Oriented Programming. Proceedings, 1998. XII, 635 pages. 1998.

Vol. 1446: D. Page (Ed.), Inductive Logic Programming. Proceedings, 1998. VIII, 301 pages. 1998. (Subseries LNAI).

Vol. 1447: V.W. Porto, N. Saravanan, D. Waagen, A.E. Eiben (Eds.), Evolutionary Programming VII. Proceedings, 1998. XVI, 840 pages. 1998.

Vol. 1448: M. Farach-Colton (Ed.), Combinatorial Pattern Matching. Proceedings, 1998. VIII, 251 pages. 1998.

Vol. 1449: W.-L. Hsu, M.-Y. Kao (Eds.), Computing and Combinatorics. Proceedings, 1998. XII, 372 pages. 1998.

Vol. 1450: L. Brim, F. Gruska, J. Zlatuška (Eds.), Mathematical Foundations of Computer Science 1998. Proceedings, 1998. XVII, 846 pages. 1998.

Vol. 1451: A. Amin, D. Dori, P. Pudil, H. Freeman (Eds.), Advances in Pattern Recognition. Proceedings, 1998. XXI, 1048 pages. 1998.

Vol. 1452: B.P. Goettl, H.M. Halff, C.L. Redfield, V.J. Shute (Eds.), Intelligent Tutoring Systems. Proceedings, 1998. XIX, 629 pages. 1998.

Vol. 1453: M.-L. Mugnier, M. Chein (Eds.), Conceptual Structures: Theory, Tools and Applications. Proceedings, 1998. XIII, 439 pages. 1998. (Subseries LNAI).

Vol. 1454: I. Smith (Ed.), Artificial Intelligence in Structural Engineering. XI, 497 pages. 1998. (Subseries LNAI).

Vol. 1456: A. Drogoul, M. Tambe, T. Fukuda (Eds.), Collective Robotics. Proceedings, 1998. VII, 161 pages. 1998. (Subseries LNAI).

Vol. 1457: A. Ferreira, J. Rolim, H. Simon, S.-H. Teng (Eds.), Solving Irregularly Structured Problems in Prallel. Proceedings, 1998. X, 408 pages. 1998.

Vol. 1458: V.O. Mittal, H.A. Yanco, J. Aronis, R-. Simpson (Eds.), Assistive Technology in Artificial Intelligence. X, 273 pages. 1998. (Subseries LNAI).

Vol. 1459: D.G. Feitelson, L. Rudolph (Eds.), Job Scheduling Strategies for Parallel Processing. Proceedings, 1998. VII, 257 pages. 1998.

Vol. 1460: G. Quirchmayr, E. Schweighofer, T.J.M. Bench-Capon (Eds.), Database and Expert Systems Applications. Proceedings, 1998. XVI, 905 pages. 1998.

Vol. 1461: G. Bilardi, G.F. Italiano, A. Pietracaprina, G. Pucci (Eds.), Algorithms – ESA'98. Proceedings, 1998. XII, 516 pages. 1998.

Vol. 1462: H. Krawczyk (Ed.), Advances in Cryptology - CRYPTO '98. Proceedings, 1998. XII, 519 pages. 1998.

Vol. 1463: N.E. Fuchs (Ed.), Logic Program Synthesis and Transformation. Proceedings, 1997. X, 343 pages. 1998.

Vol. 1464: H.H.S. Ip, A.W.M. Smeulders (Eds.), Multimedia Information Analysis and Retrieval. Proceedings, 1998. VIII, 264 pages. 1998.

Vol. 1465: R. Hirschfeld (Ed.), Financial Cryptography. Proceedings, 1998. VIII, 311 pages. 1998.

Vol. 1466: D. Sangiorgi, R. de Simone (Eds.), CONCUR'98: Concurrency Theory. Proceedings, 1998. XI, 657 pages. 1998.

Vol. 1467: C. Clack, K. Hammond, T. Davie (Eds.), Implementation of Functional Languages. Proceedings, 1997. X, 375 pages. 1998.

Vol. 1468: P. Husbands, J.-A. Meyer (Eds.), Evolutionary Robotics. Proceedings, 1998. VIII, 247 pages. 1998.

Vol. 1469: R. Puigjaner, N.N. Savino, B. Serra (Eds.), Computer Performance Evaluation. Proceedings, 1998. XIII, 376 pages. 1998.

Vol. 1470: D. Pritchard, J. Reeve (Eds.), Euro-Par'98: Parallel Processing. Proceedings, 1998. XXII, 1157 pages. 1998.

Vol. 1471: J. Dix, L. Moniz Pereira, T.C. Przymusinski (Eds.), Logic Programming and Knowledge Representation. Proceedings, 1997. IX, 246 pages. 1998. (Subseries LNAI).

Vol. 1473: X. Leroy, A. Ohori (Eds.), Types in Compilation. Proceedings, 1998. VIII, 299 pages. 1998.

Vol. 1474: F. Mueller, A. Bestavros (Eds.), Languages, Compilers, and Tools for Embedded Systems. Proceedings, 1998. XIV, 261 pages. 1998.

Vol. 1475: W. Litwin, T. Morzy, G. Vossen (Eds.), Advances in Databases and Information Systems. Proceedings, 1998. XIV, 369 pages. 1998.

Vol. 1476: J. Calmet, J. Plaza (Eds.), Artificial Intelligence and Symbolic Computation. Proceedings, 1998. XI, 309 pages. 1998. (Subseries LNAI).

Vol. 1477: K. Rothermel, F. Hohl (Eds.), Mobile Agents. Proceedings, 1998. VIII, 285 pages. 1998.

Vol. 1478: M. Sipper, D. Mange, A. Pérez-Uribe (Eds.), Evolvable Systems: From Biology to Hardware. Proceedings, 1998. IX, 382 pages. 1998.

Vol. 1479: J. Grundy, M. Newey (Eds.), Theorem Proving in Higher Order Logics. Proceedings, 1998. VIII, 497 pages. 1998.

Vol. 1480: F. Giunchiglia (Ed.), Artificial Intelligence: Methodology, Systems, and Applications. Proceedings, 1998. IX, 502 pages. 1998. (Subseries LNAI).

Vol. 1481: E.V. Munson, C. Nicholas, D. Wood (Eds.), Principles of Digital Document Processing. Proceedings, 1998. VII, 152 pages. 1998.

Vol. 1482: R.W. Hartenstein, A. Keevallik (Eds.), Field-Programmable Logic and Applications. Proceedings, 1998. XI, 533 pages. 1998.

Vol. 1483: T. Plagemann, V. Goebel (Eds.), Interactive Distributed Multimedia Systems and Telecommunication Services. Proceedings, 1998. XV, 326 pages. 1998.

Vol. 1484: H. Coelho (Ed.), Progress in Artificial Intelligence – IBERAMIA 98. Proceedings, 1998. XIII, 421 pages. 1998. (Subseries LNAI).

Vol. 1485: J.-J. Quisquater, Y. Deswarte, C. Meadows, D. Gollmann (Eds.), Computer Security – ESORICS 98. Proceedings, 1998. X, 377 pages. 1998.

Vol. 1486: A.P. Ravn, H. Rischel (Eds.), Formal Techniques in Real-Time and Fault-Tolerant Systems. Proceedings, 1998. VIII, 339 pages. 1998.

Vol. 1487: V. Gruhn (Ed.), Software Process Technology. Proceedings, 1998. VIII, 157 pages. 1998.

Vol. 1488: B. Smyth, P. Cunningham (Eds.), Advances in Case-Based Reasoning. Proceedings, 1998. XI, 482 pages. 1998. (Subseries LNAI).

Vol. 1490: C. Palamidessi, H. Glaser, K. Meinke (Eds.), Principles of Declarative Programming. Proceedings, 1998. XI, 497 pages. 1998.

Vol. 1493: J.P. Bowen, A. Fett, M.G. Hinchey (Eds.), ZUM '98: The Z Formal Specification Notation. Proceedings, 1998. XV, 417 pages. 1998.

Vol. 1495: T. Andreasen, H. Christiansen, H.L. Larsen (Eds.), Flexible Query Answering Systems. IX, 393 pages. 1998. (Subseries LNAI).

Vol. 1497: V. Alexandrov, J. Dongarra (Eds.), Recent Advances in Parallel Virtual Machine and Message Passing Interface. Proceedings, 1998. XII, 412 pages. 1998.

Vol. 1498: A.E. Eiben, T. Bäck, M. Schoenauer, H.-P. Schwefel (Eds.), Parallel Problem Solving from Nature – PPSN V. Proceedings, 1998. XXIII, 1041 pages. 1998.

Vol. 1499: S. Kutten (Ed.), Distributed Computing. Proceedings, 1998. XII, 419 pages. 1998.

Vol. 1501: M.M. Richter, C.H. Smith, R. Wiehagen, T. Zeugmann (Eds.), Algorithmic Learning Theory. Proceedings, 1998. XI, 439 pages. 1998. (Subseries LNAI).

Vol. 1503: G. Levi (Ed.), Static Analysis. Proceedings, 1998. IX, 383 pages. 1998.

Vol. 1504: O. Herzog, A. Günter (Eds.), KI-98: Advances in Artificial Intelligence. Proceedings, 1998. XI, 355 pages. 1998. (Subseries LNAI).

Vol. 1510: J.M. Żytkow, M. Quafafou (Eds.), Principles of Data Mining and Knowledge Discovery. Proceedings, 1998. XI, 482 pages. 1998. (Subseries LNAI).